SPIES

S P I E S

A Narrative Encyclopedia of Dirty Deeds and Double Dealing from Biblical Times to Today

JAY ROBERT NASH

M. Evans and Company, Inc.
New York

M. Evans and Company, Inc.
216 East 49th Street
New York, New York 10017

Library of Congress Cataloging-in-Publication Data
Nash, Jay Robert.
Spies: a narrative encyclopedia of dirty tricks & double dealing
from biblical times to today / Jay Robert Nash.
Includes bibliographical references and index.
ISBN 0-87131-790-7
1. Intelligence service—Encyclopedias. 2. Espionage—Encyclopedias.
3. Intelligence officers—Biography. 4. Spies—Biography. I. Title.
JF1525.I6N36 1996   327.12'03—dc20   95-44560

Book Design and formatting by Bernard Schleifer

Manufactured in the United States of America

9 8 7 6 5 4 3 2 1

This book is for my son Jay

INTRODUCTION

THROUGHOUT HISTORY ESPIONAGE HAS BEEN, UNTIL the coming of the electronic intelligence age, a pursuit of personal opportunity. From Biblical times to the middle of the twentieth century the lone agent has been the most potent intelligence weapon. The most effective of these were spies who acted, for the most part, without the support of a network and were thus able to avoid being betrayed by confederates, as was the case with Julius Silber, the Abwehr mole who worked undetected in the British censorship office in London throughout World War I, or Fritz Kolbe, the German OSS spy who worked in the Nazi Foreign Office, supplying Allen Dulles with invaluable information throughout World War II.

This was not the case, however, with the Black Orchestra, the German underground working against the Nazis, or the Red Orchestra (Rote Kapelle), the widespread Soviet networks in Nazi-occupied Europe during World War II. Even the best of these networks were destroyed from within, after one or more of their agents were captured then betrayed their fellow agents, a deadly domino game that led dozens, even hundreds, to their deaths.

The image of the spy that the public holds dear is one invented by Ian Fleming, John Le Carré, and others, in which the valiant agent penetrates the enemy's security single-handedly, obtaining information that saves the world from destruction. The truth is that all intelligence agencies, from the CIA to MI6, and counterintelligence agencies, from the FBI to MI5, rely on enemy nationals who have turned against their own country, and provide inside information. They do this out of a kind of universal patriotism, or for money, sex, drugs, or thrills, while others because they have been blackmailed into being agents. Billions are spent each year on these agents or double agents and what they provide is, for the most part, of questionable practical value, although occasionally a stunning intelligence coup is achieved.

Spies are not to be confused with the common or uncommon criminal. In their own eyes they are not sinister nor intentional lawbreakers. Each acts according to what he or she considers to be a moral or sensible criteria. The most challenging of spies is the patriot. His dedication is complete, his loyalty unswerving and the threat of death cannot deter him from his goal. To the enemy he is the true fanatic, and, fortunately for the enemy, he is also too embued with his own sense of purpose to fully protect him or herself from detection. This was the character of the heroic but inept American patriot spy Nathan Hale whose execution by the British during the American Revolution so incensed George Washington that he later refused to pardon the British spy John Andre, whom he sent vindictively to the gallows.

The great Soviet spymaster Richard Sorge of World War II fame, was another of these, a Soviet patriot who, after his tight little ring of spies was unearthed in Japan, lamented in his cell how he had been "defeated for the first time in my life!" Sorge's vanity, a superior attitude endemic to the personality of any first-class agent, was his undoing. Coupled to arrogance, overconfidence—the intellectual disease that invariably infects most agents who operate successfully for lengthy periods of time—corroded Sorge's operations and his own ability to function properly. It was the same overconfidence that corrupted the ambitious intelligence operations of the Abwehr in England at the beginning of World War II, a feeling that their trained agents were so expert at their jobs that most went on functioning and sending important information back to Germany almost throughout the war. In reality, almost all of the German agents were captured by Special Branch and MI5 and many of them "turned" so that any information dispatched to their German controls was doctored and of little value. German pride convinced Admiral Canaris and other Abwehr chiefs that they had succeeded when, in reality, they had failed from the beginning.

The lust for wealth motivates most spies, from ancient times to the present. Few ever make the millions gleaned by CIA traitor Aldridge Ames, although many have lived in luxury, like the notorious and blatantly obvious Mata Hari who was probably used as a decoy spy by the Germans in World War I. Greed drove Yevno Azev, the unscrupulous Okhrana spymaster who directed countless assassinations of both revolutionary and Czarist figures and was utterly without loyalty to either side. The same held true for Elyeza Bazna, the notorious "Cicero," the glib, polished valet of the British

Ambassador in Turkey who filched England's greatest secrets during World War II and was paid off by the Germans, in a final irony, with counterfeit money. Many agents dream of great fortunes but settle for ditchdigger wages, used cars, second-hand watches, trinkets, junk.

Sex is another strong motivation for some spies. Many politicians or diplomats are compromised by female ("swallows") or male ("ravens") prostitutes working with an intelligence organization (the KGB is extremely adept at such practices). After being secretly photographed, these hapless and unenthusiastic agents (the poorest kind of spies) provide intelligence to the enemy until their sources dry up and they are invariably exposed to their own side. Since the late 1920s British intelligence has been particularly plagued by a staggering number of traitors and double agents whose homosexuality seemed to serve as a collective impetus, coupled to radically leftist political convictions, in serving foreign powers, chiefly the Soviet Union.

British intelligence has long drawn its recruits from the elite of the intellectual community, especially in the 1930s from Trinity College at Cambridge, which was home to such homosexual Communists as Anthony Blunt, Donald Maclean, Guy Burgess, and Kim Philby. These and others came from prestigious, mostly wealthy families. They condescendingly sided with downtrodden workers they saw only as symbols of capitalist oppression (never having personally experienced the economic suffering of these workers). They secretly condemned the upper-class society which spawned and supported their political whims. They banded together in secret Communist cells and cemented those cells with their deeper secret. MI6 and MI5 were rent with these distracted dilettantes for forty years or more, all because the British concept of gentlemen spies demanded recruitment from "the elite" of British society. (FBI Chief J. Edgar Hoover scorned British intelligence, stating with characteristic lack of irony that it had carelessly "nurtured a nest of perverts" and therefore deserved to be victimized.)

These recruits to espionage were posturing academics from the "Old Boys" club and, as such, it was unthinkable that their backgrounds and lifestyles be too closely scrutinzed. Such investigations were restricted to the lower classes whose desperate clawing for economic survival made them suspect in the eyes of elitist British spymasters. Close examination of gentlemen was intrusive and offensive. These gentlemen possessed what the lower classes could never understand—a word of honor which stood for everything. Of course, that word of honor among the British Communist/homosexual spy network stood for nothing as it was given to a capitalist, heterosexual society in which none of the traitors believed.

A pure love of adventure has made a few spies colossal in the eyes of their peers and a public that has come to know them only through legend. One such was the inventive, dashing Sidney Reilly, one of the greatest of England's heroic agents. He thrilled to what Kipling termed the "Great Game," and always sought to accomplish what others could not. He was clever, cunning and extremely talented.

Reilly never abandoned his childhood belief in accomplishing the impossible. He often did. A superb actor, he impersonated a dockworker to obtain information on the Russian fleet before its destruction by the Japanese Navy in the Russo-Japanese War of 1904–1905. He worked in a German munitions factory so he could steal secret rearmament plans before World War I. He impersonated a German general staff officer and attended a conference over which the Kaiser himself presided, or so Reilly claimed. And he almost engineered a counter-revolution in Russia that might have destroyed the Bolsheviks, not to mention his involvement in the attempted assassination of Lenin. Reilly's own end, his entrapment in an insidious Soviet plot, was brought about by the master spy's belief in his own infallibility.

Another British agent, F. F. E. Yeo-Thomas, proved himself as heroic as Reilly. As a member of SOE (Special Operations Executive) in World War II, Yeo-Thomas parachuted three times into Nazi-occupied France, only to be captured and tortured in unspeakable ways, which produced not a single word of information for his German tormentors. Yeo-Thomas, like his counterpart Jean Moulin in French intelligence, proved that willpower could sometimes overcome all odds. But the cost was high: permanent physical injury, which finally brought about Yeo-Thomas' death after the war, or death, the price the courageous Moulin paid silently.

Men held no exclusive right to such heroism. SOE spies Odette Sansom and Violette Szabo both served as agents in France and were captured by the Gestapo. Both were sent to German concentration camps and Szabo died there under torture. A generation before them, British nurse Edith Cavell faced a German firing squad for espionage and saving the lives of hundreds of Allied prisoners-of-war.

Although there were female spies on both sides of the American Revolution, women agents came into great prominence during the American Civil War. By far and away the most effective and deadly female spy of this era was Confederate agent Rose Greenhow, a stunning beauty who wrested top secrets from high-placed Union officials and officers and whose information regarding the battle orders of General Irwin McDowell certainly won for the Confederacy its first great battle, First Bull Run (or First Manassas). Audacious and steel-willed, Mrs. Greenhow could not be broken or forced to confess and, while imprisoned, she managed to keep on spying and obtaining secrets for the South.

Greenhow's daring was matched by the valiant Belle Boyd whose legendary espionage feats for the Confederacy were later enacted on the stage (and some of her exploits, such as shooting a Yankee deserter intruding into her home, were dramatized in the pages of Margaret Mitchell's *Gone With the Wind,* for she was certainly the model for Scarlett O'Hara). The Union, too, had its espionage heroines—Pauline Cushman, the courageous actress known as the Spy of the Cumberland, and the indefatigable Elizabeth Van Lew, who lived inside the heart of Dixie, spied for the Union and aided hundreds of Yankee prisoners to escape to northern lines while convincing her Richmond neighbors that she was certifiably insane.

When these female spies were caught, they were usually treated with special consideration since the nineteenth century was still the age of chivalry, which demanded honorable conduct toward women. All that changed at the beginning of the twentieth century when espionage became a grim business. The spymasters of that day, like the enigmatic German espionage chief and teacher Elsbeth Schragmüller (Fraulein Docktor) of World War I, counseled survival above all else, advocating the most ruthless behavior. Kill or be killed is the inherent truth of modern espionage—sacrifice all, including fellow agents, for the sake of accomplishing the mission.

The spymasters of all countries and in all eras had always advocated such brutal tactics but had, in earlier days, shrouded such baseness with the notion that espionage was the adventurous pursuit of gentlemen, a game played by sensitive, educated souls, such as the British gentleman spy, Robert Baden-Powell, but, indeed, the British were exclusive in clinging to the ideals of honor among spies, long after other countries had abandoned such old-fashioned notions.

America was the most naive of all nations when it came to espionage. It had little or no effective intelligence operations until World War II. While other nations were preparing for the World Wars, spending vast fortunes on intelligence, the U.S. had only a handful of intelligence professionals. The best of these was the brilliant cryptologist Herbert O. Yardley, who headed America's unofficial "Black Chamber." In 1929, when the newly-appointed Secretary of State Henry L. Stimson learned of Yardley's operations, he closed it down with the terse and unrealistic comment: "Gentlemen do not read each other's mail."

Not until William Donovan created the OSS in World War II did the U.S. learn the significant value of intelligence. One of Donovan's top aides, Allen Dulles, would develop the CIA into the most powerful spy agency in the world. Dulles himself was most likely the finest spymaster of the twentieth century. Unlike many other spymasters trained by the military and thereby inhibited by the regimen of the ranks, Dulles came from the private sector. He was analytical, introspective, devious to the core of his being. He understood espionage from its roots and effectively used the information gathered by its branches.

After Dulles, admirals, generals, and politicians have run the CIA like a governmental bureau or an arm of the military, supervising a vast espionage organization as one would a sprawling garden. They were and are mere caretakers. Most were strutting egotists reveling in the authority of their positions as spymasters, but possessing little real understanding of their jobs. They were ineffective bureaucrats who drowned in self-importance, spent untold billions on lunatic schemes, and worst of all, turned the CIA into a vast, stumbling bureaucracy.

This is also the case with MI6 and, to a lesser degree, MI5, in England, where espionage is still conducted by upper-class gentlemen from the better schools. This has not changed since the days of Francis Walsingham, England's first great spymaster under Elizabeth I. Much has been made of the code-breaking genius displayed by British cryptologists in Room 40 at the Admiralty Offices in World War I and the brilliant deciphering done at Bletchley in World War II, where the Nazi Enigma code machine was unraveled, as well as its American counterparts at U.S. Signals Intelligence and naval intelligence who broke down the Japanese Purple Machine. Through these considerable intellectual efforts the top German and Japanese diplomatic and military codes were broken early in both wars, enabling the democracies to more quickly win the conflicts.

Yet, in spite of the great effort on the part of these cryptologists, none of their efforts would have been productive had it not been for the spies in the field who first secured the enemy codebooks and enciphering machines. In World War I, a Dutch spy, Alexander Szek, copied the German military code and passed it on to British agents at the cost of his life (which the British took to prevent him from being identified as the code thief). Moreover, in 1915, the British were actually made a gift of the top German Code Book when a copy of this invaluable document was left behind by the German consul to Persia, Wilhelm Wassmuss, while escaping British troops.

The same holds true in World War II. Polish and French underground resistance fighters obtained copies of the German Enigma machine and sent these to London where they were copied at Bletchley. The "unbreakable" codes and ciphers Enigma produced were subsequently broken, but only because the codebreakers had the actual German machines. The British, in return for the aid America provided England in 1940 (the so-called Lend-Lease program), shared the Enigma information with the U.S. and, by the time America entered the war a year later, it was able to break the Japanese Purple Machine, which had been duplicated from the German Enigma Machine.

Thus, the Ultra operations of the British and the Magic operations of the U.S. appeared to have god-like abilities in deciphering and decoding unbreakable codes and ciphers. The truth was that had not heroic field agents stolen the Enigma Machine, the Allied cryptologists might have been scratching their heads helplessly while the Axis won the war of the codes. (Ironically in the same sense, one of England's most vaunted spymasters, William Stephenson, built a pre-World War II multi-million dollar fortune on patenting a unique German can opener he stole from a concentration camp before his escape in World War I.)

Valuable intelligence information is almost always second and third hand before it reaches a destination where it can be acted upon. By then someone at the top of an intelligence agency hierarchy takes the bow for obtaining that information when the credit invariably belongs with the daring agent in the field who recognized the importance of the information and acquired it at the risk of his or her life.

The function of the lone agent, however, has been replaced in the 1990s for the most part by sophisticated listening and viewing satellites that have extraordinary electronic capabilities, pinpointing espionage targets from space thousands of miles distant. (This is the top secret Spy-in-the-Sky intelligence satellites of the U.S. which, more than any other factor, provided the Gulf War victory, and has made U.S. intelligence supreme.) Information from well-placed agents, citizens of foreign countries willing to spy on their native lands is now, for the most part, bought with enormous sums of money. The country with the most money triumphs. That is why America won all the great espionage battles of the Cold War. It paid more money, billions.

The evolution of espionage from Biblical times to the modern electronic age can be found in these pages, from one spy to another. It was my purpose to present an historical panorama of espionage through the profiles of agents over the ages. The reader will also find all the great spymasters herein, Washington's clever Benjamin Tallmadge and his impenetrable Culper Ring, Napoleon's insidious Joseph Fouché, Lincoln's dogged Allan Pinkerton,

Chiang Kai-shek's intrepid Morris "Two-Gun" Cohen, the German spymasters Walther Nicolai of World War I, Admiral Wilhelm Canaris of World War II, and Reinhard Gehlen of the Cold War. The Russian spymasters—more executioners than espionage chiefs—from Felix Dzerzhinsky and Lavrenti Beria to Yuri Andropov, all make their bloody appearances.

The Soviet field chiefs, Leopold Trepper, Rudolf Abel and many others can be found, as well as their controversial agents—Gordon Lonsdale, the Krogers, the Rosenbergs, including the professional killers of SMERSH, a political murder organization created not by Ian Fleming but by the NKVD-KGB. The unlikely spies are also present: Moe Berg, an American baseball player turned spy in Japan; Boris Morros, a Hollywood musical composer-director who spied under duress for Russia; the British bank burglar Eddie Chapman who reportedly spied and committed spectacular sabotage for the Nazis; the colorful, unpredictable Isaac Trebitsch Lincoln, who spied for everyone and anyone who paid him.

All of the major worldwide spy agencies, their techniques, and their operations can be found in these pages, along with hundreds of agents who have served their countries over the centuries for good or for evil. The reader will find herein all manner of spies representing all types of personalities and character. The best of these are single-minded individuals, early resolved to their destiny, accepting a lifestyle most would find intolerable. Their secret work cannot be shared. They have few friends, no social ambitions. They are not public figures but keep to themselves and to their work. Their passion is for obscurity; their joy is silence; their love is for the dark.

—JAY ROBERT NASH
Chicago, 1997

SPIES

ABEL, RUDOLF IVONOVICH (AKA: EMIL R. GOLDFUS)
Russian Spymaster in U.S. ▪ (1902–1971)

THE ART OF ESPIONAGE WAS NEVER BETTER practiced, at least in theory, than by Colonel Rudolf Ivonovich Abel, the KGB's top spymaster in the U.S. for nine years (1948–1957). Abel moved freely about the U.S.; headquartered in New York he supervised a vast network of Soviet spies until he was exposed by his top cut-out, or go-between. Even after Abel was arrested, the details of his espionage activities were never fully learned, and the spies he controlled—except for the two who informed on him—were never identified.

Born in czarist Russia in 1902, Abel's family was well-to-do. His father moved the family to England in 1903 and Abel lived there until 1921 when his father moved the family back to Russia to aid the Revolution. (One report has it that Abel was actually born in England under the name of William Fischer or Fisher.) As a youth, Abel moved to Scotland and when he spoke English thereafter it was always with a Scottish accent.

Abel's education in Scotland served him well. He was fluent in English, German, Polish, Yiddish, and Russian and, by the early 1930s, was selected by Soviet intelligence as a language expert. He rose to the rank of language instructor for the NKVD, the precursor to the KGB. During World War II, Abel was an intelligence officer in the Russian army on the German front. He served with distinction and proved his courage on the battlefield where he won several commendations. It was also reported that in the later stages of the war Abel was such an adroit spy that he impersonated a German officer and was able to penetrate the Abwehr (German intelligence), learning vital troop dispositions and funneling this data to Soviet commanders who used the information to achieve battlefield victories.

Following the war, the KGB reviewed possible candidates for the position of resident director of a network of Soviet spies working in America with the goal of uncovering top U.S. military secrets. Abel's name was on the list. KGB officials felt that Abel possessed all the qualities needed for the all-important spymaster post in the U.S.

Abel had a number of necessary skills. He was fluent in English and was an expert on the repair and operations of radios and radio transmissions. Abel had studied engineering and had a working knowledge of chemistry and nuclear physics. He was also an accomplished photographer and jeweler, understood codes and ciphers, and was capable of reducing complicated documents to microdot proportions. His jeweler's craft allowed him to rework watches, coins, and other small items to carry microdots. Further, Abel had spied effectively in prewar Germany and he remained unknown to the West as a Soviet agent.

Though married with two children to whom he was devoted, Abel never hesitated when told he had been selected as spymaster for America. He enthusiastically embraced the opportunity, for he was a loyal and dedicated Communist. And loyalty is the top requirement of any agent.

In many other ways, Rudolf Abel was perfect for this new job. His manner was innocuous, his personality unmemorable. A small, thin-faced man, there was nothing about him that drew attention. He dabbled in painting which gave him the usable cover as a Bohemian artist who, by nature, could not be expected to keep regular working hours. As an artist, his habits would naturally be irregular, his schedules and travels nomadic and unpredictable.

Soviet spymaster Rudolf Abel, working in his New York studio as photographer "Emil Goldfus."

Colonel Abel's studio on Fulton Street in Brooklyn replete with paintings done in his own hand.

Abel would be an "illegal" spy in America, one who assumed the identity of another, rather than having been born a native citizen or one not having diplomatic immunity. To that end, he moved to East Germany in 1946, entering a camp for displaced persons and applying for immigration to Canada under a false identity. In that unsettled era when the flotsam and jetsam of Europe sought to escape the ruins of war, it was fairly easy for Abel to be accepted as a destitute artist. Documents provided to Abel by the KGB's Center (nerve center of foreign intelligence operations) identified him as a man of German-Irish descent. He was accepted as a German émigré by Canada.

Once in Canada, Abel slipped across the U.S. border in 1948. Though he had been ordered never to contact any Soviet embassy or consulate in America, the masterspy did have contact with members of the Communist Party in the U.S. These contacts supplied him with a new identity. He was now known as Emil R. Goldfus and had a birth certificate from the city of New York to prove it. Goldfus had been a child born in Manhattan forty-some years earlier who had died at the age of two months. (This was standard procedure in providing illegal agents with verifiable identities; document spies research deaths that are difficult to trace and substitute living agents for those who died in obscurity; Soviet spy Victor Spencer did nothing but haunt Canadian graveyards in search of dead children for this purpose.)

Abel spent more than a year moving about the U.S., contacting Russian spies already in place, giving them instructions on what information to obtain and how to funnel these secrets to him. He also slowly and diligently met U.S. citizens who were dedicated Marxists or Communists or were political malcontents and converted them into new Soviet agents. At this time, and throughout the nine years he was to spend spying in the U.S., Abel never used the name Goldfus with any of his contacts. This name was used exclusively to establish his own legitimate identity as a U.S. citizen. To all Soviet agents reporting to him, Abel was only known by code names, "Mark" being the name he most consistently used.

By 1949, Abel took up residence in New York, living in slum area hotel in Manhattan. He rented a small photographer's studio in Brooklyn. In both instances, he used the name of Goldfus. The studio served as headquarters for Abel's espionage operations, although Abel did not bring any of his agents to either his home or studio. He established friendships with other artists and was generous with food, drink, and small loans. His secret agents, however, never knew of his studio. He met them in parks, the smoking rooms or men's rooms of theaters, in railway and bus stations.

Information was also conveyed to Abel by his agents in various drop zones or letterboxes throughout New York, in hollowed-out trees, under loosened concrete sidewalk slabs, in the false bottoms of doctored pay phones. Abel's agents were specifically instructed to obtain top secret military data on U.S. underwater detection devices, rocket techniques, and nuclear armaments of all kinds. Abel's own orders involved monitoring operations at the United Nations, as well as learning vital military information regarding the Port of New York. Once information was gathered, he smuggled microfilms or microdots to foreign Soviet agents or transmitted data by code through a powerful radio transmitter directly to Moscow. He also received his instructions from Moscow in the same manner. This he did after 10 P.M. on varying dates so as not to establish a regular schedule, which could be followed by U.S. tracking devices monitoring such transmissions.

Two of Abel's most productive agents were Morris and Leona Cohen, U.S. citizens and residents of New York, who had been loyal Communists for decades. In 1950, however, Cohen and his wife suddenly learned that FBI agents were closing in and they fled, eventually going to England where they assumed the names of Peter and Helen Kroger. They went to work almost immediately as Soviet agents but were exposed and sent to prison for twenty years.

Abel's spy network expanded so greatly that the spymaster had difficulty in controlling operations and collecting information. The Center in Moscow determined that Abel needed a top cut-out or intermediary to handle the information flowing to the masterspy. They sent a strange, pudgy-faced agent named Reino Hayhanen who was to act as Abel's deputy director, or top cut-out, in charge of collecting all information from Soviet agents. This would allow Abel to concentrate on relaying secrets to the Russians.

Hayhanen had been born in Russia, just on the other side of the Finnish border, which accounted for his Finnish name. He had worked as a teacher until the NKVD drafted him for the intelligence service during the Finno-Russian War of 1939. Four years later, Hayhanen had become one of the top Soviet agents in Finland, whose chief function was to ferret out anti-Russian elements who were marked for assassination.

When Abel requested an assistant, Moscow selected Hayhanen, summoning him to Moscow where he was trained in codes and photography. Hayhanen received a new identity, Eugene Nicolai Maki. A birth certificate proved that Maki had been born in Enaville, Idaho, which was true. The real Maki, whose mother was American and father Finnish, moved with his family to Estonia from the U.S. when Maki was about eight years old. In 1950, when Hayhanen assumed Maki's identity, Estonia was under Soviet control and the real Maki was either dead or in no position to object to his identity being usurped.

Following his training, Hayhanen went to the west coast port of Turku, Finland. There he worked for a while as a plumber. Though he had a Russian wife, Hayhanen married Hanna Kurikha, a Finnish girl. This act of bigamy had been ordered by the Center in Moscow to deeper plant Hayhanen's Finnish roots.

In 1951, Hayhanen showed up in Helsinki, going to the American Embassy. He produced the birth certificate of Eugene Maki, stating that he was a U.S. citizen and had been born in Idaho in 1919. He asked to be issued a permit to return to his native country, America. Some months later the permit was issued and, in 1952, Hayhanen traveled to Southampton, England. Here he booked passage on the *Queen Mary* sailing for New York, arriving on October 21, 1952. A few months later, Hanna, listed as Hayhanen's wife, followed him.

It took Hayhanen more than a year to settle in New York and he did not receive instructions to contact Abel until 1954. At that time Hayhanen was told to go to a Manhattan park on a certain day at a certain time. He was to stick a thumbtack into a sign in the park. Abel was sitting nearby so that he could identify Hayhanen later. He called Hayhanen and ordered him to meet him in the smoking room of a theater.

Once the two men met, Abel identified himself as "Mark," and gave Hayhanen instructions on collecting data from letterboxes where other Soviet agents had deposited information. A short time later Abel showed Hayhanen a special microfilm he had developed, a strip of which could be rolled into a ball without destroying the information it contained.

Abel was not pleased with his new assistant. In fact he was shocked by Hayhanen's unprofessionalism and ineptitude. The new deputy director had forgotten most of his training in codes and photography and seemed not to care about the security measures so dear to Abel. Though apprehensive, Abel helped Hayhanen lease a small shop from which to operate and trained him in the collection of data.

By 1955, Abel was exhausted with his tremendous workload and responsibilities. Moscow knew it and ordered him to return to Russia for a six-month leave. The masterspy gratefully obeyed. When the revitalized Abel returned to New York in 1956 to resume his duties he was stunned to see that his assistant had brought his carefully constructed spy network to near collapse. Hayhanen had closed his shop but had continued paying rent, which could cause suspicion. Worse, Hayhanen had failed to pick up all of the messages left by agents at letterboxes and, courting disaster, he had blithely used the same location over and over again from which to send radio transmissions to Moscow, instead of using a new suburban site for each shortwave communication.

Abel admonished Hayhanen but it seemed to have little effect. The assistant was by now a dedicated wastrel. He drank to excess and caroused through bars in search of women. He slept with prostitutes and, when drunk, thought nothing of propositioning any woman who caught his eye. Much of the money Moscow advanced for the American spy network flowed through Hayhanen's hands. The

Abel being taken into custody, the only Russian spymaster ever to be captured in the U.S.

deputy director merely used whatever funds he had at hand for his own pleasures.

On one occasion, he was given $5,000 to pay to the wife of convicted atomic spy Morton Sobell who was then serving a 30-year term in Alcatraz. When Hayhanen found that Mrs. Sobell's apartment was under surveillance by FBI agents, the deputy director drove forty-miles to a state park and buried the money. Hayhanen reported to Abel that he had paid Mrs. Sobell, and Abel informed Moscow. Next, Moscow sent another $5,000 with instructions that this money was to be delivered to Mrs. Sobell who should be immediately recruited as a spy to take the place of her absent husband. According to Hayhanen's later testimony, Abel banked this money and did not pay Mrs. Sobell, but it is likely that Hayhanen himself kept the money to fund his expensive sex revels and heroic binges.

Abel had had enough. He complained bitterly to Moscow that the Center had saddled him with a misfit who was systematically destroying all of his work through drunkenness and womanizing. In 1957, the Center finally acted, ordering Hayhanen back to Moscow. To allay his fears that he would be disciplined, he was informed that he had been promoted to the rank of major. Hayhanen told Abel he would leave for Europe but he first drove to the Bear Mountain state park and dug up the $5,000 he buried there. He then sailed for Le Havre.

Hayhanen drank all the way to France and, once there, journeyed to Paris, instead of taking the direct route to Moscow. In Paris he continued to drink and whore. Hayhanen came to believe that he would

be imprisoned or perhaps even executed when he returned to Moscow. He went on a final bender, sobered up, and then walked into the American Embassy in Paris, begging for asylum and claiming that he could expose a powerful Soviet spy network in the U.S., as well as identify its director.

At first, CIA officials disbelieved Hayhanen. Psychiatrists examined him and reported that he was alcoholic and unstable. Yet some of his information proved correct. Returned to the U.S., Hayhanen was placed in the custody of the FBI. He gave agents very little to go on, stating that he knew no Soviet agents in the U.S. by name, nor did he have any addresses. He did take agents to some letterbox areas which yielded very little.

The FBI wanted his boss but Hayhanen again came up empty. He did not know Abel's name or address but he did remember being taken by Abel to a storeroom he had rented. This was the first time Abel had violated his own strictly observed security code. At the time, Hayhanen had given him some information that required examination by apparatus Abel kept in the storeroom. He wanted his deputy present when he examined the information in case he had to question him further about it.

Hayhanen remembered that the storeroom was located somewhere between Fulton and Clark streets in Brooklyn. FBI agents scoured the area and finally located the place. The storeroom, they discovered, had been rented by one Emil R. Goldfus. This was Abel's second breach of his own security measures. He had not used a false name to rent the storeroom and given his real address.

Hayhanen's defection was known to Moscow. The Center ordered Abel to leave New York and go underground. He fled to Florida where he waited for two months, having paid his rent on his studio through this period. Soviet spies watched the studio and reported no presence of FBI surveillance. Abel felt it safe to return to New York, but no sooner had he arrived than he was arrested in Manhattan's Latham Hotel.

Charged with espionage, Abel would admit to nothing. Investigators found a great deal of incriminating evidence in one of his rooms—microfilm concealed in hollowed-out nickels, hollow pencils, and a shaving brush containing microdots, secret writing materials, a powerful shortwave transmitter. Also found were photographs of the missing American-born Soviet spies, Morris and Leona Cohen, who were known friends and supporters of atomic spies Julius and Ethel Rosenberg.

Hayhanen was granted immunity for his testimony against Abel but the prosecution needed corroboration. They found it in the form of a traitorous one-time U.S. Army sergeant, Roy Rhodes. Hayhanen recalled having met one of Abel's couriers, a man who had been recruited in Moscow where he had been assigned to the Army motor pool of the U.S. Embassy. Hayhanen knew Rhodes only by his code name "Quebec," but his knowledge of Rhodes' back-ground soon pinpointed the former sergeant who was arrested.

Rhodes also testified against Abel who was convicted. The prosecution sought the death penalty but James Donovan, Abel's court-appointed attorney, presented a brilliant and prophetic argument for his client. He appealed to federal Judge Mortimer W. Byers, saying that Abel might later talk if he remained in prison and that America might some day want to trade him for a captured U.S. agent.

Abel was sentenced to forty-five years in prison. He never talked while behind bars but he did come to be used as a trading chip for downed U-2 pilot Francis Gary Powers. On February 10, 1962, Abel was exchanged for Powers in a dramatic fashion. Abel and Powers were brought to separate sides of the Glienecker Bridge which spanned Lake Wannsee, separating West Berlin from Potsdam. The two spies stared across the bridge at each other while negotiators talked in the center of the bridge where a white line divided East from West.

Finally, two of the negotiators waved and shouted back to their own people to start the two men across the bridge. Powers paced himself with Abel who walked calmly toward him. He later recalled that "as I walked toward the line, another man—thin, gaunt, middle-aged—approached from the other side. We crossed at the same time." It was 8:52 A.M. Both men were free.

The masterspy returned to Russia where he was given a *dacha*, a small pension, and three packs of Lucky Strikes every day to support his heavy smoking habit. Many reports had it that Abel was lionized and became one of the KGB's top instructors (heading the Anglo-American "desk" at the Center). This was not true. The one-time top Soviet spy in the U.S. was mostly ignored. Since Abel had spent several years in prison, KGB bosses suspected that he might have been indoctrinated in the ways of the West or, worse, that he had been converted into an American counterspy. In fact, Abel was not publicly honored in Russia until May 7, 1965, the date of a *Pravda* edition in which his exploits were vaguely outlined. And this was more than three years after the rest of the world had bannered his exchange for pilot Francis Gary Powers.

Abel spent most of his time reading in a little cafe near KGB headquarters in Moscow, smoking, sipping coffee, and reading. He was respected but from a distance. New KGB agents feared being seen with him and passed him noddingly in the cafe. His peers paused for only moments to ask about his health. It was dangerous to consort with a man who was openly hailed as a Soviet hero but secretly suspected of being a U.S. spy.

In 1968, Abel authored his memoirs which was published with the approval of the Center. The book revealed nothing and was, as expected, only another KGB propaganda tool. The silent, thin-faced, little man went back to his cafe daydreaming. Abel died on November 16, 1971, and was buried without fanfare. So little notice was taken of his passing that news of his death did not reach the West until the following year which, perhaps, is why many reported his death as occurring in 1972.

[ALSO SEE: *The Center; FBI; KGB; Helen and Peter Kroger; Munsinger Affair (Victor Spencer); NKVD; Gary Francis Powers*]

ABWEHR
German Military Intelligence ▪ (1866–1944)

THE TERM "ABWEHR," IS AN ABBREVIATED NAME FOR the German title meaning "foreign information and counterintelligence department." This intelligence organization came into existence in 1866. At that time, Prussia established an espionage bureau to work against Austria during a war between the two nations, a struggle won by theGermans, mostly due to the fine intelligence gathered by the Abwehr.

The organization's success against Austria convinced the German high command to greatly expand its operations during the four years that led up to the Franco-Prussian War (1870–1871). Again the Abwehr performed brilliantly, obtaining, among other top secrets, all the information on chief French fortifications, which were quickly overwhelmed in later combat. Much of the credit for the Abwehr's enormous espionage victories was due to its relentless director, Wilhelm Stieber.

During World War I (1914–1918), the Abwehr was ably directed by Walther Nicolai, a spymaster who established schools for spies and controlled a vast network of agents throughout the Allied countries who, for the most part, produced consistently reliable information.

With the fall of imperial Germany in 1918, the Abwehr went temporarily out of business. For more than two years, the intelligence organization ceased to operate. Then, on January 1, 1921, under the terms of the Versailles Treaty, the victorious Allies allowed Germany to establish an army of 100,000 men. The old guard officer corps lost no time in reestablishing the Abwehr, which operated as a small department inside the Ministry of Defense.

At the Abwehr's head was placed army Colonel Erich Fritz Gempp, a crafty, diminutive spymaster who concentrated throughout the 1920s on obtaining secret data on airplanes, their innovative techniques, and new equipment. The German aim at the time was to secretly build the most powerful air force on earth. The high command knew that it would be the airplane that determined the outcome of the next world war.

By 1928, the Abwehr took over the intelligence duties for the German army, navy, and air force. When Adolf Hitler came to power in 1933, Gempp was replaced by Konrad Patzig, a naval officer, who soon ran afoul of the insidious Heinrich Himmler, Hitler's bloodhound and head of the powerful internal security agency, RSHA. Himmler, who also headed the dreaded Gestapo, and his fanatical protégé, Reinhard Heydrich (who headed the SD, *Sicherheitsdienst*, or security police) worked to have the Abwehr come under their control.

Patzig resisted Himmler's taking over the intelligence organization. This led to his replacement, on January 1, 1935, by navy Captain Wilhelm Canaris. Captain Canaris, later promoted to admiral, was a shrewd, brilliant spymaster who not only managed to keep control of the Abwehr but outfoxed the slippery Himmler at almost every turn, while, late during World War II, joined with other high-ranking German officers and officials in a dangerous plot to eliminate Hitler and make a separate peace with the Allies.

Canaris, along with his second-in-command, Hans Oster, actually helped the Allies more than injured them while supervising all German espionage, counterespionage, and sabotage. Toward the end of the war, Canaris and Oster were actually funneling the Allies almost all important German strategy and battle plans. This became evident to Hitler only after conspirators attempted to assassinate him in 1944. Canaris, Oster, and many others were arrested and executed. With the death of Canaris, the Abwehr collapsed.

[ALSO SEE: *Wilhelm Canaris; Reinhard Heydrich; Heinrich Himmler; Walther Nicolai; Hans Oster; SD; Wilhelm Stieber*]

ADAMS, ARTHUR ALEXANDROVICH
Soviet Spymaster in U.S. ■ (c.1881– ?)

HE WAS A THIN, WASTED, SPIDER OF A MAN, SO crippled with ancient rheumatism that he would sit motionless, except for the blinking of eyelids, for a half hour at a time in intense pain. At dawn, it would often take this crippled spymaster a full hour to get out of bed. Yet, when any crisis demanded, he moved with lightning speed. His name was Arthur Alexandrovich Adams, or this was the alias by which he was best known to the FBI.

Adams had many aliases during his lengthy career as a Bolshevik and, later, Soviet spy. He traveled the world for decades, gathering secrets for Russia but he concentrated his activities on the United States and

his was the first of several Soviet spy rings that began to collect vital data on the atomic bomb.

Born in Russia, Adams joined the Bolsheviks at the turn of the century. He was fond of telling how, in the abortive uprising of 1905, he was beaten so badly by thugs of the secret police (Okhrana) that he later developed his painful rheumatism. Fluent in many languages, particularly English, Adams was chosen by the NKVD (later the KGB) to operate in the U.S.

He first entered the U.S. in 1921, posing as an engineering adviser to a Russian commission. He remained in the U.S. for about a year. He popped up again in 1927, arriving in America in the role of a Russian auto expert, seeking advice on how to create assembly-line production of Soviet autos. In 1932, Adams reappeared as a buyer for a Russian trust seeking to purchase Curtiss-Wright fighter planes.

In 1938 Adams again entered the U.S., but this time as a Canadian citizen. He was then using a fake Canadian birth certificate which identified him as Arthur Adams. So effectively secret was this re-entry into the U.S., that the FBI would not know of his presence until the fall of 1943. For five years, Adams went underground, moving between New York and Los Angeles, establishing contacts with members of the American Communist Party and "fellow traveler" groups.

One of Adams' earliest supporters was wealthy Samuel Novick, a New York radio manufacturer. On December 19, 1937, just before Adams crossed the Canadian border into the U.S., Novick wrote a letter to American immigration authorities. He claimed that Adams was a skilled radio engineer and that he had employed him in Canada for ten years. This was untrue; during this time Adams had been moving about the world for the Soviets as well as spending long intervals in Russia.

Novick, who was later confronted with this untruth, would change his story, saying he first met Adams in 1938. This was also untrue. The two first met in the mid-1930s when Adams, representing the Amtorg Trading Corp., made extensive purchases from Novick's firm, Electronics Corp. of America. This same firm would fill $6 million in government contracts during the war, producing many secret radar devices. Throughout that period and earlier, Novick employed many well-known U.S. Communists.

Others had Adams on their payroll, including Eric Bernay, former advertising manager of the New Masses, who paid Adams $75 a week as a part-time engineer. Hollywood machine designer Samuel J. Wegman also paid Adams $75 a week. These payments from Wegman cost the Hollywood designer nothing since Adams had given Wegman $1,875 in cash to pay the salary. In this way, Adams could prove to anyone questioning his livelihood that he was employed by several American firms.

Payments from these persons and others were sent to Adams at the Peter Cooper Hotel in New York, which was the center of the spymaster's activities before and during World War II. In New York, Adams had strong and continuous ties to Julius Heiman, a steel importer, and Victoria Stone, who operated a posh jewelry store on Madison Avenue. Heiman, who made regular visits to Stockholm for his firm, financed Stone's jewelry business. Both met regularly with Adams.

The spymaster also maintained contacts in Chicago, particularly with scientists who were working on developing what later came to be the atomic bomb. Adams' chief contact was a flamboyant American Communist, Clarence Francis Hiskey (born Clarence Francis Szczechowski in Milwaukee, Wisconsin, July 5, 1912). Hiskey, a chemist, took his degrees at the University of Wisconsin. By the time he received his Ph.D. in 1939, Hiskey was a dedicated Communist. He had married Marcia Sand, a Communist, while in college, and his circle of friends were all members of the Communist Party.

Hiskey became a teacher and spent most of his time trying to convert students and peers to Communism. He openly condemned the American form of government as "no good," and told all who would listen that only Russia had the perfect political system, one without defects, one that did no wrong, and one that was the only salvation of the world.

After teaching at New York's Columbia University, Hiskey joined Columbia's SAM (Substitute Alloy Material) Laboratory, at the request of Nobel prize-winner Dr. Harold Urey. SAM's research was widespread, from heavy water to gaseous diffusion methods of separating out U 235. Even though a 1942 army intelligence report made it clear that Hiskey was an avowed Communist, he was nevertheless kept on at his post of division head or section chief in the SAM project. (It was later claimed that because Russia was then an ally of the U.S.; Communists were not under direct suspicion of stealing state secrets.)

In the summer of 1943, Hiskey's section of SAM was moved to the University of Chicago to work on the Manhattan Project, the building of the atomic bomb. When Hiskey took up residence in Chicago, he continued his promotion of Soviet causes, bragging that he knew important members of the American Communist Party and attempting to enlist associates and subordinates in the Communist cause. His flamboyant public posture soon drew intensified surveillance from American intelligence agencies.

Late in 1943, two CIC (Army counterintelligence) agents trailed Hiskey to a Chicago park where he met with an infirm old man to whom he handed a package. One of the agents followed the old man to a rooming house. When the elderly man left the building, his room was inspected and the packaged examined. It contained secret data involving the atomic bomb, specifically information from the K-25 plant in Tennessee, Anglo-Canadian atomic research, and top secret information involving the Metallurgi- cal Project, a part of the Manhattan Project.

The old man proved to be Arthur Adams. His permanent residence at the Peter Cooper Hotel in New York was identified and searched before Adams left Chicago. In Adams' rooms, agents found more information on U.S. atomic research. They also learned that Adams had a Brooklyn mail drop through which he had been regularly receiving infor- mation on nuclear fission research from all points of the U.S. Most importantly, agents unearthed Adams' network of spies, more than one hundred persons who were in the U.S. military, hundreds more who were Communists working in defense plants, and scores of wealthy, socially prominent Americans who served the Communist cause.

Agents continued to keep Adams and his New York contacts under surveillance, as well as Hiskey in Chicago. Hiskey proved to be an embarrassment to Army intelligence as well as the FBI. He was a middle-level member of America's most top-secret project. To arrest and prosecute him for espionage during wartime would mean to expose that project to scrutiny in a public trial. This the government could not do. It was decided to shelve Hiskey to a remote location where he could not further damage U.S. security.

Agents discovered that Hiskey had gone through R.O.T.C. while in college and was a reserve officer in the Army. Suddenly, it was determined that the Army could no longer go without the invaluable services of Clarence Hiskey. He was called up for active duty. Hiskey exploded when he learned that he was being drafted, protesting that his research role in Chicago was vital to winning the war. He also suspected that he was being discreetly put out of the way so he could no longer have access to atomic bomb secrets.

Hiskey alerted Adams. He then attempted to recruit a fellow scientist, John H. Chapin, to take his place as a spy for Adams. Chapin, who had leftist leanings, was interested enough to meet Adams before the spymaster left Chicago. At the meeting he was told by Adams that, following the war, Russia would need scientists of his caliber, that it would be willing to pay handsomely for his invaluable services. Chapin said he would think it over but, according to his own later statements, he did not join Adams' net- work nor did he ever deliver any secrets to Adams.

After the Army ordered Hiskey into uniform on April 28, 1944, the scientist was removed from the Manhattan Project and sent to Canada, then Alaska where, in the words of one official, "he was kept busy counting heavy underwear." Following this assignment, Hiskey was kept effectively away from government secrets when the Army reassigned him to Hawaii where he was busy manufacturing soap for servicemen stationed in the Pacific. (Following the war, Hiskey appeared before congressional commit- tees. He refused to answer questions about his Communist membership or if he handed over secrets. He would not discuss his relationships with Arthur Adams or anyone else.)

The far-flung operations of Adams' spy network, however, continued unmolested, although its spies were monitored by CIC agents. One of the houses closely watched was that of a prominent New York lawyer. On October 25, 1944, Julius Heiman and Victoria Stone were seen to leave this house. A short time later, Arthur Adams doddered out of the building carrying a large suitcase. He hobbled along the sidewalk in what appeared to be painful steps, pausing every so often to rest.

As he was resting, a car moved to the curb next to Adams and stopped. Adams got inside with the case and the car drove off. The vehicle was registered to Pavel Mikhailov, Soviet Vice-Consul. Agents followed the car to the Soviet Consulate. Some minutes later Adams left the Consulate. He was no longer carrying the case and he moved quickly along the street, almost in a carefree, jaunty manner.

Adams' rheumatism sometimes caused him to fall in public or even pin him to a chair for hours in his hotel room. At these times, the same physician was always called to assist him, Dr. Louis Miller. This physician was also the personal doctor of Samuel Novick, Julius Heiman, and Victoria Stone. All of these persons were under 24-hour surveillance and, it soon became apparent to the group that they were being watched. Adams realized, especially after Hiskey's abrupt conscription, that U.S. intelligence had undoubtedly pieced together his espionage web. He decided that it was time to flee the U.S.

The shrewd old spymaster was visited by one of Hiskey's one-time students who began to ask questions about Adams' involvement in atomic secrets. Adams undoubtedly sensed that the youthful scientist was probing for information on the part of the U.S. He complained to the young chemist that he was too crippled by his rheumatic condition to be running around gathering such information and that he planned to leave for Canada very soon.

This, of course, was not his plan. Adams knew the Canadian border would be closed to him. Instead, he smuggled his clothes and other items to the home of Victoria Stone. From there, using funds provided by Eric Bernay, he drove cross-country to Portland, Oregon, where a Soviet ship was about to embark. One dark night, Adams hobbled from the shadows of a pierside warehouse, heading for the gangplank of the Russian vessel.

Suddenly, FBI agents appeared out of the darkness to block his path. Adams blurted out that he was "a sick man who was going to sea for my health." The agents refused to let him board the ship. Adams shrugged and walked away. He returned to New York, holing up in the Peter Cooper Hotel where he became a recluse, seeing only a few people. He seldom left his room and it was concluded that he had probably turned the control of his network over to someone else.

The bulging dossier put together on Adams by the CIC, FBI, and other intelligence agencies was placed before President Franklin D. Roosevelt by the FBI.

The Bureau asked for an order to arrest Adams. FDR deferred the matter to the State Department which, in turn, declined to proceed against the creaking spymaster, stating that it would disturb an already fragile relationship between the U.S. and the Soviet Union. After FDR died, the Bureau tried again, this time submitting its information to President Harry Truman. The same procedure was followed with the State Department refusing to act.

Some time in 1945, although he was being watched around the clock, Arthur Adams, Soviet spymaster, vanished entirely. It was later suspected that he somehow managed to secretly board the Polish liner, *Batory*, and sail to Europe and then make his way to the Soviet Union where he eventually succumbed to his prolonged illness. Adams left in his wake a spy network that was eventually broken up, including top operatives such as Steve Nelson, one of Adams' West Coast cut-outs or liaison agents, and Rudy Baker, a Soviet spy operating in the Detroit area for years. In fact, Baker also disappeared at the same time that Adams vanished. It was thought that Baker accompanied Adams on board the *Batory*, sailing into Soviet oblivion.

[ALSO SEE: *Amtorg Corp.; Rudy Baker; Steve Nelson; NKVD; Okhrana*]

AGEE, PHILIP BURNETT FRANKLIN
CIA Case Officer in Latin America ▪ (1936–)

BEFORE ALDRICH HAZEN AMES WAS EXPOSED AS A high-ranking CIA official who betrayed the Agency and his country to the Soviets, the CIA claimed that it had never had a turncoat member. But the Agency's critics point to Philip Agee who had worked as a CIA Latin American case officer in the Agency in Mexico, a position he resigned in 1969 after twelve years of service. Agee said he was leaving the CIA for "personal reasons," but, after he left, he stated that he had rejected "my work in the CIA as a reaction against the corruption, ineffectiveness, and greed I found among the traditional political forces that we were supporting."

Thereafter Agee became a dedicated CIA basher. He moved to Cuba where he was given a house and servants and where he wrote a book about his CIA career. Agee always insisted that the Cuban government did not bring any pressure to him to write a critical portrait of his former employer, but the CIA later insisted that Agee was by then a member of the Cuban secret service, the DGI, which was an arm of the KGB.

Agee's book, *Inside the Company*, proved to be a vitriolic condemnation of the CIA, a political polemic, really, which also publicized many of the Agency's sensitive procedures and, more devastating, printed the names of hundreds of CIA employees, as well as affiliate agents and organizations. In December 1975, a publication to which Agee reportedly had ties, published the name and address of CIA operative in Athens, Greece, Richard Welch. On December 23, 1975, Welch was shot to death outside his Athens home.

The CIA blamed Agee for this death, although he denied having provided the agent's address to the publication. Agee, however, had written in the edition of the publication publishing Welch's address the following advice to foes of the CIA: ". . . the CIA people can be identified and exposed through periodic bulletins disseminated to our subscribers, particularly individuals and organizations in the foreign country in question. Photographs and home addresses in the foreign capital or Consular cities should be included . . . the people themselves will have to decide what they must do to rid themselves of the CIA."

Later, Agee was accused by Congressman Larry McDonald of betraying Polish Olympic fencer Colonel Jerzy Pawlowski as a secret agent for the West. Pawlowski was arrested by the KGB in 1976 and sent to prison for twenty-five years, convicted of being a CIA spy.

Agee, who by then was living in England, was ordered deported from that country. Agee fought the deportation order but lost and was compelled to leave Great Britain. After his American passport was confiscated, Agee battled this action all the way to the U.S. Supreme Court, which, in 1981, ruled that he no longer had the right to have an American passport.

[ALSO SEE: *Aldrich Ames; KGB*]

AKASHI, MOTOJIRO
Japanese Spy in Russia • (c.1860–1919)

BORN INTO A POOR FAMILY, AKASHI'S FUTURE appeared in the 1880s to be nothing more than thousands of other Tokyo street gangsters who lived by theft and extortion. He distinguished himself to powerful benefactors, however, by voicing right-wing political thoughts that brought him to the attention of members of the Black Dragon Society (Kokuryukai, 1881–1944).

The Black Dragon Society was a secret right-wing political organization begun in 1881 by Ryochei Uchida, a protégé of Mitsuru Toyama, one of the most sinister men in Japanese history. Toyama had formed several secret societies, with thousands of loyal members gleaned from the gangs roaming Japan's major cities. The aims of Toyama, Uchida, and their min-

ions were to control all Japanese politics, commerce, the military, and, eventually, the destiny of the nation through conquest of China and Asiatic Russia.

The Society took its name from the alternate name of the Amur River which separated Manchuria and Siberia, the Black Dragon River. It was symbolic in that the Society coveted Manchuria, as well as Siberia, all of Asiatic Russia, and Korea. Akashi was one of many recruited to the Black Dragon ranks who felt as did its leaders, that the expansionist aims of Japan were best directed north.

Akashi was groomed to become one of the Society's top espionage agents, one who swore allegiance to the Society before his country and emperor. To that end the Society sent Akashi to military school. When he graduated and joined the Japanese army, his military salary was supplemented by money from the Society. Through high-placed members of the officer corps who were also Black Dragons, Akashi rose to the rank of colonel. Following instructions from his Black Dragon superiors, he requested and was appointed to a position in army intelligence.

In 1900, Akashi served as a military attaché at the Japanese Embassies in Sweden, France and Switzerland. His job was to learn all he could about what sympathies the Western powers might have for Russia and its heavy-handed czarist regime of Nicholas II, whether or not Europe would come to Russia's aid if Japan attacked.

Akashi learned that, at best, the European heads of state were indifferent to the fate of czarist Russia, information that aided Japan's militarists in their decision to launch the Russo-Japanese War (1904–1905) to gain Manchuria. Before the war began, Akashi was summoned to Tokyo to confer with Uchida and Toyama. The Black Dragon leaders informed Akashi that he would be sent to St. Petersburg as a military attaché, working out of the Japanese Embassy.

Akashi was given specific instructions to contact known revolutionaries, Father George Gapon and Yevno Azev. He was to support their espionage and sabotage operations with money and encouragement. Further and most important, he was to learn the political and military strengths Russia possessed in east and central Asia, particularly in Manchuria and Korea where Japan meant to strike first.

Upon his arrival in St. Petersburg, Akashi immediately contacted Father Gapon and Azev. He loaned them funds and encouraged their revolutionary acts against the czar. He also spent a good deal of time attending social functions where he could learn military disposition of troops and naval forces from high-ranking Russian officials and military officers.

Aiding Akashi's efforts was an important Tartar Muslim, Abdur Rashid Ibrahim, who published a Tartar newspaper entitled *Ulfet*. Ibrahim was an adviser to the Russian government on Muslim affairs, and, as such, he had access to secret information involving czarist troop positions and naval movements in Asiatic Russia and in the coastal city of Port Arthur where the Russian fleet was berthed.

As Ibrahim learned in detail the strength of the Russian fleet and its cruise schedules, he passed this information to Akashi, who sent it on to Tokyo in the weekly diplomatic pouch. In this way the Japanese fleet was able to pinpoint the chief Russian naval targets when it attacked Port Arthur on February 4, 1904. As would be the case with Pearl Harbor four decades later, the Japanese launched a surprise attack, declaring war on Russia two days *after* it sunk the Russian fleet.

As his Black Dragon masters knew full well, much of the credit for the enormous Japanese success at Port Arthur was due to the espionage efforts of Colonel Akashi. The very day the Japanese fleet destroyed Russia's capital ships at Port Arthur, Akashi, at the invitation of Yevno Azev, was addressing a secret meeting of the Russian Socialist Revolutionary Congress in Stockholm. At this meeting, Akashi told these revolutionaries: "I am authorized by my superiors to inform you that Japan is prepared to supply arms for revolutionary uprisings in St. Petersburg, Odessa, and Kiev."

Oddly, Akashi did not know that Azev was a spectacular double agent who led the Battle Organization of the Socialist Revolutionary Party, which was dedicated to assassinating all monarchist leaders. At the same time, Azev was a masterspy for the Okhrana, the secret police that protected the monarchy of Nicholas II and who reported everything to his police superiors. Father Gapon was also a paid police informant. Both Azev and Gapon reported to the Okhrana all of Akashi's movements, speeches, and aid to the revolutionaries only hours after they took place.

The enterprising Akashi further worked with Ibrahim to organize Muslim resistance behind the Russian lines in Asiatic Russia throughout the war. Akashi returned to Tokyo in 1906, following the end of the Russo-Japanese War but he did not forget Ibrahim, arranging for Ibrahim's son to be educated in Tokyo at the expense of the Black Dragons. Ibrahim traveled to Tokyo in late 1906 and again in 1909, further cementing his links with Akashi and Japanese intelligence.

During World War I (1914–1918), Akashi was appointed assistant chief of the general staff. With General Sadao Araki, he planned and helped execute the capture of German-held Tsingtao on the Chinese coast in 1914 which encouraged the Black Dragons and Japanese militarists to plan the occupation of Siberia and, eventually, Chinese Manchuria.

Akashi would not live to see Manchuria invaded in 1931. He died in 1919 but much of his long-range espionage work later aided Japan's brutal invasion of China.

[ALSO SEE: *Yevno Azev; Black Dragon Society; George Gapon; Okhrana; Mitsuru Toyama*]

AL MUKHARABAT (AKA: THE LISTENING POST)
Iraq's Secret Service ▪ (1968–   )

SHORTLY AFTER THE BA'ATH PARTY SEIZED CONTROL of Iraq in July 1968, dictator Saddam Hussein created the Al Mukharabat, which became not only that country's secret service but an all-powerful organization that controls every facet of military, political, and economic life. Al Mukharabat, which is also known as The Listening Post and is euphemistically called the "Public Relations Bureau," conducts all intelligence-gathering operations, as well as terrorism inside Iraq and throughout the world.

Al Mukharabat methodically trains scores of assassins whom it sends on murder missions throughout the world. The targets of these ruthless killers are those who oppose the tyrannical dictatorship of Saddam Hussein. One example was the murder of General Abdul Razzak al-Naif, one-time prime minister of Iraq who was hunted down in London by an Al Mukharabat hit team and killed outside the Intercontinental Hotel in July 1978. The murder squad spent months in England tracking the victim. These Iraqi assassins form an exclusive, well-paid organization inside the Al Mukharabat, which is known as Al Hunain.

Following the Yom Kippur War with Israel in 1973, Iraq's hopelessly antiquated Al Mukharabat received superpower assistance from Russia. Iraq had become wholly dependent upon the USSR for Soviet weapons at that time and, to continue receiving these arms, Saddam Hussein concluded a secret pact with the Soviets. Its terms dictated that the Al Mukharabat be revamped according to the structure of the KGB. Iraq officers were sent to Russia to be trained in GRU and KGB espionage schools. Iraq received sophisticated Russian interrogation and intelligence-gathering equipment.

Saddam Hussein, in turn, agreed to send his terrorists to any country selected by the Soviets to carry out espionage and assassination missions on behalf of Russia. This was particularly useful to the Soviets inside nations where no diplomatic cover was available to KGB agents.

The Al Mukharabat is commanded by Brigadier General Khalil al-Wazir who carries out Saddam Hussein's orders without question. He has a fearsome reputation inside Iraq as one who routinely purges lower echelon military officers and conducts a constant reign of terror against Iraq's citizenry. Anyone heard to utter the slightest complaint about Iraq's miserable living conditions is subject to arrest and imprisonment by Al Mukharabat agents. These luckless citizens are branded dissidents and are invariably tried secretly and, most often, murdered. It is estimated that every fourth grown male in Iraq is employed as an agent for this most ruthless of secret services.

ALBANI, ALESSANDRO
Papal Spy for England ▪ (1692–1779)

As the nephew of Pope Clement XI, Albani was born and raised in wealth. Clement was a patron of the arts and a notable art collector, a penchant he developed in young Albani whose passion for classical antiquities later made him one of the outstanding collectors in Europe.

Albani rose quickly in rank and prestige in Rome. He was given command of a regiment in the papal army and took ecclesiastical orders in 1712. In 1718, he was made domestic chaplain to his uncle, Clement XI. Two years later, Albani entered the papal diplomatic corps. He served in Vienna and, when he returned to Rome, represented Austrian interests at the papal court.

Clement XI died on March 19, 1721. Though Pope Innocent XIII made Albani a cardinal, his political fortunes went into decline until Innocent died and was succeeded by Benedict XIII. At this time, Albani established a lifelong friendship with Philip von Stosch, a celebrated art collector who shared the young cardinal's love of antiquities. Stosch was a spy for the English government, which was anxious to learn the intrigues and plots hatched almost daily in the court of "James III," of the English House of Stuart, the "Old Pretender" to the British throne.

The Stuarts had attempted to reestablish the Catholic religion in England but had failed. The "Old Pretender" had taken refuge in Rome, his court-in-exile being protected by the Vatican. Stosch had subtly tried to recruit Albani's aid in obtaining information on the Old Pretender's court and the Jacobites who supported the Stuart claim to the English throne. The cardinal, however, appeared reluctant to betray Pope Benedict's allegiance to the Stuarts.

Albani himself was betrayed, he believed, by Benedict when the Pope refused his application for the post of Prefect of the Signature. Benedict had heeded warnings from a powerful court clique that Albani was not one to be trusted. This rejection drove Albani into Stosch's camp and he became a willing spy for the English, reporting in detail the plans and plots of the Old Pretender.

As one of the leading art collectors in Europe, Albani was in the unique position of meeting wealthy English travelers seeking antiquities. He learned from them the underground activities of the Jacobites and sent this information regularly to the English. Albani focused on the whereabouts of the Old Pretender, who moved about Europe. England, of course, feared that James was raising another army with which to invade its shores.

Albani established a network of spies that, in 1744, reported that James' son, Charles Edward (called "Bonnie Prince Charlie") was gathering troops to invade England. The cardinal informed the English who were ready when the dashing prince landed in Scotland in 1745. Charles Edward met with initial success in Scotland but when he met the English at Culloden and was soundly defeated. The English victory had much to do with Albani's political espionage.

Charles Edward or the "Young Pretender" returned to Europe where he sank into idleness. Albani rose further in power so that, at the request of the English, he was able to persuade the Vatican into suppressing the Jacobite royal title. Albani ended his days performing his obligations as a cardinal and pleasuring himself with his great art collection.

ALEXANDER THE GREAT
Postal Censorship Inventor ▪ (356–323 B.C.)

Halicarnassus in Asia Minor proved to be a stubborn city, refusing to submit to Alexander the Great in his conquest of Persia in 334 B.C. The wily Persian general Memmon fought off countless attacks by Alexander's men who grew demoralized. To determine which of his men could be counted as loyal, particularly those who might be selected as soldiers of the occupied territory, Alexander improvised a clever plan.

Alexander forbade all of his men to write home to their families, stating that this was a security measure. A short time later he reversed this edict. The soldiers took the opportunity to write to their

Alexander the Great who first created postal censorship to check on the morale and loyalty of his troops.

Alfred the Great (shown at right), acted as his own spymaster, disguising himself as a minstrel to learn the battle plans of his Danish enemies.

families in Greece. Couriers carrying these letters were halted a few days after they left the Greek camp, and the contents of their pouches were brought back to Alexander.

The conqueror read through the letters to discover which of his men were reliable, selecting these to remain in Asia Minor. Those who expressed discontent, Alexander sent home. Thus, Alexander became the inventor of postal censorship, a spying method that continues to the present day.

ALFRED THE GREAT
Spymaster ▪ (849–899)

DURING THE SECOND DANISH INVASION OF ENGLAND, Alfred the Great met the armies of Guthrum, and, suffering several defeats, retreated to the island of Altheney in Somerset. Here, with no more than fifty knights, the King of Wessex waited to be destroyed by Guthrum's powerful army.

In the spring of 878, the Danes languished in their vast camp, drinking and whoring. Guthrum himself was inactive and seemingly indecisive throughout the long winter. In that spring, however, he called his

commanders to his tent to convoke several councils of war. Throughout these rambling councils, the Danes gorged themselves and drank heavily. A Saxon minstrel played a harp outside the tent and sang tender love songs as these lengthy meetings ensued. Guthrum and his generals, after their meetings, dropped scraps of meat and bread into the minstrel's pouch and he scurried off, ostensibly to take the food back to his starving family.

His battle plans settled, Guthrum and his army moved toward Alfred's camp, already cherishing an unwon victory. The Danes, however, were waylaid at every point and Guthrum's army was systematically destroyed near Edington in Wiltshire. The Danish King was captured, along with his commanders and brought before Alfred who greeted them smiling, holding a harp in his hands. Of course, Alfred's rich-voiced spy had been himself, the minstrel who had learned Guthrum's battle plans by simply sitting outside his adversary's tent and warbling ditties.

ALLIED INTELLIGENCE BUREAU (AIB)
Allied Intelligence Agency ▪ (1942–1945)

THE AIB WAS A MULTINATIONAL ESPIONAGE ORGANIzation that collected intelligence data; it was also effective in committing wholesale sabotage and creating impressive propaganda during World War II. Under the direction of U.S. General Douglas MacArthur, this agency was headquartered in Melbourne, Australia, and made up of five departments, including British and Dutch espionage, sabotage, propaganda, and the Australian Coast Watchers who operated in front of and behind Japanese lines.

MacArthur left the Philippines in the Spring of 1942, ordered to Australia by President Franklin D. Roosevelt. His men on Bataan and Corregidor eventually surrendered to overwhelming Japanese forces but by that time MacArthur was building another Allied army in Australia in preparation of taking back from the Japanese the huge island-dotted area of the South Pacific they had engulfed in the first six months of the war.

To accomplish this goal, MacArthur relied heavily on the AIB which was commanded by Colonel C. G. Roberts, head of Australian intelligence. Thousands of special volunteers served as Coast Watchers. They infiltrated Japanese-held islands and sent back reports to AIB via short-wave radios. Using these reports, AIB commandos mounted devastating sabotage raids preceding MacArthur's northern advance from Australia to New Guinea and the many islands conquered by U.S. and Australian troops from 1942 to 1945.

During MacArthur's brilliantly conceived island-hopping campaigns, AIB maintained constant propaganda through radio programs, clandestine presses behind enemy lines, and leaflets dropped by airplane to discourage Japanese troops and inspire the conquered island peoples to conduct savage guerrilla activities against their Japanese foes.

The AIB-directed guerrilla movement in the Philippines was particularly effective in disrupting Japanese communications, destroying ammunition depots, ambushing small Japanese contingents, and gathering intelligence on troop dispositions and available landing areas which helped MacArthur immensely in mounting his 1944 invasion of the Philippine Islands at Leyte. Once the Philippines were secure, the AIB went out of existence.

AMANA, YOSHITARO
Japanese Spy in Panama ■ (1899– ?)

IN THE EARLY 1930s, JAPAN INCREASED ITS ESPIONAGE activities throughout the Pacific in keeping with its secret ambitions for global conquest. The U.S. had been aware of Japan's aims as early as 1928 when American agents had obtained a copy of the top secret Tanaka Plan. Baron Giichi Tanaka had, along with Japan's top militarists and with the approval of Emperor Hirohito, drawn up an elaborate scheme to invade one Pacific nation after another, until the powerful Japanese Navy reached the shores of the United States. The Tanaka Plan called for elaborate espionage operations to precede these invasions. Thousands of Japanese agents were planted in all U.S. territories, including the strategically vital Panama Canal.

In 1934, Japanese businessmen applied for a permit with U.S. authorities in Panama to construct a refrigeration plant on the small island of Taboga, just outside the Pacific entrance to the Panama Canal. (This island is not to be confused with the British-owned island of Tobago in the Lesser Antilles.) American intelligence agents rightly assumed that the refrigeration plant would be used to shield Japanese agents who could monitor U.S. military movements, air force patrols, shore and air battery dispositions, as well as the movements of U.S. warships through the Canal. The permit was refused by U.S. authorities. One of those Japanese businessmen was Yoshitaro Amana, who owned a successful store in Panama.

A few years later Amana learned that U.S. officials were so alarmed by the scores of Japanese agents blatantly operating in Panama that they were thinking of banning all foreign fishing in Panamanian waters. In 1937, Amana, heavily financed by Japanese spymasters in Tokyo, established a new company, Amano Fisheries, Ltd. He suddenly had under his control a large fleet of fishing vessels, the flagship of which was the *Amano Maru* which had been built in Japan in July 1937.

The *Amano Maru* began sailing close to U.S. coastal fortifications, its crew members photographing shore batteries. One of the crew members had been recruited by U.S. intelligence and he quickly supplied photos of the ship's interior, which included sophisticated monitoring devices and an elaborate radio room equipped with powerful, long-distance radio equipment. The vessel also had a special code room where top secret messages transmitted between Japan and the ship were encrypted and deciphered by Japanese cryptographers. In another room, Japanese mapmakers were kept busy drafting charts of Panamanian landfalls suitable to invasion craft and nearby waters that would afford hiding places for Japanese submarines.

It was also discovered that Amana had spent lavishly on the *Amano Maru*, equipping it with the most luxurious appointments, stylish bedrooms, ornate bathrooms, a galley that would have been the envy of any topflight restaurateur. The ship, indeed, was the most luxurious fishing vessel afloat anywhere.

Though aware of Amana's espionage activities, U.S. military intelligence allowed him a free hand until they decided to entrap the spy. They let it be known that the U.S. was making plans to excavate another canal through Nicaragua and that they had already begun constructing very unusual fortifications in and around Managua's military zone.

Amana took the bait and hurried to Managua, arriving there on October 7, 1937, at 8 A.M. He busily took photographs of the U.S. military zone in Managua. He then began making maps and drawings of what appeared to be heavy gun emplacements (these were dummy wooden guns set up for the occasion). A half hour later, U.S. agents closed in, arresting him. Amana was charged with suspected sabotage and taking photos in a restricted area. He was tried but acquitted.

The aggressive Amana then heard that the U.S. was constructing secret military installations in Costa Rica and he hurried to that country a few weeks later. He was promptly arrested again with camera in hand. Costa Rican officials jailed him on charges of espionage. This time, Amana was reprieved from a long prison sentence on a direct appeal from Japanese officials in Tokyo to the President of Costa Rica. He was released into the custody of Japanese consulate officials who escorted Amana to a ship sailing for Japan. The spy sailed for Tokyo where he utterly disappeared. It was believed that Amana was imprisoned, perhaps even shot, on orders of his spymasters because of his inept spying, or, more likely, because of his wild spending habits.

"AMERASIA" CASE
U.S. Security Breach ▪ (1945)

IN 1936, WHEN JAPAN WAS FURIOUSLY LAUNCHING ITS military might against China in an all-out war of conquest, the Chinese armies of nationalist leader Chiang Kai-shek and Communist chief Mao Tse-tung opposed each other in internecine conflict. Chiang was then the dominant force in China and he rightly suspected that his real long-term enemy was Mao, not the Japanese. He had secretly conducted a campaign of appeasement with the Japanese while urging his most powerful general, Marshal Chang Hsueh-liang, to hurl his ten divisions against Mao's Communist forces in northern China.

Chang argued that China would be better served if Chiang and Mao joined forces against the Japanese invaders. To convince his subordinate to follow his orders, Chiang flew to Sian and confronted Chang. The warlord was informed by Chang's officers that he was a prisoner. Chiang was held in polite custody, a kidnap victim, as it were. He finally agreed to forge a "United Front" with the Communists. Chiang's vast Kuomintang armies would join with Mao's Communist legions to resist the Japanese.

To naive Western observers, Chiang had been compelled to make this decision. It was more likely, however, that Chang's non-violent kidnapping of his leader Chiang Kai-shek had been staged to save Chiang's face, as the nationalist leader had long publicly attacked Communism and Mao. (Chang would remain at Chiang's side for the rest of his life, even accompanying Chiang into exile on Taiwan in 1948 after Mao's hordes overran all of mainland China.)

When news of the newly enacted Chinese "United Front" reached the U.S., two men quickly decided to publish a magazine that would devote itself to profiling the Chiang-Mao coalition. The founders of *Amerasia* magazine were Philip J. Jaffe and Frederic Vanderbilt Field. Jaffe, an American businessman, was the actual publisher. Field financed the publication. Jaffe, born in Russia in 1897, had grown rich by printing greeting cards.

The editorial thrust of *Amerasia* was decidedly anti-Japanese. Its writers ostensibly supported the Chiang-Mao union but Jaffe and his staff, in reality, backed the Communist cause and subtly criticized Chiang Kai-shek, criticism which increased throughout the late 1930s, while Mao was lionized. Jaffe had long been an adherent to the Communist cause. One of his closest friends was Earl Browder, leader of the American Communist Party.

Among *Amerasia*'s contributing writers were Emmanuel Sigurd Larsen, who worked in the State Department's Far Eastern Affairs and had spent most of his adult life in Asia; John Stewart Service, serving as a political adviser to the State Department as an expert on China after having spent a great deal of time at the headquarters of Mao Tse-tung; and free-lance journalist Mark Gayn, who had been born in Manchuria.

The editorial staff was as left-leaning as editor Jaffe. Kate Louise Mitchell was co-editor of *Amerasia*. A Bryn Mawr graduate, Mitchell was an ardent Communist party-liner. On the editorial board was Owen Lattimore (from 1937 to 1941) and a youthful Navy Reserve Lieutenant Andrew Roth who was Jaffe's assistant until the beginning of World War II. At that time, Roth was appointed to Naval Intelligence against the advice of security services, which reported Roth to be a "fellow traveler."

The publication never numbered more than 2,000 readers and many of these were government employees. *Amerasia* was read with avid interest by officials at the State Department, as well as agents of the OSS (Office of Strategic Services, the forerunner to the CIA). The magazine seemed to be the best-informed public source on events in Asia and the war in the Pacific, too well-informed as far as the British SIS (Secret Intelligence Service) was concerned.

In February 1945, the magazine published the text of a top secret report on British policy in Thailand, a report that could have come from OSS offices. Incensed British officials registered a complaint that wound up in the hands of OSS directors. The OSS had been aware for some time that *Amerasia* had been publishing material that appeared to have been taken from classified documents. The OSS decided to act.

Assigned to investigate was OSS agent Frank Brooks Bielaski, a beefy, bespectacled ex-Wall Street broker who had successfully handled many OSS investigations throughout the war. On the night of March 11, 1945, Bielaski and four other agents entered a dark, near empty building at 225 Fifth Avenue in New York City. They rode the elevator to the eleventh floor and, employing "deceit and subterfuge," according to Bielaski's later statements, entered *Amerasia*'s offices.

A search of the place was methodically conducted. Bielaski and associates found a room with the most modern photocopying equipment and another room with a large table over which hung special cameras for photographing documents. On the table the agents found dozens of top secret, secret, and classified documents. Behind a door the agents found a bellows-type suitcase and two briefcases. Inside of these cases more than 300 additional secret documents were discovered. These documents had been taken from the offices of the OSS, ONI (Office of Naval Intelligence), Censorship, G-2 (Army Intelligence), State Department, and British Intelligence.

The documents revealed the dispositions of U.S. submarines in the Pacific and battle reports showing the disposition of the Japanese fleet before the Battle of Leyte. Most of the secret documents dealt with

Amerasia *editor Philip Jaffe (center), shown at Communist headquarters in Yenan, China, 1937; Owen Lattimore is at right.*

Chiang Kai-shek, including highly confidential messages between President Franklin D. Roosevelt and Chiang. Dispositions of nationalist troops and Chiang's hidden arsenals were also detailed in the documents, along with State Department reports on Chiang's loss of prestige in China, as well as criticism of and opposition to his continuing leadership. All of this was fodder to a magazine devoted to undermining Chiang Kai-shek and promoting the cause of Mao Tse-tung and Chinese Communism.

Of the original copies and stats of the secret documents, 267 documents had come from the State Department, fifty from the OSS, fifty-eight from the OWI (Office of War Information), thirty-four from military intelligence, and nineteen from naval intelligence. Bielaski and his men gathered up the documents and turned them over to the FBI. The Bureau immediately placed Jaffe and his staff under surveillance but took no further action.

The FBI repeatedly asked to move against the *Amerasia* group but F.D.R.'s Administration refused to allow arrests as it had done so many times in the past regarding other suspected spies. The chief architect of the embargo on FBI action was none other than James Forrestal, Secretary of the Navy. Despite the fact that Navy Intelligence documents had been pilfered, Forrestal asked the Department of Justice to restrain the FBI, its operating investigative arm, from taking action. The Department of Justice complied with Forrestal's appeal and nothing further was done until Harry S. Truman became President following Roosevelt's death.

FBI Chief J. Edgar Hoover, who had bristled at Forrestal's do-nothing request, went to Truman and argued that the *Amerasia* group constituted a nest of spies that had to be wiped out. Truman agreed but asked that no action be taken until the upcoming founding conference on the United Nations was concluded in San Francisco. He and others were worried about the effect that such arrests might have on that fragile enclave. Finally, on June 6, 1945, FBI agents arrested Jaffe, Mitchell, Larsen, Roth, Service, and Gayn.

All were brought before a grand jury. Mitchell, Service, and Gayn spoke on their own behalf, denying any wrongdoing. Evidence against them was weak and these three were dismissed. This was not the case for Jaffe, Roth, and Larsen. Although no evidence linked these three with passing secrets to a foreign power, chiefly the USSR or China, it was clear that they had stolen, received, or possessed Government documents.

The Department of Justice realized it did not have enough evidence to convict the three men on charges of espionage. The Department thought that even the charge of possessing stolen Government documents would do little good. Robert M. Hitchcock, a special assistant in charge of prosecuting the case, took the case to court on a Saturday morning which was later termed "a surreptitious affair" in that federal court rarely sits on Saturday mornings and that this unusual time for a hearing was designed to evade normal press coverage.

Albert Arent, Jaffe's lawyer, did most of the talking before Federal Judge James Proctor, explaining that Jaffe has merely acted "from an excess of journalistic zeal." Hitchcock agreed, saying that this "in substance" was the case. Judge Proctor asked for a probation report on Jaffe but Hitchcock stated, in essence, that such a report was not worth the trouble.

Jaffe had already pleaded guilty to possessing stolen Government documents. Judge Proctor fined him $2,500 which the publisher paid on the spot. Larsen pleaded *nolo contendere* (no contest) and was fined $500. Jaffe paid this fine also. The charges against Roth were dropped for lack of evidence.

The matter did not end there. Michigan Congressman George Dondero demanded an investigation. He wanted to know why the Department of Justice had so limply pursued the case. In early 1946 a House Judiciary Committee questioned Justice Department lawyers and FBI agents about the case. The Committee wanted to know why Hitchcock had made a "deal." The attorney replied that the Government had concerns that a strong argument might be made that its agents had gotten on the trail of the stolen documents by illegal means and that no convictions at all might have been the result without making a "deal." FBI agents simply stated that it was not the agency responsible for obtaining the stolen documents, and merely carried out Department of Justice orders. J. Edgar Hoover simply put the responsibility for the entire affair back in the hands of the OSS. This kind of jockeying for position would continue between the FBI and the OSS and its successor, the CIA, until the present day.

Meanwhile Amerasia folded and Jaffe and his associates went about their various businesses. All was silent concerning the case until Wisconsin's Senator Joseph McCarthy began roaring about Red spies in the State Department. He brought back the Amerasia case again in 1950 to ostensibly prove his point. The fulminating senator so loudly condemned John Stewart Service for supporting Mao Tse-tung and the Chinese Communists instead of Chiang Kai-shek that the State Department dismissed Service in 1951. Service sued and was reinstated in 1957. By then McCarthy was gone. So was the man who had strangely acted to momentarily shield the Amerasia group, James Forrestal.

Forrestal, following the Amerasia arrests and brief hearing, began to show signs of cracking under the pressures of his duties, first as Secretary of the Navy, then as Secretary of the newly-created Department of Defense. He had been, like OSS agent Bielaski, a successful Wall Street broker, making millions during the Depression. He had a reputation as a right-wing patriot and had been appointed Undersecretary of the Navy by President Roosevelt who happened to be his neighbor in upstate New York.

A workaholic, James Vincent Forrestal was named Secretary of the Navy in March 1945, at the very time OSS agents broke into the Amerasia offices in New York. It was therefore even stranger that Forrestal, just having taken over this high office, would, as one of his first official acts, urge the Department of Justice to restrain full-scale investigation of the Amerasia group. He never gave an explanation for his actions. Moreover, Forrestal's actions became increasingly unpredictable following the war.

He publicly condemned Communism and sided with fanatical witch hunters such as McCarthy. Like McCarthy, Forrestal saw Communists behind every tree. He began to tell friends that Communists were after him. He was nervous and irritable. On April 1, 1949, Forrestal received The Distinguished Service Medal from President Truman and wept openly. Truman was disturbed at Forrestal's behavior.

A few days later Forrestal said that Communists were following him everywhere, taking his picture, that his phones were "bugged," and that he had been marked for assassination by the Communists. He appeared to be a hopeless paranoid when he checked into the Bethesda Naval Hospital to "rest." On May 22, 1949, Forrestal suddenly leaped from his bed, ran through the rooms of his hospital suite and dove through a window, falling sixteen floors to his death in a suicide that perplexes historians to this day. His self-destruction was as inexplicable as his actions in the Amerasia case had been four years earlier.

AMES, ALDRICH HAZEN (AKA: "RICK")
U.S. Spy for the Soviet Union ▪ (1941–)

NEXT TO BENEDICT ARNOLD, ALDRICH AMES PROVED to be the most infamous traitor-spy in U.S. history. As a top-level CIA official, Ames fed the Soviets information on spies he himself, the agency, and the FBI had recruited, causing many of them to be executed. He did this for money, in fact, millions. Ames rationalized his treason by egotistically demeaning the CIA and labeling modern espionage an unimportant "sideshow." His aim in the one press conference he held after being exposed in the Spring of 1994 was obvious. By downplaying the role of the CIA and, perhaps, the reasons for its very existence, Ames hoped to excuse his own lethal acts. He had no remorse or regrets at having caused the murders of the very double agents whose lives were in his safekeeping.

The creation of Aldrich Hazen "Ricky" Ames, double agent, began many years earlier in the small town of River Falls, Wisconsin, near the Minnesota border. River Falls was a farming town of no more than 3,500 people in the 1940s. Then as now, most of the residents either worked in Minneapolis or St. Paul, only thirty miles distant, or labored long days on dairy farms.

As a small boy, Ames and his friends belonged to the Cub Scouts and routinely said the Pledge of Allegiance at their meetings. He bore a distinguished name in River Falls. His grandfather, Jesse Hazen Ames had been president of River Falls State Teachers College (now the University of Wisconsin at River Falls) from 1919 to 1946. Jesse Ames helped to install his son, Carleton Ames as a teacher of European and Far Eastern studies at the college.

Carleton Ames was a recluse and a heavy drinker. He never purchased his own whiskey, but asked friends to buy him bottles so that he would not embarrass the college faculty by appearing in liquor stores and bars. His wife Rachel, an accomplished English teacher, never spoke about her husband's problems with alcohol. Carleton and Rachel Ames had three children, Aldrich, whom they called Rick, and his younger sisters, Nancy and Allison.

The professorial Carleton was fond of poetry which he often read to young Aldrich. He also enjoyed theater and directed several plays at the college. The elder Ames' affection for theater was adopted by his son who appeared in high-school plays after the family moved to McLean, Virginia. That move occurred in 1951, when Carleton Ames quite suddenly went to work for the CIA. How he came to be recruited remains a mystery.

In McLean, Rachel Ames taught English and Carleton worked at CIA headquarters, never rising above his position of mid-level analyst. He was never involved in covert operations, although he worked for a time with James Jesus Angleton, chief of CIA counterintelligence operations.

Angleton was obsessed with discovering traitors in the CIA, convinced that someone was feeding the Russians top secret information. To that end, he turned the Agency upside-down from 1954 to 1974 when he was dismissed. Though he cast suspicion on several CIA workers, Angleton never did unearth the mole he believed to be dwelling inside the heart of the CIA. That mole would be none other than the son of the man who worked for him.

Aldrich Ames was a bright student at McLean High School, considered to be "witty," and a smooth orator on the debating team. He was also thought to be a good writer. Upon graduation, Aldrich attended George Washington University, majoring in history, as had his father. Before receiving his degree, Aldrich got a job with the CIA in 1959, one arranged by his father. At the age of twenty-one, he became one of the youngest agents ever to work for the CIA. He was thought of as a "glorified office boy," who went to college part-time while working at the Agency. Ames finally got his degree in 1967.

The first important posting Ames received was to Ankara, Turkey, a glamour hot spot of international spies, a city that came close to the kind of exotic locales depicted in spy novels and movies. All of the major powers had concentrated efforts in Ankara to glean secret military information.

Ames, who had pronounced language skills and wrote detailed and proficient reports, was sent to recruit new spies for the CIA, preferably those who would work against the Soviets. He failed miserably, not able to recruit a single foreign agent even though he had an enormous amount of money at his disposal to pay for secret information. Despite his lackluster performance, Ames "exuded this feeling of superiority to everyone else," according to one of his superiors at the time whose job it was to evaluate the youthful agent.

"He was a poor case officer," the official added. "He was on a rubber rung of a career ladder." Ames'

arrogant attitude, coupled with his failure to produce results, created, in the estimation of this CIA operative, "a kind of smoldering resentment." It was then believed that Ames would never rise much beyond the kind of position held by his father. Of course, the fact that his father held a solid if unimportant position with the CIA gave Ames the image that he was destined through his connections for greater things. This was not to be.

Other CIA employees had deep resentment for Ames, whom they felt represented "the worst case of nepotism in the history of the Agency," according to one fellow worker. Recalled from Ankara, Ames was assigned to CIA headquarters in Langley, Virginia, where his specific job was to recruit Soviet officials. Ames held this post from 1972 to 1976.

At the time, the CIA projected an image across the world as an invincible, daring, and courageous agency whose agents were heroes in the mold of great spy novels. That all changed in December 1974 when it was disclosed that the CIA was spying on American citizens in violation of its charter. (The CIA has no real authority to gather information in the Western Hemisphere, this being the exclusive province of the FBI and other federal agencies.) Then came shocking revelations that the CIA had employed unsavory Mafia figures to aid in the assassination of Cuban dictator Fidel Castro and that the Agency was involved with destabilizing democratically elected governments such as Chile.

The one high-point activity of the Agency at this time was its resolve to penetrate Soviet intelligence and, for some inexplicable reason, Aldrich Ames was placed into the heart of this effort. Yet, Ames did very little to aid these new operations. He was described by one co-worker in the Soviet section at the time as "just good old Rick, who did his routine work. We all took care of him." By then, the elder Ames had died, and Aldrich Ames was looked upon as a kind of mascot. He was not required to contribute ideas and plans. He was, by virtue of his father's role, unimportant or not, "institutionalized" at the CIA.

Ames nevertheless was given all available information on Soviets in the U.S., information which would later serve him well when he decided to sell out his country. And though he had never recruited a single foreign agent or gathered any valuable information on his own, this nepotistic cog was entrusted with top-secret data on potential Russian operatives, particularly those believed to be KGB agents working in the U.S.

By 1980, Ames was working out of CIA headquarters in New York City with specific instructions to recruit agents from the Soviet bloc missions to the United Nations. In 1980, Ames married for the first time, but his marriage to Nancy Ames quickly fell apart and the couple divorced in 1985.

In that year life drastically changed for Aldrich Ames. He was posted to Mexico City where he met an attractive Colombian socialite, Maria del Rosario

Casas. Rosario, as she was called, was then a cultural attaché in the Colombian Embassy in Mexico City where Ames was stationed to monitor Cuban and Soviet espionage activity. His first recruit to the CIA was none other than Miss Casas with whom he was emotionally involved.

Ames was rated GS-14 at the Agency with a yearly salary of approximately $70,000. The woman in his life, however, came from considerable wealth, or so it was claimed. Rosario Casas came from an upper-class family which was socially and politically prominent in Colombia. Her father, Pablo Casas Santofimio, was a mathematician and Liberal Party politician who, at one time or another, had been a university dean, state governor, and member of the Colombian senate. Her mother, Cecilia Depuy de Casas, was an extrovert Bohemian, a lover of music, whose extravagant lifestyle was well known in her native town of Bogota where she "adopted" several down-and-out salsa musicians.

Although Rosario attended schools for the rich, she and her family had very little money. A lover of literature, Maria enrolled at the University of the Andes in 1969, studying philosophy and letters. Oddly, her competitive mother was not to be outdone. She enrolled in the same courses as her daughter and attended many classes with her. "They were pathologically close," a friend of that period described the relationship. "Rosario spent more time with her mother than with people her own age, and her mother dominated her."

Rosario graduated summa cum laude in 1974 and she, along with her mother, joined the faculty of the University, Bogota's most prestigious academic center. She surprised friends in 1982 by abandoning her teaching profession and a $1,000-a-month salary to become a cultural attaché at the Colombian Embassy in Mexico City. This is where she met and was recruited into the CIA by Aldrich Ames. The couple married on August 10, 1985, the very year that Ames became the highest paid spy to ever work for the Soviet Union. In 1986, Ames took his bride to his next posting, Rome. Their only son, Paul, was born three years later. Rosario Ames returned only once to Colombia, in 1991. She had become an American citizen shortly after marrying Ames and did not maintain ties with former friends and relatives in Colombia, except for her mother.

At the 1991 Colombian family reunion, Ames and his wife brought along their toddler son. Cecilia Casas introduced Ames to her friends with great pride, saying that her American son-in-law was "a generous, loving father and good husband." Her reference to Ames' generosity had, no doubt, to do with the claimed fact that Ames had already given her more than $100,000, ostensibly to purchase a home for his family as he planned to soon retire to Colombia. By then Ames was wealthy, a millionaire, possessing riches not earned at the CIA but from the pockets of his KGB spymasters. Aldrich Ames had been selling out his country for more than five years.

When Ames met and married his second wife, Rosario, he was in the enviable position of vastly enriching his life. He had been put in charge of the CIA's Soviet branch of counterintelligence in an all-out effort to recruit double agents and uncover enemy spies. The very concern James Angleton had had for thirteen years, that a KGB mole or moles were operating inside the CIA, an idea that was thoroughly abandoned when the discredited Angleton was released in 1974, had come full circle within a decade. By 1985, the CIA pursued Angleton's beliefs with a vengeance but it had placed at the helm of its probes the very man who had become that mole.

When Ames was put in charge of the CIA's counterintelligence operations in 1983, he came in contact with several KGB operatives whom he contacted. Most of these worked out of the Russian Embassy in Washington. He remained in contact with these Russian agents for the next eight years. As usual, Ames recruited not a single Russian to the CIA cause. Instead he was recruited, although he later claimed that *he* recruited himself, that he voluntarily began to turn over CIA secrets to the Soviets, a decision he made in order to obtain $50,000.

The secrets Ames had to sell were the names of Soviets working for the U.S., both in America and in Russia. Without a shred of conscience, Ames accessed the names of agents from CIA computer files and turned over their dossiers to KGB agents. Ames would arrange to deliver secret documents to the Soviets by using "dead drops," in pipes, under slabs of cement, in hollowed-out trees. He would then began to find large amounts of American currency waiting for him.

With each payment, another Soviet agent working for the U.S. was sacrificed. The FBI was the first to notice that its intelligence links began to splinter in the mid-1980s, especially when two intelligence officers at the Soviet Embassy in Washington, D.C., men the FBI had recruited, suddenly disappeared. Valery F. Martinov and Sergei M. Motorin, who, at great risk, served as double agents for the U.S., were recalled to Moscow in 1986. They were quickly tried, convicted, and executed. These were Ames' first two victims. More than a dozen would follow.

At first it was suspected that Edward Lee Howard, a CIA officer who defected to Soviet Russia in 1985, or Clayton Lonetree, who had been a Marine guard at the U.S. Embassy in Moscow and had sold secrets to the Soviets, might have turned in the two Soviet double agents but since neither man had access to their dossiers, this suspicion was abandoned.

One of the most important double agents working for the West was Colonel Oleg Gordievsky. As chief KGB officer for the Soviets in London, Gordievsky was perhaps the key channel of top secret Russian information. Gordievsky was betrayed by Ames in early 1985, it was later determined. The KGB colonel, whose CIA code name was Tickle, was recalled to Moscow. Before Gordievsky could be shot, however,

British agents from MI6 performed a daring rescue and returned Gordievsky to England.

Another KGB official betrayed by Ames was code-named Cowl. He was a Soviet intelligence officer working in Moscow and who related to the CIA how the KGB used an invisible "spy dust" which could be used to track U.S. officials. Cowl was executed. A GRU (Soviet military intelligence) officer code-named Accord who regularly provided the CIA with information was identified to the KGB by Ames. He was executed. A KGB officer who gave the CIA regular information and was code-named Fitness was executed after Ames revealed his identity.

Other Russian agents working for the CIA and whom the mercenary Ames betrayed included: Million, a code name for a colonel in the military intelligence service, executed; Motorboat, a code name for an Eastern European security officer, arrested by the KGB and vanished; Pyrrhic, code name for a high-ranking Soviet official cooperating with the CIA, arrested by the KGB and vanished; Prologue, one of the KGB's top officers working in counterintelligence, arrested and vanished. Other double agents working for the West who disappeared after Ames identified them were code-named Blizzard, Gentile, and Weigh.

Meanwhile, as CIA operatives began to be shot, the traitor himself grew rich. His Soviet contacts paid him handsomely, so much money, in fact, that he became the highest paid Russian spy in history. He accumulated more than $2.5 million through his systematic sell-out of CIA double agents. By 1989, Ames told some associates that he had inherited considerable riches through his wife's wealthy relatives and he began to spend money lavishly.

In September 1989, Ames bought a $540,000 Cape Cod house in the exclusive suburb of Arlington, Virginia, outside of Washington, D.C. His neighbors were such prominent people as former Secretary of State James A. Baker III. It was in this neighborhood that the Soviets suggested that Ames set up his dead drops for the delivery of top secret information on double agents in the Soviet Union. On other occasions, Ames drove to Georgetown where he deposited tapes, film, paper reports in a prearranged dead drop. From these same locations, he retrieved cash payments from the Soviets.

For the next three months Ames spent an additional $99,000 to improve this home, as well as purchasing $7,000 worth of furniture. He paid $19,500 for a new Honda that year and in 1992, made a down payment of $25,000 for a Jaguar with $400-a-month payments. Both he and his wife suddenly had top-of-the-line credit cards. Their bills for these cards, from 1985 to 1993, exceeded $455,000.

His phone bills were enormous, although these were most likely conversations he and his wife were having with their Colombian relatives, rather than with Ames' contacts with KGB agents. Between 1990 and 1993, Ames ran up $29,800 with Ma Bell. He paid $25,000 in tuition for his wife at Georgetown

CIA turncoat and Soviet spy, Aldrich Ames, who was responsible for the deaths of untold numbers of U.S. agents. (AP/Wide World)

University from 1990 to 1993, and he was forever looking for good stocks to purchase, buying more than $165,000 in securities between 1985 and 1993. Some of these stock purchases, it was reported, were actually purchased for him by Soviet agents. He also gave his mother-in-law several hundred thousand dollars to purchase exclusive property in Colombia where he planned to retire. Moreover, Ames deposited more than $1 million in banks in the U.S., Colombia, and Switzerland. In the case of the foreign banks, some of the deposits were made by his KGB sponsors.

Ames was careful to make small deposits only in his accounts at U.S. banks, always under $9,999, knowing that anything above this amount banks were obligated to report to federal authorities under new laws designed to prevent huge amounts of cash being laundered by drug peddlers. For instance, the Dominion Bank in Virginia, after Ames was exposed and they reviewed his bank accounts, easily determined that the CIA traitor had long been "structuring" his deposits which invariably ranged from $3,000 to $8,500.

There was little or no suspicion at the CIA regarding Ames new-found wealth. The Agency for years employed wealthy people or their sons who did not require salaries and whose ambition it was to achieve a level of importance and some excitement (without the risk which was left to others) by being involved in espionage. Casting suspicion further aside was the universally accepted fact that Ames was a bespectacled, unimaginative, nepotistic creature of the CIA's own making. He would be the very last person the Agency would suspect of treason.

Still, some at the Agency, it was later claimed by director James Woolsey, began to seriously look for a KGB mole at the CIA headquarters in the early 1990s or sooner. Suspicion fell on Ames, whose unexplained wealth and the fact that he at one time "ran" Soviet double agents who later disappeared or were executed could have been the logical traitor. There were, however, more than 200 other agents who had access to the dossiers of the double agents and the FBI and CIA began to investigate them all in a rather leisurely exercise from 1987 to 1991 when the CIA was under the direction of William H. Webster, former head of the FBI. "The investigation floundered in a sea of uncertainty," one report had it.

A joint CIA-FBI task force, however, narrowed suspects to twenty Agency people by 1991. Ames was one of these. One CIA investigator had questioned Ames new-found wealth in 1989 but it was not until two years later that Ames was directly confronted by his CIA superiors as to the source of that wealth. It was then that he explained that the money had come from an inheritance, that it had been left to him and Rosario Ames by his wife's father. In 1992 the CIA conducted an investigation in Colombia but it never unearthed the will. Robert G. Torricelli, a New Jersey congressman serving on the House Intelligence Committee, later commented that, despite its vast resources, the CIA "appeared to make no significant effort to get that will."

Meanwhile, the smug and confident Ames, knowing he was being investigated, went on doing business with the KGB as usual. He was a vainglorious and egotistical creature who truly believed he could outsmart the best minds of American intelligence agencies, that, in fact his intellect was superior to all others. In short, he held his superiors in total contempt, as he did his oath of allegiance to the United States. He would later minimize his activities as if the betrayal of others and the forfeit of their lives was routine. "These people sell each other out all the time," he was to say. And he rationalized passing information to a regime that he himself would describe as "beastly" and "nasty" by insisting that with the passing of the Cold War it was not necessary to have intelligence-gathering agencies.

During this period, Ames's background was routinely inspected through the CIA process of regular checks. He was given lie-detector tests that he passed with flying colors. Ames later bragged that such polygraph tests were easy to pass. He explained that staying up all night before the test helped so that he was tired and utterly relaxed when hooked up to the lie detector. He also smirked advice: Get to know the person making the test and be friendly to put him off guard. He recalled joking and talking casually with the polygraph operator, reminding him in oblique ways that he, Ames, had undergone many such tests, that he was a 30-year veteran with the Agency.

Not only did Ames pass the polygraph tests, but he retained access to top-secret information on all KGB double spies working for the U.S., despite his being transferred to a less sensitive post, one where he monitored information regarding international drug trafficking. Although he was under suspicion of being a KGB mole, Ames could immediately access all data on Russian double agents. During the three years he was under suspicion, another two KGB agents, a Russian nuclear technician, and a senior Soviet counterintelligence officer were betrayed by him; all four were executed.

The continued success Ames had with his espionage activities, despite the fact that he knew he was under suspicion, undoubtedly convinced him that he would never be exposed. This overconfidence undoubtedly led him to commit a blatant blunder that eventually confirmed in the minds of his superiors that he was, indeed, the KGB mole in their midst. In October 1992, following CIA procedure, Ames informed his bosses that he would be traveling to Colombia to see his mother-in-law. Instead, Ames flew to Caracas, Venezuela. This time, Ames was placed under surveillance by FBI agents who tracked him to Caracas where they documented his meeting with a Soviet contact. Three weeks after Ames' trip to Venezuela, he made bank deposits totaling $86,700.

Still, incredibly, the CIA and FBI did not act. Ames was allowed to go on contacting Soviet officials and relaying secrets to them. The FBI did wire Ames' home and placed him under surveillance. His office at CIA headquarters, however, was not searched until June 1993. At that time, investigators searched Ames' desk in Room GVO6, a basement-like office at CIA headquarters in Langley, Virginia. They found many top secret documents on paper and on diskettes where information had been copied from the main CIA computer network dealing with double agents.

The FBI later placed wire taps on Ames' home phone, computer, and FAX lines. Agents monitored his every move, and other agents sifted through the daily garbage the family placed outside for pickup. In the garbage they found torn-up notes which they pieced together. Ames had written to his KGB contacts in Washington. The FBI also found typewriter ribbons from which they were able to read several messages Ames had written to his Soviet contacts.

By February 1994, the FBI felt that it had all the evidence it needed to convict the CIA mole. Agents arrested Ames and his wife Rosario on February 21, 1994. They were taken to the local jail in Alexandria,

Virginia, and held without bail, both charged with espionage. It was a bombshell that exploded in the face of the CIA. President William Clinton immediately ordered a protest filed with the Soviet government and, five days later, ordered the expulsion of Alexander Lysenko, a Soviet official at the Russian Embassy.

Lysenko, according to the FBI, had been Ames' closest contact and was described as the resident or chief intelligence officer at the Soviet Embassy. The State Department issued a hurried, terse comment: "We do not rule out taking additional action against any other Russian diplomats who are subsequently implicated in the Ames affair." As Lysenko packed his bags to leave the U.S., Russian officials seemed to boast of the liaison with Ames.

One KGB chief in Moscow, General Yevgeny Podkolzhin publicly mourned the loss of Ames: "This spy worked for us. . . . He defended our interests over there. He unmasked our spies, Soviet spies that revealed state secrets to governments abroad. For us it was a loss of a major advantage." KGB chief spokesman Yuri Kobaladze, however, attempted to minimize Ames' treason and espionage, saying that he was at a loss to understand why the U.S. was making such "a large-scale spy mania campaign over such an ordinary case." He went on to play down the importance of what Ames had done, reminding the press that the Cold War was over. "Now we don't have any constant enemies, only constant national interest." He went on to admit that Russia had to use people like Ames to get information since it lacked the sophisticated espionage methods of the U.S. "The CIA uses satellites. We don't not use satellites. Again, it really doesn't matter how you get information. You still have to get it."

Meanwhile, Ames sat in jail, placid, refusing to say anything, even when confronted with many compromising documents which had been taken from his home, letters to his Soviet station chief requesting more and more money, promising more secrets, along with top secret documents he had routinely copied either on paper or diskette and taken home with him from work. His only concern was for his wife, he said, insisting that she was innocent, and for his 5-year-son Paul.

Rosario Ames also and persistently claimed that she had nothing to do with espionage. "I never worked for the Soviets," she told investigators from her cell. "I have no idea about it. I have very little knowledge of Rick's work or his superiors." Agents told her that they knew her own husband had recruited her as a CIA informant and that she had been paid for those services. Rosario snapped a denial: "I was never interviewed, officially hired, or met anybody else from the CIA."

The 41-year-old woman told agents that she harbored great "anger, resentment, and bitterness" toward her 52-year-old husband. Then agents confronted her with shocking evidence of her direct involvement with her husband's espionage and treasonable activities. She was made aware that agents had tracked and videotaped her and Ames on September 9, 1993, as they attended a night program at her 4-year-old's school in suburban Virginia, and how they had afterward crossed the Potomac and had driven to Garfield Street and Garfield Terrace in a residential neighborhood of northwest Washington where they were "attempting to verify through a signal site that a dead drop he [Ames] had filled that day was unloaded."

Moreover, agents informed Mrs. Ames that they had months of wiretaps from her home in which she had been recorded time and again warning her husband to be careful and to conduct his espionage with the utmost caution. Rosario Ames not only knew about her husband's secret activities but she had aided him and had liberally spent money he received from his Russian spymasters.

Ames himself refused to talk. He knew he was facing a possible death penalty and he played for time and the possibility of making a deal. He would pinpoint his bank accounts but only if his son were allowed $500-a-month expenses and his wife was set free. Authorities took pity on the innocent child and allowed the expense payments to go to Rosario's mother who would take care of the boy. Rosario, however, would not go free.

Ames kept bargaining, until it was agreed, in exchange for his full cooperation, which undoubtedly meant he would tell all he knew about his Soviet contacts and the secrets he had funneled to the Russians, that Rosario would receive a minimum sentence and that he would get life without parole, not death. In the end, Rosario Ames received a five-year prison sentence.

Before Ames went permanently behind bars in federal prison to serve out his life term, he was interviewed by the press. In long, windy, rambling, and always self-serving statements, Ames confessed his guilt but in such a way as to excuse it. He had not really betrayed his country, only an antiquated system of gathering intelligence, a system that was in and of itself morally corrupt. "I had come to believe that the espionage business, as carried out by the CIA and a few other American agencies was and is a self-serving sham carried out by careerist bureaucrats who have managed to deceive several generations of American policy makers and the public about both the necessity and the value of their work." He could certainly have been describing himself.

Ames did express regret for the grief he had brought upon his family and the child he had genuinely loved. He also apologized to "those persons in the former Soviet Union and elsewhere who may have suffered from my actions." In this typically clever statement, Ames may have been apologizing not to the families of those who lost their lives when he exposed them, but to his Russian spymasters whom he had failed and whom he later insisted were "good people." It was as if he expected the Soviets to somehow still come to his rescue.

The spy then blathered on about his motives for selling out his country, chiefly to gain money, adding that he had to go on and on with his dangerous game because of his wife, that "extravagance on her part had been and continued to be a contributing fact to my espionage." Here then, was a man who would sell out anyone, including his own wife. He did admit that he had "betrayed a serious trust."

Ames equated that trust only with that of "a corrupt government official receiving a bribe or a stock speculator acting on inside information." This was the moral foundation that shaped Aldrich Ames, the shabby rationale of the crooked money-maker. Patriotism and love of country had nothing to do with the character and being of Aldrich Hazen Ames. He was a businessman in the business of selling secrets, wholly indifferent to the more than a dozen unmarked graves outside of Moscow.

The Ames case was a disaster for the CIA, one which seriously damaged its image as a professional intelligence gathering agency and, more importantly, damaged the core of its perceived character as an effective and vigilant watchdog of the nation's international security. At present the CIA spends more than $3 billion each year to provide that security (out of an overall estimated intelligence budget of $28 billion, much of which goes to the military, the FBI, and other agencies).

Measures to prevent the Agency from nurturing another Aldrich Ames have been taken. In 1995, President Clinton signed an executive order requiring all federal intelligence employees to file regular financial statements, as well as their travel in the U.S. and abroad. Whether or not such self-serving, arrogant bureaucrats like Ames will be weeded out of the CIA is another matter. Since the employee core structure of that and other federal intelligence agencies is based on that exact character, the task may be impossible.

[ALSO SEE: *James Jesus Angleton; CIA; FBI; Edward Lee Howard; KGB; Clayton Lonetree*]

AMTORG TRADING CORP.
Soviet Trade Group and Spy Network in U.S. ▪ (1924–)

NOT UNTIL FRANKLIN D. ROOSEVELT TOOK OFFICE AS President in 1933 were diplomatic relations between the U.S. and the Soviets established and the Russians allowed to open an Embassy and consulates throughout America. Long before that time, however, the Soviets established a trade organization in the U.S. called Amtorg Trading Corp., which was located in New York City. Outwardly the organization attempted to work out trade agreements between U.S. firms and Russia but the real purpose of this sprawling corporation was to conduct industrial and military espionage.

Amtorg employed hundreds of employees, mostly American Communists supervised by Russian intelligence officers. This spy organization had counterparts in Berlin (Handelsvertretung) and London (Arcos, Ltd.), which were initially much more productive than their American counterpart. The Communist Party in the U.S. was small by comparison with that in Germany and England, and therefore the U.S. lacked a widespread spy network. Moreover, the Depression years brought more intellectuals flocking to Amtorg than the working-class recruits the Soviets preferred.

In its earliest days, Amtorg was underfinanced and struggled to obtain American industrial secrets but with little success. Until 1933, Amtorg conducted no military espionage but when the Depression deepened, American Communists flocked to the trade organization, mostly to earn a living. The corporation began hiring dozens, then hundreds, of American citizens until its ranks swelled to more than 800 employees. Soviet spymaster Arthur Adams headed most of Amtorg's espionage in the late 1930s.

American Robert Pitcoff served on the Amtorg staff between 1934 and 1939. He later testified before HUAC (House Committee on Un-American Activities), stating that Amtorg gathered industrial secrets in the glass, paper, chemical, and aviation industries. One of Amtorg's outstanding spies was Juliet Stuart Poyntz, an American citizen who traveled to Moscow in 1934 where she was trained in espionage. She returned to the U.S. and worked hard to deliver American military secrets to the Soviets and to establish a network of spies for Russia.

When the bloody party purges of 1936 were conducted in Russia at Joseph Stalin's orders, Poyntz grew disillusioned with Communism and resigned from the party. She informed some friends that she intended to write her memoirs. No one ever saw a single page of this highly anticipated document. In late May or early June 1937, Juliet Poyntz, then fifty-one, left her Manhattan apartment in the American Women's Association Clubhouse and was never seen again.

It was later stated by Carlo Tresca, veteran New York radical and editor of *Il Marello* (The Hammer) that Poyntz was abducted by Communists fearful that she would betray the Soviet spy network she had helped to create in the U.S. Tresca went further, saying that she had been smuggled aboard a ship headed for Russia and had been murdered at sea by NKVD assassins, her weighted body dumped into the waters of the Atlantic. Tresca himself was executed in 1943 at the corner of Fifth Avenue and Fifteenth Street. He was shot gangland style by an assassin later named as Carmine "The Cigar" Galante who was to become one of the most powerful Mafia leaders in New York.

The busy offices of Amtorg in the late 1920s; the Soviet trading organization in New York City was a front for widespread industrial and military espionage.

Amtorg had scores of American Communists serving as spies who developed their own network outside of the trade organization. One such was the infamous Whittaker Chambers who worked for the Communist-backed *Daily Worker*. Chambers recalled later that he met many Amtorg workers who were involved in industrial and military espionage throughout the 1930s.

Amtorg continued to spy in America throughout World War II, despite the fact that its top members were closely watched by the FBI and other American intelligence agencies. Following the war, Amtorg spies flourished. One of the top Soviet spies in America at this time was American-born Judith Coplon, who worked in the Foreign Registration Office of the Department of Justice. Coplon, stationed in Washington, worked hand in glove with a number of top Russian spies employed at Amtorg in New York.

Espionage activities by Soviet agents at Amtorg diminished considerably following the early 1950s to the extent that the Russians all but abandoned the trade organization as a viable espionage arm in the U.S., relying upon its embassy and consulates to direct such activity.

[ALSO SEE: *Arthur Adams; Arcos Ltd.; Whittaker Chambers; Judith Coplon; Juliet Stuart Poyntz*]

ANDRE, JOHN
British Spymaster in America ▪ (1750–1780)

THE ULTIMATE GENTLEMAN SPY, JOHN ANDRE WAS both honorable and courageous. His virtuous personality, however, helped to bring him to the hangman's noose, much to the regret of his British army masters, as well as his own executioners. The espionage case of Major John Andre raised a significant question which has nagged American attorneys and historians down the centuries—when is a scout a spy or a spy a scout?

London-born, Andre's parents were Swiss and French. He lived in well-to-do surroundings and received a fine education in Geneva. As a youth Andre wrote poetry and performed in amateur theater productions. He was an ardent music-lover and a fair artist who liked to sketch pretty young ladies. He worked as a clerk in his father's business in London, where he met a high-stationed belle named Honoria

British spy John Andre, a dabbler in poetry, plays, and espionage.

Sneyd who became his fiancé, but his lowly income did not allow him to marry above his place. Miss Sneyd abandoned him.

Andre decided against becoming a merchant like his father. At twenty, he gathered his funds and purchased a commission in the British army in March 1771. Posted to Canada in 1774, Andre served with distinction for a year until he was captured at St. John's by Americans. The roughneck American captors had him strip to his underwear, while starving colonials rummaged through his clothing for gold or jewels. Later Andre proudly stated that he prevented them from stealing a small locket portrait of his fiancé Honoria by popping the locket in his mouth and hiding it beneath his tongue.

In a prisoner exchange, Andre was released and joined the staff of Sir William Howe in Philadelphia. Here, in 1777, Andre was appointed aide-de-camp to General Grey. When General Sir Henry Clinton was named commander-in-chief of the British Army, Andre accompanied Clinton to New York in 1778.

Cllinton was so impressed with Andre that he promoted the young man to major and appointed him head of all espionage activities. It was Andre's job to recruit spies from colonial households, especially those who would go behind the lines of the Continental Army to gather information on Washington's troop movements, supply lines, and battle plans. There were many Tories or Loyalist colonials who yearned for the authority of King George III, and Andre found many who volunteered their services, particularly since the British paid handsomely in gold for information.

Thus, Andre, at the age of twenty-seven, found himself in the powerful position of spymaster for Great Britain in America. He approached this job as he did all others, with considerable spirit of adventure. As with all of his other pursuits, John Andre was a dilettante at espionage. When not hiring spies in New York, Andre spent most of his time writing light-hearted plays and acting in them at the old John Street playhouse. His friends thought him a fine actor.

Andre's network of spies was vast. These Loyalists posed as patriots and diligently brought any kind of information to their spymaster they thought would be of use. One of Andre's most effective agents was Ann Bates, who audaciously visited Washington at his headquarters and freely spied on him and his lieutenants.

General Clinton was pleased with Andre's efforts but less inspired by his spymaster's counterintelligence activities. Andre found it difficult to ferret out patriot spies on his side of the lines. He managed to unearth a few American agents in New York City but he was unable to outwit his opposite number, American spymaster Major Benjamin Tallmadge, whose Culper Ring operated with devastating effect in New York City and on Long Island.

All that changed on May 10, 1779, when Joseph Stansbury, a Loyalist spy and courier, arrived in New York to shock Andre with the news that an American general, Benedict Arnold, was ready to defect to the British. Arnold would not only join the British ranks but provide his former enemy with secret information, all for a price, of course.

Arnold had been one of Washington's most able commanders. He had been fiercely loyal to the American cause and had shown himself courageous and inventive in battle after battle. At Quebec Arnold had stormed the British ramparts again and again until he was dragged away with many wounds. At Saratoga, he, more than any American commander, was responsible for the collapse of Gentleman Johnny Burgoyne's British army, attacking with relentless fury until the British troops had no more will to fight.

Through a lengthy correspondence, supplemented with Tory information, Andre learned that Arnold's intent was genuine. The American general felt that his colleagues, other than Washington, were jealous of his victories and conspired against him, that members of the Continental Congress were out to destroy him. Arnold's wife, the beautiful Margaret "Peggy" Shippen Arnold, was a devout Tory and supported the British to the marrow. She fueled Arnold's anger against fellow officers and politicians and passionately urged him to betray the American cause, which she sneeringly labeled as hopeless, doomed.

In Andre's secret correspondence with Arnold, the spymaster signed his missives "John Anderson." Arnold used the names "Monk," and "Mr. Moore." The letters they exchanged were in code. Both men possessed a copy of *Commentaries on the Laws of England* by William Blackstone. They used a number system wherein the first of three numbers referred to a page in that book, the second to a line in that book, the third to a word on the line in that book.

For more than a year, Andre and Arnold wrote to each other. Most of it involved haggling. Arnold wanted to be paid handsomely for his desertion and also demanded the rank of general in the British army and a command in that army. At the time, Arnold was without any command in the American army and Clinton felt that the potential traitor had little to offer. He refused Arnold's demands.

Andre's correspondence with Arnold all but evaporated when he accompanied Clinton to Charleston, South Carolina, where the British captured the city. When Andre returned to New York with Clinton, he was greeted with more letters from Arnold. This time, the American had something to offer. By now, Arnold's fortunes had improved. Washington had placed him in charge of the American stronghold at West Point. He offered to turn over the fortress for a general's rank in the British army and £20,000.

West Point was strategically situated. Anyone holding this fortress would control the lower portion of the Hudson River. The loss of West Point would be a severe blow to Washington. Clinton approved of a plan where Andre would meet with Arnold but he cautioned his spymaster that under no circumstances was Andre to meet behind the American lines and to remain in British uniform in the unlikely event that he should be caught. The impetuous, overly-confident Andre would ignore both orders.

On September 20, 1780, Andre boarded the British sloop *Vulture* which sailed up the Hudson to Haverstraw, six miles below Stoney Point. There Andre disembarked, was rowed to shore by Joshua Hett Smith, a Tory, and waited in the moonless night. Arnold appeared shortly after midnight, September 21, 1780. Andre agreed to Arnold's terms and the traitor immediately described how the British could successfully assault and capture West Point. Arnold turned over plans of the fortress. Andre felt confident that Arnold would surrender the garrison as soon as British troops appeared.

The time of night prevented Andre from returning to the *Vulture*. He accepted Arnold's invitation to spend the night at Smith's farmhouse behind American lines. Early the next morning, while Andre and Arnold were having breakfast, they were startled at the sound of cannon fire. Andre left the second-story room where he was breakfasting, racing to a balcony with a clear view of the Hudson. His face went pale when he saw the *Vulture* weighing anchor. Farmer Smith stepped to the balcony to witness the river attack, blurting: "Why . . . why, she's on fire!" A four-pound shot had struck the vessel and smoke was billowing from her as she pulled away from Teller's Point.

Andre's escape route had been eliminated. Arnold sat down and wrote a pass for "John Anderson," signing his own name. Andre would have to take an overland route of about forty miles to New York City. Arnold told Andre that Smith would guide him back to the British lines. Smith, however, felt uncomfortable about Andre's attire, stating that he would be fired upon by roving American patrols if they spotted Andre in his British uniform. He insisted that Andre change into civilian dress. Andre reluctantly agreed to discard his uniform and don civilian clothes, but kept his expensive chamois-topped boots. Into these boots, Andre jammed the six pages of information on West Point which Arnold had given him.

Arnold then abruptly left the Smith house on horse, riding back toward West Point. Smith was not happy with his assignment, complaining of ague and the dangers involved. He, Andre, and a black slave mounted horses and rode slowly toward White Plains. Farmer Smith, a garrulous type, stopped to chat with neighbors they met along the way making Andre all the more nervous. At one point Smith got off his horse and shared swigs of corn liquor with a friendly farmer.

Andre did not stop to imbibe, but rode ahead to join the slave who was leading the way. That night, as the trio rode under the branches of a thick wood, an American night patrol commanded by Captain Ebenezer Boyd appeared out of the shadows, guns pointing. Smith smiled downward from his saddle into the light of a lantern held high by Captain Boyd.

Boyd demanded to know who the riders were. Smith affably produced a safe-conduct which read:

"Joshua Smith has permission to pass the Guards to the White Plains, and to return; he being on public business by my direction—B. Arnold."

Captain Boyd told Smith and his party to "take the Armonk Road. Less traffic. The road to Tarrytown is swarming with troops." The American captain then suggested that the trio rest for the night somewhere and resume their journey in daylight so they would not lose their way.

Smith led the way to the farmhouse of Andreas Miller, described to Andre as "a loyal Scot." The British spymaster spent an uneasy night, complaining to Smith that it was taking too long to reach his own lines. Early the next morning, Smith and his slave stopped their horses three miles from the British lines. Smith told Andre that it was too risky for him to go farther and that the spy had only a short ride around Tarrytown and described the roads to take.

Andre rode off alone on the road to Tarrytown. His brown horse clattered over the wooden boards of Clark's Kill Bridge at Sleepy Hollow, where three American militiamen were playing cards. The three—John Paulding, Isaac Van Wart, and David Williams—threw down their cards and grabbed their muskets. They wore British greatcoats which they had stolen from prisoners recently captured in a skirmish.

Seeing the British coats, Andre rode up to the men, thinking them British soldiers. "Good morning," he said cheerfully, "I hope you belong to our party."

The capture of Major John Andre.

Paulding eyed the handsome man in the saddle with suspicion. "What party?"

"The—the lower party." replied Andre, and he waved in the direction of the British lines.

Paulding, a crafty, canny person who, along with his companions, was basically a roughneck thief. He stole from both British and American victims, it mattered not to him. "We are," Paulding lied.

Andre let loose a sigh of relief. "Good. I am Major John Andre of his Majesty's Army. I have been conducting some secret and important business in American territory. I shall be glad to have your protection as far as the lines."

William held the reins of Andre's horse, asking: "How can you prove yourself?"

"I have a pass signed by the American General Arnold," Andre blurted. "It is made out in the name of John Anderson, but my own name is engraved on my watch."

With that, Andre showed the men the pass, which read: "Permit Mr. John Anderson to pass the Guards to the White Plains, or, below, if chuses . . ." Andre then flicked open the back of his watch to show his real name.

The three militiamen suddenly aimed their muskets at Andre and told him that he was their prisoner, that they were members of the "Upper Party," meaning the American army. Ever the actor, Andre laughed and told the men that he was only testing them, that he had taken the gold watch from a dead British soldier and that he was really an American officer on important business. The militiamen ignored his statements, ordering him to undress.

Andre slipped off his cloak, coat, vest, shirt, and breeches, angrily telling the militiamen: "You will bring yourselves into trouble for interfering with General Arnold's business!" When Andre removed his boots, the telltale six papers Arnold had given him fell out.

Paulding grabbed these sheafs and looked them over. "Well now, by God, what's this?" he asked. Then, after realizing that he was holding the plans for West Point, Paulding exclaimed: "By God, he's a spy!"

Andre was marched at gunpoint to the nearest American outpost which was commanded by Colonel John Jameson. En route, Andre offered his captors ten thousand guineas or "any quantity of drygoods," if the men would let him go. The three militiamen were practical rascals, however. They informed their captive that they already had the forty gold Continental gold pieces and the gold watch taken from his pockets. They militiamen also knew that they would be given Andre's horse and saddle. All of these treasures "in the hand" were more important than promises of undeliverable great riches.

Prodded by muskets, Andre was marched along sheep paths to a ramshackle set of buildings known as Sands' Mills, outside of Armonk. At dusk, he was taken before Colonel Jameson who was bewildered by the entire story. He examined the six papers and the pass signed by Arnold. Jameson could make nothing of it, believing that Andre was, indeed, "Merchant John Anderson." Jameson had just received a message from General Arnold, telling him that "Anderson" was to be sent to Arnold "as soon as he put in an appearance." (Arnold had not known that Andre was a prisoner, but had sent this message to Colonel Jameson as a precaution, in the unlikely event that Andre was captured.)

Despite the clamor of the three militiamen who insisted that Andre was a spy, the "merchant" was told to put on his clothes, was given a meal of bread and milk, then sent toward West Point and General Arnold by a detail commanded by Lieutenant Solomon Allen. Some hours later, Major Benjamin Tallmadge, the American spymaster, arrived at Sands' Mill. He was told the story of Andre's capture and that he had been sent on to General Arnold. Tallmadge could not study the six papers that had fallen from Andre's boots as these documents had been sent by Colonel Jameson to Washington. Tallmadge, however, talked to the three militiamen and quickly determined that Andre was, indeed, a spy. He was suspicious of Arnold (and always had been). Tallmadge insisted that Andre be returned to Sands' Mill.

Colonel Jameson, although he outranked Tallmadge, agreed to recall the prisoner and sent another detail after Allen's group of men. Jameson, nevertheless, was not a man to breach military protocol. He sent a messenger to General Arnold explaining the entire affair. Andre was returned to Sands Mill as a messenger sped to West Point where, the next day, he delivered the news of Major Andre's arrest. Oddly, on that very day, a prearranged breakfast with General Washington and Lafayette occurred. Arnold and his wife Peggy sat down with Washington and his devoted aide, Marquis de Lafayette, when the messenger arrived.

Arnold read the note from Jameson which announced Andre's arrest. Coolly, Arnold excused himself and went to his quarters. He then called his wife to his room and told her that Andre had been arrested. She swooned into a faint and Arnold fled. It was a contrived collapse, one wherein Washington and Lafayette discovered the unconscious woman and were considerably distracted by tending to her, giving the traitor time to escape.

Arnold rode wildly on horseback to the Hudson River where he commandeered a small, fast boat. He sailed to New York City and reached the British lines. Clinton kept his word by appointing Arnold a brigadier general in the British Army and rewarding his treason with a considerable payment, not for the delivery of West Point but for the loss of Arnold's American property.

Andre, on the other hand, was in a hopeless position. He had been caught in civilian clothes and, on September 27, 1780, was brought before a tribunal of American generals on Washington's orders, charged with being a spy. At his trial, Andre argued that he had gone behind American lines wearing his uniform but, being unable to return to the sloop *Vulture* the same way, he could not be held responsible for wearing civilian clothes when he was virtually a captive who had no way to return to British lines. He was

The hanging of Andre; he went to his death bravely.

nevertheless convicted of being a spy and condemned to death.

Clinton heard the news with shock. He sent a message to Washington asking the American commander to reprieve "my scout," and included a letter from Arnold to Washington. Arnold explained how Andre came to be wearing civilian clothes, that he, Arnold, had insisted upon the disguise, and that he, Arnold, took full responsibility. Washington refused clemency. Next, a delegation of British officers appeared at Washington's headquarters under a flag of truce to beg for Andre's life. Washington said he would spare the young adventurer if the British would exchange Arnold for Andre. When he heard the news that Andre had been condemned, Arnold went to Clinton and offered to be exchanged for Andre.

Clinton told Arnold that this was unacceptable, that he had given his word. The British general then informed Washington that he would not turn over Arnold. Andre was ordered to be hanged on October 2, 1780. The condemned spy had asked Washington for a more fitting execution, to be shot by a firing squad rather than hanging. This request was refused.

The young Andre, a victim of circumstances and his own befuddled actions, chose to die without showing the slightest bit of fear. With a muffle of drums he was escorted to the scaffold by two sub-alterns. Major Tallmadge, who much admired him, was at Andre's side. The two chatted about the fine day dawning. Andre stood on a horse-drawn cart beneath a scaffold from which a noose dangled. A blindfold was placed about the young man's eyes and the rope about his neck. An eye-witness described the next moments: "The cart moves with a sudden fitful jerk from under his feet . . . John Andre swings loose into the abyss of Eternity . . . hangs as lifeless and inert as an old meal bag, quite dead."

It remains to be asked why Washington was so adamant in his condemnation of Andre. He was aware that Andre had not intended to disguise himself as a spy when entering American lines in full British uniform and that he attempted to leave those lines in civilian dress only as a means of returning to his own lines. Some have advanced the belief that Washington was still bitter about the British hanging of American spy Nathan Hale and sought retaliation. Yet, such vindictiveness was not in Washington's character and personality.

The entire Arnold-Andre affair was one of bungled, amateur espionage that sent one man to premature death and another to eternal shame as the arch traitor of his country.

[ALSO SEE: *Benedict Arnold; Ann Bates; Culper Ring; Nathan Hale; Benjamin Tallmadge*]

KGB chief Yuri Andropov who modernized Soviet espionage and later became the leader of the USSR.

ANDROPOV, YURI VLADIMIROVICH
Soviet Spymaster ▪ (1915–1984)

BORN IN SOUTHERN RUSSIA NEAR THE VOLGA, Andropov was the son of a railway official. He took odd jobs as he worked his way through technical college and became active in the Young Communist League, the Komsomol. His party activities landed him a job as a youth leader and organizer in Karelia in the late 1930s during the Soviet-Finnish War.

As a party hack and bureaucratic cog working in Leningrad during World War II, Andropov managed to excuse himself from military duty and, unlike millions of his countrymen, never faced a Nazi bullet. He possessed no military decorations and had nothing to recommend him to higher office. Andropov, however, was clever and tenacious, clawing his way up the party ladder.

Andropov was named a counselor to the Soviet Embassy in Budapest and wormed his way to the ambassadorship just in time to witness the Hungarian uprising in 1956. It was Andropov who lured the leaders of the Hungarian Freedom Fighters to a so-called conciliatory meeting and then had them all arrested and later executed. The lure was Andropov's promise that they would be given safe conduct to the West. Moreover, Andropov then arranged to have the masses of Soviet tanks enter Budapest to create wholesale slaughter of the remaining rebels.

Such ruthlessness was appreciated by the brutal Russian leaders who promoted Andropov to higher positions. Nikita Khrushchev, the most savage of Russian leaders after Stalin, appointed Andropov Chairman of the Committee of State Security (KGB) in 1967. With this appointment, Russia now had a spymaster who was as cold-blooded a killer as he was a cunning espionage chief.

Andropov accelerated Soviet spying around the world, particularly in Europe, England, and the United States. Scores of talented spies were sent forth and as many as 105 Soviet agents were expelled from the Russian Embassy in London during Andropov's directorship of the KGB.

Khrushchev purposely misled internal dissidents. He denounced Stalinist methods and even Stalin himself, and dissidents began to surface in substantial numbers. They interpreted his actions and statements as a signal of change. Khrushchev, however, was just as ruthless a Communist as Stalin had been—dedicated to Communist dogma and violently opposed to anyone who might wish to revise its dictatorial philosophy. When the dissidents echoed Khrushchev's remarks, they were identified as opponents to the regime. Andropov had thousands of these dissidents arrested and imprisoned in the more than thirty "psychiatric prisons" he had established. He labeled those who opposed Communism as insane.

Yet, with other dissidents, particularly writers and artists who had some standing with the West, Andropov broke with the brutal ways of his predecessor, Lavrenti Beria. Instead of conducting Beria's purges, Andropov simply allowed dissidents to leave the USSR. If they were reluctant, he had them deported to the West where they could do no internal damage to the Communist dictatorship.

Andropov also disliked the shabby image of his KGB agents. He mocked their ancient, baggy, double-breasted suits, their broad-brimmed hats and wrinkled raincoats. He ordered all agents to wear Western cut suits, to get Western haircuts, and to look as modern and as well dressed as their CIA and MI6 counterparts. Some later said that Andropov got his new image for the KGB from James Bond novels; top secret policeman was a great student of Western culture, although there is no record of his ever having visited a Western country. He studied English and spoke it fluently. He then conquered German and several other languages. He also insisted that his new crop of agents be multilingual.

A firm believer in disinformation, Andropov upgraded the KGB department responsible for spreading disinformation, retitling it Directorate A. At the time he stated: "The political role of the USSR must be supported abroad by the dissemination of false news and provocative information." Much of Andropov's modern espionage ideas were culled, it was reported, from the British traitor and spy, Kim Philby, who had defected to Russia.

For many years, the spymaster promoted the KGB and his agents as ethical, clean-cut national heroes, featuring them in Russian novels, movies, and television series. Agents were depicted as decent and highly intelligent. Their opponents from the imperialistic West were portrayed as seedy, conniving thugs who stole secrets and murdered without logic and shame.

When Andropov became President of the USSR he continued to promote a self-image of being cultured and sophisticated, head and shoulders above the savage leaders who had preceded him. He was nevertheless no different than any Communist dictator. Though he talked lavishly of ending the nuclear arms race and tried to spread the belief that Russia was a nation seeking peace, he surrounded himself with his own KGB henchman to support his position of power, while he stamped out political opposition at home and aggressively promoted Communism abroad. He did not deviate until his death in February 1984. He was diehard Communist to the last gasp.

[ALSO SEE: *Lavrenti Beria, KGB; NKVD; Kim Philby*]

ANGLETON, JAMES JESUS
CIA Counter-intelligence Chief ▪ (1911–1980)

ANGLETON BEGAN HIS CAREER IN ESPIONAGE IN THE old OSS, working with his father in Italy. When President Truman disbanded the OSS, he allowed Angleton to remain in Italy, which he almost single-handedly prevented from going Communist. Angleton had maintained his friendships with left-wing groups and, particularly, with Communist leader Palmiro Togliatti. At this time, Angleton also developed deep relationships with leaders of the Jewish underground who later became the chiefs of the Mossad, Israel's secret service.

Because of these ties, Angleton entered the CIA with the clear understanding that he would head the Israeli desk. Through Angleton, the Mossad found a firm friend and much help in intelligence gathering. Most of Angleton's efforts, however, were directed at counter-intelligence. The lean, tall Angleton, appeared almost cadaverous as he marched through CIA headquarters in Virginia, attempting to ferret out defectors. He would spend endless hours studying every detail concerning a suspect.

On the international front, Angleton was obsessed with the KGB and believed that it plotted to control the world. He scoffed at the rift between Stalin and Tito, believing this was a sham as was the split between Russia and China. These were political feints to Angleton, insidious designs to make the naive West let down its guard. What convinced Angleton that

James Jesus Angleton, the CIA's chief of counterintelligence and notorious "molehunter."

there was a KGB mole or moles inside the CIA was the claim made by a KGB defector, Anatoli Golytsin, of such a counterspy. This former KGB spy, who was once described as "a charming con artist," insisted that a Soviet spy worked right in the heart of the CIA headquarters in Langley, Virginia. Angleton was the only CIA official who took Golytsin seriously. He spent thirteen years, from 1961 to 1974, doggedly pursuing this mole in a vain and often ridiculous effort.

No one seemed to elude Angleton's suspicious gaze. He dined regularly with British agent Kim Philby when Philby visited Washington. Both men could be seen regularly at Harvey's Restaurant, chatting amiably. Philby, who was then a Soviet counter-intelligence agent, later stated that "the real nature of my interest he [Angleton] did not know." This was a serious miscalculation on Philby's part. Angleton suspected him as a double agent from the start and said so to his superiors. Only when Philby defected from the British secret service did CIA chiefs admit Angleton had been correct in his suspicions.

Angleton became an institution at the CIA. His authority was unchallenged. He walked into director Allen Dulles' office unannounced at any time. When Richard Helms took over from Dulles, he permitted Angleton to continue to operate autonomously, utilizing an enormous budget. All of this came to an end when William Colby became director of the CIA. Both men had disliked each other since their days together in the old OSS.

Colby thought little of Angleton's counter-intelligence activities, believing this to be a waste of money, effort, and time. In December 1974, Colby relieved Angleton of his duties with the Israeli desk and counter-intelligence. Colby allowed Angleton to stay on with the CIA as a consultant, but expected that Angleton's downgrading would cause him to resign. When Angleton hung on, Colby leaked a story that Angleton was spying on American agents by opening CIA mail.

Believing that there was a plot against him, Angleton resigned. He made no secret of his dislike for the CIA chief, telling associates that Colby had irreparably damaged the CIA by revealing its secrets to the Church Commission and by dismantling the counter-intelligence branch, a point not lost on present-day CIA chiefs when looking back on the millionaire mole in their midst, Aldrich Ames.

The so-called "Molehunt" relentlessly conducted by Angleton would cast suspicion on more than 120 CIA employees. Eighteen of these were either demoted or fired. More than $700,000 was paid to these tainted victims as compensation in what was later dubbed the "Mole Relief Fund."

Angleton retired to fly-fishing and memories. His like has not been seen since at the CIA. He was a singular sentinel whose post is presently, ominously vacant.

[ALSO SEE: *Aldrich Ames; CIA; William Colby; Allen Dulles; Anatoli Golytsin; Richard Helms; KGB; Mossad; Kim Philby; OSS*]

ARCOS LTD.
Soviet Trade Group and Spy Network in England ▪ (1924–1927)

FOLLOWING THE RUSSIAN REVOLUTION, THE NEWLY-born Soviet Union had great difficulties in establishing diplomatic relations with other countries, particularly those in the West. In 1924, when diplomatic relations were established between England and the Soviets, the Russians also established a trade organization, Arcos Ltd. in London. Ostensibly its purpose was to develop trade between the two countries, but the real Soviet aim was to have a secret espionage organization.

Occupying two office blocks in Moorgate, Arcos staffed twice the number of personnel legally allowed. Most of the staff members spent their time spying on British industry and the armed forces. This was done, however, strictly through the sanctions of the British Communist Party, which was only a splinter political group with no real influence in the politics or decisions of the government.

Similar trade organizations had been established in Germany (Handelsvertretung) and in the U.S. (Amtorg), and these trade groups proved to be much more successful than their British counterpart. The ineffectiveness of Arcos had much to do with the disinterest in revolutionary causes shown by the British public as well as its political leaders.

For two years Arcos spied openly in Britain without obtaining any significant military or industrial information. It went unnoticed by the government until 1926 when Arcos made a bold but blundering move to foment social unrest in England. That year miners led a general strike that prompted naive Russian leaders to believe that England was ready for revolution. Moscow, through Arcos, immediately sent £250,000 to the strikers.

British government officials responded with fierce accusations that a foreign power was dramatically interfering with the domestic affairs of England. Britain's Trades Union Congress agreed, compelling the miners and other workers' unions to return the money to Russia. Many who had lobbied for the trade agreement between England and Soviet Russia felt betrayed. Further agitating the situation was the grim fact that two American anarchists, Nicola Sacco and Bartolomeo Vanzetti, were about to be executed for robbery-murder and, because of their leftist political beliefs, the Communist International began a thunderous propaganda campaign to save the two condemned men. Communist agitators, most of whom were under the direction of Arcos, harangued thousands daily in London's public squares, which led to widespread riots and arrests.

All of this was coupled by the Communists to the General Strike that they thought to finance. The Soviet Chargé d'Affaires was accused by Foreign Secretary Sir Austen Chamberlain of making propaganda and he warned the Soviet Union "in the gravest terms that there are limits beyond which it is dangerous to drive public opinion."

Home Secretary Sir William Joynson-Hicks went much further in addressing the House of Commons about Russia's attempted financing of the British strikers: "Here in our own land, as everywhere, we have the machinations of the Russian government seeking to destroy all that we hold dear. Not content with the misery of their own country, they are seeking to extend that misery to other countries, seeking to destroy civilization, seeking to destroy what they call the 'capitalist system,' and, because we are the head and forefront of civilization throughout the world, it is the people of Great Britain who have to bear the brunt of the first attack of the Soviet Union."

Winston Churchill, Chancellor of the Exchequer and leading strike breaker, became explosive. Churchill threatened to break off all trade relations with the Soviets. MI5, British counterintelligence, immediately began surveillance of the more than 300 Arcos employees who flitted freely about London, blatantly seeking confidential information on industrial formulas, equipment, and manufacturing procedures, as well classified military information.

It was not uncommon for a Russian, speaking broken English, to slip into a pub and openly quiz soldiers on leave about army posts and troop dispositions, or sailors about the movements of Britain's capital ships. MI5, working with the Special Branch of Scotland Yard, learned that N. K. Jilinsky, a chief at Arcos, was a Soviet spymaster with Moscow's espionage organization, and that his link at the Soviet Embassy was Igor Khopliakin, another chief of the Soviet spy group. When Khopliakin was replaced, his successor, L. B. Khinchuk, was denied diplomatic immunity. This so disturbed Russian officials at the Embassy in London that they sent off an urgent dispatch to Moscow, requesting the temporary suspension of all documents relating to espionage. The dispatch was intercepted by MI5.

More serious relations unfolded. A technician for the Royal Air Force was arrested on the suspicion of spying for the Russians. In his possession agents found classified drawings and calculations. The technician admitted that he had intended to deliver these secret documents to Arcos and that he had been supplying the trade organization with similar classified information for some time. Then MI5 unearthed another spy, an Englishman who had been selling secrets to the highest bidder for years until he was converted by the German Communist Party into a dedicated Soviet agent.

This agent, who worked at a British aircraft factory that manufactured military planes, had stolen top secret plans for a new British monoplane fighter, as well as documents dealing with newly-created machine-guns built by Vickers. Then, in early 1927, a top-secret RAF plan dealing with strategic aerial bombardment was suddenly missing from sealed government files.

Agents from Scotland Yard's Special Branch and MI5 went to British government officials with this story, saying that they believed the missing document could be found in the offices of Arcos. Approval was given to raid Arcos. Prime Minister Stanley Baldwin endorsed the raid which took place on May 12, 1927. Police stormed into the headquarters of the Russian trade organization at No. 49 Moorgate.

Breaking down a door in the basement, officers found two men and a woman frantically burning papers. One man was an Arcos official, the other being the chief cipher clerk at the Soviet Embassy. The clerk fought officers but was subdued. He was searched and officers found a precious list of Russian agents and "letter-box" drops (locations where messages and secret documents were exchanged) in the U.S., Great Britain, several South American countries, as well as Commonwealth countries.

This discovery justified the seizure of all documents which police took away in many trucks. Russian clerks refused to provide investigators with the combination numbers for the many heavy safes in the Arcos offices, so agents blew them open with explosives. Although the RAF document was never found (it was thought to have been burned when police were breaking down the doors), many other classified British government documents were discovered in the files, proving that the trade organization had been nothing but a cover. Stunned British leaders learned that all vital military army and navy bases, especially those at Plymouth and Aldershot, had been penetrated by Soviet agents working at Arcos.

Furious, the British government ordered all Arcos employees to leave England immediately. The Soviet Embassy was ordered closed and, on May 26, 1927, all diplomatic relations between England and the Soviet Union were severed. Not a single Russian was allowed to enter England for two years. Amtorg, the fake Russian trade organization in the U.S. fared much better. Amtorg, established about the same time as Arcos, performed widespread espionage activities in the U.S. throughout the 1920s and 1930s and was not exposed until the dawn of World War II.

[ALSO SEE: *Amtorg*]

ARMAND, MAJOR LE COMTE
Suspected French Spy for Austria ▪ (? –1918)

IN THE SPRING OF 1917 THE CRUMBLING EMPIRE OF Austria-Hungary sought to make a separate peace and step out of World War I. The new emperor, Charles (Karl), was fearful of his ally, Germany, which totally dominated the Central Powers, and dispatched an envoy to conduct secret talks with the French with the hope of taking Austria out of the conflict.

The talks progressed slowly, then stopped altogether when Charles refused give up Trieste to the Italians. The Premier of France, Paul Painlevé—realizing that French troops were on the verge of mutiny, civilians bordering on another revolution, and that the Germans were preparing another massive offensive—desperately sought to reopen talks with the Austrians. In this, his ally, Lloyd George of Great Britain, concurred.

Painlevé selected the Count of Armand, one of the richest men in France with an estimated fortune of £4 million, a young, apparently eager patriot who had served well in the Deuxième Bureau (French Military Intelligence) as his new emissary to Austria. Armand was also the personal friend of Count Nicolas Rovertera, personal adviser to Emperor Charles of Austria. Armand immediately contacted Rovertera, inviting him to his palatial estate in Fribourg, Switzerland.

The two met and conducted long negotiations to end the war between Austro-Hungary and the Allies. Throughout August 1917, both men jockeyed back and forth for better positions and by the time the hard-pressed Painlevé government fell, little had been accomplished. The new French Premier, Georges Clemenceau, called "The Tiger" because of his tenacity, asked Armand to continue his talks with Rovertera, promising to appoint the young man ambassador to some unspecified post.

Armand met again with Rovertera in Switzerland but Charles adamantly insisted that he would not give up Trieste, the eternal sticking point of the negotiations. The talks dragged on into the Spring of 1918, going nowhere.

Then, fearful that the Germans had discovered these secret negotiations, Austria's Prime Minister, Ottokar Czernin, publicly announced the fact that the secret talks had been taking place between Armand and Rovertera, all at Clemenceau's request. He stated that the talks had failed, not because his emperor refused to give up Trieste but because France would not relinquish its claims in Alsace-Lorraine.

Clemenceau roared back: "Count Czernin has lied!" and recalled Armand from Switzerland, reassigning him not to his old post at the Deuxième Bureau but to the staff of an army corps stationed in Orleans. Clemenceau came to believe that Armand had somehow sabotaged the peace negotiations although evidence to that end was never made public.

Armand carried out his duties in Orleans until one morning, when returning from his customary ride, he entered his rooms to find agents from the Sureté searching the place. When he objected, an agent smashed him in the face, knocking him down. He was threatened. He was held by several agents who stripped him of his clothes. They stated they were looking for documents that would prove him a traitor.

Finding nothing, the agents left and Armand reported the incident to his commanding general. He asked permission to go to Paris and make a formal complaint to the Minister of War, as well as demand an explanation. In Paris, Armand waited for days to see the Minister who refused an audience with him.

A few days later, the Deuxième Bureau asked Armand to come to its headquarters. Upon his arrival, Armand was met by one of his former superiors. This officer accused Armand of having "traitorous intercourse with the enemy." The Count attempted to defend himself but the officer refused to listen to his arguments. Armand was shocked into silence. Before the officer left the room, he pointed to a revolver he had left on the table, telling Armand that: "There is the only honorable course for you." The Count was left alone. A single shot rang out. He was found dead, sprawled on the table, a few moments later. Armand's relatives were then informed that he had died following an attack of influenza.

[ALSO SEE: *Deuxième Bureau; Sureté*]

ARNOLD, BENEDICT
American Spy & Traitor for England ▪ (1741–1801)

THE BRAND OF "TRAITOR" AND THE NAME OF Benedict Arnold are synonymous in the heritage of America. Arnold was the arch-betrayer of the American Revolution but, in grim irony, he was also one of Revolution's greatest patriots and heroes. No American fell further from the grace of history and the respect of his fellow men. His fall was greater than any other American traitor, for he did not collapse out of cowardice; he was the bravest of the brave. His desertion came about through envy and through the subtle, constant persuasion of a beautiful wife devoted to Great Britain, King George III, and the destruction of the Revolution.

Arnold was born in Norwich, Connecticut, on January 14, 1741. He was the second son born to Hannah Arnold; the first, also named Benedict, died in infancy. Only he and a sister, named Hannah after her mother, survived out of six births. Arnold had little formal education, serving as an apprentice in a Norwich drugstore at an early age to help support a family dominated by an alcoholic father. At the age of eighteen, Arnold joined a New York militia company and marched away to serve on the frontier during the French and Indian War. Homesick, he deserted within a few months.

A few years later Arnold went to New Haven where he became a merchant, trading pork and rum. His spinster sister joined him, keeping his scant books. Arnold was not a successful businessman. He was always running out of money and any creditor who dared to mention a debt stood the chance of being challenged to a duel. In February 1767, Arnold married Margaret Mansfield, the daughter of Samuel Mansfield, high sheriff of New Haven and one of the town's most successful waterfront merchants. Arnold prospered, opened a pharmacy, and became a well-to-do druggist. He also owned a bookstore in New Haven. Next, Arnold built himself a fine new house, a mansion really, which was purchased through profits Arnold made in trading sugar from the Indies.

With time on his hands, Arnold came to be a follower of Patrick Henry and other colonists demanding liberties from the British crown. He was at sea when the famous Boston Tea Party occurred in 1773 but he joined the American militia upon his return and, shortly after hostilities began at Lexington, he took part in the siege of British-occupied Boston in 1775.

In May 1775, Arnold was given a commission as Colonel of the militia. He was sent to join Ethan Allen and his Green Mountain Boys to take the strategically important Fort Ticonderoga at the juncture of lakes George and Champlain in upstate New York. Arnold and Allen, sharing joint command, with 130 soldiers entered the fort under the cover of darkness and surprised the British. Ticonderoga fell without a shot fired but it was one of the first significant victories for the rag-tag Continental Army and Benedict Arnold was seen as heroic as the boisterous and bold Ethan Allen.

A short time later, with about fifty men, Arnold sailed eighty miles northward to St. Johns at the mouth of the Sorel River (now Richelieu) and captured the old stone fort and about twenty British soldiers. He took a British sloop, all the stores, and a cannon and sailed southward with another victory in his pocket. A few weeks later, Arnold's wife died of a unspecified illness.

By the time Arnold reported to Commander-in-Chief George Washington, his reputation as a fierce fighter had preceded him. Washington was impressed with Arnold, believing he was one of the few men he could trust to lead men into battle and win. While Arnold waited for a new command in upstate New York, he petitioned the New York Assembly in Albany to reimburse him for the £1,000 he had spent in equipping the Ticonderoga and St. John's expedi-

Benedict Arnold, one of the great heroes of the American Revolution and America's most notorious traitor and spy.

tions. He was finally given a £195 settlement. Ever the merchant, this shortchanging rankled Arnold. He would be forever petitioning one Continental assembly or another for back pay, out-of-pocket expenses, money he never seemed to recoup. It was the same with his military standing. Though he knew he was one of Washington's favorites, he always seemed to be passed over for higher command which went to monied, socially well-connected men.

Even his victories were grudgingly given to him. Ethan Allen mentioned Arnold as his co-commander at the taking of Ticonderoga only once in dispatches. Arnold's predawn raid at St. John's was minimized. All of this rather shabby treatment embittered Arnold but he remained loyal to the Continental Army and, especially, to Washington, who was a great father-figure to him and a man for whom Arnold would do anything.

Then Washington finally approved of a plan Arnold had drawn up months earlier, the invasion of Canada and the taking of Quebec. Arnold and Richard Montgomery led two forces toward Canada in September 1775, Montgomery the western wing with 1,200 men, Arnold the eastern command with 1,050 men: mountaineers, hunters, woodsmen, crack shots all. Commanding a company of Virginia riflemen was famed Daniel Morgan. These men followed Arnold through the wild Maine wilderness in an epic trek toward Quebec. They first sailed from Newburyport, Massachusetts, to Parker's Flats, Maine, then up the wild Kennebec River, then through an entangled wilderness on the Dead River, a bruising, flesh-tearing portage-march while the food and supplies gave out.

The impossible trek to Quebec diminished Arnold's command through starvation, desertion, and death so that he had only 500 men when he scaled the cliffs to the plains before the citadel. On December 27, 1775, Arnold and Montgomery attacked in two separate columns. Dozens of Americans were cut down by withering musket and cannon fire as they dashed forward, with Arnold in the lead. Just before reaching the objective, Arnold was shot in the leg and had to be forced by his men to leave the battle, carried away while Daniel Morgan continued to lead the assault, until they were trapped in a cul-de-sac by hordes of British troops firing at them from all angles. Morgan wept as he was forced to surrender his badly mauled command.

By May the British had received reinforcements and their ships were able to move through the ice of the Sorel River. Out of 1,900 American troops, only 1,000 were fit for service and these were weak from half-rations. Quebec was simply too strong to take. The order for the retreat was given. Meanwhile, for all of his brilliance in the field, his fantastic energy, and inventiveness, Arnold watched in angry silence as junior officers were promoted above him.

Despite accusations made against Arnold in Congress for disobedience to orders and quarrels with peers, Washington made no secret of his admiration of Arnold whom he used as a stop-gap to any emergency. In 1777, when Arnold was finally made a major-general, mostly at the urging of Washington, the Commander-in-Chief sent Arnold to Trenton to guard against a British army of 20,000 led by General William Howe. So well did Arnold fortify the river passages, and disguise 5,000 troops as if they represented 20,000 by marching them constantly up and down the coastal waters for eighteen days that Howe was utterly cowed and withdrew his men by sea.

Benedict Arnold had petitioned the Congress for the reimbursement of several thousand pounds which he had personally spent during the disastrous Quebec expedition. He presented his ledgers which were hotly debated. He received only a few hundred pounds and, incensed, he resigned, brooding in Philadelphia.

With Gentleman Johnny Burgoyne, who had retaken Fort Ticonderoga, on the march, the Congress turned to Arnold and asked him to return to his rank and save the Mohawk Valley which Burgoyne's troops, aided by thousands of rampaging Indians, were ravaging. Washington himself wrote to the Congress, asking it to send Arnold northward, stating: "He is active, judicious and brave, and an officer in whom the militia will repose great confidence."

When Congress settled accounts with Arnold, paying him £2,700, the petulant patriot rode northward and into a cauldron of slaughter. He had not been officially given the rank of major general, a rank bestowed upon many others not worth his bootstraps. Other American commanders had urged him not to resign but to go northward and save the country. Arnold responded, writing a letter to Congress which stated: "No public or private injury, or insult shall prevail upon me to forsake the cause of my injured and oppressed country, until I see peace and liberty restored to her, or die in the attempt."

Arnold joined the little American army led by General Philip Schuyler, and was given the command of its left wing. Then came word that Fort Stanwix (now the site of Rome, N.Y.) was surrounded and about to fall to British troops accompanied by fierce, scalp-taking Mohawks, under the command of brutal Barry St. Leger. When news spread through Schuyler's army that Arnold was calling for volunteers to march with him to save Fort Stanwix, the troops poured from their tents, hurrahing Arnold who rode past them on horseback. He took 800 men with him at dusk, marching resolutely toward the Mohawk Valley. "You will hear from us victorious," Arnold told Schuyler in his melodramatic fashion, "or you will hear of us no more."

Arnold quickly learned that St. Leger's army of soldiers and Indians numbered almost 2,000, more than twice the size of his own. Then, providence once more came to Arnold's aid. Brought before him was a Tory youth, one Yost Cuyler who was accused of aiding the British and spying against the Americans. Arnold cleverly held an impromptu trial and condemned the youth to death. He would spare Cuyler, he said, if the youth would perform a service. Anything, agreed Cuyler. Arnold prepared the youth and sent him running in the direction of St. Leger's army.

Cuyler showed up in St. Leger's camp wearing a coat shot through, tattered by the muskets of a vanguard of a great Continental army. St. Leger's superstitious Indians asked how many Americans were approaching. Cuyler pointed to the leaves on the trees. The Mohawks panicked, grabbed what stores and blankets they could from their British allies and fled northward with a whoop. St. Leger, his force woefully depleted and demoralized, had no choice but to retreat after them. The news spread rapidly through the Colonies that Benedict Arnold had won a battle through a clever ruse and his fame shot even higher, but too high for some. Old General Horatio Gates, who had always been a supporter of Arnold, suddenly became cold, almost indifferent to him. Arnold's fame was also a threat to those holding high rank, all except Washington.

Meanwhile, his army replenished with foodstuffs, Burgoyne continued his slow march southward, heading toward Albany. Schuyler's army, now taken over by the ancient Horatio Gates, was no match for it.

Gates prepared to meet Burgoyne in the hills above Stillwater. Arnold, a superb tactician, had selected the area as excellent for defensive positions. With the Mohawk Valley relieved by Arnold, Gates' army began to swell with militia volunteers until it numbered 17,000, more than twice that of Burgoyne's. The armies met at Freeman Farm on September 19, 1777.

With great presence of mind, Arnold rode pell-mell back and forth along his own lines. Whenever he saw a weakness, he would bring up reinforcements and plug a gap in the lines. When he began to run out of reserves, Arnold sent frantic word to his superior Gates, asking for reinforcements. Three times Arnold sent runners to Gates but the cranky general did not respond.

When he refused to order a morning attack, Arnold demanded a reason. Gates would give none. Arnold stamped the floor. His face flushed red and he injudiciously spat out the words: "General, you can go to hell!" With that, Arnold returned to his troops. Gates would never forgive Arnold and, when he later sent in his official report of the battle of Freeman Farm he did not even mention Arnold's name, the man who had conducted that battle.

Again, Arnold had been grossly slighted, another wound to a memory that forgot nothing, remembered every wrong, every insult, every slander, and libel. His memory was much like the ledger books he had kept as a merchant. To him, these were unpaid debts and the accounts would have to be balanced some day.

Gates proved to be a spiteful, petty man who afterward attempted to humiliate the proud Arnold at every turn. Meanwhile, Gates made no more movement toward Burgoyne's army which sat where it was. Both armies were separated by only a few miles of woods and hills. They waited for each other to make a move.

On October 7, 1777, Burgoyne finally roused himself and ordered his troops down the Quaker Springs road, dragoons in the lead, followed by column after column of heavy-footed grenadiers, Hessians and then artillery. A spy raced to Gates to inform him of the advance. Gates ordered Daniel Morgan's riflemen to harass the oncoming columns. Meanwhile, Arnold fumed in his tent. He had been ordered to stay out of the battle by Gates. He drank considerable brandy, then raced to an officer's horse and leaped into the saddle. "No man shall keep me in my tent today!" he thundered and rode off toward the battle.

Like a thunderbolt, Arnold led a mad dash toward the heart of Burgoyne's army, the very center which was dense with Hessians and grenadiers. He and his brigades crashed into the British, tearing at Burgoyne's men with such savage fury that they fell in heaps, line after line, the center bending backward like a straining bow.

As night began to fall, one last bastion remained, the heavily fortified German redoubt. Arnold raced to it. The last rays of the sun glinted on his sword as he led his final charge straight into the redoubt, his huge bay horse sailing over logs and then dashing straight through an open sally-port where a dozen Hessians stood leveling their muskets at his heart. His men charged after him. The Germans volleyed, their bullets striking and killing Arnold's seventh horse, plunging him downward, crashing atop Arnold to fracture his leg. He managed to crawl from beneath the horse, jump upward on one good leg and withdraw two pistols, firing both at the Germans surrounding him.

Arnold's own men dashed through the sally-port and drove the Germans back, then captured those who remained. Witnesses of Arnold's last act of valor stood amazed at the man whose leadership on this day at Saratoga was later described as "still unmatched in the heroics of American warfare."

The following day what was left of the once proud and boastful British army limped northward in retreat. But the path was blocked by a division of American troops under the command of General David Fellows whose soldiers took up defensive positions at Saratoga ford. Surrounded, out of ammunition and with no hope of relief, General Burgoyne surrendered his grand army ten days later.

Arnold's superior, Gates, who never once entered the battle, took full credit for the victory, never mentioning Arnold in dispatches. Arnold slowly recuperated through the winter months. By then, the true fame he had won at Saratoga spread to Congress and, most importantly, to George Washington who, by then, held Arnold supreme above all his commanders. His brilliant triumph at Saratoga was truly the turning point in the American Revolution, one where the tide of victory swept forward the American cause.

By May of 1778, Arnold was well enough to travel to Valley Forge where Washington warmly embraced him, thanked him for saving the day and the country at Saratoga. Arnold was surrounded by admiring generals such as Nathanael Greene and Henry Knox. He accepted their kudos graciously but the fire seemed to have gone out of him. Arnold, after three years of the most fantastic military feats, was worn out, grizzled, becalmed, and he would limp for the rest of his life.

Washington's gratitude knew no bounds. He was set to reward his finest commander with an important post. He assigned Arnold to command Philadelphia, the seat of the American government. He cautioned him to be prudent, tactful, to weigh all grievances with a calm and unprejudiced mind. None of these qualities were pronounced in Arnold who was a tiger on the battlefield but wholly unsuited to a military governorship where restraint was vital to survival.

Philadelphia greeted Arnold with a great parade of which he was the center. He was cheered and then installed in the city's finest mansion, Penn House. Here, he reverted to the stodgy ways of the merchant, attempting to solve the city's sanitation problems, the shipping of goods and foodstuffs, creating provisions for Washington's army. Arnold, ever the opportunist,

Above, Margaret "Peggy" Shippen, from a pencil drawing by Major John Andre, her close friend. Right, the Shippen mansion in Philadelphia, where Arnold married his second wife, Margaret Shippen.

set up a firm that bought flour with government money at $5 per barrel and sold the same abroad at $28, taking most of the profits.

He was the guest of honor at the homes of the powerful and the rich. At one party he was thunderstruck by a beautiful blue-eyed blonde, Margaret "Peggy" Shippen. All in her family were notorious Tories, devoted to Great Britain and King George III, but that mattered little to smitten Arnold. He pursued her so avidly that her friends became his. Soon, he was giving parties in her honor, "Tory Parties" they were called, much to the disgrace of Arnold, true son of the American Revolution.

Believing that Congress had bilked him out of the fortune he had personally spent on supplying and equipping Continental soldiers through three years of war, Arnold began to line his own pockets by any means available. At the same time, in 1779, Congress had brought a court-martial against him for his privateering. He ignored these charges and married 18-year-old Margaret Shippen in a great ceremony at the Shippen Mansion. He was then court-martialed and even his mentor, George Washington, was compelled to reprimand him.

Peggy Shippen chirped night and day about the ingratitude the country had shown toward her husband, her venomous chatter prattled incessantly into his ears. He was an embittered man now, believing that he was surrounded on all sides by congressional and military enemies, even those Americans who had once called him friend.

Arnold came to believe that he would never see justice in his own country. He decided to throw in his fortune with the British, and let it be known that he would consider a commission in the British Army

and a considerable payment for changing sides. Through his wife Margaret, Arnold established contact with Major John Andre, on General Sir Henry Clinton's staff in New York. Andre, chief of British espionage, began a lengthy correspondence with Arnold. They wrote in invisible ink and in code. Arnold's missives were those of a merchant, bargaining for high military position and money.

Oddly, Andre's contact with Peggy Shippen had existed before she had married Arnold. She and Andre had exchanged more than friendly letters and, at one point, she may have been providing intelligence information to the British from American-held Philadelphia. In a Clinton letter, written in 1792, there is a reference to Margaret Shippen, stating that, in 1779, she had been paid £350 "for her services which were very meritorious."

Relieved of his command in Philadelphia, Arnold was set adrift, his coffers empty. He was a national hero without command and, as such, of little use to the British. Andre broke off his correspondence with Arnold. Then Arnold's star appeared to rise once more. Washington, ever his ally and supporter, appointed him commander of strategic West Point with full military powers. Arnold was once again a man of importance, of recognized position. He would not wait until he was henpecked into further disgrace by vile enemies in Congress, however. Arnold would sell what he had to sell to the British now and make the most of it.

Resuming his coded communications with Andre, Arnold struck a bargain with the British. He would deliver West Point in return for £20,000 and the rank of brigadier in the British army. If he failed, the British would still keep the bargain, at least the rank

Arnold's secret correspondence with Major Andre, the letter above in code, the translated copy at right, in which Arnold offered to turn over West Point for £20,000.

One of Arnold's papers found on Andre when he was captured, the disposition and numbers of troops at West Point.

Sketch of Major John Andre at the time he carried on his secret correspondence with Benedict Arnold.

in their army and, as recompense, £10,000. After months of preparation, Andre sailed on the British sloop *Vulture* up the Hudson to Haverstraw, six miles below Stoney Point. A Tory friend of Arnold's, Joshua Hett Smith, rowed out to the *Vulture* and asked for Andre, saying that he would take him to meet Arnold.

Andre was taken ashore to a place in the woods where he waited for the American general. Arnold appeared shortly after midnight, September 21, 1780. He brought with him the plans of West Point, saying that he would make sure that the British gained entry to the fort at the right time. The two spent a great deal of time talking about this terrible betrayal, as well as chatting about their mutual friends through Arnold's wife. It was by then too late for Andre to be rowed back to the British sloop and Arnold suggested that they both accompany Smith to his house to get some sleep.

At dawn both men were still chatting away when they heard gunfire and saw the *Vulture* attacked from the balcony of Smith's house, which was perched on a hill with a view of the Hudson. An American shore battery was firing on the British ship and struck it, causing a fire to break out. The *Vulture* returned fire but then got up anchor and began to sail away.

Andre appeared to have no way to escape but Arnold calmed him by saying that he could easily slip back to the British lines on horseback, that Tory Smith would guide him. Smith agreed but said he would not go with Andre as long as the spymaster was wearing a British uniform. Smith stated that he feared being fired upon. The Tory insisted that Andre change into civilian clothes. Andre reluctantly agreed and the pair set out for New York with a pass signed by Arnold.

Arnold himself mounted his horse and rode to his headquarters at Robinson House near West Point. He was visited by Washington and Lafayette who were expected for a lunch. Arnold sat down with his commander-in-chief, Lafayette, and his wife Peggy to enjoy a comfortable meal when a courier arrived. He handed Arnold a note from one of his subordinates, Colonel John Jameson. The note explained that Jameson was holding a British spy named John Andre who was traveling toward British lines with a safe conduct pass from Arnold under the name of "John Anderson." Colonel Jameson asked for instructions.

Arnold displayed extraordinary presence of mind. He asked to be excused and went to his bedroom. In a few minutes he called his wife to his side, explaining to her that he would soon be exposed as a traitor. He told he that he must flee for his life to the British. He kissed her, his young son Edward, then dashed down some back stairs. Once outside, he shouted to a servant: "Get a horse a cart horse will do! And tell his Excellency [Washington] that I've gone over to West Point . . . will be back in an hour."

A horse was brought and Arnold jumped into the saddle, then rode off at a wild gallop. Reaching Beverly Dock, Arnold dismounted and ordered his personal barge to row him to the *Vulture* which was lying off Teller's Point. One of Arnold's own officers, Colonel James Livingston, whose shore battery had fired upon the *Vulture* until it had moved out of range, stood perplexed on a hilltop, watching through a telescope as Arnold's barge approached the enemy ship. He watched as six oarsmen rowed his commander to the side of the vessel, Arnold standing at the stern of the barge with a raised walking stick above his head. To the stick was affixed a large white handkerchief.

Meanwhile, Washington was told by one of Arnold's servants that Margaret had fainted in her chambers. Washington went to her but she was delirious, so much so that a doctor had given her a sedative. Washington asked for Arnold and was told that he had gone to West Point. Washington then went himself to West Point to review the troops there and was angry at not seeing Arnold there. When his barge finally returned to Beverly Dock, Washington was greeted by an upset Alexander Hamilton who escorted him back to the Robinson House. There the whole story came out, how Andre had been captured with the West Point plans hidden in his boot, along with his confession which fully implicated Arnold.

"Who can we trust now?" sighed Washington. He later convened a tribunal which convicted Andre of treason and sentenced him to death, a fate Washington endorsed and, despite later pleas from General Clinton, refused to alter. Washington, by then his heart set against the one man he had so admired, protected and advanced, insisted that Clinton turn Arnold over to him. Only then, Washington said, would he spare the gallant Andre. Clinton refused. Arnold himself went to Clinton when he heard that

Arnold boarding the British sloop Vulture *to make good his escape to the English lines under Sir Henry Clinton.*

Andre was to die and offered to be exchanged to save the young British officer's life. Clinton would not allow it. Andre was hanged, dying bravely.

Everywhere the word spread: "Great Arnold has stolen off to the enemy!" Washington then received a letter from Arnold, telling him that he alone was responsible for his treason, that his wife, aides, and servants were innocent. Washington later allowed Mrs. Arnold and her child to be escorted to the British lines but he had nothing but contempt for Arnold, as well as his Tory friend Joshua Hett Smith. He ordered Smith arrested and jailed pending trial. But Smith, dressed as a woman, escaped the small prison and fled successfully to the British.

Clinton made much of Arnold's betrayal, holding a parade for him in New York and hosting several balls in his honor. He lodged the traitor at Number Three Broadway, a handsome mansion. British officers showed great deference to Arnold, loaning them their aides and wining and dining him. Secretly, they detested him. Clinton, however, kept his word. He appointed Arnold a brigadier general in his army, paid him the money he had demanded and bestowed upon him rent-free lodgings. He asked Arnold to raise a regiment of Tories from the American ranks to fight alongside the British.

The rest for Arnold was anticlimactic. He did manage to raise a rag-tag Tory regiment and performed some minor raids in Virginia. He marched to New London in his native Connecticut and devastated the town. In 1781, when Yorktown fell, Arnold departed for England where he lived at the edge of poverty with his wife and child. He was an anathema to the British who declined to give him a permanent commission in the Army during the wars of the French Revolution. Arnold attempted several businesses but failed miserably. He died in London of illness on June 14, 1801. Few attended his funeral. His wife died three years later and both were buried at Battersea.

Arnold left no legacy. His son Edward died of illness at age thirteen but a young daughter, Sophia did survive to marry and prosper. Her grandson, Arnold's great grandson, Theodore Stephenson, became a major-general in the British Army and served with distinction. In America, no trace remained of Arnold, the great patriot and the greater spy and traitor, except a small monument which was erected years later at Saratoga. Chiseled on its stone tablet were the words: "In memory of the most brilliant soldier of the Continental Army, who was desperately wounded at this spot, the sallyport of Burgoyne's Great Western Redoubt, 7th October, 1777, winning for his regiment the decisive battle of the American Revolution and for himself the rank of major general." The marker bears no name.

[ALSO SEE: *John Andre*]

ARTAMONOV, NICOLAI FEDOROVICH
Soviet Double Agent in U.S. ▪ (1924– ?)

IN JUNE 1959, A 35-YEAR-OLD RUSSIAN NAVAL OFFICER appeared on the beach of Oland Island off the Swedish Coast. With him were an attractive female named Ilja, a Polish physician, and a Russian sailor. The officer was Nicolai Fedorovich Artamonov. He told Swedish authorities that the woman was his girl friend and that he had tricked the sailor into helping him sail a small launch across the Baltic from the port of Gdynia.

Artamonov stated that he was in love with Ilja and that he had deserted to avoid a new posting that would separate him from the woman. He added that he was also dissatisfied with the Soviet dictatorship. The CIA stepped in and Artamonov declared that he was ready to defect and tell U.S. officials all he knew. He was flown to West Germany and then to America where he was debriefed.

Among other things, the affable Russian told CIA officials that the top Soviet command had issued instructions to officers to be ready at any moment to initiate surprise nuclear attacks on the West. Artamonov proved to be what he claimed, a well-educated officer who had received the finest training at the Frunze Naval Academy. CIA agents arranged a unique test, having Artamonov take over the controls of a U.S. destroyer. He proved to have excellent seamanship skills, although he was reluctant to give details concerning the Soviet Navy and its vessels.

For some time the CIA considered Artamonov a prize catch who eventually provided considerable information on the Soviet Navy. The good-natured Russian offered to help the U.S. in any way, including his services as a counterspy. Suspicion of the defector, however, began to surface after another Soviet defector, Anatoli Golytsin refused to meet with Artamonov. Golytsin had defected in 1961 and had met Artamonov several times on amiable terms. Then, suddenly in 1965, Golytsin denounced the young Soviet Navy officer, insisting that he was a Russian "plant" who was part of a KGB plan to deceive Western intelligence agencies and who was to supply phony secrets to the CIA.

The CIA had second thoughts about Artamonov and apparently began to use him as a double "plant," allowing him to meet with KGB agents to supply them with fake U.S. secrets. On one such mission, Artamonov was sent to Vienna at Christmas 1975. Artamonov did not return to his CIA control but utterly vanished. It was speculated that he either was forced to return or he voluntarily went back to the USSR, his role as double agent exposed and therefore finished.

[ALSO SEE: *Anatoli Golytsin*]

ASHBY, TURNER
Confederate Spy during American Civil War ▪ (1828–1862)

VIRGINIA-BORN TURNER ASHBY DESCENDED FROM A long line of soldiers dating back to the American Revolution. He lived in relative comfort, his family owning a large estate, Rose Bank. Ashby was privately tutored and later spent his time farming the estate. When John Brown raided Harper's Ferry in 1859, Ashby gathered relatives and friends and rode to the site, but by the time he arrived Brown was in custody. Ashby patrolled the Potomac for some time, in the event another insurgent group made a similar attack, and he was on hand to witness the hanging of Brown.

Ashby was not a secessionist but when Virginia left the Union in 1861, Ashby vowed to remain loyal to his native state. He joined General Thomas Jonathan "Stonewall" Jackson and soon proved to be one of the South's most brilliant cavalry commanders. When Jackson called for aid in establishing an extensive and effective espionage system, Ashby volunteered, proving himself to be a resourceful and daring spy.

In early 1861 Ashby assumed the role of a horse doctor, a subject about which he had considerable knowledge. In this disguise he worked his way behind Union lines at Chambersburg, Pennsylvania, where he easily determined troop dispositions and movements. This information allowed Jackson to properly deploy his own troops and successfully repulse several minor Union sorties.

Ashby then served as a cavalry commander for Confederate cavalry commander J. E. B. Stuart. Through skillful maneuvering of his vastly smaller cavalry forces, Ashby managed to delay Union forces so that Confederate troops under General Joseph E. Johnston could abandon Harper's Ferry and join a Confederate army commanded by General P. G. T. Beauregard at Bull Run. Johnston's troops arrived just as Union forces were about to break through Beauregard's lines and turned the battle into an overwhelming victory for the South.

Organizing a spy ring behind Union lines, Ashby was able to provide Jackson and Stuart with important information. On one occasion, however, Ashby's spies failed to detect a large Union force at Kernstown, Virginia, which led to a Confederate defeat in 1862. Ashby more than made up for this failure a short time later when he personally spied on Union forces at Front Royal, Virginia. The information he brought back to Jackson was so detailed that it enabled Jackson to correctly second-guess all Union movements and led to a smashing defeat of Northern forces.

Ashby's priceless espionage work led to his promotion to brigadier general. Union leaders, however, came to loathe the sound of Ashby's name and put a price on his head and an order that if he were found in disguise behind their lines he was to be shot on sight. This order was never carried out. While deploying a cavalry screen for Jackson's troops movements in the Shenandoah Valley, Ashy led a charge against a strong force of Union cavalry and was killed in the saddle.

ASIO
Australian Security & Intelligence Organization ▪ (1946–)

IN THE EARLY DAYS OF THE COLD WAR THE SOVIETS made a serious attempt to penetrate the government and to also secure important industrial secrets in Australia. This was made perfectly clear to Australian leaders by Vladimir Petrov, a KGB agent who defected from the Soviet Embassy in Canberra.

To counter the Soviet threat, the Australian government created the Australian Security and Intelligence Organization, ASIO for short. The organization had two branches: one was to handle all counterespionage, the other was to gather intelligence. Heading ASIO was Colonel C. G. Roberts who had been the director of the Allied Intelligence Bureau during World War II which had worked effectively against the Japanese. The chief source of the AIB's information had stemmed from thousands of coast watchers and those Australians who operated from behind enemy lines after the Japanese had overrun the islands of the South Pacific.

Now the threat was different. Instead of invading armies, Australia had to concern itself with Russian agents disguised as immigrants from Eastern Europe. These agents, once established as Australian citizens, concentrated on gathering information on Australia's successful uranium mining, this ore being essential in the construction of atomic bombs. Moreover, they attempted to penetrate the highest levels of government through servants working for Australian officials.

ASIO and its intelligence-gathering arm, ASIS (Australian Secret Intelligence Service) met with relative success until a series of debacles occurred in 1983. The first of these faux pas involved Valery Ivanov, the affable, charming Third Secretary of the Soviet Embassy. Tired of using low-level government contacts, Ivanov, on instructions from Moscow, had tried to develop "agents of influence," in Australia. To that end Ivanov cultivated a friendship with David Combe, a leading lobbyist, former Labor Party official and, most importantly, a personal friend of Bob Hawke, Prime Minister of Australia.

Ivanov was exposed and expelled as the Prime Minister, under tremendous pressure from opposition leaders, announced that David Combe was banned from having any contact with Australian government officials. The Hope Commission was then established to minutely examine the affair. Investigators for the Commission then discovered that special minister Mick Young had leaked information to a friend that Ivanov was about to be expelled.

When this was revealed, Young resigned his post. Surprisingly, Young returned six months later as a minister and a member of the government security commission. Opposition leader Andrew Peacock roared his disapproval by comparing Young's security position to that of "Dracula [being put] in charge of a blood bank."

Toward the end of 1983, ASIS chief John Ryan authorized an intelligence exercise that created heaping ridicule from critics of ASIO. The exercise simulated the rescue of a hostage held in a hotel room. Without informing local police or hotel management, Ryan's agents raced through the lobby of the Melbourne Sheraton Hotel.

The agents wore carnival masks and carried sub-machineguns, brushing aside, even knocking down guests as they stormed their way to a hotel room where they battered down the door. When the hotel manager came running to investigate the disturbance, he was manhandled and shoved aside as the agents "rescued" the mock hostage. Police were summoned and five of Ryan's agents were arrested as they left the hotel. Arresting officers stated that the agents were "under the influence of alcohol."

The result was a deafening blast from the press, the police and the politicians, particularly those who had long opposed ASIO and ASIS. The Sydney Morning Herald labeled Ryan's agents as "a bunch of stumblebums." Senator Primmer, immune to charges of slander under parliamentary privilege, called Ryan "a crook, a bureaucratic bully, a professional liar, a bad drunk and a social embarrassment." Ryan resigned.

ASIO, in February 1984, was severely regulated with new guidelines. The organization must now brief the Prime Minister and Attorney General of any espionage case from the very beginning. Detailed reports from ASIO must be submitted to the Security Committee of the federal Cabinet and all security files can be fully accessed by the Attorney General.

[ALSO SEE: Allied Intelligence Bureau]

ASSAD, RIFAAT
Syrian Chief of Intelligence ▪ (? –   )

ENORMOUSLY RICH AND RUTHLESS, RIFAAT ASSAD became the most hated man in Syria as head of Syrian Intelligence and protector of the regime headed by Hafez el Assad. Assad commanded heavily armed Defense Companies made up of members of the Alawite sect, a minority dominating the Moslem majority in Syria. Responsible for the guarding of the Presidential Palace, Assad also headed Syrian espionage, which was primarily devoted to tracking down dissidents who opposed the Assad regime.

Assad's hit teams are sent throughout the world. One of these murder squads was sent by Assad to West Germany to kill Essam El-Attar, who headed the Moslem Brotherhood and vociferously opposed the Assad government. When the killers arrived at El-Attar's home they simply knocked on the door. The intended victim's wife answered and was shot dead. The killers then fled, unapprehended.

ATLANTIC WALL BLUEPRINT
Top Secret Nazi Map of Normandy Fortifications ▪ (1943)

DURING 1943, THE ALLIES BEGAN A TREMENDOUS stockpiling of troops and war machinery in preparation of invading Nazi-occupied Europe. The main thrust of the invasion, the Nazis knew, would be somewhere along the long coast of France facing the English Channel. The Germans built an elaborate defense system along hundreds of miles of the coast consisting of underwater obstacles, tank traps, minefields, barbed wire, and some of the most formidable big gun installations ever constructed.

This defense system was called the Atlantic Wall and was thought to be impregnable, at least by Nazi generals. Normandy, which was the coastal front selected by the Allies as the intended invasion area, offered exceptionally strong defenses in the Atlantic Wall. The French resistance of underground groups in Nazi-occupied France vowed to help the Allies in the pending invasion and, to that end, resolved to unearth a plan of the Atlantic Wall so the Allies could determine its weak spots and break it. This was achieved by one resistance worker, René Duchez, a housepainter.

Duchez was hired to redecorate German headquarters in Caen. While painting an office he spotted a large map folded on top of a desk which was labeled "Special Blueprint—Top Secret." Duchez looked over the map and realized it was a map detailing all the defenses of the Atlantic Wall. While the German commander was distracted, Duchez grabbed the map and slipped it behind a mirror on the wall.

When he returned a few days later, Duchez found the map and slipped it into a bag containing his paint brushes, carrying this out of the building. The map was rushed to Paris where underground leaders verified it as genuine. It was then sent to London. The Germans remained ignorant of the missing map for some time as the officer in charge of the Caen office who had ordered the decorating had been replaced.

When the Allies landed in Normandy on June 6, 1944, they took full advantage of the German blueprint of the Atlantic Wall. Because of this information, American frogmen were able to quickly locate underwater minefields and obstacles and eliminate them before landing craft hit Utah Beach near Cherbourg. Moreover, the First Army was able to pinpoint land defenses so that it could easily overwhelm these and move inland. Praise for Duchez came after the war from General Omar Bradley who wrote: "Securing the blueprint of the German Atlantic Wall was an incredible feat—so valuable that the landing operation succeeded with a minimum loss of men and material."

AUGUSTENBORG, LON DAVID
U.S. Vice Consul in Leningrad ▪ (? –   )

IN MAY 1983 A CURIOUS STORY RAN IN *PRAVDA* WHICH reported that a Dr. Shorer, a Vice Consul working in the U.S. Consulate in Leningrad, had been apprehended as he collected secret Soviet information at a drop outside of Leningrad. The U.S. Embassy promptly responded by labeling the report false and that no Dr. Shorer worked at any U.S. consulate in Soviet Russia.

Four months later, in September 1983, Lon David Augustenborg, his wife and small daughter were taking a Sunday drive outside of Leningrad. Augustenborg was a U.S. Vice-Consul in Leningrad. The car stopped at the roadside, according to a KGB report. Mrs. Augustenborg got out of the car and went to a dead drop, retrieving a tin while her husband kept the motor running and the daughter sat in the back seat.

KGB agents then swooped down on the car just as Mrs. Augustenborg got inside. As they approached, she threw the tin into the back seat, an act later pointed to by the Soviets to prove that, along with her husband, Mrs. Augustenborg was also an accomplished spy. Against U.S. protests, Augustenborg and his family were expelled from Russia.

The KGB never identified the Russian contact supposedly in league with the Vice Consul but the Soviets did publish various documents, including code sheets and money, to allegedly prove Augustenborg's guilt. The premature story appearing in *Pravda* four months before the actual event was thought to be a warning to the U.S. and the so-called spy ring headed by Augustenborg.

AZEV, YEVNO PHILOPOVICH
Russian Double Agent ▪ (1869–1918)

NO OTHER SPY IN MODERN HISTORY EQUALED THE deception, connivance, and utter ruthlessness of Yevno Azev. He was a double agent, both espionage and assassination chief of the Russian revolutionaries at the turn of the century, as well as the masterspy for the Okhrana, the czar's secret police. He worked both sides of this dangerous fence with great skill and daring and not until his death in 1918 was it ever determined exactly which side Azev truly represented. His is one of the most fantastic stories in the annals of espionage.

Azev was born of Jewish parents in Lyskovo, Grodnensky Province, Russia, in 1869. To escape the permanent poverty to which most Russian Jews were confined, his father, Fischel Azev, a tailor, moved his family to Rostov-on-Don in 1874. This quickly developing industrial town offered opportunities to everyone and here the elder Azev opened a grocery and drapery store which, unfortunately, did not flourish.

Although fortune did not smile on the Azev family, Yevno's parents managed to send him to high school (the equivalent of junior college) from which he graduated at age twenty-one in 1890. Azev aimlessly moved from one job to another until becoming a traveling salesman. He also dabbled in politics, associating with left-wing radicals more for amusement than dedication to any political cause. In 1892 he cavalierly signed a political manifesto which fell into the hands of the secret police, the Okhrana which ordered the arrests of those who had put their names to the document.

Knowing he was about to be arrested, Azev quickly sold off a consignment of goods recently received from his employer, pocketed £85, and fled to Karlsruhe, Germany, where, in May 1892, he enrolled as a student at the Polytechnic College. Here he intended to study engineering, especially electrostatics. Azev had not selected Karlsruhe haphazardly.

Many of Azev's schoolmates from Rostov-on-Don attended the Polytechnic and most of them belonged to the Social Democratic Society which Azev joined. This political group was the largest and most moderate of left-wing organizations. In its ranks, Azev found savage anarchists, nihilists, and terrorists who advocated the violent overthrow of the czarist regime.

The money Azev had stolen from his employer in Russia began to run out. He lived at starvation level, desperately looking for funds. In early 1893, Azev hit upon an idea that would make him wealthy and, more important to his gigantic ego, one of the most secretly powerful men in Russia. He wrote to the Okhrana in Moscow, offering his services as a police agent. He would spy on his fellow Russian students in Karlsruhe, he said, and faithfully report their treasonable activities, but for a price. Azev cleverly stated in the letter that he was signing the letter with an alias, fearful that his true identity might be exposed to the Karlsruhe radicals and they would take vengeance upon him.

Azev also wrote a letter to the Rostov-on-Don police, offering the same espionage services. Again, he refused to sign his name. He nevertheless received a reply, sent to his alias and an address that was not his own. It was from the Okhrana. He was told that the Karlsruhe radicals were so small in number as to be unimportant to the Okhrana. Further, Azev was told, the Russian secret police knew all about the radicals in Karlsruhe. (This was a lie; Azev's letter was the first hint that such a group existed.)

Azev was told that the Okhrana, however, was always looking for valuable information and would pay him for such on condition that he write to its chief and sign his true name. "We have strict principles," the would-be spy was told, "and will have no

Yevno Azev, one of the most spectacular double agents in the history of espionage; he planned and executed revolutionary assassinations in Czarist Russia at the same time he was the highest paid spy for the regime's secret police.

dealings with certain people." Actually, the Okhrana had tens of thousands of spies throughout Russia, on the farms and in all the cities, and, especially, in heavily industrialized areas and in educational institutions where dissent was prevalent. It paid handsomely for information that was, for the most part, useless. Acquiring a resourceful spy who could provide important information on the plans of the leading left-wing political organizations was another matter.

The Okhrana then received another letter from Azev, still refusing to sign his name and asking that he be paid £5 a month (or fifty rubles). By this time the Okhrana had received a report from the police in Rostov-on-Don. Their investigators had identified the letter-writer as Yevno Azev. He was described to the Okhrana as a clever intriguer whose close contact with radical Jewish students living abroad could be of great use. Further, the Rostov police emphasized that Azev had always been poor, was desperate for funds and that money was his real goal in life. Properly paid, the report stated, Azev could be expected to be "zealous in his duty."

This report convinced Okhrana chiefs to immediately hire Azev as a police spy. He was enlisted into its secret ranks in June 1893 and was paid his price, fifty rubles a month. Azev did not spend the money lavishly but hoarded it. So as not to arouse the suspicions of his fellow students, he developed a shrewd plan to explain an income that did not flow from a regular job. Azev wrote letters to charitable Jewish agencies in which he begged for loans. He showed these to his schoolmates but he never mailed the letters. When he appeared with money he explained that he was receiving loans from these organizations.

To pinpoint the information the Okhrana truly sought, Azev quickly realized that he had to get close to the most left-wing radicals seeking to overthrow the Romanov regime. Azev told his fellow radicals that he was no speaker or theoretician but that he could get things done. As a man of action, he insisted, he would go anywhere in Europe to further the cause of the radicals. He was asked to take messages and set up meetings throughout Germany and in Switzerland, to help link one radical group to another. This proved to be the ideal assignment for a police spy who could then provide the Okhrana with information on a vast network of its political foes.

On one of these trips to Berne, Switzerland, in 1894, Azev met the Zhitlovskys, a man and wife who headed the Union of Social Revolutionaries Abroad. So well did Azev ingratiate himself to this couple that the Zhitlovskys endorsed him wholeheartedly and selected him to be the group's chief emissary. Azev was sent throughout Europe and in Russia to maintain contact with leaders in the movement. He was able to send detailed reports on these radicals to the Okhrana. So impressed with these reports was the Okhrana that Azev came to the notice of its infamous chief, S. V. Zubatov.

The chief of the Okhrana believed Azev made in his own image, an individual who would sacrifice anyone for a price. Since Zubatov could afford to pay more money than any other source, he believed Azev would forever be in his pocket and could be used effectively as an agent provocateur. Up to this point, provocation was a method disdained by most secret services as being repulsive to the then high-minded codes of espionage agencies.

"Azev looked at everything from the point of view of personal gain," Zubatov once wrote, "and worked for the government out of no conviction but for the sake of personal profit." In 1901, Azev was given funds and moved to Moscow where Zubatov obtained a job for him as an engineer at the General Electric Company. He was now in the heart of the revolutionary activity in Russia. To the radicals, Azev continued to preach the same crusade, terrorism and assassination.

A small minority of extreme revolutionaries embraced Azev's beliefs and he soon became one of the leaders of the group's Battle Organization which was devoted to terrorism, bank robbery, and murder. Azev actually organized several bank robberies which were carefully staged by the Okhrana itself. Zubatov gave his approval and allowed small amounts of money to be taken. In return, Azev then arranged for the perpetrators of the robberies to be caught. When these Okhrana arrests were made, Azev told his fellow terrorists that they had been betrayed by none

other than the head of the Battle Organization, Gershuni. Azev then denounced Gershuni who was arrested in Kiev. The grateful but thoroughly duped radicals then promoted Azev to the leadership of the Battle Organization.

In this powerful post Azev was able to manipulate the revolutionaries and the secret police as well. He carefully selected certain radicals to betray to the secret police. These were revolutionaries who either challenged his authority in the Battle Organization or might learn of his liaison with the Okhrana. To cement the belief the revolutionaries had in him, however, Azev actively planned the assassinations of many government leaders, including Nicolai Parlovich Bogolepov, Russia's Minister of Education who, on February 27, 1901, was shot and killed by a student who had been expelled and who was indirectly under Azev's control. Azev then denounced the killer to the secret police.

In 1902, Dimitri F. Trepov, the police chief of Moscow, came under threat from the radical elements of the Socialist Revolutionary Party. Three times assassins, all personally instructed by Azev, attempted to kill Trepov but in each instance the attack was foiled. In every instance, Azev not only sent out the assassins to murder but made sure that Zubatov knew the identities of the would-be assassins and where these men could be arrested. The arrests were made in such a way as to indicate that someone other than Azev had exposed the radicals.

The game Azev played was give-and-take. He appeared to the Okhrana as a loyal secret police spy doing everything in his power to protect the government and its leaders. At the same time, he made sure that the Battle Organization accomplished some successful assassinations. Following an assassination, Azev would then prove his expertise and usefulness to the Okhrana by exposing the assassins and making sure they fell into the hands of the secret police.

To Zubatov, if Azev could not prevent an assassination, he was unfailing in his diligence to identify and locate the guilty parties. To the radicals, Azev was the brilliant mastermind behind the murders of their hated governmental enemies but he could not be expected to protect the revolutionaries once one of the countless police spies exposed them for committing those assassinations.

In 1903, a Socialist Revolutionary murdered N. M. Bogdanovich, governor of Ufa, in Kiev. The assassination was engineered by Azev and then he saw to it that the culprit was apprehended by the Okhrana. In the following year, Nicolai Ivanovich Bobrikov, a Russian general and brutal governor of Finland was killed by a nationalist Finnish student who committed suicide before the police could grab him. The killer had been trained and sent to do his job by Azev.

By 1904, Azev had moved to St. Petersburg which was then the center of the Battle Organization's activities. At the time Azev came under the direction of the city's Okhrana chief, Gerassimov, and, indirectly,

Gerassimov's brutal boss, Vyacheslav Konstantinovich Plehve (Wenzel von Plehwe), who was the much-hated Minister of Interior. Plehve's repressive measures and savage executions of revolutionaries and dissidents had earned him the special wrath of radicals who earmarked him for certain assassination.

A professional policeman, it had been the dogged Plehve who had rounded up every member of the revolutionary group (called The Will of The People) responsible for the assassination of Czar Alexander II in St. Petersburg on March 13, 1881. Plehve had been appointed Minister of Interior after his predecessor, Dimitri Sipiagin, had been assassinated in St. Petersburg on April 15, 1902. (Sipiagin's assassination by a student, S. V. Balmashov, had also been engineered by the insidious Azev.)

Plehve had only one thought—the eradication of all revolutionaries in Russia and as many of those in Europe that Okhrana agents could reach out and destroy. He included all students and liberals in his plans of systematic extermination, being a staunch supporter of the arch-conservative educator, Konstantin Petrovich Probedonostev, chief procurator of the Holy Synod and tutor to Czar Nicholas.

Probedonostev had openly branded all liberal students as traitors to the Romanov regime and had himself been the object of no less than five assassination attempts in 1901, all of these attacks having been planned by Azev. In the final attempt on the royal educator's life, Probedonostev was seriously injured but recovered. Plehve, through Gerassimov, and his arch agent provocateur Azev, vowed to dismantle and destroy the Socialist Revolutionary Party's Battle Organization.

One of the czar's aides described Plehve as "a splendid little man for little things, a stupid man for affairs of state." Plehve began to edict severe regulations which included the banning of all political gatherings and meetings. Students were not permitted to walk together on the streets of Moscow or St. Petersburg. No one was allowed to give a party involving more than a few people unless permission of the police was first given.

Plehve was also a rabid anti-Semite. He hated Jews and took every opportunity to prevent them from getting jobs, good housing, food. He encouraged anti-Semitism by ordering his police to look the other way when mobs beat and robbed Jews. In one instance, the worst pogrom in the reign of Nicholas II was the direct result of Plehve's unwritten but boldly accepted anti-Semitic policies. A wild mob in the town of Kishenev, Bessarabia, killed forty-five Jews and destroyed six hundred homes. Plehve's police did nothing until the end of the second day.

The provincial governor was later dismissed and the government publicly condemned the incident and tried and punished the ringleaders but Plehve was kept at his post, a tacit sign by the regime that it endorsed him and his policies. The much more enlightened and liberal Count Sergius Witte met Plehve and bluntly told him that "your policies are making your own assassination inevitable."

Plehve's brutalities against the Jews drove them by countless numbers into the ranks of the revolutionaries. By early 1904 no less than a dozen different terrorist groups in Russia were plotting the minister's assassination. One of these groups, wholly unconnected with the Battle Organization headed by Azev, almost succeeded in killing Plehve but Azev learned of the plot and denounced the ringleaders who were all arrested by the Okhrana. In essence, Azev had personally saved his superior's life but then, in a fantastic turn of events, to prove himself to the Battle Organization, Azev personally planned to assassinate Plehve himself.

To that end, the master double spy planned the killing in detail. He oversaw the making of hand bombs which were to be thrown at Plehve's carriage and then selected those who were to throw the bombs. He then designated a second wave of bomb-throwers who were to go into action should the first set of assassins fail. Azev chose July 21, 1904, as the target day for the assassination. On that day, he discreetly arranged to be absent from St. Petersburg, going to Vilna on party business.

The attack was called off when Plehve's carriage was delayed along its usual route. The assassins decided that too many innocent persons would be killed if they made an attempt to murder the Minister of the Interior in a street packed with people. When Azev received this news he hurried back from Vilna and set a new day for the assassination, July 28, 1904. Before this attack, Azev went to Warsaw, Poland, again on urgent revolutionary business.

This time the plot succeeded. Bombs were hurled under Plehve's carriage as it rumbled down a St. Petersburg street, and he was blown to pieces. Okhrana chief Gerassimov immediately called in his top agent provocateur, grilling him. Azev explained that he was in Warsaw at the time of Plehve's unfortunate assassination. He pointed out that he had already saved his superior earlier in the year and was doing everything humanly possible to prevent Plehve's death but he was only one man after all and could not hope to be everywhere at all times, to unearth each and every murder plot by the countless revolutionary groups in Russia. Then Azev vindicated himself by giving Gerassimov the names of Plehve's killers who were quickly rounded up, tried, and executed.

Gerassimov was grateful. He showered money on Azev who secretly began to deposit funds in banks in far away Germany. He must have realized, at this time, that his double game could not go on indefinitely without being exposed. To gain more money, he demanded great sums from both the Okhrana, ostensibly to pay his own spy network, and from the revolutionaries to fund new, more spectacular assassinations. Much of this money went into Azev's foreign bank accounts.

In late 1904, Azev attended a high level conference of revolutionaries in Paris. He was given reports on all planned terrorist activities with instructions to pass these on to high-ranking revolutionaries in Russia. Azev sent the reports to the Okhrana. At the same time, in frenzied work, he planned scores of new assassinations. In 1905, he arranged for an anti-Semitic extremist to murder Duma member Professor Mikhail Gertsenstein, this assassination edifying the anti-Jewish leaders of the Okhrana. Azev made sure that the extremist was caught. He next designed the killing of Pavel Andreevich Shurlov, Prefect of Police in Moscow. Again, he turned in the killers.

Many of Azev's scheduled assassinations were purposely designed to fail so that he could expose the plotters to the Okhrana. Other times he would make sure that the bombs used in attacks would not go off and the culprits apprehended. When this was brought to his attention by a few of his revolutionary associates, Azev roared that he was betrayed on every side, that the bombmakers were inept and he then called for bigger and better bombs.

One of Azev's assassinations did not go awry. He carefully planned the murder of Grand Duke Sergei, Governor General of Moscow and the Uncle of Czar Nicholas II. On February 17, 1905, Ivan Kalayev, one of the most fanatical members of the Battle Organization, hurled a bomb that blew up Sergei's coach and killed the Grand Duke. Of course, Azev made sure that he had informed the Okhrana of this impending assassination but he could not learn the details of the plot, he said, until later. By then the murder had been accomplished and Kalayev was identified by Azev.

Then what Azev dreaded most occurred. In the middle of 1905, an anonymous letter was received by a member of the revolutionary council. It denounced Azev as a police spy. The Socialist Revolutionary Party convened a secret tribunal with Azev attending. He coolly sat before several judges who sifted what evidence there was to convict him. Azev's advocates, of which there were many, argued that the accusation was ridiculous. How could a man who had so brilliantly designed and executed the bold assassinations of the hated Plehve and the Grand Duke Sergei be a police spy? The charges were dismissed and Azev went back to his intrigues but with less confidence that he could overcome the next threat of exposure.

Azev attempted mightily to discover the source of the anonymous letter but failed. He surmised that this letter could have come only from one source, the Okhrana itself or one of the many police spies working for the secret police, someone who might have come to discover his identity as the Okhrana's top agent. This kind of information could only have come from Gerassimov himself or by someone who shared the highest level of the Okhrana chief's confidence. There was only one such man, Azev concluded, and that was the priest, Father George Gapon,

who stood almost as high in the Okhrana's esteem as did Yevno Azev.

Gapon came to prominence through Plehve, who, before his assassination, had cleverly established a workers' movement which would appear to seek solutions to grievances but would be secretly controlled by the Okhrana. The hundreds of thousands of workers in this movement were fed subtle propaganda which was intended to immunize them from revolutionary viruses and bolster their unwavering, almost mystic support of the czar. Gapon, who had long been a paid police spy, not out of avarice but out of patriotism, was selected by Plehve to head this movement which he called the Assembly of Russian Workingmen.

Secretly, the Okhrana funded Gapon's movement which Gapon directed not against the czar but against employers, although he preached non-violence and peaceful demonstrations. These demonstrations were always permitted by the police as they knew Gapon could control his slavish followers. Gapon himself was above the rank-and-file police spy. He had worked for years in the working class districts of St. Petersburg and he genuinely believed that his movement could better the lives of workers. He was an idealist and, as such, thought to be gullible and easily manipulated by the Okhrana.

In January 1905, workers at the Putilov steel works went on strike, mostly to protest against the mismanagement of the Russo-Japanese War in which Russia had recently been humiliated by the surrender to the Japanese of its main avenue to the Pacific, Port Arthur. The strike spread until more than 120,000 workers sought to settle their grievances against private industry.

The naive Gapon seized upon this situation, believing that he could lead a peaceful march to the czar's Winter Palace and there the benevolent monarch would receive from his hands a petition and act upon it. Gapon thought that by this one grandstanding act, he could achieve a constituent assembly, an eight-hour day, a minimum wage, universal suffrage and education, amnesty for all political prisoners, an income tax, and the separation of church and state.

Early in the morning of January 22, 1905, a Sunday, Gapon led more than 100,000 workers on a march through the icy, windswept streets of St. Petersburg, heading for the Winter Palace. The workers carried the national flag, huge portraits of Czar Nicholas II, religious banners, icons and crosses. They sang religious hymns as they marched and, as they neared the Palace, the national anthem, "God Save the Czar."

Nicholas was informed of the planned processions only a day before the marchers had been disbanded in several bloody confrontations that forever stained his image as a heartless, ruthless monarch. (This image was undeserved in many respects since Nicholas was at heart a compassionate ruler but he was indecisive and, most importantly, surrounded by ministers who constantly overreached their authority and informed the czar of their brutal acts after the fact.)

The workers on that January day followed many routes and went down many streets, finding them blocked by masses of infantry and supported by mounted Cossacks and Hussars. Some nervous officer, it was later claimed by the regime, improperly ordered his men to open fire. This led to a full-scale slaughter of the horrified, panicking workers who ran pell-mell in every direction. The troops fired blindly into their backs, shooting down helpless men, women, and children, killing ninety-two and wounding hundreds by Nicholas' own later count.

This slaughter came to be called "Bloody Sunday." The image of the czar was no longer held in the world as that of a benevolent monarch. Ramsey MacDonald, labor leader and future Prime Minister of Great Britain, called Nicholas II a "blood-stained creature," and a "common murderer." Gapon laid the blame for the mass murders at the door of the czar. He became a dedicated revolutionary. He went into hiding and promptly issued a letter addressed to "Nicholas Romanov, formerly czar and at present soul-murderer of the Russian empire. The innocent blood of workers, their wives and children lies forever between you and the Russian people. . . . May all the blood that must be spilled fall upon you, you Hangman!"

With that Gapon called upon workers to arm themselves and overthrow the Romanov regime. He began to make headway until Yevno Azev was denounced as a police spy. Azev concluded that this accusation had come from none other than Gapon who had himself been a police agent of the highest rank. Azev then began a campaign to discredit Gapon, certainly with the Okhrana's help. Gapon fled to London and became a celebrity of revolution. He was feted and lived comfortably. When this was learned by Azev he reported to the revolutionaries that Gapon was a tool of the capitalists and monarchists, that Gapon himself had arranged for the workers to be shot down.

Gapon then foolishly returned to Russia where revolutionaries shunned him. Realizing that he had lost all standing with the workers, Gapon went to the police to seek reinstatement. Gapon then informed Okhrana officials that Azev was the culprit behind all of the political assassinations in recent years and that, for a handsome price, he would betray Azev to them. When Azev heard this, he immediately arranged for Gapon to be executed by the Battle Organization. He showed his fellow revolutionaries police files on Gapon. The priest was dragged before the Socialist Revolutionary Party chiefs and condemned to death. At Azev's design and orders Gapon was then taken to an abandoned cottage in Finland and was hanged on March 28, 1906. His body was not found until early April. Azev had rid himself of his most dangerous enemy.

Revolt had been widespread in Russia during 1905. Armed uprisings had been crushed in Kronstadt,

Sveaborg, and Reval. As the workers, unemployed, hungry, and disillusioned, grew tired of revolt, the government grew stronger. Nicholas appointed Peter Stolypin Prime Minister in 1906 and he enthusiastically set up courts-martial to meet revolutionary challenges. Assassins of policemen and minor officials, many of these being Azev's recruits, were summarily tried and, within three days, were hanging from portable gallows. Stolypin's traveling courts sent more than 600 men to the gallows in early 1906. This was not considered reactionary on the part of the government which pointed out that more than 1,600 governors, army and navy officers, soldiers, and village policemen had been killed by revolutionaries.

The new Prime Minister was nevertheless branded a reactionary monster by the revolutionaries and the hangman's noose was renamed "Stolypin's necktie." Gerassimov warned Azev that many revolutionaries were planning to assassinate the new prime minister and that Azev had to take special precautions in safeguarding Stolypin's life. To that end, Azev was able to convince fellow members in the Battle Organization that any attempt on Stolypin's life at this time would result in drastic measures from the government, which would further dampen the already soggy spirits of the revolutionaries. Wait until they grew stronger, Azev counseled. Some refused to wait and broke away from the Socialist Revolutionary Party.

These diehard fanatics called themselves Maximalists and they vowed to continue widespread terrorism. The also promised to assassinate Stolypin at the first opportunity. Three of these revolutionaries quickly made bombs and, on a Saturday afternoon in August 1906, barely a month after Stolypin had been appointed prime minister by the czar, called at Stolypin's villa outside of St. Petersburg. At the time a huge reception was in progress to celebrate the prime minister's appointment and his closing down of the Duma (the Russian parliament).

When guards denied the three men permission to proceed through the gates of the villa, the revolutionaries tossed their home-made bombs into the hall. The terrific explosions caused walls to collapse and thirty-two persons, including visitors, servants, guards, and the bomb-throwers themselves, were killed. Stolypin's young son, who was playing on an upstairs balcony, was injured, as was the prime minister's daughter Natalia. Stolypin was unhurt. He had been writing at a desk in his study when the bombs exploded and was merely splashed with ink.

Azev knew he could waste no time in returning to St. Petersburg to meet with Gerassimov and explain that he had nothing to do with the attack on Stolypin. Further, he felt that the Okhrana would take widespread action against his own revolutionary group, the Battle Organization, for the bombing, and thus, the suspicions previously caste against him as a police spy would be confirmed once and for all in the minds of his fellow revolutionaries.

Gerassimov met with a highly nervous Azev who repeatedly disclaimed any responsibility for the attack on Stolypin's villa. The Okhrana chief, as cunning as was his agent provocateur, told Azev that he had his complete confidence and trust. But, just to make sure that he, Azev, would distance himself from the Maximalists, Gerassimov asked that Azev have the Central Committee of the Socialist Revolutionary Party issue a disclaimer of the bombing.

At first Azev argued that if he asked the committee to issue such a manifesto, he would come under suspicion. Gerassimov told him that he would have to use all his considerable powers of persuasion to comply and thus prove his loyalty to the regime. Azev did just that. He met with the Central Committee and argued that the revolution could not be successful without order and discipline and that such splinter groups as the Maximalists who went their own way without making their plans known to the Central Committee put all of the revolutionaries at hazard.

Since these ungovernable terrorists had put their own will above that of the Central Committee, insisted Azev, they had to be disowned publicly. Incredibly, the Committee agreed with Azev and ordered him to write a manifesto which would be widely distributed. Azev did write this manifesto, the only document he ever authored as a revolutionary. He had no choice. It was either openly denounce the Maximalists or be branded a true revolutionary by the Okhrana and hanged.

Once he had appeased his secret police masters, Azev thought to shore up his weakening stature with the revolutionaries. When someone suggested that the Battle Organization seriously considered killing Stolypin, Azev waved away the notion, saying that the prime minister could be dealt with later. (Stolypin would, indeed be assassinated, but not until 1911 and, ironically, by another police spy who was really a revolutionary, Mordka Bogrov.) Azev shocked but satisfied the Central Committee by proposing that Czar Nicholas II himself be assassinated and that he himself would arrange this highest of murders.

Azev took his time, slowly preparing for this regicide. He appointed a man named Karpovich his right hand man. Karpovich had been performing terrorist acts for several years, and had helped in the 1901 assassination of Bogolepov. Detailed plans and projects were undertaken which consumed many months. Azev was forever explaining that one plan after another had been developed, then abandoned for lack of information. He proposed that a young priest kill the czar, then a group of bombers blow up the czar's private train. When he did move some of the plots forward, he also arranged for the plotters to be arrested. Azev had no intention of killing Nicholas II for he knew that he would never be forgiven such an act by the Okhrana, no matter the excuse or explanation.

Gerassimov backed Azev in all this intricate plotting. He made sure that Azev remained above sus-picion by those on the Central Committee and in the highest levels of the Socialist Revolutionary Party in that these persons were never arrested or detained. If any of these people were accidentally arrested, Gerassimov made sure that they easily escaped. Karpovich was one of those arrested inadvertently by the secret police.

When Azev heard of this, he rushed to Gerassimov's home. Gone was the spy's cool composure. He became hysterical, insisting that the arrest of his right-hand man would compromise him with the Central Committee. "I will throw up everything and go abroad," threatened Azev. "The fate of the czar will then be in your hands."

Gerassimov promised that Karpovich would be allowed to escape and this placated the double agent. But Karpovich almost proved his own undoing. An Okhrana guard took Karpovich from his cell and put him into a carriage. The guard stopped the carriage and told Karpovich to wait until he went to a tobacconist to buy some cigarettes. Reported the guard later to Gerassimov: "I was sure that the cab would be empty upon my return but to my surprise Karpovich was quietly sitting there."

The guard then suggested that they stop at a restaurant before arriving at the next jail where Karpovich would be imprisoned. Both men went to a restaurant and, after the guard ordered meals, he went to the washroom. The guard watched Karpovich through the open door but the prisoner merely sat at the table, eating. He hesitated, apparently believing that a trap was being set for him, that he would be shot while attempting to escape. "I got tired of him," said the guard. "I thought he would never escape! What could I do if he simply did not want to take his chance?"

Karpovich finally got up and walked out of the restaurant to disappear. Azev, it was later claimed, personally murdered his aide and buried his body. Meanwhile, the double agent continued to make endless plans for the czar's murder. He complained to the Central Committee that the czar's itinerary was constantly changing and he was thus able to evade destruction.

Azev met again and again with Gerassimov. The Okhrana chief told his spy that the only matter concerning him was the safety of the czar. Azev assured him that that was his concern and then shocked Gerassimov by telling him of the czar's itinerary for the next day, information that Gerassimov himself did not know. Gerassimov assumed rightly that Azev's information came from a high-ranking official in the czar's court, perhaps one of the members of the Imperial family. He demanded to know the source of Azev's top secret information.

Azev refused, saying: "You know that I am taking every means to thwart this attempt and that I guarantee to be successful. But I am unable to give you the name of my informant because he is very highly placed and only two or three people know of our relations. If he should notice that his role is becoming known, his suspicions should fall upon me and I should be lost. . . . Please don't press it. I must have some regard for my own safety."

The next plan to kill the czar implemented by Azev in 1908, involved shooting Nicholas II while he was inspecting a new Russian cruiser, *Rurik*, before it was launched in Glasgow, Scotland. This was a terribly involved project which was confounded by locating a proper hiding place on the ship where the assassin could hide until the right moment.

In July 1908, Azev arrived in Glasgow to ostensibly arrange for the assassination but the Russian sailor volunteering for the mission backed out at the last moment. At this time, Azev knew that his days as a double agent were numbered. A member of the Socialist Revolutionary Party, Vladimir Burtzev, had long suspected Azev of being a police spy. He quietly investigated Azev's background, movements and, especially, the source of his wealth. Moreover, he was able to contact a retired police official who admitted that Azev was the Okhrana's top informant.

Burtzev put his evidence before a tribunal of the Socialist Revolutionary Party in Paris in December 1908. Azev actually appeared to defend himself. When asked if he had met Okhrana chief Gerassimov on a certain night in St. Petersburg, Azev confidently provided a bill from a Warsaw hotel for that night. The tribunal quickly discerned that the bill was forged and Azev was asked to describe his room. Azev paused, then said he could not remember the room's appearance. He was asked to return the next day but Azev never returned, neither to Paris nor to Russia.

Not until many years later, following the Russian revolution, when the Okhrana's files were recovered and inspected was Azev's role as the supreme Okhrana spy revealed, shocking the hard-boiled Bolsheviks and Communists who had once believed him to be one of their greatest leaders. Even Lenin was surprised in reading the secret police files on Azev but he made little mention of him. Lenin had also unwaveringly believed in another confederate named Roman Malinovsky who had been one of his closest friends, a revolutionary who also turned out to be an Okhrana spy.

In the years before World War I, Azev wandered about Europe, living comfortably on the proceeds of his spying efforts. Burtzev met him by accident in Frankfurt, Germany, in 1912. At that time, Azev sat on a park bench for a few minutes with the very man he knew would report their encounter and send revolu-

Master spy at play: Yevno Azev on the Riviera with one of his mistresses, 1910.

tionaries after him. Azev was ever the intriguer, reproaching Burtzev: "Had you not exposed my relationship with the Okhrana, I would have been able to assassinate the czar. You destroyed your own work and that of many others." With that Azev stood up and disappeared into a crowd.

Azev was identified in Berlin as a revolutionary in 1915, during World War I. He was interned but lived comfortably in confinement, allowed regular visits by his mistress, a woman who had gone into exile with him in 1908 and who was waiting for him when he was released in 1918. He moved into a comfortable Berlin apartment but grew ill. A member of the German Foreign Office visited him and at that time, Azev swore that, at heart, he was a monarchist and an anti-revolutionary but, as usual, this was thought to be a self-serving remark since the Kaiser's monarchy still ruled Germany with an iron hand. Yevno Azev, the most astounding double agent on record, died on April 24, 1918. Two days later he was buried at Wilmersdorf Cemetery. His loyal mistress was his only mourner.

[ALSO SEE: *Mordka Bogrov; George Gapon; Roman Malinovsky; Okhrana; S. V. Zubatov*]

BABINGTON, ANTHONY
Catholic Agent in England ▪ (1561–1586)

BORN IN RURAL ENGLAND, BABINGTON AND HIS family were secret Catholics at a time when this religion was severely persecuted by the Protestant Government of Queen Elizabeth I. When Catholic Queen Mary of Scotland fled to England for protection, Elizabeth had her imprisoned in 1568. Babington was then only a boy but he served as a page to Mary's jailer, and he became Mary's most ardent supporter. In 1580, after convincing Queen Elizabeth that he was a staunch Protestant, Babington was accepted at court and remained there for two years.

Babington nevertheless schemed against Elizabeth and her Protestant government and, in 1582, he traveled throughout Europe, organizing Catholic Englishmen of wealth and power. He planned to overthrow Elizabeth with their help and an invading Spanish army, expecting the downtrodden Catholics in England to rise up against their oppressors. At that time, Babington envisioned, Elizabeth would be replaced by Mary.

Mary received letters from Babington which he had carried from the Continent, all from English noblemen who were Catholics and who promised to rescue her. He also carried back from Mary letters to these Catholic conspirators. All the messages were written in code which convinced Mary that such correspondence was safe.

Elizabeth became aware of this treasonable correspondence through her devoted, shrewd spymaster, Francis Walsingham. After intercepting some of Mary's correspondence, Walsingham had his most talented cryptographers decipher the letters. He not only informed Elizabeth that Mary was plotting against her but, at Elizabeth's clever instigation, introduced messages of his own subtle design into the correspondence. The aim was to develop what later became known as the Babington plot until Mary and her conspirators were completely compromised.

In a surprise move, Walsingham suddenly ordered the arrest of John Ballard, one of the leading conspirators. Ballard promptly confessed to the plot, providing Walsingham with all the pieces of information Walsingham needed to prove his case against Mary, Babington, and the others. Babington went into hiding but he and other conspirators were hunted down and imprisoned in the Tower. Babington lost all of his nerve at the end and tried to shift the blame to Ballard. The other conspirators, except Mary, also blamed each other. Babington then begged Elizabeth for mercy. She responded by sending him to the block and the executioner's axe. The same fate befell the rest, including Queen Mary.

Mary's conviction of treason was based upon a single letter in which she expressed her approval of the conspirators murdering Elizabeth. The damning passage, which Walsingham insisted was in Mary's own handwriting, was undoubtedly a forgery. Walsingham had had the incriminating words inserted into one of Mary's letters, which he knew would bring about her execution.

[ALSO SEE: *Francis Walsingham*]

BADEN-POWELL, ROBERT
British Spy in Europe Before World War I ▪ (1857–1941)

LONDON-BORN BADEN-POWELL WAS THE SON OF A mathematics professor who taught at Oxford. After completing his public schooling at Charterhouse, he entered the army, excused from all training because of his brilliant test achievements.

Baden-Powell was sent to South Africa in 1887. A year later he was involved in the campaigns against the Zulus, acting as an intelligence officer for the celebrated Flying Column. In 1890, Baden-Powell was assigned to the British bastion of Malta, serving under his uncle, Sir H. A. Smyth, governor of the fortress. A short time later, Baden-Powell was named as chief British intelligence officer for the Mediterranean and was specifically ordered to gather information on Balkan troop dispositions and movements.

Baden-Powell became one of England's most accomplished if eccentric spies. His sharp ability to make and record quick, accurate observations, his skill at tracking, and his flair for amateur theatrics all contributed to his success. It would be some time before Mansfield Cumming would organize the British military intelligence system known as MI6. It was a colorful era in which such gifted amateurs as Baden-Powell practiced espionage with inventive if not outlandish disguises.

General Robert Baden-Powell, one of England's more colorful early-day spies.

During this time, the Balkans were in turmoil and tensions ran high between the old military empires of Germany, Austria-Hungary, and the Western nations of England and France. It was Baden-Powell's job to determine the military strength of the Austrians. Assuming the disguise of a lepidopterist, he scouted the fortifications in Herzgovina, a province in the Austro-Hungarian Empire (later absorbed into Yugoslavia).

Wearing spectacles with thick lenses, and carrying a butterfly net, Baden-Powell appeared to be a befuddled naturalist seeking rare specimens. In this pose, he wandered close to defense positions and was a source of amusement to the guards as he scurried about waving his net wildly in attempts to catch elusive butterflies. Baden-Powell was a talented artist who quickly drew sketches of the Austrian fortifications, cleverly concealing these drawings inside larger sketches of butterflies so that when they were inspected by Austrian censors they went undetected.

Sent to Germany, Baden-Powell learned that a huge new drydock was being constructed in Hamburg. He appeared at the location in the disguise of a consulting engineer and was able to sketch the restricted area. His report of this military installation convinced the British High Command that Kaiser Wilhelm was, indeed, preparing for war by constructing a naval base for warships.

Baden-Powell later performed intelligence work during the Boer War in South Africa and received high praise for his military defense of Mafeking which successfully resisted a prolonged siege in 1900. Seven years later, the dashing British intelligence chief established the organization for which he is best remembered—the Boy Scouts, an international institution which flourishes to this day.

Baden-Powell was to chronicle his espionage adventures in a book which did not appear until 1915, and was by then of little use to the Allies who were already at war with the Central Powers (Germany and Austria-Hungary). By then the gentleman spy world of Baden-Powell existed only in the stories told by gray-haired men in officers' clubs, sitting next to crackling fires and lifting snifters of brandy with palsied hands as they recalled the thrilling adventures of yesteryear.

BAILLIE-STEWART, NORMAN
British Spy for Germany ▪ (1909–1966)

B ORN IN LONDON AS NORMAN BAILLIE STEWART Wright, he moved with his parents to India in 1910 where his father served in the army under the British raj. His parents returned to England where Baillie-Stewart received a public school education. In 1922, he enrolled at the Royal Naval College at Dartmouth but left do to illness three years later. In

Norman Baillie-Stewart (rear of car, hands over face), arriving at court under military escort to face espionage charges in 1932.

1925, he entered the prestigious Sandhurst Military Academy, graduating in 1928, commissioned a lieutenant in the British army.

Ever posturing himself as coming from noble blood (which was not the case), he shortened his name to the more aristocratic, hyphenated spelling of Baillie-Stewart, discarding his father's last name of Wright. From that point on Baillie-Stewart lived well beyond his officer's pay and, by the time he visited Germany in 1932, he was hopelessly in debt supporting a luxurious lifestyle.

Baillie-Stewart was by then a lieutenant serving in the Seaforth Highlanders. When he got tipsy and blabbed of his financial embarrassment, an Abwehr agent contacted him. Baillie-Stewart then met the rather lethargic chief of the Abwehr, Konrad Patzig. If money was all that was needed, Patzig told Baillie-Stewart, the young officer's problems were over. Germany would pay him handsomely for some information.

Baillie-Stewart accepted a considerable cash payment. Patzig promised to send more money, all the lieutenant needed to keep himself in his comfortable lifestyle. In return, Baillie-Stewart supplied the Abwehr with some of England's greatest secrets, particulars on its new tanks and armored cars, as well as battle plans, organizations, and troop dispositions around the globe. In five months and seventeen days, Baillie-Stewart, as the only German spy then operating in England, had looted his country's top secrets.

Agents of MI5, the crack counterintelligence service founded by Major Vernon Kell in 1909, got on to Baillie-Stewart when one of his fellow officers reported the lieutenant's extravagant spending habits and the fact that he never seemed to run out of money. MI5 agents tracked Baillie-Stewart for some weeks, documenting his theft of British secrets and their delivery to Germany. He was promptly arrested, tried, and convicted, then sent to prison for five years. Baillie-Stewart was confined in the Tower of London. The British press called him "the officer in the Tower."

When released in 1936, Baillie-Stewart went straight to Germany where he lived until the end of the war. He was captured by British troops when Berlin fell and he was taken back to England. He was tried once more, this time for Pro-Nazi activities and was sent back to prison for another five years. Baillie-Stewart was freed in 1949 and relocated to Dublin, Ireland, where he lived out his life, denying to this dying breath that he was ever a spy, although the meticulous records of MI5 and the captured documents of the Abwehr following the war prove his guilt beyond question.

[ALSO SEE: *Abwehr; Vernon Kell; MI5*]

BAKER, JOSEPHINE
French Spy Against Germany ▪ (1906–1975)

THE CELEBRATED BLACK DANCER AND SINGER, Josephine Baker, was born and raised in St. Louis, Missouri, daughter of poor parents. She dropped out of school early to go to work, studying dance when she could. She then began to work small clubs that catered to black patrons but became so popular that by 1924 Baker was starring in musical revues on Broadway. The following year she went to Paris to appear in the all-black musical variety show, *La Revue Negre*.

Baker became a sensation doing her frenetic Jazz dances in scantily-clad costumes. Her success in Paris was overwhelming and she became an institution, appearing at the Follies-Bergere. No American or any other tourist visiting Paris during the Jazz Age missed seeing the fabulous Josephine Baker. She traveled throughout Europe, appearing in all the major capitals and was particularly successful in Berlin. In the mid-1930s, Baker returned to America to appear in a Ziegfeld Follies show but she was severely criticized by anti-black columnists who labelled her dancing "lewd" and "lacivious."

It was always Paris that attracted Baker and she returned to the City of Light to take up permanent residence, becoming a French citizen in 1937. In 1940, when war between France and Germany was declared, Baker volunteered for the French Red Cross. After France fell to the invading Nazis, she worked with the resistance, offering her services as a spy. She met many times with American and British agents in France, telling them what she knew of the Germans who visited the clubs in which she was appearing.

Baker was in the unique position of meeting high-ranking German officers in Paris and was able to overhear conversations which provided valuable information. Moreover, Baker was able to view first hand those French officials who were collaborating with the Germans. All of this she reported back to Allied agents.

At one point, Baker was able to learn vital information regarding Vichy French fortifications and intentions toward the Allies whom they knew were soon planning to invade North Africa. She was so helpful to the Allies in this instance that she later received a message from General George S. Patton, stating: "To Josephine Baker who helped us so valiantly." For her work with the resistance and, especially her espionage on behalf of her adopted country, France awarded Baker the Freedom Medal and the Cross of Lorraine in 1945.

BAKER, LAFAYETTE
Chief of U.S. Intelligence During
Civil War ▪ (1826–1868)

DEVIOUS, MANIPULATING, AND WITH THE HEART OF A sneakthief, Lafayette Baker became head of the Union Intelligence Service during the American Civil War. He accomplished this mighty task with pure bravado and the ability to artfully lie while unblinkingly staring into the eyes of America's greatest leaders.

Though he later claimed to be a descendant of one of Ethan Allen's "Green Mountain Boys," who had named him after the illustrious Marquis de Lafayette of American Revolution fame, no such lineage really existed. Baker was born on a farm in upstate New York. His father, a poor farmer, moved the family to Michigan when Baker was in his teens. After some brief schooling, Baker made his way to New York City where little is known of his doings, although one report has it that he became a fence for stolen goods, working hand in glove with the notorious Bowery Boys gang.

In the gold rush of 1849, Baker joined tens of thousands of nugget seekers and went to California. He did not find gold but he did find the kind of action that suited his basically brutal nature. In San Francisco he became a member of the Vigilance Committee, patrolling the fog-bound streets of the Barbary Coast at night in search of desperate criminals, or so Baker later advertised that adventurous episode of his life. In reality, he worked as a bouncer in a notorious Barbary Coast saloon and informed on his employers to the local constabulary. He was later a willing member in several lynchings.

When the Civil War began in 1861, Baker hurried back East, shuttling between New York and Washington as he sought appointments with high-ranking Union officers to offer his services as a Union spy. In New York, he managed to get an appointment with a cavalry colonel, telling this officer that he would be an ideal spy, that he had done considerable undercover work as a former vigilante in San Francisco. He enthusiastically described how he personally had meted out justice to several suspected criminals by holding three-minute trials in the streets of San Francisco, then hanging these hapless creatures from lampposts. "We don't enlist hangmen," the Union officer snorted and shoved Baker from his office.

Undaunted, in early 1862, Baker made his way to the field headquarters of General Winfield Scott, then Commander-in-Chief of the Union Army. He stood outside the general's tent, arguing with Scott's aide, insisting that he see the Commander-in-Chief on urgent business. The aide finally informed Scott that "a persistent man" wanted to see him.

Scott, then seventy-six, was a rather self-indulgent character amused by anyone possessing an eccentric personality. He was particularly impressed with flamboyant young Union officers, believing that the more arrogant and brash they were, the more likely they would be brave and brilliant in battle. Typical of Scott's proteges was George Armstrong Custer.

As usual, Scott's fancy got the better of him. He told his aide to bring in the "dark-bearded young stranger." Lafayette Baker strode into Scott's tent. He solemnly announced that he would speak to the general only after the aide left and he was alone with the Commander-in-Chief. Scott, a giant of a man who weighed more than 300 pounds, had been studying his battle maps. He threw a blanket over them, then waved the apprehensive aide out of his tent.

Baker then told Scott that he came to offer his services to him as an accomplished spy. He explained that he had lived in Richmond, Virginia, for some time and that he proposed returning to that city, now the capital of the Confederacy, to gather vital military information and bring it back.

Scott had nothing left of his intelligence service at that time operating in Richmond. A dedicated group of Allan Pinkerton's spies had been rounded up and jailed, including the inventive Englishmen Pryce Lewis and John Scully, along with the valiant "mail carrier" Timothy Webster and his erstwhile companion, Hattie Lawton. (Pinkerton was then the most famous criminal detective in America who had successfully smuggled Abraham Lincoln to Washington, D.C., in 1861 to avoid assassins planning to kill the President-Elect en route. He was later named chief of the fledgling Union Intelligence Service but he would be relieved for his failure to properly estimate Confederate troop strength and positions at the battle of Antietam.)

Scott explained to Baker that his going to Richmond would not serve the Union army's needs. He need detailed reports from the fields, how many men were in the Confederate army of General Pierre Gustave Toutant Beauregard, where were they positioned, and where were they headed? How many pieces of field artillery did Beauregard have and how much rolling stock? All of this important data could not be found in the tea rooms of Richmond, but in the field.

Baker nodded, saying that he could successfully infiltrate the Confederate lines between Maryland and Virginia and that he had the perfect disguise to accomplish what General Scott desired. With that Baker produced a tripod upon which he teetered a rather cumbersome, large black box with what appeared to be a round glass window. It was a camera, Baker announced. He would go through the lines as a southern photographer, offering to take pictures of high-ranking Confederate officers and he would thus be allowed into the camps to obtain the very information needed.

Scott liked the plan but quickly added that he could pay Baker very little money. There was no budget left for an intelligence service. Baker said he would work "for expenses only," and, if he returned with useful information, that he be rewarded with a commission in the Union Army. Scott agreed and sent Baker on his cavalier mission. From that point on, most of Baker's celebrated adventure was recorded by Baker later in his self-aggrandizing memoirs.

Using the alias of Sam Munson, Baker lugged his camera equipment to the Maryland-Virginia border and, after being stopped by Union sentries, he had to call upon Scott to save him from being shot as a spy. He was freed and renewed his perilous journey. At the time Scott asked Baker if he wanted to change his mind about being a spy. Baker shook his head and set out again for the Confederate lines. This time he crossed into Virginia but he was stopped by a Rebel patrol and was arrested as a spy.

He was taken to Richmond and thrown into a cell. Baker later claimed that he next sent a note to General Beauregard through a southern friend in Richmond. Beauregard was also informed that Baker was an itinerant southern photographer who had been captured by the Yankees after the war broke out and had worked his way southward by photographing Federal officers and their staffs. He had, the southern general was told, all the while spied on the Union garrisons, camps, and defense lines and had much to tell Beauregard.

The general ordered Baker to be brought to him. At that time, Baker gave Beauregard detailed information of Union troop movements, positions of heavy gun emplacements, and locations where ammunition and goods were stored. Beauregard's aides diligently wrote down the information but the general seemed more interested in Baker's camera and the then revolutionary techniques of photography. Very few photographers were present during the immense, bloody battles of the Civil War. The greatest of these was Mathew Brady who had been recording the terrible war from its first important battle, Bull Run, in 1861, and who also busied himself with photographing the war's key figures for the North, especially the high-ranking officers, their staffs and their loved ones. This had prompted some southern photographers to record Confederate leaders with their marvelous and mysterious black boxes.

According to Baker, Jefferson Davis, the President of the Confederacy, along with Vice-President Alexander H. Stephens, were called to the interview by Beauregard. Again, Baker claimed his innocence, begging to be set free so that he could resume his profession. Davis decreed that Baker should be allowed to do exactly that, and, after conferring with Beauregard, was given a pass which permitted him to photograph any of the southern military commanders, their troops, and camp sites, as he saw fit.

Beauregard was the first to request a photograph and he and his staff posed for Baker a short time later.

With a Confederate officer at his side, Baker was thereafter allowed to go freely into all the Confederate camps and photograph whomever and whatever he pleased. He thus recorded priceless information for the North, but not on his camera. Had the Confederates known anything about this new apparatus, they would have realized that it did not work, that it had a broken lens and that it had no glass plates upon which to record a single photograph.

For several weeks, Baker wandered freely from one Confederate military installation to another, making notes, and pretending to photograph hundreds of officers and even companies of enlisted men. He appeared in Fredricksburg, Virginia, some time later and had the mischance of meeting some officers whom he had photographed some time earlier. These officers were angry because they had not received the photos he had promised. Baker attempted to explain that he had been kept so busy taking photographs by the general staff that he had had no time to develop the pictures he had taken.

Baker was not believed and was thrown into the Fredricksburg jail to await trial on charges of espionage. By then, a professional photographer had inspected Baker's camera and had discovered it to be useless. Baker knew he would be found guilty and quickly executed. He had, however, secreted a pocket knife in his boot and, late that night, he managed to use the knife to free two loose bars on his cell, slip through the opening and make his escape. He somehow managed to get back to the Union lines to report his fantastic experiences. General Scott was so impressed with the information Baker had obtained that he made him a captain and put him in charge of his intelligence service.

At least, that was the story Baker later penned, to explain his first grand success at espionage. The truth was less spectacular. He was, indeed, captured, and taken before Jefferson Davis who did not give him a pass to photograph the whole of the Confederacy but listened for some minutes to Baker's inept lies and then pronounced him a spy and ordered him held for trial. Baker did escape from the Richmond jail, then wandered for weeks through Virginia, living in shacks and the woods, stealing food where he could find it, as he desperately tried to regain the Union lines. He was picked up in Fredricksburg as a vagrant and later held as a spy, but he again escaped, this time with the help of local prostitute whom he had been staying with, and finally managed to return to Scott's headquarters.

The tales of Baker photographing endless Confederate officers was nonsense. He had lost his camera before being picked up by the first Confederate patrol. The information regarding Confederate forces he later relayed to Scott he had learned from a Union officer he had met in the Richmond prison and all of this information was outdated by the time Baker passed it on to Scott. General Scott was an impressionable old man, however, whose whim to send the errant Baker forth into espionage without any training or experience suited his odd fancy.

Baker knew his man. He knew that the more incredible he made his report the more likely it would be believed by the doddering old Scott. Baker's fantastic tale was swallowed whole by Scott who knew very little about espionage. So impressed was he that he not only granted a commission to the conniving Baker but he warmly retold Baker's saga to several in Lincoln's administration. The man who appreciated the story most was Edwin McMasters Stanton, Secretary of War.

Stanton was a quick-tempered man of action. Although he paid lip service to the great humanity of Abraham Lincoln, to the President's compassion, decency, and kindness, Stanton himself was a bigoted, calculating person in whom dwelled a vicious bully, and, if certain historians are to be believed, the ambition of a presidential assassin. When Scott introduced the brash, young Baker to him, Stanton immediately recognized a man of his own stripe, one to whom conspiracy and collusion were second nature. He saw a man who would say or do anything to gain prestige and, more importantly, power, a man that Stanton himself could use to his own good ends.

Stanton took Baker under his own wing. He became the Secretary's personal secret agent, conducting close surveillance of those Stanton distrusted most, other members in Lincoln's cabinet, and high-ranking officers who were Lincoln's appointments. Stanton also wanted Allan Pinkerton out of the way as head of the Union Intelligence Service. Pinkerton answered only to Lincoln which Stanton resented. He, Edwin Stanton, should be in complete charge of the war, not this well-meaning but uninformed Lincoln.

At every opportunity, Stanton, through Baker's intrigues, discredited Pinkerton, and, equally, General George McClellan, who had taken over the army, brilliantly organized and trained it to a peak fighting machine but proved indecisive in battle. Baker spent much of this time discovering McClellan's mistakes and having reports of his blunders brought before Lincoln, or leaked to the Union press. Since Pinkerton was the espionage chief serving McClellan, the more mistakes the Union army made, the more blame could be shifted to Pinkerton who apparently was not providing the kind of intelligence that would allow McClellan to make decisive military moves.

Following the battle of Antietam, the bloodiest battle of the war which claimed more than 5,000 Union and Confederate lives, McClellan's image dipped drastically. His critics chorused his inability to learn of the true strengths and positions of Confederate forces under the brilliant command of General Robert E. Lee. This responsibility really fell upon Pinkerton. When McClellan was removed from command, Pinkerton was also dismissed. This was a well-rehearsed scenario by Stanton, who had long

badgered Lincoln to replace Pinkerton, arguing that Pinkerton was a detective whose ability to track down criminals had little or nothing to do with expertise in espionage.

Stanton, with Scott's backing, recommended that none other than the enterprising Lafayette Baker, descendant from American patriots and one of the greatest spies in the Union forces, head the intelligence service. Lincoln agreed and Baker, a man with no real knowledge of military espionage, was phenomenally promoted to the rank of full colonel and assumed one of the most powerful positions in the Union.

Baker's techniques were identical to those he had practiced in San Francisco as a vigilante. He terrorized, threatened, and blackmailed suspects, both Union and Confederate, to obtain information. For three years, he continued to operate a haphazard espionage system for the North but most of his information was learned second-hand from scouts working directly for Union cavalary commands. He continued to have some spies behind the Confederate lines but the best of these were originally selected by Pinkerton.

The most celebrated Confederate spies captured by the Union during this period were apprehended by those who did not work for Baker, but once they came under his supervision as prisoners, Baker conducted brutal interrogations of Belle Boyd and Wat Bowie. He woke them from sound sleeps and hectored them. He made sure they missed meals and suffered every kind of inconvenience. He deprived them of proper sanitary conditions. All of this inhuman treatment was to induce Boyd and Bowie to provide him with information. They gave him nothing. Bowie escaped from the Washington, D.C., jail from under the noses of Baker's guards and Boyd was released in 1863. Both went on to continue their spying for the Confederacy.

Most of Baker's time was spent tracking down deserters from the Union army. He also went after profiteers but only to line his own pockets. Those who refused to share with Baker their illegal spoils from the selling off of government supplies, he arrested and jailed. Baker violated Constitutional rights without fear or reservations since he was wholly backed by Stanton. He routinely made false arrests, conducted illegal searches without warrants, and blackmailed government officials into making endorsements of his almost non-existent espionage service. No one misused his authority or office more than Lafayette Baker.

One of Baker's most important duties was the protection of President Abraham Lincoln, a job at which he failed miserably. This responsibility would later become that of the Secret Service, which was created in Lincoln's last cabinet meeting in 1865. Its proposed duties were chiefly to guard the President and to detect and apprehend counterfeiters and otherwise serve the Treasury Department. Actually, Baker's intelligence service had nothing to do with the federal agency that later became the Secret Service, although Baker was to arrogantly and, as usual, mislead the public into believing that he headed that service. He entitled his memoirs: *History of the United States Secret Service.*

At one point Baker bragged that "there is no single Confederate spy or agent behind Union lines who is unknown to me and our service." Yet, flourishing within Washington, D.C. were dozens of conspirators all plotting the assassination of President Lincoln. One group met regularly only a few blocks from Baker's offices throughout the early part of 1865. Its leaders were John H. Surratt and a vainglorious actor from an illustrious theatrical family, John Wilkes Booth.

On the night of April 14, 1865, Good Friday, John Wilkes Booth went to a saloon next door to Ford's Theater in Washington, D.C., where he knew President Lincoln was watching a comedy, *Our American Cousin.* The war was officially over. Lee had surrendered at Appomattox. Yet many still sought Lincoln's death, including the diehard Booth-Surratt group. Booth was seen drinking brandy in the saloon at 10 P.M. A few minutes later the actor walked into the theater lobby, then, softly humming to himself, he climbed the stairs to the mezzanine (or dress circle), and walked behind the last row of seats to a door that led to the presidential box. The chair next to this door was vacant. The policeman assigned to guard the president, John F. Parker, who was under the command of Lafayette Baker, was not present.

Without notice, Booth went through the door, then into the box where Lincoln, his wife Mary, Major Henry Riggs Rathbone, and his fiancee Clara Harris sat watching the play. Booth stepped close to Lincoln and fired a single shot from a small Derringer pistol into the president's head. Rathbone jumped up and struggled briefly with Booth, who slashed him with a knife and then jumped dramatically from the box to the stage, a leap that broke his leg.

Instead of fleeing, Booth, ever the limelight-seeking actor, could not resist a grandstand play. As the audience erupted in panic, he raised the bloody knife and shouted: "Sic Semper Tyrannis!" ("Thus shall it be for tyrants!") With that he hobbled wildly across the stage, screaming: "The South is avenged!" Wincing with pain, Booth ran limping toward the theater's rear door. Once in the alley, he grabbed the reins of a horse held by John "Peanuts" Burrough. The boy, not knowing that the actor had just shot Lincoln, had been asked by Booth earlier to hold his horse in the back of Ford's Theater.

Once in the saddle, Booth wheeled about and raced down the alley, heading for the Navy Yard Bridge, a passage he knew would lead to freedom. No more than two minutes had passed from the time Booth had shot the President to the moment he mounted his horse and dashed away into the night.

At almost the same time Booth was firing the fatal bullet into Lincoln's head, another of the conspirators, hulking Lewis Paine (born Lewis Thornton Powell), on the pretext of delivering medicine, lumbered into the home of Secretary of State William Henry Seward and rushed up the stairs and into a bedroom. Seward lay in a heavy cast around his arm and head as the result of a carriage accident a week earlier.

Paine rushed toward Seward with a knife and began slashing at him, cutting the bedridden Seward but not fatally wounding him. The casts prevented the conspirator from delivering a mortal wound. Seward's grown sons, Frederick and Augustus, along with male military nurse, George T. Robinson, struggled with Paine who broke loose and dashed back down the stairs toward the open front door, shouting: "I am mad! I am mad!"

Paine ran to his horse cursing. Another confederate, youthful, nervous David Herold was not there as was the plan. Herold was the only person who knew where they were to meet up with Booth but when he heard the commotion inside the Seward house, he bolted, leaving Paine to find his own place to hide.

At a prearranged meeting spot, Herold caught up to Booth in Anacostia. Herold told the assassin that he panicked and abandoned Paine after he heard shouts of "Murder!" coming from the Seward house. The pair then rode quickly to Surratsville, Md., a hamlet that consisted only of a few buildings, the most important being a small hotel owned by Mary E. Surratt, mother of John H. Surratt, Booth's co-leader in the plot to kill Lincoln. Surratt, who had met with Booth only hours before the shooting that night, was not in sight.

Surratt had left the fugitives a bottle of whiskey, two carbines with ammunition, a monkey wrench, and a coil of rope. (Surratt later claimed at his trial that he had left these items at his mother's hotel two weeks earlier and not for any specific purpose.) Booth also retrieved a pair of binoculars. The binoculars, it was later claimed by Baker, had been left at the hotel by its owner, Mary Surratt, who intended them for John Wilkes Booth.

Booth and Herold rode southward. Though their destination was apparently known to them, Booth was in great pain from his broken leg. He told Herold that they would detour to the farmhouse of a physician he knew, a Dr. Samuel Mudd, who lived outside of Beantown. At about 5 A.M., the pair arrived at Mudd's home. They woke the doctor and he cut away the actor's left boot so he could set the broken ankle bone, affixing splints to it. He then bandaged the ankle and leg. Booth borrowed a razor, and, while he was shaving off his mustache, the doctor quickly assembled a crude pair of crutches for the actor. Booth then gave Mudd $25 before he and Herold once more rode off southward.

Mudd later insisted that he did not know nor recognize John Wilkes Booth, that Herold had helped the injured man into a bedroom where he lay with his face against the wall while he set and bandaged his leg. The physician also later claimed that the man he aided was wearing a red wig at the time. Though sent to prison for life, Mudd consistently maintained his innocence and his case was the subject of controversy for years to come. Mudd, however, was lying about knowing Booth. He had introduced Booth and John H. Surratt, a then accomplished Confederate spy, in the fall of 1864.

By then Lincoln had died and Edwin McMasters Stanton had taken over the government, declaring martial law. What he wanted more than anything at that moment was John Wilkes Booth, offering $100,000 for his dead-or-alive capture, preferably dead. Before Lincoln had been shot, Baker embarrassingly admitted later, he and Stanton had no knowledge of the conspiracy. Yet, within two days, all of the conspirators were in custody. Somehow, Baker knew exactly where he could find the alcoholic George A. Atzerodt whose nerve had failed him when it came time to kill Vice President Andrew Johnson. Somehow, he knew that Seward's would-be assassin, Lewis Paine, could be found in the Washington, D.C., boarding house of Mary Surratt, hiding under a bed in a third-floor room.

Somehow, the illustrious Colonel Baker knew to arrest Edward Spangler, the carpenter at Ford's Theater who had made a portable barrier for Booth so he could successfully bar the inside of the door that led to Lincoln's box once the assassin had entered this restricted but unguarded hallway. Somehow, Baker's keen but unexplained perceptions deduced that Spangler had also drilled a hole in the door leading to Lincoln's box so Booth, while standing in the outer hallway could peer into it unmolested and know when the President was most vulnerable.

The very man who was responsible for protecting the life of the President had, twenty-four hours before the assassination, no idea of the identifies of the conspirators. But then suddenly, inexplicably, almost magically, Lafayette Baker possessed all the answers within forty-eight hours, including the exact obscure escape route taken by John Wilkes Booth and David Herold. After conferring with Secretary of War Stanton, Baker called an inexperienced junior cavalry officer, Lieutenant Edward P. Doherty to his office.

Baker told Doherty that he was to take twenty-five of his best men and go in pursuit of the assassin. Also, Baker informed the startled Doherty, he would directly command this special troop but the overall command would fall upon two men, Baker's cousin, Luther B. Baker, and Colonel Everton J. Conger. Luther Baker was nothing more than a strongman thug who had for years carried out Lafayette Baker's most unsavory chores. Colonel Everton Conger also worked for Baker's intelligence service and was as conniving and secretive as his superior.

The riders left Washington by boat, sailing down the Potomac. They then disembarked and rode straight to the Garrett farm where they found Booth and Herold barricaded in a small, rickety tobacco barn on the evening of April 16, 1865. Booth refused to surrender but allowed the terrified Herold to give up. The barn was set afire and a shot rang out. Booth was then dragged mortally wounded from the blazing building. One of the troopers, Sgt. Boston Corbett, had shot the assassin.

The dying Booth, held by Colonel Conger, murmured: "Tell my mother I died for my country . . . I did my best." He asked Conger to hold up his arms so that Booth could view his own delicate hands. Conger raised the assassin's arms. Booth stared at his hands and muttered "useless, useless . . ." and died. Conger searched Booth's body thoroughly. He removed a stub of a candle, a compass, several photos of actresses, a considerable amount of money which eventually vanished, and, most importantly, an oblong, leather bound diary. It was the diary that most interested Conger, an object he had been expressly directed by Lafayette Baker to look for, seize, and immediately return to the intelligence chief.

Conger held Booth's diary, glancing through it briefly in the light of two flaming torches held by troopers. He then pocketed Booth's belongings, slipping the diary into an inside coat pocket. Conger then ordered Doherty to return Herold and Booth's body to Washington. He mounted his horse, saying that "I have urgent papers to deliver." Luther Baker ran forward, insisting that he accompany Conger. The colonel refused, and a brief argument ensued. Then Doherty heard Conger shouting to Baker that he was to stay with the troopers. With that, Colonel Conger dug his spurs into his horse's flanks and galloped out of sight.

When Lafayette Baker met Conger in Washington hours later, he nervously asked what Conger had found on Booth's body. Conger turned over Booth's effects, including the diary. Baker sat silently before Conger, then told his subordinate to witness the fact that he was going to count the exact number of pages in the diary. He proceeded to do this. Then he studied the diary at great length, making notes. Baker then told Conger that he would accompany him to see Stanton. Both men met the Secretary of War in his home. Stanton was in his dressing gown when he met with Baker and Conger in his study, taking from them all of the effects of the dead Booth.

It was obvious to Conger that Baker had wanted him present when he turned over Booth's effects so that it could never be said that he tampered with anything and that Stanton was the final and only depository of this evidence. Baker then began receiving terse orders regarding the conspirators in custody, which included Paine, Herold, Mrs. Mary Surratt, Spangler, Dr. Mudd, and two ex-Confederate soldiers Booth had at one time involved in a kidnapping attempt of Lincoln, Samuel B. Arnold, and Michael O'Laughlin.

The conspirators were tried by a secret tribunal overseen by Stanton. Paine, Herold, Atzerodt, and Mrs. Surratt were condemned to death by hanging.

Arnold, O'Laughlin, and Mudd received life terms and Spangler six years in prison. The main conspirators insisted that Mrs. Surratt was innocent, and that she was being unjustly prosecuted simply because her son, John H. Surratt, had been one of the co-leaders of the conspiracy.

John Surratt, however, was nowhere to be found. He was the one man whom Lafayette Baker had failed to apprehend, despite his infinite ability to reach out, locate, and capture all of the other parties in the conspiracy. A petition for Mrs. Surratt which begged for mercy, a commutation, was sent to then President Andrew Johnson. This petition was delayed by Lafayette Baker. Johnson never saw the petition until after Mrs. Surratt, along with Paine, Atzerodt, and Herold had been hanged in the courtyard of the old Arnsenal Building on July 7, 1865.

Try as he might, however, Lafayette Baker had little success in tracking down the elusive John H. Surratt. The conspirator fled to Canada following the assassination. He then sailed for England and then on to Italy. He was reported the following year to be a member of the Papal Zouaves, the elite guards who protected the Pope in Rome. A fellow guard turned Surratt into American diplomats at the American Embassy in Rome who arranged for his arrest on November 8, 1866. Baker was informed of this arrest and made arrangements for Surratt to be returned to the U.S. These "arrangements" were apparently shoddy in that Surratt managed to make a fairly easy escape to Egypt. He had sufficient funds to live comfortably in Alexanderia for some time until he was identified by a cousulate employee there who immediately contacted Baker and Stanton.

Incredibly, Baker, in Stanton's name, told the consulate officer not to take any action, that the famous chief of the intelligence service wanted to "look into the matter first." Realizing that Surratt might learn that he had been identified and flee once more, the diplomat took it upon his own authority to arrest Surratt and put him aboard an American ship under arrest. (The diplomat received a severe upbraiding from Stanton for his independent actions.) Surratt, despite the footdragging of his pursuers, was returned to the U.S. and stood trial on June 10, 1867.

Surratt's trial was a strange affair in which new evidence was presented and much more evidence appeared to have been suppressed. Surratt boldly admitted he had plotted with Booth to kidnap Lincoln but that he had had nothing to do with the assassination. Four witnesses stepped forth to swear that Surratt was in Elmira, New York, on the night Booth murdered the President. Surratt's defense was masterfully handled by one of the most expensive legal firms in the North. The government's prosecution seemed lame, at times indifferent. In the end, to the shock of many, Surratt was acquitted and released.

Perhaps to some the outcome was not surprising. The very lawyers who represented Surratt were close friends of none other than Secretary of War Stanton who had, on occasions past, used this legal firm for his own business. The source of payment for the high fees this firm demanded and received is still unknown. The great doubts linged for generations and they all continue to center upon Stanton and his enforcer, Lafayette Baker.

The wily Stanton and his equally shifty chief of intelligence, Baker, do not stand well under close examination of the conspracy to assassinate Abraham Lincoln. It was well known that Stanton was the harshest critic Lincoln had in his cabinet. He found the President too tolerant of the enemy which he, Stanton, had vowed to crush when the war was over. Stanton vehemently opposed Lincoln's pacification plans for the South once it had been beaten. He saw no reason to rebuild its ruined cities and reconstruct its damaged society. Even before the war ended, Stanton and others had formed a private cabal to loot the South of its goods, its crops, and, especially, its best real estate. These men wholeheartedly embraced the idea that "to the victor belonged the spoils."

The squat, angry little Secretary of War could achieve all that only if Lincoln with his "ridiculous humanitarianism" ceased to be the head of state. Stanton, like Baker, had not only acted suspiciously on the eve of Lincoln's murder but he had literally refused to provide anyone who might protect him. The President had asked Stanton to attend the theater with him that night and was told bluntly by Stanton that he was too busy, that he would be working on important matters.

On the last afternoon of his life, Lincoln walked to the Telegraph Office, the nerve center of all news, which Stanton had made his headquarters, and asked Stanton if he would "loan" him the services of Major Thomas Eckert by allowing that officer to attend the theater with him and his wife Mary. Eckert was a towering giant who bent pokers over his arm to prove his great strength. As chief of the Telegraph Office, Eckert was in charge of all the news which he directed to Stanton, not Lincoln.

Stanton brusquely told Lincoln that Eckert would also be "too busy" with work. This was the second time Stanton had lied to Lincoln's face that day. Stanton had no work that night. In fact, he had a leisurely dinner, then visited the home of Secretary of State Seward to see how badly injured he might be after the recent attack on him by Lewis Paine. He sat struggling for conversation with Seward. Both men had always disliked each other and when Stanton left Seward wondered aloud to . his sons why the Secretary of War had come to see him. Stanton, in fact, was just leaving the Seward home when Booth's bullet crashed into Lincoln's head. Stanton's man, Major Eckert, also had no business to perform that evening. He was at home shaving when the news of Lincoln's murder reached him.

There was then, only one man, John F. Parker, who could protect Lincoln. This policeman who was under direct orders from Lafayette Baker, left his post, the chair outside the door leading to the hallway and the presidential box, simply because he was bored with the play, or so he later claimed. Only a few minutes before Booth approached the door, Parker got up, walked downstairs, through the theater lobby and into the saloon next door for a drink. Booth could have passed Parker in the lobby or even seen him in the saloon to know that the way was clear.

All of those involved in tracking down Booth were handsomely rewarded by Stanton. Lafayette Baker was promoted to brigadier general and he received a substantial portion of the $100,000 reward. Colonel Conger, who had so quickly delivered Booth's diary to Baker and Stanton, received $15,000 and a fast promotion. With Stanton's help, Conger was later appointed a federal judge.

Major James O'Beirne also received $3,000 of the reward money and he, too, was promoted to the rank of general by Stanton. It was never made clear how O'Beirne came to earn this money and promotion as he was leading cavalry troops in Maryland at the time of the assassination. Upon closer inspection, perhaps it was where O'Beirne was stationed in Maryland that counted most. His men were guarding the very escape route through Maryland which Booth took, one where the assassin galloped past outpost after outpost without being challenged, stopped, or questioned.

Even strong man Eckert was handsomely rewarded by a grateful Secretary of War. Major Eckert was soon promoted. He then became Assistant Secretary of War. His star rose even higher years later when, through Stanton's efforts, Eckert became president of Western Union. Why was Eckert rewarded? He was "too busy" to sit next to Lincoln at the theater. (Had Eckert, not the frail Rathbone, been present in the box, he could have undoubtedly snapped Booth's spine in a single move.) He had more important duties at home, such as eating a huge meal, then leisurely shaving before going out "on an errand." The telegraph lines which Eckert controlled were all suddenly, inexplicably out of action and no signal could be sent from the city to announce the assassination and to alert the countryside of the escaped murderer. No cause for this massive malfuction was ever found or explained. Eckert's wires were working properly, however, when Booth reportedly sent one or more encoded wires to Washington a day later in an attempt to contact those who had sponsored his bloody action, a wire that foolishly pinpointed his whereabouts, information which, in hours, was being given to Doherty and Conger by Lafayette Baker.

In 1867, the Attorney General attempted to build a case against John Surratt. He was informed that Stanton was in possession of Booth's diary and he asked that the Secretary of War turn it over. Stanton refused. The Attorney General insisted, officially ordering him to do so. The diary Stanton relinquished was missing eighteen pages. The Attorney General wanted to know where the missing pages had gone.

Stanton said he had turned over the diary just as he had received it. Lafayette Baker and Colonel Conger were called in. Both reluctantly stated that the missing pages were present when they turned over Booth's diary to Stanton. What information did those pages contain? Some speculated that Booth had revealed the names of those who had financed his prolonged conspiracies to kidnap or kill Lincoln. (It was later learned that Booth had received large unexplained amounts of money from a New York-based firm to which Stanton had connections.)

Baker maintained his power for some time under Stanton's rule, even after President Johnson fired Stanton who refused to leave his headquarters. In this incredible political battle for power, Stanton threatened Johnson that if he wanted to go on being President, he would rescind his order. Johnson, a heavy drinker and a basically timid person, suddenly was incensed at this rank insubordination. He decreed that Stanton was dismissed. Baker tried to intervene, telling Johnson that he had accumulated enough scandal on the President to bring about his ruination and would do so unless Johnson made peace with Stanton.

President Johnson replied by openly accusing Baker of maintaining spies in the White House and of attempting to blackmail him. He fired Baker. Then both Stanton and Baker worked hard to have Johnson impeached, although their efforts were not successful. Baker thoroughly exposed his treacherous nature by testifying at the impeachment hearings in 1868. He committed perjury by insisting that certain documents would prove that Johnson had no right to hold the office of the presidency. These documents existed only in Baker's imagination, it was proved.

From that point onward, Baker's star faded as did his sanity, or so it appeared. He barricaded himself inside his home and told his few friends that a secret cabal was intent on murdering him. In 1868, Baker was found dead. It was concluded that he was either posioned to death or had committed suicide. He had left cryptic notes that pointed to a high-level conspiracy to murder Lincoln—one going far beyond that involving John Wilkes Booth.

Some years later, the President's only surviving son, Robert Lincoln, was visited by a family friend in his home. Robert Lincoln was burning papers in the fireplace. The friend tried to prevent the destruction of these historic documents, written in President Lincoln's own hand. Robert Lincoln was firm and continued tossing sheafs of paper into the fire, saying: "I must—some of these letters prove that there was a traitor in my father's cabinet."

[ALSO SEE: *Wat Bowie; Belle Boyd; Allan Pinkerton; John H. Surratt; Timothy Webster*]

BAKER, RUDY
(AKA: RALPH BOWMAN)
Soviet Spy in U.S. ▪ (1912– ?)

UBIQUITOUS AND ELUSIVE, RUDY BAKER WAS A Hungarian national who served as a Soviet spy in the U.S. in the 1930s and 1940s. Rudy Baker was not his real name and he was also known to many of his espionage contacts as Ralph Bowman or simply Al. He was a cut-out, or intermediary, who acted as an organizer of Communist spies in Detroit also served as a courier, carrying important stolen secrets from U.S. to Canadian Soviet spy rings.

It was to Baker that U.S. Soviet spy Steve Nelson sent a message in 1942 which reported that, despite great efforts, the Communists could not recruit the noted scientist, Dr. J. Robert Oppenheimer to their ranks and were thus deprived of his considerable knowledge about the atomic bomb. Baker's cover was about to be blown in 1945 and it was believed that he escaped with his supervisor, Soviet spymaster Arthur Adams on the Polish liner *Batory*.

[ALSO SEE: *Arthur Adams; Steve Nelson*]

BANCROFT, EDWARD
British Spy in American Revolution ▪ (1744–1821)

MASSACHUSETTS BORN, EDWARD BANCROFT HAD VERY little schooling before going to work in 1763 for Paul Wentworth, who owned a plantation in Guiana, South America.

In 1766, Bancroft returned to New England and, a year later, traveled to London which he would call home for the rest of his life. Bancroft studied medicine and was later elected to the Royal College of Physicians. He met and befriended fellow American Benjamin Franklin who sponsored his election to the Royal Society to continue his research into chemistry, Bancroft's passion. Franklin, who was then a representative for the colony of Pennsylvania, introduced Bancroft to the editors of the esteemed *Monthly Review*, and the erstwhile chemist-physician became a regular contributor.

Long before the Stamp Act crisis of 1765, Franklin had secretly thrown in his lot with American revolutionaries. But at that time, as one of the few foreign diplomats representing American interests in Europe, Franklin began to actively secretly spy on the British, using as his secret agent Edward Bancroft, who was then highly placed in British academic and scientific circles.

Franklin asked Bancroft to learn what British military leaders and politicians were thinking about the colonies. To Franklin, Bancroft was a staunch American patriot. To Bancroft, Benjamin Franklin was a source of considerable income, particularly when it came to being paid for his espionage information.

In 1775, Franklin met with Silas Deane, the American representative to France. At the time, Franklin recommended to Deane that Bancroft be employed as his secretary but really be used as a spy in England where his high level contacts were widespread.

Deane hired Bancroft in 1776. Bancroft regularly commuted between Paris and London, providing Deane and the American cause with British naval operations, troop movements, and strategy concerning the revolutionary armies in America. Though Deane and Franklin felt this information was useful and passed it on to Washington in America, almost all of Bancroft's reports were false, cleverly engineered by Bancroft and his old friend Paul Wentworth who had recruited Bancroft as a double agent when he first began spying in London for the Americans. It was Bancroft who reported to Wentworth and Wentworth to British spymaster William Eden.

Bancroft did this not out of any special allegiance to King George III, but out of greed. He loved money and was perfectly willing to be paid by the Americans and the British. Since the British paid him twice as much a year, £1,000, Bancroft pretended to spy for the Americans but really spied for the British. The information he gave the Americans was legitimate but so outdated by the time they received it, little could be done with it. The information Bancroft gave the British was current.

Working in Paris as Deane's secretary and known as one of Franklin's closest friends, Bancroft had the confidence of the Americans and the French. He nevertheless took great precautions when communicating with his British contact in Paris. Bancroft would write his secret information in invisible ink, then write innocent notes on the same pages, the black ink writing carefully spaced so that the invisible ink could be read between the lines.

Bancroft would then slip these messages into a bottle and place the bottle in a hole on the side of a tree located in the Tuileries gardens. A British spy would then go to these palace gardens and retrieve Bancroft's messages from the "dead drop." In this way, Bancroft was able to inform the British on January 27, 1778, that France and America had made a military alliance long before the fact was made public.

After Great Britian recognized the independence of America in the peace agreement of 1783, Bancroft was still thought to have been an effective American agent, although Franklin had been warned many times earlier that his good friend Bancroft was a double agent working on behalf of the British. Juliana Ritchie, an American woman living in France, some-

The British double agent Edward Bancroft, shown writing at table, taking dictation from Silas Deane.

Bancroft acted the double agent, reporting on political conditions to both France and England.

Eventually, Bancroft tired of "the game of the foxes," and retired from espionage to his laboratory where he concentrated on scientific projects such as developing dyeing processes. He later published some notable scientific books. His role as a double agent was not learned until many years later when a researcher rummaging through some ancient British government accounting reports, unearthed a note from Bancroft which complained that his pay for "secret information" had been late, and that he did not expect such "oversights" to occur again.

This letter was written to the offices of the British Exchequer in 1784 and it was the only time Bancroft was ever indiscreet enough to mention his espionage activities. Bancroft's letter was filed in the archives and did not surface until 1889. It was therefore more than a century before Edward Bancroft was, indeed, verified as a double agent working for the British.

[ALSO SEE: *Silas Deane; William Eden; Paul Wentworth*]

BARBIE, KLAUS (AKA: KLAUS ALTMANN)
French Spy for U.S. ▪ (1913–)

how became convinced that Bancroft was a British agent and bluntly told Franklin of her belief. On that occasion and at other times Franklin appeared to be amused and dismissed the thought. On one occasion, however, Franklin, ever the sly fox, obliquely admitted to a French noblewoman who had come to warn him about Bancroft, that he was not a complete fool, that it was sometimes wise to appear to be naive.

Franklin's cryptic remark at that time has led some scholars to believe that he knew all along that Bancroft was working for the British. The tough, old sage of American politics had known as early as 1775 that Bancroft had worked and befriended the powerful Tory, Paul Wentworth. He also knew that Bancroft often saw Wentworth when in London at a time when he was supposed to spying for the Americans. It is possible that Bancroft was given only secret information that may have been manipulated by Franklin himself and was of little use to the British. If this was the case, then both America and England used the same highly paid spy to disseminate to each other absolutely useless information.

Bancroft's espionage activities did not cease following the American Revolution. He volunteered his spy services to the French in 1789 and was sent on a mission to Ireland to learn if the Irish might revolt against British rule and cause France's then mortal enemy, England, to fight on two fronts, one in Ireland, the other in France, should war be declared. Again,

BARBIE IS BEST REMEMBERED AS "THE BUTCHER of Lyons," a dogged French collaborator who served as the Section Four leader of the Lyons Gestapo unit during the Nazi occupation of France in World War II. He was later accused of murdering 4,000 Jews and deporting another 7,500 hapless victims to concentration camps. In one instance, Barbie and Gestapo goons rounded up forty-four Jewish children on April 6, 1944, packing them into a single truck that took them to a concentration camp where they were gassed to death.

Barbie later claimed that he was only doing his duty in tracking down French resistance fighters and that he never persecuted any Jews. In 1943, Barbie was praised by his Nazi superiors for personally locating and arresting Jean Moulin, one of General Charles de Gaulle's top spymasters of the Free French in exile. Moulin was on a secret mission in occupied France when Barbie caught him; he was tortured to death a short time later. It was for this act that Barbie was tried and condemned by a French Court in absentia in 1954.

By that time Barbie had long fled French soil. Following World War II, however, the one-time Gestapo leader, remained in Lyons. To insulate himself against later charges, Barbie went to British intelligence and offered his services. He was turned over to American military intelligence officers who

Nazi agent Klaus Barbie, who tracked down Allied agents during World War II and who also sent countless numbers of Jews to death camps in Germany. (AP/Wide World)

were eager to obtain any information on European Communists. Barbie told them that he not only had extensive dossiers on German and Russian Communists in Western Europe but also had the complete list of top Communists in France. He would turn over all this information in exchange for protection against war crimes charges.

Fearing that France might follow the course of Czecheslovakia, which had been taken over in a Communist coup, the Americans agreed. Barbie was useful until 1950 when French authorities began to demand that he answer for the crimes he had committed during the war. On February 21, 1951, Barbie was given an exit visa which allowed him to sneak out of Europe and take up residency in Bolivia. (The official smuggling of wanted persons from Europe by Western powers was then called "The Rat Line.")

Living under the alias Klaus Altmann, Barbie was exposed in 1983, along with how he came to be in Bolivia. This caused the U.S. to offer a formal apology to France in August 1983. Returned to France, Barbie went on trial for crimes against humanity on May 11, 1987, was convicted and sent to prison for life.

[ALSO SEE: *BCRA; Gestapo; Jean Moulin*]

BARGHOON, FREDERICK C.
Alleged U.S. Spy in Russia ▪ (? – ?)

IN OCTOBER 1963, FBI AGENTS ARRESTED THREE KGB spies in New York. Two were released because they had diplomatic immunity but the other, Igor Ivanov, was a chauffeur and had no such immunity. He was held for trial as a spy. The KGB impulsively reacted by charging an American in Moscow, the hapless Frederick C. Barghoon, with having committed espionage.

Barghoon was completely innocent. He had served briefly as a diplomat to Russia during World War II and, in 1963, was visiting Moscow as a tourist. Barghoon was a much-respected professor of political science from Yale University. Unknown to the KGB, Barghoon was also a personal friend of then President John Fitzgerald Kennedy.

Premier Nikita Khrushchev, who was away hunting at the time, heard about his KGB men being arrested in New York and sent a fierce message to KGB headquarters in Moscow demanding action. The KGB settled on Barghoon. Since nothing incriminating could be found regarding the professor, the Soviets decided to quickly frame Barghoon.

After Barghoon visited the American Embassy in Moscow one afternoon, he returned to the Metropole Hotel, going to the restaurant for lunch. No sooner had the professor begun to eat than a KGB agent walked up to him, thrust some secret defense documents into his hand, then walked away. A security team then bounded forth to arrest the startled Barghoon. He was taken to Lubianka Prison where he was charged with espionage and held for trial.

President Kennedy was informed that his friend Barghoon had been arrested and he exploded. He immediately sent a formal protest to the Soviets and demanded the professor's release. Khrushchev by then had returned from his hunting trip. When he read Kennedy's stern message, the Soviet Premier turned in rage to Yuri Ivanovich Nosenko, shouting: "Who allowed this operation? What fools have done it?" He ordered Barghoon's immediate release.

Apparently, Khrushchev's anger was not so much that his KGB men had framed an innocent man, which was routine behavior for this wholly unscrupulous agency, but that they had had the misfortune to select a friend of President Kennedy. The "fool" who had ordered the operation was none other than Leonid Brezhnev.

BATES, ANN
British Spy in Amercan Revolution ▪ (1748–1801)

A PHILADELPHIA TEACHER WHO WAS BORN IN Pennyslvania, Ann Bates married a gunsmith who repaired British artillery. Bates and her husband developed strong loyalties to the British and were avowed Tories during the American Revolution. Bates's husband left with the British when the city was abandoned to the revolutionaries but she managed to obtain a pass to travel to New York from Philadelphia's new military commander in 1778. It was ironic that the commander who gave Bates the pass was none other than Benedict Arnold who later conducted secret negotiations with John Andre, the British spy chief who became Bates' superior.

Once in New York, Bates reported to Andre who intended to make good use of Bates' knowledge of ordnance, as well as her sex, in obtaining information about the enemy. Bates' immediate superior was Major John Drummond who ordered her to go to Washington's camp at White Plains disguised as a peddler. Bates moved freely among the Continental soldiers, selling them odds and ends.

Bates made four extensive trips to Washington's camp at White Plains, detailing the number of artillery pieces in the army, as well as troop movements, troop strength by regiment, and a comprehensive list of supplies. She also reported on the morale of Washington's troops. These reports were sent by Drummond and Andre to Sir Henry Clinton, British commander in New York City. It was Bates who arrived with the news in 1778 that Lafayette had joined Washington and had been sent to Rhode Island to await the arrival of a French fleet following a secret Franco-American alliance.

Armed with this information, Clinton doubled his garrison and strengthened the fortifications at Newport so that this bastion was able to hold out for another year against Continental attacks. Clinton also used the agile, quick-minded Bates in contacting a woman married to an important American general who was thinking of changing sides. This was Benedict Arnold and the woman was reportedly his Tory wife, Margaret "Peggy" Shippen Arnold. Bates reportedly acted as a go-between in the early stages of communication that led to Arnold's liaison with British spy chief John Andre.

Andre accompanied Clinton to South Carolina in 1780, taking Mrs. Bates with him. He reportedly used her in various military campaigns in South Carolina as a spy employing the same successful methods used with Washington's army at White Plains. In 1781, just before the collapse of the British forces, Bates and her husband sailed for England where they took up permanent residence.

[ALSO SEE: *John Andre; Benedict Arnold*]

BATZ, JEAN
Royalist Spy in French Revolution ▪ (1760–1822)

T HE LIFE OF JEAN BATZ WAS THE STUFF OF FICTION and high drama. Born to the aristocracy in Gascony, Batz began his career in the army. He was a serious student of history and economics who later wrote several pamphlets which were critical of the royal financial system. He saw in the extravagance of the French court great waste that could otherwise be put to use in bolstering the French economy.

Batz was perceived to be a turncoat royalist by the revolutionaries opposing the monarchy, particularly in his criticism of those handling the royal coffers when he became a deputy for the nobility in the states-general, France's legislature under the autocratic rule of King Louis XVI. It was in this assembly that the French Revolution of 1789 really began.

Elected to financial posts in the national assembly, the new legislative body created by the revolutionaries, Batz was disturbed to see that eonomic reform was to be overshadowed by the overthrow of the monarchy. He was, nevertheless, utterly committed to preserving Louis XVI's rule. He met secretly with the King, urging Louis to side with the nobles against the commoners. To that end, Batz became Louis' secret agent, traveling abroad to clandestine meetings with French nobles who had seen the signs of revolution and had already fled France.

Realizing that the nobility was not going to raise an army to oust the blood-thirsty revolutionaries, Batz left France and remained in exile for about a year. He decided to return to Paris where he became the leading counterrevolutionary, secretly mustering forces with which to restore the monarchy. In 1792, when the monarchy was overthrown and thousands of nobles were thrown into dungeons to await the guillotine, Batz schemed to save dozens of these forlorn prisoners.

Batz engineered many daring escapes, smuggling or bribing prisoners to freedom and escorting them in disguise to the coast where they took ship for England. In several instances, Batz and his confederates had to fight their way through barriers of revolutionaries to save these people. It was Batz who undoubtedly inspired the fictional hero, the Scarlet Pimpernel.

When King Louis XVI and Marie Antoinette were deposed and thrown into prison, Batz formed a secret cabal in Paris dedicated to freeing the monarchs. When he learned that the King was to be beheaded on January 21, 1793, Batz and his men decided that they would free the King in open combat while the monarch was being taken to the guillotine.

The plan was for Batz and his men to rush the King's carriage en route to the place of execution. By the time Batz arrived at the rendezvous, he discovered that most of his followers had lost their nerve and had fled. Desperate, Batz and a few loyal followers begged passersby to join them in saving the King but, after getting no response, abandoned the rescue attempt altogether. Batz, weeping, watched as the monarch's carriage rattled past him, escorted by a strong force of revolutionaries. Louis was executed on schedule.

Batz then turned his attentions to saving Queen Marie Antoinette and joined a plot, headed by Alexander de Rougeville, that also failed. Marie Antoinette went to the guillotine on October 16, 1793. Batz watched in horror as the monarch bravely ascended to the platform and apologized to the executioner for accidentally stepping on his foot before nervelessly placing her head beneath the waiting blade.

For two years Batz continued to intrigue against the revolutionaries. Most of his machinations involved the ruination of France's monetary system of paper money. Batz enticed several leading revolutionaries into his fraudulent financial schemes before causing the financial deals to collapse and ruin those involved. In 1795, Batz was one of the leaders of the violent insurrection in Paris which was crushed by France's new, rising strongman, General Napoleon Bonaparte who was to become emperor within a decade.

Suspected as being one of the insurrection's leaders, Batz was arrested and imprisoned. He underwent exhausting interrogations but he confessed to nothing and was eventually released. Batz continued to work for the restoration of the monarchy and his efforts were rewarded in 1814 when King Louis XVIII assumed the French throne after Bonaparte's exile to Elba. When the indefatigable dictator escaped from Elba and Louis fled Paris, Batz was imprisoned.

Batz was one of those who secretly worked to undermine Bonaparte. Following Bonaparte's final devastating defeat at Waterloo in 1815 and his permanent exile to the barren island of St. Helena, Louis XVIII resumed the throne and Batz was released from prison and honored by the King. The great intriguer retired to his country estate in Gascony where he wrote his vivid memoirs of high adventure and dramatic history.

[ALSO SEE: *Alexander de Rougeville*]

BAY OF PIGS
CIA-Backed Invasion of Cuba ▪ (1961)

FIDEL CASTRO'S TAKEOVER OF CUBA IN 1959 completely hoodwinked the American intelligence community, as well as world leaders and the public at large. Little was known about Castro's revolutionary aims, except that he had made strong representations that his was a democratic movement that would hold free elections once the dictatorship of Fulgencio Batista was overthrown. Believing this to be the case, the U.S. did nothing to aid Batista or prevent Castro from taking power.

Once this was accomplished, however, the U.S. was shocked to learn that Castro was a diehard Communist and had no intentions of bringing freedom and liberty to Cuba. He quickly established a tyrannical Communist government which was fully backed by the Soviet Union, delighted that its political idealogy had finally been firmly entrenched in the Western Hemisphere.

Castro, then as now, proved himself to be a traitor to his word. He ordered mass arrests and summary executions of all who opposed him in Cuba. He nationalized foreign businesses without compensation and demolished democratic institutions. Castro then embarked upon a savage anti-American propaganda campaign while aggressively attempting to import Communist movements to Latin American countries. In 1960, the U.S. reacted by banning all sugar imports from Cuba, its chief product, and, the following year, broke off diplomatic relations with the dictatorship.

Thousands of Cuban refugees had fled to the U.S. as Castro took over. These were the best of the country's political leaders, intellectuals, businessmen, and craftsmen. Headquartering in Florida, the exiled Cuban loudly proclaimed that they would put together an army, invade the island, and depose Castro's regime which had proved to be more represssive than that of Bastista.

Appealing to President Dwight D. Eisenhower, the Cuban exiles fround a sympathetic ear. Eisenhower conferred with CIA chief Allen Dulles who then created plans for a rebel invasion of Cuba. When John F. Kennedy became President in 1961, he embraced these plans wholeheartedly and, following approval from the Joint Chiefs of Staff, ordered that the clandestine operation proceed. The CIA then undertook to train 1,200 anti-Castro exiles at secret American bases. The so-called Cuban Brigade invaded Cuba in April 1961. The invasion was a disaster.

Richard Bissell, the CIA's deputy director of plans, conferred with Attorney General Robert Kennedy a few days before the invasion, "He told me at that time," Kennedy wrote in a June 1, 1961, memorandum, "that the chances of success were about two out of three and that failure was almost impossible . . . even if the force was not successful in its initial obejective of establishing a beachhead, the men could become guerrillas and, therefore, couldn't be wiped out and would become a major force and a thorn in the side of Castro."

The adminstration had counted on the Cuban people to rise up against the tyrant Castro but the poorly equipped, badly-trained invasion force did not establish a strong position beyond the beach. Moreover, no uprisings took place. Worse, the ammunition ships promised by the CIA did not appear to resupply the invaders who quickly ran out of ammunition. According to Robert Kennedy, the President, closely watching the situation, urged the CIA to bring the ammunition ships close to shore to suppy the invaders. This would directly involve U.S. vessels which could later identify the invasion as being directly sponsored by the U.S.

President Kennedy was in favor of direct support, if need be. Said Robert Kennedy: ". . . he'd rather be called an aggressor than a bum." Communication between CIA officers and the invaders was poor and it was soon learned that Castro's heavily mechanized forces were dealing crushing blows to the freedom fighters. The invaders called for air support. Again, according to Robert Kennedy, "Jack was in favor of giving it." Dean Rusk, ever the politically correct presidential adviser, urged the President to deny the air cover, that the U.S. had openly stated that no American forces would be employed in the covert operation and that to do so would be to make a liar out of the President.

The air cover was not provided and Casto's tanks destroyed the Cuban Brigade. Many fled to the water where U.S. destroyers later picked up about thirty exhausted invaders. Others managed to escape back to the U.S. but the Cuban Brigade was effectively destroyed. Most of its members were either killed or captured. The fiasco was later placed squarely at the door of the CIA, a failure based on its inexperience at military tactics, strategy, support, and supply.

Though President Kennedy took full responsibility for the Bay of Pigs fiasco, he blamed CIA chief Allen Dulles for not properly informing him in advance of the real chances of success or failure in the operation. So devastating was the failure of this CIA operation that it caused Dulles to resign. Reflecting upon the disaster, Allen Dulles refuted the contention of various Kennedy advisers that the 1,200 men who invaded the Bay of Pigs expected to be supported by a general uprising against Castro. Said Dulles: "We did not count on—one might hope for it, but we did not count on—an immediate uprising in Cuba."

The Bay of Pigs disaster enabled Castro to convince Soviet Premier Nikita Khrushchev to openly support Cuba with military aid which led to the Cuban Missile Crisis of 1962.

[ALSO SEE: *Richard Bissell; CIA; Cuban Missile Crisis; Allen Dulles*]

BAZNA, ELYEZA (AKA: CICERO)
German Spy in Turkey ▪ (1904–1971)

ONE OF THE MOST REMARKABLE SPIES IN HISTORY, certainly in the twentieth century, was the bold, cunning Elyeza Bazna who was to be known to the world as "Cicero." He spied for Germany during World War II at astronomical prices and delivered top secrets so shocking that the Nazis disbelieved what he put before them. Bazna's background remains much in shadow to this day.

It is known that Bazna was born in Albania at the time when it was a province of the Turkish Ottoman Empire. He moved with his family to Ankara which, after World War I, became the capital of Turkey. Bazna worked at various domestic jobs, first as a chauffeur, then as a butler, finally as a valet to political bigwigs connected to European embassies in Ankara, including that of America, Yugoslavia, and Germany. In 1943, Bazna became the personal valet of the British Ambassador in Turkey, Sir Hugh Knatchbull-Hugessen.

Elyeza Bazna, shown in later life, spied for the Germans in World War II and operated under the cover name of Cicero.

Knatchbull was a predictable and punctilious diplomat who followed his routines to the second. He was precise, unimaginative and naive in that he assumed his office insulated him against any kind of espionage.

Posted to Teheran, he was named as Ambassador to Turkey, taking up residence in Ankara. In early 1943, Knatchbull hired Bazna, a servile, smooth valet who knew exactly what to do for his master at all times. Bazna was self-taught but he was intellectually nimble in many fields and spoke several languages fluently. He was as precise in his duties as the Ambassador was in his. Knatchbull appreciated Bazna and relied upon him for all of his personal needs. Within a few months, Bazna knew the Ambassador's habits and movements which never varied. He always had his meals at exact times. He awoke every morning at the same time. He went to sleep every night at the same time. He attended social functions along rigid procedures, arriving on time, leaving on time.

Bazna diligently recorded Knatchbull's comings and goings and, in particular, noted that the Ambassador had the habit of bringing the black dispatch box from the Embassy to his bed chamber each night. The ever-alert valet noticed that Knatchbull did vary one habit. He sometimes left the box alone in the bed chamber the following day.

Bazna made a duplicate key to the black dispatch box by making a wax impression of the original. He also found Knatchbull's combination to his residency safe and thus has access to all of the British top secrets flowing in and out of Ankara. The key Bazna had made to the dispatch box was also the key to his own fortune, as well he knew, a key that would open a door to a luxurious life of ease and grace, not unlike that lived by those he had so long served, envied, and seethingly hated.

On the night of October 26, 1943, L. C. Moyzisch, a German intelligence officer stationed in Ankara, received a dramatic nocturnal visit which was to complicate his rather hum-drum life. Moyzisch received a phone call at his quarters and was told that someone was waiting to see him in a room at the German diplomatic complex. He dutifully dressed and went to the home of First Secretary Jenke. When he arrived, Jenke's wife showed Moyzisch to a small sitting room, saying that her husband had been visited by a man who had years earlier worked for him as a valet and that this man was waiting to talk to Moyzisch.

The German intelligence officer apprehensively went to the study door and opened it, walking inside. The room was dimly lit. A man sat as still as death on a sofa, his face hidden in the shadows. "Who are you?" the man said in French.

Moyzisch replied that Jenke had instructed him to talk to him, that he was a member of the German diplomatic corps. The man stood up, his face visible. He had thick black hair, a high forehead, a firm chin and a small nose. His piercing eyes were dark and they darted nervously from Moyzisch to the door and back again. Without saying a word, the man went to the door and suddenly jerked it open to see if anyone was waiting behind it. When learning that he was alone with Moyzisch, he shut the door.

The visitor sat down and spoke in a confident even voice: "I have an offer to make you, a proposition . . . for the Germans. But before I tell you what it is, I ask your word that whether you accept it or not you won't ever mention it to anyone except your chief. Any indiscretion on your part would make your life as worthless as mine. I'd see to that if it was the last thing I did." With that, the visitor raised his arm and drew his hand across his throat, signifying death. "Do you give me your word?"

"Of course I do," Moyzisch replied. "If I didn't know how to keep a secret, I wouldn't be here now."

With that the visitor explained that he could give the Germans "extremely secret papers, the most secret papers that exist . . . I will want money for them, a lot of money. My work, you know, is dangerous, and if I were caught . . ." He drew his hand across his throat once more. He then stated he wanted £20,000 sterling.

Moyzisch's poker face dropped. "Out of the question," he replied. "We don't dispose of such sums here. Certainly not in sterling. It would have to be something extraordinarily important to be worth that price." The German then told the visitor that he would first have to examine the papers before payment could be made, if it were made at all.

The visitor sat back, his face again in the shadows. Moyzisch, however could see that there was a "superior smile on his unattractive face." The visitor then said he was not a fool, that he had worked out every detail in preparation for this night. He would deliver the papers but be paid on the spot or he would sell the documents to the Soviets. He told Moyzisch that he would deliver the documents on rolls of film and that any deliveries thereafter would cost the Germans £15,000 per delivery. Moyzisch had three days to consider his offer. He would call Moyzisch's office at the German Embassy on October 30, 1943, at 3 P.M., and would identify himself on the phone as Pierre and ask if Moyzisch had any letters for him. If the answer was no, the Germans would never hear from him again.

It was past midnight when the visitor put on his coat and pulled a hat low over his eyes. He went to the door, Moyzisch at his side. He stood close to the German and said in a low voice: "You'd like to know who I am. I am the British Ambassador's valet."

With that Elyeza Bazna jerked open the door and stepped into the hallway, going quickly to the front door of the Jenke residence and slipping outside. Moyzisch followed the man but by the time he reached the street, the valet had vanished, swallowed by the night.

The next morning Moyzisch told his story to the German Ambassador to Turkey, the political schemer

Franz von Papen, former Chancellor of Germany. Papen was no stranger to espionage and intrigue. He had conducted espionage in the U.S. during World War I, had at one time been a contact for the doomed Mata Hari, and had been involved in all manner of secret political maneuvering inside the Third Reich, mostly to survive as a political entity. Von Papen had been sent to Ankara as German Ambassador to Turkey in 1939, then considered an out-of-way post for has-been politicians. But in 1943, Ankara, like the neutral havens of Bern, Switzerland, and Lisbon, Portugal, was a beehive of espionage activities by all the major powers. Von Papen enjoyed being at the center of intrigues as he was a born conspirator. When he took his post, he made sure that half his large staff were trained Abwehr spies who soon brought most of the countries in the Middle East under his surveillance.

Von Papen was nevertheless cautious after hearing Moyzisch's melodramatic tale. He told his subordinate that he could not authorize the payment of £20,000 pound sterling for information yet to be examined. Such a decision would have to be made at the highest level, by Foreign Minister Joachim von Ribbentrop himself. If this furtive valet was to become a German agent, Von Papen would not take direct responsibility. He would make sure that Ribbentrop's approval was sought and gotten first.

The Ambassador then sent a coded message to the German Foreign Minister which read:

TO THE REICH FOREIGN MINISTER, PERSONAL
MOST SECRET
WE HAVE OFFER OF BRITISH EMBASSY EMPLOYEE
ALLEGED TO BE BRITISH AMBASSAOR'S VALET TO
PROCURE PHOTOGRAPHS OF TOP SECRET ORIGINAL
DOCUMENTS. FOR FIRST DELIVERY ON OCTOBER
30TH 20,000 POUNDS STERLING IN BANK NOTES ARE
DEMANDED. FIFTEEN THOUSAND POUNDS FOR ANY
FURTHER ROLL OF FILMS. PLEASE ADVISE WHETHER
OFFER CAN BE ACCEPTED. IF SO, SUM REQUIRED MUST
BE DISPATCHED BY SPECIAL COURIER TO ARRIVE HERE
NOT LATER THAN OCTOBER 30TH. ALLEGED VALET WAS
EMPLOYED SEVERAL YEARS AGO BY FIRST SECRETARY.
OTHERWISE NOTHING MUCH KNOWN HERE.
PAPEN

No one at the Embassy expected Berlin to respond favorably to the slippery valet's proposal. To the amazement of Papen and Moyzisch, the Embassy received a coded response which read:

TO AMBASSADOR VON PAPEN, PERSONAL
MOST SECRET
BRITISH VALET'S OFFER TO BE ACCEPTED TAKING
EVERY PRECAUTION. SPECIAL COURIER ARRIVING
ANKARA 30TH BEFORE NOON. EXPECT IMMEDIATE
REPORT AFTER DELIVERY OF DOCUMENTS.
RIBBENTROP

At exactly 3 P.M., the phone at Moyzisch's desk rang. He was waiting to pick it up. A voice at the other end said in French: "Pierre here. Bonjour, monsieur. Have you got my letters?"

"Yes," said Moyzisch.

"I'll see you tonight. Au revoir."

Moyzisch went to Papen's office. Papen told Moyzisch that he was to deal with the valet who was to be called "Cicero," after the famous Roman orator because his information would hopefully prove to be "eloquent." The Ambassador told him that the courier had arrived with the £20,000 sterling. He opened a desk drawer and took out bundles of pound notes in small dominations. "Look altogether too new, these notes," Papen said. Moyzisch bundled up the money and, as he was leaving the room, Papen said in a low tone: "Remember, don't get me into trouble—or yourself either."

Returning to his office, Moyzisch placed the money in his small office safe. At a few minutes before 10 P.M. that night, he went outside and waited by a tool shed, the prearranged meeting place. Bazna stepped out of the shadows and accompanied Moyzisch to his office where he showed the German two rolls of 36mm film. When Moyzisch reached for the film, Bazna held the rolls back. "First the money," he said calmly.

Moyzisch nervously opened the safe and counted out the money. He insisted, however, that before he gave it to Bazna, that he be allowed to develop and examine the film. Bazna agreed to wait for a half hour. Moyzisch put the money back into the safe and took the film to a basement area which served as a dark room. He quickly developed the film.

The information contained on the film was, indeed, genuine top secret communications bearing recent dates. Moyzisch made the decision to pay the valet. From that point on, Bazna continued to supply Moyzisch with top secret information that he carefully photographed from Knatchbull's black dispatch box and from the residency safe. The material turned over by Bazna was a treasure trove of secrets, including the minutes of and plans of the Casablanca Conference between President Roosevelt and Prime Minister Winston Churchill; the Cairo Conference involving Roosevelt, Churchill, and Chiang Kai-shek; the Teheran Conference of Roosevelt, Churchill, and Stalin. From the details of this last high level meeting, the Nazis learned of "Operation Overlord," the planned invasion of Europe in 1944 by the Allies.

Oddly enough, Ribbentrop and the German High Command, after studying the documents Bazna provided, decided not to accept the secrets as genuine, concluding that the information was "planted" by the British SIS to hoodwink the Nazis. It was all too good to be true. Everything Bazna had provided was authentic but the suspicious Germans refused to believe it, despite the many support documents from other sources that verified the top secret reports. In other instances, the credibility of "planted" information went unchallenged. The Germans, for instance, fully accepted the bogus information they obtained through a bizarre Allied scheme which was labelled by British intelligence as "The Man Who Never Was."

The flow of Bazna's priceless information suddenly stopped in Spring 1944 when the Allies learned that there was a serious leak in the British Embassy at Ankara. The Allies learned this directly from the German Foreign Ministry itself, or, to be precise, a high-placed Allied spy, one of the few left in Germany at that time. This daring agent was Fritz Kolbe, a patriotic German who had long hated and resisted the Nazis and who worked as one of Ribbentrop's top examiners of documents in Berlin.

Kolbe had established contact with OSS chief Allen Dulles in Bern, Switzerland, in 1943 and he had provided Dulles with almost every important document in the German Foreign Office from that point onward. In early 1944, Kolbe intercepted a coded telegram from Papen in Ankara to Ribbentrop in Berlin, talking about top secret information coming from the spy Cicero and clearly stating that this information was being brought out of the British Embassy in Ankara. He immediately passed this on to Dulles who alerted British intelligence.

SIS informed Knatchbull and other British officials at the Ankara embassy that its security had been penetrated but, try as they might, investigating British agents could not determine the identity of the mysterious "Cicero." Then a secretary at the German Embassy in Ankara defected to the British. She had worked directly for Moyzisch and she had learned that the spy was Elyeza Bazna, the Ambassador's valet. Bazna was called before the red-faced Knatchbull and grilled. He admitted to nothing. To all allegations he smirked and remained silent. After sputtering indignities about such disgraceful and disloyal conduct, Knatchbull fired his valet.

Bazna shrugged, said nothing and quickly left the British Embassy. By then it mattered little to this suave, sophisticated spy. He had collected more than £300,000 sterling from the Germans, a huge fortune in those days. He went to Lisbon and booked passage for a South American country. Once in South America, Bazna opened a bank account, depositing the money in a large bank. He rented a villa overlooking the ocean, hired servants, kept a beautiful mistress and lived the high life of a gentleman of leisure. Now he had a valet who slavishly served him in a role reversal that delighted him. Bazna as Cicero had played his part well.

In grimly twisting irony, Bazna did not enjoy his new lifestyle for long. His South American bankers visited him at his villa, nervously informing him that there was something wrong with his deposit. Almost all of the British pounds he had placed in the bank were counterfeit, cleverly forged notes. Bazna was at first dumbfounded. Then, as he realized the subtle betrayal of the Germans, the master spy broke into loud laughter. His Nazi paymasters had simply forged the money and paid him off in notes as useless as they believed his information to be.

Bazna was arrested and was sent to prison but he later managed to free himself and return to Europe. Many books, including his own memoirs, and a major film, *Five Fingers*, profiled his incredible exploits, or, more accurately, that of the mysterious Cicero, a sinister phantom that still haunts the long, dark corridors of espionage. Like most spies who worked for profit alone, Bazna ended his days in miserable poverty, dying penniless in 1971, still dreaming of his halcyon cloak-and-dagger days.

[ALSO SEE: *Abwehr; Allen Dulles; Fritz Kolbe; The Man Who Never Was; Mata Hari; OSS; Franz von Papen; SIS*]

BCRA (CENTRAL BUREAU OF INTELLIGENCE AND OPERATIONS)
Gaullist Military Intelligence ▪ (1940–1945)

FOLLOWING THE DEFEAT OF FRANCE IN 1940, FRENCH General Charles de Gaulle escaped to England. From there, regularly using the radio to communicate, he called upon the French people to resist the Nazi occupation forces. This caused underground groups to band together to form the French resistance movement which was part of the Free French Army commanded by de Gaulle. Thus came into existence the BCRA, an acronym of the French title meaning "Central Bureau of Intelligence and Operations."

The BCRA was responsible for espionage in France, along with covert operations involving sabotage. The intelligence operation was headed by Andre Dewavrin whose code name was "Colonel Passy," and he, in turn, was directly answerable to de Gaulle. Working closely with the BCRA was the British SOE (Special Operations Executive) which provided the resistance fighters with supplies and also agents which were sent to France to work with the underground.

The French resistance was made up of many political factions which were at odds with each other until BCRA sent its top agent to France, Jean Moulin. This fearless Gaullist leader managed to unify all the different groups in the resistance to make the organization much more effective. Moulin was captured and executed in 1943, although he had prepared the ground work for the resistance to pave the way for the Normandy invasion in 1944. The BCRA continued to operate until the end of the war in 1945 when it was disbanded.

[ALSO SEE: *Andre Dewavrin; Jean Moulin; SOE*]

BEACH, THOMAS
(AKA: HENRI LE CARON)
British Agent in U.S. Against the Irish ▪ (1841–1894)

A NATIVE OF COCHESTER, ENGLAND, BEACH, AS A youth, longed for adventure and sought it by running away from home to France where he lived hand to mouth. Little is known of his life at this time, except that he was compelled to leave France under a cloud. He migrated to America just before the outbreak of the Civil War. Beach enlisted in the Union Army, using the alias of Henri le Caron, the name he had used in France and one which may have been tainted by some criminal activity.

Beach served with distinction throughout the war, rising to the rank of major before he was mustered out at war's end in 1865. Living in New York and elsewhere, Beach became interested in the Fenian Movement, a fraternal order of Irish immigrants in America, begun in the U.S. in 1858 by John O'Mahony, taking its name from the legendary host commanded by early day patriot Fionn mac Cumhaill. Beach learned that the Fenians planned to use the U.S. as the based from which to recruit experienced soldiers for a revolution in Ireland, to spread a worldwide propaganda campaign against the British and to collect from Irish-Americans and sympathizers considerable funds with which to finance the rebellion.

Great numbers of young Irishmen had fought on both sides of the Civil War and these the Fenians vigorously recruited to their ranks. Beach wrote in detail of this activity to his father in England who showed his letters to British officials who alerted the British secret service. Since the service had already planted numerous agents within revolutionary ranks in Ireland, it asked Beach to become its first secret agent in America with the specific task of spying on the Fenians.

Beach agreed to spy for the British and joined the Fenians under his alias, Henri le Caron. He quickly became a leader of the organization and thus had immediate knowledge of its plans, which included the invasion of Canada in 1866. Beach informed his spymasters in England of the impending invasion and when Irish contingents crossed into Canada they were quickly thrown back by British forces.

In 1867, Beach went to England where he became an official agent for the British secret service. He was trained and sent back to the U.S. By 1869, Beach had become one of the national leaders of the Fenian Movement and was so respected by Fenians that he was selected to visit the White House and appeal directly to President Andrew Johnson to aid the cause of freedom for the Irish in Ireland.

Three years later Beach was in Canada, serving on a Fenian commission which was again planning an invasion of Canada. Again, Beach informed the British and the Fenians were stopped just as they crossed the Vermont border. Beach continued his role in America as a British double agent, helping to plan rebellion with the Fenians, then informing the British to prevent the schemes from developing, much the same way the spectacular double agent Yevno Azev operated in Russia at the turn of the century.

In 1877, Fenian founder O'Mahony died and the impetus of the Fenian Movement dissipated. Other secret Irish movements such as the Molly Maguires continued to operate, committing violent acts of sabotage against unscrupulous mine owners who paid their Irish workers slave wages. The Mollies, however, were a particular problem to the U.S. and they remained the investigative province of the Pinkertons who successfully penetrated that secret society with their own double agent, James McParland.

Beach left America and went to work as a spy in Ireland for the British. His chief target was the great Irish leader Charles Stewart Parnell. Beach tried in every way to discredit Parnell and, finally, he and others devised a way to scandalize the Irish leader.

A man named Richard Pigott contacted the London *Times*, offering to sell an inflamatory letter ostensibly written by Parnell. The *Times* paid Pigott £2,500 for the letter, then a princely sum, and published its contents which condoned the assassinations of British leaders by Irish terrorists. Parnell was disgraced but the letter was proved to be a forgery in 1890. When this scandal broke, the British secret service informed Beach that it had no more need of his services. He resigned to live in obscurity for another four years.

[ALSO SEE: *Yevno Azev; James McParland; Molly Maguires; Allan Pinkerton*]

BEAUMARCHAIS, PIERRE AUGUSTIN CARON DE
French Spy Against the British ▪ (1732–1799)

G IFTED WITH CREATIVE TALENT, BEAUMARCHAIS WAS born in Paris and, at an early age, worked in his father's watchmaking shop. In his teens, he invented a watch mechanism that intrigued a wealthy widow who was a member of the royal court. So enamored of the youth was the older woman that she married Beaumarchais in 1756. He took the aristocratic name of "de Beaumarchais," from the title of his wife's estates and, through her, was named as the the official watchmaker for King Louis XV and Comptroller of the Royal Pantry. Beaumarchais then began to study music and instruments.

By 1759, Beaumarchais had become an accomplished musician and was much sought-after as a teacher. He was appointed the musical instructor for the daughters of the King at Versailles and then announced that he would devote his time to playwriting.

Beaumarchais was also an astute businessman and was paid handsomely by a financial house in Paris to represent its interest in Spain in 1764. He studied the Spanish character and customs and would use this knowledge to later produce his two most significant comedies, *The Barber of Seville* (1775) and *The Marriage of Figaro* (1784). These plays, set to music by Rossini and Mozart respectively, established Beaumarchais as a major European artist.

Beaumarchais enjoyed the luxury of the royal court and lavished a high lifestyle upon himself, one that became inaffordable. The playwright forged some financial documents to obtain money and was caught. He was found guilty of forgery but, in lieu of imprisonment and because of his social standing, Beaumarchais was deprived of his civil rights. Disgraced, the playwright sought to restore himself to favor with the government.

Lieutenant General of Police Sartines had the answer. If Beaumarchais would undertake a delicate mission on behalf of the police and, indirectly, the King, all might be forgiven. The task was to buy off an exiled one-time lover of Madame Du Barry, the King's mistress. Morande, the exiled paramour, was planning to publish a small book which would reveal in lurid detail his affair with Du Barry. Beaumarchais was sent with a sum of money to bribe the blackmailer into silence. This he did and his civil rights and citizenship were quickly restored to him.

But now that Beaumarchais had become a royal secret agent, he was again asked to perform similar duties after the death of King Louis XV, this time in hostile England. The Chevalier d'Eon had been corresponding with Louis XV before the King's death, missives that contained the King's plan for the possible invasion of England. Sartines asked Beaumarchais to go to England and obtain the King's letters before d'Eon made them public. This, too, the playwright accomplished, paying off d'Eon with a considerable sum and obtaining the letters, which were returned to Sartines.

The playwright's most significant contribution to French espionage was related to the American revolutionaries who sought France's aid in their struggle against the British in 1776. Silas Deane, representing the Americans, arrived in Paris and met secretly with France's foreign minister who agreed to then secretly aid the revolutionaries. Since France and England were not then at war, contact between the two governments was maintained in secret and the French selected as their envoy to Deane, none other than Beaumarchais.

Beaumarchais went back into business, this time establishing Roderique Hortalez et Cie (Hortalez and Co.) in Paris. This firm was an importing-exporting business but its chief activity was covertly supplying the Americans with arms, ammunition and other supplies vital to their cause. More than half of these war supplies were purchased secretly by France and its ally, Spain. The balance was bought by private sources which Beaumarchais supplied. The playwright simply implored his noblemen friends to contribute to the American cause.

The irony was that the French monarchy and aristocrats were financing a revolution against the very principles for which they stood. Their hatred of the British, however, compelled the French to support the upstart Americans. It was to Beaumarchais' great credit that he was able to keep his company in the black. He had to buy war goods from French arsenals and depots, and replenish his funds from American commodities such as rice and tobacco. If any profits could be made in the exchange, Beaumarchais was allowed to keep these but the company's debts were also his total responsibility.

Beaumarchais directed a huge fleet of commercial vessels to accomplish his goals. More than fifty large ships sailed regularly from the French ports of La Harvre, Bordeaux, and Marseilles, going to the West Indies to trade, or so it appeared, but the actual destination of these ships were American ports where they disgorged rifles, bullets, cannon and shot, uniforms, flintlocks, all the necessary tools of war. These goods were then loaded into wagons and taken to Washington and his beleaguered army. In 1777, these supplies began to flow to the American army facing John Burgoyne's British force at Saratoga and contributed greatly to the victory achieved by then America's greatest hero, General Benedict Arnold.

The war supplies continued to flow to America but Hortalez saw most of its ships return to France with empty holds. The Americans found it next to impossible to gather the rice and tobacco in payment for the arms and ammunition. Further, the Continental Congress refused to pay directly for the goods since Silas Deane had made his deal with the French in secret and he was also fearful of informing Congress because he suspected that Tory spies would uncover the clandestine pact. Deane's suspicions were well founded. His personal secretary, Edward Bancroft, was a British spy.

Hortalez appeared to be on the brink of bankruptcy but it was saved by the French nobility which made large loans to Beaumarchais to continue supplying the Americans. Beaumarchais also used every bit of his private fortune to buy arms for America. This became unnecessary in 1778 when France openly entered the war on the side of the Americans. French ships, troops, and arms eventually led to Washington's overwhelming victory at Yorktown in 1781.

Beaumarchais nevertheless continued to operate Hortalez but as a viable commercial operation which saw considerable profits from sugar trading in the

West Indies before it was closed in 1783. Six years later Beaumarchais was swept up by the French Revolution. He was distrusted by the revolutionaries, even though he had openly sided with their cause. His history was so entwined with the monarchy and the noble class that he was imprisoned.

The playwright agreed that, in return for his freedom, he would go to Holland in 1792 and return with a large cache of weapons for use by the revolutionaries. Beaumarchais failed in his mission and returned to Paris in disgrace. Because of his literary achievements, the playwright was allowed to survive in his native country but he never again regained his fortune and died in poverty in 1799. In 1834, the U.S. Congress acknowledged the great help Beaumarchais had rendered to America and bestowed upon his heirs the money that had long been due him.

[ALSO SEE: *Benedict Arnold; Edward Bancroft; Silas Deane; Charles Genevieve d'Eon*]

BEAUREGARD, PIERRE GUSTAVE TOUTANT
Confederate Spymaster in Civil War ▪ (1818–1893)

THE FIERY CREOLE BEAUREGARD WAS BORN AND BRED in New Orleans. After graduating from West Point, he joined the U.S. Corps of Engineers and served with distinction in the Mexican War. Brilliant, opinionated, Beauregard advanced to the rank of general in the U.S. Army. He was appointed superintendent of West Point only six days before the outbreak of the Civil War. He resigned his post and went south to serve the Confederacy. Placed in charge of Rebel troops at Charleston, South Carolina, it was Beauregard who gave the order to fire the first shot at Fort Sumter which began the war.

Beauregard served as an able but controversial commander throughout the war, his most outstanding contributions being made at Bull Run in 1681 and at Shiloh. At Bull Run, the Confederates won an overwhelming victory. Much credit for this victory was due to the spy network Beauregard had established in Washing-ton and Virginia. At the core of the Washington network was southern belle Rose Greenhow, who was able to learn from those in her high society set the exact plans of the Union Army as it approached Bull Run.

From Greenhow, Beauregard had learned that federal troops commanded by General Irwin McDowell would march from Washington on July 16, 1861, and attack at Bull Run the next day, and that another Union force would attempt to bottle up Confederate forces commanded by General Joseph E. Johnston in the Shenandoah Valley at the same time. Beauregard pieced this information from Greenhow to that of other spies along McDowell's route of march and then acted upon that information by ordering cavalry commander Turner Ashby, later a top rebel spy, to screen Johnston's withdrawal from the Shenandoah.

When Johnston joined Beauregard, just as the Federal troops were about to break the Confederate lines, the tide of battle turned dramatically. Within hours, the Union troops, their flanks turned and rolled up by fresh Confederate troops, panicked, fell back, then deserted the field en masse. The Union rout left the Confederates with a complete victory on July 21, 1861. Beauregard thanked Mrs. Greenhow by sending her a personal note of gratitude for her excellent, detailed espionage work.

Beauregard again used a network of spies to determine the strength of the federal army encamped at Shiloh, Tennessee, and against which was launched a fierce Confederate attack on April 7, 1862. The Union Army commanded by U.S. Grant was all but destroyed on the first day of battle at Shiloh, thanks to the efforts of Beauregard's spies which pinpointed the positions of Grant's divisions. Reinforced that night, Grant made a stubborn stand close to the banks of the Tennessee River the next day to avert a major defeat.

Following Shiloh, Beauregard served along the Georgia–South Carolina coast and did his best to stop the juggernaut attack of William T. Sherman's huge Federal army in its historic March to the Sea in 1864. By then, however, Beauregard, along with all other Rebel commanders, lacked troops and supplies to properly combat the enemy. Beauregard also lacked any sort of spy network to keep him abreast of enemy movements, a condition that existed until Robert E. Lee surrendered the tattered remnants of his Confederate Army at Appomattox in 1865 which ended the war.

Following the war, Beauregard became a successful railroad executive. He was also the director of the controversial Louisiana Lottery. Much of his time was spent by answering in print the criticism of his wartime conduct.

[ALSO SEE: *Turner Ashby; Rose Greenhow*]

BECKER, JOHANN
German Spy in Argentina ▪ (1912–1971?)

AFTER GRADUATING FROM HIGH SCHOOL IN HIS NATIVE Leipzig in 1930, Johann Becker joined the Nazi Party, believing, as did millions of others, in Hitler's credo that Germany had been wrongly punished for its role in World War I. As an ardent party member, Becker insisted that only the Nazis and Hitler could restore order to his country which was in social and economic chaos.

Johann Becker, who operated a German spy ring in Argentina in World War II.

Serving the party in minor capacities, Becker underwent espionage training after Hitler's rise to power in 1933. Four years later he was sent by the Abwehr to Argentina as a "sleeper" agent. He was financed by the Nazis to begin a business in Buenos Aires until such time that he be activated as a Nazi spy. At the war's outbreak, Becker flew back to Berlin and underwent additional training. becoming a diplomatic courier.

Becker returned to Buenos Aires and, by 1943, had set up a network of German spies there. One Argentinian closely cultivated by Becker was the swaggering, politically ambitious Colonel Juan Peron, who admired the Nazis, Becker was able to learn Argentina's intentions as a neutral country. He was also able to document arrivals and departures of Allied war vessels and commercial ships in South American waters. All this information Becker sent on to Berlin in coded messages via his shortwave radio and in diplomatic pouches. It was Becker who learned in advance from the garrulous Peron that Argentina would be entering the war on the side of the Allies in 1944.

Peron, who became president of Argentina after the war, warned his friend Becker that diplomatic relations between Germany and his country would soon be ruptured. Becker went underground while many spies in his network were rounded up and imprisoned. It was later claimed that Becker traded off his own agents to assure the fact that he would not himself be arrested. Peron could not indefinitely protect the spy and Becker was eventually tracked

down and imprisoned in 1945. Becker escaped, most probably with Peron's help, and returned to Germany where he lived out his life.

[ALSO SEE: *Abwehr*]

BEER (OR BAER), ISRAEL
Soviet Spy in Israel ▪ (1912–1968)

IN 1938, A REFUGEE FROM THE SPANISH CIVIL WAR arrived in Palestine, offering his services to the Haganah, the Jewish underground army battling to establish the free nation of Israel. He gave his name as Israel Beer, claiming to have been a battalion commander for the Republicans in Spain in their losing fight against the facist legions of Francisco Franco.

Beer fought in the Haganah and in the Israeli army during the 1948 war against the Arab nations. He was dismissed from army ranks in 1950 by Chief of Staff Yigael Yadin who later stated that Beer "could do a brilliant job of military planning but you always had to suspect his motives."

There was no secret about Beer's political affiliations, he was a Marxist and a leader in the Marxist-dominated Mapam Party. In 1954, he quit this party and joined the Mapai Party, headed by Pemier David Ben-Gurion, Isreal's greatest hero. Beer became a Ben-Gurion stalwart and protégé and he soon rose in the ranks of Israeli politics. He was assigned to write the history of the 1948 war and was given full access to the archives of the Defense Ministry. Moreover, Ben-Gurion allowed Beer to review his personal diaries.

Tall, buck-toothed, and sporting a near-shaved head, Beer was not a favorite with most Israeli leaders. He was officious and arrogant. His sneering manner offended almost everyone he met. Yet he continued to enjoy Ben-Gurion's confidence and, as such, was given one important post after another. He was appointed head of the military history faculty at Tel Aviv University. He lectured on military affairs, met visiting VIPs, and outlined Israel's military defense systems to them.

As a member of the International Association of Military Commentators, Beer was friendly with Israel's Deputy Defense Minister Shimon Peres. He also cultivated friendships with such literary giants of military history as Basil Henry Liddell Hart (*The Defense of the West*) who regularly visited him in Tel Aviv. His standing was such that he toured NATO defenses in 1958. He then lectured throughout West Germany before making a brief visit to Moscow.

Beer's image changed in 1959 when he separated from his biologist wife Rebecca and fell in love with Ora Zahavi, a woman with expensive tastes. Beer spent all his money and then began borrowing heavily from friends to keep Ora happy. He braved all for her, including a bloody fistfight with Ora's ex-husband, a taxi driver who knocked out two of Beer's front teeth.

By 1961, Beer's eccentric behavior caused Israel's secret police to shadow him. On one occasion, he was seen to meet with a known KGB agent. This prompted the police to search Beer's home. Investigators found more than sixty pounds of classified documents and correspondence. It was learned that Beer had had advance information on the Franco-British attack on Suez, learned from his contacts with the Israeli secret service. It was also determined that Beer had passed this information on to Moscow. Instead of informing Egypt of the impending attack, the Russians said nothing, coordinating their crushing attack against the freedom fighters of the Hungarian Revolution with that of the Suez attack, believing correctly that the Franco-British campaign in Egypt would divert world public opinion from the Soviet domination of Hungary.

After the discovery of the classified documents in Beer's home, a full-scale investigation into his background was conducted. It was learned that Beer had completely falsified his past. He had claimed that he had been born in Vienna, had been one of the few Jews ever to graduate from the prestigious Wierner Neustadt Military Academy, and that he had stood with the Jews of the socialist Schutzbund (militia) who fought Dollfuss' fascist troops attacking their homes in the Karl Marx Hof in February 1934. Beer had also insisted that he had been the stage manager at the elegant Berg Theater in Vienna and that he had received a doctorate in philosophy from Vienna University.

All of this appeared to be untrue. An official at the Austrian Defense Ministry reported that Beer's name did not appear on the roster of former students of Wierner Nuestadt Academy. Other sources denied Beer had ever fought in the Socialist *Schutzbund*, had worked at the Berg Theater, or had taken a degree from Vienna University or had even fought in the Spanish Civil War. Who was this man?

No one seemed to know. What was known was that he was a spy for the Soviets and had passed on countless Israeli secrets to the KGB. A shocked David Ben-Gurion groaned at hearing the news: "I am surrounded by treachery!" So upsetting was Beer's betrayal that immediately after he informed his cabinet of Beer's espionage, the Premier fainted. "We're in terrible trouble," one of the cabinet ministers remarked.

Beer's espionage activities on behalf of the KGB had been going on for a decade, according to one report, and he had apparently been a spy-for-hire in order to pay for the extravagances of his mistress. That motive was, perhaps, a sham also, for at his 1961 trial, Beer proudly stated that he had done his duty in saving Israel from becoming entrenched with the Western Powers and that it should be allied with the Soviets.

The mysterious Soviet spy who called himself Israel Beer, 1961.

The scandal hung like a black cloud over the Israeil government for months, long after Beer had been sent to prison to serve a ten-year term. The sentence was raised to fifteen years after more charges were confirmed. Beer busied himself by writing a book which justified his treasonable actions. He died of a heart attack behind bars in 1968.

By then Israeli intelligence had learned one positive thing about this most mysterious man—that he was not Israel Beer at all. The Austrian by that name totally vanished in 1938, only short weeks before Beer the imposter arrived in Palestine. The spy had employed the traditional Russian ruse of assuming the name of a missing or dead person.

[ALSO SEE: *KGB; Mossad*]

BEHN, APHRA (AKA: IMCOMPARABLE ASTREA)
English Spy in Antwerp ▪ (1640–1689)

LITTLE IS KNOWN ABOUT THE EARLY LIFE OF ENGLAND'S first professional writer, Aphra Behn, who would later be called the Imcomparable Astrea and became one of England's first female spies. It is believed by some that Aphra Behen was born near Canterbury and that her real name was Aphra Johnson. Her father may have been related to Lord Francis Willoughby, governor of Surinam, a British territory in South America, and from whom he received a business appointment in that colony. The family traveled to Surinam in 1663, but Aphra's father died of illness during the voyage. The family remained in that exotic land for six months before returning to England.

Before leaving Surinam, Aphra carried on a torrid affair with William Scot whose father had conspired to send Charles I to the executioner's block and was himself later executed. Aphra and William Scot were enamored of the popular novel *L'Astree* by Honore de Urfe and referred to each other by the names of the protagonists, Aphra being Astrea and Scot being Celedon. The two would later employ these names again, not as lovers but as code names for their spying activities.

In 1664 Aphra married a Dutch merchant named Behn, about whom there is very little information, except that he died in London of the great plague of 1665. Also during that year, England went to war with Holland over its expansionist trade progam under Charles II. Holland believed that England was intruding upon its long-established trade routes. Of great concern to Charles and his ministers was the powerful group of English officers, all republicans, who headquartered in Holland and had enlisted under the banner of Dutch leader Colonel Joseph Bampfield. One of these Englishmen was William Scot.

Scot, however, had decided to secretly straddle both sides of the fence. While swearing allegiance to Bampfield and the Dutch, he informed Charles II through his espionage chief Lord Henry Arlington that there would be an uprising in Yorkshire and the northern shires. Arlington discovered Scot's information to be correct and he was able to suppress the rebellion before it started.

Thinking to use Scot as a double agent, Arlington sent two spies to Holland to work with the errant Englishman. Scot betrayed both men to the Dutch and they were executed. Scot later insisted that the two spies had left him no choice. They had been so incompetent that they had almost revealed Scot's secret liaison with Arlington. The British spy chief knew about Scot's one-time romance with Aphra Behn and he easily recruited this devoted royalist to his espionage service.

Behn was sent to Antwerp in July 1666. From there she was to contact Scot, offer him a royal pardon if he would rejoin the ranks of the King, as well as obtain information about the movements of Dutch troops and plans. From Antwerp, Behn contacted Scot in Holland. They used their code names of Astrea and Celedon in written communications. Scot, through Behn, informed the British that the Dutch planned to sail a powerful fleet into the Thames River and set up a blockade, as well as land an invasion force at Harwich.

This vital information was inexplicably ignored and the Dutch fleet sailed into the Thames against little opposition. Behn wrote to Arlington, expressing her anger over the fact that her precious information had been ignored. Moreover, Arlington had not kept his part of their bargain by not sending Behn funds. She nevertheless continued her important espionage work. To survive she pawned her jewelry and lived on loans from friends.

At the point of poverty, Behn borrowed enough money to return to England in early 1667. When she could not return the money she had borrowed for her passage, the courageous female spy was sent to debtor's prison. After many pleas, the government responded and paid Behn's debts.

Upon her release she shunned espionage and took up the pen, writing one ribald comedy after another, including *Forc'd Marriage* (1671), *The Rover* (1677), *False Count* (1682), *The Roundheads* (1682), and her most famous tale, *Oroonoko* (1688), which was based upon her experiences in Surinam. Aphra Behn was thus immortalized not for her espionage but by becoming England's first professional female writer. England honored her by burying her remains in Westminster Abbey.

BELL, WILLIAM
U.S. Spy for Poland ▪ (1920–)

A RADAR SPECIALIST AT THE HUGHES AIRCRAFT Company in Los Angeles, William Bell was at the end of his financial rope in 1978 when he declared bankruptcy, following a failed marriage. Bell, however, was worth a considerable amount of money to Polish intelligence, which worked directly with the KGB in Moscow. Bell had clearance to secret information at Hughes Aircraft, in particular the most sensitive weapons systems then in development for the U.S. Air Force.

Bell lived at a posh apartment complex in Playa Del Rey, a fashionable beach community south of Los Angeles. Just when he was wondering how he would continue to make ends meet, Bell was befriended by a new neighbor, Marian Zarcharski, a 25-year-old executive who worked for the Polish-American Machinery Company (Polamco) which was headquartered in Elk Grove Village, Illinois, just outside Chicago. The youthful, apparently successful Zacharski, invited Bell to play tennis and the two quickly formed a fast friendship.

When Bell told Zacharski about his financial woes, he found a willing ear and a helping hand. Zarcharski advanced him some money but he asked that Bell bring him innocuous material from Hughes Aircraft, such as the company newsletter. Then, as he advanced more money, Zacharski asked for materials that outlined some forthcoming bid proposals. All of this was nonclassified material and Bell thought nothing of handing it over to his good friend Zacharski whose pretty young wife Bell had also befriended.

By May 1978, however, Bell was delivering classified documents to Zacharski and receiving thousands of dollars in cash from his friend. Bell was in the spy business with both feet. "It was a long bit by bit thing," Bell later confessed to a grand jury. "First innocent and semi-innocent and so on. And, in the end, I was in financial straits and this offered an opportunity out."

The apartment complex was then converted to condominiums and Bell told Zacharski that he wanted to buy his apartment but he could not afford the down payment. "Not to worry," Zacharski told him. A short time later Zacharski handed a plain white envelope to Bell which contained $5,000 in cash. This was followed by another cash payment of $7,000. Bell kept supplying Zacharski with weapons systems secrets.

Then, in November 1979, Zarcharski handed Bell $3,000 and told him that he was to fly to Austria and go to the Hotel Gray Bear in Innsbruck. He was to meet some of Zacharski's friends in the basement restaurant and arrange to give the contacts secrets Bell had recently stolen from Hughes Aircraft. In return, Zacharski promised, Bell would receive "big dollars." Bell dutifully flew to Innsbruck. Once inside the restaurant, he sat alone, studying other patrons. He thought that two men and a young woman were watching him. He stood up and went to a hallway and one of the men followed him, asking: "Are you Marian's friend?"

"Yes, I am."

Bell was told to go outside and begin walking up the street. A car would stop next to him and he was to get into it. Bell did as he was told and got into the car which sped into the mountains. Bell and one of the men got out of the car and walked along a mountain path. The man handed Bell $7,000 and Bell turned over a film strip of many secret documents at Hughes Aircraft. Bell had taken the photos himself with a camera Zacharski had given him. Before Zacharski's friends dropped Bell off at his hotel, they showed the American a picture of his wife and small son. They said nothing when doing this but the meaning was clear. If Bell had any thoughts of betraying them, the spies knew where they could find Bell's family.

Bell continued to supply Zacharski with secret information receiving cash and gold coins from his friend and Zacharski's contacts in Europe, more than $110,000 in three years of espionage. Bell made several more trips to Europe, delivering information on existing weapons and future weapons. In 1981, Bell went to Geneva, Switzerland, and delivered to Zacharski's people data on a "quiet" radar system that had been designed for the B-1 and Stealth Bomber. He promised that he would soon have data on the F-18 Fighter that was then being developed.

Those plans were never delivered. On June 22, 1981, FBI agents entered the office of William Bell at Hughes Aircraft, telling him that he was under arrest. He was taken to a hotel where agents showed him a photo taken of him in Geneva, handing over secrets to an agent of the Polish intelligence service. The FBI then informed Bell that they had known about his friend Zacharski for more than three years. Bureau agents had had the Polish intelligence agent under surveillance since he landed in Chicago in 1978.

The FBI had monitored his movement to Los Angles and tapped his phones there. Zacharski must have known this because he joked about agents needing "to change the tape" in his phone conversations. The firm for which Zarcharski worked, Polamco in Illinois, had been identified by a U.S. Senate committee as "the base of operations for a Polish spy network."

Zarcharski was to return to Illinois, promoted to the presidency of Polamco, Bell told FBI agents, and be replaced by another agent. Bell then offered to help the Bureau crack the entire espionage network. Zarcharski was to be kept under surveillance until his replacement had been identified as working with Bell. This was not to be. A short time later Zarcharski was arrested by FBI agents in Los Angeles. This arrest was premature, according to some authorities, because of the competition between the Chicago and Los Angeles FBI offices, each wanting to take credit for apprehending the spies.

Marian Zarcharski was tried as a spy in December 1981. Convicted, he was sent to prison for life. William Bell fared better. Since Zarcharski's conviction was largely brought about by his testimony, Bell received only eight years in prison.

BENTLEY, ELIZABETH
U.S. Spy for Soviets ▪ (1906–1963)

THE RED SPY HUNTS IN THE U.S. OF THE LATE 1940s were touched off by two former members of the Communist Party. The first was the well-known journalist, Whittaker Chambers. The other was a woman named Elizabeth Bentley. As early as 1946, the rumor mills churned by the Washington press corps had it that a mysterious, alluring blonde, a regular "Mata Hari," had confessed to being a Communist spy throughout World War II and that her espionage network included some of the most prestigious people in the government.

When Miss Bentley finally made her appearance before HUAC in 1948, she was anything but alluring and she was certainly not a blonde. She was a forty-ish, frumpy woman with brown hair and glasses. The lurid stories that she had vamped some of Washington's bigwigs into releasing classified information went to nothing as she jabbered on and on before the Committee.

Her story was oft-repeated by those Americans who had naively joined the Communist Party in the 1930s in an effort to combat fascism. Connecticut-born, Bentley graduated from Vassar in 1930. She later took an M.A. degree at Columbia University in New York. In 1933 on a tour of Italy, Bentley was

Soviet spy Elizabeth Bentley, who talked non-stop before HUAC in 1948, naming important people in the U.S. government as Russian spies.

exposed to the Black Shirt fascism of dictator Benito Mussolini. So revolted was she, she later claimed, that, upon her return to the U.S., she became "easy prey" (her own words) and was recruited by a Communist Party unit operating at Columbia.

Through this party unit, Bentley met and fell in love with Jacob Golos, an American citizen who was not only an active Communist but a spy in the pay of Moscow. After Golos suffered a heart attack in 1941 and was limited in his physical movements, Bentley assumed her lover's espionage responsibilities. By this time, she was living in Washington, D.C., and it was here that Bentley came to know Golos' espionage contacts, people in high places, she later claimed.

Bentley claimed that she had twenty contacts in Washington and they, in turn, had about thirty more well-placed men and women who fed them "secret information." These contacts, Bentley, said, were in the Army, Air Force, the State and Treasury Departments, and the OSS. The only exemptions were the FBI and the Navy. She also said that there was "a man around the White House" who had helped to place her informants in strategic posts.

After obtaining information, Bentley sent it on to Golos in New York or to his Communist contacts. Then, she believed, it went to Moscow. After Golos

died in 1943, Bentley testified that she turned over political information to Earl Browder, head of the U.S. Communist Party and her military information went to "the real Russians" via one-time government employee John Abt who held Communist meetings in his Manhattan apartment.

Bentley went on to state that in 1942, she met several times with William W. Remington who was, in her words, "in a good spot," to obtain secret information. Remington then worked for the War Production Board. He was later chairman of a Department of Commerce committee, which collected sercret information from many government agencies and departments, including the Atomic Energy Commission. The committee had the task of determining which goods would or would not be sent to Russia. Remington was dismissed from his position when Bentley named him as a Communist spy.

The contact name Bentley used in calling Remington was "Helen." To others, she used the alias of "Joan" or "Mary." Bentley claimed that she often had clandestine meetings with Remington, in a drugstore across from Washington's Willard Hotel or in a hallway of the National Gallery of Art where they would both pretend to view paintings while secret information was passed.

Remington gave Bentley scraps of paper which detailed aircraft production, she stated, and "a formula for making synthetic rubber from garbage." She described Remington at these times being "very nervous, very jittery, obviously scared to death that anybody would find out he was doing this."

J. Parnell Thomas, the autocratic head of HUAC, demanded to know the identity of "the man around the White House." Bentley replied that this was none other than Lauchlin Currie, one of President Roosevelt's closest advisers. For six years, Currie had been a White House special assistant who had twice gone to China on confidential missions. Bentley added that she never directly met Currie but that he worked with former government employee George Silverman. Both men had attended Harvard University together, and, Bentley pointed out, Silverman gave Currie's information to Nathan Gregory Silvermaster, the top Communist in Washington to whom Bentley reported.

Another important name in Bentley's list of traitors was Harry Dexter White, Assistant Secretary of the Treasury, architect of the World Bank, and, later, the International Monetary Fund. Bentley insisted that White had helped to place Communists in government posts where they could appropriate secrets on behalf of Russia. White, she said, gave secret information to Silvermaster and he, in turn, passed it to Bentley who sent it on to her contacts in New York. "Mr. White knew where it [the secret information] was going," she added, "but preferred not to mention the fact."

Silverman and a WPB employee, Victor Perlo, according to Bentley, were given information by more than thirty top Communist agents (she made sure to say that she did not believe Currie was a Communist) and these men passed information to her to send along the spy network in New York and subsequently to Moscow.

From Silverman and Ludwig Ullman, who both worked at Air Force headquarters, Bentley said she received details of the new B-29 Bomber and other new types of war planes, along with the destination of planes to various theaters of war. Throughout her long testimony, Bentley was chain-smoking. At one point she paused dramatically, lit a cigarette, and blew out a long cloud of smoke before committee members, saying in that gasp: "We knew about D-Day long before D-Day happened."

More than thirty persons were named by Bentley as either Communists or Fellow Travelers who willingly supplied secrets to the Washington and New York espionage network. Most denied ever knowing the woman. This was Currie's response who also said he never, to his knowledge, had any contact with a Communist. White denied Bentley's accusation, dismissing them with the word "fantastic." With William Remington it was another story.

Remington appeared before the committee and admitted that he had met with Bentley but he knew her only as Helen Johnson. He admitted that he had passed information to her but it was harmless data, no more than "what was available to any reporter." He denied that he was a Communist but then said that his mother-in-law was a member of the Party. He had attended some meetings of the American Youth Congress, Remington said. His wife was a dues-paying member of this organization which HUAC identified as a Communist front organization.

In defense of the Congress, Remington pointed out that many people gave their tacit endorsement of the organization by simply appearing at its meetings, and that this included the First Lady in the White House. "It was not unusual," Remington intoned, "for Mrs. (Eleanor) Roosevelt to appear at the American Youth Congress. I once had the privilege of tripping over Mrs. Roosevelt's feet at a congress meeting. She was sitting on the floor."

Bentley's statements before HUAC were both explosive and frightening, yet her wide-ranging remarks were so fragmentary and unsupported that HUAC could do little but publicize her testimony. It was pointed out that Bentley had become disillusioned with the Communists shortly after the war and had requested a personal meeting with J. Edgar Hoover, chief of the FBI, to whom she first confessed her spying activities and with whom she agreed to work in ferreting out dangerous Communists in the government. It had taken Hoover almost two years to get Bentley before HUAC.

In the end, Elizabeth Bentley's bombshell testimony, along with that of Whittaker Chambers (who did not know her, their espionage careers running parallel but never converging) brought no indictments for spying against anyone named. It did set off, however, one of the most intense spy hunts in American history, one where Communists, both real and imagined, were relentlessly sought at fever pitch.

[ALSO SEE: *Whittaker Chambers; FBI; J. Edgar Hoover; OSS*]

BERG, JACK
British Double Agent in England ▪ (1919– ?)

HALF NORWEGIAN, HALF BRITISH, JACK BERG WAS all Nazi spy, or so it seemed to his German spymasters in Oslo, Norway. Berg was short and rather portly, but there was nothing flabby about his avid belief in the fascist cause. Vidkun Quisling, the arch traitor of Norway, had recruited Berg into the ranks of his Nazi Party in Norway. Ernst Mueller, Commander of the Abwehr in Oslo, reviewed Berg's file and felt, because of his British background, that he would be an ideal spy to send to England.

Berg willingly became a German agent, undergoing intensive training as a saboteur. He was then sent to England with a Norwegian Nazi named Olaf Klausen. Both men were to randomly sabotage ammunition plants and dumps, airfields, military installations, railway lines, any site vital to England's wartime defenses. This was at a time when Hermann Goering's Luftwaffe was ceaselessly pounding London and other English cities.

A short time after their arrival in England, the saboteurs began to send reports to Mueller about their successes. Suddenly, reports of widespread sabotage in southern England began to appear in British newspapers. Berg and Klausen took credit for these devastating events. They continued to stay in contact with their Abwehr contacts, asking that they be regularly supplied by secret air drops.

Money, explosives, and equipment were dropped to the spies by fast-moving German bombers flying at low level. Their sabotage continued unmolested but, when southern England began to fill up with American troops in 1943 and security was increased, Berg and Klausen moved to Scotland where they felt their operations could be conducted more safely. Two supply drops to the spies were made in Scotland. To divert attention from these low-level drops, the Luftwaffe conducted two bombings of nearby Scottish towns which inflicted many casualties on the civilian population.

Berg and Klausen continued their espionage and sabotage operations, completing one assignment after another well into 1944. It occured to the Germans that these two agents had had phenomenal luck in evading capture but they verified the outcome of their sabotage and kept in regular contact with them through shortwave messages, closely monitoring their keystrokes to precisely identify their individual style in sending code. Reassured, the Abwehr confidently reported to Hitler that Berg and Klausen were, among some others, the most successfull spies in England.

Nothing could be further from the truth. Of the dozens of spies, in groups, pairs or as individuals, that the Abwehr had sent to England from 1939 to the end of the war, not one of them continued to operate successful espionage or sabotage operations. All of them were captured by counterintelligence agents of MI5. They were either imprisoned for the duration of the war or executed. The more cooperative were selected to act as double agents or "dummy" agents, pretending to act as successful spies for the Abwehr, completing their assignments and remaining in constant contact with their German spymasters. The sabotage they conducted, however, was staged by the British. The misinformation they sent to their Abwehr contacts was cleverly concocted by MI5.

Hugh Trevor-Roper and Major E. W. Gill who worked for MI5 had, as early as December 1939, broken most of the main codes of the Abwehr and were able to identify and thus locate the spies the Germans sent to England. In 1941, England's most gifted cryptologist, Dillwyn Knox, a director at the Government Code and Cipher School in Bletchley, was able to completely identify the keying of the Enigma Machine used by the Abwehr. From that point on, every Abwehr message was immediately decoded by MI5.

Thus Berg and Klausen were instantly identified before they paddled ashore in Scotland in 1941. They, along with all other spies sent by the Abwehr, were quickly picked up and taken to Ham, England, where, at Latchmere House, a one-time mental hospital, they were held. Each was severely interrogated and almost all of the German agents promptly cracked, confessing their roles and missions. The Abwehr had not trained any of its agents to resist shock interrogations as the Allies routinely did with their spies, most likely out of fear that such training would totally demoralize the agents before they embarked on their missions.

Berg and Klausen underwent such shock interrogations before agreeing to work with MI5 which set them up with housing, German spy apparatus, and an income. The sabotage supposedly accomplished by Berg and Klausen were staged by MI5, or, if a railway or manufacturing plant accident occured, these mishaps were palmed off as sabotage completed by the pair. Sometimes MI5 cleverly staged acts of sabotage and postured these sham explosions as the work of Berg and Klausen. (The most spectacular fake sabotage staged by MI5 was that attributed to the sensational Abwehr agent known as "Fritz," who was really a British subject and infamous criminal, Eddie Chapman.)

Klausen later proved truculent and was imprisoned. He was replaced by a British spy who by then had learned Klausen's style of sending code. The life-loving Berg, however, proved to be continuously cooperative and appeared to enjoy his role as double agent, operating in Scotland until February 1944, sending out reports to the Abwehr of blowing up buildings and installations that did not exist or had been demolished in air raids. The doctored MI5 information he sent back to Germany also mislead the Nazis into moving troops and armor to areas where no Allied threat really existed. Following the war, Berg was repatriated to Norway.

[ALSO SEE: *Abwehr; Eddie Chapman; MI5*]

BERG, MORRIS (MOE)
U.S. Spy in Japan and Europe ▪ (1902–1972)

MORRIS "MOE" BERG WAS THE SON OF RUSSIAN-Jewish immigrants. He was raised in Newark, N.J., and he loved two things in life—languages and baseball. He played baseball in high school and also at Princeton where he graduated with a degree in languages in 1923. Berg went on to play for several major league teams as a back-up catcher, notably with the Brooklyn Dodgers. During and after his sixteen-year career in baseball, Moe Berg was the most unlikely of spies, but he was also one of the most courageous and successful agents who ever worked for the OSS.

In the early 1930s, Berg was recruited by the American government as a spy. He had the perfect cover, that of a touring baseball player. In 1934, while barnstorming with an American all-star team, Berg visited Tokyo. He requested a room in his hotel that gave him a panoramic view of the city. In the morning, dressed in a kimono, Berg stepped onto the wide balcony of his room and took motion pictures and stills of Tokyo, especially the military installations surrounding the Bay, the harbor facilities, the warships sailing about and at anchor. He moved about the city like some gawking tourist but he managed to get more photos and motion pictures of Tokyo's production plants, particularly those which were already manufacturing weapons and ammunitions for its impending war with China.

This photographic record of the Japanese capital proved to be the most current available eight years later when, after Pearl Harbor, Lt.-Col. (later general) James H. Doolittle was planning his dramatic 1942 air strike against Tokyo, the first significant American counterattack of the war. Doolittle spent hours studying Berg's photos and films and his accurate attack against Japanese military installations was based upon the information supplied by the baseball player.

By 1941 baseball was a thing of the past for Berg who had gone to work for Nelson Rockefeller's Inter-American Affairs organization. He spent a great deal of time in Latin America on fact-finding missions. At the time, Berg was also used to screen various foreign businesses, particularly those owned and operated by the Japanese. So effective was Berg as a spy that General William Donovan, head of the OSS, recruited him into the ranks of his espionage organization.

Berg undertook some of the most harrowing missions "Wild Bill" Donovan and the OSS could provide. At the age of forty-one, he proved himself as physically fit as any man twenty years younger. In 1943, Berg parachuted into Yugoslavia where he met with partisans. He returned to report that Tito's forces were the most effective partisans then fighting the Nazis. He urged that the Allies fully support Tito. After Winston Churchill read Berg's report, he endorsed the plan and weapons and support units were soon sent to Tito.

In that same year Berg slipped into occupied Norway, meeting with underground freedom fighters, and located a secret heavy water plant operated by the Nazis who were attempting to build a nuclear weapon. Berg's information allowed British bombers to destroy the plant. In 1944, Berg went to Switzerland where he worked with Allen Dulles, who has chief of operations for the OSS in Europe. Berg, however, was sometimes at odds with Dulles, reminding him that his commission was direct from Donovan and that he answered only to Donavan. The two nevertheless proved to be an effective team.

From Switzerland Berg traveled several times to areas of Italy still occupied by German forces. He was able to locate several atomic scientists in Italy and later in Germany, the very scientists who later helped America develop its space and atomic programs following World War II. (Berg's exploits were later chronicled in the stirring Fritz Lang film, *Cloak and Dagger*.) It was a foot race between the U.S. and Russia as to which country could bring the scientists into their camps. Berg essentially won the race. On his information, most of the top European scientists were "liberated" by special service commandoes and brought to the West.

Following the war the spectacular Berg was awarded the American Medal of Merit, the highest decoration given to a civilian during wartime. For reasons he never explained, Berg refused to accept this most prestigious award. Berg later worked for NATO (North Atlantic Treaty Oganization) as a scientific adviser and it was reported that he continue to undertake U.S. espionage missions in Soviet block nations well into the 1960s.

[ALSO SEE: *William Donovan; Allen Dulles; OSS*]

BERIA, LAVRENTI PAVLOVICH
Soviet Spymaster ▪ (1899–1953)

A FANATICAL BOLSHEVIK FROM AN EARLY AGE UNTIL his death, Lavrenti Beria was Joseph Stalin's personal assassin as well as head of the the NKVD, precursor to the KGB. He proved to be a merciless espionage chief who relished his role as head of Russia's dreaded secret police, an espionage agency that would stop at nothing to reach its fact-finding goals.

Beria was born to peasants in the small seaside resort of Merkheuli, Georgia, on the Black Sea. He received very little education, attending local schools and graduating with an architectual degree in 1919 from a technical college in Baku. Before taking his degree, Beria was drafted into the Imperial Army and served briefly during World War I. He, like millions of others, deserted in 1917, at the time of the Russian revolution.

Joining the Bolshevik Party, Beria joined the Cheka, the secret police established by the Bolsheviks to protect the revolution against counterrevolutionaries. He was sent back to his native Georgia which was strongly anti-Bolshevik. There he served as a spy, informing on his frends and relatives, anyone who

Soviet spymaster and head of the dreaded NKVD, Lavrenti Beria.

showed disloyalty to the revolution. When the Bolsheviks took over Georgia, those pinpointed as traitors to the revolution by Beria were seized and summarily executed.

Beria's climb to power in the early 1920s was through the Cheka and later, its successor, the GPU and still later the OGPU and its successor, the NKVD. All of these organizations were responsible for internal and external espionage, counterespionage, secret police work, and various sub rosa activities. Beria compromised countless party functionaries to obtain their jobs. One of his favorite ploys was to use married women to entice his superiors and then expose the liaisons. The resulting scandals ruined his bosses and he assumed their posts.

Those Beria could not compromise, he murdered, some by his own hands, but usually through a goon squad. In 1921, at Stalin's urging, Lenin appointed Beria as head of Soviet intelligence. Stalin was, by then, indebted to Beria who had performed many murders for him. Following Lenin's death in 1924, Beria supported Stalin in his grab for power. Ten years later, Stalin named Beria a member of the Central Committee of the Communist Party. In gratitude, Beria busied himself by liquidating Stalin's opponents.

Stalin had several liquidators working for him, including Vyacheslav Menzhinsky who bossed the OGPU in the 1920s, having poisoned his predecessor Felix Dzerzhinsky. Menzhinsky was purged by Stalin in 1934 and replaced by Genrikh Yagoda, and Yagoda was deposed by Nicolai Yezhov, a bloodthirsty murderer who was the first chief of the NKVD.

Stalin realized that he had placed a fanatic at the head of the secret police, a man who wielded more actual power than Stalin himself. Stalin went to Beria and told him that Yezhov was out of control and asked Beria to murder Yezhov. In December 1938, the policeman disappeared forever and Beria took his place. One report had it that the hulking Beria personally strangled Yezhov as he sat at his desk in NKVD headquarters. To enhance his image as the new NKVD boss, Beria publicly condemned five NKVD officials in the Ukraine, stating that they had carried out senseless executions. He then ordered the officials executed.

When Russia was invaded by the Germans in 1941, Beria was named deputy Prime Minister, in charge of all security behind the Russian lines. Beria's goon squads of secret police summarily executed any soldier who malingered or appeared disgruntled. They shot tens of thousands of old Bolsheviks at the same time since, in the chaos of war, Stalin thought it the perfect time to eliminate the last of his political enemies. Those whom Beria did not execute he sent to labor camps but these became an embarrassment as the Germans threatened to overrun these camps as they pushed deep into Russia.

As the Nazi legions approached Minsk, Beria ordered the political dentention camp in that city demolished. His secret police machine gunned to death more than 10,000 prisoners, then blew up the camp with hand grenades. They torched the camp and burned the bodies. Stalin did not want a single political prisoner to survive and escape to the West and possibly mount opposition to his dictatorial regime.

At war's end, Beria streamlined the Russian espionage service, training thousands of agents for the NKVD, which became the MVD, but Beria remained as the top secret policeman. Those fortunate enough to become MVD henchmen enjoyed wealth, power, and luxury, but they also risked internal purges that had become a political way of life in a system built upon internecine struggles. The widespread espionage net thrown by Beria into the West returned countless military secrets. His budget was enormous and tens of thousands of spies throughout the world were on his payroll.

As he had with all of his other henchmen, Stalin became suspicious of Beria, believing that the secret policeman was plotting to usurp him. Stalin, at one point, called his daughter Svetlana, while she was staying with Beria and his wife. Stalin ordered her to leave at once, saying: "I don't trust Beria. He could use you as a hostage in trying to force me from my office." By 1951, the paranoid Stalin was convinced that Beria was plotting to murder him. He had Beria arrested, charging his old enforcer as "an imperial agent."

While Beria awaited trial, Stalin died. His successors had no intention of allowing Beria to take over. He was tried in secret and condemned as a traitor. Then, on December 23, 1953, "Beria the Butcher" was placed before a wall in Lubianka Prison and shot to death by a firing squad. Another story had it that a special execution squad stormed into Beria's NKVD headquarters and shot him and his top aides to death.

[ALSO SEE: *Cheka; Felix Dzershinsky; GPU; MVD; NKDV; OGPU; Genrikh Yagoa; Nicolai Yezhov*]

BERLIN TUNNEL
CIA Listening Post ▪ (1955–1956)

REINHARD GEHLEN, DIRECTOR OF INTELLIGENCE FOR the German Federal Republic, contacted CIA chief Allen Dulles in 1954, to inform him that it was possible to tap directly into top secret communication lines between Russia and East Germany. Dulles was told that a West German agent had copied and provided Communist plans for the installment of communication cables six feet underground and close to the American Sector in Berlin.

Dulles, with direct approval of President Dwight David Eisenhower, ordered the U.S. Army Engineers to dig a 300-yard-long tunnel from West Berlin to East Berlin. The tunnel was fifteen feet deep, had concrete walls and a concrete floor, and a sophisticated ventilating system. At the East Berlin side of the tunnel, an intercept chamber was constructed by the U.S. Signal Corps, which tapped into all of the communciation lines which had been buried by the Communists.

CIA agents then proceeded to monitor all messages between East Berlin and Moscow, as well as those received and transmitted by the Russian Embassy in Berlin, and messages going in and out of Russian army headquarters at nearby Zossen. This was a major espionage coup for the West that provided detailed information on Communist military and political operations for almost two years, 1955–1956.

British intelligence was informed of the secret tunnel and this led to George Blake, who worked for the British but who was really a double agent for Russia, to learn of the listening post. He informed the Communists who promptly sealed off the eastern end of the tunnel and with it the vital CIA intercept chamber.

[ALSO SEE: *George Blake; CIA; Allen Dulles*]

BERRYER, NICOLAS-RENE
French Spymaster for Louis XV ▪ (1703–1762)

A NATIVE PARISIAN, BERRYER WAS A PRACTICING lawyer who worked in the administration of Paris and later represented the crown in various matters at Poitou (1743–47). He was an arch royalist who was also a close friend of Jeanne Antoinette d'Etioles, Marquise de Pompadour. When Madame Pompadour became mistress to Louis XV, she went to Berryer and asked that he help protect her name against any scandal that might arise over her relations with the king.

Berryer agreed and Pompadour quickly persuaded Louis to appoint the lawyer Lieutenant-General of Police. His power extended throughout France and was enormous. He used a small army of agents who worked at the royal court in Versailles and in Paris, busy recording gossip and rumor regarding Pompadour and the King. So ardent was Berryer's efforts to protect the King and his mistress that he decided to screen every letter written in France.

To that end, Berryer established a *cabinet noir* ("black chamber") where scores of spies opened and read every letter sent through the French postal system. This secret postal censorship office was the first to operate on a nationwide scale. The task was not easy. In that era each letter was sealed with the individual seal of each sender. A wax impression of each seal had to be made, then the wax steamed off before the letter was opened. Once opened, the letter was read and notes were taken. A fresh seal was then made from each wax impression and affixed to the letter, resealing it before it was sent to its destination.

Fortunately for Berryer's *cabinet noir*, France was then an illiterate country and most citizens could not write at all, this skill reserved for the few who had been privileged with an education, chiefly the aristocracy, and those in business and government. Thus, the volume handled by his postal spies was not overwhelming. Berryer's postal espionage continued throughout his term as France's police chief (1747–1757). He later became Keeper of the Royal Seals, a post he held until his death.

BETTANY, MICHAEL
Soviet Spy in England ▪ (1950–   )

MI5 HAS HAD A LONG AND DISTINGUISHED CAREER AS Great Britain's counterintelligence service. It was particularly effective during World War II in gathering domestic intelligence on Nazi spies in England and apprehending almost every one of them immediately after they arrived the country. Policing its own ranks, however, became shoddy in the early years of the Cold War. One of its most blatant blunders was allowing the bumbling, oafish Michael Bettany into its ranks.

Bettany was the son of a factory worker in the Midlands industrial town of Stokes-on-Trent. He nevertheless managed to graduate from Oxford and then took a teaching job in Germany. Overweight and with constantly shifting ambitions, Bettany at one time thought of becoming a Catholic priest. While teaching in Germany, he became fascinated with Nazi idealogy but then he shifted his political allegiance to Marxism.

Even with this known scattershot philosophy, Bettany was recruited into MI5 in 1982, chiefly to rebuff critics of MI5 who claimed that the intelligence agency was exclusively staffed with agents from the upper class. In keeping the "common touch," MI5 was impaled on the horn of its own dilemma. Michael Bettany proved to be completely irresponsible, a goofy, posturing person who played at being an espionage agent.

On one occasion after he had been working for MI5 for a brief period, police stopped Bettany after he staggered drunk unto a train, offering no ticket and attempting to evade a conductor who had to chase him down the aisle of a coach. To police officers Bettany shouted: "You can't arrest me. I'm a spy!" Irrespective of this incident and many like it, MI5 kept Bettany on its payroll. He was then, inexplicably, promoted to the Russian desk, even though he had little or no background or knowledge qualifying him for that appointment.

Just as the traitorous Aldrich Ames was later tolerated and ignored as a nepotistic employee of the CIA, Bettany's shabby conduct and ineptitude were purposely overlooked on the grounds that he was a social expediency, a poor boy whose presence at MI5 was necessary to disprove any prejudice against the lower class.

In his new position, Bettany had access to information that identified all known KGB agents in England. Bettany made copies of secret documents and then attempted to make contact with the KGB. He believed, with no real knowledge, that the Russian diplomat, Arkady Gouk, assigned to the Soviet Embassy in London, was a KGB spymaster. He attempted many times to contact Gouk, phoning him. Gouk wanted no part of Bettany and told him so.

Bettany, however, was determined to become a double agent for Russia at all costs. On several occasions he went to Gouk's apartment in London and shoved secret documents through the mail slot. Each packet of top secret information had a cover letter from Bettany which blatantly stated that he wanted to spy for the Soviets and that he was an officer at MI5. When not receiving a warm reception from Gouk, Bettany contacted other Russian diplomats in London. He was rebuffed repeatedly by the nervous Soviet officials who concluded that no real traitor would act so openly and so stupidly as did Bettany and that the British were actually trying to plant Bettany in their midst as a double agent.

Ironically, it was the KGB itself that informed MI5 about its errant agent. The Russians contacted MI5 officials and told them that they had an employee trying to sell them secrets they did not want and that Bettany was intending to fly to Vienna to ostensibly meet KGB agents where he was to deliver a list of known Soviet agents in England. No Russians intended to meet its spy in Austria, MI5 was informed. In short, the KGB informed its opposition that they could not be fooled and that it was rejecting the double agent MI5 was so haphazardly attempting to foist upon them.

Of course, MI5 was incensed, mostly at its own *faux pas* at employing such a bungler. The KGB was in shock after Bettany's arrest was announced in the press, realizing that Russia had lost a priceless contact who could have provided them with a list of their own known spies and therefore it could have quickly determined which of their agents had gone undetected by MI5. In fact, Bettany had been cleared for top secret and the information to which he had access was so sensitive that even the Attorney General, Sir Michael Havers, who was to prosecute Bettany in court, was restricted from reviewing that information.

Interrogators confronting Bettany after his arrest soon realized that they were dealing with a lone wolf, one without teeth. He complained to them that his polished, uppercrust colleagues in MI5 shunned him, that they might have to put up with him in their work but he would always be treated by them as a social pariah. "Only the Soviet system can appreciate a man like me," Bettany reportedly told his MI5 inquisitors.

Brought to trial which was held *in camera*, Bettany claimed innocence but was convicted of ten charges dealing with violations of the Official Secrets Act. Lord Lane, the Lord Chief Justice, addressed the convicted spy who stood silent in the dock: "You have made treachery your course of action. It is quite plain to me that in many ways you are puerile. It is also clear to me that you are both opinionated and dangerous. You would not have hesitated to disclose names to the Russians which almost certainly would have led to death for more than one person." Bettany was sentenced to twenty-three years in prison.

The Bettany case, along with other recent breaches of British intelligence, including that of Geoffrey Prime, who worked at the secret British communications center at Cheltenham, so alarmed the CIA that it demanded that MI5 and other British agencies take immediate steps to improve its ruptured security. Prime Minister Margaret Thatcher responded by sternly ordering a prompt housecleaning of all bunglers in MI5.

[ALSO SEE: *KGB; MI5; Geoffrey Prime*]

BETTIGNIES, LOUISE DE (AKA: ALICE DUBOIS)
French Spymaster in World War I ▪ (1880–1918)

THE GERMAN ARMY INVADED BELGIUM AND NORTHern France in 1914 and before its massive columns fled countless refugees. Among them was Louise de Bettignies, a governess who spoke many languages. She had been born the seventh of eight children in Lille. Her father was a wealthy porcelain manufacturer and she received a fine education. Bettignies' social position allowed her to come in contact with wealthy aristocrats who hired her as a governess and linguist to teach their children French, German, Italian, and English. That way of life was smashed when the Germans rolled into Lille.

Escaping to England, Bettignies went to British intelligence, providing details of the German invasion. So precise were her reports that she was enlisted as a spy and returned to German-held Lille under the cover name of Alice Dubois. In Lille, Bettignies contacted many of her old friends who were more than willing to spy on the Germans, including Marie-Leonie Van Houtte who operated a shop and who assumed the cover name of Charlotte. Using the shop as a headquarters, the pair recruited others to their amateur spy ring which became known as the "Alice Service."

This ring rapidly expanded into Belgium and neutral Holland. Bettignies and Van Houtte moved freely through these countries, one selling lace, the other cheese. The Germans prohibited anyone from crossing the Belgium frontier into Holland but the two women, who insisted upon performing the most dangerous missions in their ring, crossed this border almost every week, finding unguarded areas through which to pass. With them they brought important information about the enemy which was passed along to British intelligence.

On several occasions, the pair crossed into Holland by swimming a wide canal. Actually Bettignies did the swimming, pushing Van Houtte in a wooden kneading trough through the water since Van Houtte could not swim. The ways in which Bettignies concealed her reports were ingenious and innovative in the fine art of espionage. She hid information in balls of wool, children's toys, spectacle rims, artificial limbs, sausages, bars of candy. One of Bettignies' operatives, Paul Bernard, an expert cartographer, was able to write out reports as lengthy as fifteen hundred words on the back of a postage stamp.

When the Germans tightened border security, Bettignies used young boys as couriers. One of these boys carried a coded message from Bettignies into Holland which warned the British and French of the impending German advance at Verdun, a stunning piece of espionage work for which the Alice Service is best remembered. This information helped the Allies to repulse the massive German attack, as well as minimize their casualties.

The Alice Service also busied itself with rescuing and smuggling Allied prisoners of war out of German-occupied territory. The agents sheltered these half-starved men, nursing them back to health. Then, a brilliant chemist named de Geyter who had invented secret inks, brilliantly forged German passports that the fugitives used to escape into neutral Holland. Hundreds of Allied soldiers were saved by the Service.

By 1915, the Germans became aware of the ring and began to track down its members. Bettignies disbanded her group, fearing she was endangering the lives of her friends. She and Van Houtte carried on alone, despite the fact that Bettignies grew seriously ill. Then, through an informer, Van Houtte was arrested by German counterintelligence agents as she was about to contact an agent in Brussels. Bettignies was picked up by German agents when she arrived in Tournai a few weeks later. The two women were court-martialed but would admit nothing about the Alice Service

Both women were condemned to death but were reprieved and imprisoned. The Germans had recently shot Edith Cavell, the heroic nurse who had helped so many Allied prisoners to escape. The worldwide outcry against the execution of this female had been so overwhelming that the Germans thought better of shooting two more women. Bettignies was given a 27-year term and Van Houtte was sent to prison for 15 years.

Bettignies was seriously ill at the time of her arrest and she grew worse in prison. Following the Armistice of 1918, Van Houtte was released but by then the courageous Louise de Bettignies was gone, having died in Cologne Prison on September 17, 1918. In appreciation of her valiant espionage service, the French government posthumously awarded her the Croix de Guerre. Her body was brought back to Lille where it was buried with full military honors. A statue was raised in Lille to honor the memory of Bettignies to whom hundreds of escaped Allied prisoners of war owed their lives.

[ALSO SEE: *Paul Bernard; Edith Cavell*]

BfV (BUNDESAMT FUR VERFASSUNGSSCHUTZ)
West German Counterintelligence ▪ (1950–   )

THE GERMAN NAME OF THE BfV MEANS "OFFICE for the Protection of the Constitution." This organization, smiliar to Britain's MI5, is West Germany's counterespionage agency and is part of the Ministry of the Interior. BfV is responsible for internal defense against espionage, sabotage, and treasonable acts.

The chief obligation of BfV was, until the breakdown of the Communist block countries, to prevent Communist infiltration into West Germany. The BfV has one of the most sophisticated computer systems, which contains enormous volumes of data on Communists, and, of particularly use today, worldwide terrorists and terrorist organizations, along with right-wing extremists and their groups, and this includes many neo-Nazi organizations.

Born in September 1950, the BfV was at first at odds with the West German military counterespionage agency commanded by General Reihard Gehlen. BfV's first director, Otto John, created a sensation when he suddenly vanished. He surfaced in East Germany, appearing at a press conference in which he violently attacked West Germany. John then reappeared in West Germany.

John insisted that he had been kidnapped and then brainwashed into making his anti-West German statements. He was not believed. Arrested, he was sent to prison for four years. After serving less than three years, he was released, still claiming to be innocent of treason. This scenario was repeated many times over throughout BfV's history.

Communist infiltration of the agency came about repeatedly because of the difficulty in maintaining security over the interchanging populations of West and East Germany and the rather ambiguous borders between them. The most flagrant infiltration of BfV was accomplished by the East German Communist spy, Gunther Guillaume, who managed to become an aide to West German Chancellor Willy Brandt. When Guillaume was exposed, Brandt resigned.

The headquarters staff of the BfV is large. At its peak, more than 2,000 persons worked for BfV. Its agents, however, were drawn from the same suspicious worker pool used by the police—informants. The organization averaged 3,000 arrests a year during the Cold War and more than ninety per-cent of these arrests were of Communists from East Germany. That number has been drastically reduced today.

[ALSO SEE: *Gunther Guillaume; Otto John; MI5*]

BIALEK, ROBERT
West German Agent ▪ (1911–1955)

ON AUGUST 27, 1953, A TALL, GAUNT MAN WITH dark hair walked with scores of others through the gates of the Marienfels refugee center in West Berlin. He waited in line for hours before reaching the resistration desk. When asked his name, the tall man told the clerk that he was Robert Bialek. For some moments the clerk stared in disbelief, then he summoned his superior.

Bialek was no ordinary refugee as his interrogators knew full well. He had been one of the leading Communists of East Germany, and, at one time, the Inspector General of East German Volkspolizei (People's Police). He bluntly told West German officials that he had defected because Communism had proved to be no better than Hitler's fascism and that his life was in danger.

West German intelligence officers knew from Bialek's dossier that he had fought Hitler for years, beginning in 1928, when he joined the Communist Party in Breslau as a teenager. He had battled Hitler's storm troopers in the streets and later worked in the Red Orchestra (underground) when Hitler assumed power. He had been arrested by the Gestapo and sent to prison for five years where he endured torture and unspeakable punishments.

Released by the Gestapo on his written promise that he would never again conspire against the Nazis, Bialek immediately organized another Communist underground movement in Breslau. Following the war, Bialek was hailed as one of the most important Communists in East Germany. Named secretary for the Saxon Communist Party, he was also promoted to the powerful position of Inspector General of the East German police.

Bialek rigidly operated the police according to party lines, a stickler for regulations. No one was appointed to a high position in the police unless the appointment was politically proper. As police boss, Bialek sat in the highest Communist councils and had a considerable influence on Communist policies. Unlike most who worked with the Communist leader Walter Ulbricht and Ulbricht's equally powerful wife Lotte, Bialek was no yes-man. He was a strict Marxist who voiced differences of political thought with Ulbricht.

The Ulbrichts were heavy-handed dictators who would tolerate no opposition, nomatter how slight. Bialek was eased from power. He was demoted to "cultural director" of the Lowa plant in Bautzen, a manufacturing center which produced railway cars. He was reduced even further to the rank of foreman.

Bialek stoically assumed his duties in the plant without protest. A short time later, however, the railway express cars ordered by Moscow were held up when the Russians made one design change after another, delays that cost the plant more than one million marks profit, money that was to be used to pay the workers bonuses and improve plant conditions. The Central Committee in Berlin then stated that Moscow would make good the loss of profits.

Some weeks later, the committee reneged. It reported that to keep good relations with the Soviet government it would be necessary to "strike out the excessive costs incurred in the construction" of the express cars.

An emissary from the Central Committee in Berlin addressed the Bautzen plant officials, telling them that the books had to be altered and the workers could not be told about it to prevent discontent. Bialek was asked to alter the books.

When Bialek heard this he stood up and said: "I refuse." To the stunned emissary he added: "I did not spend five years in a Gestapo prison in order to tell lies to the workers. The Soviet Union ordered the construction changes which resulted in this loss—therefore the Soviet Union should pay for it. It is a Soviet responsibility and the workers should know it."

Summoned before the Central Committee in Berlin, Bialek again refused to go along with the deception. The committee immediately expelled him from the Communist party. He was also told at the time that those who refused to obey party instructions were considered enemies of the state and enemies were liquidated. The point was clear. He was not only a political pariah in his own land but a marked man.

Bialek's disillusionment with Communism was complete when, in June 1953, Russian tanks roared through the streets of East Berlin, machine gunning down scores of workers who attempted to strike against oppressive conditions. A short time later four men who worked in the Bautzen plant visited Bialek, asking him what he made of the events occuring in Berlin.

The men told him that they wanted to know the meaning of what was behind the shooting down of defenseless workers.

Bialek told the workers: "What happened in Berlin is no different than what happened under Hitler. I regret that I have worked more than half my life for a cause that is no better than fascism. . . . This is what I thought I was fighting all those years."

The comments Bialek made that night could be used against him, Bialek knew, so he quickly arranged for his wife Inge and their young son to visit relatives in West Germany. A few days after he learned that they were safely in the West, he was summoned to police headquarters.

Bialek found himself sitting before men he had once commanded. They coldly grilled him about his meeting with the plant workers. The police chief held up a report which quoted word-for-word Bialek's statements about the Russian slaughter of workers in Berlin. "Did you make these statements?"

Bialek shrugged. "If you are going to arrest me, you might as well do it now."

"Oh, no, not now," replied the police chief. "We will not touch you. When we are ready, there are other ways. You may go."

Bialek returned home to his small apartment that night. In early August 1953, he received a visitor, an old friend who was a member of the secret police. He warned Bialek that he would be arrested in about three weeks. "The charge will be that you encouraged the Berlin revolt," the visitor said.

"Why don't they arrest me now?"

The visitor answered Bialek in a low voice, with words that sent shivers up his spine. "They are waiting until Inge returns with the child."

When the visitor had gone, Robert Bialek hurriedly made plans to defect, slipping into West Berlin a few days later to rejoin his wife and son. Allied intelligence officers met with him and asked him to help them in their espionage war with the East German Communists. He was warned that if he agreed to help the Allies, he could be in deep danger.

"I know the danger perhaps better than you," Bialek responded. He agreed to stay in West Berlin and help the Allied cause. A short time later Bialek began addressing the workers of East Germany from a West Berlin broadcasting center. His voice was beamed across East Berlin and throughout the Communist block nations. He vivisected Maxist philosophy in simple and telling terms, while profiling the East German Communist Party as a corrupt and venal organization which kept German workers slaving for Russia and their own state as a vassal nation to the Soviet Union. He recited the violent oppression of the Soviets and the countless murders and executions the Communists had inflicted upon anyone who had dared to challenge their brutal dictatorship.

For this, the Communists denounced Bialek. He was labelled a traitor, a renegade, a reactionary and a capitalist stooge. These attacks only goaded Bialek to do much more than continue his damaging broadcasts. He opened his own "office" in West Berlin and then recruited several of his own agents for a counterespionage operation sanctioned by the Allies. His network spread throughout East Germany and his information was excellent, especially in identifying Communist agents who attempted to pass into West Berlin in the guise of refugees. Bialek exposed dozens of these agents who were either members of the East German police force or KGB operatives.

Bialek became one of the most effective counterespionage agents in West Germany, according to the Allies, so effective that the enraged Communists found his presence intolerable and ordered him removed. In marking Bialek for death, however, it still remained for the Communists to lay their hands on him. They offered a huge reward to anyone willing to commit this murder. Hundreds of applicants were screened—those in prison eager to receive a suspended sentence, policemen and soldiers wanting to earn money for their families, agents looking to enhance their careers as professional assassins. A team of killers was finally selected and sent to West Berlin.

In September 1955, Bialek was approached on the Kurfurstendamm in West Berlin by a balding little man who had the appearance of an owl. At first Bialek did not recognize him, but he remembered the man when he gave his name as Paul Drzewiecki. Bialek had known Drzewiecki years earlier and also knew that he had been arrested by the East Berlin police at one time for making seditious remarks. He was a man Bialek believed he could trust.

Sitting down at a sidewalk cafe, Bialek and Drzewiecki exchanged memories and agreed to meet again soon. They met again several times and Bialek finally told his old friend that he was running an anti-Communist spy ring. Drzerwiecki volunteered to help, telling Bialek that he had a friend, Herbert Hellwiig, a one-time official in Rummelsberg Prison, who could obtain important information from East Berlin.

The next time Hellwiig arrived in West Berlin on a shopping trip, Drzewiecki introduced him to Bialek. The trio met several times at Drzewiecki's small apartment at 30 Hagowstrasse. Then, suddenly, Drzewiecki moved to new quarters, at 21 Jenaerstrasse in Wilmersdorf and he asked Bialek to meet him there. Hellwiig, and a pretty, young dark-haired woman named Christina whom Drzewiecki said was his niece, would have important information for him from East Berlin.

One night in late January 1955, Bialek went to meet Drzewiecki and his friends. A half hour after his arrival, Max Schmidt, a plumber who owned the building in which Dzrewiecki lived, pounded on the locked door of the bathroom everyone shared, demanding to use the facilities. Drzewiecki's appeared in the hallway, along with Hellwiig and Christina. Schmidt complained that their guest had been in the washroom for a half hour and he demanded they break down the door.

The door was forced open and Bialek was found on the floor, purple-faced, vomiting, choking, gasping for breath.

"He's drunk," Schmidt said.

"No, he's ill," Christina said, "We must rush him to a doctor. I'll get a taxi." With that she rushed from the building.

Drzewiecki and Hellwiig helped Bialek to his feet and half-dragged him to the street. There a black Mercedes-Benz was waiting with Christina holding the back door open. Two men sat in the front seat. Hellwiig and Christina got into the car with the semiconscious Bialek and the car sped away.

"That was no taxi," the puzzled Schmidt said to Drzewiecki, "and how did your niece find a car so late at night to take your friend to a doctor?"

Drzewiecki left the rooming house the next day and never returned. No one ever saw Robert Bialek again. His wife Inge appeared at the rooming house a few days later, telling the landlord that her husband had told her that he was going to that address. He showed her Drzewiecki's deserted room where she found Bialek's jacket. She buried her face in it, crying. She already knew what would take Allied agents weeks to learn.

Robert Bialek had been kidnapped by a special KGB squad. He was driven to East Berlin KGB headquarters. There he was tortured but he revealed nothing about his counterespionage operations. He was then murdered, strangled to death. His kidnappers and killers were given a great deal of money and medals from the Soviets "for a job well done."

[ALSO SEE: *Gestapo; KGB; Red Orchestra*]

BISSELL, RICHARD
CIA Official ▪ (1910–1994)

A PROTÉGÉ OF ALLEN DULLES, RICHARD BISSELL HAD no espionage background before joining the CIA. He had been an economist working as an administrator for the Marshall Plan in Germany and had also held a position with the Ford Foundation in Washington, D.C. Bissell's developed specialty at the CIA was reconnaissance. In 1954, Bissell supervised the U-2 spy plane project approved by President Eisenhower with aircraft operational the following year.

With the coming of the space age, Bissell foresaw the use of spy satellites and began ordering unique camera equipment to operate in these CIA spacecrafts. He was also involved in many covert operations, including a coup d'état that overthrew the Guatamalan government of Jacobo Arbenz after that country nationalized the United Fruit Company, a lucrative monopoly which controlled all the banana plantations.

Bissell's undoing came about at the CIA after the disastrous Bay of Pigs operations in an attempt to overthrow Cuban dictator Fidel Castro, a failed invasion which Bissell largely helped to mount. Part of Bissell's plans involved assassinating Castro and he entertained many bizarre murder schemes put forward by his chief adviser, the quirkish Dr. Sidney Gottlieb, an eccentric who rivaled in some ways the oddball character of Dr. Strangelove of the movie by the same name.

Assassinations of anti-American leaders of the third world were also reportedly planned by Bissell and Gottlieb. These would-be murders were aimed at General Kassem of Iraq, Patrice Lumumba of the Congo, and Dominican Republic dictator Rafael Trujillo. These bloodletting operations were eventually revealed in reports from the Church Commission which studied alleged assassination plots of foreign political chiefs.

Following the Bay of Pigs fiasco, President Kennedy, in November 1961, dismissed the venerable Allen Dulles. His protégé Bissell resigned three months later and returned to private business.

[ALSO SEE: *Bay of Pigs; CIA; Allen Dulles; Sidney Gottlieb; Gary Francis Powers; Spy Aircraft; Spy-in-the-Sky*]

BLACK DRAGON SOCIETY
Japanese Secret Assassination/ Espionage Organization ▪ (1901–   )

T HIS SECRET SOCIETY, DREADED IN JAPAN AND WITH-out by those who learned of its existence, was ostensibly founded in 1901 by Ryochei Uchida, a protégé of Mitsuru Toyama, one of the nation's most powerful men. Many years earlier Toyama had organized all criminal activities in Japan, becoming the country's crime overlord through his own secret society, Genoyosha. Though Genoyosha was fundamentally a monopoly on all criminal activities, it also sponsored Japanese militeristic aims in Manchuria.

Wanting to have an organization wholly devoted to Japanese domination of Manchuria and, subsequently, China, Toyama created the Black Dragon Society through his front man, Uchida. The credo of the Black Dragons was to foster a hatred for the white race and advance at any cost the cause of what it called Pan-Asianism, a term that veiled its true aims, the conquest of Manchuria, then China.

Following the deliberate, insidious plan mapped out by Toyama, the Black Dragons carefully selected from its bulging ranks the best candidates for higher military and polictical offices. Once entrenched, these Black Dragons began to spread their gospel of conquest through the Japanese Army and in the hierarchy of political administrations. The monarchy took no position regarding the Society, giving it sideways recognition. Japanese emperors, however, were then as they are today sacrosanct for in the predominately Shinto relgion of Japan, the emperor is a physical god on earth in human form. His edict is final and to defy the emperor is to defile Shintoism and face eternal damnation.

The defeat of Czarist forces in the Russo-Japanese War in 1905 inspired the Society to energetically lobby for a Strike North posture. The Black Dragons urged Japanese militarists to attack the Russians in Siberia, then move southward into Manchuria. The Society's very name was chosen by Toyama to symbolize its goals, taken from the Amur River which was also called the Black Dragon River, which separates Siberia from Manchuria.

The undoing of the Manchu Dynasty of China was brought about by the Black Dragons who hoodwinked insurgent Chinese leaders into believing that its aims were universally beneficial to all Asiatics. The Society actually financed the Chinese revolutionaries, advancing great sums of money to Sun Yat-sen and Chiang Kai-Shek, who formed the Chinese Kuomintang Party and their republican theories of government in the Tokyo offices of the Black Dragon Society in 1905. The Black Dragons continued to finance the Kuomintang leaders until the Manchus were overthrown in 1911.

Huge amounts of money were available to the Black Dragons through their complete control of all illegal operations in Japan, partcularly their monopoly on the opium trade. Much of the opium distributed throughout the world came from China and, through its financing of the Chinese revolutionaries, the Black Dragons were repaid by the Kuomintang, which allowed the Black Dragons to control the flow of Chinese opium.

The Manchus has energetically attempted to suppress the opium trade in China, inflicting death sentences upon major growers and peddlers. The elimination of the dynasty accomplished several ends, all desired by the Society: The Kuomintang took power, the opium trade again flourished to enrich the coffers of the Chinese revolutionaries and their backers, the Black Dragons. The establishment of the Chinese revolutionaries indebted Sun-Yat Sen and Chiang Kaishek to the Society, and, Toyama was convinced, they could be manipulated into offering little or no defense of Manchuria against invading Japanese forces.

Toyama and Uchida had been clever in dealing with the Chinese leaders. The Society was known to the Chinese revolutionaries as a criminal organization, not one of a politcal nature. Sun-Yat Sen and Chiang Kai-shek believed that the Black Dragons were only concerned with acquiring the lucrative opium trade. Once their revolution was successful, the Chinese leaders secretly concluded, they would stamp out the opium trade themselves.

Meanwhile, the Black Dragons conducted a ruthless purge of anyone inside Japan who opposed their plans of conquest. The Society had spies everywhere gathering information on Japan's military leaders and politicians. The Black Dragons received an indifferent reception from Director Abe of Japan's Political Affairs Bureau of the Foreign Office when it asked for his support in attacking Russia. Society assassins then murdered Abe on September 5, 1913.

A short time later Japan's foreign minister, Count Kato Takaakira, was attacked by a Black Dragon assassin but survived. Though not tried for the attempted murder, Uchida spent eighteen months in prison before being released. In 1923, the catastrophic earthquake that shook Japan resulted in devastating fires that all but gutted Tokyo. Toyama and the Black Dragons quickly spread the word that Koreans, whom the Society hated, had set the fires following the quake.

Mobs attacked Koreans on every street, killing hundreds. The Society used this gruesome spectacle in an attempt to convince the military that the Japanese people universally desired war with Korea and Russia. By 1932, the Black Dragons had enough power to insist that the army adopt its Strike North policy. To that end, Japanese troops invaded northern Manchuria, taking the railway center at Harbin, then moving inland to occupy most of Manchurian province of Jehol by March 1933.

By the mid-1930s, Emperor Hirohito sided with the militarists who advocated a Strike South policy, and the Japanese abandoned the long-sought Black Dragon goal of attacking Russia. Instead, Japanese armies swarmed into mainland China and throughout the South Pacific to confront Great Britain and the United States in an all-out war that ended with Japan's utter defeat. Throughout the war the Black Dragon influence declined. The Society all but went out of existence when Toyama finally died in 1944. It lingers today as an loose affiliate to the vast Japanese criminal society known as Yakuza.

[ALSO SEE: *Mitsuru Toyama*]

BLACK HAND SOCIETY
Serbian Assassination/Espionage Organization ▪ (1911–1917)

PRESENT-DAY BALKAN UNREST WAS SEEDED IN THE nineteenth century by the ancient Austro-Hungarian empire. The politically oppressive reign of the Austrian Hapsburgs brought about the slow but deadly growth of Serbian nationalism. When Austria annexed Bosnia and Herzegovina, Serbian nationalism erupted. This sudden move by Austria to absorb its neighboring countries so alarmed Serbia (which felt it was next), that many Serbian nationalist organizations came into existence. These secret military societies were bent on the destruction of the Austrian Empire and the unification of Slavic countries.

Serbian colleges and, particularly, the Belgrade Military Academy, nurtured the establishment of nationalist groups to which hundreds of young Serbs flocked. The students and young officers of the Serbian military designed assassinations and sabotage. They formed espionage arms to learn troop movements and plans of the Austrian military. In two decades the Serbian nationalist movement grew, establishing cadres of older members and constantly recruiting new members to its ranks.

One of these new recruits was a zealous and brilliant young officer named Dragutin Dimitrijevic. A Serbian patriot to the marrow, he was also ruthless and cold-blooded in his schemes to destroy the Austrians and unify the Slavs. Dimitrijevic soon became the leader of a secret Serbian group called *Ukendinjenje ili Smrt.* The group met in beer halls and boisterously proclaimed Serbian nationalism would sweep the Balkans. It planned bombings and assassinations of Austrian buildings and officials in neighboring Bosnia.

Dimitrijevic made impassioned speeches to his followers and designed banners and symbols for the *Ukendinjenje ili Smrt.* The symbols were full of sinister threats and affixed to missives sent to those who might betray their organization. These symbols included a glass of poison, a death's head, a dagger dripping blood, and, finally, the symbol later adopted as the official emblem, a black hand. The imprint of a black hand was pressed in ink and then affixed to a letter sent to anyone who might betray the organization. It meant death to those who revealed the identities of the those in the group or the existence of the group itself.

No doubt Dimitrijevic borrowed the black hand symbol from the ancient Italian extortion racket largely practiced by the Camorra, a criminal society operating for a century throughout Italy and America where it was known as the Black Hand. The Serbian nationalists, however, did not extort money from its victims, but killed anyone who stood in the way of their political ambitions. The motto of Dimitrijevic's organization was "Union or death!"

In 1903 this group selected as its first significant victims their own monarchs, King Alexander I (Obrenovic) and Queen Draga. These sovereigns, Dimitrijevic and his followers feared, were soon to form an alliance with Austria, a move designed chiefly by the much-hated Queen Draga who exercised a powerful influence on her husband, King Alexander.

On the night of June 11, 1903, Dimitrijevic assembled more than fifty of his most trusted officers at a local beer hall and, after plying them with drink and exorting them to action, led them to the Belgrade Palace in search of King Alexander and Queen Draga.

The officers shot down the guards and raced through the dreary palace, searching room by room for the monarchs who were hiding in a small dressing closet in Queen Draga's chambers.

The assassins found their quarry and hacked them to pieces with their swords, Dimitrijevic leading the pack. The bodies were thrown from the palace balcony to the front of the palace where they lay all the next morning on display to show the power of the Black Hand. Dimitrijevic and his men then put a new king on the throne and became the most powerful nationalist group in Serbia.

So powerful was the Black Hand Society that Serbia's new king, Peter Karageorgevic, appointed Dimitrijevic to chief of espionage. He later became a general on the Serbian general staff and head of all intelligence operations. The Black Hand (*Narodna Odbrana*) became the official title of Dimitrijevic's group in 1911. From that point on, dozens of Austrian officials through-out Bosnia and Herzegovenia were abducted, shot and bombed by the Black Hand Society. In the 1912–1913 Balkan wars, the Society was instrumental in expanding Serbia's borders into Macedonia, its agents performing sabotage and political murders.

When a group of college students full of ardent patriotism approached Dimitrijevic in 1914 with a plan to assassinate Arch-Duke Francis Ferdinand of Austria, the Society leader embraced them. To them he was known only under his Society code name: "Colonel Apis." He encouraged their plan, even though he knew it to be foolhardy. They would simply plant themselves in the cheering crowds anticipated in Sarajevo, Bosnia to greet the heir to the Austrian throne when he arrived on a state visit. One or more them would simply shoot Francis Ferdinand as his motorcade passed them.

None of these boys had experience in espionage or political assassination but that meant nothing to the ruthless Dimitrijevic. None had ever fired a weapon. He had them taken to a Belgrade park where they practiced firing pistols for a few days. He then armed them with pistols and bombs and sent them on their way to Sarajevo. An aide told Dimitrijevic that the group "did not stand a chance in hell of accomplishing their mission."

"I know it," replied the calculating Dimitrijevic, "but why not take a chance that one of those boys will be lucky. It costs us nothing and we could gain everything if they manage to kill that swine."

Dimitrijevic had tried several times to arrange the assassination of not only Francis Ferdinand but of Emperor Francis Joseph of Austria. On June 3, 1911, Dimitrijevic had loaned a revolver to a fanatical student, Bogdan Zeradjic, and ordered him to kill the Emperor who was visiting the Bosnian capital. Hiding behind a pillar, Zeradjic waited until the carriage in which the ancient monarch was sitting rolled into sight. He fired but, to his amazement, the weapon did not work.

To redeem himself in the eyes of the Society and Dimitrijevic, Zeradjic raced to the offices of General Marijan Veresanin, the Hapsburg governor of two provinces, and shot the official five times. He shouted: "I leave my revenge to Serbdom!" He then put the revolver to his head and sent his last bullet into it. The death of this youth upset Dimitrijevic only in that Zeradjic had failed to kill the Emperor. He was doubly upset when he learned that General Veresanin survived his wounds and he cared not a bit when hearing that the body of his assassin was dumped into an unmarked grave.

Dimitrijevic's attitude toward the students setting out for Sarajevo in 1914 was one of expediency. If the youths accomplished the assassination of Francis Ferdinand, all well and good. If they failed, well, they were expendable. He would simply try again with more assassins. It first appeared that the attempt would not succeed. Most of these naive students failed to get close to the royal carriage as it slowly rumbled over the cobblestones of Sarajevo. One of those close enough to fire lost his nerve, later saying that the Arch-Duke's morganatic wife Sophie (who had the titular title of Duchess of Hohenberg) so closely resembled his mother that he could not bear to fire at her.

This was not the case of the fanatical anarchist Gavrilo Princip. He was in an excellent position in the crowd to fire several bullets into Francis Ferdinand and his wife. Seconds after firing his fatal bullets, Princip was seized and held for interrogation. He had failed to swallow the contents of a small bottle Dimitrijevic had given to Princip and all the other youths. The bottles contained cyanide.

Princip was found guilty and sent to prison for twenty years after it was believed he was under the legal age for execution. He lingered in an airless prison cell and contracted tuberculosis, the unattended disease rotting one arm so badly that it had to be crudely amputated by a warder. He died painfully on April 28, 1918. Others in the assassination plot were executed and others were sent to prison.

Several of the conspirators confessed everything they knew, naming the Serbian Black Hand Society as their sponsor and, specifically, "Colonel Apis" as the man who armed them and sent them to murder the Arch Duke. Of course, the name "Apis" meant nothing to the Austrians. The alias thus protected Dimitrijecvic's true identity and he went on to climb even higher until he became the espionage chief for Serbia.

By then the world was at war, all because of Princip's well-aimed bullets in Sarajevo. Austria declared war on Serbia. Russia then supported Serbia, as did the Western Allies of England and France. Germany, of course, went to the side of the Austro-Hungarian empire to form the Central Powers. Millions of lives would be lost during World War I,

including that of its creator, Dragutin Dimitrijevic who was purged by King Peter I, the very man he put on the Serbian throne. Dimitrijevic was executed in early 1917, along with his top aides and the Black Hand Society effectively went out of existence.

[ALSO SEE: *Dragutin Dimitrijevic*]

BLACK ORCHESTRA
German Anti-Hitler Conspiracies ▪ *(1935–1944)*

THE COMING OF ADOLF HITLER TO POWER IN GERmany was not an overnight event. His rise was slow, deliberate and carefully planned. His brutal Nazi regime was originally organized along the lines of Benito Mussolini's black-shirted fascism in Italy. It differered in that it was more savage and bloodthirsty than any political movement before or since.

Throughout the 1920s, Hitler's Nazis paraded through the streets of German cities wearing self-styled uniforms, Brownshirts they were called, Hitler's Stormtroopers, a paramilitary organization that the government tolerated. It grew into the hundreds of thousands, made up of the social dregs of the country, criminals, perverts, right-wing malcontents, the sadistic, and the murderous, all were welcome to the Fuhrer's ranks.

As Hitler bullied his way to power with his Brownshirts, he had the tacit approval of industrialists and the regular German Army who thought their own ends best served by his political presence, even to the point of his assuming the chancellorship in 1933 following the death of the elderly President Paul von Hindenberg, Germany's venerable World War I general.

Within two years, Hitler's so-called elective office had been turned into a lifetime dictatorship. By then, some of those who had supported him, civilians and military leaders alike, realized their terrible error. Certain civilian groups and others in the military, all unassociated at the beginning, came into existence to plot against the monster who was then planning for world domination and world war, a fanatic whose maniacal ambitions would claim the lives of countless millions. The secret groups who opposed Hitler were all part of what was to become known as the Black Orchestra, a term created by Hitler's rabidly devoted Gestapo agents. "Black" meant anyone involved with anti-Hitler activities and "Orchestra" meant that a group was involved playing espionage "music" on short-wave radios.

At first these Black Orchestra groups met to plan the political replacement of Hitler but such an attempt was by then fruitless in that Hitler had banished and destroyed all politcal opposition parties. His Gestapo and SS rigidly exercised such tight security that all German citizens, nomatter their station, were looked upon as possible seditious subjects. No open display of opposition was possible by dissident forces, without facing instant arrest and either deportation (only in the middle 1930s) or imprisonment in filthy concentration camps where, by 1940, death was the only escape.

The two top German militarists who secretly opposed Hitler from the beginning of his reign of terror were Admiral Wilhelm Canaris, who headed the German military espionage service, Abwehr, and Colonel-General Ludwig Beck, who was one-time chief of the German General Staff (1935–1938). Both men hated Hitler and his regime. Beck was the nominal leader of the Black Orchestra but Canaris acted as the agent for the plotters in trying the usurp the tyrant.

On one hand, Canaris served Hitler as his espionage chief, but, on the other, he worked against Hitler whenever he could, sending covert messages to leaders of the Western Allies, especially the British, informing them of top secret meetings he had attended with Hitler. When Hitler unveiled his plans for war in 1937 to the German General Staff, Beck and Canaris informed British Prime Minister Neville Chamberlain.

They learned of Hitler's plan to annex Austria and seize Czechoslovakia in 1938 and begged Chamberlain and the Allies to intervene, to attack Hitler's untried and weak legions. Canaris pleaded with England and France to make a stand against the madman so that the Black Orchestra would be encouraged enough to somehow overthrow Hitler. He found a willing ear in Winston Churchill but Churchill was not then in power in England and Chamberlain vacillated, opting for appeasement which only encourage Hitler to take one more step toward war.

When Hitler invaded Poland in 1939, his blitzkrieg style of warfare surprised even this opponents in Germany. He met with one smashing success after another as Poland, then France, the lowlands, Denmark, Norway, and a dozen other countries fell into his hands. With each of Hitler's successes, Canaris and Beck lost ground, particularly with the military which was the only real force that had the ability to overthrow the tyrant.

Not until the Allies invaded the beaches of Normandy on June 6, 1944, were the German plotters galvanized into action. It was obvious that the Allied armies would sweep across Europe and into the heart of Germany. To all but Hitler and his diehard cronies the war was lost. Beck and Canaris activated the Black Orhestra which made feverish plans to assassinate Hitler at his military headquarters in Rastenburg, East Prussia, on July 20, 1944.

Enlisted in the conspiracy were German generals who would assume command of key areas after Hitler had been killed. These generals included Henning von Tresckow, Erich Hoepner, Friedrich Olbricht, Eduard Wagner, Hans Spiedel, Karl von Stuelpnagel, Helmuth Stieff, Field-Marshal Guenther von Kluge, Field-Marshal Erwin von Witzleben, and Germany's greatest hero, Field-Marshal Erwin Eugen Rommel, the celebrated "Desert Fox," who had earned honors for his brilliant victories in North Africa during the early days of the war, even grudging respect from his Allied opponents.

Rommel has met with Hitler and reportedly told him that unless he sought a truce with the Allies, Germany would be facing certain destruction. Hitler had refused and Rommel joined the conspirators, telling an aide that "the people in Berlin can count on me." The generals were supported by long-time civilian opponents of Hitler. These conspirators included Dr. Carl Goerdeler, one-time mayor of Leipzig and a minister in Hitler's 1937 cabinet; religious leader Dietrich Bonhoeffer; Ewald von Kleist-Schmenzin, a Pomeranian landowner and publisher who printed pamphlets against Hitler's rise as early as 1932; labor leader Julius Leber; liberals Ernst Niekisch, Ulrich von Hassell; and head of the Kreisau Circle plotters, Count Peter Yorck von Wartenburg.

The actual Black Orchestra conspirators who set in motion the plan to kill Hitler at his military retreat in Rastenburg were a number of dedicated junior officers that included Major Fabian von Schlabrendorff, Colonel Caesar von Hofacker, and the most daring of them all, Count Claus Schenk von Stauffenberg. It was Stauffenberg who was selected to carry a bomb into the conference building where Hitler was meeting with his top advisers and set it off.

Stauffenberg was an unusual-looking officer. He was missing one arm and an eye over which he wore a black patch. He had been wounded severely on the Russian front and had been decorated many times. He nevertheless despised Hitler and insisted that he be the one to set off the bomb. His presence at Rastenburg was not unusual as he was chief of staff of the Home Army and it was his duty to regularly report to Hitler.

Hitler and his retinue would have normally held the war conference in an underground bunker. Had Stauffenberg's bomb gone off in the bunker the dictator would have certainly been killed. The day of the conference, however, was hot, and the group met in a one-story building above ground and the windows had been opened to let in the fresh air. Stauffenberg arrived, gave Hitler his report, then placed a briefcase with the bomb hidden inside next to one of the large wooden blocks upon which the conference table rested. At the time, Hitler was standing next to the briefcase.

Stauffenberg left the building and waited outside to see the explosion rip the small, squat building to pieces. He immediately drove to the airport and took a training plane to Berlin where he announced that Hitler had been killed. He was wrong. Hitler had survived the bombing with only slight injuries, although several of his aides were killed or seriously wounded.

Just before the bomb exploded, Hitler had moved away from the briefcase beneath the table so that several wooden blocks absorbed the blast meant for him. The generals in Berlin, led by Beck, immediately seized control of vital buildings and communications centers, announcing that Hitler was dead. Joseph Goebbels, Hitler's chief lackey and head of all Nazi propaganda learned that Hitler was still alive and broadcast this news which convinced many fence-sitting German generals to arrest the Black Orchestra conspirators.

The coup was short-lived and the rebellion put down. Beck, Kluge, Treskow, and others committed suicide rather than face the terrible punishments they knew Hitler and the SS would mete out to conspirators they captured. Stauffenberg did not face such tortures. He, along with Olbricht, were summarily shot in Berlin by SS troops who had regained the offices of the general staff. Others were ferreted out over many months. Arrested conspirators were tortured into naming co-conspirators before they were strangled with piano wire. Then Rommel was identified as a plotter. Since his heroic stature in Germany was enormous, Hitler allowed the "Desert Fox" to commit suicide by taking poison rather than face a humiliating trial. This was the only conspirator who was shown a measure of mercy. General Treskow, chief of staff for Army Group Center in Russia heard that the coup had failed and he immediately drove to the front lines. He crawled out into no-man's-land and pulled the pin from a grenade which blew off his head.

Canaris, the erstwhile plotter and head of the Abwehr was finally identified as a conspirator. He was arrested and imprisoned and then executed. The same fate befell almost all the top conspirators who were hanged on meathooks with pianowire after they had been debased and humiliated at the kangaroo court run by Hitler's obscene judicial henchman, Judge Roland Freisler. Field Marshal Witzleben, for instance, was forced to appear in court wearing worn-out trousers too big for his lean frame. Denied suspenders or a belt, he was forced to hold up his pants while Feisler mocked him for his hobo-like appearance, chiding: "You dirty old man, why do you keep fiddling with your trousers?"

Witzleben and all the others were executed, again by hanging with piano wire from meat hooks. More than 5,000 persons, including some of those who had actually arrested the conspirators, like General Fromm, were tortured and killed in the massive hunt by the SS. One of the last to die was the crafty old spymaster, Admiral Wilhelm Canaris. No one had directly implicated Canaris but Hitler was sure that his former espionage chief had helped to mastermind the assassination attempt on his life.

When Hitler knew his own end was approaching, one of his last commands was to have Canaris

murdered. On April 9, 1945, the one-time powerful chief of the Abwehr was dragged naked from his concentration camp cell and then hanged before a large throng of hooting, jeering SS thugs. The Black Orchestra ceased to exist.

[ALSO SEE: *Abwehr; Wilhelm Canaris; Gestapo*]

BLAKE, GEORGE (GEORG BEHAR)
British Double Agent for Soviets ■ (1922–)

BORN GEORG BEHAR NOVEMBER 11, 1922, IN Rotterdam, Holland, Blake had all the advantages his wealthy parents could provide, good schooling, a comfortable home, a bright future. He studied a private school until his father, Albert William Behar, died in 1936 and then, according to his father's deathbed request, was sent to the exclusive English school in Cairo. The reason for this lay in Albert Behar's own background. His Sephardic Jewish family had cut him off from its wealth because he had married a Dutch Christian, Catherine Beijdervellen.

Albert Behar's life was fraught with danger and adventure. He had served in the French Foreign Legion and in the British Army. He later operated a successful business in Rotterdam which began to lose money a short time before his death. Ill, Behar begged his sister, who lived in Cairo, to look after his son in the event of his death. When Behar died, his 13-year-old son was sent to Cairo to live with his aunt and her husband, a wealthy banker named Henri Curiel, Sr., who raised the boy, sending him to the exclusive English School where Blake learned to speak English with a British accent.

Henri Curiel, son of the banker and cousin to Blake became the boy's best friend and strongest influence. The junior Curiel later founded the Communist Party in Egypt, then went off to Paris where he became active in several terrorist movements as well as the KGB. He was murdered in 1978 by unknown killers.

In 1938, Blake returned to Holland to finish high school in Rotterdam. He was attending classes in 1940 when the Germans invaded the Netherlands. His mother and two sisters fled to England, fearful that their Jewish history would condemn them to a Nazi concentration camp. Blake, however, a fierce patriot, remained in the Netherlands to fight with the Dutch underground. He was captured by the Gestapo and placed in an interment camp from which he quickly escaped, returning to his friends in the resistance. He was a marked freedom fighter who could best survive by joining his family in England. The resistance helped Blake escape to France; he then crossed the

Pyrenees to neutral Spain where he took passage on a steamer bound for London.

Once in England, the fugitive changed his name to Blake and joined the Royal Navy. Because of his language skills, he was accepted by SOE (Special Operations Executive) which sent espionage agents to Nazi-occupied countries in Europe to work with underground fighters against the Germans. Much to his disgust, Blake was not used for field work. His language skills were too valuable and he was assigned to a London desk job as an interpreter.

Following D-Day, June 6, 1944, Blake was commissioned as a sub-lieutenant and went with the Allies to Europe where he worked at SHAEF headquarters. He translated and interpreted secret German documents that were by then pouring into Allied hands. After the war, Blake was sent to Hamburg, heading an intelligence unit which tracked down one-time U-boat commanders. He was then recalled to England where he was mustered out of the Royal Navy. His excellent war record brought him a recommendation for a position with the Foreign Office

Blake first attended Cambridge where he studied the Russian language. In 1947, Blake became a naturalized British citizen. Once his studies were completed, Blake was officially accepted as a member of the Foreign Office. Posted as a vice-counsul to the British Embassy in Seoul, South Korea, Blake worked for chargé d'affaires Vyvyan Holt.

When the Korean War broke out in 1950, Communist troops quickly overran the city and made prisoners of Holt, Blake, and all others in the British colony. Despite the fact that North Korea had violated all diplomatic agreements, the Communists refused to give up the British diplomats. They were held for three years while the Communists painstakingly conducted deliberate brainwashing techniques on the prisoners.

Though his fellow prisoners later claimed that Blake had proved himself courageous and unyielding as a prisoner-of-war, the Communists apparently did effect his beliefs in their systematic brainwashing. An incident occured some time after Blake had been taken prisoner, when he briefly escaped the internment camp and was recaptured. He was placed before a firing squad as a spy and, just at the moment when he was about to be shot, Blake shouted in Russian: "I am not a spy! I am a civilian internee, a British diplomat! I went out of my camp at Man-po and lost my way!"

Fortunate for Blake, the North Korean officer in charge of the firing squad understood Russian and he halted the execution. He took Blake aside and the two spoke in Russian about the Communist philosophy. The North Korean officer then took Blake back to the camp and warned him not to make any further escape attempts.

The firing squad scenario, of course, may have been staged by the Communists to make themselves appear to be humane and understanding, thus winning Blake's confidence and eternal gratitude at having his life saved by those whom he had formerly viewed as the enemy. This was the turning point in George Blake's life.

Upon his release, Blake requested that the Foreign Office transfer him to MI6 so he could fulfill his deepest ambition, to become a British secret agent. His sterling record as a prisoner-of-war, as well as his excellent World War II service suggested high qualification for the job and the decision was made by MI6 to accept Blake. This was quite unusual in that British Intelligence had as a hard and fast rule that all officers of MI6 had to have complete British parentage. This was not Blake's case but the rules were waived in his instance, a decision that came to haunt MI6.

Blake went into the field as an MI6 officer in 1953. From this time until he was exposed by a German double agent, he would serve the KGB with stubborn loyalty, identifying more than forty Western agents to the Soviets, most or all of whom lost their lives, including the effective Western spymaster Robert Bialek. When posted to West Berlin in 1955, Blake's MI6 assignment was to infiltrate Soviet espionage operations. He would act as a double agent, pretending to go over to the Soviets and supply them with "safe" Western secrets, while identifying Soviet spies. He was, in reality, a triple agent, who pretended to betray the West to the Soviets but was actually betraying the West, providing the KGB not only the secrets approved by MI6 to be released but top Western secrets and the identities of top Western agents in East Germany.

Everything secret in the Berlin offices of MI6 were photographed by Blake and turned over to his KGB contacts. He simply hid in the offices until they were locked in the evening and then went to work with his camera. His most damaging espionage work was exposing in 1956 to his KGB masters the existence of the Berlin Tunnel, a joint CIA-MI6 operation ("Operation Gold") wherein a tunnel was dug into East Berlin so that CIA cryptologists could tap into Soviet military and diplomatic lines buried there. As soon as the KGB received Blake's report, they filled in the tunnel, closing down the Western intelligence operation.

Blake was not exposed as the informer but he worried much when, in 1959, he learned that Horst Eitner, who worked for Reinhard Gehlen's West German espionage operation and who, like himself, was a double agent to the Soviets, might expose him as being a triple agent really working with the KGB. Blake told his superiors that he had had enough of Berlin after three years of intensive espionage and that he wanted to be posted back to London.

His spy chiefs refused, telling him he was too valuable in Berlin to be transferred. Blake still thought Eitner might expose him at any moment. Desperate, he reported to his superiors that the Russians might be on to his role of double agent and that he risked being kidnapped, taken to East Berlin and then summarily shot, a fate Blake himself had arranged for dozens of others. MI6 reluctantly moved Blake back to London. From there, he wangled a posting to the Arabic Language School at Shemlan just outside of Beirut, Lebanon.

Blake intended to cool off in Lebenon for some time, but Horst Eitner was finally snared by MI6 and he quickly informed on Blake. MI6 was shocked but it intended to make sure that Blake did not slip through their hands. They sent one of Blake's friends from MI6 to Lebanon to suggest he take a high-paying MI6 desk job in London. Blake flew back to have what he thought would be a routine interview. He was arrested by SIS agents the minute he got off the plane at Heathrow Airport.

Blake, after many long hours of interrogation, admitted that he had been a triple agent and had fed the KGB everything he knew. Moreover, he admitted that he had embraced Communism as early as 1953 and had planned to spy for Russia from that time on. Next to Kim Philby, George Blake became the most damaging double agent to ever work out of MI6.

Blake's trial was held in secret and few details of its records are available to this day. He was found guilty. Blake was given the maximum sentence of fourteen years for each charge, forty-two years in all. He would serve less than six of those years.

Sent to Wormwood Scrubs Prison, Blake appeared to be a model prisoner. He was affable and joked with younger inmates. He liked to tell fellow prisoners complaining about their own sentences: "My dear, old lad, you will be out after a shave and a haircut." Yet, Blake had been planning an escape for some time, along with fellow prisoner, Sean Bourke. On October 22, 1967, Blake simply kicked out a weakly cemented window bar in the crumbling old prison and slipped through the opening to freedom. He then scaled a wall and dropped to a street where Bourke, released earlier, was waiting in a car to speed Blake to freedom.

Blake and Bourke hid for a few weeks in England and were then smuggled by the KGB to Moscow. Bourke eventually returned to Ireland but Blake was given a post with the KGB. The escape was ballyhooed by the Western press as having been engineered by the Soviets to snatch back one of their own in an amazing coup but this was not really the case. The simple fact was that Blake, like many another prisoner escaping from Wormwood Scrubs, had merely taken advantage of its poor security systems and gotten out by himself.

[ALSO SEE: *Berlin Tunnel; Robert Bialek; Richard Gehlen; KGB; MI6; Kim Philby; SIS; SOE*]

BLOCH, DAVID
French Spy in World War I ▪ (? –1916)

A NATIVE OF GUBWILLER IN HAUTE-ALSACE, BLOCH had volunteered to serve in the French Army at the beginning of World War I. He joined the 152nd Infantry Regiment and also volunteered for espionage work behind enemy lines, particulary near his home town which was now occupied by German troops.

On the night of June 22, 1916, Bloch, with only cursory training in espionage, was sent on a dangerous mission. He was to parachute in full uniform behind enemy lines from a low-flying fighter plane. (Spies being dropped secretly behind enemy lines by plane during World War II was almost commmonplace but during World War I, such missions were rare occurences.)

Bloch successfully parchuted to earth about twelve miles from his home town of Gubwiller but he was ordered that, under no circumstances, was he to enter the town. He was to stay on a farm, poising as a German silk merchant. He was given identity papers bearing the name Karl Sprecher, a businessman from Mulhouse. Bloch discarded his uniform and changed into civilian clothing.

With him Bloch brought six carrier-pigeons. He was to observe enemy troop movements and send a report each day by pigeon. He would be picked up on the sixth night by a plane landing at a secret field outside Merxheim. He was to signal the plane to land by sending three green flashes from his signal lantern.

All went well for five days. Bloch got off his reports without incident but he grew homesick for the sight of his elderly parents. He foolishly walked to Gubwiller but then thought better of it and began walking out of town. A German patrol ran after him and put him under arrest. He had been recognized and betrayed by an informer.

At first, Bloch denied his true identity and that he was a spy. Then his elderly father was brought before him. Block wept, embraced his father, then admitted his identity, although he refused to tell the Germans about his espionage activities. He was jailed at Ile Napoleon near Mulhouse and was later tried and condemned. Bloch was placed before a firing squad on August 1, 1916, and executed. His death went almost unnoticed by the military intelligence chiefs who had sent him ill-prepared to his fate.

Bloch was typical of many World War I spies. They received very little training and their missions were the scattershot ideas of those who cared little for the lives of their own agents. This was an age when sabrecarrying field marshals and medal-bedecked generals thought nothing of throwing away 100,000 lives in battles they knew they could not win, then retiring that night to brandy or schnapps to toast "the glorious dead." Thus, a generation of young men was destroyed along the Western Front from 1914 to 1918, including idealistic, naive spies such as David Bloch.

BLOWITZ, HENRI DE
British Spy at Congress of Berlin ▪ (1825–1903)

AN ARISTOCRAT OF WEALTHY MEANS AND A CLASSICAL education, Henri de Blowitz became a liberal journalist in France during the Second Empire of Napoleon III. His widely-read political articles were slanted in favor of Republicans running against Bonapartist candidates for the national legislature.

Blowitz had connections in high places due to his noble birth, allowing him to glean from important sources the kind of "inside" information not available to other political commentators. His incisive articles came to the attention of John Delane, editor of the London *Times*, who hired Blowitz as a European correspondent in 1871, shortly after the end of the Franco-Prussian War. He soon became Delane's top correspondent on the continent, providing one "scoop" after another through his well-placed sources.

In 1878, Delane asked Blowitz to move from Paris to Berlin to cover the all-important Congress of Berlin which was designed to ease tensions following the Russo-Turkish War of 1877–1878. The real purpose of the conference was to challenge the Treaty of San Stefano which had ended the war between Russia and Turkey and which had considerably enlarged Bulgaria at the expense of Turkey, the loser in the war. The enlargement of Bulgaria shifted the balance of power in the Balkans to Russia which greatly alarmed Austria and Great Britain.

The conference was dominated by the two leading power figures of the day, British Prime Minister Benjamin Disraeli and Germany's strong man, Chancellor Otto von Bismarck. To make sure that diplomatic talks would be completely veiled to the outside world, Bismarck ordered Germany's indefatigable espionage chief, Wilhelm Stieber to prevent all leaks of information and arrest and jail any suspects who might attempt to penetrate his iron-fisted censorship.

Blowitz easily circumvented Stieber's rigidly enforced screen by simply using his connections in securing a position for a friend as an attaché to the Congress. It was through this person that Blowitz learned of almost every important secret talk held between the attending diplomats. He reported these negotiations in full in the *Times* in unsigned articles. Bismarck was shocked and fulminated against Stieber. The German spy chief knew Blowitz was the author of the articles but try as he might, he could not identify Blowitz's source of information.

Stieber had Blowitz watched night and day in Berlin. The journalist was followed everwhere he went in the city. Not once was Blowitz seen to make contact with anyone connected with the Congress. When the journalist attended parties and fetes, he did see his attaché contact but he ignored him. The two never exchanged a word, let alone a meaningful glance. Yet Blowitz had devised a simple but effective method by which the contact passed all important information to him.

Both men went to the same restaurant each evening, sitting far apart from each other. When they entered the restaurant they placed their hats, which were the same make, color and size, on the pegs of a wall rack. When the men left the restaurant they took each other's hat. Blowitz found the detailed information from the conference each day inside the hatband of his contact's bowler.

Thus Blowitz was able to scoop the world on the most important conference of the era, even obtaining for the *Times* before it was signed, the Treaty which Bismarck had so zealously guarded, one wherein the size of Bulgaria was reduced and Russian claims given up. Throughout his life, Bismarck was nagged by the question of how Blowitz had gotten his information and when the two men met in 1883, the Iron Chancellor asked the journalist about his methods and sources. Blowitz refused to admit anything. He would protect that information until writing his memoirs in 1903. At that time he explained his prosaic hat trick, but even then he refused to identify his source of information, true to a journalistic code that continues to this day.

[ALSO SEE: *Wilhelm Stieber*]

BLUE, VICTOR
U.S. Spy in Spanish-American War ▪ (1865–1928)

A NATIVE OF NORTH CAROLINA, BLUE HAD BEEN trained at Annapolis and, at the beginning of the Spanish-American War in 1898, he was a serving officer on board the U.S. gunboat, *Suwanee*, stationed in Cuban waters. He undertook several espionage missions, the first of which was to smuggle supplies to the Cuban rebels fighting Spanish forces. To this end, Blue sailed a small boat at night to the Cuban shore where he met with insurgent General Maximo Gomez and made plans to have the supplies sent to a secret rendezvous point. The ease by which Blue arranged for the supplies to be smuggled to Gomez in Caybarien Province inspired his commanders to give him another important espionage assignment.

Blue was then given another hazarous assignment. The entrance to Santiago Harbor had been bottled up by the American fleet and a ship had been sunk at the entrance to prevent the Spanish ships from escaping. The Americans, however, needed to know how many enemy warships were still present inside the harbor.

Disguised as a Cuban fisherman, Blue and a guide paddled a small boat to the Cuban shore. The two men then had to cut their way through a dense jungle and wade through waist-high swamp waters to reach a cliff overlooking Santiago Harbor. There, at dawn, evading Spanish patrols, Blue was able to count every Spanish warship at anchor. He returned with this vital information which assured Navy commanders that no Spanish ships had escaped to attack them from the sea.

Blue was then ordered to repeat his spy mission, this time to actually chart the position of every Spanish warship. Once more the naval officer landed secretly and made his way back to the hill overlooking the harbor. He spent perilous hours detailing a chart of each and every ship in the Spanish fleet, showing their positions and pinpointing their armaments. He managed to return to the *Suwanee*.

Armed with this information, the U.S. fleet prepared to enter the harbor and systematically destroy the Spanish ships. It proved unnecessary. The Spanish fleet attempted a breakout a short time later and was destroyed. Blue received several medals for his spy missions and was promoted. He remained in the Navy and, in World War I, commanded the battleship *Texas*. In 1919, he retired with the rank of rear admiral.

BLUNT, SIR ANTHONY
British Spy for the Soviets ▪ (1907–1983)

PAMPERED WITH AN UPPERCLASS EDUCATION AND A comfortable lifestyle, Anthony Blunt embraced espionage as easily as he would later accept the honors of the country he betrayed. An arrogant intellectual, Blunt put himself and his ideas above his loyalty to England. Like most of his class, he felt himself superior to the concept of nations and thought of himself as an arbiter of political destiny.

Born in Bournemouth, Blunt was the son of a clergyman in the Church of England. He moved to Paris with his family when he was four and his father became the chaplain to the British Ambassador. In Paris, Blunt was exposed to French art which became his lifetime passion. Returning to England, Blunt was educated at Marlborough public school, then went on to Cambridge where he proved to be a brilliant student, graduating in 1932 and becoming a fellow at Trinity College. An aesthete and a politi-

Blunt at the time he was a student at Trinity College, Cambridge, and became a KGB spy.

cal dillitante, Blunt, like many of his set, followed fashionable thought in looking to the Soviet Union as the hope of the world.

Though he enjoyed all the comforts of his class, Blunt secretly denounced the uppercrust and its concepts of democracy at a time when worldwide Depression had impoverished all but the traditionally rich. Why should the few live in ease while the masses suffer, he asked, even though he was one of the few. Communism was the answer. In 1934, Blunt traveled to Moscow and there wholeheartedly embraced the Soviet system. The KGB at the time nurtured a close relationship with Blunt, seeing him as one who would rise rapidly in the British establishment and thus be in a position to pass on to them high level secrets, as well as recruit others to espionage activities.

This is exactly what happened. Blunt returned to Trinity College and there recruited some brilliant students to the Communist cause, chiefly his homosexual lover, Guy Burgess, and other homosexual academicians David Maclean and, later, Kim Philby. These self-centered men were to become the most devastating double agents in the history of Great Britain.

At the outbreak of World War II, Blunt applied for and received a commission in the British Army. He served in France until Hitler's armies overran that country. Blunt was evacuated back to England and there applied for service with MI5, England's counterintelligence. There was purpose in his desire to be an agent. He was, as an officer of MI5, in a position to obtain and pass on secrets to his friends in Moscow.

From 1940 to 1945, Blunt was a dedicated Russian double agent, passing secrets regularly to Soviet contacts in London. Many years later he stated that such activities were not treasonable in that these secrets did not harm England but he did not, at the time of

Sir Anthony Blunt when he was in charge of Queen Elizabeth's vast art gallleries.

his confession, state that in 1940 Russia was an ally of Germany and was providing the Nazis with supplies of oil, grain, and other war materials, so that by helping the Soviets then he was also aiding England's mortal enemy, Adolf Hitler.

At the end of the war, Blunt was discharged from MI5 and he immediately began to pursue his passion of art history. Within three decades he had become one of the foremost authorities in the field. The honors early heaped upon him paved the way to his fame in the world of art. In 1945, coupled to his fellowship at Trinity College, he was named surveyor of the king's pictures. He was named director of the Courtauld Institute of Art two years later. In 1950 he was named Fellow of the British Academy. He was knighted by the queen six years later. In 1960 he became professor of art history at the University of London and in 1972, he was named adviser for the queen's pictures and drawings.

Blunt later lied to interrogators when he told them that he ceased his espionage activities for the Soviets in 1945. In 1951, he learned from some of his old friends in MI5 that Maclean was about to be arrested and questioned. He contacted Kim Philby with the words "Donald is about to be interrogated." Blunt gave Philby the exact date planned for Maclean's arrest. Philby, in turn, warned Guy Burgess who packed a bag, hired a car, then drove to Maclean's country house. The two men then drove to the seaside and caught a ship for France.

Burgess and Maclean fled to France only steps ahead of MI5 agents. From there, following an escape route which the KGB had long in advance planned

out for them, the spies slipped into Russia and permanent refuge.

Blunt's career continued to soar until he was the preimminent art historian in Europe, a specialist who decreed the worthiness of such masters as Pablo Picasso. Meanwhile, the search continued for the "Third Man" who had warned Burgess and Maclean, and when Philby was identified as this man, rumors began to circulate about a "Fourth Man" who had actually sent the warning to Philby and perhaps had even coodinated the escape of Burgess and Maclean with KGB agents.

The intelligence community never gave up its search for Blunt as the "Fourth Man," and, finally, in 1964, Arthur Martin of MI5 confronted Blunt with considerable evidence that pointed to his espionage activities and his KGB liaison through his former academic friends Burgess, Maclean, and Philby. This evidence had been provided by Michael Whitney Straight, a wealthy American who had known Blunt at Cambridge in the early 1930s.

Straight, in 1963, was being considered for a sensitive post in America, as a U.S. government art consultant, a job which had been personally offered to Straight by none other than President John F. Kennedy. The position required a security clearance by the FBI. Bureau agents interviewing Straight were told by him that he had had some connection with Communism in the distant past, that Blunt had recruited him as a KGB agent when he was a student at Cambridge but, he added, he had never given the Soviets any information of real importance. The FBI immediately contacted MI5, providing the British with a record of Straight's statements.

When Blunt was shown the testimony of his American friend, he then confessed. He stated that he was the man they were looking for, the "Fourth Man," openly admitting that he had warned his friends, Philby, Burgess, and Maclean.

Blunt then struck a bargain with MI5. He would tell them everything in exchange for his freedom. The deal was struck and Blunt talked. His information was thought to be so important that he was allowed to buy his freedom with it, without prosecution or publicity. It was, of course, more than that. It would serve no purpose to expose Blunt publicly and thus sully the royal household with a great scandal. British intelligence decided for the good of the nation it would not prosecute Blunt and would shield his treason from the public. This was a morally corrupt decision in that MI5 knew that Blunt had, during World War II, passed along to the Soviets the identities of many British agents working throughout the world, and that many of these agents later vanished during the Cold War, most likely having been killed by the KGB, and thus, were victims of the lofty Sir Anthony Blunt.

Though Blunt thought himself safe from public disgrace, dogged investigators, journalists and authors kept researching and writing about the "Fourth Man." Author Andrew Boyle then published a book, *The Climate of Treason*, in which he identified the "Fourth Man," under the alias of "Maurice." (Since Blunt had never been formally charged, Boyle and his publishers were restrained by British libel laws from directly identifying him.)

Following the book's publication, in 1979, however, MP Ted Leadbitter stood up in Parliament and posed a question to Prime Minister Margaret Thatcher, asking her if she would make a statement about the conduct "of an individual . . . in relation to the security of the United Kingdom." Unlike many Prime Ministers before her who had evaded just such questions, the outspoken Thatcher did not fudge. "The name," she said, "is Sir Anthony Blunt." She went on to add: "There is no doubt that British interests were severely damaged by his activities."

A firestorm of publicity erupted. Blunt was immediately stripped of his knighthood and honors and removed from his many prestigeous posts. He retained his arrogance and smug self-righteousness, boldly calling a press conference to explain his side of the story. He attempted to excuse his joining the KGB in the 1930s as a way of serving the anti-fascist cause. He stated that Guy Burgess had recruited him to Soviet espionage when it was the other way around. "This was a case of political conscience against loyalty to country," Blunt stated imperiously. "I chose conscience." To soften his treason, he added that he had made "an appalling mistake" in betraying his country "but I did not betray my conscience." An editorial in a London newpaper answered him the next day with: "Your conscience be damned!"

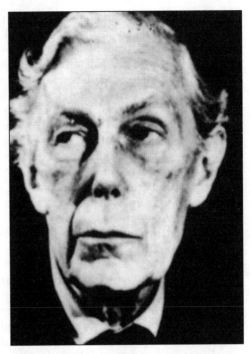

Blunt in old age, a confessed Soviet agent who had worked with KGB spies Guy Burgess, Donald Maclean, and Kim Philby to steal England's secrets for Russia.

Blunt retreated into the sanctuary of his family's money to live out a life without the limelight he so loved. He died in disgrace and silence in 1983. The treason caused severe criticism of the British intelligence agencies whose membership had been exclusively made up of upperclass individuals. MI6 responded by recruiting people from pedestrian walks of life, such as Michael Bettany in 1982. Bettany promptly began selling secrets to the KGB.

[ALSO SEE: *Michael Bettany; Guy Burgess; FBI; J. Edgar Hoover; KGB; David Maclean; MI5; MI6; Kim Philby*]

BND (BUNDESNACHRICHTENDIEST)
West German Intelligence Agency ▪ (1956–)

WHEN WEST GERMANY WAS RECOGNIZED AS A SOVereign state in April 1956, it immediately established the BND, its intelligence agency. Up to that time, all intelligence operations had been under the direction of General Reihard Gehlen, who had been Hitler's spy chief on the Eastern Front during World War II. Gehlen was named head of the BND and he quickly moved all of his agents into the new organization.

Most of these agents had served in Admiral Canaris' Abwehr and many of them had been converted by the KGB to double agents. The early days of the BND were rife with disasters. Gehlen practiced widespread sabotage and subversion behind the Iron Curtain and many of his operations failed because his organization was peopled with Russian spies.

In 1968, Gehlen was succeeded by his assistant, General Gerhard Wessell, an expert on Russian military and espionage activities. At that time, the BND was purged of old Abwehr and SS men and expanded. Top flight economists, political specialists, systems analysts, and scientists were brought into the BND to modernize its operations.

Today, the BND, is a thoroughly efficient intelligence agency that works closely with the CIA, MI6 and the Mossad. It is thoroughly computerized and has connections with and receives constant communication from a number of sources—German embassies throughout the world, scientific and cultural societies, trade delegations, emissaries to international conferences, international bank officials, travel agencies, and most international corporations. The BND's official function is "to gather information on other countries which will be of importance in the shaping of foreign policy."

[ALSO SEE: *Abwehr; Wilhelm Canaris; CIA; Reinhard Gehlen; KGB; MI6; Mossad*]

BOGROV, MORDKA
Russian Double Agent ▪ (? –1911)

LITTLE IS KNOWN OF BOGROV'S BACKGROUND. He was of Russian peasant stock and had joined the anarchists at an early age, then enlisted in the ranks of the Bolsheviks. At the same time, Bogrov went to the Okhrana, the imperial secret police, and offered to spy on the revolutionaries. As a police spy, Bogrov was an effective double agent, working with the Bolsheviks to overthrow the government and then informing on the revolutionaries before they could hatch their sabotage and assassinations, much the same way the infamous Yevno Azev had operated years earlier.

Bogrov was at heart a revolutionary intent on the destruction of the government, or so it appeared. He is best remembered for his assassination of Russia's stern Prime Minister, Peter A. Stolypin, on September 1, 1911. Only days before the killing, Stolypin accompanied Czar Nicholas II and his family on a state visit to Kiev.

The crowds in Kiev lining the streets to view the royal entourage cheered loudly as the monarchs and their children passed in resplendent carriages. When the carriage carrying Stolypin passed, there was silence, even some jeering. Much of this may have been orchestrated by the sinister Rasputin, the "Mad Monk," a self-appointed religious leader who had aided Alexis, the heir apparent, by hypnotizing him when the hemopheliac boy was seized by uncontrolled bleeding.

Rasputin had been called to the boy's side by the Empress Alexandra whenever these attacks occured and, somehow, through his mezmerizing techniques, managed to stop the bleeding, and thus the royal family became dependent upon him. The monk was nevertheless a hedonist, a drunkard, and a lacivious womanizer who seduced and raped women by the score. His shameless conduct was the scandal of the empire and, in an effort to suppress his influence at court, Stolypin had banished Rasputin from St. Petersburg, the seat of government.

This had enraged the Mad Monk who secretly went to Kiev in advance of the royal party and arranged the cold reception for Stolypin. So bold was Rasputin that he stood in the surly crowd staring at the Prime Minister as his carriage went by and, as it did, Rasputin, who claimed to have clairvoyant visions, roared: "Death is after him! Death is driving behind him!"

Stolypin did not see Rasputin in the crowd but he did notice that the carriages carrying the czar and his family were thoroughly surrounded by heavily armed guards. No protection at all had been provided for the carriage in which he and Vladimir Kokovtsov were riding. At the time, Stolypin remarked to Kokovtsov: "You see, we are superfluous."

That night and the following day, Rasputin continued to tell friends that the Prime Minister was marked for death and that he had had terrible nightmares envising Stolypin's terrible fate. So, too, did the police spy Bogrov who went to the Okhrana in Kiev some days earlier to report that an attempt would be made on Stolypin's life while he was in Kiev. In fact, Bogrov said, the assassin would try to kill the Prime Minister when he attended a performance of Rimsky-Korsakov's *Czar Sultan* at the Kiev Opera House.

Bogrov gave the secret police the names and addresses of those Bolsehviks who were involved in the plot but the culprits could not be found. That night, carrying a police pass, Bogrov entered the opera house with the special assignment of personally guarding Stolypin.

Stolypin took his seat in the first row of the orchestra. Overlooking the stage and the orchestra was the czar's box where the monarch sat with two of his four daughters, the grandducheses Olga and Tatiana. During the second intermission, Stolypin stood up next to his seat with his back to the stage. A young man in evening clothes, Bogrov, walked solemnly down the aisle to stand next to Stolypin who gave him a puzzled look.

Bogrov calmly reached beneath his cape and pulled out a Browning revolver. Just as calmly he aimed this at the Prime Minister and, at almost point blank range, fired two shots, the bullets striking Stolypin in the chest and sending him crashing to the thickly carpeted floor.

Bogrov was punched and kicked as two guards dragged him up the aisle. One man reached out and slammed his fist into the assassin's face, knocking out his two front teeth. In the lobby, a large throng surrounded him, trying to lynch him from a chandelier. Police guards rushed foward and saved the assassin, dragging him into a small room off the lobby. Here he sat bleeding from his wounds but laughing maniacally. He had totally fooled and surprised his police bosses.

"I've done my job," Bogrov sneered. "I have found the assassin!" He spread out his arms, then slowly brought his right hand close to his chest and poked it with his finger. He was then beaten unconscious before being dragged out a side door and taken to the police station were he was to await a trial that took place a short time later. Bogrov had no defense, proclaiming that he had struck down an oppressor in the name of the revolution. He was convicted and hanged. By then, Stolypin was dead. He lingered for five days, then died and was honored by the czar.

The nagging question in the minds of some at the time and historians later remaned to be asked: Why, if Bogrov truly meant to strike for the revolution, did he not shoot the czar, who presented a target almost as perfect as Stolypin, instead of a replaceable prime minister? The answer may lie somewhere in the long ago ranks of the reactionaries or Russian aristocracy who had never favored Stolypin's sweeping land reforms which had forced the nobles years earlier to give up vast tracts of lands to former serfs. Was it possible that the conniving double agent Bogrov was paid to kill Stolypin by the aristocrats who hated the Prime Minister, or even Rasputin, seeking revenge for being banished from St. Petersburg and the side of the throne?

The assassin never made it clear, only that he had struck for the revolution. He did indicate that he expected aid from some unknown source before he was hanged. Perhaps he had been promised a convenient escape by his high-placed sponsors, if, indeed, they existed. The Okhrana dossiers on former double agents were all captured by the Bolsheviks following the 1917 revolution. It was quite clear that police spies like Yevno Azev and Roman Malinowsky truly worked for the monarchy, not the revolutionaries who had been utterly hoodwinked into taking them into their ranks and elevating them to leadership. This was not the case with Mordka Bogrov. His Okhrana file was never found.

[ALSO SEE: *Yevno Azev; Roman Malinovsky; Okhrana*]

BONVOULOIR, JULIEN ARCHARD DE
French Spy in America ▪ (1749–1783)

THE SCION OF A NOBLE FAMILY IN NORMANDY, Bonvouloir served as an officer in the French Army until 1774 when he traveled to America where he learned of the great unrest among the colonialists and their hatred for British rule. He returned to France to report these conditions and was then officially appointed a secret agent with orders to return to the colonies and file regular reports on conditions there.

The French Crown still rankled over its defeat by the British in the Seven Years' War (1756–1763) and its bitter loss of French Canada. Should the Americans be successful in combating the British, the French might be presented with another opportunity to regain Canadian lands.

Bonvouloir arrived in the colonies disguised as a Belgian merchant. In Philadelphia, in 1775, he talked with Benjamin Franklin and other leading members of the insurgent Continental Congress. Franklin, Thomas Jefferson, and John Adams soon realized that the young Belgium merchant was not what he pretended to be. His indiscreet questions and his contacts in America soon had the Americans suspicious. They concluded that he was, indeed, a French spy. Instead of shunning Bonvouloir, the revolutionary leaders welcomed him.

The spy was drawn into lengthy discussions with Franklin and others in which he was subtly questioned about the possibility of France aiding the Revolution with money, military supplies, and, most importantly, diplomatic recognition of the independent colonies. Bonvouloir submitted detailed reports of these conversations in which he favorably portrayed the Americans as determined to rid themselves the British yoke and win their freedom. So convincing were Bonvouloir's reports that the French decided to aid the Americans but that aid was slow in coming.

Bonvouloir's diplomacy, however, was thought to be anything but subtle and he was recalled to France in 1776. He served with the French Army but never lived to see America win its freedom from George III of England. He died on a military expedition to India in 1781.

BOSS (BUREAU OF SPECIAL SERVICES)
Branch of NYPD

AS A SPECIAL BRANCH OF THE NEW YORK POLICE Department, BOSS was designed to monitor the activities of Cuban exiles in the city, as well as those of black militant groups, who are in contact with Cuba and China. reporting its findings to the CIA and FBI. This organization is similar to that of the Special Branch of Scotland Yard which works with England's counterintelligence agency, MI5.

[ALSO SEE: *CIA; FBI; MI5; Special Branch*]

BOSS (BUREAU OF STATE SECURITY)
South African Intelligence Agency ▪ (1950–1978)

THIS ORGANIZATION WAS LARGELY DEVOTED TO protecting white supremacy in South Africa for several decades. Its methods were ruthless and its agents were much feared. Headed by the dictatorial General Hendrick Van den Bergh, BOSS conducted ruthless campaigns against all opponents, black and white, of South African apartheid. It carried out a massive disinformation campaign against anti-apartheid leaders, burglarized the offices of Amnesty International in London and sent lethal parcel bombs to its black adversaries, killing and severely wounding many of them.

In 1978, South African Prime Minister P. W. Botha finally yielded to world pressure and disbanded BOSS, ordering Van den Bergh into retirement. It was replaced by the National Intelligence Service (NIS) but little changed. In 1983, agents of the NIS were linked with Colonel Michael Hoare's attempt to overthrow the government. Three of them were tried secretly and fined.

BOSSARD, FRANK CLIFTON
British Spy for Soviets ▪ (1912–)

THOUGH NOT AS WELL KNOWN IN ENGLAND AS GEORGE Blake, Kim Philby, Guy Burgess, and David Maclean, traitor and Soviet spy Frank Bossard proved almost as devastating to British intelligence. Bossard's espionage activities were as equally impor-

tant in that the secrets he sold were of a highly technical nature and of great value to the Russians. Money, of course, was the motive for Bossard's treason, as it had been for every wrong act he had ever committed.

Born into poverty on December 13, 1912, Bossard's carpenter father died before he was born. His widowed mother operated a general store and later a boarding house in Lincolnshire. Little Frank went to a public school but, when his mother remarried in 1923 to a penniless farmer, he was forced to go to work as a shop clerk, despite the fact that he had a keen mind and a driving ambition to attend high school and college.

Addicted to radios, Bossard built his own set at age sixteen. Bossard fancied the lifestyle of those richer than himself. He attempted to socialize with wealthy young friends and, when running out of money, forged a check. This brought him a jail sentence, six months at hard labor, in 1934.

In 1940, Bossard volunteered for the Royal Air Force. He saw action in the Middle East and by the time he was discharged in 1946, he held the rank of Flying Lieutenant. He had learned much about radar in the service which was to work to his advantange in years to come. He lectured on this subject and others at the College of Air Services at Hamble, Hampshire, and later he became assistant signals officer at the Ministry of Civil Aviation.

In 1956, MI6 recruited him, moving him as an attaché to the British Embassy in Bonn, Germany. Bossard's technical background called for him to interview all scientists, engineers, and technicians who had escaped the Iron Curtain. In dealing with these refugees, Bossard was allowed a generous entertainment allowance, one that he began to abuse, using the extra money to go on champagne binges and hire the services of high-priced call girls and statuesque club dancers.

When reassigned to London, Bossard continued to drink heavily. He ran up debts and was so short of money that, in addition to his duties at MI6, he operated a coin collection business as a sideline. In 1961, a man using the name of Gordon approached Bossard as he sat drinking in a London pub. The two chatted amiably. Bossard had little money to buy drinks but Gordon took care of that. At one of their later meetings, Gordon revealed to Bossard that he was Russian agent and that the Soviets would pay well for secret information he could provide. Bossard had no difficulty in accepting the arrangement, secrets for money. This went on for four years. Bossard provided the Soviets with the lastest information on military radar and guided missile systems.

Suddenly in the money, Bossard went on living in high style but he lavished too much cash on bar girls and other delights which brought him to the attention of MI5. Its counterintelligence agents began to trail Bossard about.

After obtaining enough evidence on Bossard, MI5

asked the Special Branch of Scotland Yard to arrest him. On March 12, 1965, as Bossard was leaving his room at the Ivanhoe Hotel, Detective Superintendent Wise stopped Bossard in the hallway. He came right to the point: "I have reason to believe that you have committed an offense against the Official Secrets Act. Will you please accompany me back to your room."

Bossard was tried at the Old Bailey on May 10, 1965, before Chief Justice Parker who, upon Bossard's conviction, sentenced the spy to twenty-one years in prison. Bossard had received about $75,000 from the Russians during the four years he spied for them, a cheap enough price for obtaining the complete details of Britain's guided missile system.

[ALSO SEE: *KGB; MI5; MI6; Special Branch*]

BOYCE, CHRISTOPHER JOHN
U.S. Spy for Soviets ▪ (1953–   )

A BOYHOOD FRIENDSHIP, DRUGS, AND SUPERFICIAL attitudes about world affairs led two American youths awkwardly into espionage in 1975. Christopher John Boyce grew up in the affluent suburb of Palos Verdes, California, the son of an FBI agent. He attended a Roman Catholic school where he met and befriended Andrew Daulton Lee. Both were altar boys and inseparable friends who helped each other with their chores after school. They played on the football squad together and, in their teens, they both developed an offbeat passion for falconry.

Of the two, Boyce was the brighter one with an IQ of 142. It was thought that he had a brilliant future but Boyce seemed indifferent to education when attending Harbor Junior College and then Loyola University. He dropped out in 1973. Much perturbed him, the war in Vietnam, Watergate, the disintegration of old standards and the family unit. He retreated into drugs, constantly smoking marijuana with his fast friend Andrew Daulton Lee. It was Lee, the son of a pathologist, who supplied the drugs; he made a fat living by buying and selling drugs.

These two came to worship only one thing—money. Boyce seemed to have little ambition which caused his father to use his influence in the old boy's network. The senior Boyce had retired from the FBI and, as is the case with most ex-agents, obtained a cushy job as the director of security for a large California firm. Through his connections, Boyce's father got him a job at TRW, an aeospace firm at Redondo Beach, California.

Beginning as a $140-a-week clerk, within five months Boyce was working in the "Black Vault," where he was required to daily change the cipher keys involving CIA satellites, the legendary "Spy in the Sky" projects. Two TRW-made spy satellites were

Christopher John Boyce, an American youth who grew up with all the advantages and sold out high-tech spy-in-the-sky secrets to the Soviets; he is shown on the day of his his arrest by the FBI in 1977.

Boyce's boyhood friend and companion in espionage, Andrew Daulton Lee, shown at the time of his arrest by the FBI in 1977.

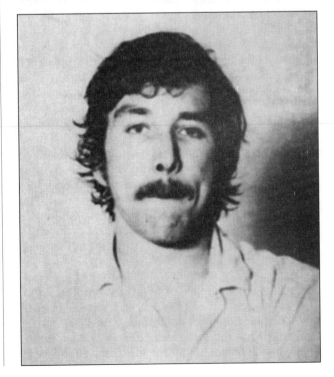

operated by Signals Intelligence (SIGENT) and they were code-named Rhyolite and Argus. To have electronic access to these satellites, Boyce needed to have top secret clearance. He got it immediately, undoubtedly because of his father's former FBI affiliation.

Rhyolite had been designed to hover 18,000 miles above Russia and China to specifically pick up the sounds of missile engines but the electronic devices on board were so sensitive that whispered telephone conversations could be monitored and recorded. Put into operation in 1972, Rhyolite sent its messages to ground stations in Australia and Great Britain. Space espionage expert Dr. Desmond Ball described Rhyolite as "perhaps the most successful development in technical development since the 'Ultra' Operation of the Second World War." ("Ultra" was the code word for the breaking of the Japanese diplomatic and military codes.)

Anyone needing to see the targeting or the messages sent from Rhyolite required a top secret clearance which had been bestowed upon Boyce. He was a 21-year-old college drop out who spent most of his off-work hours smoking pot and yet he had been entrusted with his nation's most precious secrets. In one his pot-smoking sessions with Lee, Boyce bragged about his position of trust, then added: "You know that stuff would be worth a lot of money to a foreign power."

This may or may not have given the money-hungry pair the idea of approaching the Russians, but the two devised a plan a week later. Lee would simply and boldly go to the Soviet Embassy in Mexico City to offer to sell American secrets to the Russians. In April 1975, Lee flew to Mexico City and went to the Soviet Embassy. He walked up to a guard and told him that he could obtain information which would interest Russia. He was immediately shown into an office where a middle-aged attaché greeted him, offering him vodka and caviar.

Lee sat down, drank, and ate, then told the Russian that he had a friend in a secret CIA office near Los Angeles who could provide top secrets on the U.S. spy satellites. He gave the Russian a sample of the material, a 12-inch paper tape used in the crypto machines used at TRW. On it were messages from Rhyolite. The attaché excused himself and walked out of the room. He returned to briefly chat with Lee while the information was examined. A few minutes later he left the room and when he again returned he agreed to buy whatever Lee brought to him. The attaché, of course, was the KGB spy chief in Mexico. He gave Lee an envelope containing $250, enough to cover his air trip from Mexico City to Los Angeles, and promising much more.

With that, Lee and Boyce began feeding information on the spy satellites to the Russians. Boyce smuggled the secrets out of TRW and Lee was the courier who delivered them to the Russians. With each trip, Lee returned with thousands of dollars in cash. Boyce had warned Lee not to identify him to the Russians so

Lee told the Soviets that his friend was a black man who hated America, even though the KGB spymaster kept asking Lee to completely identify the source of the information.

The KGB chief was Boris Alexei Grishin, a clever, patronizing agent who, one point, told Lee that he would pay $10,000 for every shipment of information that contained ciphers in advance that were scheduled to be installed in Rhyolite in months to come. He received this information and paid Lee as promised. In 1976, Boyce felt that Lee was cheating him out of his full share of the money which was correct. Lee gave Boyce only $3,000 out of every $10,000 he collected from Grishin.

To satisfy himself, Boyce flew to Mexico City and met with the KGB chief, dining on caviar in the basement dining room of the Russian Embassy. Boyce explained that his very important job consisted of him receiving information from the spy satellites and sending this information through cryptographic equipment to CIA headquarters in Langley, Virginia.

Grishin encouraged Boyce to continue his education and that the Soviets would be happy to finance his college education if he selected a subject that would later be suited to employment with the CIA. Boyce, impressed with the deference shown to him as someone of importance, agreed to the plan. This was typical of the Russians who had, from the 1930s, been nurturing spies around the world, advancing their careers so that later, as deeply planted moles, they were able to provide all-important information.

Before leaving the Soviet Embassy, Boyce agreed to deliver one last bulk shipment of secrets to Grishin for which he was to receive $75,000. Back at TRW, Boyce began photographing a thick top secret document which detailed the development of a covert satellite network code-named Pyramider, one which would be operated through miniature receiver/transmitters behind the Iron Curtain and in China.

This shipment was never delivered to Grishin. The unreliable Lee unexpectedly appeared at the Soviet Embassy in 1977, looking for money so he could get a fix. Before he could gain entry to the Embassy, the Mexican police arrested Lee, thinking him a terrorist. Found on him were filmstrips of classified TRW/CIA documents. The FBI was called in and Lee quickly implicated his friend Boyce who was picked up in Los Angeles. Boyce confessed that he had copied thousands of documents that Lee had delivered to the Soviets.

Both men were tried in April 1977. Boyce was given a forty-year sentence, entering a federal prison on June 20, 1977. Lee was sent to prison for life. In January 1980, Boyce escaped from the maximum federal prison at Lompoc, California. Guards found a makeshift wooden ladder and a pair of homemade tinsnips on the other side of a second 10-foot fence Boyce had scaled. He and two others went on a bank robbery spree through Montana, Idaho, and Washington before he was recaptured and convicted of charges of bank robbery, conspiracy, and firearms violations.

Boyce was returned to priston to serve out his forty-year term for espionage. When that term is completed, he will serve another 90 years for the robberies. The espionage activities of Boyce and Lee were documented in the book and movie, *The Falcon and the Snowman.*

[ALSO SEE: *CIA; FBI; KGB; Andrew Daulton Lee; Spy-in-the-Sky*]

BOYD, BELLE
Confederate Spy in Civil War ▪
(1844–1900)

BORN IN MARTINSBURG, VIRGINIA, ISABELLE BOYD was the true role model of the southern belle as portrayed later in countless books and films. Beautiful and charming, she was, however, a very determined young lady. Her prosperous store-owner father sent her to the exclusive Mount Washington Female College in Baltimore where she was taught Latin, French, music and horsemanship. She graduated in 1860 and by then she had shortened her name to simply Belle.

Returning to her home in Martinsburg, Boyd was living with her mother in the family home when the Civil War began. Her father quickly joined the army led by Thomas Jonathan "Stonewall" Jackson. Martinsburg, which was just inside the Virginia border, was occupied by Union troops in July 1861. Some federal troopers came to the Boyd's front door, demanding entrance so they could place the Union flag from a top window.

Mrs. Boyd stood in the doorway, holding the door slightly open and refusing to allow the soldiers inside. One hulking trooper shouted at the woman and smashed the door open with his shoulder. As he was about to enter the house Belle appeared in the hallway with a pistol. Without a word she fired a shot which ploughed into the trooper's head, killing him. (This scene Boyd was to later describe in her memoirs which was not lost on Margaret Mitchell who, when later writing *Gone With the Wind*, used the same scenario for Scarlett O'Hara who shoots a bruttish Union soldier who invades her home.)

Arrested, Boyd was taken before a tribunal of Union officers. When she explained that the soldier she shot was abusing her mother and violating the sanctuary of her home, the chivalrous federal officers declared that she had committed justifiable homicide and released her.

Boyd quickly collected information on the Union troops in Martinsburg and then, excellent horse-woman that she was, rode through the Union lines to

Confederate spy Belle Boyd who gathered information for Stonewall Jackson that helped him win the battle of Front Royal.

visit her father and Stonewall Jackson. Boyd delivered her information to Jackson's spymaster, Turner Ashby. She would continue to supply Ashby with vital information on Union forces in months to come. At one point, while she was caring for wounded Confederates, Union forces overran the area. Boyd brought Ashby a detailed report as to the numbers and direction of the federal troops.

Upon returning home, she was arrested and held as a spy. Allan Pinkerton, the famous detective and head of Union espionage at the time, personally interrogated Boyd and concluded that such a charming young woman could never be a spy. "There is no reason to hold her," he informed the Union commander. Boyd was released and immediately wrote out a report to Ashby which outlined Pinkerton's interrogation methods.

In 1862, Boyd was once again arrested as she rode through Union lines but she explained that she was merely out for her morning ride and was released. She then moved from Martinsburg to Front Royal to live in a small hotel owned by a relative. Union officers arrived to commandeer rooms in the hotel and Boyd was able to overhear their battle plans through air vents, a spying technique portrayed in John Ford's epic Civil War film, *The Horse Soldiers.*

Boyd then saddled her horse and rode wildly to the Confederate army, reporting to Ashby and urging General Jackson to attack Front Royal immediately, telling him that the weak Union forces could be overrun if he moved quickly before the federals blew up the bridges. Jackson accepted her story and ordered his army to march. The Confederates thundered into Front Royal, capturing the town and its garrison before the federals knew the enemy was present in force. For this victory, Jackson personally thanked his favorite spy, telling Boyd that he was grateful "for the immense service you have rendered your country today."

In 1863, Boyd made the mistake of giving a report to a man she believed was a southern sypathizer. The report was to be delivered to a Confederate commander but it was, instead, delivered to then Union spy chief Lafayette Baker, who ordered Boyd brought to Washington, D.C., where he could personally interrogate her. Boyd proved to be an unyielding prisoner. She gave the fulminating, boisterous Baker nothing.

Boyd was detained in special quarters and allowed to have a maid servant. The trunks she had brought with her were never searched, perhaps out of chivalry. They contained information that would have convicted her as a spy, as well as more than $25,000 that Boyd had been given by Confederate spymasters to use in paying for information. Baker finally gave up trying to break Boyd and ordered her to return to Confederate lines and remain there until the war was over. He told her that if he saw her again he would have her shot.

The spy went to Richmond where her exploits had long been known. She was given a hero's welcome with bands playing and crowds cheering her carriage as it was paraded through the streets of the Confederate capital. Boyd then returned to Martinsburg but undertook no more espionage assignments until 1864 when President Jefferson Davis asked her to personally deliver important dispatches to British contacts in London. She traveled to Canada and from there sailed to England but her mission, which was to urge the British to come to the aid of the Confederacy proved futile. The war ended a short time later.

Boyd published her memoirs of the war in 1865, embellishing her espionage activities with fanciful tales that were less than trustworthy. The glamourous spy was one of the most celebrated persons of the war and she capitalized upon her fame by appearing on stage in London in 1866. A gifted actress, she was a great success and she later appeared on the New York stage, a career that lasted for more than a decade.

Boyd married three times and at the time of her death left several children. In her final years, she gave stirring lectures on her Civil War experiences and though the audiences knew that much of this was fiction they nevertheless rewarded her with thunderous applause. Belle Boyd was by then, like the Civil War itself, the stuff of legend.

[ALSO SEE: *Turner Ashby; Lafayette Baker; Thomas Jonathan Jackson*]

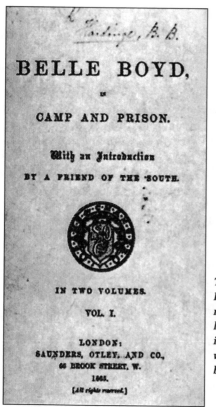

The cover of Belle Boyd's spy memoirs, published in 1865 in England, where it was a best-seller.

BREWSTER, CALEB
American Spy in Revolution ▪ (1747–1827)

A FARM BOY FROM SETAUKET, LONG ISLAND, BREWSTER became a sailor in his teens. He embraced the revolutionary cause in 1776 and led a small flotilla of boats in attacks against the British warships sailing in Long Island Sound. He soon came to the attention of General Washington's spymaster, Major Benjamin Tallmadge. Brewster was enlisted as a courier for the Culper Ring in New York.

The Culper Ring was led by Robert Townsend who lived in British-occupied New York City and was able to gather important information on British plans and troop movements through his high society contacts and commercial enterprises. Townsend used the alias of "Samuel Culper, Jr." A courier named Austin Roe then took Townsend's coded messages to Setauket and the home of Abraham Woodhull, who used the alias of "Samuel Culper, Sr." Woodhull's home looked across Little Bay to the home of Anna Strong.

Close to the shore of Little Bay, Mrs. Strong had erected a clothesline which was quite visible from Woodhull's house. If a black petticoat hung from the line it meant that the boat sailed by Caleb Brewster was anchored in a nearby cove, waiting to take Townsend's messages up the Sound to Tallmadge and Washington on the Connecticut shore. The number of black handkerchiefs hanging from the line indicated the cove where Brewster and his boat were hidden.

In this way the Culper Ring regularly sent top secret information to the American Army. Brewster's route was the most arduous and dangerous. For five long years Brewster kept his part of the spy route open and was active until the British evacuated New York in 1783. At war's end he captained revenue cutters until his retirement in 1816. Brewster then retired to his family's farm to live out the rest of his years.

[ALSO SEE: Culper Ring; Benjamin Tallmadge; Robert Townsend; George Washington; Abraham Woodhull]

BROSSELETTE, PIERRE (AKA: BRUMAIRE)
French Spy in World War II ▪ (1903–1944)

ONE OF FRANCE'S GREAT SPIES AND HEROES OF World War II, Pierre Brosselette was born in Paris to a middleclass family. He graduated with a degree in history and went to work for a socialist newspaper in the 1930s. A forceful intellectual, Brosselette became a broadcaster and propagandist for the French Socialist Party, one of the few voices that spoke out against appeasement of Hitler.

When Brosselette denounced the Munich agreement of 1938 in which Britian and France permitted Hitler to seize most of Czechoslovakia, he was shut off from the airways. To make ends meet, Brosselette and his wife opened up a bookstore/stationary shop in Paris. When France fell to Germany in 1940 and the pro-Nazi Vichy regime was established under Marshal Petain and Pierre Laval, Brosselette began publishing a clandestine newspaper attacking the French fascists of the new regime.

Brosselette's anti-Vichy reputation soon brought him to the attention of the resistance representing the London-based Free French government in exile of General Charles de Gaulle. He worked with resistance leaders in Paris and northern France from 1940 to 1942 when he fled to London after his name appeared on the Gestapo death list. In London, Brosselette was inducted into de Gaulle's BCRA (Central Bureau of Intelligence and Operations) as an assistant to Andre Dewavrin, its director. Dewavrin used the alias of "Colnel Passey" throughout the war.

Early in 1943, Brosselette accompanied Dewavrin on a secret mission to France. With them went the incomparably brave British agent and French political expert, F. F. E. Yeo-Thomas of SOE (Special Operations Executive, the British intelligence division working with resistance fighters all over Europe). Their mission was to unify the many factions of resistance fighters under the banner of de Gaulle.

De Gaulle had some concern about this mission. His two top intelligence chiefs were Jean Moulin and Dewavrin. He felt that Dewavrin was too special to parachute into France and risk being taken by the Nazis, that he knew too many secrets. Dewavrin assured his commander that he would tell nothing if captured, referring to the L-tablet he and the others always carried. This tablet contained a dose of potassium of cynanide which was fatal within seconds when swallowed.

The three men successfully parachuted into France in March 1943 and were taken to safe houses by resistance fighters. With them they carried suitcases containing revolvers, hand grenades, and a powerful radio set. Dewavrin and Brosselette met with the leaders of many resistance groups and persuaded them to unite under de Gaulle's direction. Moreover, they also convinced them not to launch an all-out insurrection which would be doomed to failure without the full military support of the Allies. Wait, they said, wait until the Allies invaded. That invasion—Operation Overlord, the planned invasion of Normany—was more than a year away. After several weeks, the three spies were picked up by at a small field by Lysander aircraft and flown back to England.

Upon the death of the heroic Jean Moulin, de Gaulle's chief representative in France, Brosselette was sent back to his native land to direct the operations of the resistance fighters. As the invasion neared, the Germans intensified their efforts to bolster coastal fortifications and increase war production. To that end, they rounded up young French men and women, especially in Paris, collecting college students like leaves and bundling them off to forced labor camps. These youths fled Paris by the thousands, hiding in the Alpine woods to the South.

One of their leaders, Michel Brault, described this flight to a resistance officer by saying: "In other words they have taken to the *maquis*." The word *maquis* means a scrub-wooded upland but it came to mean another word for the resistance: armed camps in the woods. With rampant armed resistance and sabotage occuring almost every day in France, the Gestapo and Vichy police stepped up their efforts to suppress the resistance. They arrested suspects by the thousands and lined up hundreds in front of firing squads.

Of the resistance fighters most sought by the Nazis, Brossolette headed the list along with resistance chief

Emile Bollaert. Taken to a safe house after a failed sea escape, Brosselette and Bollaert walked through the door and into the arms of secret police agents who had been tipped off by a traitor. The two men were then taken to Gestapo headquarters in Rennes and held for interrogation.

The resistance leaders awaited untold horrors at the hands of the bestial Gestapo. Bollaert would survive but Brosselette, who had lost his L-tablet, told Bollaert that he did not think he could survive Nazi torture without cracking. "I will give them nothing but my life," he whispered to his co-spy. Suddenly, he bolted for a fifth-floor window. Before he could be restrained, Brosselette crashed through the glass and sailed downward to the pavement below. He was found alive and was taken to a hospital in a coma only to die a short time later. He had revealed no secrets.

[ALSO SEE: *BCRA; Andre Dewavrin; Gestapo; Jean Moulin; SOE; F. F. E. Yeo-Thomas*]

BUNKE, TAMARA (TANIA)
Soviet Spy in Cuba ▪ (1937–1967)

THE ATTRACTIVE TAMARA BUNKE WAS A CLEVER KGB spy who used her sexual wiles to influence the direction of the Cuban revolution, especially the course taken by Fidel Castro's roving minister of espionage and sabotage, Ernesto "Che" Guevara. Her assignment led her and her lover to violent death in the cause of Communism.

Bunke was born in Buenos Aires on November 19, 1937. At that time, her father, Erich Bunke, was a professor of languages in that city. A dedicated Communist, Bunke moved his family to East Germany in the 1950s where he arranged for his daughter to study political science at Humboldt University, a Communist indoctrinational center for budding spies.

Upon graduation and through her father's influence, Bunke went to work for the East German Ministry of State Security. She willingly undertook several espionage missions which invariably involved sleeping with West German businessmen or officials who could later be blackmailed into delivering information. So successful was Bunke that the KGB inducted her into its ranks in 1961.

By that time Castro had taken over Cuba, but his brand of Communism was erratic and showed signs of becoming anti-Russian, particularly through Castro's chief adviser, Ernesto "Che" Guevara. A radical leftist all his life, Guevara was born in 1928 in Argentina. His mother was a dedicated Marxist who dominated her son, molding him into a Communist. Trained as a doctor, Guevara left Argentina upon his graduation

from medical school in 1953 rather than serve in the Army under the direction of right-wing strong man Juan Peron.

Guevara traveled throughout South and Latin America, promoting the cause of Communism. In 1954, he attempted to organize resistance to the CIA's successful ouster of Guatemala's President Jacobo Arbenz Guzman. After taking refuge in the Argentine Embassy, Guevara escaped to Mexico where he met and befriended Fidel Castro. Together they planned the Cuban revolution. Guevara acted as Castro's top military commander and, following their takeover of the country, he asserted his belief that Cuba should follow the Communist concepts of China instead of becoming a Soviet satellite. This so alarmed the KGB that they sent the most alluring agent, Tamara Bunke to Cuba. She was ordered to become Guevara's mistress and guide him into the Soviet camp.

Using the alias Laura Gutterez, Bunke went to Havana and was introduced to Guevara as an ardent Communist from Buenos Aires. Aside from the sexual attraction, Guevara was immediately bonded to Bunke as a fellow Argentine, which is what the KGB had hoped would be the effect. Bunke became Guevara's mistress and took an active role in Cuban politics.

When Castro sent Guevara throughout Latin and South America to spread the Communist gospel, Bunke went with him, taking the revolutionary name of "Tania." Slowly, Guevara's thinking began to turn more and more away from Peking and toward Moscow, undoubtedly through the influence of the ever-faithful KGB agent, Bunke.

Guevara went to Bolivia in 1967 but the peasant population there was unresponsive to Guevara's appeals. He and the few Cuban revolutionaries who accompanied him were looked upon as outsiders and they found themselves hunted as common criminals in the Bolivian wilds. To persuade local bandits to enlist in the Communist cause, Guevara paid them money and even offered the sexual delights of "Tania" to their chiefs. (Whether or not Bunke actually performed such acts of political prostitution is open to debate.)

On October 8, 1967, Bolivian army units tracked down Guevara and his band near Higueras. All were slain in a firefight. Tamara Bunke, alias Laura Gutterz, alias Tania was killed. She was found to be four months pregnant. Upon studying Guevara's diaries, it is clear that he never knew Bunke's real identity or the fact that she was a KGB agent who had successfully infiltrated the Cuban Communist hiarchy and the heart of one of its foremost leaders.

[ALSO SEE: *KGB*]

BUREAU HA
Private Swiss Intelligence Agency ▪ (1939–1945)

SEVERAL YEARS BEFORE THE BEGINNING OF WORLD War II, Captain Hans Hausamann of the tiny Swiss Army, with the tacit approval of the Swiss Government, established his own intelligence agency, named after himself, Bureau Ha. Hausamann realized that Hitler posed a threat to Switzerland and he began gathering information on the Nazis from his agents which were located in Germany, France, Italy, Austria, and the Scandinavian countries.

Operating out of a villa on Lake Lucerne, Bureau Ha worked directly for the Swiss Government. In 1939, Hausamann reported to Swiss General Henri Guisan. Should the Nazis realize that the Bureau was gathering information on Germany, the Swiss reasoned, it could always disown Bureau Ha as a private organization operating without its approval and ostensibly close it down.

Bureau Ha had two spectacular agents who unfailingly delivered throughout the war some of the most important Nazi secrets to the Allies. One was Captain Thomas Sedlacek who managed Hausamann's spy network and funneled its information to the Allies. The other was the enigmatic Rudolf Roessler (code name Lucy) who operated his own spy network in Germany and had an informant inside the German High Command throughout the war.

Roessler not only fed his information to Bureau Ha but also to a Soviet network operated in Geneva by Russian spymaster Sandor Rado that sent Roessler's reports to Moscow via shortwave radio. In 1943, German counterintelligence learned about Rado's Swiss operation and compelled the Swiss Government to close it down but Bureau Ha continued operations until the end of the war. Roessler's information and network was one of the most effective spy operations in World War II and certainly rivaled anything achieved by superspies Elyeza Bazna (Cicero) and Richard Sorge. With the collapse of Germany, Bureau Ha was disbanded.

[ALSO SEE: *Elyeza Bazna; Sando Rado; Rudolf Roessler; Richard Sorge*]

BURGESS, GUY FRANCIS DE MONCY
Soviet Spy Against Britain ▪ (1911–1963)

A FLAGRANT TRAITOR, A FLABOYANT DRUNK AND a notorious homosexual, Guy Burgess was anything but the ideal Soviet agent. He nevertheless proved to be one of Russia's most effective spies at the beginning of the Cold War. He had considerable help in achieving his treasonable ends from others sharing his offbeat lifestyle, particularly Donald Maclean, Kim Philby and, as was much later exposed, the celebrated British art historian, Anthony Blunt.

The Devonport-born Burgess had, from early youth, always wanted to join the Navy. His father had been an officer in the Royal Navy and the lore and legend of the sea became a family tradition. To that end, Burgess first attended Eton, then the naval college at Dartmouth. It was later claimed that he dropped out of Dartmouth because an eye problem disqualified him from Navy service but the real reason was that he had attempted to seduce some other youths, an affair that was hushed up.

Burgess graduated from Eton in 1930, going on to Cambridge. There, at Trinity College, he fell in with the left-wing set, the sons of well-to-do men who got drunk at poshy clubs almost every night while toasting the lower classes and vowing that Communism was the only salvation for the oppressed of the earth. In reality, none of these young men, ever had anything to do with the working class and their brand of Marxism was bottled in imported brandy. The group to which Burgess attached himself was also

Soviet spy Guy Burgess, who worked with Donald Maclean, Kim Philby, and Anthony Blunt to steal England's secrets for three decades.

decidedly homosexual. His roommate and the fellow classmate who recruited him into the Soviet ranks was Anthony Blunt who became Burgess' lover.

Other on-and-off homosexual lovers included Donald Maclean and Kim Philby. All of them would lead well-pampered lives as they first played at being spies for the KGB which early on recruited them through Blunt. Later, their traitorous espionage became serious and deeply damaging to Great Britain. Burgess, like Blunt, sought to convert any active Communist at Cambridge into a KGB spy. He was unorthodox in his approach, selecting the most handsome of young men and then attempting to sexually seduce them.

In 1934, Burgess, David Maclean, Kim Philby, and others from Cambridge took a trip to Moscow, more for social than politcal reasons. The tourist jaunt did not agree with Burgess who found the Soviet city "dreary and depressing." He remained drunk during most of his Russian stay. At one point, Moscow police found Burgess dead drunk in the Park of Rest and Culture. Inside of his coat pocket were letters of introduction to prominent Russian scholars and politicians from members of the Astor family.

Guy Burgess, like the rest of his clique, lived and prospered through his social and academic connections. Upon his return from Moscow, Burgess seemed to lose interest in Marxism. He drifted to the right (or so it appeared, although Burgess' actions in the early 1930s may have been a planned KGB scenario, for, according to Blunt's later confession, Burgess was by then a KGB spy). He joined the right-wing Anglo-German Fellowship and applied for a job with the Conservative Party.

The Conservative Party rejected him, despite the fact that his academic sponsors at Trinity had described Burgess as "the most brilliant young talent of the day." He next tried to enter civil service but was told that he had started at Cambridge too late and was too old to have a bright future in that field. Burgess worked for a while as a personal assistant to conservative MP Jack Macnamara and accompanied him to visit the Germany of Adolf Hitler. This job, too, ended abruptly when Burgess got drunk and passed out at a political dinner. Then came journalism. Through a friend, Burgess got a job as a writer for the London *Times*, a position he hated.

Then, through his connection with the historian, G. M. Trevelyan, he went to work in 1936 for the British Broadcasting System. He produced for the BBC a chatty and inconsequential political program called *The Week at Westminster*. Again, Burgess used his position to further his career, befriending many politicians who were to later help greatly in advancing his career. Among those whom Burgess cultivated at that time was Hector McNeil, a future Minister of State at the Foreign Office.

Throughout his time with the BBC, Burgess continued spying for the KGB, receiving information from John Cairncross of the Foreign Office and passing these secrets to the Russians. He went to France in 1937 and in 1939. At both times he met with another part-time lover, fellow drunk and KGB agent, Kim Philby. Philby was then working as a journalist and reporting on the Spanish Civil War (1936–1939), and who was sending information to Moscow on all he observed. In ironic fact, when Philby returned to England at the end of the Spanish Civil War, he was interviewed by none other than BBC correspondent Guy Burgess.

There is no doubt that Burgess presented, in the late 1930s, the very image of the well-educated young man in England. He was, when sober, a charming, witty, handsome fellow who made brilliant conversation and always played to the person with whom he was speaking. He had an instinct of when to say precisely the right thing. He kept a detailed ledger in which he listed all of those of political importance or those who might rise to prominent positions in the government.

Burgess made important contacts in England and throughout Europe as a BBC correspondent. He even interviewed the venerable Winston Churchill who gave him an autographed set of his speeches. As war approached, Prime Minister Neville Chamberlain, who had also been interviewed by Burgess, entrusted the BBC commentator with secret dispatches which he clandestinely delivered to French leader Edouard Daladier and Italian dictator Benito Mussolini. Chamberlain had hoped that these secret messages would help avert the war that Adolf Hitler so eagerly sought. They did not.

But Burgess' much-vaunted help ingratiated him to the British intelligence community, though it had no idea that he was feeding the Russians every piece of secret information—including copies of Chamberlain's private messages—he could obtain. Burgess used his BBC position to develop contacts with important leaders in Europe who might later unwittingly provide him with more information to give to his Soviet masters. From these sources, Burgess obtained information he sent to British intelligence, information for which MI6 paid him well.

In January 1939, Burgess again changed jobs, again through a high-placed connection. He went to work for MI6, working in Department D, a mushrooming section assigned to recruiting new agents to British intelligence. The following year, Burgess recruited none other than Kim Philby, whose impartial reporting on the Spanish Civil War had impressed many government officials. With Philby comfortably ensconced at MI6, Burgess quit the service in 1941 and went back to the BBC where he could better effect communications with his KGB bosses.

In 1944, he joined the Foreign Office with the job of handling all the news. He was able to glean countless secrets from this department for six years and send them on to the Russians. It was Burgess, secret Communist spy, who had the responsibility of releasing or not releasing news, as he saw fit, from the

Foreign Office or the British Government. Burgess then moved even deeper into the Foreign Office when he was hired by his old friend Hector McNeil who had risen to the the position of Labor Minister of State at the Foreign Office. McNeil remained permanently hoodwinked by the clever Burgess, "dazzled by his brilliance," according to one report.

McNeil was avuncular toward Burgess; he was well aware of his protégé's perverted sexual inclinations and he warned him to avoid homosexual incidents in the U.S. He also told him not to discuss racial problems and left-wing aggression. Replied the arrogant, pathologically self-confident Burgess: "In other words, Hector, you mean I mustn't make a pass at Paul Robeson." As a parting gesture, Burgess had his London apartment painted red, white, and blue, then packed his bags and went to Washington, D.C.

Waiting to greet him with open arms was his old lover and fellow KGB spy Kim Philby who was the first secretary at the British Embassy in Washington. The pair worked diligently for the Russians, sending to Moscow not only all the British secrets they could obtain but all the U.S. confidential memos that came within their grasp.

At the time, Burgess lived with Philby in Philby's home on Nebraska Avenue. Mrs. Philby hated the sight of Burgess. On many times she complained to her husband that Burgess was "supercilious, loud, habitually drunk." She also knew and despised Burgess' reputation as a flagrant homosexual. Philby said nothing and Burgess stayed on. Then Philby got word from his old friend, Anthony Blunt, that Donald Maclean, who had been under surveillance by MI5 since 1949, and was suspected as one of the sources leaking information to the Soviets, was about to be questioned. Blunt even provided Philby with the date of the upcoming interrogation—May 25, 1951. Maclean had also worked at the British Embassy in Washington until recently being transferred back to London.

Philby immediately conferred with Burgess, telling him that if Maclean was questioned, he, Burgess, would be next. It was time to warn Maclean and then disappear. Burgess then went on a wild rampage. He got roaring drunk and began racing his car at high speeds. Police stopped him and Burgess cursed them, ripping up the speeding tickets and throwing these in the air, hysterically shouting that "I have diplomatic immunity from such nonsense!"

Of course, once he was informed, the British Ambassador immediately dismissed Burgess and ordered him to return to London. This was all brought about according to plan. Burgess needed to get back to England to warn Maclean. How better to achieve this goal than to be sent back in disgrace. Back in London on May 7, 1951, Burgess schemed on how best to warn his friend. He took the simple approach. He dropped by the Foreign Office to see Maclean. He handed him a slip of paper on which was a coded message.

The message told Maclean he was about to be questioned, probably arrested, and that it was time for him to escape. Burgess arranged for the departure. It is unclear whether or not Burgess at the time planned to escape with Maclean. Some reports have it that the Soviets ordered him to leave England with Maclean, others insist that it was Burgess' own idea. Burgess returned to his apartment, packed a bag and then hired a car. He drove to Maclean's suburban home in Surrey. Maclean was waiting for him. His bag was also packed.

It was Maclean's 38th birthday but he had no time to celebrate. He said a hasty farewell to his wife and three children, hopped into the car and he and Burgess drove off at top speed. Their escape route had already been worked out by a KGB spymaster who had been contacted by Anthony Blunt. The two men drove to Southhampton. They arrived just in time to catch the 11:45 P.M. cross-Channel boat *Falaise* which was sailing to St. Malo, France.

A dockside attendant shouted to both men as they scrambled up the gangplank: "Hey, what about the car?"

Burgess grinned and waved, saying: "Be back Monday."

Neither he nor Maclean would ever be back. Both men went to their cabin and locked themselves inside. They did not leave the cabin when the rest of the passengers disembarked in St. Malo to take the train to Paris, but stayed inside guzzling a case of beer they had ordered from the steward. Some time later both men staggered from the cabin and hired a taxi to drive them fifty miles to Rennes. There they caught a later train to Paris and from there, their KGB contacts arranged for them to fly first to Czechoslovakia, then on to Moscow where they were met by KGB agent F. V. Kislytsin who had been the man to whom they had for years delivered their secrets. Kislytsin had been stationed in the Soviet Embassy in London.

Kislytsin later reported how Burgess had delivered suitcases full of British secrets to the Embassy and that, after the documents had been photographed by the Russians, Burgess lugged the secrets back to the Foreign Office to replace them in the files. Other secrets were delivered verbally by Burgess. Kislytsin coded these messages and sent them by radio to Moscow. Everything Burgess, Maclean and Philby delivered to the Russians had top priority in communication to KGB headquarters in Moscow.

The Kislytsin connection was exposed by Vladimir Petrov, a top KGB official who defected to Australia in April 1954. Petrov had been for some time one of the "control" officials who had handled Burgess, Maclean, and Philby from the time they decided to join the new world of Communism in the early 1930s. Petrov also disclosed that Mrs. Maclean and her three children who had disappeared in Switzerland on a holiday more than two years after her husband fled to Russia, was secreted into the Soviet Union to join her spouse.

"She is now living with her husband in Moscow," Petrov reported, "as he secretly continues with his work for the Soviet Foreign Ministry alongside his fellow spy Guy Burgess." The Russians paraded their star agents before Western journalists in a 1956 press conference. Both Burgess and Maclean denied ever having spied and that they were merely "peace lovers" who had become disillusioned with the West.

Both men worked at espionage in Russia. Maclean appeared to adapt but Burgess continued to drink heavily. His once chiseled handsome face became bloated. He took on weight and seemed to want to talk of his native country. He obviously missed all things British. Miserable at having to live inside a puritanical state, Burgess drank himself to death on August 30, 1963. In that year, Kim Philby, the most important spy the Russians had in the West, finally fled to the Soviet Union.

[ALSO SEE: *ASIO; Anthony Blunt; John Cairncross; Klaus Fuchs; KGB; Donald Maclean; MI5; MI6; Vladimir Petrov; Kim Philby*]

BURR, AARON
American Conspirator and Spymaster ▪ (1756–1836)

LAWYER, SOLDIER, STATESMAN AND VICE PRESIDENT OF the United States, the enigmatic Aaron Burr was many things, including a secret spymaster and a traitor to the country he once called his own. Born in Newark, N. J., Burr attended a college which later became Princeton. He founght in the Revolutionary War until 1779, rising to the rank of lieutenant-colonel. In 1782, he became a member of the bar and a practicing lawyer.

Burr's passion was politics for he believed that through election he could grasp great personal power. He championed the Democrat-Republican standard that brought him into headlong conflict with Alexander Hamilton, the standard-bearer of the Federalist Party. In 1800, Burr ran for the Presidency in a neck-and-neck race with Thomas Jefferson. The votes in the electoral college ended in a tie which was decided in the House of Representatives where the more popular Jeffereson was chosen for the office. Burr was chosen to become Vice President.

It was an uneasy position. Though friendly toward the benign Jefferson, Burr despised the President's chief advisor, Alexander Hamilton. Hamilton and Burr became bitter enemies, particularly after Hamilton blocked Burr's bid for the New York governorship in 1804 as well as vehemently opposed Burr as Jefferson's running mate in the presidential election. A heated correspondence led to Hamilton's remark that Burr was "a dangerous man and one who ought not be trusted with the reins of government."

Burr exploded, demanding a retraction. The proud Hamilton refused. Both men then sought satisfaction on the dueling ground at Weehawken, New Jersey on July 11, 1804. The famous duel resulted in Hamilton's death. His supporters claimed that Burr fired preemptorily before the signal was given, murdering Hamilton. It was then proven that both men fired about the same time, Burr a second sooner, his bullet striking Hamilton in the chest just as Hamilton got off his shot. Hamilton's supporters cried out that their champion had simply fired into the air and that the ungentlemanly Burr then took deliberate aim and killed the defenseless Hamilton.

The victor did not savor triumph. Instead, he was branded a social pariah as murder charges against him were filed in New York and New Jersey. Although he wanted to serve out his term as Vice President, Burr found himself so unpopular and, fearing that he would be jailed for the Hamilton killing, that he resigned his post and slipped out of Washington. He was by then delusional. His mind by then had hatched a grand conspiracy, one involving the huge land tract known as the Louisiana Purchase, the vast lands that stretched far beyond the Mississippi River.

Burr had long and secretly admired Napoleon Bonaparte, Emperor of France, and sought to emulate the French dictator by seizing, with the connivance of the British, the Louisiana Territory. The British had long schemed to acquire the Louisiana Territory but had been thwarted by Jefferson's purchase of the land. Burr simply planned to seize the territory with an army of adventurers supported by British troops and establish himself, like Napoleon in France, emperor of the vast western lands, a conspiracy that would, in his words, "effect a separation of the Western part of the United States."

The seeds of Burr's conspiracy had been sewed several years earlier when he befriended Senator Jonathan Dayton of New Jersey, and a wealthy Ohio Valley businessman, Harman Blennerhassett, who advanced Burr $50,000 to establish a spy network and to cover costs in advancing his land-grabbing scheme. Both Dayton and Blennerhassett were promised great fortunes and lands, once Burr had conquered the Louisiana Territory.

Supporting Burr was British Minister Anthony Merry, who resided in Philadelphia and loathed Jefferson. To Merry, Jefferson was the intellectual leader of the Revolution that saw the horrendous loss of the British colonies to the upstart Americans. Burr, Merry thought, could change all that.

The conspiracy mushroomed in Burr's mind. He believed the French living in the Louisiana Territory would join his legions and then he thought beyond those lands. Why not seize all the lands to the West, march into Mexico and make that, too, part of his kingdom? He believed the natives would welcome him warmly as a "liberator" from their oppressive rulers.

On August 6, 1804, Merry urged the British Foreign Office to embrace Burr's proposal and secretly finance the land seizure, as well as provide troops to support Burr's home grown army. Burr, nevertheless, remained for many months in Philadelphia, returning to Washington to give a rather moving farewell speech before Congress on March 2, 1805. He then met with his old friend, General James Wilkinson, whose appointment as governor of the Territory of Louisiana, had been engineered by Burr. Wilkinson was also commander-in-chief of the small Army of the United States. Burr apparently confided to Wilkinson that he would soon become the dictator of the new lands.

Burr then returned to Washington in late 1805, having dinner with President Jefferson at the White House. A few days later, on December 1, 1805, Jefferson received an urgent message from an anonymous informer, warning the President that a traitor and spy was in his midst. The message did not mention Burr by name but left no doubt as to his identity as the conspirator. The message read in part: "You admit him to your table and you held a long and private conference with him a few days ago after dinner at the very moment he is meditating the overthrow of our administration."

Much of this information stemmed from General Wilkinson, who possessed a notorious loose tongue. He had alerted Burr's enemies but it would be some time before they convinced the government of Burr's grand scheme. Further, Wilkinson, to save himself, came forth to blurt the details of the conspiracy. By then Charles James Fox became the new British Foreign Minister and, being pro-American, immediately recalled Merry.

By then, Burr's spies informed him that his plans had been revealed. He left for the Ohio Valley where his boats and supllies were being assembled, along with some armed recuits to his military expedition. Acting on Jefferson's orders, the Ohio militia seized Burr's supplies, arresting many members of the conspiracy.

Burr was then in Natchez, Mississippi, recruiting his own militia. He learned on January 10, 1807, that Jefferson had signed an order for his arrest. He fled with some of his supporters, attempting to reach Mexican-held Texas but was apprehended and returned to Richmond, Virginia, where he was brought before Chief Justice John Marshall. He was acquitted of charges of treason with the intention to wage war against the U.S. since not enough witnesses could be brought forth to testify against him. (Burr's spies had successfully spread the word that all informers would face horrible deaths.)

Burr was, however, one of the most hated men in America and he knew it. He sailed to Europe, spending his time in France and England where he continued to advance his cause of seizing American lands, thinking that he might be hired as a privateer by England or France and sent with an army to take

vengeance on the country that had ostracized him. No one was interested. Burr went to Sweden years later and penned his self-justifying memoirs.

Returning to New York in 1812, Burr opened a law office and struggled to earn a living. His daughter Theodosia Burr Alston, whom he once thought to place upon the throne of his mythical Louisiana kingdom as his "heir apparent," went to her death in 1813, when the *Patriot*, a ship on which she was sailing from Chaleston to New York, was lost in a storm off Cape Hatteras. So much was Burr still hated that a widely circulated rumor had it that the ship was not really wrecked in a gale but had been seized by pirates. When they learned that Theodosia was the daughter of the hated Burr, she was made to walk the plank.

BURTON, RICHARD
British Agent in India and Arabia ▪ (1821–1890)

RICHARD BURTON IS KNOWN TO THE WORLD AS A brilliant author, explorer and orientalist. He was also one of the most effective and dedicated spies for England in the nineteenth century. In his youth Burton appeared to be anything but the bold adventurer he was later to become. Born at Torquay, England, he was the son of a retired army colonel, a hypochrondriac who flitted about looking for the safest place to live and the healthiest way in which to live out a life he intended to prolong at all costs.

Burton proved just the opposite of his father, although his earliest ambition was to conquer languages, not geography. He studied languages night and day and, by the time he entered Oxford at nineteen, he spoke fluent French, Spanish, Italian, Portugese, German, and modern Greek. At Oxford he concentrated on ancient Greek, Latin, and the Arabic lanaguages. After two years, Burton suddenly developed a craving for adventure.

India appeared to Burton as a land of mystery, one which he decided to visit. He persuaded his father to purchase for him a commission in the army of the East India Company, a private consortium that operated on behalf of Great Britain. Burton reached India and quickly mastered its many languages and dialects. (He was to become fluent in twenty-nine languages and forty dialects before he died.)

Burton was sent with his regiment to Sind (present-day Pakistan) in 1843. General Sir Charles Napier had recently occupied this most northern of Indian provinces and he selected Burton to learn its languages, customs, as well as gather information on its dissident leaders. The gifted Burton proved that he was an excellent amateur espionage agent. Wearing

Sir Richard Burton, the famous explorer and British spy, shown in the disguise of a Persian merchant.

native disguises, he wandered through the bazaars and villages of the region, collecting information on the customs, habits, and political attitudes of the native population, all of which proved to serve the British cause well.

Also disguised as a peasant worker, his skin dyed by henna, his black hair and long black mustache making him appear to be a native, Burton labored long in the work gangs leveling the canals. He next moved from town to town dressed in worn-out clothing, presenting himself to be a dervish peddler. So convincing was Burton's disguise that he could fool the most discerning and suspicious tribal leaders, as well as his fellow British officers. In one instance he was shoved aside on a crowded street by one of his own army superiors who did not recognize him.

General Napier was delighted at Burton's detailed reports, particularly his spying activities involving the hill tribes. Because of the information his spy brought to him, Napier was able to quell much of the unrest and placate the rebellious tribesmen. So effective was Burton that Napier unofficially assigned him to investigate three reportedly homosexual brothels in Karachi. Napier felt that these dens were too close to his troops and wanted verification of their existence.

Burton visited these homosexual brothels as a Persian merchant. Upon his return he delivered confirmation of the wild rumors. So detailed was his report that even the tough old veteran Napier was shocked. The brothels were closed by the military. Napier was then replaced by a commander who disliked Burton. He used the spy's report on the brothels to ruin him, sending this on to Bombay with a statement that Burton had visited these terrible places in a disguise which was "unbecoming that of a British officer." Bombay authorities for the East India Company severely reprimanded Burton who, in 1849, left India in disgrace and ill-health.

In 1853, Burton was fit again and undertook another adventure, visiting on pilgrimage the cities of Medina and Mecca. He went again in disguise, as a merchant named Mizra Abdullah El Bushiri. He recorded his journey and the temper of the people, information which he sent to British government officials. So successful was Burton's disguise that he was fully accepted as a Moslem, allowed into the holiest of sanctuaries and given the title of Hajji and the green turban which signified that he had made the Great Pilgrimage.

In 1855, Burton published an account of his wanderings, *Pilgrimage to Al Madinah and Meccah*, which proved to be a brilliant profile of Moslem life, traditions and religion as much a classic today as is *The Seven Pillars of Wisdom*, penned by that latter day British agent and partisan leader in World War I, T. E. Lawrence.

Burton then pursued his lifelong ambition to explore Africa, leading expeditions into Somaliland and Harrar in Abyssinia. In East Africa he searched long for the source of the Nile. So legendary were his feats that the British government named him counsul of Fernando Po on the west coast of Africa in 1861. He was later appointed consul of Santos, Brazil, then Damascus from which he led exploratory expeditions into Syria, Palestine, and the Holy Land.

He retired to Trieste where he authored a six-volume translation of the *Arabian Nights*, which is considered to be his masterwork. For his incredible services to Britain, Queen Victoria bestowed upon Burton the title of Knight Commander of St. Michael and St. George a short time before his death.

[ALSO SEE: *T. E. Lawrence*]

BUSH, GEORGE HERBERT WALKER
CIA Director ▪ (1924–)

GEORGE BUSH HAD NO ESPIONAGE EXPERIENCE WHEN President Gerald Ford appointed him interim director of the CIA. Bush had been a U.S. Congressman, U.S. Ambassador to the United Nations, and a U.S. representative to China. He assumed his position at the CIA in January 1976, however, with an optimistic attitude and by-the-book procedures. It was his aim, and that of President Ford's, to clean up the image of the CIA after several years of scandals had rocked the agency.

Bush's predecessors had involved the agency in the assassination of foreign leaders. Almost immediately after Bush took over, he sent out a Presidential order to all at the CIA which stated that "No employee of the United States government shall engage in, or conspire to engage in, political assassination."

President Ford also made Bush responsible for all intelligence gathering and appointed him to a three-man committee regarding foreign intelligence. He proved to be a tough taskmaster but fair and professional. Bush is credited with doing much to reform CIA procedures as well as its badly tainted image. He served as the Agency's director until March 1977 when he was replaced by a candidate of the new President, Jimmy Carter.

The excellent performance by Bush at the CIA recommended him strongly as the presidential running mate to Ronald Reagan. Upon Reagan's election, Bush became Vice President of the U.S., a position he held for two terms, until becoming President in 1988. Bush remains loyal to supporting a strong intelligence operation. He best summed up his attitude in one statement: "We are up against a tough adversary [the Soviet Union] and we have to have the best intelligence service that money can buy."

[ALSO SEE: *CIA*]

BUSSY, FRANCOIS DE
French Spy for England ▪ (1699–1780)

AS THE ILLEGITIMATE SON OF A FRENCH NOBLEMAN, Bussy was forever on the fringe of an aristocracy that tolerated him but refused to fully accept him. He worked his way through civil service until he managed to win an appointment as secretary to the French Ambassador in Vienna in 1725. Three years later, through diligent work, he was named Ambassador in Vienna, finally arriving at the status long denied him.

By that time, however, Bussy was in serious personal trouble. He had lived well beyond his means and his debts were overwhelming. He had also by then befriended the British Ambassador in Vienna, Lord Waldgrave. In 1735, after returning to France and joining the ministry of foreign affairs, Bussy renewed his friendship with Waldgrave who offered to help him out of his financial difficulties. The price was high, money for French secrets.

Bussy began selling secrets to Waldrave. Using the code number 101 in his correspondence with the British nobleman, Bussy also relayed information on French policy and military matters in his coded correspondence. Sometimes he would meet Waldgrave in the park at Versailles at night and hand over documents. He most often gave the English spy his information verbally.

So well concealed was Bussy's espionage that he continued his spying for the British until 1749. By that time he was an undersecretary at the foreign ministry and was privy to the most secret information in France. He often took these secrets to England when on official business for the government.

The British paid Bussy so well that he not only retired all his debts but he began to live lavishly. He rented an elegant villa, staffed it with a goodly number of servants and drove about Paris in a resplendant coach. His enemies concluded that he was selling secrets to England but failed to prove it. Bussy, knowing he was being watched and that he was suspected of being a spy, suddenly ceased all espionage.

Throughout the 1750s, he kept to his business at the foreign ministry and was trusted well enough to be sent to London in 1761, with instructions to negotiate the end of the Seven Years War (1756–1763). He failed in his efforts, perhaps due to the British insisting that he resume spying for England and the fact that he utterly refused to do so. He returned to France and though the British continued to offer him great amounts of money for his country's secrets, he refused to resume his career as a spy. Bussy retired with honors in 1767 and died thirteen years later. France never learned that its trusted servant in the foreign ministry had been working for England for more than a decade.

CAHAN, SAMUEL BORISOVICH
Soviet Spymaster in England ▪ (1901?– ?)

THE IDENTITY OF THE SOVIET AGENT WHO RECRUITED the Trinity College of Cambridge spies— Anthony Blunt, Guy Burgess, Donald Maclean, and Kim Philby to name a few—has long been open to debate. Blunt and Philby later claimed that he was an eastern European named Otto. Blunt said he was a Czech, Philby claimed he was a Russian, a member of the Comintern. Historians most popularly select Samuel Cahan as being Otto the recruiter.

It was Cahan's specific chore to spot and recruit intellectual malcontents into the KGB and develop them as moles who could later be used once they had attained positions of importance. It was Cahan who certainly recruited and trained Kim Philby and was in regular contact with Blunt, Maclean, Burgess, and John Cairncross, another Trinity College graduate and traitor. Cahan operated out of the Soviet Embassy in London but he also went to the poshy nightclubs about Cambridge where he met with his youthful protégés, drinking with them and talking Communist philosophy.

[ALSO SEE: *Anthony Blunt; Guy Burgess; John Cairncross; KGB; Donald Maclean; Kim Philby*]

CAIRNCROSS, JOHN
British Spy for Soviets ▪ (1913–   )

BORN IN SCOTLAND, CAIRNCROSS CAME FROM A LONG line of civil servants. He entered Cambridge in the early 1930s to study modern languages and was almost immediately converted to Communism by Anthony Blunt and Guy Burgess who turned him over to their KGB contact, Samuel Cahan. He was was given the short course in espionage before he entered civil service.

Cairncross worked at the Foreign Office in 1936. During World War II, he worked at the Government Code and Cipher School at Bletchley, England. All important codes and ciphers used by England and the Allies were copied by Cairncross and then fed to the Soviets. He later admitted that, while at MI6, he would fill the back seat of a car with several cases of decoded German messages and then drive to London, going straight to the Soviet Embassy to make the delivery. The Russians had provided the car.

Later in the war, Cairncross worked in the London headquarters of MI6. From its offices he took the plans for Yugoslavia after the war and gave these secrets to the Russians. Following the war, he returned to the Foreign Office and the Treasury. From the mid-1930s to 1952, as he later confessed, Cairncross worked diligently as a KGB agent. He passed along secret information on the German military to the Russians during the war and, after the war, he funneled information to Donald Maclean, Guy Burgess, Kim Philby, and several Soviet contacts.

MI5 finally got on to Cairncross in 1967. Confronting him with insurmountable evidence, the spy confessed, but he stated that he had ceased being a Soviet spy some time earlier. In exchange for his information, Cairncross was not prosecuted nor was his treason and espionage made public. Incredibly, he was not removed from government service but given a "safe" job at the United Nations Food and Agricultural Organization in Rome. After his retirement, Cairncross continued to live in Italy. His treachery was not made public until 1981 when Prime Minister Margaret Thatcher obliquely referred to a man who had been persuaded to confess his treason after he was given "an indication that he was unlikely to be prosecuted."

[ALSO SEE: *Anthony Blunt; Guy Burgess; Samuel Cahan; KGB; Donald Maclean; MI5; MI6; Kim Philby*]

CANARIS, WILHELM FRANZ
German Chief of Abwehr in World War II ▪ (1887–1944)

GERMANY'S TOP SPYMASTER FROM 1935 TO 1944 was a perpetual enigma to friends, associates, historians, and even himself. As Hitler's chief of intelligence before and during World War II, Wilhelm Franz Canaris worked secretly against the Nazis to destroy them and their tyrannical leader while trying to preserve and protect his country. He failed on both accounts but his efforts were heroic and admirable. Canaris was one of the few Germans who held power and rank in the Third Reich who plotted against its maniac leaders from the beginning, a powerful force, and ofter a lone voice, inside the Black Orchestra (the German underground) which sought to defeat the Nazis.

Carnaris was born New Year's Day 1887 in Aplerbeck, a small town near Dortmund, nestled in the Ruhr Valley. (He was supposedly a descendant of the nineteenth century Greek statesman Admiral Konstantine Kanaris.) The youngest of three children, Canaris' engineer father supervised an iron works and provided well for his family. Undersized and somewhat frail, Carnaris nevertheless lived out a normal boyhood and attended a Lutheran Church regularly with his family. He had one odd quirk as a child, a deep need to know what everyone was doing. His appetite for social knowledge was insatiable, his questions endless, so much so that he earned the nickname "Kieker," which translates to "Snooper." He was a born spy.

Following public schooling, Canaris entered the Imperial Naval Academy at Kiel on April 1, 1905. He proved to be a diligent student who ranked high in his class. He kept a log or ledger which documented the behavioral patterns of those he knew, a study in human nature, more or less, which documented the habits, speech patterns, and eccentricities of all who fell beneath his scrutinous gaze. It was a continuous exercise in observation, one which is second-nature to the espionage agent.

At the outbreak of World War I, Canaris saw duty on the light cruiser *Dresden*, part of Admiral Graf Spee's squadron that sailed into the battle of the Falkland Islands against a superior British force and was destroyed in December 1914. The *Dresden* had the dubious distinction of being the only warship in the German flotilla not sunk in the action.

All were taken prisoner, including young Lieutenant Canaris. He was interned with the others on the desolate Quiriquina Island near Valparaiso. The camp was rife with escape plots but Canaris took no part in these conspiracies. He resolved to escape alone. Stealing a small, leaky boat, he rowed to the mainland shore, then exchanged the boat for a horse. He rode the animal almost to death in an impossible trek over the Andes, reaching Argentina in the disguise of a Chilean named Reed Rosas. Using this alias, he managed to book passage on a Dutch steamer, *Frisia*, which sailed for Rotterdam. (Funds for the trip and a Chilean passport were supplied by the German Embassy in Buenos Aires.)

Disembarking at Rotterdam, Canaris made his way back to Germany where he was hailed by the Navy as a great hero and promoted to the rank of captain. He was given an audience with Kaiser Wilhelm who congratulated him and bestowed upon the youthful naval officer the Iron Cross, first class. Canaris, because of his ability to avoid detection in his flight from South America, was recruited by the German intelligence service and sent on an espionage mission to Spain,

Admiral Wilhelm Canaris, chief of the Abwehr, who established one of the world's greatest espionage agencies, then turned against Adolf Hitler and was executed for plotting the assassination of the tyrant.

working out of the German Embassy in Madrid where he spied upon Allied diplomats and military officers.

In Feburary 1916, Canaris was recalled to Berlin to be trained as a U-boat commander. He first undertook a spy mission to Switzerland and then crossed the Swiss border in the same disguise that had worked so well earlier, using the Chilean identity of Reed Rosas. At Domodosolla, however, Italian police suspected him of being a spy and imprisoned him. Canaris once again escaped.

Returning to Madrid, Canaris was then picked up by a German U-boat along the Spanish coast. Once back in Germany he underwent training for U-boat service and was given a submarine command. He skippered a U-boat in the Mediterranean throughout 1917. It was during this time that Canaris, on leave home, met Ericka Waag, the sister of a fellow naval officer. He would marry her, the only woman in his life, on November 22, 1919.

As the tide of war turned against Germany, Canaris was recalled to Berlin and held a number of intelligence posts until the end of hostilities in 1918. By then the Kaiser had abdicated and Germany was awash with political chaos. Dozens of political and military factions fought for control of the government, although the weak Weimar Republic was in nominal charge. The German militarists had no intention of allowing bumbling civilians to determine the destiny of the country. To influence its political direction, the Army and Navy placed officers inside the ranks of various political organizations. Canaris was one of these. He volunteered his services to the Weimar Republic, at the secret behest of his navy commanders.

From 1931 to 1932, Canaris was back at Kiel as chief of staff of all naval operations in that area. He was then given command of the ancient battleship *Schlesien*, a post he held until late 1934. At that time, Konrad Patzig, the head of German intelligence, the Abwehr, was being replaced. Admiral Erich Raeder had selected Canaris as Patzig's replacement.

Canaris reported to the Abwehr offices in Berlin on January 1, 1935, warmly welcomed by Patzig who told him how Heinrich Himmler, head of the German internal security (RSHA) and his henchman, Reinhard Heydrich, chief of political espionage, the SD (*Sicherheitsdienst*), had been trying to make inroads on the Abwehr and usurp its authority and operations, as well as replace it altogether with their own agencies.

"I am sorry for you, Captain," Patzig told Canaris, "because you don't seem to realize what a mess you are getting into."

Canaris responded with a smile, stating: "I think I know how to get along with them [Himmler and Heydrich]."

With that, Patzig went happily to the command of the *Admiral Scheer* and Canaris sat down behind the chief's desk in the somber offices of the Abwehr. From that day until his ouster in 1944, Wilhelm Canaris became one of the most powerful men in Germany.

Canaris first disarmed his enemies, Himmler and Heydrich, flattering them and feeding their gigantic egos. He socialized with Heydrich and even bought a home next to his. He gave Heydrich's children parties and candies. Though he was not a member of the Nazi Party, Canaris made sure that he appointed a Nazi diehard, Rudolf Bamler, as chief of the counterintelligence department of the Abwehr. Of course, Canaris tightly controlled Bamler, watching his subordinate's every move. (He would later arrange to have Bamler sent to the Eastern Front in World War II. Bamler would be captured, then become as fanatical a Communist as he had been a Nazi and would later work for East German intelligence.)

The Abwehr chief placated the Nazis, whom he secretly detested as uncultured, uneducated brutes and a threat to the long-range security and well-being of Germany. He meanwhile busily built up the Abwehr with the abiding thought of making it the finest intelligence service in the world. Canaris catagorized the new Abwehr into three groups of operations. Group I conducted espionage and gathered intelligence which was vastly enlarged. Group II concerned itself with sabotage, and its agents were trained at Quenzsee in Bavaria. Group III was devoted to counterespionage operations. All three groups were directly answerable to Canaris.

Canaris chose three men to head these groups, Group I, espionage, was run by Hans Piekenbrock, a wealthy, cordial, highly-educated man whose perspectives were identitical to his chief. Helmuth Groscurth headed Group II, sabotage. He was religious and hated the Nazis, as did his chief. Group III was headed by Bamler the ardent Nazi who served as Canaris' window dressing. To the ranks of the Abwehr Canaris invited the finest young officers he could find, both from the navy and army. He made sure that all of those assuming any authority at the Abwehr were not Nazi Party members.

The Abwehr chief worked tirelessly, fourteen to sixteen hours a day, sometimes sleeping at his offices. He immediately began to screen espionage spymasters for posts abroad. He intended to have top agents in every country in the world. To aid them, he asked the huge Telefunken Company to build a special "spy radio" which it did, one called Afu, a small, easily concealed radio set with tremendous power and long-range abilities. New Abwehr departments were created almost daily, including one in Berlin which created the most sophisticated tools of espionage of the day, from invisible inks to flour that could be used as an explosive.

Canaris next cemented relations with the Foreign Ministry, persuading Foreign Minister Joachim von Ribbentrop to allow Abwehr agents into every German Embassy and consulate around the world, agents who would appear to be political attachés but who would operate independently of Embassy staffs and answer only to the Abwehr and Canaris.

New, tough codes were developed for the Abwehr by Kurt Selchon who headed the cryptographic department of the Foreign Ministry. Canaris set up revolving bank accounts under codes in all major banks throughout the world, accounts from which his agents could draw operating funds. His budget was enormous, compared to other services, ten times that of the old Abwehr. Within nine months of taking over the department, Canaris had transformed the Abwehr from a lame, lackadaisical organization to a smoothly-running, effective intelligence agency.

Canaris was promoted to the rank of admiral in September 1935. Before that time, he had already met with Italian chiefs of intelligence and signed a cooperation pact with them to share information. He next established a similar relationship with Japanese intelligence. In both instances, he preempted Hitler's own pacts with these two countries who would later join the Third Reich as the Axis Powers.

Shortly after being promoted to admiral, Canaris was summoned to a meeting with Adolf Hitler at his mountain retreat in Bavaria. The meeting was a success. Canaris knew exactly what to tell the Fuhrer and what not to tell him. He knew that Hitler was wholly disinterested in espionage and had a profound contempt for spies. He was interested in the kind of social espionage that consisted of rumor and gossip about the wealthy and the powerful. This Canaris fed him regularly to Hitler's amusement.

Hitler was interested in information regarding certain countries, particularly Austria, the country of his birth for which he had been planning an *Anschluss*, Czechoslovakia, which he planned to take over piecemeal through iron fisted diplomacy or force of arms, Poland, and France, which, of course, he planned to invade and conquer. Canaris replied that the chief of Austrian intelligence, Major Erwin von Lahousen, had secretly joined with the Abwehr and was working against his own government. (Lahousen would later become Canaris' strongest Abwehr associate, as well as a devout anti-Nazi.)

Konrad Henlein, the Sudeten-German Nazi leader, had been recruited to the ranks of the Abwehr, Canaris assured Hitler, and the agency had spies providing invaluable information from Poland and France. When Canaris mentioned England, Hitler shook his head. He wanted no German spies in England. He would solve his differences with the British, he said, through diplomacy. He had no interest at all in receiving intelligence on the United States. This country was remote and would remain neutral, Hitler emphasized, no matter what happened on the bedevilled countinent of Europe.

When Canaris concluded this trip to see Hitler, he discovered to his amazement that the Abwehr had an army of spies in the country that least concerned Germany at that time, the United States. In the early 1920s, the then Abwehr chief Colonel Erich Fritz Gempp, had established a small network of German spies in the U.S. on behalf of the German Air Force, the so-called non-existent Luftwaffe which was secretly being rebuilt.

What was needed most was information on new engineering and equipment being developed, particularly in the U.S. To that end, Gemp sent a mild-mannered, long-faced airplane mechanic, William Lonkowski, to the U.S. This was an alias and his real name was never determined. He used the name Wilhelm Schneider when he arrived in Hoboken, New Jersey, on the liner *Berlin* on March 27, 1927. He would also use the names Bill Lonkis, Willie Meller, and William Sexton in the course of his long career of espionage in America but William Lonkowski would be used most and best remembered.

Given a $500-a-month allowance, Lonkowski identified himself as having been born in Germany in 1893, being married and working as a piano tuner. As an accomplished airplane mechanic (he had served in the Germany air force during World War I), Lonkowski had no difficulty in finding work at the Ireland Aircraft Corporation on Long Island. He was soon a supervisor and had the authority to hire and fire. He hired two more spies, Otto Herman Voss and Werner Georg Gudenberg, whom he put to work at Ireland Aircraft only days after they arrived from Germany.

After planting these two moles at Ireland, Lonkowski moved on to work for several more aircraft firms, hiring new German spies to take jobs where they could filch secret information on military aircraft. Voss and Gudenberg, in turn, moved on to new aircraft plants, hiring their own agents with Lonkowski's approval. Within four years there was few secrets regarding American warplanes that this now vast espionage ring had not stolen and delivered to their spymasters in Germany.

These stolen secrets included the top secrets plans for a "fireproof plane," blueprints for "the world's most powerful air-cooled motor" being constructed by the Wright Aeronautical Company for the U.S. Army, plans taken from the Curtiss Aeroplane and Motor Company which detailed the design of a pursuit plane that could land on a ship or on water. By the time Canaris had taken over the Abwehr, its U.S. spy network had stolen almost every plan or design for every important piece of ordnance, plane, ship, or weapon in America.

Thus the Abwehr knew every detail about all the planes being built at the Sikorsky Airplane Factory in Farmingdale, Long Island, the complete specifications of scout bombers being produced at Vought Aviation, all the blueprints of Boeing and Douglas bombers, information on the construction of warships of all kinds, secret army maps, tactical air exercises, patrol plane schedules throughout the Western Hemisphere, plans of a special army night bomber and classified radio equipment being built by the Lear Corporation.

There were so many spies in the U.S., that the Abwehr could not handle them all. Some of them were self-appointed such as the ardent Nazi, Dr. Ignatz Theodor Griebl, a prominent and wealthy doctor in Yorkville, the center of Manhattan's German community. Griebl paid his own expenses and hired his own spies in a large network consisting of German-Americans eager to aid the "New Germany."

Griebl combined his network with that of Lonkowski when Canaris took over the Abwehr, offering the German spy chief literally hundreds of espionage agents willing to steal any secret at any cost. These German agents worked in the Navy shipyards in Boston and Newport News, Va., a captain in the U.S. Army who provided all new data on infantry weapons, a draftsman in a naval architectual firm in New York, an engineer in the metallurgical department of the Federal Shipping and Drydock Company of Kearny, New Jersey.

Much of the information from America was funneled through the Abwehr offices in Wilhelmshaven and to Erich Pheiffer, a Navy officer and one of the shrewdest spymasters working for Canaris. Pheiffer in turn, showed the amazing cache of information from the U.S. to his chief. Canaris not only approved of the American spy network but immediately ordered it enlarged. Contrary to Hitler's orders, Canaris made the U.S. one of the Abwehr's chief targets. The wiley admiral told his staff that "the U.S.A. must be regarded as the decisive factor in any future war."

U.S. counterintelligence, such as it was in the offices of the FBI, had no inkling that the German espionage networks existed.

One of the most diligent of Canaris' American spies was Gustav Guellich, a dedicated bachelor and teetotaler who worked as metallurgical engineer in a division of U.S. Steel. He was recruited by Griebl and was soon delivering amazing secrets such as a new polarizing foil, deck guns for warships, a new underwater sound apparatus which came to be known as sonar, and, most importantly, the secret papers of the brilliant physicist Robert H. Goddard of Clark University in Worcester, Massachusetts, papers that detailed Goddard's experiments with rocket-propelled missiles.

So dedicated was Guellich that he took several trips to New Mexico to visit the area where Goddard conducted his experiments and he viewed these rocket launchings, describing them in detail for the Abwehr. Getting the specifications for the Norden Bombsight proved just as easy for the Abwehr in 1937. Developed separately by Carl T. Norden, Elmer Sperry, and Theodore H. Barth, the device allowed bombardiers to hit targets with pinpoint accuracy. The bombsight was the military prize most coveted by Germany.

In 1937, Canaris sent spymaster Major Nikolaus Ritter to the U.S. to organize another espionage ring. By good fortune, he met Hermann Lang, who worked at the Norden plant and who was easily convinced by Ritter to smuggle blueprints from the plant piece by piece, so that within weeks, the Abwehr had the complete details of the Norden Bombsight. The American public never knew until long after the war that the Germans had acquired this most secret device. Lang was arrested and imprisoned in 1941 when the FBI swept the U.S. almost clean of Abwehr agents but by then it was too late to protect the great secrets Lang and others had stolen.

Ritter's Abwehr network in the U.S. included many top level German spies. Everett Minster Roeder, an employee at Sperry Gyroscope, handily stole for Canaris the blueprints of all the radio equipment used in the new Glenn Martin bomber. Among the many prized secrets Roeder acquired were drawings of range-finders, blind-flying instruments, a navigator compass and a bank-and-turn indicator.

Washington-based Louis A. Matzhold, foreign correspondent for the *Berliner Boersen Zeitung*, a business tabloid for wealthy industrialists, worked as an Abwehr spy with an extraordinay contact. Matzhold told Canaris that he not only had direct access to the White House but he visited President Franklin D. Roosevelt several evenings a week. His reason for being in the President's Oval Office was to entertainingly barter for the rare new European stamps he was able to procure for Roosevelt's extensive stamp collection. During these chatty visits, Matzhold picked up quite a bit of information that proved useful to the Abwehr. It is impossible to prove or disprove Matzhold's claims since all visitors to the White House were not recorded. Canaris believed Matzhold's tales because his spy's information proved mostly to be correct. Matzhold reportedly continued his friendly relationship until just before Pearl Harbor in 1941 when he was reassigned to the Orient.

Another top spy in America was an old friend of Wilhelm Canaris, Count Frederick Sauerman, who had fled to Chile in 1919 with Canaris' help. The one-time Prussian nobleman had married Freda von Maltzahn, a tall, voluptuous blonde, and had lived comfortably in Chile until Canaris asked him to move to the U.S. and spy for the Abwehr in 1934.

Assuming his mother's Scottish maiden name of Douglas, the agent and his high-living wife moved to New York and plunged into cafe society. Canaris gave the couple $1,000 each month as salary and expenses. Their assignment was to keep watch on those heading German social groups, such as Dr. Hubert Schnuch, who organized a nationwide Nazi-American group of immigre Germans called Bunaste. Schnuch was a raving tyrant who insisted that he would topple the government by force of arms and turn the U.S. into a vassal state of Germany and that he had "10,000 men all over the country, ready and willing to lay down their lives for a Nazi America."

Count Douglas and his wife followed Schnuch from one social event to another, listening to his inane speeches where he would pound on tables, shriek Nazi slogans at the top of his voice and hurl mugs of beer at anyone who dared to challenge his fantasy of a Nazified United States. Schnuch demanded and got large amounts of money from his followers in the form of dues and fees. He kept his books secret and to learn the extent of his operation, Douglas arranged a tryst between the beer-gulping doctor and his statuesque wife to whom the demagogue was laciviously attracted. "Countess Douglas" seduced Schnuch, then, after he fell into a exhuasted stupor, examined his books. She discovered that Schnuch had been embezzling most of Bunaste's funds.

This Douglas reported to Anton Haegle, Schnuch's second-in-command, who immediately exposed the thieving doctor. Schnuch packed his bags and vanished. The Bunaste group splintered and the Douglas couple went on spying for Canaris, this time moving between Washington and New York. They befriended several prominent Washington couples who invited them to high society dinners. At one dinner, in 1940, the Douglases were seated next to chief of staff General George C. Marshall. Normally taciturn, Marshall surprisingly told the Douglases that Iceland, Greenland, and the Azores would be used as air bases for the Allies.

The information was immediately reported to Canaris who passed on the information to Goering and the Luftwaffe. The important dinner guests sitting next to the affable Douglas couple never knew that they were providing Canaris with information on fighterplane range-finders, new air-cooled machine-guns, and a host of other secrets. For this information, the Abwehr paid well. The Douglases lived in luxury as did other agents working for Canaris.

Canaris targeted the Panama Canal and Pearl Harbor as the most strategic and sensitive offshore areas of U.S. security. He zeroed in on the Canal because its passage allowed the U.S. fleet to quickly cover two oceans and it was the central shipping point for vast amounts of supplies carried from one end of the U.S. continent to the other by endless cargo vessels. From the early 1930s, the Canal Zone was brimming with Japanese, Italian, and even Russian spies. The Abwehr did not establish a full-scale espionage operation in the area until early 1938.

Canaris sent Captain Hermann Menzel to the Canal. He was the Abwehr's chief of naval intelligence in Berlin, a precise, no-nonsense spymaster who quickly appointed Kurt Lindberg as resident spy director in Panama. Lindberg had been the manager of the Hamburg-America passenger line and was the German Consul in Colon. Lindberg's job was to determine the exact military strength of American forces in Panama, the number of warships and cargo vessels that went through the Canal on a daily basis, the military installations along the entire length of the Canal, and the schedules of U.S. air patrols that flew over the Canal.

Lindberg organized the German-American workers in the area into several spy rings along the Canal, men who had long-standing jobs as stevadores, crane operators, mechanics, masons, machinists. Soon information sought by Canaris was flowing to Germany. One ring was headed by Hans Heinrich Schackow, who had been trained at the Abwehr school in Hamburg. His assistant was a sexy 19-year-old secretary, Ingeborg Guttmann who acted as Schackow's courier and often compromised sea captains into her bed to obtain vital shipping information.

On the American East Coast, dozens of Abwehr spies in the late 1930s collected every bit of information requested by their spymasters in Germany. All American shipping information was collected by an Abwehr ring headed by Kurt Frederick Ludwig whose communications to his spymasters in Germany appeared to be seemingly innocuous letters to his wife in Munich. The letters were carefully coded to reveal all manner of shipping information from Boston to Baltimore. Ludwig loved fast cars and even had a powerful shortwave radio built into one of his autos so that he could contact the Abwehr while on the run.

Though Hitler had pooh-poohed the presence of German spies in America, a country which interested him not a bit, he was almost pathologically opposed to Canaris sending any spies to England, a country he oddly respected, one which he said he would subdue through the genius of his diplomacy and not through subterfuge. Yet, in spite of the Fuhrer's ban on German agents in England, an Abwehr spy was sent to that country in 1935, 45-year-old Dr. Hermann Goertz. Canaris had been pressured into sending Goertz by Luftwaffe chief Hermann Goering who wanted up-to-date reports on RAF installations.

To that end, Goertz, accompanied by a pretty, 19-year-old assistant, Marianne Emig, whom he introduced as his "typist," traveled to England in style, renting a rural cottage and telling one and all that he was completing a book about England. Goertz and Emig bicycled about the countryside photographing RAF landing bases. In some instances, Emig distracted guards while Goertz sketched the installations. One guard became suspicious and reported the couple.

The report reached Colonel Hinchley Cooke of MI5 who asked the Special Branch of Scotland Yard to keep the couple under surveillance. Goertz and Emig then hastily departed for Germany, only because the secretary had fearful apprehensions and demanded that Goertz take her home. Goertz returned alone but by this time his luggage, which he had left behind in the cottage, had been inspected and his spy gear discovered. He was arrested, charged with violating the Secrets Act and was given a four-year sentence.

When news of Goertz's arrest broke, Hitler exploded, telling Carnaris that "I don't want any wretched spies creeping about England and upsetting my plans!" He ordered Canaris not to send another spy to England unless he approved of such operations. Hitler felt that his personnel agent, Baron William S. de Ropp, would keep him informed of events in England. De Ropp was a Baltic-born (1877) nobleman whose impoverished parents had once owned vast tracts of land on his father's side and whose Russian mother was related to the Romanovs.

It was through de Ropp that Hitler felt he received his best "inside information," on England's attitude toward him and Germany, although some believed that de Ropp was a double spy really working for England. De Ropp visited England regularly to meet with the cream of British society, operating loosely as an agent of Alfred Rosenberg, who headed Germany's Political Office. The strutting, egocentric Rosenberg felt superior to all in the Nazi Party and enlarged his spy network in England without informing Canaris.

Meanwhile, Canaris' far-flung spy networks worked around the clock on Hitler's behalf. More and more the dictator came to rely on the Abwehr. In 1936, it was Canaris who secretly financed the Spanish Civil War, sending money and arms to General Emilio Mola, one of the fascist generals who supported the army rebellion of Francisco Franco, who, in 1939, took power in Spain and remained an uneasy ally of the Third Reich.

It was Canaris who secured for Hitler the secret pacts between the Soviet Union and France in 1935 and that between Russia and Czechoslovakia before these pacts were signed. In 1936, Canaris also obtained information from a high level source in the French government that if Hitler defied the Versaillse Treaty and reoccupied the Rhineland, not a single French soldier would be sent to turn back the Germans. So confident of Canaris' information was Hitler that he overruled his apprehensive generals and ordered his small occupation force to march into the Rhineland.

Shortly before the outbreak of World War II in 1939, Canaris' counterintelligence operations throughout Germany were so effective that it eliminated every British agent working for SIS, and arrested its top spymaster, Dr. Otto Krueger, who committed suicide in his cell on September 4, 1939. Two years earlier, however, Hitler had removed his ban on having German agents in England and Canaris sent scores of agents to Great Britain. One of these was Joseph Kelly who worked at the Chorley Munitions Factory and who stole designs and plans for the Germans, delivering them to Germany and then returning on a channel steamer.

Kelly, who had volunteered his services to the Abwehr for a price by boldly visiting Dr. Walther Reinhardt, the Consul General in Liverpool, was paid £30 for the secrets he delivered in Germany in 1939. His unexpected vacation to Germany, however, was not ignored by plant supervisors who alerted MI5 agents and the Special Branch of Scotland Yard. Kelly was arrested as he was returning from Germany, almost the minute he dismebarked from a channel steamer. Freshly printed pound notes were found on him.

Kelly blurted that he had won the money from a man on the boat in a poker game. Investigators saw that Kelly was chewing hard while under interrogation. An agent forced open his mouth and withdrew a wet wad of paper on which was written Abwehr codes. Kelly was convicted of espionage and given a seven-year sentence.

Another Abwehr spy in England, Donald Owen Reginald Adams, obtained the specifications of a 4.5-inch anti-aircraft gun from the Woolrich Arsenal and sold this to the Abwehr and was then detected and arrested by MI5. Though Canaris' spies kept falling into the hands of MI5 and Scotland Yard, he kept sending more and more to England, until he had obtained just about every known secret in the country, not the least of which were maps, and aerial and land photos of all docks, warehouses, harbors, oil supply areas, throughout the country.

When Hitler decided to go to war, he immediately summoned Admiral Wilhelm Canaris. Hitler and Major General Erich Fritz von Manstein, chief of staff of Army Group South, met with Canaris. Manstein showed him the detailed plans he had worked out for the invasion of Poland. An incident, however, was required. The Poles had to provoke the invasion. A plan was worked out. About 350 Abwehr men, all trained at the Brandenburg Training Camp, nicknamed Brandenburgers, would dress in Polish army uniforms and attack a small German radio station at Gleiwtiz on the Polish-German border.

At the last minute, Hitler substituted the Brandenburgers for SS men commanded by his trusted henchman and ruthless killer, Heinrich Himmler. The raid was staged by Himmler's protege, Reinhard Heydrich and carried out by Heydrich's most slavish enforcer, Alfred Helmut Naujocks. One man was killed, an inmate from a German concentration camp who was brought to Gleiwitz and murdered, a killing later blamed on the so-called invading Polish troops. The fake troops shot up the radio station, then disappeared. This "provocation" was used by Hitler to then invade Poland and start World War II.

Canaris' Brandenburgers were used to secure key passes and roadways before the Germany army advanced. These men parachuted into strategic areas, killed and captured Polish troops, then waited for the German army to arrive. It arrived with devastating fury. Within twenty-seven days Poland was defeated in the most awesome military onslaught the world had ever witnessed. It was Hitler's *blitzkrieg*, lightning war. It was achieved through the exhaustive work of the Abwehr and Wilhelm Canaris.

All of Poland's airfields had been pinpointed for the Luftwaffe by Abwehr agents, as well as all of its secret transportation routes, railroads, arms and oil dumps, armament centers, munitions areas. The Luftwaffe knew exactly what and where to bomb and thus disabled the large and modern Polish armed forces. Canaris appeared to enjoy his initial success but when he heard that Great Britian had declared war, he said solemnly: "If England comes into this, it will be the end of our poor Germany."

Up to the beginning of the war, Canaris had served Hitler and the Third Reich with considerable loyalty. When he received the reports of how SS and Gestapo murder squads had followed the army into Poland to wreak massacres, his stomach turned. So did his loyalty. The murder squads were killing Catholic priests and Polish aristocracy in appalling numbers. Canaris traveled to Ilnau to confront Hitler in his private train.

General Wilhelm Keitel, Hitler's chief of staff, stopped the Abwehr chief before he could see the Fuhrer. The normally mild-mannered Canaris was in a rage, almost shouting at Keitel: "I have information that mass executions are being planned in Poland and that members of the Polish nobility and that Catholic Bishops and priests have been singled out for extermination. I feel obliged to give you a word of warning. For such outrages the world will eventually blame the Wehrmacht, if only because it acquiesced in these unheard-of atrocities."

Keitel held up a hand to silence him. "If I were you, Herr Canaris, I would not get mixed up in this business! This 'thing' has been decided upon by the Fuhrer himself." He went on to emphasize that the Gestapo and the SS, at Hitler's direct orders, would conduct a regular "racial extermination program." (Keitel would later be tried as a war criminal at Nuremburg and executed.)

Canaris stood silent in shock and when Hitler approached him he could barely manage a greeting. He thought to protest directly to Adolf Hitler but realized the futility of challenging an order so emphatically directed by Germany's head of state. At that moment, Wilhelm Canaris decided to work against the monster he had helped so diligently to create.

England, indeed, was to prove the constant thorn in the Nazi side. At war's outbreak, more than 7,000 "unreliables" were rounded up and hundreds of Abwehr agents seeded in England in previous years were exposed, arrested, imprisoned. Astoundingly, many of Canaris best agents escaped the dragnet and were soon broadcasting their reports to Berlin. All of these agents, however, had either been turned as British double agents who would continue to feed the Germans useless information throughout the war, or were British agents from MI5 impersonating the original Abwehr spies.

As Germany prepared to move West against France and England, the Abwehr flooded Belgium and Holland with agents, gathering information for Hitler's planned invasion of those neutral countries. It worked with Major Vidkun Quisling of Norway to undermine that country's defenses in a lightning conquest of that country. Abwehr spies in Norway, Hermann Kempf and E. Pruck, had financed traitor Quisling in developing a pro-Nazi Norwegian cadre of disloyal officers. These officers would make sure that their troops did not fire on the German invasion fleet sailing into its fjords with three divisions of crack troops.

The actual invasion of Norway in 1940 was designed by Hitler to occur on April 9, 1940. Canaris, who was by then an avowed secret foe of the dictator, actually warned the Danish and Norwegian military attachés in Berlin where and when the invasion would take place but the officers received this information with disbelief, thinking the Abwehr was duping them into a false invasion date. That the Abwehr provided little or no information (on the excuse that it had not been permitted enough time) on Norway was a dismal fact. General Nikolaus von Folkenhorst, who commanded the invasion troops, was compelled to buy a guide of Norway to familiarize himself with the terrain of a country about which he knew nothing.

When the German invasion fleet entered the Oslo fjord, its commanders were dumbfounded as the Norwegian shore batteries opened up. Shells landed directly on the cruiser *Bluecher*, sinking it. The cruiser *Emdem* was badly damaged and the fleet withdrew while smug German officers waiting to greet the invaders at the docks quaked in shock, then retreated to their Embassy. When Hitler heard this

devastating news, he went berserk, ranting and raving at his general staff for its lack of preparedness.

Canaris came to Hitler's rescue, however, but not out of his own doing. His top agent in Oslo, Hermann Kempf saved the day. He managed to make a phone call to Canaris in Berlin to inform him that a small detachment of German paratroopers had seized the airport at Fornebu and were holding it. Canaris called the high command and a full German division was immediately flown to the captured airstrip. Oslo, which had resisted the invaders from the sea in the morning, collapsed because Norwegian traitors had guided paratroopers to its main airfield and was in German hands by nightfall.

France and the Lowlands were next. Thanks to Abwehr agents, who were both French and German, many French fortifications were abandoned or quickly surrendered by Nazi "fifth columnists." Many French officers belonged to pro-Nazi organizations and sabotaged defenses or surrendered without a fight. Those who did fight were beaten back to Dunkirk by Hitler's tank corps which crossed huge territories in sweeping, non-stop movements. There, more than 300,000 exhausted British soldiers and some French troops were rescued by a great flotilla of every conceivable boat and taken to England.

England was the last holdout, the final conquest in the West envisioned by Hitler's grand scheme. His generals hastily put together plans for the invasion of England, Operation Sea Lion. Landing craft of all sorts and massive amounts of troops and armor were assembled along the French coast near Pas de Calais. Canaris was told by the High Command to send scores of agents to England to prepare the way for the invasion forces. Yet, Hitler, seemed ambiguous when it came time to put his plans into action. He played with the idea of attacking the British bastion of Gibraltar from Spain. He told Canaris: "If, for any reason 'Sea Lion' would have to be postponed, I want to seize Gibraltar."

Although he ordered several companies of quickly trained agents to slip into England, Canaris devoted most of his attention to Operation Felix, the attack on Gibraltar. His attentions were also drawn to helping the Italians in Albania, dealing with a plot to overthrow King Carol of Rumania, and espionage operations in Afghanistan and North Africa.

The Abwehr agents in England met disaster at every turn and all were promptly arrested by police and soldiers. Convicted of espionage during war time, death sentences were given, and, all were hanged in December 1940 at Pentonville Prison.

There were a number of double spies who worked for the Germans but who really worked for the English. Hans Hansen was one of these, going to England in 1940 and ostensibly finding work on a farm. He would travel throughout the countryside and report by radio to Abwehr headquarters the number of barrage balloons in certain cities, the railroad timetables for supply shipments, troop dispositions, all the British activity of war. This he did faithfully from 1940 to 1945 until there existed no Abwehr headquarters to which he could send his messages.

Hansen had been a British agent all along and when he reached England, he pretended to serve his Abwehr masters, sending information to them which has been approved by his British spymasters. Hansen and others had been "turned" by MI5 and continued to play out their Abwehr spy roles throughout World War II. Ironically, the Abwehr continued to finance their activities, paying Hansen and others more than £85,000. MI5 used this money to finance its entire operation in which it hoodwinked the Abwehr into believing it had a loyal network of agents in England when none existed at all.

Once war started, the activities of Canaris' Abwehr agents were limited inside enemy countries. The most fertile espionage ground was Switzerland and here Canaris' spies did admirably well, obtaining secret information on Allen Dulles' OSS operations and even penetrating the much-vaunted Swiss intelligence service of Colonel Roger Masson. Thus, Canaris learned of President Roosevelt's clandestine meeting with Winston Churchill aboard a British warship in Placentia Bay when they formed the Atlantic Charter.

This kind of information went directly from Canaris to Hitler but the Fuhrer was seemingly indifferent to what Roosevelt and America were planning. He felt that the U.S. was wholly isolationist and would remain so, despite the machinations of "the lunatic in the White House," as Hitler and his propagandists consistently referred to F.D.R.

After the fall of France, Canaris met with Hitler to discuss a detailed Abwehr report which maintained that the giant U.S. aircraft industry could quickly produce 50,000 war planes. Hitler took one look at the report, then roared at Canaris: "Did you say fifty-thousand planes? You must be out of your mind to take such crap seriously! Fifty-thousand rubber tranquilizers maybe for the poor little babies of America, but fifty-thousand planes! Don't be ridiculous!"

Far from ridiculous was the information Abwehr spies gleaned in the very embassies and consulates of the Allies throughout World War II. In Antwerp, the U.S. Embassy employed a Belgium national, Jennie LaMarie, as a secretary. She was hard-working and conscientious and liberally filched every important document she could for the Abwehr, along with much-coveted blank American passports. In Ankara, in neurtral Turkey, Elyeza Bazna, who later be known as the notorious "Cicero," looted the British Embassy of its secrets for the Germans.

Abwehr Sabotage in the U.S. shortly before and during World War II, according to the FBI was non-existent, yet thousands of fires, explosions and other disasters befalling French and British manufacturing plants, shipping companies, cargo vessels went unexplained throughout the early period of World War II. Abwehr spies and saboteurs in the U.S., headed by

Karl Berthold Franz Rekowski and Anastase Andreyevich Vonsiatsky, reportedly brought about much of this widespread destruction. Vonsiatsky was a colorful character who reveled in cloak and dagger operations.

After marrying an American millionairess, Marion Ream, Vonsiatsky financed a Ukranian fascist party, building up a paramilitary organization on the secluded and well-guarded Ream estate in Thompson, Connecticut. He was pro-Nazi and a rabid Hitlerite who traveled about America meeting with people like German bundist Gerhard Kunze to plan sabotage. On Vonsiatsky's payroll were such notorious agents as Fedior "Firebug" Wozniak, who was considered by some to be the most infamous saboteur of World War I.

The chief Abwehr spy rings in the U.S., however, collapsed in late 1941, when William G. Sebold, a German-American who was supposed to be working diligently for the Germans, betrayed the Duquesne ring which the FBI arrested *en masse*. With direct Abwehr agents completely out of action in the U.S., Canaris shifted his attentions to Spain, his favorite espionage ground. If he could not effectively spy in America with German agents, he concluded, he would use Spanish agents.

The dictatorship of Francisco Franco was largely established due to the financing of Franco's 1936 rebellion by Canaris. Franco therefore felt a deep obligation to the Abwehr, one which Canaris called upon in 1940. He met with General Campos Martinez, head of the antiquated Spanish Secret Service, an organization that was so woefully outdated that its cryptographic procedures predated World War I. Moreover, Canaris had more German espionage agents (about 1,500) operating in Spain than the Spanish had throughout the world.

Spain, however, was a neutral country in World War II, and, as such, continued to maintain embassasies and consulates in all of the Allied countries. These would be the sources of Canaris' information. He had the full backing of Franco, who ordered all of his diplomats in the U.S. and Britain to actively spy for the Germans. They would answer to Canaris' World War I comrade Wilhelm Leissner, who operated as the Abwehr chief in Spain under the alias of Gustav Lenz.

When the Spanish diplomats proved indifferent, even truculent to spying for the Abwehr, Canaris had Leisser employ several fanatical Falangists (fascists) who had helped Franco win his civil war. Franco, from the time he took power in 1939, attempted to distance himself from his most ardent Falangist supporters. More than 30,000 of his most fanatical Falangists—the bruttish dregs of Spanish society— were formed into the Blue and Arrow divisions and, responding to demands by Hitler for aid in 1941, shipped off to the Russian front to fight alongside their Nazi counterparts. Franco expected that these most zealous of his followers, and the most difficult to control, would never return to Spain. They didn't.

A Spanish agent in England sent to the Abwehr in March 1941 a detailed report of the effectiveness of the Luftwaffe's bombing of London. In September 1941, the same Abwehr agent sent to Canaris a complete profile of the British Army which had been all but destroyed following the exodus from Dunkirk in 1940 and how it had to be completely reorganized.

As the war progressed and Germany's fortunes dipped, the Abwehr's power in Spain and Portugal diminished. However, it flourished in Shanghai, as it did in Vienna, Warsaw and Sweden. The Abwehr had a spectacular agent in Sweden, a German banker of noble but, of all things, Jewish birth. He was Baron Waldemar von Oppenheim, a member of an ancient German-Jewish family which had gleaned its wealth over the centuries in banking in Rhine province. Oppenheim, born in 1894, had served with distinction as an officer in an elite regiment during World War I, then went to work for the family's enormous and internationally successful bank in Cologne.

Like many German-Jews who thought of themselves German first and Jewish second, Oppenheim was a nationalist who gave his wholehearted support to his county. Before Hitler came to power in 1933, Oppenheim joined a Nazi banking group, which was probably a move to protect and preserve his family's increasingly tenuous banking position as businessmen, industrialists, and financial leaders in Germany, hopping onto Hitler's bandwagon. He suffered the indignity of being labeled a "second-degree bastard" by the Nazis who considered him only partly Jewish and therefore less repugnant than a full-fledged Jew. Such mindless categorizations were typical of the idiotic rascist geneologies conjured by "Ayran experts" in the Nazi Party.

Oppenheim withdrew from the Nazi Party's banking organization in the mid-1930s and busied himself with managing the international banking transactions of his family's bank in Cologne. Early in the war, however, he was recuited—bullied is more the word—into the Abwehr. Because much of his business was done in Sweden with the powerful Wallenberg family, Canaris felt that Oppenheim, a respected Jewish banker, would be the last person anyone would suspect of being a spy. After his training, Oppenheim was sent to Sweden. Through his contacts with the Wallenbergs he was able to learn about Allied convoys and arms manufacturing, especialy the production of tanks in the U.S. This information Oppenheim fed back to the Abwehr.

It was Oppenheim who provided the important report on the top secret Arcadia Conference between Roosevelt and Churchill in which it was decided that the European theater would be the focal point of the Allied war. When Canaris presented this report to Hitler, the dictator realized its significance. The Allies were, first and foremost, coming after the Nazi Third Reich and Adolf Hitler.

For several years, Oppenheim served Canaris well but he was finally allowed to "retire" as the Allies invaded Europe. He was promised that his Abwehr files would be burned but Oppenheim's dossier was seized by G-2 (U.S. Army intelligence) before it and thousands of others could be put to the torch by retreating Abwehr officials.

Canaris badly blundered, as did the whole of his vast Abwehr operations, when, in 1942, U.S. and British troops invaded North Africa. The Abwehr failed to learn about the vast convoy which sailed across the Atlantic to reach the shores of French Morocco. Canaris was too busy formulating a plan to attack Gibraltar. He personally visited the area with some of his top aides, directing intelligence gathering operations and also preparing an invasion plan. He envisioned leading the invasion of Gibraltar himself. This invasion never took place.

Events soon began to overrun the Abwehr's ability to learn about them before they happened. Allied forces in Italy had made such dramatic headway that Mussolini's legions melted away and the eight German divisions in Italy were left to fight on alone, trapped. Italian radio abruptly announced that the fascist regime of twenty-one years was over, finished.

Hitler was stunned. Canaris had told him nothing of the possible coming of this event, as had been the case of the North African invasion. But, instead of ranting against his Abwehr chief, who claimed to be ignorant of the lightning governmental moves in Italy, Hitler ordered him to save his fellow dictator, Mussolini, who had been placed under arrest. Canaris, however, had known all along that Mussolini was on thin ice and would be ousted. His agents had penetrated the conspiracy to remove the dictator and had filed several detailed reports with Canaris. The admiral did nothing and said nothing. By then he resolved to aid Hitler and the Nazis as little as possible. He believed that with the fall of Italy, the Axis would also collapse.

Canaris fed Hitler one brazen lie after another about Italy, telling the Fuhrer that the Italian army and civilians would continue to resist the Allies, when he knew that tens of thousands of Italian soldiers were, at that moment, throwing away their guns. He told Hitler that his impeccable sources in Italy assured him that the Italian government was firm in continuing the war against the Allies when he knew that the Italians were desperately attempting to distance themselves from the Germans and negotiate a separate peace with the Allies.

In the end, Hitler realized that Mussolini's ouster was genuine. He ordered German commandoes under the leadership of daredevil Otto Skorzeny to rescue the fallen Italian dictator which they did, momentarily restoring the Duce to power and prolonging the war in Italy. As each battle was lost by the Germans, Hitler's faith in Canaris waned. Eager and ambitious, Walter Schellenberg provided the

Fuhrer with a special dossier he had been building for years which showed the Abwehr's failures. On February 19, 1944, Hitler fired Canaris and replaced him with Schellenberg.

Made chief of the Department of Economic Warfare in Potsdam, Canaris busied himself with intriguing against the Nazis. After his departure, the Abwehr went into steep decline and within another year hardly functioned as a servicable intelligence agency. The little admiral continued to confuse the Nazis and save those he could from their savage reprisals. In one instance, while he was at the Abwehr, he saved seven Jews from being sent to a concentration camp and certain death by going personally to Himmler, complaining that his Gestapo was arresting his agents. The seven were turned over to the Abwehr and taught a few codes, then smuggled out of Germany.

Canaris was also one of the key figures who seriously entered the conspiracy of the Black Orchestra (underground) to overthrow Hitler in 1944. Before the military cabal attempted to assassinate Hitler on July 20, 1944, Canaris learned that Himmler suspected certain officers who were actually part of the plot. Canaris warned these men who nevertheless went ahead with the attempt which ended with Hitler suviving the bombing of his field headquarters.

Thousands were rounded up and imprisoned as suspects in the abortive assassination. One of these was Canaris. He was imprisoned and sentenced to death. Heinrich Himmler inexplicably, preserved Canaris' life, however, by sending him to a concentration camp in Flossenberg. From time to time, for no apparent reason, the dreaded Himmler would perform small acts of mercy. In Canaris' case, Himmler's actions might be explained in that he feared the one-time Abwehr chief had collected information on him and by saving Canaris would prevent any incriminating documents from reaching Hitler.

In the closing days of the war, however, Hitler, half-mad and frantic to crush all those whom he felt had betrayed him, reached out to anyone still alive he could murder. In March 1945, he personally signed Canaris' death sentence. The weary old admiral was horribly executed. He was dragged from his cell naked, paraded before hooting SS guards and then hanged, his corpse left to rot, an ignoble end to one of the great spymasters of the century.

[ALSO SEE: *Abwehr; Elyeza Bazna; Black Orchestra; Allen Dulles; Ian Fleming; Gestapo; Reinhard Heydrich; Heinrich Himmler; Tyler Kent; Simon E. Koedel; Erwin von Lahousen; Alfred Helmut Naujocks; Operation Pastorius; OSS; Nikolaus Ritter; RSHA; William G. Sebold; SIS; Otto Herman Voss*]

CARBONARI
Italian Underground Organization ▪ (1806–1831)

IN 1806, NAPOLEON'S ARMIES DEFEATED THE BOURBON monarchy and occupied southern Italy. Among his forces were certain French officers who formed a secret underground organization called the Carbonari. Its aim was to establish a republic in southern Italy by overthrowing Joseph Bonaparte, Napoleon's brother, whom the emperor had named King of Naples.

The Carbonari sabotaged French ships and armaments and attempted to create political dissension throughout southern Italy, urging violent uprisings. When Napoleon was defeated at Waterloo and exiled in 1815, the Carbonari rose but its rebellion was quickly suppressed by the Bourbon monarchy which replaced Bonaparte's regime. Again, in 1831, the Carbonari caused a widespread rebellion but this revolt was also crushed and the Carbonari disbanded.

CARRANZA, RAMON
Spanish Spymaster in Canada ▪ (1861– ?)

PERHAPS THERE EXISTS IN THE LAST ONE HUNDRED years no spymaster of any country more bumbling and incompetent than Ramon Carranza, who headed the Spanish intelligence service, such as it was, in Canada during the Spanish-American War. He was a dashing, flamboyant naval attaché in Washington, D.C., in 1898. When the American battleship *Maine* blew up in Havana Harbor, war was declared against Spain. Poloy Bernabe, the Spanish Minister in Washington, D.C., was formally handed his passports, as were all on his staff, and ordered to leave the U.S. Bernabe and staff departed for Spain via Canada, including the volatile Ramon Carranza. In Montreal, however, Carranza remained behind, stating to Canadian authorities that he was obliged to clean up some legation affairs. Those affairs involved espionage and sabotage against the U.S. government.

Renting a house on Tupper Street in Montreal and a hotel suite in Toronto, Carranza was flush with American money, paying and tipping lavishly in U.S. currency for everything. Carranza's spending habits had been extravagant in the U.S. and had brought him to the attention of the Secret Service of the U.S. Treasury, which suspected him of using counterfeit money.

A Secret Service agent rented a room next to Carranza's and overheard him talking with an ex-seaman, George Downing, who used the alias of Harry Rawlins. Downing had been born in England but was a naturalized American citizen. He had served for a time on the U.S. cruiser *Brooklyn*, and he convinced Carranza that he was some sort of naval expert and, for a heavy price, would undertake a mission to Washington, D.C. where he would learn about the movement of U.S. warships, especially those assigned to waters near Spanish territories such as Cuba and the Philippines.

Typical of the quixotic Carranza, he did not check Downing's background and had no way of knowing whether his spy recruit had any expertise in the art of espionage which he did not. He foisted several hundred dollars on Downing, promising much more after Downing obtained information on the deployment of the U.S. ships. Downing immediately took a train heading for Washington. He was followed every step of the way by Secret Service agents.

In Washington, Downing, using the alias of Alexander Cree, checked into a boarding house, then went directly to the Navy Department to visit an old friend, a cipher clerk. The friend unwittingly told him that he had just sent a coded message to the Navy Yard in San Francisco which ordered the cruiser *Charleston* to Manila, along with 500 troops and replacement equipment for warships under the command of Commodore George Dewey.

Downing scurried back to his boarding house and wrote a report of this secret information in plain English. Then, about an hour later, he stepped from the house and mailed a letter to Canada, addressed to a Frederick W. Dobson, which was Carranza's cover name. Secret Service agents asked postal inspectors to intercept the letter which they did. Downing was then promptly arrested, charged with treason, an offense in war time punishable by death, and imprisoned.

Before he was brought to trial, Downing hanged himself in his cell. When hearing the news that this spy was dead, Carranza merely shrugged and went looking for new agents. His methods were crude if not outright stupid. He placed ads in Canadian newspapers, offering to pay any Canadians "in search of high adventure" a great deal of money. A few Canadians answered the ads and they were lavishly wined and dined by Carranza, then taken to his suite where he explained his offer.

The prospective spies were to join the American army or navy. When they arrived in the Philippines or in Cuba, they were to learn all they could about the U.S. military operations against the Spanish, and then desert, going to the nearest Spanish commander to make their report. The agent would be given a gold ring with a special insignia which would identify him as a Carranza agent to the Spanish commander.

After listening to this hairbrained scheme, the few applicants quickly withdrew and Carranza was left with no would-be spies. One of the applicants was interviewed by a Secret Service agent and was told: "This fellow wanted me to join your navy, count the warships, then swim ashore and find a Spanish general to tell him about it. Can you beat that?"

Realizing that he could not recruit spies through newspaper ads, Carranza hired a less-than-reputable Canadian detective agency to find his recruits for him. The agency, after some time, produced two impoverished English sailors. Carranza bought them a huge dinner and then got them drunk on champagne. In their drunken stupors, they agreed to become spies for Spain. Carranza gave them some gold pieces and told them to report to him in the morning. When the two sailors woke up with banging hangovers, they staggered to the skipper of a British ship on which they had served and told him the whole story.

The British captain paid for the sailors' passage home to England and then informed American authorities of the plot. More Secret Service agents were assigned to watch Carranza in Canada, as well as the detective agency that was recruiting for him. Moreover, U.S. authorities began screening all telegrams sent to Toronto and Montreal from the U.S., believing that any of Carranza's recruited spies would attempt to contact the spymaster in that fashion. Their theory proved correct.

The Canadian detective agency had produced another espionage applicant named Miller. He left Montreal and traveled to Tampa, Florida, attempting to enlist at the Army camp there. Miller sent a telegram to a man named Siddall in Montreal. Agents tracked the recepient to a Montreal saloon where he worked as a bartender. Siddall admitted he had "rented" the use of his name and bar to a "rich foreigner." who was identified as Carranza. (Miller was arrested and jailed. He later died in his cell of typhus.)

Then a letter to Miller from Carranza was intercepted in which the Spanish spy chief gave Miller bold instructions on how to get the information he was seeking. The letter, along with other evidence, was presented to the Canadian government which quickly moved to oust Carranza. He was told that he had violated Canadian neutrality and was ordered to pack up and leave the country immediately. Carranza, complaining and yelling empty threats, was put aboard a boat sailing for Spain. He remains one of the most inept spymasters in espionage history, a comical figure really who had no idea of how to accomplish his mission.

CARRE, MATHILDE (AKA: THE CAT)
French Double Agent for Germany in World War II ▪ (1908–1971?)

FEW FEMALE SPIES OF WORLD WAR II MATCHED THE fantastic exploits of Mathilde Carre, who was known as "The Cat." She was a sultry Parisian, long-legged, with jet-black hair cut short in bangs, and expressive eyebrows arching over large, piercing green eyes. He mouth was wide and sensuous and her voluptuous body attracted men young and old. She used her earthy beauty to learn the secrets of the Germans, then the French, then the British, as a double, then triple spy. She gave her national allegiance to those who rewarded her best. She was a whore, a traitor, a liar, a killer and, most of all, an ingenious spy.

Born Mathilde-Lucie Belard in central France in 1908, Carre moved to Paris with her parents as a teenager. Almost at whim she married Maurice Carre and moved with him to North Africa where he became a teacher at a military school. Learning that her husband was impotent, or so she later claimed, Carre then carried on affairs with wealthy Muslims.

By the time World War II began, Carre was a notorious trollop but when she returned to France, she reformed. When France fell in 1940, Carre returned to her family. Her father, who was an engineer and had fought in World War I, receiving France's Legion of Honor, introduced her to several patriots who refused to recognize Vichy, the new French puppet government controlled by the Nazis.

One of these underground leaders was Captain Roman Czeriavski who had fought the Germans as a Polish air force fighter pilot in the short-lived Polish resistance against the German invaders in 1939. Carre was enamored of the dashing Czeriavski who established with others the Interallié, the Paris underground that worked with the British SOE (Special Operations Executive, the London-based espionage organization that supervised resistance in occupied France). Czeriavski used the code name "Armand," and quickly recruited Carre into the ranks of the Interallié.

She learned codes and how to transmit ciphered messages on a short-wave, becoming Czeriavski's top radio operator and controller of messages between Paris and London. Carre also became an expert in the use of invisible inks and could soon identify almost any German army or air force unit, along with its type of armament, battle strength, and specialty applications in the field. For a short period, Carre actually worked at the Deuxiéme Bureau in Vichy before moving back to Paris with Czeriavski and Interallié's newly established headquarters in the Rue de Baubourg St. Jacques.

Interallié soon became the largest and most effective underground espionage organizations working in occupied France. Czeriavski controlled dozens of intelligent, shrewd agents who began to supply top drawer information which Carre relayed by shortwave to London's SOE. Much of the information being fed to London came from female French spies who worked their wiles on German soldiers to get information.

One such agent was an attractive, young French spy named Christine Bouffet who worked for Interallié in Cherbourg. In early October 1941, Bouffet approached a German soldier as he sat in a cafe. He was Sergeant Hugo Bleicher, a young, handsome and ardent Nazi. He was intelligent, crafty, and ambitious. He instantly recognized the young woman as a spy and reported her to the Abwehr, telling Captain Erich Borchers that Bouffet was trying to get information on the Luftwaffe fuel depot outside of Cherbourg.

Bleicher helped Abwehr agents trap Bouffet, then aided in her interrogation. She admitted to Bleicher that she worked for a British agent known only to her by the name of Paul. On November 3, 1941, the agent was arrested. He was Raoul Kiffer, one of Czerniavski's top lieutenants. Kiffer was threatened with horrible torture and cracked, agreeing to work with Bleicher who, by then, had been absorbed into the Abwehr. He was to become one of Germany's top spycatchers.

Kiffer supplied so much information to Bleicher that he easily tracked down and arrested twenty-one of Czeriavski's top agents. Next, on November 17, 1941, Bleicher led a raid on Interallié's headquarters where he snared Czeriavski, his mistress Renée Borni, and Carre. Czerniavski admitted that he worked for the Allies but no more. Bleicher personally surpervised his torture inside Santé Prison but the brave Pole would admit to nothing. He was drugged, beaten, whipped. His fingernails and toenails were torn away, acid was splashed on his flesh, red-hot pokers seared his arms and legs. Still, Czerniavski would not talk.

Bleicher next tried Renée Borni but she spat on him, cursed him. He ignored her and went into Carre's cell. The Cat had been made aware of her leader's agony. She had been made to stand in a hallway, next to the door of the torture chamber in which Czerniavski was being brutalized. She was next and she was frightened to death. Bleicher took one look at her and then escorted her from her cell, down a corridor and, instead of into the torture room, outside to a waiting car.

The German spycatcher ordered the limousine to drive to one of the best restaurants in Paris. When Carre finished her meal, Bleicher leaned close to her and said quietly: "You have two choices. You can either be shot or work for us a double agent. If you cooperate, I will do what I can to save your friends from the firing squad. Which is it to be?"

Carre agreed to be "turned around" and become a

German double agent. Bleicher knew she craved luxury so he gave her a salary of 60,000 francs a month, a deluxe suite at the Hotel Meurice (German military headquarters) and an expense account which allowed her to dine in the finest restaurants in Paris. She quickly began to betray members of Interallié. She met with several underground members in cafes and bistros and, as soon as she went to the washroom to powder her nose, plainclothes Gestapo agents pounced on the unsuspecting resistance workers and dragged them to prison. Most were taken to concentration camps where they met horrible deaths.

Bleicher controlled Carre's at every step. Carre soon became his mistress and they moved into a spacious villa. When all the Interallié members were rounded up (almost 100 men and women), Bleicher next proposed to his spymasters that London, which knew nothing of these captures, be regularly contacted by Carre who knew all the British codes, security checks, and transmission schedules. The Abwehr agreed and Carre began transmitting messages and information as if Interallié were still in operation.

This worked so well that SOE sent another spy to France to work with an organization that no longer existed. He was Pierre de Vomecourt. Upon his arrival in France, Vomecourt sent some messages to London on the transmitter operated by Carre. Completing his mission, Vomecourt prepared to return to England. Bleicher, informed of these plans, decided to let the SOE agent get back to London so that he could report that Interallié was running smoothly. Then Vomecourt asked that Carre accompany him to brief his superiors about Interallié's operations.

When Carre told Bleicher about this proposal, the spycatcher hesitated. He then concluded that Carre could be of invaluable service to the Abwehr by collecting information on SOE. He told her to accompany Vomecourt to England. She and Vomecourt attempted to escape France by air but the plane scheduled to pick them up never appeared at the designated secret airfield. Then, on the night of February 26, 1942, a British motor-torpedo boat dashed to a Brittany beach and picked them up.

Vomecourt by then had grown suspicious of the Cat, and as the boat sped toward England the SOE agent directly confronted Carre, accusing her of being a double agent. She burst into tears and confessed everything, but quickly added that she would become a triple agent and help SOE by giving them everything she knew about the Germans.

Upon reaching England Vomecourt informed his superiors about Carre's double spying. She underwent interrogation by SOE Colonel Maurice Buckmaster, a tough no-nonsense spymaster. Carre told him everything she knew.

Buckmaster decided to use Carre in London, where she would pretend to send Bleicher important information on SOE, information which SOE would cleverly fabricate. In April 1942, Vomecourt returned to France and was captured. He was imprisoned at the fortress at Colditz where the Gestapo ruthlessly interrogated him. Buckmaster learned that Vomecourt had been taken and believed that he would reveal that Carre had turned on the Abwehr. Buckmaster was wrong. Vomecourt did not crack and spent the rest of the war in a dungeon without talking (he died in Paris in 1965).

Believing Carre had been compromised, SOE sent her to Aylesbury Prison and later moved her to Holloway Jail, the prison for women in North London. Here she languished until the war's end. In 1945, Carre was returned to France. In 1949, the Cat was charged with being a German spy and brought to trial.

Condemned to be beheaded by the guillotine, Carre's sentence was later commuted to life imprisonment. She was released in 1954 and immediately went to live in a rural area, changing her name and working on her memoirs, which Carre entitled *I Was the Cat*. Carre reportedly died in 1971, remembered as the Mata Hari of World War II, revered by no one and hated by all she served and then betrayed.

[ALSO SEE: *Abwehr, Deuxiéme Bureau; Gestapo; SOE*]

CASANOVA, GIOVANNI GIACOMO
Venetian Spy for France ▪ (1725–1798)

KNOWN TO THE world AS THE GREAT LOVER, Casanova was many other things, not least of which was a sorcerer, an occultist, and an espionage agent. The son of theater people, Casanova was born in Venice. Like his parents, he was nomadic, whimsical, and unpredictable. He became an ardent lover at an early age.

Through family friends, Casanova secured a position as secretary to Cardinal Aquaviva but he soon tired of religious court life and joined the Venetian army at Corfu. The military regimen bored the romantic Casanova who soon departed for more adventurous pursuits. He dubbed himself an abbé who heard confessions of pretty women and then seduced them. He dabbled in the occult and claimed to be a powerful sorcerer who could produce instant wealth for his clients.

For more than twenty years, Casanova wandered through the capitals of Europe, from Paris to Constantinople, supporting himself as a gambler, a violin player, a cabalist. Most of his money was made through alchemy. He claimed that he could turn iron into gold but his magician's art consisted of nothing more than slight-of-hand tricks. He returned to Venice in 1755 where he was imprisoned for practicing sorcery. He escaped in 1756 and fled to Paris where an old friend, Cardinal Francois de Bernis, who was the foreign minister to King Louis XV, employed him as an espionage agent.

Casanova's first mission was to travel to Dunkirk where a large British fleet lay anchored. At that time Dunkirk was controlled by a large garrison of British troops, the port having been ceded to England in the 1713 Treaty of Utrecht. At the time Casanova accepted his role of secret agent, however, France and England were beginning the bloody Seven Years' War (1756–1763).

It was Casanova's job to discover the exact strength of the British fleet and land garrison and report back to Cardinal Bernis.

Posing as a Venetian sea captain, Casanova traveled to Dunkirk in grand style, accompanied by many servants, coaches and trunks. Going to the best inn at Dunkirk, Casanova lavished money on everyone, ingratiating himself to British sea captains and giving them letters of introduction from some English nobles which he had taken weeks to secure before his mission. The captains were thoroughly entertained by Casanova as he talked about Venetian ships, naval architecture, and the types of maneuvers taught to Venetian sea captains. Within four days, he began to receive invitations to dine on board the British warships as an honored guest of the captains.

According to his memoirs, Casanova was thus able to learn everything he needed to know. "On every occasion," he later wrote, "I stayed in the ship for the rest of the day. I was curious about everything—and Jack [the British] is so trustful! I went into the hold. I asked questions innumerable, and I found plenty of young officers delighted to show their own importance, who gossiped without needing any encouragement from me. I took care to learn everything which would be of service to me, and in the evenings I put down on paper all the mental notes I had made during the day. Four or five hours was all I allowed myself for sleep, and in fifteen days I found that I had learnt enough."

When he reached Paris, Casanova met with Bernis and handed over his detailed report on the British forces at Dunkirk. It was reviewed by the French admiralty which paid him 12,000 francs, then a great fortune.

Casanova continued his adventures, meeting the great men of Europe who were equally charmed and puzzled by his unpredictable behavior. He acquired a title in 1759, Chavalier of the Netherlands, after he served as an espionage agent for the Dutch government, again securing information on British forces. In his travels, Casanova met the Pope, Frederick II, in Berlin where he declined a high-ranking post in 1764; Empress Catherine of Russia who was enamored of him but who condemned him after he became involved in another court sex scandal, fought a duel, and was forced to flee the country.

Back in France, Casanova befriended the great writer Voltaire and became the confidante of Madame Pompadour, mistress to the king. His other friends at this time included Europe's great mystery men, Count Saint-Germain and Count Alessandro Cagliostro (Joseph Balsamo). Both claimed to be alchemists and sorcerers wielding great spiritual powers. Both claimed they could create gold from ordinary metals and cure all diseases through their ability to hypnotize, and both were great charlatans like Casanova himself which is why he delighted in their friendships.

Casanova's fortunes dipped drastically when he returned to Venice in 1774. He again became a spy to support himself, a servant of the Venetian police. For eight years (1774–1782) he supported himself by informing on those who practiced sorcery, the very black art by which he himself had made his living years earlier. Meanwhile he wrote satires, one of which profiled Casanova's patron and was considered libelous. He was exiled from Venice in 1782. In 1785, the great lover accepted a post as librarian for wealthy Graf von Waldstein and went to live in a palace in Bohemia at Dux. Here he wrote poetry, translated the *Iliad*, penned a science fiction romance, *Icosameron*, then ended his days by writing his memoirs, *Historie de ma vie* which were not fully published until 1960–1962.

CASEMENT, ROGER
Irish Spy Against England ▪ (1864–1916)

IRISH-BORN ROGER CASEMENT WORKED DILIGENTLY FOR the British Foreign Office for years in Africa and South America. His civil service career was capped by a knighthood in 1911. Casement was nevertheless committed to the cause of Irish freedom and in his retirement, he sought to aid those who planned the Easter Uprising in Dublin in 1916.

A year earlier, Casement went to Germany and, at a prisoner-of-war camp, Limburg Lahn, met with Irish-born British soldiers who had been captured in World War I. He promised that if they would fight for Irish sovereignty, they would be freed from the camp.

Casement found only one volunteer, Daniel Bailey. An American in Germany, Robert Montieth, also volunteered. Then Casement begged his German sponsors to give him arms to take to Ireland. His sponsors had grown apprehensive of him, however, due to his constant companionship with a homosexual sailor. Reluctantly, the Germans finally turned over an impounded Norwegian cargo ship which contained 20,000 poorly-made Russian rifles and ammunition.

The ship sailed for Ireland, its arrival scheduled for the time of the uprising. It arrived too late.

Sir Roger Casement, shown at the time he worked for the British Foreign Office; he was hanged for treason in 1916.

The uprising had already been crushed. Casement, who had been ill for some time, was too weak to leave the beach. Bailey and Montieth went for help but a constable found Casement the next morning and he was jailed.

When British vessels approached the Norwegian ship, the crew scuttled the craft. With Bailey and Montieth rounded up, Casement was tried for treason, sabotage and espionage. His companions informed the British of his plans and he was convicted and condemned to death. There was a large number of supporters who wanted Casement's sentence commuted to a prison term

Public opinion reversed itself when Casement's "Black Diaries" were found in his home. He had written explicit details of his homosexual affairs over the years. When these sordid tales were disclosed, Casement lost whatever support he had. He was hanged at Pentonville Prison on August 3, 1916. On February 23, 1965, Casement's body was disinterred from the prison cemetary and taken to Ireland where it was reburied, Casement then pronounced a great Irish patriot.

CASEY, WILLIAM J.
CIA Director ▪ (1913–1987)

FEW CHIEFS OF THE CIA WIELDED SO MUCH POWER and acted with such autocratic finality as did William Casey. He relished his job, worked at it fourteen hours a day, exercising a brilliant, photographic mind. He played ruthlessly with power, operating the CIA as if it were his own foreign office through which he ruled most of the world. He was anything but impressive. He was marble-mouthed (some said purposely to disguise his statements), chewed on his tie and drooled so incessantly that the mouthpiece of his office phone had to be sanitized every day.

Casey also looked permanently unkempt. He rolled up his suits in cheap bags when he traveled and seldom had a clean shirt to wear. He left his laundry all over Washington, D.C., and never seemed to be able to locate the last wash. He popped pills into his mouth whenever he met his top men in important conferences. He mumbled when not under pressure but spoke clearly and concisely when no evasive statements were acceptable. This was his professional persona, a disarming one which left visitors to conclude that he was simply a posturing slob who had been given too much authority. He was, in fact, a shrewd and canny calculator who would stop at nothing to safeguard the U.S., or do what *he* thought was best in the interests of national security.

A lover of spy novels, Casey had lived a rather comfortable life, beginning in Queens, New York. After attending Fordham University, he became a lawyer, married happily in 1941 and was soon recruited into the OSS by William Donovan who reportedly met Casey at a cocktail party. Casey's poor eyesight prevented him from seeing field service but he so ingratiated himself to Donovan that the OSS chief made him his chief of intelligence in London. He had no real background in espionage and learned all he could from British officers he met in MI5 and MI6. He would later tell British Prime Minister Margaret Thatcher that he learned everything he knew about foreign intelligence from the British.

Following World War II, Casey went into business, becoming wealthy by publishing legal books and publications which reduced the complicated jargon of the field to simple and understandable terms, a knack Casey had possessed all his life. He was politically active, a long-time supporter of Ronald Reagan and he became Reagan's campaign manager when he ran for the presidency. In 1981, President Reagan named Casey as Director of the CIA. He went at the job like a terrier chasing rats.

First, Casey bullied and cajoled to get heavy appropriations for the CIA, so that within a short time it was super-funded. He used the money to promote one

Power broker and CIA Director William Casey, who ordered drastic covert operations that almost brought the agency to ruination.

covert scheme after another. Then he began to reorganize the CIA from top to bottom, replacing top echelon leaders and attempting to recruit brainy but down-to-earth agents. One advertisement prepared under his supervision stated that intelligence work "has less to do with cloaks and daggers than with the painstaking, generally tedious collection of facts, analysis of facts, exercise of judgment and quick, clear evaluation."

Yet Casey himself made rash judgments, and often threw studied analysis out the window, opting for the cloak and dagger, especially the dagger. He gulped scotch and pontificated, staring over his outsized Yves St. Laurent glasses, telling gullible reporters old OSS stories, those he had heard, not experienced.

In the early 1980s, Casey supervised mayhem and destruction in countries hostile to U.S. interests. He ordered that mines be secretly placed in Nicaraguan ports to thwart shipping to that country's Marxist government (which the CIA would grudgingly admit in 1984). He arranged with Saudi Arabia to assassinate Hizballah and Shi'ite leader Sheik Mohammed Hussein Fadlallah. The car bomb set off in this bloody attempt killed eighty people in a Beirut suburb but failed to injure Fadlallah (this attempt the CIA emphatically denied). He so mishandled through his top aides defecting Soviet agent Vitaly Yurchenko that the KGB spy redefected to Russia.

The most serious charges ever brought against William Casey were those uttered by Oliver North in the Iran-Contra Affair. It was Casey, North later insisted, who was the chief architect of Iranscam, the scheme by which the U.S. would secretly trade arms to Iran, ostensibly provided to Latin American insurgents allied with the U.S., in return for the American hostages held in Iran. North claimed that Casey provided a ledger for him in which to record arms transactions. North was ordered, along with his superior, Admiral John Poindexter, to assume all responsibility for the scandal.

When the scandal did break, Casey went before Congress and denied that the CIA had anything to do with Iranscam. He made the same emphatic denials to the press, all lies, according to Oliver North and, subsequently, investigative reporter Bob Woodward, who wrote a lengthy and controversial book about the scandal.

It was Woodward who later claimed to have smuggled himself into a hospital where Casey was terminally ill and got him to admit that he indeed was behind Iranscam. The CIA chief's widow, Sophia Casey called Woodward a liar, saying that he "never got in to see my husband," that she or her daughter were constantly with William Casey in the hospital room. Also, the director's room was closely guarded by CIA men.

Woodward's claims were dubious at best. William Casey was not a man to admit anything, unless trapped. He was not trapped into making any statement to Woodward. Casey died on May 6, 1987 without ever testifying in the scandal which most certainly originated with him. He was one of the worst CIA directors in the agency's history, one who operated the intelligence services of the U.S. to suit his own ambitions and ends, a trait very much in common with J. Edgar Hoover, the long time supreme ruler of the FBI.

[ALSO SEE: *CIA; William Donovan; MI5; MI6; OSS*]

CAVELL, EDITH LOUISA
British Agent in World War I ■ (1865–1915)

ONE OF ENGLAND'S GREATEST HEROINES, EDITH CAVELL started out to save lives as a nurse, inspired by Florence Nightingale, the courageous nurse who served in the Crimean War and the first woman to receive England's prestigious Order of Merit in 1907. Cavell, born to middleclass parents in Norfolk, England, entered the nursing profession in 1895.

Cavell served in many British hospitals before going to Brussels, Belgium in 1907 to become the matron of the Berkendael Medical Institute. She still held this position when German troops swarmed into Belgium in 1914. The German invasion was so overwhelming and quickly achieved that many British, French and Belgian soldiers were trapped behind the lines. Sick, some wounded, dozens of these Allied soldiers found their way to Cavell's hospital where she cared for them.

When these men were healthy, Cavell refused to turn them over to the Germans. Instead, she helped to smuggle them out of occupied Belgium to the Allied lines in France. Her efforts were coordinated by a Belgian patriot, Phillippe Baucq who furnished guides who took the soldiers from house to house until they slipped into the Allied positions.

Cavell and Baucq saved an estimated 200 or more Allied soldiers from becoming prisoners-of-war and uncertain fate in brutal concentration camps. Though German intelligence was aware that someone was smuggling the Allied soldiers out of Brussels, the source of these operations could not be pinpointed. At one point, Cavell was suspected but since no proof could be found, she was not arrested. Then, in July 1915, a member of the Belgian underground was captured with a list of all those involved in the underground operation. On the list was the name of Edith Cavell.

The nurse and Baucq were arrested on August 5, 1915. Cavell admitted to harboring soldiers. A court-martial found the nurse guilty of espionage and sentenced her to death. On August 18, 1915, She and Baucq were placed before a firing squad and shot to death. A few minutes before her execution, Cavell, in a clear voice, expressed her wonderful sense of humanitarianism, the real cause of her actions, stating: "As I stand here in the presence of Eternity, I find that patriotism is not enough."

CENTER, THE
Soviet Spy Headquarters, Moscow ▪ (1924– ?)

THE TERM "CENTER" NOT ONLY APPLIES TO THE actual headquarters of all Soviet intelligence but the specific headquarters for the GRU, which is Soviet military espionage and the KGB which applies to all other intelligence activities. The GRU dominated the Center during World War II, managing vast spy networks in eastern Europe, including the celebrated Rado spy ring. Following World War II, the KGB dominated the Center and continued as the preimminent force in Moscow throughout the Cold War.

[ALSO SEE: GRU; KGB; Sandor Rado]

CENTRAL EXTERNAL LIAISON DEPARTMENT
Chinese Intelligence Agency ▪ (1950?–)

THE CENTRAL EXTERNAL LIAISON DEPARTMENT IS responsible for China's internal and external espionage operations, working in close harmony with the Chinese Communist Party. This department has an inner core called the Central Control of Intelligence which directs the department's activities. The department does not act autonomously but is hamstrung by the Communist Party's top leaders which is mostly concerned with counterespionage and strict control of Chinese citizens. The department's agents can be found in every Chinese Communist Embassy, consulate and legation. Other Chinese spies operate through the New China News Agency. Despite China's overt peacekeeping efforts, its Central External Liaison Department works tirelessly (if not effectively) against the United States.

CESID (Centro Superior de Informacion de la Defensa)
Spanish Intelligence Service ▪ (1977–)

UPON THE DEATH OF FASCIST DICTATOR FRANCISCO Franco, Spain established a modern intelligence agency, CESID (Centro Superior de Informacion de la Defensa), which covered internal and external espionage. Most of CESID's original staff members were ex-Army officers who had served under Franco but these fascist-minded men were soon weeded out of the service. CESID proved itself effective in 1982 by exposing a cabal of right-wing military officers who were planning a coup to overthrow the government, one that was crushed by Spain's democratic forces.

The estensive political files that had been kept by Franco's former intelligence agencies (eight in all at the height of his tyrannical regime) were destroyed by CESID officials at the order of Spain's first democratically elected prime minister Adolfi Suarez.

CHAMBERS, WHITTAKER
American Spy for Soviets ▪ (1901–1961)

FOR A GENERATION, LIBERALS IN AMERICA HATED Whittaker Chambers more than any other person. That hatred stemmed from his turncoat activities as a former Soviet spy and his unwavering accusation that Alger Hiss was also a Russian agent in the 1930s. The Chambers–Hiss affair still lingers in the minds of elderly liberals and conservatives as *the* political battle of the early Cold War.

Born in Philadelphia and raised in Lynbrook (Long Island), N.Y., Chambers was the son of a journalist who often left his family to fend for itself. Chambers had to work hard as a teenager and managed to graduate high school in 1919, entering Columbia University in 1920. He wrote a play deemed blasphemous which caused his expulsion in 1922. Aimlessly, Chambers took one menial journalism job after another.

In 1925, Chambers joined the American Communist Party and went to work for its organ, *The Daily Worker*, soon becoming a senior editor. In 1931, Chambers married a dedicated Communist, Esther Shemitz who encouraged him to join an underground Communist cell, working toward the overthrow of the U.S. government. Chambers apparently used the alias George Crosley in his travels, as well as the name "Karl" after he moved to Baltimore under orders from the Communist hiararchy where he was to act as a courier of secret documents which had been stolen by Communist spies working for the U.S. government. Chambers delivered this information to a KGB agent, Col. Boris Bykov, who, in turn, sent on the documents to Moscow.

Disillusioned with the Communists, Chambers quit the Party. He sought and found other editorial work and finally found a position with *Time* Magazine. In 1939, when the Soviets signed a non-aggression pact with Nazi Germany, Chambers lost all faith in Russia, properly equating the dictatorship of Communism with fascism. Out of a sense of patriotic duty, he later stated, on the night of September 2, 1939, he went to Assistant Secretary of State Adolf A. Berle, who was in charge of U.S. security, to expose what he knew about Communist spies in the U.S.

Isaac Don Levine, a jouranlist who had carried on a private war with the Communists for years, brought Chambers to Berle, barging in on the Berles as they were entertaining guests. Berle's friendship for Levine, and the fact that Chambers worked for the prestigious *Time* magazine, caused him to listen seriously to what Chambers had to say.

For three hours Chambers sat on the lawn of Berle's Washington, D.C., house, spilling the beans on the Communist conspiracy. He detailed the activities of such men as Franklin Victor Reno, a mathematician who worked at the Aberdeen Proving Grounds and had access to bombsight secrets. Chambers urged Berle to remove Reno at once. (Reno was still working at Aberdeen in 1948 when the FBI conducted a search for him.) He identified Col. Bykov to Berle and explained how U.S. secrets were stolen by Communists in sensitive government positions and passed on to Moscow in the form of microfilm. Among the many names cited by Chambers in his lengthy conversation with Berle that night was Alger Hiss.

Berle took the statements made to him by Chambers to President Franklin D. Roosevelt who laughed, dismissing the mere idea that Communist spies had infiltrated the U.S. government and were stealing secrets on a wholesale basis. Nothing was done. Chambers went back to his job at *Time* and rose to the position of senior editor, earning a then whopping $30,000-a-year in 1948 when he became the star witness before the House of Un-American Activities Committee. On August 3, 1948, Chambers sat before the committee and began to rattle off the very information he had given to Berle almost a decade earlier.

Again, Chambers stated that Alger Hiss had been a spy for the Communists while holding high-level positions in the U.S. government between 1935 and 1937. Hiss, by then, had had an illustrious political career in Washington. He had been a brilliant lawyer who became secretary of the Nye Committee on Munitions in 1935, and had gone on to become assistant general counsel of the Solicitor General, assistant to the assistant Secretary of State, director of the political department of the State Department, a member of the U.S. delegation that accompanied President Roosevelt to the Yalta Conference, and first Secretary General of the United Nations. In 1948, when Chambers went public, Hiss was the President of the Carnegie Endowment for International Peace.

The minute Hiss heard the news, he telephoned the head of the Committee and emphatically stated that he had never been a Communist, that he had never met Whittaker Chambers and that he insisted upon making these statements before the Committee in a public hearing. He was promptly invited to do so.

On August 5, 1948, Hiss appeared, denying everything and asking that Chambers confront him. The Committee first had Chambers meet with its subcommittee in New York where he was asked to prove that he had known Hiss. Chambers related personal information about the Hiss he had known in the mid-1930s, that he called his wife Dilly and she called him Hilly, that he was an amateur ornithologist and had once told Chambers of seeing a rare bird, a pronothory warbler, that Hiss had donated an old car, a Ford, to the Communist Party, that he had sent his stepson, Timmy Hobson to a cheaper school so that he could donate more money to the Communists, that Hiss had a cocker spaniel, that he had sold bottled spring water as a boy. The details Chambers knew of Hiss' life and that of his family startled the committee which again met with Hiss.

Hiss was asked questions based on Chambers' statements about him. His answers confirmed a great deal of what Whittaker Chambers had said. Hiss also said that ever since Chambers had made his accusations, he had been searching his memory and came to realize that Chambers might have been a man he did, indeed, meet, one called George Crosley, a man who had been slovenly and had bad teeth. He assumed that Chambers had had his teeth fixed and that this had changed his appearance.

When Chambers repeated his statements on a radio program, Meet the Press, his statements were not protected by immunity as they had been when he testified before the Committee. Hiss promptly sued Chambers for slander. Meanwhile, the Committee felt it had substantiated many of Chambers' statements. It learned that Hiss had signed over his car in July 1936. Hiss had said that he had not seen "Crosley" after 1935. Moreover, the Committee learned that Hiss had drawn $400 from his bank account at the very time Chambers said he had gotten the loan from Hiss.

Then Chambers supported his statements that Hiss had stolen documents from the State Department by producing sixty-five classified documents on film. These documents had been typed on Hiss' typewriter and were accompanied by four notes in Hiss' handwriting. Why had Chambers waited so long to prove Hiss had been a Soviet agent? Chambers said he had kept the documents as "protection" against SMERSH (the Soviet assassination arm of the KGB), believing that his former Soviet masters might try to murder him.

Chambers produced even more documents to implicate Hiss, these taken from a hollowed out pumpkin on Chambers' 390-acre farm in northern Maryland, and these rolls of microfilm were later called the "Pumpkin Papers." The case came to a head on December 15, 1948 when a grand jury in New York indicted Hiss for perjury, based on his statements that he had not seen Chambers after July 1935.

Hiss went to trial on May 31, 1949. By then the FBI had tracked down the very typewriter the Hisses had had in their apartment. The State Department documents Hiss had taken home with him, according to Chambers, had been retyped by Mrs. Hiss (Priscilla Fansler Hobson Hiss), also a Communist, The typewriter was later given to a black handyman, Ira Lockey, in payment for some services he had performed for the Hiss family. The typewriter, a Woodstock 230099, was placed in evidence. According to experts, the typface of the machine matched those on the documents retyped from the State Department dossiers.

The defense claimed that Julian Wadleigh, another Soviet agent Chambers had mentioned, had been a government employee in the mid-1930s and had access to the documents Chambers claimed Hiss had stolen. Wadleigh, the defense said, could have taken the documents himself and even retrieved the four notes in Hiss' handwriting from Hiss office

Communist turned government informant Whittaker Chambers, shown in 1948 when he testified before HUAC and accused Alger Hiss of being an espionage agent.

wastebasket (though this seemed far-fetched to most).

Hiss' first trial ended on July 9, 1949, in a hung jury (eight to four for conviction). A second trial began on November 7, 1949 and ended on January 21, 1950. This time Hiss was convicted of perjury (not espionage) and given the maximum sentence of five years imprisonment. Hiss' lawyers filed an appeal which was denied. Next they demanded a new trial which was also denied. Hiss went into the federal penitentiary at Lewisburg, Pennsylvania on March 22, 1950. On November 27, 1954, Hiss was released, placed on ten month's probation.

Hiss never stopped trying to prove Chambers a liar and that his evidence was rigged. In 1980, he filed a 250-page legal brief in the Federal District Court in Manhattan which attempted to overturn his 1950 conviction and came to nothing.

Following Hiss' conviction, Chambers drifted about aimlessly, grew depressed, thought of suicide, then bolstered himself with newly-found religious convictions. He penned his memoirs and died of natural causes on July 9, 1961. In July 1984, President Ronald Reagan posthumously awarded Chambers America's highest civilian honor, the Medal of Freedom.

[ALSO SEE: *Alger Hiss*]

CHAPMAN, EDDIE
British Double Agent in England ▪ (1908– ?)

EDDIE CHAPMAN WAS A BRITISH SUBJECT BUT THE British had no pride in him. From childhood his most avid interests involved breaking the law. He was a petty thief as a teenager and, as an adult, a professional safecracker, one of England's most notorious "boxmen." As World War II approached, Chapman committed a series of sensational burglaries, breaking into safes thought to be impenetrable, and stealing considerable cash and gems.

So intense was the manhunt conducted for him by Scotland Yard that Chapman decided to go into permanent hiding. He selected the remote Channel Islands in the south but detectives tracked him down in Jersey and put him in jail. When the Germans occupied Jersey in 1940 they found Chapman pacing the narrow confines of his cell.

He was interviewed by Abwehr officials and, at that time, the scheming mind of Eddie Chapman suddenly envisioned a way in which he could obtain his freedom, as well as line his pockets. He told the Germans that he hated England. It had forced him to endure a childhood of miserable poverty, deprived him of a suitable education, and sent him into crime. He wanted revenge on this country which was indifferent to human suffering, especially his own.

The safecracker volunteered to spy for the Abwehr, if, of course, it would pay him well. Chapman's offer appealed to the Germans. They were impressed with their own research on Chapman, consulting his lengthy prison records which they had captured in Jersey. The safecracker even provided the Nazis with his own press clippings, showing them newspaper stories about sensational burglaries he had committed in the past.

Chapman was just the kind of malcontent who could be useful to them, Abwehr officials concluded, especially as a man who understood explosives which Chapman had used for years to blow open difficult safes. He would make the perfect saboteur! He was immediately enrolled in the Abwehr's spy school and was given training in sabotage. Chapman was then given a tremendous, almost impossible assignment. Captain Stephen Grunen, Chapman's Abwehr supervisor, ordered him to return to England and blow up the de Havilland Aircraft Works in Hatfield, north of London. It would be the most daring sabotage mission of World War II.

"I'll gut the damned place," Chapman promised with a sinister grin.

On the murky night of December 20, 1942, Eddie Chapman stood in the doorway of a fast German cargo plane as it swept low over the countryside near Littleport, England. He jumped on schedule and landed in a ploughed field close to the village of Welbech. Chapman quickly dug a shallow hole in the near-frozen earth and buried his chute. He then went to a wooded area to hide. At dawn, he walked to Littleport and caught a train for London.

Nothing was heard from him until December 23, when Grunen received an encrypted radio message, signed "Fritz," which was the cover name assigned to Chapman by the Abwehr. This and more messages for the next three weeks reported Chapman's progress, all of it promising. The safecracker told his Abwehr chief that he had gone to Hatfield several times and had crept close to the main power plant, "casing" the area, as he put it. He next informed Grunen that, at a quarry near Sevenoaks, he had located explosives with which to blow up the plant.

Grunen and other Abwehr chiefs awaited Chapman's next message with some anxiety. German intelligence had sent dozens of spies and saboteurs into England but none of them had ever been assigned the kind of impossible task demanded of Chapman. To the Nazis, Chapman was expendable. They thought much less of him than one of their own native agents, their own homegrown Nazi spies who risked their lives out of loyalty to Germany and Adolf Hitler.

The safecracker was working for them out of revenge and for money, a lot of money. To the Abwehr he was a traitor, a mercenary, a common criminal. If Chapman threw his life away performing an act of sabotage that most in the Abwehr thought to be "unachievable," they had lost nothing. If he succeeded, they had gained everything they half-heartedly hoped to accomplish.

"He's a lunatic and will be caught," one Abwehr official told Grunen.

"He's a clever criminal who is used to evading the law," Grunen replied. "His chances of success are improved because of this." Grunen genuinely wanted Chapman to succeed for self-serving reasons. If he did, Grunen could take the bow for enlisting the safecracker in the service of the Abwehr. Failure meant that the German spy chief's judgment was in question.

Then, on January 27, 1943, Grunen received a matter-of-fact message from Chapman: "Will attempt sabotage this evening at six o'clock." Later that night, Grunen received a second message from the safecracker, one that proudly proclaimed: "Mission successfully accomplished." The saboteur explained how he had blown the de Havilland power plant to pieces by using two time-bomb devices he had himself constructed. To each of these bombs he had attached a simple wristwatch timing device.

Grunen waved Chapman's report in the faces of Abwehr critics.

"He has done it! You called him a dirty, little thief but he has blown up the de Havilland works! In two years of war, none of *your* agents in England have achieved such marvelous results. Well, give me a thief every time!"

Still skeptical, Grunen's superiors insisted upon confirmation. To that end, the following day the Luftwaffe dispatched two JU-11 reconnaissance planes to verify Chapman's glowing report. Aerial photos were taken of the de Havilland works and were later placed before Abwehr officials in Paris. It was apparent that Chapman had done exactly what he said he had done. The photos showed wide holes in the roof of the powerplant. Debris was everywhere. Generators and other heavy equipment lay in pieces. This would cripple for some time the ability of de Havilland to produce warplanes.

In early February, Chapman again contacted Grunen, asking that a U-boat be sent to pick him up and return him to France. Grunen apologetically replied that there were no U-boats to spare. All were on important assignments. He instructed Chapman to make his way out of the country as best he could, and quickly, "now that all England is looking for you."

Chapman did not leave England immediately. He wanted to prove to his Abwehr spymasters that he was worth the £100,000 they promised to pay him, in installments, of course. He lingered in back alley London, reporting to Paris the insignias of new American divisions which were streaming into England. He also surveyed the damage the Luftwaffe was creating in its daily bombings of London. Chapman witnessed the German air raid on London on the night of January 17-18, 1943 and then radioed to Paris that the raid was ineffective. "The only thing hit were some houses near St. John's Wood close to Lord's Cricket Grounds." Then he chided: "Can't they do better?"

This message was sent to a notorious French collaborator named Maurice who monitored Chapman's radio day and night on the *Dauerempfang* waveband. It was Maurice who received Chapman's last message in mid-February 1943: "Closing transmission. Too dangerous to work. Am returning via Lisbon." It took some time to obtain forged papers but on March 12, Chapman, posing as a Portugese businessman, boarded a ship and sailed for Lisbon. From there he took a train to Paris where he was greeted with open arms by Grunen and other Abwehr chiefs.

So impressed with Chapman were the Germans that they gave the safecrackers an extravagant party at Maxim's. The safecracker reveled in his role of anti-hero. He described in lurid details how he had blown up the de Havilland works, then craftily evaded the police and British agents, always staying one jump ahead of them, moving from roominghouse to roominghouse, never remaining in the same area of London for more than a few days. "They thought they had me several times. All they had were empty rooms." Chapman went on to criticize the Luftwaffe, insisting that they hit bigger targets in their raids over London. Such savage vindictiveness once and for all convinced the Abwehr spymasters that Eddie Chapman truly hated his native land.

Chapman continued to work diligently for the Abwehr. He was valued as one of their most prized agents, one they did not wish to risk again. Chapman was taught the finer arts of espionage and sent on assignments to Switzerland, Portugal and Turkey, neutral countries where spies from both sides abounded. In Spring 1944, however, the Abwehr knew to expect an Allied invasion somewhere along the coast of France. They had to know exactly where the thrust of the invasion would be. Grunen called in his top man, Eddie Chapman, telling him that he had to return to England, learn the invasion plans and report back to him.

On June 1, 1944, Chapman slipped back to his native land. Grunen nervously awaited his report which was radioed a few days later. Somehow, Chapman had performed another miracle, He sent detailed information on where and when the Allies would land in France. The areas Chapman pinpointed were the beaches of Normandy.

The Germans did not act upon the information until it was too late to combat the massive amounts of Allied troops, armor and goods that had moved inland to secure a foothold on the Continent, a huge staging area from which the Allies launched one successful attack after another.

By then Chapman had returned to France and he later accompanied Nazi intelligence units as they retreated into the heartland of Germany. Also by then Chapman's friends such as Grunen had been expunged and the Abwehr itself dissolved by Hitler. Admiral Canaris, head of the Abwehr, had been part of the abortive plot to assassinate Hitler in July 1944. Exposed, Canaris and other Abwehr chiefs were arrested and executed. Heinrich Himmler's dreaded SS took over what remained of the intelligence service, along with the Germany military. In November 1944, Eddie Chapman also disappeared. For years afterward, he was fondly remembered by surviving German intelligence officials as one of most successful Abwehr agents of the war.

In England, however, the same Eddie Chapman was considered to be one of the shrewdest, most effective double agents to ever serve England and the cause of freedom. Every spectacular thing Eddie Chapman did on behalf of the Germans had been a sham, a setup, a fake. And only a daring, nerveless man such as Chapman, who was also an excellent actor, could have completely fooled the best minds in the Abwehr. He had considerable help from MI5.

From the moment Chapman was found in his cell in Jersey by the invading Germans, he planned to hoodwink them into believing he would spy for them. This was the only way he believed he would be released and he was correct. Moreover, he knew that they would look for a motive and his was perfect, hatred for a society that had imprisoned him. However, he had no intention of spying for the Germans, although he agreed to do exactly that.

After his brief training by the Abwehr, Chapman parachuted into England. He did not, as he later informed Captain Grunen, take a train to London. He immediately went to the tiny village of Welbech and called the police in Littleport who picked him up. The police sent him on to MI5 who were more than happy to hear his fantastic story. Chapman then volunteered to become a double agent. The safe-cracker-turned-saboteur would carry on with his Abwehr mission, MI5 agreed, and it would arrange for him to blow up the de Havilland powerplant. In return for his services, British counterintelligence promised to wipe out all criminal charges against him. Chapman, who was given the MI5 code name of "Zigzag," was also promised a considerable sum of money to get started in a non-criminal business after the war ended.

While Chapman sent messages telling the Germans of his preparations to destroy the aircraft facility, MI5 was working its own magic to make that event occur, or, to make it appear to the Germans that it had occured. To make Chapman appear authentic to the Germans, he was permitted to visit the de Havilland plant so that he could later describe the facility accurately to the Germans. He was then allowed to "steal" explosives from the quarry at Sevenoaks. When it came to actually blowing up the powerplant, however, MI5 took over.

A genius camouflage expert, Major Jasper Maskelyne, was immediately consulted. He was one of the magicians who worked in the Camouflage Experimental Station of the Royal Engineers. He had in the past created incredible optical illusions for the British military. He had comouflaged entire naval harbors and he had hidden battleships. Maskelyne and his men had actually built a dummy battleship, a fleet of dummy submarines which were launched while newsreels recorded the event, countless dummy gun emplacements along the British coast, thousands of dummy soldiers in formations that actually moved.

In the desert war against Rommel's Africa Corps, Maskelyne used mirrors to make one British tank appear to be three dozen. He had even concealed a great portion of the Suez Canal. MI5 agents told Maskelyne of Chapman's mission. They knew that the Germans would verify his claim of having blown up the powerplant. Somehow, it had to appear that Chapman had accomplished his mission.

Maskelyne and his men went to work. An enormous relief canvas was placed over the roof of the plant and painted on top of it in full color was an exact replica of the top of the powerplant, only showing gaping holes in the roof and terrible damage beneath. Next to the plant, Maskelyne manufactured out of papier-maché in one of his three camouflage plants the broken pieces of generators and other heavy equipment, along with piles of bricks, smashed furniture. All was prepared in proportionate scale so that the destruction would appear realistic when photographed from the air. Maskelyne even had the RAF photograph his camouflage from the air to check the authenticity of his huge canvas and dummy damage.

When the Luftwaffe's photos of the site were studied, Abwehr specialist declared the destruction real and that Chapman had done exactly what he had claimed to have done. Thus Chapman was fully accepted as one of Germany's most daring saboteurs.

On subsequent missions for the Germans Chapman provided his Abwehr contacts with doctored secrets which MI5 carefully prepared for him, including the information he passed on to Paris in 1944 regarding the D-Day invasion of Normandy. MI5 actually gave Chapman considerable details of the beaches close to the actual beaches where the invasion took place.

Since the codes used by German intelligence had been broken, MI5 knew full well that the Germans had already learned about Normandy and that Hitler and most of his top generals had dismissed that location as a real invasion site. Hitler believed that the Allies had provided information on Normandy to deceive him into ordering most of his divisions to that area and leave Calais and Cherbourg unprotected, areas the Fuhrer believed were the real objectives of the invasion fleet.

Hitler could not be fooled by bogus information, despite the warnings of the Abwehr. Chapman's report on Normandy was discarded, along with many other such reports. Those who sided with Hitler on this issue believed that Chapman, irrespective of his great abilities, had also been hoodwinked by the British.

In the game of counterintelligence, MI5 proved to be the victor. It had allowed their agent to tell the truth which, of course, was unacceptable, as MI5 knew it would be. When Chapman returned to occupied Europe and his German sponsors, he was again praised for his accurate report on the Normandy invasion. The congratulations were by then as meaningless as the crumbling Third Reich.

Chapman or "Zigzag," went off the roles of MI5 in November 1944. His dossier simply stated that he was no longer active for "lack of security on the part of the agent." No details were given. It was later believed that Chapman had either been identified as a British double agent or had somehow compromised himself.

One story has it that Chapman survived the war and returned to England, where he was told that his role as a British agent had to remain a secret, that his criminal records had been destroyed according to his agreement with MI5, and that he was to receive a medal for his heroic espionage work.

"Medal be damned," he reportedly stated. "You birds owe me twenty-five thousand pounds."

[ALSO SEE: *Abwehr; Wilhelm Canaris; MI5*]

CHEBOTAREV, ANATOLI KUZMICH
Soviet Spymaster ▪ (? – ?)

A MAJOR IN THE GRU, CHEBOTAREV DEFECTED IN Brussels in October 1971, going to the American Embassy, asking to be sent to America. Chebotarev was an electronic specialist who had been attached to the trade mission in Brussels. CIA officials were immediately suspicious of the defecting Russian agent.

Taken to Washington, D.C., Chebotarev was debriefed by CIA officers, identifying for them thirty-two KGB agents operating in Brussels. Moreover, he identified the Russian firms employing the spies in Brussels, including Aeroflot and Skaldia-Volga. He also disclosed that some of these agents had monitored the telephone conversations of senior Western diplomats and generals who were assigned to SHAPE and NATO.

Two months later, Cherboratov left his apartment and went for a walk. He did not return. A short time later the Soviet chargé d'Affaires notified U.S. officials that Cherbotarev had requested that he be returned to his family in Russia.

CIA officers later believed that he may have been a plant who had passed on false information to the West. Nevertheless, four of those named as spies in Brussels were expelled by Belgian authorities.

[ALSO SEE: *CIA; GRU; KGB*]

CHEKA
Soviet Secret Police ▪ (1917–1922)

F OLLOWING THE BOLSHEVIK TAKEOVER OF THE RUSSIAN Revolution in 1917, the Soviets dismantled the broad spy networks of the czarist secret police, the Okhrana, but it kept all essential functions of this organization in place, replacing the czarists with Bolsheviks and changing the name to Cheka. The official name of the organization was the Extraordinary Commission for Combating Counter-Revolution, Sabotage and Criminal Offenses by Officials.

The Russian people suffered as much under the oppressive Cheka as it had from the brutal Okhrana. The Cheka's main objective was to track down and liquidate all those who opposed Lenin and the Communist state. In many respects, the Cheka proved to be even more terrible than the Okhrana. Its leaders and agents were above the law, and, like the Gestapo in Germany a decade later, it made arrests and caused imprisonments and execution at will without having to answer for its actions. Its first director, Felix Dzershinsky, one of Stalin's closest allies, was utterly ruthless, a spymaster who unflinchingly ordered assassinations and mass murders.

Throughout the Russian Civil War, 1918–1922, the Cheka relentlessly hunted down and killed hundreds of thousands of royalists and White Russians advocating the return of the monarchy. It agents represented the worst elements of the Bolshevik and Communist parties—thugs, thieves, murderers, and sadists who killed countless victims in Cheka headquarters inside the Kremlin and in the torture chambers of Lubianka Prison in Moscow. Its successors were, in order, the GPU, OGPU, NKVD, MVD, KGB.

[ALSO SEE: *Dzerzhinsky, Felix; GPU; NKVD; OGPU; MVD; KGB; Okhrana*]

CHURCH, BENJAMIN
British Spy in American Revolution ▪ (1734–1777?)

C HURCH, BORN IN NEWPORT, RHODE ISLAND, WAS THE son of a clergyman. He was raised in Boston and attended the Latin School there, then went on to Harvard, graduating in 1754. He traveled to England where he took a medical degree and married an English subject before returning to the U.S. to practice medicine in Boston.

Church's practice blossomed and he soon lived in a fashionable home and became rich. In the Stamp Act crisis of 1765, Church spoke out loudly against the unjust taxes levied by the British on stamps. He decried the oppressive measures of King George III and was soon openly aligned with American patriots.

All of Church's professed patriotism was a sham. He was to the marrow a secret Tory, a British loyalist who became an ardent British spy, informing on his friends and the cause of the American Revolution. So well did Church act out his part that an American spy ring in Boston which kept British troops under constant surveillance welcomed him with open arms into their secret ranks in 1773. He shared the confidence of John and Samuel Adams, John Hancock and Joseph Warren, the very architects of the Revolution.

In the following year, Church was elected to the Massachussetts Provincial Congress, the political alternative to the British administration. All of what Church learned about the Patriots before and after this time, he reported in detail to Thomas Gage, British commander-in-chief and governor of Massachusetts. When Gage sent British troops to confiscate military stores at Concord on the night of April 18, 1775, he was acting upon detailed information from Church.

The spy wrote letters to Gage twice each week. These letters were written in bad French to disguise their author but they precisely listed the amount of arms available to the Patriots, where they were stored and the makeup of the militia from town to town. Fully six weeks before the first open conflict, the battle of Lexington, Church had kept Gage informed on every move the Patriots intended to make.

When the British were driven back from Lexington and Concord by the heroic and inventive Minutemen, Church celebrated with his revolutionary friends who named him to a two-man delegation to welcome General George Washington when he arrived to assume command of the Patriot forces then besieging Boston. Church promptly surveyed the fortifications Washington devised outside the city and then notified Gage by letter that Bunker Hill had been occupied by the Patriots. This was a month before the British attempted to storm this and other Patriot bastions.

With John and Samuel Adams and Hancock gone from the area, Benjamin Church became the ranking civilian Patriot in the Boston area. He wrote to Gage that he had been compelled to accept the role of courier to the Continental Congress in Philadelphia.

In Philadelphia, Church was so warmly received and held in such high esteem by the members of the Congress that he was appointed Surgeon General of the Continental Army and director of the first American army hospital outside of Boston at Cambridge. When returning to Cambridge, Church received an encrypted letter from John Fleming, his brother-in-law, a loyalist and a successful Boston printer. In the letter, Fleming stated that the British "were determined to crush this rebellion . . . For God's sake, Doctor, come to town [Boston] directly."

Church wrote back, penning a cautious reply in cipher. He may have believed that his unsigned letter might be seen by other eyes than Gage so his position appeared to be that of a fence-straddler. He stated: "For the sake of the miserable convulsed empire, solicit peace, repeal the acts, or Britain is undone. This advice is the result of warm affection to my king and to the realm. Remember, I never deceived you; every article here sent you is sacredly true."

The letter was taken to Boston by a young woman who ostensibly worked for Church but was, in reality, his mistress. She could not locate Fleming and left the letter with a Patriot woman who was puzzled by its strange code and sent it on to Washington. The general summoned Church's mistress but she would not identify the author of the letter. Then she confessed and Washington ordered Church arrested and his papers seized.

On October 3, 1775, Church was brought before Washington's officers, though, in Washington's words, he "made many protestations of the purity of his intentions." He was found guilty of "criminal correspondence" with the enemy. The offense of espionage had no set punishment in the articles of the Continental Army at this early stage of the Revolution. Church was imprisoned at Cambridge and the matter turned over to the Continental Congress.

Nothing was done. Church remained in jail until May 1776 when the British evacuated Boston. He was then ordered to later be set free as many believed that his letter did not indicate that he had been spying for the British up to that time. Church had also argued convincingly that his letter was miscontrued, although he could not deny his open statement that he was loyal to King George.

Church was released briefly on his promise that he would appear in court whenever called for trial, that he would not communicate with the British, and that he would not leave Massachusetts. On June 5, Joseph Warren wrote to John Adams, expressing his concern for his old friend's safety: "I fear the people will kill him if at large." Warren then went on to say that Church had gone to an inn at Waltham where other guests attacked him and he was saved from being lynched by local officials who held back the crowd lunging forward until Church could open a window, leap through it and run into the cover of darkness.

In late 1777, Church was exchanged for a captured American doctor and he set sail on a British schooner bound for the West Indies. The schooner vanished, most likely a victim of a storm at sea. Church's widow later went to England where she petitioned the British government for support. In her petition Mrs. Church claimed that her husband had performed "certain services" known to General Gage. She was given a yearly pension of £150.

CHURCHILL, PETER
British Spy in World War II ■ (1909–1972)

The son of a diplomat attached to the British Embassy, Churchill was born in Amsterdam and was later sent back to England where he graduated from Cambridge. He joined the British Army in 1939 just before Hitler's invasion of Poland began World War II.

Fluent in French and several other languages, Churchill was recruited by SOE (Special Operations Executive). Since he had lived for some considerable time in Europe, particularly in France, he was thought to be a perfect espionage candidate. Following training in codes and radio transmissions, Churchill was landed in southern France by submarine in January 1942. He carried considerable cash which he was to use in setting up one of SOE's first spy networks on the continent.

Churchill used the code name "Raoul" in dealing with members of the French resistance. He provided resistance leaders with money and acted as a communication conduit, transmitting messages to London from the Riviera. Much of Churchill's information was provided by a resistance group headed by Andre Giraud, a French artist whom Churchill had to sharply control; Giraud was bursting with grandiose ideas of setting up a vast intelligence network on Corsica. He was extravagant and ran his operation with little security, relishing his role as spymaster, making the dramatic most out of every clandestine meeting. Odette Sansom, a beautiful young French woman married to an Englishman, parachuted to France to aid Churchill in November 1942, becoming his permanent radio operator.

Churchill returned to London for conferences in February 1943, then went back to France, landing by parachute near Annecy on April 15, 1943. He was met by Sansom who told him the alarming news that she had been confronted by an Abwehr agent named Hugo Bleicher. This was the notorious German spy-catcher who had smashed the Interallié resistance group in Paris and who was aligned with the French double spy, Mathilde "The Cat" Carre.

Bleicher had recently arrested one of Churchill's Paris contacts, Jean Marsac, but had allowed Marsac to go free, convincing the resistance leader that he, Bleicher, represented anti-Hitler elements eager to negotiate a separate peace with the Allies. He told Marsac that he needed to get in touch with British agents in Europe working with the resistance and through them, contact Allied commanders to accomplish his ends. Marsac then put Bleicher in touch with Odette Sansom. The French agent was suspicious from the start.

When Churchill heard this story, he ordered Sansom to pack everything and prepare to flee. As they were doing so, Bleicher appeared with a large contingent of Gestapo agents and arrested them. They were taken to prison and held for three weeks before being taken to Fresnes. En route to Fresnes, Churchill and Sansom were able to communicate with each other, agreeing that they should tell the Germans that they were man and wife.

Sansom and Churchill were both tortured but they told the same story. Sansom went further. In a valiant gesture, she insisted that she, not Churchill, gave the orders to their network, that she and not Churchill, was the one who deserved to be shot. She convincingly lied to her Gestapo interrogators, saying that Churchill was not only her husband but that he was directly related to Prime Minister Winston Churchill (which he was not).

Because the Germans believed that the pair could be of use later as important relatives of Prime Minister Churchill, they spared the spies and sent them to concentration camps. Sansom was sent to the women's camp at Ravensbruck. She was rescued by American troops at the end of the war. She would later be awarded England's George Cross for her extraordinary heroism. Churchill was also liberated from another camp and lived out his life as a much-respected veteran of SOE.

[ALSO SEE: *Abwehr; Mathilde Carre; Gestapo; Odette Sansom; SOE*]

CIA (Central Intelligence Agency)
U.S. Intelligence Agency ▪ (1947–)

FOR MORE THAN A CENTURY, ALL MAJOR COUNTRIES IN the world, except the United States, developed and operated intelligence agencies. America's unwritten national code of ethics, stemming from stubborn Puritans, would not tolerate nor stoop to espionage. As late as 1929, this above-it-all attitude was summed up by Secretary of State Henry Stimson. After reviewing cryptanalysis of coded foreign documents by espionage pioneer Herbert O. Yardley, Stimson archly dismissed the information by stating: "Gentlemen do not read each other's mail."

Thus, the principal intelligence agency of the United States came into existence reluctantly. Following World War II, President Harry Truman disbanded the OSS (Office of Strategic Services), America's war time intelligence service. It was felt that there was no need for an American agency to conduct international espionage, until, of course, the Kremlin established the Cold War. Alarmed by the worldwide espionage conducted by the Soviet Union, Congress passed the National Security Act in July 1947, creating the CIA as a permanent organization of the U.S. government.

The CIA charter states that it is to operate under the control of the National Security Council (NSC), which placed it under the direction of the executive branch of the government, but it is also subject to congressional review. The CIA's chief responsibility is to "collect and evaluate intelligence," but it is also to perform "other functions and duties" as specified by the National Security Council.

The creation of the CIA was opposed most energetically by J. Edgar Hoover, director of the FBI. Hoover argued with President Truman and members of Congress that by establishing the CIA, the government would simply be duplicating efforts and information for which the FBI was responsible. Hoover was proved wrong. After the OSS was disbanded, the FBI and military intelligence provided unanalyzed, raw intelligence that was often misleading and conflicting.

To sort out the confused reports, and to better face the then apparent Communist threat, President

Truman established the Central Intelligence Group under the command of Rear Admiral Sidney Souers. This was the precursor to the CIA. When the National Security Council met for the first time on December 19, 1947, it gave an order to Admiral Roscoe Hillenkoetter, the CIA's first director. He was to supervise covert operations in Italy that would prevent the Communists from winning a general election.

Hillenkoetter and his people went to work, using military, political and economic pressure in a massive letter-writing campaign to assure a Communist defeat. This huge CIA success convinced the agency that it could be equally effective in the affairs of any foreign country in the future, setting a dangerous precedent. At its beginning the agency was staffed mostly by one-time OSS veterans whose wartime feats were daring and often reckless. These were gamblers rather than intriguers.

The CIA was not really modernized until February 1953 when Allen Dulles assumed control as director. Dulles had been the chief of OSS operations in Europe during World War II and brought a great deal of expertise to his position, although he set the pattern of CIA intervention with governments unfriendly to the U.S. From that point onward, the CIA involved itself in the internal affairs of many countries such as Iran, the Congo, Guatamala, Indonesia, Chile, and Egypt.

Its techniques were no different than most intelligence agencies, and these included bribery, blackmail, disinformation, black propaganda, guerrilla warfare, sabotage and even assassination. The agency began to excell at obtaining pure and invaluable information. It meanwhile stepped up its covert activities. In 1953, while under the direction of General Walter Bedell Smith, the CIA sent its agents into Iran to support the overthrow of Premier Mohammed Mossadegh, who appeared to be leading his country into political chaos.

The CIA became the equal to the KGB and then some when Allen Dulles assumed command in 1953. The following year the Communist-influenced regime of Jacobo Arbenz in Guatamala was undermined by CIA-supported insurgents. In 1955, the CIA supervised the digging of the Berlin Tunnel which allowed its communications experts to bug Soviet military and diplomatic phones and networks in East Berlin. In 1956, CIA agents procured a copy of a Nikita Khrushchev speech given secretly to the 20th Party Congress in the Kremlin, one in which the Soviet Premier listed the crimes of Communist dictator Joseph Stalin.

For four years, 1956–1960, the CIA directed U-2 spy planes in the skies of the Soviet Union which ostensibly ended when U-2 pilot Gary Francis Powers was shot down and imprisoned, then later exchanged for KGB spymaster Rudolf Abel. It was the CIA in 1961 which produced intelligence reports that convinced President John Kennedy to commit U.S. noncombatant "advisers" to the war in Vietnam.

And, in that same year, it was the CIA that enthusiastically spearheaded the aborted attempt to overthrow the Communist regime of Fidel Castro in Cuba by landing a poorly trained, badly supported force of Cuban exiles at the Bay of Pigs.

The CIA fiasco in Cuba caused President Kennedy to demand the resignation of Allen Dulles. (The man who had really masterminded the U-2 flights and the disaster that was the Bay of Pigs, Richard Bissell, was one of Dulles' top executives.) The following year, the CIA redeemed itself under the direction of John McCone when one of its spy planes took photos of Soviet missile emplacements in Cuba. This information was shown to the world in Kennedy's historic confrontation with Khrushchev, the Cuban Missile Crisis, in which the Soviet Premier backed down and the missiles were recalled.

When President Kennedy was assassinated in 1963, the CIA again came under severe criticism in that the assassin, Lee Harvey Oswald, had been identified earlier to the agency as a dangerous political malcontent but the CIA lost track of him. (In fairness, the doings of Oswald in the U.S. actually fell under the province of the FBI which is in charge of intelligence gathering in the Western Hemisphere; the CIA's area of responsibility is any territory outside the Western Hemisphere).

In 1964, while McCone was still at the helm, the CIA was also pillaried for aiding the insurgents who overthrew and assassinated Premier Patrice Lumumba of the Congo Republic. McCone was replaced by Admiral William Raborn (1965–1966) whose directorship was uneventful.

Raborn's successor, Richard Helms (1966–1973) concentrated on the Vietnam war, stripping CIA offices around the world to provide more than 1,000 agents in the Saigon area to the Office of Special Assistance. CIA operations during this period flourished in Vietnam, Laos, and Cambodia. The agency even operated its own air force under the banner of Air America. In America, a groundswell of opposition to the war caused President Lyndon B. Johnson, who, more than any other, was responsible for America's escalated involvement in Vietnam, to insist that Helms spy on American dissidents. Helms reportedly resisted these pressures, then conducted surveillance of political activists in direct violation of the CIA charter.

Domestic intelligence was the province of the FBI but J. Edgar Hoover refused to conduct such surveillance and the CIA assumed this illegal duty, until the revelations of Watergate forced the CIA's domestic spying into the open, albeit the agency was never proven to be directly involved in Watergate.

Helms had a strange menagerie of deputies and agents at the CIA, including dirty tricks expert Richard Bissell and James Angleton, CIA counterintelligence chief who was obsessed with discovering Soviet moles in the agency and dismissed scores of wrongly suspected CIA workers.

CIA headquarters in Langley, Virgina.

President Richard Nixon dismissed Helms in 1973, undoubtedly for his unwillingness to cover up Watergate. Nixon then appointed Helms Ambassador to Iran but he left this post when returning to the U.S. to testify before congressional committees probing the secrets of the agency. Appearing before the Senate Foreign Relations Committee, Helms was caught in the act of lying in an attempt to protect CIA secrets. He was fined $2,000 and was given a suspended two-year prison sentence.

The CIA had mud on its bureaucratic face for several years following Watergate. It was in disgrace for openly gathering intelligence on U.S. citizens. The once all-powerful agency was reduced to a whipping-boy, protrayed in books, movies and on TV as a right-wing Gestapo-like entity that was a law unto itself, an agency that was an enemy of the American public instead of its protector against subversion, treason and deadly foreign espionage.

Moreover, the CIA during this time, while William Colby was its director (1973–1976), was subject to the scrutiny of no less than seven congressional committees. It found itself hamstrung and near helpless. Even the most friendly of foreign intelligence agencies, that of Britain, Israel and Germany, were reluctant to help the CIA in fear that the newly-established Freedom of Information Act would compromise their own state secrets.

In 1979, President Jimmy Carter eased some of the restrictions placed on the CIA, allowing its then director, Admiral Stansfield Turner (1977–1981), to conduct limited covert operations abroad, including the surveillance of certain U.S. citizens in foreign countries. Carter even allowed Turner to carry on clandestine operations without informing him of those operations. Turner, however, was no freewheeling intelligence monarch. He towed the mark and welcomed the restrictions placed on the CIA.

President Carter nevertheless signed the Intelligence Oversight Act of 1980 which restricted the right of Congress to monitor the CIA to the Senate and House intelligence committees and only eight members of Congress to receive special information and even that information was to be released under extraordinary circumstances. The President had the right under the new Act to withhold certain information from these congressional leaders.

More CIA power and little or no disclosed information on its operations was music to the ears of William Casey, the new CIA chief (1981–1987) appointed by President Ronald Reagan. Casey, a self-made millionaire and President Reagan's campaign manager, was a crafty autocrat who thrived on covert activities and shared as little information as possible with Congress. During his reign, the CIA recaptured its all-powerful image. It received a twenty-five percent budget increase in 1983 (compared with an eighteen percent increase for the Defense Department in that same year), and it enlarged its staff which had been cut by forty percent during the nadir of the CIA in the 1970s.

Casey's fiefdom was the CIA headquarters located on 140 green acres at Langley, Virginia, a complex of tightly guarded buildings that cost $46 million to build. More than half of the CIA's 20,000 employees work in Langley, the rest spread throughout CIA offices in the U.S. and, in American diplomatic centers around the world. Today, as it was in Casey's era, the CIA can boast of an extraordinary work force made up of experts of every foreign language, of cryptography, chemistry, cybernetics, the most sophisticated communications systems, demography, agronomy, guerrilla warfare.

Four separate divisions form the workforce of the agency. The Intelligence Division is responsible for gathering information from published sources, speeches by diplomats, as well as from secret documents and reports throughout the world. Scientific and technical equipment and problems are handled by the Research Division. The Support Division coordinates the operations of the headquarters staff and field agents. The Plans Division supervises all covert operations.

All of these divisions were humming under the direction of William Casey. He lunged into covert operations with tireless ambition. With President Reagan's support, Casey's CIA supported the Afghan rebels against Soviet incursion, armed Iranian paramilitary groups opposing Ayatolah Khomeini's rigidly religious regime and openly supported the insurgents fighting the left-wing government of Nicaragua.

When the Iran-Contra scandal was made public, Oliver North claimed that Casey and the CIA were behind the entire operation. Casey was summoned to testify in the matter but died in 1987 before he could confirm or deny the agency's involvement.

By the late 1980s when the agency was headed by former FBI chief William Webster, and into the mid-1990s, the CIA, again came in for its share of head-thumping. It was accused of the systematic brainwashing of Canadian citizens three decades earlier in an effort to compete with brainwashing techniques developed by the Soviets, China and North Korea. It was accused of being involved in horrendous medical experiments, assassinations, and sabotage involving the deaths of many innocent citizens.

Then the worst fears of the agency were realized. In 1994, one of its long-employed desk men, Aldrich Ames, the son of a CIA executive, was exposed as a Soviet spy, the highest paid American traitor in history. To be sure, there had been other CIA turncoats, such as Edward Lee Howard who sold secrets to the Russians before fleeing to Moscow; CIA officer William Peter Kampiles who sold the Soviets a top secret manual for a CIA spy-in-the-sky satellite; CIA analyst Larry Wu-Tai Chin who had been born in Peking and spied for China for thirty years before his 1986 conviction and suicide.

None of these CIA turncoats, however, approached the devastational impact Ames had on the agency. In return for more than $2 million, Ames gave the Soviets the names of America's best Russian informants, causing the deaths of at least a half dozen or more men. Arrested and convicted of espionage, Ames made a deal, information for life imprisonment and a five-year sentence for his accomplice wife.

The CIA has yet to recover from the shock and the embarrassment of Ames, not to mention its tremendous loss of prestige. Under the present directorship of George Tenet, a cautious, closed-mouthed man, the agency is expected to maintain a more than traditional low profile as it rebuilds its self-confidence and goes about its secret business.

[ALSO SEE: *Rudolf Abel; Aldrich Ames; James Angleton; Bay of Pigs; Berlin Tunnel; Richard Bissell; William Casey; William Colby; Cuban Missile Crisis; Allen Dulles; FBI; Richard Helms; J. Edgar Hoover; Edward Lee Howard; KGB; National Security Council; OSS; Gary Francis Powers; Herbert O. Yardley*]

COHEN, ELIE
Israeli Spy in Egypt and Syria ▪ (1924-1965)

A ZIONIST ALL HIS LIFE, ELIE COHEN WAS BORN AND raised in, Alexandria, Egypt, to Orthodox Jewish parents. He attended Cairo University from 1946 to 1948. In 1951, Cohen traveled secretly to Israel and there underwent espionage and sabotage training. He returned to Cairo and was part of the team of saboteurs who attempted to blow up American business buildings in an effort to disrupt American-Egyptian relations.

Egyptian counterintelligence penetrated Cohen's cover and he was arrested which led to the Lavon Affair in Israel, a heated scandal which sought to identify the author of the sabotage in Egypt, namely Defense Minister Pinhas Lavon. Cohen managed to convince his Egyptian captors that he had no part in the sabotage and he was released. He was again arrested in 1956 and expelled from Egypt.

Cohen went to Israel where he became a full-fledged officer of the Mossad, Israel's intelligence agency and was sent to Damascus. From his Syrian contacts, particularly his high-ranking officer friends, Cohen was able to pinpoint all of Syria's military forces, the country's Russian military aid, and a water diversion scheme planned by the Syrians which would deprive the Israeli farming communities of fresh water.

Cohen also reported to the Mossad the plan

Israeli superspy Ellie Cohen, executed in Damascus in 1965.

created by Soviet advisers in which Syrian forces would cut off Northern Israel in a sneak attack. He also provided in-depth information regarding Syrian military installations, particularly the defenses of the seemingly impregnable fort that commanded the Golan Heights and regularly shelled the defenseless Israeli farming communities nearby. For three years, Cohen gathered information and sent it by short-wave to the Mossad.

Syrian counterintelligence was not, however, dormant. Syrian technicians operating sophisticated direction finders (provided by the Soviets, along with advisers) were able to locate the exact hotel room from which Cohen sent his radio messages and he was seized in 1965, arrested while he was broadcasting a message to his spymasters in Israel. This was accomplished, however, only after Syrian agents received a complaint from the Indian Embassy which reported that its radio transmissions were being interrupted by someone using a short-wave nearby. Cohen's hotel room was close to the Indian Embassy and was therefore easy to identify.

Convicted of espionage, Cohen was hanged in May 1965 in the largest square in Damascus, his gruesome execution witnessed by thousands. His work nevertheless aided the Israelis immensely when, in 1967, they stormed the Golan Heights and overwhelmed the Syrian fort. Almost every detail of the fort's defenses had been supplied by Cohen, one of Israel's most effective and valiant spies.

[ALSO SEE: *Lavon Affair; Mossad*]

COHEN, MORRIS (AKA: Two-Gun)
British Spymaster in China ▪ (1889–1970)

HE WAS NERVELESS, INTREPID, AND DARING TO THE point of recklessness. As a spymaster in China, none could compare with his acumen and thoroughness. Without any special heritage, Morris "Two-Gun" Cohen became a legend in the annals of espionage. Born in London of Polish Jews, Cohen's early life was pockmarked with mischief and petty crime, so much so that he was sent to a reform school at an early age.

Upon his release, his parents sent Cohen to Canada to live with relatives, hoping that a change in environment would settle him into lawful, successful pursuits. He became a salesman, then a carnival barker, but most of his time was consumed by his abiding passion—gambling. He grew rich enough to fraternize with social lions in Edmonton, Canada, the very people who invited Cohen to meet a strange travelor in 1910, the Chinese revolutionary leader Sun Yet-sen.

Sun was leading the revolution in China against the Manchu Dynasty, with the ambition of unifying all of China, Manchuria, Tibet and Mongolia, establishing a western form of democracy. Educated in Honolulu and Hong Kong, Sun had organized his first non-violent revolutionary group in China in 1894 and had begun lobbying the Manchus for more freedom. The dynasty was slow to respond, promising a more liberal and westernized education for all, promising a constitution and rights of self-determination.

None of this happened as promised and Sun vowed to overthrow the dynasty. He would seek any means and accept any support to achieve that end. In 1905, he and his protegé, Chiang Kai-shek, at the invitation of Mitsuru Toyama, went to Japan and struck a deal with the Black Dragon Society, the powerful, secret organization urging a Japanese war of conquest in Manchuria. In return for a monopoly of the Chinese opium trade which would fund its military ambitions, the Society financed Sun Yet-sen's Chinese revolution.

Sun now had the money but he needed weapons. He explained this dilemma to Cohen when they met and the enterprising gambler quickly assured Sun that he could provide all the guns and ammunition he could purchase. Within months, Cohen was supplying arms to Sun in China. The revolution succeeded in 1911–1912, and the grateful Sun invited Cohen to join him in China as one of his top advisers.

Cohen, however, was caught up in World War I. Following the war, Cohen traveled from England to China where he sat in the high councils of Sun Yet-sen. In 1922, Sun appointed Cohen chief of his intelligence service. He was accepted as a genuine officer of Sun's administration, rather than as a soldier-of-fortune which was the label attached to most foreigners then in China.

Counterintelligence was the chief occupation for Morris Cohen. Through a vast network of agents, both Chinese and foreigners, he was able to report to Sun the exact doings of warlords, insurgents, dissidents and political malcontents. Cohen's spies consisted of farmers in distant provinces and shopkeepers and businessmen in the cities. His networks were particularly active in Canton and Shanghai which were hotbeds of conspiracies and the headquarters for most foreign espionage operations, especially Sun's former supporters, the Japanese. One of Cohen's most active agents was a westerner who had spied for many nations, Isaac Trebitsch Lincoln, who used the cover of being a missionary to get information.

In the early 1930s, Cohen employed an amazing spy named Lionel Phillip Kenneth Crabb who was later to become Britain's most spectacular undersea spy and frogman.

Sun knew he could count not only on Cohen's detailed and corroborated intelligence reports but on Cohen's loyalty and dedication. Often as not, Cohen willingly led strike forces against rebellious groups, traveling by train and plane to distant provinces and cities to attack the headquarters of oppositionists. Some of these attacks involved pitched battles where Cohen led the way with two blazing pistols. (He went armed night and day with two holstered pistols, one on his hip, the other slung about his shoulder, thus earning the sobriquet of "Two-Gun.")

After capturing conspirators, Cohen put them through severe interrogations. He was not above using torture and he summarily executed proven spies, some of which he personally shot. It was a ruthless, wild time in China. Sun Yet-sen's government was not in control of a land overrun with warlords who dominated certain provinces with private armies of mercenaries, and foreign powers that controlled cities and towns as their own fiefdoms.

Sun Yet-sen died in 1925 and his successor, Chiang Kai-shek kept Cohen on as chief of intelligence. From 1930 onward, Cohen's counterintelligence concentrated on two major threats to Chiang's fragile government, the Chinese Communist Party which had been organized in 1921 and had been growing in power ever since, and the Japanese who had thousands of spies in China's coastal cities, all preparing for the day when Japan would invade China.

Cohen was able to penetrate the largest of these Japanese spy rings, the Special Service Organ located in Shanghai, a business front for the main Japanese military intelligence service in China, directed by a towering Japanese officer with an abnormally huge head, Major Ryukichi Tanaka. Cohen learned that Tanaka had taken as his mistress Eastern Jewel, a Manchu princess and cousin of the Manchurian boy emperor, Henry Pu-Yi.

It was through Cohen's contacts with Tanaka and Eastern Jewel that he learned of Japan's plans to invade Manchuria in 1931. He passed on this report to Chiang Kai-shek. Cohen informed Chiang that Tanaka and Eastern Jewel planned to create a disturbance in Shanghai in order to provoke Japanese intervention in that teeming city. Though forewarned, Chiang seemed powerless to prevent this incident from happening. When World War II finally broke out, Cohen undertook a mission to Hong Kong where he was captured by invading Japanese. He spent the rest of the war as a prisoner.

Cohen returned to Chiang Kai-shek in 1945 but by then he had been replaced by Tai Li as the generalissimo's chief of intelligence. Having lost his position, Cohen returned to Canada. He wrote his memoirs and lived out a quiet life, dying in London in 1970.

[ALSO SEE: *Black Dragon Society; Lionel Phillip Kenneth Crabb; Eastern Jewel; Isaac Trebitsch Lincoln; Tai Li; Mitsuru Toyama*]

COLBY, WILLIAM
CIA Director ▪ (1920–1996)

COLBY SAW HIS FIRST ESPIONAGE SERVICE AS A member of the OSS during World War II. He operated behind the German lines in France and was part of many dangerous missions, including the blowing up of a Nazi communications center in Norway which was achieved after Colby and a team of OSS men parachuted to the site.

Returning to Princeton to study law after the war, Colby then went to work for the CIA. He was station chief in Saigon from 1959 to 1962. He later ran the Phoenix Program which involved resettlement and pacification of Vietnamese villagers. The program was abused when many thousands of Vietnamese were killed or imprisoned out-of-hand as suspected Viet Cong supporters. The nightmare of this slaughter haunted Colby throughout his intelligence career.

In 1973 Colby was appointed Deputy Director of Operations, a post he assumed after returning from Vietnam. In September 1973. Colby was named Director of the CIA, a post he held until January 1976. During this period, Colby, under pressure to admit CIA "bad secrets" admitted that the agency had interferred in the internal affairs of such countries as Angola in 1975.

Colby further turned over top secret information to the Church Commission which compromised the public statements of his predecessor, Richard Helms,

CIA chief William Colby.

who was indicted for perjury. Another victim of Colby's bureaucratic housecleaning was James Jesus Angleton, who headed the CIA's counterintelligence department. Colby so disliked Angleton that he fired him. This and other arbitrary decisions earned Colby considerable criticism, even the accusation that he was attempting to dismantle the agency.

More scrutiny was directed on the CIA during William Colby's tenure than at any other time. President Gerald Ford prohibited the CIA from involving itself in the assassination of any foreign leader. Ford also established the Rockefeller Commission to investigate the agency.

The commission gave the CIA its nodding approval but stated that it had committed some unlawful acts. Frank Church who headed the congressional committee also investigating the CIA in 1975, initially described the agency as "a rogue elephant running amok." In 1976, however, the committee reported that its chairman had been too severe on an agency vital to the national interest. By then William Colby was gone, replaced by Admiral Stanfield Turner.

In late April 1996, the retired Colby paddled down a Maryland river in a canoe and mysteriously disappeared. His drowned body was identified by his wife on May 6, 1996.

[ALSO SEE: *James Angleton; CIA; Richard Helms*]

CONRAD, THOMAS NELSON
Confederate Spy in Civil War ▪ (1838–1904)

ORN IN FAIRFAX, VIRGINIA, CONRAD WAS EDUCATED at Dickinson College in Pennsylvania, graduating in 1860. He then took a teaching position in Washington, D.C., but when the Civil War started, he voiced his sympathies for the newly-born Confederacy. Allan Pinkerton, who then headed the Union espionage and counterespionage systems, identified Conrad as a Confederate sympathizer who had been scouting Washington, D.C. for the Confederate army, as well as running mail from Washington to Virginia. Pinkerton ordered him arrested.

Conrad languished in the Old Capitol Prison for two months before he was released and given a parole. He remained in Washington where he plotted to either kidnap or kill General Winfield Scott, commanding general of the Union army. When Conrad submitted his plan to Confederate leaders he was told to abandon the idea, that the Union would simply replace Scott with another general whom might prove more energetic and damaging than the obese, lethargic Scott.

Conrad went to Richmond but secretly returned many times to Washington where he developed a large spy network that fed the Confederacy vital information the helped defeat Union forces in many major battles. Conrad kept a hidden sailing boat, *The Rebel Queen*, near Port Tobacco which was used regularly by Confederate couriers to cross and recross the Potomac. One of these couriers was John Harrison Surratt, Jr., who was later to become John Wilkes Booth's co-conspirator in the fantastic plot to assassinate President Abraham Lincoln.

When Lafayette Baker replaced Allan Pinkerton as chief of Union intelligence in 1862, one of Conrad's agents managed to secure a position with Baker, one which allowed his access to the top secret military plans of the Union Army.

Thus, Conrad acquired the plans of Union General George B. McClellan for his peninsular campaign. These plans Conrad sent to General Robert E. Lee and they vastly aided that ablest of Confederate generals to soundly defeat the Union forces. The same source gave Conrad the battle plans of Union General John Pope who was moving into Virigina. Again, a Confederate courier was sent to Lee and again Lee triumphed, winning a decisive victory over Pope at the Second Battle of Bull Run (Second Manasas).

Though Union authorities began to suspect that there was a leak somewhere at the very top of Union strategy councils, they discovered nothing. Lafayette Baker was given the assignment of finding the informer. He reportedly gave this task to the very person on his staff who was the Confederate spy in Conrad's ring. This same agent, who remains unidentified to this day, learned once more of a massive Union buildup and march to the south, a Union drive to be led by General Ambrose Burnside.

Conrad met with Lee and displayed Burnside's precise battle plan, how he would cross the Rappahanock River in a forced march on Richmond, a route that would take the Union army through the small town of Fredericksburg. It was there that Lee and Stonewall Jackson and the best divisions of the Confederate army were waiting for Burnside in December 1862. Burnside wasted half his army as it uselessly assaulted impregnable Confederate positions on Mayre's Heights. This victory, more than any other, belonged to Thomas Nelson Conrad.

The turning point of the land war, the battle of Gettysburg on July 1–3, 1863, might not have been fought at all and the Union might have lost the war altogether had Thomas Conrad been able to get his top secret information to Lee's "eyes and ears," General J.E.B. Stuart. Every available man in Washington, D.C., was sent to Meade to meet Lee's invasion of the north. There were so few Union troops left in the capital that defense positions had to be taken by untrained civilians. Any substantial Confederate force could have easily captured Washington at that time and possibly ended the war.

Learning this, Conrad rode quickly through the countryside in a desperate search for the Confederate cavalary commander, General Stuart. The dashing Stuart, however, had gone off on a raid, far from Lee's army, leaving his commander without certain knowledge of Meade's whereabouts.

When Stuart did return, he was crestfallen when Conrad told him of the lost opportunity in seizing an almost defenseless Washington. "My God," moaned Stuart, "I would have charged down Pennsylvania Avenue!"

When Conrad returned to Washington, he was informed by his agent on Baker's staff that he had been identified as a Confederate spy. He joined the Confederate army, serving in the cavalry as a scout. He remained with Lee's army until its final, tragic surrender at Appomattox. Shortly after the war ended, Conrad planned the kidnapping of President Lincoln.

Conrad and his friends would hold Lincoln hostage to safeguard the lives of Confederate leaders. Before they could act, however, an associate raced up to them and warned them that the plot was discovered and all were about to be arrested. Conrad and his friends fled. A few days later another group of conspirators, headed by John Wilkes Booth, took action. Lincoln was assassinated.

Because of his sharp resemblance to John Wilkes Booth, Conrad was almost taken for the assassin. He breathed a great sigh of relief when Booth was tracked down and killed in Virginia. Following the war, Conrad became a clergyman in Virginia. He delivered speeches and sermons on the war, then wrote his colorful memoirs.

[ALSO SEE: *Lafayette Baker; Allan Pinkerton; John H. Surratt, Jr.*]

CONSTANTINI, FRANCESCO
Italian Spy for Mussolini ▪ (1895–1963)

UNSCHOOLED AND UNSOPHISTICATED, VITERBO-BORN Constantini left his village at age fourteen and walked barefoot to Rome. By luck, he got a job at the American Embassy as an office boy. The resourceful Constantini, however, used his experiences at the American Embassy to obtain a job at the British Embassy where he was to work until 1936.

Constantini performed all manner of jobs for the British, but, at the same time, he was serving Italian dictator Benito Mussolini as one of his most valuable espionage agents. His reason for spying was patriotic.

By the time Mussolini came to power in Italy in 1922, Constantini was well ensconced at the British Embassy in Rome. He had proven himself an obedient and effective servant whose responsibilities encompassed a variety of jobs.

The British Embassy staff had one important job that had to be ritually performed each day, a chore the officials found distasteful and dirty. It was the burning of each day's decoded dispatches. This work was supervised by an attaché who carefully watched Constantini feed the papers into a basement furnace and then set them ablaze.

Untrained as a spy, Constantini nevertheless knew that what he was burning might have some value to his government. He devised a plan to make sure he could obtain the decoded messages. Early one morning he stuffed the furnace with oil rags and damp paper. When he accompanied the attaché to the basement to burn the dispatches that afternoon and lit the fire, dense clouds of smoke billowed from the furnace. The attaché complained that the smoke smelled terrible and stung his eyes, not to mention the ruination of his starched collar and sharply creased pants. After a few more smoky experiences in the basement, the attaché simply had Constantini burn the dispatches alone in the basement.

From that point on, Constantini helped himself to the dispatches, burning only a few papers and taking the rest each night to the offices of Mussolini's military intelligence, giving them to Cesare Amé, who later became a general and plotted the Duce's downfall.

Constantini had no idea of what to bring Amé, as he later admitted. "I was certainly not qualified to select the material, all of which seemed to me absolutely incomprehensible." He nevertheless selected what he thought would be important documents and maintained his deliveries. "It was child's play," Constantini would remember two decades later.

Italian intelligence realized that Constantini needed espionage skills and trained him at night in their offices. Soon he was able to make wax impressions of the Embassy keys to its safes and vaults. From these he took whatever papers seemed important, carrying them to Italian intelligence headquarters where they were photographed. He then returned the papers to the safe of Ambassador Sir Eric Drummond before dawn.

One evening, while serving as night custodian of the British Embassy, Constantini managed to remove a classified 24-volume set of British code books. He smoked and drank wine for nearly seven hours while Italian intelligence officers photographed the entire set, not knowing whether they would finish the job or not before morning. Constantini just barely returned the set in time before Ambassador Drummond appeared in his office.

Mussolini delighted in reading the secret British dispatches at breakfast each day. He bragged to friends and even fellow dictator Adolf Hitler that he was able to read messages from Whitehall to Rome before Ambassador Drummond read them. The bombastic Italian dictator was fond of the art of spying since he himself had been a police informant years earlier, identifying to law enforcement officers the revolutionary groups opposed to his fascist organization.

On November 18, 1935, the League of Nations imposed sanctions against Italy for its aggressions in Africa and elsewhere. To back up those sanctions, a powerful British fleet steamed into the Mediterranean Sea, expecting to frighten the Duce into canceling his plans for conquest. Mussolini did no such thing. He defied the British and the fleet withdrew. The dictator's bold behavior was based on information supplied by the little spy, Constantini. He had obtained a copy of British Admiralty orders which clearly stated that the fleet was to merely be a show of force and was to take no action.

The spy's greatest coup occured in 1936 when Mussolini's troops were overruning Ethiopia. The Duce risked total war with England by openly invading that helpless African nation, yet he knew the British would not oppose him, thanks to a top secret British Government report Constantini had stolen from Ambassador Drummond's safe. The report stated that "no vital British interest exists in Ethiopa which would impose on His Majesty's government the necessity to resist by force the Italian occupation." (The British has already allowed Mussolini to boat thousands of invasion troops through the Suez Canal, charging the Italians approximately $2 for each trooper, a venal act for which they would later pay dearly.)

Mussolini was ebullient when receiving the secret British report. He was so confident that his legions would have a free hand and the British would never go to war with Italy that he caused the official British report to be openly reprinted in his official organ, *Giornale d'Italia*. The British Foreign Office in Whitehall responded by ordering a thorough investigation of all staff members in Italy but Constantini was not exposed. He continued working at the Embassy for another year and then quit, entering the lumber business.

This ended Constantini's career as an Italian espionage agent. He later lamented: "Out of my risky activity I gained no fortune, no material or even moral recognition. I was an inexpert spy, but I was smarter than the English."

COPLON, JUDITH
American Spy for Soviets ▪ (1922–   )

BROOKLYN-BORN JUDITH COPLON CAME FROM A middleclass Jewish family. Her father, Samuel Coplon, was a successful toy manufacturer who doted on his daughter and was known as the "Santa Claus of the Adirondacks" because he gave away thousands of free toys to country children at Christmas. After Coplon graduated from high school in 1938, she entered the elitist Barnard College for girls where she studied history and Russian culture. She found eveything about the Soviet government wonderful. By the time she graduated *cum laude* in 1943, Coplon was a petite attractive, dark-haired young woman who spoke her mind.

In 1943, Coplon got a job with the Department of Justice in New York, reportedly through her philanthropist father's connections. The FBI conducted a security check on Coplon but its agents failed to unearth the open fact that Coplon had signed editorials in her school newspaper for which she was the managing editor and which demanded a second front be established in Europe during World War II to reduce the pressue on the Russian front. Moreover, she was extremely active in exchange programs and war relief for Russia.

Coplon's work was good enough for her to receive a recommendation for promotion in 1945 when she was reassigned to the foreign agents registration section of the Justice Department. Under U.S. law, all agents, business or political, were required to register with this section. From these registrations, the FBI was able to identify suspected foreign spies. In her new post, Coplon had full access to FBI reports on foreign diplomats and suspected Soviet agents. She therefore knew what the Bureau knew, information that would be invaluable to the Russians.

So highly did KGB officials in Moscow value the reports Coplon was supplying to the Russian Embassy in Washington, that they assigned a special

Judith Coplon, who spied for the KGB inside the Department of Justice.

spymaster, Valentin Gubitchev, to act as her special contact and information conduit.

Coplon frequently left Washington, D.C. on trips to New York, ostensibly to visit her family and friends. She met no one but Gubitchev, passing on secret FBI reports to him. Some time in December 1948, the FBI received information that its most confidential reports had been showing up in the Russian Embassy and elsewhere for some time. The source of information, never identified, told J. Edgar Hoover that a female working in the Department of Justice in Washington was the purloining agent for the Soviets. The description of the woman fit Judith Coplon.

The FBI informant may have been one of Coplon's own superiors who suspected her for some time. Coplon had displayed an uncanny knowledge on the Communists and she had been promoted and given a considerable raise in May 1948 for providing her bosses with a brilliant political analysis of Soviet politics. Moreover, she had been particularly interested in seeing FBI reports on those suspected of being Soviet agents in the U.S.

Bureau agents began a thorough investigation of Coplon, learning that she had rented an apartment at 2634 Tunlaw Road, Washington, D.C. Her landlord and neighbors described her as a quiet, intellectual person who was never seen to bring home men. She later moved to Jefferson Hall, McClean Gardens,

where she took a one-room apartment, paying $34.50 per month rent. By then her sexual appetite had increased. She brought home several men, and, at one point, the FBI trailed her to the Southern Hotel in Baltimore where she spent the night with a lawyer who worked in the Department of Justice.

The agents, according to one report, "were able to achieve from their latest equipment for listening and looking through walls . . . a practical demonstration in the art of love-making." Though she would later claim that her lover throughout this period was her Russian spymaster Gubitchev, Coplon continued to see and sleep with many men. It was assumed that these brief encounters were not merely to satisfy her sexual needs but served as information contacts.

Meanwhile, though under surveillance by the FBI, Coplon continued her regular procedures in pilfering classified documents. She simply took them home and retyped the reports, then passed these on to Gubitchev. One report, a master list of suspected Soviet spies prepared by the FBI, was needed by the KGB agent. Coplon asked her chief, William E. Foley, if she could review this report, saying that she needed it for her work. By that time Foley knew that Coplan was under FBI surveillance. He stalled, calling Hoover.

The FBI director personally visited Foley, giving him a fake document involving suspected agents at the Russian trade organization, Amtorg. This document was then given to Coplon on Friday, January 14, 1949. At that moment, Coplon asked if she could have the afternoon off so she could enjoy a long weekend. Foley agreed. That afternoon, at 1 P.M., Coplon got on board a train bound for New York City. Four FBI agents also got on the train, taking seats near the spy.

When arriving at Pennyslvania Station, Coplon immediately went to the ladies room. She emerged forty-five minutes later, checked her coat in a cloak room, walked to a bookstall where she pretended to look over some editions, then went to a drugstore where she sat at the lunch counter and ate an egg salad sandwich and drank a Green River. (The preciseness of this report was based on the fact that an FBI agent was sitting next to her, eating his own late lunch.)

Coplon then walked to the subway and took a train to 191st Street in Manhattan. It was by then dark and Coplon walked down dimly lit streets only to stop at a jewelry store to stare at the gems on display. This was, the trailing Bureau men knew, an old trick. By staring into a shop window, the spy is able to view everything nearby through the reflection of the plate glass.

After peering into the window for seven minutes, a well-dressed, stocky short man with dark features emerged from the shadows of the street. He walked slowly past Coplon who had her back turned to him. She saw him in the window's reflection and turned to follow him into a nearby restaurant. Agents entered the place to see both the Coplon and the man sitting in an alcove, talking.

They constantly fed coins into a juke box, selecting noisy songs which muffled their talk. They had dinner and Coplon was seen to do most of the talking. She was excited, animated, nervous. After an hour, the couple left the restaurant. Both took the subway. As the train was about to pull out of the 125th station, Coplon's male companion suddenly leaped to his feet, raced to the closing door and squeezed through.

One FBI agent managed to follow the man who took a series of buses and taxis and finally lost the Bureau man. The FBI, however, believed that the man was a foreigner, a Slav, and, coupled to some vague reports on hand, they concluded that he was a member of the consulate-general in New York, working at the United Nations.

Bureau men were posted outside the Soviet offices until the man who had been with Coplon the previous night came outside. He was followed to his apartment at 64 West 108th Street. The building's porter was taken aside by an FBI agent who was told that the man was a Russian engineer who worked in the United Nations Architectural Department. His name was Valintin Gubitchev.

Coplon was not detained on this New York trip but by the time she had returned to Washington, Hoover told Foley that she was not to have any further access to classified documents. She was to be transferred to another department where surveillance of her would continue. When told of her transfer, Coplon became upset. She demanded to know why she was being removed from the foreign agents registration section.

"Your new position must be occupied immediately," Foley told her. "You are the only person who can do this job." Coplon quietly agreed to take the position but she was not deterred in performing duties for her Kremlin masters. She appeared every day in her old offices to help her successor. In so doing, she continued to have access to sensitive documents.

Shortly thereafter, Coplon, on February 18, 1949, again took a long weekend, taking the train to New York. This time, a female FBI agent accompanied the male Bureau agents trailing Coplon. When the train reached Pennsylvania Station, Coplon again went to the ladies washroom but this time the female FBI agent went inside with her. Nothing unusual occured, except that Coplon may have been removing documents from her purse to place in a pocket of her coat while she spent an inordinate amount of time inside a stall.

Again FBI agents followed Coplon until she met Gubitchev on a street intersecting Broadway. The two met inside a doorway for only a few minutes and were difficult to observe, although agents believed that Coplon passed some papers to the Russian spymaster before Gubitchev suddenly dashed down the street and was lost from view.

On March 4, Coplon again asked to see classified documents in Foley's department. Foley countered

KGB spymaster and Judith Coplon's lover, Valentin Gubitchev.

by asking her if she remembered the three suspected spies at Amtorg? She nodded yes. Foley told her he now had additional information on that case, including a letter from J. Edgar Hoover to the Assistant Attorney General in which Hoover stated that the three Amtorg employees had been asking questions about geophones, classified instruments that measured blast pressure and were used in atomic bomb testing. Foley left Coplon alone in his office with documents in plain sight.

A half hour later Coplon took the train to New York with FBI agents traveling with her. She again met with Gubitchev but this time the FBI agents closed in. Both spies ran but were apprehended at 16th Street and Third Avenue. They were placed under arrest and taken to Bureau headquarters. Gubitchev would say nothing. No incriminating documents were found on his person. Coplon was searched and nothing was found. But in her handbag, an FBI matron found a sealed advertisement for nylons. Opening this, the matron found copies of thirty-four top secret documents Coplon had taken from the Department of Justice offices, along with the original copy of J. Edgar Hoover's letter to the Assistant Attorney General.

The 27-year-old Judith Coplon, KGB spy, was charged with espionage and treason. Gubitchev, 32, was also charged with espionage but he claimed diplomatic immunity through the Soviet Embassy in Washington. U.N. officials stated that since Gubitchev was one of its employees he did not hold diplomatic status. He was soon given a $2,000 severance pay from the United Nations, then placed on trial with Coplon in 1950 in New York.

First tried alone in Washington in June 1949, Coplon was defended by the flamboyant Archie Palmer who enjoyed thundering rhetoric and misplaced quotations from the famous to make points no one could understand. Coplon's black-clad mother, Rebecca Coplon, who refused to believe her daughter was a spy, sat weeping in the courtroom throughout the trial.

Though the evidence against his client was overwhelming, Palmer arrogantly told reporters that his client was innocent and that he would prove it when she took the stand. On that day, Mrs Coplan sat with her daughter, holding her hand, sobbing. "Try to smile, Mrs. Coplon," Palmer told her in a loud voice. He strutted along the rail of the jury box where he had lined up throat lozenges. As he talked, Palmer popped these mints into his mouth.

No sooner had the judge and jury entered than Palmer thundered: "Judy, take the stand!"

In a strong Brooklyn accent, Judith Coplon told the jury that the government had made a horrible mistake, that she was a trusted and loyal government worker. How could the government think, she said, that she intended to give a purseful of secret documents to a Russian spy? She was not a spy, nor a Communist, she said, merely a victim of mistaken love for the scheming Gubitchev.

Coplon went to say how she had met the Russian on a Labor Day weekend in 1948 (a lie; she had met him in 1946 when he arrived in New York as her "control"). She was visiting Manhattan's Museum of Modern Art and found herself eyeing the same cubist painting as a dark-featured man who turned out to be Gubitchev. They toured the gallery together, then later began dating. Coplon told how the Russian took her rowing in Central Park, bought her dinners and gave her a box of Toll House cookies at Christmas.

"Now tell the jury how he impressed your female heart and mind," intoned lawyer Palmer.

"I thought I was in love with him," Coplon replied in a quavering voice. She went on to add that Gubitchev turned out to be a cad, a married man. She had slapped him with a rolled-up newspaper, she said, when hearing this news. She had returned to New York in March 1949, she said "to get this thing settled." Why had the couple been so furtive? Well, Coplon said without blinking an eye, they were afraid that Gubitchev's wife had hired detectives to follow them. (She knew that Gubitchev's wife lived in Russia and had never met an American detective in her life.)

Adding further to her horrors, she said, she was arrested and taken to a prison lockup where female warders had stripped her, "probed around" and "even peeked into my mouth!"

"In all your life have you ever been undressed by a strange woman?" Archie Palmer asked, attempting to display to the jury his own disgust and revulsion at such an indignity.

"Never!" replied Judith Coplon.

Then came the contents of her purse. Coplon put the blame for her having been carrying around dozens of secret documents on her one-time boss, Foley. It was Foley who told her to take Hoover's letter with her to analyze which, of course, was a lie. Moreover, she said, she was so overworked that she was compelled to take many documents home with her to analyze on her weekends.

By the time Coplon finished testifying the only believer in the courtroom was her still sobbing mother. Some time later, enjoying her publicity, Coplon sat in the press room of the federal courthouse and waited for the jury to reach its decision. She refused to talk about the trial. She talked about poets e. e. cummings and W. H. Auden. She talked about a vacation she had taken in Paris. She talked about modern dancing. She posed for pictures with her attorney, smoothing Palmer's hair and adjusting the handkerchief in the breast pocket of his suitcoat. She reveled in the photographing, striking different dramatic poses, "looking angry, looking happy, staring pensively into the distance," according to one newsman.

The jury, which had waded through more than two million words of testimony, was out twenty-six hours and returned a verdict of guilty. Judge Albert Reeves, 75, sentenced Coplon to ten years in prison the next day, saying: "I thoroughly approve of the verdict." He was reminded, he said, that "one of the great soldiers of America, Benedict Arnold, betrayed his country, and today his name is an anathema . . . Here is a young woman with infinite prospects, a great future before her . . . but she undertook to betray her country." The white-haired judge shook his head and said he could not understand why.

Palmer then sought to console his client by telling her: "It's only a verdict, Judy." As they left the courtroom, a mob of more than 500 irate people met them. Most were women, shouting. One woman yelled: "Let me get a look at the hussy!" Another screamed: "The rotten bitch ought to get a rope around her neck, that"s what! I was a yeomanette in the First World War!"

Palmer and Coplon then flew to New York to await a joint conspiracy trial with Gubitchev. The next day, with tabloid news photographers trailing her wake, Coplon took the boat to the Statue of Liberty and posed dramatically for pictures in front of the statue. The Manhattan trial was something different.

The court heard seventy-seven FBI men testify in the case. Agent T. Scott Miller had earlier testified that he had no knowledge of the Bureau tapping Coplon's phone and that of her lawyer, Palmer. He said later that he had personally seen and destroyed records of the intercepted phone conversations. He admitted that the FBI had heard itself described by

Coplon and Palmer "in burning four-letter words." Miller also admitted that he had sat through Coplon's Washington trial and had heard other FBI men deny any wiretapping.

FBI Agent Robert J. Wirth also admitted destroying some wiretap records and, though he was a lawyer, said he was "not familiar" with the 12-year-old Supreme Court decision prohibiting wiretapping evidence in federal trials. Despite all this, Coplon was convicted and received another sentence of fifteen years in prison. The case against Gubitchev was dropped and he was sent back to Russia.

Coplon never served a day in prison for her treason and espionage. In 1952 an appeal court ruled that the evidence against Coplon as prepared by the FBI was illegal in that it involved unauthorized wiretapping. Moreover, the Bureau had committed the most flagrant blunder of them all. They had arrested Coplon and Gubitchev without an arrest warrant!

The espionage career of Judith Coplon was over. Shortly after the trial she married Albert Socolov, a 41-year-old attorney who worked for the legal firm handling her defense. She settled down to tranquil domesticity as a housewife raising four children. The entire affair reflected enormous discredit on J. Edgar Hoover, who had masterminded the trap into which he thought to lure Coplon and Gubitchev.

In so doing, however, he had opened the Bureau files and its methods to public scrutiny. When he realized that all the files relative to the Coplon case would be exposed in the trials, Hoover balked, then urged the Attorney General to seek a mistrial "rather than produce these reports with consequent devastating harm to the FBI's responsibility for internal security, as well as the disclosure of as yet uncorroborated information in our files concerning individuals."

Attorney General Tom Clark knew that if Hoover did not expose those files, the federal cases against Coplon and Gubitchev would have to be dropped. The files were turned over and exposed in court during the lengthy Coplon trials. The reports came from persons of dubious reputations and many of these reports were obtained by illegal wiretaps. Most of it was based on Hoover's untried and untrue practice of identifying subversives through guilt by association.

Thus the esteemed actors Fredric March and Canada Lee, Boston University's President Daniel Marsh and CBS's Norman Corwin were identified as "outstanding Communist Party fellow travelers." The most idiotic drivel was included in these files: Helen Hayes was cited as having performed a skit in 1945 for Russian relief; Florence Eldridge (March's wife) was included because two Communists had mentioned her name in a conversation. Danny Kaye, Helen Keller, Jo Davidson, Senator Charles Tobey were all named as Communists in the FBI files because they had all been involved in addressing a peace rally in 1945.

Hoover's response was typical and traditional. He disavowed the reports for which he had a total lack of knowledge. Yet these reports, and thousands more like them, reposed in FBI files as legitimate intelligence on those considered to be enemies of the government. Such repugnant practices would not cease at the Bureau until the incredible power wielded by its totemic chief, J. Edgar Hoover, was wrenched from him by death in 1972.

[ALSO SEE: Amtorg; FBI; J. Edgar Hoover; KGB]

CRABB, LIONEL PHILLIP KENNETH
British Frogman Spy ▪ (1910–1956)

ADVENTURE, NOT FORTUNE, WAS SOUGHT BY LONDON-born Lionel Crabb. He came from a poor family and received little education. He was "Navy struck" at the age of eight and longed to go to sea, a dream he fullfilled in early youth when he joined the British merchant marine. His voyages took him across the Pacific and Atlantic. Crabb sailed to Singapore and then went to China where he was employed as a spy for Chiang Kai-shek's intelligence service which was then operated by the flamboyant and dashing Morris "Two-Gun" Cohen.

In 1940 Crabb attempted to enlist in the Royal Navy but was rejected because of poor eyesight. He returned, persuading the Navy to use him as an underwater bomb-disposal expert, a job so hazardous that Crabb was undoubtedly accepted since few other volunteers could be found. He was commissioned an officer in 1941 and, in the following year, Crabb's underwater feats became the stuff of military legend. He almost single-handedly cleared delayed-action limpet mines from the bottoms near Gibraltar and from the hulls of British warships while battling the Italian frogmen who placed these explosives.

From the feats he accomplished, it might be assumed that Crabb was a powerful frogman. He was anything but, being a poor swimmer in the bargain. Crabb had a huge head, wide shoulders and a lower body that narrowed to what one reporter described as "finlike proportions." So impressed with him were the Italian frogmen that, upon Italy's capitulation, they refused as a unit to surrender to anyone except Lt.-Commander Lionel Crabb of the Royal Navy.

"Crabbie," or "Buster," as Crabb was affectionately called, received for his heroic wartime efforts the prestigious George Medal and the Order of the Empire from the British government. He was allowed to stay in the service.

Undersea espionage was also practiced by Crabb on behalf of the British government. According to most reliable reports, Crabb secretly inspected the hull of the new Russian cruiser *Sverdlov* when it arrived in Portsmouth Harbor in honor of Queen

British frogman spy Lionel Crabb, who died mysteriously in 1956, is shown surrounded by youthful admirers.

Elizabeth's Coronation. British intelligence wanted to know how the Russian cruiser could maeuver so well with only two screws and also wanted to learn the details of the ship's underwater sonar equipment.

By 1956, Crabb's career took a nosedive. He was out of shape from heavy drinking and smoking and he found few underwater jobs. He found odd work such as being a consultant to the producers of the movie, *Cockleshell Heroes*, a job he disliked, according to one source "because it was about the Royal Marines and not the Navy." Then, in April 1956, Crabb was suddenly busy with a new and secret project which apparently coincided with the state visit of Soviet Premier Nicolai Bulganin and Party Chairman Nikita Khrushchev who arrived on board the sleek, new Russian cruiser *Ordzhonikidze* which anchored in Portsmouth Harbor, along with escort destroyers *Smotryashchy* and *Sovershenny*.

At 7:30 A.M. on April 19, 1956, Soviet sailors were surprised to see an object suddenly shoot upward between the ships and then disappear. One report had it that a diver "popped up like a cork to the surface of Portsmouth Harbor . . . the shiny, snouted figure in the rubber suit of a navy frogman. . . . Then, with a kick of his long black flippers, he dove down into the dark, dirty waters of the historic English port."

This was the last anyone ever saw of Lionel Crabb. Some time later a headless, handless corpse was found floating near the mouth of the harbor. It was presumed to be Crabb but no positive identification could be made.

Two weeks after Crabb's disappearance, Anthony Eden stood before the House of Commons and stated: "It would not be in the public interest to disclose the circumstances in which Commander Crabb is presumed to have met his death." He went on to say that "what was done was done without the authority or the knowledge of her majesty's ministers." It was then concluded that Crabb had been acting for an independent right-wiong group or a British official who had exceeded his authority. The headless body was buried under Crabb's name and there the fate of the frogman spy rested.

[ALSO SEE: *Morris Cohen; KGB*]

CUBAN MISSILE CRISIS
U.S.-Soviet Military Confrontation ▪ (1962)

FOLLOWING THE DISASTROUS CIA-SPONSORED BAY of Pigs invasion of Cuba in 1961, Cuban Communist dictator Fidel Castro asked Premier Nikita Khrushchev for heavy weapons with which to resist further American threats. The Kremlin agreed to supply such weapons, including rockets which could be launched against the U.S. The CIA redeemed itself considerably for the Bay of Pigs fiasco by learning of this agreement before Russian arms were shipped to Cuba.

President John F. Kennedy confronted Khrushchev, telling him that the U.S. would not object to small defensive rockets being used by Cuba but that the presence of large offensive missiles in Cuba could create an international crisis, perhaps war. Khrushchev assured Kennedy that Castro would receive only defensive weapons from Russia.

Russian technicians began arriving in Cuba and working in areas that restricted most Cubans. These secret sites were monitored by CIA U-2 planes. One of these planes was able to photograph launching pad sites which had been built for large missiles that could certainly reach the U.S. and other countries in the Western Hemisphere.

The gamble Krushchev took was undoubtedly inspired by Kennedy's weak posture on the Bay of Pigs, one where he chose to allow the Cubans to go down to defeat rather than involve U.S. forces. He realized his error when Kennedy, through Ambassador Adlai E. Stevenson, openly displayed the photographs of the launch pads before the United Nations, demanding that the missiles be removed. At that time, the U.S. sent a powerful fleet to blockade

Cuba and intimated that if the rockets were not immediately removed, the Soviets would be facing total atomic warfare.

Khrushchev looked for a face-saving method to escape the dilemma. He told Kennedy that he would order the missiles removed if Kennedy would remove the U.S. missiles from bases in Turkey and Greece. Kennedy said no, insisting that the missiles in Cuba be removed without conditions.

Kennedy was operating from a strong position of knowing exactly what the Russians were thinking. Oleg Penkovsky, a western spy with access to Kremlin conference results and who was working with British intelligence, told MI6 that Khrushchev and other Communist leaders felt they could not win a nuclear war in that the U.S. had a vast superiority in missiles.

In the end, Khrushchev capitulated, ordering the missiles removed from Cuba. The outcome elevated the prestige of President Kennedy as well as greatly enhanced the image of the CIA. The crisis worked devastation for Khrushchev who was so disgraced that he was portrayed by his rivals as a fulminating, bombastic clown. He was overthrown in 1964 and spent the rest of his days as a Communist nonentity.

[ALSO SEE: *Bay of Pigs; CIA; Oleg Penkovsky; Spy Aircraft*]

CULPER RING
American Spy Network in Revolution ▪ (1778–1783)

THE MOST EFFECTIVE AMERICAN SPY NETWORK OF THE Revolution was located in New York and was known as the Culper Ring. The name stemmed from the two cover names used by its leaders, Abraham Woodhull being "Samuel Culper, Sr.," and Robert Townsend using the alias of "Samuel Culper, Jr." The network was organized in 1778 when General George Washington asked his spymaster, Major Benjamin Tallmadge, to organize spies in New York City which was then occupied by a strong British force under the command of Sir Henry Clinton.

Tallmadge, who used the name of "John Bolton," as spymaster of the network, was fortunate to have inside New York the enterprising, intelligent Robert Townsend, a successful merchant who had free access to all parts of the city and was thought to be a Loyalist faithful to King George III. The meticulous Townsend wrote detailed reports in code, describing what he observed and what he heard, along with assimulating other reports from his network of spies.

One of these spies was Enoch Hale, who hated the British and sought revenge for the hanging of his patriot brother Nathan Hale two years earlier. Townsend's messages were given to a Long Island farmer named Austin Roe who regularly crossed the East River, then rode horseback to Setauket where he delivered the reports to Abraham Woodhull. In turn, Woodhull passed on the reports to a daring sailor, Caleb Brewster, who sailed his small boat across Long Island Sound to the Connecticut shore where he met with Tallmadge in Fairfield.

Only Washington, Tallmadge, Woodhull and Townsend had the key to the elaborate codes and ciphers used by Townsend, who wrote most of his secret messages with invisible inks. Townsend was particularly adept at judging troop movements, and supply shipments brought to Clinton by sea, along with warships sailing in and out of the harbor. Members of the Culper network also kept Clinton's headquarters under constant surveillance and were able to report to Tallmadge and Washington any loyalists posing as patriots who visited the British commander. In 1780, its work undoubtedly saved a French army marching to Washington's aid.

At that time, a French army under the command of Jean Baptiste de Vimeur, comte de Rochambeau, had landed at Newport, Rhode Island. Clinton learned of this force and ordered all his troops placed aboard ship. He intended to sail to Newport and defeat the French, then return to New York where he would leave only a skeleton defense force. Townsend witnessed the troops being marched to the New York docks, along with enormous supplies for Clinton's campaign against the French. He quickly warned Washington who, in, turn, planted false information in the hands of a known Tory spy.

Washington created a specious battle order which showed that he was about to attack New York City with 12,000 men. A copy of this order was then "discovered" by one of Clinton's spies who took it to the British commander. So alarmed at this impending attack, Clinton cancelled his plans to confront the French and busied himself with adding more fortifications to the city. Meanwhile, Washington met with the French army to form a formidable force that eventually overcame the British.

The Culper ring went on working for the American cause until the war's end. When the great American general Benedict Arnold turned traitor, he fled to New York City where he was made a general in the British Army. He busied himself for some time in attempting to identify Washington's spy ring in New York City. He failed miserably to learn anything about its spy chief. So well disguised were members of the Culper Ring that their true identities were not unearthed until the twentieth century, more than a century after they had conducted their successful espionage operations.

[ALSO SEE: *Benedict Arnold; Caleb Brewster; Nathan Hale; Benjamin Tallmadge; Robert Townsend; George Washington; Abraham Woodhull*]

CUMMING, MANSFIELD GEORGE SMITH
British Founder of MI6 ▪ (1859–1923)

BORN INTO A MIDDLECLASS FAMILY, CUMMING attended the Royal Navy College at Dartmouth and, upon graduation, was commissioned a sub-lieutenant. He was posted to the HMS *Belleraphon* in 1878 and for the next seven years saw sea duty in the East Indies.

Cumming married twice and, in 1885, was placed on the inactive list as "unfit for service." He suffered from severe sea-sickness, fatal to a sailor seeking promotion for duty on the high seas. He was recalled to duty in the late 1890s and undertook many intelligence missions. He was an adept spy and his reports soon won him an appointment as chief of the foreign section of the Secret Service Bureau.

In the gentle tradition of Robert Baden-Powell, Cumming undertook missions in Europe, conducting espionage through the Balkans and in Germany. He wore many disguises. One of his favorite impersonations was that of a heavyset, bearded German businessman from Bavaria. For years afterward, he kept a photo of himself in this disguise on his desk at MI6, the intelligence organization he created. He would challenge visitors to identify the man in the photo and few could do so.

The work of the Secret Service Bureau under Cumming's direction was aimed almost exclusively at Germany, chronicling its military buildup under Kaiser Wilhelm. Cumming had only a few agents other than himself and almost all of his intelligence was centered on naval activities.

One of Cummings' most important sub-chiefs was a naturalized British citizen called Max Schultz, who was a shipping executive with strong contacts in Germany. Schultz recruited some top agents who worked in German shipyards, including one man named Hipsich who stole plans of German battleships not yet built, range-finders, and fire control methods, giving these to Cumming. He, and some others were uncovered and given stiff prison sentences before World War I broke out.

In 1911, Cumming was asked to head a modern espionage agency which would serve all the military branches and high level political departments. This became the Secret Intelligence Service (SIS), renamed MI1 in 1916, and again renamed MI6 in 1920. The service was responsible for gathering intelligence overseas, from all countries thought to be hostile to Great Britain.

Cumming began to recruit agents who were mostly from the genteel class and looked upon espionage as a "game for gentlemen." Such was Compton Mackenzie who described Cumming at this time as "a pale, clean-shaven man with a Punch-like chin, a small and beautifully fine bow of a mouth, and a pair of bright eyes." He would close one of those eyes and, with the other, glare at newcomers through a gold-rimmed monocle.

Paul Dukes, who was to become, with Sidney Reilly, one of the best MI6 spies in Revolutionary Russia, later wrote of Cumming: "At first encounter he appeared very severe. His manner of speech was abrupt. . . . Yet the stern countenance cold melt into the kindliest of smiles, and the softened eyes and lips revealed a heart that was big and generous. Awe-inspired as I was by my first encounter, I soon learned to regard 'the Chief' with feelings of the deepest personal admiration and affection."

Before World War I, Cumming obtained secret information on the construction and operation on Zeppelins (dirigibles) from one of his top agents, John Herbert Spottiswoode. This agent, who claimed to have worked in a Zeppelin factory where he stole the dirigible plans, was later arrested by German intelligence agents and placed in an internment camp. He underwent such horrors that, when released, vowed he would never again work in espionage. He had a violent argument with Cumming about this decision. Cumming accused him of being disloyal and questioned his bravery. Spottiswoode called his spymaster "an old bastard" and walked out. He retired to his Scottish estate where he had nightmares about his imprisonment in Germany ever afterward.

Many of Cumming's early day agents were foisted upon him such as Bertrand Stewart, an Etonian lawyer who belonged to no less than seven private London clubs, had a large private income and who had a penchant for playing at espionage. Stewart, a territorial officer, wanted "to do something spectacular in the way of discovering German preparations for war." Cumming reluctantly sent him to Breman where, in 1911, he reportedly took secret documents from a German double agent and was promptly caught in the men's room of a restaurant where he was attempting to read the coded reports.

Just before World War I broke out, Cumming had built up MI6 spy networks in Brussels, Rotterdam and St. Petersburg. These networks continued to operate throughout World War I, providing Cumming and MI6 with valuable information on German troop movements. In St. Petersburg, Cumming's most sensational and remarkable spy, Sidney Reilly, chronicled the development of the Russian revolution. He was credited with wielding "more power, authority and influence than any other spy" in Europe.

It was Cumming's agents who obtained the German Navy's master codebook, the *Magdeburg*, and used it to quickly decipher all of the top German admiralty messages, including those of the submarine packs, throughout the war. The strict attention to detail, the accent on code and ever modern espionage equipment was all set down by Cumming. Throughout the war, he signed all of his documents and messages with the letter "C." Although this was the first letter of his last name, the initial also came to mean "Chief." In honor of Cumming, who died in 1923, all subsequent directors of MI6 have ever since signed their correspondence with the same letter.

[ALSO SEE: *Robert Baden-Powell; Paul Dukes; MI6; Sidney Reilly; SIS*]

CUSHMAN, PAULINE (HARRIET WOOD)
Union Spy in Civil War ▪ (1833–1893)

ORN HARRIET WOOD IN NEW ORLEANS ON JUNE 10, 1833, this future Union spy changed her name to Pauline Cushman at an early age.

At eighteen, Cushman went to New York where theater manager Thomas Placide was struck by the dark beauty of the 18-year-old would-be actress. He gave her a feature part in his New Orleans show and she was an instant success. She was touring cities in Tennessee in 1863, when she was asked to become a Union spy.

At one point, she visited the camp of southern General Braxton Bragg and left with his battle plans stuffed inside her boot, smuggling the plans to the Union Army of the Cumberland. She was later captured and was brought before General Bragg who ordered her tried by a military court-martial which found her guilty of espionage and sentenced her to death. Cushman's life was spared, however, when Union troops overran Shelbyville, Tennessee, where Cushman was waiting to be hanged, and set her free.

The rescue from certain death did not dissuade Cushman from undertaking another spy mission a short time later. William Truesdail, chief of the Union's army police, asked her to slip behind the Confederate lines near Nashville and report on Bragg's movements. She did, but was again captured, then rescued by Union troops under General Granger, who scoffed when he was told that Cushman was a notorious spy. He released her with a gallant flourish, saying: "On your way, you wilful, naughty girl!"

Cushman continued her spying for the North, sometimes disguising herself as a man when going behind Confederate lines. Her missions finally took their toll. She collapsed from nervous exhaustion and had to be hospitalized. Union General Rosecrans visited her in the hospital to thank her for the heroic services she had rendered to the Union. He made her an honorary "Major of Cavalry" and she was later given a resplendent uniform to go with the honorary rank, one she wore for several years after the war when making appearances as "The Spy of the Cumberland."

Making theatrical appearances for two decades, Cushman lived out her last years racked with the pain of arthritis and rheumatism. To quell the pain of arthritis, Cushman took heavy doses of morphine. She was found dead in her small room on December 7, 1893. She had mistakenly taken an overdose. When the news broke of her death, contributions allowed the body to be buried in a "handsome cloth-covered casket." More than one hundred men wearing faded blue uniforms were at the gravesite, saluting as the casket was lowered into its grave. The Woman's Relief Corps provided a marker which read: "Pauline Cushman, Federal Spy and Scout of the Cumberland."

DANSEY, CLAUDE E.M.
British Intelligence Chief ▪ (1876–1947)

FEW PEOPLE LIKED CLAUDE DANSEY. AS VICE-CHIEF of SIS (Secret Intelligence Service) during World War II, he controlled more than 80,000 Allied spies and the intelligence agencies of most foreign governments. He was a vicious, mean-spirited man with little or no regard for human life. His methods were consistently savage and he held the authority to order any disloyal agent murdered, which he did with alarming regularity.

Dansey's personality was typified by his conduct in the Boer War in which he served as a territorial officer. He was forever waking his fellow officers in their field tent by noisily filling his socks with sand which he would use as saps, storming out into the night to sneak up on Boer sentries to "bash in their heads." He had no tolerance for error and was a tyrant to his friends and associates. He was a man who bullied his subordinates. On one occasion his chauffeur, a female refugee, drove him to the rear door of the elegant Savoy Hotel in London. Dansey exploded, shouting at the driver for not having the good grace to deposit such an important person as himself at the hotel's front entrance.

Born to an army officer in London on October 21, 1876, Dansey was sent to an English boy's school in Bruges, Belgium when he was fifteen. The school was run by a bankrupt clergyman, Rev. Biscoe Wortham, who had the habit of censoring the mail of his students, the first element of espionage introduced into Dansey's life. One of the letters read by the snooping Wortham arched his graying eyebrows. It was a letter written by Dansey to a 24-year-old man named Robbie Ross, a flagrant homosexual who boasted that he had been Oscar Wilde's first lover.

Wortham questioned the then 16-year-old Dansey and the boy admitted that Ross had seduced him. The clergyman then confronted Ross who denied having sexually molested Dansey. Little came of the incident, except that Dansey forever afterward refused to write down anything if he could avoid doing so. He became secretive, almost furtive in protecting his personal life from public scrutiny. Dansey's father was incensed by Wortham's report of the seduction and withdrew his son from the school, sending him to South Africa to be educated.

Following school, Dansey was caught up in the Rhodesian-South African wars and became a territorial officer. One of his chief influences at this time was British Lt.-Colonel Robert Baden-Powell, who was in charge of intelligence during this war. Baden-Powell was an old school gentleman who practiced espionage by way of outlandish disguises and impersonations. He nevertheless impressed young Dansey as a role model. His love of adventure and intrigue led Dansey on to many other adventures such as battling bandits in Borneo. He returned to South Africa to serve as a scout in the South African Light Horse and, on November 29, 1900, became a member of the Intelligence Department.

Sent to Somaliland, Dansey headed intelligence for the local British interests and the ruling sheiks. Through diplomacy and threat, he disarmed insurgents, located rebellious tribes and provided excellent information on the politcal trouble spots in that sun-baked country. He was mentioned four times in dispatches during his five-year service period in Somaliland. He returned to England broken in health and with little prospects for the furture.

The much-hated British intelligence chief
Claude Dansey.

As World War I approached, Dansey returned to England to work in MO5, which later became MI5, the British counterintelligence service, going to work for its chief, Vernon Kell. He hated the work, believing that spying on British citizens and foreign visitors was not productive. He longed for foreign intelligence work. Throughout the early years of World War I, Dansey was in charge of authorizing the entry of all visitors to the United Kingdom, a position which rightly gave him a sense of enormous personal power.

In 1917, however, Dansey had grown so critical of Kell and had alienated others in MI5, that he moved to SIS which had been renamed MI1. He worked up the ladder through and after the war until he became vice chief and was in charge of all foreign operations, controlling a vast network of spies in Italy, Switzerland, Holland, Belgium, and Germany. As war with Hitler approached, Dansey collected a vast amount of secret military information on the Nazis.

Dansey was by then a fixture of British intelligence. His word was law. He was an intractable tyrant who regularly misguessed the Abwehr directed by the wiley Admiral Wilhelm Canaris and Heinrich Himmler's ruthless Gestapo agents who captured most of Dansey's spies in the early stages of World War II. Moreover, Dansey, who was then stationed in Switzerland, refused to cooperate with OSS chief Allen Dulles, who was also stationed in Switzerland. He did not hide his loathing for Americans. Dansey considered the American OSS as a "collection of amateurs," and only when ordered to do so by his superiors, which was rarely, did he provide the OSS with any kind of information.

The intelligence chief badly blundered in mid-1943, when an emissary for a high-level German official approached him, saying that the official was able to deliver top secrets of Nazi Germany to the British. Dansey smirked, saying that the offer was nothing more than a German ploy to place a double agent among his ranks. He dismissed the offer, refusing to even interview the official who turned out to be Fritz Kolbe, a key figure in the German Foreign Office.

Kolbe next went to Allen Dulles who accepted him as genuine and Kolbe became the most important high-level Allied spy inside Hitler's Third Reich. Even when Kolbe began sending vital information to Dulles, who shared the reports with the British, Dansey denounced Kolbe as a fake, refused to act on the reports and condemned the Americans as being foolish, naive dupes. Dansey, meanwhile, provided little in the way of good intelligence at this time and he was considered by many to be a doddering detriment to British intelligence, one who had outlived his time.

Dansey's last major operation was Operation Sussex in which he coordinated the dropping of saboteurs behind German lines just prior to the D-Day landings in Normandy in 1944. Following the war, Dansey, knighted and well-to-do, purchased a country estate in Bath and retired. His friend, British movie mogul Alexander Korda, who had worked briefly as an espionage agent for Dansey in the 1930s, made him head of his studio, Eagle Lion Films, a titular title. Within a few years, Dansey's health failed and he died on June 11, 1947, in a Bath nursing home, age seventy.

Officially, Dansey received posthumous praise, especially for his dogged supervision of the SIS division known as "Z" which was responsible for saving and smuggling back to England thousands of downed Allied pilots from 1940 to 1945. Privately, few had kind words for the British spymaster. Most of his surviving contemporaries detested him and one went so far as to say that "he gave spying a bad name."

[ALSO SEE: *Robert Baden-Powell, Wilhelm Canaris; Allen Dulles; Gestapo; Heinrich Himmler; Vernon Kell; Fritz Kolbe; OSS; SIS*]

DEANE, SILAS
American Diplomat and Spy in France ▪ (1737–1789)

CONNECTICUT BORN AND RAISED, DEANE GRADUATED from Yale and became a delegate to the Continental Congress. Congress chose him to go to France in 1776 to represent colonial interests and to secretly urge the French to support the Revolution.

Deane's chief mission was to secure arms and provisions for 25,000 revolutionary soldiers who were mostly under the command of General George Washington. This he achieved through France's secret agent, Pierre Augustin Caron de Beaumarchais, who established a fake exporting firm, the Roderigue Hortalez et Cie. It was through Deane that Washington found new and brilliant European volunteers such as Lafayette, Steuben, Pulaski, and Kalb.

Benjamin Franklin joined Deane in Paris in 1776 to help him influence the French into openly supporting the American cause. With Franklin came Arthur Lee who had been an American spy in England. Lee disliked the quiet Deane, openly accusing him of using American funds for his own purpose and for hiring a secretary, Edward Bancroft, whom Lee accused of being a British spy.

Franklin took Deane's side. Deane, in turn, believed Bancroft loyal to the Revolution which he was not, but it would many years before the crafty Bancroft was identified as a British agent. Franklin and Deane successfully negotiated an alliance with France in 1778 which ultimately decided the American War of Independence in favor of the revolutionaries.

When Deane returned to America he was not hailed as a hero but as a thief. Lee again accused him of appropriating American funds for his own use. Though Deane was eventually exonerated, his reputation was ruined by Lee's accusations. In 1780, Deane returned to Europe where he angrily denounced his American enemies and urged his friends to reunite with England. These letters were published and caused Deane widespread condemnation in America.

Upon hearing that the Constitution of the United States of America had been adopted, Deane decided to return to his native land. On the voyage to America, however, he died under mysterious circumstances. Some reports had it that he feared more public abuse and committed suicide. In 1842, Congress reexamined Deane's significant role in the Revolution and then posthumously absolved him of any wrongdoing and gave his heirs $37,000 in compensation.

[ALSO SEE: *Pierre Augustin Caron de Beaumarchais; George Bancroft; George Washington*]

DEE, JOHN
Spy for Elizabeth I ▪ (1527–1608)

WELL BORN IN LONDON, DEE WAS EDUCATED at Cambridge and continued his studies throughout Europe in the fields of mathematics, astrology, astonomy and geography. He also dabbled in the occult areas of necromancy and alchemy. When he returned to London in 1851, Dee was looked upon as a learned scholar but four years later, his preoccupation with the occult brought charges of socery practiced against Catholic Queen Mary.

He was tried and found not guilty. He returned to Europe where he became intrigued with ciphers, studying ancient codes, from the Egyptian times to that of Girolamo Cardano and Johannes Trithemius. When he returned to England, Francis Walsingham, spymaster for Elizabeth I, enlisted Dee's aid. Waslsingham used Dee to decipher the coded letters being sent to Mary, Queen of Scots, who had been imprisoned by Elizabeth. The one letter used to convict Mary and send her to the executioner's block, however, was most probably a forgery created by the treacherous Walsingham.

Thereafter Walsingham employed Dee as a English spy. He wandered about Europe, talking mysteriously to crown heads about his occult theories but really gleaning state secrets which he passed on to Walsingham in ciphered messages.

Dee spied in Spain against Philip II, and informed Walsingham of the Armada the Spanish monarch was mounting in preparation of invading England. Later,

Dee spied on the nobles of Poland in Cracow. His spying made him a rich man. Using the wealth he received from Walsingham and Elizabeth for his espionage, Dee returned to England and lived out his life in comfortable semi-retirement, serving briefly as head of Manchester College in 1595.

[ALSO SEE: *Francis Walsingham*]

DeFOE, DANIEL (AKA: ALEXANDER GOLDSMITH; CLAUDE BUILOT)
British Spy Against the Jacobites ▪ (1660–1731)

THE GREAT BRITISH AUTHOR OF *Robinson Crusoe* and *Moll Flanders* was anything but a success in life. Daniel DeFoe was so miserable a failure in business and finance that he went bankrupt and was thrown into debtor's prison. His muddled financial affairs caused him to hide under an alias (Andrew Moreton) from his creditors. To survive, the brilliant DeFoe took to spying and became so adept at it that he is thought of today as England's "father of the Secret Service."

Born and raised in London, DeFoe received a good education and, in 1683 went into business as a merchant. He joined the rebellion led by the Duke of Monmouth and narrowly missed capture and execution, a fate that befell several of DeFoe's naive, unfortunate school friends. Through his financial commitment to Monmouth, his business failed and DeFoe became a bankrupt and was thrown into debtor's prison.

Upon his release, DeFoe supported himself meagerly by writing pamphlets on religion and politics. One of his works, "Shortest Way with Dissenters" (1702), caused him to be heavily fined, pilloried, and imprisoned. A practical man, DeFoe reasoned that the only way to salvage his life was to join the government, or, more specifically, go to work for those he had been satirizing. The work he selected was espionage.

In 1703, DeFoe sent a letter to Robert Harley, who was Speaker of the House of Commons and who was considered to be one of the most promising young politicians in England. Harley, who admired DeFoe's writings, had interceded on DeFoe's behalf and secured a pardon for him from Queen Anne. Upon his release from Newgate Prison, DeFoe proposed his own position to Harley. He would travel throughout England and secretly observe the political attitudes of citizens, then report back to Harley.

Harley relished DeFoe's blueprint for his own secret service. He was deeply ambitious, coveted power and nurtured a secret self-image of being a

British novelist and spy Daniel DeFoe, shown being pilloried at the order of Queen Anne for writing an injudicious pamphlet.

spymaster. The Earl of Cowper, said of Harley: "He loved tricks, even where not necessary, but from an inward satisfaction he took in applauding his own cunning. If any man was ever born under the necessity of being a knave, he was."

DeFoe's lengthy missive proposed that he go through England county by county, organizing an army of secret agents who would list all of the gentry and detail each person's political sympathies. Harley would be given regular reports on these local leaders. Magistrates and clergymen would be profiled and their moral behavior chronicled. The many political parties would be investigated. DeFoe even promised to establish an intelligence organization in Scotland, then beset with political troubles.

Funded by Harley and others, DeFoe began his espionage in earnest in 1704, going through the southern counties of England, recruiting spies and organizing a system of secret reporting. Before departing, he wrote to Harley, stating: "I firmly believe this journey may be the foundation of such an intelligence as never was in England." At this time, DeFoe traveled on horseback, posing as a merchant and using the aliases of "Alexander Goldsmith," and "Claude Guilot." He actually bought and sold goods to authenticate his assumed identities.

Within a short time, DeFoe had organized a vast network of spies whom he chose for their intelligence and their ability to work secretly. These agents sent reports on anyone voicing anti-government beliefs. DeFoe, who maintained an office in London, diligently itemized these suspected traitors and passed on the information to Harley. He included trivial details which he felt were important to the cumulative whole, one of the cornerstones of intelligence gathering.

Harely rose to great prominence, certainly with the help of information being supplied by DeFoe. In 1706, while he was Secretary of State, Harley sent DeFoe to Scotland where negotiations were under way to form the union of England and Scotland. Harley instructed DeFoe to work for this union without appearing to do so. DeFoe went to Scotland and talked with influential citizens, sending Harley weekly reports in the form of unsigned letters. The spy was able to determine that most Scottish citizens were in favor of the union and his reports so favorably impressed his employer that Harley openly urged the negotiations forward. The union of the two countries was formalized in 1707.

DeFoe continued to enjoy Harley's sponsorship as Harley headed the government, then became the Earl of Oxford. When Harley lost power in 1714, DeFoe went to work for new masters. Following the death of Queen Anne in 1714, King George of Hanover moved from Germany to assume the British throne. George had long used spies to gather information on his enemies and Lord Townshend, his new Chief Minister, promptly rehired DeFoe as a spymaster.

DeFoe's new assignment was to learn everything he could about the Jacobites who plotted to return the Stuart kings to the throne. He was to obtain information on the "Young Pretender," Charles Stuart, also known as "Bonnie Prince Charlie," who lived in European exile but who was known to be planning an invasion of England. DeFoe reasoned that by joining the enemy he could best learn his plans. He obtained a job on the leading Jacobite newspaper, the *Weekly Journal*, owned by Nathaniel Mist. For five years, DeFoe, as senior editor, wrote all of the paper's editorials and made them so ambiguous that Jacobite opinions were obscured.

In 1720, DeFoe suddenly quit his position on the *Journal* and retired to enjoy the profits he was earning from his enormously successful novels. He quit spying for the government altogether. But years of poverty and struggle had made of DeFoe his own worst enemy. The old spymaster went into hiding, not from old enemies of his secret service days but from enraged creditors seeking him. Though he had by this time the means with which to retire all of his debts, he refused to pay his creditors. He had grown that miserly.

His son-in-law received a letter from DeFoe who was living under an alias in Greenwich, Kent, apparently on the run from a threatening creditor. The novelist complained about a "blow I received from a wicked, perjured and contemptible enemy." He signed the brief missive, "Your unhappy D.F."

DeFoe's family never saw him again. He was reported to have died in a cheap rooming house in Ropemaker's Alley in the parish of St. Giles-in-Cripplegate on April 26, 1731. The cause of his death is unknown but rumors persisted that he had been murdered by an irate creditor, or, more in keeping with DeFoe's own sense of melodrama, by a revenge-seeking Jacobite spy he had exposed a decade earlier. The creator of England's first Secret Service was buried at Bunhill Fields. No one was in attendance as his body was lowered into the earth.

DELILAH
Philistine Spy ▪ (c.1161 B.C.)

BIBLICAL SIREN, TEMPTRESS AND PHILISTINE HUSSY, Delilah worked well as a spy among the Israelites. The Book of Judges relates how Samson, a Hebrew of superhuman strength, was born to a barren Israeli woman as an instrument of Jehovah, one which would throw off the yoke of Philistine oppression. He performed great feats in his youth, such as killing an adult lion with his bare hands. He also desired a beautiful Philistine woman to become his wife.

At the wedding ceremony, Samson challenged his Philistine guests to answer a riddle, wagering heavily that they could not provide the correct response. Samson's Philistine wife wheedled the answer from him and she told her friends. When confronted with the answer, Samson realized he had been betrayed. He killed thirty or more of the wedding guests, then deserted his wife.

Samson then set fire to the Philistine crops and destroyed their vineyards and olive orchards. He fled to Judah and three thousand Philistines were sent to capture him. The Judeans, seeking to avoid the wrath of their enemies, bound Samson and turned him over to the Philistines who dragged him back to the Kingdom of Dan.

En route, taunted by a jester dwarf who carried the jawbone of an ass, Samson broke free. He overturned chariots in a narrow mountain pass called Lehigh. Grabbing the jawbone from the jester, he wielded this as a weapon with deadly force, killing more than a thousand Philistines who attempted to subdue him. The remaining, terrified Philistines fled.

The Philistines decided that the soft arms of a woman would be more effective in capturing the powerful giant than their legions of soldiers. Delilah, the younger sister of Samson's wife, was chosen to lure him into captivity. She established a camp which Samson visited. After spending some time with the giant, Delilah discovered from Samson's own lips the source of his great strength, his long, thick hair. Delilah cut his hair while he lay in a drunken stupor. Calling Philistine soldiers hidden nearby, Delilah made the giant a prisoner.

For her sexual espionage, Delilah received eleven hundred pieces of silver and was exalted by the Philistines. The great femme fatale reportedly witnessed the blinding of Samson and was present when, sightless, he was dragged into the great Philistine temple to be mocked. Placing his hands upon the two main pillars of the temple, the giant tore them from their moorings, causing all in the temple, himself, Delilah and thousands of others to be killed.

D'EON, CHEVALIER
French Spy for King Louis XV ▪
(1728–1810)

A PAMPERED FRENCH NOBLEMAN, CHARLES GENEvieve d'Eon de Beaumont, Chevalier d'Eon, possessed the feminine name of Genevieve because his eccentric mother had wanted a daughter, not a son. She dressed little Charles as a girl from age four to seven. Throughout the rest of his life, d'Eon would alternate between male and female garb. He easily passed for a woman since he was slim, had narrow shoulders and a beardless face.

Though d'Eon enjoyed his transvestite roles, he also excelled in certain masculine pursuits such as fencing. He became one of France's top swordsman while he also pursued a degree in law. He then wrote a thesis based upon the finances of Louis XIV, which was read at court and drew the attention of Louis XV. When the king discovered d'Eon's preference for female clothing, he realized he had the makings of a spy. He was recruited to the King's Secret.

At the time, Russian Empress Elizabeth was negotiating with England to support its Hanoverian king, George II, with thousands of Russian mercenary troops to protect the near defenseless Hanover from France and Prussia who were collusively plotting to invade the German province. So adroit were English emmissaries in their dealings with Elizabeth that she refused to see any French envoys who might dissuade her from accepting a half million pounds in exchange for her troops.

In the strange but clever d'Eon, Louis XV saw a way to breach the political blockade in Russia. He sent him as his special negotiator to St. Petersburgy. D'Eon traveled to see Elizabeth as a woman, using the female alias of Mlle Lia de Beaumont, and as the traveling companion of a fur trader named Douglass. Once d'Eon arrived at Elizabeth's court, he/she charmed the Empress and was granted a private interview. At that time, d'Eon discarded his female disguise and revealed himself to be the special envoy of King Louis XV, deliverying to her a letter from Louis which proposed a secret agreement.

Elizabeth was so captivated by d'Eon's disguise and daring that she seriously considered Louis' proposals and a short time later signed a secret pact with Louis not to aid George II. The treaty with Russia the English ambassadors had so confidently expected was not forthcoming. With Hanover neutralized, Louis recalled d'Eon where he bestowed upon him a large annuity and a commission in the royal dragoons. From that day forth, d'Eon was the king's favorite spy.

Louis XV sent d'Eon to England, this time as a man, to secretly learn what terms would be acceptable to the English in ending the Seven Years' War.

French spy Chevalier d'Eon, who enjoyed wearing the disguise of a woman and easily passed for one.

King Louis XV, who used the male/female d'Eon as a master spy.

A satiric portrait of the French spy Chevalier d'Eon, shown as exactly what he was to the world, half man, half woman.

his enemies in France before he gave up his office. Unless his terms were met, d'Eon threatened that he would reveal to the English all his secret correspondence with Louis XV, and the clandestine French plans to invade England. Louis XVI immediately sent his top agent, Pierre Augustin Caron de Beaumarchais, to England to negotiate the release of these sensitive documents.

D'Eon accepted the king's royal guarantee of safety, an amount of money which would be used to pay the spy's creditors, and a handsome pension. He then turned over the secret documents and returned to France. Upon his return, d'Eon was dressed as a woman, in accordance with another edict Louis had decreed. He was to live out his life in France as a female. Eight years later, d'Eon was found in violation of his agreement after he was seen riding across the grounds of his estate in his old dragoons uniform. He was ordered to never again move about unless he was dressed as a female.

D'Eon moved back to England where he lived out the rest of his life. When he lost his fortune in the French Revolution, he supported himself by opening up a successful fencing school but he cut an odd figure while teaching young Englishmen the art of swordplay. He was, at all times, dressed as a woman. Upon his death, May 21, 1810, a number of English gentlemen insisted that the 81-year-old body of d'Eon be examined to settle long-standing wagers as to whether or not he was a woman. Most lost the bet. The coroner who examined the corpse sadly reported that the clever French spy was and always had been a man.

[ALSO SEE; *Pierre Augustin Caron de Beaumarchais; King's Secret*]

D'Eon accomplished this mission by stealing papers from a drunken British officer serving the Duke of Bedford (he may have posed as a woman in getting the Englishman drunk) which revealed England's intentions.

When the war ended, Louis sent d'Eon to England as one of his ministers. He was to secretly get information from high-ranking British officers about England's armies, and deliver reports to Versaillse which also detailed England's coastal defenses. This information was needed by Louis XV who planned to invade England.

At this time, d'Eon continued to indulge his fancies, at times appearing in public places dressed as a woman. This created considerable speculation as to what gender he truly belonged. On more than one occasion, he was ridiculed for his female dress, wigs and makeup. D'Eon responded by fighting several duels which he easily won through his expert wielding of rapiers.

In 1774 Louis XV died and new King Louis XVI ordered d'Eon home. His reaction was violent. He demanded that Louis XVI bestow a considerable amount of money on him, as well as provide his written guarantee that he would be protected from

DERIABIN, PETER
Russian Intelligence Officer & Defector ▪ (1921–   )

D ERIABIN WAS LONG-TIME COMMUNIST WHO HAD served in Siberia as an NKVD officer tightening controls over the civilian population following World War II. He was ordered to Moscow in 1947 where he served in the MVD as a major. Deriabin later stated that it was at this time that he became disillusioned with Soviet Russia, having to constantly involve himself with violence and duplicity.

In 1953 he was sent to Vienna to spy on Russian diplomats stationed there, as well as supervise the network of Russian spies in Austria. In 1954, Deriabin defected to the Americans, stating that his reason was simple. He no longer wanted to spy on his own people and desired the better way of life he had witnessed the Austrians enjoying.

At the time, Deriabin was the highest-ranking Soviet intelligence officer to defect to the West. He was taken to the U.S. where he described in detail the operations of Russian intelligence. He later testified before the House Committee on Un-American activities. He exposed a number of KGB spies in the U.S., including Vladimir Pavlichenko who was working in the Public Information Office of the United Nations in New York City. In 1959, Deriabin published his autobiography and exposé of the KGB, *The Secret World.*

[ALSO SEE: *KGB; MVD; NKVD; Vladimir Pavlichenko*]

DEUXIÉME BUREAU
French Intelligence Sevice ▪ (1878–)

THE DEUXIÉME BUREAU PROVIDES INTELLIGENCE involving the fields of crime and espionage and, through its Special Services activated in times of war, counterespionage. Its chief military responsiblity is to centralize and interpret intelligence for the French high command. The Bureau was reportedly penetrated by KGB agents in 1958, according to a Russian defector code-named Martel, who also said that KGB agents belonging to a network called Sapphine had penetrated all high-level offices of Charles de Gaulle's administration. This intelligence scandal was later profiled in Alfred Hitchcock's spy movie, *Topaz.* Though investigations were conducted, no offiical report on the allegations were ever made public.

[ALSO SEE: *KGB*]

DEWAVRIN, ANDRE
(AKA: COLONEL PASSY)
Free French Intelligence Chief ▪
(1921–)

WHEN FRENCH GENERAL CHARLES DE GAULLE escaped from Nazi-occupied France in 1940, he established his Free French forces in England. He also established his intelligence department, BCRA (Central Bureau of Intelligence and Operations) which was headed by Andre Dwavrin, who used the alias of "Colonel Passy," taking this name from a subway station in Paris.

Dewavrin had been a professor at the St. Cyr Military Academy in Paris before World War II, and had led a valiant French force in Norway in an unsuccessful attempt to beat back a German invasion force, before he escaped to England to join de Gaulle. He quickly built a strong force of espionage agents and communications links working with the resistance forces in occupied France. Dewavrin was also the high cooperative link to SOE (Special Operations Executive), the British espionage agency working with French resistance fighters.

Dewavrin combined all information received from the French underground and planned operations for his own agents who were parachuted to secret areas of France to work with the French underground. He himself undertook several dangerous missions to occupied France. At one point, he and SOE agent F. F. E. Yeo-Thomas, parachuted into France to rendezvous with deGaulle's top agent, Jean Moulin, to help unite all of the various resistance groups in France.

After supervising BCRA operations in North Africa, following the Allied invasions there, Dewavrin returned to London to map out espionage operations that accompanied the Allied invasion of France in 1944. He was in the spearhead of the French division that liberated Paris that year and was chief of staff to General Joseph Koenig during the Allied drive across Europe. Following the war, Dewavrin remained in the French army and retired with honors.

[ALSO SEE: *Jean Moulin; SOE; F. F. E. Yeo-Thomas*]

DIA
(DEFENSE INTELLIGENCE AGENCY)
Central Agency for U.S. Military
Intelligence Agencies ▪ (1961–)

ROBERT MCNAMARA, WHO WAS THEN SECRETARY of Defense in the administration of President John Kennedy, created the DIA in 1961. This organization was designed to function as a clearing house of information from all of the U.S. intelligence services, except the CIA and was to house under its roof all the military intelligence groups in the U.S. It was from the first at odds with the CIA which complained that DIA was interfering with CIA operations and intelligence gathering, especially when it came to the CIA's control of Spy-in-the-Sky satellites. The rivalry and fight for budget dollars has never ceased between the two agencies.

[ALSO SEE: *CIA*]

DICKINSON, VELVALEE (VELVALEE BLUCHER; AKA: THE DOLL WOMAN)
Japanese Spy in America ▪ (1893–1961?)

BORN IN CALIFORNIA, VELVALEE BLUCHER WAS educated in Sacramento, then spent a year at Stanford University. In 1917, she moved to San Francisco where she married broker Lee Dickinson. She worked as an accountant for Japanese-Americans operating farms in California. The Dickinsons joined the Japanese-American Society which sought better relations between America and Japan.

With the failure of the brokerage firm in 1935, the Dickinsons moved to New York where Velvalee pursued her lifelong passion, working with dolls. She opened up a doll store in 1938 and also sold antiques and toys. She met with great success and soon had a nation-wide clientele purchasing her goods through a large mail-order system.

At some point during this prewar period, the Dickinsons agreed to become Japanese spies. Under the guise of searching for antiques and rare dolls, the couple traveled to the West Coast, haunting the U.S. Navy yards in San Francisco and San Diego, reporting on all the warships going in and out of the harbor.

Velvallee used her dolls in her secret correspondence with the Japanese, writing lines like "I have just received a new doll in a hula skirt," which, translated, meant that a warship had just arrived in San Diego from Hawaii. Though her husband died in 1943, Dickinson went on spying for the Japanese, sending, as before, all her correspondence through a contact in Buenos Aires. When that Japanese spy was exposed and fled, Japanese intelligence failed to provide the Doll Woman with another address.

Dickinson's undelivered letters were sent back to the U.S. where they were eventually intercepted by the FBI. Agents arrested Dickinson in her shop in 1944. "The Doll Woman," as the press dubbed the spy, was convicted of espionage and sent to prison for ten years. She was paroled in 1951.

DIMITRIJEVIC, DRAGUTIN (AKA: COLONEL APIS)
Serbian Spymaster & Founder of the Black Hand Society ▪ (1876–1917)

A FANATICAL NATIONALIST, DRAGUTIN DIMITRIJEVIC spents his entire life in unifying the Slavic states into a single country, Yugoslavia, an event that occured long after he fell before a firing squad. He was born in Belgrade, then the capital of an independent Serbia and later the capital of Yugoslavia. Dimintrijevic attended the Belgrade Military Academy (1892–1895) where he proved to be a brilliant student, receiving a commission in the Serbian Army upon graduation.

An impassioned orator and a zealot at heart, Dimitrijevic had little difficulty in establishing a cabal of young Serbian officers who formed a secret espionage organization that worked for Serbian domination of the Balkans. When it was learned that the weak-willed Serbian King Alexander I (Obrenovic) and his dominating wife, Queen Draga, intended to form an alliance with the hated Hapsburgs of the old Austro-Hungarian empire, Dimitrijevic planned to assassinate the monarchs.

Captain Dimitrijevic gathered more than fifty loyal officers in his secret society and stormed the Belgade Palace on the night of June 11, 1903. They sought out the monarchs and found them cowering in Queen Draga's secret dressing room. Dimitrijevic led the officers in hacking the monarchs to pieces and tossing their bodies from the palace balcony.

Backed by Dimitrijevic's cabal, Peter I (Karageorevic) assumed the Serbian throne and he repaid the chief assassin by promoting him to the rank of colonel and putting him in charge of Serbia's espionage operations. He actually ran two espionage organizations, one for the Serbian government and one for his own secret nationalist organization, which came to be known in 1911 as the Black Hand Society.

The Black Hand was intent on sabotaging Austrian police and military installations in Bosnia and Herzegovina, and assassinating Austrian officials in those states which had been preemptorily annexed by Austria. The Society was also designed to make sure that Serbians followed the nationalist course planned by Dimitrijevic and his henchmen. Dimitrijevic, as its head, busied himself with the assassinations of monarchs or heads of state who stood in the way of the unification of the Slavic peoples. He plotted the deaths of King Constantine of Greece, King Nicholas of Montenegro, King Ferdinand of Bulgaria. He even planned to murder Kaiser Wilhelm of Germany.

In 1914, it was Dimitrijevic, then employing the alias of "Colonel Apis" (the word "Apis" meaning "Bee") who sent Gavrilo Princip and others to Sarajevo to assassinate Archduke Francis Ferdinand, a murder that inflamed all Europe and led to World War I. Serbia, instead of ridding itself of the dangerous Dimitrijevic, promoted him to the rank of general and made him chief of all military intelligence operations.

King Peter I, however, was wary of Dimitrijevic, and believed that he, too, might be earmarked for death by the spymaster and his Black Hand Society. He abdicated at the beginning of war and named his son Alexander (Karageorevic, later Alexander I, who would also be assassinated twenty years later) as prince regent of Serbia. When the mighty armies of Germany and Austria marched into tiny Serbia, the Serbian monarchs fled with the general staff to Albania and later to Greece.

In 1916, Alexander had Dimitrijevic brought to his headquarters in Salonika and accused the spymaster of plotting to kill him and his father. In a secret trial, the spymaster and his top aides were condemned and then shot by firing squads in early 1917. Alexander felt at the time he turned on Dimitrijevic that Germany might win the war and that his dynasty would be blamed for the Sarajevo shootings. By eliminating his espionage chief and his the brutal Black Hand Society, he thought to placate the Kaiser's wrath. It was all for nothing since Germany lost the war.

Following Dimitrijevic's execution, the Black Hand Society ceased to exist. So fearful was King Alexander of its being revived that all records and documents regarding Dimitrijevic's secret trial were suppressed and it was decreed illegal to have copies of these records. Teachers uttering a single word about the Black Hand Society, or the names of Dimitrijevic/ Colonel Apis were subject to immediate arrest. Newspapers, book publishers, radio stations were also proscribed from ever mentioning the Society or its founder who was to be forgotten in his unmarked Macedonian grave.

Not until 1953 was the identity of this spymaster and dreaded assassination chief revealed and by none other than Marshal Tito, head of Yugoslavia. Tito proclaimed Dimitrijevic a national hero, restoring his "good name" to the honor rolls of Yugoslavia.

[ALSO SEE: Black Hand Society]

DODINGTON, GEORGE BUBB, LORD MELCOMBE
British Spymaster ▪ (1691–1762)

A WILY POLITICIAN, DODINGTON WAS BORN GEORGE Bubb, but adopted the name of Dodington when inheriting his uncle's vast estates in 1620. A member of Parliament, Dodington rose rapidly in the government, becoming a lord of the treasury.

His love of antiques was ostensibly used as a cover for him to travel throughout Europe in search of rare finds. In truth, he secretly met with European leaders who informed him on the movements and plans of the exiled Stuart kings of England.

On his first visit to Rome in August 1732, Dodington was introduced to Cardinal Allesandro Albani, also a lover of antiques and rare paintings. Through his friendship with Albani, Dodington was able to enlist the Catholic prelate into his services as a spy. Albani had access to the Italian court of the exiled British king, James Edward Stuart, who called himself James III and was known to his enemies in England as the "Old Pretender."

The Jacobites, who supported the Stuart claim to the crown of England, were busy plotting a return of the Stuarts. To prevent a reoccurance of the Jacobite rebellion of 1715, the English government assigned Dodington to gather from whatever high level sources in Europe he could develop (such as Albani) all information on Jacobite plans. Thus, Dodington, through Albani, learned in advance of Bonnie Prince Charlie's plan to raise the Scottish clans against England in what became a futile attempt to overthrow the government.

[ALSO SEE: Alessandro Albani]

DOIHARA, KENJI (AKA; THE LAWRENCE OF MANCHURIA)
Japanese Spymaster in World War II ▪ (1883–1948)

T HE HOARY WARRIOR CULT OF THE JAPANESE SUMURAI was deeply rooted within the personality and character of Kenji Doihara. He believed in the total Japanese conquest of the Far East and constantly harped the slogan "Asia for the Asiatics," which really meant Asia for the Japanese. Doihara was ruthlessly ambitious and desired a military career but his prospects were dim because of his low-born station in life.

At the age of twenty-one, however, Doihara hatched a plan in a mind that proved to be exceptionally cunning over the next several decades, a mind that accepted any means to achieve his ends. He would resort to blackmail, bribery, extortion, rape, assassination and mass murder, all of which would bring him to the hangman's rope. He began by enacting his first scheme to achieve military status. This meant selling his 15-year-old sister to an Imperial Japanese prince.

A camera enthusiast, Doihara convinced his sister to pose naked for him. He developed a dozen photos and selected the most sexually provocative to send to the married prince whom he knew to be a lacivious predator of young girls. The prince responded by informing Doihara that he would welcome his attractive sister into his household as a concubine, the then peculiarly acceptable position of an in-family whore.

Once the girl was settled with the prince and had become his favorite of several concubines he kept, Doihara asked his sister to ask the prince for a small reward, to arrange a military rank and post for him in China. This was granted and, in 1904, with the rank of major in the Jampanese Army. Doihara was sent as an adjutant to the military attaché, General Sigeru Honjo, in the Peking Embassy,

Doihara would spend more than a decade in China. Japanese spies were recruited by Doihara from the patrons of scores of opium dens and brothels that he secretly operated. As he had once peddled the flesh of his own sister, he peddled the bodies of his prostitutes, using them to compromise officials reluctant to cooperate with him. In greatly aiding Tokyo's plan to intervene in China, Doihara traveled throughout the Chinese provinces, usually in the disguise of a peddler, a teacher, even a missionary to learn the weaknesses of local leaders. He encouraged and financed independent warlords so as to keep China divided and the Chinese seemingly always at war with one another.

The key to invading China, Doihara proposed to his superiors, was the sparsely populated northeast province of Manchuria which could easily be attacked from the sea and from Japanese-occupied Korea. Once Manchuria could somehow be annexed by Japan, Doihara reasoned, the province could be used as a staging area to invade mainland China. There were many obstacles to be overcome. One of these was a bearlike Chinese warlord who had begun his rise to the top in the same year Doihara arrived in Peking.

He was Chang Tso-lin, who had been born in Fengtian Province in 1873. He worked as a common laborer until 1904 when he quit honest work and assembled a large band of brigands in Manchuria. He offered his services and that of his bandit brigades to the Chinese Army the following year and he was soon promoted to the rank of General. Oddly, Doihara and other Japanese conspirators in China helped Chang to achieve his rank. The warlord had also, at the same time, offered his bandit army as a mercenary force to the Japanese in the Russo-Japanese War. Although Chang's contribution to the Japanese cause was mimimal, Doihara and others believed he might be a dependable ally who could be manipulated into helping the Japanese take over Manchuria.

In 1911, the Chinese government under revolutionary leader Sun Yat-sen appointed Chang governor of Fengtian Province. The warlord was intensely loyal to Sun and was, by then, openly hostile to the Japanese whom, he announced to anyone who would listen, would some day invade Manchuria, if given the chance.

Doihara knew Chang was the man who stood in the way of Japanese empire in Manchuria, and he detailed a report which he sent to Prince Kanin, suggesting a way in which Chang could be eliminated. Kanin not only approved of Doihara's plan but personally helped in staging the assassination attempt.

As a guest of the czar, the Japanese prince inspected the crumbling Russian front in World War I. Czar Nicholas II of Russia had hoped to persuade Japan in joining the Allied Powers in overcoming Germany and Austro-Hungary. Kanin gave only sneaky lip service to this idea. His presence in Russia was a ruse to set up Chang's assassination. Returning to Japan via Manchuria, Prince Kanin arrived in Mukden Station, Manchuria, on October 15, 1916. He was met by a cadre of Japanese officers which included the plotting Doihara, along with Chinese officials that included Chang Tso-lin.

The Japanese and Chinese officials and military officers then climbed into a number of carriages and proceeded toward a restaurant where they were to attend a feast in honor of Prince Kanin's visit. As the carriages rumbled through the Japanese section of Mukden where the restaurant was located, one of Doihara's officers, Yoshiji Tatekawa, waited with several Japanese assassins holding bombs in an alleyway.

Doihara spotted his men and leaned from a carriage, pointing backward to another carriage, the one carrying Chang. As Chang's carriage appeared, one of Tatekawa's men dashed forth from the shadows, throwing a bomb. It fell short, blasting to pieces five of Chang's bodyguards and their horses. The cool-headed Chang leaped from his carriage and put on the cap of one of his dead bodyguards, then mounted a horse and rode wildly down a dark street to safety. Not knowing the warlord had escaped, Doihara motioned another of his assassins to charge Chang's now empty carriage. The second would-be assassin threw another bomb which landed on the carriage, blowing it to splinters and killing the driver and guards.

Both bomb-throwers were shot down by Chang's guards but since they were Japanese, Doihara dashed back to the carnage and, pretending to protect Chang, shot both of his own men in the head to make sure they were dead and could not reveal either their identities or the fact that they were under the spy-master's command.

Chang vanished for some time. Doihara urged Kanin to seize Mukden. The prince hesitated, sending a cable to Japanese Prime Minister Masatake Terauchi, explaining that the assassination had failed, but, in Chang's absence, he was going to order Doihara's troops to take Mukden. Terauchi fired back a cable ordering Kanin to do nothing. The time was not yet ripe to invade Manchuria, Terauchi cautioned.

Doihara's image was more public than he liked. So well-known was he in higher political circles that he was called the "Lawrence of Manchuria," a reference to T. E. Lawrence of Arabia. But Doihara was not, like Lawrence, a leader of partisans fighting for freedom. He was a calculating spymaster out to ruin China at any cost in order to bring it under Japan's domination. To that end he was given almost unlimited funds to operate his Manchurian and Chinese intelligence service which was entitled the Special Service Organ.

When more than 200,000 White Russians fled into Manchuria in 1917, to escape the Bolsheviks and their bloody revolution, Doihara welcomed these homeless, peniless refugees. He hired them by the thousands, particularly White Russian women whom he trained as spies, then placed into his myriad brothels and opium dens. He paid these women just enough to survive, addicting them to opium and using them to milk information from Chinese officials and military officers. (As part of their pay, each prostitute was given one pipe of opium for every six pipes they managed to sell to Chinese and foreign customers, but if they inveigled one Japanese into addiction, they were quickly murdered.)

By the mid-1920s, Doihara's spy network in China was vast. He employed more than 80,000 spies, made up mostly of Chines renegades and White Russian criminals who had fled the Bolsheviks. He used these agents to commit assassinations, perform sabotage and instigate widespread riots. The Chinese government was then headed by Chiang Kai-shek who knew that the Japanese were behind most of his country's unrest but he adopted a pacificistic approach to Japan, attempting to placate their demands with minor concessions. The only voice crying out against the Japanese was Doihara's old enemy, Chang Tso-lin, who ruled Manchuria with an iron hand and who curried favor from the Western Powers.

Chang was so angered at Chiang Kai-shek that he sent his armies to surround Peking and lay it under seige in 1926. Ironically, and without his knowledge, the arms and suppies his troops used at this time were supplied by Chinese who ostensibly sympathized with Chang but who were, in reality, Doihara's agents. The insidious Japanese spymaster was actually financing Chang's attempt to overthrow Chiang's government.

In Chang's absence, the Japanese began to build up a large standing army in Manchuria. Also, the Chinese Communists headquartered in Manchuria posed a considerable threat to Chiang's government in Peking. Chang's best friend, General Wu Shu-chen, who had been left in Manchuria to govern as regent, urged his leader to quit the siege of Peking and return to Manchuria to combat the growing Japanese threat.

Chang did just that, meeting with Wu and then traveling by train toward Mukden. All of this was according to Doihara's plan to finally succeed in assassinating the pesky Chang. Yoshiji Tatekawa, Doihara's agent who had failed to kill Chang in 1916, was recalled to directly supervise the new attempt. Colonel Daisaku Komoto, Doihara's top explosives expert, was directed to blow up the train on which Chang and Wu were traveling when it entered Mukden. On Chang's staff was a Japanese military adviser, Major Giga Nobuya, who was also traveling with the warlord on the train.

Nobuya's presence symbolized the contradictory nature of Oriental reasoning. Although Chang denounced the Japanese as the natural enemies of China, he allowed one the Empire's officers to travel with him, acting out the pretense that he intended to stay on good terms with the Japanese despite his vow to destroy them. Oddly, Chang also knew that Nobuya was one of Doihara's top agents. What Chang did not know was that Prince Kanin was still determined to see Chang assassinated and this time, in 1928, he had the full approval of Emperor Hirohito to kill the warlord. (Hirohito had by then come to power in Japan and was the chief architect behind the plotting of World War II. The Emperor and Baron Giichi Tanaka had devised in 1927 a detailed plan of conquest for all Asia—the Tanaka Plan—although a rigid conspiracy made it appear that Hirohito was being pressured into war by a cabal of Japanese militarists. This was, at best, silly to any intelligent Japanese in that the national religion, Shinto, demanded total obedience to the Emperor whose will could not, under eternal damnation, be challenged. Only the West, even to this day, accepted the Emperor's role in World War II as titular.)

As Chang's train roared toward Mukden on the night of June 4, 1928, explosives expert Komoto planted three huge cans of blasting powder beneath the tracks over which Chang's train would travel. At that moment, Chang sat drinking beer in his private, lavishly appointed lounge car and playing mah-jongg with none other than the Japanese spy Nobuya. "Our arrival in Mukden may be delayed somewhat," Chang told his Japanese adviser.

"How so," asked Nobuya.

Chang grinned knowingly. "It has come to my attention that foreign assassins are planning to blow up this train." He searched Nobuya's face for a reaction.

The Japanese major stared in silence at his host.

"They will blow up the wrong train," Chang added in a calm voice, nonchalantly continuing the game of mah-jongg. "Another train identical to this one has been placed on the track in front of us. Unfortunately, my youngest wife [his fifth] is on board that train, the very one which will be blown up."

Nobuya shook his head but said nothing. The head-shaking was a signal to one of Doihara's men who was a steward in the car and had overheard Chang's remarks. The steward immediately walked between cars and, as the train slowed for a curve, leaped off. He sent a message ahead, warning Doihara's dynamiters that the first train into Mukden and was a decoy, and that they were to blow up the second train.

At dawn, the first train entered Mukden without incident. Then Chang's train came barreling toward the city. Chang and Nobuya were still drinking beer. Nobuya excused himself, saying he had to relieve his bladder. He grabbed a heavy blanket, then walked to the last car and stepped outside onto the observation platform where he lay down, covering himself with the blanket. A few minutes later, Captain Tomiya Tetsuo, another Doihara assassin, standing at an underpass, watched as the train started to pass. When Chang's car began to roll over the tracks under which the black powder was buried, Tetsuo depressed a plunger which set off a mighty explosion that blew the car off the tracks, shattering it and killing Chang, Wu and dozens of others in the lounge car.

Major Nobuya slipped off the blanket and jumped from the observation platform. He sauntered down the siding to see the bodies of Chang and others being removed from the wreckage. He then said in a rather sarcastic tone: "Ah, how dreadful!" A few minutes later Nobuya was wiring the news to Doihara which made the spymaster so delighted that he immediately began a three day drinking party with his officers to celebrate the death of a mortal enemy.

Blame for the assassination was placed by the Japanese on two disaffected Chinese soldiers who were found next to the wrecked train, bayoneted to death. A third Chinese soldier managed to escape, going to Chang's son and telling him in detail about Doihara's plot against his father. The son, Chang Hsueh-liang, who had long earlier adopted the appeasement policy of Chiang Kai-shek toward the Japanese, kept the plot secret, fearing that exposure would cause an open war between the Japanese and the Chinese to break out.

Nine days after warlord Chang had been killed, a jubilant Emperor Hirohito gave a feast in the royal palace for the all espionage officers involved in murdering Chang such was his level of "non-involvement" in Japanese aggression of foreign lands. He was particularly delighted with the overall planning of this coup by Doihara who was promoted to the rank of colonel and given even more authority and funds with which to speedily arrange the invasion of Manchuria.

This occured in September 1931, when Doihara created what was later euphemistically called the "Manchrian Incident," a tactic which the Nazis would utilize eight years later when attacking Poland and beginning World War II. In the evening of September 18, 1931, Doihara entered his espionage command center outside Mukden, the headquarters of the Special Service Organ. This was a two-story building of Doihara's own design, one with reinforced concrete and surrounded by guards.

Inside, a large communications center buzzed with activity. Officers stood by at phone lines that connected them to all of the Japanese garrisons along the South Manchurian Railroad, the so-called Kwantung Army. (The Japanese had built the railway and owned it.) Seeing that all was ready, Doihara went to one of the finest teahouses in Mukden to entertain local Mandarins, preparing his announcement that he would be the "Mayor of Mukden" the next day.

Meanwhile, Doihara's saboteurs gathered north of Mukden along the South Manchurian railway, wiring up forty-two cubes of yellow blasting powder on the embankment. They carefully placed the powder five feet from the tracks so that the explosion would throw up considerable dirt but not damage the Japanese-owned rails. At 10:20 P.M., the explosives were detonated, which created a large whole in the earth but left the tracks undamaged.

The explosion was used as an excuse to blame the nearby Chinese garrison of an "unprovoked attack" on the Japanese rail line. As soon as the explosion took place, Special Service Organ headquarters was contacted. Doihara's men then called to all the Japanese garrisons in the area and ordered them to attack the barracks of Chinese troops which was located only 300 yards from the mock bombing.

Huge siege guns which had been captured from the Russians in the 1905 Russo-Japanese War, had been secretly mounted along the rail line and these opened up on the barracks and compounds where Chinese troops were asleep. It was a slaughter. Hundreds of unsuspecting Chinese soldiers were blown to pieces. Hundreds more where attacked by Japanese troops who bayoneted their victims in their beds. Within a half hour, more than half the towns along the railway were in Japanese hands.

Yoshiji Tatekawa, Doihara's henchman in the 1916 and 1928 plots to kill warlord Chang Tso-lin, was by then a major-general and was on hand to supervise the military takeover of Mukden. When the explosion occured, several of his officers appeared at a teahouse where Tatekawa was roused from his sleep. Dressed in a kimono, he was told that the young officer cadre had arrived to protect him from Chinese aggressors. He yawned, then said he was going back to bed with his geisha.

Once inside the bedroom, Tatekawa hurriedly got into his uniform, then slipped outside through a back entrance where another group of his officers whisked him away in a touring car. He later claimed, as did his testifying geisha, that he was asleep when events were taking place that night in Mukden, but many eye-witnesses later swore that they saw Tatekawa outside the walled city of Mukden that night, sabre in hand, screaming "Banzai!" and leading fanatical charges against near-defenseless Chinese troops.

As the attacks continued, Doihara, informed his Japanese superiors that all was going according to plan. Lt.-General Honjo, at his headquarters in Port Arthur, 250 miles to the south, was awakened in the hot tub where he had been sleeping. He was told of the situation and he immediately took responsibility in ordering a full-scale attack by the entire Kwantung Army against the Chinese. He quickly dressed and then moved his headquarters to Mukden the following day.

The War was over by noon the next day. Honjo's 20,000 disciplined Japanese troops quickly overwhelmed a Chinese force of more than 200,000. The Chinese army, however, was made up of green troops on orders not to fight the Japanese if they were confronted. They retreated toward the Sungari River, leaving all of southern Manchuria in the hands of the Japanese. Doihara had achieved the greatest coup of his career, creating an incident which put Manchuria into the hands of his country at a loss of only two Japanese soldiers (400 Chinese were killed).

The Japanese had startled the world by the obviously staged "Manchurian Incident." When foreign observers and newsmen went to investigate the site of the explosion, they were turned away by armed Japanese troops who told them that no one could go into the "dangerous" area until repairs were made.

It was then pointed out that the railway line had not been blown up as the Japanese insisted, since an express train had rolled over the very stretch of track the Japanese said had been destroyed only a few minutes after the explosion and had reached Mukden without any passengers reporting an explosion. Doihara then provided an "eye-witness," one of his paid Chinese stooges, who insisted that he had seen the explosion go off and that the train had "rocked and swayed," before just managing to clear the track that was destroyed.

The day General Honjo arrived in Mukden to establish his military headquarters, he was greeted warmly by the new Mayor of Mukden, Kenji Doihara, who, within four months, broadened his Special Service Organ spy network throughout every town and village of southern Manchuria. He hired thousands of new agents, both Chinese and European. One of the white foreigners he employed was a former Italian Blackshirt, Amleto Vespa, who had gone to China in the late 1920s and had earned his living as a mercenary, police chief, and, especially, an expert in espionage.

Vespa worked for war lord Chang Hsueh-liang when Doihara identified him as a spy. The Japanese spymaster ordered Vespa to join the Special Service Organ in February 1932. Vespa was suddenly serving a new master he both hated and feared. Doihara told Vespa that he would pay him well but that if he failed to do as instructed, his family, then living in Mukden with Vespa, would be interned, perhaps liquidated.

Doihara tested Vespa, ordering him to obtain information the Japanese spymaster already possessed. When Vespa delivered the proper information, Doihara turned him over his "chief," a Japanese civilian who spoke perfect English. Vespa, who published a book about the Japanese spy service in 1936, never learned the man's name or true identity. The authoritative manner in which this civilian spymaster spoke, casually deprecating Doihara, has led historians studying Vespa's published claims to believe that the civlian was no less a personage than one of the many Japanese princes who belonged to the cabal that surrounded Emperor Hirohito.

Vespa continued working for the Japanese, operating the Japanese spy service in Harbin, northern Manchuria, until 1936 when he wrote his book which he used to blackmail the Japanese into releasing his family, who joined him in Peking. The Japanese did not, however, keep their word about paying him the considerable funds promised for his espionage activities. To earn enough money to enable him and his family to escape China in 1936, he sold the book to a publisher.

The most shocking aspect of Vespa's revelations had to do with Japan's systematic creation of nationwide Chinese dope addiction. "Japan is poor," his nameless spymaster told him. "The Japanese Army in Manchuria cost millions every day." To get the funds necessasry to support his expensive war machine, Emperor Hirohito, through a business cabel he directed, sold monopolies of opium distribution province by Chinese province. The cabal also sold franchises controlling from town to town, the traffic in heroin, prositution and gambling. Doihara was one of those who arranged for the sale of these monopolies in human misery and death.

The buyers were mostly cold-blooded Japanese businessmen in the Japanese sectors of northern China. "After they moved into Manchuria," one account reported, "mass graves besides the garbage dumps outside all the major cities were kept open for the daily disposal of overdose victims cleared from the streets each morning." Tens of thousands died through this insidious purging of China, as envisioned and accomplished by Doihara and his peers.

Instead of world powers accepting the Japanese military presence in Manchuria on grounds of provocation, most countries condemned Japan, saying it had no authority to rule. Japan's answer was to set up a puppet Chinese emperor in Manchuria, a figurehead who was manipulated into fronting for the Japanese by Kenji Doihara and his enterprising agents. The victim was Henry Pu-Yi, the young pretender to the Manchu throne who was directly related by blood line to the old Chinese dynasty which had been wrecked by the half-mad dowager empress Yehonala.

On September 30, 1931, only twelve days after Doihara's fabricated "Manchurian Incident," one of the spymaster's agents appeared in the small villa occupied by Pu-Yi in Tientsin, the second city of northern China. The villa itself was paid for by the Japanese who had "sponsored" the titular boy emperor in expectations of having him serve some useful purpose in the future. That purpose was at hand.

Pu-Yi was asked to accompany the agent to Japanese headquarters. Once there, he was told that his fellow emperor, Hirohito, invited him to give up his shabby, rented villa, and go to Mukden in Manchuria where he would be placed on the Manchu throne; he would be pronounced emperor of all

China. Pu-Yi said he would consider the proposal, but he found it hard to conceal his excitement.

To expedite Pu-Yi's decision, Doihara called on his scheming female spy, Eastern Jewel, who was related to the boy emperor, ordering her to fly from Shanghai to Tientsin. Doihara minced no words with Eastern Jewel. She was to terrorize Pu-Yi into accepting the Japanese proposal. Eastern Jewel first plied her old devices, sex, sleeping with Pu-Yi, an act to which the pretender's opium-addicted wife Elizabeth was completely indifferent.

When this did not work, Eastern Jewel had Doihara's men phone and send letters to Pu-Yi, threatening him with death. Pu-Yi consulted with Doihara who had flown from Mukden to aid his femme fatale spy. The cunning spymaster became avuncular and played the role of protector. He shortly reported that the threats were coming from agents of war lord Chang Hseuh-liang, arch foe of Pu-Yi. The threats became real, with poisonous snakes found in the pretender's bed, discovered by Eastern Jewel who had actually placed them there. Then a basket of fruit was delivered to the boy emperor, but inside the basket was found two bombs which Japanese guards difused just in time to save Pu-Yi's life. The bombs, Doihara reported, had been examined by his explosives experts and they had discovered that these bombs had come from Chang's arsenal.

At the same time, Doihara ordered riots staged in the Japanese Concession area of Tientsin. His agents attacked Japanese shops and businesses, the terrorists loudly proclaiming hatred for Pu-Yi and those who protected him. Doihara then made a great show of allegiance to Pu-Yi by calling out elite Japanese troops to protect the pretender's villa. Standing in front of the villa, Pu-Yi behind him, Doihara shouted to his men: "You are to sacrifice your lives to the last man before a single hand is placed upon the emperor."

Utterly terrified, Henry Pu-Yi was convinced that Chang meant to kill him and agreed to go to Mukden to assume the throne. With that, Doihara escorted the boy emperor to his convertible parked outside the villa and stowed him away in the trunk. The emperor's chauffeur was so rattled at Doihara's insistence to drive faster that he smashed into a telephone pole which caused Pu-Yi to receive a nasty blow to the head. When the car pulled up behind a Japanese-owned restaurant, Doihara opened the trunk to find the prentender in a daze.

Doihara slipped a Japanese army coat over the youth, placed a private's cap on his head, then placed him inside a Japanese staff car which roared off to a dock in the British Concession. In the moonlight, Henry Pu-Yi and Doihara got aboard a small motor launch, the pretender hiding in the bilge. Next to him was a large drum containing high octane gas which Doihara intended to ignite and blow Henry Pu-Yi to pieces should they be discovered.

The launch went down river toward the China Sea, skirting the Chinese coastal batteries. At one point, searchlights illumined the launch and Chinese sentries ordered the boat to go to shore for inspection. Doihara himself was at the helm. He cut the motors, drifted past the checkpoint then turned on the motors and sped off with the sentries sending bullets whistling past his head.

At the mouth of the river, Pu-Yi was smuggled onto a Japanese freighter which sailed off for Port Arthur. From there, Pu-Yi, treated regally, was taken to Mukden to live in an austere mansion which passed for a palace and to remain until the end of the war a puppet of the Japanese, as well as a virtual prisoner of spymaster Kenji Doihara.

All of the elaborate Japanese machinations to cover their seizure of Manchuria meant nothing to the West which branded Japan an aggressor nation. In 1933, refusing to give up Manchuria, Japan, with Hirohito's full approval, withdrew from the League of Nations. Japan then moved on Jehol, then Mongolia. Doihara again was sent ahead to create dissension, riots and internecine warfare between warlords. Using Pu-Yi as a role model, Doihara placed another puppet at the head of Mongolia, Prince Teh.

Eight years later, Doihara had risen to the rank of major general in the air force, flying having been one of his lifelong passions. He split his time heading an air force corps and supervising his intelligence networks. So powerful had Doihara become that he sat in the exclusive private council of Prime Minister Hideki Tojo and voted, on November 4, 1941, to attack Pearl Harbor.

It would be another seven long, harsh years before Kenji Doihara and the military cabal that pursued Japanese aggression would be brought to justice. He was tried with Tojo and others in 1948 and found guilty of so many war crimes that it was impossible to list them all. All were sentenced to be hanged, not shot as would have been a more honorable samurai death.

Doihara waited for death in Sugamo Prison. Some of his relatives visited him to receive from his hand some hair and nail cuttings which they took away with them to later enshrine in a memorial. Then, on December 23, 1948, Doihara followed Tojo and six others into the death chamber, climbed heavily onto a scaffold and was sent through a trapdoor to the ignominious death he so richly deserved. Doihara was the only spymaster of modern times to ever be executed for his crimes against humanity.

[ALSO SEE: *Eastern Jewel*]

DONOVAN, WILLIAM JOSEPH (AKA: WILD BILL)

OSS Director ▪ (1883–1959)

WILLIAM J. "WILD BILL" DONOVAN WAS THE STUFF of heroic legend. For forty years he was a preeminent figure in the American establishment, having distinguished himself in two world wars. In World War I, he led the the valiant soldiers of the old "Fighting 69th" New York Irish brigade (165th Infantry). That force's record in France was astounding in that it fought and was victorious in more battles than any other unit of the American Expeditionary Army under General John Pershing. And it lost more than two thirds of its men achieving that record.

At war's end, Donovan wandered weeping through the empty billets of his lost generation of soldiers, then murmured to his brother Vincent: "When I think of all the boys I have left behind me who died out of loyalty to me . . . it's too much." That same loyalty would be demonstrated by those who served Donovan in World War II when he headed the OSS (Office of Strategic Services).

Donovan, who participated in the heavy hand-to-hand action, was severely wounded and received the Congressional Medal of Honor. When he and what was left of the old 69th returned from France and marched down the streets of New York, he was lionized before the world, as was his regimental chaplain, the unforgettable and equally heroic Father Francis Duffy whose battle-garbed statue still stands in New York's Times Square.

Donovan was born in Buffalo, New York on January 1, 1883. His middleclass family could not afford to send him to college so Donovan worked his way through Columbia University, earning a law degree in 1907. He operated a successful law firm and organized a regiment of cavalry in Buffalo as part of the National Guard. Donovan rose to the rank of captain. He married Ruth Rumsey in 1914.

Donovan's reputation as a fair-minded, intelligent lawyer, one who could accomplish difficult tasks with seeming ease, brought him to the attention of the Rockefeller Foundation in 1916. The Foundation asked him to travel to Europe, without compensation, in setting up war relief supplies and medical attention for the displaced persons of Poland. He accepted with alacrity. When arriving in England, however, Donovan was informed by British naval authorities that Germany's blockade of the seas would prevent the Rockefeller supplies from getting to Poland. Donovan then joined the Belgium Relief organization, headed by future president, Herbert Clark Hoover, to feed ten million starving refugees in Belgium

This was Donovan's first introduction to espionage. Before going behind the German lines to bring food to the starving, displaced Belgians—American was neutral in 1916—Donovan met in London with a Canadian officer working for British intelligence, William Samuel Stephenson, who would later be known under the code name "Intrepid." It was this meeting, one which Donovan denied to his dying day but was evident in Stephenson's biography and Donovan's correspondence, which started Donovan on the road to being a spy.

He received some brief espionage training in London before going to Belgium and it is believed that while Donovan was working to aid refugees, he also gathered information on German supplies, troop reserves and other important military information. This he managed to pass to the British before their great offensive which resulted in the devastating battle of the Somme where the British lost 420,000 men in killed, wounded and missing—60,000 on the first day of the offensive—the "flower of British manhood," as it was later stated.

It was alleged that without Donovan's information, the British might have lost considerably more men. It was Stephenson, assigned to Washington, D.C. in 1940, who would put forth the strongest recommendation that Donovan head America's first full-fledged intelligence agency, the OSS. Just as the Somme offensive took place, Donovan was suddenly recalled to the U.S., his old cavalry unit activiated and ordered to join General Pershing in an expeditionary mission into Mexico in pursuit of the bandit Pancho Villa who had raided the small town of Columbus, New Mexico.

Villa had lead a force of 1,500 Mexicans on the raid, in search of cash and supplies to fuel his revolution in northern Mexico. He had attacked the U.S. Army camp of the 13th Cavalry, killing nine U.S. citizens and eight troopers. The cavalry had pursued Villa, killing fifty of his men inside the U.S. and seventy more inside Mexico. Now, Pershing was to lead a full-scale punitive invasion of Mexico in an undeclared war against Pancho Villa.

Donovan put his cavalry through severe training at McAllen, Texas. He got his men up one hour before any other unit and ordered them to sleep one hour after all other units were in bed. He double-drilled them, forced them to hike and march on greater distances than any other commander would expect. He was unpopular which he knew but he was unconcerned. He had been to northern France and seen the rigors of deadly warfare. He also knew that America would eventually become involved and he wanted his troops trained as well as they could be, to be as tough as the veteran front-line Germans. This he achieved.

The "Border Days," as Donovan later referred to this experience, proved to be some of the happiest of his life. He loved the rough and tumble life, the banjo campfire parties, eating carrot stews on the mesas under the stars. The discipline of his troops was superb and he had never been in better physical condition. After six months of unsuccessfully chasing the

America's first real spymaster, William J. Donovan, founder of the OSS, precursor to the CIA; Donovan was one of the great heroes of World War I and for forty years one of the reigning members of the American Establishment.

will-of-the-wisp Villa, Donovan and his unit were withdrawn from Mexico, one of the last U.S. forces to return from the expedition.

No sooner did he return than Donovan, commissioned a major, was named to head the 69th New York Irish battalion which became the 165th Infantry in the Rainbow Division. Again, Donovan proved to be a severe taskmaster in training his tough New Yorkers. They were boated to France and went into action for the first time on February 18, 1918 at Luneville. One of Donovan's men was Joyce Kilmer, who had worked for the New York *Times* and was considered one of the finest American poets of the day. Donovan promoted Kilmer to the rank of sergeant and made him his intelligence clerk.

Donovan instructed Kilmer to keep a running daily logue of everything heard and seen along his front. Dutifully, Kilmer described unusual smoke formations, noises of digging (underground tunnels for German sappers laying mines), rockets exploding from the German lines, their colors and configurations, artillery fire and the type of shells used, the sound of German patrol dogs. All of this seemingly trivial information was extremely useful to American military intelligence. By studying such information,

the Americans could determine how the Germans were reinforcing their trenches, laying mines (which meant a defensive posture instead of mounting an offensive), different colored rockets and flares which would signal forthcoming artillery barrages. Kilmer would be killed, a loss deeply felt by Donovan, as were those of all of his men.

Following an eight-day epic battle which resulted in an American victory, Donovan and only one half of his regiment survived. For this action Donovan was to receive the Distinguished Service Cross and, subsequently, the Congressional Medal of Honor. A few days after this battle, regimental chaplain Father Duffy, overheard three of Donovan's doughboys arguing in a trench as to the worthiness of their commander. Said one: "Well, I'll say this—Wild Bill is a son-of-a-bitch, but he's a game one!"

By the time the doughboys returned from France, Donovan, along with Sergeant Alvin C. York, Captain Eddie Rickenbacker and General John Pershing, were the four great heroes of World War I. Although there were many who wanted Donovan to run for the presidency in 1920, he refused any chance at political office and went into private law practice in Buffalo, N.Y. In 1920, Donovan was appointed U.S. Attorney for the Buffalo district. His main chore was enforcing the unpopular Prohibition law. He eagerly prosecuted dozens of rum-runners and sent them to federal prison.

In 1925, Donovan became Assistant U.S. Attorney General under his Columbia University mentor Harlan Fiske Stone. One of his chores was to help clean up the Department of Justice and its Bureau of Investigation which had corrupted by the Teapot Dome crooks in the administration of President Warren G. Harding. One of Donovan's first jobs was to review the work and background of J. Edgar Hoover, who had been temporarily named to head the Bureau of Investigation, after William J. Burns had been removed from that office.

The Bureau, its name having been changed to the Federal Bureau of Investigation (FBI), had, under Harding's regime, been corrupted by several agents working for Burns, men like Gaston Bullock Means, an agent whose job with the Bureau in the early 1920s, consisted of blackmail, bribery and other dirty deeds on behalf of the venal Attorney General Harry M. Daugherty and his cronies. Hoover cleaned his own house, purging the bureau of these boondogglers. In turn, Donovan studied Hoover's background and new procedures and then gave him the approval that led to Hoover's permanent appointment.

J. Edgar Hoover, who was to become the all-powerful director of the FBI, had very little contact with Donovan. The two never became friends and were never seen together throughout their long careers in Washington. Not until Donovan's appointment to head the newly-formed OSS in 1940 did J. Edgar Hoover again significantly appear in Donovan's life, and he came not as an old friend but a wiley, vicious antagonist.

Donovan served the Justice Department until 1929, when he returned to private practice, successfully arguing many cases before the U.S. Supreme Court. He ran as a Republican against Herbert Lehman for the governorship of New York in 1932, and was soundly beaten. Again, Donovan returned to private practice, becoming one of the most successful appeals lawyer in the country. He prospered but suffered a great tragedy in 1940 when his 22-year-old daughter Patricia, a student at George Washington University, was killed when her car overturned in a rain storm. She was buried at Arlington National Cemetery, an honor given to her as the daughter of a Medal of Honor winner.

Dononvan had doted on his daugher, his only child, and her death caused his hair to turn white almost overnight. Two month's after the death of his daughter, Donovan received a call from William Samuel Stephenson, who was in New York City, having just arrived from London. He was one of the leading British intelligence figures of the day and operated under the code name Intrepid. His job was to convince President Roosevelt to aid England in its war against Germany and he asked Donovan to help. Through Donovan's friend, Secretary of the Navy Frank Knox, President Roosevelt approved of a clandestine trip Donovan was to make to England.

With government credentials and a letter of credit for $10,000, Donovan flew to war-torn England. There he met with King George VI and Prime Minister Winston Churchill, the British chiefs of staff and the war cabinet. He also conferred with British spymaster, Colonel Stewart Menzies, chief of SIS (Secret Intelligence Service).

Menzies confided to Donovan a great many secrets, even the details of its most secret operations, the British code and cipher service which operated under the name of Ultra. This was extraordinary for the usually close-mouthed Menzies but he had been obviously instructed to cooperate in every way with Donovan in the hopes that Donovan would do his utmost to urge FDR to aid England. Even more extraordinary was the fact that England's top secrets were imparted to a private citizen on a temporary state visit.

Donovan returned to the U.S. to report to President Roosevelt that England would continue its fight against Hitler but that it desperately needed the tools of war, particularly destroyers, having lost many such warships in its sea battles for control of Norwegian waters. A short time later FDR responded by establishing his so-called "Lend-Lease" deal with England, giving that country fifty old American destroyers on the absurd condition that, after having used them, England would return this warships to the U.S.

Oddly, the British intelligence system had vastly overrated Donovan's political standing in Washington. In a secret memorandum, Sir Alexander Cadogan, undersecretary of state for England, sent a note to the British foreign secretary which described Donovan as a man who could turn the tide for England. According to Cadogan, Stephenson had convinced Menzies that Donovan had "Knox in his pocket," and that if Churchill would be completely frank with Donovan in future talks, Donovan "would contribute very largely to our obtaining all that we want of the United States."

Donovan did return to England to meet with Churchill who candidly outlined his plan for the defeat of Nazi Germany. Then Donovan was given a V.I.P. tour of the British war stations from North Africa to the Middle East, all conducted by the SIS. During this tour, Donovan visited many heads of state, acting unofficially for FDR, attempting to persuade neutral countries from joining the Axis Powers. All through this period, Donovan, with the urging of his British intelligence friends, formulated a plan to create a new super intelligence agency for America, one which would collect, collate and evaluate all military intelligence. The agency would be organized similar to England's SIS.

When Donovan put forth this plan to Roosevelt, a storm of protest broke about his head from U.S. military leaders. General Sherman Miles, head of the army intelligence wrote to Chief of Staff, George C. Marshall that he considered the formation of a new superintelligence agency "very disadvantageous, if not calamitous." J. Edgar Hoover of the FBI was enraged at the thought that Donovan might create an agency competitive with the FBI. He personally went to Roosevelt to complain about the idea.

Secretary of War Henry L. Stimson wrote in his diary that Hoover "goes to the White House . . . and poisons the mind of the President" about Donovan's plans. General Marshall noted Hoover's incessant badgering of Roosevelt to discard any notion of activating Donovan's plan, calling the FBI Director "very childish," "petulant," and "more of a spoiled child than a responsible officer."

Actually, Hoover had planned to have just such an intelligence agency spring from his FBI domain, one in which he would create a worldwide system of "legal attachés" (FBI officers) in every U,S, embassy, consulate and legation. As it was, when the OSS came into existence over his vitriolic objections, Hoover had to be content with getting all areas of the Western Hemisphere only as his absolute jurisdiction in gathering information, although the FBI was ordered to cooperate with the OSS (and its successor, the CIA), providing all intelligence it had on hand in those areas to the OSS when requested to do so.

This was easier said than done, particularly when dealing with the possessive, self-aggrandizing Hoover who became incensed at anyone who thought to enter the criminal investigation or intelligence fields which he believed were his private fiefdoms. He remained the eternal foe of Donovan's for his invasion into the intelligence field, albeit much of the FBI's early work in the area was woefully incompentent, and nonproductive. So envious of any OSS activity was Hoover that he made ridiculous accusations against Donovan.

In 1942, Hoover carped that Donovan had more than ninety OSS agents operating in South America when Donovan had but one and that agent had been given permission to pick up some papers in Mexico by the New York branch of the FBI. Hoover had his agents put together dossiers on all of those who might exercise authority over him, from Presidents to members of Congress, from cabinet members to agency directors. He maintained a very large file on William Joseph Donovan which was crammed with rumor and gossip but not a single indictment of misbehavior.

In an article appearing in a 1941 edition of Collier's Magazine, an FBI spokesman reassured citizens that the FBI was cooperating with the OSS by sending it all the intelligence it had collected. Said the FBI agent in a snide fashion: "Donovan knows everthing we know except what we know about Donovan." This, of course, clearly implied that the FBI was maintaining a file on Donovan. Hoover nervously followed up this article by sending a letter to Donovan in which he flatly denied that the FBI maintained a dossier on the OSS director. This was a lie, but J. Edgar Hoover's entire career was pock-marked with inconsistencies, misrepresenations and outright lies. Such conduct was his hallmark.

Roosevelt was very much in favor of a superintelligence agency, but, at first, he thought to name his boyhood chum, Vincent Astor to head such an agency. The wealthy Astor had been Roosevelt's social spy in Washington for years, reporting the gossip and rumor of cocktail parties and fetes. He was totally unqualified for such a position. Donovan, on the other hand, was one of the few Americans who had a perfect grasp of world matters, and the best intelligence system in the world at that time, SIS. He had the support of Frank Knox, Secretary of the Treasury Henry Morganthau, Jr., and Winston Churchill, along with all of the leading British intelligence chiefs (with the exception of the venomously anti-American Claude Dansey).

Donovan had already submitted his concepts of the proposed intelligence agency. He insisted that "intelligence operations should not be controlled by party exigencies. It is one of the most vital means of national defense. As such it should be headed by someone appointed by the President, directly responsible to him and no one else. It should have a fund solely for the purpose of investigation and the expenditures under this fund should be secret and made solely at the discretion of the President." With this statement, Donovan had layed the cornerstone idea for not only the OSS but the CIA which was to follow.

The organization Donovan envisioned came into being as the COI (Office of Coordinator of Information) on June 18, 1941, when Roosevelt announced its formation and Donovan at its head. Agents and workers for this new service were recruited by Donovan from the Ivy League, Wall Street and media. His first lieutenant, so to speak, was playwright Robert E. Sherwood, who was a friend of Donovan's. Sherwood was made head of the propaganda arm of the new organization, called FIS (Foreign Information Service) and large offices in New York were rented. Within a year more than 800 journalists, writers and broadcasters were employed by FIS.

Another branch of the COI, the Research and Analysis department, had as its chief recruiter Archibald MacLeish. He drew heavily from the Academy and from the field of journalism. James P. Warburg, the New York banker, joined this staff, as did Wallace Deuel, correspondent for the Chicago Daily News. Donovan recruited Thomas A, Morgan from the Sperry Corporation; James Roosevelt, one of the President's sons; Estelle Frankfurter, daughter of U.S. Supreme Court Justice Felix Frankfurther; Atherton C. Richards, who owned a goodly portion of Hawaii; film director John Ford and film producer Mirian C. Cooper.

Six months after the U.S. went to war with the Axis Powers, the COI came under the supervision of the Joint Chiefs of Staff on June 13, 1942, and its name was changed to the OSS (Office of Strategic Services). As Roosevelt had warned Donovan, the military commanders tried to absorb the various branches of the OSS but Donovan was able to resist such moves and kept his organization intact and under his direct control. Before the OSS was disbanded, more than 60,000 persons would be employed in its many services.

Many OSS agents performed the same duties as the British SOE (Special Operations Executive), going behind enemy lines to work with underground and resistance fighters, in Europe, the Middle East and throughout Asia and the Pacific. OSS agents swarmed into French North Africa in advance of the Allied invasion, preparing the way by meeting with Vichy French officers and convincing many to welcome rather than resist the Allies.

One of those resisting OSS overtures was French Admiral Jean Darlan. He had earlier told the Allies that if they appeared with a well-equipped force of 500,000 men, he would abandon Vichy and side with them. When learning that the Allies were headed for Algiers, Darlan did just the opposite, ordering his men to resist. The embarrassing situation was settled when Fernand Bonnier de la Chapelle, shot and killed Darlan in his offices on December 24, 1942.

An investigation by French officials soon had it that the OSS was behind the assassination. Suspicion was cast upon William A. Eddy, OSS chief in Algiers, and his right-hand man, Carleton S. Coon whose job it was to train Free French fighters in the ways of sabotage. These Frenchmen belonged to a paramilitary organization called Corps Franc. Bonnier, Darlan's assassin, had been a member of the Corps Franc. Though neither OSS man was accused openly of being involved with Bonnier's murder of Darlan, both quickly left Algiers. Coon went to work with a British SOE operation in Tunisia, using the identity of a British officer who had recently been killed. When he returned to the U.S. he met with Donovan, submitting a report which urged political assassination as an OSS procedure, one which was not adopted.

Though accusations were flung about, the assassination of Admiral Darlan was never proven to be an OSS-sponsored act. Bonnier, who was a Gaulist and monarchist, had apparently acted out of his own accord. At the same time the North African invasions took place, Donovan's best spymaster, Allen Dulles, arrived in Bern, Switzerland (with two unpressed suits and a $1 million letter of credit) to organize OSS operations there. He was to provide invaluable information on military and political operations inside Italy and Germany.

Dulles was indirectly in touch with Germany's spymaster, Admiral Wilhelm Canaris, and he established a spy network equal to and eventually superior than the long-standing British networks headquartered in Switzerland. The American spymaster was also in contact with most of those inside Germany's underground, euphemistically called the Black Orchestra. It was Dulles who accepted Fritz Kolbe as a genuine top spy inside of Germany after the British spymaster Claude Dansey denounced Kolbe as a Nazi "plant." Kolbe proved to be the most important German spy working for the Allies during World War II.

At the same time that Donovan was supervising worldwide OSS operations behind enemy lines, operations in neutral countries such as Switzerland, Portugal, Sweden, he was also directing a host of operatives in Washington, D.C. who spied upon the embassies of many countries who were reportedly neutral. Few persons could devote as much time, sixteen hours a day, to his exhausting tasks as did Donovan, then in his sixties. Moreover, he had to contend at the same time with sniping from military intelligence chiefs such as the vainglorious, back-shooting General George Veazey Strong, head of Army Intelligence and General Marshall's hand-picked hatchet man.

Strong was forever writing sarcastic and demeaning memos about Donovan and the OSS. He had at his disposal, where the OSS did not, the military intelligence services of Magic, the American computerized system of intelligence analysis which was to break the Japanese codes, and Ultra, the British counterpart, which had broken the German codes almost at the beginning of World War II and continued to superbly analyze information through its computer system Colossus, developed toward the end of the war.

To discredit OSS efforts at every opportunity (and waste valuable time doing it), Strong compared Donovan's intelligence data with that produced by Magic and Ultra to show OSS failings. He could not, however, replace the human factor which was the hub of OSS operations and which produced, in the end, raw information from which genuine high-level intelligence was gleaned.

Donovan continued to be personally on hand to oversee many OSS operations. He was present at the Allied invasion of Sicily and at the OSS operations around Bari, Italy. He was present at the Normandy invasion in 1944 and closely supervised his massive OSS operations carried out behind German lines shortly before the Allies landed. Donovan's agents, many of them spectacular heroes, felt that they could do no less than "the chief." One of these was the courageous Moe Berg, former baseball player, who parachuted into Nazi-occupied Yugoslavia for the OSS to meet with Tito and report that the Allies should support the guerrilla leader which they did.

The OSS had proven its worth countless times over during World War II, and, given the Communist aims at the end of that conflict, Roosevelt believed that there was a future for the organization in the years to come. On October 31, 1944, he sent a note to Donovan, asking that he provide a report on an American intelligence agency in the postwar period. Donovan drew up a plan for a revamped OSS to continue its intelligence gathering duties and submitted this to Roosevelt. The President's death the following year, however, delayed these plans.

When President Harry S. Truman came to power, he believed that there was no need to have a world-wide American spy network now that the war was over, a view he would later change when confronted with the Russian menace. Truman disbanded the OSS on September 20, 1945, a month after the Japanese surrender and the official end of the war. Donovan retired a major general.

The OSS went silently out of business but by the time of its demise, it had earned the respect of intelligence communities throughout the world. Of its 16,000 agents and subagents in the combat zones, more than 2,000 of them had won medals for gallantry. Donovan had lost only 143 men and women. About 300 had been captured and imprisoned. It was a remarkable record of limited casualties, far less than Donovan had lost in World War I. Donovan's personal contribution was vast, and, as usual, valiant.

Donovan retired to private life but helped to create the CIA (Central Intelligence Agency) in 1947. He served as Ambassador to Thailand in 1953–54 before going into permanent retirement. In January 1959, a huge portrait of Donovan was hung in the lobby of CIA headquarters in Langley, Virginia. The oil painting showed an erect, commanding figure wearing the uniform of a major general, his chest bedecked with ribbons topped by the blue Medal of Honor. Donovan attended the ceremeony. He was ill at the time; in fact, he was dying.

"Wild Bill" gazed at his portrait and suddenly his bent frame came to life. One report had it that "the bowed head came up, the jaw hardened, the sagging body stiffened to attention. Straight as a soldier, the general about-faced and strode down the corridor and through the foyer, and climbed without help into the car." He died a month later, on February 8, 1959. When President Eisenhower heard the news he remarked: "What a man! We have lost the last hero!"

[ALSO SEE: *Morris Berg; Black Orchestra; Wilhelm Canaris; CIA; Claude Dansey; Allen Dulles; FBI; J. Edgar Hoover; Fritz Kolbe; Gaston Bullock Means; Stewart Graham Menzies; OSS; SIS; SOE; William Samuel Stephenson; Ultra*]

DOUBLE-CROSS SYSTEM
British Misinformation Program in World War II ▪ (1941–1945)

OPERATED BY MI5 THROUGHOUT WORLD WAR II, THE Double-Cross system involved the complete compromise of German agents in Britain. Some of the Abwehr agents were allowed to continue operating as German spies but all the information they sent to their Nazi spymasters was controlled by MI5.

The most effective results of the Double-Cross system was seen in Operation Bodyguard, the masterwork of MI5. One of MI5's best double agents, Luis Calvo, a Spaniard using the code name "Garbo," convinced the Abwehr that the invasion of Europe would be launched from southeastern England and directly at Pas de Calais.

Supporting this notion was a dummy army commanded by U.S. General George Patton who traveled about the area inspecting endless rows of tanks, troops and planes which looked real from the air but upon closer inspection proved to be of wood, cardboard and rubber So convinced was Hitler that the invasion would, indeed, come at Pas de Calais, that he concentrated his forces at this point, which allowed an easier landing of the Allies on the beaches of Normandy.

[ALSO SEE: *Abwehr; Wilhelm Canaris; Eddie Chapman; Ultra*]

DOWNEY, JOHN THOMAS
American Agent in Manchuria ▪ (1931–)

DOWNEY WAS NOT ONLY UNLUCKY BUT UNWISE IN that he need not have undertaken the mission which caused his capture and imprisonment. A first-year student at Harvard Law School, Downey was recruited by the CIA and trained as a spy instructor to Taiwanese agents who were to be sent into Manchuria during the Korean War. Nothing in Downey's orders called for him to accompany the

agents in a flight to Manchuria but he decided to go on the first run to gain experience.

A cargo plane loaded aboard Downey, Richard George Fecteau, another CIA operative, and nine Taiwanese agents on November 29, 1952, flying from Seoul, Korea to Manchuria. The plane was to set down at a secret airstrip, disgorge its Taiwanese passengers and pick up others, then return to Seoul. The plane, instead was shot down. The Taiwansese were killed but Downey and Fecteau were captured and taken to Tsao Lan-Tze Prison (Grass Basket Prison) in Peking.

Downey was publicized by the Communists as "the arch-criminal of all the American prisoners," but he was not placed on trial until 1954. He was convicted of espionage and given a life sentence. Fecteau was sentenced to twenty years. When Downey confessed everything his captors demanded, his leg irons were removed and he was later well-treated, used as a showpiece by the Communists. He and Fecteau were allowed to see family members and were even taken on a tour of China to impress upon them how well the Communist system was working.

The CIA was embarrassed at the capture of the two men. It flatly denied that the men worked for the agency. The U.S. government first announced that the two men had been lost at sea in an accident. When the Communists published photos of the men, U.S. officials insisted that the men were civilian employees working with the army. Not until March 12, 1973, were Downey and Fecteau released, and only after President Richard Nixon acknowledged the fact that both men had been CIA agents.

DOWNING, GEORGE
British Spy in Holland ▪ (1624–1684)

BORN IN DUBLIN, IRELAND, DOWNING MOVED WITH HIS family to Massachusetts in 1638 where his father practiced law. He graduated from Harvard in 1642, and returned to England to join Oliver Cromwell in the great rebellion against Charles I. Three years later, Downing went to Scotland, acting as a spy for Cromwell.

Following service in Parliament in 1656, Downing was appointed ambassador to The Hague in 1657. He spent more time spying on English loyalists living in Holland, along with Dutch politicians and military men than attending to his diplomatic chores. He sent his coded reports in diplomatic pouches to Cromwell's spymaster John Thurloe.

Relations between Holland and England were strained following the First Dutch War of 1654-56, and it was thought that the Dutch might be plotting another war. Downing told English diarist Samuel Pepys that he had dozens of spies in The Hague and many of these were the servants of Johan de Witt, head of the Dutch government.

Through these spies, Downing supplied Thurloe with reports detailing de Witt's oral conversations with his top advisers. He also secured secret documents from de Witt's office. The information he sent to Thurloe was of little value to Cromwell who died in 1658. Within two years his commonwealth was dissolved and Charles II was restored to the throne of England.

Downing swore allegiance to the new king, was knighted and amassed a fortune. He left to the government priceless London property, including Downing Street, now famous for housing the residence of English prime ministers.

DREYFUS, ALFRED
French Officer Accused of Spying for Germany ■ (1859–1935)

THE DREYFUS AFFAIR INVOLVED A HORRENDOUS miscarriage of justice and brought shame and disgrace to the government of France. It was fraught with spies, counterspies and political corruption so vast and venal that it took France's greatest men to expose France's greatest villains before the victim was grudgingly exonerated. The victim was Alfred Dreyfus, a French Jew born in Mulhouse, Alsace. When Germany annexed Alsace in 1870, following the Franco-Prussian War, the Dreyfus family moved to Paris.

While Dreyfus' brothers continued to operate their father's successful manufacturing plant, Alfred dreamed of becoming a soldier, entering the Ecole Polytechnique. An excellent student, he became an artillery expert, graduating with the rank of lieutenant. Dreyfus was assigned to the Fourteenth Regiment of Artillery in 1880. He was promoted to first lieutenant and married Lucie Hadomard in 1889. The marriage produced two children.

Dreyfus proved to be a superb, conscientious officer. He lived better than most army officers in that he supplemented his pay with income from his father's business. Promoted to the rank of captain, Dreyfus underwent rigorous training after being nominated to the staff college. He graduated third in his class but his dossier was stained by an anti-semitic remark made by a French general who expressed concern in having a Jew on the French General Staff.

The remark was ignored and Dreyfus was appointed to the General Staff on January 1, 1893. He served a year of probation and was deemed a model officer. At this time, certain members of the General Staff became alarmed when learning that information on certain French fortifications and newly-created French weapons had fallen into the hands of the Germans.

This information came by way of a French spy named Bastian who worked as a maid in the German Embassy in Paris. She had reportedly taken a document from the waste basket next to the desk of Lt.-Colonel Maximilian von Schwartzkoppen, military attaché at the German Embassy. This memorandum, or *bordereau*, found its way into the hands of Major Hubert Henry of the Statistical Section of the French Intelligence Bureau. Henry took the *bordereau*, which was unsigned and torn into four pieces, to the General Staff.

Studying the document, general staff officers concluded that, since it contained information on French artillery emplacements, the *bordereau* had been written by someone on the general staff who was an artillery expert. Suspicion quickly focused upon Captain Dreyfus, not out of any logical conviction or evidence, but out of petty envies, peevish offenses and outright bigotry. Officers came forward to denounce Dreyfus as the traitor and German spy. These officers disliked the accused because he was humorless, or distant in that he socialized only with his family or a few friends, or, mostly, because he was a Jew.

So-called handwriting experts then stated that the *bordereau* had been written by Dreyfus. When it was pointed out that the handwriting of the memorandum and that of Dreyfus were completely dissimilar, the experts nodded yes, exactly. Dreyfus, the experts insisted, knew he was writing a document that might later prove him to be a German spy and therefore he disguised his handwriting.

Dreyfus, utterly confused, was arrested on October 15, 1894. He was imprisoned and an order signed by General Auguste Mercier charged him with high treason. His court-martial occured on December 19–22, 1894. It was a kangeroo court where Dreyfus' guilt had been predetermined by a cabal of French officers who hated Jews, the worst of these being the head of the court, General Mercier. Major Henry testified that a "person of integrity," whom he would not name because of national security, had told him that Dreyfus was the traitor and the author of the infamous *bordereau*.

Contrary to French law, attorneys for Dreyfus were denied the right to examine the so-called "evidence" against their client, again under the flimsy excuse of protecting national security. The "evidence" that convicted Dreyfus remained in a sealed envelope which Major Armand du Paty de Clam turned over to the court. The court refused to disclose its contents. (Paty de Clam was the officer who had originally dictated the contents of the memorandum to Dreyfus, having him write out the same document and then used the wholly dissimilar writing of both documents to claim that Dreyfus was the spy.) Dreyfus was sentenced to life imprisonment in "a fortified place." He was ordered to be publicly humiliated for betraying his country.

Thousands of anti-semites paraded before government buildings and public places, whipped into a frenzy by equally anti-semitic French newspapers,

A rare photo taken of the wrongly convicted Alfred Dreyfus (first officer seated on platform at right) during his 1894 court-martial for treason and espionage.

screaming their rage over the fact that Dreyfus was not to be executed. For weeks, the anti-semites paraded through the streets of Paris by torchlight, demanding the death of Dreyfus.

January 5, 1895, was the date scheduled for Dreyfus' public degradation. Emasciated and sickly from sleepless nights in prison, Dreyfus was marched into a military square where General Darras raised his sword to signal the beginning of the public humiliation. Shouted Darras: "Dreyfus—you are unworthy to wear the uniform! In the name of the French people, we deprive you of your rank!"

With that, a towering sergeant stepped before the convicted man and ripped away the gold braid epaulets from his uniform. Next he tore away the stripes from his trousers. Then he snatched away the hard-earned medals and decorations pinned on his coat. His kepi hat was snatched and the stripes on it torn away, as were the numbers on his high collar which signified his military unit. Even the brass buttons from his coat were pulled off. The final degradation consisted of the sergeant taking away Dreyfus' sword and breaking it in half over his knee, then throwing it to the ground.

Dreyfus was then marched about the square for all to witness his shabby appearance. He finally found his voice and shouted: "In the name of my wife and my children, I swear that I am innocent! I swear it! Long live France! You are degrading an innocent man!" Dreyfus halted briefly before a group of newsmen, imploring: "You will say to the whole of France that I am innocent."

Crowds hissing hate pressed against the high iron fence surrounding the courtyard. "Kill him!" came the shout, and "Execute him!" and "Death to the Traitor!" With shoulders bent, Dreyfus was ushered into a police van. The cashiered Dreyfus was then sent, on January 17, 1895, to the hellish French penal colony of Devil's Island, off the coast of French Guiana, a barren rock that had once served as a home for lepers.

Dreyfus lived inside a small stone cottage with barred windows. He was watched day and night. He was permitted to walk about a treeless half acre in the afternoons. The harsh climate and bad food made him ill. Most of the time he suffered from fever, indigestion and dysentery. He was to live in silence, without visitors. His mail was heavily censored and even his guards were not permitted to talk to him. Alfred Dreyfus was to be ignored, forgotten.

Only Dreyfus' family and a few close friends refused to forget him. They continued to believe him innocent. So did one officer, a man who proved to be the bravest Frenchman of them all. He was

Lieutenant-Colonel Georges Picquart, a member of the general staff who had been troubled by the entire Dreyfus affair. Since there were persistent rumors that Dreyfus had been railroaded, the general staff ordered Picquart to conduct a reinvestigation into the case, but it was made clear to him that the investigation was to result in affirmation of the conviction.

Picquart was a diligent, conscientious officer who took his duties seriously. Defying orders not to inspect certain documents too closely, Picquart examined the *bordereau* again and again, comparing it to the handwriting of several French officers. He was able to determine with certainty that the author of the memorandum and the traitor and spy on the French general staff was Major Ferdinand Walsin Esterhazy. Without hesitation, Picquart went to the general staff to report that Major Henry had instantly recognized the handwriting of the *bordereau* as that of Esterhazy, his close friend, and that to save Esterhazy, he had accused the innocent Dreyfus.

Moreover, Picquart pointed out, long after Dreyfus had been sent to Devil's Island, French secrets had continued to flow to the Germans and this Picquart also proved. He offered in evidence handwriting samples of Esterhazy which he had obtained in August 1896. With the naked eye, it was clear that Esterhazy's writing and that of the memorandum were identical.

Picquart's statements were like thunderbolts to his superiors, General R. C. F. de Boisdeffre, chief of staff; General Baptiste Billot, war minister; and General Charles-Arthur Gonse, deputy chief of staff. Angrily, they hurled back Picquart's evidence, refusing to accept any of it, branding it "inadmissable." Picquart was told that he had conducted "the wrong investigation." The general staff was not interested in any evidence that had to do with the case which did not exclusively involve the man's conviction. Dreyfus had been identified by the general staff to the world as the French traitor and German spy. Any new evidence to the contrary would utterly compromise the integrity of the general staff.

Picquart was told in the harshest terms to cease his investigation into the affair. Stubbornly, Picquart warned his superiors that if the general staff did not reverse its decision concerning Dreyfus, it risked exposure by others who might discover that the French high command had known all along that Dreyfus was innocent and that it had criminally protected the real traitor and spy, Esterhazy.

The high command refused to alter its decision and Picquart was strongly warned to cease his involvement with the Dreyfus case and return to his duties, or else he might face "serious consequences." Esterhazy was secretly confronted by officers of the general staff who collusively decided to send him out of the country to perform useles missions. His assistant and friend, Major Henry, then created more forgeries in a haphazard attempt to disprove Picquart's evidence.

Meanwhile, Mathieu Dreyfus, continued to battle for his brother's exoneration. When he learned of Picquart's discoveries, he made them public, naming Esterhazy as the spy. The general staff was trapped by its own machinations and was compelled to order a court-martial for Esterhazy which occured on January 10–11, 1898. The hearing was a farce. Esterhazy was asked a few vague questions to which he gave vague answers. He was then promptly cleared of all charges. This flagrant cover-up prompted Emile Zola, the leading French journalist of the day to publicly denounce a military caste system that protected its own corrupt members, and the government that backed the general staff.

In a momentous publishing event, on January 13, 1898, Zola's celebrated article, *J'Accuse*, addressed to Felix Faure, the then president of the French Republic, was published on the front page of the powerful newspaper, *L'Aurore*. Zola was fearless. He knew that he was risking criminal charges and possible imprisonment. He nevertheless accused the government and several generals of committing criminal acts when covering up the guilt of Esterhazy in an effort to save their own reputations, of illegally convicting Dreyfus and of compounding their offenses through lies, forgeries and the outright destruction of evidence. The great French author, Anatole France, called Zola's valiant and masterful attack "a moment in the conscience of mankind."

Zola's denunciation caused the scandal to be exposed to the world and France reeled in turmoil over the corruption of its government. But Zola's attack did not uproot and destroy the villains. The general staff answered by having Zola charged with libel. He was convicted and his name was struck from the ranks of the Legion of Honor. The militarists attempted to degrade him in the same way they had degraded Dreyfus. To protect his family from more persecution, Zola moved to England where he remained for a year.

France's greatest writers rallied around his cause. Jean Jaures, Leon Blum, Georges Clemenceau, Anatole France and others incessantly pressured the government through a nagging press until Dreyfus was recalled from Devil's Island and retried. Major Henry, realizing that he was about to be exposed as the protector of the real traitor, Esterhazy, killed himself by cutting his throat. Drefus' second trial, at Rennes, from August 7 to September 9, 1899, was a sensation. More than 3,000 journalists from throughout the world attended. Thousands of citizens choked the streets surrounding the courthouse, arguing the case with each other. Fights and near-riots broke out.

The general staff was ramrod stubborn. It completely refused to admit is guilt in wrongly convicting Dreyfus and covering up its blatant frauds and collusion in the case. Again, Dreyfus was convicted "with extenuating circumstances." The world was in shock. Most had come to believe that Dreyfus was innocent. To mollify critics, French President Emile Loubert, issued a hedging decree which pardoned Dreyfus.

Dreyfus had no triumph and he would not be appeased. He insisted on complete vindication and continued a long, painful and expensive legal campaign which, in 1906, resulted in the French Court of Appeals quashing the verdict at Rennes. The court announced that Dreyfus was completely innocent of the crimes of treason and espionage. He was ceremoniously restored to the French Army and promoted to the rank of major. Further, he was awarded the Cross of the Cavalier of the Legion of Honor.

Serving with distinction in World War I, Dreyfus was promoted to the rank of lieutenant-colonel and named an Officer of the Legion of Honor. He then retired and, after a long illness, died in 1935, and is remembered as one of France's most heroic figures. He enjoyed one final triumph. He had outlived the real culprit, Esterhazy, by one year. Esterhazy, after being exposed at the turn of the century, fled to England where he later admitted that he had been the long-ago traitor and spy for the Germans. He died penniless, without friends, and in utter shame, in 1934.

DRIBERG, THOMAS
British Double Agent ▪ (1905–1976)

DRIBERG WAS EDUCATED AT LANCING AND OXFORD and was recruited in his youth by MI5 to penetrate the Communist Party in England. He joined the Young Communist League and he eventually penetrated Communist Party Headquarters. He became a well-known journalist, writing a column in Lord Beaverbrook's *Daily Express*. All the while, he collected information on British Communists and turned this over to MI5.

Driberg's duplicity was discovered by the KGB in 1941 and he was expelled from the Communist Party. He became a member of Parliament in 1942 and again in 1945. Throughout this time, Driberg continued to provide information to MI5. He traveled to Moscow in 1956 to meet with his old friend, Guy Burgess, traitor and KGB spy who had defected to Russia. His aim was to write a book about Burgess.

At the time, Driberg was Chairman of the British Labor Party. He was, unknown to most at that time, a practicing homosexual. When in Moscow, he participated in homosexual affairs which were secretly photographed by KGB agents. The KGB then ostensibly blackmailed Driberg into acting as a spy against his Labor Party and the British government. He agreed, but insisted upon being paid. The Russians gave him thousands of pounds, asking him to provide disinformation about Soviet Russia in his book about Burgess. Driberg agreed.

Upon his return to England, Driberg turned over most of the money he had received from the KGB to

MI5, telling his British spymasters everything the Russians had asked him to do. Oddly, when the galley proofs of the Burgess book was ready, Driberg made sure that both the KGB and MI5 received copies. Both made annotations and suggestions with MI5 having the last editorial word, spreading its own disinformation. Driberg's role of double agent continued until his death in 1976. A year earlier, he was raised to the peerage as Lord Bradwell.

[ALSO SEE: *Guy Burgess; KGB; MI5*]

DRONKERS, JOHANNUES MARINUS
Dutch Spy for Germany in World War II ▪ (1896–1942)

A DUTCH POSTAL CLERK, DRONKERS HAD BEEN ACTIVE for many years in the National Socialistische Beweging, a group of Dutch Nazis headed by Adrian Mussert with widespread operations throughout Holland. This political party also served the Abwehr well, with each member acting as a spy involved in espionage and sabotage operations prior to the Nazi invasion of the low countries in 1940.

Following the Nazi occupation of Holland, several of Mussert's most fanatical followers volunteered to act as spies in England. One of these was Dronkers. After receiving brief Abwehr training, Dronkers was told to flee Holland, posing as a refugee. Using that cover, he was to go to England and to the Dutch government in exile, offering his services to broadcast anti-Nazi propaganda over Radio Orange, the BBC service sponsored by the Dutch government in England.

On May 18, 1942, the British trawler *Corena* was patrolling the north sea when it spotted a small craft bobbing in high waves. Plucked from the leaking boat were three Dutchmen who were taken to Field Security in Harwich where they were segregated and separately interviewed. The two younger Dutchmen, de Langen and Mulder, appeared to be genuine refugees, but 46-year-old Johannues Dronkers drew suspicion to himself by his exaggerated behavior.

Dronkers, upon arrival in England, knelt on the ground and kissed it, then went on to slavishly babble his gratitude at being rescued and taken to a land of freedom. At one moment he wept uncontrollably, at another he sang and shouted praises to God for his deliverance. He continued in this manner for many hours, appearing ridiculous even to the two men who had accompanied him. The other two refugees stated that they had joined Dronkers at the last minute after learning that he was being smuggled out of Holland in a small boat.

Dronkers was next taken to the R.V.P.S. (Royal Victoria Patriotic School) in Wandsworth. This was the headquarters of MI9, which was the escape and evasion division for foreign refugees which was supervised by MI5, counterintelligence. Here, thousands of refugees fleeing from Nazi-occupied Europe were intensely interviewed to determine whether or not they were German spies. Dronkers was interviewed by the Dutch Security Service of the Dutch government in exile.

Interviewing Dronkers was a shrewd intelligence officer of the Dutch Security, Colonel Oreste Pinto, later known as one of the best spycatchers in the business. Pinto remembered how Dronkers "burst into my room like a whirling dervish, waving his arms and skipping to and fro, shrieking in his cracked voice an old Dutch patriotic song." He was impressed with Dronkers' appearance, a tall, thin man with premature white hair. Pinto later described "the skin so tight over his cheekbones that they seemed about to burst through."

Dronkers continued his outlandish behavior until Pinto ordered him to calm down and describe how he had organized his escape. The refugee then went limp, as if releasing his hysteria, and calmly explained that he had gotten involved in black marketeering in Holland and that the Gestapo learned of it. He knew that the offense for trading in the black market was death so he fled to Rotterdam and went to the Cafe Atlanta where he hoped to meet a member of the Dutch resistance. He was fortunate to encounter a man named "Hans," Dronkers said, who provided him with a small boat. Just as he was sailing for England, Mulder and de Langen, two young men he had met through "Hans," asked to join him.

Pinto suspected Dronkers as being a spy but played a waiting game. He kept him on hand for more than two weeks. At one point, Dronkers asked permission to broadcast from Radio Orange which was beamed to Holland. He wanted to send messages to his friends in Holland, urging them to resist the Germans. One report has it that Pinto brought him before a microphone and allowed Dronkers to read from some short scripts he had prepared himself. Unknown to Dronkers, the microphone was dead but the messages were recorded and were analyzed by Ultra, which had broken the German codes. Dronkers' messages had been, indeed, in German code and contained the cover message "safe arrival."

Dronkers was then informed by Pinto that he was believed to be an Abwehr spy. The Dutch colonel went on to tell Dronkers that he was very familiar with the Cafe Atlanta in Rotterdam, and that it was a place where Abwehr spymasters met frequently with their agents.

"Sir," said the weeping Dronkers, "in the name of the God I worship and in the name of my dead father whom I loved and who is assuredly in Heaven, I swear to you solemnly that I am faithful to my country . . . I am not a spy."

Then Pinto brought another interrogator into the room, a man named Adrianus Vrinten, also a member of Dutch Security. Vrinten had been a detective in Holland before the war and had investigated Mussert's Dutch Nazis on behalf of the Dutch Justice Department. "I know who you are, Dronkers," Vrinten told the man. "You were a leading Party member when we first met in Holland and you are now a German spy."

Dronkers sagged in his chair, then admitted being an Abwehr agent. He insisted, however, that he had been coerced into espionage, that the Germans had threatened to kill his wife unless he spied for them. Pinto then gave Dronkers the names and addresses of two Abwehr agents, one in Stockholm, the other in Lisbon, to whom Dronkers was to send his reports.

Surprised, Dronkers admitted everything but he was eager to know how Pinto had discovered his contacts. Pinto held up the Dutch-English dictionary Dronkers had been carrying when picked up. Pinto had for several days and nights closely examined the 700-page book, discovering tiny pinmarks under certain letters which revealed the identities of Dronker's Abwehr contacts.

With this Dronkers gave up all pretense and confessed his complete and willing involvement in his spy mission to England. He was charged with espionage and went to trial at the Old Bailey before Justice Wrottesley in Central Criminal Court on November 13, 1942. He was found guilty and condemned to death. His appeal was denied and he was hanged on December 30, 1942, in Wandsworth Prison.

Before his death, Dronkers wrote letters to King George, Winston Churchill and Queen Wilhelmina of the Netherlands who headed the Dutch government in exile. In these carping missives, he complained about his treatment at the hands of Oreste Pinto, telling these august world leaders that they "were harboring a Himmler."

[ALSO SEE: *Heinrich Himmler; Ultra*]

DRUMMOND, NELSON C.
American Spy for Soviets ■ (1934–)

NELSON C. DRUMMOND HAD THE DUBIOUS DISTINCtion of being the first black American ever convicted of espionage. He was a Yeoman First Class stationed at U.S. Naval Headquarters in London where he worked as a clerk having top secret and Cosmic (NATO) security clearances. A chronic gambler and pub-crawler who was forever in financial difficulties, Drummond's name was passed to a Soviet spy by a "spotter agent," reportedly an English barmaid.

The KGB agent invited Drummond to a pub and bought him drinks all night long. When picking up the tab, the agent asked the sailor if, for a price, he could get him a Navy ID card so a friend could make purchases at the Navy Exchange. Then the agent offered the money-strapped Drummond $250 in cash.

Drummond agreed to obtain the ID card. Before Drummond pocketed the money, the wiley KGB agent asked him to sign a receipt for the cash. Drummond shrugged and did so. From that point onward, Drummond belonged to the Soviets. His Russian spymasters were able to threaten to expose him through the receipt should he ever fail to provide information they wanted. Drummond went on supplying the KGB all the classified documents he could obtain, being paid small amounts of money.

Reassigned to duty in the U.S. in 1958, Drummond resumed his contact with the Soviets and continued to supply them with classified documents from various stations in his tours of duty, in Boston, Norfolk and Newport, Rhode Island. From 1962, until he was arrested and tried for treason and espionage in 1964, Drummond supplied Soviet agents with many classified operating manuals and defense files which he stole from the Newport Naval Base. He turned over these documents, he later admitted, to Russian diplomats who worked for the Soviet Mission of the United Nations.

FBI surveillance of suspected Soviet spies apparently led to Drummond's identification. He confessed his espionage, telling interrogators that he had been paid a total of $20,000 by the Soviets. He was convicted and sent to prison for life. Drummond's damage was deep. An estimated $200 million had to be spent in revising procedures, manuals, plans, and personnel he had compromised.

DST (Direction de la Surveillance du Territoire)
French Counterintelligence Service ▪ (1910–   )

The DST, similar to MI5 in England, is dedicated to detecting and arresting foreign spies in France. Added to its tasks in the 1970s was the responsibilities for counter-terrorism and counter-subversion. Controlled by the Interior Ministry, the DST is traditionally made up of ex-police employees.

The organization often uses a police service, Renseignements Generaux, which has extensive files on political and trade militants and foreigners to supplement its own huge files which are all computerized. The DST reportedly has the largest phone-tapping division in Europe, located near Les Invalides in Paris.

DUBBERSTEIN, WALDO (AKA: DOOBIE)
CIA Offficial and Spy for Libya ▪ (1908–1983)

A RESPECTED BIBLICAL SCHOLAR AND ARCHEOLOGIST, Waldo Dubberstein long-served the CIA as its resident expert on the Middle East. Quiet, retiring, Dubberstein also sold CIA secrets to the notorious spy Edwin Wilson, who, in turn, sold them to Libya. Though he had considerable property and cash, Dubberstein nevertheless turned spy for money so that he could support his 70-year-old wife and his 32-year-old German mistress in two luxury apartments in the Washington, D.C. area.

After Wilson was exposed, Dubberstein was indicted but never went to trial. On April 30, 1983, Dubberstein went to the basement of his mistress' apartment, sat down in a chair wearing a three-piece suit and a hat, then placed a recently purchased shotgun to his mouth and pulled the trigger, blowing away a goodly portion of his head. He left a note on the floor which read: "I am not guilty."

[ALSO SEE: *CIA; DIA; Edwin Wilson*]

DUEBENDORFER, RACHEL
Polish Spy for Soviets ▪ (1901–1973)

BORN IN WARSAW AND RAISED IN DANZIG, Duebendorfer was the Jewish daughter of a merchant named Hepner. She joined the Communist Party in 1920 and became a political fanatic and Soviet agent. While spying on the Polish government throughout the 1920s, she also married and divorced. Her Russian spymasters ordered her to take up permanent residence in Switzerland.

From 1934 to 1944, Duebendorfer worked in Bern, living with Paul Bottcher, a German journalist, also in the pay of the Soviets. Their spymaster was Sandor Rado who operated a vast and effective Soviet spy network throughout Switzerland and in Germany and Italy. In Rado's network, Duebendorfer operated under the code name "Sissy," but she also maintained direct contact with spymasters in Moscow, using another code name unknown to Rado. Apparently, she was also spying for the Kremlin on Rado and his associates, reporting on their continuing loyalty and effectiveness as Russian agents.

Duebendorfer was a cut-out or go-between, maintaining contact with all of Rado's agents, coordinating their reports to the central office in Bern. Her most important coup was recruiting Christian Schneider (code name "Taylor") in 1942. Schneider served as the cut-out to the spectacular Soviet spy, Rudolf Roessler (code name "Lucy"), who became the key source of information on German the German military during World War II.

It was Duebendorfer who excitedly went to Rado on June 17, 1941, with information from Lucy, reporting that more than a hundred German divisions were at the Polish border and were about to invade Russia. Stalin, however, reviewed these priceless intelligence reports and dismissed them out-of-hand. He had signed a non-aggression pact with Hitler two years earlier and he refused to believe that Hitler would break his word, a decision that cost countless Russian lives.

In 1943, Swiss counterintelligence broke up Rado's network. Duebendorfer was arrested the following year but escaped from prison in 1945. She fled to Paris and then to Soviet-controlled Eastern Europe where she died.

[ALSO SEE: *Sandor Rado; Rudolf Roessler*]

DUKES, PAUL
British Spy in Russia ▪ (1889–1967)

LONDON-BORN DUKES WAS THE SON OF A CLERGYMAN. He went to school in Surrey, and, following his graduation from Charterhouse in 1909, went to St. Petersburg to study music at the conservatory. He intended to make music his life career and got a job at the Imperial Marinsky Opera, as an assistant to conductor Albert Coates. In 1916, Dukes left the Marinsky Theater to take a position with the Anglo-Russian commission. His job was to study and report on the Russian press. Dukes then went to work for the foreign office with a "roving commission," in 1917, the year of the Russian Revolution. At one point in 1917, Dukes was in Samara, ostensbily working for the American YMCA, but his duties, other than "training Boy Scouts," were never explained.

In 1918, Dukes became a British spy, one who loved intrigue, and thought of espionage as "high adventure." He was first summoned to London where he met with British spymaster Mansfield Cumming, who later stated that Dukes was his "top mate [spy]" in Russia. After brief training in invisible inks and codes, Dukes returned to Russia. He traveled throughout the country, employing many disguises and aliases, using forged identification papers. He observed the chaos the revolution had brought and encouraged England to side with the White Russian forces attempting to overthrow the fragile government of the blood-thirsty Bolsheviks.

Dukes was made spymaster in Russia. He was a gifted agent in that he was clear-headed, acted decisively and knew well the people and the language

British agent Paul Dukes, who spied on the Bolsheviks during the Russian Revolution, shown in disguise.

of Russia. He established contact with the National Center, the organization that represented the interests of the White Russian monarchists who had armies in the field battling the Bolsehviks. Using money from Cumming, Dukes helped finance widespread espionage, sabotage and insurrection against the Reds. At one point, however, Dukes had to use promissory notes in that the money he received from England was badly counterfeited.

Much of Dukes' activities were directed toward rescuing prominent White Russians from prison and smuggling them out of the country through Finland. Working with MI1c (a branch of the intelligence service which dedicated itself to aiding refugees), Dukes was able to save hundreds of lives. He also worked with Augustus Agar, a lieutenant in the Royal Navy stationed in Finland who operated a torpedo motorboat squadron near Helsinki. Dukes supplied information on Russian warships to Agar which allowed him to lead a wild attack resulting in the sinking of Russian battleships and a cruiser.

Meanwhile, using disguises, Dukes managed to join the Communist Party, the Red Army, the Cheka (secret police), and the Comintern, extraordinary feats in and of themselves. He was thus able to report on the strategy and tactics of Lenin and Trotsky, as well as troop movements and battle orders of the Red Army. Spies for the Cheka, however, were able to identify the top leaders of the National Center in 1919 and they arrested its chief, N.N. Shchepkin on the night of August 28–29, 1919, along with dozens of other White Russian spies, and a courier from

Admiral Kolchak, head of the White Russian armies. In the following month more than a thousand agents of the National Center were arrested. Shchepkin and sixty-seven others were executed.

Dukes had been identified by the Cheka but its detectives could not find the elusive spy. Dukes fled to the Finnish border where he attempted to contact Lt. Agar, but failed. To avoid detection from spies at the Kronstadt forts, Dukes crossed nearly impossible terrain to reach Lake Luban and then escaped by foot into Latvia.

When he reached Reval, Dukes injudiciously confided some of his adventures to White Russian friends. These tales suddenly burst into the headlines of the Latvian press. "The fat was in the fire," Dukes later stated. "The Finnish and Swedish papers promptly quoted the story, and, long before I reached London, I realized that Red Russia was closed to me, perhaps forever."

So elated with Dukes and Agar was Cumming that he arranged for both men to meet King George V. They related their adventures to the King who awarded the Victoria Cross to Agar. Dukes was a civilian, and therefore, the King explained, could not receive England's highest decoration given to members of the military. King George then told Dukes that he considered the spy as the greatest of all soldiers, and added that he had an award in mind for him. That award came in 1920 when Paul Dukes was knighted, becoming the only British agent to receive knighthood as a direct reward for espionage.

[ALSO SEE: *Cheka; Mansfield Cumming*]

DULLES, ALLEN WELSH
OSS and CIA Chief ▪ (1893–1969)

ALLEN DULLES WAS THE CONSUMMATE SPYMASTER. HE was a large, burly man, with an unkempt appearance, rumpled white hair, a bristling mustache and, to give him that academic image, round-rimmed glasses and a smoking pipe in hand. He was outgoing and loved to tell spy anecdotes without ever mentioning names or giving anything away. Unlike the scowling British spymasters of old, like Mansfield Cumming, who was inspirational only to a few of his agents, and Claude Dansey, who inspired no one, except with hatred, Dulles delighted in parties where he talked freely and charmed almost all who fell beneath his benign gaze.

But Allen Dulles was inwardly cagey and crafty. He had an inordinate ability, which was painfully learned, to size up strangers and know how to quickly use them to his advantage, or, more specifically, to the advantage of the American intelligence agencies for which he so long labored. His attitude was consistently avuncular.

Dulles would patiently listen to anyone offering information, smile, nod, encourage, then listen some more. All things considered, Dulles was one of the finest spymasters America ever had, despite his well-publicized failures. His victories were enormous, saved countless lives and kept countries free, though certainly most espionage triumphs are as fleetingly remembered as the winners of picnic sack races.

Born and raised in Watertown, New York, Dulles was the son of the pastor of a Presbyterian Church. His older brother, John Foster Dulles (1888–1959), was to become President Dwight D. Eisenhower's secretary of state (1953–1959, considered to be the most powerful secretary of state in U.S. history).

Allen Dulles entered Princeton in 1910 and received his bachelor's degree in 1914. He was awarded his master's degree in 1916 and immediately entered the diplomatic service. He was sent to Bern, Switzerland to work under State Department senior official Hugh Wilson. His job was to collect political information on Germany and the Austro-Hungarian empire at a time when America was still neutral and war was being waged.

Dulles' real job was to serve as a spymaster. He was later to state: "That's where I learned what a valuable place Switzerland was for information and when I became interested in intelligence work." It was also in Bern where Dulles learned an important lesson. He had the opportunity to meet a then fairly obscure Russian revolutionary, Nicolai Lenin but skipped the meeting. He later resolved that never again would he ever disregard any source of possible intelligence.

Wilson and Dulles, working out of the American Embassy, built up a wide-ranging, loosely-organized espionage network of American expatriates and European refugees who had fled Germany and the crumbling Austro-Hungarian empire. One of Dulles' best informants was the American biologist, Dr. Henry Haviland Field. (Ironically, more than two decades later, Field's son Noel, an ardent Communist, would work for the OSS, betray the West, and, in turn, be compromised by Dulles in one of his cleverest and cruelest spy schemes.) Following Germany's defeat in 1918, Dulles joined his older brother, John Foster Dulles, and David Bruce as members of President Woodrow Wilson's staff at the Versailles Peace Conference. In 1922, he was assigned to the State Department where he headed the division of Near Eastern Affairs.

During his Washington period, Dulles married the daughter of a Columbia University professor. He was caught up in the social whirl of the Coolidge Administration and at one party he met a resolute assistant attorney general named William J. Donovan, the celebrated "Wild Bill" Donovan of World War I fame. Their friendship was to last until Donovan's death in 1959.

Although he was assured of a fine future at the State Department, Dulles was dissatisfied with his

Allen Dulles in 1942, when he headed the OSS in Bern, Switzerland, controlling a vast spy network throughout Europe.

Allen Dulles, right, in 1943, at his Bern flat with Gero von Schulze Gaevernitz, his chief contact with the underground in Germany, which was known as the Black Orchestra.

meager salary as well as a new assignment to the American Embassy in China, a post which Dulles considered to be too remote to serve as a stepping stone to a higher position. He quit the State Department in 1927 and joined Sullivan and Cromwell in New York, an international law firm where his brother worked. That same year, Dulles was the legal advisor to the American delegation attending the Geneva Disarmament Conference.

Attending a second disarmament conference in 1933, Dulles met his old friend Hugh Wilson, then the American Minister to Switzerland. Both of them observed the fanaticism rampant in the German delegation, all of these represenatives being Nazi cohorts of the newly-elected German Chancellor, Adolf Hitler.

In 1941, while attending the Republican national convention in Philadelphia, Dulles again met William "Wild Bill" Donovan who told him he was organizing an intelligence service and wanted him to be part of the organization. Dulles said he would be very interested in joining such a service. In October 1941, Dulles, along with Hugh Wilson, agreed to enter Donovan's intelligence agency, then called COI (Office of Coordinator of Information).

One of Dulles' first jobs was opening offices for COI in New York City. He chose the 25th floor of 30 Rockefeller Plaza and busied himself with obtaining eviction notices against the American Guild of Organists, the Van Dam Diamond Corporation and the Rough Diamond Corporation. He paid the evicted tenants $10,000 in compensation and then signed leases for the space, paying a rental of $35,737, along with yearly maintenance costs of $3,532. From that point onward, Dulles had carte blanche from his boss Donovan. To Dulles, his operations were "practically unlimited in concept or financial scope."

There was a very good reason why the site was chosen by COI chief William Donovan. One floor below COI offices in New York were the offices of the United Kingdom Commercial Corporation, William Stephenson, president. Stephenson was Donovan's good friend and one of the top British intelligence officials, working in the U.S. to gain support for England.

By January 1942, only a month after America had entered the war, Dulles' COI offices in New York were buzzing with activity. After conferring with Donovan, Dulles launched intelligence projects all over the world. But much of Dulles' COI operations was concentrated on Germany, not Japan, in keeping with Churchill's insistence that the European theater of war take precedence over the war in the Pacific. Churchill was Donovan's close friend. Extensive files were created which profiled every leading Nazi in Germany, this information assembled by Baron Wolfgang von Zu Putlitz, a former German counsel in the Hague who had gone over to the British. The neighbor downstairs, Stephenson's SIS (British Secret Intelligence Service) had provided the Baron. (Zu Putlitz would, in 1954, be identified as a Communist spy in East Germany, involved in the defection to the Communists of Otto John, chief of West Germany's counterintelligence.)

Next, Dulles created a Special Activities Desk which was headed by Arthur Goldberg and Donald Downes. This COI division proposed using German emigres to help the Black Orchestra, those inside Germany working against the Nazis. This project was short-lived in that many of the emigres selected to "front" for the COI were left-wing radicals, such as Dr. Karl Frank, or right-wing reactionaries, like Gottfried Treviranus.

Dulles as head of the CIA in 1961 with a silhouette of President Kennedy superimposed at left, indicating sealed lips for silence and secrecy regarding the disastrous Bay of Pigs invasion in Cuba.

In late 1942, Dulles asked to be relocated to Bern, Switzerland, where he had had his first strong taste of espionage. By selecting Switzerland, Dulles knew that he was choosing not only a remote post but one that would virtually leave him marooned. By the time he went to Bern in 1942, Dulles was virtually shut off from OSS offices in London and Washington. He was surrounded by a sea of fascists, Italy and its fiefdoms on one side, Germany and occupied France on the other. There were only two lines of communication to the West for Dulles, the telegram for coded messages, and the telephone for non-sensitive information.

This suited Dulles well. If he could not openly contact his superiors, they, in turn, could not contact him. He would have a free hand to develop his own intelligence network. He would literally be his own boss and he would have to establish his own reputation as a spymaster without the help of the vast staffs and systems OSS enjoyed in London, Washington and elsewhere. Dulles knew that Switzerland, as had been his experiences in World War I, was the center of espionage activities and that this would be the country to which all of those working against the Nazis would gravitate. His problem, of course, was in selecting the right spies and not double agents planted by the Germans.

Dulles did not fear Admiral Canaris of the Abwehr, who, by then, was making overtures to the West concerning a separate peace, along with leading figures of the Black Orchestra (the resistance movement inside Germany). These would be his best sources of information. But Heinrich Himmler's Reich Security, the SD, SS and Gestapo had their own agents who would stop at nothing, even inside the neutral borders of Switzerland where they operated in great numbers. Those coming forward with offers to spy in Germany

for Dulles might well come from these treacherous sources.

From the moment the 49-year-old Dulles arrived in Berne, carrying a small bag containing two unpressed suits and a few other personal items, along with a Letter of Credit for $1 million, he was furtive and clever about his role in Bern. He was officially listed as a "Special Representative of the United States of America." He rented the garden apartment at Herrngasse 23 and used this as his office. On the first night of his arrival, Dulles went to the street and removed the electric light bulbs from the street light outside his house so that guests could visit him nocturnally without being seen to enter his apartment. Throughout the war, Dulles made sure that street lamp never functioned.

Only hours after Dulles arrived in Bern, British intelligence offered its help in the form of Edge Leslie of MI6 and John McCaffrey of SOE. Dulles politely thanked them but went his own way, saying he would establish his own staff somehow. He pressed into service several American businessmen who had been stranded in Bern when the French borders had been closed by the Nazis following the invasion of North Africa. A representative of an American bank secretly bought foreign currency for OSS operations. An executive of Standard Oil provided information on petroleum reserves available to the Nazis and their secret locations. This information later aided the U.S. Army Air Force in its bombing raids, particularly in attacks on the Ploesti oil fields in Rumania.

Many ex-Weimar Republic leaders Dulles had known in the 1920s and 1930s were living in exile in Switzerland and the OSS spymaster took full advantage of their contacts in Germany and the occupied countries when establishing his spy network. These included Gero von Schulze-Gaevernitz, a naturalized American banker whose father had been a Weimar administrator; Dr. Wilhelm Hoegner, one-time Munich prosecutor who had prosecuted Hitler for the 1923 putsch; Noel Field, a one-time State department official who acted as a courier between Dulles and the Communist underground in Europe.

The most important contact Dulles then had with the Black Orchestra, the secret cabal of generals and politicians plotting Hitler's downfall in Germany, was the phlegmatic, close-lipped Hans Bernd Gisevius who worked at the German Consulate in Zurich. Gisevius had worked with British intelligence for a brief period but MI6 dropped him, suspecting him, as it did all Germans, of being a double agent. Dulles had no qualms in using Gisevius. The German agent later stated that "Dulles was the first intelligence officer who had the courage to extend his activities to the political aspects of the war."

Gisevius met with Dulles many times to provide useful information. He told Dulles that the anti-Nazi groups he represented wanted to eliminate Hitler and then sign a separate peace with the U.S. and England in order to prevent the Soviets from seizing goodly portions of Germany. Dulles also used as an agent the quirkish Adam von Trott zu Solz, who worked in the German Foreign Office. Trott was a leader of the Kreisau Circle, another Black Orchestra group inside Germany.

Dulles had great expectations for the Black Orchestra but England, especially Winston Churchill at that time, although he radically changed his view in the post-war years, insisted that no peace settlement could be achieved without the participation of Russia, then a staunch ally of the Western Powers. Moreover, Dulles OSS operation, so thickly populated by German dissidents, unnerved Churchill and British intelligence. MI6 and SIS chiefs in London became resentful of Dulles' seeming unwillingness to follow their lead and to be dominated by their procedures.

Subtly, such British spymasters as Claude Dansey went out of their way to discredit Dulles' intelligence operations and attempted to show that the quality of his information was decidedly inferior, if not useless. This they did by evaluating Dulles' data through Ultra, which had developed a giant computer system which analyzed the worthiness of information. By 1944, Ultra had built and was operating a huge computer system it called Colossus.

Though this computer system did, indeed, break the German ciphers and was excellent in analyzing military information, it did not replace the human spy and could not compete in the field of supplying political and social intelligence. It could also not compete with the kind of superlative secret information Dulles provided through the best Allied spy in Germany, Fritz Kolbe. This man was highly placed as an intelligence official in the German Foreign Office and had access to Germany's most current top secrets.

Kolbe first approached the British and was rebuffed, labelled a German double agent. Dulles, however accepted Kolbe, and used all of his information which proved to be invaluable. British intelligence, especially the American-hating Claude Dansey, exploded in arrogant rage (which had always been a deadly British weakness in the intelligence field). How dare this upstart Dulles accept as a genuine agent a man whom the British had declared a double agent, a plant? Dansey and other British spymasters consistently denounced Kolbe as a fake but his information proved them disastrously wrong, and it proved Allen Dulles as a shrewd, successful spymaster.

Throughout 1943, Dulles also busied himself with aiding insurgents and dissidents in Italy. OSS operations in Italy helped to topple dictator Benito Mussolini. Meanwhile, Dulles was in close contact with the German conspirators who attempted to assassinate Hitler in 1944 and failed with the conspirators slaughtered by the SS. This was Dulles' greatest disappointment. By 1944, at the time of the Battle of the Bulge, Dulles concentrated his efforts in sending hundreds of OSS agents, both American and Europeans who spoke flawless German, behind enemy lines in Scandinavia, the Lowlands, and Germany, to conduct chaos, sabotage and all manner of subversion. Aiding the infiltration operations of the OSS at this time was a wealthy, 32-year-old New York tax lawyer named William Casey who would some day become chief of the CIA.

In early 1945, Dulles entered into talks with representatives of SS General Karl Wolff, who intended to surrender all German units still fighting in Italy. These talks, code-named SUNRISE, were endorsed by President Roosevelt, who fended off sharp notes from Stalin who objected to separate surrenders by German commanders when the Soviets were not present. When Roosevelt died, President Truman, fearful of offending Moscow, ordered Dulles to break off the negotiations with Wolff. Dulles expressed bitter disappointment. He believed that the Russians wanted the talks to terminate so that they could seize key cities in northern Italy.

Dulles' top Geman agent, Fritz Kolbe, contacted the spymaster in April 1945, sending information about a German intelligence unit which had preserved all its records on the Eastern front and had a widespread spy network in place throughout Russia. This unit was headed by a sharp German spymaster, General Reinhard Gehlen, who was later to head West German intelligence. Gehlen, who had led his team to the Alps to surrender to the Allies, offered to make his espionage network available to the Americans.

Dulles and Donovan seriously considered this proposal, knowing that it would take years and millions of dollars to establish just such a network. Gehlen offered extensive microfilm on his unit's complete records. The German spymaster's proposal was accepted and one of those who facilitated the absorption of Gehlen into Western intelligence operations at that time and immediately after the war was OSS agent Richard Helms, who would later direct the CIA.

Dulles had moved to Berlin where he was the OSS chief in the American Zone of occupied Germany. He worked closely with Gehlen's new German intelligence organization in identifying KGB spies, as well as hunting down Nazi war criminals. Dulles also attended the Potsdam Conference that year where he conferred with President Truman and informed him that Japan, still at war, had sent envoys to Switzerland to secretly extend peace feelers. These envoys, Dulles reported, would negotiate a conditional peace. Truman refused; it would be unconditional surrender or annihilation.

That war, of course, was ended when Truman, relying on intelligence reports that told him that more than a million American lives could be lost in attempting to capture mainland Japan, ordered the dropping of atomic bombs on Hiroshima and Nagasaki. Truman also by that time considered the OSS obsolete. He naively concluded that America, now that it had won the war, had no more need of a worldwide espionage system. He completely failed to

Allen Dulles, the grand old spymaster, at the time of his retirement from the CIA.

see the Communist threat, despite the fact that Donovan, Dulles and many other intelligence chiefs had warned him of Russia's plans to overrun all of Europe and Asia.

Truman disbanded the OSS in 1945 which left Allen Dulles without a job. He returned to private practice but he could not resist the allure of intelligence work, especially when Truman, realizing his misjudgment of Russia' Cold War aims, established the CIA in 1947. Dulles joined the agency and became deputy director in 1951. By 1953 he became its autocratic director and ushered in the most sweeping American intelligence operations in history. Dulles, backed by his brother, John Foster Dulles, who was then Secretary of State, virtually did as he pleased and answered to no one in the Eisenhower administration.

Dulles planned and set in motion spectacular espionage operations, including interference in the affairs of many third world countries, assassinations of political enemies of the U.S., the digging of the Berlin Tunnel which allowed the CIA to monitor Soviet networks, and the operation of high altitude U-2 spy planes, which resulted in the shoot-down of CIA spy pilot Gary Francis Powers. The capture of Powers was used by Soviet Premier Nikita Khrushchev to cancel his planned summit meeting with President Eisenhower.

In 1961, Dulles' star fell. He strongly advised President John Kennedy that the CIA-backed invasion of Cuba at the Bay of Pigs would prove successful and bring about the destruction of Communist dictator Fidel Castro. When the invasion turned into a disaster, an onslaught of criticism buried Dulles, who then resigned from his post at the CIA. In retirement, Dulles wrote extensively about intelligence but defended the old OSS and championed the CIA, stating that neither agency ever circumvented orders from the President and remained within the regulations of their charters. Dulles insisted that the CIA never constituted "an invisible government" and was an important and responsible organization that had faithfully and successfully protected the security of the United States. Before leaving the CIA, he was present to officially open the resplendant new CIA headquarters in Langley, Virginia, and inspect the luxurious suite of offices that were to be his own, offices in which he never worked. Allen Dulles died eight years later, respected throughout the world as the most talented and celebrated American spymaster in history.

[ALSO SEE: *Abwehr; Bay of Pigs; Berlin Tunnel; Black Orchestra; Wilhelm Canaris; William J. Casey; CIA, Mansfield Cumming; Claude Dansey; William J. Donovan; Noel Field; Reinhard Gehlen; Otto John; Fritz Kolbe; OSS; Gary Francis Powers; SIS; William Stephenson; Ultra*]

DUNLAP, JACK
American Spy for Soviets ■ (1928–1963)

ONE OF AMERICA'S MOST SECRET ORGANIZATIONS, the NSA (National Security Agency) was thought to be unpenetrable by foreign agents. Its security was said to be ironclad, its tight-lipped officials unapproachable. The KGB had for some time targeted the NSA but found no way to obtain its secrets until it discovered Sergeant Jack Dunlap, a beer-drinking clerk-messenger with five children, a tired wife and mounting bills.

Louisiana-born Dunlap was a career army man. He enlisted in the U.S. Army in 1952 and served with distinction in Korea. Remaining in the service, Dunlap rose to the rank of sergeant and was assigned to the NSA in 1958. He was given top secret messages to carry to NSA officials before they had been put into code. Moreover, Dunlap was given a top-secret clearance to view these "raw" uncoded messages.

Somehow learning of Dunlap's sensitive position, a KGB agent approached the sergeant in 1958, bluntly telling him that he would be paid handsomely for the contents of the pouches he was carrying. Dunlap did not hesitate and began selling the Russians copies of all the documents he carried about. His method was reportedly simple. Before delivering the documents, he slipped them under his shirt, drove to a rendezvous in Washington, D.C., had his contact make copies or photograph them, then returned them to the pouch and went on to make his delivery.

By June of 1960, he bought two Cadillacs and a Jaguar. Next, Dunlap acquired a statesque blonde mistress, paying her expenses. It was later estimated that Dunlap was receiving from the Soviets between $40,000 and $50,000 a year. When neighbors asked about his new riches, Dunlap said that he had inherited a plantation in Louisiana.

NSA security paid no attention to Dunlap's new lifestyle. The spy brought attention to himself in 1963. He was about to be transferred to another post which would cut off his access to documents. To continue making money from the Soviets, Dunlap believed that he could stay on at NSA by simply not reenlisting when his tour of duty expired. He would then go to work for the agency as a civilian.

After being mustered out, Dunlap applied for work at NSA as a civlian. As such, he required a new clearance and, unlike the military working for NSA, he was compelled to take a lie detector test. He was given a polograph test which he failed. Dunlap learned that NSA and Army intelligence were both looking deeply into his background.

Dunlap, fearing exposure, opted for suicide. The nature of Dunlap's death did not deter the Army from burying him with honors at Arlington National Cemetery. Then the spy's wife, Diane Dunlap, discovered a large number of classified documents in their home and turned these over to NSA which then pieced together Dunlap's traitorous activities, although it was never learned exactly how many documents Dunlap had turned over to the Russians, a vexing and costly problem for America's most secret organization.

[ALSO SEE: *KGB; NSA*]

DZERZHINSKY, FELIX
Soviet Spymaster ■ (1877–1926)

BORN IN VILNA, LITHUANIA, DZERZHINSKY BECAME a leftist radical in his late teens and worked with the underground to plot the overthrow of the czar's regime. He was arrested in 1897 for political agitation and sent to Siberia, escaping from a concentration camp there two years later. In 1900, he was again arrested and sent to Siberia and, in 1902, he again escaped.

Going to Berlin, Dzerzhinsky continued to conspire against the czar. He returned to Poland in 1905 to participate in the failed revolution and was captured by the Okhrana and was sent to prison for seven years. Released in 1912, Dzerzhinsky was arrested for political agitation and sent to prison to serve another nine years. He was released, however, in 1917, when the Bolsheviks led their revolution and opened the prison cells of all of those loyal to their cause.

Lenin looked upon Dzerzhinsky as a revolutionary hero and named him head of the Cheka, the newly-formed secret police which would evolve into the GPU, OGPU, NKVD and, finally, the KGB.

A police photo of Felix Dzerzhinsky when he was imprisoned for revolutionary activities in Russia.

Dzerzhinsky at the time he headed the first Soviet spy service, the Cheka.

As head of the Cheka, Dzerzhinsky became the founder of the feared Russian intelligence and terrorist organization. It was Dzerzhinsky who organized agents to spy on dissidents within Russia, as well as establish a terrorist network that pinpointed, then tracked down and assassinated exiled White Russians opposing the Communist regime. He was tireless in his efforts, maintaining a brutal, punitive posture toward anyone unlucky enough to be arrested by his thug agents. He devised countless tortures until finding the most effective in getting victims to talk.

After leaving the then OGPU in 1921, Dzerzhinsky became commissar of transport and reorganized Russia's railroad system. In 1924, he became director of the Soviet Economics Council. Dzerzhinsky, much to the relief of the Russian people, as well as Communists fearful of his wrath, died on July 20, 1926 of natural causes, only to be replaced by another monster, Vyacheslav Menzhinsky. Stalin later named a large intersection in Moscow as Dzerzhinsky Square to commemorate the memory of Russia's first Communist spymaster.

[ALSO SEE: *Cheka; GPU; KGB; NKVD; OGPU*]

EASTERN JEWEL
(AKA: YOSHIKO KAWASHIMA)
Chinese Spy for Japan ▪ (1906–1948)

BETRAYAL WAS AN ART FORM FOR EASTERN JEWEL. The Chinese-born Tartar princess was corrupted early by the Japanese, adopted their Bushido code of conquest, and used her wits and her body to take vengeance on the land of her birth. Perhaps more than any other single person in the Orient, Eastern Jewel was directly instrumental in starting World War II.

Eastern Jewel's father was Prince Su, the Manchu monarch of Inner Mongolia who claimed descendancy from Emperor Nurhachi who founded the dynasty in 1616. Chinese princes had at their courts Japanese advisers who had bullied their way into positions of consultants. These were military men who planned on the eventual conquest of China, as the princes well knew. They feared these swaggering officers because of their recent victory over mighty Russia in the Russo-Japanese War in 1905. From that time on, Japanese envoys to Chinese courts were tolerated and shown pointed respect out of abject fear.

Prince Su's Japanese adviser was Naniwa Kawashima who had eyed the pretty Eastern Jewel since her birth in 1906. He had asked Su for the honor of raising the child as his own, a request that was routinely granted in 1914, when the girl was only eight. She was taken to Japan where her name was changed to Yoshiko Kawashima. She was sent to primary school and taught judo and fencing.

Death claimed Prince Su in 1921 in Port Arthur. His wife, told that she had no official status once her husband had died, committed suicide. When told of these events, Eastern Jewel merely shrugged. She was indifferent to her Chinese heritage, in fact, had been taught by her Japanese masters, to hate the land of her birth. By then she had given her heart, soul, and body to Japan.

Eastern Jewel later bragged about how, at the age of fifteen, she had been raped by her Japanese grandfather and her adoptive father, and had had, at her adoptive father's insistance, several affairs with Japanese officers. She also later told the old story of unrequited love, that a young Japanese officer named Yamaga, for whom she had deep affection, had rejected her. She, in turn, having a large dowery, revenged herself by taking countless lovers (if that can be called revenge).

By 1927, the Japanese military family ruling Eastern Jewel ordered the 19-year-old girl to marry the son of a Mongol prince, a rather nondescript youth named Kanjurjab. Through this marriage, the Japanese would have another foothold inside Mongolia, a land also coveted by Japan. The couple were wed in Port Arthur but the marriage lasted only four months.

Eastern Jewel had had enough of married life and, in 1928, she deserted her husband and left Mongolia, traveling to the teeming Chinese coastal towns, before returning to Tokyo to live in the Chinese student quarter where she called herself Yang Kuei Fei, the name of a legendary Chinese imperial concubine who, like Helen of Troy, brought about the ruination of an empire. Here she seduced and abandoned several lovers, then inveigled a member of the Japanese Diet to take her to Shanghai.

When Eastern Jewel had milked this gullible old man of all his funds, she left him, looking for another rich lover. The scheming dragon lady had little trouble attracting just such a person. He was a barrel-chested Japanese officer, Major Ryukichi Tanaka. He had an enormous head and sported a thick, flowing black mustache. He was rich and exercised considerable power as chief of the Special Service Organ, the Japanese intelligence service in Shanghai. Eastern Jewel attended a party in Shanghai, dressed in her usual garb—riding breeches, shiny, black knee-high boots, military jacket and riding crop. She flicked the crop at Tanaka and he silently followed her into a back room where, without a word, she attempted to make love to him.

Tanaka drew back, insisted upon knowing who she was. When Eastern Jewel outlined her background, the spymaster shook his head. He could not have sex with a Manchu princess, he said apologetically. He was a mere line officer in the Japanese army and she was socially above him. Eastern Jewel laughed and departed. She called at Tanaka's office a short time later, however, continuing to pursue him. They both had one thing in common, she pointed out, a fetish for boots. The spymaster let down his military guard and Eastern Jewel seduced him. She had been right about the boots. According to one report, Tanaka "loved to wear high black boots and she insisted that he wear them always. The boots scuffed the polish of the brightest dance floors of Shanghai, and ended each evening dangling over the end of a bed." Not just "a bed," but Eastern Jewel's bed.

Tanaka not only took Eastern Jewel regularly to his bed, but he enrolled her into his spy service. By putting her on the payroll of the Special Service Organ, he was simply obtaining enough money to keep his mistress in high style. When he learned of her total devotion to Japan, he decided to make her one of his legitimate agents. He sent her to a special school to learn English, which Tanaka felt would prove an asset in her espionage work.

In 1931, Tanaka received orders to create disturbances in Shanghai to allow an incursion of Japanese troops into the city. To that end, Tanaka gave Eastern Jewel about $10,000 in American currency, instructing her to hire Chinese thugs to attack Japanese businesses. A short time later, the agent provocateur accomplished her assignment. Dozens of Chinese street gangsters, using a list of businesses and homes owned by Japanese residents in Shanghai provided by Eastern Jewel, barged into offices and houses, brutally beating the inhabitants and destroying everything in sight.

As planned by Tanaka and his superiors, which included Emperor Hirohito, the grand architect of World War II (Tojo and other military officers were merely scapegoats), the abuse of Japanese businesses and residents by Chinese gangsters provoked a Japanese invasion force, conveniently offshore, to land thousands of troops. These Japanese troops ostensibly went to the rescue of their own people in the Japanese enclave but this was merely an excuse to take over the city. World leaders, however, quickly saw through the primitive ploy and demanded that Japan withdraw its troops, which it reluctantly did.

By then Eastern Jewel had drawn a new assignment from her Japanese spymasters. Tanaka received specific orders from his superior in the north, Colonel Kenji Doihara (later executed as a war criminal) to send his mistress to Tientsin where she was to convince her relative, the deposed boy emperor, Henry Pu-Yi to move to Mukden where Doihara and his Japanese bosses whould install him as their puppet to support their takeover of Manchuria. Eastern Jewel flew immediately to Tientsin where she moved into the small villa housing Pu-Yi.

Henry Pu-Yi was ripe for Japanese picking. As the last of the Manchu emperors, he longed for the ancient splendors and authority of the old palaces and courts. He felt resentful at his being shunted aside by the new republic established by Dr. Sun Yat-sen and Chiang Kai-shek. He knew that the Japanese were using him but he also knew that without his Japanese sponsors, he would have no status at all. When Eastern Jewel arrived, she immediately warned Pu-Yi that his life was in danger, and, unless he moved to Mukden, where he could assume the throne of China with the help of his good Japanese friends, he would undoubtedly be assassinated.

Pu-Yi did not believe her and told her that Mukden was a primitive little town with no nightlife or excitement. He could never move to such a dreary place.

(He did not mention the fact that though he paid respect to his Japanese sponsors, he greatly feared them, and believed that once he moved to Mukden he would be in their complete control.)

Undaunted, Eastern Jewel resorted to more terrifying ploys. She placed poisonous snakes in the emperor's bed and "discovered these horrid reptiles" herself, just as she was undressing, preparing to tryst with Pu-Yi, for she had often had sex with the lascivious boy-emperor in the past. When the snakes did not provoke a decision, a more potent threat appeared. A basket of fruit was sent to Pu-Yi from an anonymous friend. Eastern Jewel was the first to partake, discovering (as she knew she would) two bombs hidden beneath the bananas and apples.

Pu-Yi went white-faced, calling for his Japanese guards. They rushed in on cue, led by one of his court officers, a Japanese captain who was a member of Doihara's Special Service Organ. Making much show of removing the bombs, the captain later returned to tell the now terrified Pu-Yi that the bombs had been examined by experts at the Japanese enclave in Tientsin and they had reported that the bombs had been made at the arsenal of Chang Hsueh-liang, warlord of Manchuria and arch foe of Henry Pu-Yi.

Still the boy-emperor hesitated, frustrating the plans of Kenji Doihara and associates who were on the verge of creating an "incident" in Manchuria, the fake sabotage of the Japanese-owned Manchurian Railway. Before this plan could be put into action, Doihara wanted Pu-Yi enthroned in Mukden to endorse the Japanese invasion of Manchuria, ostensibly to protect Japanese interests, the same tactic Eastern Jewel had employed in Shanghai. To hurry Pu-Yi's decision, Doihara himself appeared in Tientsin and had Eastern Jewel brought to him for conference.

The two had never before met. Eastern Jewel's entrance into Doihara's office in the dead of night was calculated to impress upon the spy chief that she was a dramatic master of disguise, worthy of any top agent in the employ of Japan. She entered the outer office dressed as a Chinese gentleman, refusing to give her name. Doihara had the visitor brought to him as he was doing paperwork, his gun close to him on the desk.

"Your name, please?" Doihara said.

"My name is of no importance," replied Eastern Jewel in her deepest voice. "I have come to help you."

"You speak like a eunuch," snorted Doihara. "Are you one of Pu-Yi's men?"

When she laughed, Doihara stood up, moved quickly around his desk, withdrawing his sword and pointing it at her. "Very well then," said Doihara, "if you will not tell me who you are, let's see what you are." Delicately flicking the point of his sword, Doihara, as he related with relish to friends later, cut one string on the front of her robe after another, then, while she continued to smile at him, flicked the robe open to reveal her petite, female body. "I saw that she was a woman," Doihara concluded, "so I conducted a thorough investigation and determined that I had not put even the smallest scratch on any part of her white skin."

Following their lengthy tryst, spymaster and spy put together a plan that they felt would finally compel Pu-Yi to go to Mukden. It was the old provocation tactic again. This time, Eastern Jewel hired Chinese terrorists to attack the Japanese guards protecting Pu-Yi at the very entrance of his villa. The commotion brought the boy-emperor to the foyer where he witnessed his guards hard-pressed to drive off the attackers.

At this point, Pu-Yi immediately opted for Mukden. Doihara later stated that he smuggled the boy-emperor into the trunk of his car and, after a wild ride and a trip down the river, managed to get him aboard a Japanese ship which took him to Mukden. On the other hand, Pu-Yi might have still hesitated and Doihara, at his wit's end, simply kidnapped Pu-Yi.

Once in Mukden, Pu-Yi was installed on a throne that had no meaning, except to give the Japanese the excuse that their invasion of Manchuria was at the request of Emperor Pu-Yi, a request made to "preserve peace." Pu-Yi would remain a virtual prisoner of the Japanese until after World War II, when, homeless, throneless, wifeless, he wandered through China and its then civil war, only to be identified finally by the Communists and, after a long imprisonment and indoctrination, be released to die in obscurity.

For her part in the Pu-Yi operation, Eastern Jewel was commended by her Japanese spymasters who rewarded her by giving her the rank of commander and allowing her to wear the full dress uniform of a Japanese officer. She reveled in this role. In 1932, during the phony war she had helped launch between Japan and China, she celebrated the ruthless bombing of Shanghai by the Japanese air force. She flew in Japanese fighter planes over burning Shanghai viewing the monstrous destruction of human lives and property, laughing and applauding the terrible sight. She later walked through the devasted streets of Shanghai, in the company of Japanese officers, joking, and indifferently stepping over the dead bodies of brutally slain women and children. No Chinese who saw her then would ever forget the sight of the smug, gloating Eastern Jewel.

After Peking fell to the Japanese, Eastern Jewel went to the capital to take up permanent residence with orders from the Special Service Organ to spy on the inhabitants. Establishing her headquarters in the finest hotel, the spy let it be known that, for a price, she could intercede with her Japanese friends and save the lives of those accused of sabotage, espionage or collaboration with the enemy, meaning Chiang Kai-shek. Eastern Jewel simply selected wealthy businessmen, ordered them to meet with her, and then told them they were under suspicion but that she could protect them for a fee.

As the tide turned against Japan, Eastern Jewel began to indulge in her most sordid sexual fantasies, taking on a number of bed partners, sometimes as many as a dozen at one time. On other occasions she slept with members of her own Japanese guards. She sent her guards to haunt the local theaters as she was attracted to handsome, young actors.

At war's end, Eastern Jewel was no longer the sensual, alluring woman that had enchanted so many men. She was a haggard, bloated ruin, suffering from syphilis and many other veneral diseases. Her body, covered with open sores, was simply rotting to death and the sight of her sickened those who viewed her on the street, as she drove about in a broken-down army vehicle that had been abandoned by retreating Japanese troops.

When Chinese troops recaptured Peking, Eastern Jewel went into hiding, changing her name and taking up residence in a hovel. She used up all her money by paying for protection but she was finally identified by one of her many abandoned lovers who led Chiang's police to the broken-down shack where she lay on a dirty cot. Taken before a military tribunal, she was tried for treason, espionage and numerous war crimes.

Said her chief prosecutor: "This woman deserves death as a traitor but most of all because she rode in Japanese airplanes over bombed-out villages and laughed." Eastern Jewel claimed she was a Japanese soldier and if she were to be executed, she demanded that she be given the military honor of a firing squad. This was denied. She was led to a wooden block and, like the countless thousands slain by her Japanese friends, she was beheaded by the sword.

[ALSO SEE: Kenji Doihara]

EDEN, WILLIAM (LORD AUCKLAND)
British Spymaster in American Revolution
■ (1744–1814)

AN ARISTOCRAT WHO STUDIED AT ETON AND OXFORD, Eden entered Parliament and then headed several government offices before his appointment in 1776 to the Board of Trade and Plantations. One of Eden's government roles was to supervise surveillance of American diplomats in Europe seeking aid, arms, and alliances in combating the British during the American Revolution.

Establishing a vast network of agents throughout Europe, Eden received reports from every major capital where American envoys were seeking aid for their revolution. One of Eden's best agents was Paul Wentworth, a loyalist from New Hampshire stationed in England but who was responsible for the surveillance of Americans in Paris.

With Americans Benjamin Franklin, Arthur Lee and Silas Deane in Paris was a secretary named Edward Bancroft. He had been deftly recruited as a British spy by Wentworth who had once been Bancroft's employer. Wentworth paid Bancroft considerable sums for information on the activities of the American envoys and was able to learn in advance that the French planned an alliance with the patriots in 1778.

Following the Franco-American alliance of 1778, Eden himself went to America where he attempted to negotiate the Americans back into the arms of the British Empire. He urged British General Clinton to "win over" the Americans, but, of course, this was by then an unrealistic, if not utterly naive posture. The Americans, once backed by France, had every chance of winning their freedom and would tolerate no talks involving their capitulation. It was only long after the British capitulated that Eden accepted "the terrible loss of the colonies."

[ALSO SEE: *Edward Bancroft; Silas Deane; Paul Wentworth*]

EDMONDS, EMMA (AKA: FRANKLIN THOMPSON)
Union Spy in Civil War ▪ (1841–1898)

DEEPLY RELIGIOUS, EDMONDS WAS A FARMER'S daughter, born in New Brunswick, Canada. She read her Bible daily and dreamed of becoming a missionary when she relocated to the U.S. Instead, she got a job selling religious books throughout New England and the upper Midwest, going from town to town dressed in men's clothes and being accepted as a man. (Ladies in those days did not work at such jobs.)

Edmonds despised slavery, considered it immoral, and when the Civil War began, she enlisted in the Union Army as a man, using the alias "Franklin Thompson." Despite the close billeting quarters, she somehow managed to go undetected for two years (albeit she later claimed that she served first as a nurse and then as a soldier). She reportedly fought in several major battles from 1861 to 1862, Bull Run, Antietam, Fredericksburg. During the Peninsular Campaign in 1862, she volunteered to work as a spy.

Working under cover while dressed as a man—her superiors did not know she was a woman at that time—she went to Yorktown and freely investigated the Confederate defenses. At that time, using burnt cork to darken her skin, she posed as a black man. She was pressed into service as a slave, helping to build fortifications. She secretly drew sketches of these

defense positions, placing the illustrations inside her shoes.

A few nights later, Edmonds slipped through the picket lines and brought her information to General George McClellan who, acting on reports, was able to capture the city. The spy next went among the Confederates in the garb of a woman, her natural sex. Again, she supplied McClellan with excellent information. When Edmonds' unit was transferred to Kentucky, she continued her spying activities around Louisville but had to quit the service after becoming ill.

Upon her recovery, Edmonds discarded her long impersonation as a man and married Linus H. Seelye. She wrote her memoirs following the war and the book was a run-away best seller, making Edmonds wealthy. By 1882, she was impoverished and applied for a soldier's pension. Even though she had already revealed her impersonation of a male in her book, army authorities took exception to her claim. Then many of her former comrades came forth to support her story and the pension was granted. In 1898, shortly before her death, Emma Edmonds was honored as the only woman to ever be officially received in the veteran's organization known as the Grand Army of the Republic.

ERICKSON, ERIC
Spy for the U.S. in World War II ▪ (1889–196?)

BORN TO AN IMPOVERISHED FAMILY IN BROOKLYN, New York, Erickson decided early to be a self-made man. Hard-working, he worked at many jobs throughout his school years. He went to Texas and labored in the oil fields until he saved enough money to enter Cornell University in 1917. When America entered World War I, Erickson enlisted. Following the war, he went back to school, became a Cornell football star, and received a degree in engineering.

Working for Standard Oil and a number of other oil firms in the Far East during the 1920s, headquartered for some time in Shanghai, his business took him to Stockholm. He made friends there among the business community and soon moved his operations to Sweden. He renounced his American citizenship and became a naturalized Swedish subject in 1936.

In 1939, Laurence Steinhardt, the then American ambassador to Russia, arranged for a dinner with Erickson in Stockholm. Steinhardt knew that Erickson had done business with German firms and had solid relationships with oil industrialists, some of whom were members of the Nazi Party. He also knew that Erickson had often voiced his democratic views.

Steinhardt came directly to the point. He wanted Erickson to act as a spy for American intelligence, to learn and report everything he could about the German oil industry and its synthetic oil production which was vital to the war operations Hitler had been so long in planning. Erickson agreed and he was put in contact with OSS spymasters in Stockholm. He was given a short course in espionage. The minimum OSS training period was thirty-eight hours, at which time the student was taught the use of tiny cameras, codes, and ciphers. With this accomplished, Erickson was then instructed to publicly befriend the Nazis.

This Erickson knew would brand him a turncoat, even in his own neutral country of Sweden, which was mostly sympathetic to the Allied cause. Only Erickson's young, new bride, and his best friend, Prince Carl Bernadotte, the nephew of the Swedish King, knew of the deception. Bernadotte accompanied Erickson to Germany many times after that while the businessman began cementing his "Nazi friendships." So convincing was Erickson's pro-Nazi pose that his friends and relatives in Sweden shunned him as a collaborationist.

Working with a few German industrialists and businessmen who were part of the conspiracy, Erickson made scores of trips to Germany between 1941 and 1944. He gathered priceless information on Germany's oil refineries, which he turned over to his OSS contacts. The hazards were great. Gestapo agents tracked him on his visits to Germany. Though Erickson knew that he was under constant surveillance, he went about his oil business as well as the business of spying.

One of his closest confederates was a woman. While visiting her, Gestapo agents suddenly rushed in and arrested them both. Both were confined at Gestapo headquarters where both told a prearranged story, that the attractive woman was a high-priced prostitute and Erickson one of her clients.

The Gestapo accepted the story, or seemed to, especially when Erickson's background was checked and his close association with high-level Nazis was verified. The woman, however, had been under suspicion as being a spy. The Germans concluded that Erickson was simply a businessman seeking sexual gratification but the woman was a spy. While Erickson watched from a prison window, the woman was taken outside to a courtyard and summarily shot by a firing squad. The Nazis studied him at that moment and he appeared to be unperturbed at the horrific sight, although he was inwardly quaking with fear and anger. He was released.

The Allies stepped up their bombing of Germany and Nazi-occupied countries in 1943, but had difficulty in locating the oil refineries that kept Hitler's war machine moving. Erickson was told by his OSS spymasters that he had to locate the key refineries. He concocted a fantastic scheme and took it to the most fantastic Nazi of them all, Heinrich Himmler, head of the Gestapo and SS, the most feared man in Europe, a mass-murderer unparalleled in recorded history.

Himmler was also a practical bureaucrat who thought only to further Hitler's mad ends in any way possible. He was, by 1943, virtually in charge of everything and everyone inside the countries still dominated by the Nazis. When Erickson was given his audience with the cold-blooded little Deputy Fuhrer, he explained that he had an investment opportunity that should interest Germany.

Erickson and his wealthy German business friends, he said, planned to build a huge oil refinery in neutral Sweden, safe from Allied bombers. This plant, when running at peak capacity, could deliver all the oil Germany might need. If he went ahead with his plans, he explained, he would want an exclusive contract with the Germans.

Erickson then pointed out that he had few friends in Sweden because of his long association and loyalty to Nazi Germany. He also pointed out to the Gestapo chief that his name was on the Allied blacklist, a fact that Himmler already knew and one that endeared Erickson to his cold heart. As they talked, Himmler came quickly to believe that Erickson was an opportunist who had thrown in his lot with the Germans after they had scored lightning success through blitzkrieg invasions. He was also impressed in the detailed blueprints for the proposed Swedish oil refinery that Erickson had taken pains to prepare and submit for examination. Erickson then explained that, before he and his partners put up their millions to build the plant, he would have to inspect present oil refineries and receive from experts and technicians in the field, all important information on operations in order to better build a highly productive refinery.

In the end Himmler fully embraced Erickson's plan and gave him a top level Gestapo pass, waiving all security clearances and requirements. The pass authorized Erickson to travel anywhere in the Reich or occupied territories, to investigate any oil refinery operation he wanted to see, and to get from experts any information he desired in preparation of building the proposed refinery in Sweden. He was also given an order signed by Hitler that provided automobiles for Erickson and unlimited gas coupons.

Before leaving on his deluxe spy tour, Erickson was shocked to run into a man he thought long dead, a German oil executive he had known in the early 1930s, a rabid Nazi. The executive was shocked to see Erickson in Germany. Erickson asked him to have a drink and the two men went to a bar where the Nazi, with squinting, suspicious eyes, said: "I am very curious to hear how one day you're working hand in glove with the goddamned Jews and the next day you're hooked up with our side against your own people, the Americans!"

Erickson kept cool. He told the Nazi that it was simply good business to have joined the Germans, and that he was a businessman first and always.

He told the man that he had been on the Allied blacklist for years after establishing friendships with German Nazis. He then played his trump card, showing him his newly-signed Gestapo papers, which bore the name of Heinrich Himmler. This seemed to convince the Nazi that Erickson, was, indeed, to be trusted. He then explained that he was late for an appointment.

Erickson followed the man, or rather stalked him, knowing the Nazi was about to turn him in to the Gestapo. When the Nazi stopped at an outdoor phone booth, Erickson realized that he was calling the Gestapo. He moved next to the booth and heard the man about to report him. At that moment, Erickson withdrew a large penknife he carried and got into the both behind the man, stabbing him to death. Then he fled.

In the months to follow, the intrepid spy toured almost every major oil refinery in Germany and the occupied countries. He obtained detailed plans of oil operations and these quickly wound up in the hands of the OSS, MI6, and, subsequently, the Allied air forces, which then bombed the refineries out of existence. The bombings caused a shortage of oil so accute that the German army and air force was nearly brought to a halt after the Normandy invasion. Lack of oil caused the surrender of more than 300,000 German troops in the Ruhr Valley, the last real threat in the West against the Allies. Following the war, General Dwight D. Eisenhower attributed the Allied victory to the destruction of the German oil industry and almost all of the credit for that destruction was due to one man, Eric Erickson.

It would be some time, however, before Erickson's tarnished image was cleaned up. The true nature of his work for the Allies was eventually revealed and he was hailed as a hero, rather than the traitor he was thought to be. A suspenseful and superlative film, *The Counterfeit Traitor*, with William Holden essaying the role of Erickson, proved to be an immense success.

[ALSO SEE: *Gestapo; Heinrich Himmler; MI6; OSS*]

ERNST, KARL GUSTAV
German Agent in World War I ▪ (1871–1930)

NOT TO BE CONFUSED WITH THE NAZI SA CHIEF who was exterminated by Hitler in 1934, Karl Ernst was one of Germany's most daring agents prior to World War I. Though born in Hoxton, England, Ernst's parents were German, his father being a surgical-instrument maker. He was raised to believe that Germany was his true fatherland and that

is where his sympathies remained, even though he continued to live out his life in England.

Ernst opened a barbershop at 405A Caledonian Road in London in 1899. Beginning in 1909, the shop was patronized mostly by German officers who were either stationed in England or vacationing there. Some of these officers were members of the German intelligence service assigned to England and supervised by Gustav Steinhauer, a one-time private detective, who reported directly to Colonel Walther Nicolai, who headed Kaiser Wilhelm's intelligence service.

The barbershop on Caledonian road became Steinhauer's "letter box" to which all German agents in England sent their reports. Ernst, in turn, sent these reports to Steinhauer in Berlin, addressing the spymaster as "Frau T. Reimers," his cover name. In addition to sending Steinhauer the reports Ernst received from German agents, he appended his own bits of information.

MI5 (then known as MO5) was responsible for all counterintelligence in England and one of its agents was assigned, in 1911, to shadow Captain von Rebeur-Paschwitz, who was known to be connected with German naval intelligence. The navy captain was trailed to the barbershop on Caledonian Road. Vernon Kell, head of MI5 at the time, thought it curious that the German officer would go so far out of his way to get a haircut at a cheap, dirty little out-of-the-way shop.

Kell's agents began to investigate the background of the proprietor, Ernst. They reported that the little shop received an enormous amount of mail, mostly from the seaports about England. The letters were intercepted and, after decoding, proved to be from German agents residing in all the major port cities. Their secret reports dealt with the movements and strengths of the British fleet.

MI5 agents then tediously identified the letter-senders, twenty-six of them, all having German backgrounds. The British adopted a wait-and-see attitude. If the German agents were rounded up at that time, it was believed that Nicolai would simply replace them with another ring that might not be as easy to identity and destroy. MI5 did, however, alter all the letters slightly so that the reports being sent on to Rebeur-Paschwitz provided little useful information or data.

The day war was declared, Kell notified his agents to accompany officers of Sir Basil Thomson's Special Branch of Scotland Yard in rounding up the German spy ring. They went into action on August 5, 1914, the second day of the war, rounding up twenty-two of the agents; four of them, including Otto Weigels at Hull, escaped. From that time until the end of World War I, Nicolai had no effective espionage ring in England. The enterprising barber Ernst, who had begun it all six years earlier, was one of the first to be arrested. He was tried on charges of treason and espionage and sentenced to seven years in prison. At his trial, he admitted his guilt and complained that the Germans to whom he had been so devoted had paid him no more than £1 per month for his services as a spy.

[ALSO SEE: *Veron Kell; MI5; Walther Nicolai*]

ESTERHAZY, FERDINAND
French Spy for Germany ▪ (1847–1934)

ESTERHAZY HAD BEEN BORN IN FRANCE BUT HIS ancestors were Hungarian. Little is known of Esterhazy's past and he was asked no questions when he joined the French Foreign Legion as was the tradition. After serving in North Africa, Esterhazy was reassigned to the regular French Army when the Franco-Prussian War (1870-71) created an unusual demand for officers.

After completing a secret mission in 1881, Esterhazy was promoted to the rank of major and assigned to the Second Bureau (French military intelligence), working with the general staff. Stationed at the War Ministry in Paris, Esterhazy, though married with children, indulged his womanizing ways. He had more than one mistress to appease his insatiable sexual appetite and these costly courtesans soon caused Esterhazy to field about in search of more money than his army salary provided.

All Esterhazy could sell to obtain that money were the secrets of his country. He went to his old acquaintance, Colonel Maximillian von Schwartzkoppen, who was the ranking military attaché in the German Embassy in Paris, and offered to sell French military secrets in 1890 (or before, the date of his initial treason remains uncertain). For a number of years, the spy filched classified documents at the Ministry of War and turned them over to the Germans, receiving handsome payments. The French general staff slowly realized that there was a leak of information somewhere and suspected the traditional enemy, the Germans.

A French counterspy managed to obtain a job as a maid in the German Embassy and, on September 1, 1894, retrieved a *bordereau* (memorandum) from a waste basket in Schwartzkoppen's office, taking this to the Ministry of War. Major Hubert Henry of the Second Bureau, looked at the memorandum and immediately realized that it was written in the hand of his good friend Esterhazy. To protect his friend, Henry put the blame on an innocent man, Captain Alfred Dreyfus, an artillery officer attached to the general staff.

Dreyfus was court-martialed. His attorneys were not allowed to examine the document in question and other so-called "evidence" supplied by Henry. Further, Alphonse Bertillon, considered to be France's top expert in criminal identification (bertillonage) and a self-proclaimed hand-writing expert, positively identified the notorious memorandum as having been written by Dreyfus. Convicted in a flagrant miscarriage of justice, Dreyfus was sent to Devil's Island.

Two years later, a conscientious officer, Colonel Georges Picquart, investigated the Dreyfus case and was able to determine that Esterhazy was the real spy. He brought his evidence to the general staff, which suppressed it and assigned Picquart to a remote post in North Africa. The scheming Henry took Picquart's place on the general staff. To discredit the evidence Picquart had offered, Henry forged several documents which further implicated Dreyfus.

Then members of Dreyfus' family learned of the Picquart investigation. This was brought to the attention of the press and the hue and cry began all over again. Esterhazy then played his highest card, demanding a court-martial to clear his name, believing that the general staff would never convict him. To do so would mean that it would have to admit its collusion in wrongly convicting Dreyfus and then covering up the matter. Esterhazy was tried in 1898 and found innocent.

Then the great French journalist Emile Zola took up Dreyfus' cause, writing a sensational article, "J'Accuse," which was openly printed and accused the French government of criminally convicting Dreyfus and covering up lies, forgeries and misrepresentations. Zola was convicted of libel and had to leave the country for a year to avoid persecution. The affair would not die.

Henry's documents were exposed and he was interrogated. He finally broke down and admitted creating a fraudulent case against Dreyfus. The wrongly-accused man was brought back from Devil's Island and reinstated in the army with honors. Esterhazy fled to England to live out a miserable life in poverty. To earn money, he published his confession in which he admitted writing the *bordereau* but he claimed that a superior officer, who was by then dead, was the real traitor. Esterhazy died in London, despised, penniless, cursing "that Jew Dreyfus" to the day of his death in 1934, one year before the noble Dreyfus died and was buried as a hero of France.

[ALSO SEE: *Alfred Dreyfus; Second Bureau*]

FARNSWORTH, JOHN S.
American Spy for Japan ▪ (1893– ?)

JOHN FARNSWORTH WAS NOT THE ALL-AMERICAN boy but he was close to it. Born and raised in Cincinnati, Farnsworth came from a middle-class family. After graduating with honors, he pursued his boyhood dream of entering the U.S. Navy. He arranged to meet his local congressman who interviewed Farnsworth and was so impressed with him that he secured for him an appointment to Annapolis in 1911.

Farnsworth graduated in 1915 close to the top of his class. A brilliant student, he made an excellent officer when going to sea. He served on a destroyer during World War I. Following the war, Farnsworth was sent back to Annapolis in 1922 where he studied aeronautical engineering. He furthered these studies at the Massachusetts Institute of Technology in 1923.

Upon leaving MIT, Farnsworth, promoted to lieutenant commander, was assigned to the Navy station at Pensacola, Florida, where he taught naval aviation. He was later sent to Norfolk, Virginia, where he commanded a navy squadron of fighters. The handsome, charming Farnsworth was soon drawn into high Virginia society, meeting and marrying a girl from a blueblood family. The social strata in which they lived demanded an expensive home and expensive restaurants and nightclubs.

Getting deeper and deeper into debt, the desperate Farnsworth borrowed money from an enlisted man. The sailor demanded the return of his money and Farnsworth refused. The seaman made an official complaint, which brought about Farnsworth's court-martial. He was found guilty and dismissed from the Navy, given a dishonorable discharge in 1927. Farnsworth's life went to pieces. His wife divorced him and he began drinking. He attempted to obtain civilian jobs with ship lines and aviation firms but his military record came to light and he was consistently turned down. Next, he went to the governments of several countries—Brazil, China, Peru, Russia—and all rejected his application. He finally applied for a job with the government of Japan.

A Japanese representative interviewed Farnsworth in Washington, D.C., at his private suite in the Alban Towers, telling him that they had no room for a technical adviser but that, perhaps, Farnsworth might be interested in working for Japan in another capacity? Farnsworth asked what that meant. It meant getting important information on the U.S. Navy, he was told, and secretly putting that information into the hands of the Japanese representative, Commander Ichimiya, a naval attaché in the Japanese Embassy.

Suddenly, John Farnsworth was flush with money. He remarried and moved into a luxury suite at the New Willard, one of Washington's best hotels. He was seen at the best restaurants and nightclubs, flashing rolls of one hundred dollar bills. He was earning that money by providing U.S. Navy secrets on new warships, equipment, communications systems, and other data to the Japanese.

Though he was not directly working for the Navy, Farnsworth was able to obtain his information from old friends still in the Navy. He visited their homes and haunted their offices, telling them that he still hoped he would be reinstated in the service. He would then go on to ask seemingly innocuous questions about navy operations, a not uncommon habit of many ex-servicemen who are emotionally tied to the military. Through gossip, rumor, chit-chat, and an occasional unclassified report, Farnsworth was able to obtain information that would lead him to classified documents he simply stole from the offices of friends.

He traveled up and down the eastern seaboard, visiting navy friends in Boston, New York, Philadelphia, Baltimore, and Norfolk, Virginia. When staying at hotels, he made long distance calls only to Washington, not to his wife, but to Ichimiya and a man named Sata, who was listed as a correspondent for the Japanese news service, *Domei*, but who was really part of Japan's intelligence network in the U.S., as were all Japanese visiting America at that time, whether or not they were part of diplomatic legations, businesses, exchange students, or simply tourists.

No Japanese was given a visa to go to the U.S. from 1927 on unless they traveled for the specific purpose of espionage, irrespective of their cover activity. It was in 1927 that Emperor Hirohito finalized his plans with his military henchman to launch invasions in Asia in the 1930s, the initial schedule of this world conquest drawn up by Baron Giichi Tanaka in what later became known as the Tanaka Plan, a document that was obtained by the West. This plan was publicized and the Japanese promptly denounced it as a forgery, insisting it had no plans for global conquest (which was essentially true, all Hirohito wanted was all of Asia and the Pacific).

The Tanaka plan was dismissed by the West as a hoax but its reality was reflected in the budget the Japanese government assigned to its intelligence operations. In 1934–1935, the Japanese Secret Service was given a budget of $4 million, while, at the same time, Great Britain's SIS had a budget of $800,000, and the U.S. spent $50,000 on intelligence. The Japanese increased its budget for espionage throughout the 1930s and right up to the eve of World War II. In 1938–1939, Japan spent $25 million on intelligence, but, for the same period, Great Britain spent $1 million and the U.S. $240,000. The Western nations, following World War I, were, at best, indifferent to maintaining extensive espionage and counterintelligence systems. Of course, as Germany and Japan well knew, good intelligence gathered in advance, years, perhaps decades in advance, could determine the outcome of any war.

From the perspective of spies like John Farnsworth operating in the 1930s, practicing espionage was not a dangerous profession. He and other American spies for Japan and Germany knew that, at that time, the penalty, if they were caught, would consist of a few years in prison. With these risks in mind, they operated in the open, almost casually, taking few precautions. When Farnsworth filched documents from the offices of his navy friends, he had them copied by commercial firms, telling them that he was a Navy officer and needed to have copies of the documents quickly.

He was never challenged, and, though the documents were clearly seen to be classified, no one thought to report Farnsworth. His spying came to the attention of the ONI (Office of Naval Intelligence) only because someone thought to file a routine report. This occured in early 1934 when Farnsworth visited the office of his friend, Lieutenant Commander Leslie Gehres, a member of the Navy Examining Board. After chatting a few minutes, Gehres had to leave his office. When he returned he called his meeting with Farnsworth short, saying he had to attend to some duties. Farnsworth left and a short time later Gehres needed to consult a highly classified booklet, *The Service of Information and Security*, a document that had been issued to only a restricted number of officers. The booklet was missing.

Gehres searched his offices for the booklet and then questioned his staff. Then he remembered Farnsworth's visit and called him, asking if he had taken the booklet. Farnsworth nonchalantly admitted that he had, quite by accident, that he had picked it up when retrieving a folded newspaper he had been reading. He said he would return the booklet the next day, which he did. A short time later, Gehres, a by-the-book officer, made out a routine report and sent it to ONI. The report was read with some curiousity by Captain William Puleston, chief of ONI.

Puleston looked into Farnsworth's background, and, upon reviewing his dishonorable discharge and subsequent and unsuccessful search for work,

Ex-U.S. Navy officer John S. Farnsworth, who stole secrets for the Japanese in the 1930s.

decided to investigate. He discovered that Farnsworth was living in luxury and always had a lot of cash on hand, although his bank account showed only a small balance. This was inconsistent with what Gehres later told Puleston, that when Farnsworth visited him, he complained about being unemployed and was still hoping that the Navy would take him back.

The ONI had only a small staff, which would not allow Puleston to keep Farnsworth under suveillance. He called J. Edgar Hoover at the FBI and the Bureau agreed to tail the ex-officer. For two years, agents dogged Farnsworth but were unable to learn how he kept himself in money. He spent most of his time at his hotel, in his suite, at the hotel restaurant, or in the bar. He never seemed to run out of one hundred dollar bills.

When he did venture out of the hotel it was to take short trips to visit friends still in the Navy. Agents followed him about but could not learn what Farnsworth was doing. Then, while Farnsworth was visiting friends in Annapolis, the agents were able to learn about Farnsworth's Japanese contact. At the time, Farnsworth went to the naval academy to see his old friend Lieutenant Commander James E. Mather and his wife, staying at the Carvell Hall Hotel.

Agents tapped Farnsworth's hotel phone and waited. He made only one call, to an unlisted number in Washington, D.C. He used an alias when making the call. The man answering did not identify himself but he appeared angry, saying a few words in English with what agents determined was a decided Japanese accent, before hanging up. The agents checked the number and learned that it was the residence of Commander Ichimiya in the Alban Towers.

When Farnsworth returned to Washington, agents went to see the Mathers. They discovered in their interview with this couple that Farnsworth had acted strangely when coming to their home. He was in a nervous state, appeared gaunt and red-faced, the result of too much drinking, they concluded. Instead of the affable and charming old Farnsworth, he appeared desperate to have information on a new destroyer, the U.S.S. *Baddlitt*, which had been recently commissioned. He had pumped Mather for information on the *Baddlitt*'s guns, equipment, and communications but Mather had avoided giving him direct answers. When Mather stepped from the room for a few minutes, Farnsworth, Mrs. Mather told agents, turned to her and said in an almost frantic voice: "Please tell me about the *Baddlitt*! I've just got to know!"

The Mathers had sent him on his way without giving him information, other than idle gossip, but the agents concluded that Farnsworth had gotten enough data to report to Ichimiya. When they later began to investigate Ichimiya, they learned from hotel maids at the Alban Towers that they were not permitted to enter two rooms in the Japanese officer's suite. The maids also complained that an acrid smell drifted from under the doors of these rooms. From the description, it was concluded that the strong odor was from chemicals used in developing photos.

Then, suddenly, Ichimiya was no longer living at Alban Towers. His suite was now occupied by another attaché to the Japanese Embassy, Commander Akira Yamaki. Agents followed Yamaki and discovered that he regularly dined with Sata, the so-called newsman from *Domei*, but that the two never met except in restaurants and afterward went to their homes alone. Then, one night, an agent trailed Sato from his home to the rear entrance of the Alban Towers where Sata visited Yamaki at four o'clock in the morning. Farnsworth, on the other hand, was never seen to meet with Yamaki. Agents began watching the rear entrance to Alban Towers and, on March 15, 1936, their patience was rewarded.

On that day, Farnsworth appeared in the bar of his hotel in late morning. He began sipping his usual Scotch and soda, and whiled the time away by reading that day's Washington *Post*. His eyes were suddenly drawn to an article about an ex-Navy man named Harry Thompson, who had been arrested on the West Coast, charged with spying for the Japanese. Farnsworth downed his drink and headed for the Alban Towers. Agents saw him go through the rear

entrance of the hotel and he was followed to Yamaki's suite where he spent some time.

What happened inside the suite was later related by Farnsworth. He watched as Yamaki paced the floor "like a caged tiger."

"It's terrible, terrible!" Yamaki exclaimed, referring to the arrest of Thompson. He spun about and angrily said to Farnsworth: "You should not have come here. Go away! See that no one notices you leaving. Drop everything you are doing and do nothing until you hear from me."

The smug Farnsworth shook his head, saying "just because they've caught this idiot doesn't mean they have anything on me. I'm surprised that you used an uneducated yeoman who had no training and no sense."

"The risk is too great," Yamaki shot back. "This is one of the greatest blows Japan has ever suffered."

"Come now, Commander," Farnsworth said, attempting to minimize the Thompson arrest.

Yamaki was firm. "It is true. Now go, please, and remember, you are to do nothing until you hear from me."

Farnsworth then told Yamaki he needed money. The spymaster went to his safe, withdrew three one hundred dollar bills and handed this to Farnsworth who left with what would be the last payment he would receive from the Japanese for his spying activities. (It was later estimated that Farnsworth had been paid by the Japanese about $50,000 a year from 1933 to 1936, a vast sum during the Great Depression.)

When Farnsworth left the Alban Towers, FBI agents checked the bank account of Commander Arika Yamaki and learned that he received a considerable amount of money beyond his regular salary from the Japanese Embassy in Washington each month, and that as soon as this money was transferred to his account, he withdrew all the money above his normal salary in the form of one hundred dollar bills. This, then, was what Yamaki paid to Farnsworth for his spying efforts.

The FBI continued its investigation, interviewing officers and enlisted navy men who had unwittingly turned over a great deal of information to Farnsworth in past years, including reports on the effectiveness of almost every large gun mount in the navy, as well as vital data on the aircraft carriers *Saratoga* and *Ranger*. The FBI finally reported to ONI and other federal authorities that it had enough evidence to arrest Farnsworth. They were ordered to continue surveillance and not to arrest the traitor.

Meanwhile, Yamaki adamantly refused to pay another dime to Farnsworth, telling him to "never call us again." Sata was sent to New York to actually work as a newsman and Yamaki closed down his operations at the Alban Towers and returned to Japan. When Farnsworth learned that Harry Thompson had been given the stiff sentence of fifteen years in prison, he went on a bender. When he sobered up, he realized he was dead broke. He had another scheme to earn considerable funds. He went to the National Press Building on Fourteenth Street and then rode the elevator to the offices of the Universal News Service, a Hearst operation.

Farnsworth talked to John Lambert, Washington Bureau chief, who then turned him over to Fulton Lewis Jr. To Lewis, Farnsworth spewed forth a fantastic story. He said that he had been employed by the Japanese as a spy to glean the secrets of the U.S. Navy, but, he added, with the twist he had concocted, he had only pretended to be a spy in order to determine the extent of Japanese intelligence and to penetrate their spy network in the U.S. He went on to say that he felt that if he did a good enough job at his self-assigned task, he would be reinstated in the Navy. He then said he would provide Universal the whole story for $20,000.

Lewis played for time. He said he could not authorize such a payment but if Farnsworth would return the next day, he would have an answer for him. When the spy left, Lewis called the FBI. Agents were waiting for Farnsworth when he returned the following day and arrested him. He was charged with espionage and tried in February 1937. He insisted he was innocent but, after seeing the massive evidence prepared by the FBI and placed against him, he changed his plea to "no contest." Farnsworth was sentenced to four to twenty years in federal prison on February 23, 1937.

[ALSO SEE: *FBI; SIS; Harry Thompson*]

FAUCHE-BOREL, LOUIS
French Royalist Spy ▪ (1762–1829)

A FRENCH PRINTER, FAUCHE-BOREL PRINTED ROYALIST pamphlets and broadsheets during and after the French Revolution of 1789, and continued doing so, despite fierce opposition. He published the Declaration of Pilnitz in 1791, which was an overt threat by the king of Prussia and the emperor of Austria to restore King Louis XVI by force of arms if the French did not re-instate their monarch. In 1795, Fauche-Borel acted as an undercover agent for the royalists, spying on the revolutionaries while attempting to convince revolutionary generals like Charles Pichegru to go to the aid of the king.

Fauche-Borel was unsuccessful and was eventually thrown into jail by the revolutionaries. He was set free in 1804 when Napoleon's Minister of Police and spymaster, Joseph Fouché, released him on his promise to spy for Bonaparte in Germany. The royalist, however, had not changed his beliefs and, once safe in Germany, he openly denounced Bonaparte and lobbied for the restoration of the Bourbon kings.

Fouché thought to lure Fauche-Borel back to Paris in 1807 by sending an agent with the news that a secret committee of royalists wanted to meet with him. Fauche-Borel sent his nephew, Charles Vitel, in his place and he was promptly seized and executed. The royalist could not be inveigled back to France and did not return to his homeland until Bonaparte was exiled to Elba. When Bonaparte returned during the Hundred Days, Fauche-Borel was trapped in Paris but he survived. Following Bonaparte's crushing defeat at Waterloo, with the monarchy restored, Fauche-Borel resumed his printing business.

[ALSO SEE: *Joseph Fouché*]

FBI (Federal Bureau of Investigation)
U.S. Law Enforcement and Counterintelligence Agency ▪ (1908–)

THE PRESENT DAY FBI CAN TRACE ITS LINEAGE BACK to the congressional creation of the Department of Justice on March 3, 1871. With a $50,000-a-year budget, it had one agent on staff for the "detection and prosecution of crime." For the next thirty years it concentrated chiefly on violations of the Indian Intercourse Act.

Encouraged by President Theodore Roosevelt, Attorney General Charles Bonaparte issued an order that created a permanent investigative force that was answerable only to the attorney general.

This force was made up of agents from the Secret Service, other law enforcment agents and a group of "examiners," who were basically accountants. The agents concerned themselves with banking fraud, bankruptcy, antitrust, land fraud, and naturalization. This force was not named until Attorney General George W. Wickersham called the force the "Bureau of Investigation." Its first official director was Stanley W. Finch.

The Bureau's investigations were chiefly financial, its agents examining for errors and corrections documents produced by other federal employees— U.S. attorneys, federal marshals, clerks of federal courts, and U.S. commissioners. In 1910, agents actively began criminal investigations concerning federal offenses, the first of these being violations of the White Slave Traffic Act, which was passed in that year.

Not until 1917, when America entered World War I, did the Bureau become involved in counterintelligence activity, enforcing the Espionage and Sabotage Acts passed that year. The Bureau was responsible for running down spies and saboteurs but their methods were crude and some of their agents were so eccentric as to be unbelievable. Gaston B. Means was one of these.

On April 12, 1912, Alexander Bruce Bielaski replaced Finch as director, and he, in turn was replaced by William Allen, who was acting director in 1919. In July 1919, William J. Flynn became director and he was replaced by the noted private detective William J. Burns on August 22, 1921. At the height of the Teapot Dome scandal of the Harding Administration, Burns resigned and, the next day, May 10, 1924, Harlan Fiske Stone appointed a young lawyer, J. (John) Edgar Hoover, to head the Bureau. He was to remain in this position until his death in 1972, a reign of forty-eight years, dying as one of the most powerful men in America.

When Hoover became director, he commanded a force of more than six hundred employees. Of these, 346 were investigators, the rest being forensic experts, accountants, clerks, and support personnel. Nine field offices had been established in 1920, headed by superintendents who were renamed by Hoover as "Special Agents in Charge." To his credit, Hoover cleaned house, weeding out corrupt agents like Means who were political appointees, and abolishing the seniority system of promotion, substituting instead appraisals for promotion based on employee performance.

Hoover set new recruitment standards, stipulating that new agents had to be between twenty-five and thirty-five years old, and were required to have either a law or accounting degree. The new director and his hand-picked aides established a forensic laboratory and identification system that eventually became the finest in the world, the latter having more fingerprint cards on file than any other investigative repository. New agents were required to undergo rigorous physical training and a new manual specifying high standards, rules, and regulations was given to all agents, the bible by which they were to live.

The name "Bureau of Investigation" was changed to the "United States Bureau of Investigation" on July 1, 1932, and changed again on July 1, 1935 to the "Federal Bureau of Investigation," (FBI) as it is known today. At this time, the Bureau had already taken jurisdiction of all federal kidnapping and extortion cases. Hoover and the Bureau remained in the background until the early 1930s. The Bureau received tremendous publicity in its wars with the Depression-era gangsters and independent bank robbers, and was celebrated in its dogged pursuit of such wild bank robbers as John Dillinger, Charles Arthur "Pretty Boy" Floyd, George "Baby Face" Nelson (Lester Gillis), the bloodthirsty Ma Barker and her sons Arthur ("Dock") and Freddy, George "Machine-Gun" Kelly, Alvin Karpis, and a host of others.

This was the era in which FBI agents were given the name "G-Men," and Hoover spent a good deal of his time promoting the gangbuster image of the Bureau. Though it was responsible for counterintelligence in the U.S., the Bureau did not spend a good deal of time tracking down German, Japanese, and Russian spies who operated in America during the 1930s. It did manage to track down and identify navy turncoats and spies Harry Thompson and John Farnsworth, but it failed miserably to penetrate large spy rings, especially in Hawaii where the Kuhn spy ring operated so successfully that it provided the Japanese with all the necessary information to conduct its sneak attack on Pearl Harbor on December 7, 1941.

In World War II, the Bureau proved efficient in rounding up German and Japanese spies and saboteurs, but much of the credit for the apprehension of these spies can be attributed to the ineptitude of the spies themselves, such as the bumbling eight German saboteurs who were landed by submarine to perform impossible sabotage in what the Abwehr labelled "Operation Pastorius." Much of the CIA-FBI contentions against each other originated at this time. The FBI insisted that its counterintelligence domain included all of the Western Hemisphere and it took issue with any activity conducted in the U.S., South and Latin America by the OSS (precusor to the CIA) and its chief William J. Donovan. Conversely, the CIA later claimed that Hoover was invading its fields of operation by attempting to place FBI agents inside American embassies abroad to collect intelligence under the guise of being diplomatic attachés.

Following World War II, the FBI and Hoover concentrated on Soviet espionage with a vengeance. So intense was Hoover's campaign to ferret out Russian spies that he was later criticized for ignoring the rise of the criminal syndicate. Hoover, however, emphasized Bureau hunts for "Red Agents," and he was the power behind HUAC (House of Un-American Activities Committee) and the information provider to the uncontrollable Senator Joseph McCarthy who led the witch (red) hunts of the late 1940s and early 1950s.

The Bureau was nevertheless effective in tracking down Soviet spies like the Rosenbergs, Judith Coplon, and Rudolf Abel, although, in the Coplon case, agents overreached themselves to the point where Coplon went free. Under Hoover's direction, the Bureau, it was later revealed, conducted 238 burglaries (called "Black Bag Jobs") of fourteen "target organizations" from 1942 to 1966. Hoover continued to authorize thereafter only burglaries of foreign embassies to obtain codebooks for the NSA (National Security Agency) so that it could read diplomatic traffic.

With the death of J. Edgar Hoover in 1972, the Bureau came under the direction of a number of new chiefs, the latest being Louis Freeh, who have modernized the Bureau and expanded its activities in counterintelligence. It was the FBI that ran to ground the American traitor and Soviet mole inside the CIA, Aldrich Ames, in 1994. Critics of the Bureau, however, claim that the FBI should have detected this spy long years earlier and prevented his passing of information to the Soviets, information that brought about the executions of Russians who were actually working for the Bureau.

[ALSO SEE; *Rudolf Abel; Aldrich Ames; CIA; Judith Coplon; William J. Donovan; John Farnsworth; J. Edgar Hoover; Bernard Kuhn; Gaston Bullock Means; OSS; Ethel and Julius Rosenberg; Harry Thompson*]

Heinz Felfe, head of counterintelligence for the Gehlen Organization in West Germany, served as a double agent for the KGB.

FELFE, HEINZ PAUL JOHANN
German Double Agent for Soviets • (1918–   )

DRESDEN BORN FELFE WAS THE SON OF A POLICEMAN. He attended local schools, then joined the Nazi Youth Party and then the Nazi Party itself in 1937. Before the outbreak of World War II in 1939, Felfe was a member of the Nazi secret service and by 1943, he was working for the Gestapo, the Nazi secret police headed by Heinrich Himmler. After brief service in Switzerland, he moved to Holland and, in 1944, as a member of the SD (SS security service), fought a ruthless campaign to wipe out the Dutch underground.

When the Third Reich collapsed, Felfe was arrested by British intelligence and interned in Canada. He was released in 1946 on condition that he work with MI6, helping to identify Soviet agents in the Cold War years. He first went to work for the Ministry of All German Affairs, identifying Russian agents who migrated from East Germany.

He rose quickly, becoming an official in the Federal Republic of Germany (West Germany) in 1949. Two years later he entered the West German intelligence service headed by former Nazi intelligence chief Reinhard Gehlen, the BND. For a decade, Felfe worked assiduously for Gehlen's service, becoming head of the Russian desk. Ironically, Felfe had long been a Soviet double spy, recruited to the Russian intelligence service by an old friend, Hans Clemens, who had served with Felfe in the SS. In fact, when Felfe took over the Russian desk, he made Clemens his right hand man, and Erwin Tiebel, another friend from his Nazi days, was also enlisted as a Soviet agent.

Felfe had turned traitor for money. The Russians paid him so much cash that he was able to purchase a luxurious ten-room manor house in West Berlin, employ servants, enjoy the best of food and wine, and the company of the most expensive harlots in West Germany. The house in which Felfe resided had four rooms crammed with short-wave radios and spy equipment.

A defector from East Germany, Gunther Maennel, exposed Felfe and his many Soviet double agents in 1961, a scandal that shook the Gehlen organization and helped greatly to bring down the government of the venerable Konrad Adenauer. Felfe was tried in July 1963 for espionage and treason and convicted, given fourteen years in prison. He served six years and was then exchanged for West German prisoners. Felfe moved to East Germany and then Russia.

[ALSO SEE: *Reinhard Gehlen; Gestapo; Heinrich Himmler; SIS*]

FIELD, NOEL HAVILAND
American Spy for Soviets • (1904–1968)

HARVARD TRAINED FIELD WENT TO WORK FOR THE State Department in 1926, and befriended the leaders of left-wing causes and those in the Comintern who were stationed in Washington. As the son of Dr. Henry Haviland Field, the American biologist who proved so helpful to Allen Dulles's espionage activities during World War I, Field also went to work for Dulles in 1942, as a courier between OSS and emigre Communists who had fled fascism and were living in Vichy, France.

Following the war, Field moved about eastern Europe and finally took a teaching post in Prague in May 1949. He suddenly disappeared while living at the Palace Hotel. His wife Herta and brother Hermann went in search of him and also promptly vanished. In September 1949, Field suddenly re-appeared as the chief prosecution witness against Laszlo Rajk, the Hungarian Foreign Minister who had been charged with treason and planning to overthrow the Communist government.

Next the Czech Communist leader Rudolf Slansky was tried and condemned to death, and again Field's name was involved. It appeared that whomever had come into contact with him was in danger. The claim—planted by Allen Dulles—that he was head of American intelligence in Europe at that time was, of course, ridiculous. He supported the brutal Russian suppression of the 1956 Hungarian uprising and acted as an adviser to the hard line Communist regime that took over, remaining in that role until his death in 1968.

[ALSO SEE: *Allen Dulles; Frank G. Wisner; OSS*]

FLEMING, IAN
British Intelligence Officer in World War II ▪ (1908–1964)

THE CREATOR OF THE FICTIONAL BRITISH AGENT JAMES Bond was himself a British agent, but Fleming never personally experienced the adventures so vividly described in his later spy novels. Fleming was born in London, his family part of the upper-class, his father being a member of Parliament. Educated at Eton, he entered the military academy at Sandhurst in 1926 but he departed before receiving his commission.

Journalism was Fleming's first love and, after a literary apprenticeship of freelancing, he got a job with the London *Times*, going to Moscow as its foreign correspondent. Returning to London in 1933, Fleming worked for financial institutions. At war's outbreak in 1939, he joined British naval intelligence and served with a navy commission in Washington in 1941. Using the code name "17F," Fleming worked with William Stephenson of SIS in coordinating joint British and American intelligence operations. In 1942, he befriended OSS chief William J. Donovan and prepared for Donovan's OSS an extensive report on intelligence operations and procedures.

When returning to London, Fleming took command of a Royal Marines unit just in time for the Allied invasion of France in 1944. Fleming's specific assignment, once in France, was to locate enemy codes and new weapons and report this information back to SIS. In 1945, Fleming was discharged and almost immediately returned to journalism, publishing his first Bond novel in 1953. In the action-packed stories to follow, Fleming identified a lethal and all-powerful terrorist organization as SMERSH, which was not an invention but the actual name of the execution arm of Soviet intelligence. Fleming's novels were enormously successful and made him fabulously wealthy, so rich that he lived in a villa on the Riviera where, until he died, he sat in the sun and penned tales of dastardly and heroic spies of the long-ago.

[ALSO SEE: *William J. Donovan; OSS; SIS; SMERSH; William Stephenson*]

FOOTE, ALEXANDER ALLAN
British Spy for Soviets ▪ (1905–1958)

OPPORTUNITY WAS NOT A WORD KNOWN WELL TO Alexander Foote. He was born in Liverpool to a working-class family that struggled to keep food on the table and a roof over its head. Foote wore second-hand clothes and barely managed to get a minor education. He worked at odd jobs while he gave his loyalties to left-wing political groups. In 1936, after joining the RAF and then going AWOL, he went to Spain to fight with the International Brigades supporting the legal government, which Falangist (fascist) General Francisco Franco sought to overthrow.

Assigned to the British battalion, Foote was in charge of transport for more than two years and saw little action. He returned to London before the war ended in a fascist victory. At the time, a Soviet agent in London met with Foote and asked if he was interested in accepting a dangerous assignment. The adventurous Foote agreed, not really knowing where he was going or what was expected of him. He was told to go to Geneva where he would meet with a Soviet agent.

Foote went to Geneva and stood outside the Post Office until a woman walked up to him. She was Ursula-Maria Hamburger, who used the code name "Sonia." Her real name was Ruth Kuczynski and she was the daughter of a reputable German-Jewish economist who had fled Nazi Germany and was living in Oxford.

Sonia and Foote exchanged passwords and she took him to a small cafe and bought him coffee, then shoved an envelope across the table to him. It contained in code his instructions, as well as expense money. He was to immediately leave for Munich, Germany, where he would gather information on certain German politicians. At the end of three months, he was to return to Geneva with his reports.

This Foote did, and when he returned to Geneva, his reports were read, then thrown away. He was told that the Soviet spy network in Geneva already knew what he had been sent to collect but that he had passed the test so well that he would be taken into the network. His assignment was to work as Sonia's radio operator and to that end Sonia trained Foote in the use of wireless radios and codes, as well as the general business of spying.

Stationed in Lausanne, Foote worked for Sonia until she was reassigned to England. Foote's new boss was a Hungarian-Communist, Sandor Alexander Rado, a wild adventurer who had been successfully operating a Soviet spy ring in Switzerland. His communication with Moscow, however, was old-fashioned. All of his coded messages had been sent by courier but this became too difficult as World

War II lengthened and Rado was ordered to send everything by wireless.

At that time, Rado relied completely on Foote to send all of his important communications to Russian intelligence. Most of Rado's information stemmed from his own network in Switzerland and inside Nazi Germany but through his agents, Rachel Duebendorfer, code name "Sissy," and Christian Schneider, code name "Taylor," he came in contact with the most effective Allied spy in World War II, a man who operated out of Lucene and used the code name "Lucy." This was Rudolf Roessler who provided information on the German army, its movements and plans far in advance of their actual reality, and he appeared to never be wrong. (His source, never identified, could only have been at the very top of the German High Command; most intelligence chiefs later concluded that that source was Wilhelm Canaris, head of the Abwehr, German intelligence, who had been secretly working against Hitler since his invasion of Poland in 1939.)

When sending his messages to Moscow, Foote employed the code name "Jim," a name that came to the attention of the Swiss intelligence service (BUPO), which was attempting to break up all Allied spy networks in Switzerland under the pressure of Heinrich Himmler's Gestapo and SS. Then two former Russian agents, George and Joanna Wilmer, openly denounced Foote to Swiss intelligence. Rado, however, was unknown to the Swiss authorities. He went into hiding in Bern, telling Foote that he was now Moscow's resident director.

On the night of November 19-20, 1943, just as Foote was in the middle of sending his regular traffic to Moscow, Swiss agents began banging at the door of Foote's apartment at 2 Chemin de Longeraie. At that moment, Foote broke off his transmission to Moscow, seized all his important papers and codebooks and set them ablaze in a waste basket. Just as the agents broke through the door, Foote smashed his radio set so thoroughly that it could not be repaired.

Taken into custody, Foote underwent exhausting interrogations but he told the Swiss nothing. He spent ten months in prison, at the end of which, he was told that if he admitted that he had been spying for Moscow, he would be allowed to go free on bail, pending his trial by military tribunal. He refused. The Swiss then told Foote that he would be released on bail without conditions. Paying 2,000 Swiss francs, Foote stepped from prison in 1944, promising to be on hand for his trial.

Evading Swiss agents trailing him, Foote slipped out of Switzerland and joined Rado in Paris. The Hungarian spymaster was jittery; it was through his negligence that his spy ring had been exposed—he had used his mistress, Margaret Bolli, as an agent and she had compromised him by unwittingly bedding down with an Abwehr agent, one Hans Peters, who had kidnapped her.

Rado contacted his spymasters in Moscow from Paris and was told to report to Moscow immediately. On January 6, 1945, the two spies were flown out of France in a Russian war plane, which, because of the dangerous war zones, had to be diverted to Cairo. When the plane touched down at Cairo, Sandor Rado went into the men's room at the airport and vanished. He knew that he was to be punished for his failure in Switzerland and thus chose to disappear.

Foote nevertheless went on to Moscow. To verify his continued loyalty to the Soviets, Foote asked for a new assignment. The Center waived its rule that they could not use any spy who had been arrested for at least five years after that spy's release, and gave Foote a new identity. He was now Major Granatov and he was to fly to Argentina where he would establish a new GRU spy network.

In March 1947, Foote flew to Berlin where he waited to change planes for the trip to Argentina. This was a flight he never intended to make. Foote had seen first hand what the Soviets were all about and his deep resentment at being mistreated in Moscow, coupled to his new belief that the Soviet system was as dictatorial as that of the Nazis, convinced him to defect. While waiting at the Berlin airport, Foote slipped away from his Russian aides and went to the British sector, where he told his story.

Foote spent the rest of his days as a clerk in England, but it was later claimed that he had been an SIS plant, recruited in 1936 for Claude Dansey's "Z" group of double spies. Foote, at Dansey's urging, went AWOL from the RAF to Spain so he could establish his Communist background and thus be acceptable to Rado's Soviet network.

[ALSO SEE: *Abwehr; Wilhelm Canaris; The Center; Claude Dansey; Rachel Duebendorfer; Gestapo; GRU; Heinrich Himmler; Ruth Kuczynski; Sandor Rado; Rudolf Roessler; SIS*]

FOUCHÉ, JOSEPH (DUC D'OTRANTE)
French Police Minister and Spymaster ▪ (1759–1820)

FEW MEN OF THE NAPOLEONIC ERA WERE AS FEARED and despised as Joseph Fouché. He was one of those who shouted loudest in voting to behead King Louis XVI, and he was responsible for atrocities committed against suspected Loyalists during the French Revolution. His name is synomymous with police oppression and the most vile acts of political espionage.

Born on May 31, 1759, Fouché's parents insisted that he dedicate his life to the Catholic Church. He studied with the Order of Oratorians and became a teacher in its schools. When the French Revolution

Napoleon's sinister spymaster and police chief Joseph Fouché, who was, after Bonaparte, the most powerful man in France.

broke out in 1789, Fouché, however, found his true vocation. He was a born radical and revolutionary, joining the Jacobin Club in Nantes in 1792. He was elected a representative to the National Convention in Paris which was to take over the government.

In the following year, Fouché's voice rang out inside the halls of the National Convention, demanding with others that King Louis XVI should be executed. Further, he discovered a nest of Loyalists in Lyons and personally led a punitive expedition to that city, arresting suspects at will and summarily executing them.

Everyone feared Fouché, all but the leader of the Reign of Terror, Maximilien de Robespierre, who had been Fouché's sponsor and friend. Fouché realized that the man who stood in the way of his great ambitions was Robespierre and he headed a plot that eventually overthrew him in 1794. He next backed Napoleon Bonaparte who took control of France and, as a reward for his services, appointed Fouché as his Minister of Police.

Fouché would occupy this powerful position for two terms (1799-1802; 1804-1810). The French police force was then an extensive organization, made up of outcasts, misfits, rogues and criminals who saw the force as an opportunity to advance and enrich themselves, not unlike Fouché himself. These truly, were the dregs of France, the brutes and killers who reveled

in the endless executions of nobles and persecution of the middle class, which had supported the monarchy. Bonaparte wanted a police force that not only kept order but one that would serve as an intelligence service, spying on all citizens so that the emperor would know what was occuring at all times.

Fouché's spies were recruited from the prisons for the most part, and were given a so-called Test of Fidelity. Those about to be charged with criminal felonies were told that their police records would not be acted upon if they worked as spies for the police. In other instances, Fouché's men entrapped honest citizens into committing crimes and then told these victims that they would not be prosecuted if they spied for Fouché.

The policeman and spy chief was also a master of spreading disinformation. He once attempted to lure back to Paris an important exiled Loyalist, Louis Fauche-Borel, by spreading information that a powerful group of Loyalists were waiting to act on his orders where no such group existed. Fauche-Borel sent instead his hapless nephew, Charles Vitel, whom Fouché arrested and who was later executed. He also established a counterespionage service within the French army to determine the loyalty of Bonaparte's soldiers, from private to grand marshal.

Spymasters in the future studied the habits and practices of the Frenchman, how he used double agents; employed any kind of entreaty to gain information, from money and political appointments to indirect threats; his use of propaganda and misleading information; his files, which were meticulously kept up-to-date. For his diligence and loyalty, Napoleon rewarded Fouché with a dukedom but when the emperor seemed to be losing his political advantages, Fouché secretly contacted Louis XVIII, who was in exile, attempting to establish a friendly relationship with him so that he could secure a place with the monarchy in case Napoleon was overthrown.

When the emperor was sent into exile to Elba, Fouché rushed to the reinstated King Louis but was rebuffed. He was reminded by the king's ministers of his vote a decade earlier to execute King Louis XVI. Bonaparte returned to again seize power but was defeated at Waterloo and his final abdication was urged by Fouché, which earned from the again reinstated Louis an appointment as the Minister of Police. This time Fouché hunted down Bonapartists until royalists who could not forgive his past oppressions forced his resignation. He was then tried for his part in the regicide of Louis XVI and convicted. Fouché was sent into exile. He wandered about Europe but found little welcome anywhere. He died in a cheap rooming house in Trieste on Christmas Day, 1820. Many writers later used Fouché as the role model for evil characters in their novels, such as Dumas' *The Count of Monte Cristo*, and Hugo's *Les Miserables*. He usually appeared as a police chief or police spy, oppressing the innocent out of sheer joy at having the power to do so, acid portraits that would have undoubtedly pleased the scheming Fouché.

[ALSO SEE: *Louis Fauche-Borel*]

FRANCKS, WOLFGANG
German Spy for Turkey in World War I ▪ (1881– ?)

GERMAN BORN FRANCKS WAS AN ADVENTURER AND an entrepreneur. Little is known of his early life. At one point he was a sheep rancher in Australia's outback, at another he was a merchant in Bombay, India. Still later he was working as a newsman in Cape Town, South Africa. In all of these places and others, he cultivated the English language. By the time World War I began, he spoke English as would a genuine Etonian.

Returning to Germany, Francks served in an artillery battalion until 1916 when he volunteered to go to the Middle East as an intelligence agent. After his espionage training, Francks was sent to Palestine, which was then controlled by Turkey, a member of the Central Powers.

Francks arrived in Palestine with a trunkful of British officer's uniforms. He was able to impersonate to perfection the high-born general staff officer with uppercrust accent or the swaggering territorial officer with marked colonial accent. He enacted both as he ventured into Egypt and the British camps. On one occasion he boldly slipped into a British encampment dressed in a colonel's uniform, curtly informing sentries that he was conducting an unannounced tour on behalf of General Allenby.

He was shown about the camp by officers who readily provided him with a complete inspection of their equipment, supplies, ammunition, and troops on hand. Francks got this information to the Turks within twenty-four hours. On another occasion, dressed as a military police officer, Francks misdirected a huge convoy of supply trucks into enemy territory where they were promptly captured by the Turks.

In addition to his many impersonations, Francks was a telephone equipment expert. As such, he was able to tap into telephone lines and listen in on British staff conversations. In other instances, he made calls to field posts, countermanding with the voice of stiff British authority the orders of the day, which resulted in confusion and gaps in Allenby's battle lines when units went off to the wrong positions.

Though the general staff and even Allenby knew that information was being leaked, the blame was put upon "a number of agents impersonating our staff officers." There was no "number" of spies, only Francks. So genuine did Francks appear that not once in dozens of impersonations was he challenged. Even those having superior rank eagerly bowed to his demands for information.

Despite his spectacular efforts, Francks was helpless against Allenby's inexorable march to Jerusalem, which he captured in 1918. As Turkish resistance crumbled, Francks returned to Germany in time to witness the abdication of the Kaiser and the surrender of his warlords.

FREDERICK THE GREAT
Prussian King and Spymaster ▪ (1712–1786)

WHEN FREDERICK ASSUMED THE THRONE OF Prussia in 1740, he immediately launched the War of Austrian Succession (1740-1748), and then the Seven Years' War (1756-1763). Throughout his long reign, Frederick established an espionage system unequalled in Europe. He drew his agents from all levels of society, diplomats, generals, politicians, clergymen, merchants, and tradesmen, paying them according to their social status, and even blackmailing those unwilling to spy on his behalf.

As such, Frederick's spy service was his first line of defense as well as his first line of attack. The system worked effectively because the monarch himself was its actual spymaster. His espionage organization was the role model for many to come.

FRIEDMAN, ELIZEBETH AND WILLIAM FREDERICK
American Cryptologists in World War I and World War II ▪ (1893–1980; 1891–1969)

WILLIAM FRIEDMAN IS REMEMBERED AS ONE OF THE great cyptologists of the twentieth century and he alone was responsible for breaking the Japanese master code known as Purple. Born in Kinishev, Russia, Friedman was the son of a postal worker who migrated to the U.S. in 1892 to live in Pittsburgh. Going to work at the Riverbank Laboratories outside of Chicago in 1915, Friedman began to concentrate on crytography, a field of study that had intrigued him since childhood.

In 1917, Friedman married Elizebeth Smith, who was also a cryptologist working at Riverbank. Together, the couple devoted their efforts to the breaking of codes and ciphers. Both worked in Washington,

William and Elizebeth Friedman, shown in 1958 with some of their many cipher machines.

America's most brilliant cryptologist, William Frederick Friedman, shown in 1930 when he was chief of the U.S. Signal Intelligence Service; it was Friedman who broke the allegedly impenetrable Japanese code called Purple, an enormous contribution to Allied victory.

until Friedman was sent to France in 1918 to work as a code-breaker on the staff of General John J. Pershing, head of the American Expeditionary Forces. After the war, Friedman was made chief of the Signal Intelligence Service.

In the late 1930s, American intelligence came to realize that war with Japan was inevitable and stepped up its counterespionage activities. Many of the American spies working for Japan in the U.S. who had been captured had turned over top secrets to Japanese agents. These secrets, American agents learned, had been relayed to Tokyo via Japanese consulates through a unique coding system. Friedman was asked to work on the Japanese master code known as Purple, which was considered to be unbreakable.

Like the German code Enigma, the Japanese code Purple was produced through a twin typewriter system wherein an operator could type in plain language on one typewriter while the other typewriter automatically translated the message into code, the message having been processed through rotors arranging random cryptographic signs. Friedman spent endless days and nights studying the astronomical number of electronically guided combinations to finally arrive at a finite translation.

Thus, American intelligence was able to intercept and read the coded Japanese messages sent between Japan's representatives in Washington and its military masters in Tokyo in the long hours preceding the attack on Pearl Harbor. U.S. intelligence experts,

Friedman at their core, were able to translate the Japanese orders to break off negotiations on December 7, 1941, which clearly indicated Japan's intent to go to war, although the messages did not pinpoint Pearl Harbor as the site of the first sneak attack.

Friedman visited the British code-breaking operations at Bletchley in 1941. He exchanged information on his code-breaking techniques that had penetrated Purple for the British information on how they had broken the German code Enigma. From that point onward, the Americans and British high commands were able to obtain detailed information on all major German and Japanese military and naval operations before they occured.

In the Pacific, the ability to quickly translate Purple codes brought about many decisive American naval victories, including the battles of the Coral Sea and Midway. American cryptographers were able to read the battle orders of the Japanese admirals as they were communicated from fleet to fleet.

Following the war, Friedman remained with the American intelligence service, becoming in 1952 the chief cryptologist for NSA (National Security Agency). In addition, he and his wife applied their great cryptographic talents to literary detection. In 1957 they authored *The Shakespearean Ciphers Examined*, in which they dismissed the claims of those who insisted that Francis Bacon actually wrote the works of William Shakespeare by minutely comparing the literary styles of both writers.

After decades of dealing with incredible pressures involved with mind-exhausting code-breaking, Friedman's health began to fail in the late 1960s. He died in 1969, one of the great unsung American heroes and the greatest cryptologist of his era.

During World War II, Elizebeth Friedman was one of the top cryptologists working for OSS and was the person who broke the code used by the Japanese spy Velvalee Dickinson, known as "The Doll Woman." Elizebeth Friedman retired after her husband's death in 1969 and lived on until 1980.

[ALSO SEE: *Velvalee Dickinson; OSS*]

FUCHS, KLAUS
German Spy for Soviets ▪ (1911–1988)

OF ALL THE ATOMIC SPIES WORKING FOR THE SOVIETS, the most important and dangerous was the scientist traitor Klaus Fuchs. He did not spy for money or personal gain. He did not spy out of any extravagant emotion such as revenge. His motive was ideological, or so he maintained all his life. His ability to turn over the A-bomb secrets in public places to Harry Gold and others was made easy for him through shoddy security and an unwillingness to

Klaus Fuchs, the British scientist who turned over America's atomic bomb secrets to the Russians in 1945; he proved to be the most dangerous, damaging spy of the era.

believe on the part of intelligence officials that a respected scientist would betray his country and place the world in jeopardy. Any cursory check of Fuch's background would have convinced the most novice counterintelligence agent that he was too much a risk to have ever worked on the A-bomb. That background was apparently never checked; if it was, it was ignored.

Fuchs was born in Russelheim, a small town near Heidelberg, Germany. His father, Emil Fuchs, was a Lutheran pastor who became a Quaker in 1925 and who rigidly maintained a thick religious atmosphere at home, and who denounced Adolf Hitler as an evil opponent of the Social Gospel. Fuchs adopted his father's anti-Hitler posture as a teenager and joined the Communist Party when he was a student at the University of Kiel. He lived in England from 1933 to 1940, while his father continued to resist the Nazis.

Fuchs took his Ph.D. in Bristol and his Sc.D. in Edinburgh. Throughout this time, he maintained his Communist Party membership. When Great Britain went to war with Germany, Fuchs was arrested as a suspected German agent, although he was not. He was sent to Canada where he was interned. It is most likely that Fuchs, miserable at his treatment in

Fuchs at the time of his release from a British prison; he was immediately deported to East Germany where he went to work on atomic research for the Soviets.

the internment camp, and certainly at his most vulnerable, was approached at this time by a Soviet agent who asked that he supply Russia with any secrets he might be able to obtain should he be recruited as a physicist in England's war effort.

This is exactly what happened. Fuchs's file was reviewed and his pronounced anti-Nazi sentiments, which he often voiced, convinced British officials that he was not a risk as an enemy alien. Moreover, Fuchs was a brilliant physicist, a cateogry of scientists of which England was then in short supply. He was recruited to work on various projects and moved to Glasgow. A short time later, Fuchs was sent to the University of Birmingham to work with Professor Rudolf Peierls, who was also a German refugee and who was a former friend of Fuchs. In all likelihood, Peierls personally requested that Fuchs join him in his research.

Working with Peierls and others on the Tube Alloys Project—a euphemism for atomic bomb research—Fuchs required a security clearance, which he got without incident. He was also required to become a British citizen, which he did without protest in early 1942. Almost at the same time, Fuchs contacted Semion Kremer, secretary to the military attaché at the Soviet Embassy in London. He had resolved to secretly provide the Russians with all the secrets on atomic research, convincing himself that this was morally correct in that Russia was also

fighting the Nazis and, as a member of the Allied Powers, had the right to know what America and England knew about the A-bomb. To that end, for the eighteen months he worked in England, he gave Kremer a copy of his monthly reports while he worked in Birmingham.

In December 1943, Fuchs was sent to America, to continue his atomic research at Columbia University in New York. Kremer instructed him to meet another Soviet agent once he arrived. Dutifully, Fuchs, as instructed, went to a specific street corner carrying a tennis ball in his hand. He would recognize his Soviet contact by looking for a man wearing a pair of gloves and carrying another pair of gloves, as well as a book with a green binding. To this agent, Harry Gold, Fuchs regularly turned over his detailed notes on atomic research.

Gold would continue to be Fuchs' contact man for the two and a half year period in which the physicist worked for the U.S. and England, and, secretly, for Russia. When Fuchs was transferred to Los Alamos, New Mexico, to continue his work on the "Manhattan Project," the actual construction of the Atomic Bomb, Gold was reassigned to the area. Week after week, Fuchs met with Gold to give him hundreds of handwritten pages that meticulously set down the involved technical details of the atomic bomb, including test results, manufacturing methods, and guidance on theory.

Fuchs was a spectator at the test explosion of the atomic bomb at Los Alamos. Following the dropping of the bomb at Hiroshima and Nagasaki, the Japanese surrendered and the scientists in New Mexico decided to have a party to celebrate the end of the war. Fuchs volunteered to drive into Santa Fe to buy the liquor. Once in Santa Fe, Fuchs went to a bar and met Harry Gold for the last time. They sat in a booth and Fuchs handed over his final report, and also dictated what he had seen in the Los Alamos explosion, as well as the results of the Nagasaki and Hiroshima bombings.

In the middle of 1946, Fuchs and the other British scientists, returned to England. The physicist was named chief of the theoretical physics division of the Atomic Energy Establishment at Harwell, working with Dr. Cockroft. At the time, he was again given a security clearance, despite the fact that Fuchs had reestalished his contact with Soviet agents and was feeding them all the top secret information he could provide from Harwell.

The Soviet contact in 1947 was Ruth Kuczynski who operated under the code name "Sonia." Kuczynski had long been a Soviet agent in various parts of Europe. She had headed a Soviet spy ring in Switzerland in 1939, when recruiting the British double agent, Alexander Foote, as a radio man for the Sandor Rado spy ring. Sonia became more and more demanding until Fuchs came to believe, or so he later claimed, that Russia was not using his information for the good of mankind but for its own selfish and sinister ends. He failed to meet with Sonia and soon, he cut off all contact with the Soviets,

In 1949, however, the FBI conducted sweeping investigations in the U.S., snaring a bevy of Soviet spies. It was at that time that one of these Russian spies described to Bureau agents a brilliant British physicist who had worked at Los Alamos and who had provided the details of the A-bomb to him. This information was sent to British intelligence in 1949. Fuchs became an immediate suspect but no hard evidence could be produced to cause his arrest.

Oddly, Fuchs himself brought on his own investigation. He asked to see the security officer at Harwell and, in a private interview in which he appeared extremely nervous, explained that his elderly father had been recently appointed to a teaching position at the University of Leipsig in East Germany. Would the fact that his father was now working for a Communist-sponsored school compromise his position at Harwell, Fuchs wanted to know.

The security officer said he would send in a report and let Fuchs know whether his clearance would be affected by his father's appointment. MI5 was informed of the interview and, suspecting Fuchs for some time, took this opportunity to confront the scientist. One of their best interrogators, William Skardon, visited Fuchs and employed an approach for which he was celebrated.

Fuchs as a Soviet scientist, a short time before his death behind the Iron Curtain in 1988.

Skardon was never accusatory, always friendly, appearing to be sincerely sympathetic. He had several meetings with Fuchs, until a friendship had been established. A lonely, introspective man, Fuchs finally unburdoned himself to Skardon, confessing his espionage activities in great detail while his MI5 "friend" listened sympathetically.

He was placed on trial and astonished prosecutors and the public alike by claiming that he really had been living two lives, and that his mind was governed by "a controlled schizophrenia." He spoke of having a mind that had two separate compartments (as did Aldrich Ames, the CIA traitor, some forty years later), one that was loyal to the West and one that was ruled by his Marxist philosophy.

All of this was psychological gobbledygook to Lord Chief Justice Goddard, who, following Fuchs' conviction, gave him fourteen years in prison, the maximum sentence. He was sent to Wormwood Scrubs prison where he was made the librarian. After nine years, Fuchs was released and he immediately went to East Germany where he was appointed by the Soviets to head the nuclear research institute at Dresden where, it was claimed, the physicist would work on atomic research for "peaceful purposes only."

A short time later Fuchs married for the first time, to Greta Keilson, a German woman he had known since childhood. Nothing more was heard of Fuchs until 1988 when news stories announced his death of natural causes. He was, undoubtedly the most important of all the atomic spies, a new type of agent who did not spy for money (although he once took £100 as a "symbolic payment"), a spy ruled by technology and ideology, the kind of spy most difficult to catch. Fuchs' own statements, however, did allow the FBI to catch his counterparts in the U.S. His confession was revealing in that it led to the identification of his American contact man, Harry Gold, who, in turn, led to David Greenglass, who, in turn, led to America's most infamous atomic spies, Ethel and Julius Rosenberg.

[ALSO SEE: *Alexander Foote; Harry Gold; David Greenglass; Sandor Rado; Julius and Ethel Rosenberg*]

FUNSTON, FREDERICK
American Spymaster ▪ (1865–1917)

FUNSTON WAS A MAN OF ACTION, AN ADVENTURER, sometimes a daredevil. He epitomized the bold and daring American officer of the Teddy Roosevelt era. In addition to his many military talents, Funston had an instinctive knack for espionage, establishing and controlling vast networks of spies in Cuba and later in the Philippines.

Born in New Carlisle, Ohio, Funston began his career as a journalist, working for newspapers in Kansas City. He was also a botanist who worked for the Department of Agriculture in Washington, serving as a special agent to investigate the abuses of federal lands. As such he led expeditions to Alaska and Death Valley. On these occasions, he fought salmon pirates, renegades, and land thieves.

So effective was Funston that the U.S. government sent him to Cuba in 1896 as an adviser to the Cubans in their on-going rebellion against Spain. For two years, Funston helped the rebels in planning their attacks, as well as establishing a network of spies in every town and village who reported on the movements of Spanish troops. After participating in twenty-three pitched battles, he was finally captured with some Cuban rebels, but not before he made a fight of it, wounding several Spanish soldiers with his sword and revolver. He was captured and taken before Spanish General Nicolau Valeriano Weyler (called "The Beast" for his many atrocities against the Cubans).

"What are you, an American officer, doing in Cuba?" Weyler demanded.

"I'm a tourist," Funston replied as he rewrapped a bandage around his hand which had been slashed in the sword fight. "And I don't care much for the kind of welcome you extend to visitors."

"You're a spy," hissed Weyler. "I should have you shot!"

"I'm an American officer!" Funston spat back. "Shoot me and in a week you'll be tasting the steel bayonets of our marines! You can't bully us like you do these poor Cubans, Weyler!"

Weyler's face grew red as he exploded: "Do you realize who you are talking to?"

"Do you realize that you're talking to the United States of America?" With that, Frederick Funston turned on his heel and marched with a befuddled escort of Spanish guards from the room, as Weyler stood open-mouthed in shock.

One of Weyler's aides recommended that Funston be executed. "No," Weyler said. "Send him back to the United States. One war's enough."

Funston was expelled from Cuba in 1898. He became a colonel when joining the Kansas Volunteers and was then sent to the Philippines during the Spanish-American War. This was a war decreed by President William McKinley after the U.S. battleship *Maine* was blown up in Havana Harbor in 1898, but the real power behind the administration and the launching of the war was the forceful Theodore Roosevelt, then Assistant Secretary of the Navy. It was Roosevelt who sent a cable to Commodore Dewey in Hong Kong, telling him to attack the Spanish fleet anchored in Manila Bay, stating: "You must capture vessels or destroy." In a short time the Spanish were overwhelmed and the Philippines were annexed as a colony, as were Hawaii, Guam, and Puerto Rico, one-time Spanish lands now in the hands of the U.S.

The Filipinos, however, expected to assert their full independence, which, under a treaty signed in 1899, gave them that independence from the U.S. in 1946. Until that time the Philippines would have American territory status. Filipinos under the leadership of Emilio Aguinaldo, however, disputed the treaty and began a prolonged rebellion against the U.S. The American troops stayed in the Philippines, and more were added, all under the command of the country's first governor, General Arthur MacArthur, the father of America's great World War II commander, General Douglas MacArthur.

Colonel Frederick Funston was ordered to stamp out Aguinaldo's forces and capture its fiery, inspired leader. This was a job easier ordered than performed. The Filipino was a wily jungle fighter whose techniques centered about ambush and sabotage, which Funston quickly learned while battling insurgents around Manila. He countered Aguinaldo's tactics by setting up large espionage and counter-espionage networks throughout Luzon. He accomplished this by taking captives, interrogating them at length, and then converting them into spies.

Moreover, many of Funston's spies were recruited from the Filipino middle class, which quietly sided with the Americans, preferring the protection of the U.S. to a sudden independence that would leave the Philippines without a world power army and navy to defend itself against predatory nations such as Japan. One by one, Funston raided insurgent pockets and destroyed or captured the enemy in large numbers. Aguinaldo, however, continued to elude him.

More than 75,000 American troops were tied up in Luzon in an attempt to track down the dwindling guerrilla band that followed Aguinaldo from one hidden camp to another. Funston's spies then reported in March 1901 that the guerrilla leader was hiding in northern Luzon, but the exact location could not be pinpointed.

Using his network of spies, Funston was able to narrow the hiding spot to a small area in one province and then led an expeditionary force to the village. Creeping up on the encampment at night, Funston and his men dashed forward, capturing the force by surprise. Funston himself dove through a hail of gunfire and into a hut where, revolver in hand, he captured Aguinaldo.

Funston, at the age of thirty-five, was hailed as a hero. When he returned to the U.S. he was promoted to brigadier general and given the Congressional Medal of Honor. Stationed in California, Funston again came into the limelight when San Francisco was rocked and almost destroyed by a devastating earthquake on April 18, 1906. After a quake of 8.3 on the Richter Scale, the city was torn in half and then burst into flames that the fire department could not control with almost every water main broken. Block by block, the city burned and Funston, who lived in a large mansion on Knob Hill watched the flames creep toward him through binoculars.

Reports then reached him that thousands of hooligans and roughnecks had fled their burning shacks in the Barbary Coast and had poured into the business district, looting, and sometimes killing those who stood in their path. Funston, ever the man of action, did not waste time by consulting the civilian authorities. He immediately declared martial law and ordered his troops from the Presidio garrison to march into the city. He gave orders for his soldiers to search at bayonet-point through the ruins for looters and to "shoot them on sight."

Dozens of thugs were shot as Funston's troops fanned out through the city. The general had not lost his touch with espionage. He ordered some patrols to don civilian clothing and pretend to be refugees so that they could better approach looters. In this fashion dozens more looters were caught red-handed and taken to the nearest lamppost where they were promptly hanged, a sign for each placed about the neck which read: "Hanged for looting."

In 1914, Funston was again called to action. He was ordered to occupy Mexico's chief port, Vera Cruz, to protect the many American businesses and citizens living there who were threatened by Mexican revolutionaries under the command of Venustiano Carranza. Funston landed with a brigade and the city remained under American control for almost a year. He would have pulled his troops out earlier had it not been for the spies he sent into the Mexican camps to learn that many in the city, including more than 300 nuns and priests, had been put on Carranza's execution list for having earlier supported Victoriano Huerta, the previous dictator of Mexico.

One story reported that Funston himself, not able to resist his insatiable urge for adventure, dressed as a Mexican peon with wide, floppy sombrero and a serape draped about him, and, pretending to be drunk, staggered into Carranza's main camp outside the city. He squatted outside an open window to overhear Carranza's officers toasting to future deaths they planned for their enemies inside Vera Cruz.

Funston advised President Wilson of the situation and Wilson refused to evacuate American troops until Carranza guaranteed the safety of Vera Cruz's citizens. This Carranza eventually did and the Americans embarked for the U.S. Funston made a point of taking along many of those who had been at the top of Carranza's death lists, a copy of which Funston had himself somehow obtained.

By 1916, Funston was a major-general, considered to be the most able army commander in the U.S., when Mexican revolutionary leader and bandit Pancho Villa raided Columbus, New Mexico, on February 27, 1916, in search of guns and horses. His band killed civilians and American soldiers stationed at the garrison. General John J. Pershing was selected to lead the Expeditionary Force into Mexico to punish Villa. His superior, Funston, was ordered to oversee the operation. Pershing's troops were recalled in 1917. At that time, Frederick Funston was preparing for another great adventure; he had been informed that he would be leading the Expeditionary Force to France as America entered World War I. He would not have that honor. Two weeks later Frederick Funston was dead of a heart attack. His subordinate, John J. "Black Jack" Pershing went to France in his place.

FURUSAWA, TAKASHI
Japanese Spymaster in U.S. ▪ (1891– ?)

HAD IT NOT BEEN FOR AN ACCIDENT IN A LOS Angeles street in October 1933, one of Japan's most active spymasters might never have been detected. A young Japanese language student named Torii was struck by a car and killed. He had been carrying a briefcase. The body was removed to the morgue where Torii was identified as a Japanese naval officer.

A few hours later, the phone rang at a police station. The caller identified himself as a Dr. Takashi Furusawa, asking about the dead Torii. He was particularly interested to know if the deceased had been carrying a briefcase. When told that he had, Furusawa asked if the briefcase was safe and had it been opened. Yes, the briefcase was safe and would be turned over to the Japanese consulate, Furusawa was told, and, no, it had not been opened. The Japanese doctor gave a noticeable sigh of relief before he hung up.

The desk sergeant found the call curious and mentioned it to his superior. The police decided to open the briefcase. Inside they found copies of classified documents belonging not to Japan but the U.S. The FBI was called and agents also inspected the case.

After the contents of the case were photographed, the briefcase was sent on to the Japanese consulate, along with Torii's effects. Then the FBI turned to look at the ubiquitous Dr. Furusawa. Checking into the doctor's background, the Bureau learned that he had graduated from Stanford University and had lived in San Francisco for some time. Furusawa had moved to Los Angeles in 1930 where he had opened a medical center, which was also his residence, at 117½ Weller Street. The doctor was very close to all of the Japanese officials and military attachés at the Japanese legation and was extremely active in many Japanese-American social and fraternal groups, as was his beautiful, articulate wife, Sachiko.

Outwardly, Furusawa appeared to be an upstanding citizen, a highly respected professional and a prominent member of the Japanese social set. Yet, the FBI found it more than curious that Furusawa's clinic on Weller Street, which was a well-equipped and staffed nursing home, never had a registered bed patient, although dozens of people streamed in and out of the place. Most of these visitors were Japanese and they came from all parts of the U.S.

Sachiko Furusawa was also extremely active at this time. She was the founder of the Los Angeles Branch of the Women's Patriotic Society of Japan. This organization was, the FBI knew, an espionage front. Its Los Angeles offices were located at 7425 Franklin Avenue, which was the residence of the Japanese consul.

FBI agents, meanwhile, were able to identify most of the visitors to Furusawa's clinic as suspected spies, including one visitor in particular, Count Hermann von Keitel, a high-ranking naval officer and member of the Abwehr. During his two-day stay at Furusawa's clinic, Keitel was visited by dozens of Japanese military attachés who came from legations in San Francisco, Seattle, Portland, in fact every major seaport along the western seaboard where U.S. Navy stations were located.

It was determined that all of the attachés visiting the Furusawas were bringing to them classifed documents stolen from the U.S. Keitel, who had arrived from New York and who operated under the direction of Abwehr spymaster George Gyssling, the German vice-consul in New York, had brought to Furusawa a number of espionage reports from Japanese spies operating in the East. These agents were Roy Akagi, who managed the New York office of the Japanese-owned South Manchurian Railway, and Chuzo Hagiwara, chief of the Japanese news agency *Domei*, located in New York.

This behavior went on throughout the 1930s. The FBI repeatedly asked for permission to arrest the Furusawas, believing they had more than enough evidence to convict them and many of their contacts of espionage. Permission to do so was consistently denied by Department of Justice officials who believed that if the Furusawa operation was closed down, another would simply spring up elsewhere, one that might take considerable time to locate. The cat-and-mouse game continued almost to the time of Pearl Harbor in 1941. Only weeks before the Japanese sneak attack, the Furusawas packed up their belongings and, in the dead of night, drove to Long Beach. Frustrated FBI agents watched as they went aboard a Japanese ship and vanished forever when the ship steamed out to sea. The fact that Furusawa knew that he had been under close surveillance was evident when, just as the ship was pulling away from the dock, he appeared at the railing and looked down to see several FBI men standing in the shadows. He raised his arm slowly, mockingly, and waved farewell.

[ALSO SEE: *Abwehr*]

GAPON, GEORGE
Czarist Police Spy ▪ (1870–1906)

APON WAS BORN IN POLTAVA, IN THE UKRAINE. HE received a religious education at an Russian Orthodox seminary and took holy orders in 1895. Sent to St. Petersburg, Gapon was assigned to duties at one of the city's many churches. His duties brought him in direct contact with the oppressed workers. While preaching the Social Gospel, Gapon, though politically naive, concluded that the workers would have to agitate to better their conditions.

An effective orator, Gapon preached social reform instead of religion. He lectured the workers about the need to abstain from drinking and gambling, to better themselves by rejecting all vice. He lobbied for better conditions at factories, but he also reminded his followers that they owed their allegiance to their church and to the czar, Nicholas II. His credo was later summed up by one historian as "God save the czar and the eight-hour day."

In 1903, unions secretly organized by the Okhrana under the direction of S. V. Zubatov, had caused industrialists and government officials to panic. Zubatov was disgraced, but the Okhrana still clung to the belief that it could manipulate the workers by having its agents organize and control the workers. To that end, Okhrana chiefs approached Gapon, who had made a favorable name for himself among the working community of St. Petersburg.

Gapon was easily recruited, believing that the Okhrana represented the czar he claimed to revere. He accepted large amounts of money to organize his Union of Russian Factory Workers, and to especially bring into that organization the most revolutionary of those workers, so that they could be subdued and controlled.

Gapon did exactly that, earning a great respect from workers and revolutionaries alike, although none knew at the time that he was a police spy.

To the Russian and foreign revolutionaries infesting St. Petersburg in 1904, Gapon was one of the pre-eminent revolutionary leaders. The clever Japanese spy, Motojiro Akashi, learned of Gapon and, as a military attaché assigned to the Japanese Embassy in St. Petersburg, sought out Gapon, offering him money and arms, encouraging him to lead a full-scale revolution. Akashi's motive, of course, was to aid Japan in creating internal chaos in a country it planned to attack in the upcoming Russo-Japanese war.

Abandoning his priestly duties altogether, Gapon began to play a double game. He encouraged foreign powers and revolutionaries outside of Russia to provide him with money with which to build his union into a potent revolutionary movement, when all the while he took money from the Okhrana to suppress his own movement. V. K. Plehve, the ruthless Minister of Interior, not only authorized the Okhrana to go on supplying Gapon with funds, but he added more money to the priest's coffers to organize a national union, The Assembly of Russian Workingmen. (Only weeks after Plehve authorized additional payments to be made to Gapon, he was blown to pieces by a bomb hurled by an assassin who was, incredibly, under the instructions of Okhrana spy Yevno Azev.)

In response to the disastrous Russo-Japanese war, which resulted in the surrender of Russia's only Pacific outlet, Port Arthur, the workers at the Putilov Steel Works went on strike in January 1905. During the four-day strike, Gapon fumed and fulminated against the industrialists, feeling that their refusal to respond to workers' demands was placing the czar in jeopardy, that Nicholas would be unfairly blamed for any civil unrest that might result.

Gapon was by then a man who could have easily been diagnosed as deranged. Certainly, his perceived dual role of secret protector of the throne through his Okhrana position and his leadership of hundreds of thousands of oppressed workers, gave him a grandiose idea of self. He thought that only he could, at that moment, avert a national crisis, a bloody calamity that threatened to envelop and destroy the ancient monarchy he so revered. Gapon, rich with the contributions of police funds, huge donations from foreign espionage operations, and money from all of the European revolutionary groups, was the man of the hour, a leader who possessed more power than the government itself.

Making one impassioned speech after another, Gapon went from meeting to meeting, enlarging support for the striking unions. He increased his demands upon employers and the government. His Okhrana bosses feared that he was out of control, which he was. Gapon chose to lead the workers, not control them. He was completely carried away by his fanatical sense of purpose. It was his mission, he told his followers, to save the country and the Czar. He would personally lead hundreds of thousands of workers to the Winter Palace and there, as he envisioned it, the czar would emerge to stand on the royal balcony and approve of the petition. He even envisioned himself being invited to stand on that balcony next to his sovereign and, somehow, be instantly named as a special minister to the people, becoming the real power behind the throne and the savior of his country. All contact with reality was gone; Gapon thrilled to his own fairy-tale image.

The priest labored to write five closely written pages of demands, which included an eight-hour day, a minimum wage of one ruble a day (50¢), no overtime, a constituent assembly, universal suffrage and education, amnesty for all political prisoners, an income tax, and the separation of church and state. With the petition written, Gapon, on January 21, 1905, wrote a letter to Nicholas II, announcing the fact that he and the workers would appear before him the next day. He wrote: "Sire! Do not believe the Ministers. They are cheating Thee in regard to the real state of affairs. The people believe in Thee. They have made up their minds to gather at the Winter Palace tomorrow at 2 P.M. to lay their needs before Thee . . . Do not fear anything. Stand tomorrow before the people and accept our humblest petition. I, the representative of the workingmen, and my comrades, guarantee the inviolability of Thy person. Gapon."

This letter may never have reached the Czar, but it was seen by Okhrana chiefs who became exeedingly alarmed. Only two days earlier, on January 19, 1905, the Czar had visited St. Petersburg to perform an ancient religious rite, the Blessing of the Waters. He had ridden through the streets and had been loudly cheered but while he was standing at the banks of the Neva, a cannon used in the imperial salute somehow let loose a live charge, which exploded near the Czar. Nicholas was unhurt but a policeman standing nearby had been killed. Okhrana agents were still investigating this incident and were unable to determine whether it was an accident or part of a plot to kill the Czar.

Now they learned that their once trusted Gapon was about to lead a march on the Winter Palace involving more than 100,000 disgruntled workers. The Czar was not at the Winter Palace. He had left St. Petersburg two days earlier and was at the family retreat, Tsarskoe Selo, fifteen miles outside the city. He was given some brief information about the planned march, however, on the night of January 21, 1905.

The next morning, January 22, 1905, which would be remembered as "Bloody Sunday," Gapon appeared, a little man with a pointed black beard, dressed in priestly robes. He began to lead a huge procession estimated to be between 120,000 and 200,000 men, women, and children. The marchers moved slowly forward in well organized, peaceful columns. They carried the national flag and portraits of the Czar, along with religious ikons and placards. They sang "God Save the Czar," as they moved innocently toward the Winter Palace.

Reports are varied as to what happened next. Many of the streets down which the marchers moved were blocked by mounted Hussars and Cossacks. Infantry with bayonets affixed to their rifles blocked others. The palace guard in front of the Winter Palace appeared in three long lines, guns at the ready. One report had it that officers loudly barked orders to the crowds to desperse, ordering them to return to their homes. Other reports had it that no such commands were given and that the troops simply opened fire, some at a distance of only twenty yards from the lines of helpless workers.

Bullets smacked into bodies as the crowds turned in panic and ran. Gapon, unhurt, fell to the ground, which was hard-packed with snow. Wind and snow swept the streets and the open area in front of the Winter Palace. The troops kept firing, and hundreds fell, staining the snow with their blood, an image that would never be forgotten. The official count had ninety-two killed and several hundred wounded but the death toll was most likely five times that number with thousands wounded. The slaughter was senseless and gave cause to the revolutionaries to believe that Nicholas II was a ruthless oppressor of his own people. Gapon was now one of these.

The priest went into hiding and emerged a short time later as a wild-eyed revolutionary seeking the violent overthrow of the Romanov regime. He sent a letter to the czar that read: "Nicholas Romanov, formerly czar and at present soul-murderer of the Russian empire. The innocent blood of workers, their wives and children lies forever between you and the Russian people . . . May all the blood that must be spilled fall upon you, you Hangman!"

Gapon then issued a call to the workers to arm themselves, seize the government, and purge the monarchy. In his frenzy for revenge, the priest denounced the Okhrana and all the police spies he could identify, including Yevno Azev. Some workers did obtain weapons and planned to attack small garrisons but suddenly Gapon fled the country, no doubt because he had been warned that he would be executed if caught by police and even some radical elements of the revolutionary groups that were controlled by Azev. The priest's open attack on Azev was worse for him than his bombast against the Czar. Azev was the more powerful man.

When Azev learned that Gapon had reached London and was being feted by liberal leaders, he spread the word that the priest was the tool of the capitalists and monarchists and that it had been Gapon who had urged the Cossacks to shoot down his own workers in order to spread terror and revolution. The priest in exile was showered with funds by wealthy liberals and he soon fell into a dissolute life. He went to Paris, then the Riviera where he was seen in the company of expensive whores. He gambled at Monte Carlo and threw money about carelessly.

Gapon was also courted by exiled Russian revolutionaries as a prized or coveted possession. He was the man who had unhinged order in Russia for the first time and had created an event, unwittingly or not, that had placed the Czar in the light of a bloodthirsty murderer. He had joined the Socialist revolutionaries, becoming a member of the Russian Socialist Democratic Labor Party, which had at its axis the Socialist Revolutionary Party, which was secretly controlled by the Okhrana spy Azev, the very man Gapon had denounced and who was now planning the priest's demise. Azev was a man who planned far in advance. Long before Bloody Sunday, he had assigned a leading Socialist revolutionary, Pinhas Rutenberg, to stay at Gapon's side.

Rutenberg, who was unaware of Azev's ties to the Okhrana, lay with Gapon in the blood-splotched snow before the Winter Palace, having thrown the priest to the ground at the first volley fired by the palace guard. He had helped Gapon escape to England and had remained at his side, even through Gapon's bender of drinking, gambling, and whoring. He also steered Gapon to Geneva where the priest met several times with Lenin. In a later statement, Lenin recalled Gapon as having made "an impression on me of a wise and enterprising person undoubtedly devoted to the revolution, although, unfortunately, without a sustained revolutionary philosophy."

Georgy Plekhanov and others believed that Gapon might still be an *agent provocateur* for the Okhrana. Lenin, nevertheless, clung to Gapon as a raw but genuine revolutionary. Lenin, however, was never a good judge of those who had been labeled traitors to his cause, as was the case with Roman Malinovsky, an Okhrana spy who had been sent into his midst to obtain information for the Czarist government. Even when Malinovsky was denounced as such by party members, Lenin refused to believe it. It was the same with Gapon.

His head swimming with self-glory, the little priest injudiciously returned to Russia in early 1906. He soon found it impossible to resume his role as revolutionary leader. He had missed his chance by fleeing Russia and his profligate ways, the very sins he had preached against to his followers and had then embraced, had thoroughly discredited him.

Gapon, desperate, then went back to the Okhrana, attempting to negotiate favor with the secret police. He said that, for a high price, he would prove to them that their ace spy, Azev, had arranged for countless assassinations in the past. When this was reported to Azev, he, in turn, went to Rutenberg, and ordered the priest to be executed.

Rutenberg, however, wanted to be sure. When next he spoke with Gapon, the priest told him that Azev and the Battle Organization was working against the revolution and on behalf of the Okhrana (the first part was true), and that it should be betrayed to the secret police. He asked Rutenberg to join him in selling out this terrorist group. Rutenberg said he would consider the matter and, on March 28, 1906, he inveigled the priest to a meeting across the Finnish border. The two men met in a room inside a small cottage. The room was divided by a thin partition. On the other side of the partition sat members of the Socialist Revolutionary Party, waiting to listen in on Gapon's conversation with Rutenberg, as Rutenberg had planned.

When Gapon arrived, he was in a nervous state. He immediately got to the point, telling Rutenberg that he had arranged a large amount of cash from the Okhrana to be paid to Rutenberg in return for information on the Battle Organization. "Twenty thousand rubles isn't bad money," Gapon wheedled. "I can't think why you are behaving like such a fool." George Gapon, at that moment, had come full circle, from police spy to inspired revolutionary to police spy.

Rutenberg shook his head at the proposition. "I can't stomach the idea. Many of the men are innocent revolutionaries and if they are caught with the traitors, they will be hanged."

"That's their bad luck," snorted Gapon, all humanity vanishing from his character. "The Okhrana is clever enough to make sure that you will never be identified as the informer."

Rutenberg could stand no more. He walked to the door that led to the room where the revolutionary judges sat and flung it open. The judges in the other room, many of them Gapon's former friends, had heard everything. These men rushed into the room and seized the priest, manhandling him, punching and kicking him, shouting "Traitor! Spy!" Gapon fell to his knees, clutching at his former friends, begging them for mercy.

Rutenberg, once Gapon's closest friend, stepped from the room, sobbing. Gapon was held upright and a rope was placed about his neck. He struggled fiercely but his hands were then tied. He was placed beneath a hook extending from a beam in the ceiling and then hauled upward. The little priest kicked wildly, struggling for air, then jerked spasmodically and died. Rutenberg stepped inside to see the horrible sight of Gapon's tongue protruding its full length from his mouth, turned black, and his eyeballs popped from his skull. The revolutionaries then solemnly filed from the cottage, leaving the priest's body to swing creakingly from the hook. It would not be found until the following April.

[ALSO SEE: *Motojiro Akashi; Yevno Azev; Roman Malinovsky; Okhrana; S. V. Zubatov*]

GCHQ (Government Communications Headquarters)
British Signals Intelligence Organization ▪ (1914–   )

BASED AT CHELTENHAM, ENGLAND SINCE WORLD War I, the GCHQ is the top secret British signals intelligence organization responsible for the breaking of enemy codes and ciphers. In World War I, the GCHQ was responsible for breaking as many as 1,500 German military codes and ciphers. In World War II, GCHQ expanded to include the Code and Cipher School at Bletchley where its cryptologists, in what was called the Ultra Operation, broke the code of the German Enigma Machine in 1939, which allowed the British to read all important coded enemy messages throughout the war. In 1947, the U.S. and Great Britain signed an agreement to share all important information between NSA (National Security Agency) and GCHQ. This agency presently stores all of its information in vast computer warehouses.

GEHLEN, REINHARD
German Spymaster ▪ (1902–1979)

GEHLEN BEGAN AS A CAREER GERMAN OFFICER who graduated to intelligence, miraculously emerging from the crushed Third Reich to become the great spymaster in post-war Berlin when it was the hotbed of espionage between the Soviets and the West. The son of an army officer who later became a successful publisher, Gehlen was born in Erfurt, Germany. After graduating officers' candidate school, Gehlen joined the artillery in 1921.

In 1942 Gehlen was promoted as a lieutenant colonel to head intelligence for Foreign Armies East, the German military forces in Russia. His superior was Colonel Adolf Heusinger who found Gehlen a superb spymaster. (In postwar Germany, Gehlen would later find a place for Heusinger in his West German intelligence organization.) Gehlen's unit worked separately from the SS and SD, collecting an enormous amount of information on Russian partisans and regular troops.

Of particular interest to Gehlen was the Soviet officer corps. In-depth profiles were produced not only on the high-ranking officers but on those who would replace those military leaders in years to come. The Soviet codes and ciphers were systematically categorized, then broken.

Russian intelligence methods of infiltration, interrogation, use of covers, letterboxes, dead drops, all the techniques of espionage were chronicled in precise terms and on an encyclopedic basis. All Communist politicians received the same kind of deep profile treatment. Gehlen was a demanding, exacting spymaster and his records later proved how extensive and encompassing was the work of his unit.

Gehlen cultivated a vast network of spies, mostly recruiting Russians with German backgrounds and who thought of themselves as Germans. He planted these spies behind enemy lines and in every major city in Russia, as well as territory already occupied by Nazi troops, in Poland, Prussia, the Baltic cities. His intelligence reports were accurate and dependable and helped the Germans in their tactical retreat from Russia after the fall of Stalingrad, but Gehlen and no one else could aid the maniac Hitler in his relentless drive for self-destruction.

Hitler had never liked Gehlen. As head of German military intelligence (FHO) on the eastern front, Gehlen never minced words in his reports, which were read by Hitler himself. The Fuhrer tersely commended Gehlen's precise reports but he was constantly annoyed by Gehlen's dim view of the eventual conquest of Russia by Germany. This began in the summer of 1942 when Gehlen assessed the Russian will to fight to the death and predicted in one report the eventual Battle of Stalingrad and that this was a key city the Russians would never give up.

By early 1945, Gehlen, at his headquarters in Zossen, had risen to the rank of major general and he realized that the war was lost. Hitler, in his eyes, had gone mad, having dismissed the best of his generals and, in particular, the grand old man of German intelligence, Admiral Wilhelm Canaris. The Fuhrer had ordered the murder of more than 5,000 high-ranking officers and politicians whom he suspected of being part of the Black Orchestra (German underground) and the failed plot against his life in 1944. In the past he had warned Gehlen that his incisive intelligence reports were too heavily laced with "a virulant pessimism." Hitler, by April 1945, dumped Gehlen, telling his generals that the spymaster "is an unreliable defeatist."

Gehlen was unperturbed. As usual, he had a plan to not only survive but rise again as an important intelligence chief in the post-war years. His vast, deep knowledge of Russia, its leaders, its intelligence, would be of great use to the Allies. To achieve that end, Gehlen had all of his files put onto microfilm and then led the leaders of his unit toward the Alps where, in the earth beneath a hut near Lake Spitzing in Upper Bavaria, he and his men buried fifty large steel boxes, the archives of their intelligence unit. Gehlen and his men then sought out a contingent of American troops and surrendered to them.

Eventually, Gehlen was interviewed by officers of the CIC, the American Army's counterintelligence corps. He informed them that he was able to provide the Allies with a vast repository of intelligence on the Soviets, information the West would soon desperately need. None of the CIC officers shared his view.

More American officers interrogated Gehlen, coming to the conclusion, in Gehlen's words, "that I was not a valuable prisoner." A few days later, Gehlen was herded with other prisoners into the back of a truck and driven to a prison at Wiesbaden.

Gehlen was not long forgotten. In May 1945 both the Russians and the Allies set up separate commissions, searching for German intelligence officers, especially their cache of information and, in particular, the chief of the FHO, Reinhard Gehlen. CIC officers were notified and their records revealed that Gehlen had been sent from the Wiesbaden prison to a concentration camp at Oberusel in the American zone. Gehlen was then brought before American General Edwin L. Sibert, one of the liberators of Paris in 1944 and head of all military intelligence in the American zone.

Gehlen, in essence, told Sibert that Stalin would never allow Poland, Czechoslovokia, Bulgaria, Rumania, Hungary and the Baltic states to escape occupation by Soviet troops and that he planned to spread communism throughout Germany to purge the country of its national socialism. Stalin would risk war with the West to achieve his ends, Gehlen insisted. Sibert listened patiently, then replied with a single sentence: "You know a lot about the Russians, General."

The FHO chief then told Sibert that he could prove his claims through the intelligence he and his men had accumulated during the war. Gehlen wrote out a 129-page report for Sibert that detailed Russian military and political aims, and then turned over the 50 steel boxes that had been hidden in Bavaria. It was a treasure trove of eye-opening information, which detailed current strengths, composition, and deployment of Soviet divisions, thousands of air photographs pinpointing Soviet rail junctions, military fortifications, and armament plants, as well as figures on armament production, morale reports on the Red Army and the Russian people as a whole.

So impressed were Sibert and his superior, General Walter Bedell Smith, that Gehlen was given the green light to set up his intelligence unit and begin spying for the West. A short time later Gehlen and his top officers—Heinz Herre, Albert Scholler, Horst Hiemenz, and Konrad Stephanus—were sent to the U.S.

Gehlen and his staff met with OSS director William J. Donovan and his European chief Allen Dulles, who both agreed with him that Russia was the dominant threat to world peace. It was obvious that while America was rapidly disarming in 1945, Russia kept its six million-man army intact, and kept its 50,000 tanks and 20,000 aircraft operational. The Soviets could not disarm and execute conquest of Eastern Europe.

Not until February 1946, however, did Gehlen return to Europe to seriously begin his espionage

One of the shrewdest spymasters for the Third Reich and post-war West Germany, Reinhard Gehlen, shown when he was chief of intelligence for the German armies in Russia in 1944; he turned over his entire spy network and archives to the Americans at the close of WW II.

operations against the Russians, working in tandem with Hermann Baun who had already been putting together his own intelligence unit under Sibert's approval. The delay in Washington was the American reluctance to initiate espionage against its former ally, Russia. But when the Soviets invaded northern Iran, their aims were clearly that of an aggressor and Gehlen was given the green light.

The Gehlen Organization, as it became known, was funded with $7 million and operated in the Soviet zone of Eastern Germany. Gehlen's own headquarters at Pullach evaluated the information culled from tens of thousands of willing spies. Who were these armies of the night that flocked to Gehlen's banner? They came from the tattered ranks of German prisoners-of-war who were released over a period of several years following World War II. Gehlen's men interviewed each and every one of these men, writing out details of their concentration camp experiences.

Those who had been stool-pigeons or who had turned propagandists for the Soviets were eliminated. Those who had special knowledge of the Russian

Spymaster Reinhard Gehlen, shown after he had retired as chief of West German intelligence; his career was smashed by a Soviet double agent, Heinz Felfe.

military and civilians and who proved loyal to the West were enlisted as agents.

Other agents, thousands of them, were already in place. These were Gehlen's "sleeper" agents in Russia, Poland, the Baltic states, in Rumania, Bulgaria, Hungary, Albania, Czechoslovakia and, especially in East Germany. Gehlen's service operated under the auspices of the U.S. until the establishment of the Federal Republic of Germany when Gehlen's organization was absorbed into the West German government. His bureau was known as "Org" to its members but officially it was called the Federal Intelligence Service, and, in 1956, the BND.

Gehlen's operations were chiefly directed against the East German Ministry of State Security and the SSD, the Communist political police. The SSD was headed by Ernst Wollweber, a crusty old German Communist organizer turned spymaster. Wollweber so hated Gehlen and rankled under Gehlen's many intelligence triumphs over him that he put a "dead or alive" price tag of one million marks on Gehlen. It was never collected. One of the reasons why Wollweber despised Gehlen was because Gehlen had planted his agent, Walter Gramisch, on Wollweber's personal staff.

One of Gehlen's great strengths was that he had dedicated agents holding high-level positions in East Germany, men like Lieutenant Colonel Siegfried Dombrowski who worked for Communist intelligence. Walter Gramisch, who headed the shipping and ports section of the East German Ministry of Shipping was one of Gehlen's most productive agents.

Even bettter positioned was Hermann Kastner, Deputy Prime Minister of East Germany who operated for Gehlen under the code name "Helwig" and supplied Gehlen with reports that detailed all East German Cabinet meetings.

For more than twenty years Gehlen's organization provided one spectacular coup after another. It identified the existence of SMERSH as the execution arm of the KGB, it helped the CIA to dig the Berlin Tunnel so the West could splice into security telephone lines and listen in on top-level Communist conversations. It was an agent of Gehlen's who secured for the CIA the copy of Nikita Khrushchev's secret speech to Communist Party members that denounced Joseph Stalin. Gehlen also obtained information in advance of the Six Day War in the Middle East in 1967.

There were failures. Gehlen did not warn the West that the Berlin wall would be built. (He did say in his memoirs that he had reported that the Soviets would quickly move to prevent the mass exodus of East Germans to the West and that they were stockpiling building materials.) A significant defection, that of Hans Joachim Geyer in 1953, caused dozens of Gehlen's East German informants to be compromised.

Throughout the 1950s and 1960s, Gehlen expanded his organization until he became the most powerful man in Europe. His agents operated in the U.S., England, France, in the Middle East (working with both the Egyptian secret service and Israel's Mossad). Then, in 1963, disaster struck the Gehlen organization. Heinz Felfe, who had worked for Gehlen for more than a decade as an agent, was exposed as being a double agent who was really in the employ of the Soviets.

The scandal broke over the head of the venerable Konrad Adenauer, chancellor of Germany and one of Gehlen's most ardent sponsors (Adenauer called him "my dear General"), who was compelled to resign. Gehlen would continue at his post for another five years but his prestige had been diminished. He retired in 1968, replaced by one of his old subordinates, Lieutenant General Gerhard Wessel. Gehlen died of natural causes eleven years later. He is remembered today as the spymaster's spymaster, one of the greatest intelligence chiefs in history.

[ALSO SEE: *Abwehr; Berlin Tunnel; BND; Wilhelm Canaris; CIA; William J. Donovan; Allen Dulles; Heinz Felfe; Gestapo; Hans Joachim Geyer; KGB; Mossad; OSS; SD; SMERSH*]

GERHARDT, DIETER
South African Spy for Soviets ▪ (1935–   )

A S A YOUTH LIVING IN SOUTH AFRICA, GERHARDT'S life was miserable. His father, a German architect, expressed right-wing views that, to the authorities, smacked of Nazi philosophy. He was interned, and a stigma was cast over the family.

Gerhardt harbored a deep-seated hatred for his country ever after and, by the time he was a 25-year-old navy lieutenant, he decide to injure South Africa as he had been injured, and get well paid in the bargain. At that time, in 1960, while attending a weapons training course in England, Gerhardt took a day off and went to London. He took a taxi to the Russian Embassy and, after meeting with a GRU agent serving as a military attaché, offered his services as a spy.

A short time later Gerhardt divorced his English wife, Janet, and married Ruth Johr, a match that appears to have been made by the GRU, as Soviet intelligence always preferred man and wife espionage teams. Gerhardt was hamstrung in delivering reports to his Soviet spymasters in that there existed no Soviet or Eastern Bloc country maintaining diplomatic relations with South Africa. The spy could contact his Soviet spymasters only two ways, through radio communications or through courier. Often enough, Gerhardt accompanied his wife on trips to Geneva or to Vienna to visit relatives. Once in Vienna, they flew to Moscow where Gerhardt received espionage training and equipment.

For twenty-three years, Gerhardt assiduously spied for Russia, and during that time he rose to the rank of commodore, becoming a close friend of the Prime Minister and other important South African leaders. Every South African secret worth knowing was delivered to the Soviets by Gerhardt, including the West's contingency plans to use Simonstown, South Africa's most important port, as the main oil route during any international crisis. He also delivered detailed operations information on Silvermines, the elaborate and sophisticated electronic listening center, an organization similar to America's NSA (National Security Agency) and one that was responsible for plotting all air force and maritime movements throughout the South Atlantic.

Since Gerhardt was in a high-ranking position, he was privy to the secrets of the western allies. He was able to obtain and turn over to the Russians reports on British warship development and weapons systems, and the French Exocet missile.

Gerhardt's espionage activities were not uncovered by any western counterespionage agents, but by the Soviets themselves, or, specifically, one Soviet spymaster who was known only as "Boris" when he defected. A GRU desk official, Boris identified Gerhardt to the CIA as one of Russia's best-placed spies. The CIA, in turn, informed MI5 in England. When South African Security Services were told about Gerhardt, its chiefs were too astonished to believe the report concerning their top naval officer.

CIA and MI5 agents decided to close down Gerhardt's operations in January 1983 while he was in New York, attending a mathematics course at Syracuse University. He was by then collecting American secrets and was thought to be ready to turn these over to a GRU agent. Before that happened, the American and British agents barged into Commodore Gerhardt's hotel room on Ninth Avenue, arresting him for espionage. With Gerhardt at the time was a fellow student who had been attending the same course, an FBI agent who had been feeding information to the CIA about Gerhardt's spying activities.

Confronted with overwhelming evidence provided by Boris, Gerhardt broke down and confessed. In his lengthy statement, he revealed how he had provided the Soviets with scores of candidate spies in the British navy, a revelation that greatly alarmed MI5. He had, he explained, found his applicants through the British press. While serving as a South African naval attaché in London, he took out ads in the newspapers that invited technicians in the Royal Navy to join the South African Navy, which, at that time, was about to commission a modern fleet of submarines.

Hundreds of applicants flocked to Gerhardt to be interviewed for jobs that paid a great deal more than what they were making. Gerhardt cleverly had these applicants fill out forms that asked why they wished to leave the Royal Navy. Those that answered that they were either discontent or were in need of money, were selected by Gerhardt. He turned over more than a hundred of these applications to GRU contact man, Mikhail Nikolayev, who, as usual, paid Gerhardt a heavy sum in pound notes. The Russians were glad to pay for what ammounted to "a list of potential spies," according to one MI5 official.

For the Gerhardts, espionage was a well-paying business. Although the exact sum was never fixed, it was estimated that they made an average of between £100,000 and £200,000 a year from the Russians. He and his wife were tried before the South African Supreme Court, a trial held *in camera*. Both were found guilty of high treason and sent to prison for life.

[ALSO SEE: *CIA; GRU; MI5*]

GESTAPO
German Secret Police for Third Reich ▪ (1933–1945)

IN WHAT WAS ALMOST HIS FIRST OFFICIAL ACT, Adolf Hitler, after becoming the chancellor of Germany in 1933, established a secret police force, the Gestapo (a contraction of the German words for "secret state police") to assure the control of the country by the Nazi Party. Though originally designed as an internal police force, the Gestapo soon became an effective and dreaded counterintelligence agency.

On April 26, 1933, Hermann Goering, Hitler's right-hand adviser, officially established the Gestapo as a secret police force in Prussia to replace the old Prussian political police known as Department IA. Goering's original designation for this force was the Secret Police Office, in German the *Geheimes Polizei Amt*, or GPA, but this was too similar to the GPU of the Soviet Union. A postal employee then making up a franking stamp for this new force, suggested that Goering call the new organization the *Geheime Staatspolizei*, the Secret State Police, or, in abbreviated form, the Gestapo.

The most frightening thing about the Gestapo was, that as a secret state police force, it operated above the law. Goering used the Gestapo as his personal terror weapon, deploying this force of sadistic thugs to enforce his own decrees, meting out beatings, torture, and murder at will. The Gestapo was originally made up of Germany's worst social elements, police officers who had been dismissed for brutality, army officers who had been dismissed for gross misconduct.

These agents had deep histories of persecuting those condemned by the Nazis—Jews, Catholics, or liberal politicians. Many of the Gestapo's early-day members came from the gutter ranks of the SA, Ernst Roehm's Brown Shirts or stormtroopers. They were blackmailers, extortionists, pimps, homosexuals, rapists, most with long criminal records. These were the men Goering wanted, asked for, and got.

Goering appointed Heinrich Himmler as deputy chief of the Prussian Secret Police in April 1934. This placed the Gestapo under Himmler's direct command. He expanded the Gestapo's responsibilities as the police arm of the equally dreaded SS, Himmler's own creation. (The SS was a sinister and mysterious organization that came to control all police and counterintelligence agencies in Germany, as well as provide the elite army divisions that spearheaded Hitler's invasions and military operations. The Gestapo and the SS were identical in the kind of personnel both employed: fanatical Nazis whose allegiance was only to Adolf Hitler.)

Himmler insisted that the Gestapo, like the SS, have a completely free hand. To that end, in 1935,

he pressured the Prussian Supreme Court to rule that the Gestapo's orders and actions were not subject to judicial control. The Third Reich made this official on February 10, 1936, when it decreed that the Gestapo was placed above all laws of the land.

Further, civil liberties in Germany were suspended by a notorious Nazi law instituted on February 28, 1933. Under this edict, the Gestapo operated at will. Its agents did as they pleased, arresting and imprisoning whomever they chose or for whatever reason. Anyone daring to ask questions about a person picked up by the Gestapo (many of whom simply vanished) were told that the suspect had been placed in the status of *Shutzhaft*, or "protective custody," a catchall phrase for any charge the Gestapo later cared to invent.

Himmler himself was named as chief of all secret police in Germany in June 1936, operating under the Ministry of the Interior. In addition to using the Gestapo to hunt out Allied spies, political malcontents and members of the Black Orchestra (the German underground working against Hitler), Himmler used Gestapo agents to create dossiers on German leaders Himmler disliked or vied with in the reach for more and more power. It was the Gestapo that proved, under Himmler's direction, that Field Marshal Werner von Blomberg, a member of the army's high command and Hitler's Minister of Defense, had married a prostitute, and, having violated Nazi rules, was dismissed from his important post.

The white-haired, 60-year-old Blomberg, an early-day Hitler supporter, was disliked by Himmler who thought he had too much power, so the history of Blomberg's wife, Erna Gruhn, was unearthed by the Gestapo to prove her a common whore. The woman was a typist in Blomberg's office at the time he met her and he had no knowledge of the fact that her mother had operated a brothel. Josef Meisinger, a Gestapo agent and one of Himmler's henchmen, admitted before his execution as a war criminal in Poland in 1947, that Blomberg's wife had no record as a prostitute and he used her mother's background to blacken the young woman's name so that Blomberg would be disgraced and dismissed.

Next came General Werner von Fritsch, commander-in-chief of the Germany Army, the top soldier of the land, whom Himmler knew hated the Nazis and was constantly making contemptuous remarks about him, Goering, Goebbels, and others. In January 1938, the Gestapo produced a dossier that stated that Fritsch, a lifelong bachelor, was a homosexual and had had relations with a number of male prostitutes. This was supported by the statements of a Hans Schmidt, a degenerate blackmailer who preyed upon homosexuals in Berlin. Fritsch vehemently denied the charges, which were cause for dismissal, but the ever bold Himmler brought Schmidt in front of Fritsch and Hitler at the Chancellory Building.

Schmidt shuffled in front of Hitler, gave Fritsch a glance, then said that he had seen Fritsch meet with a notorious male prostitute named "Bavarian Joe" in the Potsdam railroad station in Berlin and had witnessed homosexual acts between the pair in the men's room. Schmidt then went on to say that Fritsch had been paying him blackmail money for years until he, Schmidt, was sent to prison for another offense. Fritsch could not believe his ears. He was too incensed to answer the charges. Hitler interpreted Fritsch's silence to signify his guilt. He asked for Fritsch's resignation. The general refused, demanding to be tried under military law.

While awaiting trial, Fritsch, unlike almost all victims of the Gestapo, had at his disposal the means through which to prove his innocence. Army intelligence, working with certain officials with the Ministry of Justice not yet then under the control of Himmler and his Gestapo, discovered that Schmidt had, indeed, been blackmailing a homosexual officer, but not Fritsch. His victim had been a captain of cavalry, Rittmeister von Frisch. The Gestapo knew this but when it arrested Schmidt, its officials, including Himmler, ordered Schmidt to point his finger at the wrong man, at Fritsch.

Army officials were then able to take control of not only Schmidt but of Frisch who had also been arrested and detained by the Gestapo. The army kept these two under lock and key to await the military tribunal, confident that Himmler and the Gestapo would finally be shown up for what they were, blackmailers. Himmler and the Gestapo were compromised as was Hitler. The Army vowed that if Fritsch did not receive a fair trial, it would seize the government and throw out the dictator. (Had it done so, the world might have been spared World War II and its awful devastation.)

The Army never got the chance. Hitler realized his dilemma. Fritsch, if brought to trial, would be exonerated and he, along with the Gestapo, Himmler, and Reinhard Heydrich of the SD, who had also prepared fake files in the Fritsch case, would be in disgrace and could lose power. To extricate himself from the mire of the Gestapo's blundering, Hitler simply announced on February 4, 1938, he was assuming command of all the armed forces of Germany. As the head of state, he had the legal right to assume that command.

Fritsch, and sixteen other senior generals, the only real opposition to Hitler left in Germany at that time, were relieved of their commands, and forty-four other high-ranking officers who had shown little enthusiasm for the Nazis were transferred to minor positions. In the end, the Gestapo and Himmler had won, but only through the heavy-handed tactics of Adolf Hitler, the only person in Germany exercising power over them.

Dr. Hjalmar Schact, Hitler's Minister of Economics, was a ruthless autocrat, a usurous banker and a declared foe of Himmler who dared to tell the Gestapo chief that he and his secret police had "better stay out of my way." Gestapo agents were immediately sent to bug Schact's home and offices with hidden microphones. Agents then recorded Schact's every word, especially anything critical of the Third Reich or Hitler's cronies, and this was then placed before Hitler, year after year, until the Fuhrer finally dismissed Schact.

The Gestapo was Himmler's secret police force, which also functioned as an arm of the SS in that it made arrests and detained persons before the SS determined the fate of that person. The Gestapo conducted widespread counterintelligence. Since anyone advocating the political overthrow of the Nazi Party was considered a criminal, espionage and civil crime could be interpreted by the Gestapo as one in the same charge.

Himmler's Gestapo spies operated throughout Germany and in the countries the Nazis occupied. They were fairly efficient in tracking down Allied agents and breaking up underground cells and resistance groups, yet their duties were so widespread that the same counterespionage agents were kept busy hunting down shopkeepers, factory workers and civil servants who casually complained about the government. They assumed the role of a "thought police," chasing disgruntled citizens instead of foreign agents and thus their energies were debilitated, their aims distorted and their overall counterintelligence awash with the trivial and inconsequential. The art and science of espionage was replaced by obsessive witchhunting.

The Gestapo, like its perverse parent, the SS, collapsed with the fall of the Third Reich in 1945. Its chief, Himmler, was captured but to avoid conviction as a war criminal (which he certainly was), committed suicide by swallowing poison. The image of the Gestapo to this day is twin to that of Hitler and his ruthless, maniacal gang, sinister and all things evil.

[ALSO SEE: *Reinhard Heydrich; Heinrich Himmler; SD*]

GEYER, HANS JOACHIM
German Spy for Soviets ▪ (1923–)

THE CASE OF HANS JOACHIM GEYER IS UNUSUAL IN the annals of espionage in that it is perhaps the only instance where an author of spy thrillers turned actual secret agent. (Ian Fleming was a British agent many years before he became the author of the James Bond novels.)

Geyer used the pseudonym of Henry Troll in writing a series of cheap spy novels that featured an agent named John Kling. He began to act like his protagonist and, incredibly, came to enter the real world of espionage. In 1951, Geyer applied for work with the Gehlen Organization and he was offered a job as an investigator in East Germany the following year. Geyer's job was to seek out and enlist possible spies in the Communist sector who would work for Reinhard Gehlen.

Somehow, in 1953, Geyer was recruited to the ranks of East German counterintelligence, the SSD. He became a double spy, controlling Gehlen agents during the day, and breaking into Gehlen's offices in West Berlin at night to filch secrets and lists of Gehlen spies in the East, which he turned over to Soviet spymasters. Geyer, however, also began to live out his fantasies as a super spy, playing the role of his own protagonist, John Kling, putting on airs, acting mysteriously.

He tried to impress young women with his role as spymaster. In October 1953, Geyer was told to hire a secretary for his branch. He interviewed several applicants. One young, attractive woman became alarmed at his mysterious behavior. She told her story to her cousin, a detective, who paid a call on Geyer.

On October 29, 1953, the West German detective rang the bell at Geyer's apartment house. Finding him gone, he told the superintendent who he was and that he would return later. When Geyer came home and heard this news, he rushed to his apartment where he hastily gathered files stolen from the Gehlen Organization, then locked his door and leaped from a window into a back garden, fleeing to East Berlin.

As soon as Geyer was in the hands of his Communist spymasters, the SSD sent out squads to arrest Gehlen agents, all those identified by double agent Geyer. More than sixty of the West's best agents in East Berlin and in the Communist zone were taken into custody, including members of the Ministry of Reconstruction, leading functionaries of the Communist Party, an editor of the *Berliner Zeitung*, and several high-ranking East German police officers.

Gehlen's agents were embittered and disillusioned by the Geyer defection. Gehlen himself admitted that security had been lax in that Geyer should never have been recruited. Geyer's defection caused other West German agents to go over to the Soviets but most of Gehlen's widespread organization remained intact.

[ALSO SEE: *Ian Fleming; Reinhard Gehlen*]

GIMPEL, ERICH (AKA: EDWARD GEORGE GREEN)
German Spy in U.S. ▪ (1910– ?)

A TACITURN, TOUGH NAZI, ERICH GIMPEL, ALONG with William Colepaugh, landed on American shores toward the end of World War II, in a last gasp effort of the Abwehr to provide in-depth intelligence from the U.S. A native of Merseburg, Germany, Gimpel was always obsessed with radios. Following his graduation from high school, he studied high frequency transformers. Next he went into the radio business.

Gimpel's expertise led to his employment in 1935 by Telefunken, the largest radio corporation in Germany. He was sent to Peru but a few years later he returned to Germany as a dedicated Nazi intent on aiding Hitler to win his wars. He enlisted with the Abwehr as a spy. After his espionage training, Gimpel was sent back to Peru, operating out of Lima. He paid regular visits to the German legation there to turn over reports on ships entering and leaving the harbor.

In 1942, when Peru joined the Allies, its agents picked up all German operatives in Lima, including Gimpel. He was interned but managed to be repatriated by claiming that he was Swedish. Sent to Sweden, Gimpel was smuggled back to Germany. He went to work in a Hamburg radio factory until it was destroyed by Allied bombing. In 1943, he went back to work for the Abwehr, this time as a courier, carrying messages between Berlin and Madrid.

Gimpel's life changed drastically in the following year when he was suddenly elevated from common courier to superspy, all as a result of the Abwehr's desire to appease Germany's ally, Japan. The Japanese had been lobbying Admiral Canaris at the Abwehr to launch some spectacular espionage efforts in the U.S., although Canaris knew this was, by January 1944, a losing proposition. Germany and Japan were already losing the war and no amount of espionage, sabotage, or any other kind of covert activity could turn the tide back.

Canaris was relieved of his command by Hitler in February 1944, but Lieutenant Colonel Higati of Japanese intelligence in the Japanese Embassy in Berlin insisted that the Abwehr "send agents to America under the German-Japanese espionage agreement." Not until November 1944 did the Abwehr act, and then only after the Japanese, now desperate as the American forces moved ever closer to their homeland, implored the Germans to act. Abwehr II, which was the sabotage arm of German military intelligence, was given the futile assignment. Two agents were rather haphazardly chosen, one being Gimpel, the other American-born William Curtis Colepaugh.

Born in Niantic, Connecticut, Colepaugh's mother was German and throughout his uneventful youth, he heard from his mother a litany of praise for everything German. He attended Admiral Farragut Academy in Toms River, New Jersey, then went on to the Massachusetts Institute of Technology where he failed his studies and left to suddenly work for Hitler's Third Reich as a spy.

Colepaugh was by then an ardent admirer of Adolf Hitler and everything Nazi. He went to the German legation in Boston where he offered to spy for the Germans. His proposal was accepted and he was soon earning a small weekly wage to report on shipping going in and out of Boston Harbor. This low-paying work was abandoned by Colepaugh when America

The Abwehr spy school, Park Zorgvliet, outside of The Hague, where Erich Gimpel and William Colepaugh received their training as German agents before being sent to America to perform one of the most peculiar missions of World War II.

Tough, taciturn Erich Gimpel, Nazi spy under arrest; he was sentenced to death by hanging but later was reprieved.

entered the war in 1941. He joined the U.S. Navy but was soon discharged for consistently and loudly expression pro-German views.

With millions of men entering the armed forces, there was suddenly a desperate need for seaman to serve in the merchant marine. Colepaugh's background at the Farragut naval academy helped him find a berth on board an American cargo vessel. For three years he served on American and British merchant ships but he was shunned by his shipmates who resented his glowing comments about Hitler and Germany. In 1944, Colepaugh served as a messboy on board the *Gripsholm*, a German ship that, before the war, was infamous for having a crew that was mostly made up of Abwehr spies. When the vessel anchored in Lisbon, Portugal, Colepaugh suddenly jumped ship. (He was undoubtedly encouraged to do so by Abwehr spies still serving among the crew.)

Colepaugh went to occupied France and there applied at the Abwehr for a job as a spy. His background was checked and he was accepted, mostly because he was a native American and could possibly be used some day as an agent in the U.S. He was sent to the Abwehr espionage school in Holland. It was there that Colepaugh met Erich Gimpel.

Both of these men were selected to go to the U.S. as spies. Their mission was so peculiar that its Abwehr planners had to admit to themselves that they had concocted the wild scheme only to meet their obligation to the Japanese. Gimpel and Colepaugh were to be smuggled into the U.S. Once there, they were to read newspapers, listen to the radio, and do other

Gimpel's co-spy, American-born William Colepaugh who got drunk and blabbed his mission to a friend which resulted in an FBI capture of both spies.

research that would allow them to determine the effect of German propaganda on the 1944 presidential election between Franklin D. Roosevelt and Thomas E. Dewey.

Gimpel, who would be the team leader, was to serve as the radio operator, camera operator, and contact with Berlin. Although he could speak English, his decided accent was a drawback. Colepaugh, therefore, would do all the talking once the pair reached the U.S. Gimpel was given the cover name "Edward George Green" and Colepaugh would operate under the cover name of "William Charles Cauldwell." They were given $60,000 in new American currency and a bag of diamonds that they could, if needed, convert into more cash. They were to buy equipment in America that Gimpel was to use in building a radio system that would reach Germany.

From Kiel, the two spies were taken by submarine across the Atlantic, both wearing German Navy uniforms, until they approached American shores. At the last moment, they changed into civilian clothes bearing American labels. At 11 p.m., November 29, 1944, the German submarine surfaced in a blinding snowstorm three hundred yards from the coast of Maine, at Frenchman Bay. The spies were placed into a rubber boat and paddled by two German sailors to Crabtree Point where they disembarked and the boat struggled back to the submarine, which quickly vanished.

The two men went to Bangor, Maine, and from there took a train to Boston. The pair then traveled to New York City where they stayed in the best hotels, lavishly spending the Abwehr's money. Gimpel then insisted that they find an apartment and begin to work for their German spymasters. Colepaugh shrugged, pointing out that the chief reason for their mission no longer existed. The election was over and Roosevelt was the winner.

Gimpel did not intend to desert his duties. He insisted they rent an apartment, which they did. Gimpel began to assemble and build a radio set and ordered Colepaugh to spy on ships in New York harbor. Instead, Colepaugh enjoyed himself, going to movies, nightclubs, and expensive brothels. Then Colepaugh, ever the shiftless lout, told Gimpel that their roles in America were useless, that Germany was going to lose the war and no information they collected would change matters. Worse, Colepaugh nervously pointed out, they were spies and, if caught, would be hanged.

Gimpel snorted his contempt for Colepaugh and ordered him to continue chronicling the vessels in New York Harbor. He would soon have his radio operational, he told Colepaugh, and they could begin sending messages to Berlin. "As soon as you do that, the Army will pick up your signal and find us," Colpaugh stated. Gimpel said, no, that would not happen, that they would be constantly on the move once he began sending and thus thwart the Signal Corps' direction-finding equipment.

Colepaugh had heard enough. He went out and got drunk, then visited an old friend in Richmond, New York. Half tipsy, he told his friend that he was spying for Germany and he flashed a money roll thick with hundred dollar bills. The friend called the FBI and Colepaugh was arrested. He quickly informed on Gimpel who was found by agents, buying out-of-town newspapers at a Times Square newsstand. Both men were in custody thirty-three days after they had landed in America.

The pair faced a military tribunal at the historic U.S. Army post on Governor's Island in New York Harbor. From where both men sat, they could see from a window the Statue of Liberty. The slack-chinned Colepaugh begged understanding of the court. He only worked for Germany because his life at home was so miserable, he whined. He admitted that his life in Germany had also been miserable. Gimpel, ever the hard-spirited Nazi, said nothing. The court then returned its verdict: Death by hanging. President Harry Truman, who assumed the presidency after Roosevelt's death, commuted the sentences to life imprisonment in 1945, a short time before both men were to go to the gallows. They were later released and were heard of no more.

[ALSO SEE: *Abwehr; Wilhelm Canaris; FBI*]

GISKES, HERMANN J.
German Spymaster ▪ (1896– ?)

BORN IN THE RHINELAND, GISKES WAS RAISED A Catholic. He joined the German Army during World War I and served in the Alpine Corps. Following the war, he actively fought attempted coups by Communists to take over the government. From 1924 to 1934, Giskes was a successful wine salesman, but he returned to the army in 1934, accepting a commission.

By 1937, Giskes had joined the Abwehr, and was considered to have the talents of a spymaster. The following year he was sent to The Hague in Holland, which was swarming with spies from all the major powers. Giskes concentrated on breaking the strong British network that had been built up for more than twenty years by SIS.

Of particular interest to Giskes was the mysterious death of Captain Hugh Reginald Dalton, the brilliant SIS chief in Holland who operated the most effective spy ring in Europe. Dalton had blown out his brains in his villa outside The Hague on September 4, 1936. It was several months before Giskes learned that Dalton had been siphoning off money from an SIS slush fund. When discovered by a subordinate, he killed himself rather than pay the blackmail demanded by the assistant.

Who was the subordinate, Giskes wanted to know. The SIS knew it was John William "Jack" Hooper, a naturalized British citizen who had been born in Holland. SIS spymaster Claude Dansey wanted to have Hooper murdered and his body dumped into a canal but he was overruled by calmer heads. Hooper, who had admitted that he had demanded a share of the money Dalton had been filching, was told by SIS that he was no longer in their employ. He vanished. Then Dansey and other SIS chiefs thought better of having Hooper wander about Holland where Abwehr agents might pick him up.

The SIS began to search for Hooper but Giskes got to him first. Hooper quickly confessed his background with SIS to Giskes, and cheerfully accepted money to work for the Abwehr by informing on the dozens of British spies in Holland, Belgium and Germany. Giskes bought everything he could from Hooper but, by April 1939, the Abwehr counterintelligence chief concluded that Hooper had no more to give him. He told Hooper that the Abwehr no longer required his services.

Then Hooper played his last card, telling Giskes that he knew the identity of the ace agent of the SIS in Germany, a respected naval engineer who had worked for British intelligence for twenty years and was still England's top spy in Europe. Giskes was so impressed that he offered a princely sum of 10,000 guilders sterling to Hooper for that identity. Hooper then promptly gave away Dr. Otto Krueger, who had been recruited by the SIS in 1919 in Hamburg.

Krueger had served in the German Navy during World War I, and was unemployed and vague about his future when he was approached by British agents to work for SIS. He accepted and went on the SIS payroll, remaining there for the next twenty years. During that time Krueger, a naval engineer, grew wealthy with a private business that saw lucrative contracts with the Reichsmarine. He was in the unique position of reviewing almost all of the German Navy's top secrets.

Soon Giskes had a full dossier on Krueger who was one of Germany's most respected naval engineers. He had been elected to the board of directors of the powerful Federation of German Industries. He held honorary degrees from the most esteemed engineering institutes in Germany. Giskes assigned a half dozen of his best Abwehr agents to shadow Krueger night and day.

In late June 1939, Giskes' efforts were rewarded. Krueger went to Hamburg where he visited the Blohm and Voss Shipyards. He also stopped by the German Naval Station to see old navy friends and to confer with them about new armaments for German battle cruisers. Then he journeyed to The Hague where his every movement was recorded by Abwehr counterspies. On some occasions, Giskes himself took to shadowing the prim and proper Dr. Krueger. All seemed above board.

Krueger checked into a hotel and remained in his room every day, all day. He could be heard tapping on a rented typewriter for many hours each day. A waiter who served Krueger was one of Giskes' men and, when Krueger was out of the room in the evening, he searched the room but found nothing, no scribbled notes, no reports. "He keeps it all in his head," Giskes concluded. He was correct in this assumption. Krueger committed everything he saw to a photographic memory, then typed out carefully what he had seen and turned over almost every major secret of the German Navy to SIS. This had been his meticulous espionage procedure for two decades.

On his first evening at The Hague, Krueger, at nine thirty, left the restaurant and was driven to a seaside villa outside of Scheveningen. He had left the villa a little after midnight and was driven back to his hotel.

Who owned the villa, Giskes asked. His agents replied that its owner was a wealthy Belgian, August de Fremery. No information could be produced on this mystery man. Giskes and Traugott Protze, another Abwehr chief, racked their brains and searched their files but they could find nothing. Then Protze talked with Folkert Arie Van Koutrik, who had been a British spy and had gone over to the Nazis.

Koutrik recognized the name of the villa owner immediately. "Of course, it's Hendricks." The rich Belgian was none other than Captain Jan Hendricks, known as "John" to his confederates, one of the top British agents for SIS. Hendricks had been second-in-command under the tragic Captain Dalton and he was now the top SIS spymaster in Holland. On July 7, 1939, Krueger returned to Hamburg and was promptly arrested. He confessed everything and was thrown into a concentration camp from which he did not emerge.

Giskes had scored his first major counterespionage coup for the Abwehr. His next would occur in 1942–1943 in a plan of his own invention that he entitled Operation North Pole. In late 1941 Giskes learned that SOE had sent teams of agents into Holland by parachute. One of the first agents dropped into the Dutch country-side was a radio operator named Hubertus Lauwers, who moved into an apartment in a suburb of The Hague. Abwehr agents pinpointed the location of the apartment through direction finding and arrested him.

Lauwers followed his SOE training instructions. He was to show some resistance to being converted as a double agent and then agree. He was then to send whatever messages to London as ordered by the Germans but he was to insert a prearranged signal that would indicate that he had been captured, this being a deliberate mistake in every sixteenth word. Lauwers did exactly that in several messages but SOE failed to catch his warning signal. As time passed and Lauwers continued to allow himself to be used by the Abwehr, he realized that SOE was not picking up on his hidden warning signal. In three separate transmissions he managed to slip the word "caught" into his messages. Still SOE failed to get the signal.

Giskes by then had been scooping up SOE agents by the dozens. As they parachuted into Holland, they were met by Abwehr agents posing as Dutch resistance fighters. The Abwehr agents cleverly disarmed the SOE men, telling them that they might run into German patrols and be searched so they would have to disarm. They then told the SOE agents that since London had mixed up some messages and identifications, they needed to know their true identities. The SOE men provided this information and were then taken into custody and thrown into Haarlen Prison.

Meanwhile, Giskes was able to turn some of the foreign-born SOE men to act as double agents and they kept sending messages to London as if the Dutch operations were going smoothly. For almost two years Giskes was able to maintain his grand deception. SOE kept pouring men and equipment into Holland. All fell easily into German hands, including 570 parachuted containers having radio equipment, Sten guns and a half million rounds of ammunition.

Two SOE agents, Peter Dourlein and J. B. Ubbink, managed to escape Haarlen Prison on August 29, 1943, but they did not reach England until December to tell the shocking tale of how the Dutch SOE operations had long been controlled by Giskes and the Abwehr. It would be several months before uncompromised SOE operations were resumed in Holland but there was no way to minimize the enormous setback created by the inventive Giskes in his Operation North Pole, the meaning of which was by then humiliatingly clear to SOE; it had been sending their agents into oblivion.

Giskes had the distinction of being the last Abwehr officer to put into action the final German counterintelligence operation of the war. This was Operation Heinrich, in which forced laborers were allowed to escape to allied lines in 1944, carrying misleading information on German troop movements. The German spymaster was captured by Allied troops in 1945 and was held until 1948, although he was never officially charged with war crimes. He was finally released after Dutch authorities reported that his conduct in their country during World War II was "in accordance with international law and the unwritten laws of humanity."

[ALSO SEE: Abwehr; Claude Dansey; SIS; SOE]

GOLD, HARRY
American Spy for Soviets ■ (1912–1972)

GOLD WAS A KEY CONTACT MAN AND COURIER FOR Soviet espionage in its feverish hunt for information on the atomic bomb during World War II and immediately afterward. His was a pivotal role, and, thanks to a tremendous error on the part of his controlling spymaster, he became the identifiable link to several super spy rings that were unearthed in the U.S. and in England.

Born to Russian-Jewish parents in Bern, Switzerland (original name Golodnotsky), Gold immigrated with his family to the U.S. as a small boy. He attended the University of Pennsylvania, specializing in chemistry. He was a competent scientist whose real interests lay in left-wing politics.

By 1935, as was the case with many radical leftists in the U.S., Gold had become a dedicated Communist, believing that the Soviet system was the only salvation for the common man plagued by the Great Depression. Gold then held important jobs that allowed access to secret industrial information. This he passed on to the Russians. When Nazi Germany invaded Russia in 1941, Gold became one of the most important Soviet spies in America. His role of spy changed in 1944 to that of contact man and courier.

At that time, Anatoli Yakovlev arrived in New York as General Consul for the Soviet legation. He was also the GRU's top spymaster, whose chief assignment was to obtain all of the top-secret information involved with the development of the atomic bomb. He chose Gold to act as the contact man to Klaus Fuchs, a high echelon British scientist working on the Manhattan Project. Gold never knew Fuchs' name nor Fuchs his. For that matter, Gold never knew the true identity of his spymaster; to him Yakovlev was known only as "John."

KGB courier Harry Gold (shown center, shackled in custody), who passed atomic secrets from scientist Klaus Fuchs to Russian spymasters in 1945.

When the two men met for the first time in 1944, Fuchs was carrying a tennis ball and Gold a book with a green cover, the items by which they identified each other. This would be the first of eight meetings between the two men. When Fuchs was assigned to the atomic research center in Los Alamos, New Mexico, Yakovlev directed Gold to go to Santa Fe where he was to remain in contact with the British scientist.

On each occasion, Fuchs gave Gold large packages containing almost every detail on the atomic bomb. So successful was Gold that Yakovlev decided to have him act as a contact man and courier with other Soviet spy rings who were also filching atomic secrets. In making this decision, the Russian spymaster overreached himself and made the fatal error of linking separate spy rings through Gold. Time, however, was a large factor in Yakovlev's decision; the Soviets were demanding all the information on atomic and nuclear reseach and, in an effort to speed up the process of collecting data, he employed his best courier, Gold.

Gold reveled in his role. He would later boast of the key part he played in stealing atomic secrets. He was no longer a cog in the vast machinery of espionage. He was important, vital, necessary. He not only obtained and delivered secrets from Fuchs, but also from Mortin Sobel, who was working on rocket research at General Electric Laboratories, and from David Greenglass, an army machinist at the Los Alamos testing area. From Greenglass, Gold was able to deliver exact drawings, sketches, and blueprints of the atomic bomb.

These networks continued to operate until 1946, a year after the end of World War II. At that time, Fuchs returned to England to continue atomic research. Greenglass was discharged from the U.S. Army. Then, all of Yakovlev's networks slowly unravelled when British intelligence was warned by the FBI that Fuchs was a spy.

By that time, the FBI had already identified Gold and had placed him under surveillance. When Fuchs was shown Gold's photo, he stated: "That is my American contact." This was the same manner in which Gold later identified Fuchs, following his arrest. Gold quickly confessed and named Greenglass, Sobel and the Rosenbergs as his fellow traitors and atomic bomb spies. Although Gold had never met the Rosenbergs, he said he knew about them and his testimony was strong enough to convict Greenglass. That conviction led to the eventual trial and execution of the Rosenbergs.

Gold himself was convicted and given a thirty-year prison sentence. He served almost two thirds of it, being paroled in 1965. Moving back to Philadelphia, Gold died there seven years later, penniless, despised. Of little consolation to Gold was the fact that the Kremlin had awarded him the Order of the Red Star.

[ALSO SEE: *FBI; Klaus Fuchs; David Greenglass; GRU; Julius and Ethel Rosenberg*]

GOLYTSIN, ANATOLI
Soviet Spymaster ▪ (1923–   )

IN DECEMBER 1961, THE STATION CHIEF OF THE CIA in Helsinki, Finland, was suddenly surprised by a visit from a Russian who was accompanied by his wife and child. He announced that he was a major in the First Directorate of the KGB. His espionage target was NATO. With that he announced that he wanted to defect, giving the promise that he could identify hundreds of Soviet agents working in the West.

Golytsin was able to tell CIA officials exactly where NATO information had been leaking. He began by providing a list of KGB agents in Helsinki, promising to identify KGB agents throughout the world. He and his family were taken to the U.S. where James Angleton, head of the CIA's counterintelligence supervised Golytsin's interrogations.

Though Angleton became a Golytsin supporter, others at the CIA believed the Russian was an *agent provocateur* who had been planted to spread disinformation. Much of the distrust emanated from Golytsin's behavior. He was arrogant, quarrelsome, and temperamental. Angleton demanded Golytsin provide proof of his claims. The KGB spymaster then identified three Soviet agents in the U.S. who would begin to spread disinformation about him in an effort to discredit his information. These agents were found by the CIA.

British intelligence agents visited CIA headquarters at Langley, Virginia, to meet with Golytsin and were astonished at the information he provided to them, identifying three top Soviet agents working in England. These agents were also apprehended. Moreover, Golytsin was able to provide information on the notorious British spy Kim Philby that was not then known. The Russian spy visited England to work more closely with MI5 and MI6 but his cover was blown in an article published by the *Daily Telegraph* and, fearing assassination by KGB agents, he immediately returned to the U.S.

[ALSO SEE: *James Angleton; CIA; MI5; MI6; Kim Philby*]

GOTTLIEB, SIDNEY
(Joseph Scheider)
CIA Chemist ▪ (1918–   )

ALTHOUGH HIGHLY RESPECTED AS A CHEMIST AND AN academician, Dr. Sidney Gottlieb was considered by his foes to be a dangerous crackpot who experimented with mind-altering drugs and use of poisons for the purpose of political assassination. To some in the CIA, Gottlieb perfectly fit the stereotype of the mad scientist.

Gottlieb's real name was Joseph Scheider and he was a native of the Bronx. He received his Ph.D. in chemistry from Cal Tech and joined the CIA in 1951, working his way upward through the Technical Services Staff (TSS), until he headed the Chemical Division. The chemist was by then a favorite of Richard Bissell, head of the CIA's "dirty tricks" department. Gottlieb also found a place in the impersonal heart of future CIA director Richard Helms, despite the fact that he was undoubtedly the most eccentric person on the CIA payroll.

Living on a fifteen-acre farm outside of Washington, Gottlieb, as a cover, sold Christmas trees and raised goats. He had an abiding belief that only goat's milk was healthy to drink. He drank it all the time as did his wife and four children. The chemist milked his own goats each day before going to CIA headquarters. He walked with an awkward gait, having a clubfoot. Despite this handicap, Gottlieb was a square-dancing enthusiast.

In addition to the clubfoot, Gottlieb also struggled to overcome another handicap—severe stuttering. Bissell and Helms, however, always seemed to understand and appreciate Gottlieb's often bizarre chemical schemes. In the mid-1950s, he advanced the wild theories that LSD could be used to the CIA's advantage.

Gottlieb was given the green light to go ahead with experiments and to that end, through established foundations working with the CIA, he provided large amounts of money to university laboratories. These labs experimented with LSD, working with volunteers, to see if the drug could be manipulated for CIA purposes. Those purposes were outlined by Gottlieb to labs: "a. Disturbance of Memory; b. Discrediting by Aberrant Behavior; c. Alteration of Sex Patterns; d. Eliciting of Information; e. Suggestability; f. Creation of Dependence."

By the early 1960s Gottlieb was involved in far more serious chemical projects, chiefly the use of poisons by which the CIA could effect the assassination of Third World leaders who were considered a threat to the national security of America. Not the least of these foreign politicians was Fidel Castro. Gottlieb received instructions from Richard Bissell to create a method of poisoning Fidel Castro. The chemist busily inserted poison into Havana cigars Castro was known to smoke and these were sent to the Cuban dictator but apparently never arrived.

Undaunted, Gottlieb tried a poisoned wetsuit, which Castro never wore. He also rigged a conch shell to explode when Castro was swimming underwater and was attracted to it, the dictator being a collector of such shells. The shell was never planted. The chemist also planned to assassinate General Kassem of Iraq by planting a poisoned handkerchief in his suit pocket but this plan also failed.

The planned assassination of African leader Patrice Lumumba, was even more macabre. At the time, Lumumba, a charismatic leftist, was Prime Minster of the Congo (now Zaire). In September 1960, Gottlieb feverishly labored to construct a sort of quick-and-easy assassination package, which included a lethal biological agent that Gottlieb never identified. The chemist went to Fort Detrick in Maryland, where he studied a list provided by the Army Chemical Corps, selecting an agent that would cause tularemia (rabbit fever), brucellosis (undulant fever), anthrax, smallpox, tuberculosis, and Venezuelan equine encephalitis (sleeping sickness). This agent was mixed with toothpaste and placed in a tube that would be slipped into Lumumba's traveling kit, although Gottlieb was uncertain as to whether or not Lumumba actually brushed his teeth.

Along with several other poisoned objects, Gottlieb included in his murder kit rubber gloves, hypodermic needles, and gauze masks. He then got on a plane and flew to Leopoldville where he personally delivered the package to CIA station chief Lawrence Devlin, instrucing him to kill Lumumba. The whole fanatastic scheme never went into action; Lumumba's Congolese enemies did the job for the CIA by murdering him on about January 19, 1961.

Gottlieb's bizarre murder techniques were still being put together by as late as 1973 when Bissell's "dirty tricks" department was exposed. Richard Helms then ordered Gottlieb to destroy all of his records relating to LSD experiments and assassination methods. The loyal chemist destroyed these documents and his years of strange research. He left the agency but later admitted his lethal doings for the CIA when testifying in Washington. As a whole, the career of Dr. Sidney Gottlieb reads like a science fiction tale or as dark a fantasy as portrayed in the black comedy film *Dr. Strangelove*.

[ALSO SEE: *CIA; Richard Bissell; Richard Helms*]

GOUZENKO, IGOR
Soviet Spy in Canada ▪ (1919–)

GOUZENKO WAS NOTABLE IN THAT HE WAS ONE OF the first important Soviet spies to defect just after World War II. His defection is likened by many historians to the real beginning of the Cold War, or the startling revelations he made signaled that beginning. Gouzenko was born outside of Moscow, in Rogachov. His father gave his loyalty to the Czarist forces then known as the White Russians and vanished during Russia's civil war.

Wearing a hood during a 1945 interview shortly after his defection from the Russian Embassy in Ottawa, Canada, is Igor Gouzenko; his were the first important revelations of widespread Soviet networks in the U.S. and Canada.

After attending school in Rostov-on-Don and Verkne Spasskoye, where his widowed mother began teaching school in 1926, Gouzenko joined the Komsomol, the Communist Youth Movement. In 1937-38, he studied art and architecture in Moscow and was recruited by the NKVD (later the KGB) in 1939 as a cipher and code clerk. Following the invasion of Russia by the Nazis in 1941, he saw service in the front lines as an intelligence officer.

Gouzenko served almost two years in the hellish battles for Russia and was suddenly reprieved from the likelihood of death when, in 1943, he was sent to Ottawa, Canada, as a cipher clerk working in the Russian Embassy. In reality, Gouzenko was a lieutenant in the GRU who had been ordered to spy on Canadian officials, as well as send secret messages back to Moscow.

Canada was the first free country Gouzenko ever visited. He was astounded at the amount of liberties granted civilians, so much so that he envied the Canadians and, at the same time, grew to despise the dictatorial Communist regime. By September 5, 1945, Igor Gouzenko had had enough of the GRU. He left Room 12 (cipher and secrets room) of the Soviet Embassy, his briefcase stuffed with files and documents, all of which would prove the existence of a large Soviet spy ring operating throughout Canada.

The first place Gouzenko went to was the offices of an Ottawa newspaper. Editors listened to his story, looked at some of his documents, then showed him the door. They could not believe the tale. This was still an era in which Russia was perceived by the West to be a staunch ally which had helped win World War II.

Gouzenko returned home to his wife and small son. He realized that it would only be hours before the files were found missing. Soviet strongarm men would be looking for him and his family. Frantically, he made the rounds of government departments the next day, but he was dismissed as either a crank or a lunatic. He went back to the newspaper and he was again rebuffed.

That night Gouzenko and his wife and child remained locked inside their small apartment, the lights off. A knock was heard at the door. The occupants did not answer. A man on the other side of the door called out Gouzenko's name. The defector recognized the voice as the chauffeur from the Embassy. He did not answer and, finally, the caller went away.

Desperate, Gouzenko went outside on his balcony which faced that of the adjoining apartment. He signaled to his neighbor, Sergeant Main of the Royal Canadian Air Force, that he needed to talk to him. Main listened as Gouzenko told him that he was frightened for his wife and boy. He explained what he had done and begged for help. Main gave it to him, insisting that the Gouzenkos stay in his apartment that night. The next day, Main arranged for the Gouzenkos to move to another apartment while he contacted police.

Two officers interviewed Gouzenko and told him that they would keep the apartment complex under surveillance in case the Soviets showed up. They did. Close to midnight, Main heard the sound of banging in the hall. He stepped outside to see four men breaking down the door to the Gouzenko apartment. Main ran to a window and gave a signal to a policeman waiting below. Officers rushed upstairs to find the four men wildly ransacking the Gouzenko apartment.

Police detained the men, asking for their papers. They handed over passports that identified them as employees of the Soviet Embassy. They said they had the permission of a fellow Russian to enter the apartment to retrieve some important papers. The officers called in an inspector who looked over the suspects and then ordered them to remain on the premises while he contacted his superiors. When the inspector left, the four men brushed aside the dumbfounded policemen and departed.

The next day, September 8, the Soviet Embassy contacted the Canadian Department for External Affairs to complain about how their employees had been treated, how the Ottawa police had ignored their diplomatic immunity. Soviet officials then demanded that Gouzenko, whom they described as a "capital criminal," had stolen funds from the Embassy and that they wanted him arrested and turned over to them so he could be taken to Moscow for trial.

The Royal Mounted Police then entered the picture. Gouzenko, a day earlier, had contacted the Mounties and had left several documents with them. These papers were examined and inspectors soon realized that Gouzenko was not a crank but a genuine defecting Soviet agent. The papers were described as detailing "the largest and most dangerous spy-plot known in the Dominion in peace or war."

Gouzenko and his family were given sanctuary in Canada and put under protective custody. His documents included a great deal of index cards listing scores of Soviet agents, with anecdotal information on all of them, notes that read "is afraid," and "takes money." The defector had also taken a goodly number of pages from the casebook of the Soviet spymaster in Ottawa, Colonel Nicolai Zabotin. Canadian officials were stunned. The Prime Minister immediately notified President Harry Truman in the U.S. and Prime Minister Clement Atlee in England.

Sweeping arrests were made in Canada, especially of those who were in the Canadian Communist Party and were serving as outright spies. Other agents were Communist sympathizers such as Fred Rose, who was a member of the Canadian Parliament, and Sam Carr. Gouzenko's information exposed the British nuclear scientist Dr. Alan Nunn May, who was arrested as a Communist spy. The domino theory became reality. May's arrest led to Klaus Fuch's arrest and confession. That exposure led to an unraveling of a vast number of American Communists who had helped steal the atomic bomb secrets for the Soviets—Harry Gold, David Greenglass, Julius and Ethel Rosenberg.

What shocked the innocent West at the time was that Gouzenko's information proved that Soviet Russia controlled the Communist parties throughout the Western World and used them as espionage agencies. The Soviets presented a stony silence to it all. They immediately ordered all espionage links to Communist parties and memberships to be severed.

Gouzenko spoke out from his cover over the years since he first struggled to tell the world about the vast Soviet plot. He condemned British intelligence for not acting sooner on his information in the case of Klaus Fuchs, pointing out that when he first provided his information, Fuchs' name was prominent in the documents yet MI5 waited almost five years to finally arrest Fuchs. He also pointed out that MI5 had been infiltrated by the KGB as early as 1942. At that time, while serving in Moscow's KGB headquarters, Gouzenko remembered, he had been shown by a friend, Lieutenant Lev Lubinov, a recently decoded telegram from London that came from a KGB mole inside MI5.

It was later conjectured that the KGB spy in MI5 was Roger Hollis, later Sir Roger Hollis who had been Director General of MI5 from 1956 to 1965. As late as 1983, Hollis' true role was still being questioned, even by Prime Minister Margaret Thatcher who neither denied nor affirmed the accusation. It was just as difficult to identify many of the spies listed in Gouzenko's original documents when Canadian authorities began their 1945 investigation.

Many of the agents in Canada were simply identified by cover names and it took months to match these names to actual persons. During this time Colonel Zabotin continued his clandestine operations in a secret wing of the Soviet Embassy at 285 Charlotte Street, Ottawa. Only when Soviet agents began to be arrested, did Zabotin close down his operations. He was recalled to Moscow, along with his entire staff. Zabotin was then arrested and sentenced to serve four years in prison at hard labor. He had been convicted of not realizing that he had a malcontent, Gouzenko, working for him.

Gouzenko went into deep cover, still afraid of eventual retaliation by the KGB. He remained securely protected by the very force that first recognized his genuine defection and, fortunately for the world, the authenticity of his documents, the Royal Canadian Mounted Police.

[ALSO SEE: *Klaus Fuchs; Harry Gold; David Greenglass; GRU; Roger Hollis; KGB; Alan Nunn May; MI5; Julius and Ethel Rosenberg*]

GPU
Soviet Intelligence Agency ▪ (1922–1923)

MADE UP FROM THE INITIALS OF THE RUSSIAN words for the State Political Board, the GPU was the successor to the Cheka (1919–1922), the secret police established by the Bolsheviks. With sweeping arrest powers, GPU members were mostly immune to regulations or governmental controls. Unlike the autocratic Cheka, the GPU was somewhat limited in that it could make political and criminal arrests but had to conform to local police procedures.

The GPU was nevertheless as dreaded an organization in Russia as the Gestapo was in Nazi Germany. It practiced widespread intimidation, torture, and the mass murder of anyone opposing Communist dictators Nicolai Lenin and Joseph Stalin. The GPU, which operated as an internal and external espionage agency, later gave way to the OGPU, the NKVD, the MVD, and the KGB.

[ALSO SEE: *Checka; Gestapo; KGB; NKVD; OGPU*]

GRANVILLE, CHRISTINE (KRYSTYNA SKARBEK; AKA: PAULINE ARMAND)
Polish Spy for England in World War II ▪ (1915–1952)

ONE OF THE BRAVEST AND MOST INVENTIVE ALLIED spies in World War II, Christine Granville (born Krystyna Skarbek) became a legend by saving the lives of her fellow agents through sheer nerve and will power. Born in Warsaw and into wealth, Granville was the daughter of Count Jerzy Skarbek, a Polish aristocrat. Her mother was the daughter of a powerful Jewish banker in the Goldfeder family.

Following her education in a Warsaw convent, Granville married a writer named Georg Gizycki in 1938. The couple went to Kenya where her husband was working on a book when the Nazis invaded Poland in 1939. Granville immediately went to London where she was recruited for SOE (Special Operations Executive) by George Taylor, an Australian who helped to develop that organization.

SOE's mission was to work with underground resistance groups opposing the Nazis. To that end, after receiving espionage training, Granville (a cover-

The SOE spy Christine Granville, murdered in 1952; she managed to free British agents from Nazi prisons in WW II through incredible bluff and bravery.

name given to her by SOE), was sent to Budapest and from there to her native Poland. Her mission was to spread propaganda that England had not deserted Poland and would continue its war with Germany. Granville, who had been an excellent skier before the war, made her way with a few friends across the Tatra Mountains into Poland, skiing most of the way.

Granville made contact in Warsaw with Stanislaw Witkowski, head of an independent underground organization working with SIS. Obtaining information from him on German troops occupying Poland, Granville returned to London. She made this arduous trip twice again. On her third trip to Poland, she and others were stopped by guards at the border. Granville managed to throw a rucksack filled with incriminating documents into a river but she could not explain a large amount of money she was carrying.

Boldly, she told the guards: "You have two choices. Either take the money and let us go or turn us and the money over to your superiors." The guards took the money and released Granville and her friends. On her third trip into Poland, Granville was able to smuggle out many Polish men of fighting age

who found their way to London to join the Polish Army in exile, as well as British prisoners of war who had been captured in France in 1940 and had been sent to internment camps in Poland.

Slipping back to then neutral Hungary, Granville took refuge in Budapest but the Nazis had identified her and demanded that Hungarian police turn her over to them. She and an associate were arrested but Granville pointed out that she was related (though distantly) to Admiral Horthy, Regent of Hungary. The Hungarian police released her and her fellow spy. She made her way back to London via Istanbul. With her she brought photos smuggled out of Poland that showed massive German armor along the Polish-Russian border, along with reports that insisted the Germans would soon invade Russia.

This was startling information to all but a select few who already knew of this impending invasion since MI6 had broken the German codes. Granville next parachuted into southern France in 1944, reporting to Colonel Francois Cammaerts, who commanded the *maquis* in the Rhone Valley, an armed force estimated to be more than 10,000 freedom fighters. Granville was used as a courier by Cammaerts, using the cover name of Pauline Armand. She took messages and plans that could not be transmitted by radio to Cairo, repeatedly parachuting back into the Vecors area where Cammaerts and his *maquis* operated.

At one point, Granville crossed the Alps into Italy and persuaded hundreds of Russian and Italian troops to desert their German allies, leading these men into Switzerland. She went back to Italy and this time convinced several hundred men serving in Polish units supporting the Germans to desert. On both occasions, she was detained by German guards when crossing the border. Granville, an excellent actress, convinced them on the first occasion that she was nothing more than a peasant girl visiting relatives and she was permitted to pass. When she was stopped by two German soldiers the second time, she raised and opened her hands, revealing two grenades, one in each hand. The Germans fled.

Granville then heard that Cammaerts, along with a British agent, Xan Fielding, and a French Major named Sorensen had been arrested at Digne and placed in the local prison, all of whom were correctly suspected of being Allied spies. She immediately went to Digne where she reportedly convinced the Nazi prison commandant that the Allies were not far from the prison and if her friends were not released, the commandant would be shot by the invading Americans, a threat that caused the release of the prisoners. This story is apocryphal.

The truth is that Granville met with two high-placed Digne officials, Albert Schenck, an Alsatian, and Max Waem, a Belgian, who served as liaison officers between the French prefecture and the German SD (*Sicherheitsdienst*), who controlled the Digne prison. She told them that she was

General Montgomery's niece (using the same important ploy she had successfully used in Hungary), and that she was willing to pay the price for the release of her friends. Moreover, she warned, when the Allies won the war, they would be looking for collaborators to punish, men exactly like Schenck and Waem.

Brazen though Granville was, she was on dangerous ground. Schenck and Waem could have simply ordered her shot immediately by their Nazi associates. Instead, the two officials demanded that she write out a statement that they had helped her release the British agents, which she did. They then demanded a payment of two million francs. Granville contacted London and the money was dropped by parachute the next night.

The following night, Cammaerts, Fielding, and Sorensen were roughly dragged out of their cells and marched out of the Digne prison. All three men believed they were about to be shot. Instead they were taken to a car waiting near the prison and shoved into the back seat. Christine Granville was behind the wheel, smiling triumphantly. She paused to give her startled fellow spies some brandy and cigarettes and then drove them to freedom.

At the end of the war, Granville was stranded in Cairo. SOE abandoned her and she managed to borrow enough funds to reach London where she held a variety of jobs, operating a switchboard at India House, then selling dresses at Harrods. Then, in 1951, she got a job as a stewardess on board the liner, *Winchester Castle*, sailing between England and South Africa and Australia. Her superior was a steward, 41-year-old Dennis George Muldowney, a small strange little man afflicted with schizophrenia.

Muldowney became passionately enamored of Granville, following her about, begging her attention. She rebuffed him politely. Muldowney pestered her to the point where Granville quit her job, moving back to London, living in a small hotel in Kensington. Muldowney, to be near her, quit his job and took a job as a porter at the Reform Club in Westminster. He repeatedly called on Granville who finally ordered him to leave her alone and never again attempt to see her.

On the evening of June 15, 1952, Muldowney went to Granville's hotel and when he spotted her walking down the stairs and entering the hotel foyer, he grabbed her. "Get him off of me!" Granville cried out. A hotel porter came running but was too late. The 37-year-old Granville lay dead, stabbed through the heart.

Muldowney was arrested and tried at the Old Bailey before Justice Terence Donovan on September 10, 1952. He entered a plea of guilty, even though he knew the consequences. Sentenced to death, Mudlowney was hanged at Pentonville Prison on September 30, 1952. His victim was by then in her grave. Buried in the coffin with Christine Granville, valiant and indefatigable spy, were the medals she had so well earned in World War II—the French Croix de Guerre and from Great Britain, the George Medal for Special Services and the Order of the British Empire.

[ALSO SEE: *SIS, SOE*]

GREENGLASS, DAVID
U.S. Spy for Soviets ▪ (1922–)

DAVID GREENGLASS IS THE PIVOTAL FIGURE OVER which still rages the argument concerning the guilt of Julius and Ethel Rosenberg, convicted U.S. traitors and Soviet spies who were executed for their treason and espionage. It was Greenglass' testimony that sent his sister Ethel and her husband Julius to the executioner.

Born in New York, as was his sister Ethel, Greenglass was a rather lackadaisical student. In his late teens, he joined the Young Communist League where he met his future wife Ruth. He attended the Polytechnic Institute of Brooklyn where he failed his courses. He half-heartedly attempted to make up his courses through night classes at the Pratt Institute and then went into the U.S. Army in 1943.

David Greenglass, who turned over atomic secrets to the Russians through his relatives, Ethel and Julius Rosenberg; his testimony later helped send the Rosenbergs to the death chamber.

Greenglass received technical training and received various assignments as a machinist of only mediocre talents. In 1944, he was inexplicably sent to Los Alamos to work on the Manhattan Project, the development of the atomic bomb. This was fortuitous for Julius Rosenberg, who headed up a Soviet spy ring that was controlled by Anatoli Yakovlev, the Soviet General Consul in the New York legation.

According to several reports, Rosenberg had, before World War II, recruited his brother-in-law Greenglass, as a Soviet spy and when he learned of his Los Alamos posting, he instructed Greenglass to obtain all the information he could on the atomic bomb, telling the rather naive Greenglass that it was only fair that this top U.S. secret be shared with America's then ally, Soviet Russia.

Yakovlev then arranged for Harry Gold, a Communist courier, to meet several times with Greenglass in New Mexico to retrieve nuclear secrets stolen by the machinist. Although they both claimed that they never knew each other's name, Gold and Greenglass identified each other by matching the halves of a Jell-O box (raspberry flavor), a tactic designed by Julius Rosenberg. Greenglass later stated that he also used his wife Ruth as a courier, giving her secrets that she took to the Rosenbergs, who, in turn, delivered them to Yakovlev.

The last packet of secrets Greenglass delivered to Gold included a rough sketch of the plutonium bomb later dropped at Nagasaki, as well as details of its trigger mechanism. In 1946, Greenglass was honorably discharged from the Army. He went into business with Julius Rosenberg but the partnership split apart in 1949, due to quarrels. These arguments, for the most part, Greenglass later insisted, were centered about Rosenberg's insistence that Greenglass continue to spy for the Soviets.

Greenglass, full of remorse and extremely fearful of being apprehended, now that the Cold War between the West and Russia was a grim reality, told Rosenberg that he would no longer spy for Russia. A short time later, the British Communist scientist Klaus Fuchs was arrested as a Soviet agent, admitting that he had turned over atomic bomb secrets to a pudgy-faced man addicted to wearing pin-stripe suits. He did not know this man's name but identified his photo when it was shown to him. The Soviet courier was Harry Gold.

When Gold was arrested, he, in turn, confessed and named Greenglass as another Soviet spy from whom he had collected secret data on the atomic bomb. (Yakovlev had committed the cardinal espionage sin of using the same courier to link separate spy rings he was controlling, and thus establish for counterintelligence an identifiable chain of spies.) When Greenglass was arrested, he identified the Rosenbergs.

Greenglass gave evidence against Julius and Ethel Rosenberg, telling the jury in their case that he was with them when they learned that Harry Gold had been arrested. Julius Rosenberg and Greenglass' sister, Ethel, told him: "You'll be next!" They gave him $1,000 and told him to flee with his wife to Mexico. The jury believed Greenglass and convicted the Rosenbergs who were later executed.

Critics of the Rosenberg trial have pointed out that Greenglass perjured himself to save his own life and that of his wife, that he cut a deal with the FBI before the trial and before he received his own sentence, and that only ten days before the Rosenbergs were tried, he provided new, more strongly damaging evidence against his own sister, Ethel. Greenglass was sentenced to fifteen years in prison. His wife was set free.

After serving ten years of his sentence, Greenglass was released. In an interview at that time, Greenglass told newsmen that it would be reasonable to protect a wife rather than a sister. To escape the wrath of those who still charged that he had bargained away his own flesh and blood to save his life, Greenglass changed his name and vanished.

[ALSO SEE: *Klaus Fuchs; Harry Gold; Julius and Ethel Rosenberg*]

GREENHOW, ROSE O'NEALE
Confederate Spymaster in Civil War ▪ (1817–1864)

O F ALL THE FEMALE SPIES IN THE AMERICAN CIVIL War, Confederate agent Rose Greenhow stands out as the most spectacular and the most effective. She was one of the most beautiful women of her era, courted by important politicians of Washington, and befriended by a future president. Her high social position gave her access to the country's most guarded secrets, information that allowed Confederate generals to win many of the early battles of the war.

Born Rose O'Neale in Montgomery County, Maryland, she was raised in the genteel tradition of the Old South, taught all the social etiquette required of female southern aristocrats. In her teens, already a breathtaking beauty, Greenhow was placed with a maiden aunt, a Miss Hill, who operated the exclusive Congressional Boarding House in Washington. She was soon the center of attention by young men and old at receptions, balls, political fetes, and dinners. Her sister, Ellen Elizabeth O'Neale, married Dolly Madison's nephew, James Madison Cutts.

So strikingly beautiful was Greenhow that she was the source of endless gossip by Washington women much less her physical equal. Her beauty was striking. Fair-skinned, Greenhow had jet black hair, dark eyes, and strong facial features. She was tall, graceful, and always knew exactly what to say and when to say it. One of her most ardent admirers was Cave Johnson who was later to become postmaster general for President Polk. He and many others deluged Greenhow with flowers, dinners, carriage rides, and endless attention but, in 1835, the belle of Washington married a quiet physician and historian, Dr. Robert Greenhow, who worked in the State Department.

Through her husband, Greenhow came to meet the leading southern politicians of the day, R. M. T. Hunter, the leading politician of Virginia; the fiery John C. Calhoun who taught her his philosophy of State's Rights; South Carolina's Robert Barnwell Rhett, the leading advocate for secession; and Jefferson Davis, who was to become the first and only president of the Confederate States of America.

Calhoun later hired Greenhow's husband to run some of his newspapers, in Petersburg, Virginia, later in Richmond. These papers were really powerful propaganda organs for Calhoun's State's Rights issue. By the time America verged on civil war, Rose Greenhow was an entrenched southern patriot, a matronly mother of two children who still set male hearts beating wildly. A Washington general described her at this time as "famous for her beauty, brilliance of conversation, aptitude for intrigue and regal bearing." One of those smitten by Greenhow was Pennsylvania Senator James Buchanan who was to become President and continue writing to Greenhow, signing his letters "your ancient and devoted friend."

In 1857, Greenhow and her two daughters accompanied her husband on a trip to California on State Department business. Dr. Greenhow accidentally fell down a grating and was killed by the fall. Greenhow sued the city of San Francisco and was awarded a large sum of money. She returned to Washington wearing a mourning dress, and she would continue to wear black until the day of her death. Further tragedy visited Greenhow when her daughter Gertrude died of an illness, leaving her alone with her daughter Rose.

The widow was again courted by dozens of admirers who visited her two-story, richly appointed house. One who came most regularly was James Buchanan, who was by then President. Greenhow was often the President's guest for dinners and gay balls and she was described at this time by the New York *Herald* as "The queen of Buchanan's rose-water administration."

As the country moved toward war, Greenhow continued to host parties for both southern and northern politicians, but she made her views clear, that she was a southerner first, last, and always. In March 1861, southern soldiers were leaving their northern posts, preparing to join the Confederacy. Greenhow's good friend General P.G.T. Beauregard, a Creole from Louisiana, resigned his position as superintendent of West Point. Hundreds more did the same, including a young lieutenant from Virginia named Thomas Jordan.

Union troops running pell-mell before advancing Confederate troops at the Battle of Bull Run; the resounding southern victory was due to information supplied by Rose Greenhow, one of Washington's high society belles.

Jordan knew that Greenhow was probably the best-placed southerner in Washington and, after meeting with her, he proposed that she spy for the Confederacy, acting on behalf of General Beauregard. She accepted. She was to address all her secret correspondence to Jordan who assumed a cover name of Rayford with a Richmond, Virginia, address. Jordan, a handsome, dashing officer, also recruited another Washington socialite, Mrs. Augusta Heath Morris, to enlist in the cause of the South as an agent. She was to serve as one of Greenhow's couriers.

After the South fired on Union-held Fort Sumter in Charleston, South Carolina bay (the first shot was reportedly fired by Beauregard himself), Greenhow was instructed to learn the battle plans of the Union Army. In early July 1861, she did exactly that, getting the battle order and marching routes of the Union Army as planned by its commander, General Irwin McDowell. Exactly how Greenhow obtained this

The Confederacy's most daring and accomplished espionage agent, Rose O'Neale Greenhow, shown in custody with her daughter; she would later drown while trying to get information to Jefferson Davis from a storm-tossed ship off the North Carolina coast in 1864.

Beauregard ordered Fairfax Court House abandoned by Confederate troops and sent a request for General Joseph E. Johnston at Harper's Ferry to reinforce his troops, which were already digging in at Manassas, which the North called Bull Run. When McDowell's overconfident troops reached Bull Run, they were met by Beauregard and, a little while later, Johnston, who sent his 20,000 troops by rail to support the Creole general.

The Union Army was all but destroyed, its panicking survivors fleeing for their lives as victorious Confederate troops gave hot pursuit. The rout of McDowell's men streamed back across the Potomac and to Washington. The Union defeat was complete and Beauregard immediately acknowledged in a ciphered message to Greenhow that she deserved much of the credit for the Confederate victory.

On August 11, 1861, she was able to send Jordan a report several pages long, detailing the complete Washington defense system. Every fort in the Washington area was described in detail by Greenhow, along with the number of guns, their caliber and range; weakspots in the earthworks; regiments identified by state origin and their strengths; the level of troop morale; number of officers and their experience; the political beliefs of the officers; the number of muskets issued to each regiment and the number of shots and grape issued for each weapon; the number of mules for freight-hauling available and the condition of the animals; itemized lists of wagons, ambulances, and stores for each fort. This was the kind of information that won battles and the southern officers looking over Greenhow's reports knew it.

McDowell, in disgrace after the battle of Bull Run, had been replaced by General George McClellan, a stickler for organization. He rebuilt the Army of the Potomac into a huge fighting force. Aware that information had been leaked from Washington to the Confederates, McClellan intended to put a stop to any effective espionage by recruiting Allan Pinkerton, of the famous Pinkerton Detective Agency, as his spymaster and head of the newly established Secret Service.

Pinkerton was no cavalier who would shun suspicions of a lady. He soon realized that Rose Greenhow was probably the top Confederate spy in Washington. He ordered his agents to watch her night and day, trail her wherever she might go. Pinkerton himself undertook to trap the lady spy. On the night of August 21, 1861, Pinkerton, accompanied by three of his top men, William Ascot, Sam Bridgman and Pryce Lewis went to Greenhow's house on Sixteenth Street. (Lewis would later be condemned as a spy by the Confederates and who would, to save his life, betray Pinkerton's finest agent, Timothy Webster.)

The four men stood in the doorway of St. John's Church, watching the house during a thunderstorm. When Pinkerton saw a lamp lit in the parlor, he and his men moved across the street, standing in some

priceless information was not revealed until some years later. She got it from Senator Henry Wilson, of Massachusetts, who chaired the Committee on Military Affairs. Wilson, a long-time dinner guest at the Greenhow home, had provided the plans after his hostess expressed an interest in government plans to "defeat the rebels."

This plan was sent in detail to General Beauregard, delivered to his Virginia headquarters by Betty Duval, the daughter of a Washington socialite and friend of Mrs. Greenhow. Betty Duval had hidden the plans in her long tresses. When it was delivered to Jordan, Beauregard's adjutant, he was delighted to read Greenhow's confident words: "McDowell with 55,000 men will advance this day from Arlington Heights and Alexandria on to Manassas via Fairfax Court House and on to Centreville."

high bushes beneath a parlor window, dripping in the sheeting rain. Pinkerton took off his boots and climbed onto the shoulders of Lewis and Bridgman, peeking into the window. He watched Mrs. Greenhow as she sat on a sofa reading a book. Then the agents heard the sound of approaching footsteps. Pinkerton dropped down and the men hid in the bushes, watching a young Union officer go into the house.

Pinkerton, again standing on the shoulders of his men, saw Greenhow warmly greet the officer and, according to his later report, take from him a military map. He heard the officer describe in precise detail the strength of each fortification shown on the map. (The spymaster later stated that his "blood boiled with indignation" at the sight and sound of this treason.) He watched as Mrs. Greenhow led the young officer to another room. They returned about an hour later "arm and arm." There was no doubt, if Pinkerton's report was to be believed, that the handsome widow had performed a sexual tryst with the officer in return for his delivery of the vital map.

The officer was escorted to the front door by Greenhow while the agents hid crouching in the bushes. Pinkerton later stated that he heard what "sounded like a kiss." Then, as the officer left, Pinkerton told Lewis and Bridgman to watch the house while he and Ascot went after the traitor. The officer suddenly realized that two men were behind him and he broke into a run, Ascot and the bootless Pinkerton racing after him. Ascot fell down and Pinkerton slipped and splashed his way through the muddy road, struggling to keep up with the young officer.

Both agents trailed the officer to his military quarters but were stopped from entering by a guard. When they insisted upon being admitted, Pinkerton and Ascot were arrested and thrown into jail. The head of the Secret Service refused to identify himself but he did send a note to Thomas Scott, Assistant Secretary of War, who arrived at the jail a short time later and arranged for the release of Pinkerton and Ascot.

There was some confusion as to the identity of the Union officer who had turned over the map to Greenhow. His name was purposely distorted by Pinkerton, it appears, so that he could keep this man under surveillance. The officer, who was later arrested by Pinkerton and thrown into prison where he committed suicide on December 3, 1862, was Captain John Elwood of the Fifth Infantry.

Pinkerton took his time in arresting Mrs. Greenhow. On August 23, 1861, he surrounded her house with a bevy of agents but he still did not move. Mrs. Greenhow left her home at 4 P.M. to take her usual afternoon promenade and two agents followed her at a discreet distance. She knew that she was being followed but she intended to keep a rendezvous with one of her couriers, a female Washington socialite, so that she could pass on the warning she had received from General Beauregard two days

earlier, that she and many others were on Pinkerton's "prescribed list" of espionage suspects and would be arrested "at any moment."

The fact that Rose Greenhow did not flee to Richmond but chose to remain in Washington to alert her fellow agents and thus risk capture attests to her dedication to the southern cause. She had already managed to warn William Preston, the Union's Ambassador to Spain, who was then in Washington. Preston promptly slipped through the Union lines and reached the safety of Richmond. A friend in the diplomatic corps met Greenhow during her walk and she allowed him to escort her to a friend's house where "a child was ill."

Upon her return walk home, Greenhow met with her courier. The females appeared to be chatting innocently. The agent, however, handed Mrs. Greenhow a slip of paper with a ciphered message on it. The spy then appeared to cough and raised her hand to her mouth, popping the paper inside and swallowing it. The agent told Greenhow that her house was surrounded and that two Union agents were waiting at her front door to arrest her.

With great presence of mind, Greenhow told the agent to wait on the corner across from her house. "When you see me raise my handkerchief," she said, "it will be a signal that I have been arrested. Inform the others."

The agent nodded, walked across the street to the corner, and waited. Greenhow then walked to her house and up the stairs to the entrance where she was met by Allan Pinkerton and one his agents.

"Are you Mrs. Greenhow?" Pinkerton asked formally, even though he knew who she was.

"Yes," she responded. "And who are you?"

Pinkerton's voice was calm: "I have come to arrest you, ma'am."

"By whose authority, sir?" Mrs. Greenhow replied, head held high.

"We have sufficient authority, ma'am." Pinkerton told her.

"Produce your warrant," she demanded.

Pinkerton grew red faced and angry at her regal attitude. "My warrant is the Secretary of State and the War Department!"

With that, Mrs. Greenhow raised her handkerchief to her lips, the signal to her agent, and opened the door, going inside. The agent saw the signal and hurried away to warn the others in the Greenhow ring. Pinkerton followed her inside after giving a wave to his men who "swarmed into the house like bees into a hive," Greenhow later reported.

They began searching everywhere for incriminating evidence. Some of them merely grabbed what they thought to be valuable and pocketed the items. Mrs. Greenhow demanded that they replace lace doilies and expensive bric-a-brac. At that moment, her precocious eight-year-old daughter Rose, hearing the news, ran through the hall, then outside where she escaped the clutches of agents, screaming at the top of her voice: "Mama has been arrested! Mama has been arrested!"

Little Rose then climbed a tree in front of the residence and shouted the same litany to startled passersby: "Mama's been arrested! Mama's been arrested!" It took two agents to climb the tree after her and bring her down, then carry her kicking and screaming back into the house.

At that moment, Lily Mackall, one of Greenhow's agents, appeared at the front door. She had not been warned to stay away and when she entered she was promptly put under arrest. She explained that she was merely making a social call but Pinkerton told her that she would be detained until he and his men determined that she was not part of "this nest of spies." As the agents tore the house apart, rummaging through closets, drawers, looking under beds, into hat boxes, behind wall pictures, the two women slowly, carefully walked about the place. Greenhow and Mackall picked up several pieces of paper, including a blotter that had part of Greenhow's encrypted messages on it, and secreted these in their bosoms or in their stockings.

The agents nevertheless were able to find a huge amount of documents that certainly evidenced Mrs. Greenhow's espionage operation, all of which later wound up in a large steel box in the National Archives, marked "Civil War Papers, 1861–65; Greenhow. Captured Correspondence." Many letters and notes had been torn up and were later pieced together. They showed Mrs. Rose Greenhow to be a woman of far-reaching influence and power. They came from presidents, senators, congressmen, members of cabinets, ambassadors, judges, generals, admirals, and officers of all ranks. There were letters from blockade runners and spies, adventurers and outright lunatics.

The most damaging were scraps of paper that, once pieced together, proved that Rose Greenhow controlled more than fifty spies, most of them women, in five states, some stationed as far as Texas. Information was found on many Union military installations, and the disposition of regiments, brigades, even divisions, as current as a week before her arrest.

A great deal of correspondence was made up of loveletters from ardent admirers. Several of these were Rose Greenhow's actual lovers. The woman had been conducting simultaneous affairs with a half dozen high-placed men, somehow juggling her schedules to tryst with them, sometimes a male visitor each night for a month, sometimes two males visitors in the same night, at different hours. It appeared that the widow's sexual commitment to the South was unbounding and tireless, although many of her lovers were swains who loved her from afar.

Mrs. Greenhow was kept a prisoner in her home, which had been labelled "a clearing house for spies," for a week. This was not an era in which ladies of refinement were sent to jails and placed into cells.

The government was in a quandry about what to do with her. Her home was officially made her prison by government decree on August 30, 1861.

By this time, Union soldiers under the command of a lieutenant, were ordered to guard the house. The young officer in command was soon smitten by Mrs. Greenhow and gladly ran errands for her, buying her groceries and flowers. One by one, those of Mrs. Greenhow's couriers and agents who had not been warned or had not fled, were rounded up and imprisoned in Mrs. Greenhow's house. These included Miss Mackall, Mrs. Augusta Heath Morris, and Mrs. Philip Phillips, wife of a former senator from Alabama, her two daughters, and her sister, Mrs. A. Levy.

The reason why Mrs. Greenhow and her agents were being handled so delicately was obvious. The Confederate spymaster had tremendous political connections, not the least of which was her brother-in-law, James Madison Cutts, second comptroller of the Treasury; his son, James Madison Cutts Jr. was a highly-placed Washington attorney, and also an aide to General Ambrose Burnside; another relative by marriage who was the adjutant to General H.W. Halleck; almost all of the influencial women in Washington were Mrs. Greenhow's close friends and these included the very wives of the men who found it next to impossible to prosecute her. These politicians and diplomats held high offices in Lincoln's cabinet and they secretly pressured Pinkerton and his superiors to release Greenhow and her agents, fearing, no doubt, that they might be implicated in her espionage.

As weeks dragged by, Greenhow became an even greater celebrity. Articles appeared in northern magazines and newspapers that praised her wit and beauty. *The National Republican* called her "the beautiful Rebel of Sixteenth Street . . . the fascinating female spy . . ." Additional guards had to be ordered to control the large crowds that gathered each day outside the Greenhow residence to silently stare at the upper windows of the house, expectantly waiting to see Greenhow appear.

When guards discovered a Confederate plot to free Greenhow, the government acted, ordering her and her daughter from her house and to quarters at the Old Capitol Prison. Mrs. Greenhow's new confines were anything but comfortable. The sprawling red brick Old Capitol Prison was in terrible condition when Greenhow entered its forboding walls. Dust was everywhere. The walls had rotted out and it was alive with vermin and rats. Its window panes were broken and wooden slats had been nailed across missing windows. Inside its dank cells languished Union deserters, Confederate soldiers and spies, contraband and blockade runners, crooked contractors, and common criminals. Food consisted of half-cooked rice, fatty pork, and moldy beans, all of it swimming in tepid grease.

Superintendent William P. Wood welcomed the

famous spy, escorting her and her daughter to a small room on the second floor. It had a single window that overlooked a dreary courtyard. A high board fence blocked any view to the street. Secretary of State Seward had personally selected this room for Greenhow to make sure that she could not signal to anyone in the street. Inside the room was a bed, chair, sewing machine, and a looking glass. Mrs. Greenhow was allowed to keep her pistol but Wood made sure she had no bullets. The reason for this was never explained but it was assumed that should she be sexually molested by any of the unruly guards, she would have, at least, the empty pistol to wave as a warning.

Through five bitter months, Mrs. Greenhow warred with prison officials. Her female agents who had also been confined at the prison, were released one by one, no charges ever having been brought against them. Their confinement, like Greenhow's, however, had been sustained by the lack of the sacred writ of habeas corpus, suspended by President Lincoln's order. Incredibly, Rose Greenhow still managed to send encrypted messages to Richmond, usually through bribed guards or departing prisoners but her information was shallow.

While Greenhow and her daughter continued to wait in the prison, petitions asking that she be released crossed Seward's and Stanton's desk almost every day. They were ignored. Mrs. Greenhow's spirit was not broken. She made her stay a nightmare for Superintendent Wood.

Washington officials, some time in April 1862, agreed that Mrs. Greenhow should be released, although General McClellan insisted that she be detained until the war ended. He wrote to Pinkerton: "She knows my plans better than Lincoln." At the end of May, however, Seward, Stanton and others had had enough of the fiery spy. She was told to pack up her belongings, that she and her child would be taken to Fortress Monroe and from there be sent to Richmond. She was escorted from the prison by a military guard of honor and taken to the Washington train depot where thousands had gathered to cheer her.

Men removed their hats and women wept as the grand Confederate spy of Washington sailed away. In the salon, the captain of the ship appeared to offer Mrs. Greenhow champagne and sandwiches. As the Union captain turned politely away, she loudly toasted Jefferson Davis and the Confederacy.

On June 6, 1862, Mrs. Greenhow and her daughter arrived in Richmond to wildly cheering crowds. She withdrew from her bosom a large Confederate flag she had sewn in prison and she displayed this throughout the triumphant parade. She was greeted by General Winder and that night she dined with President Jefferson Davis.

After a tour of Fort Sumter and other Confederate battlefields, Mrs. Greenhow was asked by the government to act as a courier to Confederate diplomats, James M. Mason and John Slidell, who were in London attempting to woo the British government into entering in the war on the side of the Confederacy. In July 1862, she and her daughter sailed on the *Phantom*, a fast ship that outdistanced the Union blockade vessels attempting to catch her. She was taken to Bermuda, then on to Paris where she placed her child in a convent school. She met with Matthew Fontaine Maury, the Confederate commissioner in France who arranged an audience between Greenhow and Napoleon III.

At this meeting, Mrs. Greenhow charmed the emperor in the great gaslit hall of the Tuileries, asking him to aid the South in any way that would serve the interests of France. Napoleon was courteous but noncommittal. In London, much pomp and ceremony was extended to Greenhow. Mason and Slidell escorted her to the court of St. James where she met Queen Victoria who was delighted at the spy's grace and wit.

To convince Europeans to side with the Confederacy, Greenhow then wrote a brilliant piece of propaganda, *My First Year in Prison, and the Abolition Rule at Washington.* The book was a bestseller. Taking a large house in Mayfair, Greenhow was the toast of London.

In September 1864, when the fortunes of the Confederacy were dipping, Mrs. Greenhow decided to return to Richmond. Carrying $2,000 in gold and important dispatches for President Davis, she boarded the *Condor*, a fast merchant vessel. The dispatches, it was later reported, contained a secret agreement between England and the Confederacy that would bring Great Britain into the war against the Union.

On the night of September 30, 1864, the *Condor* attempted to run the Union blockade off the coast of Wilmington, North Carolina, but ran into a raging storm. With a Union warship in pursuit, the British vessel managed to reach the mouth of the Cape Fear River where it crashed into the wreck of a blockade runner, *Nighthawk*.

The *Condor* wildly rolled and pitched. Huge waves engulfed her as Admiral Hampden saw from the stern that several Union gunboats were fast approaching. As the *Condor* creaked and wallowed on the sandbar, Greenhow ran on deck with a shawl wrapped about her head. She, too, saw the Union warships bearing down and shouted in the gale to Hampden to lower a boat and give her a pilot so she could make for land and avoid capture.

Hampden refused but Greenhow, drenched by waves, her black dress clinging to her tall, shapely form, ordered him to do her bidding. Like many a man before him, Hampden bowed to her wishes, saying "it's against my better advice, madam." A boat was lowered, and Greenhow, accompanied by serveral officers, got into it. With her, Mrs. Greenhow carried her dispatches and the mailbags. The boat struggled to reach shore, the men straining at the oars. As it neared the beach a tremendous wave crashed over it, upturning the boat and throwing the occupants out, sucking them back to sea in the undertow. Some of the men fought against the current and, exhausted, managed to collapse onto the beach.

It was some time later, when these men revived, that they began searching for Greenhow. At dawn the next day, a Confederate soldier found the woman lying on the beach, dead. He found a small bag wrapped about her wrist. Upon opening it, her gold slipped out. He collected the gold and pushed the corpse back into the water. It washed once more to the beach a few hours later and was found by Thomas E. Taylor who later authored *Blockade Running*. The body was taken to Fort Fisher where its burial was supervised by the commandant, Colonel William Lamb.

The body of the heroic spy was cleaned and clothed by the ladies of the Soldier's Aid Society, and thousands came to view it at the Seaman's Bethel where it lay in state. For decades, those still alive, told of how they had seen Rose Greenhow in death and that she was "more beautiful than any living woman."

A few hours later a weeping, nervous Confederate soldier appeared before Colonel Lamb. He tossed gold pieces onto Lamb's desk, saying: "Colonel, there is one of two things I must do. I stole the money from Mrs. Greenhow's body. I must either give it up or go crazy." The soldier was dismissed without punishment. The woman had worked her magic posthumously on yet another smitten man.

In the afternoon of Saturday, October 1, 1864, the body of Mrs. Rose Greenhow was carried in a long funeral procession through the streets of Wilmington, a guard of honor accompanying her horse-drawn casket, which was draped with a huge Confederate flag. Thousands of soldiers marched behind it, Admiral Hampden and many Confederate officers leading the way to Oakdale Cemetery. A squad of Confederate soldiers fired their muskets over her grave as the guns of Fort Fisher boomed in her honor.

The whole South grieved the loss of the indomitable, heroic spy, whose beauty was legend and whose spirit was unconquered. It was remembered at the time that Rose Greenhow had sworn that if she died on northern soil she would rise from her grave and crawl as a ghost back to the sacred soil of the South. That trip was not necessary.

A great white stone was later placed above the grave of Rose Greenhow, purchased by the Ladies Memorial Association of Wilmington. It bears the legend: "This monument commemorates the deeds of Mrs. Rose Greenhow, a bearer of dispatches to the Confederate government. She was drowned off Fort Fisher from the blockade runner 'Condor' while attempting to run the blockade on September 30, 1864. Her body was washed ashore at Fort Fisher Beach and brought to Wilmington."

[ALSO SEE: *Lafayette Baker; Pierre Gustave Toutant Beauregard; Allan Pinkerton; Timothy Webster*]

GRU (Glavnoye Razvedyvatelnoye Upravlenye)
Soviet Intelligence HQ for Red Army ▪ (1920–   )

ESTABLISHED IN 1920 DURING THE RUSSIAN CIVIL war by Leon Trotsky, the GRU was the center of intelligence for the Russian Army's general staff, although it was subordinate to the KGB. Its first chief, Yan Berzin, was shot in 1937 as part of Joseph Stalin's nationwide purge of suspected political enemies. Though it was ideally supposed to work hand in glove with the KGB, generals heading the GRU have often clashed with the much broader intelligence network, which has been run by Communist functionaries of far-reaching power.

Almost every Russian legation stationed abroad had in its midst a GRU officer, invariably assigned as a political attaché. These spymasters operated their own espionage networks apart from that of the KGB but were required to share all information with its parent organization. The Soviet spy network that operated in Canada after World War II was operated by the GRU, from which ranks Igor Gouzenko defected in 1945. The greatest spies to ever work directly for the GRU were World War II agents Rudolf Roessler in Switzerland, the enigmatic Richard Sorge who operated in Tokyo and was executed by the Japanese, and Rudolf Abel, the spymaster who operated successfully for many years in America after World War II.

All GRU agents have been officers graduated from the Russian Army Academy. Although the GRU trained its own men, they were first approved and also trained by the KGB. The GRU operated at 19 Znamensky Street in Moscow, an ornate palace once owned by a wealthy czarist merchant.

The GRU was divided into four divisions—training, information, operations, and auxiliary, with twenty-four sub-divisions making up the many geographical sections of the world where the agency operated. Its members were subject to investigation by the KGB. The most damaging defector from the GRU was Oleg Penkovsky, who enlighted the West on GRU's widespread operations and techniques.

[ALSO SEE: *Rudolf Abel; KGB; Oleg Penkovsky; Rudolf Roessler; Richard Sorge*]

GUILLAUME, GUNTHER
German Spy for Soviets ▪ (1927–   )

WHEN GUNTHER GUILLAUME ESCAPED FROM East Berlin into the West, he was a one-time captain in the East German Army. He decried the oppressive Communist regime and vowed that he would work against the Soviets. To that end he became a staunch Social Democrat, his views right of center. The stout, double-chinned, pudgy-faced Guillaume impressed Willy Brandt who believed him to be invaluable in helping to ferret out Russian spies and oversee West German intelligence. Brandt's dedication to Guillaume, both as a friend and political associate would cause his downfall. From the beginning, Guillaume was a Soviet double agent. He had been trained by the KGB in a Kiev military academy and was an adept spy when he pretended to defect to the West.

Guillaume became one of three of Brandt's personal assistants. His job was simply to review all important papers that came to Brandt before passing them on. This he did, after making copies of everything and then passing these secrets on to the Soviets at prearranged letter drops, or secretly meeting with his Soviet case officer, or by using his wife Christel as a courier to East Berlin where she excused her trips by explaining that she was visiting relatives.

In 1973, a Russian defector, Vadim Belotzerkovsky, sought asylum in France. He told French intelligence that he had seen Guillaume on television, sitting next to Brandt during press conferences and that he was a KGB spy.

Brandt was informed of this situation. He feigned continued friendship with the spy, even inviting him on a vacation trip to Norway in 1973. West German intelligence then informed Brandt that it intended to arrest Guillaume. The spy was taken into custody in April 1974 as he got off of a plane from France, following a holiday trip. The next month, the energetic, optimistic Brandt, realizing that he had been thoroughly compromised by the Soviet spy, wrote to the president of the West German Republic: "I accept political responsibility for negligence in connection with the Guillaume espionage affair and declare my resignation from the office of Federal Chancellor."

Guillaume was quickly tried, convicted, and sentenced to thirteen years in prison. He served only eight years, being released in 1982. He was then exchanged for a number of West German agents and political prisoners.

[ALSO SEE: *KGB*]

HALE, NATHAN
American Spy in Revolution ■
(1755–1776)

HAILED AS AMERICA'S FIRST ESPIONAGE AGENT, Nathan Hale was a great patriot but an inept spy. A Connecticut farmer's son, Hale graduated from Yale in 1773. He began teaching school but upon hearing of the fight at Lexington in 1776, he quit his post and joined the American army.

He participated in the siege of Boston and was promoted to the rank of captain, serving in Knowlton's Rangers.

When the British under General William Howe invaded Long Island, N.Y., Washington retreated to Manhattan. He asked Colonel Thomas Knowlton to provide him a volunteer to spy on the British. Hale immediately volunteered. Washington told the untrained Hale to make his way behind the British lines on Long Island and determine his opponent's strength and movements.

Hale changed his uniform for civilian clothes and slipped through the British lines, telling those who questioned him that he was a school teacher. He took detailed notes and made sketches of the British formations, their supplies and reserves, then began to make his way back to the retreating Washington, following the British troops who invaded Manhattan on September 15, 1776. On September 21, Hale was stopped and questioned by a British patrol and was determined to be a spy after his notes and sketches were found on him.

How this came about is still a mystery. Some claim that Hale was caught in a lie or that he simply, foolishly told the British he was a spy, or was turned in by a relative in which he had confided his true mission. Nothing is known for sure. He was imprisoned and condemned. It was his naive thought that since he carried no weapon and wore no uniform, he could not be considered a combatant or soldier

The courageous American spy Nathan Hale is shown dressed in civilian clothes, gathering information from British troops in Manhattan in 1776; he was caught and hanged a short time later, his last patriotic words inspiring the American cause: "I only regret that I have but one life to lose for my country."

and was therefore immune to military punishment. He had no conception of what really happened to captured spies.

Awaiting execution, Hale demonstrated great courage, so much so that he irked British Provost Marshal Cunningham by not begging for mercy or the chance to inform on his fellow Americans. Hale wrote several letters, one to his sweetheart whom he had planned to marry, another to his brother Enoch (who would later join the American spy network known as the Culper Ring), and to his superior, Colonel Knowlton. He gave the letters to Cunningham but the brutal British commander tore them up in the spy's presence. When asked later by another British commander why he had done this, Cunningham barked: "The rebels ought not to know that they had a man in their army who could die with that much firmness."

Hale was taken to the scaffold and hanged on September 22, 1776, only one day after his capture, an execution that was decreed by Sir William Howe himself. Hale's epitaph was taken from one of his last letters, a line that Hale borrowed from Joseph Addison's then popular play, *Cato*: "I only regret that I have but one life to lose for my country." Those stirring words became Hale's and an eternal American call to arms for patriots in all ages.

Washington was informed of Hale's execution a few days later when Captain Montressor, of the British Royal Engineers, came through the lines under a flag of truce. Montressor simply informed Washington that a spy named Nathan Hale had been summarily hanged, without giving the American commander-in-chief any details. When Washington learned of those details, he became incensed. His bitter memory of Hale's unappealed execution undoubtedly still rested in Washington's mind years later when he refused to reprieve the British spy, Major John Andre, sending him to the scaffold for his work of espionage with the traitor Benedict Arnold.

Hale's untimely death, however, did confirm in Washington's mind the absolute need to use trained, experienced spies in the future. He made it strict policy thereafter to employ only those who were properly schooled in the art of espionage, which, no doubt, resulted in his own highly effective military intelligence service under the command of Benjamin Tallmadge and the successful Culper Ring in New York, which operated throughout the war and provided Washington with consistent invaluable information.

[ALSO SEE: *John Andre; Benedict Arnold; Culper Ring; Benjamin Tallmadge*]

HALL, WILLIAM REGINALD (AKA: BLINKER)
British Spymaster in World War I ▪ (1870–1943)

HALL CAME FROM A LONG LINE OF DISTINGUISHED British naval officers. Raised in Wiltshire, his father, Captain William Henry Hall, was made the first director of the Foreign Intelligence Committee (FIC) in 1883. Entering the Royal Navy, Hall served on several warships, rising to the rank of captain and commanding the battle cruiser *Queen Mary* at the outbreak of World War I. Ill health forced him to give up his command when the war was only three months old.

Hall, however, was promptly named director of naval intelligence at age forty-four. He was a shrewd spymaster with inexhaustible energy. He looked like a character out of the British satirical magazine *Punch*, a large, prematurely bald man with a protruding hooked nose. He had since youth a facial twitch that unnerved anyone in his presence, and this produced high-speed blinking that earned him the sobriquet of "Blinker."

Hall's first move was to tightly organize and consolidate the Navy's cryptography section, moving it into Room 40 of the old Admiralty Building in London. It became famous for its ability to monitor German diplomatic and military codes and break their ciphers.

The Magdeburg codebook, which detailed the operating ciphers and codes of the German Navy, had been captured early in the war and Hall's cryptographers used it against all transmissions of the German fleets. Every German squadron, for instance, was required to regularly radio its position. These communications were intercepted by Room 40 and decoded so that the British knew the position of every German ship, from battle cruiser to submarine almost throughout the entire war.

It was Hall's policy to share Navy information with all other British intelligence operations. To that end, he exchanged data with Vernon Kell's MI5, Mansfield Cumming of MI6, and Basil Thomson of the Special Branch of Scotland Yard. Though Hall supervised a host of naval intelligence operations, it was Room 40 that proved to be his prize operation, one that made any surprise attack by the German fleet impossible. It was Room 40 that intercepted German Navy battle orders in December 1914 that called for raids along the British coast and led the British fleet to intercept the German warships and drive them off.

The greatest coup by Hall and Room 40 involved the notorious "Zimmermann Telegram," a coded message intercepted by Room 40 on January 17, 1917, from German Foreign Minister Zimmermann to the President of Mexico. The decoded message bluntly

Sir William Reginald "Blinker" Hall, head of British naval intelligence during World War I; his operations intercepted the notorious "Zimmermann Telegram" on January 17, 1917, a coup that helped Hall to convince President Wilson to go to war against Germany.

proposed that Mexico and Japan join Germany in a war on then neutral United States. Zimmermann boldly proposed that if Mexico attacked the U.S., it could regain its lost territories. Germany, then, would be free of any interference from America in crushing the forces of England and France. Three months later, on April 6, 1917, the U.S. declared war on Germany.

Following World War I, Hall entered politics and was elected a member of Parliament. Throughout the 1920s and 1930s, he traveled in the U.S. giving lectures on his intelligence gathering experiences, information much sought after by American intelligence chiefs such as William J. "Wild Bill" Donovan. Another of Hall's admirers in the U.S. was Franklin Delano Roosevelt, who had been Assistant Secretary of the Navy in World War I, and was impressed with Hall's intelligence operations. When World War II broke out, he was too old for the intelligence service but he nevertheless became an active member of the Home Guard, a post he held until his death in 1943.

[ALSO SEE: *Mansfield Cumming; William J. Donovan; Vernon Kell; MI5; MI6; Special Branch; Basil Thomson; Zimmermann Telegram*]

HARDINGE, HENRY
British Spymaster ▪ (1785–1856)

BORN IN KENT, HARDINGE WAS A CAREER OFFICER who served with the Duke of Wellington throughout the Peninsular War between Britain and France (1808-1814). Hardinge acted as chief of Wellington's espionage operations, enlisting Spanish nationals as agents. These agents, motivated either out of patriotism or by payment, reported on the movement and strength of French forces. One of the spymaster's agents managed to steal the code book of Marshal Andre Messena, which allowed Hardinge to quickly decipher intercepted French dispatches. Wellington thus learned of French battle plans. This priceless information brought him victories at Salamanca in 1812 and Vittoria in 1813.

The British spymaster was also instrumental in aiding Wellington to win the momentous battle of Waterloo on June 6, 1815. Colonel Hardinge had collected considerable information from royalist spies working for him, including Napoleon's battle plans that clearly showed how the French Emperor would feint at Maubeuge, then hurl his main force toward Mons. Armed with that information, Wellington established a defense position that proved to be impregnable.

Knighted, Hardinge entered Parliament. When Wellington became prime minister in 1828, Hardinge served as secretary of war under his old chief. The spymaster later served in India and Ireland before retiring.

HAREL, ISSER
Israeli Spymaster ▪ (1912–)

BORN ISSER HALPERIN IN VITEBSK, RUSSIA, HAREL moved with his family to Latvia in 1922 and to Palestine in 1929 where he changed his name to Harel. Joining the underground organization Haganah at an early age, Harel was a dedicated Zionist. He joined the British auxiliary forces in the mid-1940s, fighting the Nazis, but at the same time, he gathered intelligence for the Haganah against the Arabs and the British who then controlled Palestine.

So effective was Harel that he became head of Haganah intelligence by 1944, continuing in that capacity until Israel became a sovereign nation in 1951. At that time, Prime Minister David Ben-Gurion reorganized Israeli intelligence, creating the Mossad, the country's official intelligence agency, and naming Harel as its chief. Harel tirelessly worked to make the Mossad one of the finest organizations of its kind in the world, establishing excellent relations with the CIA. He personally directed the capture of Nazi war criminal Adolf Eichmann in 1960 in Buenos Aires.

In 1963, two Mossad agents were arrested and jailed for violating Swiss laws by threatening German scientists allegedly working with Egypt. Always a champion of his men, Harel defended their actions so emphatically to Ben-Gurion that he was asked to resign. In 1965, Harel became security adviser to Levi Eshkol, Isreal's new prime minister, but he resigned a year later, again over policies. Harel then permanently retired.

[ALSO SEE: *CIA; Mossad*]

HARNACK, ARVID
German Spymaster for Soviets ▪ (1901–1942)

BORN IN DARMSTADT, GERMANY, HARNACK CAME from a long line of intellectuals, his father being Otto Harnack, the historian, his uncle, Adolf Harnack, a celebrated theologian. After graduating from the University of Berlin in 1926, Harnack went to the U.S. to study economics at the University of Wisconsin on a Rockefeller grant. He met an American woman of Jewish descent, Mildred Fish, and married her. Upon his return to Germany, he completed his economics studies at the University of Giessen.

It was while he was at Giessen, known for its left-leaning faculty, that Harnack came under the Communist influence. He visited Moscow in 1932 and was easily recruited to the Party and to the KGB as a spy for the Soviets. Though an avowed anti-Nazi, Harnack went to work in the German ministry of economics, supplying the Russians with secret information on Hitler's government. He worked in unison with his friend Harro Schulze-Boysen, who also hated the Nazi regime and who served in the German ministry of aviation.

These were two of many who made up what the Gestapo termed the "Rote Kapelle," or the Red Chapel or Red Orchestra, a strongly unified Communist underground spy network, controlled by Moscow. This network spread its tentacles throughout Germany, France, Holland, Belgium, and Switzerland. In Germany there existed two branches of Rote Kapelle, the larger in Berlin and another operation in Hamburg.

After Germany invaded Russia in 1941, Harnack was able to wire to Moscow plans of German offenses on the Eastern Front, as well as intended use of homefront troops and details of Germany's major industrial plants and their products. Additional Russian agents who were native-born Germans were dropped by parachute near Berlin. They brought with them miniature transmitters and money and were hidden in the homes of Harnack, Schulze-Boysen, and others. These agents gathered information, transmitted messages, and sometimes carried back voluminous data to Moscow.

The Abwehr's counterintelligence finally captured one of these agents and forced him to transmit messages to Moscow, enabling the Germans to thereafter capture almost all of the Russian agents parachuted near Berlin. The Red Orchestra nevertheless continued to function.

A Red Orchestra message coming from its branch in Brussels was interecepted in 1942 that mentioned Schulze-Boysen by name. The German Luftwaffe lieutenant was arrested, along with Harnarck and most of the leaders of the spy network. All were tried and condemned by a military court.

[ALSO SEE: *Abwehr; Red Orchestra; Harro Schulze-Boysen*]

HARPER, EDWARD DURWARD JR.
American Spy for Poland ▪ (1935–   )

AN ELECTRONICS ENGINEER, HARPER FIRST MADE contact with Polish intelligence on a 1979 trip to Geneva. Through his second wife, Ruby Louise Schuler Harper, who was the executive secretary to the president of Systems Control, Inc. and Systems Control Technology in Palo Alto, California, Harper was able to obtain classified information on the Minuteman missile systems and other strategic weapons. Harper passed this information on to a Polish spymaster named Zdzislaw Pryzchodzien and, over a period of about three years, received more than $250,000.

FBI agents, who had been investigating the Harpers for some time, arrested Harper on October 15, 1983, charging him with espionage and treason. His wife had died the previous June. Harper was convicted and sent to prison for life on May 15, 1984.

HAUKELID, KNUT
Norwegian Spy for Allies • (1917–   )

HE TWIN BROTHER OF ACTRESS SIGRID GURIE, Haukelid was a leader of the Norwegian underground during World War II. He, more than any other, was responsible for preventing the Germans from producing and shipping heavy water (deuterium oxide) in their race to develop the atomic bomb.

Norsk Hydro, Norway's hydroelectric authority, had established in the mountainous valley near Rjukan, a plant dedicated to producing heavy water. When the British SIS informed Prime Minister Winston Churchill of this in 1942, he called his cabinet together. An immediate decision was made to send thirty specially trained engineer troops to Rjukan to destroy the plant. This was an SOE operation.

The men were sent in gliders but the mission proved to be a total failure. The glider mission disaster called for new action. In England, SOE (Special Operations Executive), which coordinated underground efforts in Nazi-occupied Europe, located some Norwegian refugees who volunteered for espionage and sabotage missions in their country, chiefly covert operations against the Norsk Hydro plant. Members of the Norwegian underground were smuggled back into Norway, one of these being Knut Haukelid, a daring, adventurous young man who was a born leader. SOE built a replica of the plant and had their Norwegian agents familiarize themselves with every nook and cranny of the place, in prepartion to blowing it up.

Knut Haukelid led a team of Norwegian agents by parachute into Norway in early 1943. The agents crossed the hazardous mountain passes on skis, then slipped into the plant, overpowering the guards and planting an explosive that damaged the plant and caused heavy water production to be shut down for several months.

By 1944, with Hitler screaming for new super weapons, German scientists resolved to speed up development of the atomic bomb by removing the entire Norwegian heavy water plant to Germany. To that end, all the heavy water produced to date was placed in large drums. These drums would be placed on the ferry, which would carry them across Lake Tinnsjo to a waiting train, which would carry them to the sea and then, by ship, to Germany.

Learning of this, Haukelid and his men got aboard the ferry the night before the Germans arrived, planting an explosive that was timed to go off just as the ferry reached the point of the lake where its waters were deepest. The bomb went off exactly as planned and the ferry sank with the drums of heavy water in the deepest part of Lake Tinnsjo, thus disabling the German scientists from completing their atomic bomb development. Haukelid's story and that of other heroic Norwegian resistance fighters was told in the film *The Heroes of Telemark*.

[ALSO SEE: *SOE*]

HELMER, FRITZ
German Spy in Russia • (1886– ?)

ELMER JOINED THE ABWEHR SHORTLY BEFORE World War I. Speaking fluent Russian, he was sent to Moscow, posing as a businessman. He learned that Russian Minister of War, General Vladimir Sukhomilov, was in deep debt. Though despised by the regular officers of the Russian Army, particularly the czar's cousin and commander-in-chief, Prince Nicholas Nicolaievich, the fat little general had the czar's ear. Knowing all this, Helmer instantly ingratiated himself to Sukhomilov when first meeting him, promising lucrative investments that he would make on the general's behalf, returning considerable profits in return for information on certain Russian products. Sukhomilov gladly provided the data on seemingly innocuous items such as cars, tractors, trucks. Helmer paid him handsomely. Then the spy asked for military information and the Minister of War complied without hesitation.

Urging Sukhomilov to cooperate with Helmer was the general's sensuous wife who had been seduced by Helmer and had arranged the first meeting between Helmer and her husband. For her continued support, Madame Sukhomilov demanded and received Helmer's sexual attentions. In 1916, when the czar's armies were deteriorating, Helmer learned from Sukhomilov exactly where the Russian troops would be positioned in a major offensive planned through Galicia. Informing the Abwehr, Helmer personally went to a strategic bridge to be used in the Russian advance and, alone, blew it up.

At the time of the armistice in 1918, Helmer was in Latvia. With the collapse of the Kaiser's government, he was no longer employed and fielded about for opportunities. At that time, he met Hasso von Manteuffel, a millionaire Junker obsessed with the Soviet takeover of the Baltic states. He financed Helmer who organized Latvian troops, taking them into action against Soviet forces invading Latvia. Raising thousands of fresh troops from the Latvian peasantry, Helmer put together a formidable army, equipping it with machine guns and armored cars, which were paid for by Manteuffel.

Unemployed officers of the defeated Wehrmacht flocked to Helmer's banner, including eight German generals and twenty colonels. He then led his army into northern Latvia, clearing out the Soviets. His forces moved into Estonia where they quickly defeated an Estonian army. Helmer then ran out of money and began paying his troops in his own scrip, bills that bore his image in a bedazzling general's uniform.

Allied forces, however, were sent to the Baltic states to rid themselves of this pesky spy-turned-general. Helmer's army was routed and he escaped to Copenhagen in the disguise of a beggar. When Helmer heard that rebels had taken arms against the French in Morocco, he offered his services to Abd el-Krim.

The Arab leader informed Helmer that he would be welcome in aiding him in driving out the French forces. Helmer, using an alias, and the cover of a German correspondent, crossed Germany and France and arrived in Morocco. French troops, however, ambushed the convoy in which Helmer was traveling. He was wounded and taken prisoner. He was to be charged once he had been released from a hospital.

Helmer escaped before the French could place him on trial. A short time later, French authorities in Paris were notified by German officials that Helmer was in custody in Berlin, awaiting trial for plotting to overthrow the government. The record of this spectacular spy and military entrepreneur is thereafter blank.

[ALSO SEE: *Abwehr*]

HELMS, RICHARD McGARRAH
Chief of CIA ▪ (1913–   )

CIA Chief Richard M. Helms who was victimized by Watergate, among other political catastrophies.

HELMS WAS PART OF THE CIA DURING THE AGENCY'S most covert period. Through such devious CIA associates as Richard Bissell and Sidney Gottlieb, Helms witnessed attempts to assassinate third world leaders via bizarre murder schemes and wild plans to interfere with the national interests of many foreign governments.

Helms came from well-to-do parents, attending prep schools in Switzerland and Germany. After receiving his degree from Williams College, he joined the UPI staff in Berlin in 1935. A short time later, Helms scored a journalistic coup by obtaining a lengthy interview with German dictator Adolf Hitler. In 1938, Helms returned to the U.S., becoming the advertising manager for an Indianapolis newspaper. He joined the Navy in 1942 and served in New York as a fund-raiser for the Naval Relief Society. He was then reassigned to anti-submarine operations.

In August 1943, due to his experiences in Nazi Germany, Helms was accepted into the ranks of the OSS and went to work for Allen Dulles. He worked for OSS in England and France and, unlike many other OSS agents, Helms stayed on after VE day. Although the OSS was dismantled by President Harry Truman in 1946, Helms remained at his post in Germany, as a station chief for the Central Intelligence Group, the precursor to the CIA, and then for the CIA.

Helms worked with Reinhard Gehlen's West German espionage operations and advised Washington in the early stages of the Cold War that the Russians had established a worldwide espionage network and were intent on using any and all means of covert operations to accomplish world domination of communism. Returning to Washington, Helms served in CIA middle-management, watching his superiors fall by the wayside, Lyman Kirkpatrick from polio, Frank Wisner from a nervous breakdown (he later killed himself), Allen Dulles from the Bay of Pigs disaster.

Following the Bay of Pigs fiasco in 1962, Helms was made Director for Plans at the CIA and served in this capacity until 1966 when he was named Director. It was Helms' bad luck that he became chief of the agency at a time when President Lyndon B. Johnson was obsessed with Vietnam. The controversy still rages over whether or not Helms advised Johnson to stay out of Vietman. If so, he was unsuccessful in convincing Johnson to keep out of the attritional war in southeast Asia. (It would be next to impossible to stop Johnson's crusade, especially after Johnson's encounter with the Holy Ghost, or so it was reported, that spirit personally directing him to send 500,000 American soldiers to Vietman, or so it was later claimed.)

Helms was also compromised by Watergate, which involved the CIA's aid to an ex-CIA man, E. Howard Hunt (Helms' favorite spy novelist). When it appeared that the CIA would be directly drawn into the

Watergate affair, Helms did his utmost to protect the agency, a posture that President Nixon interpreted as treacherous, and one that caused Helms to be fired by Nixon on February 2, 1973.

The firing of Helms was not unexpected. Helms had never been considered a leader or director, only a caretaker. More trouble was in store when Helms appeared before the Foreign Relations Committee, prior to his assuming the ambassadorship to Iran. He swore at the time that the CIA had no part in attempting to overthrow the government of Chile under President Salvador Allende.

Evidence supplied by CIA officials succeeding Helms proved him to be a liar. Helms was found guilty of perjury in 1977. He was fined $2,000 and given a two-year prison sentence, which was suspended.

President Ronald Reagan, however, attempted to rehabilitate Helms' much-tarnished reputation in 1983 by awarding him the National Security Medal. Helms, by then a consultant on Middle East investments, remarked: "I have no feelings about remorse or exoneration."

[ALSO SEE: *Richard Bissell; CIA; Allen Dulles; Reinhard Gehlen; Sidney Gottlieb; Frank Wisner*]

HEREWARD THE WAKE
Saxon Spy Against Normans ▪ (? –1071?)

DURING THE NORMAN CONQUEST OF ENGLAND, THE leader of the Saxon resistance was Hereward, who was called "The Wake," for his ability to escape Norman traps. Hereward conducted a prolonged guerrilla war with the Normans, which was successful due to Hereward's ability to obtain intelligence on the enemy. Like Alfred the Great, Hereward acted as his own spymaster. Appearing in many disguises, even as a woman, he entered Norman camps, learned the strength and intentions of the enemy, and later led devastating attacks on the Normans. Hereward's forces were betrayed by the monks at the Ely monastery in 1071 and were destroyed. It remains uncertain whether or not Hereward was killed at that time.

[ALSO SEE: *Alfred the Great*]

HEYDRICH, REINHARD TRISTAN EUGEN (AKA: THE HANGMAN)
German Spymaster in World War II ▪ (1904–1943)

HEYDRICH WAS ONE OF THE MOST RUTHLESS NAZIS of Hitler's Third Reich. He was born in Halle, Germany, on May 7, 1904, the son of an actress and an opera singer who was reportedly Jewish, a fact Heydrich concealed through his blatant anti-Semitism. When he graduated high school, Heydrich joined the Free Corps, a right-wing militant organization that expressed a pronounced hatred for Jews. Through his connections with the Corps, Heydrich was accepted as a naval cadet at Kiel in 1922. In July 1923, while serving on the training ship *Berlin*, he met Wilhelm Canaris, later chief of the Abwehr.

By 1926, Heydrich had been promoted to the rank of sub-lieutenant and was sent to the Naval Signal School, excelling in mathematics and navigation. Promoted to lieutenant, Heydrich served on the flagship *Schleswig-Holstein* in 1928. He was not well-liked by his superiors, peers, or subordinates. He was aloof, superior, and barked his commands like a martinet. He placed any seaman he disliked on punishment. Though he acted like an arrogant Prussian Junker, Heydrich went to great lengths to conceal the identities of his parents, particularly his Jewish mother.

By that time Heydrich flaunted a fake background that conformed to the Nazi concept of the Aryan superman—he had become a Nazi Party member early on—and he made a great impression on Heinrich Himmler, Hitler's private policeman, when the two met. Heydrich was the physical epitome of the Aryan—tall, lanky, blonde-haired, and blue-eyed. He had a long, thin, pointed nose. His chin was also pointed. To one contemporary, everything about the man was pointed, like the tip of a spear.

Heydrich was attracted to the daughter of an I. G. Farben director in 1930. He seduced this underage girl and when she told him that she was pregnant, he refused to marry her, saying that he would never wed a female who had given herself to him before the proper nuptials. Her father, a man of great wealth and influence, went to his friend, Admiral Erich Raeder, complaining about Heydrich.

Raeder summarily cashiered Heydrich in April 1931. The grounds of his dismissal from the German Navy was listed as "impropriety." A short time later, Heydrich married a tall, bosomy blonde, Lina Mathilde von Osten, who was a great admirer of Heinrich Himmler. On June 14, 1931, Lina arranged for Heydrich to meet her friend Himmler. Himmler, at the time, was looking about for a man he could trust to become head of his Security Service. After twenty minutes of listening to the Jew-hating Heydrich,

Himmler concluded that he had found his man.

Heydrich, as head of the SD (*Sicherheitsdienst*), a secret police inside Himmler's secret police (SS), was assigned to spy on Nazi Party members, reaffirming their loyalty to the Party and to Adolf Hitler. He became the most dreaded man in Germany.

Heydrich's power increased as Germany invaded and conquered one European country after another. The SD moved in and established its iron-fisted authority over the citizens of these countries, identifying them according to religion and race. Of course, it was Heydrich's job to identify the Jews whom Hitler had long planned to exterminate. It was also Heydrich's job to bring about Hitler's "final solution" to the Jewish "problem" by directing the mass murder of the Jews (an estimated six million) in Nazi concentration camps.

Heydrich, throughout the many years he bloodied his hands with countless victims, professed a love of the fine arts, especially music. He would return to his posh Berlin home after ordering the deaths of hundreds, if not thousands each day, to sit with his family and play the violin, not unlike Nero's mad lyre-playing at the burning of Rome.

By 1941, Heydrich was plotting Himmler's ouster and gathering more power. He was named Acting Protector of Bohemia and Moravia and most of Czechoslovakia. He sent hundreds of suspected political malcontents to prison and ordered the executions of thousands of other Czechs without trial.

To eliminate this murderous beast, the Free Czech government in exile in London, ordered a top notch assassination squad to parachute into Czechoslovakia to kill Heydrich. Eight Czech freedom fighters, on May 27, 1942, waited for Heydrich's touring car to leave Heydrich's villa and go through Prague to Hradcany Castle where the offices of the SD and Gestapo were located. When the car passed a certain point, one of the freedom fighters threw a bomb, which struck the Mercedes touring car. The driver was injured, as was Heydrich who received a splinter in the back. He stood up in the car, then collapsed. On June 4, 1942, Heydrich died of septicemia. Hitler and Himmler exploded at the news, saying that the Reichsprotector had been the victim of a Jewish plot.

In Berlin, 152 Jews were immediately murdered in retaliation. The small Czechoslovakian town of Lidice was destroyed in a massive reprisal. All of the men and boys of the town, 172 of them, were trucked to an open field and shot to death. All the town's 195 women were sent to concentration camps. The children were placed in German homes to be raised as "good Nazis." Not every Nazi was horrified at the news of Heydrich's assassination. Sepp Dietrich, a rabid Nazi and leader of a Panzer division, upon hearing of Heydrich's demise, sneered and snorted: "The hog has finally gone to the butcher!"

[ALSO SEE: *Wilhelm Canaris; Gestapo; Heinrich Himmler; SD*]

HIMMLER, HEINRICH
German Police Chief and Spymaster ▪ (1900–1945)

NO OTHER MAN WAS AS FEARED IN THE THIRD REICH as Heinrich Himmler. Next to Hitler, his power was absolute. As head of the SS and the Gestapo, Himmler and his sadistic henchmen began arbitrarily arresting tens of thousands of political opponents, Jews, Catholics, anyone Hitler's regime designated as unfit for German society. By 1945, when World War II ended, Himmler, more than any other Nazi, was responsible by one account for the horrific mass murder of more than eleven million persons.

This arrogant, strutting little man who wore an imitation Hitler mustache, was born on October 7, 1900, in Munich, Germany, graduating high school in Landshut. He served in the German Army during World War I, but saw no action. While in the army, Himmler spent most of his time training to be a machine gunner. He then attempted to enter an officer's training course but was rejected. Himmler would later lie in claiming to have been an officer leading men on the Western Front.

Following the war, Himmler received a diploma in agronomy from the Munich Technological College in 1919. He went to work on a poultry farm (which later earned him the sobriquet of "chicken farmer") but ill health forced him to quit. In 1923, drifting about and looking for a future, Himmler wandered into a Munich meeting hall where he met Ernst Roehm, who had formed the National Socialist Workers Party whose chief speaker and nominal leader was Adolf Hitler.

Himmler quickly fell under Hitler's spell and became his most ardent advocate. He blindly accepted every utterance made by Der Fuhrer. He wholeheartedly embraced Hitler's anti-Semitic philosophy. He joined the Party and became one of its core functionaries, willing to accept any chore assigned to him. He was, at best, a bureaucratic clerk. A calculating man with a sneaky nature, Himmler took part in the Munich Beer Hall Putsch on November 9, 1923, carrying an old Imperial German flag and marching with Roehm to take over the War Ministry. Himmler thought at the time that Roehm, not Hitler, might emerge as the Party leader and he was prepared to back Roehm.

When the Putsch failed and Hitler and Roehm were imprisoned, Himmler attached himself to Gregor Strasser, the then top Nazi functionary at large. He became Strasser's secretary, receiving 120 marks a month. Himmler gave endless speeches in cramped meeting rooms and on street corners throughout Bavaria in 1924, condemning the Jews, Communists, democrats, and liberals for creating the punitive

Versailles Treaty under which Germany struggled to pay off its impossible war debts.

The methods Himmler used were blunt. He stood on a makeshift podium surrounded by strong-arm thugs screaming his racial slurs, appealing to the most rabid racists, the most brutal malcontents. Thousands flocked to the Nazi banner. So successful was Himmler that he moved to Berlin to begin organizing more Party chapters. By that time, Hitler had been released from prison and assumed the role of the Party leader. By now Himmler became a slavish follower of the Fuhrer.

Women were rarely seen with Himmler, although, unlike Roehm and others in the brown-shirted SA, he was not a homosexual. In 1926, he met Margarete "Marja" Boden, a statuesque, blue-eyed blonde who was the daughter of a wealthy landowner. She epitomized for Himmler the perfect Aryan woman. They married on July 3, 1928. A devout Nazi, Marja Himmler was ecstatic over her husband's appointment by Hitler as head of the SS on January 6, 1929. From that point onward, Himmler began to develop a secret police force that was loyal only to Adolf Hitler and to himself.

Himmler was a man dedicated to detail. He was methodical and unimaginative, suspicious of everyone surrounding Hitler. He distrusted Goering, Goebbels, and other Party leaders and was constantly scheming to usurp their power while pretending to support them. After Hitler came to power, the Gestapo passed from Hermann Goering's authority to Himmler. In 1934, Himmler's first important assignment from his demented leader was to eliminate Ernst Roehm and the leaders of the powerful SA.

Himmler's picked SS troops were used to arrest and summarily execute Roehm and his top lieutenants. As Hitler's high executioner, Himmler rounded up tens of thousands of Jews, political opponents, and others in Germany in the 1930s, placing these hapless victims in concentration camps from which they would never emerge. Throughout the war, Himmler's camps would house millions who were shot and gassed to death under his direction.

There was nothing Hitler could not ask of his most lethal servant. It was rumored with conviction by many Party members that Himmler had murdered Hitler's niece and lover, Geli Rebaul in 1931 when the attractive young woman attempted to leave Hitler and pursue a stage career in Vienna. There was no question of morality in Himmler. He murdered at will and applauded the effective methods developed by his ruthless subordinates—Reinhard Heydrich, Ernst Kaltenbrunner, and Adolf Eichmann—which accelerated the deaths of Jewish prisoners. He paraded through concentration camps, viewing the thousands of starving inmates with disdain, complaining of the stench from their unwashed bodies, then impatiently ordering them executed. He called them "lice . . . vermin . . . slave scum."

Ever broadening his power, Himmler established the SD (security service) early on, appointing the Jew-hating Reinhard Heydrich as its chief. The Gestapo and SD were used to spy on civilians and Nazi Party members. His agents were above the law and they arrested, imprisoned, and murdered suspects at will. In the concentraton camps, Himmler's "doctors" took to mutilating helpless prisoners under the guise of conducting "medical experiments." This involved the sterlization of "socially unfit" men and women, the freezing or burning to death of children to test tolerances, the administering of lethal injections to determine how long it took a person to die, the gassing of other prisoners to determine how long it would take them to choke to death.

The monsters conducting these experiments, among many, included Dr. Karl Gebhardt, hanged as a war criminal on June 2, 1948; Dr. Fritz Fischer, sent to prison for life; and Dr. Joseph Mengele, called the "Angel of Death," who murdered countless thousands in his insane experiments and who escaped to South America after World War II.

Though Himmler practiced espionage on his own people and those in conquered countries, it was not until 1944, when his sly adversary, Admiral Wilhelm Canaris was removed as director of the Abwehr, that Himmler took over foreign espionage and counterintelligence. His spies operated on all fronts and throughout the world. They were especially adept at infiltrating resistance groups in France, Belgium, and Holland.

In 1942, when learning that his henchman Reinhard Heydrich had been assassinated in Prague, Himmler ordered the village of Lidice and all of its inhabitants destroyed. He was terribly effective as an executioner but as a military leader Himmler was, at best, inept. His SS divisions serving on the Eastern Front were unreliable and scorned by the regular German Army. When Hitler was trapped in his Berlin bunker at the close of the war, he turned over the direction of his military forces to Himmler, naming him his heir. Himmler uselessly squandered the remnants of the army, then attempted to negotiate a separate peace. When Hitler heard of this, he denounced his once fanatical follower and named Admiral Karl Doenitz as his successor.

Himmler, meanwhile, went into hiding, attempting to flee Germany in disguise. He shaved off his mustache and donned a patch over one eye. He dressed in the uniform of a common policeman, assuming the role of Heinrich Hitzinger, a man he had ordered murdered so as to assume his identity. He was nevertheless identified after being captured by the British. While he was standing in a prison cell, stripped naked, a physician began to examine his mouth. Himmler turned away and crunched down on a vial of cyanide. He collapsed, dying in fifteen seconds. The naked little body was wrapped in camouflage netting, taken to a freshly dug hole in the ground, and dumped into it. The hole was filled up and no marker was placed.

[ALSO SEE: *Wilhelm Canaris; Gestapo; Reinhard Heydrich; SD*]

HIRAYAMA, CHOICHI
Japanese Spy Against Russia ▪ (1869–1924)

BORN INTO POVERTY IN TOKYO, HIRAYAMA WORKED as a rickshaw boy until he was taken in by the Black Dragon Society in 1897 and trained to be a spy. The Society was fiercely devoted to driving Russia from its far eastern lands.

Hirayama was sent to the Japanese spy school in Sapporo on the island of Hokkaido where he learned the Russian language and espionage techniques. He was then sent to the town of Iman in Siberia which straddled the trans-Siberian railroad. Posing as a merchant, Hirayama opened a general store. He befriended some Russian women married to staff officers and learned much about troop dispositions, military stores, and battle plans for the expected war with Japan.

Further, Japanese and Chinese agents from all over Siberia, Mongolia, and Manchuria came to Hirayama's store to leave their reports that the little storekeeper sent on to his spymasters in Tokyo. So valuable were Hirayama's reports that they were used by Japan's high command in its plans to attack the Russians at Port Arthur and for the great sea battle of Tsushima in 1905, both proving to be crushing victories for Japan. He was sent to Manchuria in 1922 to work for the Special Service Organ in Mukden under Kenji Doihara but ill health forced him into retirement.

[ALSO SEE: *Kenji Doihara*]

HISS, ALGER
Alleged Spy for Soviets ▪ (1904–   )

HISS WAS BORN IN BALTIMORE AND WAS EDUCATED at public schools. At the age of three, his father committed suicide but this tragedy seemed not to have left any lasting impression upon him. He attended Powder Point Academy in Duxbury, Massachusetts, then went on to Johns Hopkins University where he graduated in 1926. He graduated Harvard Law School in 1929 and went on to serve as a law clerk for Supreme Court Justice Oliver Wendell Holmes. In that same year Hiss married a divorcee, Priscilla Fansler Hobson.

During the early 1930s Hiss practiced law in Boston and New York. He then went to work in

Whittaker Chambers testifying before the House Un-American Activities Committee, naming Alger Hiss as a Communist spy; Hiss sits two rows behind Chambers (third from left), laughing at his accuser's statements.

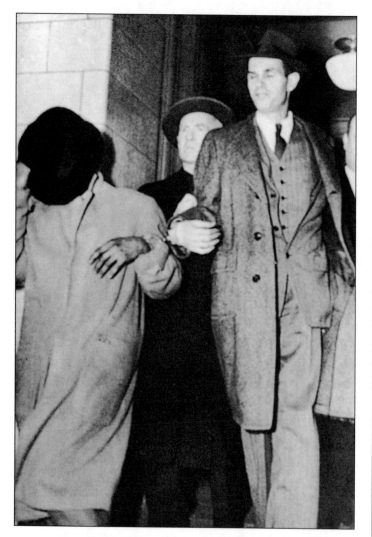

Alger Hiss (right), leaving court after his conviction for perjury; he is handcuffed to a black offender hiding his face with a hat.

Washington, first with the Agricultural Adjustment Administration (1933–1935), also serving at that time, 1934, with the Nye Committee which was investigating arms manufacturing. He worked for the Department of Justice (1935–1936), and then the State Department (1936–1945).

Hiss had risen high by the time of the Yalta Conference between Roosevelt, Churchill, and Stalin. He attended the conference as the chief aide of Secretary of State Edward R. Stettinius. Moreover, Hiss had been the executive secretary of the Dumbarton Oaks Conference, which established the United Nations in 1944. His professional and private life appeared to be impeccable. Yet high-placed American officials had years earlier received disturbing reports about Alger Hiss.

As early as 1939, journalist Whittaker Chambers accused Hiss of being a Communist spy when he met with Adolf Berle, Assistant Secretary of State.

Chambers, a longtime member of the Communist underground in the U.S., told Berle at the time that Hiss, his wife, and his brother Donald Hiss were all members of that underground. Berle found Chambers' story too fantastic to be true and did nothing. At this time, William C. Bullitt, American Ambassador in Paris, reported to Stanley Hornbeck of the State Department and Hiss' superior, that he had learned from French intelligence that both Alger and Donald Hiss were Soviet agents.

Unlike Berle, Hornbeck acted on Bullitt's information. He confronted Hiss with the charge. Hiss denied any such activities. Though Hornbeck accepted the denial, the FBI, in 1944, followed up the report by interviewing Hiss. Again, Hiss denied having anything to do with the Soviets and said he had no sympathy whatsoever with communism. The allegations would not die. In 1945, Igor Gouzenko, a Soviet cipher clerk, defected to the West in Ottawa, Canada, turning over concrete evidence to prove that a vast Soviet spy network existed in Canada and the U.S. Gouzenko himself stated that an assistant to the Secretary of State in Washington was a Soviet agent. He did not give a specfic name but, by process of elimination, the FBI pinpointed Hiss.

Hiss was not at the time confronted with the Gouzenko report but the Bureau kept him under surveillance. In 1946, James Byrnes, the new Secretary of State under President Truman, heard the rumors about Hiss and confronted him, pointedly asking him if he had ties to the Communists. No, Hiss emphatically replied. He repeated his denials to the FBI when again interviewed by agents.

In 1946, Hiss left the State Department, becoming the President of the Carnegie Endowment for International Peace in New York. Hiss retained his important post until 1948, when his old nemesis Whittaker Chambers reappeared.

Called before the House of Un-American Activities, Chambers admitted that he had been a Communist agent and that Alger Hiss was also a Communist who had worked with him in spying on the U.S. in the early 1930s. At first Chambers was disbelieved but he demonstrated such an awesome memory for the detail of Hiss' private life and that of his family that opinion began to turn.

Hiss himself testified, angrily denying that he ever knew Chambers. He then hazily recalled meeting Chambers under a different name. Chambers told how he had lived with the Hiss family on and off between 1934 and 1938 and that Hiss had even given him the family car. Hiss admitted that he had given Chambers a car but not in the year Chambers had claimed. Chambers went on to say that Hiss stole documents from the State Department and that his wife typed up copies of these classified reports, turned them over to Russian agents, then returned the originals to the State Department files.

Chambers repeated his accusations on the radio program, *Meet the Press* after which Hiss sued him for slander. Chambers countered by providing documents he had hidden for years for just such an event. The documents were copies of stolen State Department reports which bore Hiss' handwriting. A grand jury then indicted Hiss on two counts of perjury, for denying he knew Chambers in 1938 and that he had never handed over documents to Chambers. Two trials ensued, the first, in 1949, ending in a hung jury. The second trial in 1950 saw Hiss convicted and he was sent to jail.

After serving four years in the federal penitentiary at Lewisburg, Pennsylvania, Hiss was released. He claimed that he had been victimized by the FBI which had tapped his phone as early as 1945 and had used what they had heard to frame him through Chambers. He attempted to vindicate himself throughout the 1980s but was unsuccessful. The Hiss-Chambers affair is debated to this day, with conservatives taking Chambers' side, and liberals claiming that Hiss was framed.

[ALSO SEE: *Whittaker Chambers*]

HISTIAEUS OF MILETUS
Greek Spy Against Persia ▪
(Sixth Century B.C.)

HERODOTUS, THE FATHER OF GREEK HISTORY, relates the tale of Histiaeus of Miletus, who opposed the invasion of Scythia in 513 B.C. by Persian King Darius I. As an envoy to Darius, Histiaeus became the Persian king's hostage. Learning that Darius planned to occupy Ionia, Histiaeus hit upon a unique method by which to warn the Greeks.

Histiaeus called his most loyal slave to his chambers where he shaved the man's head, writing a message to his allies on the bald pate. He then ordered the slave to wear a cap until his hair grew back. Once the hair was grown back, Histiaeus sent the slave to Ionia where the Greeks shaved the slave's head and read the message. When revolution broke out in Ionia, which was part of Histiaeus' plan with his Greek allies, Darius sent Histiaeus to Ionia to suppress the revolt. Thus Histiaeus freed himself and was also able to bring his report of Darius' plans to the Greeks.

HOLLIS, ROGER
British Spymaster for MI5 ▪ (1905–1973)

HOLLIS WAS CHIEF OF MI5 FROM 1956 TO 1965, at the height of the Cold War. While in this powerful position and earlier, it is quite possible, according to accusations made after Hollis left his position, that he was a double agent, giving the Soviets everything he knew about British intelligence.

Born in Taunton in Somerset, Hollis joined MI5 in 1939. For the next six years he worked on the Russian desk. A born bureaucrat, Hollis was promoted to deputy director in 1953 and director three years later. After being knighted by the queen, Hollis retired in 1965. When he died in 1973, Hollis was eulogized as a heroic figure of British espionage.

He was anything but, according to later findings. In 1980, author Chapman Pincher claimed that Hollis had been a Russian mole inside MI5 for years and had passed on to the Soviets all he could send them, which was everything British intelligence possessed. A storm of accusations followed. It was revealed that while a student at Oxford, Hollis had befriended notable Communists such as Claude Cockburn.

When Hollis quit Oxford, he got a job with the British-American Tobacco Company which sent him

British spymaster Roger Hollis, one-time head of MI5, who was accused of warning Soviet agent Kim Philby that he was about to be arrested, a charge not proven.

to Shanghai. There he socialized with the Soviet spymaster Richard Sorge, the American Comintern agent Agnes Smedley, and Soviet agent Ruth Kuczynski who later helped to establish a Russian spy ring in Switzerland during World War II. When Hollis contracted tuberculosis, he went to Switzerland for a cure but he took the trans-Siberian railroad to Moscow first. It was at this time, it was concluded, that he received further espionage training and instructions to join British intelligence when returning to England and serve as a deep mole.

Hollis first attempted to join SIS in 1938 but was rejected, the reason being ill health, or so it was later claimed. He was accepted the following year by MI5, showing what some thought was an "excessive amount of zeal" in joining the service. In 1945, the West was shocked to learn that Igor Gouzenko, a cipher clerk in the Russian Embassy in Ottawa, Canada, had defected, exposing a vast Soviet spy network. Hollis was the man chosen to go to Canada to debrief the defector.

Kim Philby, the Soviet double agent working in MI6, was supposed to perform this chore but was busy hushing up another Russian defector. In Hollis' debriefing of Gouzenko he was told that there was an important Soviet mole deep inside MI5. Hollis never reported Gouzenko's statements.

Still later, it was said that Hollis was the man who, in 1963, warned his good friend Kim Philby that he was about to be interrogated by MI5, information which caused Philby to leave Cairo and defect to Russia. In that same year Hollis refused to give Prime Minister Harold Macmillan information on Russian spy Yevgeny Ivanov who had been at the center of the scandal involving him, John Profumo, Christine Keeler, and others. Hollis was also supportive of the traitor and Soviet spy Sir Anthony Blunt when Blunt was granted immunity in exchange for his confession in 1964.

Sir Roger was under such a cloud of suspicion that he was brought into MI5 offices where he was grilled by his successor, Sir Martin Jones. Hollis repeatedly denied having anything to do with Soviet espionage and Jones let it go at that. A decade later, Prime Minister Margaret Thatcher admitted that Hollis had been interviewed but that he had been cleared of any wrongdoing. Hollis peers later recalled how he had been called "Mr. Inertia," due to his unwillingness to take action. It is a matter of record that MI5 under Hollis' direction was lame in catching Soviet agents and those that were caught were identified by defectors to the CIA.

It was later stated that the Soviets had spread the gossip, rumors, and disinformation about Hollis to undermine MI5. This, however, could hardly explain MI5's poor record under Hollis' direction, his strong association to Communist friends, his obvious cover-up of Gouzenko's information and a host of other more than coincidental events that pointed to him as the Soviet agent who got away.

[ALSO SEE: *Anthony Blunt; CIA; Igor Gouzenko; Ruth Kuczynski; MI5; MI6; Kim Philby; SIS; Richard Sorge*]

HONEYMAN, JOHN
American Spy in Revolution ■
(1730–1823)

HONEYMAN WAS A VETERAN OF THE BRITISH ARMY, having fought at Quebec in 1759 when it was captured by General James Wolfe. He later moved to Philadelphia where he met George Washington. Years later, when defeated Americans retreated past his New Jersey farm in 1776, Honeyman went to Washington's headquarters and volunteered his services as a spy. Honeyman posed as a Loyalist thereafter, selling cattle to the British while obtaining information on enemy troops, supplies, and warships entering and departing New York harbor.

Honeyman learned that the Hessian troops were disorganized and poorly led. He went to Washington with this report and it, more than any other, convinced the general to attack Trenton, N.J. To assure victory, Honeyman returned to Trenton and told Colonel Johann Rall, the commanding officer, that Washington's army was all but destroyed and in a long retreat away from New Jersey. Rall ordered his men to relax and enjoy their Christmas celebrations.

Washington then crossed the Delaware on Christmas night, 1776, taking the Hessians completely by surprise and capturing the town and its rich stores. This spectacular spy work by Honeyman was not known until some time later. In the meantime, to protect Honeyman's cover, Washington publicly branded him "a notorious Tory."

Honeyman's home was attacked several times by patriots and his life and that of his family was threatened. Washington finally sent a letter to the patriot elders of Griggstown, New Jersey, explaining that Honeyman and his family were to be treated fairly. Honeyman's espionage activities for Washington thereafter are lost to history, but it is known that he lived a long and prosperous life, much respected and hailed as a great patriot after the Revolution.

FBI chief J. Edgar Hoover (right), shown in the mid-1930s with his then top agent, Melvin Purvis; Hoover fought against the creation of the OSS and its successor, the CIA; his spycatching had more to do with happenstance than expertise.

HOOVER, J(OHN) EDGAR
Director of FBI ▪ (1895–1972)

NO OTHER AMERICAN LAW ENFORCEMENT OFFICIAL IN the twentieth century wielded as much power as did J. Edgar Hoover. His influence on eight presidents and the U.S. Congress was enormous. His name is synonymous with the FBI, which he headed for five decades. The Bureau's headquarters building in Washington is named after Hoover. His imprimateur is everywhere to be found in today's FBI. A superlative bureaucrat (if such can exist), Hoover established the best forensic laboratory in the world and the identification systems organized by him inside the Bureau have yet to see an equal.

Yet Hoover was a poor administrator of the power he possessed. He abused it, often putting himself above the law, ignoring the civil rights of citizens he was honor-bound to protect. He connived to maintain his power and assembled illegal files on individuals he subtly blackmailed. He would tolerate no criticism of the FBI or of himself which he propagandized as invincible. (The author, who was the first to publish a biography of Hoover, the only such book published during his lifetime, personally felt the wrath of the Director for daring to expose his misuse of power.)

Born in Washington on January 1, 1895, the youngest of three children, Hoover's devoutly religious parents taught him to read the Bible every day. Throughout his schooling, he remained apart from gangs and had few friends. Upon his graduation from Brent Public School he went on to Central High School (1909–1913). He entered George Washington University in 1913, studying law. His father, Dickerson Hoover, was a civil servant with a limited income, causing Hoover to work in the Library of Congress to defray college expenses.

Hoover did not excell in sports. In college he attempted to play football but quit after a drop-kicked football flattened his nose. He did not have but a small circle of friends and eschewed the limelight. He nevertheless proved to be an excellent debater and graduated with honors with a law degree in 1916. He obtained his master's degree the following year and immediately went to work for the Department of Justice at $990 a year. It would be his home for the next fifty-five years.

In 1917, he went to work for John Lord O'Brien, special assistant in charge of war work for Attorney General Thomas W. Gregory. Hoover's first assignments dealt with ferreting out German spies from the ranks of innocent immigrants.

Heading the Enemy Alien Registration section of O'Brien's office, Hoover's job was to determine which of the arrested immigrants were innocent and which might qualify as legitimate suspects of espionage. This put the 22-year-old Hoover in a weighty position of power. He alone determined who was to be branded a potential spy or not. From that moment on, Hoover's acute sense of personal power would never leave him. He fed on it and, in the end, it would consume him.

By 1919, a year after World War I had ended, America was aflame with the "Red Scare." This was the time of the Russian revolution and its resultant civil war. Bolsheviks were seen hiding behind every American tree, seeking to violently overthrow the U.S. government. There was at the time, no single Russian intelligence network operating in America. Disorganized anarchist and Bolsehevik groups did plot to disrupt the government; one ring of anarchists did plan a number of assassinations of high-positioned political leaders.

The ring's poorly organized attacks began on June 2, 1919, when two witless anarchists placed a home-made bomb on the front doorstep of the Washington home of Attorney General A. Mitchell Palmer. The bomb exploded prematurely, destroying the front of the house and killing both anarchists. A bloody foot of one of the bombers was blown across the street to land on the stoop of the home occupied by Franklin D. Roosevelt, then Secretary of the Navy. It was soon learned that the ring had sent out thirty-eight similar bombs in the mail or by personal delivery to congressmen, senators, judges, administration officials, and business leaders. They injured no one, except the servant of one target, Senator Tom Hardwick of Georgia.

The result was a "Red Scare" that panicked most of the nation, and, in particular, Washington officials. Hoover's work in Enemy Alien Registration brought him to Mitchell's attention and he was immediately named to head the Justice Department's General Intelligence Division (GID). Then twenty-four, Hoover had little or no idea of what he was dealing with and to quickly gather insight about the enemy he went to the library. He steeped himself in the works of Karl Marx, Frederick Engels, Lenin, and Leon Trotsky. Within a few weeks Hoover emerged from the scriptorium with the firm belief that he was the leading American expert on the evil machinations of the radical left.

Hoover's eye-opening crash-course in communism convinced him that a "Red Menace" indeed existed and that it posed the most serious threat to American democracy. This belief would remain Hoover's abiding and obsessive passion for the rest of his life. Palmer ordered widespread, random arrests of anyone suspected of being a Marxist or anarchist. As these radicals were rounded up, Hoover prepared briefs against the top leftist agitators, chiefly Emma Goldman and Alexander Berkman. They were brought to trial and quickly convicted of treason and subversive activities.

Goldman, Berkman, and 245 other radical leftists were immediately ordered deported to Russia. Hoover took this as a personal triumph and, on December 2, 1919, was delighted in escorting the radicals to the gangplank of the departing ship, the creaking steamer *Buford*, which the press had dubbed "the Soviet Ark." As the ship pulled away, Hoover contemptuously waved farewell. Emma Goldman sneered from the railing of the ship and thumbed her nose. Alexander Berkman shook his fist and shouted: "We'll come back and when we do we'll get you bastards!"

A week later Hoover submitted a lengthy report to Palmer that detailed the Communist plot to violently overthrow the government. Palmer was so unnerved by Hoover's alarming report that he ordered another series of sweeping arrests of members of the Communist Party of America and the Communist Labor Party.

Beginning on January 2, 1920, more than 2,500 persons were arrested. Agents wildly broke down doors to seize aliens. Many of these hastily appointed federal agents acted without warrants and without checking proper identities. This resulted in dozens of innocent people being taken into custody. Another 446 persons were convicted of treason and deported but the display of raw power had unnerved the press. Members of Congress denounced Palmer as a tyrant who illegally ordered arbitrary arrests without evidence or foundation.

While Palmer bombastically defended himself, the mole-like Hoover went on ferreting out suspects, going unnoticed. For months he went on compiling dossiers and directing GID agents to scour the countryside for Reds. So effective was Hoover's work thought to be that he was transferred to the Bureau of Investigation on August 22, 1921, and awarded a $4,000 yearly salary. By this time he had changed his name (not officially) from John Edgar Hoover to J. Edgar Hoover. He did this after learning that another Washington resident, a spendthrift with creditors hounding him, had the name of John Edgar Hoover.

What Hoover did exactly at the Bureau at this time is not known, but he did spend a great deal of time spying on the then director, William J. Burns, who had once been a famous detective and had operated the celebrated Burns Detective Agency. He also spied on other agents such as the ubiquitous Gaston Bullock Means.

Hoover learned that Means was a go-between for oil tycoons like Harry Sinclair and Secretary of State Albert B. Fall, arranging secret meetings between these people, along with huge bribes in exchange for clandestine agreements to turn over oil-rich government lands to the oil interests. He later lambasted Means in a formal complaint to Burns, labeling Means amoral and an opportunist.

No womanizer, the only female of any importance to Hoover was his mother with whom he lived. Further, he never drank, did not socialize, ate in quiet restaurants, and had but a few friends. One of these friends, Larry Richey, was an aide to Secretary of Commerce Herbert Hoover. When President

Harding died and Calvin Coolidge became President, he fired Harry M. Daugherty and replaced him with conservative Harlan Fiske Stone as Attorney General. Stone knew Burns was inept and looked about for a replacement. The name of J. Edgar Hoover was suggested by Herbert Hoover after Richey recommended his friend.

Stone interviewed Hoover who said he would accept the job as Bureau chief only if he had a free hand to get rid of the corrupt agents such as Means and the political patronage system. He insisted that all agents be lawyers or accountants and that he have absolute control. Stone approved and, on May 10, 1924, J. Edgar Hoover, age twenty-nine, became head of the Bureau of Investigation.

For seven years Hoover concentrated on cleaning up the Bureau, which became the Federal Bureau of Investigation. He established an expanding fingerprint division until it contained one third of the adult population of the U.S. He began a forensic division that became the envy of law enforcement agencies worldwide. Hoover's agents were trained through its own FBI academy in martial arts and the thorough methods of detection. He established codes and regulations that strictly controlled the complete conduct of his agents.

By the early 1930s, Hoover was faced with a crime wave created by the Great Depression, and his force spent most of its time chasing down bandits such as John Dillinger, Charles Arthur "Pretty Boy" Floyd, the Barker clan, and others. Hoover by then had become publicity conscious and to bolster his yearly budget from Congress, he stressed the invincibility of his "G-Men," a term he invented. Throughout this period, Hoover utterly ignored the rise of organized crime in the U.S. (denying almost to his dying day that such an organization even existed, even though he knew better). He also ordered his agents to conduct surveillance of known Communists, still believing that the greatest threat to the U.S. was the "Red Menace."

With the coming of World War II, Hoover began to work closely with the British Secret Intelligence Service (SIS), which had its U.S. clandestine headquarters at Rockefeller Plaza in New York, run by British spymaster William Stephenson. British intelligence, in 1940, then worked clandestinely with the U.S. and Hoover since America had yet to enter the war against the Axis Powers. At first, the FBI chief, under the watchful eye of President Roosevelt and England's Prime Minister Winston Churchill, extended enormous help to Stephenson's operation, which would grow to a force of 2,000 persons working in the U.S.

The Director's insistence on control began to dominate his relationship with Stephenson. The British believed that Hoover, well-intentioned or not, could not set aside a policeman's mentality and that his heavy-handed methods proved more of a hindrance than a help. The British, for instance, provided information to Hoover through one of their double agents,

Dusko Popov. Through his Nazi connections, Popov learned that the Japanese intended to attack Pearl Harbor. The FBI Chief thought little of the information, chiefly because he regarded Popov as a playboy. He dismissed Popov's warnings because of the spy's sexual prowess. According to Hoover, Popov "had a liking for bedding two girls at a time." Hoover's obsession with the sexual activities of others would, throughout his long career, prejudice his evaluations of usable information.

With the establishment of OSS (Office of Strategic Services), the American intelligence service of World War II, new problems arose with J. Edgar Hoover. The FBI chief deeply resented the creation of OSS and, in particular, its energetic director, William J. Donovan. Hoover opposed the creation of OSS from the beginning, saying that it would compromise FBI intelligence procedures and operations, particularly in the Western Hemisphere. He was forever objecting to the existence of OSS agents operating in any area outside of its headquarters. In one instance, Hoover formally complained to President Roosevelt about OSS agents operating in South America, which led to a direct and bitter confrontation with Donovan.

Hoover's counterintelligence operations during World War II were generally effective and, in some instances, provided startling and productive results. It was Hoover's FBI laboratory that cracked what the director called "the enemy's masterpiece of espionage," this being the Abwehr's development of the microdot, known as the *Mipu* or *Mikropunkt*. A Professor Zapp at the Dresden Institute developed a process of reducing a sheet of paper to the size of a postage stamp, and then, by photographing the reduced image through a reversed microscope, reducing the document once more to the miniscule size of a dot on a typewriter's "i."

In August 1941, a suspected Nazi agent arrived in the U.S. and his briefcase was examined by the FBI. Nothing incriminating was found at the Bureau lab in Washington until a technician held up one of the sheets of paper found in the briefcase before a light and saw a tiny gleaming dot inside the typewritten words. The dot was carefully lifted and examined under a powerful microscope to reveal a secret letter of instructions to the spy. Thus the mystery of the microdot was solved.

In pre-war America, Hoover continued to assign a good number of his agents to keep a staggering list of "Reds" under surveillance. He also kept agents on the trail of many suspected Nazi agents and collaborators.

Much of the success Hoover had in cracking Nazi spy rings prior to World War II came from information provided by other Allied intelligence agencies or through sheer accident. Both elements were involved with pinpointing Germany's top spymaster in the U.S., Major Ulrich von der Osten. William Stephenson's intelligence service in the U.S. had intercepted several messages Osten had written under an alias and sent these along to Hoover for analysis.

The Bureau immediately began a search for the German spymaster but were unable to identify or locate him until Providence took a hand.

At 8:45 P.M., on March 18, 1941, Osten and one of his agents, Kurt Ludwig, stepped into the street at Times Square in New York after having dined at a nearby Child's Restaurant. Two cars suddenly crashed, one hitting Osten. He was rushed to a hospital and died the next day. The stunned Ludwig called his spymaster's hotel, The Taft, where Osten had been staying under the name of Don Julio.

Ludwig explained to the hotel manager that "Mr. Julio has met with a serious accident" and that he would stop by shortly to pick up the victim's luggage. The hotel manager asked Ludwig to identify himself and the spy panicked, quickly hanging up the phone. Suspicious, the manager contacted the FBI. Agents inspected the dead man's effects and soon discovered he had been Osten. Moreover, phone numbers found in the dead man's belongings led to the identification of Ludwig and his spy ring in New York.

The FBI stepped up its counterintelligence activities so that by June 29, 1941, Hoover was to jolt the public with an announcement that his Bureau had conducted "the greatest spy roundup in a series of sudden raids." His agents picked up spymasters Hermann Lang, Everett Roeder, and the unbiquitous Frederick Joubert Duquesne. Much of the success for Hoover's smashing of the top German spy rings in the U.S. had to do with a youthful German-American William G. Sebold who had been asked to spy for Germany and who had gone to the FBI and then acted as a double agent for Hoover.

When war did come, Hoover's success against German saboteurs was considerable but this was due mostly to the ineptitude of the Nazi agents such as the unfortunate eight German spies landed by submarine in the Abwehr's abortive Operation Pastorius. These saboteurs were identified by alert U.S. citizens who provided FBI agents with enough information to track them down. Hoover personally interviewed all eight German saboteurs, striking deals with two of them who turned against their colleages. Six were executed. The two providing Hoover with information were spared.

In many instances, Hoover "turned around" German spies so that they became double agents, sending out messages from America to Germany, information that was controlled by Hoover and his men. One German agent, however, was clever enough to deceive the FBI chief into believing that he had switched his loyalties and was serving as an American agent acting as a German agent in sending false messages to the Abwehr throughout World War II. In reality, he fooled Hoover and the FBI. He did send out fake messages but he also sent out real and valuable information and almost right up to the time that Germany collapsed in April 1945.

This spy, who worked alone and with great diligence, was Walter Koehler, a Dutchman who had spent many years working in the U.S. as a jeweler. Koehler had worked for the Abwehr in World War I, and served as a "sleeper" agent in the U.S. between the wars. He had returned to Holland in 1941 and then pretended to flee Nazi oppressors the following year, returning to the U.S. Koehler had by that time been given courses in nuclear research since the Abwehr knew the U.S. was spending a great deal of money in developing some kind of nuclear weapon. It was Koehler's job to learn everything he could discover on America's nuclear weapons program and report this to Germany.

Koehler was given a large sum of money and then sent to Madrid. He was originally ordered to go to Argentina, then back to the U.S. When in Madrid, Koehler discovered the route to Argentina blocked. He then formulated his own ingenius plan to penetrate the U.S. He went to the American consul in Madrid and told them a simple but shocking story.

The fat little man wearing thick-lensed glasses told the consul that he was employed by the German secret service. "They are sending me to the United States on a special espionage mission," he said in a calm voice. He then went on to admit that the Abwehr wanted him to establish a secret radio station and transmit reports on troop movements to Germany via shortwave. To prove his claim, Koehler showed the consul his spy kit, including a manual for the construction and operation of a wireless set, secret inks, ciphers, his call letters, and a prayer book on which his code was based. He also displayed chemicals for the making of secret inks and a powerful magnifying glass to be used to read documents reduced by microphotography.

More convincing still, Koehler produced $6,230 in U.S. currency and traveler's checks which the Abwehr had given him. He also displayed some jewelry, gold coins, and rare stamps which he was to have used to barter for more cash. Koehler swore that as a Catholic and a Dutchman, he hated the Nazis and then he proposed that he be sent to the U.S. to carry out his mission for the Germans but that he would really serve as an agent for the U.S. The consulate contacted the FBI and Hoover personally reviewed Koehler's story. The FBI chief believed the tale and asked the State Department to grant Koehler a visa. Hoover then dispatched a terse message to the consulate in Madrid: "Send him along."

In August 1942, Koehler embarked for New York on board a Portugese ship sailing from Lisbon. FBI agents were waiting at dockside to meet Koehler but were shocked to discover that he was not on board. He had been taken off the ship when it was off the coast of Florida by the Coast Guard after the ship had sent an urgent message that one of its passengers was seriously ill with pneumonia.

Agents finally located Koehler in a Florida hospital and, after he was nursed back to health, took him to a secluded estate on Long Island, New York. In a large mansion ringed with guards and police dogs,

FBI agents set up Koehler's radio station. Three FBI men, all trained in German linguistics, worked eight-hour shifts while pretending to be Koehler. Their first message was sent to Germany on February 7, 1943, one that contained bogus information, of course. For two years the messages from Long Island to Hamburg continued with the Germans fully accepting Koehler as their top agent in the U.S., one that sent completely reliable information.

Hoover later stated that "week by week we fed the Germans military and industrial information (cleared with the armed services) for the most part true." The information contained ship movements in U.S. ports, classified weather reports, names and types of warships in drydock for repair, and, in particular, the insignia of troops being transported from New York. The Germans were pleased with the information and sent him greetings on his birthday, Christmas, and New Year's Day. The FBI agents operating his key, all trained to have the same touch, gave the same kind of cheery response.

Hoover was elated. He had completely fooled the Abwehr. "We wanted to find out whether any other spies were operating in America," he later said. Hamburg might tell Koehler to get in touch with them. We wanted to know how the Germans paid their operatives in the Americas. And, most important, we wanted to mislead the High Command by feeding it false information. We succeeded on all scores." This was not the case. Only long after the war when Abwehr documents were inspected, was it learned that Koehler, not the FBI, had succeeded in accomplishing his mission. The number of actual transmissions made by the FBI to Germany on Koehler's behalf was 115. Yet Abwehr files later revealed that 231 messages had been received from Koehler. Also, the cipher which Koehler had identified as being assigned to him by the Abwehr and the one used by the FBI agents for two years was the same as those in 115 messages received in Hamburg but another 116 messages from Koehler were in an entirely different cipher.

These 116 messages contained the real information the Germans expected and got. From the beginning, Koehler's story had been planned by the Abwehr. They had concocted the plan for Koehler to go to the American consul and admit that he was an Abwehr spy. He was to cooperate but once inside the U.S., he was to conduct espionage completely apart from that enacted on his behalf by the FBI. This he did, gathering information and slipping messages to a German spy who picked up the coded messages and then returned to Rochester, New York, where they were transmitted to Abwehr offices in Paris.

The Abwehr knew that the FBI messages were fake but that those coming from Rochester were real. Moreover, if Koehler had to transmit pressing information, he simply slipped down to New York docks at night, went aboard Spanish freighters and had the ship's wireless operator send his messages. Koehler funded much of his own operations. He had not turned over all the money given him, but had kept about $10,000 in U.S. currency.

Koehler had never been taken to the Long Island mansion where the FBI operated his phony radio station. He was placed in comfortable rooms at a midtown Manhattan hotel and was given a job in a radio repair shop. It was in this shop that Koehler received information from other German agents still active in the U.S. throughout World War II. Although Koehler was originally kept under surveillance, this coverage was dropped after a few months. Hoover simply could not spare the men to watch him and other "turned agents" night and day. Moreover, from the response the FBI agents in Long Island received from Hamburg, Hoover's ruse had worked completely, or, at least, he thought so.

Koehler did fail, however, in obtaining information on nuclear weapons being developed in the U.S. The security surrounding the Manhattan Project was so intense he was never able to penetrate the screen. That was left to British scientist and Russian spy Klaus Fuchs and others. Koehler survived the war as the most successful triple agent in Abwehr history (or that of any other agency for that matter), a clever little man who completely hoodwinked J. Edgar Hoover.

There were many who attempted to do the same thing following World War II. These were Hoover's arch foes, the Soviet spies. Throughout the Cold War, Hoover concentrated on tracking down Red spies and his agents were instrumental in snaring such important Russian agents as Judith Coplon and Rudolf Abel. In 1956, Hoover established Cointelpro (counterintelligence programs), which were chiefly aimed at domestic espionage. These programs involved wiretapping anyone suspected of subversive activity, as well as infiltrating political groups by FBI informers. (Hoover always felt that FBI agents themselves should never perform undercover activities since they might more easily be compromised or corrupted.)

From 1961, the Bureau's Cointelpro programs were expanded to include those demonstrating against the Vietnam War. Hoover considered such anti-war demonstrators a threat to national security as he did any vocal black leaders such as Martin Luther King, the advocate of non-violent protests. Hoover tapped King's phone and made much of the black leader's reported sexual escapades, attempting to ruin King's reputation by spreading the scandal that he was a womanizer.

At the same time, Hoover took an obsessive interest in any black movements that seemed to threaten national security, particularly the paramilitary Black Panther Party which trained its recruits in marching drills and adopted a militia-type posture.

Cointelpro came under severe criticism by 1970 with critics claiming that Hoover was violating constitutional and civil rights by spying on U.S. citizens.

With pressure mounting, the director disbanded Cointelpro in 1971. By that time, Hoover had been exposed as a neurotic who felt that Moscow was behind every protest in America, a bigot who refused to accept minorities and women into the FBI, and, worse, a scheming conspirator who kept files on upstanding Americans with the intention of using the information contained therein as a form of blackmail to further the FBI's ends.

On the night of May 1, 1972, J. Edgar Hoover dined at the home of Clyde Tolson, his lifelong friend and Associate Director of the FBI. He then returned home to retire. His housekeeper, Annie Fields, made him the usual breakfast the next morning, toast, soft-boiled eggs, and coffee. He did not come downstairs to eat it. Fields found him sprawled in his pajamas on the bedroom floor, dead of a heart attack. The most powerful man in America for almost fifty years was given a state funeral. He was in death far from the young reformer who openly dedicated himself to establishing the Federal Bureau of Investigation as a powerful instrument of justice. In one interview near the end of his reign, Hoover summed up his own character of dictatorial power, stating that "law and order is first, justice is incidental."

[ALSO SEE: *Rudolf Abel; Wilhelm Canaris; Judith Coplon, William J. Donovan; FBI; OSS; William G. Sebold; SIS; William Stephenson*]

Ex-chief petty officer Harry Houghton of the Royal Navy; he sold secrets to KGB agent Gordon Lonsdale.

HOUGHTON, HARRY FREDERICK
British Spy for the Soviets ▪ (1906–)

BRITISH-BORN HOUGHTON JOINED THE ROYAL NAVY in 1922 and rose to the rank of chief petty officer before being mustered out in 1945. Houghton went to work at the Navy's Underwater Weapons Establishment in Portland. Also working at the same post was Ethel Elizabeth "Bunty" Gee with whom Houghton formed a close relationship, despite the fact that he was married.

Houghton and Gee were contacted by a Soviet diplomat who was later identified as Russian spymaster Gordon Lonsdale. The Soviet agent asked for information on British submarine detection. At the time British and NATO technology in underwater technology was far in advance of the Russians. Both Houghton and Gee passed the information on to Lonsdale in return for several hundred pounds. Lonsdale gave the information to Peter and Helen Kroger (also known as Cohen), an American couple who had an apartment in London where they transmitted information to Moscow via shortwave radio.

Houghton was anything but discreet when it came to spending the money he earned through

espionage. A naval security officer witnessed some of Houghton's sprees and found it strange that the ex-chief petty officer could have so much money on a meager salary and navy pension. He called this to the attention of Scotland Yard's Special Branch, which put Houghton and Gee under surveillance.

In early 1962, officers from MI5 and the Special Branch, led by Detective Superintendent George Smith, pounced on Houghton, Gee, and Lonsdale as they were meeting near London's Old Vic Theater. At that moment Gee was turning over a shopping basket to Lonsdale that contained a tin filled with microfilm and four large Admiralty files. The developed film produced several hundred photographs of British warships, including specifications for the atomic submarine *Dreadnought*.

The Krogers were also arrested and all five were placed on trial and sent to prison. After serving eight years, Houghton and Gee were released. They were then married and Houghton later published his version of the Portland espionage case. Lonsdale and the Krogers were exchanged for British subjects who had been held as spies in Russia.

[ALSO SEE: *Helen and Peter Kroger; Gordon Lonsdale*]

Frumpish, middle-aged Ethel Gee, being escorted by police to her trial for espionage; she provided her lover Harry Houghton with secrets she stole from British admiralty offices.

HOWARD, EDWARD LEE
American Spy for Soviets ■ (1952–)

ALDRICH AMES WAS NOT THE FIRST CIA AGENT TO sell secrets to the Russians. That dubious honor went to Edward Lee Howard, a drug-taking, heavy-drinking adventurer who, despite his suspicious background, was accepted by the CIA and trained to occupy an important position in Moscow, even though Howard had admitted to a CIA colleague that he had contemplated selling American secrets to the Russians.

Howard joined the CIA in 1981. In his application to the CIA, Howard admitted that he was a "moderate" drinker and he had confided that he had occasionally used drugs—marijuana, cocaine, Quaaludes, LSD, and hashish. None of this caused his rejection by the agency, which concluded that his education, overseas experience, and expertise with firearms made him a good candidate. He was eventually trained for special duty with the CIA's Soviet/East European division, the sacrosanct SE that ran all of the agency's spies in Russia and the Eastern block and was headed by Burt Gerber.

Following his intensive training, Howard was about to be assigned to a position in Moscow, one of the most sensitive assignments the CIA could make. He was thoroughly briefed as to all of the important agent contacts the CIA had in the Moscow area, as well as important espionage operations the CIA was then conducting behind the Iron Curtain. A short time before Howard was to be sent to Moscow, CIA officials learned that Howard had a drinking problem. He was ordered to take a polygraph test that revealed Howard was using drugs and was involved with petty theft. The decision was made to force Howard into resigning.

The CIA apprehensions were to become a nightmare. By ousting Howard, the agency made a bitter enemy. He next did the very thing they had feared, contacting the Soviets and going to Europe several times where he met with Russian agents and divulged whatever he knew about his aborted Moscow assignment, including names of U.S. agents.

In September 1984, Howard openly admitted to CIA officials that he had once stood outside the Soviet Embassy in Washington with thoughts of contacting the Russians and selling them all he knew of the CIA's SE operations in Moscow. (By then, Howard had long been in contact with the Soviets; in 1983, knowing that the FBI had no surveillance on the Soviet consulate located on Phelps Place in Washington, he simply walked into the building and left a note that stated that he was a disgruntled CIA man and wanted to talk to someone.)

Despite the red flags, CIA officials did not alert the FBI so that Howard could be put under surveillance.

Edward Lee Howard (photo taken in 1983), former CIA agent who sold information to the Soviets, then fled to Russia in a daring escape.

They thought they could handle the temperamental Howard themselves, not realizing that he had already enriched himself by hundreds of thousands of dollars by selling secrets to the Russians.

Then, on August 1, 1985, the world's intelligence community was shaken by a bombshell. Vitaly Yurchenko, the top KGB official in Moscow, defected to the West. Yurchenko's job had been to supervise all KGB espionage operations in the U.S. and Canada. Yurchenko simply walked into the U.S. Embassy in Rome and asked for a CIA officer, saying that he was seeking asylum in America. Taken to a safe house in Virginia, Yurchenko immediately began to tell CIA officials that they had two traitors in the midst of the American intelligence community.

The first double agent pinpointed by Yurchenko was an operative for the super secret NSA (National Security Agency), which specialized in codes and electronic surveillance throughout the world. This agent had actually walked into the Soviet Embassy in Washington when Yurchenko was stationed there. The Russian did not reveal the agent's name but his information quickly helped to identify Ronald W. Pelton, who was arrested by the FBI and later convicted and jailed for espionage.

Yurchenko then said that a CIA agent who bore the KGB code name "Robert" had met with Russian officials in Austria in the Fall of 1984 and had turned over secrets and had received large sums of cash. He did not know "Robert" personally, Yurchenko said, but he did know that this agent had been specially trained for a post in Moscow but had been suddenly removed before being sent to Russia.

Horrified, the CIA quickly realized that "Robert" could be none other than Edward Lee Howard. Yurchenko's alarming information dovetailed with recent CIA setbacks in Moscow. The chief of station there had been sending in disturbing reports that many of the agency's operations had been "blown." In one recent incident, CIA agent Paul M. Stombaugh, Jr., who had diplomatic cover, had been expelled from Russia for conducting espionage. Six weeks later, one of Stombaugh's nationals, Adolf G. Tolkachev, a defense researcher, was arrested and later executed for treason. Other CIA agents fell victim to the KGB, all turned over by the traitorous Howard.

CIA reaction was one of shock, dismay, and silence. Agency officials, to avoid embarrassing the CIA, decided not to inform the FBI, which was responsible for all counterintelligence inside the U.S. Howard still lived in America, residing in Santa Fe, working as an economic analyst for the New Mexico State Hospital. By contacting the FBI about Howard, the CIA would have to admit that it had known its own agent was a security risk and had done nothing about it. On August 7, 1985, CIA officials finally faced the music and informed the FBI's Phil Parker that it had identified "Robert" as Edward Lee Howard.

The day before, August 6, Howard inexplicably flew to Zurich and then went to Vienna. It was later assumed that when Yurchenko defected, Howard, among other KGB informers who would be compromised by the Russian spymaster, was contacted by the Russians and that he flew to Europe to meet with his Russian caseworkers, receive cash, and prepare for his own defection. Nevertheless, he returned to his New Mexico home without the FBI knowing he had been out of the country.

Howard's home was placed under FBI surveillance and he was tailed to and from work, in fact everywhere he went. But Howard had been well-trained by the CIA. He was an expert in detecting such surveillance and spotted the FBI agents jogging in baseball caps near his house, the low-flying small planes buzzing overhead, and the vans parked across the street, behind the tinted windows of which he knew were surveillance cameras and listening devices. He went about his business as usual, secretly making plans for his wife and child and preparing to make his escape.

The FBI could do little more than watch him. They had no hard evidence of his treason. Yurchenko had never met him and could not identify him as "Robert," and everything that had happened—the compromised American agents and operations in Moscow—all of this was circumstantial. Not having enough evidence to arrest him, the FBI decided to jolt a confession from Howard by directly accusing him. They called him to the Santa Fe Hilton Hotel in mid-September 1985. This is where the Bureau had established the headquarters for the special surveillance detail assigned to Howard.

Howard sat in a hotel room surrounded by agents who tried the direct approach. "You're a Soviet agent, we know it," one of the FBI men told him.

"It's not true," Howard replied.

"We know what you did," another FBI agent joined in.

"No, I did nothing," Howard lied.

"You're lying," said another agent.

Of course he was lying, but Howard knew the Bureau had no hard evidence against him or he would have been arrested much earlier. A few days later, Howard made his plans to escape. He and his wife drove about, even knowing that they were being followed by FBI agents, looking for a good "jumping off" place. This was part of their CIA training, how to make good an escape by having one person drive the other to a remote spot, the escapee rolling out of the car while it was still in motion and a dummy quickly replacing the missing person in the passenger seat next to the driver. The CIA had provided an instantly inflatable dummy for such purposes but Howard had had to surrender this item, called "the jib," when he was forced to resign from the agency. He would have to make his own dummy.

To that end, Howard affixed a white Styrofoam head his wife used for wigs to a broom. To the broom he attached a hanger. Then he put a wig on the Styrofoam head and a jacket on the hanger. His replacement was ready. Next, to make sure that FBI men listening to his phone conversations would believe he was still at his Santa Fe home, instead of in flight, Howard made a tape recording, telling his wife Mary how to use it after he had fled.

Gathering about $1,000 in cash, 10,000 Swiss francs, his American Express card, and passport, Howard also pocketed his TWA getaway card which the CIA had ironically provided to him and which he had not bothered to return. He kissed his little son Lee goodbye, then tearfully left the boy with a babysitter as he and his wife got into their 1979 red Oldsmobile. They drove off and soon realized that no FBI tail was on them. Oddly, as they left their home on Verano Loop, the lone FBI agent inside the van parked across the street did not see them go.

Embarrassed FBI officials later claimed that the agent inside the van was a novice, newly assigned to the field and that he was not looking out of the van's window but at a monitor showing the house from a camera viewing the Howard home from the van. The monitor at that moment, the FBI said, was presenting "reflection and glare. The sun is very strong in the desert." The Howards were gone and the FBI knew nothing about it, still believing their quarry was inside his house.

The Howards drove out of town, onto Interstate 25, then on to the Old Santa Fe Trail, stopping at Alfonso's, a restaurant. Though Howard knew he was not being tailed at the time, he made a call to his home to talk to the babysitter, telling her that he and his wife were at Alfonso's. "I wanted the FBI to know

where I was at the time," Howard later said. But the agents did not react. The call was monitored like all incoming and outgoing calls to and from the Howard house but the listening agent botched the message. He thought that Howard was still in the house making an *outgoing* call.

The Howards finished their dinner, got back into the car and drove along several roads until they came to the appointed jump-off place they had previously selected off the Camino Corrales. Howard popped the dummy up from the floor of the car, opened the door of the car as it made a turn and rolled out and into a deserted spot with high grass.

As the car sped away, his wife at the wheel, Howard looked at the retreating Oldsmobile. The dummy was in place, looking exactly like a live passenger, himself. Mary Howard arrived home at dusk. The FBI agent on duty in the van was amazed to see the Howard car returning, Mary Howard driving the car into the attached garage. A short time later Mary called the psychiatrist her husband had been seeing, knowing it was after work hours and that the analyst's phone answering machine would be on.

When she heard the recorded message, she left the message as her husband had instructed, his own pre-recorded voice on a tape machine, one which had Howard saying that he would see the psychiatrist next week. Ironically, this was the same psychiatrist whose bills were being paid by the CIA as a sop to their ex-employee for forcing his resignation. The FBI did get this message straight and concluded that Howard was still in town and inside his house. By that time, however, the fugitive was in flight to Tucson, Arizona, nursing an arm that later turned black and blue as a result of his leap from the moving car.

Before taking flight, Howard had gone to his office, typed out his resignation and had left this on the desk of his superior, Phil Baca. Just as he was doing so, FBI agents entered the home of William Bosch, a former CIA agent who had been forced out of the agency about the same time as Howard. Bosch admitted that he had not only kept in touch with Howard but they had taken recent road trips together during which they exchanged secrets they knew about the CIA and then "jokingly" Howard proposed going to the Soviet Embassy in Mexico City and selling the KGB information.

"This was a proposal for an espionage partnership," a CIA official later stated, "a classic attempt to recruit a subagent." The FBI thought so, too. In fact, with Bosch's testimony to back them up, the FBI now felt it had enough evidence to arrest Howard. Since it was the weekend, however, they would have to wait until Monday to obtain an arrest warrant, or so they later claimed.

Howard did not expect his boss, Phil Baca, to show up at his office until Monday to find his resignation. Baca, however, stopped by the office on Sunday to retrieve some papers and found the resignation. He had earlier been contacted by the FBI and had been asked to inform them of anything unusual involving Howard. Baca went home and called the FBI office in Santa Fe, leaving the message that Howard had quit his job. Still, the FBI in Washington did not know this until Monday when agent Phil Parker was told that Howard had disappeared.

Howard by then was on a flight crossing the Atlantic, going to Copenhagen. He later traveled about Europe, went to Helsinki, then Canada, South America, then back to Europe. Six months after he had fled, he walked into the Soviet Embassy in Budapest and was greeted warmly by his KGB case-workers who sent him to Moscow where he was given an apartment, a country retreat, and a comfortable salary for selling out his country.

His wife Mary was never charged. She later admitted to FBI agents that her husband had met with KGB agents in Vienna, provided secrets, and was paid. She also admitted that Howard had a numbered Swiss bank account and, upon checking, the Bureau discovered that it contained about $150,000. Moreover, Mary Howard later led FBI agents to a tin ammunition box buried in the desert. It contained part of the payments Howard had received from the KGB, gold Krugerrands, bars of silver, and U.S. currency, all amounting to more than $10,000. This was only one of several such boxes Howard had buried in the desert, the FBI conjectured, but it was the only box they found.

Howard was later interviewed by a Western journalist in Moscow. He insisted that he had not been a spy for Russia. He had fled the U.S., he said, because he had gotten drunk in New Mexico and fired a bullet through the roof of a man's car and that he was facing a long prison sentence for this and other petty crimes. "I didn't want to spend one day in jail,"

Howard said. He was afraid of being sodomized by fellow prisoners. It was better, much better, Howard reveled, to live out his life in Moscow than behind bars in America, even for one day.

[ALSO SEE: *Aldrich Ames; CIA; KGB; Ronald W. Pelton*]

HVA (Hauptverwaltung Aufklarung)
East German Intelligence ▪ (1956–1989)

EAST GERMANY'S HVA WAS BEGUN UNDER THE COVER organization of the Institute of Economic Research. It was headed by sharp and ruthless General Markus Wolf who convinced East German leaders that it was easier to steal industrial secrets than spend the money and time to develop new technology. It was Wolf who placed emphasis on using female agents above males. He trained and placed hundreds of female clerk typists inside the businesses and government agencies of West Germany. These female spies brought him endless secrets from the West.

HVA trained thousands of male agents, sending them to posts in Scandinavia, Ethiopa, and South Yemen. One of its agents, Gunther Guillaume, became an aide to Willy Brandt and, when he was exposed, thoroughly discredited the charismatic West German leader.

[ALSO SEE: *Gunther Guillaume; Markus Wolf*]

IMRO (INTERNAL MACEDONIAN REVOLUTIONARY ORGANIZATION)
Macedonian Terror Group ▪ (1893–1934)

SIMILAR TO THE BLACK HAND SOCIETY THAT operated in Serbia, IMRO was a nationalist secret society that worked for Macedenonian independence. Founded before the turn of the century, IMRO used undercover agents to spread dissent, riot, and rebellion against the Turks who ruled Macedonia. Turkish repression followed until the terror campaign on both sides spilled into the war of 1897 between Greece and Turkey. Macedonia was then divided after World War I, sections of the country going to Greece, Bulgaria, and the newly established country of Yugoslavia.

IMRO revived with great strength in the early 1920s. Its terror operations were chiefly directed against Yugoslavia in an attempt to regain Macedonian territory taken by that nation. In 1923, IMRO agents successfully led the violent overthrow of the Bulgarian government. For the next decade, IMRO spies were everywhere in the Balkans, fomenting unrest and sedition. The society finally collapsed after its leaders began in-fighting, which led to ineffective factionalism.

[ALSO SEE: *Black Hand Society*]

INAYAT KHAN, NOOR
Allied Spy in France in World War II ▪ (1914–1944)

BORN IN MOSCOW, INAYAT KHAN WAS THE daughter of a Sufi missionary. Her father was Indian, her mother American. In 1915, one year after the beginning of World War I, the family fled to the West, settling in France.

Then the Germans invaded France for the second time in the century, panzer armies smashing through stationary French defenses in 1940. Inayat Khan escaped to England and joined the Women's Auxiliary Air Force. In 1943 she joined SOE (Special Operations Executive), the British espionage service working with the undergrounds in countries occupied by the Nazis, chiefly in France.

Trained as a radio operator, Inayet Khan was sent to Paris where she was accepted fully as a French citizen because of her flawless use of the language. Using the code name "Madeleine," Inayat Khan operated her shortwave radio in a small apartment at 40 Rue Erlanger, regularly sending out reports on resistance operations, where Allied planes were to drop arms and supplies by parachute, and the doings of SOE agents throughout France.

Inayat Khan used the cover name of Jeanne-Marie Regnier and worked closely with Henri Garry, a French lieutenant and head of the spy network called Cinema. This network used as its headquarters the National School of Agriculture at Grignon, northwest of Versailles. To this school Inayat Khan regularly peddled her bicycle to deliver and retrieve messages for transmission to London.

On July 1, 1943, she was late in arriving at the school. Seeing about eighty SS and Gestapo agents pouring into the building, Inayat Khan left her bicycle at the side of the road and crept through the hedgerows to witness the Nazis collecting the underground workers. She escaped back to Paris where she reported the raid. More devastating raids ensued until most of SOE's best agents and hundreds of resistence fighters were in custody. It appeared that the counter-intelligence section of the Abwehr had developed expert spies of their own and had penetrated SOE security.

Chief of SOE operations Maurice Buckmaster realized that it was only a matter of time before the Germans located Inayat Khan and he ordered her to return to England, telling her in a coded message that he would send a special plane for her in a night landing. The spy refused, saying that now that the Nazi raids had drastically depleted SOE ranks there was no one to handle radio traffic.

For three more months she stayed at her post. Ever alert, Inayat Khan changed her lodgings frequently during this time, careful to transmit late at night and for brief periods only. After sending a few transmissions to London, she would again move to a new apartment. Her insistence on staying in France took great courage since Inayat Khan, her SOE caseworkers in England knew full well, was terrified of being captured and interrogated. During her training she had undergone mock interrogation and after these exhausting sessions, she appeared pale and trembling.

Inayat Khan nevertheless proved to have steel nerves. Once when traveling on the Metro while carrying her transmitter a German soldier sat down next to her. He noticed the case she was carrying and asked what it contained. Without a pause, the spy told him that "it is part of the machinery for a film projector." The German told her to open the case. She did and he inspected it. After looking over the transmitter, the soldier nodded, saying she was right "because of all the little bulbs." He apparently knew nothing of radio transmitters or film projectors.

On another occasion Inayat Khan was fixing a wire that served as her radio antenna to a tree, running this to the window of her apartment. A German officer appeared and asked what she was doing. "A clothesline," she responded dryly. The officer helped her place the wire to the tree, then walked away.

In mid-October 1943, Gestapo agents were contacted by a French woman whose name was never learned. This woman lived close to Inayat Khan and reported her radio operations. She was paid £500 for her betrayal. The Gestapo swept down on the spy, arresting her while she was in the act of sending out a transmission to London.

There was no question as to Inayat Khan's guilt but she would admit to nothing and reveal nothing under severe interrogation. To the Gestapo commander, she said: "I prefer to be shot immediately." Instead she was confined to the top floor of Gestapo headquarters on the Avenue Foch. Making contact with two other SOE agents also held there, Inayat Khan made plans to escape. The trio did manage to leave the building and appeared to be making their escape when an air raid warning sounded. Gestapo guards checked the cells of all the prisoners and discovered Inayat Khan and the two men were missing. They were quickly recaptured.

Listed as a dangerous prisoner, Inayat Khan was transferred to Pforzheim Prison in Germany where she was ordered to be kept in chains. The commandant thought this harsh and, exceptional for a German prison warden, ignored the order and allowed the spy to move freely inside her cell. On September 13, 1944, she was transferred to Dachau with three other female British agents. All were executed a short time later. Noor Inayet Khan was posthumously awarded the George Cross.

[ALSO SEE: *Abwehr; SOE*]

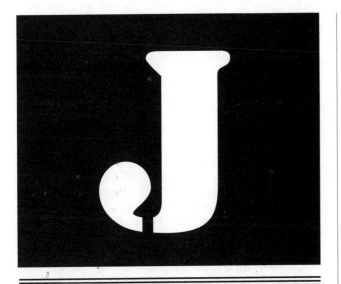

JACKSON, THOMAS JONATHAN (AKA: STONEWALL)
Confederate General and Spymaster ▪ (1824–1863)

ONE OF THE MOST BRILLIANT FIELD COMMANDERS fighting for the Confederacy (whom General Robert E. Lee called his "right arm"), Thomas Jonathan Jackson earned his celebrated nickname at the first battle of Bull Run in 1861. When the Confederate line wavered, General Bernard Bee rallied his troops by pointing to a hill where Jackson and his men stood ready to repel Union troops. "Look!" shouted Bee, "there stands Jackson like a stone wall!" He was Stonewall Jackson ever afterward.

An amazing strategist and tactician, Jackson was also a superb spymaster who strongly believed in espionage as an effective tool in winning battles. The Confederate victory of First Bull Run was achieved, Jackson knew full well, because of the precisely correct information supplied by rebel spy Rose Greenhow. In his lightning victories in the Shenandoah Valley in 1862, Jackson employed many spies, particularly Turner Ashby, cavalryman, scout, and master spy. Ashby's excellent information allowed Jackson to destroy one Union army after another.

Ashby knew well exactly what Jackson wanted to know about the enemy, repeated to the spy by Jackson on several occasions: "The position of the enemy's forces, his numbers and movements, what generals are in command and their headquarters, especially the headquarters of the commanding general."

Belle Boyd served Jackson well as a spy. The daring rebel agent rode through Union lines to Jackson's headquarters to warn him that Union troops were advancing on his position at Front Royal, their numbers and the direction of their march. Fully accepting her report, Jackson acted on her information immediately and soundly defeated the Union force.

Jackson's successes were increased when he joined Robert E. Lee's forces to devastate the Union army of General Ambrose Burnside at Fredericksburg in December 1862, and utterly smash Union armies at Chancellorsville the following year. During this battle, however, Jackson, always at the forefront of the fighting, went so far in front of his own advancing lines that he was mistaken for a Union officer and was fatally shot by his own pickets.

[ALSO SEE: *Turner Ashby, Belle Boyd, Rose Greenhow*]

JOB, OSWALD
British Spy for Germany ▪ (1885–1944)

BORN IN BROMLEY, KENT, ENGLAND, JOB RESETTLED in France after he finished his education. He taught English to members of aristocratic families in a language school in Paris, one which he owned. When the Germans overran France in 1940, Job was interned as an enemy alien, placed in a civilian camp at St. Denis, just outside Paris.

In October 1943, Job suddenly appeared at the British Embassy in Madrid. He was emaciated, frail, and weak from malnutrition. Job told interrogators that he had escaped St. Denis and detailed his background.

British security cleared Job and he was given a small apartment in Bayswater in London and a small income from National Assistance. He appeared to live quietly but, like all repatriated British subjects, Job was kept under surveillance by MI5.

Agents noticed one peculiarity in Job's otherwise normal routines. He wrote a great number of letters every day, mailing these as Red Cross letters to friends still imprisoned at St. Denis. The letters were examined and appeared to be innocent until they were sent to MI5 laboratories. All were discovered to contain writing in invisible ink, information obviously directed to German intelligence that was made up of gossip and tidbits of information about British and American military forces, equipment, and naval data.

Job was arrested and charged with espionage and treason. It was learned that his story was true but that he had omitted the fact that while at St. Denis, he had gone to the Nazis and struck a bargain. If released, he would be willing to spy for the Abwehr. A large amount of cash was deposited in a French bank in his name, money he could claim after he served as a spy in England, his assignment being to send information on the impending Allied invasion of France.

Job was convicted of treason and sentenced to death. He was hanged at Pentonville Prison in London on March 16, 1944.

[ALSO SEE: *Abwehr; MI5*]

JOHN, OTTO
German Agent for Soviets ▪ (1909–1997)

THE SON OF A CIVIL SERVANT, JOHN WAS BORN IN Treysa, Germany, where he attended high school. He went on to the University of Frankfurt and attained a law degree in 1933. At that time Adolf Hitler had just risen to power and John became an ardent anti-Nazi. John may have joined the Communist Party at this time. He obtained a job with Germany's top civil airline Lufthansa where his departmental chief was Klaus Bonhoeffer whose brother, Pastor Dietrich Bonhoeffer was a leading member of the Black Orchestra, the secret cabal planning to oust Hitler and his Nazi thugs.

John became an energetic member of this anti-Nazi conspiracy. At the onset of World War II, John, exempt from military service because of his important job as legal adviser to Lufthansa, was able to travel widely and he acted as a courier and contact man for the anti-Hitler forces. As such he worked with the British SOE (Special Operations Executive), MI6, and the American OSS, keeping these Allied intelligence services abreast of his group's activities when visiting neutral Lisbon and Madrid.

In 1944, John informed the Allies that an attempt to assassinate Hitler would be made but the attempt failed. Thousands were arrested and summarily executed, including one of John's brothers, Hans John. John himself escaped, flying to Madrid, then to Lisbon where SOE agents smuggled him to England. He later served as a translator at the Nuremberg Trials of Nazi war criminals in 1945–1946.

So well entrenched with Allied prosecutors was John that they helped him set up a lucrative legal practice in London in 1949, one where he acted as a consultant on German and international law. At this time he married Mrs. Lucie Mankowitz, an opera star who sang under the name of Lucie Manen. He continued to serve Allied prosecutors in preparing cases against German military commanders of World War II, including field marshals Runstedt, Manstein, and Brauchitsch.

The following year, West Germany's President Theodor Heuss, one of John's old friends, appointed him director of the Federal Internal Security Office, which was later retitled the Bureau for the Protection of the Constitution (BfV). It was John's paramount duty to control Soviet espionage in West Germany. Since John's experience in counterintelligence was limited, the organization was slow in developing into an effective agency. In 1954, however, John submitted a report that would vastly overhaul the BfV.

On July 15, 1954, John and his wife Lucie traveled from Bonn to West Berlin to attend the tenth anniversary of the July 20th assassination plot against Hitler. Five days later, John attended the ceremonies. At 7:30 P.M. that night, John left the Hans Schaetzle Hotel alone, going to the home of Dr. Wolfgang Wohlgemuth, a surgeon John had known during the war. The reason for his visit to the physician was to obtain a certificate that would enable one of John's friends to obtain a pension.

What happened next was the subject of hot debate between East and West. John claimed that after he arrived at Wohlgemuth's apartment, he found the doctor just finishing dinner. He was given a cup of coffee and then accompanied Wohlgemuth to his office. As the physician was driving to the office, he told John that he suddenly remembered that he had to retrieve some important papers.

John objected, saying that he was already late for his own dinner appointment. At that point, John said, he grew sleepy and then blanked out. He awoke lying on a couch in a dark apartment. His coat and shoes were missing.

John could see an open door and beyond that a lighted room where three Russians and a huge female nurse were talking at a table. He called out and one of the Russians came to him. John asked for a glass of water. This was given to him. Then John asked: "Where is Dr. Wohlgemuth?"

"Operating at the hospital," the nurse told him.

"What do you want of me?"

"You are to work for us," one of the Russians said. John concluded that the Russians were all KGB agents.

He was then taken to Garba on the Black Sea and interrogated at length but the questions posed by his inquisitors, John later insisted, were routine and did not involve the national security of the Federal Republic of Germany.

Taken to the headquarters of the East German Committee for German Unity, John was given an office and two secretaries. He was ordered to write articles about German reunification (under the Communist banner, of course), and he was also to write letters attacking any anti-Communist articles that appeared in the West German press. Albert Norden, chief of the committee, knew well that John had served as an anti-Nazi propagandist in England during World War II, and expected him to produce top-flight propaganda for the Soviets. This was not the case. John's writing ability was poor.

Though he appeared to be pleased with his new lifestyle, John was all the while planning his escape back to the West, or so John later claimed. Allowed the freedom of visiting the press club, John made contact with Hendrick Bonde-Hendricksen, a Danish journalist, telling the newsman that he planned to escape from the University Library where he had been researching a thesis on international civil law.

On December 12, John was driven to the rear entrance of the library so that he could momentarily retrieve some papers. The KGB men were off-guard and simply nodded to John who went into the building, walked to the front entrance and stepped outside and into a waiting car driven by Bonde-Hendricksen.

A few minutes later the car was at the Brandenburg Gate checkpoint. The guard spotted the Danish license plate and waved Bonde-Hendricksen and his passenger through to West Berlin. John was then taken to Walm, near Bonn, where he was met by the federal prosecutor and others who immediately began interrogating him. He told the tale of abduction and compulsory servitude, but, to his amazement, he was arrested and charged with treason.

Dr. Wohlgemuth did not testify at John's trial but he did supply a written statement, claiming that John met with him to complain of his impotence in combating the rise of Neo-Nazism in West Germany. Wohlgemuth stated that John met with him in his surgery and went voluntarily to East Berlin where he met with high-ranking Russian leaders.

No other evidence was at hand in John's trial. Thus, the defection of John, or his abduction at the hands of the Soviets, was to be decided either on the word of Otto John or Dr. Wohlgemuth. The West German court opted to believe Wohlgemuth. It dealt with John severely, doubling the sentence demanded by the prosecution, giving John four years at hard labor in prison.

When relaeased, John relocated to Austria and quit public life. He wrote a book ten years later in which he claimed that his abduction most likely had to do with his former association with British double spy Kim Philby, that he had known Philby in Spain during the Spanish Civil War. John wrote that his Russian kidnappers constantly questioned him about Philby who had, by that time, not been exposed as a Soviet agent. The Russians were unsure about Philby who had served as their super mole inside SIS. John was convinced that the Soviets had abducted him to determine the loyalty of their master spy, Philby.

Years later Russian intelligence officers defecting to the West signed sworn statements that John had, indeed, been kidnapped. Western intelligence leaders, however, remained suspicious, believing that the Russians were attempting to vindicate one of their own spies so that he would again be accepted by the West where he could do more damage. East German spymaster Markus Wolf admitted in 1997 that John was drugged and kidnapped by Wohlgemuth and the KGB.

[ALSO SEE: *BfV; Black Orchestra; KGB; MI6; OSS; Kim Philby; SOE*]

JOHNSON, ROBERT LEE
American Spy for Soviets ▪ (1920–1972)

An American Army sergeant stationed in Berlin, Johnson married an Austrian national. Hedwig Johnson urged her husband to somehow make more money by contacting the Russians to see if he could sell them any secrets. Johnson contacted the KGB in Berlin in 1952.

U.S. Army Sergeant Robert Lee Johnson, who peddled American secrets out of a top-secret courier station in Paris.

KGB officials patiently heard him out, then proposed to pay him for whatever small secrets he might be able to steal from U.S. Army headquarters in Berlin. They trained him secretly in West Berlin, providing Johnson with spy cameras and showing him how to take photos of documents. Johnson then introduced a fellow soldier, Sergeant James Mintkenbaugh, to his KGB caseworkers. Mintkenbaugh also became a Soviet agent.

Johnson eventually finished his tour of duty and returned to the U.S. Mintkenbaugh showed up in 1956 to reactivate Johnson for Soviet spy work, convincing him to reenlist and attempt to get himself stationed to an important post in Europe. He did exactly that, asking that he be assigned to SHAPE, a target of Russian intelligence. This did not happen. Instead, Johnson was given a post at the Armed Forces Courier Station in Paris at Orly Airport.

The Russians were jubilant. This had been one of their prime espionage targets. Up to that time, the Orly Courier Station had proved to be impenetrable. Now, the Soviets would have a spy inside the very center that dispatched all the important secrets between the Pentagon and U.S. Army commands throughout Europe.

On orders from his caseworker, Johnson volunteered for weekend guard duty, the most unpopular duty hours. He soon discovered that for several hours every Saturday night he was utterly alone at the Orly center. It was at this time that he accessed the security vault, withdrew several packets of information from the vault and turned these over to KGB agents waiting in the parking lot outside.

The Russians quickly took the packets to a special photography center where they made copies of all the

James Allen Mintkenbaugh, who was recruited by Johnson to spy for the KGB and who later reactivated Johnson as a Soviet agent.

ultra-secrets and then, within two hours, rushed the packets back to Johnson who returned them to the vault. The information gleaned by the Soviets was invaluable—U.S. contingency plans for international crises, cryptographic materials, codes, ciphers, troop dispositions and roster lists of American agents in Europe, and up-to-date reports on NATO and Soviet military strengths and weaknesses.

Johnson continued to raid the Orly security vault, making seven successul hauls before he was posted back to the U.S. in April 1963. He was reassigned to the Pentagon where he continued to obtain information for the Soviets, but nothing could match his work in Paris.

Though he had been paid well by the Russians, Johnson began to drink even more heavily. His marriage went to pieces when his wife Hedwig underwent a nervous breakdown. Nagged and threatened by his wife, Johnson went on a bender in October 1964 and staggered onto a bus heading for Las Vegas, mostly to escape the hellish nightmare of his home life.

When Johnson failed to appear at his post, FBI agents investigated his disappearance. They interviewed Hedwig Johnson who broke down and, in a rambling statement, described her husband's spying activities. Johnson sobered up in Las Vegas. He was broke and his nerves were shot. He turned himself in to the local police and was soon arrested and tried for treason, along with Mintkenbaugh. Both men were convicted and, in July 1965, were given twenty-five-year prison sentences. In 1972, Johnson's son Robert, who had served in Vietnam, visited his father in prison and, for what he later described as "personal reasons," suddenly produced a knife and stabbed his father to death.

[ALSO SEE: *FBI; KGB*]

JOSHUA
Spy for Moses ▪ (c.2400 B.C.)

THE FIRST REFERENCE TO SPIES IN THE OLD TESTA-ment of the Bible is made to Joshua, the son of Nun. Joshua, a young military leader of the Israelites, was ordered by Moses to scout Canaan in preparation for its occupation by the Jews who had been grudgingly released by Ramses, Pharoah of Egypt. It was Joshua's task to determine if Canaan had good or bad land, whether or not crops would grow upon the soil, and to gather its fruit and return it to the then wandering Jews.

Joshua was also to learn what kind of people lived in Canaan and the strength and numbers of their armies and bastions. Leading twelve other agents, Joshua and his men went throughout Canaan, returning to report to Moses that the place was truly a land "of milk and honey."

Caleb, one of Joshua's spies, reported that the many tribes of Canaan had formidable armed forces but that they could be overcome. Doubters rose and argued not only against moving to Canaan but urged that Moses and his brother Aaron be deposed as leaders. A rift between the Jewish factions led to the doubters wandering into hostile countries (some reports saying for forty years) while Moses led his people toward Canaan.

Joshua and Caleb making contact with a spy in Canaan, gathering information on the strength of a walled city.

K

K'ANG SHENG (CHAO YUN)
Intelligence Chief for Communist China ▪ (1899– ?)

BORN IN SHANTUNG PROVINCE TO A RICH AND powerful landowner, K'ang Sheng was born Chao Yun, a name he renounced when becoming a Communist to repudiate the bourgeois reputation of his family. He attended Shanghai University in the 1920s, becoming a Communist at that time. Upon graduation, he became a Communist labor organizer, working for the Communists in Shanghai from 1925 to 1933. At the time, he conducted counterintelligence operations against Nationalist agents working for Morris "Two-Gun" Cohen and Tai Li.

In 1927, K'ang Sheng joined the Communist intelligence organization and soon rose through the ranks to a prominent position. By 1933, he was a confidant of Mao Tse-tung who sent him to Moscow where he was trained in the art of espionage. By 1940, he was directing a huge network of spies against the Japanese invaders, as well as the Nationalist Chinese under Chiang Kai-shek.

Following World War II, K'ang Sheng directed all his activities against the Nationalists, chiefly his shrewd counterpart, Tai Li. In 1945 an airplane on which Tai Li was traveling blew up and K'ang Sheng was credited with ordering one of his fanatical agents to carry a bomb on board, one which was self-detonated. With the fall of Chiang Kai-shek's government in 1949, the Nationalists retreated to Taiwan against which K'ang Sheng continued his espionage efforts.

During the 1950s, next to Mao himself, K'ang Sheng became the most powerful man in China. He cemented relationships with the KGB in Moscow but this soon deteriorated. He later conducted widespread counterintelligence operations against the KGB inside China and throughout the Communist bloc nations.

K'ang Sheng devoted a great deal of time in obtaining atomic secrets for China and he lured or abducted many Chinese nuclear scientists back to China where the Communists developed their first atomic bomb. Following Mao's death, however, K'ang Sheng lost power and slipped from public view. His fate was never determined but one report has it that he was murdered by his political enemies and secretly buried.

[ALSO SEE: *Morris Cohen; KGB; Tai Li*]

KAO LIANG
Chinese Communist Spy ▪ (1929–   )

THROUGHOUT MAO'S ERA IN CHINA, THE TOP Communist agent was Kao Liang who traveled throughout the Far East in the guise of a correspondent for the New China News Agency. Wherever he went, Kao Liang gathered intelligence information for Mao's government while financing covert operations that undermined the CIA and KGB. In turn both agencies kept him under surveillance.

Posing as a journalist for the New China News Agency, a front for Communist China's intelligence, Kao Liang, shown arriving in New York at the UN Building, traveled the world as his country's top spy.

Working under the direct instructions of Communist China's spymaster, K'ang Sheng, Kao Liang bought information from Third World government officials and financed open rebellions such as the pro-Chinese Communist uprising in Zanzibar in 1964. In keeping with Mao's edict to subvert Africa to communism, Kao Liang financed rebellions in Kenya, Réunion, and Mauritius in the 1960s. He later became ineffective after being publicly identified as a secret agent.

[ALSO SEE: *CIA; K'ang Sheng; KGB*]

KASTNER, HERMANN
West German Spy ▪ (1886–1957)

THE SON OF A WEALTHY LANDOWNER IN SAXONY, Kastner attended the University of Leipsig where he obtained a law degree. He became a professor of law and throughout the Nazi era in Germany he became celebrated as a defender of anti-Nazis who were brought to trial. Before the end of the war Kastner was arrested by the Gestapo but he managed to survive until freed by Allied troops.

Following the occupation of Saxony by Russia, Kastner worked in the Ministry of Justice in East Berlin and joined the economics commission in 1948. He had by then long given up on communism and had been in contact with West German spy chief Reinhard Gehlen, agreeing to spy for the West. He rose rapidly in the Communist Party hiarchy until he was appointed deputy prime minister under the all-powerful and ruthless Walter Ulbricht, first secretary of the Communist Party of East Germany.

Kastner attended all secret sessions of the Party held by Ulbricht and was able to take home a complete set of the minutes of these meetings, which he copied before secretly returning the cabinet documents. These secrets were easily delivered to the Gehlen organization in West Berlin by Mrs. Kastner who simply drove through several Communist checkpoints on her special pass as the wife of an important Communist leader, ostensibly to shop in the better stores of West Berlin. From 1949 to 1953, Kastner was able to keep Gehlen and the West German Government (the Federal Republic of Germany) completely informed of all Communist intelligence activities.

Suspicion was cast on Kastner by East German agents after they discovered serious information leaks regarding cabinet meetings but the Russian high command in East Germany ignored the accusations leveled against Kastner whom they considered a dedicated Communist and proficient statesman. Then a double agent working in West Berlin defected to the East and Gehlen immediately warned Kastner that this spy would soon expose him as a Western agent.

Kastner and his wife hastily packed their bags (Mrs. Kastner taking her jewels with her) and were smuggled by Gehlen's agents to Bonn. Kastner resumed his law practice and also taught legal classes. He died of a heart attack in 1957.

[ALSO SEE: *Reinhard Gehlen; Gestapo*]

KATHIGASU, EDITH
Allied Spy in Malaya ▪ (? –1948)

A EURASIAN, EDITH KATHIGASU WAS LIVING IN THE small town of Ipoh in Malaya with her physician-husband Addon and their 4-year-old daughter Dawn when the Japanese invaded in 1941. They fled to the interior, where they started a small farm and urged their neighbors to "grow more food" for the Allies and the guerrillas resisting the Japanese.

Kathigasu also operated a clandestine radio over which she informed the British on Japanese troop movements and operations. She also sheltered and nursed British soldiers escaping the Japanese onslaught, as well as wounded guerrillas. The Japanese learned of Kathigasu's espionage activities through an informer. She and her daughter were captured and tortured but neither gave their tormentors any information.

Flown to England after the war, the spy was given an audience with King George who gave her the George Medal for civil heroism. She also received intense medical care, undergoing many operations, but doctors could not mend her broken body. Kathigasu wrote her biography shortly before her death in 1948. She was too weak to finish the last fifty pages, dictating this to a stenographer, telling the press that it was important that "the world know what kind of people these Japanese people are. Already memories are growing short."

She died a few days after completing the book. Kathigasu's body was buried in the small village of Lanark, Scotland.

KATZ, OTTO
Cheka Agent ■ (1900–1952)

THE SON OF A WEALTHY GERMAN MANUFACTURER, Katz (shortened from Katzenellenbogen) studied literature, befriended Franz Kafka, and decided that he possessed literary talents that he did not. He convinced his father to back several of his plays, which failed miserably. After spending two million marks on his son's vanity productions, Katz's father retired. He later lost his fortune in the widespread inflation created by the inept Weimar Republic government.

By then Katz junior was also penniless, but Communist friends suggested that he travel to Moscow where Russian intelligence might take him into its ranks. He did, becoming a Cheka agent, the Cheka being an internal security police force that monitored the activities of Communists in Russia and throughout Europe.

Katz's first assignment from Moscow was to keep one man—Willi Muzenberg, a wealthy Jewish Communist who headed the Communist Party in Germany—under surveillance. Katz went to Paris when the Nazis overran France in 1940. Muzenberg had by then been arrested by order of Marshal Petain and imprisoned. Katz's assignment from the Center was to free Muzenberg.

This he accomplished by bribing guards at a concentration camp near Paris. He personally escorted Muzenberg toward the city but the fugitive never lived long enough to revisit Paris. His body was found hanging from a tree a day later. It was clear that Katz had executed Muzenberg on orders from Stalin who was fearful of what the former German Communist might reveal if he remained in custody. The execution of Muzenberg had all the earmarks of the Russian assassination bureau known as SMERSH which, by then, Katz had joined as a special agent.

Remaining in Paris, Katz used the cover name of Andre Simone. He used this name when going to the American Embassy in Lisbon a short time later, asking for a visa to visit the U.S. He arrived in New York and immediately traveled to Hollywood where, the FBI learned quickly, he attempted to organize actors, writers, and producers into Communist cells. The FBI was about to arrest Katz as an emeny agent but he was warned and fled to Mexico where he remained until 1943, when he traveled to Moscow.

At the end of World War II, the Red Army flooded into Czechoslovakia and with them came Otto Katz, then a colonel of the NKVD, but still acting as a Cheka agent. It was his mission to ferret out disloyal Communists. Hundreds of suspects fell into his net and were imprisoned. Many simply vanished. By 1948, Katz was chief of the Czech Government Information Service, a cover for his Cheka activities. In this role, Katz undermined the work of Czech Foreign Minister Jan Masaryk who, like Willi Muzenberg years earlier, was accused of treason and committed suicide, a death that Katz himself arranged in his wild bid for power.

Moscow by this time had grown extremely suspicious of Katz who acted independently and operated at will. In 1952, at Moscow's bidding, a great purge of the Czechoslovakian Communist leadership took place. Among those arrested was Katz, who was taken into custody under his alias, Andre Simone, his occupation then listed as a journalist working on the staff of *Rude Pravo*, the official Communist newspaper in Czechoslovakia. He was tried and condemned as "an agent of Jewish bourgeois nationalists," and he was hanged. Only after the execution, was his real name, Otto Katz, released to the West.

[ALSO SEE: *The Center; Cheka; NKVD*]

KAUNITZ, WENZEL VON
Austrian Spymaster ■ (1711–1794)

BORN INTO THE AUSTRIAN ARISTOCRACY, KAUNITZ joined the diplomatic service of Archduchess Maria Theresa in 1740. He became Ambassador to France in 1750 and three years later became chancellor of Austria. It was Kaunitz who engineered the "diplomatic revolution" of 1756, which, through artful persuasion, brought France to Austria as an ally against Prussia and its iron-fisted ruler, Frederick the Great.

For forty years Kauntiz remained one of the most powerful figures in Europe, much of his influence supported by his wide-ranging espionage networks. He established postal stations throughout the Holy Roman Empire and at each station his spies carefully opened all mail, read the contents, recorded important information, then resealed the letters, and sent them on for delivery. In this manner, Kaunitz was the best-informed spymaster in Europe, receiving all diplomatic and military information culled from tens of thousands of letters.

Another successful intelligence ploy used by Kaunitz was to plant dozens of his own spies as couriers for Frederick the Great's diplomats and military leaders. He thus read secret dispatches even before they reached Frederick. Learning of this espionage operation, Frederick matched wits with Kaunitz by planting double spies in the ranks of his courier system so that he was able to supply Kaunitz with a great deal of misinformation.

When Joseph II became emperor of Austria, Kaunitz remained in his all-important position but when Austria switched allegiance to Prussia during the French Revolution his power waned and his spy network crumbled. He resigned in 1792, dying two years later.

[ALSO SEE: *Frederick the Great*]

KEENAN, HELEN
British Spy for South Africa ▪ (1945–)

IN 1967, HELEN KEENAN, A TYPIST WORKING FOR British Prime Minister Harold Wilson at 10 Downing Street, London, suddenly quit her job. A suspicious officer from Scotland Yard's Special Branch, which worked closely with MI5, decided to interview Keenan. The secretary quickly confessed that the real reason she was leaving her job was that she was upset in having smuggled minutes of Wilson's cabinet meetings to a South African man named Norman Blackburn. She said that she had met Blackburn at the Zambesi Club and had become involved with him.

Scotland Yard's Special Branch wasted no time in arresting Blackburn who identified himself as an intelligence officer working for the South African Intelligence Service, called BOSS, and that he had been delivering the material supplied by Keenan to a Rhodesian intelligence officer at a secret rendezvous in Dublin. Both Blackburn and Keenan were tried and convicted in July 1967. Blackburn was given five years in prison. Keenan received a six-month sentence.

[ALSO SEE: *BOSS*]

KELL, VERNON
First Chief of MI5 ▪ (1873–1942)

FEW MEN WERE BETTER SUITED FOR COUNTER-intelligence than Vernon Kell. Born on November 21, 1873, in Yarmouth, England, to a wealthy family, Kell learned Polish and English as a small child. By the time he graduated Sandhurst in 1892 and received his commission, Kell spoke many languages fluently and was immediately assigned as an interpreter to important missions abroad.

He went to Moscow in 1898 where he quickly mastered the Russian language. Reposted to his regiment in Cork, Kell met Constance Scott, daughter of a rich Cork landowner. They were married on April 5, 1900. Later that year he was sent to China, serving with

General Vernon Kell, first chief of MI5; he brilliantly shut down German espionage at the start of World War I, but Churchill fired him in World War II for his inability to stop Nazi sabotage.

frontline Western Powers troops in crushing the savage Boxer Rebellion, which had threatened to annihilate the European legations in Peking.

In 1902, Kell returned to London where he was promoted to captain and assigned to the German desk at the War Office. Kell was by 1907 held in such high esteem that he was placed on the Committee of Imperial Defense.

In 1909, two years after the establishment of Britain's Secret Service Bureau, a counterintelligence service, orginally designated MO5, was created and Vernon Kell was selected to be its director. MO5, a title that was to last until 1916 when it was changed to MI5, began small.

To learn techniques, procedures, and establish operations, Kell quickly linked himself to Mansfield Cumming, director of the Secret Intelligence Service (SIS or MI6); Basil Thomson of the Metropolitan, Police; Reginald "Blinker" Hall of Naval Intelligence, and Patrick Quinn, chief of Scotland Yard's Special Branch, which would make all official arrests for MI5 since Kell's MI5 had no powers of arrest.

Many of the German spies were purposely not rounded up until just after England declared war on Germany in 1914. Kell waited until the last second so that his agents could arrest the entire network in one fell swoop. Among those caught in the net were Karl Ernst, who operated a barbershop as a front for a mail drop center, Dr. Armgaard Graves; Heinrich Grosse; Frederick Gould; and George Parrott, a Royal Navy gunner working with the Germans.

Throughout World War I, Germany sent many spies to England but almost all of them were tracked down and imprisoned. Some of them were executed. It was Kell who directed the hunt for Germany's top spy in Great Britain, Karl Lody. This German agent used a fake American passport to enter England and successfully spied on several military installations in Scotland before he was tracked down in Ireland.

Kell's career was distinguished throughout World War I and into the 1920s and 1930s. He rose to the rank of major-general and was considered to be one of the world's top counterintelligence chiefs. Under his direction MI5 gathered information on Communist and Nazi spies throughout the 1920s and 1930s. (In one incident Kell's MI5 raided the Communist spy front named Arcos Ltd., and an international incident was created.) By the time war came in 1939 and Winston Churchill assumed power in England, Kell's days were numbered.

Churchill demanded action from MI5 and when he did not receive reports as he expected, he blamed Kell for dragging his feet. He also told confidantes that Kell's methods were old-fashioned and that he was not keeping pace with Wilhelm Canaris' Abwehr. (One unofficial report had it that Churchill was still miffed at Kell for denying him a security report he requested when Churchill was out of power in the 1920s, and that he was seeking revenge for the slight.)

Then a disastrous event occured on October 14, 1939, shortly after war between Germany and England had been declared. A German submarine helmed by Captain Gunther Prien picked its way around the Navy's anti-submarine defenses in the Orkney Islands, penetrating the Royal Navy's anchorage at Scapa Flow. Prien sent a torpedo into the battleship *Royal Oak*, which quickly went down for the Deep Six, taking 834 men with her.

Rumors had it that a German spy, undetected by Kell's MI5, had provided Prien with information on how to penetrate the Navy defenses. This was later proved to be a myth; there was no German spy, but Kell was nevertheless blamed for the disaster by Churchill who was then First Lord of the Admiralty. Then an explosion at a munitions factory in Churchill's constituency, the Royal Gunpowder Factory in Waltham Abby in January 1940, which killed five persons, was attributed to Nazi sabotage that Kell's MI5 had not detected or prevented.

Again, Churchill blamed Kell, even though Scotland Yard's investigation of the explosion did not prove sabotage of any kind. Churchill apparently used the Scapa Flow sinking and the Waltham Abby explosion as the reasons for dismissing Kell on May 25, 1940. So embittered was Lady Kell, who managed a serviceman's canteen, that she called the staff together and snapped: "Your precious Winston has sacked the General!" Kell retired to a small rented cottage in Buckinghamshire where he died, broken-hearted, on March 27, 1942.

[ALSO SEE: *Abwehr; Arcos Ltd.; Wilhelm Canaris; Mansfield Cumming; Karl Ernst; Reginald Hall; Karl Lody; MI5; MI6; SIS; Special Branch; Basil Thomson*]

KEMPEI TAI
Japanese Secret Police ▪ (1936–1945)

FOLLOWING THE 1936 ARMY MUTINY IN JAPAN, ONE which was reportedly staged on orders from Emperor Hirohito to make it appear that he was merely a pawn in the hands of war-mongering militarists, the Emperor established the Kempei Tai. Hirohito, who secretly directed the military cabal planning world conquest, ordered Lieutenant General Nakajima Kesago to head Kempei Tai, specifically stating that this secret police force was to keep order in Tokyo and throughout Japan and all lands conquered by Japan's invading armies.

Kesago was, in the words of one historian, "a small Himmler of a man, a specialist in thought control, intimidation and torture." Kesago had been a ranking member of the Japanese military intelligence organization since 1921. Even the most ruthless of Japanese commanders considered him "sadistic." He would later be given command of the notorious 16th Japanese Army, which overran Nanking, China.

It was Kesago who presided over the terrifying "Rape of Nanking" in 1937, delighting in the countless atrocities committed by his men, horrors which he himself detailed and directed: myriad rapes; murders; the tossing of Chinese babies onto the bayonets of his drunken, bestial soldiers, the barbarous executions of tens of thousands of captured Chinese soldiers who were lined up, hands tied behind their backs, as they were brutally murdered in bayonet practice.

Kempei Tai quickly expanded its operations, monitoring every move made by foreigners visiting Japan before World War II. It also spent vast sums in propaganda among Japanese citizens, warning them to be alert to foreign spies, circulating millions of posters, flyers, and pamphlets that urged distrust of all persons who were not Japanese. Anti-spy days were declared in which hundreds of thousands of people ranted and raved against foreign suspects, bringing to Kempei Tai officials any kind of evidence, no matter how trivial, that might implicate foreigners in espionage.

Hardly a shop or business in Japan did not display Kempei Tai posters that warned of spies in their windows. Kempei Tai monitored all radio programs, newspapers, and periodicals, as well as all public speeches, propagandizing against possible espionage agents. Through this relentless campaign, the Japanese people as a whole were whipped into fanatical distrust and hatred for all foreigners, a xenophobic passion that later led to mass genocide on the part of Japanese troops fighting on all fronts.

The Japanese people did not admire the Kempei Tai but feared it. Any citizen could be arrested without stated reasons and be charged with espionage, secretly imprisoned, or even be executed. Few Japanese ministries had any real control of the Kempei Tai. Oddly, the Ministry of the Navy exercised more control than any other, but mostly on military matters because the Kempei Tai was essentially organized as a combat arm of the Army.

All of the agents selected by Kempei Tai were recruited from the army and had to have at least six years of military service before they were accepted into the ranks of the counterintelligence organization. The ability to speak and learn new foreign languages, especially English, was sought in agents, as well as detailed knowledge of foreign countries, their people, habits, customs, political inclinations. Of the 70,000 agents—half this number being officers—working for Kempei Tai during World War II at least one third of them spoke English and most of these had spent some time in the U.S.

Kempei Tai maintained several training schools where candidates were rigorously educated for one year in foreign languages, law (and how to skirt its applications), espionage, and counterespionage techniques. Classes detailed how to perform unarmed combat (jujitsu, judo, and other martial arts), the use of invisible inks, ciphers and codes, shadowing suspected spies, even a class on how to enter and leave buildings without being observed.

Kempei Tai members had special privileges, higher pay, and enjoyed considerable power. They were allowed to wear military uniforms or civilian clothes. On their uniforms they wore the insignia of a flower-like star surrounded by leaves. This same insignia could be found on a button worn behind the lapel of a civilian suitcoat.

Kempei Tai regulated the sale of all explosives, drugs, arms, electrical equipment, anything that might be used by enemy agents, including those rare Japanese citizens that spied upon their own government. It had hundreds of thousands of informers who either volunteered information to protect or better themselves or were blackmailed into supplying information.

As the most powerful organization in Japan at the close of World War II, General Douglas MacArthur, when taking over the reigns of the Japanese government in 1945, made it his personal business to thoroughly dismantle Kempei Tai.

He exposed Kempei Tai leaders, who were held up in public disgrace as true oppressors of their own people, before sending them to prison or obscurity. Fifty years later, however, this insidious organization had been remodeled into "business" organizations that train Japanese businessmen in the wiley art of undermining all foreign businesses in order to maintain the sharp competitive edge.

KENT, TYLER GATEWOOD
American Spy for Nazi Germany ▪ (1911– ?)

BORN IN MUKDEN, MANCHURIA, TO AN AMERICAN diplomat of considerable wealth, Tyler Kent enjoyed a carefree youth. He traveled widely with his family and was privately tutored until entering the exclusive St. Albans School in Washington, D.C., graduating in 1927. He went on to Princeton, graduating in 1932 with a degree in history. Through his father's connections, Kent joined the American diplomatic service and was sent to Moscow in 1933.

After serving six years in Russia, Kent took a position in the American Embassy in London, working as a code clerk. As World War II loomed, Kent met an attractive Russian emigré, Anna Wolkoff, whose parents operated a tearoom in South Kensington. Enamored of Wolkoff, he began attending her political discussion groups and soon endorsed her fanatical anti-Semitic views.

Anna Wolkoff was the daughter of one-time Czarist Russian Admiral Nicholas Wolkoff, who fled Russia with his family when the Bolsheviks overthrew the Romanov dynasty in 1917. The couple opened an innocuous tearoom where their daughter began holding political meetings twenty years later. Anna Wolkoff had adopted the views of right-wing leaders, such as Captain Archibald H. M. Ramsey.

The 29-year-old Kent was not only politically captivated by the 38-year-old Wolkoff but was emotionally involved with her. She drummed into him her beliefs that Hitler was correct in branding all Jews as enemies of any civilized country and that the impending war was really "the Jew's war." By the time Kent met her, Wolkoff had already attracted the attention of MI5 whose agents kept her under surveillance.

Wolkoff had long since dropped the pose of political agitator. She actively sought intelligence information from employees in the British War Office, one of whom being Joan Miller. After hearing of this request, Miller went to MI5 and was asked to provide doctored information to Wolkoff while infiltrating her discussion group and to obtain information on Ramsay and other right-wingers who supported Hitler.

Tyler Kent, shown with his mother at his trial, stole secrets from the American Embassy in London for the fascists.

Meanwhile, Wolkoff easily convinced Tyler Kent to obtain secret information from the U.S. Embassy in London, which she passed along to Nazi agents. Kent delivered all cables between President Roosevelt and Prime Minister Churchill. These ultra-secret communications, which demonstrated Roosevelt's support of England against Germany, despite the fact that America was then neutral, were delivered by the Italian Embassy to the German Ambassador in Rome, Hans Mackensen.

Learning that Mackensen and subsequently Hitler himself were reading the highly secret Roosevelt-Churchill correspondence, MI5 approached Ambassador Joseph Kennedy, revealing their findings. Kennedy waived diplomatic immunity for Kent and a squad of agents from Special Branch, accompanied by an observer from the Embassy, raided Kent's apartment in Gloucester Place on May 20, 1940. Kent was caught by surprise before he could dispose of many Embassy documents he had stolen.

Arrested, Kent and Wolkoff were placed on trial. Kent by that time had been fired from the American diplomatic service by Kennedy. He was convicted after the stolen U.S. documents were placed in evidence. Kent was sentenced to seven years in prison. Wolkoff was confronted by the testimony of Joan Miller and was convicted and sent to prison for ten years. Before leaving the dock, Wolkoff screamed that she would kill Joan Miller when released. At war's end, Kent was released but immediately deported to the U.S. where he soon disappeared.

KGB (COMMITTEE FOR STATE SECURITY)
Soviet Intelligence Service ▪ (1917–)

THE WORLD'S MOST DREADED INTELLIGENCE SERVICE, Soviet Russia's KGB, has been known by many names since its inception following the Russian Revolution of 1917. At that time, Communist leader Lenin reorganized the old czarist secret police, the Okhrana, changing its name to Cheka (Extraordinary Commission for Combating Counterrevolution and Espionage), which lasted until 1922. The Cheka, as a Bureau, however, continued on for many years inside the ever-expanding intelligence service that later became known as the KGB.

The Cheka was renamed the GPU (State Political Administration, 1922–1923). When the USSR was formally adopted as a country, the GPU was renamed the OGPU (United States Political Administration, 1923–1934). The organization known as Cheka, GPU, and OGPU was headed by Felix Dzerzhinsky, a ruthless, murderous Bolshevik. Following Dzerzhinsky's death in 1926, the organization expanded quickly to possess total power in enforcing Stalin's merciless edicts, including the forced collectivization of all lands. In this process, millions of Russians were displaced and millions more were simply killed by OGPU murder squads.

In 1934, the organization's name was again changed to the NKDV (People's Commissariat for Internal Affairs, 1934–1946), headed by a sadist named Genrikh Yagoda, Stalin's hand-picked hatchet man. Under Yagoda, the NKVD assumed total control over all industry, professional occupations, unskilled workers, farmers, all media, all police forces. It controlled the everyday lives of all living in Soviet Russia.

Yagoda, next to Stalin, was the most powerful and most feared man in Russia. He murdered those whom Stalin wanted eliminated, until the ever paranoid Stalin had Yagoda shot in 1936 as a subversive, replacing him with the equally barbarous Nicolai Yezhov, called "The Bloody Dwarf," whom Stalin had shot in 1938. Stalin's close associate, a murderer and rapist, Lavrenti Beria, then assumed command of the NKVD, remaining in power after Stalin's death.

During Beria's reign, the NKVD became the MVD (Ministry of Internal Affairs, 1946–1954), and, a year after Stalin's death in 1953, became the KGB. Its headquarters is located at the Center, and it is the most important division of Russia's intelligence core, supplemented by the GRU (Chief Intelligence Directorate of the General Staff of the Red Army), which handles military intelligence but is under the overall supervision of the KGB.

The KGB is all powerful in that its operations include all foreign and domestic espionage. It acts without legal restrictions or regulations against the Russian people. Its SMERSH division is a strong-arm branch that metes out punishment and assassination to any Russian branded a traitor or any informer, defector, or Communist not following the Party credo, irrespective of whether or not these hapless victims reside in Russia.

Entrapment of foreign diplomats is a favorite KGB ploy, and it invariably involves sex. This was the manner in which the KGB compromised British Ambassador to Moscow Sir Geoffrey Harrison in 1968. The Ambassador became enamored of a sultry, statuesque Russian woman named Galya who worked as a maid in the British Embassy. She was, of course, a KGB plant. Shortly after the pair trysted in a Leningrad apartment, Harrison was shown photos taken of him and Galya having sex.

Harrison was informed that unless he provided the KGB with information they were seeking, the photos and the affair would be made public. Instead of cooperation, Harrison returned to London and confessed his affair to MI5 officers. He retired with full pension. Though this entrapment attempt failed, many before and after were successful.

One such was the compromising of the French Ambassador, Maurice Dejean. The Dejeans arrived in Moscow from Paris in 1955, eager to make friends with any high-ranking Soviets. They were greeted by many who claimed to be stellar Russian leaders but these were either KGB officers or KGB spies. One of them was Lieutenant General Oleg Mikhailovich Gribanov, who took the name of Gorbunov.

Dejean confided to Gribanov/Gorbunov that he appreciated attractive women and the Ambassador's path was suddenly lined with sulty, bosomy females. The women, called "swallows" by their KGB bosses, were provided by KGB agent Yuri Vasilevich Krotkov. Krotkov introduced Dejean to a number of Russian film actresses, one of whom was named "Lora." While Dejean was making love to "Lora" her supposed husband burst through the bedroom door to threaten public court action, a scenario that was nothing more than the age-old badger game.

Later that night a nervous Dejean confided his dilemma to Gribanov/Gorbunov who warmly assured his friend that he would use his considerable influence to hush up the husband. He informed Dejean a short time later that he had taken care of the matter and that the French Ambassador had no worries. The grateful Dejean then began giving information to Gribanov, unwittingly or not. The KGB pimp of this affair, Krotkov, then attempted to seduce Dejean's wife and, failing this, compromised another French diplomat with one of his KGB whores.

Colonel Louis Guibaud, the French air attaché, however, did not cooperate. Instead of providing information to the KGB to have *his* affair suppressed, he blew out his brains. Krotkov later visited London in 1963 and, while attending a reception for Soviet authors and artists, he slipped away to British intelli-

gence where he said that he was defecting because of his remorse in the Guibaud affair. In that same year, Gribanov was informed that a KGB spy had been caught in New York. Desperate to have an American spy to exchange for the Russian, he ordered his men to find an American espionage agent.

All the KGB agents could come up with was an American teacher, Frederick C. Barghoon, a professor from Yale University who was a tourist in Moscow. Gribanov was told that Barghoon, unfortunately, was not a spy. "Make him a spy!" barked Gribanov. Barghoon was arrested but it turned out that he was a personal friend of President John F. Kennedy, who lodged a formal protest with Nikita Khrushchev, who, embarrassed and full of red-faced anger, upbraided Gribanov and ordered him to release Barghoon immediately.

Diplomats the KGB could not sexually compromise into providing information were the subject of constant surveillance, beginning with sophisticated listening devices that were cleverly concealed in foreign embassies. In 1975, the American Embassy in Moscow, always the top target for Soviet bugging, was implanted with a new and highly sophisticated communications system that could be activated only by high intensity rays beamed through the Embassy windows. In shooting these rays into the Embassy, KGB technicians inadvertently (or so it was later assumed) caused Ambassador Walter Stoessel to be infected with radiation poisoning.

Stoessel returned to Washington where he recovered from the overdose of radiation, a condition that became hazardous to all diplomats serving on Soviet territory as KGB eavesdropping and counter-eavesdropping devices became more and more complicated. Sometimes, the reasons for branding Americans as spies was simply to show continued espionage activities against Russia in order to prove that the Revolution was in constant danger of being undone. Such was the case of Martha Petersen, who was part of the American diplomatic corps in Moscow. KGB agents reported that she was caught retrieving a secret message from a dead-letter box. She was expelled.

The same fate befell Richard Osborn, First Secretary from the economics section of the U.S. Embassy. The KGB announced Osborn's arrest in May 1983, saying that he was caught red-handed while transmitting messages from a radio to a Marisat communications satellite. When the Embassy demanded proof, that the KGB show the copies of the secret messages, the Soviets smirked and reported that Osborn's notes had been destroyed when he quickly dissolved them in water. Osborn, his wife Mary, and their two children, were expelled from Russia.

Many of the ranking KGB officials who summarily ordered the compromising of diplomats or their arrests were far less sophisticated than those who developed KGB spy technology. They were, for the most part, brutes, thugs, and murderers who had done

Lubianka Prison in Moscow where all KGB prisoners were held and interrogated.

U.S. envoy to the United Nations Henry Cabot Lodge displays the inside of the Seal of America from the U.S. Embassy in Moscow to show how the KGB planted a microphone inside of it.

Stalin's bidding from the time of the Revolution until the dictator found no more use for them. Such was Boris Nicholaevich Ponomarev, who had been a KGB functionary since the days of the Cheka and who arranged for the betrayal of Dubcek in Czechoslovakia in 1968. Ponomarev headed the international department of the KGB that was responsible for intelligence operations in Soviet bloc nations for years. He undoubtedly planned to assume the directorship of the KGB but was passed over for Yuri Andropov, a younger man. By that time Stalin was long entombed in the Kremlin.

Not dissimilar to Ponomarev was Sergei Kruglov, one of Stalin's most trusted assassins and a one-time member of SMERSH. Kruglov had been a constable in the Red Militia during and after the Revolution. He rose to the rank of colonel and was made commander of the Kremlin Guard. In the 1920s and 1930s, Kruglov was known as Stalin's "triggerman," executing or assassinating anyone Stalin selected. He was a ranking member of the Cheka and yet he survived five of his chiefs. It was claimed he had personally shot Cheka bosses Yagoda and Yezhev on Stalin's orders and that he may have caused the mysterious deaths of three other Cheka chiefs.

It is known that Kruglov personally shot Marshal Tukhachevsky, Chief of the General Staff of the Red Army, who was part of the great army purge of 1937. For this bloody service, Kruglov was made an "honorary" lieutenant general and Deputy Commissar for Internal Affairs. He also had a hand in directing the widespread SMERSH operations that led to the assassination of Leon Trotsky who, more than any other person, was the guiding light of the Communist Revolution of 1917, and whom Joseph Stalin hated more than any other person on earth.

During World War II, Kruglov was so trusted by Stalin that the Russian dictator insisted that he alone make all security arrangements for the Yalta, Teheran, and Potsdam conferences. At the time, the Western Powers rewarded Kruglov with the Legion of Merit from the U.S. government and an honorary knighthood from the British Empire. Upon Stalin's death Kruglov was made Minister of the Interior and that Ministry was combined with the Ministry of State Security.

KGB boss Lavrenti Beria, one of Kruglov's old friends, continued to openly support him but he distrusted the old killer and he suggested that Kruglov might have accumulated too much power. In April 1954, the Committee for State Security was detached from Kruglov's Ministry of the Interior and placed under the command of General A. I. Serov, who would later head the KGB. Thus, Kruglov was outmaneuvered from taking over Beria's position. He was quietly dismissed in 1956 and faded from view.

KGB agents have been the best trained spies in the world and, despite the number of them who defect, proved to be utterly dedicated to their nefarious tasks. Next to the Soviet military, the KGB has commanded a staggering budget, billions of dollars each year to maintain its enormous headquarters staff, tens of thousands of field agents, and staggering technical support staffs. The CIA's John McMahon reported to Congress in 1982 that the KGB was then spending between three and four billion dollars a year to create disinformation, propaganda, and outright forgeries such as the fake letters between President Ronald Reagan and King Juan Carlos of Spain in which Reagan reported that his own advisers were opposed to Spain's inclusion in NATO, a KGB fabrication.

One KGB victim was Russian leader Boris Yeltsin, who was found drunk and dripping wet by aides in a Moscow police station in 1990. Yeltsin said the KGB tried to drown him.

[ALSO SEE: *Yuri Andropov; Frederick C. Barghoon; Lavrenti Beria; Cheka; CIA; Felix Dzerzhinsky; GPU; NKVD; OGPU; Okhrana; SMERSH; Genrikh Yagoda; Nicolai Yezhov*]

KHOKHLOV, NICOLAI
SMERSH Assassin ▪ (1923–)

BORN IN NIZHNII NOVGOROD (NOW GORKY), Khokhlov was the son of a printer who had fought for the Red Army during the Civil War of 1918–1920. After his parents were divorced, Khokhlov was taken to Moscow by his mother and stepfather. He joined the Komsomol (Communist Youth Movement) in 1938 and, by 1941, the second year of World War II, he was working for the Ministry of State Security, which focused its espionage activities outside of the U.S.S.R.

Khokhlov's secret desire was to become a movie director. He had performed bit parts in plays and films and had earned a reputation on the variety stage as an "artistic whistler." When the Nazi armies closed in on Moscow, Khokhlov volunteered for front-line duty but was rejected because of bad eyesight. He was later recruited to fight rear-guard guerrilla action in the event that Moscow had to be abandoned.

From that point on, Khokhlov was to remain with the KGB's SMERSH section, functioning as an assassin. In 1942, the enterprising Khokhlov was brought before Lieutenant-Colonel Pavel Sudaplatov, who commanded SMERSH. He was complimented for his speedy execution of Wilhelm Kube, the Nazi Gauleiter of Minsk and was then ordered to go to Ankara and assassinate Franz von Papen, the German ambassador to Turkey. According to Khokhlov's later testimony, he refused the assignment, claiming that his inability to speak Turkish would prove him ineffective for the assignment.

When the Red Army advanced into Rumania in 1945, Khokhlov, assuming the identity of Stanislaw

Lewandowski, a displaced person, followed in its wake. His job was to work against any intelligence operations conducted by the Allies in Rumania, chiefly the OSS. He stayed in Rumania throughout the 1940s, taking Rumanian citizenship in 1947.

Khokhlov continued to perform KGB assignments without hesitation and he rose to the rank of captain. SMERSH considered him to be one of its top assassins and, in October 1953, he was selected to perform a very special murder mission. He was summoned by Colonel Lev Studnikov, commander of SMERSH'S murder squads. (Though SMERSH had been technically disbanded in 1946, it continued uninterrupted operations under a different name within the MVD/KGB; in 1953 this "terror and diversion section" was headed by the taciturn Alexander Panyushkin who had been the Soviet Ambassador to the U.S., 1947–1952.)

Studnikov ordered Khokhlov to arrange for the assassination of Igor Georgi Okolovich, the director of NTS (Society of National Unity), a powerful anti-Soviet organization headquartered in Frankfurt, Germany. This society had proven extremely effective in spreading anti-Communist propaganda throughout the ranks of the Red Army and among Communist officials in Austria and Germany. The KGB considered Okolovich the intellectual and spiritual leader of NTS and as such, he was classified in their files as "the most dangerous enemy of the Soviet regime." The order for his assassination had been personally signed by Prime Minister Georgi Malenkov and First Secretary of the Party, Nikita Khrushchev.

Khokhlov traveled to East Berlin, going to the SMERSH training school at Karlhorst where he selected two East Germans, Hans Kugovits and Kurt Weber, to act as his assistants in the assassination of Okolovich. The murder team selected a number of bizarre murder weapons that had been designed by SMERSH, including what appeared to be an ordinary pack of cigarettes but what was really an electric gun that fired pellets filled with potassium cyanide, a highly toxic substance that, after entering the bloodstream, causes death almost instantaneously.

During this time, however, the SMERSH agent did something he had never done before. He confided the details of his mission to his young wife Yanina, a beautiful blonde he had recently married.

Yanina Timashkevits was a brilliant construction engineer and a Roman Catholic. Her family had somehow managed to preserve its Christian faith, despite the ruthless efforts of the Communists to exterminate all religions in the Soviet Union. After marrying Yanina, Khokhlov began to regret his work for SMERSH. He had, through her influence, attempted to quit SMERSH but his superiors refused to reassign him to other duties. He had even refused a recent murder mission. He and his wife knew that to refuse a second assassination assignment, that of Okolovich, would mean his death, that of his wife, and their one-year-old son. They both decided that the only way out

SMERSH assassin Nicolai Khokhlov (right), shaking hands with Igor Okolovich, the man he was assigned to kill in 1954.

was for Khokhlov to go on the mission but to defect to the Americans in Frankfurt before Okolovich was killed.

"Do you realize what awaits you and the boy if I go West?" Khokhlov asked his wife.

"I know and that does not alter my decision."

On February 8, 1954, Khokhlov received his orders to depart immediately. When he arrived in Frankfurt ten days later, however, the assassin had second thoughts about confronting the Americans with the plot. Instead, dramatically, he went directly that night to the apartment of his intended victim. Okolovich opened the door to see a middle-aged, pudgy-faced man wearing glasses. He spoke in a mild, even voice.

"Are you Herr Okolovich?"

"I am," replied Okolovich.

"Then I must talk to you privately. It is most important."

Okolovich invited the visitor inside and offered him a cup of tea. This was declined. Then, switching from German to Russian, the stranger announced: "I am Captain Khokhlov of the MVD, and I have been ordered to kill you."

Though startled, Okolovich was not too surprised. SMERSH operatives had only a week earlier violently kidnapped Dr. Alexander Trushnovich, the director of NTS in Berlin. Okolovich then proposed that Khokhlov accompany him to U.S. Army headquarters, which he was only too happy to do. CIA agents quickly interviewed the defecting SMERSH agent, the first from his murderous cadre to ever go over to

Khokhlov (left) at a news conference with American journalists, detailing how SMERSH murdered Soviet political opponents around the world.

the West. He informed them where his two East German assistants could be found and both men were quickly picked up. They happily agreed to defect to the West with their boss Khokhlov.

Six weeks later, Khokhlov met with American newsmen, telling the whole incredible story. The impact of his defection and the revelation that SMERSH actually existed staggered the West. Up to Khokhlov's defection, only unsubstantiated rumors existed about SMERSH and Western intelligence agencies had tended to dismiss these reports as "Hollywood fantasies." The extensive report made to the CIA by Khokhlov, however, proved SMERSH to be all too real—his CIA dossier was, by the time he appeared publicly, almost four feet thick.

Khokhlov begged the U.S. to somehow intervene and save his wife and child. Efforts were made by U.S. officials to secure the release of Yanina Khokhlov and her son, but, on June 2, 1954, it was learned that she, her little boy, and her 14-year-old sister had been arrested and imprisoned by the KGB. After that, all that came from Moscow was a terrible silence.

The defecting Khokhlov knew what it meant. He, on the other hand, was not silent. He began to talk non-stop, racking his memory for every detail concerning KGB operations. He provided the Western

intelligence agencies with hundreds of names of Soviet agents and their headquarters, networks, ciphers, codes, and letter-drops throughout Europe. Scores were arrested and KGB operations were thoroughly disrupted for more than a year while the Center in Moscow frantically scurried to find replacements for those spies who had been identified by Nicolai Khokhlov, a spy who finally found his conscience.

[ALSO SEE: *CIA; KGB; OSS; SMERSH*]

KING'S SECRET
French Intelligence Service under Louis XV ▪ (1740s–1760s)

Louis XV ESTABLISHED HIS OWN INTELLIGENCE SERvice in the 1740s in an attempt to influence the election of a Polish king. He conspired with his French Ambassador to Poland, Charles Francois de Broglie, to place a French candidate on the Polish throne. Throughout Poland de Broglie employed an intelligence network of spies, which came to be known as the King's Secret.

In the attempt to place the French candidate—Louis Francois de Bourbon, prince de Conti—on the Polish throne, the King's Secret service was expanded until French undercover agents, throughout Europe, provided Louis with information on his enemies. Louis insisted upon directing his own intelligence agency, but often compromised his ministers and military leaders.

One of the most effective agents for the King's Secret was the bizarre Charles Genevieve d'Eon (a spy attired in female garb) who persuaded Empress Elizabeth of Russia to adopt friendly relations with France and thus removed Russia from siding with Louis' enemies. Following the death of Louis, the King's Secret was no longer an effective organization.

[ALSO SEE: *Charles Genevieve d'Eon*]

KNUTH, ANNA MARIA
German Spy for Soviets ▪ (1906–1954)

ATTRACTIVE AND TALENTED, ANNA MARIA KNUTH was an actress without work following World War II. The German film industry was a wreck. In 1948, she befriended Heinko Kunze, a former Prussian officer and art historian who operated an antique shop in Berlin. Kunze loaned money to Knuth and slowly worked on her to join a group of Soviet spies that included Kunze; his mistress, Luise

Former actress and Soviet spy in West Germany Anna Maria Knuth is shown at her trial in 1953; she is in a deck chair, already dying of cancer.

Frankenberg; and one-time Polish cavalry officer, Gregor Kowalski. This network was known as the Kolberg Ring and busied itself with recruiting displaced East Germans into their ranks.

Maria Knuth proved herself an excellent agent. She lured American and British officers into the Berlin antique shop, compromised them, and extracted important information that she dutifully passed on to spymaster Kowalski. So successful did she become that she was provided with more funds with which to rent a handsome villa outside of Cologne. This was used as a love nest where more Allied officers and West German officials were compromised and milked for information.

Knuth was promoted, and ordered to take over the Frankfurt operation, which she did, proving herself to be one of the best Soviet spies in the West. In 1950, she was ordered to penetrate the newly-established Amt Blank, a West German intelligence network organized to identify Soviet spies in the West. Knuth boldly went to Amt offices and applied for a secretarial job but was turned down because she did not know shorthand. Knuth later came to the attention of West German spymaster Reinhard Gehlen who thought to trap Knuth.

In 1952, a Dr. Petersen, claiming to be a West German agent opposed to German rearmament, was introduced to Knuth, offering to work for the Kolberg Ring. Although she was warned that Petersen might be a Gehlen agent, Knuth accepted him as genuine, especially when she learned that he worked in the offices of West German Chancellor Konrad Adenauer. In fact, Knuth was so enamored of Petersen that she became his mistress.

Petersen dutifully supplied Knuth with high-grade information, which she passed on to Kowalski and the Soviets. All of it, however, was counterfeit intelligence, cleverly concocted by Gehlen who had, indeed, planted Petersen. By 1953, Petersen had learned everything there was to know about Knuth and the Kolberg Ring. All of its members were rounded up by West German police, including Knuth who was caught red-handed collecting coded letters from Kowalski in a Cologne post office.

Colonel Kowalski escaped into East Germany but his network was smashed, all of his agents, including Knuth being quickly convicted and sent to prison. Maria Knuth did not survive for long. By the time she was arrested she had already contracted cancer and she died two years later from the disease in the prison hospital.

[ALSO SEE: *Reinhard Gehlen*]

KOEDEL, SIMON EMIL
American Spy for Germany •
(1882–1949?)

BORN IN WURTZBURG, GERMANY, KOEDEL MIGRATED to the U.S. on April 4, 1906, appearing with the flood of German immigrants swarming to America. He served in the U.S. Army, and was promoted to the rank of corporal before being discharged in 1909. Koedel became a naturalized citizen in 1912, living a quiet hard-working life. He married, inherited a stepdaughter, and was later divorced. At the outbreak of World War I, Koedel returned to Germany and offered his services as a spy in America.

He was accepted by the Abwehr and, after a short course in espionage, was sent back to the U.S., equipped with radio, binoculars, invisible inks, and a code book. His job was to report on American shipping, especially supplies to England. Back in the U.S. in 1915, Koedel roamed the docks of New York, carefully noting the merchant ships destined for British ports. This information, along with cargo lists of each ship, was radioed to Germany every few days.

No one interferred with Koedel at this time since the U.S. was not at war. Moreover little or no security existed on the docks in New York harbor and Koedel easily learned about cargoes, shipping routes, departure and arrival times. The harbor lights of New York soon worked their magic on Koedel who sent a message to his spymasters in Germany, requesting that he be sent to England to collect information. He assured them there would be no problem in traveling since he could use his American passport.

Abwehr officials gave their approval and soon Koedel, drawing a German captain's pay, booked passage on a luxury liner sailing for Southampton. MI5, however, suspected Koedel of being a German agent and he was met by agents who detained him. He had asked too many questions of fellow passengers regarding British defenses. Not having enough evidence to jail him, the British deported Koedel back to America. He was undeterred, and sailed for Europe within a few weeks. He managed to reach Germany where he worked with military intelligence until the end of the war. He returned to the U.S., via Ireland, his citizenship still intact.

Throughout the 1920s, Koedel kept in contact with the Abwehr who sent him small monthly stipends and kept him in reserve as a "sleeper" agent. With the rise of Hitler, Koedel returned to Germany, arriving at the Abwehr headquarters in Bremen in 1936. He met with Johannes Bischoff, who would be his control, along with Niko Bensmann. He also met R. A. Hambourg who maintained a residence in Milan, Italy, which Koedel would use as a mail drop. Also introduced to Koedel was Waldemar Othmer, an American citizen who lived in Trenton, New Jersey.

Othmer, who would take up residence in Norfolk, Virginia, would be Koedel's back-up man and was responsible for coast-watching from Baltimore to Cape Hatteras. Koedel would be responsible for New York harbor and occasional trips to Boston. After a refresher course in the art of spying, Koedel returned to the U.S. to rent a luxurious apartment on Riverside Drive in New York. Though he retained his rank of captain in the German Army with a salary of $200 per month, the Abwehr gave him a special expense account that exceeded $2,000 a month.

With such riches, Koedel could show himself as a successful businessman, although his business was exclusively that of espionage. He was responsible for sending regular reports on American shipping but he was also ordered by the Abwehr to provide data on the defense industry in the U.S. He accomplished both jobs easily. He scouted New York harbor daily, observing all departing and arriving ships. He obtained detailed cargo lists from a dock official whom he paid handsomely.

Details on American armament and munitions Koedel surprisingly received directly from the War Department. In 1937, he simply applied for membership in the American Ordnance Association, a confidential organization of American armament and munitions manufacturers closely tied to the Ordnance Division of the War Department. In his application to the AOA, Koedel stated that he was a chemical engineer and a large stockholder in defense industries such as Curtiss-Wright and Sperry Gyroscope. He enclosed his 1909 honorable discharge papers from the U.S. Army. His application was accepted by L.A. Codd, Secretary of the AOA, who wrote back: "You can be justly proud of your service to our country." As a member of AOA, Koedel was placed on an exclusive War Department mailing list, receiving all releases involving ordnance, a treasure trove for any agent.

As an AOA member, Koedel could attend any membership meeting, many of which consisted of lectures on new American weaponry and were held behind closed doors because of the classified nature of the information imparted by armament speakers. He also had free access to any private or government munitions or weapons plant. All he had to do was show his AOA membership card.

Membership in AOA demanded clearance by the FBI but apparently the Bureau rubber-stamped Koedel's membership card after simply checking his clean service record. The Bureau apparently had no record of his World War I espionage activities for Germany. The British SIS never filed a formal report on its deportation on Koedel in 1917. Knowing this, Koedel, ever bold, began writing letters to various members of the U.S. Congress, using the stationery of the American Ordnance Association.

Koedel sent letters to the chairmen of the military and naval affairs committees of both houses of Congress in which he again described himself as a large investor in various defense firms, telling the recipients that he was concerned with "the interest of our nation's preparedness and security." Senator Robert Rice Reynolds of North Carolina, who was a member of the Senate's Military Affairs Committee and later its chairman, was so impressed with Koedel's letters that he invited him to pay him a visit in Washington.

The nervy Koedel went to Washington and cemented a friendly relationship with Reynolds that lasted for many years. At this and other meetings, Koedel volunteered security measures that should be taken at defense plants against possible spies. The agent shrewdly took the same tack when writing letters to L.A. Codd, who edited the AOA journal. In one letter, Koedel complained that one article went too far in revealing information and that more caution should be exercised when publishing information about munitions factories. Further, Koedel sent Codd regular recommendations on how security could be improved at various defense plants he visited. He even went so far as to write the War Department directly, warning that defense plants in America were lax in providing proper security. In each instance, he received letters of thanks from high-ranking officials.

All of this letter writing served to build Koedel's contacts and establish himself as an acceptable entity in the defense industry, which he had never been. Had any official bothered to check his holdings in the companies in which he claimed stock it would have been discovered that he owned not a single share in any of these firms. No one checked.

He attempted to gain entry to secret U.S. military installations, on the premise that he wished to inspect their security devices and measures. Twice in November 1939, he was turned away by sentries at Edgewood Arsenal in Bel Air, Maryland, where the U.S. Chemical Warfare Center was located. He played the peevish citizen, insulted by the rebuff, lodging a strong letter of complaint at AOA headquarters in Washington. AOA phoned the War Department and actually obtained permission for Koedel to inspect the arsenal, which he promptly did.

Upon his arrival at the arsenal, he was greeted by high-ranking officers who gave him the deluxe tour. During this tour, when not observed, Koedel peeled off labels from boxes of special weapons stacked on railroad cars and slipped these into his pocket. He took mental notes of every type of armament he was shown and all of this information he sent to the Abwehr that night from his hotel at Havre de Grace, Maryland.

Koedel included in his huge report a tremendous amount of technical and scientific information. He provided statistics of the arsenal's storage facilities and an itemized list of new developments in armament laboratories. In this detailed report, one of more than six hundred Koedel was to send to the Abwehr over the war years, he stated: "The major suppliers of the arsenal are Baker in Philipsburg, the General Chemical Co., and a factory in Lodi, New Jersey.

However, its biggest source of raw material is the firm Eimer & Amend, located between 18th and 19th Streets on Third Avenue in New York, controlled by German-American interests. Penetration probably possible."

The Abwehr was astounded and staggered by Koedel's report. None of their hundreds of trained agents in the U.S. had been able to supply this kind of quality information, yet Koedel did it with incredible ease, although he never informed his spymasters that he accessed such information as a member of AOA. He demanded more money, a lot of it, and he got it, as much as $5,000 to $10,000 a month. He continued to shock his spymasters with astounding, irrefutable classified documents.

Another Koedel coup involved the destruction of the German pocket battleship *Admiral Graf Spee*, which was severely damaged in the battle of the River Platte by British cruisers. The *Spee* limped into Montevideo Harbor where the British bottled up the ship. Its captain scuttled her and sent her to the bottom to avoid capture. Hitler demanded details but received an incomplete report. A few days later Koedel sent a detailed report of the warship's demise, one that was presented to Hitler. How did Koedel obtain this report? He simply requested it as a member of AOA, which had sent a special delegation of experts to Montevideo to make up the detailed report.

The most urgent of Koedel's reports—those perishable reports on eastbound ships that had to be flashed to lurking U-boats—were sent via cable from the German Consulate in New York, prior to America's entry into World War II. Many of Koedel's bulkier reports, and this comprised the majority of his communications to Germany, had to be sent by mail. To make sure that his mail went uncensored, Koedel used a clever ploy. He received each week, some times twice weekly, regular classified reports from the War Department. These arrived in large brown envelopes, printed with the words "War Department, Washington, D.C." A large official-looking stamp on each envelope read "Official Business." All of the envelopes were addressed to Mr. Simon E. Koedel, 660 Riverside Drive, New York, N.Y."

After receiving an envelope, Koedel would steam it open, review the contents, add his own report, then reseal the envelope, cross out his own name and address and write in the name and address of his mail drop in Milan, Italy. He would then mail these official-looking envelopes, believing that they would pass the censors without molestation.

Koedel was right in his assumption. Not one of his hundreds of envelopes was ever opened. They were passed straight on to Milan by U.S. postal authorities who never questioned an envelope bearing the address of the U.S. War Department. In this fashion, the American government was handing over its secrets to Nazi Germany!

No challenge seemed too great for Koedel. He was one of many Nazi agents who received an urgent request for information on certain French ports that the Germans anticipated using after their conquest of France. They wanted to know if the ports of Nantes, La Pallice, and La Rochelle could handle large tankers and colliers. Koedel replied in detail within a short time—long before any Abwehr agents in France responded. He simply contacted his friend Senator Reynolds and told him that he was making arrangements for shipments to France and needed to know the capabilities of these ports.

Senator Reynolds was only too glad to help. He contacted the U.S. Maritime Commission who, at the Senator's request, sent on the details to Koedel who, in turn, sent the information to the Abwehr. Through Reynolds and his other Washington contacts, Koedel obtained weekly breakdowns of war materials being sent to England, which was then at war with Germany.

Koedel's spying became intensive. He visited a half dozen army installations in a few months, sending detailed reports on each fort's training specialty, number of men trained each month, and their eventual assignments. He supplied detailed reports on not only all merchant shipping in and out of New York but on U.S. warships, new weapons, supplies being sent to England. His voluminous reports staggered the Abwehr, which had been feeding the data to Hitler himself.

The German dictator was so pleased with Koedel's work that he personally ordered that the spy be promoted to the rank of major and that he be given all the funds necessary to carry out his work. (This was unusual for Hitler in that he was always skeptical of data obtained through espionage and often told his Abwehr chief, Admiral Wilhelm Canaris, that information produced by spies "amounted to nothing more than a lot of crap!")

When America entered the war against Germany, the FBI cracked down on the many Nazi spy networks active in the U.S. Almost every German agent was rounded up with only a few exceptions. One of these was Simon Koedel. The reason why he evaded capture was mostly due to the fact that he had very few contacts with other Abwehr spies working the U.S. Never a part of a network, there remained no one to inform on him. He continued throughout most of the war to live in his luxurious Riverside Drive suite of rooms, sending out priceless espionage reports.

As the tide of war turned against Germany, Koedel's fanatical belief in the Third Reich became his undoing. He brooded over the battles lost by the Germans and began fulminating against the United States, the country to which he had sworn allegiance and the country he had so cleverly betrayed. Bitter, sensing failure, Koedel began to go to pieces.

Inexplicably, Koedel wrote a letter to Major General Morris B. Payne of the 43rd Division, Connecticut National Guard, telling him that no matter how many battles the U.S. won, Germany would win the war. He added this bit of vitriol:

"The average American is a double-crosser, a chronic draft-dodger and crooked at heart." These traits, Koedel insisted, Americans "carried into the Army." This letter was turned over to the FBI, which began to investigate Koedel's background in depth. Bit by bit, letter by letter, including Koedel's cleverly engineered membership in the AOA and the information he had been receiving for years from the War Department all conspired against the spy.

Then a shoeshine man who worked on the Staten Island Ferry named Carmine d'Andrea came forward and told the FBI that Koedel had regularly taken the Ferry and had spied on docks with binoculars. He had, d'Andrea insisted, taken notes and the bootblack had asked him what he planned to do with them. "I'm sending them back to Germany," Koedel replied sarcastically. He then asked d'Andrea if he would like to serve Italy the same way he, Koedel, was serving Germany. The bootblack declined.

These two incredible and arrogant blunders caused Koedel's arrest on October 24, 1944. On March 1, 1945, with Germany only weeks away from utter capitulation, Koedel was convicted of "conspiracy to commit espionage." He was sent to the federal penitentiary at Milan, Michigan, to serve fifteen years but he was released a year later, deported back to his native Germany, which lay in ruins. He reportedly died a vagrant three years later.

[ALSO SEE: *Abwehr; Wilhelm Canaris; FBI; MI5*]

KOLBE, FRITZ
German Spy for Allies in World War II ▪ (1903– ?)

THE GREATEST ESPIONAGE DISCOVERY OF THE OSS during World War II was a German official who worked in the heart of the Nazi Foreign Office in Berlin and who was willing to spy for the Allies. At first this man was utterly disbelieved when, in mid-1943, he approached British officers of MI6 who were stationed in neutral Switzerland. Through an emissary, Fritz Kochertaler, the official stated that he had always opposed Hitler and his regime and that he had repeatedly attempted to contact the Allies, offering to spy for them.

The official claimed to be well-placed to receive and send top-secret information from Berlin and he told the British that a Nazi agent was working "close to Churchill," and was sending Allied secrets to the Abwehr in Berlin by way of Stockholm. The British intelligence chief, Claude Dansey, fearful of double agents, dismissed the offer out of hand, a decision that forever discredited him.

Next came the Americans. On August 23, 1943, the official sent Kochertaler, an emigre German doctor, to see OSS official Gerald Mayer who was then working with Allen Dulles in Bern, Switzerland. The physician stated that his friend was a high-placed official in the Wehrmacht (German Army) liaison section of Germany's Foreign Office in Berlin and wanted to pass top-secret information to the Americans. Mayer was skeptical but he arranged a meeting that night with the German official, who was somewhere in Bern, and himself and Allen Dulles.

Dulles and Mayer sat in Mayer's small apartment until midnight. The visitor appeared on schedule, a small man of forty with a balding head. Quiet and reserved, he identified himself as Fritz Kolbe. He had worked as a bureaucrat for the State Railways in Berlin and later held diplomatic posts in South Africa and Spain. He insisted that he had always been opposed to Hitler and the Nazis but that, up until now, had no way to contact the Allies.

Kolbe went on to say that he had had difficulty in getting to Switzerland and had initially gone to the British but they had turned him away. "They think me a Nazi plant, no doubt," Kolbe mused. In his Foreign Office position, Kolbe explained, he saw every important secret document flowing from the Army through the Foreign Office and that he had access to all the most sensitive records of Foreign Minister Joachim von Ribbentrop. Kolbe was also privy to the top secrets of the Abwehr, Germany's intelligence agency headed by the wiley Admiral Wilhelm Canaris. Top echelon Abwehr agents worked throughout the world in embassies, consulates, and legations under the guise of attachés, and much of their espionage information was sent to the Abwehr via the diplomatic channels of the Foreign Office, which allowed Kolbe to examine and copy at his discretion any document he thought would be useful to the Allies.

To prove his claim, Kolbe surprised Dulles and Mayer by producing a roll of microfilm and handing this to Dulles, telling him that it contained 186 pages of documents that he had photographed from the German diplomatic files. He worked directly for Dr. Karl Ritter, Kolbe quietly explained, who was the Foreign Office's liaison officer with all the armed services. Ritter was privy to all the war plans, troop movements, the Luftwaffe's activities, the secrets involving all Nazi submarines, and the operations of German occupation forces throughout Europe.

Dulles asked Kolbe if he was a member of the German underground working against Hitler of which the OSS had been aware for some time. He said he was not, that he knew of a few dissidents, but that he basically worked alone. Then Dulles leaned close to Kolbe and said: "We have no way of knowing that you are not an *agent provacateur*."

The German was unruffled. "You would be naive," he intoned, "if you did not suspect that. I cannot prove at this moment that I am not. If I were, however, I would hardly have been so extravagant to bring you the contents of so many documents. Two or three

would have sufficed. Gentlemen, I hate the Nazis. To me they are the enemy. I have a similar feeling about the Bolsheviks. They both menace the world. But we are in the middle of a war and this is no time to bargain. Try to believe that I am a patriotic German with a human conscience and that there are others. All we ask as payment for our services is help and encouragement and support after the war."

Kolbe left at 3 A.M., promising to remain in contact with the OSS men. After he left, the Americans closely studied the documents Kolbe had left and concluded that, indeed, they represented genuine secret Nazi information.

They decided to use Kolbe as much as possible as a spy in Ribbentropp's Foreign Office. Kolbe was given the cover name of George Wood, undoubtedly because of Dulles' rapping on the wooden table. He would prove to be the most valuable spy the Americans had in the heart of the Third Reich, a man who operated for the OSS under the noses of Hitler and his henchmen.

Kolbe went back to gathering information for the Allies but he was unable to leave for Bern again until October. This time he did not strap an envelope containing microfilm to his leg as he did before his August trip to Switzerland. He ingeniously slipped the secrets directly into the courier pouch, next to the legation packet he was to deliver.

During the course of his train trip to Switzerland, he was searched several times but the diplomatic pouch went untouched. When Kolbe reached Bern, he simply removed the packet containing the secrets he was to deliver and slipped this into his coat pocket, delivering the legation packet and then going on to meet with Dulles once more.

Kolbe's second trip to Switzerland was full of hazard. The train normally took eighteen hours to travel from Berlin to the Swiss border. Now that Allied planes were bombing all rolling stock in Germany daily, the trains mostly moved at night and it could take days to get to Switzerland. Only Hitler's private express train, *Sonderzug*, was equipped with anti-aircraft guns to fend off air attacks. All other trains had to stop when Allied planes appeared.

When reaching Basel, Switzerland, he stood before a Nazi official and coldly answered questions, stating that he was on a diplomatic mission for the Foreign Office. He placed the diplomatic pouch down on the interrogator's desk. The official opened the pouch and took out a large envelope. It bore the official Nazi seal, red wax with the insignia of the swastika affixed over the lip of the large envelope. The official knew not to violate the seal which had been affixed in Berlin. Putting it back in the pouch, he let Kolbe go on his way.

Sweating, Kolbe went to the men's room in the train station. He locked himself into a stall. He took out the large envelope, broke the seal, then slipped his own envelope into his pocket. Kolbe placed a smaller envelope, also bearing the Foreign Office seal—this was the legation packet he was to deliver—back into the pouch. He had taken pains in Berlin to place both envelopes, the legation packet and his smuggled secrets, into a large envelope that he had had sealed by a security officer. Thus, Kolbe had cleverly created a "false bottom" inside the pouch in which to smuggle Nazi secrets right under their noses.

When reaching Bern, Kolbe dutifully delivered the legation packet. He then contacted his physician friend who arranged to have him picked up by Gerald Mayer that night as he stood on the Kirchenfeld Bridge, which spanned the Aare River. Mayer picked him up shortly before midnight and drove to the home of Allen Dulles. There the OSS chief delightedly met with Kolbe who turned over his new batch of secrets.

Among the information Kolbe had brought along was a report that the Nazi envoy to neutral Ireland was equipping a secret radio station that could contact Nazi submarines as to the whereabouts of Allied convoys. One report came from occupied France, from Nazi collaborator Pierre Laval who offered a plan to arrest and execute all relatives of those in the French resistance.

Another report was from the German Embassy in Madrid. This coded message was deciphered to reveal that fascist dictator Francisco Franco had broken his pledge to the Allies to remain neutral, and that he was smuggling tungsten, used to temper steel, to the Nazis in orange crates. Another current report came from the German Embassy in Buenos Aires that pinpointed a huge convoy about to leave an Atlantic port and the route it would take to England.

As a result of Kolbe's deliveries to Dulles, the convoy was rerouted before it entered the waters where Nazi wolf packs were waiting to intercept it, thus saving tons of war goods and countless lives. An Allied oil embargo was quickly decreed against Spain for its smuggling of tungsten to Germany. All of this was with President Franklin D. Roosevelt's solid approval. He had seen Kolbe's documents right from the beginning and concurred that they were genuine and that Kolbe be accepted as the most important OSS spy in Germany, despite the fact that Claude Dansey, assistant chief of Britain's MI6, a notorious anti-American, continued to discredit and demean Kolbe and his information.

Superb as Kolbe's information was, Dulles asked if there was a faster way to get his information rather than waiting for the spy to travel by train every three months to Switzerland. Kolbe said he had been thinking about just that problem. He would send coded messages through third parties who would send greetings to relatives in Bern. These greeting cards would contain an intricate cipher Kolbe had worked out, based upon some of his favorite musical numbers.

Before leaving, Kolbe asked Dulles for a better camera, one that could photograph many documents in a single roll of film. OSS provided a tiny camera that took dozens of photos in a single roll.

Once Kolbe had returned to his Berlin offices, he began channeling information to Dulles through third parties, one being a regular courier traveling to Switzerland, another being a retired Foreign Office employee who bought a small mountainside home above Lake Constance in the Bavarian Alps near the Swiss border. Kolbe managed to smuggle rolls of film to Switzerland in watch cases. Few watchmakers were then operating in Germany and Swiss-made watches were best repaired in Switzerland.

The Allies asked Kolbe to determine whether or not their bombing of German cities had slowed war production. He quickly sent information pinpointing plant production figures, which had diminished considerably since the daily Allied bombings of the Third Reich had begun. Kolbe was also able to send information that proved that public morale in Germany was devastatingly low because of the bombings.

Kolbe's flow of information was invaluable and also included top-secret information regarding Germany's ally, Japan. He sent to Dulles a complete battle order of the entire Japanese fleet that the U.S. Navy was able to use in confirming that it had, indeed, broken the Japanese military code and led to several successful American naval engagements.

On July 20, 1944, a serious attempt on Hitler's life was made by the strongest element of the Black Orchestra, the German underground plotting to elmininate the dictator. When nothing was heard from Kolbe after the July assassination attempt, Dulles assumed that Kolbe had been caught in the Gestapo and SS nets thrown out to snare conspirators and that he had been executed. To Dulles' surprise, he heard once more from Kolbe some weeks later. The dedicated spy had survived the purge and continued to send valuable information for the duration of the war; more than 1,600 priceless documents that certainly saved countless lives and helped to shorten the war in Europe. Kolbe survived the war and began a successful business under a different name. Then all information on his whereabouts ceased and this greatest of Allied spies during World War II utterly vanished.

[ALSO SEE: *Abwehr; Black Orchestra; Wilhelm Canaris; Claude Dansey; Allen Dulles; MI6; OSS*]

KONO, TORCHICHI
Japanese Agent in America ▪ (1887– ?)

IN 1940, THE WORLD'S FAIR IN SAN FRANCISCO offered myriad marvels for a fascinated public. The Fair also offered many sideshows to amuse patrons, including the "Candid Camera Artist's Model Studio," operated by Al Blake, an old-time silent film actor and novelty performer. Amateur photographers could enter the Studio at the Fair and, for a small fee, photograph the attractive models posing inside.

Blake had created the idea for the exhibit and was operating it when he spotted a middle-aged Japanese gentleman enter with a camera hanging from his neck. He paid his fee and took several photos of the girls. When his time was up, he began to walk out but he stopped and approached Blake.

"Do you recall meeting me, Mr. Blake?" the Japanese gentleman asked.

Blake looked at him blankly. Then the man introduced himself as Torchichi Kono, reminding Blake that they had first met in 1917 when Blake was appearing in a silent film, *Shoulder Arms*, starring Charlie Chaplin. Kono had been Chaplin's valet. They began chatting, exchanging their experiences since their first meeting. Blake told Kono that he had served in the Navy but had gone back to show business, that he was making extra money by posing in store windows next to mannequins. Blake's ability to stand perfectly still had earned him the sobriquet of King of the Robots. Window shoppers were asked to guess which of the dummies in the window was Blake.

Kono heard him out, nodding, smiling. Then, he said: "It is a pity that you are not still in the Navy. If you were, you could make a good deal of money, much more than posing in store windows." He then left before Blake could say another word.

Blake did not again see Kono until running into him on Santa Monica Boulevard in Hollywood in March 1941. Remembering what Kono had said to him a year earlier, Blake walked along with Kono, telling him that his appearances at music halls were becoming so infrequent that he was thinking of rejoining the Navy to earn a regular salary. Kono responded by asking Blake if he had any friends still serving in the Navy, anyone who might help speed his reenlistment.

Nodding, Blake said, yes, and fabricated a friend named "Jimmy Campbell" who was serving on the battleship *Pennsylvania* stationed at Pearl Harbor. That night, Kono phoned Blake and asked him to meet him the next day in front of a furniture store. The next morning, Blake went to the rendezvous and stood by the curb. A large sedan drew alongside and Kono was in the back seat, opening the door. Blake got in and the car drove off.

At the wheel was a man introduced to Blake as Mr. Yamamoto who immediately began to question Blake as they drove through the Hollywood hills. Yamamoto then said: "I am very interested in your idea of rejoining the American navy but please tell me about your friend Jimmy Campbell who is stationed on the *Pennsylvania*."

"If I get any information for you," Blake told Yamamoto firmly, "definite arrangements must be made, and I'm talking about money."

For some moments Yamamoto said nothing. Then he replied: "Are you prepared to go to Hawaii right away?"

"I'm prepared to go anywhere right away if the money is right," said Blake.

"I will make all the proper arrangements for such payments," Yamamoto reassured Blake. "All you need do is go to Hawaii and persuade your friend Campbell to give me information."

Blake nodded and Yamamoto drove back to the rendezvous in Hollywood. Blake got out of the car and was told that he would receive a call within a few days. That night, Blake realized that he was being tailed by Japanese agents. They stood outside of his apartment, front and back. They followed him when he drove down the street. They were everywhere. (These were members of the Kempei Tai, the Japanese secret police.)

Now Blake became extremely nervous. He realized that he was in serious trouble, that he was dealing with spies and that his fake story about a fake friend on board the *Pennsylvania* had landed him in a great dilemma. He immediately went to ONI headquarters where he met with Lieutenant Leo P. Stanley. He told Stanley the whole fantastic story. Stanley asked him to play along with the Japanese and Blake agreed. Stanley told Blake that ONI would arrange to have an agent placed on board the *Pennsylvania* to impersonate Campbell.

ONI checked out Kono's background. They discovered what Blake already knew, that he had been Charlie Chaplin's valet, but they found out much more. Since that time, Kono had become extremely wealthy.

Kono lived in a luxury apartment on Bronson Street and had his own servants. He owned two luxury cars and had a substantial bank account, the source of his funds undetermined. He nevertheless made large deposits regularly into his account. ONI also learned from the FBI that the Bureau had kept him under surveillance since 1934, along with a host of other suspected Japanese spies who reported, as did Kono, to a known Japanese spymaster, Dr. Takashi Furusawa who ran a clinic on Weller Street in Los Angeles. Kono made many trips to this clinic, sometimes in the middle of the night.

Furusawa's clinic, ironically, never had any medical patients, only many visitors, all Japanese. On one occasion, FBI men tailed Kono when he took the Super Chief to Chicago. From Chicago he took the

Broadway Limited to New York, Bureau men following him. Once in New York, Kono went directly to the apartment of Count von Keitel, a known Nazi agent. From New York, Kono traveled to Washington, D.C., where he visited Commander Yoshiashi Ichimiya, who was a naval attaché at the Japanese Embassy. Kono then returned to New York, met with Keitel, and then traveled by train back to Los Angeles.

Yamamoto, FBI agents reported, was another Japanese spy whose real name was Itaru Tachibaka, a commander in the Japanese Navy who had arrived in the U.S. in 1930 and had attended the University of Pennsylvania where he had studied American history and American foreign relations. He then went to Los Angeles where he became a student at the University of Southern California in Los Angeles. He spent most of the 1930s traveling up and down the Pacific coastline meeting prominent Japanese businessmen. Kono and Tachibaka had been meeting for several years and were both part of the same spy network controlled by Dr. Furusawa.

Blake, meanwhile, received a call from Yamamoto who instructed him to book passage for Honolulu on board the liner *President Garfield*, which was to depart from San Francisco. This Blake did, calling Lt. Stanley at ONI to inform him that he was leaving for Hawaii. Before the ship sailed, FBI agents trailed Kono and Yamamoto to a shop where they held a whispered conversation while they tried on hats. Yamamoto then went to the Japanese consulate while Kono went to Furusawa's clinic on Weller Street.

That night Kono and two other Japanese men emerged to drive to a brothel named the Red Mill. After several hours they emerged, got into their car, and drove to San Francisco just in time to catch the *President Garfield*. Blake was already on board. He was watched throughout the voyage by the Japanese agents.

Once in Honolulu, Blake quickly made contact with the ONI agent pretending to be the mythical Jimmy Campbell. Both men met with the Japanese agents and "Campbell" answered all their questions on the armaments of the battleship *Pennsylvania* and other warships anchored at Pearl Harbor. Blake then returned to Los Angeles where he was given the balance of the money due him. Some months later the Japanese attacked Pearl Harbor and one of the battleships singled out for destruction by Japanese dive bombers was the *Pennsylvania*, which was then in drydock.

By that time, the FBI had lost complete track of Kono, one-time valet and full-time spy, as well as his superior, Yamamoto, and almost every one of Dr. Furusawa's vast spy ring, including Furusawa himself.

[ALSO SEE: *FBI; Takashi Furusawa; Kempei Tai*]

KRIVITSKY, WALTER G. (SAMUEL GINSBERG)
Polish Spy for Soviets ▪ (1899–1941)

KRIVITSKY IS FAMOUS FOR BEING THE FIRST HIGH-ranking GRU agent to defect to the West, a decision that cost him his life. Born Samuel Ginsberg, a Polish Jew in Galicia, which was part of the then Hapsburg Empire, he and his family suffered terribly from the rampant semi-official anti-Semitism in Austro-Hungary. To avoid racial persecution, he changed his name to Walter Krivitsky. In 1912, he joined an underground political movement working to overthrow the Hapsburgs.

After studying the works of Karl Marx, Krivitsky became an avowed Communist and, by 1917, he took part in Lenin's revolution in Russia, earning a place in Communist intelligence. Following Lenin's death, Krivitsky displayed his loyalty to Stalin and rose even higher in military intelligence, being posted to the Netherlands in 1935 where he acted as the head of all Soviet military intelligence (GRU) for western Europe with the rank of general. Using the alias of Dr. Martin Lessner, Krivitsky posed as an Austrian dealer of rare books and maintained offices in The Hague, which had been called "The Spy Capital of the World," due to its neutrality during World War I.

Krivitsky's faith in Stalin remained unshaken until his good friend, Ignace Reiss, who was also a director of Soviet intelligence in Europe, explained the true ruthless nature of Stalin and how he planned to placate Hitler and woo him into signing a non-intervention pact. Reiss told Krivitsky that he was breaking with Stalin and communism.

In 1937, Krivitsky, who had moved his headquarters to Paris, heard that Stalin's murder squads (SMERSH) were seeking to kill Reiss; they finally tracked him down and killed him in Switzerland. SMERSH had also recently kidnapped White Russian General Miller, head of the Federation of Czarist Army Veterans, and had most likely murdered him. Then, in late September 1937, Krivitsky himself was ordered to return to Moscow. He knew what that meant, that as a friend of Reiss he would be branded a traitor and summarily murdered. Krivitsky went to French government officials and asked for asylum. This was granted and he turned over a great deal of information on Soviet intelligence and counter-intelligence operations.

Fearing that SMERSH agents would find him in Paris, Krivitsky traveled to the U.S. where he provided American intelligence with a complete description of Soviet espionage operations. He wrote a book exposing the ruthless Stalin and OGPU operations (this was ghosted for him by an American writer). The autobiography, entitled *I Was Stalin's Agent*, was published in 1939 and became a best-seller. It was one of the most reliable records of OGPU (KGB) operations at that time.

British intelligence had been aware of Krivitsky since the mid-1930s and SIS had kept his bookstore and art gallery in the fashionable Celebestraat in The Hague under surveillance. SIS agents had followed Krivitsky as he went to the French Ministry of the Interior to seek asylum and watched him later sail for America. In January 1940, Jane Sissmore, a lawyer and MI5 agent, interviewed Krivitsky but apparently attached little importance to the defector's statements, even when he talked about how Soviet agents had recruited quite a number of Cambridge students into the KGB ranks and that a British journalist had been sent to Spain to ostensibly cover the Civil War but whose real KGB job was to spy against France.

MI5 did not pursue these unnamed British agents working for the KGB, but had they properly addressed Krivitsky's allegations and probed deeply, they would have no doubt unearthed the whole rotten barrel of apples grown at Cambridge—Burgess, Maclean, Blunt, and Philby (the British journalist serving in Spain as a Soviet spy was no doubt Kim Philby)—which would have saved British counterintelligence a good deal of embarrassment, not to mention the loss of many state secrets, some decades later.

Sissmore did manage to collect enough information from Krivitsky to have MI5 identify a British subject working as a cipher expert in the British Foreign Office who was regularly feeding the OGPU information. This was Captain John Herbert King. Two MI5 agents, William Codrington and T. A. "Tar" Robertson caught up with King at the Bunch of Grapes Pub on Curzon Street. They bought him one glass of whiskey after another until the spy was in his cups. Drunk, sorrowful, King admitted spying for the Soviets, that he had been working for them since 1935 when he had been stationed in Geneva as a member of the British delegation to the League of Nations.

King was tried *in camera* at the Old Bailey on October 18, 1939, and was found guilty of violating the Emergency Powers Act. He was sent to prison for ten years. Not a bit of this appeared in the British press or was ever made public until June 1956 when the British Foreign Office admitted King had been prosecuted in 1939. Released after the war, King was the only spy captured on the strength of Krivitsky's information but many more might have been identified to prevent the loss of future secrets had MI5 treated this important defector with something other than a routine, cursory interview.

Krivitsky did not enjoy his freedom from Stalin's iron grasp for long. A maid in the Bellevue Hotel in Washington, D.C., entered the defector's fifth-floor room on Sunday morning, February 9, 1941. Walter Krivitsky, late major general of the GRU/OGPU (KGB) was found dead, shot in the head. His death was ruled a suicide but it is most likely that he was assassinated by dedicated SMERSH killers.

[ALSO SEE: *Anthony Blunt; Guy Burgess; KGB; Donald Maclean; MI5; Kim Philby; Ignace Reiss; SIS; SMERSH*]

KROGER, PETER AND HELEN
American Spies for the Soviets ▪ (1910– ?); (1913– ?)

BORN MORRIS COHEN IN THE BRONX IN 1910 OF Russian-Jewish parents, Kroger graduated high school in New York, then went to the University of Illinois where he met and married Leona (or Lona) Petka of Adams, Massachusetts. Both became Communists at that time. After receiving his degree in science, Kroger went to Spain to fight in a Communist brigade against Franco in the Spanish Civil War, using the *nom de guerre* of Israel Altman. He returned to the U.S. following the collapse of the Republic and hired out as a guard at the Soviet pavillion during the 1939 World's Fair in New York. He worked for the Russian-sponsored Amtorg Trading Corp. in New York until 1942, before serving in the U.S. Army in World War II.

American-born Soviet agents Peter and Helen Kroger (Cohen), who first spied in the U.S. with the Rosenbergs and Rudolf Abel, then in England as part of Gordon Lonsdale's spy network.

A short-wave transmitter hidden inside a space-heater that was found in the Kroger home.

The Krogers, a name by which this espionage couple is best known, were part of the Soviet spy network in New York City involving Julius and Ethel Rosenberg and the stealing of atomic secrets that were passed on to Soviet agents, and another KGB network run by Russian spymaster Rudolf Abel. Warned that the Rosenbergs were about to be arrested by the FBI in 1950, the Krogers hurriedly fled.

The couple next surfaced in London as the Krogers in 1954. (They had taken the name of a couple, Peter and Helen Kroger, who had died much earlier in New Zealand, a long used identity-change tactic employed by the KGB; they had used the name of Cohen in the U.S.)

It was not until November 1960 that MI5 picked up the trail of the Krogers in London, identifying them with the Soviet network operated by Gordon Lonsdale who had been delivering secret information he had obtained by British traitor Harry Houghton, who, in turn, had been getting top-secret data from his girlfriend, Ethel Gee, an employee at the Admiralty Underwater Weapons Establishment in Portland, England.

MI5 agents kept the Krogers under surveillance until Lonsdale, Houghton, and Gee were arrested in early January 1961. Agents then went to the Kroger home and confronted the pair, arresting them.

A search of the Kroger home yielded a motherlode of espionage equipment, including cipher pads on quick-burning paper, ciphers, code books, sophisticated photo equipment, a device for reading microdots, a specially-built Ronson lighter containing a coded message inside, and numerous other items.

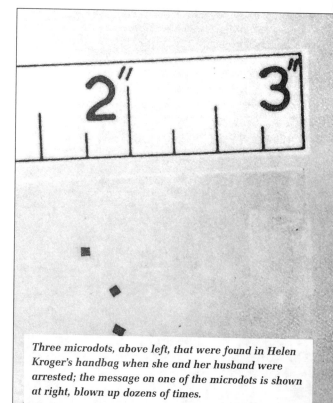

Three microdots, above left, that were found in Helen Kroger's handbag when she and her husband were arrested; the message on one of the microdots is shown at right, blown up dozens of times.

After a week of digging, agents found a powerful transmitter capable of sending in rapid bursts. There could be no doubt that the Kroger home was the communications center for sending information to Moscow. (Twenty years later, the new occupants of the Kroger home dug up a second high-speed Soviet radio transmitter in the back yard.)

Fingerprints taken from the Krogers were sent to Washington where the FBI identified them as belonging to Morris and Leona Cohen, who were still wanted in the Rosenberg case. Instead of returning the Krogers to the U.S., the British authorities tried and convicted them of espionage. They were sent to prison for twenty years.

Though the British did not hold the Krogers in the highest espionage esteem, the Russians certainly did. The KGB went out of its way to secure the release of the couple by engineering a fake arrest of British lecturer Gerald Brooke, who was visiting Moscow and who was accused of distributing subversive literature. By seizing Brooke, the KGB had a bargaining chip that they played when offering to exchange the hapless lecturer for the Krogers.

U.S. authorities stepped in, stating that the Krogers were U.S. citizens and could not be bartered for a British subject, and that if they were to be released, they had to be extradited to the U.S. for their part in the Rosenberg conspiracy. The Russians claimed that the Krogers were Polish citizens, not Americans, and the British, more eager to regain Brooke than to appease U.S. officials, accepted that claim. The Krogers were exchanged for Brooke in October 1969. They vanished a few years later.

[ALSO SEE: *Rudolf Abel; Amtorg; KGB; Harry Houghton; Gordon Lonsdale; MI5; Julius and Ethel Rosenberg*]

KUCZYNSKI, RUTH (URSULA-MARIA HAMBURGER, RUTH BREWER, "SONIA")
Soviet Spymaster ▪ (1907– ?)

OF ALL FEMALE SPIES IN THE TWENTIETH CENTURY, Ruth Kuczynski remains the most enigmatic. A dedicated Communist all her life, she operated spy rings for the Soviets in China, Switzerland, and England. Born in Germany, Kuczynski was the well-educated daughter of a prominent German-Jewish economist, Professor Rene Kuczynski, who fled Germany when Hitler came to power and took up residence in Oxford, England, where he taught economics and befriended some of Britain's most distinguished political leaders.

Ruth Kuczynski married Rudolph Hamburger, who was a Soviet agent, had two children, and reset-

tled in Shanghai, China, about 1933. She was by then a KGB spymaster who controlled a ring of Soviet agents in China, at the same time the celebrated Soviet agent Richard Sorge was operating there. Chinese intelligence, headed by Morris "Two-Gun" Cohen, identified Kuczynski and her agents and she was arrested in 1935. She managed to escape and flee to Switzerland with her two daughters, living in Montreux.

In an effort to penetrate the Soviet spy rings SIS knew were operating in Switzerland, they planted their own double-agent, Alexander Foote, with the Russian agents. Foote first made contact with a sultry, black-haired woman with a shapely figure named Ursula-Maria Hamburger who also employed the alias of Ursula-Maria Schultz. This, of course, was Ruth Kuczynski, who had long established a Soviet spy ring throughout Switzerland. She then went under the code name of "Sonia."

The Kuczynski spy ring's activities were then wholly directed against Hitler's Third Reich. It was Foote's job to obtain the information Kuczynski's ring and other Soviet rings in Switzerland were acquiring through a vast spy network known as the Red Orchestra and relay this information to SIS in London. Although Russia was at the time an ally of England, Stalin shared no information with his allies.

Through Kuczynski, Foote came to meet Sandor Rado, who controlled the largest and most effective Soviet network in Switzerland, including that of Rudolf Roessler, whose code name was "Lucy," and who, next to OSS agent Fitz Kolbe, proved to be the most effective Allied agent in World War II, providing astounding but accurate high-level information on the Nazi war machine.

Spectacular Soviet agent Ruth Kuczynski (shown with her young son Micha) spied in China, Switzerland, and England, where she handled Klaus Fuchs, the British scientist who turned over atomic secrets to her.

Ruth Kuczynski's brother Jurgen, who operated a left-wing bookstore in London and also spied for the Soviets.

In 1939, it appeared to Foote that Kuczynski had become utterly disillusioned with Soviet Russia after Stalin and Hitler signed their infamous Non-Aggression Pact. She nevertheless continued to work for the Soviets, increasing her efforts when Hitler finally invaded Russia in 1941. When the Soviet rings in Switzerland were finally identified and Kuczynski was about to be arrested, she married Len Brewer, an Englishman and Communist, and went to England, ostensibly to retire from espionage altogether.

This was not the case, however. She had married Brewer on orders from the Soviets in order to gain reentry into England where she was to become the caseworker of atom-bomb scientist, Klaus Fuchs, who had been recruited into the Communist Party in England by none other than Brigitte Kuczynski, Ruth's younger sister, also a dedicated Communist and KGB spy. In fact, the entire Kuczynski family had been spies for Russia since the time they fled Nazi Germany. Ruth's father, Professor Rene Kuczynski, esteemed as a shrewd expert on the Third Reich, obtained a great deal of information from British leaders like his good friend, Sir Stafford Cripps, then a member of the War Cabinet. Kuczynski also passed this information on to Moscow.

Even Ruth's outgoing brother Jurgen Kuczynski was a KGB spy. When William J. Donovan of the OSS wanted to establish contact with the German underground, he opted to contact German Communists inside the Third Reich and one of his agents, Lieutenant Joseph Gould, simply walked into Kuczynski's left-wing political bookshop and bluntly asked to talk to someone representing the Free Germany Committee. Kuczynski was delighted to steer Gould to his KGB network. (British intelligence later claimed that it had warned Donovan that this was dangerous, that the Communists might be tomorrow's enemies, but Donovan shrugged off the notion. The job at hand was winning the war against the Nazis and his OSS would use anyone to accomplish that goal. The British, it was claimed, then concluded that the OSS was a short-term organization, one that would not outlast the war. In this SIS officials were correct.)

Throughout the war and afterward, Ruth Kuczynski continued to serve as Klaus Fuch's spymaster. He had turned over atomic secrets to Harry Gold in the U.S. when he was working on the Manhattan Project and this information had been sent on by Gold to Soviet agents, but once Fuchs had returned to England, he continued to supply secrets to Kuczynski until he was exposed and arrested. Kuczynski did not come under suspicion until some time later, when she was linked with not only Klaus Fuchs but Sir Roger Hollis, one-time chief of MI5. It was said that Hollis had known Kuczynski in China and later in Switzerland and that he had actually been recruited by her into the KGB ranks. Hollis was later confronted with this allegation and utterly denied ever knowing the spectacular Kuczynski.

Both Ruth and Len Brewer successfully fled to East Germany. In 1977, Ruth Kuczynski published her memoirs, *Sonia's Rapport*, a rather self-aggrandizing autobiography that added nothing new to information already on file.

[ALSO SEE: *Morris Cohen; William J. Donovan; Alexander Foote; Klaus Fuchs; Roger Hollis; KGB; Fritz Kolbe; MI5; OSS; Sandor Rado; Rudolf Roessler; SIS; Richard Sorge*]

KUHN, BERNARD JULIUS OTTO
German Spy for Japanese ▪ (1895– ?)

THE DEVASTATING JAPANESE SNEAK ATTACK ON PEARL Harbor, December 7, 1941, was not a success by accident. Japanese intelligence had worked long and hard to pinpoint which capital ships would be at anchor in the harbor that day, as well as the exact locations of U.S. airfields and military installations throughout the island of Oahu. Among the small army of Japanese spies in and about Honolulu that had provided information on the American base was a German agent in the direct employ of Japan, Dr. Bernard Julius Otto Kuhn, along with his wife Friedel; his daughter Ruth, age twenty-four; and even his son Hans, age thirteen. All the Kuhns worked for Japan and all of them were spies.

Born into a working-class family, Kuhn joined the German Navy at age seventeen in 1912. He relished authority and was an early supporter of Adolf Hitler's Nazi Party. It mirrored his own peculiar values—a hatred for Jews and all nationalities other than German, an intolerance of organized religion, and a gnawing desire for supremacy. He joined the Party and served as a functionary, befriending the enigmatic Heinrich Himmler, Hitler's ruthless secret policeman, and urged his oldest son Leopold to work as a secretary for Dr. Paul Joseph Goebbels, Hitler's propagandist who would later head all German media.

With the rise of Hitler, Kuhn was given a job with the Gestapo by his good friend Himmler. Kuhn was invited to many social functions sponsored by Goebbels' Ministry of Propaganda, as was Leopold. On one occasion in 1933, Leopold attended a social affair at the Ministry, taking as his date his 17-year-old sister Ruth. A lovely, charming girl, she soon caught the eye of the lecherous Goebbels.

Though married, the dwarfish, club-footed Goebbels was an ardent womanizer who was not without charm. After meeting Ruth Kuhn, he invented small jobs for her in order to make her one of his many mistresses. Ruth was not without sophistication and wile. She knew that a liaison with Goebbels would further her family's position. She was correct.

General Karl Haushofer, a friend of the Kuhn family, was head of the geopolitical department at Berlin University. This department was really a spy school where agents were trained for service with the Abwehr and the German Foreign Service headed by Joachim von Ribbentropp. Since 1914, General Haushofer had developed close relations with the Japanese intelligence service. In early 1935, the Japanese asked Haushofer if he could provide them with Europeans who might work with them. The Japanese, outside of oriental communities, had difficulties in using their own agents due to quickly identifiable racial features. Thus they desperately sought to fill the ranks of their intelligence service with Caucasian spies who could more easily infiltrate Western circles.

The proposition was made to not only Bernard Kuhn but to his entire family. The Kuhns accepted the deal. Kuhn met with Japanese navy intelligence chief, Captain Tadao Yokoi, in Berlin and haggled a contract that called for his espionage services at $2,000 a month with a $6,000 bonus at the end of each year, a contract for two years, to be renewed each year thereafter with regular raises. Friedel and Ruth Kuhn were also to receive salaries.

Kuhn then traveled to Tokyo where he met with Japanese spymaster Kanji Ogawa, along with other staff officers of the Japanese Navy. Kuhn discussed intelligence plans and was given his family's assignment. The Kuhns were to travel to Hawaii. Kuhn and his family members were to collect all kinds of data on the American fleet stationed at Pearl Harbor, as well as all military installations throughout the islands, regularly sending this information to Japanese contacts at the Japanese consulate.

In 1935, the Kuhns took a comfortable home in Honolulu where Friedel opened a beauty salon and her husband went to work on his history of the Hawaiian Islands. Friedel Kuhn was a plumpish bespectacled woman who encouraged her American customers, mostly the wives of Navy and Army officers, to talk freely in her shop. She projected the image of a responsible mother and devoted wife whose family's interests always came first. She was forever talking about the large meals she insisted on personally making for Dr. Kuhn, her beautiful daughter, and her small son, Hans. (Leopold had remained in Germany as Goebbels' private secretary; he would later be killed on the Russian front.)

Ruth Kuhn was very popular with single American Navy officers. Beautiful and outgoing, the charming young girl was sought after by dozens of ardent Americans. They played tennis with her, took her sailing and to dances. They also unwittingly provided her with a good deal of information about the American Pacific fleet, the types of warships at anchor at Pearl Harbor, their departures and arrivals. Ruth Kuhn was particularly enthralled with U.S. aircraft carriers and not only learned everything about those carriers stationed at Pearl Harbor but was even escorted by proud navy officers through several of them on Sunday afternoons.

In 1939, Otojiro Okuda, the Japanese consul in Honolulu, met with the Kuhns, requesting that the family move closer to Pearl Harbor itself. They took a house on a hill that overlooked the main harbor, which they could survey through binoculars. Mrs. Kuhn moved her beauty salon to Pearl Harbor and she and Ruth both pumped customers for information about the naval base. Moreover, 11-year-old Hans was trained to ask sailors countless questions about their warships. He, like his sister, was taken on board destroyers, minesweepers, cruisers, battleships, and carriers to look around.

Hans Kuhn had been trained to remember all important details about the ships he toured and immediately upon his return home, he rattled off these details to Ruth who detailed the reports in code. By March 1939, the Japanese had equipped the Kuhns with a radio transmitter having a range of about 100 miles, enough to reach Japanese submarines that were, from 1940 on, lying submerged to receive these coded messages. The submarines, in turn, relayed Kuhn's information to Japan.

U.S. agents were uncertain whether the Kuhns were spying for Germany or Japan. They monitored the comings and goings of family members but, due to a shortage of manpower to cover the myriad spies in Hawaii, did not place Kuhn's home or Friedel's beauty parlor under constant surveillance. Kuhn

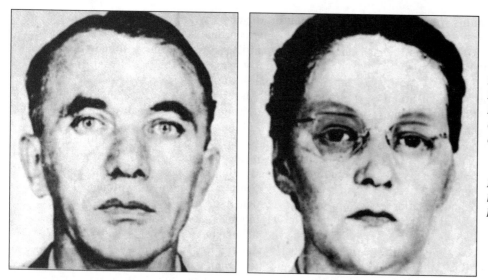

Nazi spy for Japan in Hawaii, Bernard Kuhn, who reported the hits made by Japanese dive bombers on U.S. battleships at Pearl Harbor on December 7, 1941.

Friedel Kuhn, who aided her husband by reporting navy gossip picked up in her Honolulu beauty parlor.

continued to feed his Japanese contacts with information through the summer and fall of 1941, meeting at his home or at clandestine places with Takeo Yoshikawa and even Nagao Kita, the Japanese Consul General. Years later, the Japanese insisted that Kuhn acted contrary to their orders, that he was strictly a "sleeper" agent and conducted espionage from 1935 right up to the attack on Pearl Harbor on December 7, 1941, at his own initiative but this was to save the considerable loss of face the Japanese experienced when confronted with planning the sneak attack against the naval base years in advance.

The official Japanese position on Pearl Harbor was that this attack was not planned until only a short time before it actually took place. Japan was compromised, it later insisted, through the bungling of its representatives in Washington, D.C., who were supposed to announce the opening of hostilities to U.S. authorities before the attack—albeit only hours before the attack, which would still reserve the element of surprise for its fleet.

The truth is that the Japanese diplomats in Washington, D.C., were not informed of the attack until after it was launched. All of this was according to the insidious plan worked out long in advance by Japanese leaders with the enthusiastic approval of Emperor Hirohito himself. Kuhn was part of that long-range plan. Why else would Japan have been paying a mere "sleeper" agent more than $50,000 a year for six years, not to mention equal amounts paid to his wife and daughter, as well as supply him with special transmitter radios, code books, and other spy apparatus from 1939 onward?

As the deadline for the attack grew near, Kita asked Kuhn to scout the American Navy base closely. This he did on November 28, 1941, spying on each warship and pinpointing its anchorage. He reported personally to Kita at the Japanese consulate two days later to show a map of Pearl Harbor and exactly where the American ships were located. This included two

aircraft carriers (which, fortunately, were sent on patrol shortly before the attack), seven battleships, six cruisers, forty destroyers, assorted auxiliary ships, and twenty-seven submarines.

Two days later, on December 1, Kuhn put into effect a system by which the Japanese could receive instant information on the movement, if any, of those warships. He worked out a signal code with Okuda whereby he would send light signals from a small window in the attic of his home, which was perched on a hill directly overlooking Pearl Harbor, to the Japanese spy in the consulate. This signaling system was tested.

Six days later, the Kuhns were ready. It was near dawn on December 7, 1941. Ruth Kuhn stood at one window of the attic with binoculars, surveying the American fleet spread out before her. Her father stood at another window with a signal light, ready to flash the information she called out to him. Below, in the house, Friedel Kuhn and 13-year-old Hans were busy packing suitcases, not with clothes or household belongings, but with wads and wads of money, American, Japanese, and German, which they had collected over the years from their spying activities.

They waited anxiously, as did Kita and other Japanese officials standing at the windows of their consulate, ready to receive the light signals from the Kuhn house high up in the hills. At 7:55 A.M., Ruth Kuhn trained her powerful Zeiss binoculars on the eighty-six ships (some reports say ninety) lying at anchor in the harbor. She then scanned the skies over Pearl Harbor to the northeast and almost at the same time a steady, distant drone of plane motors could be heard, she shouted to her father: "They are coming!"

Kuhn stood with a large signal light at another attic window. "All I hope," he said, "is that they managed to get the submarine inside the defenses." The Kuhns were to accompany Kita and his staff in escaping Pearl Harbor in one of the Japanese submarines that were hidden outside the harbor the previous night.

Ruth Kuhn could see a huge formation of Japanese planes coming toward her from the mountains to the northeast—353 war planes in all.

A formation broke off and went toward Wheeler and Hickam Fields. The night before the Kuhns had sent a message to Kita that the American planes on these fields had been foolishly grouped closely together, wingtip to wingtip, so that they could be more easily guarded against saboteurs who had been reported in the area. This tactic allowed the Japanese divebombers to quickly destroy the fighters and bombers en masse.

Another formation of Japanese planes veered toward the U.S. Navy Airfield at Kaneohe Bay. The largest formation kept coming straight for Pearl Harbor. Suddenly, the Kuhn's wooden house shook from the explosions in the Harbor. The windows rattled. China fell from cupboards and smashed on the kitchen floor. Friedel and Hans Kuhn sat on the sofa, holding each other. Ruth Kuhn, coolly and precisely recorded the carnage she viewed through her binoculars, calling out to her father each successful bomb and torpedo unleashed by the Japanese planes: "Direct hit on battleship . . . cruiser struck amidships and burning . . . destroyer burning . . . another destroyer exploding . . ."

Ruth Kuhn marveled at the carnage brought by the Japanese planes circling and diving on the helpless ships below them. She reported how well each flight performed, the accuracy of their bombing, how low to the water the torpedo planes flew before unleashing their torpedoes. Suddenly a gigantic, roaring explosion shook the entire area and seemed as if it would shake the Kuhn house from its foundation. Peering through her binoculars, Ruth Kuhn gasped, then gave a shout of delight: "It's the *Arizona*! It blew up! Direct hits down her stacks! It's gone, the *Arizona* is gone! There's nothing left of it!" (At that moment 1102 American sailors died with the battleship *Arizona*; they are still on board as the *Arizona* rests at Pearl Harbor today, a national memorial, a battleship never removed from the registry of the U.S. Navy.)

Some minutes after Dr. Kuhn had flashed the information about the *Arizona* to the Japanese consulate, another voice, a strange one, was heard in the attic. "Put up your hands!"

Kuhn and his daughter turned from the windows. Two military intelligence agents stood before them, guns in their hands. As the bombs kept exploding in the harbor, the Kuhns were ushered downstairs to the sitting room where another agent was guarding Friedel and little Hans Kuhn. The agents had seen the light signals from some distance (the Kuhns had been signaling the Japanese consulate for an hour and a half through the two major attacks on the harbor).

The agents realized that the signals were coming from the Kuhn house, which was on the list of suspected espionage sites and they drove quickly to the place where they caught Dr. Kuhn and Ruth red-handed as the secret servants of Japan.

By then the Japanese attack was over. Forty Japanese planes had been shot down and three Japanese subs had been sunk. One of these was the vessel on which the Kuhns and their Japanese spymasters were to escape. Instead the Kuhns were placed on trial, charged with espionage.

At the Kuhn trials, many ugly truths were exposed, including the fact that J. Edgar Hoover's FBI had badly handled its counterintelligence responsibilities at Pearl Harbor. The Bureau, as well as military intelligence, knew very little about the workings of the Japanese spy network in the islands, only that it was controlled through the consulate and that Kita was undoubtedly directing all espionage. Beyond that, they failed to fully identify Japanese agents who had long worked in the area. They *suspected* the Kuhns but never obtained evidence of their espionage until it was too late. They had never figured out Kuhn's coded messages, undoubtedly because these codes were of Kuhn's own invention and departed radically from the regular Japanese codes that the American military had earlier deciphered.

When U.S. intelligence agents stormed into the Japanese consulate and ransacked the place, along with the Kuhn home, they were unable to later interpret codes and maps that had not been burned by the panicking Japanese spies. FBI agent Shivers later insisted that the Japanese planes had tenaciously dive-bombed the battleship *Utah*, mistaking it for the carrier *Saratoga*, because the maps provided by Kuhn showed the carrier at that anchorage position. This was not the case. Kuhn had carefully drawn the overhead silhouette of a battleship at that anchorage, not an aircraft carrier.

Kuhn had dutifully scouted the entire fleet between December 1 and December 6, the six days referenced in his final message when using the word "six," and he knew the exact position of each vessel, especially the battleships, and by name, priority information desired by the Japanese. During the trials of Dr. Kuhn, Ruth, and Friedel Kuhn, each claimed to be the leader of the family espionage ring. Dr. Kuhn was finally believed to be the spymaster and it was he who drew the most severe sentence, death. Ruth and Friedel Kuhn were each given 50-year prison terms. The sentences were passed down in October 1942.

A few hours later, Dr. Kuhn volunteered to provide all he knew about Japanese espionage operations. It was an obvious effort to save his life. Authorities agreed to reduce his sentence to life if he talked. Kuhn talked, explaining his every move and that of his wife and daughter since their arrival in Hawaii in 1935. The family members were released following the war and returned to Germany where they faded from view. Ruth Kuhn was last seen alive in West Germany in the middle 1970s and then no more.

[ALSO SEE: *Abwehr; FBI; Gestapo; Heinrich Himmler; J. Edgar Hoover*]

LAELIUS
Roman Spymaster ▪ (? –160 B.C.?)

DURING HIS WAR WITH CARTHAGE IN 203 B.C., Scipio Africanus, the Roman general, found it difficult to determine the defense system devised by Hannibal, particularly that held by a large force of Numidians. To play for time, Scipio asked for a truce, bringing to the compound where the peace talks would be held a number of slaves and civilians and a few military aides. Among the slaves was one of Scipio's ablest generals and his spymaster, Laelius.

It was Laelius' job to somehow escape the confines of the compound and get inside the Numidian defenses, yet he and his men were so closely watched he found this task impossible. Scipio prolonged the truce talks to the point where the Numidian King Syphax began to suspect he was being stalled and said that he would break off talks within twenty-four hours.

Hearing this, Laelius quickly devised a plan. He had noticed flies swarming about the horses of the Roman entourage so he and his slaves caused the animals to stampede into the Numidian defense system, chasing wildly after them and ineptly attempting to corral the animals. In so doing, Laelius and his men had time to note every detail of the defenses and by the time they had rounded up the horses they had the information they were seeking.

Shortly after the truce ended, Scipio attacked the Numidian position, knowing exactly where its weak points lay. His men overran Syphax's men and position, causing the Numidians to flee. The Carthaginians were left with inferior forces, causing the great Hannibal to ultimately lose the battle of Zama to Scipio in 202 B.C., the final defeat of Carthage, which became a Roman vassal state. It was Laelius, Scipio's spymaster, who commanded the cavalry at Zama, which helped to decide the great Roman victory.

LAHOUSEN, ERWIN VON
Abwehr Spymaster in World War II ▪ (1897–1955)

BORN IN AUSTRIA TO AN ARISTOCRATIC CATHOLIC family, Lahousen was part French (his full last name was Lahousen-Vivremont). He attended the University of Vienna and he served in the Austrian Army in World War I. Following the war, he received further training at the Austrian staff college and then rose in the ranks until, in 1933, he headed Austrian military intelligence in eastern Europe. A clever man, Lahousen never revealed his true political views. During the mid-1930s, he cooperated with the French in working toward the defeat of Hitler and, at the same time, worked with Admiral Canaris of the Abwehr to advance Hitler's land-grabbing schemes. When Hitler annexed Austria in 1938, Canaris invited Lahousen to join his Abwehr as head of Abwehr II, the department responsible for sabotage and sedition. He accepted and, a year later, he brilliantly created a number of sabotage teams to work inside Poland and provoke an incident that would allow Germany to invade the country. Hitler took the assignment away from the Abwehr and gave it to Heinrich Himmler's SS, although the SS enacted all of Lahousen's plans with great success.

Himmler, of course, took the credit for duplicating what the Japanese had originally done in Manchuria where intelligence agents of the Special Service Organ under Kenji Doihara faked a bombing attack against the Japanese-owned Manchurian Railroad. Instead, the SS troops, wearing Polish uniforms, attacked a small German community, and wrecked a radio station just across the Polish border.

It was Lahousen's fine-tuned intelligence that had created that lightning conquest. As head of Austrian intelligence he had put together an enormous amount of information on the Polish military, its train and truck routes in supplying troops; its airfields, camouflaged hangars, secret fuel depots; its nationwide communications and control centers; its key bridges, hidden artillery, and munition dumps.

Though he had served Hitler well, Lahousen was in no way loyal to the Fuhrer. He enthusiastically shared a basic dislike for Hitler with Canaris and his right-hand aide, Hans Oster. This dislike grew quickly to intense hatred until Lahousen was plotting with Canaris, Oster, and others in the Black Orchestra to overthrow the tyrant.

Lahousen was not interested in operating an effective sabotage organization for Hitler. It is a fact that he slowed down his operations, muddied them up with interminable requirements and paperwork. His agents were, for the most part, not the highest level of spies but those whom Lahousen took personal pains to select for complicated missions—plodding

Nazi fanatics he was not sorry to lose. Their unsophisticated procedures, cursory training, naive perception of British counterintelligence was all fostered by Erwin von Lahousen and it led to their quick capture by an MI5 that lauded itself on its brilliant snaring of German spies when, in truth, they were casually dumped into the yawning mouth of the British lion.

Typical of Lahousen's inept saboteurs was 61-year-old Ernst Weber-Drohl, a one-time vaudeville strongman who had toured Irish cities in 1907. The old performer was taken to Ireland by U-boat and then left to do his own damage to English installations. Weber-Drohl did nothing except spend most of his Abwehr money in tracking down an old mistress and seeking two illegitimate sons.

Next came Dr. Hermann Goertz, a failed 45-year-old lawyer who claimed to have special knowledge of Ireland and knew nothing of the country. He and his mistress were smuggled into Ireland, meandered about the countryside, got drunk, and were arrested sixteen days later on May 22, 1940. In 1942, Lahousen, at Canaris' request, planned and executed Operation Pastorius, a mission wherein eight bumbling, wholly unskilled German saboteurs were landed on U.S. shores by submarines and were quickly rounded up, six of them being executed, the other two imprisoned.

No spymaster in history ever repeatedly sent out such bungling agents to accomplish sophisticated missions as did Lahousen (and Canaris who approved of all these hapless adventures), unless failure was the objective. In 1940, Lahousen sent three agents to Scotland. He ordered them not to travel by train once inside the country but to use bicycles. The spies were landed by rubber dingy from a seaplane, then abandoned to their fate. Lahousen's technical division had prepared these spies so inexpertly that it would appear to any novice that the German spymaster wanted them to be caught.

One had been given a flashlight which bore the marking "Made in Bohemia." Another was carrying German sausages. Another had a British registration identity card that had been prepared by the Abwehr credentials division, normally an extremely meticulous organization. The card bore the date "1940," but the "1" was written with a long tail, a handwriting feature that no English office would ever employ but one typical of European letterwriting.

These spies, too, like all the rest sent to England, were rounded up.

The same was true of America. On June 6, 1940, Karl Franz Rekowski, who had once been a wholesale paper salesman in the U.S., returned to America as a Lahousen-selected Abwehr spy. He claimed to have strong contacts with exiled I.R.A. leaders in New York and believed he could activate them as effective saboteurs. To that end, Lahousen had given him $200,000. Rekowski sent back voluminous reports, naming many Irish leaders working to destroy America on behalf of the Abwehr. He included newspaper clippings of various disasters, such as the September 12, 1940, explosion, at the Hercules Power Plant at Kenvil, New Jersey, which killed fifty-two persons and injured another fifty, as proof of his success.

Rekowski, however, like many another con artist, had merely swindled the Abwehr. There was no network of I.R.A. men blowing up power plants and munition dumps. Rekowski had made up the names and had merely clipped reports of real accidents from newspapers, passing these off as acts of Abwehr-financed sabotage. It seemed not to matter to Lahousen and to his chief, Canaris. They both knew that Hitler was unconcerned with espionage activities in the U.S. and in England and the money, spies, equipment, and support costs extended in one ridiculous operation after another went unreported and unknown. Early on, Lahousen had readily agreed to follow Canaris' subversive dictate to "sabotage our sabotage."

By early 1944, Lahousen was actively participating in the plot to assassinate Adolf Hitler. Though Canaris fell into disrepute with Hitler, and the Abwehr was all but dismantled by the time the plotters were ready to act, Lahousen had not been molested by Himmler's SS. He had access to Abwehr sabotage equipment and explosives and it was he who supplied the sophisticated bomb that was carried into Hitler's field headquarters in East Prussia on July 20, 1944 by conspirator Count von Stauffenberg. The bomb exploded but Hitler received only minor injuries.

Thousands paid with their lives for the attempted assassination, including Stauffenberg, Oster, and, subsequently, Admiral Canaris. Lahousen escaped punishment, managing to survive the war. He testified against Nazi leaders at Nuremberg in 1946, and then went into retirement, dying in 1955.

[ALSO SEE: *Abwehr; Black Orchestra; Wilhelm Canaris; Kenji Doihara; Heinrich Himmler; SIS*]

LA REYNIE, GABRIEL DE
French Spymaster ▪ (1625–1709)

BORN IN LIMOGES, FRANCE, LA REYNIE'S GRANDFATHER and father were magistrates and he followed them in this profession. Cardinal Mazarin brought him to Paris where he was later appointed chief of police by Louis XIV. Paris at that time was awash with crime, political intriguers and revolutionaries, poorly staffed and equipped hospitals, crumbling prisons, disease-infested neighborhoods, and a road system that was in complete disrepair. All of this became La Reynie's responsibility. Being an excellent organizer, he soon cleaned up the hospitals and prisons, repaired the roads, curbed the epidemics and established an elaborate and effective spy network that reached into every criminal haven.

So effective were La Reynie's spies that, like Eugene Francois Vidocq after him, La Reynie knew every criminal in the city, along with their plans. Thanks to La Reynie's spy network, Paris became the safest city in Europe.

The most famous case handled by La Reynie was euphemistically called the Affair of the Poisons. It involved Catherine Montvoisin, born Catherine Deshayes, who was popularly known as La Voison. She made poison her business, selling it to those wishing to dispose of unwanted spouses and lovers. Her customers, La Reynie discovered in 1679, were mostly aristocrats, chiefly female. The police chief's investigation led to the door of Madame de Montespan, the king's mistress. When Louis XIV received this report, he ordered the investigation closed.

La Reynie continued in his role of police chief—the first in Europe—until 1697 when he retired. He had organized the first real police department of any city and his procedures would be improved upon decade after decade by law enforcement officials to come. His spy network became the role model for every undercover operation in the future.

[ALSO SEE: *Eugene Francois Vidocq*]

LAVON AFFAIR
Israeli Espionage Operation ▪ (1954)

TAKING ITS NAME FROM PINHAS LAVON, ISRAELI Defense Minister, this abortive espionage operation involved Israeli agents who bungled a spectacular mission aimed at bringing the U.S. into confrontation with Egypt. The mission was reportedly designed and ordered by Pinhas Lavon (1904–1976).

Lavon, born in Warsaw to a merchant family, attended Lvov University in the 1920s, then departed for Palestine, working for Israeli independence as a dedicated Zionist. Upon Israel's recognition as an independent state, Lavon was appointed Minister of Agriculture by Prime Minister David Ben-Gurion in Israel's first cabinet (1948–1953), later becoming Minister of Defense.

Lavon continued in that role when Moshe Sharett became Prime Minister in 1954. In that year, it appeared that the U.S. was beginning to favor Egypt over Israel. President Dwight D. Eisenhower seemed very friendly toward Egyptian strongman President Gamal Abdul Nasser.

To counter this political situation, eleven Israeli agents living in Egypt, apparently under orders from Israeli military intelligence (headed by Colonel Benjamin Gibli) planned to blow up American buildings in Alexandria and Cairo, the blame for which would then be fixed upon Egyptian nationalists. This plot was designed to thoroughly rupture American-Egyptian relationships. It backfired when one of the Israeli provocateurs—he is known only by his cover name of Paul Frank—proved to be a double agent working for Colonel Osman Nouri, the shrewd chief of Egyptian counterintelligence. Frank informed on the other agents.

Except for their operational chief, Colonel Dar, who escaped, the spies were captured and placed on trial. Two were executed, one commited suicide, and the rest were sent to prison. The responsibility for this fiasco was placed at the door of Pinhas Lavon, who immediately denied having ordered the mission. He insisted that the agents had been under the direction of Israeli military intelligence, the Mossad, and that he knew nothing of it.

To protect his name, Lavon demanded an official inquiry. Sharett ordered a commission to investigate the matter but nothing could be determined. The investigation reported that Colonel Gibli testified he had received verbal orders to proceed with the mission and that Lavon had given him those verbal orders. Lavon denied ever giving any orders to Gibli.

The Lavon Affair, as it was afterward called, left the Defense Minister in disrepute. He resigned in February 1955. His supporters openly accused Israeli Chief of Staff Moshe Dayan of conspiring against Lavon and that he was the real culprit in the bungled Egyptian mission. Another commission determined that Dayan was innocent of leading a conspiracy against Lavon.

Still another commission was ordered to investigate the Lavon Affair in 1960 by David Ben-Gurion who had returned to power as Prime Minister. The commission, headed by Chief of Staff General Chaim Laskov, reported that Lavon had not issued the order and that it was most likely a directive from military intelligence, although the commission did not identify the person responsible. Ben-Gurion rejected the findings of the commission and refused to reinstate Lavon.

So divided was public sentiment that Ben-Gurion was forced to resign and reorganize his cabinet before resuming office in 1961. Lavon gave up the attempt to vindicate himself and went into permanent retirement. The Lavon Affair remains today a subject of controversy.

[ALSO SEE: *Mossad*]

LAWRENCE, T.(THOMAS) E.(EDWARD)
British Soldier & Spy in World War I ▪ (1888–1935)

T. E. LAWRENCE WAS A MAN OF INCREDIBLE VERSATIL-ity and independence. He was charismatic, sensitive, and kind. He was also a brilliant military tactician, political diplomat, and spy. A born leader, Lawrence was also capable of betraying a people whom he came to admire and love, the Arabs, a people he led for several years in a whirlwind guerrilla war against ruthless Turkish forces in World War I.

Born in Tremadoc, Wales, Lawrence moved with his family to Oxford, England, where he attended high school and then went on to the university. He graduated with honors in 1910 with a degree in history. Two dark secrets always loomed in the creative mind of T.E. Lawrence. The first was the fact that he was illegitimate, at least in the sense that his father and mother lived together and bore five sons without ever being married. The second secret, discovered at about the same time by Lawrence was that he had a decided preference for the company of males. He never developed a strong relationship with any female.

Following college, Lawrence pursued a career in archeology, going to the digs at Carchemish on the Euphrates in 1910. He accompanied a British team of archeologists who were discovering ancient Hittite and Assyrian artifacts. He remained in this area for four years. Lawrence occupied his time with more than archeology. He scouted the region for some distance, mapping the uncharted terrain in the event that Britain might some day be militarily involved there.

The area was part of the old Ottoman Empire controlled by the Turks, and Turkey was expected to join Germany and Austro-Hungary in an impending war. Lawrence, reportedly on orders from the British Secret Intelligence Service (SIS), accompanied Leonard Woolley and Captain S. F. Newcombe to Sinai, which was also under Turkish control. They mapped the entire area, using their archeological expedition as a cover, much the same way German tank commander Erwin Rommel was reportedly sent to Egypt in the early 1930s in the disguise of an archeologist to map out supply routes in preparation for an Italian-German attack years later.

Lawrence's team charted the terrain as far south as Aqaba, mapping possible attack routes and defense positions. Lawrence and his group published their archeological findings under the title of *The Wilderness of Zin* in 1914. The lengthy, detailed espionage report prepared for SIS was submitted in secret.

T. E. Lawrence, the great desert leader of World War I, who served as his own chief of intelligence in scouting enemy positions, a tactic that brought about a nightmare experience that altered his life. (AP/Wide World)

At the onset of the war in 1914, Lawrence went to work for the Foreign Office in London as a mapmaker. The following year he was sent to Cairo to serve in intelligence, his knowledge of Arabic dialects allowing him to interrogate prisoners of war. In 1916, the Arabs under King Faisel I revolted against their Turkish masters in Arabia and Lawrence was sent to Faisel as an adviser. His role was to coordinate Arab and British attacks on Turkish strongholds. It was a difficult assignment as Lawrence had to serve as a British spymaster, a liaison officer exercising sensitive political diplomacy with the Arabs, and a military adviser who wound up actually leading the Arabs in their guerrilla attacks against the Turks.

Faisel brought Lawrence to a fierce tribal leader, Ouda, a chieftan who by his own admission had killed at least seventy-five Arabs; he did not count his Turkish victims since he felt them of no account. Promising Ouda gold and other spoils, Lawrence convinced the Arab chieftan to attack Aqaba, which was taken in 1917. Lawrence, of course, knew exactly how to attack this Turkish stronghold, which was heavily fortified but from the sea only. Following maps and charts he had made years earlier of the area, Lawrence led Ouda and his bedoins through a narrow strip of land to successfully attack and capture the city.

The British military objectives were Jerusalem and, far to the north in Syria, Damascus. In disguise, Lawrence scouted the terrain, railway routes, and Turkish military installations to these cities. At one point, he traveled by rail to Damascus where he moved about freely, documenting the disposition of Turkish forces and then rode back to his Arab forces to complete another hazardous spy mission. Arranging with General Allenby to supply the Arabs with gold, guns, rations, and other war materials, Lawrence led the Arabs in many attacks against the Turks, repeatedly blowing up railway lines and successfully attacking troop and supply trains.

Then, Lawrence was captured at Deraa in November 1917 while conducting another spy mission. He had passed himself off as a Circassian while trying to determine the strength of the Turkish garrison there. The Turkish commander attempted to rape him and when he resisted, the officer pressed a fold of Lawrence's flesh together at the ribs and inserted a bayonet into the fold and turned it. Bleeding, Lawrence was then taken away by three men who beat his back with a whip; he bore the scars until his death.

Lawrence was then pinned down by two men while he was sodomized by the man whipping him. He was again sodomized by the Turkish commander. The next day he was released, not having told the Turks anything of his real identity or of his connection with the Arab revolt. Lawrence later led his forces back to Deraa, capturing the place and seeing to it that his torturers were summarily executed. So vengeful was Lawrence over his ghastly experience in Deraa, it was said, that he showed little mercy to the Turks thereafter. At one point, he and his Arabs came upon a retreating column of Turkish troops. Rather than allow the Turks to surrender, Lawrence ordered them annihilated.

The British under Allenby captured Jerusalem from the Turks in 1917 and then, with Lawrence and the Arabs separately advancing northward, the thrust toward Damascus was made the following year. It was the Arabs who took the city in 1918. Lawrence was present when the city was taken and, for a while, acted as its governor. He then met with Allenby who was accompanied by British and French officials. Allenby told Lawrence that the Arabs would not be granted complete independence, that England and France would actually rule Syria and all other lands freed from the now vanquished Ottoman Empire. In light of Lawrence's promises to Faisel and other Arab leaders to the contrary, he was thoroughly compromised. (Faisal would be made king of Syria in 1920 and later Iraq, but would serve as a puppet of the British and French.)

Lawrence begged British and French officials to grant the Arabs the independence they had fought for and earned. This was denied. Syria would be ruled by the French. In a frenzy, Lawrence later wrote and lectured against this policy but to no avail. Disgusted, he left the army, throwing away everything. He joined the Royal Air Force as an enlisted man, using an alias. When he was identified and released, he joined the Royal Tank Corps, again as an enlisted man and again using an alias, but again his fame overcame him. He was identified and released. He later was allowed to rejoin the Royal Air Force, serving as a Colonel. In later years he worked as a mechanic, developing high-speed motor launches that were used for sea rescues.

Lawrence chronicled his desert experiences in World War I in his brilliant and poetic *The Seven Pillars of Wisdom*, a memoir of nomads and a desert land long since vanished. The work was liberally sprinkled with insightful if not imperialistic thoughts and ideas concerning the ubiquitous and often mystical world of the Arabs of that era, a tough, dedicated civilization that survived through simple discipline decades before it was utterly corrupted by the riches of oil.

Lawrence's book made of him an international celebrity. So did American journalist Lowell Thomas, who had first written about Lawrence when he was serving in the desert. (Since Lowell Thomas' first biography, *With Lawrence In Arabia*, more than 50 biographies of Lawrence have been published. His fame is so widespread that a first edition of his *The Seven Pillars of Wisdom*, published in 1926 and autographed by him, recently sold for $40,000. The film, *Lawrence of Arabia*, starring Peter O'Toole as the much-troubled English hero, further spread the legend of Lawrence and his war in the desert.)

The love of speed offered a peculiar form of escape for Lawrence who took to racing his motorcycle at high speeds down narrow, twisting country roads. In 1935, while returning home from a village after mailing a letter, he drove his cycle at top speeds. Rounding a bend, he suddenly saw two delivery boys on bicycles. He swerved to avoid them and crashed into a tree.

Critically injured, Lawrence lingered for six days in a hospital before dying at the age of forty-six. Thousands attended his funeral, including many of those who had served with him in Arabia and other parts of the world. Winston Churchill, one of Lawrence's greatest admirers, was there, telling the world that T. E. Lawrence "would live forever in history."

[ALSO SEE: *SIS*]

LECLERC, JULIEN
French Royalist Spy ▪ (1762–1839)

NORMANDY-BORN LECLERC WAS A MONARCHIST AND Catholic who became a priest at about the time of the French Revolution. When the revolutionaries defied King Louis XVI, Leclerc became a royalist spy, using the cover name of "Boisvalon." He scouted the dangerous dens of the revolutionaries, learned their plans, and then reported this information to Louis' aides, as well as royalists in exile to whom he sent voluminous letters.

Following the execution of Louis XVI in 1792 and his son, Louis XVII in 1795, Leclerc attached his allegiance to comte de Provence who lived in exile and assumed the title of Louis XVIII. Even when Napoleon Bonaparte came to power, Leclerc continued his royalist spying, sending his information to French monarchists in exile, as well as the British whom he knew were in favor of restoring the French monarchy.

In 1803, when Bonaparte moved large forces to the French coast in what appeared to be a massive preparation to invade England, Leclerc, financed by French noblemen and the British government, traveled to the area, establishing a vast espionage network along the coast. He sent a small army of spies into the French camps to report on numbers of troops, supplies, equipment, cannon, and any news of French barges that might be used for the Channel crossing.

The spies reported to Leclerc and he wrote letters to his contacts in England, employing invisible ink in his letters in case they might be intercepted. His letters were delivered by French fishermen who met British warships patrolling the Channel waters.

Throughout Bonaparte's reign as emperor, Leclerc continued to spy and plot against him, establishing another network in Germany. It was not until Bonaparte's fall at Waterloo, final abdication, and permanent exile to St. Helena in 1815 that Leclerc saw the restoration of the French monarchy. When Louis XVIII was safely on the throne of France, the ardent Leclerc returned to his native country.

LEE, ANDREW DAULTON
American Spy for Soviets ▪ (1952–   )

THERE WAS VERY LITTLE PURPOSE TO THE LIFE OF Andrew Daulton Lee. Adopted by a well-to-do doctor in Palos Verde, California, he was given every opportunity. He graduated from high school in 1970 and then went on to junior college but found academic life boring. He began to use drugs and then, to support his expensive habit, became a drug pusher.

He was arrested for possession of marijuana in 1971 but he received a suspended sentence.

Entering Whittier College, Daulton made a feeble attempt to rehabilitate himself. He soon dropped out and returned to drugs. He served a jail term in 1974 but when released he had learned nothing. He immediately went back to drugs. At this time he learned that his childhood friend Christopher Boyce had recently obtained a job at TRW at Redondo Beach, California, working inside the Defense and Space Systems Group and had access to all the top-secret data relating to CIA space satellites.

Lee easily convinced Boyce to sell the classified information to the Soviets since they had both adopted the hippie attitude of condemning America as a failed government and a hopeless society. Since Lee had been to Mexico City on many drug-buying trips, he arranged for the secrets Boyce stole from TRW to be bought by KGB agents at the Soviet Embassy in Mexico City. Boyce stole the documents and Lee regularly delivered them, being paid handsome sums, not all of which he evenly split with his partner.

The spying continued until 1977 when, stoned on drugs, Lee created a disturbance outside the Russian Embassy and was arrested. He was found to be carrying filmstrips of TRW secrets. Mexican police notified the FBI and returned Lee to the border where he was turned over to Bureau agents. Boyce was arrested a short time later after Lee implicated him. Lee was given a life sentence, Boyce forty years.

[ALSO SEE: *Christopher Boyce*]

LE QUEUX, WILLIAM
British Spywriter & Agent ▪ (1864–1927)

LONDON-BORN LE QUEUX HAD AN ENGLISH MOTHER and a French father. He was privately educated in England and Italy, later studying art in Paris. He then went to work at the London *Globe* and became its foreign editor in 1891.

In 1893, Le Queux quit his job and began writing thrillers and mystery books. He was a success and his income allowed him to travel throughout Europe where he often performed special assignments for the British government, particularly at the turn of the century.

As one of the first to see the clear threat of Kaiser Wilhelm's war-thrusting Germany, Le Queux became alarmed at the apathy of the British government, as well as the public. In 1908, he wrote and published *The Invasion of 1910*, which clearly indicted Germany as the aggressor in a coming war.

Traveling throughout Europe, he performed some secret missions for the then newly created SIS, apparently working with Mansfield Cumming. One of his missions was to disguise himself when visiting a gun factory in Germany. He later submitted reports on new German weaponry to British intelligence.

In 1910, Le Queux published a provocative book entitled *Spies of the Kaiser*, which incensed Wilhelm who branded the author a dangerous enemy of Germany. Before World War I, the Kaiser's agents reportedly trailed Le Queux in London to the point where Scotland Yard provided several guards to protect him against assassination. Le Queux's undercover work came to a halt, unlike that of other authors such as Compton Mackenzie and Somerset Maugham who carried out secret missions for SIS.

Following World War I, Le Queux enjoyed enormous success from his thrillers and continued living his lavish continental lifestyle until his death in 1927.

[ALSO SEE: *Compton Mackenzie; Somerset Maugham; SIS*]

LEYDS, WILLEM
Dutch Spymaster in South Africa ▪ (1859–1940)

BORN IN JAVA AND EDUCATED IN HOLLAND, LEYDS attended the University of Amsterdam where he graduated with a Ph.D. in law in 1884. He met Paul Kruger, President of the Transvaal Republic, who asked him to take a position with his government. Within four years, Leyds rose to the position of state attorney.

Leyd's key responsibility was creating and overseeing the Transvaal intelligence network in the Cape Colony where the British were planning military operations against the Dutch Boers in Transvaal. Boer spies in the Cape were equipped with codes and ciphers Leyds had designed. He funded their covert operations along with supporting Boers running for election. He also spent huge sums in propaganda attempts to sway public opinion toward the Boers in Europe, funding newspapers and magazines that favorably profiled the Boers.

In 1902, the Boers were finally defeated and Kruger fled into exile, leaving Leyds without a government to represent. Leyds retired from public life and wrote history books on the Boers.

LIDDELL, GUY
British Spymaster ▪ (1892–1958)

LIDDELL SERVED IN THE BRITISH ARMY'S FIELD ARTILLERY during World War I, earning the Military Cross. In 1919, he went to work for Basil Thomson, head of Scotland Yard's Special Branch. His assignment was to identify political extremists living in England, chiefly Communists. Liddell worked closely with Vernon Kell, head of MI5, and Hugh Sinclair at SIS, which had, since the Bolshevik Revolution of 1917, been conducting widespread espionage operations in the Soviet Union, believing that the eternal menace to Western nations was communism.

In 1927, after Kell's organization aggressively identified Soviet spies in the celebrated Arcos raid, Liddell joined MI5, going to work in its "B" division, which was responsible for all British counterintelligence. His superior at that time was an old-line army officer, Brigadier General A. W. A. Harker, who had been serving since 1910. Liddell was considered brilliant, mysterious, and vain. He was short and balding, nurturing the few remaining strands of hair on his head.

Liddell's above-it-all image (his protective friends said it stemmed from shyness) had him staring vacantly into space and never into the eyes of those he met. He would, at such times, pluck nervously at some hair on his head. Liddell's only preoccupation was playing the cello and he was considered the best amateur player in England, sometimes holding musical soirées at his home.

T. A. Robertson and Richard White, who both later became MI5 stalwart chiefs, were trained by Liddell, and greatly aided him in his tireless investigations of Communists and Nazis in England during the late 1920s and throughout the 1930s. Liddell's major counterespionage case developed in 1937 when he unearthed a female Nazi spy, 51-year-old Jennie Wallace Jordan, of Dundee, Scotland. Jordan was the widow of a German who had died in the Kaiser's army in World War I. She ran a beauty parlor and used this as a front for a letter-drop, receiving and dispatching secret messages from Nazi spies located throughout Europe and even in the U.S.

Liddell's division was so efficient that it was able to pinpoint all of the Nazi agents sending messages to Mrs. Jordan, including a top Abwehr spy in America, Guenther Gustav Rumrich, who had been personally selected for his mission by Admiral Wilhelm Canaris. Liddell personally went to Washington to present the incriminating evidence to J. Edgar Hoover. The FBI subsequently tracked down Rumrich and other spies connected to the Jordan network.

At the onset of World War II, Liddell's counterintelligence division was kept busy tracking down Nazi spies. With the firing of Vernon Kell by Winston

[ALSO SEE: *Abwehr; Arcos Ltd.; Anthony Blunt; Guy Burgess; Wilhelm Canaris; Vernon Kell; Donald Maclean; MI5; Special Branch; Basil Thomson*]

British intelligence chief Guy Liddell, who joined Vernon Kell's MI5 in 1927 and was a good friend of Soviet spies Guy Burgess and Anthony Blunt; Liddell was suspected of warning Blunt that Burgess was to be arrested, although this was never proven.

LINCOLN, ISAAC (or IGNATIUS) TIMOTHY TREBITSCH
Hungarian Spy-for-Hire ▪ (1872 or 1879–1943)

Churchill in May 1942, Harker was replaced and Liddell was put into Harker's position to head the "B" division of counterintelligence.

Liddell was ably assisted in his wartime duties by Edward Henry Maxwell Knight. The two organized a vast network of MI5 agents in combating Nazi spies in England. Most of their "agents" were really informants, thousands of them, from racetrack touts to shopkeepers, who became the eyes and ears of MI5.

Following the war, everyone in the British intelligence community expected Liddell to take over MI5. But Prime Minister Clement Attlee distrusted that community and chose Sir Percy Sillitoe to head counterintelligence. Liddell was made Deputy-Director General in 1946. He continued to serve in that post until 1953 when he accepted a post with the Harwell Atomic Energy Center.

By that time, the traitorous activities of Guy Burgess had come to light. Liddell had been a close friend of Burgess' and, as it proved later, with Anthony Blunt, the aging art historian and KGB spy who had recruited students at Cambridge in the 1930s into the Soviet spy system. It was Blunt who warned Burgess and Donald Maclean in 1951 that they were about to be arrested as Soviet agents, but who warned Blunt? Some later said it was Liddell, although no one ever proved that claim. Liddell died of a heart attack in 1958.

COLORFUL AND UNPREDICTABLE, FEW PEOPLE EVER really knew Isaac (or Ignatius) Timothy Trebitsch Lincoln. Those who did professed later to be utterly mystified by him. He was an adventurer who knew no loyalties, except to himself. At one time or another he was a political spy—an espionage agent for many nations—often feeding information to both sides. This human chameleon was also a journalist, religious leader, member of British Parliament, forger, Buddhist monk, and mandarin. Charming, witty, a linguist and business entrepreneur, Lincoln traveled throughout Europe, England, America, and the Far East. He counted as friends European kings, Chinese princes, American statesmen, as well as low-life confidence men, cat burglars, and prostitutes.

Born with the name Trebitsch in Paks, outside of Budapest, Hungary, Lincoln's father was a successful Jewish shipbuilder, his business located on the Danube. As a child, Lincoln received an exceptional private education that included learning many languages.

Then, in 1896, apparently with the police on his heels for some minor offense, Lincoln hastily departed Hungary and journeyed to England. With little money in his pocket, Lincoln found shelter in Whitechapel, the Jewish quarter of London that had been the prowling grounds of Jack the Ripper only eight years earlier. There Lincoln met the Rev. Epstein, who represented a society that attempted to convert Jews to Christianity.

After a short period in which he was accused of stealing small amounts, Lincoln fled to Germany. In Hamburg he studied theology and was baptized in the Methodist Church. From Hamburg, Lincoln went to Canada where he officially converted to Lutheranism, studied for the ministry, and seduced a ship captain's daughter. Confronted with his sexual transgression by the girl's father and seminary officials, Lincoln admitted that, indeed, he had fallen in love and intended to marry the girl.

Following the marriage, Lincoln and his wife traveled to remote timber and mining camps in Canada, serving as Lutheran missionaries. Lincoln was a magnificent orator with a stentorian voice and he was hailed as one of the most dynamic religious speakers in the country at the Halifax International Missionary Exhibition. He came to meet provincial governors, statesmen, and business tycoons.

Lincoln tired of Lutheran dogma, however, and switched to the Anglican church, again studying for the ministry. On Christmas Day, 1902, he was ordained an Anglican minister by no less a personage than the Archbishop of Montreal. Within three months, Lincoln complained that his religious duties had exhausted him. He left Canada, traveled to Hamburg, Germany, and then went back to England. Lincoln then wrote to the Archbishop of Canterbury, requesting a license to officiate in England. This was granted.

Quitting his post in Kent in 1905, Lincoln went to York where he took up teaching in a Quaker school. He met Quaker leader and cocoa millionaire Seebohm Rowntree who was a prominent member of the Liberal Party.

Rowntree was so impressed with Lincoln that he made him his private secretary and assigned him research projects. Lincoln diligently worked for his mentor Rowntree from 1906 to 1909, the longest period of any time in his life that he kept a single job. There was a purpose to Lincoln's diligence. He had learned all he could from Rowntree, using his mentor's political connections to establish himself as candidate of the Radical Party in Darlington. To that end, he also officially changed his name to Lincoln and became a naturalized British citizen. He was known as Trebitsch-Lincoln or simply Lincoln.

Funds for the campaign were supplied by Lincoln himself, money, it was later claimed, he had purloined from Rowntree's ample coffers, although no one could ever prove the misappropriation. To almost everyone's surprise, Lincoln was elected to Parliament, making his first speech before the House of Commons on February 23, 1910. Fellow members thought little of Lincoln except as an object of mirth; his decided accent was mimicked and mocked.

After losing his seat in Parliament, Lincoln became a contributing writer for several London newspapers. He next decided to go into the oil business, convincing the gullible Rowntree to loan him money, and, through Rowntree, he also obtained considerable funds from the London Joint Stock Bank. Investments in European oil proved disastrous and Lincoln went bankrupt. He went back to journalism, serving as a foreign correspondent in covering the Balkan Wars of 1912-1913. Lincoln saw that he could make money by selling information, so he became a paid spy for Bulgaria. When he realized that he could earn money from both sides, he offered his espionage services to Turkey.

The Bulgarian secret service discovered Lincoln's role as a double agent and arrested him, throwing him into a Sofia prison. His release, strangely enough, was brought about by the intervention of Walther Nicolai, chief of German military intelligence. Why Nicolai would arrange the release of this peculiar Englishman has never been fully explained, but it was conjectured that Lincoln was either already a spy for the Germans in the Balkan Wars, his true espionage role, or that he agreed to spy for the Germans in England once he returned to his adopted country.

When Lincoln returned to England in August 1914, on the eve of World War I, he immediately applied for a position with British intelligence but SIS turned him down. This rejection caused Lincoln to develop an almost pathological hatred for the British. The would-be spy then went to Rotterdam, ostensibly to find out from the German Consul how his mother-in-law was faring in Hamburg. To that end, Lincoln met with Lieutenant-General von Ostertag in The Hague on December 29, 1914. Lincoln knew Ostertag from his days when the German official had been a military attaché in the German Embassy in London before the war. Ostertag was, as the SIS knew, also the chief of the Abwehr in Holland when Lincoln met him at The Hague.

Upon returning to England, Lincoln went directly to the chief of naval intelligence, Reginald "Blinker" Hall, to state that he had obtained a copy of the German code that all Abwehr agents used. He turned over a code that SIS, after quick analysis, concluded he had made up himself, one that was absolutely useless.

Naval intelligence stalled Lincoln for a few weeks before he was brought before Admiral Hall. The navy intelligence chief, who believed Lincoln was acting as a double agent and had been in the employ of the Abwehr since 1912, told him that he was playing a dangerous game, that "the sooner you turn your back on England, the better it will be for you."

Lincoln, stunned, did not delay. He sailed for America the very next day on board the steamer *Philadelphia*. He arrived in New York on February 9, 1915. He immediately went to the German consulate and offered his services as a spy but the Germans, apparently, had reservations about him and declined. Next, Lincoln began writing venomous articles about the British government that appeared in many German-American newspapers.

To stifle Lincoln's virulent propaganda, British officials demanded his extradition to face the criminal charge of forgery. After protracted negotiations, this was granted by the U.S. government. He was arrested on August 4, 1915, and sent to England. Once in England, Lincoln was tried in 1916 and convicted, then sent to prison for three years.

Released in 1919, Lincoln was deported to Hungary where Béla Kun was conducting a reign of terror. Lincoln left for Germany. There he announced that he was an ardent monarchist and he gave public speeches urging the restoration of the Kaiser. He even traveled to Amerongen where the Kaiser lived in exile and attempted to gain an audience with the deposed monarch but was rebuffed.

Going to Vienna and then Budapest, Lincoln attempted to interest Hungarian officials in a monarchist takeover of the country but he was rebuffed. He went to Italy where he joined the Black Shirts of Benito Mussolini. As an ardent fascist, Lincoln was reported to have been involved in the abduction of Geocomo Matteotti, the only important politician in Italy opposing Mussolini. On June 10, 1924, Matteotti was kidnapped by six men as he left his office in Rome. His remains were not found until two months later.

Many of those involved with this political assassination, which had been directly organized by Mussolini, as it was determined following World War II, fled the country at the time. One of these was Lincoln, who first went to Chile and then to China. He was found there in the mid-1920s as the political adviser to Wu Pei Fu, a warlord. He admitted to an American correspondent for the New York *World* that he had been a double spy in World War I, but that he had given up all those "ungodly pursuits," and had found peace in China as a Buddhist monk. He had finally found his true religion, Lincoln insisted.

In China, Lincoln was anything but pious. He actually served as an intelligence agent for the Chinese government in Peking and later in other parts of the country, working under the direction of Chiang Kai-shek's spymaster, Morris "Two-Gun" Cohen. By 1926, however, Lincoln had quit China and had moved on to Ceylon where he was known as Dr. Leo Tandler. At the time it was reported that he was spying for China or Japan or both. It was then that Lincoln learned that one of his sons had been convicted of murder in England and was about to be hanged.

Lincoln contacted British authorities and asked for permission to visit England in order to say goodbye to his son before he was executed. This was granted and Lincoln traveled to England via France where he either lost his money in a card game or was robbed. Destitute, he had to borrow more funds and by the time he got this money and returned to England, his son had been hanged. He returned to Europe, moving from one capital to another, buying arms for China as the representative of Chiang Kai-shek, negotiations for which he concluded in 1927.

Lincoln returned to China, taking up residence in the teeming city of Shanghai. He called himself Abbot Chao Kung, proclaiming himself to be a Buddhist preacher, leader, and healer. He established a large and opulent monastery and had three Buddhist monks attending him, along with six "Bhikshunis," or begging girls. The monastery was, in fact, an espionage headquarters that Lincoln operated for Japanese intelligence for the ubiquitous Colonel Kenji Doihara of the Special Service Organ. Lincoln's monks were agents, and his begging girls were street informers. Lincoln gathered much information for Japan during the years prior to the Japanese invasion of China and continued in that capacity until his death.

Even Lincoln's death was initially shrouded in mystery. Radio Tokyo sorrowfully announced on October 7, 1943, that the "revered Abbot Chao Kung" had died after an unsuccessful operation to save his life. He had been stricken by an unspecified illness, Tokyo declared. The "illness" was a Japanese dagger driven into Lincoln's back by one of Doihara's assassins, sent after the Japanese learned that Lincoln, his loyalties forever unpredictable, had concluded that Japan would lose the war and had gone back to Chiang Kai-shek as a spy for China.

[ALSO SEE: *Abwehr; Morris "Two-Gun" Cohen; Kenji Doihara; Walther Nicolai; SIS*]

LIPINSKI, WACLAW
Allied Spy in Poland ▪ (1897–1948)

A POLISH PATRIOT, LIPINSKI FOUGHT AGAINST THE Germans when they invaded his country in 1939. When Radio Warsaw was bombed into silence, Lipinski repaired it and kept it operating for the duration of the short war—twenty-seven days—so that it could keep broadcasting hourly bulletins and Chopin's *Polonaise Militaire*. After the Germans occupied Poland, he fled but returned in 1942 to work with the underground as a spy for the Allies. He arranged for arms and supplies to be parachuted to the Polish underground and kept London updated on sabotage operations conducted by the partisans.

Lipinski was captured and tortured by the Gestapo but would not reveal any information about the underground. He was later released and, in 1944, he advised Bor-Komorowski, the underground leader, against the abortive uprising. Radio Moscow had urged the underground to rise up and openly combat the Germans in Warsaw, promising that it would send several Russian divisions only a few miles distant to their aid.

"They are lying," Lipinski told Bor-Komorowski. "The Germans are too strong for us and the Russians know it. We will be slaughtered without their help. They know that, too. They won't come to our aid. They want the Germans to kill us off, so they won't have to deal with us after the war. They want us dead and Poland in their pocket." Despite Lipinski's accurate prediction, the underground rose and was crushed by German panzer divisions.

When the Russian divisions finally did sweep through Poland, they remained, refusing to leave until the country had been turned into a Communist fiefdom. Lipinski remained in Poland, working toward the ouster of the Communists and a return of Polish democracy. He openly defied the Communists until 1947 when he was arrested by KGB agents, charged with being a spy for the Allies. The Communists claimed that Lipinski had been regularly delivering secret information to the American and

British embassies in Warsaw. Six other anti-Communists were arrested with Lipinski and they quickly "confessed."

Not Lipinski. He was kept in an unheated cell inside Mokotow Prison for a year, refusing to admit that he worked for the Allies, insisting that he was a Polish patriot. When he was brought to trial in 1948, he stood defiantly in the dock as false charges were rattled off by the Moscow-directed prosecution.

As the trial dragged on, the Communists paraded one stooge after another to testify to the defendant's treason and espionage. On the last day of the trial, knowing what the outcome would be, Lipinski asked to see his grown son for the last time. This was granted, in fact, Lipinski and his son were chatting up to the moment the court reconvened. Lipinski stood up and stoically listened to his sentence: Death. He was executed a short time later.

[ALSO SEE: *Gestapo; KGB*]

LODY, KARL HANS
German Spy in England ▪ (1879–1914)

BORN AND RAISED IN BERLIN, LODY SERVED IN THE German navy until retiring with the rank of lieutenant. He moved to New York in 1900 and obtained a job with the Hamburg-America line. Lody's position was that of a guide to rich tourists taking around-the-world cruises. Given promotions, salary increases, bonuses, and handsome gratuities from tourists grateful for his attentiveness, Lody lived a comfortable life. All that changed in the summer of 1914.

Lody, knowing war could erupt any moment, suddenly left the tour and went to Berlin. He offered his services to the navy but he was found to be physically unfit for sea duty. Because he spoke fluent English, however, he was sent to Gustav Steinhauer of German naval intelligence. At that time, Steinhauer was facing disaster. British counterintelligence, MI5, headed by Vernon Kell, and Scotland Yard's Special Branch, headed by Basil Thomson, had only weeks earlier pinpointed the entire German spy network in England and had arrested all of Steinhauer's agents.

The German navy needed a spy in England immediately. Steinhauer needed to know the location of the British fleet and its number of warships. Once Lody had gotten this information, Steinhauer told him, he could depart for America and resume his career as a tourist guide, with no further obligation to Germany. Lody accepted the assignment. He was given a crash course in espionage and then traveled to Norway on a fake American passport bearing the name "Charles A. Inglis." As an native of America, a neutral country friendly to England, it was believed by Steinhauer

The hapless German spy Karl Lody when he was an officer in the German navy in the 1890s.

that Lody would go unquestioned as a visitor. From Norway, Lody traveled to Scotland, arriving in Edinburgh in early September 1914.

Scouting the Firth of Forth, Lody found the greater part of the British fleet at anchorage. He counted the ships, noted the types of warships and quickly sent a telegram to his contact, Adolph Burchard in Stockholm, Sweden.

Lody brought attention to himself simply because he had been poorly trained. He had no ciphers, codes, or secret inks. He had no sense of self-security and did not bother to check if anyone was ever following him. He blithely rented a room on the Scottish coast, hired a bicycle, and rode about the coastline, showing particular interest in the naval base at Rosyth. Though he pretended to be an American tourist, his behavior seemed odd. He appeared to be too interested in the British navy and all of his questions were centered about warships anchored nearby.

MI5 time had agents monitoring Lody's letters to Burchard and to a Karl I. Stammer in Berlin. Only one of them was permitted to go to its destination. Letters addressed to him from Germany were also confiscated before he received them. Not until September 7, 1914, did Lody realize that he was being tailed.

The experience sobered Lody. He left Scotland so quickly that his trackers lost all sight of him. A few weeks later he resurfaced in London. He was identified after appearing at a military installation, asking blunt questions about how army artillery had prepared against Zeppelin bombing attacks. Agents from Special Branch and MI5 dogged Lody's trail every minute thereafter. He returned to Scotland where he scouted more navy installations. Lody then traveled to Liverpool where he drew sketches of the defense works along the Mersey River. Then, he sailed for Dublin. He was arrested upon his arrival and taken back to London, where he was jailed in the Tower of London, the traditional prison for spies and traitors.

On October 30, less than two months after he had arrived in Edinburgh, Karl Hans Lody faced a military court martial. He received a death sentence.

On the night before he was to die, Lody wrote a letter to his family in Stuttgart, saying: "My watch is run down and I have to go through the dark valley, like many of my brave comrades in this dreadful war of nations. A hero's death in battles is certainly more beautiful, but this is not vouchsafed to me; I am to die here in the land of the enemy, alone and unknown.

Lody in 1914, after having been condemned as a spy; he was shot to death in the Tower of London only a few days after this photograph was taken.

The consciousness that I am dying in the service of my country makes death easy for me to bear. I have had just judges. They have condemned me for conspiring to betray their plans. I am to be shot tomorrow, here in the Tower. Goodbye."

On the morning of November 6, 1915, Lody was taken to the moat of the Tower. He was calm and courageous to the end. Before the blindfold was placed over his eyes, Lody said to Provost Marshal, Lord Athlumney: "I don't suppose you would care to shake hands with a spy?"

"No, I don't think so," replied Lord Athlumney. "But I shall be proud to shake hands with a very brave man."

Seconds later, Lody was dead. Robert Baden-Powell, who had been a British agent a generation earlier when espionage was a much less sordid occupation, later reported that "in the Lower House of Commons they spoke of him [Lody] as a patriot who had died on the battlefield for his country." As the war progressed, the world of espionage was dominated by agents who did not possess the noble virtues of Karl Lody. They were, for the most part, desperate creatures for whom patriotism was nothing more than a naive impulse.

[ALSO SEE: *Robert Baden-Powell; Vernon Kell; MI5; Basil Thomson*]

LONDON CONTROLLING SECTION
British Disinformation Center in World War II ▪ (1941–1945)

CONSISTING OF A SMALL BUT EFFECTIVE WORKFORCE, London Controlling Section, LCS, was headed by Colonel John Bevan, and it worked in cooperation with MI5, MI6, SOE, and, to a lesser extent with Allied intelligence organizations such as OSS. Its job was to spread disinformation, to hoodwink the Germans into believing armies, planes, tanks, paratroopers existed where none did.

LCS spread disinformation on the Allied landings in Sicily and Italy in 1943 so that German intelligence was gulled into believing the invading forces would arrive where they did not. It was also very effective in planting false information that there would be an Allied invasion of the Balkans so that many German divisions were diverted to that region and could not participate in repulsing the Allied invasion of Normandy in 1944.

LONETREE, CLAYTON J.
American Spy for Soviets ▪ (1962–)

A WINNEBAGO INDIAN FROM ST. PAUL, MINNESOTA, Clayton J. Lonetree has the dubious distinction of being the first U.S. marine ever convicted of espionage. He was at the core of what was termed the "sex for secrets" scandal that rocked the U.S. Marine Corps in January 1987.

At age eighteen, Lonetree enlisted in the Marine Corps and proved to be a model enlisted man. He later went into training at the Corps' elite Security Guard Battalion School, graduating in September 1984. This is one of the most rigorous and demanding schools in the U.S. military and less than fifty percent of those entering graduate. The school provides intensive training in anti-terrorist tactics, espionage, and counterespionage.

Guards such as Lonetree—who was assigned to the U.S. Embassy in Moscow and later to the U.S. Embassy in Vienna—have access to highly sensitive material and have the keys to safes where such material is kept. Lonetree was assigned to the U.S. Embassy in Moscow in 1985. He served there for seventeen months before he was restationed to the U.S. Embassy in Vienna, rising to the rank of sergeant.

On December 14, 1986, a nervous Lonetree went to CIA officials in Vienna and told them that he had turned over classified information to a KGB agent that he knew only as "Uncle Sasha," a man introduced to him by his Russian girlfriend, Violetta. Lonetree was immediately arrested and put through intense interrogation by the U.S. Naval Investigative Service (NIS). Spying for the KGB apparently began for Lonetree after he met a sexy Russian woman named Violetta at the annual Marine ball held in the residence of the U.S. Ambassador in Moscow in November 1985.

NIS investigators swarmed over the case, more than 100 of them, in a global search for spies within the Marine guards at all U.S. embassies. Arrested in the nine-month NIS investigation (which would cost more than $100 million), was Corporal Arnold Bracy, an enlisted man, who signed a confession in which he stated that he acted as "lookout" at the Moscow Embassy while Lonetree served as a guide to KGB agents touring the embassy building so they could plant bugs in various rooms, and that the floor plans of the embassy's most sensitive areas were provided to the Soviet agents.

Bracy later claimed that he was coerced into signing the confession, which he was not permitted to read, and that immediately after doing so, a jubilant NIS agent jumped to his feet and shouted "We've caught another spy!" All charges were later dropped against Bracy who left the service. Lonetree, however, altered his statements to say that he had given Sasha low-level classified documents from the Vienna Embassy, never anything from the Moscow Embassy and that he never accompanied any KGB agents into any U.S. Embassy.

As the scandal spread, NIS was accused of blowing the incident out of proportion, that it had been gripped by "spy mania." Moreover, Marine Lieutenant-Colonel Michael Powell, who had served as Bracy's lawyer, insisted that it would have been impossible for any Marine Guard to escort KGB agents through U.S. embassies without being detected by other guards on duty or the tightly-controlled security alarms electronically reporting such intrusions.

In the end, Lonetree was convicted of turning over secrets to the Soviets and was given a 30-year prison sentence in November 1987. For cooperating with investigators, Lonetree's sentence was reduced to twenty-five years in May 1988. He served ten years as a model prisoner and was released in early 1996.

LONSDALE, GORDON ARNOLD (KONON TROFIMOVICH MOLODY)
Soviet Spymaster in England ▪ (1922–1970)

BORN IN RUSSIA, LONSDALE WAS SENT TO LIVE WITH an aunt in California at age seven in 1929. He lived there for nine years, learning English so well that he spoke the tongue like a native. He returned to Russia in 1938 and immediately joined the Communist youth movement. After fighting in

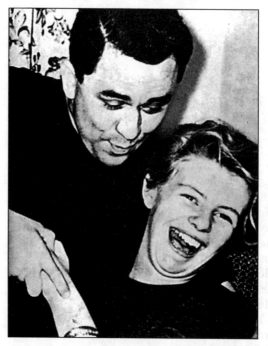

Lonsdale as a London playboy, shown with one of his many girlfriends.

Top, right, a flashlight found in Lonsdale's apartment, one in which he kept rolls of film containing secret documents instead of batteries.

Bottom, right, a circular lighter found in Lonsdale's apartment; when the wooden base and cover were removed, a code pad was found inside.

Below, the powerful radio transmitter used by the Krogers to send Lonsdale's secrets to Moscow.

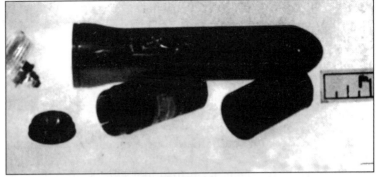

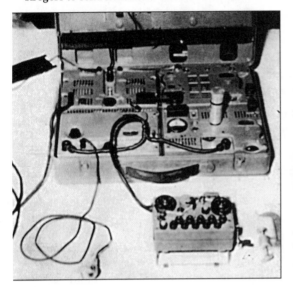

The Soviet spymaster known in England as Gordon Lonsdale; he ran a KGB network that successfully stole British Admiralty secrets in the late 1950s.

World War II, Lonsdale was accepted by the KGB and was trained as a spy, and then sent to Canada in 1954 with a fake passport and the alias of Gordon Lonsdale. A year later he arrived in London in the guise of a successful Canadian businessman.

Lonsdale opened up substantial bank accounts and rented a luxury apartment in Regent's Park. He made friends easily and talked of opening up an importing firm to distribute amusement games in Europe. He was regularly seen at London's best nightclubs with an attractive woman on his arm.

All of this was, of course, a front. Lonsdale was in England with a specific mission to accomplish for the KGB, to learn all he could about Britain's underwater detection devices. His contact was Harry Houghton, a one-time chief petty officer in the navy whose girl friend, Ethel Gee, worked at the Admiralty Underwater Weapons Establishment in Portland. Gee stole naval secrets, gave them to her alcoholic boyfriend Houghton who turned them over to Lonsdale.

In 1961, the agents pounced on the trio, arresting Lonsdale, Houghton, and Gee outside the Old Vic theater. The British agents confiscated a shopping bag Houghton and Gee had handed over to Lonsdale. It contained undeveloped photographs of 212 pages from *Particulars of War Vessels*, a classified British

navy document, drawings for some of the navy's latest ships, and fifty-eight pages of Admiralty fleet orders.

Peter and Helen Kroger were also arrested and all five were placed on trial, convicted, and sent to prison. Lonsdale received a 25-year prison term.

The spymaster served less than four years in prison, released in 1964 when he was exchanged for Greville Wynne, an Englishman accused of spying in Russia in the Penkovsky Affair. Hailed as a hero upon his return to Moscow, Lonsdale received two medals, the Red Star and the Red Banner. He then wrote his memoirs, with the help of British defector Kim Philby, publishing this fanciful tale under the title *Spy*, a specious, lying document that was made into a specious, lying film by the Soviets. In October 1970, Gordon Lonsdale collapsed in a small garden behind his Moscow apartment, dying of a heart attack as he was assiduously picking mushrooms.

[ALSO SEE: *Harry Houghton; KGB; Peter and Helen Kroger; MI5; Special Branch*]

LOTZ, WOLFGANG
Israeli Spy in Egypt ▪ (1921–1993)

THE SON OF A GERMAN THEATRICAL DIRECTOR, LOTZ was born in Mannheim, Germany. His actress mother, however, was Jewish and she fled Germany before World War II, taking her son to Palestine. He spoke perfect German and fluent English, which made him important as an interrogator of German POWs for the British Army during World War II. Following the war, Lotz joined Haganah, the Israeli underground, and when Israel attained its independence, he joined the regular army.

Lotz was soon part of the Israeli intelligence service who put his fluent German to good use. He was sent to Egypt where he posed as a former member of Rommel's Africa Corps. After ingratiating himself to other German refugees in Egypt, Lotz began to meet important Egyptian government officials. From them he learned much about Eygpt's military forces, as well as the German scientists who were working to build up the country's armaments, particularly Egypt's use of rockets.

Using a small radio transmitter hidden in his bathroom scale, Lotz sent coded messages to Israeli intelligence for almost five years. But Egyptian direction-finding vans eventually pinpointed his radio transmissions and he was arrested and tried. The Egyptians were unsure of Lotz' true background, believing him to be a rogue German working for Israel. Instead of being executed, Lotz was sent to prison for life in 1965. He was released three years

later, exchanged for 500 Egyptian officers who had been captured in the "Six-Day War" of 1967.

Upon his release, Lotz went to Tel-Aviv with his German-born wife. He wrote a book entitled *Champagne Spy*, which saw moderate success. The spy's fortunes declined rapidly after the death of his wife, Waltraud. He was interviewed while living in Munich in 1978, complaining that he was living in near poverty, with only the small $200-a-month pension paid to him by the Mossad.

[ALSO SEE: *Mossad*]

LOUVOIS, MARQUIS DE (FRANCOIS LE TELLIER)
French Minister of War & Spymaster ▪ (1641–1691)

AN ARISTOCRAT, LOUVOIS'S FATHER HAD BEEN Minister of War under French kings Louis XIII and Louis XIV. He worked with his father until replacing him as Minister of War in 1666. Louvois introduced many reforms into the French military, including regulation uniforms, the bayonet, and a promotion system based on merit. Moreover, he established a widespread, effective spy network throughout Europe.

Louvois hired thousands of spies to feed him any kind of information they thought useful. Invariably these spies worked in and about the royal households of many countries as maids, riding masters, music teachers, anyone who might learn throne-room gossip. Louvois also developed an intricate internal spy system in which informers inside the Army guaged the loyalty of troops and their commanders.

The spymaster spent many hours analyzing his myriad reports with a cadre of espionage specialists. The results allowed Louis XIV to conduct warfare better than enemy nations and was the source of France's political and military strength for several decades.

LUCIETO, CHARLES
French Spy in World War I ▪ (1879– ?)

ON APRIL 22, 1915, DURING THE PROLONGED AND bloody battle of Ypres in Belgium, the Germans unleashed a new and terrible weapon on the Western Front. They brought large cannisters to the front-line trenches and, waiting for a wind blowing toward the enemy lines, opened these containers to allow poison chlorine gas to sweep forward. The result was devastating. Thousands of Allied troops were killed, blinded, or permanently disabled. The German success, however, was short-lived. When they attempted to release the poison gas again, the unpredictable Flanders wind shifted, sending the lethal gas back upon their own troops.

The Germans stopped the use of poison gas until they could find a way to safely use it on the enemy without causing risk to their own forces. French intelligence knew it would be only a matter of time before the Germans perfected their terrible weapon at the massive Krupp war plants in Essen. To learn as much as possible about the poison gas experiments at Krupp, the French dispatched their best agent, Charles Lucieto.

Lucieto spoke perfect German and easily passed himself off as a German salesman. He took a hotel room in Essen. He soon learned that guards working at the Krupp plant in Essen drank mostly in one bar and he became a regular patron at the place. One elderly security guard he befriended began to talk freely about the experiments Krupp was conducting with poison gas. The guard informed Lucieto that German engineers had constructed special artillery shells containing poison gas. Large field pieces could fire these shells from a great distance and, upon exploding, the shells would automatically release the poison gas.

The result of Lucieto's espionage coup was that the Allies quickly supplied their troops with gas masks and were themselves busy making artillery gas shells. From that point onward the Germans, realizing that gas masks rendered their new weapon ineffective and that the Allies would retaliate with poison gas if such weapons were used, gave limited use to poison gas.

LYALIN, OLEG ADOLFOVICH
Soviet Spy in England ▪ (1937–)

A HIGH-LIVING, WOMANIZING KGB OFFICER, LYALIN defected in London to MI5 in the early 70s, on the provision that he would be granted asylum, along with a statuesque blonde secretary, Irina Teplyakova. Lyalin was an officer in the KGB's Department Five, which was responsible for sabotage.

Lyalin blithely informed MI5 that he had been sent to England, attached to the Soviet trade mission at Highgate, with specific instructions to destroy the super radar station at Fylingdales on the Yorkshire moors that was operated under British and NATO direction and had cost £45 million to establish. The Soviet defector also began to identify scores of KGB Department Five operatives in the West.

Moscow denied everything but the Lyalin defection and subsequent revelations that Moscow was preparing to go on a war footing by destroying key Western defense systems such as the radar complex at Fylingdales caused party leader Leonid Brezhnev and KGB chief Yuri Andropov to panic. They immediately called back to Moscow all of their Department Five agents such as Valeri Kostikov who hastily left Mexico City. Other Soviet agents departed Athens, Bonn, Paris.

Lyalin had not operated alone. He identified all of those in his sabotage ring, including two Cypriot tailors and a Malaysian named Siroj Abdoolcader. All were arrested. Following their confessions, they were convicted and sent to prison. In retaliation for the British ouster of an unprecedented number of their diplomats, the Soviets expelled eighteen British officials and diplomats from Moscow. But it was only window-dressing. The KGB had suffered a major setback from which they would not recover for some years. Lyalin and his sultry secretary went into hiding, fearfully waiting for SMERSH agents to track them down.

[ALSO SEE: *Yuri Andropov; KGB; MI5; SMERSH*]

A tape recorder, transmitter, code sheets, hollowed-out flashlight batteries, and hollow pencil containing film were only a few of the items turned over by Soviet spy Oleg Lyalin when he defected to the West.

MACDONNELL, ALASTAIR RUADH
Scottish Spy for England ▪
(1724?–1761)

T HE SON OF THE MOST POWERFUL CLAN LEADER IN
Scotland, Macdonnell supported the claim of
Prince Charles Edward Stuart (known as
"Bonnie Prince Charlie," or the "Young Pretender")
on the British throne. Those who endorsed Stuart also
supported the restoration of the Catholic religion in
England. They were known as Jacobites.

In 1750, the prince secretly visited London in disguise where he met with a group of conspirators led
by Lord Elibank, a Scottish clan leader. The plotters
planned to lead a group of 400 Scottish highlanders
and French officers in a surprise attack on the palace
and kidnap King George II on November 10, 1752.
After George was in custody, the clans would rise and
join with troops from Sweden under the command of
Marshall Keith, a Jacobite leader.

One postponement after another took place until
one of the plotters, Dr. Archibald Cameron was captured. He was tried and convicted of treason, then
hanged, although little or no evidence of his direct
involvement in the plot could be obtained. Other clan
leaders were arrested and jailed. It was then learned
that Alastair Macdonnell, the son of the clan leader,
had betrayed the plot. He had been serving as a spy to
Henry Pelham, British secretary of state, collecting
considerable sums for naming the plotters.

Macdonnell remained on Pelham's payroll until
1760. By that time, Bonnie Prince Charlie had given
up all hope of ever reclaiming the throne of England
and accepted his permanent exile.

MACKENZIE, EDWARD MONTAGUE COMPTON
British Spy in Greece in World War I ▪
(1883–1972)

T HE DISTINGUISHED NOVELIST AND CRITIC COMPTON
Mackenzie was, like Somerset Maugham,
Graham Greene, and Ian Fleming, a spy for his
government. During World War I, Mackenzie served
as the British Marine officer in charge of military
intelligence in the eastern Mediterranean. A love of
adventure led Mackenzie to cement a strong friendship with Mansfield Cumming, head of England's
secret service, the SIS.

Mackenzie served briefly as a spy in Athens in
1916 and later wrote of those experiences in his book,
Greek Memories, published in 1932. The book caused
an uproar in the British intelligence community, particularly among ranking members of MI5 and with its
then chief, Vernon Kell. The author was charged with
publicizing secret information he had learned while
"in the service of the government," and violating the
Official Secrets Act, specifically, revealing the identities
of those with whom he had worked sixteen years earlier.

Mackenzie's lawyers pointed out that the trial was
a farce in that most of the agents the author had mentioned, such as Captain Christmas, had been dead for
a decade. Defense lawyers also pointed out that one of
those mentioned by Mackenzie, Sir C. E. Heathcote-
Smith, had himself compromised his own position
with SIS in that he had included the same information Mackenzie had related in his *Who's Who* entry.

The entire trial was a farce but to save the face of
the blustering intelligence leaders, Mackenzie was
persuaded to plead guilty and pay a minimal fine of
£100 and £100 in costs. He did, but never forgave
those who had embarrassed him in the trumped-up
trial. *Greek Memories* was withdrawn from publication but Mackenzie had his revenge by writing and
publishing a savage satire, *Water on the Brain*, in
which he profiled British intelligence chiefs as petty
and paranoid, ridiculing their penchant at playing
at security to advance their self-important image as
keepers of the flame.

[ALSO SEE: *Mansfield Cumming; Ian Fleming; Vernon
Kell; Somerset Maugham; SIS*]

MACLEAN, DONALD DUART
British Spy for Soviets ▪ (1913–1983)

DONALD MACLEAN, LIKE HIS FELLOW CONSPIRATORS, Guy Burgess, Kim Philby, and Anthony Blunt, was a dilettante, a homosexual, a dabbler in the fine arts, and a dedicated Soviet spy for most of his adult life. Born in London, Maclean was raised as the pampered son of a Scottish politician, Sir Donald Maclean, a distinguished member of Parliament.

The political epidemic of the day was communism, espoused by many radical teachers, including some at Gresham's, Maclean's school. Maclean came to believe early on that the Russian Revolution was a noble adventure and that resulting communism in Russia would some day spread throughout the world to save humanity from oppressive capitalism. Moreover, it was at Gresham's that Maclean developed sexual liaisons with other boys. Following his graduation from Gresham's, Maclean went on to Cambridge where he immediately fell in with Guy Burgess, Kim Philby, and Anthony Blunt.

Through Blunt, Burgess, and Philby, Maclean was introduced to a Soviet spymaster in England who had recruited the others as KGB spies. Maclean, too, became a willing spy, telling his caseworker that he really wanted to go to the Soviet Union and work there. He was persuaded to stay in England, to graduate from Cambridge, and to take a place in the Foreign Office where he could obtain secrets that would help the Soviets.

Upon his graduation in 1934, Maclean did exactly that, easily obtaining a position at the Foreign Office on the strength of his father's reputation, albeit the elder Maclean had died two years earlier. He worked his way up the ladder and soon held important positions at the Foreign Office which allowed him to feed secret information to his Soviet spymaster in London. Although a practicing homosexual (more so, it seemed, when he was drunk), Maclean was attracted to Melinda Marling, the "liberated" daughter of an American oil executive. The couple married in 1940 in Paris and barely escaped capture by invading Germans. Maclean continued to work in London at the Foreign Office until 1944, reporting every secret he learned to his Soviet bosses. He was then appointed first secretary to the British Embassy in Washington.

Serving on the Combined Policy Committee, which supervised all plans for the development of atomic energy and the atomic bomb being developed in New Mexico, Maclean was in an excellent position to obtain and deliver these secrets to the Soviets. He also used a diplomatic pass to the Atomic Energy Commission to obtain further secrets. His spying for the Russians continued after World War II was over. Twice each week, Maclean would bundle up the

British diplomat and Soviet agent Donald MacLean, shown as a resident of Moscow after his defection.

many documents he had stolen and take them by train to New York where he delivered them to the Soviet consulate.

By 1948, however, Maclean's constant haunting of the Atomic Energy Commission offices came to the attention of the CIA, which had his pass cancelled. Then Maclean was suspected of being a Soviet agent through CIA monitoring of the traffic sent to Moscow from the Soviet consulate in New York. A cipher clerk made an error and transmitted Maclean's information in a simple code usually reserved for lower-grade traffic.

James Angleton, the CIA's counterintelligence chief, analyzed these intercepted transmissions and concluded that Maclean was a Soviet agent. He informed MI5 in England but the British were reluctant to accept Angleton's conclusions. In September 1949, Maurice Oldfield, who later became chief of SIS, casually told Kim Philby that there was probably a Soviet agent in the British Embassy in Washington. Philby warned the Soviets who ordered Maclean to stay where he was and to continue to supply them with secrets.

Maclean, aware that he was suspected, began to drink heavily. Maclean was ordered home in 1951. He was pronounced fit and, incredibly, was assigned to head the American desk at the Foreign Office.

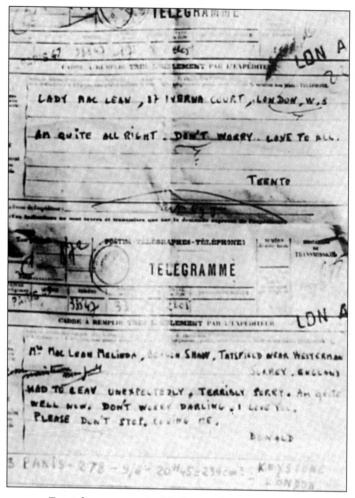

Two telegrams sent by Maclean to his mother and wife after his hasty defection to Russia.

By then the CIA had definitely pinpointed Maclean as a Soviet agent and, apparently applied considerable pressure on MI5.

On May 25, 1951, the very day MI5 was scheduled to confront Maclean, the suspect, along with Burgess, drove to Southampton and scrambled up the gangplank of the S.S. *Falaise*, the channel ferryboat heading for St. Malo. Maclean and Burgess arrived in France, then fled to Russia, proclaiming themselves defectors.

Maclean was honored by the Soviets who made him a colonel in the KGB where he instructed future spies in the ways of espionage. He was given a handsome salary, a luxury apartment (by Moscow standards), and a dacha outside of the city where he spent much time gardening when not drinking. His wife Melinda finally joined him in Moscow but she became romantically involved with Kim Philby, who had also defected, and then left for America.

On March 6, 1983, Donald Maclean died of a heart attack in his Moscow apartment. He was sixty-nine and utterly alone. He had stated to some friends a short time earlier that he had become completely disillusioned with communism and longed to see the English countryside once again. Following his death,

Maclean was cremated and his ashes were later returned to England where they were buried.

[ALSO SEE: *James Angleton; Anthony Blunt; Guy Burgess; MI5; Maurice Oldfield; Kim Philby; SIS*]

MAC NALLY, LEONARD
Irish Spy for England ▪ (1754–1820)

IN 1754, THE IRISH PLANNED A REBELLION TO FREE Ireland from England. British spymasters, however, planted spies among the Irish revolutionaries, one of these being Leonard MacNally. Dublin-born, MacNally was the son of a merchant who had gotten a law degree. He willingly went into the pay of the British, joining the United Irishmen led by Wolfe Tone.

As a ranking member of the organization, MacNally was able to inform the Anglo-Irish administration in Dublin of every step the Irish society took toward revolution. When the Irish did rise in 1798, the British, much to the credibility of MacNally's information, were able to crush the rebellion quickly. Those Irish rebels arrested were, ironically, represented with great zeal by MacNally. Because of this, the great Irish leader Robert Emmett confided in MacNally, telling him that the best time for Ireland to strike for its freedom was when England was at war with a foreign power. In 1803, Britain went to war with Napoleon Bonaparte. Thus occupied, Emmett concluded that England would be too weak to fight on two fronts. He led a rising that year but it failed and Emmett went into hiding.

Emmett hid in the home of Sarah Curran, his fiancee, and the daughter of MacNally's law partner. Curran told MacNally that her betrothed was hiding in her home, and, after visiting with the Irish rebel, MacNally went to the British and gave him away. Arrested and imprisoned, Emmett and his followers still had no idea that MacNally was a traitor and informer. MacNally actually defended Emmett against a charge of treason and lost the case. Robert Emmett went to the gallows. MacNally retired to write plays, thought of by the Irish as a patriot until the day he died. Long after, the truth of MacNally's real role as a British spy was revealed.

MAENNEL, GUNTHER
German Spy for U.S. ▪ (1931–)

MAENNEL WAS A MEMBER OF EAST GERMAN intelligence who was turned by a member of the Gehlen organization in 1959. Captain Maennel thereafter supplied West Germany and the CIA with important information on Soviet espionage. He brought with him an impressive array of secret information on Soviet intelligence.

Maennel immediately identified a number of treasonable West German officers who worked at NATO but who served as Soviet spies. He also said that there was a double agent working for the Soviets in the heart of the Gehlen organization in its Pullach headquarters. This agent was later identified as Heinz Felfe who headed counterintelligence for West Germany. Felfe was arrested.

Further, Maennel identified a spy network in England led by Armin Grosz and Eric Hills that had worked with Gordon Lonsdale and the Krogers. This ring was smashed by MI5. Maennel then repaid the CIA (which had paid him an estimated $50,000 for his services and a $20,000 bonus when he defected) by pinpointing an American officer, Captain Joseph Kauffmann of the U.S. Air Force, as a Soviet agent. Kauffmann had served in West Germany and had sold the East Germans key information on Allied radar installations, as well as U-2 spy plane operations once he was restationed in Greenland. Kauffmann was arrested and sent to prison for twenty years.

[ALSO SEE: CIA; *Reinhard Gehlen; Peter and Helen Kroger; Gordon Lonsdale*]

MALINOVSKY, ROMAN
Russian Revolutionary and Police Spy ▪ (1878–1918)

LIKE YEVNO AZEV, ROMAN MALINOVSKY SERVED TWO masters, the revolutionaries of Russia and their arch foe, the Okhrana, the Imperial secret police. He was a double spy and a police *agent provocateur* but he was less spectacular than the amazing Azev. What is astounding about Malinovsky is that the supreme Russian revolutionary leader Lenin, even after he learned that Malinovsky had been a police spy, refused to publicly disown him.

Born in Poland in 1878 of peasant working stock, Manlinovsky moved to St. Petersburg as a young man. There he worked as a metal turner. Stocky, ruddy-faced, and always animated, Malinovsky easily won friends and he was soon involved in the trade unions.

At the same time, Malinovsky craved the finer things of life and he took to stealing. He was caught breaking and entering and was sent to prison in 1899.

Released in 1902, Malinovsky returned to trade union activities. He had plenty of money, however, since by then he had volunteered his services to the Okhrana and had become a police spy. His assignment was to report on all revolutionary activities and treasonable actions by his fellow trade unionists. By 1907, he had become the Secretary of the Metal Workers Union in St. Petersburg. He proved himself to be an excitable, impassioned worker and orator who could whip a crowd into a frenzy.

Moving to Moscow, Malinovsky worked directly with Police Chief Beletsky, and he named his own price for information on the Social Democratic Party, which was then a coalition of the Menshevik and Bolshevik factions. Malinovsky centered his activities with the Mensheviks and reported all their doings to the police.

The workers who followed Malinovsky adored him, called him "the great Roman," and they talked of him as one of the future leaders of Russia. Lenin instantly took a deep liking to Malinovsky. Here was a peasant worker who sprang from the very soil of Russia. Malinovsky's oratory was aflame with aggressive action, simplistic and inspiring. Lenin persuaded Malinovsky to change sides, quitting the Mensheviks for the Bolsheviks and urged him to run for election to the Duma. Malinovsky agreed, vowing eternal loyalty to Lenin.

Malinovsky had a serious problem, however, in running for the office of deputy. No one could seek election who had a criminal record. Malinovsky had been convicted of rape and three burglaries. After consulting with Chief of Police Beletsky, Malinovsky's record was expunged. Beletsky ordered Malinovsky to not only run as a Bolshevik but to do his utmost in taking over the leadership of that party in the Duma. He succeeded in doing just that, of course with the help of the Okhrana, which arrested Malinovsky's rival candidates.

Once elected, Malinovsky became the Okhrana's highest paid spy, receiving 500 rubles a month. At the first session of the Duma, Lenin chose Malinovsky to read the Bolshevik Party's program. This document, written by Lenin and other top party leaders, was first sent by Malinovsky to his Okhrana bosses who suggested a few changes, which Malinovsky made without objection from Lenin.

As leader of the Bolsheviks in the Duma, Malinovsky made speeches and proposed legislation that was always edited by his secret police bosses, restructured and softened, sometimes conciliatory to the oppressive Czarist regime it claimed to so violently oppose. This raised suspicions among certain revolutionaries, including an editor of *Pravda* who hinted that Malinovsky was a tool of the government, perhaps the police. The editor, Chernomasov, stated that revolutionary leaders Jacob Sverdlov (who would later personally supervise the mass execution of the czar and his family in 1918), Josef Stalin, and others had been arrested and sent to Siberia just after having contact with Malinovsky. (Indeed, Malinovsky had informed on Stalin, Sverdlov, and the others.)

Malinovsky's response was a raging denial in which he accused *Pravda* of libel. He filed suit and won. The publication was ordered to pay Malinovsky a fine and that fine was collected by the very police who secretly employed Malinovsky. Moreover, Malinovsky learned that Chernomasov was also a police spy out to enhance his own financial position with the Okhrana by becoming Malinovsky's replacement. Malinovsky insisted that the Okhrana get rid of Chernomasov. The editor was forced to resign.

Meanwhile, Malinovsky's Okhrana salary grew larger. He was also given an almost unlimited expense account. When he made donations to the Bolsheviks, he was allowed to deduct the contributions as expenses. He even loaned money to Lenin, it was claimed, money supplied by the revolutionary's most ardent foe, the Okhrana.

The seeds of suspicion had nevertheless been sown that the earthy peasant Malinovsky was in the hire of the police. Lenin refused to accept such talk, labeling it vicious rumor. To quell party fears, however, Lenin set up a special investigative committee to look into the matter. It cleared Malinovsky with all involvement with the police. The report was given to Malinovsky by Lenin himself who continued to trust the spy with all party secrets and told him that he trusted him implicitly. Malinovsky promptly sent the report of his own exoneration to the police, demanding another raise.

Though Lenin continued to support Malinovsky, he was undoubtedly too cunning a man to truly believe that his protégé was innocent of the mounting charges. The evidence seemed apparent that Malinovsky had engineered the arrests of Stalin and Sverdlov but he himself had been so thoroughly compromised by his own liaison with Malinovsky that he could do little else than whitewash the peasant worker he had so publicly embraced.

But the secret police concluded that its top spy was siding with the enemy, that he was truly a revolutionary who, in the end, would throw in his lot with Lenin. It was decided to end his services. The Okhrana gave him a huge final payment of 6,000 rubles and suggested that he leave the country for his own well-being.

On May 8, 1914, Malinovsky handed his resignation to the Chairman of the Duma and fled the country, going to Galicia. Lenin was in shock, writing to a friend: "Do you know what M-sky has gone and done? We are going out of our minds with this idiocy."

During World War I, Malinovsky was imprisoned by the Germans but Lenin remained in touch with his protégé. Following the war and the Russian Revolution, Malinovsky remained abroad, spending his Okhrana money but he suddenly and inexplicably returned to Russia in 1918, even though he knew that the Bolsheviks had obtained all the Okhrana files that proved him to be a long-standing police *agent provocateur.*

Upon his arrival in Russia, Malinovsky was arrested and charged with treason. He undoubtedly counted on Lenin's aid, believing that his old political sponsor would come to his rescue as he had so protectively in the past, despite his admission that he had, indeed, been a police spy. Lenin did not appear in court. Malinovsky was condemned and, a short time later, was shot to death by a firing squad.

[ALSO SEE: *Yevno Azev; Okhrana; S.V. Zubatov*]

MALRAUX, ANDRE
French Spymaster ▪ (1901–1976)

THE FRENCH WRITER, PHILOSOPHER, AND POLITICIAN served as a spymaster in World War II. Malraux joined the French underground, using the cover name of "Colonel Berger." He directed a large spy network in southern France that was headquartered in Périgord. Malraux planned all espionage and sabotage in the area and proved to be so effective that his *nom de guerre* was placed on the Gestapo's wanted list.

Malraux remained at large for three years. He was captured in 1944 but managed to escape and later participated in the Allied drive to free Paris and then France. Following the war, Malraux became Minister of Information. A loyal supporter of Charles de Gaulle, Malraux saw service with de Gaulle throughout the general's political career, retiring when de Gaulle did in 1969.

MAN WHO NEVER WAS, THE
British Intelligence Ruse in World War II ▪ (1943)

FOLLOWING THE SUCCESSFUL ALLIED INVASION OF North Africa, American and British leaders conferred to plan their next invasion, which would either be in Greece or in southern Italy. Prime Minister Winston Churchill favored Italy, calling it "the soft underbelly of the Axis," and convinced President Roosevelt that the next strike would be in that theater. This presented a grave problem for Allied intelligence, which realized that the Abwehr knew Italy would most probably be the next Allied target. How then to dissuade the Germans from that conviction?

British intelligence slowly developed a plan, wryly dubbed Operation Mincemeat. British naval intelli-

The fake identity card planted on the body of "Major William Martin," a corpse that posthumously fooled the Abwehr in a brilliant British intelligence operation.

gence officer, Lieutenant Commander Ewen Montagu conceived of the idea of using the body of a British officer to convince the Germans that the next Allied thrust would be in Greece. To that end, Montagu met with England's preeminent pathologist, Sir Bernard Spilsbury. Montagu described his plan to Spilsbury, saying that he wanted to have a body found, which appeared to have recently been in an aircrash at sea. That body would be set adrift close to the coast of Spain where Montagu hoped it would be found. Spilsbury provided the proper condition that just such a corpse should have.

Next Montagu searched for the right body, finding the fresh corpse of a 38-year-old man who had died of pneumonia and had liquid in its lungs, a condition which could easily be attributed to a body floating in water as a result of an aircrash at sea. Spilsbury examined the corpse and told Montagu: "You have nothing to fear from a Spanish *post-mortem*; to detect that this young man had not died after an aircraft had been lost at sea would need a pathologist of my experience—and there aren't any in Spain."

Montagu obtained permission to use the body from the relatives of the deceased, then gave it a new identity. The dead man was renamed Major William Martin of the Royal Marines, attached to the staff of Louis Mountbatten, Commander-in-Chief of Combined Operations in the Mediterranean theater. Papers, which would identify him as an expert on certain types of landing craft, were planted in a watertight briefcase that would be chained to his wrist. He also carried a top-secret coded letter from General Archibald Nye to General Harold Alexander in which Nye stated that the Allies hoped to convince the Germans that they would attack Sicily, instead of

their true military objective, Greece. Of course, just the reverse was true.

Martin was also given a personal identity. He would carry letters from his father, from his bank manager, and two love letters from his girlfriend "Pam." He even carried a photo of the girl, along with a receipt for a diamond ring and the stubs of two recent London theater tickets. Thus prepared and preserved, the body was placed aboard the British submarine *Seraph*, which sailed from Holy Loch in northwest Scotland on April 19, 1943.

On the night of April 30, the *Seraph* surfaced just long enough to put "Major Martin" overboard, a short distance from the beaches of Huelva, Spain. British intelligence knew that an Abwehr spy operated in that area with the full cooperation of Spanish authorities, who were, like himself, dedicated fascists. The body, floating with the help of an inflated Mae West, drifted onto the beach, and was found by a Spanish fisherman.

On May 3, 1943, the British Embassy in Madrid notified London that Martin's body had been found at sea and had been given a military funeral. No mention was made of the black briefcase that had been attached to the dead man's body or the secret papers it contained. Montagu then asked a British attaché at the Madrid Embassy (who had not been informed of the ruse) to contact Spanish authorities to see if the briefcase and other papers had been found with the body. This was done and ten days later Spanish officials turned over the briefcase and the papers.

Had the Germans accepted the disinformation carried by Martin? Montagu and other naval intelligence officials did not know for some time. Intercepted messages to the Abwehr, however, confirmed that the

Spanish had turned over the documents to the Germans who had copied them before they were returned to the British. Operation Mincemeat was a resounding success, as proved by Hitler's strengthening of German garrisons in Greece where the next invasion was expected by the Nazis. (Asbolute proof that Operation Mincemeat wholly deceived the Germans was found in captured Abwehr files after World War II.)

Sicily was ignored by the Germans. A short time later American and British troops under Generals Patton and Montgomery invaded and conquered the island, leading to the invasion of mainland Italy at Salerno. Montagu's plan was one of the masterpieces of intelligence in World War II, an espionage *coup de main* that undoubtedly saved thousands of Allied lives and hastened the end of the war.

MANN, HORACE
British Spymaster in Italy ▪ (1701–1786)

MANN'S APPOINTMENT TO A DIPLOMATIC POST IN Florence, Italy, in 1737 had but one purpose, to establish contact with Cardinal Alessandro Albani who was spying on the exiled Jacobites planning to ursurp the British throne. Mann met and corresponded with Albani who related all of the conspiracies at the Court of James Stuart, or James III, called the "Old Pretender," and his son, Charles, called the "Young Pretender," and "Bonnie Prince Charlie." It was a secret message from Albani to Mann that warned the British of the clan uprising of 1745, led by Charles, and allowed them to prepare an army to crush this rebellion. With the collapse of the Jacobite movement to restore the Stuarts to the throne of England, Mann concentrated on collecting Italian art and his voluminous correspondence with British writer Horace Walpole—forty years of letters between two men who never met.

[ALSO SEE: *Alessandro Albani*]

MARE ISLAND SABOTAGE
German Sabotage of U.S. Navy Yard ▪ (1917)

NO ONE EVER IDENTIFIED THE GERMAN SABOTEURS who exploded a U.S. munitions dump on Black Tom Island, New Jersey, on July 30, 1916, causing a $22 million loss. This was not the case in the German sabotage of the U.S. Navy Yard in San Francisco the following year. Abwehr spy and saboteur Kurt Jahnke thought it clever that he report his own sabotage to U.S. authorities before he and others blew up the U.S. Navy Yard at Mare Island in 1917.

In this manner, Jahnke reasoned, he would never become a suspect. A tremendous explosion tore the Navy Yard to pieces a short time later, leaving many dead, including sixteen children. Authorities in Washington had no trace of the man who had reported the sabotage before it happened, except a vague clue that he had fled to Mexico, then a safe haven for German agents. The German government, desperate for aid from any source as World War I ground on and its war effort waned, was attempting to entice Mexico to its side and into its war.

On January 16, 1917, German Foreign Minister Arthur Zimmermann sent a coded telegram to German Ambassador to Mexico von Eckhardt in which he proposed that Mexico, in the event that the U.S. did not remain neutral, attack its northern neighbor. In return, Germany would provide the impoverished Mexican government with huge funds and all the arms and military support it might require.

This wire was intercepted by British intelligence and forwarded to Washington, D.C. On April 4, after many American ships had been sunk by wanton U-boat attacks, the U.S. declared war on Germany. The Bureau of Investigation, the precusor to today's FBI, along with U.S. military intelligence and the ONI (Office of Naval Intelligence), actively sought out German spies and saboteurs.

In its efforts to identify the Mare Island saboteurs, officials contacted Paul Altendorf, a colonel in the Mexican Army. Unlike most Mexican officials at that time, Altendorf was pro-American.

Altendorf agreed to act as a counterspy on behalf of the U.S. in investigating the Mare Island sabotage. He began by haunting Mexico City bars and he turned up Jahnke, a heavy drinker. In his cups, Jahnke admitted that he was the public-spirited citizen who had informed the authorities in San Francisco that there was a plot to blow up the Mare Island station. He then bragged that he was the saboteur who blew it up.

"If you blew it up," Altendorf said, "then why did you report it beforehand?"

Jahnke grinned. "By reporting the plot, I became the last person they would suspect of creating the explosion." The burly, droopy-eyed Jahnke then boasted of his being an explosives expert. "There isn't anything or anyone I can't blow up!"

Altendorf bought drink after drink, telling the slobbering Jahnke that he, too, hated the United States and offered help in any effort that would injure the Americans. Jahnke took the bait, saying that he had done the Mare Island job with another German saboteur and spy, Lothar Witzke (sometimes called Wittke), who was also hiding out in Mexico City, under the alias of Pablo Waberski. Witzke needed help in crossing the Mexican border back into the U.S., Jahnke said. Altendorf immediately offered his aid.

Witzke was guided to Nogales, Arizona, by Altendorf but as soon as he entered the U.S., American agents appeared and arrested him, charging him with the Mare Island sabotage. Found on Witzke was a letter in code, which was sent to American cipher expert Herbert Yardley who soon deciphered the message that had been signed by the German Ambassador to Mexico, von Eckhardt and was addressed to all German consulates in Mexico. It read: "Strictly secret. The bearer of this is a subject of the Empire who travels as a Russian under the name of Pablo Waberski. He is a German secret agent."

Witzke was convicted and sentenced to be hanged, the only German agent in World War I to be sentenced to death. The sentence was later reprieved by President Wilson. Following World War I, he was deported to Germany where he was greeted as a hero, given the Iron Cross, first and second class. Jahnke was also detained but he managed to escape and return to Germany.

An important link in the sabotage ring, including those who had blown up the Black Tom Island stores, was another German agent, a woman who was identified only as "Victorica." One of the many German immigrant suspects being watched by the agents was the young sister of a factory worker. She appeared to be very religious, going to St. Patrick's Cathedral on Fifth Avenue every day. An agent followed her into church to see her place a folded newspaper on the pew next to her. When she left the church, a tall, well-dressed man sat down in the pew and picked up the newspaper, which the agent could clearly see was folded about a packet of letters.

The agent trailed the man to the Nassau Hotel in Long Island. He watched as the man sat in the lobby for a few minutes. Then he walked out, leaving the newspaper behind. In a few seconds a tall, strikingly beautiful blonde woman in her mid-thirties appeared. She went to the lobby chair where the newspaper nestled and picked it up, including the letters inside of it, then went to her suite. The agent discovered that the stunning blonde was registered at the hotel under the name of Maria Vussier. She was confronted a few days later and admitted that she was the "Victorica" being sought by the American agents.

Her real name was Maria von Kretschman. She was the 35-year-old daughter of Baron Hans von Kretschman, a German general. Through her coteries of German aristocrats she had earlier come to meet Colonel Walther Nicolai, chief of German intelligence who immediately recognized her value as a spy. She possessed several academic degrees and spoke several languages fluently, including English. Nicolai recruited her into his service about 1910.

The alluring female spy developed a heroin addiction that Nicolai may have initiated himself to make her more dependent upon him, a ploy often used by spymasters. Some time in 1912 she married an Argentine citizen, Manual Gustave Victorica (thus the code name), who was also one of Nicolai's spies.

Kretschman later went to Antwerp where, at the beginning of World War I, she operated a German spy network, which was identified by British agents who dubbed its leader "the beautiful blonde woman of Antwerp." SIS, however, lost track of her for some time until they received a report that she was operating somewhere in the U.S.

Kretschman had actually sailed for America on Jaunary 1917, quickly establishing contact with other German agents. She was well-supplied with cash, more than $50,000 to finance sabotage operations. She had taken the precautions taught her at Nicolai's spy school, moving from one hotel to another every few days and having her coded letters received at mail drops where her real identify was unknown. She felt that she had covered her tracks so well that she would never be detected but American agents nevertheless caught up with her.

The spy admitted that she was the Abwehr agent who had been supplying the chemicals used in the making of explosives that had been used in the last two years to destroy docks, munitions plants, and the Mare Island facility. She had been under a terrific strain, she said, and, in breaking down before the agents, she confessed that she had conducted her espionage activities with the unwitting help of Catholic priests. She had asked several clergymen to order religious statues for her from a special shop in Zurich, Switzerland.

When these statues arrived at the church, the priests would contact Kretschman and she would retrieve them. Inside of the statues were vials containing chemicals that had been specially prepared by the Abwehr laboratories, chemicals to be used to make explosive devices. The lovely lady spy was tried, convicted, and imprisoned but her dependency upon heroin was so accute that she was kept at Bellevue Hospital where she died in 1919.

This was not the fate of Witzke and Jahnke. During World War II, Witzke headed Section II (sabotage) at the Hamburg branch of the Abwehr. He was in charge of all sabotage in England. After World War I, Jahnke traveled to China as an Abwehr spy, joining the household staff of Dr. Sun Yat-sen. He also worked with many Chinese warlords and even trained Chinese spies at the Whampoa Military Academy and, at the same time, secretly worked for the Japanese secret service in Manchuria, taking commands from Kenji Doihara, the Japanese spymaster later hanged as a war criminal. He later returned to Germany to become an aide to Rudolf Hess but, in reality, Jahnke was an Abwehr agent spying on the much-distrusted Hess. In gathering information, Jahnke answered only to Walter Schellenberg who later replaced Admiral Canaris as head of the Abwehr in the closing stages of World War II.

Jahnke's star faded when Rudolf Hess made his inexplicable and dramatic flight to England in 1941 to sue for a separate peace (or something like that). Schellenberg and Heinrich Himmler, an arch foe of

Hess from the early days of the Nazi Party, prepared detailed reports on Jahnke that stated that Jahnke was in league with the British SIS and that he was, in fact, a British spy. Instead of being arrested, Jahnke was placed under close surveillance by Himmler's Gestapo and SD agents working for Reinhard Heydrich. He vanished after World War II.

[ALSO SEE: *Abwehr; Wilhelm Canaris; Kenji Doihara; Reinhard Heydrich; Heinrich Himmler; Walther Nicolai; Walter Schellenberg; Herbert O. Yardley; Zimmermann Telegram*]

MARLOWE, CHRISTOPHER
British Spy ▪ (1564–1593?)

THE CELEBRATED ENGLISH DRAMATIST WAS BORN IN Canterbury, the son of a shoemaker. A brilliant child, he was allowed to attend the King's School. He went on to Cambridge where he graduated in 1584. He then began to pursue his master's degree but his studies were mysteriously interrupted in 1857. That interruption was the undertaking of an espionage assignment.

Marlowe had met and befriended Francis Walsingham, who served as secretary of state to Elizabeth I. Walsingham was a crafty, cunning man who established a vast and effective spy network for the protection of his sovereign. He detected many conspiracies and smashed plots to overthrow Elizabeth, including the Throckmorton Conspiracy of 1583, the Anthony Babington plot of 1586, and through his spies he learned of the planned invasion of the Spanish Armada in 1587. In that same year, when Marlowe vanished from Cambridge, Walsingham was attempting to detect another conspiracy against Elizabeth headed by her own sister, Mary Queen of Scots.

At the time, Mary was being held prisoner in London by Elizabeth but Mary's uncle, the Duke de Guise, leader of a Catholic faction in France, sought to free Mary and place her on the throne of England. Knowing that the Guise plot was being developed at a Jesuit seminary in Rheims, France, Walsingham selected several young men to enter the seminary, acting as spies.

The Jesuits at the time were carefully recruiting English students whose loyalty was to the Catholic religion, which had been persecuted in England by Elizabeth and which would be restored as the state religion if Mary were to take the British throne. One of the student spies chosen by Walsingham was the adventurous, enterprising Christopher Marlowe.

Traveling to Rheims, Marlowe loudly denounced Protestantism and Elizabeth and was accepted by the Jesuits with open arms. He became part of the conspiracy and soon learned the identities of all the key members involved in the plot. Marlowe quickly fed these names to Walsingham who had the plotters arrested. Elizabeth's spymaster then faked Mary's writings to incriminate her directly with the conspirators, bringing about her execution.

When Marlowe returned to England, however, officials at Cambridge were ready to expel him for being absent without an explanation for so long a period. Walsingham and other government agents interceded on Marlowe's behalf and he was allowed to complete his studies.

Marlowe's association continued with Walsingham, both as an informer on Catholics in England and as Walsingham's lover. The homosexual relationship continued over some years while Marlowe penned some of the finest plays ever produced in England to that time—*Tamburlaine the Great, Edward II, Dr. Faustus*—until he was murdered in a drunken tavern brawl on the stormy night of May 30, 1593.

The details of Marlowe's death, like much of his life, remain shrouded in mystery. The 29-year-old dramatist was dining at the Eleanor Bull's tavern in Deptford, later a suburb of London. He had entered the tavern with three companions, Nicholas Skeres, Robert Poley, and Ingram Frizer. All were in Walsingham's employ as spies. The four young men drank a great deal and Marlowe suddenly dove for Frizer's dagger, pulling it from its scabbard and slashing Frizer on the forehead.

Frizer struggled with Marlowe and took the dagger from the playright's grasp and drove it into his skull, killing him with one wound above the eye. Frizer and the other two men claimed self-defense which was accepted by authorities. Marlowe's death, however, remained a mystery. To the few eyewitnesses present, the fight seemed staged and Marlowe's body was quickly removed from the tavern before his fatal wound was closely examined by any competent medical authority.

All of this gave rise to the belief that Marlowe had not been killed, that his death had been feigned so that he could disappear and serve as a truly anonymous spy for his lover Walsingham. It was then rumored that Frizer had killed Marlowe so that he, Frizer, could take Marlowe's favored place with Walsingham. It was then pointed out that Marlowe had recently been arrested and jailed for making atheistic statements and that he had been released on bail, pending a trial that could have resulted in his execution.

Walsingham, it was claimed in this scenario, had contrived the murder and that another body was substituted for Marlowe's and buried in its place. Marlowe then sailed to France to live comfortably on a private income provided by Walsingham. It was while living out a long anonymous life, it was later claimed by some, that Marlowe wrote all of the plays later attributed to William Shakespeare.

[ALSO SEE: *Francis Walsingham*]

MARTIN, WILLIAM H.
American Spy for Soviets ▪ (1930–   )

BORN IN COLUMBUS, GEORGIA, MARTIN WAS RAISED in Ellensworth, Washington. He seemed to be an all-American boy. He was an obedient child at home and became a good chess player in his youth. He played the piano with a good deal of talent and he amazed his friends when exercising his hobby, hypnotism. He excelled at math and science when attending the University of Washington. He dropped out a year later and joined the U.S. Navy.

Martin was trained as a cryptologist and was then assigned to the naval base at Yokosuka, Japan. There he met Bernon F. Mitchell, a native of Eureka, California. Like Martin, Mitchell had gone to college for one year, attending Stanford University before joining the navy. Martin and Mitchell developed a fast friendship that later grew into a homosexual liaison.

When both left the service, they joined the super secretive NSA (National Security Agency), which concentrated its intelligence-gathering in the fields of communication, chiefly monitoring Communist military and diplomatic nets throughout the world and cracking the codes employed by the Soviets. Martin and Mitchell became cryptologists after supplementing their background with additional college training.

Both men secretly joined the Communist Party in 1958, and they took unauthorized secret trips to Mexico and to the Communist-controlled Cuba of Fidel Castro in 1959. By the following year both men began openly criticizing U.S. intelligence-gathering operations, sneeringly condemning the American U-2 flights over the Soviet Union in 1960. Their superiors did nothing about such inflammatory criticism in the heart of the NSA. In July, Martin and Mitchell took their summer vacations together as usual and did not return.

In September both men suddenly appeared on Moscow television in a KGB-staged press conference. They read copies of statements they said they had left in safe deposit boxes in America. The statements renounced their American citizenship and denounced the United States as a war-mongering country that used any illegal means to gather intelligence.

The event was labelled "Traitor's Day in Moscow," by the NSA, which stated that homosexuality was the root cause of the defections. Martin and Mitchell remained in Russia and, after the KGB milked them of all the NSA secrets they could divulge, they were pensioned off to tiny Moscow apartments and the monthly wages of ditch-diggers.

MATA HARI (MARGARETHA GEERTRUIDA MAC LEOD, née ZELLE)
German Spy in World War I ▪ (1876–1917)

THE MOST CELEBRATED FEMALE SPY IN HISTORY WAS also one of the most inept agents in the world of espionage. But when it came to the notorious Mata Hari, her accomplishments were counted in the bedroom and on the stage, not in the recorded annals of secret intelligence. She was a creature of her own imagination. Her wild fancies finally engulfed her in terrible adventure and led her before a French firing squad on October 15, 1917.

The enigmatic Mata Hari struck down by bullets that day had nothing to do with the little Dutch girl born Margaret Gertrude Zelle on August 7, 1876, in Leeuwarden, Holland. Her parents, Adam Zelle and Antje van der Meulen, were wealthy. Her father owned a successful hatter's business and he and his wife lavished attention and gifts on their only daughter. Her mother died when she was fourteen, however, and her father sent her to a convent school.

Graduating at eighteen, Margaret met within a few weeks a dashing Dutch officer, Captain Rudolf MacLeod, a man of forty whose uncle was an admiral and who bragged of his frequent visits to the court of The Hague where he chatted with Queen Wilhelmina. The couple married in 1895 and left for Java where MacLeod was serving as a colonial officer. They made their home in Banjoe-Biroe, a Dutch East Indias settlement that was anything but idyllic. It was a

The World War I German spy Mata Hari shown adjusting a headdress of her own design.

The dancer/spy Mata Hari when she was the rage of Paris.

place of squalor and uncomfortable climate, unbearably hot and rain-soaked.

MacLeod's image of the handsome, dashing husband soon vanished. He drank incessantly, while his wife struggled against boredom and labored through a difficult pregnancy, which had begun before the nuptials. Worse, MacLeod kept a string of native girls as mistresses, bringing these women into his home at all hours of the day for quick assignations. When Margaret gave birth to her son Norman on January 30, 1896, MacLeod, according to her bitter statements in divorce court later, was having sex with a native girl in the next room. The boy later died, poisoned by an embittered servant.

MacLeod then proposed that Margaret and he operate a badger game. He would arrange through intermediaries for wealthy plantation owners in Java and Sumatra to visit his wife. While the visitor was having sex with her, MacLeod would suddenly barge into the bedroom to play the outraged husband. Both MacLeod and Margaret would then blackmail the victims for heavy payments. Margaret later summed up this sordid episode of her life by sarcastically repeating MacLeod's oft-stated philosophy that "man is an animal! Let's make the most of it."

In her divorce proceedings, Margaret claimed that she was little more than a naive, confused young woman who was easily manipulated by her calculating spouse. "My husband picked wealthy men as suitable objects for blackmail," her petition stated. "One gentleman was a great admirer of my eyes and I led him on as I was told . . . I was able to collect several thousand guilders."

Awarded custody of her daughter, Margaret received only a small court-ordered settlement from MacLeod. Placing her child in the home of a relative, she spent most of the settlement money on dancing lessons. She had resolved to support herself as an Oriental dancer, and intended to emulate the dances she had seen performed in Java, those that emphasized the arms, legs, and eyes, which Margaret felt were her best physical attributes. To make her body supple and lithe, she performed strenuous acrobatic exercises.

In October 1903, she believed she was ready to astound the world with the mystical dances of Shiva (or Siva) and traveled to Paris to make her reputation. Her ambitions were dashed by failure. No one would hire her. The tall, long-legged beauty, however, found work for a while as a stripper in some low-life clubs.

For most of the following year, Margaret was a common streetwalker. By late 1904 she was servicing ten to twenty men a day in a cheap bordello. She contracted a venereal disease and a Dr. Bizard was summoned to examine her. (Ironically, this same physician would become her mentor in Saint-Lazare Prison while she awaited a firing squad.)

Returning to Holland, Margaret pressed all she knew, friends, and family members, for cash. With a substantial amount of money, Margaret returned to Paris with a new wardrobe and took an expensive suite of rooms at the luxurious Hotel Crillon.

The woman was no longer Margaret Getrude Zelle. She was Mata Hari, a stage name she had created, one that meant "Eye of the Morning," or "Child of the Dawn," whichever definition Margaret cared to give. Acting as if she were a member of visiting royalty, Mata Hari summoned the entrepreneurial nightclub owner, Emile Guimet, to her Crillon suite.

Guimet went out of curiosity, being told by a courier that "the most exotic dancer in the world wished to see him." He was greeted by a tall, sloe-eyed brunette who exuded sultry sex with every move of her curvacious body. Guimet was captivated, enthralled by a woman he thought was the most sophisticated, worldly female he had ever encountered.

Guimet fell in love with the siren, making her the dancing star of his nightclub and his mistress as well. Guimet presented Mata Hari to high society Paris in a stunning nightclub debut in 1905. Audiences and critics alike swooned over Mata Hari's exotic, interpretive dancing. They heaped praise upon her for her undulating prowess as she shed one veil after another with swirling precision, ending her act with shuddering, quivering nakedness.

Everywhere the dancer appeared she was mobbed by rich men begging her to take their wealth in exchange for her sexual favors. Police had to be called to put down riotous crowds when Mata Hari appeared at the Casino de Paris, the Olympia, and the Folies-Bergere. She was by then called "the red dancer," after the many red veils she would shed while dancing the Dance of Love, the Dance of Sin, the Dance of Death.

Leaving Paris for two years, the dancer toured the capitals of Europe—London, Vienna, Rome, Berlin. Fame and fortune were dumped into her coffers. To men everywhere, Mata Hari became the smoldering symbol of sex. She knew it and capitalized on it at every turn. She was summoned to perform privately before Crown Prince Wilhelm in Berlin. The Prince and the dancer had a brief but passion-filled affair during which Wilhelm gave Mata Hari diamonds and emeralds worth more than $100,000.

When Emperor Wilhelm objected to his son's liaison with the courtesan, the Prince flaunted the dancer in public. On one occasion, he had the dancer at his side on a Berlin parade ground while he reviewed the royal guards. In 1907, he escorted the dancer into his officers' mess where he ordered her to perform naked on the tables before his salivating men. Some time later Wilhelm tired of the dancer and turned her over to his future brother-in-law, the Duke of Brunswick. Within months, she had stepped down another notch to become the mistress of Berlin Police Chief Traugott von Jagow.

A beefy, bald man, Jagow would later become the adjutant of Colonel Walther Nicolai, head of German intelligence (*Nachrichtendienst*) during World War I.

Although he could not afford her extravagant lifestyle, Jagow's love for Mata Hari was genuine and remained for the rest of her life but her association with him would, indeed, cost the dancer her life. Though she drew an allowance regularly from Jagow, the dancer continued her many affairs with European diplomats and aristocrats.

By 1912, however, Mata Hari had risen to great heights as a legitimate ballet dancer. She had never forsaken ballet, which she practiced painfully each and every day, exercising for several hours in a ballet exercising room that she had constructed in her villa.

She scored great successes at the Paris Opera Ballet and also in the ballet theaters of Madrid, Vienna, and Berlin. In 1912, she appeared at La Scala in Milan and rendered a magnificent performance of the classic ballet *Bacchus and Gambrini*, one which dispelled all doubts of her most severest critics about her dancing abilities.

Like all in her profession, the dancer kept a bulging scrapbook of clippings praising her and her performances. Unlike other dancers, she kept a second scrapbook, much thicker, which contained hundreds of letters from Europe's most powerful men, all of which were compromising, along with copies of her own profane, obscene letters to them. Undoubtedly, these letters made up her insurance policy, correspondence that could easily be converted to blackmail.

The year 1912 was pivotal for Mata Hari. She not only scored her most triumphant artistic successes at that time, but decided on a new career packed with adventure, excitement, and danger. She had decided to become a spy. Exactly how she slipped into the dark shadows of espionage is uncertain to this day. The accomplished spymasters of Europe would minimize her activities in this realm. The British joked about her ineptitude, the Germans dismissed her as ineffective. Only the French branded her so devastating as to be equal to a whole German army.

Jagow was the inspiration for this new career. The ever faithful lover invited Mata Hari to lunch in a private room of a Berlin restaurant some time in 1912. Jagow by then had become one of Nicolai's spymasters for German military intelligence, which was already preparing for war with France and England. The German came bluntly to the point.

The spymaster proposed that the dancer go on using her boudoir as a source of money, but that she get information in the bargain. Jagow told her that he would supply her with a list of clients who would pay her handsomely—he told her the fee should be 30,000 marks per night—and that she was to pry state, political, and military secrets from these lovers.

The spy was by then designated as a German agent under the code number of H.21. The prefix *H*, learned later by Allied intelligence, applied only to German spies recruited *before* August 1914, the beginning of World War I. As such, Jagow arranged for her to attend important diplomatic parties and receptions in all of the capitals of central and western Europe, even North Africa. In the German embassies in Amsterdam, Paris, Madrid, Vienna, Cairo, the dancer met and seduced high-ranking diplomats and military officers who mixed their bedroom babble with information about troop movements, munitions dumps, espionage operations, naval maneuvers, warships, new artillery weapons. All of this Mata Hari or H.21 dutifully reported in eyebrow-raising detail to Jagow.

When the war began, Mata Hari was well-positioned to spy for Germany, a country that she is said to have adopted and one that secretly granted her citizenship. Jagow then ordered the dancer to return to France via her native Holland. Once she arrived at her villa in Neuilly, she would receive further instructions. Mata Hari went to Amsterdam but found the French border closed to her. Only those with special passes were permitted to cross.

Undaunted, the spy went to the French consulate in Amsterdam, pleading non-belligerency. "My home is in Neuilly," she said. "My friends are there. My career is in France." To a French official she showed letters she had received from high-ranking French politicians and military officers. The consul agreed to prepare a pass for her. While she waited, the ever sexually active dancer seduced the richest Dutch trade merchant in Amsterdam. She learned from him the number and embarkation dates of food ships leaving Holland for England, and subsequent rerouting to France. The spy delivered this information to Major Sprecht, a German intelligence officer in Amsterdam, and he sent it on to Jagow.

Agents did watch the dancer as one important Foreign Office official after another dined with her, went to her hotel suite, and slept with her. But these officials were much too important to be questioned by the police. Further, nothing Mata Hari did suggested that she was a spy. Her mail was inspected and nothing incriminating was found. What investigators did not know was that she was told much by her paramours, how the French armies were supplied, where troops were positioned, even where recruits to act as reinforcements were being trained.

This information the spy sent to Jagow in Germany inside the diplomatic pouches of certain neutral countries with the cooperation of diplomats in the embassies of those countries. When French counter-intelligence was about to close its dossier on Mata Hari, agents turned up evidence that brought more suspicion upon the dancer. Jules Cambon, department chief of the French Foreign Office and a close friend of the dancer, arranged for Mata Hari to receive a pass to travel to the village of Vittel which was near the front lines.

Although French agents watched her day and night for almost seven months they could not collect any evidence against her. All they reported was that she worked tirelessly in nursing wounded men. Most of these, however, were officers whom the dancer subtly pumped for information. The wounded men gladly told her all she wanted to know about a great French offensive that was going to be mounted in that sector, which later became known as the battle of the Somme.

Jagow later received this information from the spy when she returned to Paris. A huge German army lay in wait for the French attack and smashed the French armies, slaughtering more than 200,000 men.

Captain Georges Ladoux of French counter-intelligence then thought to jolt the spy into an admission by having her brought to his office where he bluntly accused her of being an agent for Germany. "Madam," Ladoux intoned, "you are under suspicion by all the Allied Powers. You are to be deported, returned to your native Holland."

Mata Hari knew that deportation would end her career as a German agent. She thought to outwit the French officer by offering to spy for France. "I can be extremely useful," she promised. "I have access to German military matters." Then she asked that she be sent to German military headquarters. "I will obtain any secret intelligence the French General Staff might require."

Though she thought she was being clever, the spy had made a fatal mistake. She had all along denied that she knew anything of espionage and yet, to prevent her deportation, she offered to expertly perform the acts of a professional spy. Ladoux pretended to be persuaded that Mata Hari would do anything for her "beloved France." He agreed that she could spy against the Germans, but not at Stenay where she originally proposed to go.

Ladoux ordered the dancer to travel to occupied Brussels. Then came a report from British intelligence that told the French that one of its agents had been captured and killed in Brussels. The agent, the British said, had been betrayed by a woman who answered the description of Mata Hari. Now convinced that the dancer was working with the Germans, Ladoux ordered that Mata Hari was to be arrested the moment she returned to France. The Germans had all but given up on Mata Hari. She was no longer beautiful, nor sultry. Her sallow complexion had hardened and she now bore a decidedly wrinkled and well-lined face. She appeared gaunt, emaciated. Everything about her seemed severe, including her attitude and personality. She was shrewish and demanding.

Also, the Germans knew that their spy had been identified as such many months earlier. She was too notorious now to be used with any kind of effectiveness. Realizing that she was no longer the beau ideal of espionage, Mata Hari went to other foreign powers, offering her services as an agent but she was rebuffed. Returning to the Germans in Madrid, the spy demanded that she be paid for her services and that she receive another assignment. A nervous Captain von Kalle contacted Jagow in Berlin.

Jagow was irked and resigned to the fact that Mata Hari was now expendable. He sent a wire to the

German Embassy in Madrid that agent H.21 was to return to France where, through a neutral legation, she would be paid 15,000 pesatas. French intelligence intercepted this message and quickly identified agent H.21 as Mata Hari. Agents trailed her back to Paris where she registered at the Plaza-Athenée Hotel on the avenue Montaigne. She collected her check but oddly did not cash it.

On the morning of February 13, 1917, Commissioner Priolet, in the company of his secretary and two gendarmes, burst into Mata Hari's suite to find the spy in bed, eating her breakfast. Priolet ordered her to dress. As she silently did so, her rooms were searched and the check for 15,000 pesatas was discovered. The spy was unperturbed. As she was leaving her rooms, she swooped up several bunches of wild violets and thrust them into the arms of the startled Priolet.

Mata Hari was taken to the crumbling prison fortress of Faubourg Saint-Denis where she was kept in a padded cell to prevent possible suicide. The French expected to get information from the dancer before eliminating her. She languished in her cell until brought to a closed military trial, which occured on July 24–25, 1917. So secretive was this hearing that armed sentries were placed outside the doors with strict orders to shoot anyone who came closer than ten paces.

Colonel Semprou of the Guard Républicain acted as president of the court. Lieutenant Andre Mornet represented the Commissioner of the Government (Judge-Advocate General) and acted as the prosecutor. Also in attendance was Major Massard of the Deuxiéme Bureau. Mata Hari was represented by a brilliant lawyer, Edward Clunet, who so enthus-

iastically undertook the case that he became the spy's devoted champion.

Semprou opened with a damning statement: "On the day that war was declared you had breakfast with the Prefect of Police [Jagow] at Berlin and then drove with him through a shouting crowd." Dressed all in black, Mata Hari was unperturbed, calmly responding: "It is true. I had met the Prefect in a music hall where I danced. That is how we came to know each other." She added the titillating tidbit that Jagow had come to inspect her scanty costume after receiving complaints that it revealed too much of the dancer's body.

"A little later the Prefect charged you with a mission and gave you thirty thousand marks," intoned Semprou.

"That is true," the dancer replied softly. "He was the man and gave me thirty thousand marks. But not for the reason you impute. He was my lover."

"Hundreds of thousands of marks were paid to you—"

"As a courtesan, yes! I confess it, but never a spy!" The dancer had lost her composure. She learned forward as if pleading with the officers of the court who sat ramrod stiff in front of her. "Harlot, yes, I am that! But traitoress—never!"

Then Semprou presented the court's real evidence: "At the order of German Headquarters you were notified in Madrid that you were to be paid 15,000 pesatas, money waiting for you here in France, and you came to France and collected those funds."

Mata Hari for the first time appeared frantic. She shook her head and said: "I was the mistress of Kalle, head of German intelligence in Madrid. That payment was a love debt, that's all."

Mata Hari at her most alluring; the exotic dancer was a rather incompetent spy who was shot by the French in 1917.

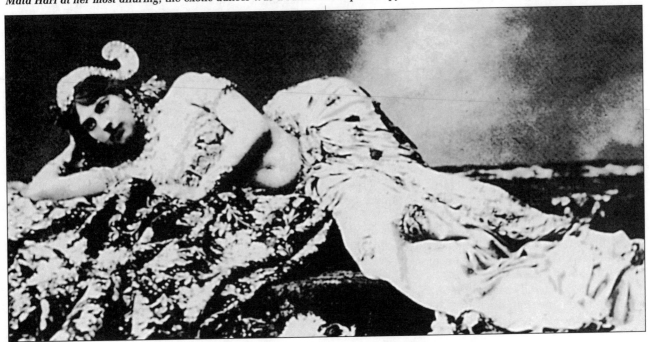

Semprou then drove home his point like a dagger into her heart: "But that remittance was sent to the order of H.21. That is a number on the list of German spies. That was your number. That is what you were known as—not as a mistress, a lover, a harlot. That was the pay of a spy. You, madam, are H.21, an agent in the employ of the German intelligence service. And that is what you have always been since long before this war began."

The dancer was trapped and knew it. She was shattered at the evidence. Her body trembled. Her doe-eyes blinked uncontrollably. Her mouth quivered as it delivered a final answer: "That . . . that is not true! I'm telling you that—it was—it was to pay—to pay for my nights of love. It—it is my price. Please believe me, gentlemen."

The court deliberated for a half hour. Then Mata Hari was ordered to stand and hear its verdict. The president of the court stated in an emotionless voice that she had been found guilty of espionage against France. He then said: "Margaret Gertrude Zelle—you are condemned to death."

Stunned, the dancer muttered: "It's not possible. It's not possible."

On the day before the scheduled execution, she maintained a confident, almost cheerful air.

Also on that day, Sister Léonide was present with Dr. Bizard in the dancer's cell. The nun had been instructed to be Mata Hari's cellmate and watch the prisoner closely so that she would not harm herself before the sentence was carried out. At one point, to cheer up the condemned spy, Sister Léonide said to Mata Hari: "Show us how you dance." The spy rose from a small bed, smiling. She loosened her robe and began to slowly dance about the cell.

At 4 A.M. the following morning, Commandant Julien came into the cell. He asked Sister Léonide to wake the spy. The condemned woman put on her warmest gown and chatted calmly as she dressed. "It is cold. I slept so well. Another day I would not have forgiven them for waking me so early. Why do you have this custom of executing people at dawn? In India it is otherwise. It takes place at noon. I would much rather go to Vincennes [the place of execution] about three o'clock after a good lunch. Give me my nice little slippers, too. I always like to be well shod."

After powdering her face, the spy cocked her head at Julien and announced: "Gentlemen, I am ready."

She was escorted into a large touring car, which sped off toward Vincennes, arriving there at 5:40 A.M., the car driving up to the firing range where twelve picked soldiers of the Fourth Regiment of Zouaves awaited her. Dr. Bizard quickly poured a small glass of brandy for the dancer and she drank this down. Then she lifted her skirts and stepped from the car and began marching toward a post staked in the middle of the rifle range.

An officer offered her a blindfold, which she refused. When he attempted to tie her waist to the post, the dancer waved him away. She smiled and held that smile as the twelve riflemen, standing twelve paces away from her, fired their bullets into her body. As the spy slumped to the ground, an officer walked up to her, placed a pistol behind her ear and fired a bullet into her brain, the traditional *coup de grace*.

No one came forth to claim the body.

[ALSO SEE: *Deuxiéme Bureau; Vernon Kell; MI5; Walther Nicolai; Special Branch; Basil Thomson*]

MAUGHAM, (WILLIAM) SOMERSET
British Agent in World War I ▪ (1874–1965)

BRITISH WRITER SOMERSET MAUGHAM, WHO admired the honesty of the working people but who sought the luxury of the rich, served as a spy for England during World War I, and a reluctant one, at that. Planning to become a physician, Maugham worked as an intern while reading omnivorously. He kept a "writer's notebook," about what he termed "life in the raw," particularly in the slums of Lambeth where he worked briefly as an obstetric clerk.

That career was abandoned when, in 1897, Maugham published a very successful novel, *Liza of Lambeth*, a book he wrote more for his own amusement than with any thoughts of enriching himself. It accurately and sympathetically portrayed "the low life" of Lambeth, drawn from his own experiences, and was, as the French term it, a *succes de scandale*. Riches flowed from this work, so much so that Maugham decided on a full-time writing career. He wrote not only successful novels but well-received plays and also short stories. In 1915, Maugham published what was later heralded as his masterpiece (and would eventually sell more than 10 million copies), *Of Human Bondage*.

By the time this book appeared, the 41-year-old Maugham was an ambulance driver in France, having volunteered for service when World War I broke out in 1914. He corrected the proofs for *Bondage* in a small hotel in Malo, near Dunkirk, between driving shifts. He was also torn between two loves by then, that of his beautiful mistress, Gwendolyn Maude Syrie Wellcome, daughter of philanthropist Thomas John Bernardo, and that of a handsome young American homosexual, Gerald Haxton.

One of Syrie's female friends (she had many male lovers other than Maugham), was the mistress to Captain John Wallinger (later Major Sir John Wallinger), who had been an officer of Army Police in India and who was a good-natured but rather naive officer in SIS. In 1915, Wallinger was given the task of restructuring the British espionage force working in Switzerland where most of the English spies and their foreign agents had been exposed and arrested.

Wallinger was dining with his mistress, Syrie, and Maugham one evening in London when he suggested to the writer who was then home on leave that he serve as an agent in Switzerland. The idea intrigued Maugham although he had little respect for Wallinger.

With a little hesitation, Maugham accepted the assignment to Switzerland. He was equipped to deal with a number of foreign agents working for the British in that he spoke fluent French, acceptable German, and had the perfect cover, a famous writer living abroad so that he could "write a play in peace and quiet in a neutral country." Maugham made his way to Lucerne where his first assignment was to contact an English spy who had a German wife. The agent was suspected of being a double agent who was really working for the Germans.

Maugham not only made contact with this agent but convinced him to go to France where he was seized and shot as a spy. This episode was later recounted in Maugham's short story, "The Traitor," a story that first introduced his enigmatic fictional spy, Ashenden. While building up his espionage contacts, Maugham did manage to write a play, *Caroline*, which was loosely based on his affair with Syrie Wellcome. The play opened on February 8, 1916, and played to packed houses.

The character Ashenden, drawn from Maugham's own experiences and based on his own subtle character, would appear in later Maugham stories and a full blown novel, *Ashenden*, in 1928. At one point, when Maugham's friend Winston Churchill complained that his Ashenden stories broke the Official Secrets Act, the author burned fourteen original manuscripts of the Ashenden stories and did not publish more on his fictional spy until the 1928 novel.

In one Ashenden tale, Maugham recounted his own espionage routine while living and working in Geneva: "He saw his spies at stated intervals and paid them their wages; when he could get hold of a new one he engaged him, gave him his instructions and sent him off to Germany; he waited for the information that came through and dispatched it; he went into France once a week to confer with his colleague over the frontier and to receive his orders from London; he visited the market-place on market-day to get any message the old butter-woman had brought him from the other side of the lake; he kept his eyes and ears open; and he wrote long reports which he was convinced no-one read, till having inadvertently slipped a jest into one of them he received a sharp reproof for his levity. The work he was doing was evidently necessary, but it could not be called anything but monotonous."

The "old butter-woman" to whom Maugham referred was an elderly woman from French Savoy who crossed over the lake to sell butter, eggs, and vegetables in the Geneva marketplace. She was an SIS

Author Somerset Maugham at the time he became a World War I British spy.

agent who carried notes from Maugham's "control" to the author and from Maugham back to "control," exchanging these notes when Maugham bought vegetables from her at the Geneva marketplace. He later wrote of her: "Indeed this old lady looked so bland and innocent, with her corpulence, her fat red face, and her swirling good-natured mouth, it would have been a very astute detective who could imagine that if he took the trouble to put his hand deep down between those voluminous breasts of hers, he would find a piece of paper that would land in a dock an honest old woman (who kept her son out of the trenches by taking this risk) and an English writer approaching middle age."

Maugham's function was that of a relay man, sending on messages from SIS chiefs in France and London to British agents located in Germany, specifically the towns of Mainz, Trier, Frankfurt, and Koblenz. Maugham was warned that he had several fake agents in his midst, men who claimed that they went to Germany but who did not really leave Switzerland, providing SIS with bogus information they created from reports in German newspapers, along with gossip picked up in Swiss pubs. One of these was an agent named Bernard who apparently threatened Maugham with a gun when demanding more money for his services, a scene which Maugham transferred to one of Ashenden's fictional adventures.

Maugham's Ashenden stories were innovational and fresh, to be sure, and they truly changed the course future spy fiction writers took in portraying agents and espionage. Until Ashenden appeared, the public knew spies only through the flamboyant novels and stories of E. Phillips Oppenheim and William LeQueux. These writers portrayed spies as romantic adventurers whose everyday lives were punctuated by death-defying feats and narrow escapes. This was not the spy fiction of Somerset Maugham. His spy Ashenden was methodical, dealing with hum-drum reports and enduring a rather monotonous life that was sprinkled with sudden threats of death.

Ashenden was drawn as a cynical, detached agent, a middle-aged hero with a wry sense of humor, a characterization that was later embraced by the most successful of spy writers, Eric Ambler, Graham Greene, and John Le Carré, the latter admitting that his most memorable character, Alec Leamas of *The Spy Who Came in from the Cold*, was based upon Maugham's Ashenden. Le Carré later wrote of Maugham as "the first person to write about espionage in a mood of disenchantment and almost prosaic reality."

Maugham's own life was certainly more dramatic than that of his alter ego, Ashenden. Though his mistress Syrie had many lovers, her husband, Sir Henry Wellcome, named Maugham as the correspondent in his divorce, which was granted on grounds of adultery. While the divorce proceedings were going on—which oddly enhanced the stammering writer's image rather than destroying it, writers then popularly believed to be exempt from conventional social conduct—Gerald Haxton, Maugham's homosexual lover, was indicted on several counts of gross indency. Haxton was acquitted and left for America. He returned three years later but was deported as a security risk; he was thought to be in the employ of a foreign intelligence service, one not named.

All of this brought too much attention on Maugham who resigned from the SIS in February 1916. He moved back to Geneva where he sporadically continued working as an unpaid secret agent for SIS while writing plays and stories. He realized he was ineffective as a spy and ended his relationship with Wallinger in May 1916, replaced by Edward Knoblock, an American who was also a playwright. By this time Maugham concluded that his days as a spy were over but he was to reenter the espionage arena once more, surprisingly entrusted with a mission that could have had world-shaking consequences.

Maugham married Syrie Wellcome in May 1917 in Jersey City. In the following month he received a call from William Wiseman of the SIS who had been gassed on the Western Front in 1915 and had entered the SIS to head its offices in New York. There Wiseman had monitored pro-German activities and attempts to sabotage war shipments to England. Wiseman explained to Maugham that the war in

Russia was going badly and the West feared that if the Russian war effort collapsed one of the many political internal forces assailing the Czar's shaky government would take over and sue for peace with Germany, allowing the Germans to shift enormous forces on the Eastern Front to the Western Front and overwhelm the democracies.

"The long and short of it," wrote Maugham later, "was that I should go to Russia and keep the Russians in the war." Maugham was stunned. He was a successful playwright and author but he was no diplomat and understood little of Russian politics or its chaotic social situation. He knew that a socialist, Alexander Kerensky, had taken over the government and that Czar Nicholas II and his family were being held incommunicado.

Maugham accepted the assignment only on the provision that he receive a substantial salary and expenses, remembering how he had worked for meager wages as an agent in Switzerland. SIS and the American government each provided Maugham with $75,000 to use in support of Kerensky with the promise of more funds to come. Maughan arrived in Petrograd in August 1917. He was received coldly by the British Ambassador, Sir George Buchanan, who thought that Maugham was unacceptable as a secret agent and special envoy.

Finding it difficult to get an audience with the much-harrassed Kerensky, Maugham busied himself by setting up a Slav press bureau headed by Thomas Masaryk who would, following World War I, become president of the newly-created Czechoslovakia. He was able to rekindle his association with one of his former mistresses, Alexandra "Sasha" Kropotkin, the daughter of former anarchist Prince Peter Kropotkin, who had been living in exile in London where Maugham had met her.

Alexandra Kropotkin was a favorite with the Kerensky government and it was she who introduced Maugham to Kerensky after the writer gave a sumptuous party at the Medvied, Petrograd's finest restaurant, where Kerensky was the guest of honor. Maugham gave a party at the restaurant once a week, providing Kerensky and his ministers with the best vodka and caviar available, impresssing the Russian leader with the wealth at his disposal.

Maugham informed Kerensky that the West was willing to finance his government and perhaps might even provide armed forces to make sure that Russia stayed in the war. Kerensky did not respond directly to this proposal but simply went off on political tirades. Maugham later wrote: "I think Kerensky must have supposed that I was more important than I really was for he came to Sasha's apartment on several occasions and, walking up and down the room, harangued me as though I were at a public meeting two hours at a time."

Kerensky appeared to have no specific plan to keep Russia in the war. He was more concerned with Bolshevik plots, and those from the right led by White

Russian General Lavr Konilov, to seize his government. Conditions in Russia worsened and Maugham, desperate to save the situation for the West, wired Wiseman on October 16, 1917, that he would need $500,000 to finance a program of propaganda and covert action to keep Kerensky in power.

While waiting for a reply, Maugham, on October 31, was summoned to Kerensky's office where Kerensky gave him an urgent secret message to deliver personally to Lloyd George, Prime Minister of England. In it, Kerensky begged for guns and ammunition so that his troops could continue the war against Germany (as well as put down the Bolshevik attack that was expected at any minute). Failing to receive help from the West, Kerensky stressed to Maugham, "I don't see how we can go on. Of course, I don't say that to the people. I always say that we shall continue [the war] whatever happens, but unless I have something to tell my army it's impossible."

The reason why Kerensky did not convey his message through official sources was because he did not trust the British and American ambassadors to fully grasp the political situation he was facing. He saw them as identifying "with the old regime," that of the czar. Before Maugham left Kerensky suggested that both ambassadors be replaced quickly.

Immediately traveling to Oslo where a British destroyer was waiting for him, Maugham sailed to Scotland. There he boarded a train that had been held for him and, on the following morning, he was at 10 Downing Street to meet with the Prime Minister. Maugham was terrified that his stammer would ruin any convincing plea he might offer on behalf of the Kerensky government, so when the stern-faced Lloyd George entered the room, the author/spy merely handed him a carefully-written note he had prepared in advance, one that summarized the desperate situation and Kerensky's urgent request for guns and ammunition.

Lloyd George studied the note, then handed it back to Maugham, saying: "I can't do that."

Stunned, Maughan managed to ask: "What shall I tell Kerensky?"

"Just that I can't do that," replied the Prime Minister matter-of-factly. He seemed annoyed and added tersely: "I'm afraid that I must bring this conversation to an end. I have a cabinet meeting I must go to." Lloyd George shook Maugham's hand and politely said goodbye.

Kerensky's government was overthrown on November 7, 1917, and Kerensky himself fled Russia just ahead of Bolshevik assassination squads hunting him. He managed to slip over the Finnish border dressed as a woman. Maugham's secret mission ended and so, too, did his role as a secret agent and spy. He would go on to write excellent books such as *The Moon and Sixpence*, 1919, and *The Razor's Edge*, 1944. In the 1920s, he moved to the south of France, buying a villa on the French Riviera where he lived until 1939 when Germany threatened France. He returned to that villa to live out his life, which ended on December 15, 1965, when he died in a Nice hospital.

Maugham's brief service as a secret agent remained a distinctive memory for him, one that elevated his sense of excitement and the idea that he was doing something important. While trying to save Kerensky's government (naive as he and the British government were at that time in dealing with the insidious Bolsheviks), he emphasized the importance of his work when writing from Russia in 1917 to a friend: "It seems incredible that one of these days we shall all settle down again to normal existence and read the fat, peaceful *Times* every morning and eat porridge for breakfast and marmalade. But, my dear, we shall be broken relics of a dead era, on the shelf all dusty and musty."

MAY, ALLAN NUNN
Soviet Spy in England ▪ (1912–   )

A NATIVE OF ENGLAND, MAY ATTENDED TRINITY College at Cambridge, that hotbed of Soviet spies that spawned the likes of Donald Maclean, Kim Philby, Anthony Blunt, and Guy Burgess. He received his Ph.D. from that institution, working as a physicist. May had joined the Communist Party while at college and a short time later became a Soviet agent.

In May 1942, the physicist was assigned to the secret Tube Alloy Project, working at the Cavendish laboratory in Cambridge. In January 1943, May was

British scientist Allan Nunn May, who stole atomic secrets for Russia.

sent to Canada, working on atomic bomb research in Ottawa. Once there, he was contacted by a Lieutenant Angelov, a representative of a Russian spymaster, Colonel Nikolai Zabotin. May, while using the cover name "Alek," began to funnel information to Angelov who used the cover name of "Baxter" when they met.

In January 1944, May visited the atomic research labs in Chicago where he met and highly impressed Major General Leslie R. Groves who was in charge of the ultra-top-secret "Manhattan Project," a cover name for the development of the atomic bomb.

In the following April, May again journeyed from Canada to Chicago, spending two weeks on a minor experiment at the Argonne Laboratory where the original atomic pile using graphite was located, along with a later pile employing heavy water as a slowing-down material. He was back in August 1944 to meet with officials at the Chicago laboratory on setting up a pile in Montreal where atomic research was ongoing but nowhere near as successful as that occuring in the U.S.

May's fourth visit to the U.S. in 1944 occured between September 25 and October 30. During that period he conferred with top nuclear scientists about the construction of the atomic bomb but only a few details of these meetings were ever made public. It is certain, however, that all of May's visits to the U.S. were contrived so that he could steal information on atomic research and pass these secrets to the Soviets.

May was badly paid for his traitorous espionage. When he handed over the first plutonium sample to Angelov, he received $200 and two bottles of whiskey. The second sample he turned over profited him $500. These were the only two known payments May received but he went on spying for the Soviets against Russia's World War II allies.

When Igor Gouzenko fled to the arms of Canada, exposing the vast Soviet spy rings in Canada and the U.S., May immediately opted to return to England where he promised he would continue his espionage efforts for Russia. Before he left, May made arrangements with Zabotin to contact another Soviet spymaster in front of the British Museum in London on October 17, 1945. May, for whatever reason, failed to keep that appointment, one that was known to MI5.

May returned to teaching, lecturing in physics at King's College. His tranquil world was disturbed on February 15, 1946, the day in which all of the suspects on Gouzenko's spy lists were rounded up. On that day Lieutenant Colonel Leonard Burt, who headed up the Special Branch of Scotland Yard, which worked hand-in-glove with MI5's counterintelligence operations, called on Dr. May at Shell-Max House in London where the scientist was then working.

Burt was polite, stating that he was making some routine inquiries and, in the course of their tea-sipping conversation, he informed May that he knew he was supposed to meet someone outside the British Museum but that he did not keep the appointment. He waited for some minutes while the scientist

thought over the implications. May then dully announced: "I decided to wash my hands of the whole business."

Before Burt could formally arrest him, May surprised the spycatcher by telling him he was going to write out a confession immediately. With that, the always precise May hastily wrote out a statement and signed it, turning this over to Burt. It was a clever way in which May correctly believed he could avoid making any revelations other than admitting to his own treason and violation of the Official Secrets Act.

Thus, Allan Nunn May explained that he had given secret information to a foreign power that was allied with England and America in a common cause, claiming he had violated no laws and had maintained his ethical belief that no one country, especially the U.S. (for which he had a decided hatred), could alone possess such a terrible weapon as the atomic bomb. He stuck to this story, refusing to name names or give any information other than what he revealed in his confession, which had been apparently well thought out in advance of his possibly being identified as a Soviet agent while following strict espionage procedures through his unwillingness to compromise the Russian spy networks in which he so secretly labored.

May demanded a jury trial, which began on May 1, 1946, and in which his lawyer portrayed him as "a man of honor who had only done what he believed to be right." Cleverly, May then pleaded guilty, before evidence could be presented against him. His confession, then, contrived to portray him as a hero, was all that remained as a document of his treason.

May was sent to Wakefield Prison in Yorkshire, and released in January 1953. He was followed from Yorkshire to the home of his sister-in-law in London by a horde of newsmen but he refused to make any comment.

May afterward vanished behind the Iron Curtain. It was later contended that this mysterious little scientist was the most effective Soviet agent the KGB ever recruited and could have been a spymaster himself, supervising the spy efforts of Klaus Fuchs, England's most notorious turncoat in atomic research.

[ALSO SEE: *Anthony Blunt; Guy Burgess; Klaus Fuchs; Igor Gouzenko; KGB; Donald Maclean; MI5; Kim Philby; Nikolai Zabotin*]

McCARTHY, JOSEPH RAYMOND
American Spyhunter ▪ (1908–1957)

U.S. SENATOR JOSEPH McCARTHY, FROM WHOM THE term "McCarthyism" stems, gave America a four-year witch-hunting nightmare it will never forget. Born in Grand Chute, Wisconsin, McCarthy had a rather pedestrian youth and an unspectacular beginning in politics. He rose to become a state circuit judge in 1940, a position he held for two years. He served in the air force in the Pacific theater during World War II, earning the nickname "Tailgunner Joe." In 1946, with considerable support behind him, he was elected a U.S. senator from Wisconsin.

Beginning his freshman year in the Senate in 1947, little was heard from McCarthy until 1950. He then erupted like a volcano, spewing forth sweeping allegations and widespread accusations of Americans thought to be working for the Communist domination of the world. A heavy drinker, McCarthy had a mercurial personality, one susceptible to the suggestion of conspiracy. Knowing this, the master of Washington conspiracies, FBI Chief J. Edgar Hoover, began to feed his own apprehensions into the bombastic politician.

To be sure, Americans acting as Soviet agents such as the Rosenbergs, David Greenglass, Harry Gold, Judith Coplon, and others gave vent to the belief that Russian spy networks honeycombed the U.S. The allegations of Whittaker Chambers against Alger Hiss and others firmly entrenched the conviction that the American government was awash with Soviet spies. Hoover played on these public facts and their attendant fears with McCarthy, intimating to the politician that the State Department and even the CIA (which Hoover had always envied and opposed as competitive with his FBI) were crawling with Russian spies.

McCarthy was suddenly holding press conferences, waving sheafs of paper that purported to list the names of countless spies in the U.S. government. He named some names and set off incredible panic in the American film community, throughout business, industry, and even in the media. He was forever on the front pages of America's newspapers labeling this or that person as a Communist agent.

Many suspects were summoned before the House of Un-American Activities Committee to answer McCarthy's charges. Some were guilty of Communist affiliations but most were innocent persons who had merely flirted with Communism at one time or another. That mattered little to the witch-hunting McCarthy who became obsessed with exposing Soviet agents. To be accused by McCarthy was to be instantly ruined and by 1952 everyone knew it. "McCarthyism" swept the nation like an unchecked plague.

It was obvious to CIA Director Allen Dulles that it would only be a matter of time before the victim-searching McCarthy got around to his agency. He made preparations by putting Lyman Kirkpatrick and Richard Helms in charge of CIA defenses. Those inside the agency who might be considered security risks for any reason were let go.

One CIA employee McCarthy selected for branding as a Communist sympathizer was Cord Meyer. He had a superlative service record, having lost an eye as a Marine officer battling the Japanese for Eniwetok Island in the Pacific. Following World War II, Meyer had become president of the United World Federalists, an organization working for a world federation. He was also active at that time in the work of the American Veterans Committee. When Communists attempted to take over these organizations, Meyer quit the groups and later joined the CIA.

After McCarthy pointed accusingly at Meyer, the CIA officially denied his allegations. Meyer submitted a 100,000-word document that the agency helped him prepare and one that precisely detailed his life, as well as demonstrated his lifelong opposition to communism or any other form of dictatorship. Meyer was nevertheless suspended but was reinstated through the help of influential friends. He became one of the most powerful men in the CIA.

McCarthy steamed on, raging wildly about Communist spies to the point where his maniacal diatribes branded him an unstable grand inquisitor. Anyone who opposed his brutish methods was labelled a Communist by McCarthy and when, in 1954, he branded high military officers as disloyal, President Eisenhower openly opposed him. His full censure by the U.S. Senate followed that same year and McCarthy was eliminated as a political force. He remained in office, drinking himself into stupors and dying in 1957.

McCarthy never did produce the documented lists of the "thousands of spies" he claimed were infesting the U.S. government. But then, his mentor, J. Edgar Hoover, who had promised to supply that information to him for years, never provided those lists. As Hoover knew full well, they didn't exist. Hoover used McCarthy as a pawn in his drive to expose those he mistrusted or those he believed would threaten his own power, as well as support his own mania for the "Red Menace." J. Edgar Hoover was the true author of "McCarthyism."

[ALSO SEE: *Whittaker Chambers; CIA; Judith Coplon; Allen Dulles; FBI; Harry Gold; David Greenglass; Richard Helms; Alger Hiss; J. Edgar Hoover; Julius and Ethel Rosenberg*]

McPARLAND, JAMES
U.S. Labor Spy ▪ (1844–1919)

McPARLAND (OR McPARLAN) WAS ONE OF THE most successful labor spies in American history. Like the men he spied upon, McParland was an Irish immigrant. After arriving in Chicago from Ulster, he worked as a wagon driver, lumberman, store clerk, and barkeeper. The Great Chicago Fire of October 9, 1871, burned his saloon to the ground and McParland applied for a job at the Pinkerton Detective Agency. He had known Allan Pinkerton in earlier years and the detective had just the job for him.

The Philadelphia Reading Railroad had hired Pinkerton to crush a violent Irish secret society known as the Molly Maguires. The Mollies had been disrupting commerce, blowing up trains shipping coal, as well as the mines themselves in Pennsylvania in an effort to improve the lot of Irish coal miners. Pinkerton's assignment to McParland was to infiltrate the Mollies and identify their leaders so they could be brought to justice.

In 1873, McParland, posing as "James McKenna," an itinerant worker with a criminal past, roamed the mining towns of Pennsylvania. He was admitted to the fraternal Ancient Order of Hibernians and this gave him entry into the inner circle of Molly leaders.

McParland met the most fierce and dedicated labor terrorist of the era, John "Black Jack" Kehoe, the 43-year-old leader of the Mollies. McParland got work in a mine so he would work alongside Kehoe and others.

Not until 1876 did McParland's labor espionage bear results. In that year dozens of Mollies were rounded up and McParland, discarding his pose as "McKenna," testified against the ringleaders. Because of his testimony, Kehoe and nine others were convicted and hanged for their crimes.

Public opinion was strongly divided. There were those who championed Pinkerton and his man McParland as courageous defenders of the American way. They had exposed and crushed a lethal and criminal secret society bent on anarchy. Others believed that Pinkerton was nothing more than a stooge for the robber barons who oppressed immigrant workers and that McParland, instead of being a hero, was nothing more than an *agent provocateur*.

History had the final decision. In 1979, a century after his execution, John Kehoe received a full

Molly Maguires going to the gallows in 1877.

posthumous pardon because, the courts decided, his conviction had been obtained through collusion between the coal companies and the Pinkerton Detective Agency. Yet, a century earlier, McParland was hailed as a hero and, as a reward for his services, was appointed to head the Pinkerton office in Denver. It would be another thirty years before McParland again came into public prominence.

At that time, January 1905, the Western Federation of Miners was thought to be behind a campaign of sabotage and terrorism that had taken the life of Idaho Governor Frank Steunenberg who had sided with mine owners in their labor disputes. Harry Orchard, a labor terrorist, had been arrested, sticks of dynamite, dynamiter's tools, and a sawed-off shotgun found in his room.

McParland was assigned the task of compelling Orchard to confess. He had Orchard placed in solitary confinement, then interrogated him for days until Orchard confessed, naming his sponsors as labor leaders William D. "Big Bill" Haywood, Charles H. Moyers, and George A. Pettibone. These men were arrested and later faced sensational trials. Clarence Darrow defended the labor leaders in an exhausting trial and won their acquittal, despite Orchard's lone testimony against his former bosses. Orchard himself was sentenced to death but his sentence was commuted to life imprisonment.

[ALSO SEE: *Allan Pinkerton*]

MEANS, GASTON BULLOCK
U.S. Spy and Swindler • (1879–1938)

FEW AMERICAN SPIES APPROACHED THE FANTASTIC exploits of Gaston Means, who was a spy by instinct and a con man at heart. The fourth child of William Gaston and Corrallie Bullock, wealthy North Carolina landowners, Means left the University of North Carolina in 1898 a year before taking his degree. He became a salesman or "drummer" for a large textile firm, traveling throughout the East Coast. In 1910, Means grew tired of sales and sought adventure by becoming a detective in the employ of the famous William J. Burns.

To Burns, the ever-inventive Means was "the greatest natural detective ever known." Means also felt that he was one of the most underpaid detectives working for the Burns Detective Agency and to augment his meager income in August 1914, the beginning of World War I, he went to Captain Boy-Ed, a naval attaché at the Germany Embassy. Means had known Boy-Ed for some years, learning that the German was really a spymaster. He easily convinced Boy-Ed to hire him as a spy.

Means told Boy-Ed that he could provide the Germans with important information on Allied shipping and to "embarrass British commerce," as he later quaintly put it, through his contacts as a detective for Burns. He was hired at the weekly salary of $700, which was shortly increased to $1,000 a week, a princely sum in those days. Always the entrepreneur, Means offered his services to U.S. Army intelligence, saying that he would spy on the Germans, for a price, of course, and transport secret documents to any destination desired. U.S. intelligence paid him about the same as the Germans were paying him. With his inflated income, Gaston Means lived high and handsome, renting a spacious Park Avenue apartment in New York and wining and dining expensive chorus girls.

Impersonating the spies of three countries, Means dreamed up the most incredible stories to thoroughly confuse his employers. At one point, Means showed up with a number of empty trunks, informing Army intelligence that he had unearthed several trunks of secret documents but before he could bring them to headquarters at least a half dozen agents from an unspecified country jumped him, making off with the secrets and leaving him with the empty trunks. One report had it that "the flaw in this story was that the trunks weighed the same when delivered without documents as they did when supposedly crammed with secret papers."

Means supposedly quit the employ of the Germans when America entered World War I in 1917 and became an exclusive spy for the U.S. Later, this most flamboyant spy involved himself in stealing a $150,000 inheritance of a wealthy widow, Maude King, whose suspicious death was found a suicide; officials suspected Means but they could not prove murder. He went on to become an agent for the Bureau of Investigation under the administration of William J. Burns, a cover for his work as a bagman for the corrupt Harding Administration. He made payoffs and bribes for politicians illegally selling off government lands.

J. Edgar Hoover, who would become chief of the FBI in 1924, despised Means and knew him for the charlatan he was. By that time, Means had moved on to greener pastures. Means had stolen the diaries of Nan Britton, mistress of the married (and by then deceased) President Warren G. Harding. He helped Britton write a scandalous book, *The President's Daughter*, which claimed that Harding had sired an illegitimate daughter through his liaison with Britton. The outlandish Means went further, writing another book, *The Strange Death of President Harding*, in which he claimed that, after learning about her husband's affair with Miss Britton, Mrs. Harding murdered him by poisoning.

Means would attempt any scam, no matter how outrageous it might be. He sold protection to bootleggers, saying that he was a Prohibition Agent who could make sure their rum-running boats would not be stopped by the Coast Guard for a handsome slice of their profits. When he learned that Mrs. Finley Shepherd, a wealthy woman in Tarrytown, New York, had established a committee to combat communism, he wrote her a letter threatening to destroy her and her entire family, signing this black missive: "Agents from Moscow."

Means then turned up at Mrs. Shepherd's doorstep, introducing himself as the world's greatest counter-intelligence agent. He had learned that she was being threatened by murderous Russian agents. He, Gaston Bullock Means, would track down these vultures and bring them to justice. Mrs. Shepherd glady paid Means $1,000 to seek out the Communist agents. After mulcting her out of a small fortune, he reported that he had finally trailed the Soviet thugs to their lair in New Jersey and shot them all dead. Their bodies, all fifteen of them, were layed out in a Newark warehouse. Would Mrs. Shepherd care to view the corpses before they were shipped back to Moscow for burial? No, she would not, said Mrs. Shepherd, thanking the great spyhunter before he waddled his heavyset body away with a wide smile pushing up his dimpled cheeks.

Using the same scam against firms and wealthy individuals, Means was able to pocket tens of thousands of dollars. This went on until 1932 when Means seized upon the tragedy of the Lindbergh kidnapping to make his biggest score. The small son of Charles A. Lindbergh, America's greatest flyer, was kidnapped and police seemed helpless to recover the child and track down the abductors. Means heard that social gadfly Evalyn Walsh McLean, owner of the Hope Diamond and one of the world's wealthiest women, wanted to help find the child.

Means offered the heiress his services and was paid handsomely to go on wild goose chases. He finally told his employer that he had found the nest of kidnappers and that they had agreed to release the child for $100,000. She gave him the cash, plus $4,000 for his own expenses. Nothing happened. When Means told McLean's lawyers that the deal had fallen through they demanded the return of the $100,000. Means looked puzzled. "Why, don't *you* have it?" he said. "I gave it to a representative of your firm. Funny, too. When I demanded a receipt, he only shrugged. May I now have a receipt for the $100,000?"

This ploy did not work with the lawyers nor in court where Means was convicted of cruelly swindling the heiress. He was sent to prison to serve a fifteen-year term. While serving his term, Means contacted J. Edgar Hoover, offering to solve a number of sensational unsolved federal crimes. Hoover responded with two words: "Not interested." The FBI chief was interested enough in finding out what Means had done with the McLean money before he was sent to prison.

Hearing that Means had suffered a heart attack and might die behind bars, Hoover sent two agents to see him at the Medical Center for prisoners in Springfield, Missouri, on December 12, 1938. The two agents sat at Means' bedside. The heavyset ex-spy, ex-detective lay flat, sheets to his armpits, his large pink hands folded over his ample chest.

"We heard you buried the McLean money, Gaston," one of the agents said.

"Where did you bury it?" inquired the other.

Means arched an eyebrow. "What's in it for me?"

"If you cooperate, maybe, when you get well, we can get some time taken off your sentence."

Means closed his eyes, smiled weakly, and sighed: "Not interested." He then promptly died.

[ALSO SEE: *FBI; J. Edgar Hoover*]

MENZIES, STEWART GRAHAM
British Spymaster ▪ (1890–1968)

BORN IN LONDON ON JANUARY 30, 1890, MENZIES was the son of wealthy John Graham Menzies and Susannah West. He went to Sandhurst and then into the army, joining the Grenadier Guards. During World War I, he served in France and was injured in a 1915 gas attack.

Unable to serve on the front lines, Menzies entered British intelligence and served with distinction. He remained in the SIS (which later became MI6) after the war. In 1939, only three months after the outbreak of World War II, Menzies was named chief of the British Secret Intelligence Service.

In addition to an expanding intelligence service, Menzies also supervised the Government Code and Cipher School at Bletchley. Menzies gave great importance to codes and through his personal efforts (by going to Poland in 1939 to retrieve a captured German Enigma code machine), the top German codes were broken. This breakthrough, along with that of American William Friedman's breaking of the Japanese code, greatly contributed to the Allied victory. (The breaking of the Enigma machine codes allowed SIS to decrypt as many as 100,000 top-secret German messages a month by 1943.) In that he loved the obtaining of intelligence rather than its analysis, he was much like his American counterpart, Allen Dulles, whom he met when Dulles was an OSS chief in Switzerland and who later headed the CIA.

A club man who was married four times, Menzies lived a rather lonely life with few intimates. He was credited with being one of the few intelligence chiefs who could maintain a working relationship with the demanding Winston Churchill during World War II.

Following the war, however, Menzies found his position considerably weakened by the traitorous actions of Guy Burgess, Donald Maclean, and Kim

British SIS director Stewart Graham Menzies.

Philby. He resigned his post a short time after these Soviet agents were exposed in 1956, and he went into permanent retirement, dying on May 29, 1968.

[ALSO SEE: *Guy Burgess; CIA; Allen Dulles; William Friedman; Donald Maclean; MI6; OSS; Kim Philby; SIS*]

METTERNICH, CLEMENS VON
Austrian Spymaster ▪ (1773–1859)

BORN IN COBLENZ, METTERNICH STUDIED INTERnational relations at the University of Strasbourg, with the intent of following his father's footsteps who was a diplomat for the then mighty Austrian Empire. He became one of the finest diplomats serving the court of Emperor Francis II during the French Revolution and the rise of Napoleon Bonaparte.

A monarchist to the core, Metternich despised the leaders of the French Revolution and their savage executions of the aristocracy and the royalty. Because of this, he had an abiding hatred for all revolutionary theories and beliefs. He nevertheless proved to be a worthy opponent of the wiley Napoleon when he became the Austrian foreign minister in 1809.

Bonaparte had dissolved the Holy Roman Empire and was the most powerful man in Europe. Through his own secret intelligence service, Metternich was kept abreast of Napoleon's every move and much of the information his agents gathered helped to eventually bring down the tyrant.

Metternich's spy network also worked excellent results for him at the Congress of Vienna (1814–1815) which, following Napoleon's permanent exile to St. Helena, rearranged the map of Europe. The Austrian spymaster had all of the visiting members to the Congress watched day and night. His agents collected information on the heads of state attending the conference, especially the mystical and unpredictable Czar Alexander I of Russia.

By learning Alexander's secret desire for a "holy alliance" of European nations, Metternich was able to ingratiate himself to the Czar and persuade him, as well as all the other important heads of state, to accept his plan for a balance of power in Europe. For the next thirty years Metternich remained one of the most powerful men on the continent, his vast espionage network thriving until 1848 when a revolution in Austria forced him into exile.

MfS
East German Intelligence ▪ (1950–1989)

ESTABLISHED IN APRIL 1950, THE MfS FUNCTIONED as a vast and effective espionage network until the collapse of communism throughout Eastern Europe. Organized along the lines of the KGB, the MfS functioned as a surrogate to Soviet intelligence. Headquartered in East Berlin, the spy network was headed by the tough, shrewd General Markus Wolf, and it employed more than 5,000 agents throughout Germany at the peak of its powers.

The espionage activities of MfS were directed chiefly at West Germany and NATO. The impact of this expensive and sometimes unwieldy intelligence agency was never greater than in the late 1950s. In 1959 alone, almost 3,000 MfS agents were seized in West Germany.

[ALSO SEE: *Marcus Wolf*]

MI5
British Counterintelligence Agency • (1909–)

ONE OF THE MOST EFFECTIVE COUNTERINTELLIGENCE agencies in the world, MI5 (Military Intelligence, Department Five) was established in 1909 with Vernon Kell as its chief, a post he retained until 1940. MI5 is responsible for national security and operates much like America's Federal Bureau of Investigation. It is unlike the FBI in that it handles no criminal cases and has no authority to make arrests. All arrests decreed by MI5 are made by Scotland Yard's Special Branch, which also presents all evidence in court on MI5's behalf.

Although its functions can be traced as far back as the time of Daniel Defoe's country-wide spy system, MI5 was officially created as a department of military intelligence, stemming from the Haldane reforms of the British War Office in 1905. So much squabbling over control of military intelligence ensued that, on August 23, 1909, MI5 and SIS (Secret Intelligence Service, later called MI6) were created as separate departments. Despite their military labels, both MI5 and MI6 were removed from the War Office and came under the control of the Foreign Office.

Vernon Kell, the agency's first director, suggested MI5's creation, outlining how it was to control all national counterintelligence, while SIS was to handle all foreign intelligence. At that time, Kell had convincingly shown his superiors how Germany, in preparation for war, had already begun to establish a spy network in England. Kell demonstrated the vital need to establish a counterintelligence agency to deal with this spy network.

For more than thirty years Kell was the guiding light of MI5. He worked closely with Basil Thomson of Scotland Yard; their association produced dramatic results as they rounded up innumerable spies in England.

Unlike MI6, which can more easily cover its errors through silence, MI5 has been extremely vulnerable to criticism, because its operations are linked to internal affairs that can be scrutinized by the media. Most of MI5's problems occured after World War II when the press was able to penetrate some of its operations through breaking political scandals.

The defections of Guy Burgess, Donald Maclean, and Kim Philby raised suspicions that MI5's Director-General, Roger Hollis, a long-time friend of the defectors, had warned them that they had been identified as Soviet spies and allowed them to flee behind the Iron Curtain. Although Hollis was never charged with being part of that conspiracy, he resigned his post shortly after the scandal broke. It fell to Hollis' successor, Edward Martin Furnival Jones, to confront Hollis with MI5's suspicions. After interrogating Hollis, Furnival Jones was convinced that his former colleague was innocent.

In 1961, the Portland Spy case exposed MI5 operations to public view. The press obtained the details of a Soviet spy network headed by Gordon Lonsdale, who had access to Admiralty top secrets.

Another devastating public setback for MI5 was the notorious Profumo Affair. Following in the wake of the Portland Case, it was discovered that Secretary for War John Profumo, through a pair of high-class hookers, was associated with Soviet agent Eugene Ivanov. Scandal tracked MI5 into the modern era of electronic communications when Geoffrey Prime, a member of the British signals intelligence turned Soviet agent.

On the other hand, MI5's many successes have not been publicized and have been taken as silent triumphs. In times of crisis, the agency has performed with great effectiveness. It successfully smashed the German spy rings in England in the First and Second World Wars and, on the whole, proved more than a match for Soviet networks operating in England throughout the Cold War.

[ALSO SEE: *Guy Burgess; Daniel Defoe; FBI; Roger Hollis; Harry Houghton; Vernon Kell; Peter and Helen Kroger; Gordon Lonsdale; Donald Maclean; MI6; Kim Philby; Geoffrey Prime; Special Branch*]

MILITARU, NICOLAI
Rumanian Spy for Soviets • (1927–)

THE MUCH-HATED COMMUNIST PUPPET GOVERNMENT of Rumania, headed by Nicolae Ceausescu, was peopled by high-ranking Soviet agents, not the least of whom was the conniving General Nicolai Militaru. Ceausescu, who secretly allied himself with terrorist organizations headed by Libya's Muammar Qaddafi and the PLO's Yassir Arafat, was unknowingly and constantly under Soviet surveillance.

It was Militaru's job to monitor Ceausescu's political conduct and report to Moscow if the Rumanian tyrant deviated from party dictates. One of Ceausescu's favorite generals, Militaru had been a member of the Central Committee of the Rumanian Communist Party since 1969 and commander of the Bucharest region since 1970.

Militaru had Ceausescu's complete trust and was about to be named Deputy Minister of National Defense when Rumanian spymaster Ion Pacepa, chief of the Rumanian DIE (the equivalent of the KGB or CIA) unearthed the general's collusion with the Soviets. Pacepa presented his evidence against Militaru to Ceausescu just when the Rumanian dictator was about to sign the decree making the general Deputy Minister of Defense.

Militaru was removed from his posts and went into retirement but he was not further punished. Ceausescu feared that if he had the general murdered—as was the dictator's usual reaction to those who opposed him—the Soviets would retaliate.

Not until after Ceausescu's removal a decade later, in 1989, did Militaru reemerge. By then Rumania had disavowed communism but Militaru, during the anti-Ceausescu protests, had quickly taken control of the army, which backed the demonstrators, a subtle move dictated from Moscow to oust the tyrant Ceausescu while secretly keeping a Communist toehold in the Rumanian government. Militaru remained in high-ranking positions, feeding the Soviets secret information until the country finally abandoned communism altogether.

[ALSO SEE: *Muammar Qaddafi*]

MI6
British Intelligence ▪ (1911–   )

MI6 (MILITARY INTELLIGENCE, DEPARTMENT SIX) evolved from the British Secret Intelligence Service (SIS), which was established in 1911 under its first director, Mansfield Cumming whose initial "C" became the pseudonym for the head of the service (and later satirized by Ian Fleming in his James Bond novels). It operates much the same way America's CIA functions, as an organization responsible for gathering intelligence on a worldwide basis, conducting all manner of espionage against enemies or potential enemies.

Also like the CIA, MI6 has no jurisdiction within Great Britain, the responsibility of handling counter-intelligence belongs to MI5. In reality, MI6 or SIS dates back to Elizabethan times when Sir Francis Walsingham became the first British spymaster, ferreting out plots, conspiracies, and intrigues against his sovereign, Elizabeth.

Oddly, there is a polite pretense that MI6 does not really exist, although this ultra-secret organization is supported by enormous government funds, as much as £70 million a year. MI6 came into its own under Cumming, a shrewd spymaster of the old school who stopped at nothing in obtaining secrets vital to British security. Cumming, who had a wooden leg, enjoyed startling his agents. On occasion, to get the attention of an agent or aide, he would suddenly drive a knife into his wooden leg to emphasize a point. Those not knowing of his disability were dumbfounded at the sight of seeing the knife protruding from Cumming's leg while he went on blithely talking.

The efficiency of MI6 is not easily evaluated because of the super-secret operations it conducts. During World War I, MI6 or SIS proved to be very effective, uncovering and exposing a vast German spy ring headed by Gustav Steinhauer and, for the most part, outwitting the military spies throughout the world that were directed by German spymaster Walther Nicolai. The organization's image was tarnished in World War II when two of its agents were abducted at Venlo in the Netherlands in 1939 through a clever Abwehr ruse conducted by SD spymaster Walter Schellenberg.

So embarrassing was the Venlo Incident, as it came to be called, that MI6's covert operations in Nazi-held European countries during World War II were turned over to the newly-created SOE (Special Operations Executive). MI6 fared better during the Cold War but it saw many setbacks when the KGB outwitted its schemes. One of its finest Cold War coups was the way in which MI6 was able to obtain top secret documents from Oleg Penkovsky, a colonel of Russian military intelligence at the Center in Moscow.

MI6, however, bore the stain of compromise when, in 1963, one of its much-valued agents, Kim Philby, defected to Russia before he was publicly revealed to have been a double agent for the KGB, one who had, with fellow traitors Donald Maclean and Guy Burgess, been stealing British secrets for decades. Because of Philby's success in turning over MI6 secrets to the Russians, the organization was thoroughly revamped.

As late as the 1980s, MI6 was under severe criticism, chiefly because it was an old boys' club of uppercrust gentlemen who were recruited from elitist colleges that had proven suspect as to their political affiliations and patriotic fidelity. Labor politician Roy Hattersley stated at that time: "The failure of the security services' present organization stems largely from inbreeding, limited field of recruitment and its traditional attitudes, and the complacency that comes from the feeling that since its entire administration is cloaked in secrecy, its organizational failures can always be swept under the carpet."

Prime Minister Margaret Thatcher, however, did not yield to special "outside controls" of MI6, such as the watchdog committees that oversee CIA operations. Her policy was unbending: MI6 would answer only to the Cabinet in order to preserve the services' integrity. MI6 did, however, adopt a more liberal attitude in its recruitment, selecting young applicants from a broader academic spectrum, emphasizing the need for those fluent in foreign languages.

[ALSO SEE: *Abwehr; Guy Burgess; Wilhelm Canaris; CIA; Mansfield Cumming; William J. Donovan; Ian Fleming; Donald Maclean; MI5; Walther Nicolai; OSS; Oleg Penkovsky; Kim Philby; Walter Schellenberg; SIS; SOE; Venlo Incident; Francis Walsingham*]

MIXED BUREAU
Allied Counterintelligence in World War I ▪ (1914–1918)

THE BRITISH AND FRENCH INTELLIGENCE AND COUN-terintelligence services mounted a combined operation called the Mixed Bureau in 1914 that screened all refugees fleeing from the German advance into Belgium and northern France in 1914. Headquartered in Folkstone, on the Kent coast of England, across from Pas de Calais, the Bureau's agents skillfully examined refugees and picked out German agents in the fleeing masses, as well as gleaning a good deal of valuable information on German troop movements. The Bureau also selected and trained several Allied agents who performed priceless service during World War I, notably the heroic Louise de Bettignies.

[ALSO SEE: *Louise de Bettignies*]

MONAT, PAWEL
Polish Spy for Soviets ▪ (1920–   )

BORN IN GALICIA, MONAT WAS INDUCTED INTO THE Russian Army when Russia seized his country as part of the 1939 Non-Aggression Pact it signed with Hitler's Germany. He fought the Germans throughout World War II and helped to liberate Warsaw. Following World War II, Monat attended staff college and then entered Polish intelligence.

In 1955, Monat was sent to the Polish Embassy in Washington as a military attaché with the KGB assignment of spying upon U.S. military installations. While in the U.S., Monat was impressed with the freedom enjoyed by U.S. citizens, the free press, and the freedom of speech. Though he continued his espionage in New York where he controlled pickups and drops from other agents in the New York Public Library, Monat resolved to defect to the West.

After returning to Warsaw in 1958, he wangled a visit to Vienna in the following year. At that time he went to the American Embassy, asking for asylum. He was taken to the U.S., provided the CIA with all he knew about Polish intelligence, and was then given a new identity before disappearing somewhere in America.

MONTGAILLARD, COMTE DE (MAURICE ROCQUES)
French Spy in Napoleonic Era ▪ (1761–1835)

FEW SPIES WERE EVER AS BOLD AS THE DOUBLE-dealing Comte de Montgaillard, a secret agent who changed sides so quickly and so many times it was almost impossible for those who dealt with him to know if he was friend or enemy. A native of Languedoc, France, Montgaillard had a shady past. He was born Maurice Rocques of low peasant ancestry but he had a quick wit and an inventive mind. An adventurer with a glib tongue, Montgaillard did not believe the French Revolution would be successful. He opted to become a spy for the doomed King Louis XVI, planning to spirit the King and Marie Antoinette out of the country before they could be executed.

As a royalist agent, Montgaillard soon learned that he had chosen the wrong side. When the King was imprisoned, he fled Paris along with thousands of other royalists and was condemned in absentia by the revolutionary tribunal in Paris. A master of compromise, Montgaillard offered to spy for the revolutionaries, convincing their leader, Maximillien de Robespierre, that he could be of service. During Robespierre's reign of terror, Montgaillard went to London where he pretended to be an escaped royalist.

After an interview with British Prime Minister William Pitt, Montgaillard was accepted as a royalist and was entrusted with a mission to Louis Joseph de Bourbon, prince de Condé, the leading French royalist in Europe who maintained an army on the Rhine. His assignment was to persuade revolutionary French generals to side with Condé. One of these was General Charles Pichegru who had fought for the Revolution but quickly grew disenchanted with its violent attempt to wipe out the nobility.

Condé allowed Montgaillard to select his own agents to approach Pichegru and he sent Louis Fauche-Borel, an ardent royalist, to see the general in an attempt to win him back to the cause of monarchy. Fauche-Borel failed to convince Pichegru to change sides and Montaillard, playing both sides, exposed his own agent to the revolutionaries as a royalist spy.

Montgaillard finally concluded that the royalists were ineffective and could not regain power. He returned to Paris and again announced his loyalty to the Revolution. As a revolutionary spy, Montgaillard went on betraying royalists who were led to the guillotine. When Napoleon rose to power, Montgaillard sided with the Corsican, becoming an agent for Joseph Fouché, Bonaparte's police chief and spymaster.

Montgaillard flourished thereafter, being granted a yearly salary of 14,000 francs as a spy for Fouché. When Bonaparte was defeated and driven into final exile, Montgaillard, ever the survivor, swore his allegiance to King Louis XVIII, somehow managing to convince the royalists that he had remained loyal to the monarchy and had worked on its behalf for the more than two decades it was out of power. He was given a handsome pension. The revolution of 1830, which permanently unseated the Bourbons, also spelled the end of Montgaillard's comfortable life. He was thoroughly distrusted as a renegade who swore allegiance to any side that was winning and he ended his days in miserable poverty.

[ALSO SEE: *Louis Fauche-Borel; Joseph Fouché*]

MOODY, JAMES
American Spy for England ▪ (1744–1809)

MOODY WAS A NEW JERSEY FARMER WHO REMAINED a secret loyalist at the beginning of the American Revolution. He refused to swear an oath to his state in 1777, which caused him to be watched as a possible traitor to the revolutionary cause. He came into the open when fleeing to the British lines, joining the ranks of a brigade led by another New Jersey Tory, Courtlandt Skinner.

When it was apparent to his neighbors that Moody had not only joined Skinner at Staten Island but was recruiting other loyalists in New Jersey, state officials confiscated his farm and branded him a traitor. He earned that title with a vengeance. In 1778, Moody led a small contingent of men into upstate New York, far behind American lines, to contact Tory frontier fighter Colonel John Butler, with whom the British had lost contact.

Moody found Butler and returned to report that the Tory force under Butler was continuing to attack American outposts and encampments. In the following year, Moody raided American settlements in New Jersey, his men burning towns and capturing supplies and livestock. The daring Moody also became a spy, accepting the most dangerous missions. At one point, disguised as a bearded revolutionary soldier, he slipped into George Washington's camp to learn American military plans.

In 1780, Moody tried to kidnap New Jersey Governor William Livingston, but the plot collapsed after one of Moody's men was captured and revealed the abduction plan. Before Moody could return to British lines he was tracked down and captured in Englishtown. Imprisoned, he faced certain death as a spy but during a violent rainstorm he was left unattended and escaped the small jail in which he was being held.

Returning to British lines, Moody remained undaunted. He continued to lead savage raids into American territory and his name became synony-mous with that of Simon Girty, Benedict Arnold, and other traitors and renegades. He specialized in waylaying American mail couriers and, on one occasion, managed to obtain dispatches from Washington to Jean Baptiste de Vimeur, comte de Rochambeau, who headed the French Army in America, allied with Washington's forces.

As the British cause began to collapse, Moody continued to scheme against the Americans. He planned to enter Philadelphia and steal all of the official papers of the Continental Congress, including the Declaration of Independence but before he could act, the Patriots learned of the plot and put the documents under heavy guard.

After Cornwallis surrendered at Yorktown in 1781, Moody realized he had no future in America. He sailed to London in the following year where he penned his autobiography, concentrating on his wild exploits during the war. It did not sell well and in 1784, Moody made an impassioned appeal to the British government, asking reimbursement for the loss of his lands in America, forfeited because of his unswerving loyalty to the crown. He was given a large parcel of land in Nova Scotia, which he farmed successfully until the day of his death fifteen years later.

MOORE, EDWIN G. II
American Spy for Soviets ▪ (1921–   )

WORKING AT THE CIA IN ITS MAPMAKING AND logistics section, Moore retired in 1973 after twenty-two years of service. During that time, Moore had taken considerable secret materials from CIA headquarters and stored these documents in his $120,000 Bethesda, Maryland, home. Some time after his retirement, or perhaps earlier, Moore attempted to contact Russian officials at their Washington Embassy to make arrangements to sell them the documents he had stolen.

In 1976, Moore made a clumsy attempt to sell the looted secrets by leaving a package on the grounds of a Washington apartment house where Russian officials lived. The Soviets looked at the package and thought it might be a bomb. They turned it over to the FBI and agents found a note from Moore addressed to the Soviets in which he demanded a $200,000 payment for his stolen CIA secrets.

Moore was arrested December 22, 1976, and charged with espionage. Eight large crates containing CIA documents were found in his home. He was sentenced to life imprisonment and was also ordered to undergo psychiatric examination. Moore maintained his innocence throughout the trial and after he was sentenced, saying throughout that he had been a pawn of the CIA.

MORAVEC, FRANTISEK
Czech Spymaster ▪ (1895–1966)

AS A CITIZEN OF THE NEWLY-CREATED CZECHOSLO-vakia following World War I, Moravec attended the Prague Military Academy, received a commission, and went to work for Czech military intelligence. He spent years working in counterintelligence against Communist Russia and Nazi Germany, both with ambitions to conquer his country. He survived the takeover of Czechoslovakia in 1938 by Germany and, after World War II, that of Soviet Russia.

In 1948, Moravec, who was by then director of Czech military intelligence, was utterly surprised when a group of Russian secret agents murdered Czech foreign minister Jan Masaryk, son of the country's first president, Thomas Masaryk. The lightning Soviet coup was completed quickly as Communists took power. Realizing that his days were numbered, Moravec fled his country, taking refuge in the U.S. where he revealed the methods of Soviet covert operations.

MORROS, BORIS
American Spy for Soviets ▪ (1895–1963)

A RUSSIAN JEW BORN IN ST. PETERSBURG, MORROS was a child prodigy on the cello, his father a teacher, his mother a singer. So accomplished was Morros that he performed before Czar Nicholas II and his family. Following the Russian Revolution in 1917, Morros' musical career came to a halt. He immigrated to the U.S. in 1922 where he resumed that career, going to Hollywood where, in 1930, he went to work for Paramount Studio.

In 1935, Paramount made Morros its musical director. A year earlier he had, against his will, he later said, become a secret agent for Soviet Russia. In 1934, Morros went to Leningrad to visit his parents and was told by Vassili Zubilin, head of the NKVD in the U.S., that unless he spied for Russia, his parents might be liquidated as enemies of the state.

To that end, Morros used music talent scouts as Soviet agents in Germany during Hitler's reign. These agents gathered information on German troop movements, arms manufacturing, and diplomatic secrets, sending all this to the NKDV. In 1942, Morros was instructed to cooperate with Alfred and Martha Dodd Stern, wealthy New Yorkers who were rabid anti-Nazis and Communists working secretly for Moscow. (Martha Dodd Stern was the daughter of William E. Dodd, one-time American ambassador to the Third Reich.)

In 1944, Jack Soble replaced Zubilin as head of the U.S. spy ring and Morros would also work with his pyschiatrist brother, Dr. Robert A. Soblen (both were Lithuanian Jews who Americanized their family name, Sobolevicius, each spelling it differently). To the ring were added other spies, including Jacob Albam and George and Jane Zlatovsky. The ring's spies worked for Morros' independent film company (which he had established in 1939) or firms owned by others in the ring, so they would have covers. Members also acted as couriers, taking messages to Moscow or other European capitals.

Morros later claimed that the ring was not very effective and, for the most part, the secret information it relayed to Moscow was the kind of data that could be obtained in scientific magazines and reports available to the public. By 1947, Morros, swept up by patriotism and worried that he might be exposed, went to the FBI, revealing all he knew about the Soble ring. The Bureau asked him to become a counterspy and he accepted, providing the FBI with all he learned.

The members of the ring were later indicted or arrested in 1957, with Morros appearing in court to bear witness against them. Jack Soble and his Russian-born wife, Myra Soble, and Albam were sent to prison. Robert Soblen was convicted of espionage and while on bail fled to Israel but was deported back to the U.S. While stopping over in England, he committed suicide. The charges against the Sterns were dropped in 1979 since all of those who could testify against them, including Morros, were dead.

[ALSO SEE: *FBI*]

MOSSAD
Israeli Intelligence ▪ (1951–)

BEFORE ISRAEL CAME INTO BEING AS A NATION, many freebooting organizations functioned as intelligence services for the not-yet-born country. In 1948, after Israel was recognized as an independent nation (the first to do so being the U.S.), its first prime minister, David Ben-Gurion, announced the reorganization of the various intelligence agencies. In 1951, he further defined these organizations into three distinct groups, military intelligence, counterintelligence (Shin Beth), and the most far-reaching, the Mossad.

Known as the Institute or the Institution, the Mossad is more important to the Israeli government than the CIA is to the U.S. government. It has the power to deal with countries with which Israel has no diplomatic relations. The chief of the Mossad reports to the Prime Minister and none other. Its budget, reported to be enormous, is kept secret. The name

Mossad has a great historical significance to the Israelis; an organization by the same name was responsible for smuggling thousands of displaced Jews into Palestine during the 1930s and 1940s.

At the heart of the Mossad is its much-vaunted Special Operations section, which is responsible for its dedicated missions against Israel's enemies and its relentless pursuit of war criminals who have harmed the Jewish people in any land. In 1960, the Mossad scored its first much-publicized victory when its agents, led by Isser Harel, located the Nazi war criminal Adolf Eichmann in Argentina, kidnapped him in the streets of Buenos Aires, and surreptitiously smuggled him back to Israel where he stood trial. Eichmann was condemned in a show trial (the accused stood in a glass case in court) for his part in the mass murder of millions of European Jews in the Nazi death camps of World War II and hanged in 1962.

Like Isser Harel, the Mossad has been fortunate to have many brilliant agents who, unlike the legions of spies for other countries, are motivated by a fierce patriotism and devotion to Israel. One of these was Shulamit Kishak-Cohen, a Jewish woman and the mother of seven who lived in Beirut. She was responsible in the 1940s for smuggling countless Jewish refugees into Palestine, over the objections of her merchant husband.

Known as Shula Cohen, the smuggler became a Mossad agent in the early 1950s and operated under the code name of "Pearl." She traveled to Israel where she was trained in the artcrafts of espionage, then returned to operate out of Beirut. While raising her large family, she managed to provide the Mossad with state and political documents from Lebanon and Syria, these secrets obtained through her social contacts.

Shula Cohen's information proved so valuable that the Mossad provided her with considerable sums to purchase favors and secrets. They even financed a Beirut nightclub, the Star, so that it could be used as a meeting place for Mossad agents. The Cohen ring was eventually penetrated by a bright Lebanese intelligence officer and several members, including its female spymaster, were arrested and tried. Cohen was labelled "the Mata Hari of the Middle East," although this attractive housewife was nothing more than a proper married woman who efficiently acquired secrets for her country.

Convicted and condemned to hang, Cohen's sentence was commuted to a seven-year prison term. Following the Six Day War in 1967, Cohen and her family members were exchanged for the many Lebanese soldiers captured by the Israelis. Shula Cohen opened a flower shop near the King David Hotel in Jerusalem. There were many such heroic Mossad agents, including the courageous Elie Cohen, who was hanged in Damascus, and Wolfgang Lotz, the "champagne spy." And there were scores of Mossad spies never known except through their exploits, such as the stealing of the gunboats at Cherbourg and the penetration of the terroristic PLO.

The Mossad has always had the cooperation and aid of America's CIA. In fact, a special relationship has always existed between the two intelligence organizations. When the Mossad was in its infancy, the CIA helped train its agents with the latest espionage methods and provided it with sophisticated equipment. Today the Mossad is as well-equipped as is the CIA and its electronic and microchip operations equal any other power. It has a tremendous brain trust of mathematicians and cryptographers.

Western powers are supplied by the Mossad with constant information on Arab terrorists entering Europe and the U.S., so much material, in fact, that at one point the French complained that it did not have enough men to keep track of the terrorists. Particularly effective is the Mossad's special army unit, called the Sayaret Matkal, or the General Staff Reconnaissance Unit. About 200 men make up this unit, which is never mentioned publicly and is referred to as simply "The Guys." It was this unit that conducted the 1973 assassination raids in Beirut and the rescue of Jewish hostages at Entebbe in 1976.

Since Israel is always on alert against many enemies, its position is one of constant survival and to maintain that survival the Mossad does not hesitate to employ assassination. This rigid posture has sometimes backfired as in 1973 when Mossad agents killed an innocent Moroccan waiter in Lillehammer, Norway, mistaking him for Ali Hassan Salameh, the terrorist who engineered the Olympic massacre of Jewish athletes in Munich. The Mossad is not infallible. The Yom Kippur War of 1975 caught Israel off guard because the Mossad had failed to provide its leaders with information on the Arab military build up for that conflict.

Many of Israel's top political leaders began their careers in the Mossad. Major General Yitzhak Hofi who had served in the Israeli Army for many years and had been the Northern Front Commander in 1973, was appointed director of the Mossad the following year and held that post until 1982. It was Hofi who had made contacts and arrangements with the Gemayel family of Christian phalangists that carried out the massacres in PLO camps in Beirut in 1982, a slaughter that brought down world criticism on the Mossad.

Chaim Herzog, Yitzhak Shamir, Menachem Begin, and Yitzhak Rabin, who was assassinated by a right-wing Jewish fanatic in 1995, had all been members and leaders of the Mossad at one time or another in their notable careers. Because of the leadership, dedication, and professional effectiveness of the Mossad it remains, in the estimation of espionage experts, one of the best of the top five intelligence agencies in the world.

[ALSO SEE: *CIA; Elie Cohen; Isser Harel; Lavon Affair; Wolfgang Lotz; Victorino Ninio; Sylvia Raphael*]

MOULIN, JEAN
French Spy and Resistance Leader in World War II ▪ (1898–1943)

FRANCE'S SUPREME SPY, RESISTANCE LEADER, AND underground chief of World War II was Jean Moulin. Moulin was born and raised in Beziers in the south of France, the son of a teacher. He entered the University of Montpellier in 1917, then served in the French Army on the Western Front the following year. After World War I, Moulin returned to school and took his law degree in 1921. He became a civil servant, working in the local government of French Savoy the following year. He proved to be an excellent administrator and soon rose in rank. By 1939, when World War II began, he was the prefect of Chartres.

In 1940, the German juggernaut overran France, which sued for peace through the newly created collaborationist government of Marshal Henri Philippe Pétain, a hero of World War I. There were many in France who were angered by Pétain's quick capitulation and vowed to fight on. One was the tall, youthful General Charles de Gaulle who managed to reach England with many of his men after the fall of Dunkirk.

Others, like civil servant Moulin, remained in France. As the Germans occupied most of France under the terms of the country's surrender, they acted like the conquering barbarians of old, taking what they pleased.

One of France's greatest espionage heroes, Jean Moulin, legendary French underground spy of World War II who was caught, tortured, and murdered by the Gestapo in 1943.

A contingent of German armor roared into the village of Luray in the Chartres District, some of them barging into the house occupied by an elderly woman, Madame Bourgeois and her daughter. The old woman shouted at the German soldiers, shaking her fist at them.

Two of the Germans seized her, dragged her outside, and tied her to a tree, then shot her to death before the horror-filled eyes of her screaming daughter. The soldiers then ordered the daughter to leave her mother's corpse tied to the tree for twenty-four hours as a warning to others who might resist their authority. If not, they warned, she, too, would be shot.

News of this atrocity quickly reached Prefect Moulin. He immediately called German headquarters, protesting the murder and demanding that the two soldiers responsible be arrested and held for trial. Late that night two German officers marched into Moulin's office and ordered him to get into a waiting car. He was to meet with their commanding general who had information for him.

Moulin never saw the general. He was taken to the office of a junior-grade German officer who shoved a "protocol" before him, demanding that he affix his signature to it. It was a declaration that the murder of the old woman and other war crimes committed in the district had been committed by French Senegalese troops. The document described a massacre in a nearby village, which included the raping of women and the bayoneting of children to death.

Moulin stared at the declaration in amazement. He told the German officer that no such massacre had happened, that he, as prefect, would have been notified as to such a horrendous crime and that he had not received any such notification. He then asked that the Germans produce proof for such a charge. The German officer nodded to a soldier standing nearby. The soldier stepped forward and smashed his rifle butt into Moulin's jaw, knocking him down.

Bleeding, his teeth loosened by the blow, Moulin was then beaten before being dragged to a cell. As the door was thrown open, Moulin could see a Senegalese soldier crouched on the dirty floor of the cell. Like Moulin, he, too, was bleeding after having been beaten. One of the German guards jeered: "Since you love niggers so much, we've given you one to sleep with." He was then thrown into the cell.

Knowing that it would only be a matter of time before the Germans returned to beat him again until he signed their false document, Moulin decided that death was preferable to dishonor. He found some shards of glass on the floor of the cell, left there after an air raid had blown out all of the building's windows. Clutching one of these, he quickly drew it across his throat, moaned, then sank into a pool of his own warm blood.

The Senegalese soldier cried out and guards ran to the cell. A German officer realized that the sudden death of a prefect might be hard to explain. He ordered Moulin taken to a hospital where his wound was closed. While recuperating in the

Charles de Gaulle, leader of the Free French forces in World War II; Jean Moulin was his chief deputy to the French underground.

hospital, Moulin received from the Ministry of the Interior a letter that informed him that he had been removed from his position as prefect. Able to speak only in a hoarse whisper, Moulin escaped from the hospital, and, using false identities, went underground, attempting to reach London to join Charles de Gaulle. He would bear a horrible scar on his throat, one he covered with a long muffler, until the day he was murdered by the Nazis.

As he tried to make his way out of the country, Moulin saw everywhere the competent, jaw-jutting Germans in their smart uniforms, exercising precise authority, shoving back hordes of French soldiers in dirty uniforms. He felt shame and sorrow. The French Army had surrendered in just four weeks. Marshal Pétain had whined over the airways on June 17, 1940, that the new French government at Vichy would cooperate with the Germans in every way and he asked that his countrymen do the same thing.

On June 15, 1941, Moulin reached Marseilles, attempting to find a guide to take him to Spain and from there to London where he could join de Gaulle. On that day, however, he was introduced to Henri Frenay, a French Army Officer who had refused to surrender to the Germans. Frenay told Moulin that there were then tens of thousands of underground resistance fighters representing many factions and political parties. These groups, Frenay suggested, should be organized under the unifying symbols of "the Cross of Lorraine and de Gaulle."

Frenay proposed to organize all of these underground resistance groups under a common banner. He wanted Moulin to serve as the point man or contact person to de Gaulle, establish an effective communication link via an underground radio network with de Gaulle in London. Moulin was also to provide through de Gaulle's Free French organization in England money, arms, ammunition, equipment, everything necessary to a vast espionage network in occupied France, one that would eventually enlist more than two million patriotic French citizens. (It is estimated that more than five percent of France's population were members of the active resistance.)

Moulin then went to the American consulate in Marseilles where he introduced himself to consul Hugh Fullerton as Joseph-Jean Mercier, professor of law at New York University. He had a false passport (provided by Free French fighter, Major Henri Manhès). He wanted to travel to London to join the Allied Forces. Fullerton issued Moulin an American visa without question. At the time, the U.S. was not at war with Germany and any European wanting help from American embassies and consulates to aid the Allied cause promptly received it. (Knowing this, some German agents used this argument to persuade unwitting American officials into issuing them U.S. passports or visas to enter the U.S. where they conducted espionage operations.)

Traveling to Lisbon, Moulin then asked the British consul to approve his traveling to London. Much more wary than the Americans, the British put him off until the SIS determined the true identity of "Joseph-Jean Mercier." After a month, he was allowed to go to London but he was by then identified as Jean Moulin. He arrived at Bournemouth where the British flattered the French patriot, attempting to have him work with their own intelligence operation. Moulin, however, insisted on seeing de Gaulle. He was finally sent to London where de Gaulle's chief of intelligence, Colonel Passy (real name Andre Dewavrin) met with him. Passy had already studied Moulin's impressive dossier that his spies in France had supplied.

Passy proposed that Moulin become de Gaulle's liaison officer with the resistance groups in France and Moulin happily accepted. He would report directly to Passy all underground operations that he would help to coordinate with Free French intelligence, then called SR (*Service des Renseignements*). Moulin accepted and then met with de Gaulle, giving the Free French leader a full report of underground conditions and operations in occupied France.

De Gaulle informed Moulin that he had been selected to be his personal envoy to all resistance groups and that he was to centralize their activities. Moreover, Moulin was to be the chief political and military leader of the resistance, answerable only to de Gaulle and various members of his Free French contingent. Moulin's authority was limited to southern France while Passy was to supervise all of Nazi-occupied France.

On the night of January 1, 1942, Moulin, accompanied by a radio operator, Joseph Monjaret, and

One of Moulin's spies sabotaging a French railway track over which German troops were transported, circa 1942.

Raymond Fassin, who was to serve as his liaison officer to Frenay's underground groups, was flown in a British Armstrong-Whitley bi-motor to Arles where all three men parachuted to earth. They successfully landed with radio equipment and, after a close shave with two suspicious gendarmes, the spies traveled to Marseilles.

Moulin and Frenay met clandestinely and Moulin was accepted by the underground as de Gaulle's representative. From that point on, Moulin organized a communications system that fed information on the Nazis and all resistance operations to Monjaret who then radioed this information to de Gaulle in London. Those underground groups in the north were, at first, less inclined to accept de Gaulle as their supreme leader, arguing that the real fight was in France, not in England.

Supplying Frenay with 250,000 francs, Moulin, whose code name was "Max" (Frenay's was "Charvet"), began visiting underground groups in Marseilles, Avignon, Lyons, and Paris. He managed to convince all resistance groups to work under one authority, which came to be known as the National Council of the Resistance. The chief purpose of the resistance, as outlined by Moulin, was to prepare for open warfare in support of the Allied armies that would return to France.

After several trips to London and back, all filled with close encounters with Nazi agents and soldiers, Moulin was using up his nine lives as a secret agent and he knew it. On May 7, 1943, he wired London that he believed Vichy and German agents were closing in on him. So intense was Moulin's sense of doom that he asked de Gaulle to send another officer who could replace him should he be arrested. On June 16, one of de Gaulle's best aides, Claude Bouchinet Serreulles, parachuted into France and met with Moulin who fully briefed him on the vast underground network.

On June 21, 1943, Moulin was in Lyon, going to an afternoon meeting with some of the leaders of the resistance. He went to a small villa in the hilly suburb of Caluire. Only a few minutes after Moulin entered the villa with some of his men, the place was surrounded by Gestapo agents led by the notorious Klaus Barbie, who had been seen some days earlier with René Hardy, a resistance fighter who was also at the meeting. The villa served as a clinic operated by Dr. Dugoujon and the resistance fighters were to simply act as some of his patients. Innocent patients were present in the villa's waiting rooms.

Barbie, a small, wiry man, led the Gestapo men into the villa where they slapped, punched, and kicked Moulin and his men, as well as unwitting patients, slamming them against walls and handcuffing them. No cuffs were put on Hardy; a Gestapo agent shouted that they had run out of cuffs. Hardy was bound by a chain.

Gloating at the capture, Barbie called some of the resistance fighters by their underground code names. He wanted to brag that he knew all about them and he did since he had spies inside the resistance group. Dr. Dugoujon burst into the waiting room only to be slapped and handcuffed. As he stood against a wall next to Moulin, the resistance leader whispered to the physician: "My name is Jean Martel."

The always suspicious Moulin had taken the precaution of having another doctor write a letter to Dr. Dugoujon in which he stated that Moulin's name was Jean Martel, that he suffered from rheumatism and needed to be examined by a specialist. Moulin had the letter on him when handcuffed by Barbie's Nazi thugs. Suddenly, the prisoners heard several pistol shots outside.

It was Hardy, or so he later said when tried for treason and collaboration following World War II. He had been led by the chain to a waiting guard where he broke free, grabbed a pistol, and shot at his bewildered guards, leaping over a stone wall and running down a wooded hill to freedom. The Germans did not pursue him since they had so many prisoners to guard, or so it was later reported. To those who suspected Hardy of giving Moulin away, the escape was staged by the Gestapo to make Hardy appear innocent and to allow him to go back to other resistance leaders in preparation of betraying them.

The resistance leaders were taken to a prison where Barbie continued to gloat, telling them he knew that he had bagged the Chief of the Resistance, the infamous Max, which was Moulin's cover name. It soon became evident to the prisoners, however, that Barbie did not know which of his prisoners was Max. Barbie knew how to find out that identity. He had the prisoners taken one by one to the basement chambers of Gestapo headquarters where they were put through the most painful torture. Finally, two days later, on the night of June 23, 1943, one of the underground men broke and identified Jean Martel as Moulin. Barbie never identified the traitor.

Moulin refused to admit his true identity or give Barbie and his goons any information. He was mercilessly tortured. Hot needles where shoved under his fingernails. His fingers were forced through the narrow space between the hinges of a door and a wall and then the door was repeatedly slammed until the knuckles broke, and the skin broke, with blood gushing forth.

Screw-levered handcuffs were place on Moulin and tightened until they bit through his flesh and broke through the bones of his wrists. He would not talk. He was whipped. He was beaten until his face was an unrecognizable pulp. A fellow prisoner, a barber named Christian Pineau, was summoned to shave Moulin who lay on a bench in an open courtyard. Pineau later described the resistance leader as "unconscious, his eyes dug in as though they had been punched through his head. An ugly blue wound scarred his temple. A mute rattle came out of his swollen lips."

Moulin regained consciousness for a few minutes and begged for some water. Pineau pleaded with a heavily armed German guard to give him some. The guard dumped the soapy water the barber was using and filled a pan with fresh water that Pineau gave to Moulin, a few swallows before the spy again collapsed into a coma. He remained in this coma when he was shown to other resistance leaders who were being interrogated at Gestapo headquarters. Barbie had ordered Moulin put on display in an office. His unconscious form sprawled on a chaise longue. His face was yellow, his breathing heavy, his head swathed in bandages. It was the last time Moulin was seen alive.

Barbie realized that the extraordinary Jean Moulin would never talk. In July 1943, Barbie also realized that his prize prisoner was about to die and, to avoid having this death attributed to him, he transferred Moulin to a German prison. Moulin either died en route or shortly after he arrived, it is not known for sure. Moulin's body was returned to Paris where it was cremated and his ashes buried. In 1964, Jean Moulin's remains were reburied in the Panthéon, the resting place of France's greatest heroes. At a special ceremony honoring him at that time, Andre Malraux, the celebrated French writer and one-time resistance fighter, called Moulin "the champion of the people of the night."

The man who most likely betrayed Moulin, René Hardy, was tried twice after the war, the second trial ending with a hung jury. Moulin's murderer and the killer of countless Jews and resistance fighters, Klaus Barbie, vanished after World War II and was tried and condemned in absentia. He was found living in Bolivia in 1983 and was returned to France where he was tried and, on July 4, 1987, was sent to prison for life, France having abolished the death penalty.

MUKHABARET EL-AAM (GIA)
Egyptian Intelligence Service ▪ (1952–   )

ORGANIZED BY GERMAN SPYMASTER GENERAL Reinhard Gehlen, Egypt's intelligence agency, commonly called the General Intelligence Agency (GIA), this organization is responsible for gathering all intelligence relative to Egyptian security on a worldwide basis. It acts independently of the Egyptian military, which has its own intelligence agencies.

The Mukhabaret El-Aam has a vast network of spies throughout the Middle East and specializes in wiretapping and bugging anyone suspected of being an enemy of Egypt (even allies are thus treated). Under President Nasser, the organization came to symbolize raw oppression as it operated without any governmental authority other than Nasser.

Officers of this agency, particularly Colonel Nouri Osman, who penetrated the Israeli spy and saboteur ring in 1954, have proven to be equal to the best minds that direct Israel's Mossad, the super intelligence agency of the Middle East.

Though Anwar Sadat promised to reform this agency, he made little headway before he was assassinated. This agency is generally ineffective outside of the Middle East, but it is thorough and ruthless in all its operations, particularly inside Egypt.

[ALSO SEE: *Lavon Affair; Mossad; Victorino Ninio*]

MUNDAY, ANTHONY
Elizabethan Spy ▪ (1560–1663)

BORN TO A LONDON BOOKSTORE OWNER, MUNDAY was schooled in literature and became a minor playwright and poet. He earned more money in the service of Francis Walsingham, spymaster for Elizabeth I. After some brief training, Munday was sent to Rome to infiltrate the English College where young Catholic Englishmen were reportedly being trained to return to England and secretly work for the restoration of the Catholic faith.

Fearing that he was about to be identified as an Elizabethan spy, Munday returned to London suddenly. During 1582 he helped track down the English students from Rome as he knew many of them on sight. As a reward for his treachery, Munday was appointed to the staff of Topcliffe, the chief official torturer. He proved to be a ruthless interrogator. At the same time, he continued having his rather humdrum plays produced, mostly through government sponsorship.

[ALSO SEE: *Francis Walsingham*]

MUNSINGER AFFAIR
Canadian Sex-and-Espionage Scandal ■ (1960–1963)

CANADA WAS ROCKED BY A SEX-AND-ESPIONAGE scandal in the early 1960s, all centering around Gerda Munsinger, an attractive vamp born Heseler in Königsberg (now Kaliningrad in Russia). Her father was a leader in the Communist Party and indoctrinated his daughter early so that by 1947 she was an ardent Communist and a Soviet spy, working in West Germany.

Keeping her married name, the KGB agent somehow managed to get into Canada and began affairs with top government officals in the administration of Prime Minister John Diefenbaker. One of these was the associate minister for national defense Pierre Sevigny who sponsored Gerda for Canadian citizenship in 1960. The Mounties reported her to be a security risk and moved to have her expelled from the country. She went to East Germany in 1961. Sevigny resigned his post in 1963.

Meanwhile, the Diefenbaker administration was unseated in an election that saw liberal Lester Pearson become Prime Minister. During this time a lonely little misfit of a man, Victor Spencer, came to prominence. He had been recruited as a KGB spy in 1956 by Soviet agents acting on behalf of Russian spymaster Lev Burdiukov, who was attached to the Soviet Embassy in Ottawa. From 1960 to 1963, Spencer flew to Ottawa seven times to meet with Burdiukov and two other KGB agents, Rem Krassilnikov and A. E. Bytchkov.

Spencer's chief assignment was to visit Canadian cemeteries and take photographs of tombstones ("ghoul work"), particularly those of children who had died in infancy. KGB researchers used these photos to verify the obituary notices in old newspapers. They then produced false documents for their "illegals," spies who assumed the adult identities of long-dead children whose birth certificates could be verified by government officials who would never think to check on their premature deaths. (This was the manner in which Soviet spies Peter and Helen Kroger assumed several identities while spying for Russia in Australia and England.)

Canadian counterintelligence received a report of Spencer's haunting cemeteries and he was arrested. He quickly admitted his spying activities and implicated his Soviet spymasters.

The out-of-office Conservative Party quickly used the Spencer case to attack Pearson's Liberal Party, saying that it had completely mishandled the spy case and that it had been much too lenient on Spencer. Pearson retaliated by stating that ministers in the previous Conservative Government had dallied with a blonde KGB spy named Gerda Munsinger. The Munsinger scandal then exploded.

The Toronto *Star* found Gerda in Munich where she openly admitted that she had trysted with several Canadian ministers. The Conservatives then charged that Pearson had instituted a Communist witchhunt similar to that conducted by U.S. Senator Joseph McCarthy.

The scandal was almost as infamous as England's sex-and-espionage blowup, the Profumo Affair. Ironically, Victor Spencer, the bumbling KGB agent who began the whole thing, died of cancer while the Commission was digging up its scandal sheet dirt.

[ALSO SEE: *KGB; Peter and Helen Kroger; Joseph McCarthy*]

MUUS, FLEMMING B.
Danish Spymaster in World War II ■ (1916–)

RESISTANCE TO NAZI OCCUPATION IN DENMARK WAS inconsequential until a superb spymaster named Flemming Muus was parachuted into the country near Randers in March 1943. An agent sent by SOE (Special Operations Executive), Muus quickly organized Danish resistance so that it became an effective intelligence gathering organization.

He sought and got the cooperation of Danish royalty, convincing the royal house that sabotage had to be performed regularly to thwart Nazi military movements. He also went to the Danish police, risking exposure from possible collaborationists, and developed a strong liaison with law enforcement officers.

Police regularly informed Muus and his agents as to planned Gestapo raids against resistance hideouts. He organized sabotage of key German military installations and his espionage network was vast, sending information to London on all German political and military operations.

Muus was identified in the fall of 1944 and was compelled to turn over his operations to Ole Lipmann who replaced him. Muus returned to London as a highly lauded SOE spymaster. He was, however, criticized after World War II for not keeping an adequate record of his expenses, some of his enemies even claiming that he had misappropriated espionage funds for his own use, but the charge was never proven against this courageous and effective spymaster.

[ALSO SEE: *SOE*]

NAICHO
Japanese Intelligence ▪ (1960?–)

FOLLOWING ITS DEFEAT IN WORLD WAR II, JAPAN WAS never again to become a military super power. It does maintain, however, a small military organization, as well as four intelligence organizations, the most important being NAICHO, which is responsible for national security. Most of NAICHO's small budget is spent on signals intelligence. From all points of its many islands, NAICHO radio-monitoring stations track electronic communications in Russia, Korea and Communist China. Further, NAICHO spends a good deal of money buying reports from private institutions and journalists.

NATIONAL SECURITY COUNCIL (NSC)
U.S. Supervisory Intelligence Group ▪ (1947–)

FOUNDED IN 1947 UNDER THE NATIONAL SECURITY Act, the NSC is made up of the senior members of the U.S. government, the armed forces, and the intelligence community, under the direction of the President. It is considered to be the most powerful group in the U.S. Decisions of the NSC are made on intelligence briefings chiefly supplied by the director of the CIA, and they result in government policy.

In 1955, the NSC established the 5412 Committee (later called the Special Committee, the 303 Committee, and the Forty Committee), which was responsible for approving all covert intelligence operations through the President. The Committee is made up of members of the State Department, the Defense Department, and the CIA.

[ALSO SEE: *CIA; NSA*]

NAUJOCKS, ALFRED HELMUT (AKA: HANS MULLER)
SD Agent Provocateur ▪ (1908– ?)

A BRAWLING, CUNNING KILLER, ALFRED NAUJOCKS was the perfect SS-SD specimen. A rabid Nazi, he would perform any service for his SD boss, Reinhard Heydrich, from kidnapping to assassination, from forging documents to staging a fake invasion of German soil that Adolf Hitler could use as an excuse to begin World War II. Naujocks was daring, reckless, and utterly without scruples or mercy. He was one of the most fantastic of all German *agent provocateurs.*

A resident of Kiel, Naujocks studied engineering at the University of Kiel but he neglected his studies to join the Nazi Party, becoming a fanatical follower of Hitler and soon joining the brown-shirted Storm Troopers. As part of this brutal security force, Naujocks joined scores of other devoted young Nazis in street battles against Communists, and, during a fierce skirmish, had his nose flattened by a Communist youth wielding an iron bar.

In 1931, Naujocks joined Heinrich Himmler's black-shirted SS. Three years later he had risen to some prominence as an aide to SD leader Reinhard Heydrich. Though he strutted the image of an intellectual interested in history and philosophy, Naujocks revelled in undertaking unsavory assignments from his mentor, Heydrich, particularly those that appealed to his brutal, murderous nature. He was also enthralled with espionage, and he functioned as an agent-at-large for the SD's foreign intelligence division, a fledgling organization that busied itself with sub rosa sabotage rather than the gathering of intelligence.

Hitler's one-time follower, Otto Strasser, had defected from the Nazi Party and was attempting to set up his own right-wing movement through his Schwarze Front, which was headquartered in Prague, Czechoslovakia. From Prague Strasser lambasted Hitler and his policies over a clandestine radio, spreading anti-Nazi propaganda into the very heart of the Third Reich. This Heydrich and the SD found intolerable. The "black radio" had to be eliminated, Heydrich concluded and he ordered his top henchman, Naujocks, to kidnap the station's chief operator, Rudolf Formis, and bring him to Berlin for judgment. Formis had been the chief technician for Radio Stuttgart, a brilliant operator of transmitters who suddenly became Heydrich's obsessive goal.

On January 10, 1935, Naujocks met with Heydrich and helped his chief formulate a plan. By then SD direction finders, though technically crude, were able to pinpoint the location of the "black radio," determining that the station was fifteen to twenty miles southeast of Prague. Naujocks, using the alias of Hans

Muller, disguised himself as a trader of dry goods. He was accompanied by his voluptuous blonde girlfriend, Edith Kasbach, a gym instructor in Berlin. They leisurely drove a newly-purchased Mercedes across the border into Czechoslovakia.

Within a short time, Naujocks located Strasser's "black radio" in the small town of Dobris. Formis was living at the Zahori Hotel and Naujocks and his mistress took the room next to the radio operator. Taking a wax impression of Formis' room key, Naujocks had a duplicate made, then sent a wire to his SD chief Heydrich that stated a single word: "Found." He then waited patiently for more orders.

On January 23, 1935, Naujocks received Heydrich's instructions to destroy the radio, and, if possible, seize Formis and return him to Berlin. That night Naujocks stood at his hotel window and sent a signal with his flashlight. He then dropped a rope and up it climbed another SD agent, Werner Goetsch, a hulking thug whose specialty was strangulation. The two men left Naujocks' room and crept down the darkly lit hotel corridor until they stood before Formis' room. Naujocks inserted the duplicate key into the doorlock but as he did so, sounds from inside the room were heard. Formis was not gone, as the SD men suspected.

Instead of leaving, Naujocks boldly knocked on the door.

"What do you want?" shouted Formis.

"Hotel service, sir," replied Naujocks. "We forgot to leave you fresh soap when the room was made up earlier."

When Formis opened the door, Naujocks and Goetsch rushed forward, knocking the radio operator backward. Formis drew a revolver as did the SD men. The nerveless Naujocks fired first and Formis fell to the floor dead. The shots alerted the hotel staff and several servants came on the run. Naujocks placed a phosphorous charge on Formis' radio transmitter and ignited it just before running from the room with Goetsch. Both men bounded past startled hotel employees, shouting that a maniac killer was loose. They made good their escape but when Heydrich learned of the botched kidnapping he exploded in rage, accusing Naujocks of reducing sophisticated secret service work to the kind of showy gangsterism seen in Hollywood movies.

Naujocks, however, not only remained with the SD but he continued to share a favorite position with Heydrich. The SD chief knew that he could count on Naujocks to complete future missions with ruthless dedication, even though his henchman might create more human gore than necessary. The next SD operation in which Heydrich involved Naujocks instigated a bloodbath in Soviet Russia that all but wiped out the hierarchy of the Red Army, or so Heydrich later claimed.

By 1936 the SD had established its own foreign intelligence operations, much to the consternation of the Abwehr and its leader, Admiral Canaris. Through SD agents Heydrich learned that opposition against

Stalin was mounting in the Russian officer corps and that Marshal Mikhail Nicolaevich Tukhachevsky headed the cabal. Information was fed to Heydrich's agents by General Skobline, a Russian emigre who reported that the most able of Soviet generals, Tukhachevsky, who had crushed the Kronstadt revolt in 1921, and had in the mid-1930s completely reorganized the Red Army from disjointed militia formations into a modern fighting organization, was ready to usurp the dictatorial Stalin.

Heydrich suddenly envisioned a master plan in which he schemed to eliminate the entire officer corps of the Red Army and thus enfeeble Stalin's ability to conduct warfare, as well as rid Hitler of certain high-ranking German generals who opposed him. He ordered his henchman Naujocks, who had been working in the SD document division, to prepare elaborate forged documents and letters that showed Tukhachevsky and his fellow officers in correspondence with intriguing Wehrmacht officers, all conspiring to not only rid Russia of Stalin but Germany of Hitler.

According to Heydrich and Walter Schellenberg—an SD intelligence officer who would later replace Wilhelm Canaris as head of the Abwehr—Eduard Benes, President of Czechoslovakia, advised Stalin of the existence of the documents. Stalin had long suspected Tukhachevsky of seeking to usurp him through the powerful officer corps the Marshal had established. Stalin sent an NKVD representative to Berlin to negotiate the release of the documents. Schellenberg later stated that the Soviets paid 3,000,000 rubles for the forged documents but the currency later proved to be well-executed forgeries as well.

It was later stated that Stalin was not taken in by Naujocks' forgeries but had long decided to purge the handsome, popular, and powerful Tukhachevsky. The Marshal and seven top Red Army generals were arrested, tried, and condemned to death on June 11, 1937. Then Stalin unleashed a staggering bloodbath in which half of the entire Red Army officer corps, more than 35,000 top-ranking men, were liquidated or cashiered, ninety percent of the generals, eighty percent of the colonels.

Heydrich was jubilant, claiming that he had severed the head of the much-feared Red Army, a claim that was believed by Winston Churchill and Nikita Khrushchev and one that was seriously profiled in the film Canaris. Moreover, Hitler, who knew the documents and letters were forgeries, held them up as legitimate and used them to get rid of two of the highest-ranking Wehrmacht officers who opposed his mad schemes for conquest. He confronted General Werner von Blomberg and Field Marshal Walther Brauchitsch with the forgeries and demanded their resignations, which he got.

Naujocks rose in stature at the SD because of this vaunted coup and he became Heydrich's most trusted agent. His next important assignment would prove catastrophic for humanity. He would be the linchpin in the grim machinery that started World War II and would cost 55,000,000 lives.

In 1938, Hitler met with Himmler and Heydrich to develop a way in which his troops could preemptorily invade Czechoslovakia. It was Heydrich, the alert student of world history, who remembered how their friends, the Japanese militarists, had traditionally employed provocative incidents to make it appear that they had been forced into acts of aggression.

Heydrich reminded Hitler how well these Japanese-inspired "incidents" worked to excuse Japan's aggression and he proposed that the same technique be employed to excuse Germany's invasion of Poland. The remote German radio station in Gleiwitz on the German-Polish border in Upper Silesia would be attacked by marauding Polish invaders, said Heydrich. The radio station would be seized, Polish propaganda shouted briefly over the airways, and some precious German blood would be spilled to prove the naked aggression of the rogue Polish government. This blatant aggression by Poland would leave Hitler no choice in retaliating with a full-scale attack against the Poles.

The deviousness of the plan appealed to Hitler's sneaky nature and he ordered Himmler and Heydrich to make preparations. Though the operation was first thought to be assigned to the Abwehr, its principled chief, Admiral Canaris, might pose a problem. At the last minute, the mission was turned over to Heydrich's SD agents and murder squads from Himmler's SS.

On August 10, 1939, Heydrich met with Alfred Naujocks to outline the fake attack against the Gleiwitz radio station. "Merely for the sake of appearances," Heydrich informed Naujocks, "we must place the blame for forthcoming events on other shoulders." He then told him that Himmler would be supplying the Polish invaders for the fake attack at Gleiwitz, a dozen or more concentration camp prisoners who would be dressed in Polish uniforms and who would be given drugs before they were shot to death by German troops heroically defending the soil of the Fatherland. One of these prisoners would also be dressed in a German uniform so as to provide to the world a "victim" of naked Polish aggression. Heydrich chortled as he described these hapless victims under Himmler's code word: "Canned goods." Dr. Herbert Mehlhorn, who administered the SD under Heydrich, would provide through Gestapo chief Heinrich Mueller the concentration camp prisoners who were to be used as human guinea pigs for Hitler's launching of World War II.

Naujocks selected five of his toughest men, along with a Polish-speaking SD agent and then went with his group to Gleiwitz where they took rooms in two hotels and waited. After he had been given the code words, Naujocks was to make his attack. He later recalled (in a signed affadavit during the 1946 Nuremberg Trials where he awaited judgment as a war criminal): "My instructions were to seize the radio station and hold it long enough to permit a Polish-speaking German who would be put at my disposal to broadcast a speech in Polish. Heydrich told me that this speech should state that the time had come for conflict between Germans and Poles. . . . Heydrich also told me that he expected an attack on Poland by Germany in a few days."

The *agent provocateur* and his men waited patiently in Gleiwitz for fourteen days. Naujocks scouted the radio station, noting that the transmitter was located on a remote, rural road outside of Gleiwitz and that it was surrounded by six-foot-high wire netting. The station and adjacent living quarters were unguarded. Heydrich, meanwhile, organized similar fake attacks along the German-Polish border to take place at the same time the Gleiwitz station was being "attacked" by the fake Polish troops.

While Naujocks and his men waited, Heydrich altered his plan. He ordered 150 SS men to don Polish uniforms; they would be the "invaders," while the concentration camp prisoners would be dressed in German uniforms and represent the "victims." Hitler, at the the same time, briefed his generals and ordered his forces to assemble near the Polish border.

After several postponements and a few bloody clashes brought about prematurely by overeager SS men confused about schedules, the Gleiwitz operation was authorized by Heydrich, who learned that Hitler would invade Poland on September 1, 1939. He called Naujocks at his hotel in Gleiwitz at 4 P.M. on August 31, 1939, saying in his high-pitched metallic voice: "Call back." When Naujocks called Heydrich back, he heard the words: "Grandmama is dead."

By 7:45 P.M., Gestapo chief Mueller ordered several trucks carrying the corpses of the concentration camp prisoners to depart for the border. The bodies were placed in strategic places. Most of these victims were drugged and then shot by the SS men dressed as Polish soldiers. One of the victims was placed at the gate of the Gleiwitz radio station that Naujocks and his men reached shortly before 8 P.M.

Naujocks and his men, with guns drawn, rushed into the station. An engineer named Foitzik stood mouth agape as the SD squad rushed inside shouting and firing pistols into the ceiling. He thought that the inmates of a lunatic asylum had escaped. Said Naujocks later: "We fired our pistols in the broadcasting room. We loosed off a couple of warning shots into the ceiling in order to make a bit of shindy and frighten people."

Station personnel were handcuffed and then taken to the celler and locked up. Then Naujocks was faced with a dilemma. He did not know how to stop the broadcast in progress and get his Polish-speaking propagandist on the air. He discovered the "storm microphone," a special microphone that allowed announcers to break into broadcasts to alert listeners to impending storms. Switching this on, Naujocks motioned to his Polish-speaking aide to begin his anti-German diatribe. This he did for about four minutes while Naujocks and the others shouted and fired their weapons to make it all sound as if a pitched battle was taking place.

Then, with a wave, Naujocks led his men out to waiting cars. He stepped over the man laid out at the gate, kneeling beside him to see that he was still breathing but that he had been shot and was bleeding to death. "I did not see the gun wounds," Naujocks later stated, "but a lot of blood was smeared across his face." He and his men then drove toward Berlin.

The next day, Adolf Hitler appeared before the Reichstag to explain to his stooge audience that German armies were pouring into Poland in retaliation for the aggression of "Polish regular soldiers [who had] fired into our own territory." Thus, Hitler, through Himmler and Heydrich, had created his own "incident" that ostensibly provoked him into beginning World War II. As German Stukas screamed down on Warsaw and German panzers dashed across Poland, foreign press members were shown the dead Germans killed by the attacking Poles, these being the assassinated concentration camp prisoners.

Naujocks was not inactive. Heydrich sent him to Czechoslovakia a few weeks later to commit various acts of sabotage to undermine the Nationalist government that was resisting Nazi occupation. He and other SD men blew up several factories, blaming these explosions on dissident workers opposed to the regime, which promptly collapsed, allowing the government to go wholly into the Nazi camp. Naujocks' next assignment involved a confrontation with British intelligence.

Only a few months before Heydrich brainstormed the Gleiwitz incident, he and Himmler had hatched another plan to infiltrate British intelligence, inveigling two of Claude Dansey's top SIS officers, Captain Sigismund Payne Best and Major R. H. Stevens, into a scheme to contact a German underground that did not exist. Heydrich believed that he could draw the British agents into a plan whereby he could learn of SIS operations in Europe.

Best and Stevens, after meeting with several so-called Black Orchestra (German underground) representatives, were to redezvous in Venlo, Holland, on November 9, 1939, where they would be given the full details of German underground operations and the identities of the high-ranking German army officers who intended to depose Hitler. The man waiting to greet the German agents was Walter Schellenberg, then one of Heydrich's rising stars in the SD and who who would later replace Admiral Wilhelm Canaris as head of the Abwehr.

On the night of November 8, 1939, the evening before Schellenberg was to meet with the British agents in Venlo, Hitler attended a gathering of his old 1923 Beer Hall Putsch cronies in Munich. He and other top Nazi leaders joined hundreds at the Burgerbrau Keller to salute the Brown Shirts of yes-teryear. Unlike such previous occasions, Hitler and the Nazi bigwigs departed early. Eleven minutes later a bomb went off that tore the beer hall to pieces, killing eight and wounding sixty-two others.

Himmler, who was responsible for the Fuhrer's security, immediately seized an opportunity to explain the explosion as an assassination attempt upon Hitler's life, telling the Fuhrer that British intelligence was behind the plot. (An unemployed mechanic, George Elser, was later charged with setting the bomb. He may have been plucked from one of Himmler's concentration camps to serve as a scapegoat, one who reportedly stated under torture that he was in the employ of British intelligence.)

The stunned Hitler accepted Himmler's claims and flew into a rage, unleashing a night-long diatribe against the British. Knowing that Schellenberg was meeting with the two SIS agents in Venlo the next day, Hitler ordered the British spies arrested. When agents Best and Stevens arrived in Venlo the next day, Walter Schellenberg was waiting for them at a outdoor cafe. Parking their car behind the cafe, the British agents began to step from the auto, preceded by Lieutenant Klop, a Dutch intelligence officer working with them.

A car packed with SD agents roared up to the British agents. The SD men, led by Alfred Naujocks, jumped from the car. Klop drew a revolver as did Naujocks and both men began firing as they stoically advanced toward each other. Klop fell first, mortally wounded. Naujocks ordered his SD men to seize Best and Stevens who were thrown into the SD car, along with the wounded Klop (who later died in prison). Schellenberg, Naujocks, and the SD men, along with their prisoners, then sped back to Germany.

Though Best and Stevens never admitted having anything to do with the Munich bombing, they were nevertheless kept imprisoned for the duration of the war. The Venlo Incident was a tactical triumph for German intelligence, although it brought Heydrich little insight into SIS operations, other than some of its agents could be duped. Again, the daring Naujocks performed with nerveless aplomb, although Heydrich began to feel uneasy about his favorite thug. He saw Naujocks as a reckless gangster who opted for violence and mayhem instead of secrecy and subtlety.

In May 1940, when Hitler moved against France and the Lowlands, Naujocks again appeared on the borders, this time with German troops disguised as Belgian and Dutch soldiers whose task was to infiltrate enemy territory and seize key bridges and hold them until German panzer forces arrived. As the war progressed, Heydrich tired of Naujocks' reckless attitude. He reassigned the wild adventurer to the documents section of the SD where Naujocks busied himself with making forged passports. Still, Naujocks could not resist developing a wild scheme to wreck the British economy, a plan he called "Operation Bernhard," one that called for dropping billions in forged British banknotes over England.

Heydrich dismissed the scheme as too fantastic, even for him, and, to rid himself of Naujocks and any future embarrassment he might bring to the SD, ordered his henchman to join an SS regiment and serve in the bloody war of attrition in Russia. Wounded, Naujocks was later assigned to a post in Nazi-occupied Belgium. In 1944, he was working there as an economic administrator but his real mission was to liquidate resistance leaders. In the closing days of the war he often flew to Denmark with SD murder squads where he hunted underground leaders.

As Germany began to collapse, Naujocks slipped back to Belgium where he surrendered to American forces. He was held for trial as a war criminal and attempted to save himself by providing information on the dead Heydrich and the fantastic SD operations prior to and during World War II. Realizing that he might still be condemned, Naujocks escaped from the special camp where accused war criminals were being held and he was not seen again. He remains one of the most bizarre and spectacular *agent provocateurs* during World War II.

[ALSO SEE: *Abwehr; Wilhelm Canaris; Kenji Doihara; Eastern Jewel; Gestapo; Reinhard Heydrich; Heinrich Himmler; NKVD; Walter Schellenberg; SD; Venlo Incident*]

NELSON, STEVE (STEVE MESAROSH)
U.S. Spy for Soviets ▪ (1903– ?)

BORN STEVE MESAROSH IN CHAGLICH, YUGOSLAVIA, Nelson became a Communist at an early age and, during the 1930s, received his schooling at the Lenin Institute in Moscow, becoming a top NKVD espionage agent. He served as commissar and Lieutenant-Colonel of the Abraham Lincoln Brigade during the Spanish Civil War (1936–1939), and later moved to the U.S., assigned by the Communist Party to organize on the West Coast.

Nelson became chairman of the San Francisco chapter of the Communist Party before World War II, and he moved freely among liberal-leftist political circles, recruiting members from the academic community, particularly teachers and students at Berkeley, California.

Though Nelson appeared to be consumed with recruiting new party members, his chief assignment from the Russian Consulate in San Francisco was to discover atom bomb secrets from the Radiation Laboratory. Nelson's primary source of secrets from this scientific group was a research chemist named Joseph Woodrow Weinberg.

Weinberg would later be instrumental in passing to Nelson many elements of atomic research but Nelson's real goal was to snag the top atomic research

scientist in America, Dr. J. Robert Oppenheimer. Nelson had an ironic contact to Oppenheimer, the scientist's wife, Katherine Puening Harrison.

This woman had appeared in Spain during the bitter Civil War. She was seeking her husband who was serving on the Loyalist side. Nelson had met her at that time and told her that her husband was not only dead, killed during a battle, but had, indeed, died in his arms. Nelson then made arrangements for Mrs. Harrison to return safely to the U.S.

Upon her return, Mrs. Harrison enrolled at the University of California where she studied mycology and it was also there that she later met and married Dr. Oppenheimer. Nelson planned to use his contact with Mrs. Oppenheimer in recruiting the scientist to his espionage cause. Further, Nelson was already close friends with Oppenheimer's younger brother, Dr. Frank Oppenheimer of Stanford University who had gone to work at the Radiation Laboratory in 1941. Frank Oppenheimer and his wife were both members of the Communist branch at Palo Alto.

Nelson met Dr. J. Robert Oppenheimer at the scientist's Berkeley residence at several social occasions. It is not believed that he directly discussed the scientist's atomic research at these times. It is known that Nelson directed one of his contacts at the Radiation Laboratory, who, in turn, asked one of Oppenheimer's associates to approach the scientist.

Oppenheimer was approached by Prof. Haakon Chevalier, who told Oppenheimer that since Russia was an ally of the U.S., it was entitled to "technical data that might be of assistance to that nation," meaning information on atomic reseach. Oppenheimer responded by bluntly informing Chevalier that he considered efforts to obtain this top-secret information treasonable. He dismissed Chevalier and went directly to Major-General Leslie R. Groves, the military commander of the Manhattan Engineering District Project (or the Manhattan Project), and reported the meeting with Chevalier. (Nelson sent a report to Communist spy and courier Rudy Baker that Dr. J. Robert Oppenheimer could not be recruited into his spy ring.)

At the same time Oppenheimer was named chief of the Los Alamos operations, Steve Nelson received a nocturnal visit at his Berkeley home from a scientist named "Joe." (It was later assumed that this person was Joseph Weinberg.) During the midnight meeting, the scientist read a complicated formula slowly, which Nelson diligently copied.

A few days later Nelson phoned Peter Ivanov, the Soviet Vice Consul in San Francisco to arrange for a meeting in the park situated on the grounds of St. Francis Hospital. There Nelson passed on the formula to Ivanov. Two days later Vassili Zubilin, third secretary of the Russian Embassy in Washington, arrived at Nelson's home and gave him ten bills of unknown denomination.

In later years, Weinberg, who was suspected of actually passing on the vital formula for the A-Bomb (before the Rosenbergs), appeared before the House of Un-American Activities Committee and refused to answer any questions. He was later indicted for perjury but this indictment was subsequently dismissed.

Nelson also appeared before HUAC and stated that he did not know Joseph Weinberg. He was kept under constant surveillance and, in 1952, he was brought to trial in Pennsylvania where he was convicted of sedition and sent to prison.

[ALSO SEE: *Rudy Baker*]

NICOLAI, WALTHER
German Spymaster in World War I ▪ (1873–1934)

A LEGENDARY SPYMASTER, WALTHER NICOLAI CAME from middle-class parents and had to work his way up through the ranks. After earning his commission, Nicolai was sent to Russia as an observer of the Czar's army in 1896. His detailed report of the cumbersome, ill-led, ill-equipped, and disorganized Russian forces led to his promotion to captain and an appointment to the War Academy in Berlin in 1901. He graduated three years later and was assigned to military espionage.

In 1913, Nicolai was ordered to join the General Staff in Berlin where he was appointed director of military intelligence, the Abwehr, with the rank of lieutenant-colonel. Until the appearance of Admiral Wilhelm Canaris, Nicolai would be the most famous Abwehr chief in the annals of German espionage. He was a shrewd manipulator of agents who understood well their strengths, weaknesses, and motivations.

Almost immediately, Nicolai faced an intelligence scandal that rocked German-Austrian relations. His counterpart in the Austro-Hungarian Empire, Colonel Alfred Redl, it was revealed, not only headed Austrian military intelligence but was a double agent secretly serving Russia. Redl had been bought for a great deal of money and had turned over to Russian intelligence a vast amount of information regarding his spy networks, along with what he knew of Nicolai's operations.

Nicolai's reaction was to dismiss most of his spies in the field and even those on his own headquarters staff whom he suspected of cooperating with Redl. He rebuilt his entire organization, personally selecting and training his top aides, and carefully culling military men, as well as trusted civilian men and women to work inside his tightly-controlled spy networks. On occasions, Nicolai indulged himself by using wild-eyed adventurers as agents such as Isaac Trebitsch Lincoln.

Lincoln was used in Turkey by Nicolai but the unpredictable agent was arrested in Bulgaria and charged with being a double agent, spying for

The astute and ruthless German spymaster Walther Nicolai, head of the Abwehr during World War I.

Germany and Turkey. Nicolai used his considerable influence to have Lincoln released. He may have used this agent again but he kept the colorful Lincoln at arm's length. Nicolai preferred to have his top spymasters deal directly with the thousands of agents who worked for the German networks Nicolai established in Belgium, Russia, and France. He also had some agents working in America such as Maria von Kretschman, the heroin-addicted daughter of a German general who figured prominently in the sabotaging of U.S. military installations at the beginning of World War I, notably Mare Island.

As he was later to write in his book, *Secret Powers*: "In the German military intelligence service, it was a cavalry officer, and an exceptionally cultured woman who proved most competent in dealing with the agents, even with the craftiest and most difficult characters." The unique woman to whom Nicolai referred was Elsbeth Schragmüller, whose true identity was not learned until long after World War I. She was known by many names—Fraulein Doktor, the Queen of Spies, the Big Boss (la Grande Patronne), the Black Cat, the Red Tiger.

Schragmüller, who was given a post by Nicolai in the German censorship system, later became an efficient teacher at the Abwehr's spy school in Antwerp. Her graduates went on to become some of the best agents Germany had along the Western Front, as well as behind the lines in all the Allied countries, except in England.

German spies like Karl Hans Lody (poorly trained, quickly apprehended, and executed in England at the beginning of the war), were not the responsibility of Walther Nicolai. All German espionage conducted in England during World War I was directed by German naval intelligence. Its chief, Gustav Steinhauer, was considered to be a miserable failure as a spymaster. He sent one young man after another to his death after brief, even shoddy, training and with little knowledge of how to accomplish impossible missions.

Organization and training were Nicolai's hallmark. Most of the agents trained at his schools went on to perform useful espionage work without losing their lives. Nicolai's dedication to the craft of espionage was summed up by Captain Ellis M. Zacharias, deputy director of U.S. Navy Intelligence during World War I: "He [Nicolai] was a ruthless and unscrupulous spymaster devoted to Secret Service with the unconditional devotion of an ascetic monk."

The "cavalry officer" mentioned by Nicolai as being one of his best spymasters of German agents was none other than the beefy but meticulous Traugott von Jagow, one-time Police Chief of Berlin, who became Nicolai's adjutant at the Abwehr. Jagow ran many networks and scores of spies, constantly evaluating their work by systematically reviewing their missions. He had an encyclopedic mind that could recall almost every one of the spies under his command. His most exotic spy, however, performed her espionage in the bed chamber and proved to be high-strung, demanding, and, in the end, so inept as to make Nicolai's Abwehr look absurd. That spy was Mata Hari.

As the war drew to a close, Nicolai's once vast spy networks shriveled, then collapsed along with Germany itself. Nicolai held onto his position until turning over what was left of the Abwehr to Colonel Erich Gemp in 1921, who, in turn, was replaced by Admiral Wilhelm Canaris, the craftiest espionage fox of them all. Nicolai did not admire the Nazis or support Hitler's rise to power. He wrote his memoirs and kept in touch with old comrades. Hitler reportedly detested Nicolai and once commented that the retired spymaster had given away secrets in his memoirs. Nicolai's death in 1934 is shrouded in some mystery. One story had it that he was murdered by Nazi thugs during Hitler's widespread purge of enemies, real and imagined.

[ALSO SEE: *Abwehr; Wilhelm Canaris; Isaac Trebitsch Lincoln; Karl Hans Lody; Mare Island Sabotage; Mata Hari; Alfred Redl; Elsbeth Schragmüller; Special Branch*]

NINIO, VICTORINO (MARCELLE)
Israeli Spy in Egypt ▪ (1927–   )

ONE OF THE MOST ILL-CONCEIVED MOSSAD ADVENtures was its Operation Suzanna, a disaster for Israeli espionage. It began in 1951 when Colonel Abraham Dar, using the cover name of John Darling, arrived in Egypt. Posing as a British businessman, his real business was the reorganization of an Isreali spy network that had been systematically dismantled by the Egyptian secret service, Mukhabaret El-Aam, under the ruthless guidance of President Nasser.

Dar's new recruits were all Egyptian Jews, none with any espionage experience. With little or no training, Dar enlisted a number of eager, youthful spies, breaking a cardinal rule of the Mossad (or any other secret service for that matter) by enrolling agents who all knew each other socially. Obviously, all the Egyptian spymasters had to do was unearth one in this group and that would lead to the unraveling of the entire network and that is exactly what happened.

One of Dar's first recruits was an attractive 24-year-old Olympian athlete, Victorino Ninio who was called Marcelle. The Israeli spymaster became Marcelle's lover and through her, he enlisted many more agents. Marcelle used her high-society contacts to obtain information for Dar, as well as provide him with new recruits. These included the 27-year-old, blonde-haired, blue-eyed Paul Frank, who eventually replaced Dar when he was recalled to Tel Aviv.

It was to the nervous, almost manic Frank that Operation Suzanna was entrusted. His control, Motke Ben-Tsur, met with him in Paris and outlined an almost lunatic plot. Frank and the network established by Colonel Dar would begin a reign of terror in Alexandria that would spread to Cairo and throughout Egypt. The network's agents were to firebomb important American and British institutions and places of business and make it appear that Nasser was behind the terrorism. They would set all Egypt aflame and then begin assassinating its top leaders, including the dictator Nasser.

Going to Alexandria, Frank contacted Philip Nathanson, a 19-year-old agent selected by Dar. He was then put in touch with Victor "Pierre" Levy, Robert Dassa, Samuel "Jacques" Azar, and the vivacious Marcelle who was a friend to all of these ardent but inexperienced spies. The radio operator selected for Operation Suzanna was Elie "Alex" Cohen but he was off on another assignment (Cohen would prove to be one of Israel's most heroic agents in a future mission).

Levy was designated as radio operator by Frank. In July 1954, the group set off a number of bombs in Alexandria and Cairo. Newspapers and television reports heralded the terrorist campaign without fixing responsibility. Then 19-year-old Philip Nathanson attempted to blow up a movie theater in Alexandria but the small bomb went off prematurely in his shirt pocket, blowing him to the sidewalk. Coincidentally, Captain Hasan el Manadi of the Egyptian Secret Service was on hand. He tore off Nathanson's shirt and stamped out the flames, but he discovered the remains of the explosive materials inside Nathanson's eyeglass case and immediately arrested the saboteur.

The entire network was quickly identified since all knew each other. When brought to trial, all of the defendants pleaded guilty. On January 29, 1955, Azar and Dr. Moshe Marzouk were sentenced to death. Marcelle, who was not involved with the actual bombings, and the others drew long prison terms. Azar and Marzouk were executed on February 2, 1955. Marcelle, after serving fourteen years, was repatriated to Israel in a prisoner exchange following the Six Day War in 1968. She was greeted as a national heroine and later married Colonel Eli Boger in a wedding attended by then Prime Minister Golda Meir.

Operation Suzanna was a public disaster for Israel and though it was never proven, Israeli Defense Minister Pinhas Lavon was blamed for ordering the terror bombings in Egypt. He was removed from office and though he attempted to vindicate himself many times, he remained guilty by suspicion. Israel's greatest spymaster, Isser Harel, also had suspicions. He believed that the flamboyant Paul Frank was somehow behind the Egyptian roundup of Israeli agents involved in Operation Suzanna.

Frank, upon returning to Israel, claimed that he barely escaped alive from Egypt. Frank was given another assignment and went to Germany.

Harel sent his own men to shadow Frank who was seen to meet with Egyptian Army officers in Europe. When Frank finally returned to Israel in 1958, he was secretly tried the following year, accused of betraying the Egyptian network and stealing secret documents. He was convicted on all counts and sent to prison for twelve years. After his release, Frank went to live in the U.S.

[ALSO SEE: *Elie Cohen; Lavon Affair; Mossad; Mukhabaret El-Aam*]

NKVD (PEOPLE'S COMMISSARIAT OF INTERNAL AFFAIRS)
Soviet Secret Police ▪ (1934–1946)

THE DREADED SECRET POLICE OF SOVIET RUSSIA CAME into existence in 1934 as a new name for the OGPU (1923-1934). Little other than the name changed. As with its predecessor, NKVD chiefs and agents had no obligation to obey any standing civil laws. It answered only to dictator Joseph Stalin who edicted mass arrests and murders through this oppressive agency.

It was in the NKVD era that Stalin launched his massive purges of political opponents, as well as widespread collectivism that saw the extermination of millions of Russian nomads, gypsies, and "undesirables," as designated by the ruthless Stalin. The NKVD conducted arbitrary arrests, conducted torture, committed mass murder, and sent myriad victims into Siberian exile.

The NKVD was headed by a number of blood-thirsty chiefs, not the least of whom was Genrikh Yagoda and his successor, Nicolai Yezhov, who personally murdered his mentor, Yagoda, at Stalin's orders, only to be executed by his successor, the hulking killer, Lavrenti Beria who was to head the KGB, successor to the NKVD in 1946.

[ALSO SEE: *Lavrenti Beria; Cheka; GPU; KGB; OGPU; Genrikh Yagoda; Nicolai Yezhov*]

NOSENKO, YURI IVANOVICH
Soviet Spymaster ▪ (1926–)

TWO MONTHS AFTER PRESIDENT JOHN F. KENNEDY was assassinated in Dallas on November 22, 1963, Yuri Nosenko, a major in the KGB strolled into the American Embassy in Switzerland and asked for political asylum. Nosenko had been a deputy director at the American section of the VIIth Department of the KGB. His job in Moscow was to deal with Americans visiting Russia. One of those Americans, Nosenko quickly admitted at his first interrogration, had been Kennedy's assassin, Lee Harvey Oswald.

CIA officials, who moved Nosenko to its Virginia headquarters in 1964, continued to grill the KGB spymaster about Oswald. He informed his CIA interrogators that he had inspected Oswald's application for Soviet citizenship during his 1959 visit. Nosenko stated that he reported to his superiors that Oswald was mentally unstable and, under no account, should he be employed in any espionage activities on behalf of Soviet Russia.

Nosenko went on to say that Oswald married a Russian woman but he was ignored by Russian authorities; he grew depressed and attempted to commit suicide by slashing his wrists. It was a feeble attempt to get attention, Nosenko claimed. After his wounds were healed, Oswald left Russia and returned to the U.S.

CIA officials found Nosenko's story too pat to be believed, especially since his defection came on the heels of Kennedy's assassination. They suspected that this was a cover story the KGB had invented to derail any American suspicion of KGB involvement with Oswald and the assassination. Nosenko was confronted with these suspicions. He shrugged, then admitted that the Russian hierarchy had panicked after the assassination, believing that America would think Oswald had been a hired KGB assassin. Exactly, countered the CIA agents, and that is why the KGB sacrificed Nosenko, sending him over to the enemy to pose as a defector to defuse the idea.

Nosenko shrewdly pointed out that if the KGB did use an assassin to kill Kennedy, it would have employed an anonymous and professional assassin, not a mentally disturbed loud-mouth like Oswald whom they knew had had a high public profile as a political leftist and agitator and a security file as such with the FBI and the CIA. Some CIA officials argued that that is exactly why Oswald was chosen as a KGB agent. Because of his demeanor and recorded political background, the U.S. would dismiss him as having been selected by the Soviets to kill Kennedy.

While this seemingly endless debate went on, Nosenko was treated like a prisoner. He was housed in a special 10-foot-by-12-foot specially constructed "vault" with windows on all sides so that he could be constantly watched. The KGB spymaster was held in this confinement, except for exercise excursions, for three-and-a-half years.

CIA officials eventually accepted his story about Oswald and other information. They gave him a new identity, a new house, and hired him as a consultant at $38,325 a year. In the end, the CIA concluded that the KGB wanted nothing to do with Oswald after he had attempted to kill himself. Said one former CIA official: "They feared that the KGB would be accused of murdering an American tourist [Oswald] at a time the Kremlin was trying to reduce East-West tensions."

[ALSO SEE: CIA; KGB]

NOURI, OSMAN
Egyptian Spymaster ▪ (1917–   )

A tough and uncompromising spymaster, Colonel Osman Nouri headed Egyptian counterintelligence during the 1950s, devoted to supporting the political aims of President Nasser. It was Nouri who detected the ill-conceived espionage and sabotage plot on the part of Egyptian Jews to blow up U.S. and British buildings in Egypt in order to embarrass Nasser with the West.

Working with Mukhabaret El-Aam, Egypt's intelligence agency, Nouri was able to set up his own spy networks in Europe. To accomplish this considerable feat he received aid and contacts from Reinhard Gehlen, chief of West German intelligence. Many of Nouri's agents were ex-Nazi intelligence agents whom he met through Gehlen.

Nouri placed agents in Iraq and Syria, the two most militant countries in the Middle East, to work with their intelligence agencies in plotting against Egypt's enemies, chiefly Israel. Nouri and his agents gathered the intelligence on Yeman, which allowed Egypt's invasion of that country and the overthrowing of the Imam. An utterly ruthless spymaster, Nouri advocated any means to secure confessions and information, including brutality, blackmail, and torture. He was later appointed Egypt's ambassador to Nigeria where he successfully combated the Mossad in preventing Israel from establishing a widespread influence in Africa.

[ALSO SEE: Reinhard Gehlen; Lavon Affair; Mossad; Mukhabaret El-Aam; Victorino Ninio]

NSA (NATIONAL SECURITY AGENCY)
U.S. Signals Espionage Agency ▪ (1952–   )

ESTABLISHED IN 1952 BY PRESIDENT HARRY TRUMAN, the NSA is the most secret of American intelligence agencies and it seldom makes an appearance in the media. Its chief function is deciphering messages sent through all forms of sophisticated communications. The NSA was formed to unify all of the U.S. cryptographic agencies existing in the armed services, as well as those in the intelligence services and diplomatic corps.

The three armed services, the FBI, and the CIA all contribute and share in the efforts of the NSA, which was originally headquartered in Fort Meade, Maryland. This ultra-secret organization employs a vast army (approaching 100,000 at last count) of computer experts, satellite and electronic technicians, programmers, and analysts, and, for the most part, cryptographers who brilliantly decipher the codes of foreign powers.

Housed within the Defense Department, the NSA's director reports to an Assistant Secretary of Defense who, in turn, reports to the Secretary of Defense. The Secretary of Defense is a member of the National Security Council, which he briefs. The Council in turn, answers to the President.

In addition to deciphering and decoding, the NSA operates a vast worldwide electronic eavesdropping network through armed forces and intelligence agencies. Throughout the free world and inside Communist countries and other nations ruled by dictatorships, the NSA has operatives monitoring military and diplomatic networks, copying coded messages that are then transmitted back to the NSA for decoding or deciphering. The messages of friends and foes alike are monitored, deciphered, and analyzed.

Prosaic written and telephoned messages are taken into the agency, as well as all forms of electronic messages. NSA's four code-breaking departments handle commercial, military, and diplomatic messages as well as those sent by individuals who, for whatever reason, may be under electronic surveillance. Special sections are dedicated to sophisticated types of electronic espionage—Elint handles electronics intelligence, Radint covers radar intelligence. Comint is an NSA term that applies to all communications intelligence.

Only three serious breaches of security in NSA history have occurred. The first involved Jack Edward Dunlap, a sergeant who functioned as a chauffeur, and who managed to sell secrets to the Soviets before committing suicide in 1958. The second involved William H. Martin and Bernon F. Mitchell, two homosexual cryptographers who defected to Soviet Russia in 1960, causing the agency to completely overhaul its organization and institute a rigid internal security force, the Office of Communications Security.

The third breach of security that damaged the NSA came from an indirect source, James William Hall III. A native of Sharon Springs, N. Y., Hall, following his high school graduation, joined the army at eighteen in 1976. He was trained as an analyst of intercepted encrypted radio and telephone traffic culled in the field by ASA (Army Security Agency) operatives, information which is funneled to NSA through Army G-2. In 1977, Hall was given a top secret clearance.

Hall rose to the rank of warrant officer and, from January 1981 to January 1985, he was stationed in West Berlin as a senior analyst of electronic communications for Army G-2, deciphering coded messages sent by Soviet diplomatic and military nets. He lived off base with his wife and two children and, in 1982, he began selling the KGB information on COMINT (U.S. Communications Intelligence), collecting an estimated $100,000 to $200,000 from his Soviet spymasters. For this money, Hall delivered detailed data on the army's most up-to-date equipment and methods in electronic eavesdropping.

Undetected, Hall returned to the U.S. in May 1987, stationed at Fort Huachuca, Arizona, before being sent to Fort Stewart, Georgia, where he went on selling secrets to his Soviet control, Huseyin Yildirin. From January to July 1988, Yildirin reportedly paid $40,000 to Hall for stolen COMINT secrets. Hall then began spending money, buying a new house and car. His spendthrift ways alerted superiors and, subsequently the FBI.

On December 20, 1988, an undercover FBI agent, posing as a KGB spymaster, paid Hall $30,000 for secrets he stole at Fort Stewart. Hall was then arrested as was Yildirin. Hall was sent to prison for forty years and fined $50,000 and Yildirin was also imprisoned. The damage, however, had already been done with the KGB acquiring information on the most sophisticated electronic surveillance used by the ASA/NSA, almost all of which had to be altered and reconstructed at a staggering cost.

The NSA, unlike the CIA, invariably has a high-ranking military man as its director. Typical was Lieutenant-General Lincoln D. Faurer, a U.S. Air Force officer who became the NSA chief in 1981. Faurer had served as chief of intelligence of the U.S. European Command in Germany and had been deputy chairman of the NATO military committee in Brussels.

The NSA's budget is certainly much larger than that of the CIA or the FBI combined. Its operations are so vast and its staff so large that only the President and the National Security Council know how many billions the agency spends each year. A similar but considerably scaled-down version of NSA exists in England, the Government Communications Headquarters in Cheltenham, with which the NSA works closely.

[ALSO SEE: *CIA; Jack Edward Dunlap; FBI; National Security Council; William H. Martin*]

NUT, BERNARD
French Spymaster ▪ (1937–1983)

A LIEUTENANT-COLONEL IN THE FRENCH COUNTER-intelligence service, Nut was found dead in February 1983, his body sprawled in the snow of a mountain in the French Maritime Alps. Nut's car, a Peugot 305, was parked nearby on a mountain road. Six feet from the body was found a Smith and Wesson .357 Magnum with three chambers empty. One of its bullets had been fired into the back of Nut's head.

Despite the blatant fact that Nut had been murdered, French authorities inexplicably decreed his death a suicide. There was no evidence or note to indicate this. On the contrary, Nut's background suggested that he was murdered. His most likely assassins were either Russian or Bulgarian.

A few days before Nut's murder, his name was mentioned in a report concerning the arrest of Soviet spy Viktor Pronin. Nut had apparently captured the KGB spy who had crossed into France through the lightly guarded Italian border, the path taken by most Soviet agents. Pronin, who used the cover of an Aeroflot official stationed in Rome, was found to be in the possession of microfilm detailing Western defense plans.

Moreover, Nut had aided Italian intelligence agents in exposing the Bulgarian connection to the attempted assassination of the Pope in 1981. Outside of SMERSH operations, few revenge killings occur in espionage but in Nut's case, he may have been the exception. He mentioned to his family that he was going to a hush-hush rendezvous on the night of his murder. His killer or killers were most likely Soviet agents retaliating for the capture of Pronin or Bulgarian spies whom he had compromised in his investigation of the papal assassination plot.

[ALSO SEE; *KGB*]

OFFICE OF POLICY COORDINATION (OPC)
U.S. Covert Group ▪ (1948–1952)

ESTABLISHED IN JUNE 1948 BY THE NATIONAL Security Council, the Office of Policy Coordination was staffed by reckless adventurers. Many agents in OPC were former OSS agents and thrived on outlandish missions, the more impossible the better. One of the first covert operations conducted by OPC was to spread unrest in Communist countries. To that end, OPC agents went into Albania where they tried to start a revolution. Their operation was a dismal failure and most of the agents were captured. It was later claimed that the British intelligence agent turned double spy for Moscow, Kim Philby, was responsible for identifying many of the OPC agents for the Albanian secret service.

Critical of OPC were CIA agents in that agency's Office of Special Operations who planned dirty tricks, assassinations, and about the same thing that OPC was attempting to accomplish. When OPC was dismantled in 1952, many of its agents were absorbed by the CIA's Special Operations department, which acted in the same kind of irresponsible manner. Most of these agents were fired for creating the disaster that became known as the Bay of Pigs, a covert operation designed to unseat Cuban Communist dictator Fidel Castro, but one that completely backfired and cost CIA director Allen Dulles his job.

[ALSO SEE: *Bay of Pigs; CIA; Allen Dulles; National Security Council; OSS; Kim Philby*]

OGPU (All Union State Political Board)
Soviet Secret Police ▪ (1923–1934)

THE SOVIET SECRET POLICE, EVOLVING FROM THE GPU (1922), was headed by a ruthless, savage chief named Felix Dzerzhinsky. Though bound by civil law, Dzerzhinsky and his fellow OGPU agents ignored any legal restrictions and did as they pleased, arresting and torturing anyone suspected of being an enemy of the Communist state. The OGPU concentrated on tracking down counterrevolutionaries, as well as importing thousands of spies to the West to establish espionage networks, spread communism, and disrupt democratic governments.

[ALSO SEE: *Felix Dzerzhinsky, GPU; KGB; NKVD*]

OKHRANA
Czarist Secret Police in Russia ▪ (1881–1917)

THE CHIEF REASON FOR THE EXISTENCE OF THE Okhrana, the monarchist secret police in Russia, was to protect the Czar. (The word "ochrana" means "guard.") In its protection of the Czar, his family, officials, and top military leaders, the Okhrana, in another form, had existed since the days of Ivan the Terrible in the sixteenth century. The latter-day Okhrana was officially organized in 1881 by Czar Alexander III.

With enormous funds at its disposal, the Okhrana hired thousands of spies to infiltrate the peasant and worker populations where the seeds of political unrest invariably found root. These spies informed on those advocating rebellion or revolution and the radicals were then picked up and thrown into prison but were most often executed. The fortunate ones, like Joseph Stalin, were sent to Siberian labor camps. Others, like Count Leo Tolstoy, were harrassed and shadowed (as Tolstoy recounts in his memoirs) for expressing liberal opinions.

At the turn of the century the Okhrana became the most powerful and dreaded secret police and intelligence-gathering organization in the world. It employed spies throughout Russia and all over Europe. These agents spied against suspected enemy nations as well as Russian immigrants in foreign countries and any radicals preaching the overthrow of the Russian monarchy. They also practiced terrorism and, as designated by the Okhrana chiefs, assassination of the Czar's most dangerous enemies.

By the 1910s, Russia's working classes were in turmoil, starving and radicalized to revolution. The sinister Okhrana chiefs and chief spymasters like Yevno Azev planned and executed drastic counter-revolutionary measures. Many revolutionary groups were formed and led by men who were really Okhrana spies. In this way the Okhrana knew almost every active revolutionary and could quickly identify and arrest them. Failed revolutionaries like Father George Gapon, and Lenin's hand-picked man, Roman Malinovsky, were driven into the arms of the Okhrana, betraying their fellow conspirators for money.

But for all of its conniving, back-stabbing, and double-dealing, the Okhrana's policies eventually failed when the social fabric of Russia fell apart in 1917 and the government was seized by actual revolutionaries, first led by Alexander Kerensky, then by Lenin and his Bolsheviks and Communists. It was in that year that the Okhrana collapsed. Its chiefs and spymasters were either tracked down and executed or they fled to Western Europe.

The Communists delighted in seizing and publicizing Okhrana records, revealing the identities of the spies who had worked for them. They replaced the Czarist secret police with one of their own, the Cheka (Extraordinary Commission for Combating Counterrevolution and Espionage), which protected the dictatorships of Lenin, Stalin, and their Communist successors. The Cheka immediately launched repressive measures that soon developed into mass terrorism, a system of internal espionage and ruthless oppression that would not lose its stranglehold on Russia until the collapse of communism in 1989.

[ALSO SEE: *Yevno Azev; Cheka; George Gapon; Roman Malinovsky*]

ORLOV, ALEXANDER (LEON FELDBIN; AKA: ALEXANDER BERG)
Soviet Agent ▪ (1895–1973)

SON OF A JEWISH BUSINESSMAN IN MINSK, RUSSIA, Orlov (born Leon Feldbin) was trained in Jewish schools but abandoned his religion and family when he embraced communism. He took part in the Russian Revolution of 1917 and was an officer in the Red Army during the Civil War against the White Russians, 1918–1920. Following the Communist victory, Orlov entered the legal professon, becoming a ferocious prosecutor of those dragged into kangeroo courts as enemies of the state.

As such, Orlov caught the eye of Felix Dzerzhinsky, the ruthless chief of the OGPU (All Union State Political Board, 1923-1934), the pre-decessor of the GPU, NKVD, and KGB. Orlov enlisted with the OGPU and became one of Dzerzhinky's most ardent deputies. From 1926 to 1936, Orlov strengthened the OGPU by traveling throughout Western Europe where he established many Soviet spy networks with young Communists he personally recruited to the Soviet banner.

In 1936, Orlov was sent to Spain as an adviser to Communists fighting within the ranks of Loyalists opposing the usurping Falangists of Francisco Franco. When it appeared that the Spanish Republic was doomed, Moscow ordered Orlov to have the Republic's gold sent to Russia for safekeeping before Franco's legions could seize it. Orlov persuaded the Republican government to ship its gold to Russia, promising that it would be returned once Franco was defeated.

The overly trusting Republicans ordered all government gold shipped to the port of Cartagena where Orlov supervised the loading of hundreds of millions of dollars of the precious metal onto a fleet of Russian vessels waiting in the harbor. He accompanied this gold fleet across the Mediterranean, through the Black Sea to Odessa, and then by train to vaults in Moscow.

Stalin expressed his thanks but Orlov became suspicious of his leader when many of his former revolutionaries and agents began to disappear. They were summarily arrested, secretly tried, found guilty of "counterrevolutionary activities"—a catchall phrase of Stalin's kangaroo courts—and secretly executed. Orlov had returned to Russia to witness Stalin's purge of anyone he thought might oppose him in the future.

Fearing for his life after a cousin was shot by a Stalin purge squad, Orlov smuggled his family out of the country, then fled to Paris where he defected to the Canadian Embassy. He was allowed to emigrate to Canada and later went to the U.S., living in Cleveland under the alias of Alexander Berg. He wrote several books attacking the Communist regime of Stalin and detailing the operations of the OGPU.

[ALSO SEE: *Felix Dzerzhinsky; GPU; KGB; NKVD; OGPU*]

OSLO SQUAD
Norwegian Underground Group in World War II ▪ (1940–1945)

ONE OF THE MOST EFFECTIVE RESISTANCE GROUPS in Norway during the Nazi occupation of 1940–1945 was the Oslo Squad, which worked under the direction of the Central Leadership of the Home Front, the national underground organization. The Squad was led by a daring resistance fighter named Gunnar Sonsteby (code name Kjakan or No. 24). Under his direction the Squad conducted military and political espionage and sabotage. In 1944, Sonsteby and his men had destroyed sophisticated tabulating machines that identified the 80,000 Norwegian men who were to be called into Nazi forced labor. The result was that the Germans were able to call up only 300 men for compulsary labor.

One of the Squad's most effective operations was the seizure of more than two tons of documents housed in Oslo's Department of Justice and Police Headquarters, information that would prove the actions of traitors and Nazi war crimes. Just before the Allies occupied Norway, the Central Leadership concluded that the files would be destroyed by the Nazis to protect themselves against war crime trials after the war.

OSS (OFFICE OF STRATEGIC SERVICES)
U.S. Intelligence Service in World War II ▪ (1942–1945)

PRIOR TO WORLD WAR II, AMERICA HAD NO OVERALL intelligence system beyond that operated by the armed forces. To coordinate secret information of all types at the start of U.S. involvement in World War II, President Roosevelt, on January 13, 1942, created the Central Office of Information and placed General William "Wild Bill" Donovan at its head. Donovan, a World War I hero, quickly organized a vast network of experts in all intelligence fields. The oranization's title was changed a short time later to the Office of Strategic Services, or OSS. The agency was responsible for espionage and sabotage in countries occupied by the Germans, Italians, and Japanese. It became legendary through the feats of its agents.

Donovan was a tolerant spymaster, allowing his agents a great deal of freedom in accomplishing their missions. He encouraged inventiveness, even recklessness. More than 13,000 men and women worked for the OSS during World War II. They parachuted or were smuggled into all the countries occupied by the enemy to work closely with underground units, the SOE, and the SIS, as well as other national intelligence agencies operated by Allied countries.

One of the most effective operations conducted by the OSS was its preparations for the Allied landings in North Africa in 1942. OSS agents deftly negotiated terms with Vichy French officials to make sure that no French warships in African ports would be given over to the Germans who then occupied most of France. Moreover, they were able to place scores of agents in North Africa, ostensibly as monitors of foodstuffs going to refugees. These agents spent most of their time recording the movements of German warships and aircraft through the Mediterranean, while placating indecisive French officials and military commanders in preparation for the Allied landings.

When American and British troops did storm the beaches, OSS agents were waiting for them to lead them through minefields and direct them to the strategic objectives. OSS agents performed the same kind of incredible feats in preparation of the 1944 Normandy landings. The agency's agents were also effective in China, 1943–1945, working with Chiang Kai-Shek in discovering weaknesses in the Japanese war machine.

In 1943, OSS agents, with Donovan's approval and without informing the Joint Chiefs of Staff, broke into the Japanese Embassy in Lisbon, Portugal, in search of documents and codebooks. They managed to obtain information that was, for the moment, valuable, but in the long run, this covert operation, which was quickly discerned by the Japanese, was devastating to U.S. military intelligence.

Though U.S. military intelligence had broken the Japanese "Ultra Code" in early 1942 and continued to monitor all important military and diplomatic messages throughout the war, the OSS break-in caused the Japanese to change its entire military attaché code, or that used by its intelligence service.

General Douglas MacArthur, Supreme Commander of South Pacific Operations, refused to allow the OSS to operate in his theater of war, preferring to rely upon the intelligence provided to him from the Army's G-2. The most truculent opponent facing the OSS was J. Edgar Hoover, chief of the FBI, who thought Donovan's OSS to be an upstart agency that might usurp his own power and the jurisdiction of the Bureau, even though FDR constantly assured Hoover that the OSS mandate was to operate outside the Western Hempishire, a regulation that later applied to the CIA, which succeeded the OSS.

British intelligence during World War II was, on the other hand, extremely cooperative with Donovan who visited SIS chiefs in 1940 to confer about his aims in establishing the OSS. He was shown the complete operations of the SOE (Special Operations Executive), which worked with the underground resistance fighters in occupied Europe. So impressed was Donovan that he modeled the OSS organization after the SOE. The British gave Donovan full cooperation, much more than might otherwise have been given in any other time, in that England was then desperate to draw the U.S. into the war against Germany.

At the end of World War II in 1945, President Harry Truman disbanded the OSS, believing that America had no more need of a super intelligence agency. This attitude quickly changed, however, when the Soviet Union was perceived to be a very real threat to the security of the U.S. and the world, causing the creation of another intelligence agency in 1947, the CIA.

[ALSO SEE: CIA; William J. Donovan; FBI; J. Edgar Hoover; SIS; SOE; Ultra]

Abwehr deputy director Hans Oster, who, with his chief Canaris, plotted the overthrow of Adolf Hitler and was executed for his efforts.

OSTER, HANS
German Spymaster in World War II ▪ (1888–1945)

BORN IN DRESDEN, OSTER WAS BROUGHT UP IN the strict Protestant faith, which he never abandoned. He entered the Army and quickly rose in rank, being an excellent administrator. When Hitler came to power in Germany in 1933, Oster immediately aligned himself with high-ranking officers of the Wehrmacht (the German Army) who secretly opposed the dictator. He continued this secret resistance as Admiral Canaris' deputy at the Abwehr, plotting against Hitler and the heads of his secret police—Himmler of the Gestapo and Heydrich of the SS and SD. He was joined in his conspiracies by Canaris and fellow Abwehr spymaster Erwin von Lahousen.

Not only did Oster protect the Wehrmacht from the prying eyes of the Gestapo and the SS/SD, but he secretly aided Jews attempting to flee the secret police. In 1942, one of Oster's Abwehr officers, Lt. Joseph Müller, and a state attorney working for the Central Abwehr office, Dr. Hans von Dohnanyi, had processed a good deal of money through Munich banks on behalf of the Abwehr. This money, SS officials learned, was being funneled to Jews who had been taken into the Abwehr as agents and were being sent to Switzerland to spy for Germany, or, at least, that was Oster's story.

In reality, Oster, Canaris, and others were trying to save these Jews from extermination. Oster, the SS suspected, had been working for years against Hitler's regime, organizing members of the Wehrmacht's general staff in an effort to oust or eliminate the dictator. The Abwehr from top to bottom was peopled with anti-regime conspirators, but getting evidence against them proved difficult for Himmler and Heydrich. Moreover, Himmler had given strict orders to his men that the German Army never be criticized.

Since the Army was in league with the Abwehr, it was difficult for the Gestapo and the SS to outwardly accuse Canaris or his chief of staff Oster with any wrong doing. The Gestapo turned the matter over to the Reich Military Court, which immediately sent Dr. Manfred Roeder to Abwehr headquarters. Roeder had rooted out many members of the Communist underground, known as the Red Orchestra (Rote Kapelle).

On April 5, 1943, Roeder marched into Dr. Dohnanyi's office and found papers identifying the escaped Jews. Worse, he discovered notes Dohnanyi had kept that described meetings between himself, Müller, and Oster with many anti-regime conspirators such as Pastor Dietrich Bonhoeffer and their attempt to mediate a separate peace with the Allies through the offices of the Vatican.

When this came to light, Canaris had no option but to dismiss Oster. Dohnanyi, Müller, and Bonhoeffer were arrested and thrown into prison. Oster remained free to continue his plotting. He was instrumental in having a bomb secretly placed on board Hitler's private plane in 1943, but the contraption malfunctioned and failed to explode. He was again at the center of the group that planned Hitler's death in what was called Operation Valkyrie on July 20, 1944.

On that day Colonel Claus Graf Schenk von Stauffenberg, Chief of Staff to the Commander-in-Chief of the Replacement Army, entered Hitler's command headquarters in his military retreat at Rastenburg, East Prussia (called the Wolf's Lair). He placed a bomb at a conference table that exploded but it did not kill the dictator. Almost all of the conspirators, including Oster, were rounded up and sent to concentration camps. More than 5,000 people were executed, including Oster.

[ALSO SEE: *Abwehr; Black Orchestra; Wilhelm Canaris; Gestapo; Reinhard Heydrich; Heinrich Himmler; Erwin von Lahousen; Red Orchestra*]

OWENS, ARTHUR GEORGE (AKA: JOHNNY)
British Double Agent in World War II ▪ (1899–1961?)

BORN AND RAISED IN WALES, OWENS WAS THE product of a poor family. He became a salesman and traveled throughout Europe in the 1930s when Hitler had just come to power. SIS asked Owens to become a spy for England. He did, working under the code name of "Johnny" and collecting information on Germany's secret plans to rebuild its armed forces.

By 1937, however, Owens went over to the Germans who paid better than British intelligence. Two years later he was trained by the Abwehr as a radio operator in an electronics-intelligence school in Hamburg. He continued to pretend to spy for England, however. SIS officials closely examined the information Owens supplied to them and concluded that it was so superficial as to be fake information.

When Owens returned to England just before the outbreak of World War II, he was confronted with SIS suspicions that he had become a double agent and was really working for the Abwehr. He admitted that he had, then agreed to continue in his role as a German spy, but that he would send on by radio to his Abwehr spymasters the disinformation created by MI5 and SIS.

Owens played a cat-and-mouse game with both the Abwehr and SIS, sending disinformation to Germany but also, as SIS suspected, sending valid secret information. By the end of 1941, SIS believed Owens was too much of a security risk to allow him to continue contacting Germany. The Abwehr also suspected him of double-dealing by that time since one of their agents entrusted to his guidance had been arrested by Special Branch.

Owens was finally arrested by Special Branch and MI5 officers and sent to prison where he remained until 1945. Upon his release, Owens went to Ireland where he reportedly died under an assumed name. In the end, no one knew for which side Arthur Owens really spied.

[ALSO SEE: *Abwehr; MI5; SIS; Special Branch*]

PACK, AMY THORPE (AKA: CYNTHIA)
U.S. Spy in World War II ▪ (1910–1963)

BORN IN MINNEAPOLIS, AMY THORPE MARRIED Arthur Pack, a secretary at the British Embassy in 1930 and traveled widely around the world with her husband. In 1937, she and her husband were stationed in Warsaw where the attractive blonde became the center of attention at fetes and receptions. Suddenly, European diplomats were confiding state secrets to her, which she reported to MI6.

British intelligence ordered her to pump as much information from these diplomats as possible. In a short time, Pack was able to state that Hitler would demand an agreement in Munich in 1938, one in which he would seize a goodly portion of Czechoslovakia. Pack drew from memory for MI6 agents a map of that country with the new German borders. She had been shown the German map by a high-ranking German officer, one of her admirers. Her information proved to be painfully accurate.

Returning to Washington in 1940, Pack was visited by William Stephenson, chief of MI6 in New York. He was coordinating intelligence operations between Britain and the U.S., working closely with William J. Donovan who was to head the OSS. Using the cover name "Cynthia," she agreed to spy on the German, Italian, and Japanese diplomats still stationed in Washington.

Through a naval attaché in the Italian Embassy, Pack was able to obtain the top-secret Italian Naval Code, which she photographed before it was returned. The code went to MI6 and it did much to help the British fleet locate and sink many Italian warships in the Mediterranean. Grateful as Stephenson was for this priceless information, he asked Pack to undertake another mission almost immediately, one much more dangerous. She was to somehow get into the French Embassy and learn what the Vichy government planned for its armed forces, particularly in Africa where the French still maintained a powerful fleet.

She approached the French press attaché, Captain Charles Brousse, an outgoing anti-Nazi with whom she formed a friendship. Through Brousse, Pack gained entrance to the French Embassy. He convinced a night watchman that she was Brousse's mistress and that she would be visiting him. An outside door was left unlocked for several nights.

On one of those nights, Pack slipped into the embassy with one of Stephenson's agents who was a locksmith. The locksmith was able to unlock the door to the code room and Pack quickly got into a safe and found the French naval ciphers Stephenson was seeking. Pack handed these ciphers to another MI6 agent through a window. This agent dashed to an office where the ciphers were copied and returned to Pack who replaced them in the safe and left the Embassy with the locksmith.

Although she had no way of knowing it, the French naval ciphers Pack had obtained vastly aided the American invasion of North Africa in 1942. The ciphers clearly stated that the French were to scuttle their ships if threatened either by the Allies or the Nazis. When Pack's husband later died, she married Brousse and moved to France where she died of cancer in 1963.

[ALSO SEE: *William J. Donovan; MI6; OSS; William Stephenson*]

PAKHTUSOV, YURI
Soviet Spy in U.S. ▪ (1954–)

DURING THE REAGAN ADMINISTRATION THE KGB and Russian military intelligence, the GRU, stepped up their espionage activities in the U.S., so much so that the White House, over a period of time, ordered the expulsion of 105 Russians from Moscow's UN Mission. The Soviets retaliated by expelling a number of American diplomats.

By 1989, the Bush administration had set a firm policy of monitoring the activities of Soviet envoys. One such was Lt. Col. Yuri Nikolayevich Pakhtusov, a military attaché in the Russian Embassy in Washington. Two months after his arrival from Moscow, the GRU agent approached an employee of an American firm that developed security programs for the U.S. government.

Pakhtusov offered the employee considerable cash payments for the delivery of these programs. The employee, whose name was never divulged, went to the FBI. Agents recorded the GRU spy's movements for the next few days and his expulsion was then demanded. After Pakhtusov was expelled, the Soviets expelled American Lt. Col. Daniel Van Gundy from the U.S. Embassy in Moscow, claiming that he had attempted to take photos of restricted military installations.

[ALSO SEE: *FBI; KGB*]

PAPEN, FRANZ VON
German Spymaster ▪ (1879–1979)

Diplomat Franz von Papen; he served as a German spymaster in two wars. (AP/Wide World)

A MEMBER OF THE JUNKER CLASS, FRANZ VON Papen WAS born on a rich Westphalian estate. In 1915 he went to the German Consulate in New York City. Papen's job was to act as a spymaster in New York, directing German agents in preventing American supplies from reaching England, which was then at war with Germany. The agents, under Papen's direction and using considerable funds that he supplied, set up fake American armaments firms, which took all the orders they could get from the Allies. The guns and equipment they promised, however, were interminably delayed and never delivered.

Other dummy firms Papen controlled bought up all the gunpowder available, ostensibly for the use of making grenades and artillery shells to be sent to England. The powder was simply hoarded so as to keep it out of the hands of Britain. Though successful, many of Papen's espionage activities were severely compromised through the incompetence of his associates.

Heinrich Albert was one of these. Albert, a commercial attaché in the Consulate, foolishly forgot his briefcase on a New York elevated train. It was seized by an American intelligence agent. The briefcase contained a number of incriminating documents that were later published in the newspapers and served to embarrass Papen and the entire German diplomatic corps. Worse, Papen quarreled constantly with Franz von Rintelen, who had been sent from Berlin to oversee sabotage in the U.S.

Rintelen was a foolhardy madman, according to Papen. At their first meeting together, Rintelen informed Papen that he had made several unique bombs that he planned to use to blow up American freighters taking supplies to England. He would also immediately launch a terrorist campaign across the U.S., blowing up warehouses and U.S. military installations.

This was not Papen's kind of espionage. He feared that Rintelen's wild sabotage would endanger his own mission. Several U.S. merchant vessels were sabotaged and Rintelen was the funding source behind the Mare Island explosions.

Papen's response to all this was to cable the Abwehr, demanding that Rintelen be recalled.

Rintelen was ordered back to Germany but he was taken from a Dutch ship (the Netherlands then being a neutral nation) when it stopped at Southampton. Papen's message to the Abwehr about Rintelen had been decoded by British naval intelligence agents working under the direction of Reginald Hall.

The Abwehr respected Papen but it also demanded that he supervise sabotage now that Rintelen had been removed. Papen refused to have his agents commit such acts in the U.S., but he did send a group of saboteurs to Canada to blow up strategic parts of the Canadian Pacific Railway in order to prevent Canadian troops from reaching ships sailing for England. Canadian police and the Royal Mounted Police were able to track down the saboteurs before they could do any damage.

Meanwhile, Papen spent a good deal of time having forged papers prepared for German nationals in the U.S. wanting to return to Germany to fight for their homeland against the Allies. This, along with the Canadian misadventure, came to the attention of U.S. authorities who declared him *persona non grata* and demanded that he return to Germany. Papen packed his bags and went home. For a short period of time in 1917, Papen served as a military attaché in Spain where he reportedly was in contact with the doomed German spy, Mata Hari. In light of his less than successful mission to the U.S. and his lackluster services in Spain, Papen was assigned to remote duty in Palestine in 1918, as a spymaster for the Turks in their war against the British, chiefly the tracking down of Arab guerrillas under the command of T. E. Lawrence. Again, he was unsuccessful.

Following the war, Papen rose through the political ranks to become Chancellor of Germany in 1932, a position for which he was wholly unsuited. He proved to be a weak pawn for Hitler. Hitler distrusted the intriguing Papen and wanted him out of the way. In 1939, he appointed him ambassador to Turkey, neutral in World War II. In that capacity, Papen conducted a vast spy network in Turkey, as did the Allies.

In 1943, through a German clerk in his embassy, Papen was introduced to an Albanian named Elyeza Bazna, who worked as a valet for the British ambassador in Ankara and offered, for huge sums, to steal important secrets for the Germans. After confirming Bazna's claim, Papen approved of the deal, giving Bazna a codename that the world would later associate with high espionage—"Cicero."

Papen paid Bazna enormous amounts of money in British bank notes, but Papen never realized that the notes, which were sent to him from German Foreign Minister Joachim von Ribbentrop, were all forgeries. The information the wiley little valet gave Papen was so important that the Germans found it impossible to believe. He supplied them with the actual records of meetings between Churchill and Roosevelt at Casablanca, as well as information from the Allied high command regarding the planned invasion of Europe. The Germans even learned from Bazna the codename "Overlord," but could not discern its meaning (the invasion of France in 1944).

Turkish intelligence then learned that there was a serious security leak in the British Embassy but they could not identify the spy among the English. An OSS agent, Fritz Kolbe, a German national working in Ribbentrop's Foreign Office in Germany, filched a cable sent from Papen to Ribbentrop in which Bazna's name was mentioned. He passed this on to OSS spymaster Allen Dulles in Switzerland, who, in turn, notified Claude Dansey of British Intelligence.

Papen, following the war, returned to a devastated Germany. He was arrested and tried for war crimes in the Nuremberg trials in 1946. He was sent to prison and, following his release, he wrote his memoirs, attempting to justify a lifetime of double-dealing and intrigue.

[ALSO SEE: *Abwehr; Elyeza Bazna; Allen Dulles; Claude Dansey; Reginald Hall; Fritz Kolbe; T. E. Lawrence; Mare Island Sabotage; Mata Hari; MI6; Walther Nicolai; OSS; Franz von Rintelen*]

PAQUES, GEORGES
French Spy for Soviets ▪ (1914–   )

ONE OF THE STRANGEST OF SPIES TO TURN OVER VITAL information to the Soviets was Georges Paques, a well-educated French civil servant who insisted at his 1964 trial that he was not a low-life spy but a private diplomat who had been preserving world peace through his espionage.

An intellectual and a teacher, Paques served in Algeria after World War II and it was here, as early as 1944, that he came into contact with NKVD agents who cultivated him. In 1958, he became an official to the joint chiefs of staff of the French Defense Ministry. Then Paques obtained a position with NATO, his credentials allowing him to rise to the position of Deputy chief of NATO's press and information department. As such, Paques had access to NATO top secrets, which he began passing to the Russians.

Paques' espionage came to an end when Soviet spymaster Anatoli Golytsin defected in 1962 and began identifying Western agents working for the NKVD and KGB. Paques had been one of his agents when the Soviet spymaster had specialized in penetrating NATO security. Golytsin was able to provide DST, French counterintelligence, with copies of NATO documents that Paques himself had signed.

Paques's 1964 trial was the first to appear in the French Security Court, which had been newly created by President Charles de Gaulle. The defendant presented himself not as a traitor and NKVD spy but as a patriotic Frenchman who had done nothing more than try to preserve world peace by giving the Russians top secrets. The court did not agree. He was convicted and sent to prison for life.

[ALSO SEE: *Anatoli Golytsin; NKVD*]

PARIS AGENCY
Monarchist Spy Network in French Revolution ▪ (1791–1797)

AT THE START OF THE FRENCH REVOLUTION, THE Spanish Ambassador in Paris, acting for the jeopardized Louis XVI and his queen, Marie Antoinette, organized a royalist espionage network known as the Paris Agency. Its aim was to collect information on revolutionaries that could be used to convince other European monarchies to intervene in the Revolution and save French monarchs.

The Agency lost considerable support when Louis XVI and Marie Antoinette were beheaded in 1793. When Louis XVII, their son, was murdered in 1795, the claimant to the French throne, Comte de Provence took the title of Louis XVIII but he did not inspire a great deal of royalist support. The most sinister and brutal revolutionary leader, Maximilien de Robespierre fell from power in 1794. This momentarily revived the activities of the Agency, but Robespierre was replaced by a five-man Directory bent on giving power to Napoleon Bonaparte, not the restoration of the monarchy.

In 1797, the Agency recruited new agents who soon proved to be revolutionaries who exposed the network and were responsible for the round-up of the few royalist agents with the courage to remain in Paris.

PELTON, RONALD
U.S. Spy for Soviets ▪ (1942–)

PELTON WORKED FOR THE NSA IN A MINOR CAPACITY, joining that ultra-secret agency in 1965. He resigned in 1979 and the following year he established contact with the KGB. Pelton delivered whatever secrets he had stolen from NSA files to the Soviets and continued his contact with them for the next five years, receiving small sums for his information. The Soviets at the time may or may not

Ronald Pelton sold NSA secrets to the Soviets after he retired from that ultra-secret organization.

have found Pelton's information useful but it was customary for the KGB to continue liaisons with any American citizens who might later be useful to them, keeping them on the dole, promising more money in greater sums to come, always to come. Pelton was one of these. He was finally unearthed by federal agents, tried and convicted in 1986. Pelton was sent to prison for life.

PENKOVSKY, OLEG
Soviet Double Agent ▪ (1919–1963)

THE SON OF A CZARIST OFFICER WHO FOUGHT THE Bolsheviks in the Russian civil war, Penkovsky was born and educated in Ordzhonikidze. From 1945 to 1948, Penkovsky attended the Frunze Military Academy in Moscow and was then assigned to the GRU, military intelligence.

Penkovsky's first espionage assignment was in Ankara where, in 1955, he served as a military attaché in the Soviet Embassy. He spied on Turkish military installations, as well as those of the U.S. in Turkey. The following year he returned to Russia and studied military engineering. The GRU and the KGB considered Penkovsky, who had always carried out instructions to the letter, to be one of its most reliable agents.

Penkovsky, however, felt that Soviet Premier Nikita Khrushchev was irresponsible, a thug at heart who could bring the world to nuclear disaster. He was also disillusioned with communism and its obvious aim to dominate the world. In 1961, Colonel Penkovsky was designated to lead a Soviet trade delegation to London, but his real mission was to operate a KGB spy network.

When British businessman Greville Wynne arrived in Moscow to arrange for the Soviet delegation's visit, he met with Penkovsky. Wynne was startled to hear Penkovsky tell him that he wanted to talk to Western intelligence officers once he arrived in London. Wynne, who had served with British intelligence, set up this meeting, which occured almost immediately after the Soviet delegation arrived in London.

Penkovsky told CIA and MI6 officers that he wanted to help the West and, after convincing them that he was sincere, his offer was accepted. He was to be a double spy, pretending to conduct Soviet espionage while sending reports to the West. In 1961 and 1962, Penkovsky proved to be a wide, deep, and flowing river of secret Soviet information for the West. He passed along to the CIA and MI6 Soviet secrets involving Russia's overall military aims, plans, and espionage operations around the world (and identifying scores of Soviet agents), armaments, missiles, even details on Russian space satellites.

The Soviet GRU mole for the CIA, Oleg Penkovsky, at his trial in Moscow; he was later executed as an example to his fellow spies.

chev in the Cuban Missile Crisis. Moreover, minutes of a war council meeting that Khrushchev presided over, in which the Soviet Premier decided to back down from Kennedy, were sent on to the CIA by Penkovsky, one of the Agency's greatest espionage coups.

The KGB slowly came to realize that a highly positioned Soviet official was feeding the West information. Penkovsky was finally pinpointed and arrested. Wynne was arrested in Soviet-controlled Budapest, Hungary. (He would spend a year in prison before being released and sent back to England.)

In 1963, Penkovsky was tried and convicted in a show trial after prosecutors spent six months putting together evidence to convict him of treason and espionage. A few days after Penkovsky's conviction, *Izvestia* reported that Penkovsky had been shot to death.

[ALSO SEE: *CIA; Cuban Missile Crisis; GRU; KGB; MI6*]

PERI, MICHAEL A.
U.S. Spy for Soviets ▪ (1968–)

A NATIVE OF LAGUNA NIGUEL, CALIF., SPECIALIST 4th Class Michael Peri disappeared from his post at the U.S. Army base in Fulda, West Germany, on February 21, 1989. Peri resurfaced twelve days later and was held in custody. Army investigators immediately suspected the intelligence specialist of handing over secrets to the Soviets.

By mid-March 1989, investigators had assembled enough evidence to charge Peri with the theft of stolen classified information. The classified documents Peri turned over to the Soviets specified the order of battle for U.S. tanks and helicopters. Peri, an expert on Warsaw Pact radar equipment, had been assigned as an electronic signal interceptor of the S-2 intelligence section of his unit, the 11th Armored Cavalry Regiment, then responsible for the front-line defense of the border between East and West Germany.

At first Peri claimed innocence. He then changed his plea to guilty when facing court-martial. He admitted giving the East Germans classified data, stating: "I really didn't have a plan. My primary reason was to leave behind all the frustrations and problems at work. Everything had been wrong. I wasn't enjoying myself. I wanted to start over somewhere else." He said that he had been looking at intelligence maps showing Russian troop dispositions and simply wanted to see what they looked like.

Peri had been considered a model soldier and had been promoted several times. Because of that he had been given a substantial workload and had not been permitted to join his unit on a survival training

(The Soviet double agent delivered more than 5,000 photographs to the CIA and MI6 over an eighteen-month period.)

The manner in which Penkovsky delivered information to MI6 when he was in Moscow was prosaic but effective. He strolled along Moscow's Tsventnoy Boulevard and sat down on a bench next to Mrs. Ruari Chisholm whose husband was Penkovsky's control at MI6. The Russian double spy simply handed a box of candy to the Chisholm children. Under the candy was microfilm. Penkovsky, using the Western code name "Alex," took great quantities of top secret Soviet documents out of KGB and GRU headquarters each night and photographed them in his small flat overlooking the Moscow River. He used a Minox camera that MI6 had provided him. Sometimes, Penkovsky met with Wynne and simply handed him dozens of rolls of film.

Penkovsky's information about Russian missiles (or the lack of them for an all-out war) armed President Kennedy in his showdown with Khrush-

mission. His workload would also delay his planned furlough to Spain. In short, Peri was in a fit of temperamental pique when he decided to give away his nation's secrets. He drove to the East German border, climbed a fence, and was shortly picked up by two East German sentries who turned him over to KGB interrogators.

The East Germans, after taking his disk packed with U.S. secrets and interrogating him in several safe houses in Berlin, allowed him to return when he got homesick. "I couldn't handle leaving my parents behind, my friends behind," Peri said. "Taking what I had coming was better." By returning voluntarily, Peri's sentence was thirty years in prison instead of life.

[ALSO SEE: *KGB*]

PERLET, CHARLES
French Spy in Bonaparte Era ▪
(1769–1828)

A PRINTER BORN IN GENEVA, PERLET MOVED TO PARIS and opened a small publishing firm. During the French Revolution he published pamphlets that sided with King Louis XVI. His published royalist views caused Perlet to be sent into exile in French Guyana in 1797. He was allowed to return to France in 1804 on the proviso that he become a Bonapartist spy, working for Napoleon's spymaster and police chief, Joseph Fouché.

Fouché wanted to lure royalist spy Louis Fauche-Borel back to France and he used Perlet and his former royalist reputation to accomplish that end. Perlet began corresponding with Fauche-Borel in 1806, stating that he respresented a powerful underground committee dedicated to the restoration of the monarchy and he asked the royalist agent to come to Paris to meet the committee members. The cautious Fauche-Borel sent his nephew, Charles Vitel, instead. The hapless Vitel was arrested and executed in 1807.

After this ruthless entrapment, Perlet was known to royalists as a Bonapartist agent and he was shunned by those seeking to restore the monarchy. When Napoleon met defeat and the Bourbons regained the throne, Perlet, financially adrift, attempted to make money by publishing a tract that portrayed Fauche-Borel as a spy for Fouché. Fauche-Borel sued Perlet and won in 1816. Broke and discredited, the scheming Perlet fled to Geneva where he successfully blackmailed King Louis XVIII for large sums of money, after having secured documents that would have proved embarrassing to the monarch.

[ALSO SEE: *Louis Fauche-Borel; Joseph Fouché*]

PETROV, VLADIMIR
Soviet Spymaster in Australia ▪
(1907–1966)

T HE OFFSPRING OF PEASANTS, PETROV (BORN Shorokhov in Siberia) received little schooling before going to work as a blacksmith's apprentice in 1919. He joined the Communist youth movement, Komsomol, and finished high school under the party's indoctrination. So imbued with communism was Petrov that when he joined the Soviet Navy in 1930 he used the name Proletarsky to signify his support of the proletariat.

In 1933, Petrov was recalled to Moscow and allowed to enlist in the OGPU, the then Soviet intelligence organization (later called the KGB). He served in China as a spy in 1937 and returned a year later to work in the OGPU cipher section to which he was named director a few years later.

By 1943, the cryptologist spy had risen to the rank of major and had adopted the name he would finally

KGB director of espionage in Australia Vladimir Petrov, who defected along with his wife, the objective of SMERSH assassins.

use, Vladimir Petrov. Sent to neutral Sweden, he immediately established a spy network, working out of the Soviet Embassy in Stockholm. Following the war, Petrov returned to what was now KGB headquarters, where he remained until 1951 when he was sent to the Soviet Embassy in Canberra, Australia, ostensibly as a consul but really as a spymaster.

Petrov's assignment was to establish a sophisticated Soviet spy network and launch a full-scale espionage campaign against Australia. His wife Evdokia, a cipher clerk, also went to Australia to work with him. Though liberally supplied with funds, Petrov found his task next to impossible. Too few government contacts could be found who were willing to provide him with information.

KGB chief Lavrenti Beria became extremely critical of Petrov, bullying and lambasting him in coded cables, accusing him of failing his party and his country. Petrov grew embittered against the Soviet regime. Suddenly Beria was arrested and executed. Petrov was recalled to Moscow. He knew what awaited him since he had been Beria's hand-picked man and was thought close to the KGB chief. Petrov contacted Mikhail Bialogusky, a Polish refugee whom he had befriended and whom Petrov rightly believed was a member of the Australian intelligence agency.

Petrov asked the Australians for political asylum on April 5, 1954, the very day Petrov expected his replacement from Moscow to arrive. Petrov defected and brought a great number of documents, exposing Soviet spying. It was a severe blow to the KGB, which, of course, denied everything. The KGB also took action against Evdokia Petrov, who was by then a ranking KGB official in Australia. Petrov had not told his wife he intended to defect.

Mrs. Petrov was arrested at the Soviet Embassy and escorted under guard to the airport in Sydney. She was being sent back to Moscow, presumably to answer charges for her husband's defection, an act she apparently knew nothing about, even though that day's papers carried the news. Alerted by the press, an angry Australian crowd assembled at the Sydney airport, shouting and threatening the guards who literally pushed Mrs. Petrov onto a BOAC Constellation, so hard that she lost one of her high-heeled shoes and had to walk barefoot to her seat.

The plane flew off toward Darwin, the next stop. During the flight, a Russian-speaking stewardess asked Mrs. Petrov if she had seen the newspapers reporting how her husband had begged her to join him. She had not. She went to the women's lavatory where the stewardess read the appeal from the newspaper, translating it for Mrs. Petrov. She nodded, then stated that she wanted to stay with her husband.

The pilot contacted Darwin and, when the plane landed, Australian police and intelligence officers, along with Petrov were on hand. After speaking with her husband, the KGB agents began to tug at the woman. She shouted in Russian that she wanted

asylum in Australia. The KGB men began pushing her across the tarmac to the waiting plane. Then the Aussies reacted. They grabbed the KGB guards and disarmed them, taking the Walther automatics both men carried. (They were thought to be SMERSH agents under assignment to execute Mrs. Petrov at the first opportunity.)

Both Petrov and his wife later appeared before the Royal Commission investigating Soviet espionage in Australia and showed in detail how the Russian spy network had operated. The information supplied by the Petrovs included details on the flight and defection to the Soviet Union of British intelligence agents Guy Burgess and Donald Maclean. The Petrovs then went to live on a small farm under assumed names.

[ALSO SEE: *Lavrenti Beria; Guy Burgess; KGB; Donald Maclean; SMERSH*]

PHILBY, HAROLD ADRIAN RUSSELL (KIM)
British Spy for Soviets ▪ (1912–1988)

FEW BRITISH TRAITORS AND COUNTERSPIES HAVE earned such national revulsion as did Harold "Kim" Philby. Vain, arrogant, cynical, and oozing with self-confidence, he was a clever spy who reveled in outwitting the British intelligence agencies for whom he worked. He was a dedicated Marxist who preferred the tyranny of communism to Western democracy at any cost, including his own citizenship and reputation.

Philby, like many of his co-agents in British intelligence, never really had to work for anything. He was born into an upper-class family at Ambala, India, where his father was a high-ranking civil service officer. (He was early on nicknamed Kim after the boy hero of the Kipling novel, which, as if in grim prediction of Philby's later secret profession, was focused upon espionage in nineteenth-century India.)

After graduating the prestigious Westminster school in 1928, Philby went on to Trinity College at Cambridge from which he graduated in 1933. Trinity was the first building block in Philby's construction as a spy and Soviet double agent. It was here that he met young men who, like himself, would become the secret servants of Moscow—Anthony Blunt, Guy Burgess, and Donald Maclean, among others.

Early on they all secretly swore their allegiance to communism and were recruited early as NKVD spies, although the ever-cautious Philby never actually joined the Communist Party. Using a motorcycle purchased with money supplied by his father, he took his college vacations in France, Austria, and Germany where he said he would study political conditions "in countries ripe for revolution." In 1932, Philby

Britain's arch-traitor and double agent for Russia, Kim Philby, shown at the time he worked for British intelligence in World War II.

lications so as hide his Communist beliefs. When the Spanish Civil War broke out, Philby got a job as a correspondent for the London General Press, a small news agency, to cover the war. He was really being sent to Spain by the Soviets to spy on the Falangists rebelling against the Republic. Philby, as well as Burgess, had aligned themselves with the right-wing Anglo-German Fellowship, attending formal dinners that raised funds for Nazi groups and where swastikas were prominently displayed on the long dinner tables. Their membership in such a group had been dictated by the NKVD as a perfect smokescreen for their real political convictions.

Philby, because of his membership in the Anglo-German Fellowship group, was approved as a journalist and welcomed at Franco's headquarters. He moved from one city to another as it was conquered by Franco, prying information loose from cooperative Falangist commanders and sending this information across the lines to Communist contacts, information that Moscow thought most valuable.

When the Republican cause collapsed in 1939, the London *Times* hired Philby as their German correspondent. He was in an excellent position to spy on the Nazis for the Soviets. He was thought of as a right-wing journalist with Nazi sympathies and was welcomed to the inner circles of high-ranking Nazi officials and German generals.

Philby was back in England at the outbreak of war between Britain and Germany but he was off with the

went to Germany to witness the upheaval resulting from the election of Franz von Papen as chancellor, and the election of Nazis to the Reichstag.

Philby's "study" of the political situation there was to take part in street fighting at every opportunity. He joined the Communists in fighting Nazi Brown Shirts and returned to Trinity with a gash on his forehead that he boasted was the result of a storm trooper smashing him with a steel rod. Philby later returned to Germany to befriend Communist propagandist and publisher Willi Münzenberg, helping him set up a phony World Peace Congress with a gullible and duped Lord Robert Cecil at its head. (This organization was sharply profiled in Alfred Hitchcock's superb espionage film, *Foreign Correspondent*, 1940.) Münzenberg and Louis Dolivet (an alias for NKVD spy Ludwig Brecher) were the Congress' secretaries.

By then Philby and his friends were deeply committed to communism, recruited by active Communist Party chiefs Roy Pascal and Maurice Dobb. Others like John Cornford recruited Michael Straight, Maclean, Burgess, Philby, and Peter J. Astbury were thought to be good candidates as NKVD moles; it was apparent that they were all willing to spy on England, a country they had secretly abandoned in their first year at college.

Upon his graduation, Philby went into journalism, seeking to be employed by politically moderate pub-

Soviet spymaster Anatoli Gorsky (alias Gromov), one of Kim Philby's many handlers during the British agent's long and notorious espionage career.

British Expeditionary Force, which was sent to France. By then he was thought of as a seasoned war correspondent and was shown every courtesy by the British high command. He also gained access to military secrets that he most certainly sent on to his Communist spymasters.

When France fell, Philby returned to England once more where, despite his one-time membership in the Anglo-German Fellowship (many members having been detained for the duration of the war), was courted as an ideal candidate for the British Secret Intelligence Service, the vaunted SIS. Maclean and Burgess also obtained important government jobs that gave them access to secrets. All fed their Soviet controls every piece of classified information they could obtain.

Philby's most important contribution to SIS was to put MI6 agents in touch with the Soviet network operated by Sandor Rado in Switzerland (with the NKVD's approval), which resulted in SIS receiving valuable information on the German military. Burgess, on the other hand, was able to provide MI5 (where he worked from 1939 to 1941) with the iden- tification of Tyler Kent, a code clerk in the American Embassy, and Anna Wolkoff, who had been sending the secret correspondence between Roosevelt and Churchill to the Abwehr. Burgess, like Philby, got his information from Soviet spymasters.

Philby later entered SOE (Special Operations Executive), a British espionage network working with the undergrounds of Nazi-occupied countries). At first, Philby and his Soviet spymasters thought this would be an excellent opportunity to obtain information on underground movements where future Soviet spies could be recruited. He was not to be sent into the field, however, because he had already been identi- fied by the Abwehr through his membership in the Anglo-German Fellowship.

Toward the close of the war, England and, to a lesser degree, the U.S. came to distrust its ally Russia, realizing that Stalin's post-war plans included the seizing of central European countries as they were liberated from the fleeing Germans. Churchill wanted the Soviets closely monitored. Philby seized upon this, offering to establish an anti-Communist desk inside SIS. His SIS superiors realized that Philby had been in contact with high-ranking Russian officers in England and elsewhere, strictly in his SIS duties (as far as they knew). They approved of Philby's plan, which delighted his Soviet control, Anatoli Lebedev who had replaced Boris Krotov, a KGB spymaster who had long controlled the British spy.

Philby called his new agency "SIS, section 5," no doubt in mocking imitation of MI5. His offices on Ryder Street were one floor below that of the American OSS. William J. Donovan and Allen Dulles of the OSS came often to the building and sometimes conferred with Philby who happily established these contacts to later infiltrate OSS and its successor, the CIA.

One of the detailed reports Philby provided SIS was the complete background on a Russian spy named Boris Krotov who had operated in England for years. Unfortunately, Philby stated to his SIS superiors, Krotov had recently departed for Moscow. It must have appealed to Philby's twisted sense of humor that he was chronicling the espionage career of the very Soviet officer who had been the control for Burgess, Maclean, and himself, among many others. Of course, Philby did not mention his own group of Soviet agents in his sanitized Krotov report. He knew that anyone later researching Soviet espionage in England would begin with his report, which never mentioned the Trinity spies. Philby was thus able to conveniently and cleverly sweep his own spy tracks under a heavy carpet that he himself had woven.

Because he was seen as a foremost authority on Soviet espionage, Philby, following World War II, was selected to go to Turkey, which had been neutral dur- ing the war, and report on possible Soviet incursions into that country that might threaten Britain's Middle East oil interests, as well as the Suez Canal. In February 1947, Philby went to Istanbul as an acting first secretary of the Foreign Office. His Soviet con- trol, Lebedev, was overjoyed that Philby's assignment was to spy on Soviet agents in Turkey, Syria, Iraq, and Lebanon. His contact was no less a personage than Sergei Alexandrovich Vinogradov, the Soviet Ambassador to Turkey and an old friend of Philby's— they had met in Vienna in 1933.

Yuri Feoktislov, a Soviet spymaster who had operated for a quarter of a century in the area, became Philby's Soviet control. Istanbul was then swarming with American, British, and Russian spies. The Turks also had their own agents, one of whom being Ismail Akhmedov-Ege who had been one of Stalin's handpicked spies and who had risen to the rank of colonel in the GRU. He had returned to his native Turkey in 1942 in the guise of a Tass correspondent. He spent his time spying on Franz von Papen's agents and, along with an old-time Soviet agent, A. M. Solovyev, was part of the abortive attempt to assassi- nate von Papen outside of his embassy in Ankara. Akhmedov-Ege watched Philby closely in Istanbul, perhaps knowing long earlier that he was a Soviet double agent. He nevertheless did not reveal any information on Philby until he went to work for the CIA in 1951.

Another threat to Philby was more immediate. Konstantin Volkov, the Russian consul-general in Turkey, contacted British intelligence officers, saying that he wanted to defect and that he knew of British agents in Istanbul who were working for the Russians. When Philby heard about this he took over Volkov's case. Philby acted before Volkov could (believing the Russian was about to betray him); he contacted the KGB, then stalled the recovery of Volkov until SMERSH agents could seize the would-be defector and rush him back to the Soviet Union where he was liquidated.

Philby's double game accelerated in Istanbul. As part of his Foreign Office duties, he regularly met with nationalist leaders attempting to wrest back control of Albania from the Communists who had seized the country in 1945. Through these contacts, Philby was able to learn about the planned nationalist raids into Albania. He passed this information to Lebedev and when the nationalists crossed into Albania the Communists were waiting for them, killing or capturing scores of these patriots.

When the CIA and SIS later planned a covert invasion of Albania, Philby and Burgess obtained advanced information on this operation and passed it along to the Soviets who foiled the Anglo-American mission. Philby then prepared documentation on the Soviet counterespionage thrust, which he gave to SIS but, unfortunately, it was too late. The loss of Albania had already been conceded by the Americans and British. As usual, however, Philby was lauded for his outstanding though untimely intelligence reports.

In 1949, he was sent to Washington as the first secretary to the British ambassador. His job was to act as a liaison officer between the CIA and MI6. Moscow was again overjoyed. The Soviets now had an agent at the very core of Western espionage operations. Burgess arrived in Washington a year later and he worked closely with Philby to funnel Western secrets to the Soviets, including top-level data on NATO and atomic research. By 1951, however, the double spies began to go to pieces. Philby, always a heavy drinker, began to make mistakes, failing to pass along information to his Soviet controls in Washington because of hangovers and homosexual liaisons. Burgess was by then an alcoholic and his drunken behavior soon caused him to be recalled to London.

Then Philby heard from Blunt that MI5, long suspicious of Donald Maclean, was about to arrest Maclean and his on-and-off lover Burgess. Philby notified Burgess. In a dramatic on-the-spot act, both Burgess and Maclean suddenly fled England, going to Moscow, a defection that shocked the Western espionage establishment. Burgess and Maclean, smug in their ability to escape, held a press conference in Moscow on February 12, 1956 in which they lambasted Western democracies as corrupt and oppressive, the reasons they gave for their decision to defect.

Philby was safe for the moment; however, the Soviet-Turkish spy, Akhmedov-Ege, had gone over to the CIA, bringing a dossier on Kim Philby that identified him as a deep mole for the Soviets. When Philby returned to England he was confronted by MI5 with this information. He coolly agreed to a long interrogation in which he flatly denied any Soviet ties. His argument was that he was being pilloried because Burgess and Maclean had been college chums but that he was not guilty merely because of association.

Percy Sillitoe, head of MI5, went after Philby with a vengeance but SIS chief Stewart Menzies thought

Kim Philby in 1955 at a press conference, still denying he had betrayed his native England.

that Philby was still a loyal and gifted British agent who was being maligned because of the actions of some of his friends. Playing the indignant and insulted hero, Philby resigned from the Foreign Office and rented a London apartment. He dabbled in real estate and other business dealings, mostly in Europe. His family estate provided funds, as usual. Meanwhile, some British politicians believed that Philby was the unidentified "third man," who had warned Burgess and Maclean.

Other politicians, believing in Philby's SIS record, supported the spy, including Prime Minister Harold Macmillan who publicly stated that Kim Philby was an upstanding British citizen who had heroically served his country. Such endorsements caused SIS to recall Philby to service, although he was not given any post of significance. It is staggering to think that a suspected double agent was so sanctioned but MI6 chiefs may have thought to keep Philby close so as to better keep him under surveillance. Moreover, a common belief today among intelligence communities is that British intelligence simply did not want to bring Philby to an open trial. Such a trial might reveal British spymasters to be gullible and naive members of a "good old boys" club who had been duped by a shrewd Soviet double agent that they themselves had nurtured, promoted, and fawned over.

Hard suspicion was again directed at Philby on September 12, 1962, when William John Christopher Vassall, a clerk in the Admiralty Office was arrested

Philby, who defected to Russia in 1963, is shown walking the streets of Moscow, where he died in 1988.

on espionage charges. He had been named as a Russian agent by Soviet spymaster and defector Anatoli Golytsin, who had also named Kim Philby.

On January 23, 1963, Philby deserted his family and fled to Soviet Russia. While his wife Eleanor waited for him at a dinner party, Philby walked through a heavy downpour to a dock in the Beirut harbor and boarded the Polish cargo ship *Dalmatova,* which sailed for the Russian port of Odessa. Philby was kept for many months in Kuybishev on the Volga, a thousand miles from Moscow and his friends Burgess and Maclean. By the time he reached Moscow, Burgess was dead of a heart attack at age fifty-two. The cause was heavy drinking.

Philby did see Maclean on occasions but longed to have his wife and children join him. They did, with the tacit approval of British intelligence. Eleanor Philby left her husband in 1965, going to the U.S. About the same time, Philby began living with Melinda Maclean who had also joined her defecting husband and then deserted Maclean in favor of the wittier Philby.

Philby was held up as a model Communist by the Soviets who gave him a desk at KGB headquarters and the title of general. He was given the Order of Lenin which he proudly showed to British friends visiting Moscow. (He also kept the Order of the British Empire, which had been bestowed upon him in 1946.) He did not elaborate on the feats he performed for the KGB that earned him this high Russian medal. Those "heroic acts" involved betraying scores of Western agents and defectors, such as Konstantine Volkov, and bringing about their murders at the hands of Soviet assassins.

To one and all, he continued to deride his native country, England. He did not consider himself the arch traitor Britain knew him to be. "To betray you must first belong," he stated a few months before his death in May 1988. "I never belonged." Kim Philby then added: "I want to be buried in the Soviet Union, in this country which I have considered to be my own since the 1930s." He got his wish, with full military honors. None mourned in England.

[ALSO SEE: *Abwehr; Anthony Blunt; Guy Burgess; CIA; William J. Donovan; Allen Dulles; Anatoli Golytsin; Tyler Kent; KGB; Donald Maclean; MI5; MI6; NKVD; OSS; Sandor Rado; SIS; SMERSH*]

PICQUART, GEORGES
French Intelligence Officer in Dreyfus Affair ▪ (1854–1914)

ALSATIAN BORN, PICQUART'S FAMILY SWORE ITS loyalty to France after that country lost the province to Germany following its defeat in the Franco-Prussian War (1870–1871). Entering the French Army, Picquart proved to be an able soldier and he attained the rank of Lieutenant-Colonel and was appointed to the Ministry of War where, in 1895, he was named head of French counterintelligence.

In his new capacity, Picquart began to reinvestigate a sensational case. He had been troubled by the conviction of Captain Alfred Dreyfus as a German spy.

According to certain French officers, Dreyfus, an artillery expert attached to the General Staff, had given secret information on French military installations and armaments to Lt.-Col. Max von Schwartzkoppen, the military attaché (and resident spymaster) at the German Embassy in Paris. The only evidence used to convict Dreyfus was a suspicious document, or memorandum called a *bordereau* in which classified information on French artillery was contained. This document had been retrieved from Schwartzkoppen's office by a maid who was really a French spy. The writing on the *bordereau* was identified as being Dreyfus'.

Picquart knew that one of the reasons why Dreyfus had been so ruthlessly prosecuted was due to the fact that he was a Jew, the only Jew, in fact, on the General Staff, and that many high-ranking French officers were virulently anti-Semitic. Moreover, Dreyfus came from a wealthy family and had independent means, which allowed him to live in comfort far beyond that enjoyed by officers superior to him in rank, a condition that angered many of Dreyfus' commanders.

After closely examining the *bordereau* once more, Picquart was able to identify the real author of the *bordereau*, Major Ferdinand Esterhazy. In the original investigation, Major Hubert Henry identified the handwriting of the *bordereau* as that of his close friend, Esterhazy. To save the real spy, Henry falsely fixed the blame on the innocent Dreyfus. In August 1896, Picquart took his findings to his superiors, General Raoul C. F. de Boisdeffre, chief of staff; General Jean Baptiste Billot, war minister; and General Charles-Arthur Gonse, deputy chief of staff.

Picquart pointed out that Dreyfus should be immediately released from Devil's Island where he had been sent for life and restored to his military rank, and that Esterhazy and Henry should be charged with treason and espionage. The generals refused to a accept Picquart's overwhelming evidence. They ordered him to cease his investigations.

The courageous Picquart stood alone. Still he persisted, saying that secrets were still flowing to Germany from Esterhazy and unless the French high command did not arrest this traitor, there was every chance that someone else might expose these spies before the high command and embarrass the French government.

None of Picquart's arguments had any effect on the proud generals. Picquart and members of Dreyfus' family, however, forced the issue and Esterhazy was brought to trial on January 10–11, 1898. The prosecution presented no evidence against him, including that so laboriously produced by Picquart. He was cleared of all charges.

Incensed by this injustice, France's greatest writer, Emile Zola wrote and published, on January 13, 1898, in the widely-read *L'Aurore* his classic *J'Accuse*, an article he addressed to the French Republic. Zola accused the French high command of perverting justice, covering up and destroying evidence, creating forgeries, committing perjury, and purposely imprisoning an innocent man. Zola's brave attack caused the country to erupt into controversy so violent that riots ensued. He himself was convicted of libel and his name stricken from honor rolls. He went into exile in England.

Picquart was also punished for his courageous efforts. He was sent to a remote post where he could cause no more public outcry. The writers of France, however, banded together for the most part and began a relentless campaign to vindicate Dreyfus. Finally, he was brought back from Devil's Island and retried at Rennes in 1899. Again, thanks to the unbudging high command, he was convicted, a verdict that shocked the country for by then most French citizens believed Dreyfus to be innocent.

The court added that Dreyfus was guilty "with extenuating circumstances." French President Emile Loubert then pardoned the cashiered captain but Dreyfus insisted that he receive full vindication. Major Henry was by then dead, having cut his throat in prison while awaiting his own trial for forgery and perjury. Esterazy had fled France and was living in England. Dreyfus fought on and, in 1906, the French Court of Appeals quashed the Rennes verdict and announcing Dreyfus innocent. He was restored to the Army with the rank of major and would serve France well during World War I, earning the Legion of Honor and the rank of lieutenant-colonel. Dreyfus died in 1935, his name respected throughout France. Esterhazy died a year earlier in England, penniless, embittered, hated by all. Georges Piquart, the intrepid French officer who dared to face the wrath of the French high command, died in 1914.

[ALSO SEE: *Alfred Dreyfus; Ferdinand Esterhazy*]

PINKERTON, ALLAN
American Spymaster ▪ (1819–1884)

FROM CHILDHOOD, ALLAN PINKERTON LONGED TO BE a policeman like his father who served on the police force in Glasgow, Scotland, where Pinkerton was born. Instead, he apprenticed to a cooper at an early age, continuing this trade when he emigrated to America in 1842. It was while working in Illinois—chopping wood, according to his own account—that Pinkerton discovered a gang of counterfeiters. He notified authorities and helped capture the gang. This incident spread Pinkerton's reputation as a sleuth and he became a deputy sheriff in Kane County, Illinois, in 1846. The following year he held a similar post in Cook County, which encompassed the sprawling, growing city of Chicago.

In 1850, Pinkerton joined the Chicago Police Department as its first detective. He was so successful

Detective Allan Pinkerton (left), shown with President Abraham Lincoln (center) in 1862, became the Union's first spymaster.

in tracking down wanted criminals that he quit the force about two years later and opened up Pinkerton's National Detective Agency. The detective carefully chose his men from the ranks of police forces and trained them in the arts of detection. His business flourished as the Pinkertons became known for almost always getting their man.

How Pinkerton got his man was often unique. On one occasion he hired a detective who so closely resembled a murdered bank teller that he could have been the dead man's twin. Pinkerton had this detective openly follow the suspected killer, a man named Drysdale. So unnerving was the image of the man he had killed that Drysdale confessed, then committed suicide.

Pinkerton's clients soon numbered large shipping firms and railroads for which he provided heavily armed guards to protect goods and gold shipments. To project the ever-vigilant image Pinkerton envisioned for his agency, he created a memorable logo—a wide open eye with the words "We Never Sleep" arching over it.

In 1860, Abraham Lincoln was narrowly elected President. He was much-hated in the South where he was known as an abolitionist (although he was not). Groups of southern conspirators decided that Lincoln

would never take office and planned to assassinate him when he was en route to Washington for his inauguration. Somewhere along the route of the newly laid Philadelphia-Wilmington-Baltimore Railroad, the conspirators would board the presidential train and either kidnap or kill Lincoln. Hearing of this plot, the railroad's president, Samuel Felton, called in Pinkerton.

The detective, along with his two best operatives, Timothy Webster and Henry Davies, went to Baltimore where he believed the plotters were headquartered. Using the alias E. J. Allen, Pinkerton, and his men infiltrated the southern conspiracy.

Davies learned that the Baltimore plotters were in collusion with Baltimore Police Chief, George P. Kane, a strong southern sympathizer. Kane had promised the plotters that the police would do nothing to interfere with an attempt on Lincoln's life.

Davies immediately informed Pinkerton that an assassin had been chosen but there was no way of identifying him among the conspirators. Then Webster reported that he had learned of a second group of conspirators who planned to destroy the railway line to Washington once Lincoln's death had been announced. Lincoln, meanwhile, had begun his long journey toward Washington, arriving in Philadelphia on February 21, 1861, with a private secretary and six friends.

Although Pinkerton had no idea as to the exact location where the assassin would strike, he concluded that it would be somewhere in Baltimore, along the short stretch of track that linked separate railway lines, one where the train cars were actually pulled by horses through the streets of the city. This would be the area where an assassin could best have access to Lincoln.

When Lincoln departed for Baltimore, he was accompanied by a woman posing as his sister. She was Mrs. Kate Warne. When the train left Philadelphia, Lincoln was escorted by Pinkerton to a sleeping car at the rear of the train. The detective had positioned dozens of his best detectives under the command of Webster and Davies along the route, stationed at key bridges and other places where the conspirators might attempt to destroy the track. As the train moved southward, Pinkerton stood on the rear platform of the last car, noting the flickering lanterns waving an "all's safe" at these key positions.

When the train reached Baltimore and the cars were horse drawn from one terminal to another, no incident occured. By then Pinkerton had completely confused the plotters by releasing a press report to the newspapers that Lincoln would be arriving on a later train. The President-Elect arrived unharmed in Washington to take his oath of office on time.

Lincoln was forever grateful to the vigilant and enterprising Pinkerton and showed that gratitude when he asked the detective to establish an espionage network for the Union shortly after the Civil War began. Pinkerton selected his most trusted men and sent them to the South to report on Confederate troop movements, arms manufacturing, supply depots, and even the morale of enemy soldiers and civilians. He himself ventured many times behind enemy lines, as well as organizing a counterintelligence network in Washington.

Union counterintelligence was not effective, however, against the Confederate's most daring and clever spy, Rose Greenhow, whose high-level military information on the Union plan of attack in the first great battle at Bull Run was given to Confederate General P. G. T. Beauregard, enabling him to achieve an enormous victory. Pinkerton finally exposed Greenhow as the top southern spy in Washington, causing her to be imprisoned for some time but, though he interrogated her endlessly, he could not obtain her confession. She was finally released through her influential Washington friends. Pinkerton also failed to detect Belle Boyd as a Confederate spy when he interviewed her but his top agent, Timothy Webster, proved to be an excellent spy behind enemy lines.

Pinkerton had early on formed a deep friendship with Union General George McClellan. The association was so close that Lincoln came to feel that Pinkerton's espionage agency worked more for McClellan than the President. When McClellan's star fell, so too did Pinkerton's. He was replaced in 1862 by a colossal charlatan, Lafayette Baker, who headed what was later called the Secret Service (not to be confused with the present-day Secret Service, which is a branch of the U.S. Treasury Department). Baker was a self-seeking power broker who used the federal espionage service for his own ends and that of his real master, Secretary of War Edwin Stanton, who was most likely involved in Lincoln's assassination in 1865. Baker would go slightly mad following the war, claim killers were hunting him, and die a mysterious death.

Pinkerton, on the other hand, flourished following the Civil War. His agency expanded, opening offices in New York and Philadelphia, but the headquarters remained in Chicago. Pinkerton detectives were used by large businesses, the railroads, and millionaires seeking protection. He was later portrayed as a tool of big business, even when his agency was hired by banks and railroads to track down and capture the notorious Missouri outlaws, Frank and Jesse James and the Younger brothers who rode with them.

The Pinkertons failed miserably at that task, two of its detectives carelessly tossing a bomb into the window of the James farm and killing Jesse's eight-year-old half-brother Archie and injuring his mother so badly that she lost an arm. This enraged America's most famous outlaw to the point where he tracked the detective in Chicago, following him about but failing to kill him since, as he later told friends, he was in the company of his wife. "I know God some day will deliver Allan Pinkerton into my hands," Jesse James added but this was not to be. James was killed by Bob Ford, one of his own band.

One of the most controversial Pinkerton detectives was James McParland, who infiltrated the Molly Maguires in Pennsvylania where the Mollies were sabotaging mines in order to better their miserable working conditions. McParland identified the ringleaders of this Irish secret society, sending many of them to the gallows and earning the reputation for the Pinkertons as an agency that labored to protect land-greedy railroad magnets, brutal mine owners, and robber barons in general.

The Pinkertons did have some outstanding successes in tracking down east coast bank robbers and master thieves such as Adam Worth. When Pinkerton died in 1884 his left his dynastic detective agency to the care of his sons William and Robert Pinkerton who successfully moved it into the twentieth century.

[ALSO SEE: *Lafayette Baker; Belle Boyd; Rose Greenhow; James McParland; Timothy Webster*]

POLLARD, JONATHAN JAY
U.S. Spy for Israel ▪ (1954–   )

THE YOUNGEST OF THREE CHILDREN, POLLARD'S father was a noted microbiologist who taught at Notre Dame in South Bend, Indiana. A National Honor Society member, Pollard entered Stanford University and majored in political science.

From childhood, the Pollards had instilled in Jonathan a deep respect for Israel, repeatedly saying that "this land is a Godsend for Jews." He had heard countless stories about brave Israelis fighting for liberty and vowed that when he grew up he would aid Israel. While at Stanford, Pollard falsely claimed that he had dual citizenship in the U.S. and in Israel and he even bragged to classmates that he was a secret agent for that country, a member of the Mossad.

Though he dramatically saw himself as a romantic espionage figure battling imaginary enemies on behalf of Israel, Pollard decided against migrating following his graduation, abandoning a long-stated ambition. Instead, he entered the Fletcher School of Law and Diplomacy at Tufts University in Boston to work on a graduate degree. It was here that he began to activate his private daydreams, informing on foreign students to the CIA.

Pollard then applied for a job with the CIA but was turned down because of his occasional drug use while in college. U.S. Navy intelligence, however, hired him as a research specialist in 1979. Working in Washington, Pollard grew resentful over what he thought was a prevalent anti-Semitic attitude among his fellow workers. In 1982, he attended a meeting between U.S. Navy intelligence officers and officials of Israeli intelligence and came away believing that the U.S. was unfairly withholding secrets that were vital to the security of Israel, America's ally.

Two years later Pollard took action. A friend called him at that time to rave about an Israeli hero whom he had recently met, Colonel Aviem Sella, one of Israel's top war aces who had fought in four wars and who had led the celebrated Israeli air strike that had wiped out Iraq's nuclear reactor in 1981. At Pollard's insistence, the friend arranged for a meeting between him and Sella.

Sella contacted superiors who approved of a "walk-in," meaning that the Israeli pilot would entertain a confidential meeting with someone, Pollard, who literally walked in from the street with secret information to impart. Once approved, Pollard met with Sella on May 29, 1984, in the coffee shop of the Washington Hilton Hotel. Pollard, who had already been checked by the intelligence arm of the Israeli Defense Department, came right to the point, telling Sella that his aim was to aid Israel "strengthen its defense capability" by supplying U.S. secrets.

The wily Sella gave his tacit approval and met once again with Pollard a short time later. Pollard offered him forty-eight documents, which Sella carefully examined.

From that point onward, Pollard dumped a staggering amount of U.S. classified documents into the hands of Israeli intelligence. The spy had no difficulty in smuggling out the secrets, more than 1,000 classified cables and messages and 800 documents, many of them labelled top secret. He simply signed for them and was allowed to take them home. U.S. intelligence later estimated that the motherlode of secrets Pollard sold to the Israelis, while being paid $2,500 a month, would occupy a space six feet by six feet by ten feet.

A good deal of these secrets involved Soviet-made weaponry that had been supplied to Arab countries that were openly hostile to Israel. Some documents pinpointed the locations of anti-Israeli terrorist training camps and headquarters. This information allowed Israel to conduct an air strike on October 1, 1985, which destroyed the headquarters of the Palestinian Liberation Organization in Tunisia.

The money kept flowing as long as Pollard kept stealing the secrets. The Israelis could not get enough; they asked for more and more. Their greed for information was boundless. It was later speculated that had not the Israelis demanded such a heavy volume of classified material from Pollard, the espionage looting might have gone on undetected.

But Pollard was taking home suitcases packed with classified material, which finally alerted FBI agents who began to look into his background and contacts. Pollard himself realized he was being followed. Then FBI agents and interrogators for the Naval Investigative Service brought Pollard in for questioning. They wanted to know why he was taking so many sensitive documents from his office to his home. He was analyzing their contents, which was his job, he said. He presented himself coolly as a dedicated intelligence researcher.

The FBI did not act. The Bureau was not sure if Pollard was a spy or not but they followed him night and day, waiting for him to make contact with representatives of a foreign power. Knowing this, Pollard and his wife decided to make a break for it. Their plan was simple. They would drive to the Israeli Embassy and ask for asylum, that they be sent to Israel where they would apply for citizenship and take up residence. To that end, the couple got into their green Mustang on November 21, 1985, and drove to the Israeli Embassy. With them they carried their birth certificates and marriage license. Anne Pollard held the family cat Dusty in her arms and had even brought along the animal's vaccination record.

Pollard and his wife drove confidently into the courtyard of the Israeli Embassy but, in minutes, were shocked to learn that no officials would speak with them. Pollard began to argue with an Israeli security officer, demanding that Israel give him and his wife political asylum. The security officer then ordered both of them to leave the embassy. Dejected, the Pollards got back into their car and drove home. FBI agents following them now realized in shock that the foreign power to whom Pollard had been funneling secret information was Israel, American's close friend in the Middle East.

Pollard and his wife were arrested and charged with espionage. The news stunned both America and Israel. Friendly allies on the surface, it was quickly concluded that Israel had seriously violated espionage protocol and risked damaging its special relationship with the U.S. What most found incredible was the fact that Israel resorted to such tactics since it regularly and routinely exchanged information with the U.S. that was vital to the interests of both countries.

Pollard immediately cooperated with U.S. prosecutors, naming names and providing a detailed list of documents he had turned over to Israeli agents. It was his position that he was not spying *against* the United States but *for* Israel, a country to whom he owed his religious and emotional allegiance. Nonsense, said Secretary of Defense Casper Weinberger in a 46-page memorandum to the judge presiding over Pollard's case in 1987. Pollard was simply a dangerous and destructive spy who had betrayed his country for money, despite the image of heroism he used in veiling his espionage.

Convicted, Pollard was sent to prison for life; his wife, Anne, drew a five-year term for collusion and abetting. Israel, meanwhile, worked hard to repair the political damage, although each month, reportedly to this date and until he is released, his spy pay continues, $2,500 each month being deposited in his name in an Israeli bank, money he can claim once he is released and relocates to Israel.

In 1994, attorneys representing Pollard appealed to President Clinton for leniency, asking that their client be released since his plea-bargaining agreement with prosecutors had been violated. The lawyers argued that Pollard had cooperated fully with U.S. investigators on the expectation that he would receive a lighter sentence than life imprisonment. Clinton rejected the plea.

[ALSO SEE: *CIA; FBI; Mossad*]

POPOV, PYOTR SEMONOVICH
Soviet Spy for U.S. ▪ (1916–1959)

IN THE SPRING OF 1953, AN AMERICAN DIPLOMAT stationed in Berlin got into his car to find a note sitting on the seat next to him. It was from Lieutenant-Colonel Pyotr Popov, of the GRU, who brazenly offered his services to the CIA. The CIA was suspicious that the Soviets were attempting to plant a double agent within its midst. It moved cautiously, contacting Popov through George Kisvalter, one of the agency's top handlers of Soviet defectors.

Kisvalter, Russian-born and a man of precise decisions who spoke four languages, was extremely successful in controlling Popov in Germany (as he would be when later handling Soviet mole Oleg Penkovsky). He learned that Popov hated the Soviet regime ruling his country, particularly the KGB, and would do anything to undermine its operations and authority. As a mole, Popov proved invaluable to the CIA, which out of necessity shared the double agent with MI6.

Through subtle persuasion, Kisvalter got from Popov a list of 370 Soviet "illegals," spies operating in the West without the cover of diplomatic immunity. The names of these agents were supplied in the form of cryptonyms, which were then fixed to the identities of Russian agents. Several GRU rings were thus smashed by the CIA, MI6, and the Reinhard Gehlen spy organization operated on behalf of West Germany.

Few CIA and MI6 officials actually knew of Popov's existence (his identity was not shared with the Gehlen organization since that agency was rightly suspected at the time of being riddled with Soviet double agents). Popov had promised Kisvalter that he would continue to work as a mole once he was ordered back to Moscow after his assignment in East Germany was over in 1955.

Before leaving East Germany, Popov again took the unusual form of contacting Western agencies through a written coded note that he simply handed to a member of the British military mission on tour in East Germany, requesting that the note be delivered to the CIA. It was not; instead the British officer handed Popov's note to the station chief of MI6 in West Berlin who ordered his agents to send the note along to the CIA, which they did.

Once back in Moscow, Popov was handled by Russell Langelle, a CIA operative who had diplomatic cover. Langelle worked out a clever system of communication with Popov. The GRU agent would meet with Langelle in Moscow but never at the same location twice. His letter drops were also never used more than once. For three years Popov successfully passed top-secret information to Langelle until, in 1959, KGB agents suddenly arrested both men as they were exchanging papers on a Moscow bus.

Langelle was charged with espionage and expelled from Russia. Popov's fate was horrible beyond imagination. After a speedy trial and conviction, he was taken to a basement boiler room of the KGB building and, while his fellow GRU officers were forced to watch, he was slowly fed alive into a roaring furnace. Only the KGB could conceive of executing a human in such a devilish fashion.

The CIA had lost its most important mole in Moscow and was puzzled as to how he had been identified. KGB officials announced that the trap had been sprung because its agents had been following Langelle about for three years, suspecting him of espionage. When he was finally seen several times with Popov, the Soviets simply arrested both men. This was untrue.

From the time Popov returned from East Germany to his new GRU post in Moscow, KGB officials knew he was working with the CIA. They knew it because the MI6 agent in West Berlin who received Popov's note and sent it to the CIA also sent that information to the KGB. He was George Blake, one of the most sinister and damaging double agents inside MI6. Not until another Soviet agent defected, Michael Goleniewsky, would Blake be identified as an arch traitor and the Soviet mole and be brought to justice.

[ALSO SEE: *George Blake; CIA; Reinhard Gehlen; GRU; KGB; MI6; Oleg Penkovsky*]

POWERS, GARY FRANCIS
U-2 Spy Pilot for U.S. ▪ (1929–1977)

U-2 pilot Gary Francis Powers facing a Soviet tribunal after his capture in 1960.

AT ABOUT 11 A.M., ON MAY 1, 1960, THE INHABITANTS of a small village outside the city of Sverdlovsk heard the ripping sound of a jet plane flying at extremely low level. They rushed from their homes to suddenly hear an earth-shaking crash and see a plume of smoke curling upward in the distance. Above them was a tiny speck descending into the discernable form of a man dangling from a parachute. Several men ran to the parachutist as he landed, knees buckling, struggling with the lines of his chute.

The parachutist stood up, attempting to unbuckle the chute. He was of medium height, stockily built, with close-cropped brown hair graying at the temples and a noticeable birth mark on the left side of his neck. He was a strange sight to the villagers. He wore an odd-looking uniform, a steel-colored suit, a white helmet painted with the number 29, and brown boots. A long-barreled pistol and a knife were holstered on a belt slung about the man's waist. When the villagers asked the dazed airman who he was he replied in a strange language. He was Gary Francis Powers.

When he was turned over to KGB officers, Powers told an English-speaking officer that he had a terrible headache. A physician was summoned who gave him some aspirin. Then the pilot was taken to Moscow where he disappeared for three and a half months inside the labyrinthine bowels of KGB headquarters.

Then, at a show trial decreed by Nikita Khrushchev to show "the insane aggressiveness of the U.S.," to quote the Soviet dictator, Powers was brought into a Moscow court on August 17, 1960, charged with espionage. He stepped into a dock in Moscow to face a grim-faced hostile Soviet tribunal.

He wore a baggy, double-breasted Russian-made suit, a white dress shirt, and a rather loud tie. His square-jawed face was immobile, revealing nothing.

Powers' relatives had flown to Moscow to be on hand. His wife Barbara, 25, dressed in funereal black, entered the court with two lawyers. His father, 55-year-old Oliver Powers, a one-time coal miner from Kentucky who had taken up shoemaking after an accident, entered the court holding tightly to his wife, Ida. He had not been outside of his native hill country since making a visit to Atlanta and Washington in 1935.

Ida Powers took one look at her son standing stoically in the dock and began to weep. Oliver Powers placed his arm around her, saying naively: "They'll know he's a good boy like he's always been. We'll have him back real soon." He was wrong. The U-2 pilot, on trial for violating Soviet air space so that he could photograph Russian defenses, would not again be free until early 1962.

When Powers faced the Soviet tribunal, however, he knew he was on trial for his life, that the Russians had no tolerance for spies and routinely shot them. Facing him was Roman A. Rudenko who had been chief Soviet prosecutor at the Nuremberg war crimes trials. Powers had been interrogated endlessly before his trial; he had cooperated and his prosecutors knew well the answers he would give.

The public questioning began routinely enough, with Rudenko saying: "What is your profession?"

"Pilot," Powers droned back.

"What place of work?"

"Detachment 10-10 at Adana, Turkey."

"When did you receive the order to fly over Soviet territory?"

"In the morning of May 1 [1960]."

"Where did you receive the order to fly to the Soviet Union?"

"In the town of Peshawar in Pakistan."

Powers gave his answers in the flat accent of Pound, Virginia, his home. He was a southerner to the bone, born in Burdine, Kentucky, thirty-one years to the day of his trial. Powers' background was naked before the tribunal, his court-appointed lawyer, Mikhail Grinev, laying out the pilot's past as if opening his college yearbook at Milligan College, from which Powers graduated in 1950. He had joined the Air Force and was trained as a fighter pilot.

In 1956, with the rank of captain, he entered an espionage campaign that involved pilots selected by the CIA to fly U-2 spy planes at high altitudes over the Soviet Union, photographing nuclear test explosions, military exercises, or any other operations that might pose a threat to the West. Using the cover story that these pilots were working for the National Aeronautics and Space Administration (NASA), they were secretly trained, as was Powers, for three months in a secret Nevada desert base before being assigned duty at another base in Incirlik, Turkey.

Powers served at Incirlik for four years. His wife was allowed to live with him in the area while he conducted many spy missions. In late April 1960,

Powers was instructed to fly to a base in Peshawar, Pakistan, where, in a few days, he would undertake another U-2 spy plane mission, flying over the Soviet Union at an altitude of 68,000 feet. He was told that no Soviet plane or ground-to-air missile could reach that height so he would be perfectly safe. Following his mission, he was to fly to Bodo, Norway, and land at an American base.

Of course, that is not what happened, as the Soviet court knew full well. Prosecutor Rudenko was particularly interested in having Powers admit that he had been shot down by a Soviet rocket. (This was a directive from Khrushchev himself who wanted to be able to claim that Soviet air space was impenetrable.) Powers would not give Rudenko what he wanted, but he knew enough not to openly contradict the inquisitor.

"I have no idea what happened," he said. "I heard and felt a hollow-sounding explosion. It seemed to be behind me and I could see an orange-colored light." U.S. officials listening to this description believed that Powers' plane had not been hit by a Soviet missile but had suffered a jet flame-out, which is often accompanied by a jolting explosion of gases at the plane's tail.

Painful expressions were also visible on the faces of Rudenko and other prosecutors when Powers stated that he had been flying over Russian air space for four years, conducting several reconnaissance missions each year. Obviously, Russian air space was not inviolate.

There was no question as to Powers' admitting his responsibility. He began the trial by answering the 4,000-word indictment by quickly stating: "Yes, I am guilty." He then added, as if reading from Soviet promptor cards: "I understand that, as a direct result of my flight, the summit conference [between Soviet

A U.S. U-2 spy plane like the one Powers flew over Soviet air space; it was part jet and part glider, able to reach extreme altitudes and remain there for nine hours. It has an 80-foot wingspan, twice the length of its fuselage.

The immense Moscow courtroom selected for Powers' show trial; Powers stands in the dock at right, closely guarded.

and U.S. diplomats] did not take place and President Eisenhower's visit was called off. I am sincerely sorry that I had anything to do with this."

General Victor Borisoglebsky, presiding judge of the three-man tribunal, could not restrain his eagerness to insert more Soviet propaganda and indictment of the West, interjecting with:

"Did you not think that your flight might provoke armed conflict?"

"The people who sent me should think of these things," Powers coolly replied.

"Did you do your country a good service or an ill service?"

A thin smile crept about the corners of Powers' mouth. "I would say a very ill service." He had apparently given Borisoglebsky an oblique criticism of the U.S., but Powers meant, according to what he told this author in 1970, that because he had failed and was captured he had performed an "ill service," not because he undertook the mission.

Powers admitted that, as a U-2 pilot, he was paid $2,500 each month, $1,000 more than his usual Air Force pay, a statement that caused the poverty-level Russian audience to gasp. This admission also allowed Rudenko to profile Powers as a hired spy. The capturing of the pilot, emphasized the prosecutor, "unmasked completely the criminal aggressive actions of the U.S. ruling quarters [and the] savage man-hating ethics of Allen Dulles and company, placing the dollar, this yellow devil, higher than human life."

Powers admitted all he could safely admit, even telling the court that his commanding officer was Colonel William Shelton and that "six civilian pilots" made up the U-2 spy team. He did not know how the cameras on his plane worked, he stated. He merely pressed some buttons and pulled some switches when reaching certain coordinates. When asked how long Shelton had briefed him before he took his last flight, Powers replied almost casually: "I barely had time to study my maps."

Rudenko pointed out that he was captured with two unmarked survivor maps and a printed plea in fourteen languages that read: "I need food and shelter. You will be rewarded." How did he come to have this printed information, the prosecutor wanted to know. "Someone must have stuck them in my pockets," Powers snapped back.

Reporter James Morris of the Manchester *Guardian* was present, later stating that Powers "presented himself as a poor, deluded jerk . . . a part that I suspect did require much playing. But there are moments when he is suddenly master of the court, summoning from some unsuspected source of strength a remnant of good old-fashioned down-to-earth American guts."

This fortitude was exhibited repeatedly. In one instance, Rudenko pointed out that the American Catholic Cardinal Spellman had visited Powers' air base in Turkey, sneering: "So Cardinal Spellman is interested in military bases."

"I would say that Cardinal Spellman was interested in military personnel, not military bases," Powers shot back.

Defense attorney Grinev did little more than parrot the prosecutor's condemnation of his client and further indict the U.S., at one point shouting: "The defendant should be joined in the dock by his masters who attend this trial invisibly." Grinev did take Powers' wife and parents aside before the trial to tell them that "social factors are very important with our judiciary."

In what amounted to a plea for mercy instead of a defense, Grinev told the court that his client's family lived in near poverty in the hill country of America where its members hardscrabbled a day-to-day existence. He emphasized that Powers had gone to work for the CIA only because of the "mass unemployment," in the U.S. He asked that Powers receive only a seven-year sentence, instead of the harsh 15-year prison term demanded by prosecutor Rudenko. Never once did the defense attorney attempt to prove his client innocent.

In the end, Powers was sentenced to ten years confinement, three years in prison and seven years at hard labor at a work camp where he was scheduled to study the Communist system. Following the trial, Powers met briefly with his family. They were all served tea and caviar sandwiches. Then the U-2 pilot was led from the room and to his cell where he waited until he was exchanged for KGB spymaster Rudolf Abel on February 10, 1962. At that time, Powers and Abel faced each other at the ends of the Glienecker Bridge, which spanned Lake Wannsee, separating Potsdam from West Berlin. Both began walking toward each other and freedom. Powers paced himself with Abel.

"As I walked toward the line [the official white border line painted in the middle of the bridge]," remembered Powers later, "another man—thin, gaunt, middle-aged—approached from the other side. We crossed at the same time." Powers and Abel did not speak. Powers turned his head slightly to look at the Soviet spy but Abel did not glance in his direction, merely peered straight ahead at the KGB men waiting for him on his side of the bridge.

Following Powers' capture and trial, the CIA cancelled its U-2 missions, or it said it did, developing quickly a safer, more effectively accurate system of aerial surveillance, monitoring by satellite, its Spy-in-the-Sky espionage program. For Nikita Khrushchev, the Powers incident was a highwater triumph for the Soviets. He personally went on Russian television to display what he claimed were infrared photos taken at high altitude by cameras in Powers' plane, which the Soviets had reclaimed. This was contra-

Soviet Premier Nikita Khrushchev boasts of the capture of Powers while holding aloft photos of the gold coins taken from the U-2 pilot's pockets.

dicted by Khrushchev himself who also claimed that a Soviet rocket had blown Powers' plane to bits. As he held up the photos, the Russian leader stated: "The pictures are quite clear, but I must say that ours are better."

Then Khrushchev held up a poison needle and said that this is what Powers was supposed to have used on himself to avoid being captured. He added: "Everything alive wants to live." He reveled in showing items that had been taken from Powers' air suit pockets, French francs, Italian lire, Russian rubles, two gold watches and seven gold rings. "What was he going to do," scoffed the premier, "fly to Mars and seduce Martian women?"

Powers returned to the U.S. where he was considered a hero. He wrote a best-selling book, his memoirs, in 1970 and then entered commercial aviation. He was tragically killed in 1977, crashing in a helicopter he was flying for a Los Angeles television station.

[ALSO SEE: *Rudolf Abel; CIA; KGB*]

POYNTZ, JULIET STUART
U.S. Spy for Soviets ▪ (1886–1937?)

ONE OF THE MOST SENSATIONAL DISAPPEARANCES of the late 1930s was that of Juliet Poyntz, a 51-year-old teacher and one of America's ten top Communist leaders. From best information, she was one of the more celebrated murder victims of SMERSH, the assassination arm of the NKVD.

While still a teenager, Poyntz left her home town of Omaha, Nebraska, and moved to New York. She attended Barnard College where she returned as a teacher some years later. Receiving a fellowship from the General Federation of Women's Clubs, she went to England where she studied at Oxford University and the London School of Economics. She returned to New York and, in 1909, Poyntz became an ardent member of the Socialist Party. Four years later,

Juliet Poyntz, who quit communism, denounced Stalin, and threatened to expose the spy network she established in the U.S. shortly before she vanished, most probably a victim of SMERSH assassins in 1937.

despite her political views, which were by then decidedly Communist, she married Dr. Frederick Franz Ludwig Glaser, an attaché to the German consulate in New York.

Poyntz had married this man for only one purpose, to spy on German operations in the U.S., sending this information to Russian revolutionaries in Europe who were then planning the overthrow of the Czar's regime. Following the Russian Revolution of 1917, Poyntz became an enthusiastic member of the Communist Party. By the mid-1920s, Poyntz was one of the most trusted members of the party in the U.S.

GPU and OGPU spymasters in Moscow had such faith in Poyntz that they assigned her delicate espionage missions, which she carried out in Europe and in China in the early 1930s. She also ran for the office of New York State Attorney General on the Communist ticket. She lost but was undeterred. In 1934, she was summoned to Moscow where she received intensive training at NKVD headquarters in the fine arts of espionage. She returned to the U.S. with the assignment of establishing a spy network in America.

Poyntz tackled this job with great energy and enthusiasm, enlisting and training dozens of Communist spies. Then everything went sour in 1936. At that time, Stalin launched his widespread purge trials of old line Bolsheviks, a blatant method of exterminating any possible political opposition in the future. Poyntz rebelled. She denounced Stalin and his NKVD stooges as genocidal killers. She also denounced communism as a savage and murderous political system, telling one and all that she intended to write her memoirs, an exposé of all she knew to be wrong, corrupt, and illegal in the dark Communist world. Some time in late May or early June 1937, she utterly vanished.

Poyntz was last seen walking out of her Manhattan apartment at the American Women's Association clubhouse, taking nothing but the clothes on her back. Her disappearance was not officially noted until her attorney, Elias Lieberman, announced the disappearance. Lieberman said he had searched his client's rooms and found her clothes and valuables present. Her bank account, containing $10,500, was untouched and intact. (The money was later awarded to Poyntz's sister, Eulalie Poyntz, when Juliet Poyntz was officially declared dead in 1944.)

New York's Missing Persons section of the NYPD searched for the woman with considerable vigor, barging into Communist cell meetings and examining the records of Communist Party headquarters and party newspapers. They found nothing. Then Carlo Tresca, editor of an anti-facist newspaper, *Il Martello* (The Hammer), told officials that he believed Juliet Poyntz had been kidnapped and killed by Soviet agents because of her outspoken remarks against Stalin and the Soviet Union.

Tresca pointed to the case of Ignace Reiss, a prominent Russian Communist official who became disillusioned with the party and defected to Lausanne, Switzerland, where he was later assassinated by SMERSH agents. Although Tresca, who was himself later assassinated, never named the persons he thought responsible for Poyntz's disappearance, some of his closest associates later insisted that he had told them that two ubiquitous SMERSH agents, George Mink and Hugo Marx had kidnapped Poyntz, taken her to a Russian merchant ship sailing out of New York, and killed her while on board, dumping her body into the waters of the Atlantic.

[ALSO SEE: *NKVD; Ignatz Reiss; SMERSH*]

PRIME, GEOFFREY (AKA: ROWLANDS)
British Spy for Soviets ▪ (1938–   )

BORN AND RAISED IN STAFFORDSHIRE, ENGLAND, Prime had an unhappy childhood. He was sexually assaulted by an adult relative but still managed to adjust into a clever youth who had technical skills. He attended a technical school before joining the RAF where he applied himself and soon rose to the rank of sergeant. He took a Russian language course and was posted to West Berlin. Lonely and with a deep sense of isolation, Prime daydreamed about the Soviet Union, mistakenly believing that the regime represented the oppressed peoples of the world.

Prime suddenly made a decision to work for the Soviets. He made contact with the KGB by simply going to a Soviet checkpoint in Berlin and handing a note to a Russian officer. Two KGB agents contacted him a short time later.

Knowing that Prime's enlistment was about to run out after twelve years in the RAF, the Soviets encouraged him to use his training to get a job with British Government Communications Headquarters (GCHQ), a source of great communications secrets. Prime did exactly that, obtaining a job at GCHQ in September 1968, where he translated electronic communications intercepts and then sent them on for analysis at Cheltenham, the nerve-center of British communications intelligence.

Taking a vacation to West Berlin, Prime slipped into East Berlin where he underwent more espionage training and was given a complete spy kit that was contained in the false bottom of a briefcase. Inside were invisible inks and specially prepared writing pads on which he was to record his secret messages. He was also given £400 to be used in the purchase of a short-wave radio and a tape recorder. Once back in England, Prime went to work photographing Cheltenham secrets, which he sent on to his control in East Berlin in the form of microdots. He also made contact with his handlers through short-wave broadcasts in coded messages made up of figures and numbers in groups of five increments.

Meanwhile, Prime rose in stature at Cheltenham, becoming a highly regarded translator and processor of signals intelligence (SIGENT). He was transferred to the Center at Cheltenham in 1975, and was asked to work on intelligence information provided by a spy satellite named Rhyolite, which was a CIA operation funneling Spy-in-the-Sky intelligence to the American NSA, British intelligence, MI6, and the Cheltenham electronic nerve center. So sophisticated were the spy satellites that they could monitor all forms of phone conversations and electronic messages inside the Soviet Union. The CIA, through TRW, manufacturers of the satellite, had almost perfected an even more sophisticated satellite, Argus, which was about to go into operation.

Prime excitedly contacted his KGB handlers with this news and, at their request, flew to Vienna to confer with them. The KGB agents gave Prime a small sum of money when he arrived but were not startled to hear about the spy satellites since Soviet agents in Mexico were already receiving news about the Spy-in-the-Sky apparatus from two American amateur spies, Christopher John Boyce who worked at TRW and was filching the blueprints for the satellites, and Andrew Daulton Lee, his drug-taking friend, who was delivering these plans to KGB spymasters in Mexico City.

What Prime's handlers wanted now was the actual information being delivered by these satellites. Prime delivered and quickly, particularly since he was now able to access almost all of the information the satellites were producing after being promoted to section chief at Cheltenham. When he learned that Boyce and Lee had been caught in America and sent to prison, Prime became nervous and seriously thought about accepting the Russian offer to defect. He stayed on at Cheltenham, nevertheless, undoubtedly opting to spy for the pay it brought him. Then, he suddenly resigned his post but took 500 secret documents with him out of the Cheltenham offices before leaving.

Prime, however, had more serious problems to address when he returned to London. In addition to his secret espionage life, Prime conducted a secret and decidedly perverted sex life. He was a pedophile who preyed upon little girls. In a card index he kept, Prime had a list of more than 2,000 small girls that he had assembled from local newspapers. He annotated the cards with notes about his telephone calls to girls and visits he made to their homes in hopes of finding them unprotected.

In April 1981, Prime attacked one little girl with a knife but her screams drove him off. The police in West Mercia were able to get an accurate description of the assailant and, armed with a police sketch and the description of Prime's car, went to the spy's home. Police questioned him but he denied everything. After detectives left, Prime, completely unnerved, confessed not only his sexual perversion to his wife but also admitted that he had been a spy for Russia for more than a decade.

Rhona Prime urged her husband to go to the police. When Prime went to police headquarters, he admitted his sexual crimes but he did not mention his espionage. His wife, however, felt it her patriotic duty to inform officials that her husband was a spy. Prime was charged with violating the Secrets Act and tried in November 1982. He was sentenced to thirty-five years in prison for espionage and three years for his sexual offenses.

As a result of Prime's actions, Benson Buffham of the NSA went to London to confer with British intelligence and establish methods by which the agencies could better screen those involved with espionage data. Among other procedures, both agreed that all of those involved would be given lie-detector tests before being exposed to sensitive information.

[ALSO SEE: *Christopher Boyce; CIA; KGB; Andrew Lee; MI6; NSA*]

PRIOR, MATTHEW
British Spymaster ▪ (1664–1721)

BORN IN DORSET, PRIOR ATTENDED WESTMINSTER School in London where he befriended classmate Charles Mantagu, who later became earl of Halifax. They continued their friendship at Cambridge, which they both attended. In 1688, Prior was named a fellow of St. John's College, the same year in which James II was overthrown and fled to Europe as William III took the British crown. From that moment, conspiracies, led by the Jacobites, were formed to plot the return of the Stuart kings.

Prior, meanwhile, established himself as a shrewd young diplomat, as well as a minor poet, and rose quickly in the new government with the considerable help of his friend, Halifax. He was posted to The Hague where he acted as secretary to British officials who signed the Treaties of Ryswick in 1697, which ended the War of the Grand Alliance, that of England, Spain, Holland, and the Holy Roman Empire against France. As part of the treaty terms, Louis XIV of France agreed to quit his support of James II and to recognize William III as the legitimate British monarch.

The Jacobites nevertheless found a home in France where they continued to intrigue on behalf of James II. When Prior was assigned to the British Embassy in Paris as secretary to the ambassador, his chief duty was to spy on the Jacobites and report their activities to London. Organizing a spy network, Prior sent his agents to Rheims where the exiled James held court. Here he discovered a number of Jacobite spies,

including Englishmen who traveled between France and London. His information allowed English officials to find and arrest the Jacobite agents.

Prior's agents also spied on Louis XIV and his court, attempting to determine whether or not he would honor the Treaties of Ryswick. He soon learned that Louis XIV planned another expansionist conflict, which came to be known as the War of the Spanish Succession (1701–1713). Though James II died in the first year of that war, his son and grandson carried on attempts to regain the British throne through the powerful Jacobite movement. Prior continued to effectively use his spies against the Jacobites in Europe. When William III died, Queen Anne assumed the throne and Robert Harley, one of her more abler ministers, became England's spymaster, working with Prior in Europe and Daniel Defoe in England.

When Queen Anne died, Prior's Tory supporters vanished and he was impeached by Robert Walpole and imprisoned (1715–1717). While in jail he composed poetry, the most memorable being *Alma, or the Progress of the Mind* (published in 1718). Prior died before the Stuarts quit their claim to the English throne and the Jacobite movement that he had undermined through clever espionage eventually collapsed.

[ALSO SEE: *Daniel Defoe*]

PROJECT JENNIFER
CIA Operation to Recover Sunken Soviet Sub ▪ (1974)

IN 1968, A SOVIET SUBMARINE WITH ATOMIC MISSILE capability (fired from its conning tower), after a series of explosions, sank in the Pacific. In 1974, the CIA commissioned billionaire Howard Hughes, of Hughes Aircraft and other enterprises, to salvage the submarine in order to discover its secrets. Hughes' Summa Corporation built a special salvage ship, the *Glomar Explorer*.

The Hughes vessel was equipped with a "moon pool" into which a 209-foot derrick could lift salvaged material up to 800 tons in weight. Refrigeration facilities were installed to handle up to 100 bodies. When the *Glomar Explorer* set sail for the spot in the Pacific where the submarine had gone down, its officers carried booklets containing American and Russian burial services.

The results of this CIA operation, dubbed Project Jennifer, were never fully detailed. One report had it that only the front part of the submarine's hull was salvaged; it contained the bodies of seventy Russian sailors who were buried at sea after full naval ceremonies. Another report has it that the conning tower, the real object of the search, was brought up with one or more Russian missiles still intact and that this prize of the deep was worth more than the untold millions spent for the Hughes salvage vessel.

There was an additional benefit to this espionage operation. The *Glomar Explorer*, after completing its mission, was used to establish a precedent, being the first ship to conduct deep-sea mining for minerals.

[ALSO SEE: *CIA*]

PURPLE MACHINE, THE
Japanese Cipher Machine in World War II ▪ (1937–1945)

AMERICAN INTELLIGENCE WAS UNDERSTAFFED AND underfunded during the late 1920s, so much so that the cryptology department known as the Black Chamber under code wizard Herbert O. Yardley was shut down in 1929. Yardley had performed excellent decoding work in World War I, but there seemed to be no more need for such code-breaking.

The need for this service increased dramatically as Japan began its Far Eastern conquest of China and covetously eyed the islands of the Pacific, chiefly Hawaii. The Japanese realized that Western ears were listening to their electronic messages and sought to create an unbreakable code. To that end, Japanese intelligence secured a copy of the Enigma machine from their German allies in 1937, and, using it as a model, created its own super codemaking machine, one later dubbed "Purple," for reasons still unknown.

The new coding machine was almost a duplicate of the German Enigma, two typewriters joined by a plugboard through which a maze of wires ran into each typewriter. A code clerk adjusted four rotors to a specific alignment of letters, then typed a plaintext onto one typewriter as the other typewriter automatically enciphered the same message. As the typing continued, the rotors automatically shifted the alignment of letters to vary the code. To retrieve the plaintext, the method was reversed by typing on the second machine to send electrical impulses through the wires and rotors to the first machine.

When U.S. interceptors first picked up code generated by Purple, American cryptologists were baffled. The Japanese knew that their enemies would have to build an identical machine to break their code and they believed that task impossible. It was, until America's master code-breaker, William Friedman, painstakingly built an identical Purple machine in 1938. The Japanese used Purple to transmit all of its high-level military and diplomatic messages prior to Pearl Harbor.

Unfortunately, though the U.S. Navy read and quickly decoded every one of these messages, particularly those sent to Japanese diplomats in Washington in early December 1941, it could not determine precisely where the Japanese Navy would strike. Not once in the messages sent to the Japanese Ambassador in Washington was the name Pearl Harbor mentioned, let alone the Hawaiian Islands, nor any other military objective scheduled for Japan's sneak attacks that began World War II.

Thus, America knew Japan would attack but it did not know where, until the American fleet was almost completely destroyed by Japanese war planes at dawn, on Sunday, December 7, 1941. Through decoded Purple messages, the U.S. Navy was able to determine when and almost where the Japanese fleet would be thereafter.

This resulted in America's decisive sea victory, the battle of Midway, where four of Japan's first-line aircraft carriers were sunk, breaking that country's naval back. It was also through decoded Purple messages that an air flight by Admiral Yamamoto was discovered and American war planes enabled to shoot down the Japanese admiral's plane, a crash in which Yamamoto was killed. Throughout the war, the Japanese were so confident that their Purple machine was invincible that they never changed its basic design and thus their military leaders never knew that the Allies knew their innermost thoughts and plans.

[ALSO SEE: *William Friedman; Herbert O. Yardley*]

QADDAFI, MUAMMAR
Libyan Dictator and Spymaster ▪ (1942–)

Libyan strongman and spymaster Muammar Qaddafi

IN 1969, QADDAFI, A YOUNG AND TREACHEROUS LIBYAN army officer, engineered a lightning coup d'etat, which saw him take over Libya and quickly institute a reign of terror throughout the Arab world. President Reagan aptly described him as "the most dangerous man in the world." He would stop at nothing to advance the cause of what he called "Islamic Unity." He established a vast network of spies and saboteurs throughout the Middle East and Africa, attempting to overthrow many governments. His agents successfully conducted a coup in Sudan and were almost as successful in Zaire.

Qaddafi's agents spread terror in Iraq, Tunisia, and North Yemen. The dictator made Libya a training camp for terrorists, including those of PLO leader Yasir Arafat. The U.S. rightly accused him of creating "state-sponsored terrorism."

Born in a goat-skin tent, the son of a Bedouin farmer in the province of Fezzan, Qaddafi belonged to the Berber tribe of Ghadaffa. His father and uncle were imprisoned for opposing Italian colonialists and he grew up with a hatred for all Europeans. He was inspired as a youth by the 1952 uprising in Egypt led by military strong man Gamal Abdel Nasser, and he later copied Nasser's political platform, which demanded the unification of all Arab peoples.

In 1959, Qaddafi organized a secret cabal of revolutionaries dedicated to the violent overthrow of King Idris Senussi I, ruler of Libya who was thought to be a British puppet. Qaddafi graduated from the University of Libya in 1963 and, two years later, he graduated from the military academy at Benghazi, receiving an army commission. He further trained in England at Beaconsfield where he became an expert at radio communications. Returning to Libya in 1966 a lieutenant, he served in several outposts.

Throughout all these years, he stayed in contact with the revolutionary cell he had established and continued plotting the overthrow of King Senussi.

Winning the support of the army, Captain Qaddafi staged a bloodless coup on September 1, 1969. The 27-year-old Qadaffi immediately established a private terrorist group he called the Revolutionary Command Council (RCC), made up of those young men who had earlier joined his revolutionary cell. The RCC wasted no time in exporting terrorism, supporting the terrorist attacks in Rome and Vienna in 1985. He ousted the 20,000 Italian nationals living in Libya, abolished the U.S. bases in his country, and all but declared war on Israel, the nation he hated most.

In 1986, Qaddafi's terrorist groups caused the U.S. to anchor a fleet off Libya. The dictator sent patrol boats against it and two were blown up, along with a shoreland missile site. In retaliation, on April 5, 1986, Qadaffi's terrorists blew up a cafe in Beirut that was frequented by U.S. military personnel. On April 14, U.S. Air Force B-11 bombers attacked several strategic military installations inside Libya, destroying a barracks where the dictator was said to be living at the time. More than 100 Libyans, including two of Colonel Qadaffi's sons, were killed in the attack.

A stunned Qadaffi emerged safe some time later, touring his country to show his people that he had survived. His reputation did not, especially among the Arab nations that concluded that siding with Qadaffi meant risking war with the world's super power. The dictator has since carried on many clandestine operations and continues to peck away at U.S. prestige. He still allows terrorist groups to train in Libya, hiring renegade foreigners to instruct terrorists in the methods of espionage and sabotage.

One of these was ex-CIA agent Edwin Wilson, who was later sent to prison for thirty years for illegally dealing with Libya. Another was the notorious Carlos, a Venezuelan assassin who taught Libyan murder squads how to bomb, shoot, and stab victims to death. At this writing, Qadaffi's world standing has not changed.

[ALSO SEE: *CIA; Edwin Wilson*]

QUISLING, VIDKUN ABRAHAM LAURITZ JONSSON
Norwegian Conspirator and Traitor ▪ (1887-1945)

QUISLING'S NAME IN NORWAY MEANS THE SAME AS that of Benedict Arnold in America: Traitor. A crafty, conniving politician and army officer, Quisling operated a secret cabal that arranged for Hitler's troops to invade his helpless country in 1940.

A graduate of the Norwegian Military Academy, Quisling served as a military attaché in Petrograd in 1918–1919. He grew to admire the ruthless operations of the Bolsheviks and, when returning to Norway, he approached the Labor Party, which was controlled by Communists, and suggested he organize a paramilitary organization called The Red Guards that would protect the party and advance its interests with strong-arm methods.

The Communists distrusted Quisling, knowing he was a former army officer and thinking him to be a plant. They rejected the proposal and Quisling, incensed, swung drastically to the right. He entered politics and became Norway's Minister of Defense, 1931–1933, just when Hitler was taking over the German government. So enthralled was Quisling with Hitler's Nazi philosophy that he quit his post and—with Hitler's secret financial backing—founded and organized his own fascist party.

Quisling openly lobbied for official alliances with Nazi Germany and Mussolini's Italy but Norway made no such pacts, its pacifist population rejecting fascist beliefs. Quisling then established through his party a network of spies who gathered information on Norwegian military installations, its small Navy, and its government. Quisling personally took this information regularly to Hitler with whom he secretly conferred in Berlin.

Hitler early on told his slavish follower Quisling that he planned to invade Norway but knew that such an invasion might prove disastrous unless Quisling and his spies provided detailed information on landfalls and anchorages in Norway's treacherous fjords. At one point, Hitler told Quisling: "It is ironic that I have to march against the two countries for which I have always had the greatest respect—England and Norway."

Quisling assured Hitler that he had his full cooperation in aiding German invaders take over his country. Still a major in the Norwegian Army, Quisling then enlisted the aid of fascist Norwegian admirals and generals who promised that they would take no action against invading German warships and troops.

On April 5, 1940, Hitler summoned Quisling to a secret meeting in Berlin. He told the traitor that Germany would invade Norway three days later. "They will meet no opposition," Quisling assured the German dictator. On April 8, a German fleet sailed past the Norwegian forts overlooking the landing areas. Not a single gun was fired. The Germans landed unopposed, except at Oslo.

King Haakon VII fled to the north country to lead a small guerrilla campaign that would persist throughout the war. Hitler rewarded Quisling by making him the puppet premier of Norway but he was so detested by his own people that Quisling was removed from office a short time later. When Norwegian resistance stiffened, Hitler brought Quisling back to power, naming him Norway's sole political leader on February 2, 1942.

Quisling proved to be as ruthless as any Nazi commander, ordering the arrest of Norway's Jews for relocation to German concentration camps and certain death. He ruled the country with an iron hand, relentlessly tracking down resistance leaders and underground operations, ordering all those who resisted Nazi rule to be executed. He worked closely with the Gestapo but saw little success in rounding up the country's Jews. Only 760 Norwegian Jews were snared by Quisling's dragnets. The rest were hidden by underground forces or smuggled to neutral Sweden or even to England.

Though Quisling witnessed the collapse of Nazi Germany, he refused to abdicate his position. Even when he learned of Hitler's suicide, the Nazi puppet dictator clung to power. His government collapsed on May 8, 1945, and Quisling was arrested. He was tried for treason and absurdly defended himself in court by claiming to be "the saviour of Norway."

Quisling was found guilty and sentenced to death. He was placed before a firing squad on October 24, 1945. At the moment, he refused a blindfold and told his executioners in a loud voice: "Don't let your conscience trouble you in later years! You are acting under orders and doing your duty, like myself!" With that he was promptly shot to death.

[ALSO SEE: *Gestapo*]

RADO, SANDOR (ALEXANDER RADOLFI)
Soviet Spymaster in World War II ■ (1899–1981)

BORN ALEXANDER RADOLFI AND EDUCATED IN Budapest, the son of a wealthy Jewish businessman, Rado joined the Communist Party when he was a student at the University of Budapest. So entrenched was Rado in the Communist Party in 1919 that he was named a commissar and took part in the coup that briefly took over the Hungarian government that year with the adventurer Béla Kun at its head. When the Communists were driven out, Rado fled to Russia, where he lived for several years, marrying fellow Communist exile Helene Jensen.

Rado received espionage training from the NKVD in 1931. The following year he was sent to Germany, where he posed as a clerk in the Russian Embassy in Berlin. His real work was to spy on the Nazis, who were then clubbing their way to power. On several occasions, Rado organized armed Communist resistance to Hitler's storm troopers, which resulted in many bloody street battles.

Rado was earmarked for death by the Nazis, both as a Communist and a Jew, and, when Hitler took power in 1933, he was ordered by the NKVD to move to Paris to escape Nazi death squads looking for him. In Paris, Rado founded Geopress, a publishing house specializing in producing maps and reports on current events. This was, of course, a cover. Rado continued to feed his Soviet spymasters information on the French and German military.

By 1936, Rado was considered to be one of the top Soviet spies in the West. He was inducted into the GRU, Russian military intelligence, and sent to Switzerland and named Resident Director of all Soviet intelligence in that country.

Rado established a reliable espionage network in Switzerland over the next few years, one which he dubbed DORA (an anagram of his real name). To recruit top-notch agents, Rado used an experienced handler and spy, Ruth Kuczynski (AKA: Ursula-Maria Hamburger), a British subject who later became a handler for atomic bomb spy Klaus Fuchs. Using the code name "Sonia," Kuczynski recruited an expert radio man, Alexander Foote, who traveled from England to Switzerland. Foote, unknown to Rado, was an SIS plant. Everything Rado's group discovered and gave to him to radio to Moscow he also passed on to British intelligence.

In Bern, Rado's cut-out, or go-between, was Rachel Duebendorfer. This clever woman, using the code name "Sissy," made contacts for Rado, who preferred to remain behind the scenes. From the late 1930s, Rado's spy network, numbering dozens of diligent agents, proved to be Moscow's best source of information on Nazi Germany. When France fell in 1940, DORA remained an accurate source of military secrets.

At about this time, Rado began sending priceless information on German military operations. This data came from an agent whom Rado knew only as "Lucy," a spy so secret that only two of Rado's own cut-outs, Duebendorfer and Christian Schneider ("Taylor") knew his real identity. He was the ubiquitous Rudolf Roessler, who worked out of Lucerne and who, next to Fritz Kolbe and Richard Sorge, was probably the most accomplished spy in World War II. Information provided by Roessler stemmed from both the Black Orchestra, disaffected Germans working secretly against Hitler, and the Red Orchestra, Communist networks inside Germany and throughout Nazi-occupied Europe.

Moscow was startled by information from Rado in late 1941 which gave detailed battle plans for Germany's invasion of Russia. Unfortunately, Soviet intelligence could not convince dictator Joseph Stalin that Hitler actually meant to invade Russia, any more than could Soviet masterspy Richard Sorge, who had learned the same information while operating an effective Soviet network inside Japan.

Rado and his agents continued to supply Moscow with the most amazing information, detailed battle plans of the invading German army, down to the division level, informing the Center when and where attacks could be expected. The GRU came to believe that Rado had agents in the heart of the German high command. Some of this information was really coming from British SIS, through its Ultra code-breaking operations. Ultra had broken the German Enigma codes and was able to read much of what the German high command sent in cipher. SIS determined that it would share this information with England's ally, Russia, but since it did not want Moscow to know about its breaking Enigma and be compelled to share *that* information also, it was best to funnel the information through its planted agent, Foote, who then

Spymaster Sandor Rado, who operated the Soviet espionage ring DORA in Switzerland during World War II.

sent on the data to the Center in Moscow as if it had been generated by Rado's own network.

When Ultra was able to decode Enigma codes that showed the German army was mounting a massive attack against Kursk, where most of the Soviet army was then deployed, Foote received this information and it was sent to Moscow in such detail to show the exact order of the German battle plan that it staggered Soviet intelligence. This time, however, Stalin acted on the information and the Russians were ready for the German onslaught, destroying many Wehrmacht divisions.

Through 1941 and 1942 and into the early part of 1943, Rado's spy network was unequaled in performance. Rado himself, however, demonstrated anything but the rigid discipline required of a spymaster. He enjoyed the good life, staying in a luxurious villa with his family and dining in the better hotels and restaurants. He also drank excessively.

Two of Rado's agents resented his spendthrifting ways and his authority. They were also suspected of being double agents, working for Nazi agents who infested neutral Switzerland. These two agents informed their Nazi handlers about Rado and soon the German government was demanding of the Swiss government that DORA be dismantled and its agents arrested. The Swiss had adopted an attitude of laissez-faire toward Allied espionage, knowing full well that Allen Dulles was operating an American espionage ring inside Switzerland, as was the SIS. But Rado's agents, it was felt, had made their presence too well known in the country and jeopardized Switzerland's shaky relations with Germany. In October 1943, to avoid a diplomatic scandal, Swiss counterintelligence arrested several members of Rado's network.

Rado, typical of his behavior when under pressure, panicked and told Foote that he was going into deep cover. Foote escaped to France, where he helped liberate that country from the Nazis. There Foote met Rado and his wife. They had left Switzerland only a few weeks beforehand. Both received orders to report to Moscow. The Center wanted to know how DORA came to be closed down by the Swiss authorities. Rado was terrified that he would be blamed for the collapse of most of his network. "They will think I betrayed my own agents. I know them, I know how they are," he told Foote. Nevertheless, on January 6, 1945, Rado and Foote left in a Russian aircraft which took a circuitous route to Moscow. In order to avoid the air battles still raging over Germany, the plane first flew to Cairo. It would then proceed to Moscow.

The passengers and crew had to stay two nights until some parts of the Russian plane were replaced. Rado shared a room with Foote, explaining that he feared for his life once he arrived in Moscow. Foote argued with him, saying that he could not be blamed for two of his own agents betraying DORA. Sandor Rado fell silent, appearing to be deeply depressed. He then left the room and Foote never saw him again. When the Russian plane was prepared to continue its journey, Rado could not be found.

Spies for the Centre soon unearthed the cowering spymaster. He was hiding out in a small Cairo hotel in the disguise of a colonel in the Red Army, using the alias of Itgnati Kulichev. GRU agents arrived and forced Rado onto a plane that took him to Moscow. For many years it was believed that he had been liquidated at the orders of KGB boss Lavrenti Beria, whose son had been sent home by Rado after having proved ineffective as a spy in Switzerland. Beria, it was said, took his revenge for Rado's disgracing his son.

The truth was that Rado was not tried and executed. He resurfaced in Budapest in 1955, where he taught cartography at his old alma mater, Budapest University. He published his rather tame and carefully edited autobiography in 1971. He died at age eighty-two on August 20, 1981.

[ALSO SEE: *Black Orchestra; Rachel Duebendorfer; Alexander Foote; Klaus Fuchs; GRU; Fritz Kolbe; Ruth Kuczynski; Red Orchestra; Rudolf Roessler; Richard Sorge; SIS*]

RAHAB THE HARLOT
Spy in Jericho ▪
(Fourteenth–Thirteenth Century B.C.)

WHEN JOSHUA THE SON OF NUN MADE HIS PLANS to conquer the strong fortress of Jericho, he sent two spies into the city to learn its weak points. The spies, about to be captured, fled to a brothel owned and operated by Rahab the Harlot. She hid the two, telling searching soldiers that, indeed, two strangers had come to her but had left the city. She encouraged the soldiers to pursue them, which they naively did.

Returning to Joshua's spies, Rehab asked that when Joshua took the city, her contribution to his espionage be remembered and that none of her relatives be killed and that they be allowed to keep their possessions. The spies gave their word that this would be done. Rahab's house was next to one wall of the city. She made ropes of flax and let both men down over the wall with these.

Before leaving, one of the spies told her that when she heard the armies of Joshua storming the city, she was to lock her family inside her house and wrap a piece of scarlet cloth, which he gave her, on a window.

The spies, according to the tale, kept their word. Joshua ordered them to go into the city when the first of his troops rushed the walls and retrieve Rahab and her family members. This they did, bringing the harlot and her relatives to the camp of the Israelites before the city and all of its inhabitants were destroyed.

[ALSO SEE: Joshua]

RAPHAEL, SYLVIA
Israeli Spy ▪ (1938–)

WHEN THE MOSSAD TARGETED ARAB TERRORIST Ali Hassan Salameh for extermination, attractive and sophisticated Sylvia Raphael was one of the agents sent to perform the assassination. She and five other Israeli agents flew to Lillehammer, Norway, in July 1973. Salemeh was thought to be the terrorist who had slaughtered the Israeli Olympic athletes in Munich during the 1972 games.

Through a wrong identification, the Israeli team killed a Moroccan waiter named Ahmed Bouchki instead of the much-wanted Salemeh. Raphael and a fellow agent, Abraham Gehmer, were arrested when they attempted to leave Norway using false Canadian passports. Raphael identified herself as Patricia Roxbourgh.

The sultry agent was defended by Anneaus Schjodt, one of Norway's finest attorneys. Though sentenced to five and a half years in prison, Raphael was released in twenty-two months, thanks to Schjodt's untiring efforts. When the amateurish agent was released she immediately married Schjodt.

[ALSO SEE: Mossad]

RB-47
U.S. Spy Plane ▪ (1960)

WITH A CREW OF SIX, A U.S. RB-47 SPY PLANE flew from a base in England to the Barents Sea in the Arctic on July 1, 1960. The mission of this flight was to use the sophisticated communications system on board to electronically survey the Russian coast and coastal waters. A Russian fighter plane spotted the plane and shot it down. Two survivors, Captain Freeman Olmstead, the co-pilot, and Captain John McKone, navigator, were picked up by the Soviets.

Russian premier Nikita Khrushchev denounced the U.S. for sending a spy plane into Soviet air space, saying that Olmstead and McKone would be imprisoned as spies. President Eisenhower replied that the U.S. flight was properly conducted over international waters and demanded the release of the flyers.

A short time later, two Soviet spies, Igor Melekh and Willi Hirsch, who had been on the FBI suspect list as active Soviet agents in the U.S., were arrested and jailed. As was the case with U-2 spy plane pilot Gary Francis Powers, who was exchanged for Soviet spymaster Rudolf Abel, the RB-47 flyers were exchanged for Melekh and Hirsch in 1961.

[ALSO SEE: Rudolf Ivonovich Abel; Gary Francis Powers]

RED ORCHESTRA (ROTE KAPELLE)
Soviet Spy Networks in World War II ▪ (1939–1943)

WITH THE RISE TO POWER IN GERMANY OF ADOLF Hitler in 1933, the Soviet Union, long recognizing him and his Nazi Party as a political and military threat, organized many separate espionage rings inside Germany. These often vast intelligence networks were expanded to Nazi-occupied countries during World War II and were made up of Communist agents working for Moscow.

The Abwehr soon learned from secret broadcasts made by Soviet agents that Moscow referred to their radio transmitters as "Music Boxes," and the operators as "Musicians," thus the German label, "Red Orchestra" or *Rote Kapelle* in German.

The original leaders of the Red Orchestra were two outstanding Soviet spies, Harro Schulze-Boysen and Arvid Harnack. A member of the German Junker class, Harro Schulze-Boysen was an intelligence officer for the German Ministry of Air and had access to the top Nazi secrets. Associating himself with Harnack shortly before Hitler's invasion of Russia in 1941, the two built a solid spy network which broadcast regularly to the Center in Moscow. Their top agents at the time were Alexander Erdberg and Adam Kuckhoff.

Harnack was also exceptionally well-placed to accomplish his espionage, holding a position in the German Ministry of Economics. Kuckhoff was a prominent writer and theater producer. His wife, Margarete, worked inside the race policy department of Nazi theorist Alfred Rosenberg. Others who consistently contributed valuable information that was sent to Moscow included Horst Heilmann, a cryptologist working in the coding department of the Wehrmacht signals division; Herbert Gollnow, who worked in German military counterintelligence; Johann Graudenz, who provided aircraft brakes to the Luftwaffe and had access to all of Hermann Goering's airfields; and Gunther Weisenborn, an official with Joseph Goebbel's national radio system.

The Red Orchestra also had spies in the German Ministry of Labor, the Ministry of Propaganda, the Foreign Office (where OSS spy Fritz Kolbe operated independently for Allen Dulles) and the city administration of Berlin. The Center had independent agents in Germany but these spies were rare.

One such German agent for the Soviets was the aristocrat Rudolf von Scheliha, a hedonist, womanizer, and spendthrift. He had married a wealthy woman but his taste for expensive mistresses depleted his own and his wife's fortunes so that he decided to sell Germany's secrets to maintain his extravagant lifestyle. At first he sold secrets to the British, but when SIS learned that Scheliha was selling the same information to Moscow, it dropped him from its espionage rolls. The Center, however, continued to use him, paying enormous amounts of money for military and industrial secrets, but only after Moscow sent one of its top spymasters, Victor Sukolov, to verify Scheliha's position and data.

Sukolov sent back a favorable report on Scheliha, requesting that a radio specialist, Kurt Shulze, be parachuted into Germany to assist the high-living Scheliha. Sukolov's report, however, was intercepted by a German listening post. Abwehr specialists, with the help of Johann Wenzel, a Dutch SOE agent who had gone over to the Germans, were able to decode Sukolov's message and learn from it that the Center was sending, in addition to the radio operator, Shulze, another agent, Heinrich Koenen, who was to blackmail Scheliha into continued cooperation with Moscow.

Knowing all this, the Gestapo arrested Ise Stöbe, Scheliha's assistant, and planted their own agent in Stöbe's apartment to impersonate her. When Koenen arrived he told the woman he thought was Scheliha's assistant that Moscow expected her boss to continue providing secrets or he would be exposed to the Gestapo. At that moment, Gestapo men stepped from hiding in the apartment and told Koenen that "the Gestapo already knows." Arrested, Koenen joined the real Stöbe in prison. Though tortured, Stöbe loyally refused to implicate Scheliha. Koenen, however, told the Germans everything they wanted to know about the luxury-loving Scheliha, who was then arrested and, along with Stöbe, shot to death on December 22, 1942.

The Red Orchestra, despite these setbacks, continued to send Moscow vital information. Its agents informed the Center the exact troop movements for the German Army battling in Russia, the specific air attacks planned against British convoys carrying supplies to Murmansk, the amounts of fuel being supplied to German troops in Russia, the monthly German aircraft production figures, all priceless information that greatly aided the Russians in fighting Hitler's legions.

The Abwehr knew that the Red Orchestra was effective and they identified many of the top spymasters, such as Leopold Trepper, who was known as the grand chief. Trepper traveled throughout Germany, Belgium, Holland, France, and Switzerland, coordinating the many Red Orchestra operations, including that of Sandor Rado in Switzerland and even that run by the energetic Ruth Kuczynski in England. Yet, the Germans found it next to impossible to track down leaders like Trepper.

When German agents were able to pinpoint Wenzel's radio transmissions in Belgium, they seized the spy, telling him that unless he agreed to be "turned," and send out disinformation created by the Abwehr to Moscow, he would be shot. He not only agreed but informed on many of the Red Orchestra's leaders. This was how the Gestapo was able to arrest Schulze-Boysen and his wife in Berlin on August 30, 1942, and Harnack and his wife on September 3, 1942. Even the grand chief Trepper was located through Wenzel's treachery. Except for Rado's operation in Switzerland, most of the Red Orchestra operations ceased to exist by early 1943. Rado was also shut down that year when two of his agents betrayed his ring.

The penalty paid by these Germans spying for Russia was severe. Hitler himself took a deep interest in the trial, which brought fourteen Red Orchestra leaders to the dock. Included were the Schulze-Boysens, the Harnacks, Hans Copp, Kurt Shulze, Gehrts, Heilmann, Graudenz, Gollnow, a couple named Schumacher, and Ericka von Brockdorf.

Eleven of the spies received death sentences. Mildred Harnack and Brockdorf were given long prison terms. Those executed faced a horrible end. They were thrust onto meathooks while alive, the hooks penetrating their throats; they dangled in agony until dying. To the incensed Hitler it was unthinkable that Germans would spy against their country. He was also enraged that the two women spies, Harnack and Brockdorf, had escaped execution. "Those who have come within the shadow of treason have forfeited their lives," he informed the German court, which slavishly changed its sentence for Mrs. Harnack and Brockdorf to death. They were quickly beheaded.

[ALSO SEE: *Gestapo; Fritz Kolbe; Ruth Kuczynski; Sandor Rado; Harro Schulze-Boysen; SOE; Leopold Trepper*]

REDL, ALFRED
Austrian Spymaster ▪ (1864–1913)

FEW MEN WERE MORE POWERFUL IN THE OLD Austro-Hungarian empire than Colonel Alfred Redl, chief of military counterintelligence (*Kundschaftsstelle*). Outwardly he appeared to his

Austrian spymaster Alfred Redl, homo- sexual, money- hungry, he proved to be a double agent, arch-traitor, and one who made it easier for World War I to begin.

superiors to be the model spymaster, conscientious, with a penchant for detail, and a fanatical loyalty to Emperor Franz Josef. Inwardly, he was a shrewd and calculating person, whose secret homosexuality was insatiable and whose lust for money knew no bounds. For these two reasons he became his country's arch traitor before the begining of World War I.

Redl, though poor, was allowed to attend military school, graduating in 1882. He was given a commission in the Austrian Army and quickly rose through the ranks. In 1899, he was a military observer stationed with the Russian Army. Throughout his youth, Redl had been fascinated with espionage and in 1900 his boyhood dream came true; he was appointed to Austria's military counterintelligence corps by General Baron von Giesl.

By the following year Redl had become chief of counterintelligence in Vienna. He immediately began modernizing Austrian intelligence techniques. He introduced photography and fingerprinting into his agency. Anyone shown into his office was secretly photographed by hidden cameras no matter what position he might take in Redl's office. The arms of the chairs and the cigarette box Redl invariably offered guests were coated with a fine powder to trap fingerprints. Voice recordings of guests were made by hidden recording machines. It was Redl who introduced the "Third Degree" method of interrogation of suspected spies, having blinding lights flood the faces of those being grilled.

Unknown to his superiors, Redl pursued several homosexual liaisons with members of the the Austrian nobility. He patronized notorious homosexual clubs in Vienna and lived in luxurious apartments. Though well paid, Redl's salary could not afford the expenses of such a lifestyle. He decided to sell his country's secrets to support his fleshpot liaisons. Having made friends with several high-ranking Czarist officers while stationed in Russia, he went to them in St. Petersburg, offering to sell them Austria's contingency war plans. They bought the plans for a princely sum in 1902 but, in the following year, the Austrian Foreign Office realized that the Russian high command possessed these plans, although it had no idea who had turned over the secret documents to the Russians.

Redl, as chief of counterintelligence, was ordered to find the spy or spies. Ironically, he then went in search of himself, frantically trying to conceive of a method by which he could escape undetected. He confided his dilemma to his Russian contacts. The Russians believed the spymaster was too valuable as an information source to be exposed. They gave Redl the names of several lesser Austrian spies working for them. These then were the unhappy agents detected and exposed by Redl.

By breaking the alleged spy ring, Redl was applauded by his duped superiors. He became director of all espionage for Austria in 1907 and by

1909 was conferring with his German counterpart, the enigmatic Walther Nicolai, head of the Kaiser's intelligence operations. From what Nicolai told him, Redl was able to piece together substantial secret information about German forces and this, too, he sold to the Russians, sending his information in coded letters to Okhrana agents.

In 1912, Redl was again promoted, made chief of staff to General Giesl, who commanded an army corps in Prague. When he assumed this duty, he immediately began supplying the Russians (as well as the intelligence bureaus of France and Italy) with information on those Austrian forces. He continued his high living and secret homosexual debaucheries, believing that he was so well placed that he would never be detected as a double agent. His replacement as counterintelligence chief, however, was Captain Maximilian Ronge, who had avidly studied Redl's methods and soon began to improve on them, paying particular attention to the postal censorship Redl had originally established.

Ronge expanded this censorship by adding several hundred more postal censors so that almost every piece of mail entering or leaving the Austrian empire was read and analyzed. Two of the most interesting letters examined by Ronge's Black Cabinet (postal censorship office) arrived at the Vienna Post Office on March 2, 1913. They were both addressed: *Opera Ball, 13, Post Restante, General Post Office, Vienna.* Both were post-marked from the small town of Eydtkuhnen in East Prussia on the German-Russian frontier.

Since both of these envelopes were never claimed they were returned to the post office in East Prussia unopened. A few days later they returned to Vienna, but this time they were sent inside another, larger envelope which came from the German spymaster, Walther Nicolai, addressed to his then counterpart, Ronge. The Austrian counterintelligence chief saw that the two letters contained only money, about 14,000 Austrian kronen in all ($2,700).

Ronge had the envelopes of the two letters resealed and then took them to the general delivery station at the Vienna Post Office. He had a wire installed at this cage, one which led to a nearby police station. Ronge instructed the clerks on duty at the general delivery cage to be alert for anyone calling for the two letters. Should that person call, the clerk was to press a button attached to the wire which would ring a bell in the police station. The clerk was to take his time in handing over the letters, waiting until agents could arrive from the police station to arrest the caller.

Ronge kept his agents at the police station around the clock, day after day. Weeks went by and still no one called for the envelopes containing what was then a great deal of money. Then, eighty-three days later, in the Saturday afternoon of May 24, 1913, the bell in the police station began ringing.

The claimant of the letters containing the cash was none other than Colonel Alfred Redl, former chief of intelligence and now chief of staff of the Eighth Army in Prague. Ronge himself soon appeared at the Post Office. He took the receipt signed by Redl and returned to his offices. There he took from a shelf a forty-page, hand-written document that Redl had prepared for Ronge before turning his post over to him, one in which Redl summarized for his replacement his best-kept secrets in tracking down spies. Ironically, Ronge used the handwriting in the report to compare with the postal receipt. In both instances, the handwriting was the same.

Ronge did not conclude, however, that Redl was a traitor. He had received money but he could be acting on behalf of Austrian military intelligence. What nagged at Ronge was the fact that the letter to Redl had come from Eydtkuhnen, which was a hotbed of spies, mostly Russian spies. Then one of Ronge's agents appeared holding pieces of scrap paper. He was exhausted, he said, having followed Redl through half of Vienna. He explained that Redl must have realized he was being shadowed so he stopped and tore up some papers, then walked on, apparently believing that the agent would stop to examine the bits of paper. He did not, but continued following Redl. Some minutes later he lost the spymaster but had the presence of mind to return to the spot where Redl had thrown the paper scraps to the cobblestones.

The agent collected the paper and reported back to Ronge. Carefully, Ronge and his men put the pieces of paper together. On them they found written in Redl's hand a receipt for the payment of money to a Lieutenant Hovora, an officer in the Uhlans, and three more receipts for letters which had been sent to addresses in Lausanne, Warsaw, and Brussels.

Again, Ronge reached for a "blacklist" of addresses for foreign powers where their secret agents could send mail, a list that had been prepared by Alfred Redl himself. All three addresses taken from the scraps of paper were on the list. Redl was, indeed, a double agent. Ronge immediately notified his superior, General August Urbanski von Ostromiecz. Shocked, Ostromiecz called General Conrad von Hotzendorf, commander-in-chief of the Austrian Army. Agents were meanwhile assigned to follow Redl everywhere.

Later that night Ronge and three of his most trusted officers went to Redl's hotel and entered his suite unannounced. Redl was sitting at a writing table, scribbling. He rose and, in the courtly manner of old school officers, bowed to the waist. He then said: "I know why you have come. I have spoiled my life. I am writing letters of farewell."

Ronge faced his old superior and said quietly: "It is necessary to ask the extent and duration of your— activities."

Redl nodded. "All that you wish to know will be found in my house in Prague." He then added: "I would appreciate the loan of a revolver."

None of the officers carried weapons. Ronge told one of his aides to retrieve a weapon. He, too, was imbued with enough old-world chivalry to allow his former superior what was then considered to be an honorable end for a disgraced soldier—suicide. When the aide returned he handed Redl a Browning revolver.

The spymaster nodded, then wrote on a piece of paper: "Levity and passion have destroyed me. Pray for me. I pay with my life for my sins. Alfred. 1:15 A.M. I will die now. Please do not permit a post-mortem examination. Pray for me."

At that moment, Ronge and his aides left Redl's suite. They went to an all-night cafe and ordered coffee, waiting tensely for several hours, sending a police detective to Redl's suite every half hour to see if the spymaster had had nerve enough to end his nefarious career.

Each time the detective went to the suite, he found Redl still alive. At 5 A.M., when he entered again, he saw Redl crumpled in front of a full-length mirror. He had placed all of the lamps in his room about him, undressed and, apparently while looking at his naked body, fired a bullet into his troubled brain. It was thirteen hours from the time when Redl had picked up the two money-stuffed envelopes at the Vienna Post Office.

One of the letters Redl had left was addressed to his brother, the other to his good friend General Giesl. Neither contained incriminating statements. Redl's home in Prague was searched the next day. The findings clearly showed how Alfred Redl had made the Russians pay for his secret information. He had purchased no less than two large houses in Vienna and a vast estate outside the city. He owned four of the most expensive autos made in the world.

In the basement of Redl's mansion in Prague, searchers found one hundred and sixty dozen bottles of the finest champagne. A great deal of cash was also found and thousands of secret documents, letters to Russian handlers and Okhrana spymasters, cases and cabinets brimming with incriminating documents, as well as long list of several thousand names and addresses—the most flagrant homosexuals in Vienna, Prague, Paris, Brussels, and Berlin.

Though Hotzendorf had ordered Ronge that only a few persons were to know about Redl (whose body was removed from the Hotel Klomser in secret), and that the scandal was not to reach the ears of Emperor Franz Josef, the suicide and treason of the spymaster was soon blared in the press. A porter at the hotel talked and so did a private locksmith in Prague who, incredibly, had been hired to break into Redl's home.

It all came out. Redl had been spying for more than a decade for Russia. He had aided Okhrana spies caught in Austria by arranging for their escapes. He had identified Austrian spies in Russia and they had paid with their lives. Alfred Redl had caused the deaths of several hundred men, as well as his own, in his climb toward wealth. There were a number of other countries who benefited from Redl's espionage, including Serbia, Austria's archenemy. Redl had

been in constant contact with the Serbian Black Hand Society, a secret nationalist federation plotting assassination. Some of the information Redl provided to the the the leader of that sinister group, Dragutin Dimitrijevic, resulted in the murder of Archduke Franz Ferdinand the next year in Sarajevo, an event, more than any other, that plunged Europe into World War One.

[ALSO SEE: *Black Hand Society; Dragutin Dimitrijevic; Walther Nicolai; Okhrana*]

REILLY, SIDNEY GEORGE (SIGMÚND GEORGIEVICH ROSENBLUM)
British Spy in Russia ▪ (1874–1925?)

ENGLAND'S MOST PUBLICIZED AND LIONIZED SECRET agent to this day is Sidney Reilly. It was claimed that he "wielded more power, authority, and influence than any other spy." He was also a professional assassin, expert at "poisoning, stabbing, shooting, and throttling." Energetic, unpredictable, self-confident, and decidedly ruthless, Reilly loved money, women, and power. He possessed, it was reported, "eleven passports and a wife to go with each of them."

Born in Odessa, Russia, on March 24, 1874, Reilly was the bastard son of a rich Jewish landowner and contractor in Russian Poland and the wife of a czarist officer. Though he used his father's name, Rosenblum, he had no official name. He was an inmaginative youth who received the equivalent of a grade-school education and was thereafter self-taught. Curious and greedy for knowledge, Reilly became an avid reader and linguist who later spoke seven languages fluently. By the age of nineteen he realized that Russia held no future for him and he stowed away on a merchant vessel sailing for Brazil.

There Reilly took all manner of jobs to survive, loading vessels as a dockworker, cooking for construction crews, cutting new roads into the jungle and, for a while, was employed as a bouncer and doorman in a whorehouse. In 1895, Reilly was hired as a cook for an expedition led by three British intelligence officers who planned to explore a jungle-bound territory. When the group was attacked by cannibals, Reilly amazed the officers by grabbing one of their revolvers and shooting several of the attackers dead and then driving off the rest.

The British officers were so impressed with Reilly, particularly with his language abilities, that they asked him to go to England on their return voyage. Reilly, always the opportunist, leaped at the chance. He was given cursory training in espionage and was sent to Russia to gather some information. He accomplished his assignment and was given a permanent berth with the Naval Intelligence Department, or NID.

Following a brief affair with author Ethel Voynich, Reilly met and married Margaret Thomas, a rich and attractive young widow. He also changed his name at that time from Rosenblum to Sidney George Reilly, taking his last name from that of his wife's maiden name. It was also at this time that he became a British citizen, a requirement of the Secret Service employing him.

During the Boer War, Reilly was sent to Holland by NID to obtain secret reports on arms shipments being sent to the Boers in South Africa. He was a master of disguises and on this mission he impersonated a Russian arms buyer, which allowed him to inspect the various Dutch plants manufacturing weapons. Reilly's quick espionage successes established him as one of England's most daring and accomplished agents. He loved adventure and risk and preferred playing a lone hand, the espionage style of agents in his era.

Reilly would not flinch from any assignment, no matter how impossible it might appear. Of course, he was always provided with huge amounts of cash to bribe his way to secrets. He also enjoyed a salary reported to be almost as much as the chief of the intelligence service. Reilly was, in reality, a luxury-loving womanizer. Despite claims to the contrary, he had no more respect for England than he did for his mother country Russia. He was a spy for hire and had another country paid him more, he would have given that country his services.

In his subtle contempt for his spymaster employers, Reilly took any chance, any risk to accomplish missions that heaped more glory and, most importantly, money on him. If his work served England, all the better. Reilly's audacity was one of the keys to his consistent successes. After completing his assignment in Holland, Reilly was sent to Persia, where the Shah had recently authorized an Australian businessman the right to grant concessions to Persia's newly-discovered and vast oil deposits. Germany, France, Russia, and England were all vying for those rights, which were held by William Knox D'Arcy.

Reilly heard that D'Arcy was about to grant the oil concession to the French. He rushed to this meeting, and, unannounced, barged into D'Arcy's offices dressed as a priest. He implored D'Arcy to postpone signing until he told the Australian about an orphanage charity that was about to collapse unless financially aided. The distracted D'Arcy stepped into another room with Reilly where the spy quickly convinced the Australian that his duties lay with mother England, not France, convincing D'Arcy to grant the oil concession to Great Britain. This agreement gave birth to the Anglo-Persian Oil Company that later became known as the giant British Petroleum Co., Ltd., or B.P.

Reilly's NID spymasters next sent him and his wife in style to Port Arthur, on the Liaotung

England's superspy, Sidney Reilly, whose espionage exploits were the stuff of high drama and adventure fiction, most of it real.

Peninsula, the naval base of the Russian Far Eastern Fleet. His bank account brimming with British money, Reilly, to cover his real mission, bought into a timber company, becoming a partner. A short time later he was named the manager of Compagnie Est-Asiatique, a Danish company in which he heavily invested. His positions, of course, were covers. Reilly spent most of his time identifying and sketching the Russian warships at Port Arthur, the times of their arrivals and departures, their armament and its effectiveness, and the morale of their crews. He also studied the coastal defenses and the dispositions of land troops.

All of this information Reilly sent back to London. While staying on in Port Arthur, Reilly reportedly became a triple spy, sending information not only to his British spymasters but to those in Russia and Japan, gleaning a great deal of money from the intelligence agencies of these countries.

One report had it that Colonel Motojiro Akashi, Japanese spymaster and chief of staff of Japanese forces in Korea, who had met Reilly in St. Petersburg during Reilly's first assignment to Russia, convinced the British agent to provide him with information on the Russian fleet at Port Arthur, paying him an unspecified large sum of money. Akashi had been an enterprising spymaster, going to St. Petersburg at the turn of the century to financially underwrite many

Russian revolutionaries and radicals, from Yevno Azev to Father George Gapon.

Agents of the Okhrana, the czar's secret police, had kept close track of Akashi, even when he returned to the Far East, and when they learned that Reilly was in league with Akashi, Okhrana spymasters paid Reilly for information on Japanese war plans. Japan and Russia were then on a collison course toward war. Shortly before the Russo-Japanese War broke out in 1904, Reilly departed for England, a wealthy man.

British intelligence could find no fault with their spectacular agent. In 1909, when SIS (Secret Intelligence Service, later MI6) was created, it inducted Reilly, who immediately became the pet spy of SIS chief Mansfield Cumming. The SIS chief came to admire Reilly but with reservations, saying that he was "a man of indomitable courage, a genius as an agent but a sinister man who I could never bring myself wholly to trust."

England's intelligence eye in 1909 was glued to Germany. The Kaiser was building a gigantic war machine, they knew, but British intelligence had no idea what kind of weapons were being forged inside Germany's sprawling war plants. Reilly was sent to find out.

He traveled to Germany and got a job as a welder inside one of the huge Krupp armaments plants. He soon realized that he could not photograph any of the plans in the drawing office, which was heavily guarded. Reilly noted that fewer guards were on duty at night so he volunteered for the company fire brigade that required that he work the night shift.

A few nights later Reilly crept up on the foreman of night security and strangled him to death. He then knocked out and tied up another guard before breaking into the drawing office. He simply stole the plans and escaped by train and boat to England with German agents hot on his heels.

Upon his return, Cumming gave Reilly another important task. He was to learn everything he could about German naval and military power. This time he would go to Russia, where he would establish himself as a distributor of armaments. He was given an enormous amount of money with which to set up this cover. When he arrived in St. Petersburg, Reilly realized that the best way to learn the strength of the German fleet in the Baltic Sea was to view it from the air. He cleverly sponsored air races for Russian aviators near Riga and soon flew in a flimsy plane over the sea, photographing German war vessels.

The air races made Reilly a great favorite with the social elite in St. Petersburg and Moscow. Through these social connections, Reilly came to meet the object of his search, a man named Massino, who was assistant to Russia's Minister of Marine. Through Massino's attractive wife, Nadine, whom the handsome Reilly seduced, the spy was able to learn that Blohm and Voss, the large naval manufacturers in Germany, were actively seeking to get the contracts for rebuilding the fleet Russia had lost in its war with Japan.

Reilly next bought into a small company, Mendrochovich and Lubensky, which had exclusive contracts to sell railway cars to Germany. He went back to Massino and convinced him to persuade Blohm and Voss to name his firm, Mendrochovich and Lubensky, as their St. Petersburg agents. Thus, after Blohm and Voss received the Russian contracts to rebuild the Czar's fleets, the German firm sent all of its designs, which Reilly knew were patterned after the German fleet, through his firm. As the agent for Blohm and Voss, Reilly passed along the designs to the Russian Minister of Marine but not before he photographed every detail in the designs, sending these revealing graphics to SIS in London.

Cumming was stunned. Reilly, through his own masterful invention, had engineered himself into a position where the Germans were actually handing him their most secret naval designs. It was one of the greatest espionage coups of that era and it established Reilly as a spy without equal. It also enriched Reilly a great deal in that he received the commission as agent for the government contracts. (SIS or chiefly Cumming gave tacit approval to Reilly's own entrepreneurial ventures; whatever funds he earned on his own in the line of duty he was allowed to keep. All Cumming wanted was results that benefited England.)

The spy stayed on in Russia, lavishing luxury upon himself. He bought a small palace and peopled it with liveried servants. He drove around in a long touring car, as well as fancy carriages. To his bed came Nadine Massino and many other comely Russian socialites, even women from the Russian royal bloodline. When his wife, Margaret, heard of his good fortune, she traveled to Moscow, confronting her husband as he was trysting in bed with Nadine Massino. Enraged, Reilly ordered her to leave Russia immediately or he would kill her. Terrified, Margaret left the country.

Reilly had decided that he would marry Nadine, but Margaret presented a problem. He didn't bother to divorce his wife; he merely arranged to make it appear that she had died. The spy bribed the editors of several papers to plant a bogus story about a Russian railway wreck in which several people had been killed, including his wife. He thus convinced Nadine he was free to marry. He next gave Massino a large sum of money to divorce Nadine.

Before the couple went to the altar, Reilly went into the armaments business. When the Central Powers and the Allies went to war, Russia was woefully underequipped. It possessed more men than any other nation but it lacked weapons. Reilly was asked to buy those weapons. He went to the U.S. and purchased armaments, then to Japan, where he bought more armaments with the help of his spymaster friend Akashi. Meanwhile, he had completely deserted Cumming's SIS, which infuriated the British spymaster.

In 1916, Reilly was in New York, where he continued to purchase arms on behalf of the czarist government in Russia. Nadine Massino joined Reilly in New York after taking a circuitous escape route from Russia. The couple married. Since Reilly had never divorced Margaret, he was now a bigamist, an offense that troubled him not. He and Nadine settled down in Manhattan for a brief period but Reilly grew nervous. He wanted action (and money). He contacted Cumming, who urged him to return to the service. Within a week, Reilly was back in England to accept another espionage assignment.

Since he spoke German like a native, he was sent into Germany several times to obtain information on enemy troop dispositions. He joined the German Army as an officer. He actually served with German troops on the Western Front while sending details of German plans to Cumming via carrier pigeon. At one point, Reilly, by his own account, impersonated the chief of staff to Rupert of Bavaria. As such he attended a top-level planning conference with the German high command, a meeting in which Kaiser Wilhelm himself presided. Those plans, too, went back to the British.

After spending eighteen months in Germany, Reilly resurfaced in England, recalled by Cumming for an ultra-important mission that had been decreed by no less an authority than Prime Minister David Lloyd George. The Prime Minister saw that by 1917 Russia was about to collapse through revolution. Alexander Kerensky had taken over the government, but he had kept Russia in the war. SIS had sent several agents to help finance his trembling administration, including the author Somerset Maugham. Then the Bolsheviks under Lenin and Trotsky seized the government, secretly negotiating with the Germans to pull out of the war.

The Germans had recently developed a close relationship with Lenin, having allowed him and a delegation of Bolsheviks to travel to Russia across German-occupied territory in a sealed train for the very purpose of taking over Russia. If Russia were to pull out of the war, more than a million German soldiers could abandon the Eastern Front and be sent against the Western Front.

All this was evident to Britain's Prime Minister Lloyd George. Russia had to stay in the war, he insisted. To that end, Cumming selected his best agent, Sidney Reilly, telling the spy that he was to spend whatever necessary and commit any action required to make sure Russia went on fighting. The master spy left for Russia, where he met with Robert Bruce Lockhart, the British general consul to Russia, a sort of roving ambassador for Britain, who had established shaky ties with the new Kerensky government but had difficulty in communicating with the insidious Lenin and calculating Trotsky.

The Bolsheviks stunned England by signing a peace treaty with the Germans at Brest-Litovsk on March 3, 1918. But this did not deter Lockhart, who believed that counterrevolutionary forces in Russia could overturn the Bolsheviks and bring Russia back into the war and tie up German divisions on the Eastern Front. At that time, Lockhart changed from diplomatic envoy to conspirator, organizing counterrevolutionary movements, it was reported, with the aid of the the master spy Reilly

Reilly, with the code name S.T.1, left for Russia in April 1918, loaded with SIS cash. Cumming told him to deal with Lenin if he could. The master spy tried to do exactly that, arriving before the gates of the Kremlin in Moscow on May 7, 1918. With an air of authority that cowed the Kremlin guards, Reilly demanded to see Lenin immediately. He was taken before one of Lenin's aides, Vladimir Bonch-Brouevic, who called Lockhart.

Once Reilly appeared before the British consul, Lockhart exploded, dressing him down for his attempted bold confrontation with Lenin. He threatened to send Reilly back to England immediately. The spy then began to talk slowly and was, according to Lockhart "so ingenious in his excuses that in the end he made me laugh."

Reilly then assumed the guise of a Greek from the Levant (he spoke Greek fluently) and, after acquiring another mistress, moved into a luxurious apartment in Moscow and began to plot the extermination of Lenin. He worked for a time in liaison with another SIS spy, George A. Hill, who was called "Jolly George" (code name I.K.8) and who later rose to the rank of general. Hill kept his distance from Reilly for unknown reasons. He had taken a different approach, first believing that the Bolshevik revolution could be undone, then abandoning this idea for appeasement tactics. He befriended Trotsky and actually helped Dzerzhinsky in developing the Cheka (the forerunner to the GPU, OGPU, NKVD, and KGB), which became even more ruthless in its persecution of suspected enemies of communism than the very organization it replaced, the Okhrana, the dreaded czarist secret police. (Hill ostensibly helped the Cheka develop its counterintelligence against German operatives inside Russia.)

Meanwhile, Reilly came to the conclusion that the best way to get rid of the Bolsheviks was to kill their leader, Lenin. He began to bribe Lenin's special Lettish bodyguards. Two of their officers agreed to act "when the time was right." Before the Letts could act on behalf of Reilly (and Lockhart, if one is to believe the later propaganda spread by the Bolsheviks that the British consul was directly involved with the plot), a bizarre set of events occurred in Moscow. On August 30, 1918, Moisay S. Uritsky, chief of the Petrograd Cheka, was shot and killed by L. Kenigiessev, identified by the Bolsheviks later as a Socialist Revolutionary student. Also killed that same day in Petrograd was V. Voladarsky, chief of Bolshevik propaganda. His killers, like that of Uritsky, were identified by the Bolsheviks as Socialist Revolutionaries.

The next day, while Lenin was addressing workers in a Moscow factory in Moscow that made hand-grenades, a dark-haired woman wearing a faded black dress and clutching a handbag approached the driver of Lenin's large touring car, Stepan Gil, who was waiting for Lenin to emerge from the factory.

"Has Lenin arrived?" the woman asked Gil.

The chauffeur had received strict orders to never identify who might be the passengers of his auto, especially the ever-furtive Lenin. Gil's evasive response was "I don't know who has arrived."

The woman smirked. "You're his chauffeur. How is it you don't know?"

"Why ask me?" said Gil. "There are so many speakers nowadays, it is impossible to keep track of them."

The woman, later identified by Cheka thugs as Fanya Kaplan-Roid, called Dora, went into the factory, going to the machine shop where Lenin was speaking from a rostrum, and sat down at a table, where she chain-smoked cigarettes. She appeared to be disinterested in Lenin's speech, which was an attack on capitalists in the United States. Some near her took note of the dark circles under the woman's eyes and how she nervously glanced about.

Following the speech, Lenin walked slowly from the factory toward his car, stopping to listen to some women complain about how food was being distributed. Lenin agreed that some of the people in charge of provisioning had been guilty of black marketeering, "but it will certainly be put right," he added.

Then Lenin walked through the crowds to the entrance of the building. A man named Novikov reportedly pushed back some people so that Dora Kaplan could get close to Lenin. Without a word, she whipped out a Browning pistol and quickly fired three shots. Two of the bullets struck Lenin, one striking and breaking Lenin's left shoulder and injuring the arm, the other piercing his left lung and exiting through the neck. Had the second bullet deviated one millimeter in either direction, it would have struck the heart and Lenin would have been dead.

Dora Kaplan fled down the street, Gil the chauffeur drawing his own pistol and running after her. When she disappeared into the crowd, he turned to see everyone fleeing from the place where Lenin lay crumpled on the ground. Gil was the only one who went to him.

"Did they get him?" Lenin asked. He apparently had no idea that he had been shot by a woman.

"You musn't talk," Gil cautioned. "It will only make you tired."

A man in a sailor's suit then ran from the factory. He kept one hand in his pocket, and the other he motioned frantically in the air, as if trying wave Gil away from Lenin. The man's features were contorted and to Gil he appeared to be insane.

Gil covered Lenin with his body and brandished his pistol, aiming it directly at the sailor, who kept coming. "Halt or I'll fire!" Gil shouted. The sailor suddenly stopped, and, looking about as if appraising the dangerous situation, then ran off on the heels of the fast-fleeing crowds. Gil thought that this man was part of the assassination plot, assigned to administer the coup de grace to Lenin. Gil later described the sailor as "dark complexioned, medium height, dark and penetrating eyes, long straight nose." Easily, he could have been describing Sidney George Reilly.

A woman appeared in the courtyard, screaming: "Don't shoot! Don't shoot!"

Gil realized that she thought *he* was the assassin and she was begging him not to shoot Lenin again. Then three men came running from the factory. Gil pointed his pistol at them, shouting: "Who are you? Halt or I'll fire!"

The men identified themselves as factory committee members, loyal Bolsheviks all, they insisted. Gil recognized one of the men and then asked them to help him with Lenin, who was breathing heavily. "You'll have to take him to the nearest hospital," one of the men said.

"No, I'm taking him home," Gil replied.

Lenin whispered as the men were putting him into the car: "Home, home."

With Lenin slumped in the back seat, a factory worker beside him, Gil drove the car at top speeds, reaching the Kremlin but not stopping at the Troitsa Gate to show his papers. He merely shouted "Lenin!" and drove on to Lenin's apartment building. Lenin was half-carried, mostly shoved up a flight of stairs to his apartment, where Lenin's trusted physicians attended to him. The reason Gil had not taken Lenin to the hospital was obvious; he did not (and neither did Lenin) want to risk putting Lenin in the care of a doctor who might be an anti-Bolshevik. The bullets were never removed from Lenin, who lived with them until his death in 1924.

As Lenin recuperated, Bonch-Brouevic stayed at his side, issuing orders for Lenin and keeping the Bolshevik hierarchy informed of the leader's progress. In fact, even before Lenin's physicians were summoned, Bonch-Brouevic called Trotsky and all of the other Bolshevik leaders to make sure that they and their troops were at their posts to fend off a counter-revolutionary takeover of the government. Lenin to the Bolsheviks, despite their claim of "boundless love" for him, was expendable. This attitude was not perceived by Reilly, who naively believed that if the head of the snake was cut off the reptile would die.

The Bolshevik leaders placed the assassination attempt at the door of the Socialist Revolutionaries. The man identified as "Novikov," was a sheer fabrication to make it appear that Dora Kaplan was part of a conspiracy. When the woman was finally tracked down and imprisoned before being shot without a trial, she was identified as a Socialist Revolutionary. She was anything but. Kaplan had been an anarchist who had spent many years in a czarist prison, where she had gone insane. She had been released at the time of the 1917 revolution but she was unable to make the distinction between Czar Nicholas II and Lenin. They were both the same to her.

Kaplan was interrogated by Cheka chief Dzerzhinsky in a sub-basement cell of the Cheka building on Lubianka Square. He could discover no plot. She would not say where she had obtained the Browning pistol nor how she came to shoot Lenin or why. Kaplan gave no answers. Dzerzhinsky, Lenin's right-hand executioner, decreed that Kaplan should die and issued the order to Pavel Malkov, Commandant of the Kremlin.

Malkov was ordered to kill Kaplan himself and he did so, taking delight in strangling the woman to death. Malkov later stated: "All kinds of fables and nonsense tales are in circulation: that Kaplan allegedly remained alive, that Lenin allegedly cancelled the verdict at the last moment. There are even 'eyewitnesses' who 'met' Kaplan either in the Butirki Prison, or in Solovkii, or in Vorkuta, and I don't know where else. These fairy tales were born of a petty bourgeois urge to represent Lenin as a kindly fellow who graciously forgave enemies their evil deeds. . . . No, nobody annulled Kaplan's death sentence. On September 3, 1918, the sentence was carried out, and I carried it out, I, a Communist, a sailor of the Baltic fleet, commandant of the Moscow Kremlin, Pavel Dmitrievich Malkov—with my own hands!"

Throughout the panic that ensued after the assassination of Uritsky and the attempt on Lenin's life, the Bolsheviks insisted that their political enemies had brought these murderous acts about. They pinned the blame on the Socialist Revolutionaries so they could track down the leaders and imprison or execute them out-of-hand. They then discovered Reilly's Lettish plot when two Lett officers confessed that the British spy had bribed them to turn on Lenin, but they insisted that they had merely played along to learn that the scheme had been hatched by none other than British consul Bruce Lockhart, a conspiracy termed the "Lockhart Plot" by the Bolsheviks. The Bolsheviks moved in on Lockhart while he was attending a symphony.

Reilly suddenly appeared in Lockhart's box to tell him that the Letts had betrayed him and that it was every man for himself. Before Lockhart left the theater he glanced back to see the British spy swallowing bits of paper that might incriminate him if he were to be captured. (Reilly would later tell Cumming that he had no intention of ever assassinating Lenin or Trotsky. His plan, he said, was to thoroughly discredit them in the eyes of their followers through ridicule. He planned to kidnap them, strip them naked, and parade them through the streets of Moscow on a chain! Moreover, Reilly mused, the assassination of Uritsky and Kaplan's attempt on Lenin was most probably engineered by the Bolsheviks themselves so as to provide an excuse to eliminate their political enemies.) Lockhart was arrested in the apartment of his mistress, and later released.

Robert Bruce Lockhart, British diplomat, who was arrested and charged with being part of Reilly's plot to kill Lenin and change the course of Russian history.

Reilly did resurface before Lockhart left Russia. He met with the British official to say that he intended to stay on in Russia to work for the defeat of the Bolsheviks. He believed that there were enough anti-Communist forces to overcome the ragged legions of Lenin. He did not accomplish that task. Instead, he barely managed to stay one step ahead of pursuing Cheka agents. Several of his associates and mistresses were arrested before Reilly paid 60,000 rubles to be smuggled on board a Dutch freighter. In a brief trial held in Moscow that year, Sidney Reilly was found guilty of conspiring against the Bolshevik regime and the life of Lenin. He was condemned to death *in absentia*.

British spy George Hill also realized that he was facing overwhelming odds in combating the Bolsheviks. Eighteen of his top spies had been arrested and executed following Kaplan's attempt on Lenin's life. Hill, along with Lockhart, who had been under house arrest in Moscow, and Ernest Boyce, another SIS spy, were allowed to return to England in October 1918, exchanged for Soviet official Maxim Litvinov and other Russian envoys who had been detained in England in retaliation against the Bolshevik custody of Lockhart.

When Reilly finally managed to return to England, he immediately lobbied Cumming to have the British

Foreign Office use him to continue the fight against Bolshevism. He was convinced, he said, that he was the one man to bring down Lenin's regime. The Foreign Office was disinclined to add to their muster a man as flamboyant and uncontrollable as Reilly. He stayed on with SIS, loosely connected but unsevered as an agent.

In 1919, Reilly allied himself with Boris Savinkov, a conniving, clever anti-Communist terrorist who swore that he could raise a mighty army that would overthrow the Bolsheviks. Reilly took Savinkov to see Winston Churchill, who was mightily impressed with the terrorist. During the Russo-Polish war of 1920, Savinkov fought with his old friend, Polish Marshal Pilsudski, and by September of that year he had put together an anti-Bolshevik corps of 30,000 well-trained officers and men. This force, Savinkov proposed to the British, would be used to "push forward into Soviet territory collecting a huge snowball of anti-Bolshies."

The march of anti-Bolsheviks into Russia did not take place. Anti-Bolshevik forces already inside Russia were supported by the British but they carried on a losing civil war with the Bolsheviks— White Russian armies led by General Anton L. Deniken, General Lavr Kornilov, and Admiral Alexander Kolchak—until these monarchists were defeated in 1922. During that time Reilly continued to promote Savinkov as the only man who could truly redeem Russia. To make a living, however, the spy entered into several business dealings with a former military intelligence officer, General Edward Spears.

When it appeared that he had lost all support, Savinkov was suddenly elated to discover a wealthy group of White Russian monarchists in Paris who had formed the Monarchist Union of Central Russia (MUCR), which was also called the Trust. Its representatives told Savinkov that it would financially back his revolution if he were to go to Russia and meet with underground MUCR leaders. Savinkov did exactly that on August 27, 1923. He was immediately arrested by MUCR representatives who turned out to be GPU agents of Felix Dzerzhinsky. The Trust, although it did have several genuine though unwitting monarchist members, was a ruse created by the devious Russian spymaster to lure the hated Savinkov back to Russia.

Reilly's own fortunes had collapsed. He was almost broke, having been set adrift by Spears, who, after several years of enduring Reilly's wildly unsuccessful business schemes, severed their relationship. Reilly had also spent a great deal of money in a prolonged and unsuccessful litigation against an American firm that had reneged on a huge commission due him.

The super spy had borrowed money from all of his former friends in the SIS and no longer had a relationship with British intelligence, Cumming having been replaced by Hugh Sinclair, who believed Reilly was little more than a seedy adventurer. In March 1925, Reilly admitted in a letter to Ernest Boyce, his one-time fellow spy in Russia, that "my own personal affairs . . . as you know, are in a hellish state." He added with a tinge of self-pity: "I was fifty-one yesterday and I want to do something worthwhile, while I can."

Then Boyce, who was then the SIS chief in Helsinki, wrote to Reilly to tell him that he had been in contact with representatives of the Paris Trust (which had lured Savinkov back to his death in Russia, a fact unknown to Boyce or Reilly). Boyce was convinced that the Trust was extremely powerful and had the contacts, money, and secret forces to bring about a radical change in Russia. Through him, Reilly came to meet several of MUCR representatives, agreeing to go to Russia to confer with the Trust's leading council members.

Like Savinkov before him, the once great spy was easily hoodwinked. He crossed the Finnish border on September 25, 1925, and was taken to a villa outside Moscow two days later to meet with council members who were really OGPU agents.

The spy was interrogated and then told that the death sentence imposed upon him *in absentia* in 1918 would be carried out. The once nerveless spy panicked. He wrote a desperate note to OGPU chief Dzerzhinsky, according to later Soviet accounts, in which he begged for his life in exchange for priceless information he could provide Soviet intelligence. Reilly's note read: "After prolonged deliberation, I express willingness to give you complete and open acknowledgement and information on matters of interest to the OGPU concerning the organization and personnel of the British Intelligence Service, and, so far as I know it, similar information on American intelligence and likewise on Russian émigrés with whom I have had business."

Dzerzhinsky did not respond. Some time in November 1925, Sidney George Reilly was placed before a villa wall outside of Moscow and shot to death, his body dumped into an unmarked grave. Since that time, several authors have attempted to perpetuate the myth that Reilly not only survived but went on to become the top adviser to the chiefs of the Soviet intelligence agencies, living on for years in Russia. Nothing could be farther from the truth. The spy's luck, contacts, and money had run out. He still believed, perhaps up to the very moment he faced his firing squad, that his brand of lone-wolf espionage, his brazen, old-fashioned methods could somehow overcome a fanatical, murderous enemy he truly did not understand. The Bolsheviks of his day did not barter. The Bolsheviks did not deal. They only killed.

[ALSO SEE: *Motojiro Akashi; Yevno Azev; Cheka; Mansfield Cumming; Paul Dukes; Felix Dzerzhinsky; George Gapon; GPU; Somerset Maugham; OGPU; Okhrana; SIS*]

REISS, IGNACE (OR IGNATZ; LUDOWIK PORETSKY)
Polish Spy for Soviets ▪ (1899–1937)

REISS WAS BORN LUDOWIK PORETSKY IN GALICIA. Early on, Reiss was enamored of socialism and went to Vienna to join radical socialists in 1917 in hopes of ending the war. By 1919, Reiss had joined the Polish Communist Party, going to Moscow to live the following year.

Reiss actively supported the Communist cause during the Russian Civil War and when he returned to Lvov in 1922 he was a GPU spy. While attempting to obtain Polish military secrets, Reiss was caught and sent to prison for five years. Upon his release, he returned to Moscow, where he received more espionage training. In 1932, Reiss was sent to France as the resident director of the OGPU.

By 1936 much of Reiss' ardent political faith in communism had faded, mostly due to Stalin's ruthless purges of old Bolsheviks in the infamous Moscow trials. He formally resigned from the OGPU and then, in July 1937, boldly wrote a letter to Stalin which he distributed to the European press. In one portion of his letter, Reiss stated that "he who remains silent at this hour makes himself an accomplice of Stalin and a traitor to the cause of the working class and of socialism . . . I am finished with everything, to Lenin, to his teachings and his cause. I am returning to freedom."

Stalin exploded, summoning Nicolai Yezhov, chief of the NKVD, and ordering Yezhov to send not one but three SMERSH assassination teams to France to kill the impudent Reiss. Yezhov, a perverted dwarf who was once described by Stalin as "a drunken sot," and who would be himself murdered on Stalin's orders two years later when Lavrenti Beria replaced him, quickly assembled three groups of killers.

Overseeing the murder squads was Colonel Mikhail Shpigelglas, a deputy chief of the foreign division of the Center. The three teams were assembled but only one was sent after Reiss, this being led by Roland Abiatt (or Abbiate), an old-time illegal who was then using the alias Francois Rossi, and included Etienne-Charles Martignat, who lived in France, and an Italian NKVD agent, Gertrude Shildbach.

Abiatt knew it would be difficult to locate the clever Reiss, who had immediately gone underground with his wife and small son after issuing his open denouncement of Stalin. He knew that no resident director who defected had ever lived very long to tell about it. Abiatt employed an ardent young Communist, Renata Steiner, who had met Reiss and befriended him in the early 1930s. Through friends of Reiss' wife, she located the fugitive in Holland and kept him under surveillance until Abiatt's team arrived.

By then, however, the wily Reiss had vanished. He resurfaced in Paris, where Abiatt located him in August 1937. He and the other SMERSH agents closed in on Reiss' apartment but when they broke inside they found their quarry had once again escaped. Then Abiatt discovered that Reiss and his family had fled to Switzerland. He and Steiner went to Bern on August 28, 1937, where Abiatt had reserved rooms at Hotel City. By then Steiner still had not learned why Abiatt was searching for Reiss, or, at least, that is what she claimed when arrested for Reiss' murder.

Reiss by then was resigned to his fate. He hurriedly began writing his memoirs, which he intended to publish as an exposé of the brutal Stalinist regime in Russia. He knew that he would never live to finish the book but he did secretly meet with Lev Sedov, Trotsky's son, to verbally indict Stalin as a mass murderer. Meanwhile his killers were drawing ever closer.

Getrude Schildbach, one of Reiss' old friends, visited the villa where he was staying and convinced him to take a ride with her and her friend, someone she said who could arrange for Reiss to escape to America. She made a phone call and soon her friend, Abiatt, arrived by car.

Reiss got into the car next to Abiatt, who was driving. Schildbach, after leaving the gift of a box of chocolates for Mrs. Reiss and her child, got into the back seat of the car, which then sped off in the direction of Lausanne. As the car neared Chamblandes, Abiatt pulled the car to the side of the road. Schildbach leaned forward from the back seat, looping a long scarf over Reiss' neck, pulling him backward so that he reached over his head in the struggle. At the moment, Abiatt pulled out a revolver and emptied it into Reiss, killing him. The SMERSH agents dumped their victim's body alongside the road and drove away.

The next morning, September 4, 1937, Steiner had breakfast on the terrace of her hotel in Territet. She read in the morning paper a report that the body of an unidentified man had been found on the road to Lausanne and thought nothing of it. She continued to wait for a call from Abiatt but it never came. On September 8, Steiner took a train to Bern, going to Hotel City, but there was no trace of Abiatt, whom Steiner knew only as Rossi, or so she later said.

Next Steiner went to the garage where she had rented a car, asking if it had been returned by her friends. The clerk on duty seemed a bit startled to see her. He asked her to wait while he checked, then returned to ask Steiner to step into the office to collect her deposit. While she was waiting, a Swiss police car suddenly drove into the garage and officers jumped out, arresting her for being an accomplice in the murder of Ignace Reiss.

Steiner, realizing that she had been wantonly used in the SMERSH assassination, gave the police a full and detailed report, describing Abiatt, or Rossi, and the Italian Communist agent Schildbach. She was later imprisoned for a brief period while Swiss police conducted a desperate search for the killers. Abiatt and Schildbach, however, had gotten completely away. When Stalin heard that Reiss had been exterminated, he ordered that the SMERSH agents be given a large bonus.

Then he was informed that Reiss' wife and son had survived. Neither of them had taken a piece of the candy the kindly Schildbach had left for them. The candy had been dosed with strychnine. Stalin ordered the bonus cancelled. In Paris, one of Reiss' closest friends, also a Polish Jew who had worked his way up the Communist ladder and Soviet intelligence service with Reiss, received a message from the Center only a few days after Reiss had been liquidated. He was Walter G. Krivitsky, resident director of the GRU in Paris.

Krivitsky knew that, as Reiss' friend and associate, he would be killed as soon as he returned to Moscow. Packing voluminous materials on his subversive activities, Krivitsky immediately defected, asking for asylum from the French government. This was granted. Krivitsky then managed to get to England, then America, only a few jumps ahead of SMERSH agents. He did what Ignace Reiss could not, writing his memoirs and exposing in print for the first time the full horrors of the Stalin regime. He, like Reiss before him, did not escape the long arm of SMERSH. Krivitsky was found murdered in his Washington, D.C., hotel room in 1941.

[ALSO SEE: *Lavrenti Paulovich Beria; Walter G. Krivitsky; NKVD; OGPU; SMERSH; Nicolai Yezhov*]

REVERE, PAUL
American Patriot and Revolutionary Spy ▪ (1735–1818)

PAUL REVERE WAS EULOGIZED IN A STIRRING POEM by Henry Wadsworth Longfellow, one which told of his wild and exciting ride through the night to warn that British troops were about to march on Concord and Lexington to disarm the Minutemen. Though full of historical inaccuracies, Longfellow's paen of praise to Revere was correct. He did make a ride that fateful night in 1775 but others completed his task.

Revere was born in Boston. His parents were Huguenots and he was apprenticed to his father, who was a leading silversmith. In 1756, Revere answered the British call to arms as a colonial volunteer in the French and Indian War. Following many adventures, he returned to Boston, where he resumed his trade as a silversmith, becoming one of the most famous in that trade.

From youth, Revere expressed patriotic views, openly voicing his opposition to British rule in the colonies. He joined the Patriots as early as 1770 and commemorated the "Boston Massacre," a clash between drunken rebels and British troops, with a magnificently etched copper plate, and proceeded to make copies of the skirmish. Revere actually obtained a vivid sketch of the clash on King Street which had been done by Henry Pelham, an eyewitness. He used this sketch for his original engraving from which he made and sold countless copies, gleaning a handsome profit. Pelham later complained that Revere never paid him a cent for his sketch.

Joining the Sons of Liberty, a clandestine revolutionary group in Boston, Revere took part in the notorious "Boston Tea Party" of 1773, when a gang of patriots thinly disguised as Indians threw £10,000 worth of British tea into Boston Harbor as a protest against excessive British taxes.

A skilled horseman, Revere volunteered to act as a courier for the revolutionaries and often rode great distances to warn inhabitants of British military moves, such as his ride to Portsmouth, New Hampshire, to warn a band of patriots under the command of John Sullivan that British troops were about to take action there. Sullivan, with Revere at his side, in the first real act of rebellion, broke into a British military bastion and seized all the arms and gun powder available, denying these stores to British troops, which arrived a short time later.

The chasm between the colonials and the British military widened. London ordered more troops into Boston, which was then the hotbed of rebellion. Operating from his silversmith's shop, Revere organized a spy network throughout the city. His agents strolled the streets and British campsites, recording the number of soldiers, their equipment and arms, and their lines of supply from the harbor. All this was taken back to Revere who prepared detailed reports which he submitted to John Hancock, head of the Committee of Safety.

Outside of Boston in the little towns and villages of Massachusetts, the patriots began assembling secret militia. British spies, of course, were also at work, noting the secret meetings and assembling of arms by the patriots. These British spies were Tories such as Benjamin Thompson. Inside Boston, in fact within the very ranks of the leading patriots, was another Tory spy, Benjamin Church, who called John and Samuel Adams, Joseph Warren, and John Hancock his friends.

By 1775, both patriots and British were prepared for open conflict. British General Thomas Gage was hesitant to take any action against the patriots, warning London that if the leaders were arrested, as they suggested, open conflict would surely ensue. Called an "old woman" by his troops, Gage insisted upon written orders "to march into the countryside," where he was to seize all arms and military supplies hidden by the rebels. (Tory spy Benjamin Church had provided the British with a detailed list of locations where these military stores were secreted.)

When Gage received written orders to mount an offensive against the patriots, he slowly and reluctantly began assembling his troops in Boston. On April 16, 1775, Revere learned of the plan through one of his spies and warned Hancock and the other leaders, who immediately left Boston, going into the countryside to assemble the militia. It was on that night that Revere told William Conant, a rebel living across the Charles River, that he should look for a lantern signal in about two nights, the scheduled time for Gage's troops to leave Boston—"one if by land, two if by sea." The signal would appear in the tower of the Old North Church.

On the night of April 18, Revere and others climbed to the belfry of the church and hung two lighted lanterns to indicate to Conant and the Patriots in Charlestown that British troops were coming by sea; Gage was sending his troops across the Charles River in small boats. The Committee of Safety then ordered Revere and William Dawes to ride through the countryside and sound the alarm.

Dawes left first, slipping through the fortifications at Boston Neck and alarming the countryside. Then Revere departed. He was rowed by two friends across the Charles River to Charlestown, where he obtained a horse and began his historic ride, shouting from the saddle: "Alarm! Alarm! Gage is coming! British troops are coming!" (He did not, as is often quoted, shout: "The British are coming!" The colonialists were British subjects and thought of themselves as British.)

Just outside of Charlestown, two British officers jumped into the road, one grabbing the reins of Revere's horse. The silversmith kicked the officer in the face and sent him reeling, then spurred his horse forward and escaped. Revere arrived at Lexington, where he warned Hancock and Samuel Adams, who were in hiding there. Then Dawes, who had taken a longer route, arrived, along with Dr. Samuel Prescott, who was then courting a girl in Lexington. The three men then spurred their horses to the outskirts of town to continue spreading the alarm, heading for Concord.

Suddenly a mounted British patrol blocked their path. Dawes turned his horse about and dashed back to Lexington, escaping. Prescott gave his horse a violent kick and jumped a fence, running through open countryside and on to Concord, where he warned the Patriots of Gage's coming. Revere, however, was trapped and arrested, his horse taken away. After talking with the British officer in command, Revere convinced him that he and his friends had been out drinking and his friends had merely been startled and ran away, thinking the British soldiers, not distinguishable in the darkness, might be highwaymen. The officer accepted the story but kept Revere's horse. The silversmith walked back to Lexington.

When Revere arrived back in Lexington he encountered the Reverend William Gordon, who told him that Captain John Parker and about seventy militiamen had assembled on Lexington green. Suddenly, Revere heard firing and, as Gordon was later quoted: "he, having nothing to defend himself with, ran into a wood where he halted, and heard the firing for about a quarter of an hour."

At Lexington, not Concord, "the shot heard 'round the world," was fired. It was never determined which side fired that fateful shot. Both sides blamed the other. Eight Patriots and no British were killed. Parker and his men then fled and the British continued toward Concord, where several hundred Patriots met them at the North Bridge. The Patriots sent a withering volley into the ranks of the British troops, which reeled backward and began retreating.

During the retreat, thousands of farmers from throughout the countryside came running, firing at the British from behind trees and stone walls. Many of these Minutemen were veterans of the Canadian and Indian wars and knew how to fight in wooded and hilly terrain. The British paid a heavy toll, running out of ammunition in their bloody retreat, which almost turned into a rout until British reinforcements led by Hugh Percy arrived. The humiliating retreat, involving between 1,500 and 1,800 British troops, continued all the way back to Boston. The British losses involved 73 dead, 174 wounded and 26 missing. About 100 Patriots had been killed. The American Revolution had begun. Percy, who hated the colonials, nevertheless gave them their due, saying: "Whoever looks upon them as an irregular mob, will find himself much mistaken."

Although he continued some espionage activities, Revere devoted much of his time to the printing of Continental currency, and the seals of America and the state of Massachusetts. At the war's conclusion in 1783, Revere returned to silversmithing, his work considered to be the best found in the United States to this day. He later operated a copper mill and produced plating for American warships such as "Old Ironsides" (the *Constitution*), as well as constructing boilers for steam vessels designed by Robert Fulton.

[ALSO SEE: *Benjamin Church; Benjamin Thompson*]

RICHELIEU, CARDINAL (ARMAND-JEAN DU PLESSIS)
French Statesman, Cardinal, and Spymaster ▪ (1585–1642)

PARIS BORN, RICHELIEU WAS A JUNIOR MEMBER OF the French aristocracy. After entering the clergy, he became Bishop of Lucon in 1607. Politically ambitious, he gained the favor of Marie de Medici, mother of King Louis XIII, who brought him to court and influenced his appointment as secretary

French Cardinal Richelieu, the spymaster who ran France.

of state for foreign affairs in 1616. Though he fell from favor, Richelieu regained his political stature when he was made a cardinal of the Catholic Church in 1622. Two years later he became prime minister under Louis XIII, a post he tenaciously held until his dying day.

From the day of his appointment, Richelieu began to establish his own espionage network, which he funded from government coffers, an enormous treasure chest that allowed him to put thousands on his payroll. Richelieu's spies worked both for the King and the Cardinal, but mostly for Richelieu. In addition to spying on the nobility to determine plots against the crown, Richelieu's agents spied on his foremost enemies at court, those resentful of his powerful position and who intrigued to have him replaced.

Such was the conspiracy headed by the queen mother and some of her supporters, who feared that the very man they had promoted to the position of prime minister was now so powerful that he might usurp the throne. They plotted to have Richelieu replaced. Learning of this from his spies, the bold Cardinal burst into a palace meeting where his fate was being discussed. He confronted the conspirators and suavely persuaded the King that he should keep his post for the benefit and safety of France.

Louis XIII kept him on and never again was Richelieu's authority challenged.

Richelieu's top agent was a Capuchin friar, Francois Leclerc du Tremblay, who traveled to the smaller states of the Holy Roman Empire to spread discontent against Ferdinand II, the Hapsburg emperor. Throughout the Thirty Years' War (1618–1648), Richelieu's agents were able to undermine the military might of Austria, then France's greatest political rival.

A master at double-dealing, Richelieu maintained relations with Austria while secretly backing Gustavus Adolphus of Sweden to invade the Hapsburg empire in a war that so weakened Austria that France emerged as the strongest empire in Europe. Tremblay was the instrument by which Richelieu was able to remove Austria's greatest general, Albrecht von Wallenstein, from the active list in 1630. Tremblay had wormed his way into the confidence of Ferdinand II, convincing the monarch that Wallenstein's abilities were overrated. When Adolphus' armies gobbled up many Austrian provinces, Ferdinand returned Wallenstein to his position but by then it was too late to recover the lost lands.

Almost all French teachers of dance or fencing who went abroad were invariably Richelieu's hand-picked spies, working in the courts of other kings and countries, relaying information to Richelieu through a network made up of tens of thousands of spies. This vast army of agents remained in place and continued to work for France even after the death of the "Gray Eminence," as Richelieu was called. He was replaced by an equally cunning spymaster, Cardinal Mazarin, who removed Tremblay as his chief aide, replacing him with Ondedei, the Bishop of Fréjus.

RICHER, MARTHE
French Spy in World War I ▪
(1889–1949?)

THE DAUGHTER OF A FRENCH BREWER IN BLAMONT, in the province of Lorraine, Richer's maiden name was Betenfeld, which suggested a German heritage. In 1901, Richer studied German at a school in Nancy and, after studying three more years, became a dressmaker, opening her own shop in Paris in 1906.

With her business a success, Richer spent time learning how to fly, one of her girlhood ambitions. She became an accomplished aviator and one of the first females in France to receive a flying license. In 1914, the year World War I began, she married Henri Richer, another flyer, who was killed in action the following year. Three months after her husband's death, the patriotic Richer went to Captain Ladoux, chief of French military intelligence, and volunteered to spy for France.

Ladoux sent Richer to spy on the German colony in the Spanish town of San Sebastian. She arrived in early 1916 and met a Dr. Stephan, who shortly admitted that he was an Abwehr spy, asking her to become an agent for Germany in France. Richer said she would consider the proposal but only if the proposition came from Stephan's chief, Baron Hans Kron, a German naval captain and an attaché in the German Embassy in Madrid.

Stephan arranged for the meeting. Kron was instantly smitten with the attractive Richer and, a short time later, made her his mistress. The ever-enterprising Abwehr chief Walther Nicolai informed Kron that Richer had to earn her way and ordered her to go to Paris, where she was to obtain the production figures of the great Schneider armaments firm. Before leaving Madrid, Kron instructed his agent how to use the latest German invisible ink, packaged in tiny capsules. After one of these capsules—the size of a flower seed—was dissolved in plain water, it would produce "enough secret ink to write a book," according to Kron.

Once in Paris, Richer reported to French counterintelligence. At first, her handlers doubted she had actually become the mistress of the arch-conservative Kron. She removed all doubts when picking out his photo from French intelligence files, as well as providing information on his relatives in Germany.

Some weeks later Richer returned to Madrid, providing Kron with information on the Schneider works, data which had been skillfully counterfeited by French counterintelligence. This was sent on to Nicolai, who accepted the information as genuine. A few days later Richer accompanied Kron on a visit to inspect the German submarine U-52 that had developed engine trouble and had been interned in Cadiz.

Richer made a detailed description of the submarine, which she sent to her French handlers, ironically using the very invisible inks Kron had given her in her message, which she signed "Alouette" (lark), her code name. Kron next sent Richer to Buenos Aires to contact the many German agents there.

Not for some months did Richer return to Spain. When she arrived she told Kron that she had been detained by Allied agents and had destroyed the instructions before they could be discovered. She described a hair-raising escape back to Europe, sailing on a Portuguese vessel under an alias. Kron accepted her story and Richer went on living with him and plundering German secrets, which she dutifully sent to French intelligence.

In 1918, Richer tired of the pretense. Also, she had developed a genuine affection for Kron. Before returning to France, she inexplicably told him of her role as a double agent. He could do little about this since the war had come to a close.

[ALSO SEE: *Abwehr; Walther Nicolai*]

French agent Marthe Richer, who spied against Germany in World War I.

RICHTER, KAREL RICHARD (AKA: FRED SNYDER)
German Spy in World War II ▪ (1912–1941)

During 1941, the Abwehr grew desperate to smuggle German spies into enemy England. Hitler, in the third year of World War II, had all but given up on invading England but ordered Admiral Canaris, chief of the Abwehr, to flood the country with spies to learn English military strength and its national will to win the war. Many Abwehr spies were already in England, sending a great deal of information to Germany. Unknown to the Abwehr, MI5 had remarkably captured all of the German spies and had turned them around so that they were actually sending out disinformation to Germany, which British intelligence carefully concocted. In some instances, MI5 lured more German agents to England.

Two of these Abwehr spies were parachutists, the first being Josef Jakobs, a 43-year-old meteorologist from Luxembourg who broke his ankle when parachuting into a field near Ramsey in Huntingdonshire on the night of January 31, 1941. He was found limping along a road and quickly searched. His papers, which identified him as George Rymer, were obvious forgeries and his ration book had not been used for a month. He was turned over to MI5. British interrogators soon heard Jakobs' confession that he was a spy who was deliverying bundles of counterfeit pound notes to another German agent who had already been turned by MI5. Jakobs was tried, found guilty, and sentenced to death. On August 14, 1941, he hobbled from his cell in the Tower of London and faced a firing squad of eight soldiers, who promptly shot him to death.

The second parachutist sent by the Abwehr to England arrived in spring. He was even more inept and inexperienced than Jakobs. He was Karel Richard Richter, age twenty-nine, and his mission was to deliver a new valve for a radio operated by an Abwehr spy who was already working for MI5 as a double agent (Wulf Schmidt, who had been captured in September 1940 and went on operating as an Abwehr spy in England under the direction of MI5 until May 1945, the very end of the war in Europe). Tall, thin, and red-headed, Richter came from Kraslice, Czechoslovakia, a predominantly German community in the Sudetenland where he went to school.

On the early morning of May 14, 1941, Richter descended by parachute into a field near Tyttenhanger Park, London Colney. After hiding his parachute and supplies in a dense hedge, Richter waited until nightfall before he began walking along a country road. A truck pulled up alongside of him and the driver asked for directions. Richter merely shrugged, giving a brief, mumbled reply that hardly sounded English. The driver went on down the road, stopping when he encountered war reserve policeman Alec J. Scott, a constable on a bicycle. The truck driver asked for directions and got them. Then he told Scott about the stranger on the road behind him, "a bit of a suspicious character." Richter was detained.

A search of Richter uncovered a Swedish passport that bore his photo and the name Karel Richter. Oddly, Richter was found to be wearing three pairs of underwear and two pairs of socks. When asked to explain this unsual garb, Richter only shrugged. Police quickly concluded he was a spy and summoned agents of MI5 and Special Branch. To these agents, Richter admitted that he was a German agent.

The hapless Richter was imprisoned at Canon Row Police Station in London, adjacent to Scotland Yard. He was tried at the Old Bailey in October and was convicted and sentenced to death by hanging. On December 10, 1941, Richter was led to the scaffold but when he reached the trapdoor, the spy suddenly began to violently struggle with his guards. Four guards and the executioner, Albert Pierrepoint,

grappled with Richter for some minutes until they finally tied his hands with a leather strap. Yet, he continued to fight for his life in what was later described as "an extraordinary free-for-all . . . to the dismay of those gathered to watch the proceedings."

Pierrepoint finally yanked the lever and Richter plunged downward but, horrifying all present, the rope slipped from under the spy's chin and caught at his nose. The first and second vertebrae of Richter's spinal column audibly snapped, causing his instant, gruesome death. MI5 was later criticized for entrapping an inexperienced, naive German agent and sending him to his death, as if for no other reason than to increase its victorious toll of captured Abwehr spies.

[ALSO SEE: *Abwehr; Wilhelm Franz Canaris; Gestapo; MI5; Special Branch*]

RINNAN, HENRY OLIVER
Norwegian Double Spy for Nazi Germany ▪ (1898–1945)

NEXT TO VIDKUN QUISLING, THE MOST NOTORIOUS traitor and Nazi spy in Norway during World War II was Henry Oliver Rinnan. He slavishly served the German cause not only for the money it paid him but because he truly believed in Hitler and his Nazi philosophy. Inventive and canny, Rinnan organized an effective and lethal spy network that disrupted British espionage and sabotage in occupied Norway for years, causing the deaths of countless SOE and Norwegian agents.

Norway's undergound was active throughout the war and produced countless heroes whose heroic feats and incredible stamina became the stuff of legend. Typical was underground leader Jan Baalsrud, who trained with the British SOE before returning to his native Norway to undertake several sabotage missions. One of the missions proved to be a disaster, all of the agents killed or captured except Baalsrud, who escaped into a frozen wilderness in northern Norway. He survived avalanches, frostbite, and gangrene.

To avoid detection from Nazi alpine troops searching for him, Baalsrud lay in a sleeping bag for twenty-seven days. When his toes became frostbitten and turned gangrenous, the spy doused his feet with brandy as an anaesthetic and a disinfectant before cutting off his own toes with a penknife. Found by a Norwegian resistance group, he was carried by sledge up a 3,000-foot mountain and was finally delivered to safety by Lapps herding hundreds of reindeer into neutral Sweden.

One of those pursuing the courageous Baalsrud was the dogged Rinnan, who had vowed to track down every resistance fighter in Norway, along with the SOE spies who aided them. His organization was large and dedicated and some of his agents even infiltrated the Home Front, the chief resistance movement. Knowing this, Norwegian freedom fighters sought to kill Rinnan, sending their own agents from Milorg, the Army resistance movement, to find and liquidate him. None were successful.

So vast was Rinnan's spy network that he knew within hours almost every covert operation planned by the Allies. At one point, the British thought to mount a large assault in northern Norway. Arms and supplies for this military incursion were sent ahead of the troops, smuggled from the Shetland Islands by a flotilla of small fishing boats, which landed spies and the weapons in foggy fjords.

Rinnan's spies learned about the arrival of the SOE spies only hours after they had landed. In reprisal and to prompt suspects into informing on the agents, the Gestapo seized thirty-four Norwegians at random and shot them. This only stiffened Norwegian resolve and, of the many SOE groups landed in this operation, only one man, a radio operator, and a few rifles, were found by the Nazis.

Milorg and the Home Front realized that Rinnan had become so well entrenched with the district that the area was given up as lost to the resistance. Rinnan remained a thorn in the side of the resistance to the very end of the war when he himself became the hunted one. He led Allied agents on a wild chase through Norway but was finally apprehended, tried, and executed.

[ALSO SEE: Gestapo; Vidkun Quisling; SOE]

RINTELEN, FRANZ (OR FRITZ) VON
German Spymaster & Saboteur in World War I ▪ (1885–1949)

WALTHER NICOLAI, DIRECTOR OF THE ABWEHR, chose Rintelen to go to the U.S., which was then a neutral country, and sabotage merchant vessels transporting supplies and war materials to England and France. He was a charming, handsome young man who, before the war, had lived for some time in New York, where he had been a director of the Deutsche Bank.

Arriving in America in April 1915 (using a false Swiss passport that identified him as Emile V. Gasche), Rintelen reported to Franz von Papen, who, like Rintelen, came from the German aristocratic Junker class. Papen, who had conducted espionage for Germany in Mexico before being assigned to duty in the U.S., was responsible for all covert German operations in America.

When Rintelen enthusiastically described how he planned to blow up American supply ships, harbors, and warehouses, the normally reserved Papen grew alarmed. In fact, he panicked, telling an aide that he thought Rintelen might be unbalanced and that the espionage network he had so carefully pieced together in the U.S. and Canada might be on the verge of exposure through the machinations of a certifiable madman. Papen glumly listened as Rintelen showed him plans for bombs that he himself had constructed.

Rintelen proudly described his pipe bomb: One end of the pipe was filled with sulphuric acid, the other end, separated from the first by a copper plate, contained picric acid. He had attached a timing device to the pipe, the saboteur said, that would determine how long it would take before the sulphuric acid ate through the copper plate, ignite the picric acid, and set off the pipe bomb with a terrific blast. He then detailed another bomb to Papen, one which was to be fixed to a blade on a ship's propeller. The strutting saboteur predicted that he would sink a million tons of shipping in a few months. (Rintelen's bombs proved useful to British explosives experts in World War II; they built their "limpet" bombs and mines along the lines of Rintelen's original creations.)

Papen, horrified at Rintelen's proposal, viewed covert operations as subtle, well-planned plots. The wild schemes of Rintelen, he felt, would jeopardize his own spy networks. "Impossible," Papen groaned later to an aide. "The man [Rintelen] is crazy. You should have seen him when he talked of setting off his bombs. His eyes blazed, and he cackled like a lunatic!" Papen moved to stop Rintelen's operations.

The next meeting between the two spymasters—Nicolai having provided Rintelen a group of German saboteurs answerable only to him—was almost as explosive as one of Rintelen's infernal machines. Papen reminded Rintelen that he was the resident director of all German espionage and sabotage in America. "You are not to conduct any sabotage here," ordered Papen. He then added: "At least until I have consulted Berlin."

The proud Rintelen bristled, snapping back: "I do not take my orders from you! I will mount my attacks against the targets which have already been chosen by *my* superiors in Germany!" With that Rintelen stormed off to wage his secret war against Allied shipping.

Of course, Papen and Rintelen had the same superior in Berlin, Walther Nicolai, a crafty spymaster who often played both sides against the middle to see if better results could be achieved. When Papen sent Nicolai a long, coded letter, stating that Rintelen was a threat to the whole German spy network in America, he received no response. Papen perservered, sending more messages, urging Berlin to recall the "irresponsible" Rintelen. Finally, Nicolai relented and gave Papen the authority to send Rintelen back to Germany.

Rintelen, meanwhile, had resumed the same kind of high living he had enjoyed before the war. He used his old financial business as a cover and even gave speeches on international banking.

Using the alias E. V. Gibbons, Rintelen established as a front an export-import business, then started a wine business, for which he used the cover name of Edward V. Gates (he had an unexplained penchant for using aliases with the initials "E.V.G."). Using considerable funds provided by the Abwehr, Rintelen spread unrest through American labor unions that dealt with the manufacturing and shipping of American-made weapons to Europe, managing to create work stoppages at the Remington arms plant and at the General Electric plant in Schenectady, N.Y. Through an American associate, David Lamar, he established the Laborer's National Peace Council, which attempted to pressure the U.S. Government into passing legislation that would prohibit the shipment of arms to belligerents.

The saboteur's main efforts were centered on the manufacturing of bombs that were conducted on a German vessel, which had been interned in New York harbor. The bombs were planted in the cargo holds of merchant ships carrying supplies and arms to England and were timed to explode when the ships reached the mid-Atlantic. According to one report: "The devices worked only too well; at least thirty-five ships were destroyed."

The Bureau of Investigation under the direction of William J. Burns (the predecessor of the FBI, which was later directed by J. Edgar Hoover) learned of Rintelen's activities but found it next to impossible to do anything about him and his organization since, incredibly, there then existed no federal statutes covering espionage and sabotage. The Bureau discovered that Rintelen had attempted to buy 300,000 rifles while using a false name. Burns notified the New York offices of SIS, which then assigned several British intelligence agents to follow Rintelen night and day. Though he knew he was being followed, Rintelen displayed nothing but confidence to his superiors in Berlin and to Papen.

When Rintelen next met with Papen he bragged how he and his agents had damaged and sunk a number of British and American supply ships, as well as having done serious damage to several U.S. harbor facilities with his specially designed bombs. (There is evidence that Rintelen, in addition to blowing up many cargo ships en route to England, provided money and explosives to the German saboteurs reponsible for the Mare Island explosion, which seriously damaged the U.S. shipping facility.)

Before the reckless Rintelen went further, Papen told him that he had received authority to order him to cease operations immediately and return to Berlin. Demanding proof, Rintelin was shown Nicolai's decoded order to that effect. Seething, the saboteur nodded, clicked his heels, and obeyed. A few days later Rintelen booked passage for Europe, sailing from New York on the Dutch liner *Noordam* on August 3, 1916. Papen dutifully sent a coded message to the Abwehr in which he identified the ship in which Rintelen was sailing.

When the *Noordam* docked in Southampton before going on to the continent, officers of Scotland Yard's Special Branch and MI5 agents went aboard and detained the German saboteur in his stateroom. The ship was held for fourteen hours while Rintelen (again using the Swiss passport and the alias of Emile V. Gasche) was searched. His trunks were also searched and, in the false bottom of one of them, agents found incriminating documents. He was taken from the ship in handcuffs. Rintelen was dumbfounded as to how British authorities knew that he was traveling on that ship. Later, he concluded that the vindictive Papen had sent his message about Rintelen's sailing in the clear so that British authorities knew to arrest him. This was not the case.

What Rintelen did not know, nor did Papen or the Abwehr, was that British naval intelligence under the command of Reginald Hall had broken the code used by Papen and was thus able to identify the ship on which Rintelen was sailing. Rintelen was imprisoned in England and then, when America entered the war, extradited to the U.S. where he was found guilty of conspiracy to foment strikes. He was sent to the federal prison in Atlanta to serve a one-year prison sentence. In February 1918, he was convicted of a fire-bomb conspiracy and received an additional eighteen-month term and a fine of $2,000. In November 1920, President Wilson commuted his sentence and he left the U.S. on December 31, 1920.

He did not return to Germany but went, instead, to England, where he lived out his life. Rintelen was no doubt apprehensive about returning to a Germany he had so miserably failed. He later became very friendly with Admiral Hall of naval intelligence and it is said that he provided Hall with all of his bomb designs, which the British later adopted and modified in developing naval explosives and mines. Rintelen tried many times to become a British citizen but was rejected and lived on in London as a stateless person. He offered his services to British intelligence at the beginning of World War II but was rejected as a security risk. Instead, the miserable Rintelen was interned on the Isle of Man, released when the war ended in 1945. By then he was no longer considered "the mad saboteur."

[ALSO SEE: *Abwehr; FBI; Claude Dansey; William Reginald Hall; J. Edgar Hoover; Vernon Kell; Mare Island Sabotage; MI5; Walther Nicolai; Franz von Papen; Special Branch*]

RITTER, NIKOLAUS VON
German Spymaster in World War II ■ (1897–1965?)

RESPONSIBLE FOR ALL GERMAN ESPIONAGE IN THE U.S. and Great Britain (under Admiral Canaris) during World War II, Nikolaus von Ritter was a man of many faces and fantastic ideas. He was born in the Rhineland, the son of a university professor, receiving a top-notch education. After graduating from the University of Cologne in 1924, Ritter entered the textile business. In 1927, Ritter expanded his business to America and went to manage his New York branch. He remained there until 1937, when the Depression ruined his market, and he returned to Germany.

Fluent in English, Ritter volunteered to the Abwehr and was instantly accepted by Admiral Wilhelm Canaris, who, after training him, sent Ritter back to the U.S., appointing him resident director over the sprawling, unwieldy German spy networks in America. Ritter selected only those Germans or German-Americans whom he felt he could trust to do their duty and keep silent. One such agent was Hermann Lang, an inspector in a factory that produced the top-secret Norden bombsight, a sensitive American invention that provided pinpoint accuracy in high-altitude bombing. In 1937, Lang made copies of the blueprints for the bombsight and gave them to Ritter, who passed them on to the Abwehr. This proved to be one of Ritter's most spectacular espionage coups.

As was the case with all secrets Ritter delivered to Canaris in Germany, he used couriers who worked for the Hamburg-America steamship line. Almost all of the shipboard employees worked for German intelligence in one form or another, from the hairdressers in the female salons to the stewards and restaurant busboys. From these crews, Ritter was able to select many talented agents who would interchange themselves for Germans living in the U.S., take jobs in American manufacturing plants producing weapons and war materials, steal secrets, then replace the persons who had taken their positions on board the Hamburg luxury liners.

Using the code name Dr. Rantzau, Ritter sailed on the Hamburg-America ships regularly between the U.S. and England and then on to Germany, organizing his networks of spies in Great Britain as well as in the U.S. Ritter's network in England was thought by the Abwehr to be superlative by the beginning of World War II, with such top spies as Arthur George Owens, a Welshman who used the code name Johnny, Dusko Popov, and Eddie Chapman.

These spies continued sending what appeared to be useful information by shortwave for the duration of the war. Ritter never knew, however, that the dozens of German spies in England feeding him and the Abwehr information had all been turned, and were actually working for MI5 and England, that the information they were sending to Germany was all carefully created disinformation that aided the Allies, not the Nazis.

In America, the same double-cross system was employed when his top agent, William Sebold, was turned by J. Edgar Hoover and the FBI, so that he not only passed on useless information to the Abwehr but betrayed the top echelon of Ritter's spy network, testfying against Hermann Lang, Everett Minster Roeder, and the craftiest of the lot, Frederick Joubert Duquesne.

By the end of 1941, Ritter's top spies in America were in prison or dead. Though his network in England was thought to be effective, it was bogus. Ritter's failure in America caused him to be eventually moved from the Abwehr to the Luftwaffe as part of that service's intelligence operations. At the end of the war, Ritter became a businessman.

[ALSO SEE: *Abwehr; Wilhelm Canaris; Eddie Chapman; FBI; J. Edgar Hoover; MI5; William G. Sebold*]

RIVINGTON, JAMES
British Spy in American Revolution ■ (1724–1802)

RIVINGTON WAS A FAIR-WEATHER SPY DURING THE American Revolution, siding first with the British when it appeared that they would triumph, then the Americans when it became evident that they would endure and clutch ultimate victory. Born in London, the son of a publisher, Rivington adopted his father's profession but bad investments caused him to nearly bankrupt his father's business in 1760. To escape debtors, he went to America, where he purchased a small printing plant and began publishing books and pamphlets, distributing these works through bookstores he established in Boston, New York, and Philadelphia.

Prior to open hostilities between British and American forces, Rivington attempted to be fair to both sides but when war broke out in 1775, his editorials took a decided British stand. This incensed the Patriots, a group of them breaking into Rivington's shop and destroying his presses. Terrified, he fled to England.

In 1776, Rivington returned to New York, then under British occupation. He carried with him the title of king's printer and established a pro-British newspaper, the *Loyal Gazette*, later changed to the *Royal Gazette*. Rivington's editorials and columns thundered against the Patriots, the Continental

Congress in Philadelphia, and George Washington. By 1779, however, the publisher was less inclined to libel the revolutionaries since they had won some decisive battles and it appeared that they might actually win the war.

Rivington became a secret spy for Washington in 1779, the same year in which he went into business with Robert Townsend, buying a coffeehouse with Townsend. Townsend himself had been a spy for the Patriots throughout the Revolution. Though he pretended to be a Loyalist, Townsend led the most successful American spy network in New York, the Culper Ring. Though Rivington had a change of heart and began to send Washington information about British troops in New York, he apparently never knew that Townsend was one of Washington's top spymasters.

In 1781, Rivington was so bold as to purposely lead General Sir Henry Clinton into making a disastrous decision, one that cost the British the war. At that time, Washington was preparing to move his army south to Virginia, join up with French forces, and attack British General Cornwallis at Yorktown. He could not withdraw from New York, however, where he had long besieged the British, without Clinton learning of this maneuver. To solve his dilemma, however, Washington turned to Rivington, who had long since been accepted by Clinton as a devoted Loyalist and effective British spy.

When the publisher came to him and told him that Washington was martialing a huge army to attack New York, Clinton listened but did not respond. Then Rivington published the actual battle plan Washington was about to employ in his attack on New York and this, indeed, convinced the British general to ignore reports that Washington was instead marching to Virginia. Clinton held his forces in New York, leaving Corwallis to face the Americans and French alone and subsequently surrender his entire army, which brought the war to a close.

The end of the war did not signal the end of Rivington's troubles. When the Patriots reclaimed New York, he was attacked as a diehard Loyalist and was almost lynched. He was dramatically saved at the last moment, however, by Major Benjamin Tallmadge, Washington's head of intelligence, who had ridden into New York ahead of Washington's troops to protect those who had secretly served the Patriot cause. Tallmadge announced that James Rivington had been an American spy who had greatly aided Washington's army. The publisher not only survived but enjoyed a successful and peaceful life until his death twenty-one years later.

[ALSO SEE: *John Andre; Benedict Arnold; Culper Ring; Benjamin Tallmadge; Robert Townsend*]

ROESSLER, RUDOLF (AKA: LUCY)
German Spy for Allies in World War II ▪ (1897–1958)

ONE OF THE MOST EFFECTIVE AND DEVASTATING spies in World War II, certainly one who equalled the exploits of Richard Sorge and the sly Elyeza Bazna (Cicero) in producing top secret documents, Rudolf Roessler was also the most secretive, a mole so deep in Germany that even his own spymasters did not know his true identity.

Born on November 22, 1897, in Kaufbeuren, Bavaria, a small town near Munich, Roessler was raised in strict Protestant surroundings. His father was an official with the Bavarian Forestry Commission and provided a comfortable livning for the Roessler family. Roessler was educated in Augsburg at the Realgymnasium, attending school with a gifted classmate, Bertholt Brecht.

Seeing service with the German Army in World War I, Roessler entered journalism after the war, going to work as a reporter in Augsburg and later moving to Berlin, where he became a literary critic. He moved inside the artistic world of writers and painters. His close friends included the novelist Thomas Mann and the poet Stefan George, both of whom would later be put onto Hitler's death list, their books burned, their images tarnished as branded enemies of the Third Reich.

With the collapse of the economically inept Weimar Republic and the rise of Hitler in 1933, Roessler, who detested the Nazis, relocated to Switzerland, moving to Lucerne, where he established a publishing house, the Vita Nova Verlag. The 36-year-old German who established his literary presence in Lucerne was not an imposing figure. He was small and slender with thinning hair and spectacles. He was nervous and, despite being a chronic asthmatic, he was a chain smoker, and was never without a burning cigarette.

A dedicated anti-Nazi, Roessler was never a Communist. In fact, he hated any kind of political dictatorships. He was politically conservative but most of all, he was a German patriot. His small publishing firm was successful enough for Roessler to travel broadly but most of his trips were between his native Germany and Switzerland. He was in touch with others in Germany who felt the way he did about Hitler, many of these persons occupying important positions within the government, German nationals who spied against Hitler's regime and who were loosely connected with what the Gestapo had labeled the Black Orchestra, the German underground working to usurp the dictator.

No one at Allied intelligence who received Roessler's priceless information during World War II, nor those in the Red Orchestra who also received secrets from him, ever knew his sources, although one of Roessler's top informants was certainly Hans Oster, Deputy Director of the Abwehr, Admiral Canaris' right-hand man until he was exposed and arrested by the Gestapo.

In 1936, however, Roessler contented himself with striking back at the Nazis through a small Catholic-sponsored publication, *Die Entscheidung* (The Decision) for which he wrote articles under the pen name Arbiter. One of the group sponsoring the magazine was an ardent anti-Nazi, Xavier Schnieper, who was also a Marxist.

Schnieper and other close friends came to realize that Roessler possessed an extraordinary gift; he retained in exact detail all information that interested him, especially in military and political fields. He kept "records" in his head the way a file clerk would arrange an index file and could rattle off the details of troop movements down to the company level, or the smallest detail in a report which he may have only glanced at, or facts relative to the manufacturing of munitions, tanks, and planes.

In early August 1939, Roessler visited Schnieper, telling him that he had just returned from Germany and he knew that Hitler was about to invade Poland and that Europe would be plunged into war. Further, he stated that he represented friends "in top posts, friends who think in the same way as I do, politically and ideologically, all of them people from the right, from the conservative circles. They told me: 'We will keep you informed about everything important that happens and we will give you details. You are the living embodiment of our conscience. Deal with our information as you see best for the future of Germany.'" This extraordinary statement was not lost on Schnieper, who had been commissioned an officer and assigned to the Bureau Ha, an unofficial Swiss intelligence agency that collected data on Germany.

Roessler began feeding his high-level information to Schnieper and the Bureau Ha as soon as the Germans invaded Poland in 1939. He was able to provide the Allies, through Bureau Ha, almost the precise battle plans of the German armies as they went into France, Holland, and Belgium. He provided the exact time the Germans would invade Russia and this information was also given to the Soviet intelligence organization operated by Sandor Rado. When Stalin received this information he refused to believe it, just as he ignored a similar report from his agent in Japan, Richard Sorge.

Roessler never communicated directly with Rado but went through his friend Christian Schneider, who, in turn, gave Roessler's information to Rachel Duebendorfer, a Rado operative who only knew Roessler as "Lucy." The Soviets were first skeptical about Roessler's information but finally came to depend upon it. From him the Soviets were able to learn the strength and composition of all German forces on the Eastern Front, their locations, and battle plans, as well as Hitler's own strategy. Equally impor-

Rudolf Roessler, one of the most outstanding Allied spies of World War II.

tant, Roessler was able to tell Moscow via Rado what the Abwehr knew about Russian positions, strengths, and plans—information that could only have come from Oster or Canaris himself.

German agents in Switzerland knew that clandestine radio operations there were being beamed to Moscow and when they finally pinpointed some of Rado's spies, a formal protest was lodged with Swiss authorities. To save face and to counter the threat of a German invasion, the government ordered the arrest of all those in Rado's organization in 1943. Rado himself escaped but others were captured and imprisoned, along with Roessler, who was jailed for a time, then tried, and found not guilty of espionage. By that time Germany had collapsed.

Following the war, Roessler's publishing business suffered such financial reverses that, to make money, he began selling information about the Allied occupation forces in post-war Europe, information that, essentially, could be found in Western newspapers and magazines. Arrested, he was again tried for espionage by Swiss authorities and this time he was convicted. He spent a year in jail before returning to his Swiss publishing firm.

[ALSO SEE: *Abwehr; Black Orchestra; Elyeza Bazna; Bureau Ha; Wilhelm Canaris; Rachel Duebendorfer; Alexander Foote; Gestapo; Hans Oster; Red Orchestra; Sandor Rado; Richard Sorge*]

ROOM 40
British Naval Intelligence Headquarters in World War I ▪ (1914–1918)

A T THE OUTBREAK OF WORLD WAR I, THE GERMAN military began transmitting coded messages that were structured in cipher unknown to British intelligence. British Admiral Henry Oliver quickly assembled a contingent of cryptologists under the direction of code expert Alfred Ewing. A month after Ewing and his cipher analysts went to work on the German code, Reginald Hall replaced Oliver. Hall moved Ewing's group into Room 40 of the Admiralty Building.

From that point onward, Room 40 represented British naval intelligence and all of its operations, albeit that the actual work that went on inside that room was dedicated to the breaking of enemy codes. Aiding the cryptologists were three startling events, the first, in 1914, being the sinking of a German cruiser by Russian warships. A surviving Geman sailor was picked up by the Russians and on him was found a copy of the German naval code book, which the Russians turned over to British intelligence. That same year a chest was retrieved from a sunken German submarine by a British trawler. It contained a copy of the German naval attaché code book which was used by Germany's Foreign Office when sending messages to its embassies throughout the world.

In 1915, Wilhelm Wassmuss, the German consul in Persia (now Iran), fled his consulate in Bushire so hastily in escaping British troops that he left behind a trunk containing a copy of the German diplomatic code. Armed with these top secrets, Room 40 was able to decipher all of Germany's top codes by applying variations to the original.

The greatest triumph of Hall and his men in Room 40 occurred in 1917 when they broke the code of the notorious "Zimmermann Telegram," one in which Germany blatantly offered Mexico large spoils if the Mexican Government would go to war against the U.S. More than any single event, the revelation of this German plan by British intelligence helped to bring the U.S. into World War I, the deciding factor in favor of the Allies. Room 40 also reported in 1918 that the sailors in the German Navy had mutinied and this brought on the Kaiser's abdication and the surrender of Germany.

[ALSO SEE: *Reginald Hall; Zimmermann Telegram*]

ROSENBERG, JULIUS AND ETHEL
U.S. Spies for Soviets ▪ (1918–1953; 1915–1953)

B EFORE THE SENSATIONAL CASE OF CIA TURNCOAT Aldrich Ames in the early 1990s, the most celebrated espionage case in American history was that of Julius and Ethel Rosenberg. Though the Rosenberg case is hotly debated to this day, there can be no doubt for anyone carefully examining the evidence that these two were Soviet spies who helped to steal atomic secrets for Russia. The debate hinges on whether or not the amount of secrets they helped to steal warranted their executions.

Both Julius and Ethel Rosenberg were born to Jewish immigrants and grew up in New York. Raised in the orthodox Jewish faith, Julius had been trained to become a rabbi but he abandoned his family's ambitions for him and, instead, embraced Marxism. Attending City College in New York, he received a degree in electrical engineering. At the time he attended college, Julius became a card-carrying member of the Communist Party, a fanatical hard-line Stalinist.

Ethel (Greenglass) Rosenberg, two years Julius' senior, graduated high school during the Depression. She attempted to make a success in the fine arts through dancing, drama, and music but had no real success. She found her expression through radical left-wing protests and strikes in the 1930s. She and Julius met at a workers' fund-raising meeting. They married in 1939.

In 1940, Julius Rosenberg became a civilian employee with the U.S. Signals Corps. According to most reports, he was then, along with Ethel, actively spying for the Soviets. By 1943, Julius withdrew from open party activity in preparation for more dedicated espionage, working for Soviet spymaster Anatoli Yakovlev, who was attached to the Russian Consulate in New York but whose assignment was to steal the atomic bomb research then being conducted in the U.S.

Ethel's brother, David Greenglass, had been, for unexplained reasons, sent to Los Alamos, New Mexico, to work on the Manhattan Project. Here, at the suggestion of Julius Rosenberg, Greenglass stole secrets concerned with the making of the atomic bomb.

Rosenberg then arranged for Harry Gold (real name Golodnotsky), a courier working for Yakovlev, to retrieve stolen secrets from his brother-law Greenglass in New Mexico. Gold was also at that time picking up atomic secrets from British scientist Klaus Fuchs, who was working in Los Alamos. According to later documentation, Greenglass was only one spy who fed the Rosenbergs American secrets that they, in turn, passed on to Yakovlev throughout World War II. At one point, in January 1945 while he was on leave in New York, Greenglass went to Rosenberg's New York apartment and handed his brother-in-law a sketch of the lens mold which detonated the atomic bomb.

By that time, Rosenberg was no longer merely a conduit of secret information but served as a principal or control who recruited and handled KGB spies on behalf of Yakovlev. He was careful in recruiting new spies, selecting these agents from his family and close friends, those he felt would not be so willing to betray him and his wife. (How active Ethel Rosenberg was in Julius' espionage is debated to this day; it is known that she knew full well his activities and cooperated fully with him to achieve his ends.)

In 1945, Julius was discharged from his position with the Signals Corps after it was learned that he was suspected of being a Communist. Rosenberg was more than indiscreet in his rather loud endorsements of Soviet Russia. The following year, Rosenberg and Greenglass went into business together, a shaky partnership that lasted until 1949, when the two men split up. They constantly quarreled, Greenglass later stated, because he did not want to go on spying for the Soviets against the U.S., while Rosenberg insisted he do so.

In 1950, the FBI learned of Fuchs' treason through information supplied by Russian defector Igor Gouzenko, and informed British intelligence. Fuchs was arrested in England and quickly identified a photo of Harry Gold as his contact man who carried the secrets he stole to the Soviets. Then Gold was arrested and he informed on Greenglass who, in turn, named the Rosenbergs as his control agents.

The FBI arrested the Rosenbergs as they were listening to the radio show *The Lone Ranger* with their two young sons. One of their confederates was also arrested, Morton Sobell, a college classmate of Julius Rosenberg who had fled to Mexico after hearing that Harry Gold had been arrested. Sobell had been extradited and went to trial in federal court in New York with the Rosenbergs on March 5, 1951. They, along with Gold, Greenglass, and Yakovlev, were charged with violating the Espionage Act of 1917.

Judge Irving R. Kaufman, one of the judges for the Southern District of New York, presided over the trial. The prosecution was headed by U.S. District Attorney Irving H. Saypol. The defendants were represented by top criminal lawyer Emanuel H. Bloch and his father Alexander Bloch. O. John Rogge held a watching brief for Greenglass, who had already pleaded guilty. The Rosenbergs and Sobell pleaded not guilty.

David Greenglass' wife Ruth took the stand to testify that Julius Rosenberg asked that she go to Los Alamos in 1944 and obtain classified documents from her husband. He assured her, she said, that her husband, who was already a Communist Party member, would want to help Russia, then an ally of the U.S., obtain information on the atomic bomb.

The information Ruth Greenglass brought back to the Rosenbergs from her husband entailed the names of the scientists working at Los Alamos, the general layout of the restricted areas, numbers of employees,

Ethel and Julius Rosenberg, who stole atomic secrets for the Soviets and were executed.

and the types of experiments taking place there, all of which Mrs. Greenglass had put to careful memory.

When Greenglass came home on leave in January 1945, Ruth continued, they went to the Rosenberg apartment and were introduced by the Rosenbergs to a Mrs. Siorovich, who, according to Rosenberg, might become a contact person or courier visiting Greenglass. With that Rosenberg took a Jell-O box and tore it in half. He gave one half to Mrs. Greenglass, who was planning to revisit her husband in Los Alamos, and the other, he said, would be produced as a form of identification by the contact agent who would pick up secrets stolen by Greenglass.

The contact person showed up in June 1945 in Albuquerque, New Mexico. He went to the residence where the Greenglasses were living and showed them the other half of the Jell-O box, saying "I come from Julius." He was Harry Gold. Greenglass gave Gold secrets he had stolen at Los Alamos and Gold gave him $500 cash. Ruth Greenglass then stated that she and her husband had maintained a close relation with the Rosenbergs right up to May 1950 when Julius burst into their apartment with the news that Gold had been arrested as a Soviet agent.

Despite the warnings, the Greenglasses remained in New York, and David was pinpointed by Gold. FBI agents arrested David Greenglass on June 15, 1950. When David Greenglass took the stand, he repeated his wife's testimony, except to point out that he did not actually know what it was that he was working on in Los Alamos until Julius Rosenberg told him that it was the atomic bomb. In January 1945, Rosenberg told him that the experiments in Los Alamos dealt with "fissionable material at one end of a tube and on the other end a sliding mechanism with fissionable material, and when the two were brought together under tremendous pressure nuclear reaction was accomplished." This description generally fit the uranium bomb dropped on Hiroshima.

In September 1945, Greenglass returned to New York and gave the Rosenbergs a ten-page analysis and a sketch of the atom bomb. This information delivered by Greenglass applied to the plutonium bomb which was dropped on Nagasaki. Harry Gold was next. He admitted to being a Communist and spy since 1935, to his connection with Klaus Fuchs, and how he had acted as courier with other spies such as Greenglass.

The defense put Julius Rosenberg on the stand. He admitted that he had been discharged from the Signals Corps because he was *suspected* of being a Communist. He would not admit that he was a Communist or ever had been. He denied everything else, taking the Fifth Amendment several times. Ethel Rosenberg also denied everything. Morton Sobell did not testify.

The jury took about eighteen hours to reach a verdict, guilty for the Rosenbergs and Sobell. Judge Kaufman later sentenced Sobel to thirty years, pointing out that his espionage was of a lesser degree than that of the Rosenbergs. He sentenced the Rosenbergs to death.

The fight for the lives of the Rosenbergs then ensued. President Truman received a petition for executive clemency on January 11, 1953, but he refused to commute the sentence. When recently-elected President Eisenhower received a similar plea, he, too, refused clemency. Eisenhower thought that the Rosenbergs had committed a hideous crime that involved "the deliberate betrayal of the entire nation, and could very well result in the death of many, many thousands of innocent citizens."

A last ditch appeal to the U.S. Supreme Court failed and Julius and Ethel Rosenberg went to the electric chair on June 19, 1953, at Ossining (Sing Sing) Prison in New York. Julius entered the death chamber first, his thin, black mustache shaved off. He wore a T-shirt. Three shocks of 2,000 volts were sent through his body and a few minutes later he was pronounced dead. His body was removed and his wife Ethel walked into the same room wearing a print dress with white polka dots. She sat in the same chair and died in the same manner. Neither made statements.

Throughout their two years in prison the Rosenbergs, while exhausting appeals, portrayed themselves as victims of anti-Semitism, although they had been prosecuted by a Jewish attorney and sentenced by a Jewish judge. Ethel Rosenberg had nothing good to say about the brother whose testimony had sent her and her husband to the death house. "I once loved my brother," she said from her prison cell, where she spent time singing folk songs, "but I'd be pretty unnatural if I hadn't changed."

The Rosenbergs were the first Americans to be executed for espionage. Ethel Rosenberg was the second woman to be executed, after Mary Surratt, who was connected with the Lincoln assassination, at the dictate of a federal edict. To the very end, the Rosenbergs insisted that they were innocent. Following their deaths, Pablo Picasso did a sketch of the pair sitting in twin electric chairs and holding hands, a rather distasteful piece of artwork which was published as a form of protest in *L'Humanité*.

[ALSO SEE: *FBI; Klaus Fuchs; Harry Gold; Igor Gouzenko; David Greenglass; J. Edgar Hoover; KGB*]

RSHA (Reichssicherheithauptamt)
Security Department of Nazi Third Reich ▪ (1939–1945)

IN 1939, NAZI DICTATOR ADOLF HITLER GATHERED all of his police and security agencies under the command of Heinrich Himmler, including the Gestapo, the SD, the SS, and the RSHA (standing for the German title which means "Reich Central Security Office"). Himmler, in turn, appointed a clinical killer, Reinhard Heydrich, to head the RSHA, which directed the Gestapo (the secret police), the SD (civilian intelligence), and the regular criminal police (*Kriminalpolizei*).

The RSHA had limitless power and was answerable to no one but Adolf Hitler, and it was to Hitler and his Third Reich that it owed its single allegiance with the sole purpose of protecting and perpetuating the dictatorship. Heydrich proved to be a ruthless exterminator of those considered to be political or military enemies of the Third Reich. Within the framework of RSHA was Office VI, headed by Adolf Eichmann, who was responsible for the shipment of countless persons, mostly Jews, to concentration camps and eventual execution.

When Heydrich was assassinated in 1942 by Czech partisans in Prague he was replaced by an equally oppressive director, Ernst Kaltenbrunner. In 1944, the Abwehr was taken over by the RSHA and came under Kaltenbrunner's control, after Canaris and others were purged following the plot to assassinate Hitler. The RSHA was disbanded at the end of World War II and Kaltenbrunner was convicted of war crimes and executed.

[ALSO SEE: *Abwehr; Wilhelm Canaris; Gestapo; Reinhard Heydrich; Heinrich Himmler; SD*]

SALEMEH, ALI HASSAN
Palestinian Agent and Terrorist ▪
(1943?–1979)

THE SON OF SHEIK HASSAN SALEMEH, A PALESTINIAN leader who was slain by an Israeli bomb in 1948, Ali Hassan Salameh vowed revenge as a youth for the taking of his father's life. After finishing his schooling, he underwent a six-week espionage-sabotage course in Cairo, trained by agents of Egyptian intelligence. He took still more training with the Saika, a Syrian-backed guerrilla organization, and then went to Moscow in 1972, where he received still more instruction from the KGB.

By that year, Salemeh had been named the senior intelligence officer of Fateh, the Palestinian terrorist and espionage organization, operating out of Beirut. Well-paid, he indulged his passion for silk shirts and suits tailor-made on Saville Row in London. He was also the military director of the terrorist group known as Black September which was led by Abu Iyad.

It was this group, directed by Salemeh, that kidnapped and killed eleven Israeli athletes at the Olympic games in Munich, Germany, in 1972, a heinous crime labeled the Munich Massacre. This mass killing prompted the Mossad to send revenge agents to Europe to seek out and kill those Arabs responsible, especially Salemeh, these groups operating under the ominous title of the "Wrath of God."

Mossad agents thought they had located the cosmopolitan terrorist chief in Lillehammer in Norway and sent a team of assassins there. The agents wrongly identified Ahmed Bouchki, a Moroccan waiter, as Salemeh and shot him to death. Two of the agents were caught and imprisoned, one of these being the attractive Sylvia Raphael.

The Mossad, however, did not relent, its agents continuing to pursue Salemeh. One one occasion he was wounded and barely escaped but he was finally killed in January 1979 when he was blown up by a car bomb in Beirut.

[ALSO SEE: *Mossad; Sylvia Raphael*]

SANCHEZ, ILYICH RAMIREZ (AKA: CARLOS, THE JACKAL)
Venezuelan Terrorist and Agent ▪
(1949–   )

THE SON OF A WEALTHY VENEZUELAN LAWYER AND ardent Communist, Sanchez, like his brothers, shared one of Lenin's names. He was sent into a Communist underground cell by his father when he was fourteen and then went to Fidel Castro's Cuba, where he was trained as a Communist agent and terrorist by experts in the Cuban DGI (Direccion General de Inteligencia). At the time, Sanchez, known to his fellow trainees as "Pudgy," or "Fatty," impressed KGB General Simenov, who was overseeing DGI training in Cuba.

Invited to the Soviet Union, Sanchez went to Moscow and attended Patrice Lumumba University, a third-world clearinghouse for candidates slated to be KGB agents or future leaders that would favor the Soviets. After attending the best anti-Western espionage schools, Sanchez launched his bloodthirsty career as one of the world's fiercest terrorists, known everywhere as the dreaded "Carlos."

Allying himself with the PFLP (Popular Front for the Liberation of Palestine), Sanchez directed many terrorist operations, the most spectacular occurring on December 21, 1975, when he led a group of six heavily armed guerrillas into an OPEC conference in Vienna, Austria, holding eighty-one members hostage. He demanded safe passage out of the country in the name of the "Arm of the Arab Revolution."

Austrian negotiators were able to effect the release of forty-one Austrian hostages. The other African, South American, and Arab delegates accompanied Sanchez and his men on a flight to Algiers and then to Tripoli, where they were released after the Shah of Iran and King Khaled paid a $50 million ransom for their release. Sanchez then vanished inside Libya, which was ruled by fellow terrorist and spymaster Muammar Qaddafi.

In 1982, Sanchez was almost killed in Beirut when Palestinian guerrillas were driven from the city by Israeli forces. He then went permanently underground, remaining the most sought-after terrorist in the world.

[ALSO SEE: *Muammar Qaddafi*]

SANSOM, ODETTE (BRAILLY)
French Spy for Allies in World War II ▪ (1912–   )

BORN IN AMIENS, ODETTE BRAILLY WAS THE daughter of a banker who joined the French Army at the beginning of World War I and who was killed two years later in 1916 at Verdun. She was convent-educated in Saint Sens and, at age nineteen, married an Englishman, Roy Sansom, moving to England with him in 1932. The couple had three children.

In 1940, after the British evacuated Dunkirk during the fall of France to the Nazis, the War Office requested all French-born residents in London to provide photos of their towns and provinces. Odette came forward, offering her family photo album, which contained many photos of the French Channel coast, particularly the Boulogne area. British intelligence needed these photos to prepare bombing missions and secret landings along the coast made by small fishing vessels and from submarines.

It was quickly apparent to British intelligence agents interviewing Odette that she would make a perfect agent for SOE (Special Operations Executive). She was asked to join SOE, train as a radio operator, and be sent to France, where she would work with the French underground. Though she had three small children, Odette enthusiastically volunteered in 1942. After finishing her training, she was taken by submarine to southern France, where she rowed ashore near Cannes on the night of October 30, 1942, to make contact with British agent Peter Churchill, who was in charge of all SOE operations in southern France.

Operating under the code name "Lise," Odette's mission was to bring Churchill money and to act as his radio operator. So expertly did she perform that Churchill asked London for permission to have her stay on as his permanent assistant.

In 1943, through the treachery of a French double agent, Churchill and many in his organization were captured and imprisoned. They had been trapped through the machinations of Hugo Bleicher, a fanatical Nazi agent who knew well how to turn French underground fighters into German double agents. It was Bleicher (known as Colonel Henri, although he never rose above the rank of sergeant), who penetrated Churchill's network with the help of a French turncoat.

When Odette and Churchill were taken to a Gestapo prison for interrogation, both underwent tortures. Throughout fourteen hideous interrogations by Nazi thugs, Odette was branded on the base of the spine with a white-hot iron and had several of her toenails ripped out with pliers, but she refused to talk. Moreover, she not only convinced her Nazi interrogators that she, not Churchill, was the leader of the SOE group, but that Churchill was the nephew of British Prime Minister Winston Churchill (which he was not). This undoubtedly preserved Churchill's life. He, in turn, told the Nazis that Odette was his wife. As such, she was treated with some deference when she was sent to the women's camp at Ravensbrück.

Both Churchill and Odette, housed in separate camps, were spared execution as Allied troops closed in, their captors believing that they would receive leniency if they preserved the lives of those related to Winston Churchill, a ruse Odette had perpetuated throughout captivity. After the war, Odette attended the 1946 war crimes trials in Hamburg, where she testified against German females who had served as guards at Ravensbrück, detailing their cruelty and atrocities against prisoners. Four of these women were later executed. One of these bestial female guards was Irma Grese, who took pleasure in torturing and murdering helpless prisoners.

Odette's husband had died and, after returning to England, she married her SOE commander, Churchill, a union that ended in divorce in 1955. The courageous Odette was awarded England's prestigious George Cross for her wartime service. A stirring film, *Odette*, released in 1951, retold the spy's heroic story. Odette herself acted as technical adviser on the film.

[ALSO SEE: *Peter Churchill; Gestapo; SOE*]

SAVAK (Sazamane Etelaat va Amniate Kechvar)
Iranian Security and Intelligence Service ▪ (1956–1979)

SAVAK, THE SECURITY AND INTELLIGENCE AGENCY for the Shah of Iran, was created with the considerable help of the CIA and the Mossad in 1956. Intended as a security force that would bolster the Shah's dictatorship and its close association with Western powers, Savak was initially led by General Teymur Bakhtiar, a feudal chieftain upon whom the Shah became more and more dependent as assassination attempts increased.

Savak's power also increased to the point where it oppressed the Iranian people and dealt ruthlessly with any political opponents. "Savak is everywhere," stated one report. "Every high official, every state secretary, even each minister has a Savak shadow who monitors everything he does and has the right to inspect his every move." Savak's agents were not restricted to Iran, but traveled throughout Europe and the Middle East, seeking out Iranian students and political dissidents who opposed the Shah, intimidating or killing them.

The brutality, torture, and murder exercised by the Savak was, in a large part, the cause of the revolution that eventually overturned the Shah, a rebellion led by Islamic fundamentalist Ayatollah Ruhollah Khomeini, who had been living in exile in Paris. When the rebels seized all of the government buildings in Teheran, the raging mobs vented their hatred on the headquarters of the Savak in the Komiteh Building. The structure was utterly wrecked, its files dumped into the street and its torture instruments destroyed and burned. The Savak's last commander, General Nematollah Nassiri, a sadistic killer with yellowish eyes and a pock-marked face, was trapped on the rooftop of the Komiteh Building, where he was shot to death, then hacked to pieces. The Khomeini regime ushered in another security force that was as criminally bent as its predecessor.

[ALSO SEE: *CIA; Mossad*]

SAVARY, RENE
French Spymaster in Napoleonic Wars ▪ (1774–1833)

A NATIVE OF THE ARDENNES IN FRANCE, SAVARY joined the army in 1790, just after the French Revolution began. He fought well on the Rhine in 1798 and received many promotions. Fighting in the Egyptian campaign in 1800 under Napoleon Bonaparte, Savary, then a general, became one of Bonaparte's closest confidantes. He was unswervingly loyal to Napoleon in victory and defeat and was a favorite at court after Bonaparte became emperor in 1804.

After holding several military and diplomatic posts, Savary was named Duke of Rovigo in 1808 by Napoleon. Two years later, Bonaparte became apprehensive about his conniving, clever chief of police and spymaster, Joseph Fouché, believing that Fouché had become too powerful. He sacked the chief and replaced him with Savary.

There was much to recommend Savary to this post. As early as 1799, he had carried out covert missions for Napoleon and had brought into the French military intelligence service one of the greatest spies of that time, Karl Schulmeister.

When Savary entered Fouché's offices he was thunderstruck to find that his predecessor's files were empty. Fouché, embittered at his dismissal, had taken his voluminous records, including the lists of thousands of police and military spies, and hid them. When Savary and Napoleon demanded the return of the files, Fouché told them that he had destroyed them. He was obviously playing a dangerous game, one wherein he felt that Bonaparte, seeing that his police and espionage office

was useless without Fouché's records, would reinstate him in order to regain years of intelligence information.

Fouché guessed wrongly. Savary managed to find a list of spies overlooked by his predecessor and he quickly summoned these agents, interviewed them carefully, and retained the best of them. The list which Savary used was one chronicling the duties of Fouché's third-rate agents but through these contacts, the general was able to identify most of the top spies who had worked for France. He thus rebuilt the French espionage network inside of a year.

French intelligence under Savary was almost as effective as it had been under Fouché. The spymaster was able to ferret out countless conspiracies and plots to unseat Napoleon, as well as determine military strengths and plans of opposing European countries.

When Bonaparte was sent into exile on Elba, the ever-loyal Savary worked hard to arrange for the emperor's triumphant return to France, providing the ship on which Napoleon sailed from his island prison. Savary and the Old Guardists emotionally welcomed their commander when he stepped again on French soil and served him until his disastrous defeat at Waterloo. (Here Savary's intelligence collapsed, his agents failing to detect the strength and position of Prussian troops under the command of Field Marshal Gebhard Blücher, who fell upon Napoleon's exhausted command just as Wellington was about to be overwhelmed.)

Bonaparte was sent again into exile on the barren island of St. Helena. The loyal Savary begged to go with his commander but the Allies refused, believing that the enterprising spymaster might find a way to once more return his emperor to France. Savary himself was banished but returned to France, writing his memoirs in 1828 and winning the good graces of the restored Bourbon monarchy so that he was once again restored to a command in the French army, holding this post until he died.

[ALSO SEE: *Joseph Fouché; Karl Schulmeister*]

SAXE, MARSHAL (HERMANN MORITZ COMTE DE SAXE)
French Spymaster ▪ (1696–1750)

T HE SON OF AUGUSTUS I OF SAXONY (LATER Augustus II of Poland), Saxe, though illegitimate, was recognized by his father, who raised him at his court. Saxe entered the military and proved to be an excellent military leader, first opposing King Louis XIV of France in the War of the Spanish Succession (1701–1713), serving with Prince Eugene of Saxony in Flanders (1709–1710). Four years after being entitled the count of Saxony, Saxe, to further

Marshal Saxe of France, who wrote the classic primer on espionage.

his military career, joined the French, fighting against the Poles and Russians (1725–1727).

Saxe was promoted to the rank of general by Louis XV because of his victories in the War of Polish Succession (1733–1735). He later rose to the rank of marshal of France, then, in 1747, achieved the highest rank to be held, marshal-general of France. He more than earned the title during the War of the Austrian Succession (1740–1748) when he soundly defeated the British and their allies at the Battle of Fontenoy in 1745 and in the following year at Brussels, Antwerp, Mons, and Raucoux. In 1747, he invaded Holland and defeated the duke of Cumberland at Lauffeld, capturing the fortress of Bergen-op-Zoom.

As a military commander, Saxe was a shrewd and astute spymaster who held high the power of military espionage. In each of his military campaigns he used vast spy networks, his well-paid agents culled from the ranks of his enemies. These agents supplied Saxe with information on troop movements, strengths, morale, and the amount of loyalty soldiers had for their superiors. Saxe later wrote a military treatise, *Mes Révieres*, which was published in 1756–1757, considered to offer one of the best analysis of military intelligence.

Saxe advocated spending as much money as needed for agents, particularly buying information from spies living in the immediate battlefield area who had long-standing familiarity with the terrain and inhabitants. He established a spy network in the camp of the enemy, especially in the commissary, where the stores of food would indicate the length of the campaign anticipated by the enemy. Another rule he followed was making sure that his spies never knew each other's true identity unless certain situations dictated otherwise. His strongest precaution was to be alert for spies too willing to serve, an indication that they could very well be double agents. Though such theories seem prosaic today, Saxe was the first recognized espionage spymaster to put his theories into print, which long served as a guide to other spy chiefs over the decades.

SCHELLENBERG, WALTER
German Spymaster in World War II ▪ (1900–1952)

BORN IN SAARBRÜCKEN, SCHELLENBERG'S FATHER manufactured pianos and provided a comfortable middle-class income for his family. When he saw that Hitler would take power in Germany, he joined the Nazi Party and served the Third Reich in many legal positions until, in 1939, he became a deputy director of the SD (Security Police), which operated under RSHA, headed by the dreaded Reinhard Heydrich.

Intelligent, sophisticated, and cunning, Schellenberg cultivated relationships with Abwehr chief Admiral Wilhelm Canaris and Gestapo and SS head Heinrich Himmler. In a flight to Vienna in a small plane, Himmler had carelessly leaned against the door, which was about to open. Without a word, Schellenberg reached forward, grabbed Himmler by the tunic, and yanked him forward, saving his life. Thereafter, Himmler favored the glib Schellenberg, calling him by a pet name, "Benjamin."

As a liaison officer coordinating espionage activities between the SD and the Abwehr, Schellenberg also established a rapport with the Abwehr's Canaris. The German intelligence chief looked upon Schellenberg with a paternal eye and knew that even though Schellenberg was a Nazi, he would not betray him. When asked by a diehard Nazi in Ribbentropp's Foreign Ministry if Canaris could be trusted, Schellenberg instantly replied that the intelligence chief's loyalty was not to be questioned.

It was Schellenberg, however, who, at the directions of his RSHA chiefs, arrested Admiral Canaris for his suspected involvement in the July 20, 1944, attempt on Hitler's life. He had long dreamed of having one central intelligence agency in Germany, which he would head. Schellenberg had fancied himself one of the most astute spymasters in Europe, ever since he ensnared two British SIS agents in Holland in 1939 at the beginning of the war in what was later termed the Venlo Incident.

Nazi spymaster Walter Schellenberg, who compromised MI6 in a clever entrapment scheme in 1939.

Schellenberg learned in 1942 that members of the Black Orchestra and the Red Orchestra, underground espionage networks working against the Nazis, were obtaining top secret military and diplomatic information. He could not penetrate most of these networks, but he did discover that the most effective Red Orchestra network was located in neutral Switzerland. He met with General Henri Guisan, Switzerland's top commander, telling him that he knew the network was operating in that country, without mentioning names, and that if the Swiss did not close down this information channel to Moscow, Germany might well think of invading the country. This was, of course, a colossal bluff but the Swiss believed him and, to preserve their neutrality, most of the operatives working under Sandor Rado, including the superspy Rudolf Roessler, were arrested, although most of these agents were later released.

By 1944, Schellenberg attempted to create a uniform German secret service under RSHA, absorbing the old Abwehr and keeping on all of its members except those in top positions. By then Canaris, who had been released, joined OKW intelligence and was then rearrested and imprisoned, and other Abwehr leaders, such as Hans Oster, were either in jail or had been summarily executed for plotting against Hitler.

Though outwardly Schellenberg appeared to be staunchly loyal to the Nazi regime, he realized by 1944 that Germany could not win the war and through his Ausland-SD, he attempted to conduct secret negotiations to conclude the war between the Allies and his chief Heinrich Himmler. This came to nothing, and, with the collapse of Germany in 1945, Schellenberg, along with what was left of his espionage network,

went into captivity. He was tried at Nuremberg for war crimes and received a six-year sentence. Released in 1950, he wrote his memoirs, which claimed that German intelligence had established a vast and reliable spy network in England in World War II, never realizing that MI5 had compromised and turned each and every Nazi agent in England.

[ALSO SEE: *Abwehr; Black Orchestra; Wilhelm Canaris; Gestapo; Reinhard Heydrich; Heinrich Himmler; MI5; Hans Oster; Sandor Rado; Red Orchestra; Rudolf Roessler; RSHA; Venlo Incident*]

SCHRAGMÜLLER, ELSBETH
German Spymaster in World War I ▪ (1887–1940)

ELSBETH SCHRAGMÜLLER WAS ONE OF THE MOST accomplished German spymasters in the World War I Abwehr. A petite, blonde-haired woman with large, blue eyes (which earned her the nickname of "Tiger Eyes"), she was uncompromising and precise in everything she did.

The only known photo of Germany's lone female spymaster, Elsbeth Schragmüller, who ran an Abwehr spy school in Antwerp in World War I.

Schragmüller was blatantly portrayed as a femme fatale in a film about her life, Fraulein Doktor, *with Suzy Kendall (left) enacting the role of the German spymaster, shown here appeasing the lesbian lust of Capucine, playing a scientist with secrets to impart.*

Born in Westphalia, Schragmüller attended the University of Freiburg, graduating in 1913. She was by then fluent in Italian, French, and English. When World War I broke out the following year, the young woman began writing letters to Abwehr chief Walther Nicolai, imploring him to take her on staff. After reading several dozen such appeals, Nicolai, to get rid of what he thought was a pest, obtained a post for Schragmüller at the Censorship Bureau in occupied Brussels.

German censorship officials noted that the diligent young woman had a knack for intelligence. She worked twice as hard as anyone in her section and was able to provide details of military importance from the mail she read. General von Beseler, commanding the German army in Belgium, was so impressed with Schragmüller that he sent her to the Special Intelligence Corps at Baden-Baden for training.

Schragmüller proved to be an excellent student, graduating at the top of her class. Though she wanted to be sent on missions behind enemy lines, her superiors valued her too highly to risk her life in anything but the most important of such missions. She was sent, instead, to Antwerp where she was to teach at a newly established espionage school. She was to train agents to penetrate French coastal towns and English Channel cities.

Relentless and demanding, Schragmüller soon proved that she was an indefatigable teacher. She insisted on performance and washed out many students who showed the slightest signs of academic weakness or low spiritual resolve. Espionage was a science to Schragmüller, not a haphazard adventure of luck and circumstance.

She was the first to promote the widespread use of the sacrifice, a procedure which entailed identifying a genuine spy in the network in order to preserve another agent of far greater value. Selecting an agent for a sacrifice was based on several factors. Some of these agents are so destined from the time of their training, spies who are so inept that they will unintentionally betray themselves and thus divert attention from the professionals in the network. Mata Hari, in her final years of service to the Abwehr, was considered a sacrifice.

Those suspected of being disloyal were purposely betrayed by double agents so as to enhance the image of their expertise and increase a sense of trust with those they were really attempting to spy upon. Of course, Schragmüller did not invent the sacrifice. The Okhrana, the czarist secret police, had employed this technique for thirty years earlier in Russia, and so had the insidious Colonel Alfred Redl, the Austrian spymaster, at the turn of the century.

The dictums of this Elsbeth Schragmüller were rigid and were later adopted by just about every espionage agency in the world:

Collection of information: "Never develop an *idée fixé* about some item of intelligence you think you can or must obtain. This will lead you into making yourself conspicuous by your inquiries. Collect every bit of information you can, but without showing special interest in any of it."

How to record information: "Always record the information you collect if you cannot absolutely trust your memory, but record it in terms of absolute innocence. Figures and dimensions you must report may best be remembered as items of personal expenditure. You have seen on a visit to Chantilly ten heavy naval guns on lorries, ready for mounting. You remember this item, however, as the excellent fish dinner you had in Chantilly which cost you ten francs."

Destroying evidence: "If you burn a letter, do not believe you have made it unreadable and do nothing more about it. Microscopic examination can reveal writing or printing on ash. You must pound the ashes to fine powder and scatter it to the winds. Merely tearing up paper into small scraps is almost as dangerous as leaving it whole. Even putting small scraps down a lavatory is no real precaution. Such scraps must be thrown away in segments at different locations."

Communication techniques: "Avoid any temptation to be too clever or original about methods of communication, unless you are quite sure that your invention is really new. Rely rather on proven methods."

Foreign language use: "Conceal whatever linguistic gifts you have so that others will be encouraged to talk more freely in foreign tongues you understand within your earshot."

Conduct: "Never talk or behave mysteriously. There is only one circumstance in which you may do so: A person who has really something important to communicate and is half-ready to do so, can often be fully persuaded by being told something—preferably wholly fictitious—in a confiding way, with a slightly mysterious air, for he will be flattered by it."

Almost all of Schragmüller's agents sent their reports by cipher through Geneva, Switzerland. The secret script she received, either handwritten or by wireless, was in a code that was changed every week on orders of the spymaster. When an agent performed well, he or she was rewarded with double or triple the regular pay, or bonuses amounting to twelve or fifteen thousand francs. These amounts were dutifully placed in bank accounts held in Germany and in safekeeping for the spies who expected to enjoy these grim profits following the war.

But she could misuse agents as well. One of her agents compromised a French girl, Marguerite Francillard, luring her into German espionage. Schragmüller's agent used the love-smitten girl as a courier, sending her back and forth with information between Paris and Geneva, until she was thought expendable. Her address in Paris was given to Allied intelligence and she was arrested and executed by a French firing squad at Vincennes on January 10, 1917.

Allied intelligence learned about Schragmüller's school and were so awed by the legends concerning this spymaster that they attached to her all sorts of fantastic missions, lurid plots, impossible schemes in which tens of thousands of Allied troops lost their lives. She became in the eyes of her enemies a horrid and Machiavellian monster. The French called her "Mademoiselle Doctor," "Queen of Spies," and "la Grande Patronne" ("the Big Boss"). The British dubbed her "Tiger Eyes," "Terrible Doctor Elsbeth," "Black Cat," "Red Tiger," and "Fraulein Doktor." (She had earned a Ph.D. at the University of Freiburg, therefore the sobriquet of "Doktor.")

Schragmüller reveled in her lifestyle, once remarking to an aide: "I would not exchange my profession for a throne." After the the war, her superior, Walther Nicolai, who once believed she was worth no more than a post in the censorship office, stated that "in the German military intelligence service, it was a cavalry officer belonging to an old family, and an exceptionally cultured woman, who proved most competent in dealing with the agents." The "woman" was Elsbeth Schragmüller. To an Allied counterpart, the perception of the woman spymasters was somewhat different: "Her work was, in her eyes, romantic and intellectually a stimulus and a joy, but it dripped blood."

Allied intelligence hunted her after Germany capit-

ulated but could not find her. She had been careful to avoid having her photograph taken and no one really knew her true name, except Nicolai and a few other top-ranking German intelligence officers. She returned to Germany, going to Munich some time in the 1920s, where she became a lecturer, a position she held until her death in 1940 during World War II. By then she had severed all contacts with her former intelligence associates. Her only companion in later years was her mother.

[ALSO SEE: *Abwehr; Walther Nicolai; Okhrana; Alfred Redl*]

SCHULMEISTER, KARL LOUIS
French Spy in Napoleonic Wars ▪
(1770–1853)

THE SON OF A LUTHERAN CLERGYMAN, SCHULMEISTER was an Alsatian, born in Neu Freistett on the banks of the Rhine. He quit his religious education to take up smuggling—ferrying contraband at night between France and Germany. He operated a store in Strasbourg, and chatted freely with French soldiers who patronized his place. Thus he was able to learn the schedules of their river patrols and evade them. So well did Schulmeister know the Rhine that he was able to snare many a French aristocrat attempting to flee the guillotine during the French Revolution.

Napoleon's top spy, Karl Louis Schulmeister, a daring agent who impersonated aristocrats to obtain secrets from the Austrians.

Above, the Duke d'Enghien, who was captured through the efforts of master spy Schulmeister, is shown facing a French firing squad.

Left, Schulmeister's lavish estate in Alsace, purchased with the enormous proceeds of his espionage, was blown to pieces by Austrian artillery in 1813, an act of vengeance taken against Napoleon's agent, who had almost wrecked the Austrian empire.

In 1799, René Savary, a colonel in Napoleon's legions, met Schulmeister in Alsace and was so impressed with the glib-tongued young man that he enlisted him in the French intelligence service. He undertook many undercover missions in Germany and, by 1804, he was the top spy working for Napoleon's spymaster, Joseph Fouché. In the following year, Bonaparte himself selected Schulmeister for a daring and next-to-impossible mission. He was to go to Vienna and somehow infiltrate the Austrian military intelligence system. The bold spy decided he would start at the top.

Schulmeister employed a disguise that to him had been a self-created image since childhood. As a youth, the Alsatian had, for reasons of vanity or much needed self-esteem, deluded himself that his severe and demanding minister father was not his father after all. He sincerely believed that he was the illegit-

imate son of a dashing Hungarian nobleman who had seduced his mother. The spy entered Vienna with great pomp, arriving in an elegant coach with liveried servants and trunks of fine clothes. He soon passed the story that he was a Hungarian aristocrat who had been expelled from France by Napoleon after defending the Austrian cause to the French emperor.

Next the spy wrote several letters to General Karl Mack, commander of the Austrian army on the Danube, offering his services as an intelligence agent and saying that he had a large number of secrets about the French army to impart to him. Mack summoned the young man to his headquarters, where he granted him an interview. Schulmeister so impressed the Austrian general that Mack appointed the French agent to his general staff and, a short time later, made him head of intelligence for the Austrian army.

Thanks to Schulmeister's audacious posturing, Napoleon now had an agent not only within the ranks of the enemy but one who actually controlled the intelligence of the opposing army just before the battle. The master spy informed Mack that Bonaparte's army was on the brink of rebellion since the troops had not been paid in months, disinformation that convinced the Austrian commander that he was facing a disorganized army turning to rabble. Schulmeister, on the other hand, was able to provide Napoleon with Mack's battle plans and an exacting profile of the Austrian commander that showed him to be overconfident.

Bonaparte played his part in this ruse. He made it appear to Mack, who occupied the strategic city of Ulm, that his troops were deserting by the thousands. When the French began to withdraw, Mack believed Schulmeister's story completely. French morale had utterly collapsed. He boldly led his 30,000-man force out of Ulm in pursuit of the retreating French, but as he did so, he was amazed to see French forces under Marshal Ney attacking his front instead of slinking away in retreat. Then, on his flanks, appeared the forces of Soult, Marmont, Dupont, Lannes, and, finally, the grand cavalry under Marshal Murat. He was surrounded and soon surrendered his entire command.

Schulmeister was allowed to "escape" French troops ringing Ulm and fled back to Vienna, where he attempted to convince the Austrian and Russian monarchs then conferring there that all was lost because of Mack's incredible blunder, attacking against his advice. There was nothing to do but sue for peace. Austrian intelligence, such as it was, determined that Schulmeister was an agent of France. He was about to be arrested when Murat appeared outside Vienna and quickly accepted the Austrian surrender. The battle of Austerlitz followed a short time later and proved to be Bonaparte's most sterling victory, one that ended Austrian resistance.

For a short period Schulmeister efficiently served Napoleon as Vienna's chief of police. In 1808, he went to Germany to spy on the Prussian princes conspiring against Napoleon, setting up a large and effective spy network at Erfurt in Prussia.

Time and time again, the master spy provided intelligence that allowed Bonaparte to win great battles. He also fought in those battles, being wounded many times. Bonaparte, as he did many times, rewarded his inventive agent with a great amount of money but refused to give Schulmeister what he craved most—the award of the Legion of Honor. Napoleon told him that that honor was reserved only for his soldiers, telling him that "gold is the only suitable reward for spies," even though he was the greatest spy of his era.

When Bonaparte married Marie Louise, an Austrian archduchess, in 1810, Schulmeister's star went into decline. The new empress hated the master spy for having humiliated her father five years earlier.

She insisted that her husband dismiss his favorite agent. He did and Schulmeister went into retirement, purchasing two vast estates in France. With the collapse of Napoleon's armies in 1813, Austrian troops invaded Alsace and, in retaliation for the spy's work against Austria, his villa was pounded to pieces by cannon fire.

Napoleon went into exile but returned from Elba and Schulmeister openly supported him. Then came Waterloo and Bonaparte's final defeat and exile. The master spy was arrested and saved himself only by paying a ransom that equaled almost all of his personal fortune. He attempted to regain his losses through speculations but all failed. Penniless, Schulmeister was granted the concession of a tobacco kiosk in his home town of Strasbourg, where he lived on for four more decades, selling blends and regaling customers with wild espionage tales that no one believed.

[ALSO SEE: *Joseph Fouché; René Savary*]

SCHULZE-BOYSEN, HARRO
German Spymaster for Soviets in World War II ▪ (1910–1942)

BORN IN KIEL, SCHULZE-BOYSEN WAS THE SON OF a German naval officer and was related to Grand Admiral von Tirpitz. He attended school in Duisburg, at which time he was a member of a conservative anti-Nazi group. He attended the University of Freiburg, 1928–1930, then the University of Berlin, 1930–1931, studying law. The following year, he joined a progressive political group and was later arrested by the Gestapo for expressing opposition to Hitler. His aristocratic family, however, managed to have the charges dropped.

Schulze-Boysen was still adamantly opposed to the Nazis when family members used their influence to get him a job in the press department of the Air Ministry. In 1936, he married Libertas Haas-Heye, the granddaughter of Prince Philip von Bulenberg, who was from the Junker class like himself. His wife was also liberal and urged him to continue his opposition to the Hitler regime but to operate secretly. To that end, he established his own underground spy network and worked closely with another led by Arvid Harnack, a dedicated Communist. These and other espionage groups would later be labelled the Red Orchestra by Himmler's Gestapo and the RSHA.

Important information, particularly on the Luftwaffe, passed through Schulze-Boysen's hands daily and, when Hitler dispatched the Condor Legion—squadrons of dive bombers used to test Stuka performance—to Spain to fight for Franco during the Spanish Civil War, he passed secret air force data to members of the Spanish Republic. Though never a Communist, the spy worked closely with Soviet networks and began giving information to an NKVD agent in the Soviet Embassy in Berlin in 1936. This agent, Alexander Erdberg (or Erdmann, a cover name), worked closely with Soviet spymaster Bogdan Kobolov.

Erdberg named Schulze-Boysen to head up his own network, supplying him with codes, ciphers, invisible inks, and other espionage apparatus, instructing him to work with Harnack's group and a network under the leadership of Adam Kuckhoff. Between these three groups, more than 200 agents, mostly members of the old Communist Party in Germany, worked to supply the Center in Moscow with information. Schulze-Boysen's group operated under the code name "Choro."

Just before Hitler decided to invade Russia, Schulze-Boysen was promoted to the position of liaison officer to the chiefs of staff of the Luftwaffe. In this capacity, he had direct access to aircraft production; the number of active aircraft; locations of fields for bombers and fighters, fuel depots and reserves for aircraft; the number of pilots, crews, and ground support personnel available; and the overall strategy of the German air force. This made him an invaluable spy for the Center in Moscow.

When the Germans invaded Russia in 1941, Schulze-Boysen's group was responsible for the gathering of secret information. Harnack's group had the job of assigning the information into code and another group in Brussels was responsible for transmitting the information to Moscow. For that purpose, before he left Berlin, Erdberg delivered to the three spy networks several transmitters, the code, and code key, as well 10,000 marks.

All went well with these networks until 1942, when Abwehr agents were able to pinpoint the Brussels transmitter used by the Red Orchestra group. One of its members turned informer and double agent, identifying Schulze-Boysen, Harnack, and others. The Gestapo did not move immediately against the underground groups. A wiretap was placed on Schulze-Boysen's phone and in this way German counterintelligence was able to pinpoint more than one hundred members of his group and that of Harnack's. On August 30, 1942, Gestapo agents arrested Schulze-Boysen and then rounded up several hundred more members of the Red Orchestra. The leaders were tried, found guilty of espionage, and executed. Their executioners hung them on meathooks.

[ALSO SEE: *Abwehr; Gestapo; Heinrich Himmler; Red Orchestra; RSHA*]

SD (Sicherheitsdienst)
Nazi Party Intelligence Department ▪ (1931–1945)

HITLER'S ELITE GUARD, THE SS, HAD AT ITS INTELLIgence department the SD, which was also known as the Security Service. The SD, as well as the SS and the Gestapo, was directed by Heinrich Himmler. This organization had only 100 full-time employees in 1933, with as many part-time workers, and its intelligence-gathering was vague but centered mostly on spying on Nazis holding official or important posts. Though snubbed and ridiculed by party members, the SD eventually mushroomed into a vast internal spy network.

In 1934, the SD was attached to the Gestapo, and the following year it came under the direction of Reinhard Heydrich, Himmler's right-hand henchman and eventual commander of the RSHA. The SD was responsible for the safety of Hitler and all high-party officials, as well as investigating any German thought to oppose Hitler. It had sweeping arrest powers and could summarily send anyone to the death camps. As such, it became as feared as the Gestapo and the SS.

Inside the SD could be found whatever intellectuals remained within the National Socialist Party. These were essentially young men born between 1900 and 1912, "the flotsam from the wreckage left by the social disintegration that had overtaken the German middle class in the early 1930s," according to one historian. They hated the decadent democracy represented by the Weimar Republic that had brought Germany to economic ruin and felt that only National Socialism and Hitler could save their country. They also felt that all of their leader's closest associates were nothing more than "little Hitlers," who had to be closely watched lest they usurp the genuine Fuhrer.

Many SD men were law students or lawyers who had been weened on the philosophy that state power was to be held in the highest esteem. Among the SD's early high officials were Otto Ohlendorf, Dr. Werner Best, Dr. Herbert Mehlhorn, and Gunter D'Alquen. Later, robot functionaries like Adolf Eichmann joined the SD, men who carried out any order, no matter how illegal, heinous, or criminal.

Dr. Werner Best was the original guiding light of the SD, a lawyer whom Heydrich, his replacement, hated. Best had his own slogan printed in large letters and hung on the wall of his SD office. It read: "In the long run factual work gets the better of any enemy." Heydrich took one look at that sign and sneered to Best: "That may be good enough for the civil servants who come here in the course of business. But for real life that bureaucratic principle is nonsense." Heydrich despised Best as he did all attorneys, fond of quoting his Führer's statement: "I shall not rest until every German realizes that it is a disgrace to be a lawyer."

In the middle to late 1930s, Heydrich eased out the lawyers and brought his yes-men into the SD, like his no-nonsense deputy Siegfried Taubert. Heydrich also put the SD directly under his authority in the RSHA and then built up its staff until it numbered tens of thousands of spies, who busied themselves spying on any German suspected of disloyalty to Hitler. In 1937 alone, the SD carried more than 50,000 informers on its payroll.

The slightest infraction or suggested infraction could cause an SD spy to submit a report on a German national. Typical of the millions of reports found in SD files after World War II was one dated January 26, 1938, in which an SD spy noted the behavior of German nationals, sailing in a German ship on a holiday cruise in Italian waters: "One of the holidaymakers, Fritz Schwanebeck, born March 30, 1901, resident Mückenberg-Ferrosiedlung, makes a bad impression; when the [German] national anthem was sung he adopted a sloppy attitude, evidencing a complete lack of interest." This man was to be closely watched thereafter.

Teachers and professors—Hitler hating the academic class—were secretly investigated by so-called genealogical SD experts to prove, with no evidence, that they had Jewish origins. If even a trace of Jewish blood could be proved, the subject was arrested and packed off to a death camp.

The SD also published its own newspaper, the *Schwarze Korps*, which took pains to share some of its secret investigative work with the public, not to inform but to terrorize. The SD maintained a postal censorship office that read every letter posted in Germany. It sometimes published these letters in its newspapers to show that no one could express a private thought without the SD knowing about it. Businessman Wilhelm Stapel, a conservative, wrote a letter to a friend in which he expressed the thought that those of his political bent could only support Hitler "with a shudder." This letter was published and Stapel realized for the first time that his mail was monitored and that he was a marked man.

As the Third Reich expanded into other countries, the SD was imported to these lands, where it concentrated on rounding up Jews and others designated as "undesirable" by the Nazis and packing them off to concentration camps, a chore that eventually become the SD's main function. By the end of World War II, the SD was completely dismantled. Its members burned their identification papers, uniforms, photos, and anything else that would suggest that they had ever been associated with this terrorist organization. In 1946, the Nuremberg war crimes tribunal declared that merely being a member of this dreaded organization was a criminal act.

[ALSO SEE: *Gestapo; Reinhard Heydrich; Heinrich Himmler; RSHA*]

SDECE
French Counterintelligence (1958–   )

WHEN FRENCH INTELLIGENCE WAS REORGANIZED IN 1958, the SDECE came into existence. Its chief function is to collect intelligence information throughout the world, similar to the American CIA, while its internal counterpart, the DST, handles all counterintelligence within France, similar to the American FBI. Controlled by an intelligence committee, the SDECE is answerable to the premier of France. It has three distinct departments—espionage, counterespionage, and covert operations. No activity of the SDECE is to be conducted within France, which is the strict province of the DST.

Not to be confused with the Second Bureau (French military intelligence), the SDECE supposedly has never been penetrated by a foreign intelligence such as the KGB. There is little way of knowing if this is truly the case since the SDECE, like its British counterpart, MI6, has no public posture in France.

What is known is that there has been internecine wars at SDECE involving its top-ranking officers. Typical of this on-going problem was Colonel Alan de Gaigneron de Marolles, who headed the super secret agency's covert operations until he resigned in September 1980. He gave "technical reasons" as the cause of his departure but most believe he resigned because he could no longer bear the in-fighting at SDECE. Marolles and the SDECE had aided President Anwar Sadat of Egypt in secret military actions against President Qaddafi of Libya in 1977 and had directed covert disturbances in Benghazi two years later.

Similar to the kind of "smear" files J. Edgar Hoover of the FBI notoriously kept on American politicians, the SDECE maintained files on liberal or left-wing French politicians for years. This was the case with the right-wing SDECE director Count Alexander de Marenches, who had run the agency for ten years until he resigned when Socialist premier François Mitterrand took office. He destroyed many files before leaving office, including dossiers on Mitterrand. In 1982, this organization was retitled DGSE.

[ALSO SEE: *DST; Muammar Qaddafi*]

SEBOLD, WILLIAM G. (WILHELM GEORG DEBROWSKI)

U.S. Double Agent in World War II ▪ (1899- ?)

ONE OF THE MORE SURPRISING ESPIONAGE TALES TO come out of World War II involved a man without any purpose, a drifter who barely survived in the backwaters of middle European society. He had no particular ambitions except to find a decent job, marry, and return to his adopted country, America, where he hoped to live out a peaceful existence. Instead, he was plucked from the flotsam of Europe and coerced into taking over the most important Nazi spy ring in the U.S. He called himself William G. Sebold.

Born Wilhelm Georg Debrowski in the soot-laden city of Muehlheim, an industrial town in Germany's Ruhr Valley, he grew up with scant education but a decided knack for anything mechanical. Tall and heavyset, he looked older than his fifteen years in 1914 when Germany went to war. Like many his age, he saw the war as a great adventure and a way in which to escape the poverty of his home. He enlisted, lying about his age, and somehow survived four grueling years in the trenches of the Western Front.

For three years after the war, Sebold tried to find employment but was given only odd jobs, from cleaning hotel washrooms to part-time machine shop work, making only enough money to feed himself. He wore his old uniform until it fell from his back in pieces, then stole an old suit of clothes and briefly went into the smuggling business, a short-lived occupation, for he was inept as a thief. Caught, he was given a short jail sentence.

Upon his release in 1920, Sebold could think only to escape the ruins of Germany. He went to Hamburg on foot and managed to find a berth as an apprenctice seaman on a freighter. He worked hard and, out of natural curiosity, learned all he could about the ship's wireless operations. Sebold sailed the world's oceans for two years, no different than many of his generation who were rootless, lonely, post-war wanderers.

In 1922, the freighter on which Sebold was serving docked in Galveston, Texas. On shore leave, he was impressed with this first visit to America, particularly the free and easy ways of its citizens and their opulence. He decided then and there to adopt the U.S. as his country. Jumping ship, he began to tramp throughout the Southwest, finally drifting into southern California. He learned what he could about machinery, his hobby and passion. By 1938 his skills were such that he obtained a job as a mechanic in the San Diego division of the Consolidated Aircraft Company.

By then Sebold had married and had also become a citizen, using the name William G. Sebold. He developed a stomach ulcer, however, and argued with his wife. Miserable, he reverted to his old habits and took to the road, going to New York, where the ulcer caused so much pain that he was taken to Bellevue Hospital for an operation. Upon his release, his thoughts were only of his mother, two brothers, and sister in Germany. He decided he would spend his convalescence with them and, in February 1939, he boarded the *Deutschland*, a Hapag liner sailing for Hamburg.

When disembarking at Hamburg, Sebold was stopped by two men, agents of the Gestapo. They took him to a small office near the wharf and questioned him, learning that he had been a mechanic at Consolidated Aircraft. He was permitted to continue his journey to Muehlheim, where he happily reunited with his family. Throughout that summer he recuperated at his family's home and when war broke out between England and Germany in September, he decided it was too dangerous to sail back to the U.S. He remained in Muehlheim, where he got a job constructing turbines.

A short time later he received a letter from Dr. Otto Gassner in Duesseldorf. It was written on Gestapo stationery. Gassner had contacted Sebold after reading a routine report from the two agents who had earlier interviewed Sebold. They had stated that Sebold was "a German-American aviation mechanic of possible interest for some undercover work in the U.S.A." Gassner thought so, too, and invited Sebold to visit his offices, telling him in the letter that he believed that there might be some considerable advantages for him if he would serve Germany.

Sebold was apprehensive but believed that because he was a naturalized American citizen, he was beyond the reaches of the Gestapo. He gave no response. Gassner sent another letter to him and Sebold answered by stating he was not interested in hearing any propositions from him. A third letter arrived, one which contained an unmistakable threat. Gassner wrote that the "pressure of the state" would be applied to Sebold if he refused to "cooperate." He went on to give a more sinister description of "the burial shift," which "we'll give you when you are laid out."

Taking a train to Dusseldorf, Sebold met with Gassner but still balked at working with the Gestapo. Gassner told him he had no choice, tossing a file onto his desk for Sebold to inspect. It was his old police dossier describing his conviction and imprisonment for smuggling in 1920. Gassner pointed out that Sebold had not told American authorities about his police record when applying for U.S. citizenship (which would not have been granted as convicted felons were barred from becoming American citizens).

"We are trying to accommodate you," the oily Gassner intoned. He tapped the police file with a beefy finger. "If this information found its way to America, your passport and citizenship would be

A photo of Nazi spy Frederick Joubert Duquesne, part of the Abwehr spy ring in the U.S. before World War II; this photo was taken by a hidden FBI camera in the offices of double agent William G. Sebold (shown with back to camera) while Duquesne's conversation was also secretly recorded.

canceled." He lit a cigar and blew large smoke rings past Sebold's immobile face. "You should know that if that happened, the state would then consider you an undesirable." He continued to blow smoke rings. "What a disgrace that would be for Germany! One of its own sons going to another country and then kicked out on his ass for covering up crimes! We'd have no choice but to send you to a concentration camp. Then we'd be compelled to look deeper into the private lives of your brothers and your sister—what kind of pasts to they have, eh? Perhaps your mother—"

"I accept your proposition," Sebold broke in, "whatever it is, one hundred percent."

Sebold was sent to the Abwehr office in Muenster, where a Dr. Rankin interviewed him. (Rankin was an alias for Abwehr deputy Nikolaus Ritter, who had established a widespread spy ring in the U.S.) Rankin told him that German intelligence wanted him to operate a clandestine radio in the U.S. He would be given information collected by German agents in America and he would send this on by shortwave to Hamburg. He would have to undergo three months of training.

"I was planning to return to the States to take care of my wife. If it takes that long, I'd better make some arrangements to send her some money."

"We'll take care of that," Rankin assured him.

"I think I'd better do it through the American consul in Cologne," Sebold said. "That way we'll avoid all suspicions."

Rankin gave his approval and Sebold, given money by Rankin to send to his wife, went to Cologne, where he asked to see the American consul. When ushered into the presence of the U.S. official, he explained that he had been pressured into becoming an Abwehr spy and how his spymasters, after he received his espionage training, planned to send him back to America as an agent, a radio operator dealing with other German spies in the U.S.

The official lost no time in contacting Washington. J. Edgar Hoover at the FBI was told about Sebold and he encouraged a plan wherein Sebold was to complete his training and sail for America. He would be contacted by FBI agents and told what to do next. Sebold left the consulate in Cologne and dutifully reported to the Abwehr training school in Hamburg.

Before he was to sail back to America, Sebold was given the names and addresses of five top German agents in New York. These agents would be supplying him with information that he was to send back to Hamburg on his shortwave. The first of these spies was Frederick Joubert Duquesne, Ritter's top agent in America at the time.

Duquesne had been in the pay of the Germans since World War I. A native of South Africa, Duquesne had been arrested by the British in the Boer War as a spy and imprisoned in Bermuda. After his release, he was a foreign correspondent for French and American newspapers, reporting from the Far East, where he served as a spy for the Japanese in China. He resurfaced in London in 1915 as a German agent during World War I.

He then sailed undetected to New York, where he worked with Abwehr sabotage expert Franz von Rintelen, blowing up transport ships en route to England. He then returned to South Africa and then back to the U.S., where, in the mid 1930s, he went back onto the Abwehr payroll as a spy for Hitler's Third Reich.

The identities of several other Abwehr spies in New York were revealed to Sebold. They were Edmund Heine, head of the Ford Motor Company's distribution arm for England; Everett Minster Roeder, an engineer at the Sperry Company; a German bundist who spent his off-work time recording the British ships leaving New York harbor; Hermann Lang, who worked as an inspector in the plant that built the Norden bombsight (and stole the blueprints for this top-secret item two years earlier, delivering them to Ritter); and the tragic Lily Barbara Stein, an attractive young Jewish woman whose parents had committed suicide the day the Nazis marched into Vienna following the 1938 Anschluss and who, with the help of the enigmatic Admiral Canaris, had fled to New York to avoid being sent to a concentration camp. Stein acted as a courier within the network.

Sebold memorized the names and addresses of his American contacts and then checked his baggage and papers. He had been given a new passport with the name William G. Sawyer, along with a background to go with his new identity. A small transmitter was hidden, disassembled, in his luggage, along with invisible inks and other spy apparatus. He was given $1,000 in cash and was told by his control, Heinrich Sorau (Herman Sandel), that another $5,000 would be delivered to him once he arrived in New York.

Sailing from Hamburg on the SS *Washington*, Sebold arrived in New York on February 6, 1940. At first, he lived at the Y.M.C.A. on Manhattan's 63rd Street. Ranken had suggested taking a room there, saying "most of the crooks in America stay there." He then opened an office in the Knickerbocker Building on 42nd Street, operating under a firm called the Diesel Research Company. He set up his transmitter in a house in Centerport, Long Island. A short time later, Sebold contacted the agents on his list. They came to his office, received their instructions, gave him their information, and Sebold transmitted the messages in code to Germany.

Everything Sebold did, however, was monitored and directed by the FBI. U.S. agents had picked him up immediately after his ship arrived in New York. He turned over all of the documents, ciphers, and Abwehr instructions to German agents, as well as $910 of the $1,000 Sorau had given him and went on the FBI payroll at $50 per month and expenses. His office was outfitted with a partition behind which agents stood and filmed each interview Sebold had with Duquesne, Lang, Roeder, and Stein, along with other agents.

The Bureau allowed the network to flourish, except that the information it collected and delivered to Sebold for transmission was altered before Sebold sent it on by shortwave to Hamburg. The FBI even added genuine information that was essentially useless, such as secret military plans that had been aborted. For sixteen months the charade went on, until, on July 30, 1941, J. Edgar Hoover ordered the entire network closed down and its members arrested.

FBI agents took Duquesne, Lang, Roeder, Stein, Heine, and twenty-eight other Nazi agents into custody, holding them for trial on charges of espionage. The trial began on September 2, most of those charged pleading not guilty. The evidence against them, however, was overwhelming, particularly the films taken of them in Sebold's office by FBI agents, along with their recorded statements.

William G. Sebold then appeared in court to directly and courageously testify against them. All were convicted and given an average of fourteen years in prison. It was the end of the Nazi spy networks in America. Sebold was given the thanks of his adopted country and faded into American society with a new name and a new life.

When Adolf Hitler read of this espionage fiasco, he went into one of his usual tirades, berating the "dirty business" of the Abwehr to Admiral Canaris' face. Canaris, as was his custom at such times, said little, except that he would "discipline" the Abwehr spymasters in charge of the ruined American network. Nikolaus Ritter was then dismissed from his post and reassigned to a meaningless job. In Washington, FBI chief J. Edgar Hoover gloated over his triumph: "Let them send their spies to America, all they can send. We have room for all of them in our prisons."

[ALSO SEE: *Abwehr; Wilhelm Canaris; FBI; Gestapo; J. Edgar Hoover; Franz von Rintelen; Nikolaus von Ritter*]

SECOND BUREAU
French Military Intelligence ▪ (1870–)

ESTABLISHED AT THE TIME OF THE FRANCO-Prussian War, the Second Bureau is a processing center for information collected by French intelligence and counterintelligence inside Special Services. The Bureau analyzes reports and draws conclusions and suggestions, passing their own reports on to the general staff for decisions.

The Second Bureau has proved to be one of the most active intelligence barometers of the Western powers. It accurately estimated the military strengths, movements, and strategy of the Kaiser's armies on the Western Front in World War I, and doggedly kept track of Germany's secret and illegal rearmament programs during the late 1920s and particularly in the 1930s after the rise of Hitler.

Its prediction of the time and place of the German invasion of Poland in 1939 was largely ignored by the French and British military. Worse, the Second Bureau accurately detailed the time and place of the German invasion of France the following year, even pinpointing the sectors of the so-called "invincible" Maginot Line where the Germans would break through. Again, the French general staff did nothing.

When France fell, the Bureau became the tool of the puppet German government at Vichy where Marshal Philippe Pétain ruled in the name of the Nazi conquerors. Many of the Bureau's top leaders, however, secretly sided with de Gaulle's Free French forces operating out of London and fed information to the Allies, working with them until France was liberated in 1944.

SECURITY INTELLIGENCE SERVICE
Canadian Security and Counterintelligence ▪ (1981–)

AFTER A GOVERNMENTAL COMMITTEE CONCLUDED IN 1981 that the Royal Canadian Mounted Police had abused its counterintelligence authority through illegal trespassing, wiretaps, and other transgressions, the Security Intelligence Service was created to assume those responsibilities. The new agency was authorized to supervise internal Canadian security, operate national counterintelligence, and collect antiterrorist intelligence.

SEMENOV, GREGORY M.
Russian Spymaster for Japan ▪ (1890–1946)

ONE OF THE MOST UNSAVORY, DOUBLE-DEALING White Russian leaders to come out of the Russian Revolution, Gregory Semenov was a Cossack chief in Siberia when the Provisional Government of Alexander Kerensky commissioned him in 1917 to raise an army to fight against the Germans. Semenov did raise a huge army, one which he called the "Special Manchurian Detachment," but, instead of fighting the Germans, it was used for Semenov's own purposes, mostly to take over and control land in Siberia and Manchuria.

Following the October Revolution, Semenov's army fought with those of Admiral Alexander Kolchak and other White Russian forces against Boshevik forces fighting in Siberia, ostensibly to restore the monarchy of Nicholas II, who by then had been forced to abdicate and was being held prisoner, along with his family, by the Bolsheviks at Ekaterinburg.

Although he promised the truly royalist Kolchak to make every effort to take Ekaterinburg and free the Romanovs, Semenov did little more than consolidate his own power and prepare to defend his own provinces east of Lake Baikal, his headquarters being at Chita. At the time, he used hundreds of spies who worked not only inside the Bolshevik forces but also within the "friendly" White Russian forces. In this way, he was able to learn when and where the Bolsheviks would attack and was able to cut off their supply lines, especially routes taken by supply trains on the Trans-Siberian Railway.

When the American Expeditionary Forces landed in Siberia to aid the White Russians, Semenov gave orders to his agents to spy on the U.S. forces, as well as steal their supplies. He also refused to work with or aid the Americans. When the U.S. forces began shipping supplies exclusively to Kolchak, Semenov had these shipments intercepted and brought to his headquarters. The U.S. branded Semenov a renegade and a thief, and other White Russian leaders disavowed him.

The overwhelming red tide in Siberia forced Kolchak's collapse in 1919 and the admiral's execution at the hands of the bloodthirsty Siberian Bolsheviks on February 7, 1920, the same hierarchy of killers who ruthlessly murdered the czar and his family in 1918 (on secret orders from Lenin).

The British had also intervened in the Russian Civil War, urging the many anti-Bolshevik forces to form a united front, which, for a short time, was done, these forces headquartering in Omsk. Semenov, however, showed no allegiance to this force, but drew closer to the Japanese, who supplied him with money, munitions, arms, supplies, and military advisers from their secret service known as the Special Service Organ in Manchuria.

So blatant were the Japanese in disrupting Allied operations through Semenov in Siberia that the U.S. government lodged a formal protest, demanding that they cease financing the Siberian brigand. The Japanese ignored the ultimatum. The Reds, however, decided the issue, overwhelming Semenov's forces at Chita. With a small band of followers, the Cossack leader fled to Manchuria and the protection of the Japanese. He set up headquarters at Dairen, where he was protected by Japan's Kwantung Army, operating an independent fiefdom and remaining a thorn in the side of the Soviets for the next twenty-five years.

For the next two decades, Semenov ruled with puppet authority in Dairen, using his people as spies throughout Manchuria for the benefit of the Japanese. These hapless White Russians went into Siberia, Asiatic Russia, and even European Russia to gather information on Soviet troop movements, camps, positions, and battle plans through the 1930s and throughout World War II. In this way, Semenov fed his Japanese masters information and retained his titular hold on Dairen.

Following the collapse of the Japanese military machine in 1945, Semenov and his closest commanders were seized by the Soviets and brought to trial the following year in Moscow. Before a kangaroo court, Semenov admitted to countless crimes against the Soviets. He confessed that he had attempted to murder Lenin in 1917, that he had raised an army of 50,000 men with Japanese help during the Civil War and that he destroyed countless villages and murdered myriad Bolsheviks in the Trans-Baikalia region. He confessed that he had established spy schools in Dairen and in other Manchurian towns where his agents plotted the seizure of Asiatic Russia.

The Soviet tribunal found him guilty of espionage and war crimes and sentenced him and five of his top aides to death. The aides would be given the deaths of soldiers by facing a firing squad. The Soviets reserved a special vengeance for Semenov. He was taken to a cell in Lubianka Prison on August 30, 1946, and hanged.

SEROV, IVAN
Soviet Spymaster ▪ (1905–1963)

AFTER A LONG AND BRUTAL CAREER AS AN OFFICER IN the Red Army, Serov, who was responsible for the massacre of 15,000 Polish officers in the Katyn Forest during World War II, was appointed chief of the KGB by Georgi Malenkov in 1954. Two years later, Serov went to England to prepare for a state visit by Nikita Khrushchev and others. His reputation as "Ivan the Terrible" caused him to be so harshly attacked by the press that he was recalled to Moscow.

In 1958, Khrushchev removed Serov from his KGB post after learning that the spymaster had failed to detect conspiracies against the premier's regime. After being assigned to some nonessential posts, Serov disappeared in 1963. It was presumed by Western intelligence agencies that he was secretly liquidated on orders of Khrushchev.

Mass-murderer Serov was replaced by Alexander Shelepin, who had headed the Komsomol, the Young Communist League, shaping the minds of twenty million youngsters, before Khrushchev appointed him to head the KGB, despite the fact that he had no experience in the intelligence field.

[ALSO SEE: *CIA; KGB; Bogdan Stashinsky*]

SHEVCHENKO, ARKADY
Soviet Spymaster ▪ (1931–   )

THE HIGHEST LEVEL SOVIET DIPLOMAT TO DEFECT by 1978, Shevchenko was the first deputy to Foreign Minister Andre Gromyko, working at the United Nations in New York. He also supervised a spy network in the U.S. and had grown accustomed to the good life. Before defecting, he drove a hard bargain, demanding a huge financial settlement, which was paid before he sought political asylum. He abandoned his wife and children who were taken back to Moscow while Shevchenko was kept at a CIA safe house. The defecting spymaster was able to pinpoint the KGB agents spying inside the U.N. and elsewhere in the U.S., as well as detail Soviet negotiating techniques and policy-making.

[ALSO SEE: *CIA; KGB*]

SIGLER, RALPH J.
U.S. Army Counterintelligence Agent ▪ (1930–1977)

ONE OF THE STRANGEST SPY TALES OF THE 1970S ended in April 1977 when Ralph Sigler, a warrant officer in U.S. Army counterintelligence, was found dead in a Jessup, Maryland, Holiday Inn. Electrical wiring torn from a lamp had been wrapped around his upper arms and plugged into a wall socket. Even though officials claimed that Sigler's death was a suicide, it was apparent that he had been tortured and then electrocuted to death. Exactly who murdered Sigler—the KGB or the CIA—remains part of the mystery to this day.

Sigler had loved his work, had longed to be a spy since his youth. Born in Czechoslovakia, Sigler had joined the U.S. Army when he was seventeen. He became an electronics specialist and rose to the rank of warrant officer by 1968 when he was stationed in Germany. He was married and had assumed special duties that involved spreading disinformation to KGB agents with whom he met regularly in Switzerland.

American agents (most likely from the CIA) monitored Sigler's meetings with the KGB, as he turned over doctored secrets and received regular payments. After one rendezvous in 1969, the double agent returned home with $3,000 in twenties and fifties which the Soviets had given him. As was the case with more than $100,000 he received from his Russian handlers, he turned the money over to his superiors.

Returning to the U.S., Sigler was stationed at Fort Bliss, Texas. From this post he went regularly to Mexico, where he met with Soviet agents in 1973. It was in that year, according to his wife, that he returned home one night to sit dejectedly in front of a television set, staring vacantly. His wife asked him what was wrong and Sigler responded: "I don't like what they made me do this time. They made me sell my country. I don't like that. It's getting too deep, what I have to do for them." He requested regular duty in Korea and spent a year there before returning to the U.S. and his wife in 1974.

In that year, Sigler resumed his double-dealing with the Russians, taking a vacation with his wife in Switzerland. His Soviet handlers apparently became suspicious and insisted that Sigler take a lie-detector test. He took the polygraph test and apparently passed with flying colors. Sigler returned to the U.S. with his wife and a thick wad of money from the Russians, which he routinely turned over to the Army.

In 1976, Sigler showed signs of strain. He was again meeting with KGB agents in Mexico and worried that he might not return, telling his wife to call his Army superior if he did not return, warning her that "you can't trust anybody anymore. They have a conspiracy among their own people."

Some time later that year a colonel whom Ilse Sigler did not know picked up her husband at home and drove to White Sands several times. In March 1976, Sigler traveled to San Francisco where *both* the Soviets and U.S. agents insisted upon giving Sigler polygraph tests. By this time, Sigler was suspected by both sides as working for the other. One later report had it that Sigler had begun to improve his reports to the Soviets by giving them actual information from files at Fort Bliss, where he was then stationed, either to convince them that his information was genuine or because he had actually been turned and had gone over to the Soviets. The Soviets, on the other hand, had learned that most of Sigler's information in the past had been bogus and that they were now convinced that he was a CIA plant. Sigler was in a no-win position with both sides.

Sigler failed the U.S. polygraph test and was ordered to report to Fort Meade, Maryland. It was the last time his wife saw him alive. She later reported that she believed the CIA had learned that her husband was writing a book about his espionage career, and that the agency had ordered him killed. She later filed a multimillion-dollar suit against the Army, FBI, and CIA. Ilse Sigler claimed in her suit that several Army officers "either murdered Ralph J. Sigler or placed him in a position of extreme danger and failed to protect him and that such failure on the part of the defendants resulted in the death of Ralph J. Sigler in violation of the Fifth Amendment." The suit was later dropped and Sigler's fate remains a mystery.

[ALSO SEE: *CIA; FBI; KGB*]

SILBER, JULIUS (OR JULES)
German Spy in World War I ▪ (1874–1933)

JULIUS SILBER HAS THE DISTINCTION OF BEING THE only German spy in England who went undetected throughout World War I. He achieved this goal only because he insisted that his German spymasters not connect him with any other German agent in Britain. In so doing, he was not unearthed by Vernon Kell's MI5 and Special Branch when all of the identified members of the Abwehr and German naval intelligence networks were arrested. Silber was a lone wolf and the information he passed on to his spymasters in neutral Holland proved invaluable to the Germans.

Born in Silesia of German parentage, Silber had to quit school to support himself, becoming a salesman. He traveled to South Africa, where he improved his English. During the Boer War (1899–1902) he served the British military as an interpreter and was so helpful in interrogating Boer prisoners-of-war that he received a certificate of recommendation from his British employers. Silber went to America following the war and remained there until 1914 when World War I broke out. He had become so fluent in English that he could have passed for a native American.

Although Silber had not returned to Germany in more than a decade, his sympathies were decidedly with the Fatherland. A few days after war broke out between England and Germany, he went to the German Embassy in Washington and offered to work in England as a spy, although his experience with espionage was extremely limited. Despite these shortcomings, the Abwehr approved of his application and he traveled to England via Canada. Once in London, he applied for a job in the Censorship Office, using the recommendation given to him by the British in the Boer War to secure his job. Because of his proficiency in understanding foreign languages, he was soon promoted to a supervisory position.

Silber was adamant in telling his control in Holland that under no circumstances was he to be linked with any German spy networks in England. Silber knew that by remaining separate from such espionage rings there would be no way for British counterintelligence to identify him. He operated through only one control in Holland, who knew him only through his code name.

As a censor responsible for mail going to southern Holland, which included Rotterdam, Breda, Eindhoven, and Tilburg, Silber was given the Suspect List of those addresses in Holland that British intelligence considered to be "safe houses," places where German intelligence received information. He was also given a list of "safe houses" maintained by SIS, to which British agents sent information. Silber did

War Office,
Whitehall. S.W.1.

5th July, 1919

Dear Silber,

At the termination of the Postal Censorship
I wish to thank you for the work you have done in my
Directorate.

The Censorship has inevitably worked to a
large extent in the dark, and the public has even now
little appreciation of the pressure which this weapon
has enabled us to exert on the enemy, or of the part
it played in winning the war.

You may, however, be sure that in the General
Staff there is no lack of appreciation of the importance
of the work to which you have given your services.

Yours sincerely,

Major General,
Director of Military Intelligence

J.C.Silber Esq.,
5, Amberley Street,
Liverpool.

A letter of commendation received by Julius Silber from British intelligence for his services as a postal censor, a position Silber used to successfully spy for Germany throughout World War I.

nothing for a few months, carefully planning his moves. As was the case with all censors, he opened and read letters, made or did not make deletions, then resealed the letters and sent them on for delivery, after stamping each letter *Passed by the Censor*. After a letter was thus stamped, no one else saw the letter, other than the recipient.

Silber began sending secret information to safe houses maintained by the Germans. Much of the information he obtained came from secret messages sent to British safe houses, which he intercepted, read, and copied. He then sent the information on to a German "safe house." Later, Silber sent his messages to German intelligence by using "window" envelopes. He would write his message using a transparent "window" where an address in Holland was shown, posting the letter in London. He would then intercept his own letter, remove the original letter he had written, then insert one containing a secret message, reseal it, stamp it, and send it on.

German control asked Silber to send on the list of those German safe houses which British intelligence had identifed. He refused, saying that if he did so, and these addresses were changed, suspicion might be turned in his direction. Though this incurred the wrath of his Abwehr supervisors, Silber's caution protected him against being exposed.

The diligent spy not only sent thousands of messages to German intelligence, he aided the German war effort by destroying important mail being sent to the U.S. On more than one occasion, he deliberately smudged or distorted important production blueprints for weapons so that they were unreadable. On other occasions, he delayed important government mail by rerouting it, or held it up until requests for confirmation were answered. Silber went on sending secret messages to the Germans and disrupting important British communications for four years.

One one occasion, Silber went far beyond his usual modus operandi. He became a field agent to confirm what he had discovered in censoring what was otherwise an innocent letter from a young English woman to a friend in Holland. At the time, Silber knew that the Germans were puzzled at the failure of several U-boats to return to base. Silber thought he might have the answer after reading a young woman's letter in which she confided to a friend: "At the moment we are happy to have my brother Philip living with us. While he is at sea we are always extremely worried for his safety, but he has been put on a shore job at Devonport and is likely to remain there for several months. It's something to do with refitting old ships. He doesn't say very much, but, as you know, he is a gunnery officer. He has permission to live at home, as we are so near Devonport."

Following his suspicions, Silber took a short vacation and traveled to the coastal town of Devonport. Silber then returned to London having solved the mystery of the missing U-boats. The British, he had learned, had been refitting old freighters into what they called Q-boats, arming these vessels with heavy guns and camouflaging them, knowing that it was the practice of U-boats to allow a freighter sailing without escort to disembark its crew into lifeboats before sailing close to the prey on the surface and sinking it with gunfire.

The Q-boats, disguised as helpless frieghters, had hoodwinked U-boat commanders into believing that they were helpless, putting some of its crew members into lifeboats but keeping gun crews on board and in hiding. When the German submarine drew close to sink the armed freighter with surface guns, the camouflage was drawn away on the Q-boat and the heavy guns opened up, sinking the U-boat. When Silber reported this British naval tactic, the Germans no longer allowed the crews of freighters to escape. They did not surface but merely sent their torpedoes into the commercial ships, sending the vessels and their crews to the bottom in what became unrestricted sea warfare. Silber had scored his greatest coup but he was also responsible for unleashing one of the most devastating types of sea warfare in history.

At the time of the Armistice, Silber, on the surface, appeared to have been a tireless and conscientious censor, so much so that he was given a commendation from the British military. After the war, he returned to

Germany. In 1932, Silber wrote his memoirs which, after publication, shocked British intelligence. MI5 had to admit that it had never detected this adroit German agent so successfully spying in its midst.

[ALSO SEE: *Abwehr; MI5; SIS*]

SINON
Greek Agent in Trojan War ▪ (c.1215 B.C.)

AFTER TEN YEARS OF LAYING AN UNSUCCESSFUL SIEGE to Troy, the frustrated Greeks concocted a plan to smuggle a small force behind the walls of the seemingly impregnable city. Then, suddenly, the Trojans looked beyond their walls to see the Greeks constructing a huge wooden horse. They observed the Greeks laboring on this towering structure for some days. One morning, however, the Greeks, their war machines, horses, and campsites had disappeared. All that remained was the wooden horse.

Rushing through the gates of the city, the Trojans flocked to the wooden horse, wondering why the enemy had left the structure behind. At that moment, a group of Trojan soldiers appeared, dragging a prisoner in chains. It was Sinon, who bemoaned his fate, bitterly crying out that the Greeks had abandoned him to the fierce Trojans. He was taken before the ancient Trojan king, Priam, who talked to the sobbing youth. Why had he been left behind by his comrades, Priam wanted to know.

Sinon explained that he had been a squire to Palamedes, who had been slain because he insisted upon continuing the war. The Greeks then consulted the Oracle of Delphi to learn that by stoning Palamedes, they would reap nothing but ill luck. Their priests told them that they had to appease the gods and to that end they built the huge wooden horse and left Sinon behind as a human sacrifice.

The hapless Greek then explained that he had been tied to a post outside the city but, after the Greeks departed, he had broken free, only to be captured by a Trojan patrol. Priam accepted Sinon's story and pardoned him. The Trojans then dragged the huge horse into the city, tearing down part of a wall so that it could be pulled behind the fortress. That night the Trojans feasted, drank, and fell into orgies and exhaustion.

From inside the belly of the horse came a group of Greek warriors who crept to the gates and opened them, letting the Greek army inside. Ulysses, according to legend, led his Greeks throughout the city, slaughtering the Trojans and torching the city. Thus the lies of Sinon, Ulysses' artful spy, brought an end to the Trojan War.

SIS (Secret Intelligence Service)
British Intelligence ▪ (1909–   )

ALTHOUGH THE BRITISH SECRET SERVICE HAS BEEN in existence since the days of Wellington, the present-day MI6, or SIS, first came into official existence in 1909 as the Secret Intelligence Bureau. This most secret organization, answerable only to the prime minister and his appointees, never publicized its existence, let alone its current directors. SIS chiefs were simply referred to as "C," which is the case to this day. Not until the 1980s did the British press violate the standing tradition when they revealed the names of Sir Arthur Franks and Colin Frederick Figures as directors of SIS (MI6).

SIS has the responsibility of collecting intelligence throughout the world that is considered vital to Britain's security. It maintains agents everywhere, invariably stationed in British embassies as military or cultural attachés. SIS works closely with America's CIA, and, to a lesser degree, the French intelligence service.

Since SIS files, as well as its history, is kept in top secrecy, it is difficult to assess the agency's effectiveness, except to say that in World War I and World War II, this organization functioned with splendid effectiveness, except for some occasional fiascos such as the Venlo Incident in World War II, in which two SIS agents were lured into capture by the SD's enterprising Walter Schellenberg. The agency was further embarrassed and ridiculed for not detecting a group of Trinity College spies who thoroughly compromised SIS for two decades following World War II. These SIS turncoats included Anthony Blunt, Guy Burgess, Donald Maclean, and Kim Philby.

During World War I, SIS chief Mansfield Cumming proved to be an excellent spymaster. Under his direction, the SIS most often outwitted its German counterpart.

SIS critics have repeatedly pointed out that the organization has suffered greatly from a sort of in-breeding wherein its leaders and agents have been traditionally selected from upper-crust schools and from among the gentry where alcoholism, homosexuality, and other social weaknesses prevail. To overcome that image, the SIS in the 1980s began recruiting its agents from a broader area of academia, although that policy also held dangers. Some of these recruits proved too eccentric or unreliable to conduct proper SIS business.

SIS, or MI6, has not had the best of relationships with MI5, the British counterintelligence service, particularly during the Cold War period (1946–1992). Such MI5 stalwarts as the brilliant William Skardon, a one-time Metropolitan policeman before becoming the best interrogator MI5 ever had, thought that those working for SIS were little more than brigands. After the defections of Burgess and Maclean, he referred to British intelligence as "the enemies." It was Skardon who expertly manipulated A-bomb spy Klaus Fuchs into confessing his treason and espionage. He was also responsible for the exposure of the notorious Soviet spy ring headed by Gordon Lonsdale and Peter and Helen Kroger.

[ALSO SEE: *Anthony Blunt; Guy Burgess; CIA; Mansfield Cumming; Klaus Fuchs; Peter and Helen Kroger; Gordon Lonsdale; Donald Maclean; MI6; Kim Philby; Walter Schellenberg; Venlo Incident*]

SMERSH
Soviet Assassination Division of KGB ■ (1917–   )

EVER SINCE THE BOLSHEVIK REVOLUTION OF 1917, a division of Soviet intelligence has been responsible for seeking out and blackmailing, kidnapping, or killing anyone who opposed the Communist regime, especially defecting Russians or Russians opposing the regime who live abroad. Non-Russians who have proved to be particularly antagonistic to the Soviets have also been selected for action by SMERSH, a phrase meaning "Death to Spies!" (*Smert Shpionam*). This slogan is said to have been coined by Stalin and certainly reflected his own murderous character.

SMERSH is actually the Ninth Division of the KGB, which is dedicated to Terror and Diversion, led and staffed by the most fanatical Communist killers. Its sophisticated murder techniques were found in the novels of Ian Fleming and others but they grimly existed in reality. Though the title SMERSH ceased to be used by the KGB after 1948, the organization continues to exist. SMERSH was originally created into five separate sections.

The first section works inside the Red Army, ferreting out dissident soldiers and summarily executing them. The second section of SMERSH collects information and, during wartime, is responsible for dropping agents behind enemy lines. The third section is responsible for collating and disseminating information and issuing orders. The fourth section investigates suspects and has the authority to make arrests. The fifth section is made up of three-man tribunals of high-ranking Soviet officers who hear cases and pass judgment. All sentences by the tribunals are final and, if execution is ordered, it is carried out immediately.

SMERSH (now called Department V of the First Chief Directorate, which is hidden inside the internal security department of the Army, also called CUKR) is responsible for ruthlessly murdering tens of thousands of people in the last eight decades. Many world leaders, including Roosevelt and Churchill, who were guarded at the Teheran Conference by SMERSH agents, knew of its existence but the agency was not made public until the defection of KGB Captain Nicolai Khokhlov in West Germany in 1954. Khokhlov himself was a SMERSH agent sent to murder Georgi Okolovich on orders from Nikita Khrushchev. Okolovich was a staunch opponent of the Communists, a leader in NTS, an anti-Soviet émigré organization headquartered in Frankfurt.

Khokhlov, an experienced killer, had received special training for his mission; he was to murder Okolovich with a miniature poison pellet gun. The assassin suddenly changed his mind and then defected to the CIA, exposing SMERSH operations as well as identifying two other SMERSH killers in Western Europe, who were promptly arrested.

After Khokhlov's defection, two other SMERSH agents, Peter Deriabin and Bogdan Stashinsky, also defected. Both one-time assassins detailed the workings of SMERSH. All of these assassins were equipped with sophisticated murder weapons. Stashinsky was equipped with a small tube that sprayed prussic acid.

One of the most active early-day SMERSH agents in the West was American-born George Mink. A native of Philadelphia, where he drove a taxi in the early 1920s, Mink joined the Communist Party in 1926, becoming a trade-union organizer for the Marine Workers Union, which reportedly had a direct link to Joseph Stalin. By 1927, Mink was sending reports directly to Moscow. He was summoned to Moscow in 1928, where he underwent his SMERSH training and in the following year he undertook his first assassination assignments throughout Europe.

In 1931, he was in Berlin, where he met a journalist who was to later describe him as "a short, strongly-built, dapper young man, with a small cruel mouth, greenish-brown eyes and irregular teeth." Mink was then stalking Hans Wissenger, a spy who had been controlling three GPU couriers working on the Hamburg-America line and who had exposed them to German authorities. Wissenger had been ordered back to Moscow and had refused. Mink was then assigned to kill him.

On May 22, 1932, Mink—along with Hugo Marx, another SMERSH assassin—located Wissenger and shot him to death in his apartment in the Muehlenstrasse. The murder is listed in Berlin's police files to this day as unsolved. Mink got away completely and reportedly killed at least another half dozen people by 1935 when his luck ran out. He and another American KGB assassin, Nicholas Sherman, were arrested in Copenhagen and charged with espionage. They were both sent to prison for eighteen months, reportedly for stalking a Russian businessman who had fled the Soviet Union.

Released in 1936, Mink returned to Moscow, where he was reportedly seen in the company of Juliet Stuart

Poyntz, one of the leading American Communists who vanished the following year. According to Carlo Tresca, a rabid anti-Communist and anti-fascist editor in New York, Poyntz was ordered killed after she openly denounced Stalin and communism. George Mink, Tresca told friends, was the man who was her contact and KGB control and he arranged for a hurried meeting with her. At that time, Mink lured her into a car in Central Park. He drove north and stopped alongside a lonely road where he strangled Poyntz to death, burying her body in a woodland near the estate of President Franklin D. Roosevelt in Dutchess County. (Informant Tresca was himself murdered in 1943 as he strolled down a New York street. His assassin was later identified as Mafia boss Carmine "The Cigar" Galante, who had accepted a SMERSH assignment to murder Tresca for a one-time fee of $50,000.)

Next, Mink went to Barcelona, where, using the alias of Alfred Herz, he joined the anarchist brigade so that he could get close to Professor Camillo Berneri, an anti-Stalinist who had so angered Stalin by his virulent statements about the Soviet leader that the Russian dictator was seized by a screaming fit of rage, calling in his KGB chief to order Berneri's execution. So beside himself was the distempered Stalin that he could barely manage the assassination order—he was reportedly foaming at the mouth at the time. Berneri and an aide were found shot to death and the bodies were mutilated. Mink, alias Herz, vanished from the rolls of the anarchist brigade a few hours later.

Throughout the 1930s, SMERSH agents roamed throughout Western Europe, seeking out fallen-away Communists. They tracked down and shot Ignace Reiss, who had been the resident director of the KGB in France and who had denounced Stalin for his bloodbath purges in Russia. Reiss' close friend, Walter Krivitsky, the first ranking GRU officer to defect, testified as to the ruthlessness of SMERSH and was himself tracked down to a Washington hotel room and murdered.

The most celebrated SMERSH assassination was that of Leon Trotsky, who had led the Bolshevik revolution of October 1917 in Russia with Lenin. He had been exiled from Russia in 1929 by his nemesis, Joseph Stalin, but had conducted an intense propaganda campaign against the Russian dictator. Stalin had ordered Trotsky murdered.

Trotsky had moved to Mexico in 1937 and by 1940 he was living with his wife, Natalya, in Coyoacan, a suburb of Mexico City. He resided in a fortified bastion with the walls around his small villa and the entrance gate guarded around the clock by ten heavily armed Mexican policeman. A squad of Trotskyites supplemented his personal bodyguard. Also, armed guards in a watchtower scanned surrounding property through binoculars. Trotsky felt that it was only a matter of time before SMERSH agents caught up with him. A short time earlier, his personal representative, Rudolf Klement, had been tracked down in Paris and murdered by Soviet killers.

On May 24, 1940, twenty heavily armed men led by David Alfaro Siqueiros, a Mexican painter and ardent Communist who had accepted the SMERSH assignment to murder Trotsky, attacked the exile's compound with machine guns and bombs but Trotsky and his family survived. Siqueiros went into hiding and was allowed to leave Mexico in 1942, becoming a resident of Chile, where he lived out his life, described by a local official as "an uncontrolled element considered half mad."

Jaime Mercader, on the other hand, was a SMERSH agent who embodied cold, calculating reason. For almost a year, Jaime Ramón Mercader del Rio Hernandez, using the alias of Frank Jacson, had been stalking Trotsky, worming his way into the confidences of the exile's friends. He was the son a Spanish businessman and a Cuban Communist mother. Mercader had fought in the Republican Army during the Spanish Civil War and had been recruited into SMERSH by Leonid Eitigon, a KGB/SMERSH handler and one of his mother's many lovers. He had posed as a French journalist, using the cover name of Jacques Mornard, and attended the Fourth International Conference of Communists in Paris, a largely Trotsky-inspired group.

In Paris, Mercader seduced Sylvia Agelof, an American social worker whose sister had once been Trotsky's secretary. When Agelof returned to the U.S. she took Mercader with her. At that time he traveled on a Canadian passport under the name of Frank Jacson, the same passport he used to enter Mexico where, through Agelof, he was introduced to Trotsky.

He stayed in contact with Trotsky, paying several social calls to the Coyoacan bastion. At one point, he told Trotsky that he had written a white paper based on Trotsky's political philosophies and asked the exile if he would be so kind as to to read it. Trotsky agreed, fixing an appointment for August 20, 1940. Mercarder arrived at Trotsky's complex that day with the manuscript. He was also carrying a thirteen-inch dagger, a pistol, and an Alpine ice ax, which he concealed under a topcoat draped over his arm.

Trotsky warmly greeted Mercader, took his manuscript, and sat down at his desk to read it. Trotsky, after turning a few pages, realized that the manuscript was gibberish. He looked up quizzically at his guest. Mercader leaped from his chair and swiftly brought the ice ax crashing down onto Trotsky's head, splitting the skull. It was, however, not a killing blow.

Falling to the floor, Trotsky cried out in pain, which immediately brought Joseph Hansen and Jake Cooper, his two American bodyguards, into the room. Hansen and Cooper dove at Mercader, knocking him to the floor, where they began beating him into unconsciousness. Bleeding from the gash in his head, Trotsky asked them not to kill Mercader, croaking: "He has a story to tell."

Rushed to a hospital, Trotsky lived for another twenty-four hours. Mercader was by then imprisoned, claiming that he had killed Trotsky to defend the honor of his mistress, Sylvia Agelof, whom Trotsky, he claimed, had seduced. Agelof strongly denied having had any sexual contact with the Communist leader and condemned Mercader as a SMERSH assassin. There was much confusion as to exactly who Mercader was. He insisted that he was Jacques Mornard and, as such, he was finally tried on April 17, 1943, and found guilty of assassinating Leon Trotsky. He was sent to prison for life in the Juarez Penitentiary in Mexico City.

After seventeen years as a model prisoner, Mercader was released on May 6, 1960. He went to Prague, where he worked as a journalist, then moved on to Moscow, where he received the "Order of the Soviet Union," a tacit admission by the Kremlin that he had performed a great political service for the Soviet Union by assassinating Trotsky. Some time later, Mercader moved to Cuba, where he died in 1978, still using the alias Jacques Mornard.

Often in foreign countries, SMERSH will use professional criminals and killers to perform its abductions and assassinations, paying them enormous sums of money for their services. By employing professional criminals, kidnappings and liquidations appear to be criminal acts and not political coups, thus clouding the motives and redirecting suspicion from the Soviets to lawbreakers. This was the case of Carlo Tresca, where an American gangster, Carmine Galante, was handsomely paid to kill a SMERSH victim.

The same was blatantly evident in the case of Dr. Walter Linse, a prominent West German lawyer and acting president of the Association of Free German Jurists. Under Linse's direction, the Association exposed the outrageous crimes committed by the Soviets under the guise of Communist law, and sought to offer victims aid against arbitrary KGB arrest, secret trials, and false imprisonment or confinement in labor camps. Linse's reputation as a staunch anti-Communist was such that SMERSH received orders to have him kidnapped in West Berlin and removed to East Berlin, where he could be held in permanent custody and cause no more political damage.

To that end, SMERSH used four infamous criminals who were all serving long prison sentences in East Germany: Harry Liedtke, 22, who had been imprisoned for robbery and assault; Herbert Novak, 27, imprisoned for life for murder; Joseph Dehnert, 22, a burglar; and Erwin Knispel, 27, who had been imprisoned for no less than eighteen separate serious crimes.

On July 7, 1952, Liedtke went from East to West Berlin, where he got into a taxi driven by Wilhelm Woiziske. He told Woiziske to drive to the Senefelderplatz in East Berlin. Knowing West Berlin cab drivers were reluctant to go into the Soviet sector, Liedtke offered Woiziske a twenty-mark tip. A few moments after passing the checkpoint, Liedtke leaned forward and placed a carton of American cigarettes next to Woiziske and the grateful Woiziske murmured his thanks for the tip. When the taxi reached the Senefelderplatz, however, several German policemen rushed to the taxi, yanking Woiziske and Liedtke from the car, one of the officers shouting: "So you're the smugglers of American cigarettes."

Taken to East German police headquarters, Woiziske was locked up in a basement cell but he was not interrogated. It became obvious later that Liedtke's use of the taxi had only one purpose, to borrow the cab's West Berlin license plates. Those plates were affixed to another car that had no difficulty in passing the checkpoint into West Berlin early the following morning, July 8, 1952. The car contained Liedtke, Novak, Knispel, and Dehnert. The four men drove to the residence of Dr. Linse, who lived in the American sector of West Berlin at 12a Gerichstrasse in the suburb of Lichterfelde.

Linse, a prompt person, stepped as usual from his apartment house at precisely 7:30 A.M. and began walking toward his office, puffing on his pipe. As he came abreast of the car in which the four men sat, Liedtke and Dehnert got out and Dehnert went up to Linse holding an unlighted cigarette. He asked the doctor for a match. Linse fumbled in his pockets and, as he did so, Liedtke slipped behind him and struck him a heavy blow on the head with a blackjack.

Dr. Linse, however, was tougher than expected and stood his ground, pushing the kidnappers away. Liedtke then grabbed the doctor around the waist and Dehnert clasped the victim's legs together, and they carried him to the car, attempting to toss Linse into the back seat. The doctor put up a fierce struggle until Novak pulled a pistol and shot Linse in the leg. He collapsed into the back seat, Liedtke and Dehnert falling on top of him.

Knispel, who was at the wheel, drove off at such a terrific speed that he ignored the fact that Dr. Linse's legs were protruding from the open rear door of the car. The car raced down the Drakenstrasse with a van in hot pursuit. The driver of the van had witnessed the abduction and was pursuing the kidnappers, a wild chase that soon included a West German police car.

Seeing that they were being pursued, the kidnappers leaned from the windows of their car and tossed tetrahedral nails to the cobblestones, believing that these would puncture the tires of the pursuing vehicles and bring them to a halt. The pursuers, however, managed to avoid the nails and began gaining on the kidnap car. Morning rush-hour crowds then provided an avenue of escape for the East Germans. Maneuvering the car between clusters of pedestrians, Knispel managed to turn down a sidestreet and escape pursuit. The car then disappeared into East Berlin.

Woiziske, the cab driver, was taken from his cell a few hours later. An East German official apologized to him, saying that it had all been a mistake. The license plates had been reaffixed to his taxi, which was returned to Woiziske, who then drove back to West Berlin to tell authorities of his strange experience. The CIA and Reinhard Gehlen of West German intelligence soon pieced together the method by which SMERSH had abducted Dr. Linse.

The Western press soon trumpeted the bold kidnapping and American officials lodged a formal protest with the Soviets. The Russians said they knew nothing about Dr. Linse or his disappearance. Western officials kept up demands for the return of Linse for eight years. Then, in June 1960, the Russian Red Cross perfunctorily informed the West German Red Cross that "Walter Linse died in a Russian prison camp on December 14, 1953."

In the case of Vladimir Poremsky, a leader of NTS and an ardent Soviet opponent, a real cigarette smuggler in East Berlin, Wolfgang Wildprett, was used for a SMERSH assassination assignment. On Christmas day, 1954, Wildprett appeared at Poremsky's door in Frankfurt. He held a newpaper photo of his victim in one hand and in the other a Walther P38 aimed at the startled Poremsky.

The SMERSH assassin did not fire. Pocketing the weapon, he said: "I'm here to kill you, but I don't trust them [his SMERSH handlers]. If I kill you, then they will tell me to murder somebody else. Then one day the police will arrest me, and put me in prison with a big pile of deutsche marks I can't spend." Poremsky arranged for his reluctant killer to defect to the West, where he settled down under an alias. "So he didn't kill me," Poremsky later said. "I like Wildprett, and I still see him sometimes. In fact, I went to his wedding."

SMERSH remained undaunted. Despite defecting killers in their ranks, the agency developed a number of particularly vicious methods of murder, undoubtedly to allow their assassins less chance of being identified and apprehended. One victim of these new murder weapons was Horst Schwirkmann, a skilled West German technician working in the West German Embassy in Moscow. Schwirkmann was a debugging expert who "swept" his embassy clean of KGB listening devices. When unearthing a listening device he fed into its microphone a high voltage that undoubtedly sent a terrific shock into the ears of KGB listeners.

More frustrating for Soviet bugging experts, no doubt, was Schwirkmann's discovery and dismantling of a sophisticated electronic device which had been secreted in the embassy's decoding room, one which immediately broadcast to the KGB all messages being typed before they were automatically cyphered. The newly developed device allowed the Soviets to break West German diplomatic codes by comparing cyphered messages with those picked up in the clear.

So irritated with Schwirkmann were KGB officials that they ordered SMERSH to kill him. The West German was stuck in the buttocks by an agent as he moved through a crowd of tourists at the Zagorsk monastery outside Moscow in 1964. The stricken technician was rushed to the U.S. Embassy, where a full-scale medical clinic was maintained. Here, doctors learned that Schwirkmann had been injected with nitrogen mustard gas. He was treated and, after a painful recuperation period, the SMERSH victim survived.

Georgi Markov, who received the same treatment, was not as fortunate. A brilliant Bulgarian journalist who lived in exile, Markov detested the Soviets and said so in broadcasts over the BBC and Radio Free Europe. He described in detail how the Communist regimes in Bulgaria and elsewhere practiced terror and murder. The Bulgarian bloc nation had become the most oppressive of all the Soviet-dominated countries. It lashed out viciously at anyone opposing the regime, using SMERSH agents out of Moscow for their purposes.

At the request of the Bulgarian KGB, SMERSH unsuccessfully attempted to murder Boris Korczak, a suspected Polish double agent living in Virgina and reportedly working for the CIA. Vladimir Kostov, a Bulgarian living in exile in Paris, was also attacked by SMERSH agents but he, too, survived. Two other Bulgarians who had defected, a rocket technician living in Vienna and a newspaperman, had been liquidated by SMERSH operatives.

Korczak had been jabbed in the back by a sharp instrument wielded by an unidentified passerby. He developed a high fever and was delirious for three days until he recovered. In September 1978, Georgi Markov stood waiting for a bus on Waterloo Bridge. A man in the crowd jabbed his thigh with the pointed end of an umbrella. He apologized for what seemed to be an accident and scurried away. Hours later Markov lay dying. The umbrella had actually fired a pinhead platinum pellet containing ricin—a poison made from castor oil plants—into Markov's leg. Within hours Markov developed a high fever and then died of heart failure.

SMERSH believed it had developed the ultimate murder weapon with the use of ricin. The poison is almost undetectable and invariably leads to cardiovascular collapse, a condition that any unsuspecting doctor would simply attribute to a common heart attack. Although it is claimed that SMERSH went out of existence with the collapse of Communism in Russia, the agency still exists.

[ALSO SEE: *CIA; Reinhard Gehlen; Otto Katz; KGB; Nicolai Khokhlov; Walter Krivitsky; Juliet Stuart Poyntz; Ignace Reiss; Bogdan Stashinsky*]

SOE (Special Operations Executive)
British Intelligence Organization in World War II ▪ (1940–1945)

THE SOE CAME INTO BEING AFTER THE FALL OF France, on July 16, 1940, when a British intelligence committee in London organized Special Operations Executive "to coordinate all action by way of subversion and sabotage against the enemy overseas." SOE's first chief was Dr. Hugh Dalton, Minister of Economic Warfare, who had been told by Prime Mininster Winston Churchill to "set Europe ablaze."

Organized resistance to the Nazis occupying European countries was already in place. SOE's job was to finance, supply, and direct operations and supplement the resistance groups with SOE agents expert in espionage, as well as electronics, explosives, and communications technicians. Fortunately for SOE, it had a number of brilliant officers who understood well the conduct of irregular warfare and guerrilla action, such as J. C. F. Holland, Colin Gubbins, George Taylor, Bickham Sweet-Escott, Harold Perkins, and Maurice Buckminster.

SOE worked very closely with American intelligence during World War II, the OSS and its colorful director, William J. Donovan, and his equally brilliant deputy, Allen Dulles. Thanks to the efforts of Canadian millionaire and SIS deputy in New York, William Stephenson, who had befriended Donovan much earlier, the ties between the OSS and the SOE became umbilical, an effective relationship that often, when working together in joint operations, proved more than a match for Admiral Canaris' Abwehr.

The British and French agents trained by SOE and sent to occupied countries to work with underground groups against the Nazis were some of the most courageous and inventive spies in the history of espionage. These included Malcolm Munthe; Douglas Dodds-Parker; Peter Wilkinson; Anthony Quayle, who later became a distinguished actor; Christine Granville, whose life ended in tragedy; Peter Churchill and Odette Sansom, who were both captured by the Gestapo and spared only because the Nazis believed Churchill was related to the prime minister; and the most dashing of them all, F. F. E. Yeo-Thomas.

Most of the agents working in SOE were not military officers but mountain-climbers, explorers, linguists, geographers, yachtsmen, adventurers of all kinds, but some were merely housewives, like the fabulous Odette, who felt it their patriotic duty to help defeat the Nazis in any way possible. SOE agents served in all of the Nazi-occupied countries, from Poland to Scandinavia, from France to Belgium and Holland, from Italy to Yugoslavia and Greece. SOE spies could also be found in North Africa and in the Pacific islands of the Far East, in China, Burma, Thailand—everywhere the Allies were fighting the Axis powers.

There is no doubt that SOE was instrumental in making the Allied landings in France a huge success and that the organization not only supplied but stimulated the resistance movements throughout Europe until the Allied armies were able to once again free those countries. Most SOE agents were wartime spies, not professional espionage agents, and most of them were motivated by patriotism.

[ALSO SEE: *Abwehr; Wilhelm Canaris; Peter Churchill; William J. Donovan; Allen Dulles; Gestapo; Christine Granville; OSS; Odette Sansom; SIS; William Stephenson; F. F. E. Yeo-Thomas*]

SORGE, RICHARD
Soviet Spy in Japan ▪ (1895–1944)

BORN IN BAKU, RUSSIA, RICHARD SORGE WAS RAISED a German and became one of that nation's leading foreign correspondents. He was sent to Japan in the early 1930s, ostensibly to spy for the Germans, but Sorge had, by then, been recruited by the NKVD. While sending the Abwehr accurate but fairly useless information, he sent the real product of his double agent labors to Moscow. He became a spymaster himself, one so effective that all of Russia's top secret intelligence flowing from the Orient in the 1930s and into World War II was obtained, analyzed, and passed on to Moscow by Sorge.

A superb actor, clever, and accurately perceptive, Richard Sorge became one of the great spies of the twentieth century. The life of Richard Sorge was the stuff of high drama and real danger, a lifestyle in which the spy reveled. Success, however, led Sorge to believe himself invincible, an arrogant, intractable conviction that eventually led him to disaster and execution.

Sorge's mother, Nina Kobeleva, was Russian, his father, Wilhelm Sorge, a German mining engineer who moved to Russia in 1894 to find lucrative employment in the Baku oilfields. Sorge was born on October 4, 1895, in Adjikent, the youngest of nine children. In 1898, the Sorges moved to Berlin and here Sorge and an older brother were raised. Sorge became an ardent German nationalist and when World War I erupted in 1914, he was one of the first to enlist, leaving school at the age of nineteen and joining a student battalion of the 3rd Guards, Field Artillery.

In March 1916, Sorge was severely wounded while helping to repel a Russian attack. Shrapnel had broken both of his legs and he was sent to a Berlin hospital. He was promoted to the rank of corporal and given the Iron Cross, first class, but Sorge's fighting days were over. His wounds would cause him to limp for the remainder of his life. While recovering from his wounds, Sorge read the works of Karl Marx. He had long known about this radical political writer, his paternal great uncle having been Marx's personal secretary.

The war had shaken Sorge's belief in the Kaiser's Germany and his youthful nationalism had crumbled. Enrolling at the University of Berlin, Sorge studied economics, later attending the universities of Kiel and Hamburg. He graduated from the University of Hamburg in 1920 with a Ph.D. in politicial science.

On the day of his graduation, Sorge joined the German Communist Party. He obtained a job teaching history at a Hamburg school but the headmaster quickly learned that Sorge was not only teaching communism to students but recruiting members to the Communist Party during school hours. He was dismissed. Sorge then went to work in a coal mine but his constant recruitment of coal miners to the Communist banner caused him to be fired. The German police had by then marked Sorge as a Communist spy.

Only a few hours before his impending arrest, Sorge learned that police were closing in, and he hastily slipped out of Berlin on an eastbound train, using an alias. He arrived a few weeks later in Moscow, where he was met by Dimitri Manuilsky, then head of intelligence for the Comintern. Manuilsky realized that the intellectual, crafty Sorge would be excellent material for Soviet intelligence. Sorge was immediately recruited as a novice espionage agent, and went to work learning the spy trade. In the process, he became fluent in French, Russian, and English.

Sorge returned to Germany and married Christiane Gerlach, the ex-wife of his college mentor. After wedding in May 1921, Sorge and Christiane Gerlach took a house in Solingen, in North Rhine–Westphalia. Christine continued to study for her doctorate while Sorge wrote articles for the *Voice of the Mineworkers*, an organ of the Communist Party.

Sorge also spent a great deal of time lecturing on economics and philosophy, which he used as a smokescreen, combining his journalistic chores with underground Party operations. His wife had no knowledge of his espionage activities. In October 1922, Sorge visited members of the Central Committee of the Communist Party in Berlin. He received instructions to relocate to Frankfurt and gather intelligence there about the intellectual and business community, as well as recruit more members to the Party.

Sorge enjoyed his new social position in Frankfurt. He hosted all-night parties to which flocked writers, journalists, and artists. He played the role of savant political scientist while traveling about Germany on clandestine missions for the Party. These missions

Soviet spymaster Richard Sorge, one of the greatest espionage agents of the twentieth century, shown here in 1928 in Norway.

had a single purpose—to stir up political revolution. In October 1923, at the urging of Moscow, Communists in Germany attempted to overthrow the government but this uprising was quickly and ruthlessly put down. Sorge had helped to coordinate the revolutionary outbreaks, but after the Communists had been crushed, he quickly retreated to his role as journalist.

Late in 1923, D. B. Riaznov, an esteemed Russian scholar and head of the Marx-Lenin Institute in Moscow, arrived in Germany, seeking original documents written by Marx. Sorge provided him with original letters Marx had written to his great uncle, Frederich Albert Sorge. This endeared him to Riaznov, who later introduced Sorge to top Russian leaders, particularly those in the intelligence community.

Using student passports, Sorge and his wife traveled to Moscow, where Sorge was embraced by Party leaders. In March 1925, he was officially given Communist Party card number 0049927. He then took an oath to the Party and to the exclusion of all other countries and parties. He was assigned to the OMS section of the Orgburo, which had been established in 1922 and was officially known as the Organization Bureau, which controlled all clandestine and covert activities abroad and was linked directly to the Central Committee. The highly secretive OMS section was responsible for gathering all intelligence, as well as organizing all subversive and illegal operations outside of Russia.

Sorge was so thoroughly dedicated to his duties with OMS that he ignored his wife, and they soon divorced. In the next few years, Sorge spent his time on OMS missions throughout Europe and America.

In 1930, Sorge was transferred to operations controlled by the GRU, Red Army intelligence, going to work in the Fourth Bureau, one of six sections of the Red Army's Directorate of military intelligence. His chief in the Fourth Bureau was the legendary General Yan Karlovich Berzin, a colorful commander who had been in the forefront of the Bolshevik revolution of October 1917. Berzin personally selected Sorge for espionage missions abroad, but this time the already accomplished spy was sent to the Far East.

At that time the Soviets had all but given up hope for instigating full-scale revolution in western Europe. Their focus then centered upon China. Although Chinese Communists had been thoroughly routed by China's new nationalist strongman Chiang Kai-shek, who ruled from Nanking, Berzin and other Soviet savants felt that China was ripe for a full-scale Communist revolution. Such a social upheaval, the Soviets reasoned, would tip the balance of world power in their favor.

In extensive briefings, Berzin instructed Sorge to travel to Shanghai and into the interior of China. He was to learn all he could about Chiang's military power and his financial resources, and gather information on Chiang's most influential backers, along with dispositions of his troops and the factions opposing him. Moreover, Sorge was to learn the true attitudes of the British and American governments toward Chiang and whether they would support the nationalist leader if he were opposed by Communist insurgents.

He arrived in Shanghai in January 1930. This cosmopolitan city was a polyglot community of Chinese and international citizens. The foreign colonies were large and mixed. The city teemed with the rich and the poor, and trades and businesses of all kinds flourished. Shanghai had been selected by the Soviets as the perfect Chinese city for its espionage agents to gather information, a city that could be manipulated into urban revolution. Sorge met with the German Consul-General in Shanghai, explaining that he had come to China to study its agriculture and agrarian methods. For this purpose, he pointed out, it was necessary that he travel widely through China. He was given a number of contacts and then set off through the countryside, staying first for some months in Canton, making contact with Communist underground cells and gathering intelligence, then moving through the south of China.

Sorge was back in Shanghai by November 1930. At that time he met and befriended a fellow traveler, Agnes Smedley, an American who was a correspondent for the *Frankfurter Zeitung* and who had been endorsed by Sorge's spymasters in Moscow. Smedley, a mannish female and a political malcontent who was a native of Missouri, in turn, introduced Sorge to a Japanese journalist, Hotsumi Ozaki, who was Smedley's lover and a special correspondent for Japan's biggest daily newspaper, *Asahi Shimbun*. Sorge, then using the alias of Johnson, passed himself off as an American. It was not until some time later that Ozaki would learn Sorge's true name.

Educated in Japan's finest schools, including Tokyo Imperial University, Japan's Harvard, Ozaki studied German, the tongue in which he communicated with Sorge. Like Sorge, he had read the works of Marx in his youth and became a secret leftist, although he maintained, through his family, his links to the Japanese high command and Japanese intelligence. Ozaki would prove to be Richard Sorge's most reliable source of secret information in the fourteen years to come.

In Shanghai Sorge met with Ozaki regularly in Smedley's apartment and in restaurants. The pair exchanged ideas and soon developed a deep friendship. Neither ever probed into their private lives, which they kept separate from each other. Ozaki proved to be extremely helpful in Sorge's fact-finding mission in China. A dedicated leftist, the Japanese journalist provided Sorge with scores of important contacts in the Chinese Communist underground. Information Sorge received from these contacts was coded and then given to Max Klausen, a Communist merchant seaman and radio operator.

The plans of the Sorge ring were thrown into turmoil when the Japanese invaded Manchuria in September 1931. Sorge was uncertain as to how the various political factions in China would react to this new threat. It was evident to him that relations between Japan and the Soviet Union were strained to the point where hostilities between the two nations might soon occur.

Sorge met with a friend of Ozaki's, Teikichi Kawai, who worked as a correspondent for the Shanghai *Weekly*. He quickly absorbed Kawai into his circle, sending him on a mission to Manchuria, instructing him to find out if Japanese militarists there planned to invade Northern China. He was also to determine how the inhabitants were reacting to Japanese occupation and, especially, what the Japanese and Chinese in the area thought about the Soviet Union. Within a few weeks, Kawai returned to Shanghai to deliver a detailed report to Sorge of conditions in Manchuria. A few days later Kawai was arrested by Japanese police who maintained order in the Japanese enclave in Shanghai and kept strict surveillance on their own nationals. As would be the case with almost all of Sorge's spies, Kawai proved his loyalty to his chief by telling nothing to the agents of Kempei Tai (Japanese secret police). He was soon released without ever mentioning Sorge or his mission in China.

Soviet spymasters in Moscow at this time were doubting Sorge's real value to them. They had assigned another spy, Ruth Kuczynski, one of the NKVD's cleverest agents, who also used the cover of a journalist, to report on Sorge's progress. Though married, Kuczynski, a sensuous brunette, was always ready to employ her feminine wiles on behalf of the Communists, she being a fanatical follower of Marx and Lenin. Meeting Sorge at the Shanghai press club, Kuczynski reportedly struck up a relationship with Sorge that became briefly more intimate, though she learned nothing from him.

Meanwhile, Moscow began carping about what it considered to be extravagant operating expenses and salaries for the Sorge ring but its doubts were soon dispelled. On January 28, 1932, the Japanese invaded Shanghai under the pretext that Japanese nationals in their enclave had been attacked by Chinese insurgents. The attacks had been staged by Eastern Jewel, who had paid gangs of Chinese criminals to attack the Japanese and thus create the necessity for the invasion.

As Japanese troops battled the 19th Chinese Route Army in the streets and suburbs of Shanghai, Sorge learned from his contacts at the Japanese consulate that Japan's incursion was only the preliminary act to a full-scale war which Japan intended to launch in gobbling up all of China. Members of his ring fed him information on Chinese troop dispositions at the time and Sorge himself witnessed the vicious street fighting in Shanghai between Japanese and Chinese troops. His long, detailed report in which he analyzed the inferiority of Chinese troops as to morale, equipment, and leadership and the excellent condition and leadership of Japanese troops impressed GRU in Moscow.

Ozaki was recalled to Japan in early 1932, but the loss of the Soviet spymaster's most important link to high-level Japanese information was supplanted by many other contacts he had made, especially Kawai. Ozaki may have, at this time, been suspected of being a spy either for the Soviets or, more logically, the Kempei Tai or Special Service Organ, as his abrupt departure suggested. Chinese intelligence, headed by the indefatigable Morris "Two Gun" Cohen, believed Sorge was a Soviet spy but its agents could not prove it.

Sorge was too clever for his pursuers. For the next nine months he diligently applied himself as a journalist, writing lengthy, well-composed articles of a decidely right-wing nature for his German newspaper. His published works cemented his relationship with the German Military Mission to Chiang Kai-shek. So impressed with these articles were the Germans that they arranged to have Sorge invited to Chiang's headquarters in Nanking, where he met the generalissimo.

Chiang was friendly and outgoing toward Sorge. He viewed the man, on the advice of his spymaster Cohen, as an acceptable double agent, one whose leftist contacts in Shanghai suggested he was a Soviet spy but who, in reality, had merely set up these contacts to appear as such. Sorge, according to the Chinese *and* the Japanese secret police and intelligence services, was really a German agent pretending to be a Soviet agent pretending to be a working journalist.

Sorge, of course, knew that he was suspected of being an agent for the Abwehr and he did much to promote that perception. In reality, of course, Sorge was never anything more or less than the top Soviet spymaster in the Far East, a role he would continue to faithfully enact until his exposure and execution.

In December 1932, Sorge was recalled to Moscow. General Berzin and other high-ranking Soviet intelligence chiefs hailed him as a brilliant spymaster, one who had with apparent ease obtained deep and useful information concerning Japan's military aims, as well as Chiang Kai-shek's military power and sources of equipment and arms, along with an overall perspective of foreigners and Chinese toward the Soviet Union.

After being feted and decorated, Sorge was allowed to pursue his own interests. He began writing a book about Chinese agriculture. He met an attractive young woman named Yekaterina Maximova, whom he married. Sorge did not have enough time to either finish his book or enjoy his new marriage. Summoned to General Berzin's office, he was told that the Fourth Bureau had a new assignment for him. Japan was the one nation in the world, because of language problems and fierce native patriotism, thought to be impenetrable as far as the gathering of any real intelligence. The Fourth Bureau and the GRU chiefs of the Red Army believed that since Richard Sorge had penetrated Japanese and Chinese intelligence in Shanghai with such excellent results that he might be the one man to run an effective Soviet spy ring in Japan.

Sorge himself later related that his mission to Japan was "to study very carefully the question of whether or not Japan was planning to attack the Soviet Union. This was for many years the most important duty assigned to me and my group. It would not be far wrong to say that it was the sole object of my mission to Japan."

The mission originally specified that Sorge would spend only two years in Japan to learn if he could actually conduct espionage activities in a security-conscious country where spies were routinely ferreted out by secret "thought" police (the unofficial title of the Kempei Tai). The naturally furtive Japanese were always alert and on guard against foreign intelligence probing, this unswerving attitude coupled to a traditional distrust of all foreigners.

So that Sorge would have absolute control of his ring, it was decreed that he was never to have more than four persons in his cell. Besides himself, he was to be allowed a single Japanese contact, a wireless operator, and a European. Most important, Sorge was to have no contact whatsoever with the Japanese Communist Party or with the Soviet Embassy in Japan. He was to wholly disassociate himself with any leftist-leaning groups and appear to be a German journalist with decided sympathies for the fascist states of Germany, Italy, and Japan. He was given the code name of "Ramsey," and, on May 17, 1933,

Sorge left Moscow for Berlin. He had serious bridge-building to perform in Berlin before he could move on to Japan. The Nazis had come to power with Adolf Hitler as chancellor only a short time earlier. All of the secret police dossiers were now in the hands of the Gestapo.

Sorge knew that his own early history of Communist activities were to be found somewhere in German police files. Once in Berlin he hastily and nervously began to shore up his past by obtaining references from those of the right-wing who never knew about his Communist background. With these references and those from editors of German newspapers for which he had written while in China, he was able to present a self-portrait of a German dedicated to the advancement of Hitler, the Nazis and Germany. On June 1, 1933, Sorge applied for a German passport, emphasizing in his application his father's acceptable German background.

Somehow the Gestapo overlooked, ignored, or could not find evidence of Sorge's leftist past in Germany, such as there was of it to examine. It is also possible that a Communist mole in the Gestapo destroyed any records dealing with Sorge's former Communist affiliations. His passport finally in hand, Dr. Richard Sorge, German journalist, took passage for Japan, arriving in Yokohama on September 6, 1933. Once in Yokohama, Sorge lined up his other three contacts, a wireless operator named Bernhardt who used the alias of Wendt, a Yugoslav Communist named Branko Vukelic, who worked as a photographic technician and a correspondent for the French news agency Havas in Tokyo, and a Japanese painter, Yotoku Miyagi.

None of these new Sorge associates were fully trusted by their superior. Bernhardt was a heavier drinker than Sorge and the spymaster often found him so drunk that he could hardly manage to transmit messages. Vukelic was a frail person whose commitment to communism seemed equally anemic. Miyagi, like Vukelic, was vague in his commitment to the Soviet cause.

Sorge met secretly and separately with his three contacts. In a Tokyo art gallery, while pretending to study paintings, he sat next to Miyagi and told him to obtain certain political and military information. The 30-year-old Miyagi, though willing and intelligent, was a poor conduit of information on Japan's military and political plans. He had lived in the U.S. since he was sixteen and he had no real understanding of lifestyle and policies in Japan. He earned a living by selling paintings but made few important contacts among government officials. Most of the information he passed along to Sorge was useless, gleaned from Japanese newspapers which Miyagi read religiously each day.

Where Miyagi disappointed Sorge, Bernhardt angered the spymaster with his seemingly purposeful negligence. Drunk most of the time, Bernhardt seldom transmitted the reports Sorge put together from his

own findings while masquerading as a journalist. Bernhardt had set up two transmitters in Yokohama, one in his own home and one in a small house occupied by Vukelic and his wife, Edith. Less than half of the messages Sorge brought to Bernhardt, however, were actually transmitted and even the film Sorge gave Bernhardt to send to Moscow by courier was often misplaced or never delivered at all.

When Sorge confronted the timid Bernhardt, the radio operator replied: "The frequent sending and receiving of messages will be tantamount to inviting discovery by the police." Sorge called him a coward and later angrily wrote to his superiors: "A man who engages in espionage work must have some courage." He demanded that Bernhardt be replaced and soon the wireless operator was on his way back to Moscow.

Vukelic, on the other hand, proved himself useful and was effective in photographing documents Sorge had stolen or borrowed. Sorge realized that he also needed a Japanese contact who could penetrate high-level sources in the gathering of important information. To that end, he sent Miyagi to contact Ozaki, his journalist friend during the time of his mission to Shanghai. In the spring of 1934, Miyagi called the Tokyo offices of *Asahi,* where Ozaki was working as a journalist. Ozaki was first suspicious until Miyagi told Ozaki that he was calling on behalf of an old friend of Ozaki from Shanghai days, the journalist Ozaki had known as "Johnson."

At that point Ozaki told Miyagi he would do anything and everything he could for Sorge. Ozaki, for his part, would accept no money from Sorge for the valuable information he passed on to him. The Japanese journalist, although a secret liberal, was not a member of the Japanese Communist Party. He was above suspicion and operated out of genuine concern over his country's military aims of unscrupulous aggression and conquest. He supplied Richard Sorge with information because he sincerely believed that his actions might keep Japan out of war.

Sorge's information from contacts at the German Embassy, coupled to what he received from Ozaki, and his perceptive evaluation of this information soon produced detailed reports that accurately portrayed Japanese military and political activities. The Fourth Bureau was delighted with its master spy in Yokohama. Sorge, meanwhile, delighted in his ability to hoodwink the much-vaunted Japanese secret police, who had identified and classified him as a fascist journalist who acted as a spy for Germany, a friendly power and soon to be a partner to Japan's own aims of world conquest. Sorge was therefore freely permitted to move about Japan without anything other than occasional or cursory surveillance. "I think that I am managing to lead them all by the nose," he wrote to General Berzin.

Sorge's old friend Kawai then returned from China and settled in Tokyo. Kawai, after leaving Shanghai in 1932, had gone north to Tientsen, where, in 1933, he infiltrated Chinese Communist cells, ostensibly for the Japanese secret service, Special Service Organ, but, in truth, he played a double-dealing game like Sorge, and was really feeding the Communists information about Japanese intelligence. Upon his return to Japan in 1935, Kawai took up residence in the Tokyo home of Isamu Fujita, a top agent in the Japanese espionage service, one of the plotters who had carried out the spectacular 1928 assassination of Chinese warlord Chang Tso-lin.

Oddly, Kawai served his host Fujita by spying on the young idealists in the Japanese Army who plotted the abortive coup of 1936, while feeding information to Miyagi, who passed it on to Sorge. Sorge was frustrated, however, at having voluminous information he was not able to transmit to Moscow since he had gotten rid of the alcoholic Bernhardt. He decided to personally deliver a full-scale report of conditions in Japan and traveled to Russia via the U.S. He had the full cooperation of Japanese and German officials since they believed he was on a fact-finding mission in the U.S. for Germany.

Sorge did pick up some valuable information from U.S. Communists, passing this along to his Nazi contacts in Berlin before secretly returning to Russia. When he arrived in Moscow, however, he was shocked to see that a reign of terror was being conducted by Joseph Stalin, who was purging the Party of all the old Bolsheviks. Stalin had removed General Berzin from the Fourth Bureau, replacing him with Geneal Semyon Petrovich Uritsky, who had, in 1921, led a famous cavalry charge across the frozen waters of Kronstadt to suppress a naval mutiny.

Sorge met with Uritsky in the summer of 1935, bringing with him a chart that detailed all of the various militarists in Japan, from Hirohito (who pretended to be merely the titular emperor but who, in truth, directed the Japanese military toward world war) down through all the ranks. This chart had been laboriously constructed by the painter Miyagi based on information supplied by Ozaki. It listed the names of hundreds of Japanese officers. The chart indicated those who favored a strike south against the British and Americans, and those who wanted to strike north against Russia. Sorge reported that Japan would move across China in 1936 and would not attack the Soviet Union. He backed up his contention by demonstrating to Uritsky the disposition of Japanese troops and how they were massed for a China strike which would preclude assembling more troops to attack Russia. Uritsky and his superiors were impressed.

Sorge insisted that Ozaki be officially accepted as a member of his ring and that he be provided a new wireless operator immediately. To all this Uritsky agreed. Max Klausen, who had been Sorge's diligent wireless operator in Shanghai, was assigned to the Tokyo ring. Klausen had been sent to Germany, where, as part of the Red Orchestra, he successfully spied upon Nazi politicians. He happily accepted the assignment to Sorge, and arrived in Japan on November 28, 1935. He immediately set up a blueprint shop to copy plans for architects and contractors, a cover for his espionage activities.

Sorge arranged to meet Klausen every Tuesday at the Blue Ribbon bar in Tokyo, where he would give him information to send on to Moscow. Sorge picked this bar because it was always packed with foreigners and was noisy. Klausen spent most of his waking hours building a new wireless set while secretly obtaining copper wire for the tuning coils, and more tubes than what he had originally smuggled into Japan. By February 1936, Klausen's set was operational, established in the home of Gunther Stein, the Tokyo correspondent of the London *News Chronicle*, who was sympathetic to Sorge's operations but knew little about the ring. Klausen, however, was so gifted a printer of blueprints that his shop actually began to make money from the many orders he received from large construction companies and manufacturers. He even fulfilled orders from the Japanese Army.

Suddenly, without any kind of warning, the Sorge ring came close to annihilation at 5 A.M. on January 21, 1936. Japanese detectives of the secret police who had maintained surveillance on Kawai broke into Kawai's residence, rushed into his bedroom, and yanked him naked from his bed. He was hustled outside to a car, and then to the airport, where he was thrown aboard a plane that flew to Hsinking in Manchuria.

Here the startled Kawai was charged by Japanese officials with being a Communist spy who had spread propaganda for the Soviets and the Chinese Communists in Manchuria. Savagely beaten for five days, Kawai refused to give his captors any information. The police learned nothing of the Sorge ring in Yokohama and Tokyo. Kawai was then thrown into jail and held until June 1936. He was then released and, some years later, returned to Japan, his resolve to aid Sorge all the more strenghtened by the brutal experience.

Also in 1936, dramatic events shook Japan that caused Richard Sorge to be sought out by German officials in Tokyo. A year earlier, young militarists in Tokyo had ostensibly made a move to control the military destiny of Japan. On July 16, 1935, Lieutenant-Colonel Saburo Aizawa visited the Tokyo offices of Major General Tetsuzan Nagata. Aizawa was angered over the fact that General Jinzaburo Mazaki, who had been Inspector General of Military Education for Japan and an advocate of launching a full-scale war against China, had been removed by more peace-loving officers, including General Nagata. Once inside Nagata's office, the berserk Aizawa drew his sword and hacked General Nagata to death.

The diehard nationalist was placed on trial but one closed to the public. It dragged on month after month. On February 26, 1936, hundreds of young military officers, none over the rank of captain, took control of most of the important military and political installations in Tokyo. All were supporters of Aizawa. They demanded that the Japanese Army purge itself of liberal, peace-loving officers such as the assassinated Nagata. Several military officers opposing the insurrectionists were murdered, along with some officials. The insurgents were later confronted by troops and capitulated. Thirteen of the leaders, along with Aizawa, were quickly convicted and executed.

This crisis caused deep alarm among the international community in Japan. The Germany Embassy summoned Sorge, who conferred with several officials. He told them that he believed the affair was the result of two factions of Japanese militarists who held opposing viewpoints as to which direction to take in the conquest of foreign lands. Mazaki, the deposed Inspector General, was a war hawk who wanted to attack China. Nagata and his clique wanted to avoid war at all costs, and another military faction wanted to strike north against the Soviet Union.

Aizawa was not a rebel, according to Sorge, but a veiled messenger of the Emperor. He traced Aizawa's connections to Hirohito's uncles and brothers and thus concluded that Aizawa truly represented the Emperor. Aizawa had struck down Nagata, who opposed Hirohito's ambition to invade China. He also willingly sacrificed his life by silently meeting execution, as did thirteen others leading the 1936 revolt without ever revealing that Hirohito himself had been the architect of the mock rebellion, one which was meant to warn all those opposed to Hirohito that assassination would be their fate if they did not follow the imperial design of conquest. Of course, Hirohito could not himself overtly make his plans public so his most fanatical officers demonstrated his will by eliminating opposition at the cost of their own lives, a sacrifice that, in their incontrovertible religious belief, would allow them into the highest strata of Shinto heaven.

So convincing was Sorge that he became known as the western savant on Japanese affairs. High-ranking German officials shared with him their most secret information regarding Japanese military movements and political machinations. Sorge would analyze this information for the Germans and then pass on the information to the Soviet Union. Through Eugen Ott, who was to become the German Ambassador to Japan, Sorge learned that Japan and Germany were secretly preparing a special pact in which both countries would aid each other in their future aggressions. So intimate did Ott become with Sorge that he asked Sorge to edit his top-secret reports to Berlin and shared with Sorge reports he received from Germany regarding Japanese affairs. Sorge appeared cooperative but he took pains to copy each and every document Ott gave him to review. He then passed copies of these documents on to the Fourth Bureau so that his Soviet masters possessed up-to-date top secret information regarding impending events affecting the security of the Soviet Union. So effective did Sorge become that he became a legendary spymaster within the Fourth Bureau.

Sorge not only predicted Japan's strike into the heart of China, but he also predicted that the Chinese-Japanese war would drag on for years, and again he would be proved correct. On July 7, 1937, the Japanese provoked a skirmish with Chinese troops at the Marco Polo Bridge outside Peking, this being enough of an excuse for Japanese troops to invade China, a war that would last eight long and bloody years, until its end in August 1945. Much of Sorge's insightful evaluations were based upon exhaustive reports he received from Ozaki, who had, by that time, established contacts with the highest Japanese authorities, becoming a confidant of some of Prime Minister Prince Konoye's top aides from whom he learned the inner directives of the imperial throne room.

By May 1938, Sorge's drinking increased to a dangerous level. One night, after drinking for hours with Prince Albert von Urach, an official in the German Embassy in Tokyo, Sorge mounted his motorcycle to return home. He roared through the empty Tokyo streets, somehow lost control of the cycle, and slammed into the wall of the U.S. Embassy. Although badly injured, Sorge managed to call Klausen to the spot. Before fainting and being removed to a hospital, Sorge was able to give Klausen secret documents he had stolen that night from the German Embassy, along with a large amount of U.S. currency. When he emerged from the hospital, Sorge bore terrible facial scars which distorted his face into what was later described as a "Japanese mask . . . of almost demoniacal expression."

No sooner was Sorge recovered from his wounds than a fresh crisis loomed. Soviet General G. S. Lyushkov, a senior officer of the NKVD, and the Soviet Frontier Forces, suddenly defected to the Japanese in June 1938. Lyushkov brought with him detailed maps and data that identified all of the Soviet military dispositions in Sibera. The defecting Russian, in a show of great cooperation with the Japanese, pinpointed all defense positions maintained by Russian troops along the Manchurian border. The reason for Lyushkov's defection was clear to the Japanese. He was on Stalin's purge list and he had fled to the arms of the Japanese to escape the dictator's wrath. Though he discussed with the Japanese at length the internal disorders of the Soviet Union and the ongoing Stalinist purge, Lyushkov could shed no light on Soviet spies in Japan. He had had no relationship with the Fourth Bureau, Moscow assured the anxious Sorge. The Sorge ring remained a mystery to the Japanese secret police.

It was later claimed that the Japanese had, for some time, known about Ozaki, Sorge, and his other associates. Reportedly, certain top-level information was purposely given to Ozaki to pass on to Sorge and then Moscow—information Hirohito wanted Stalin to possess, mostly intelligence that would assure Stalin that Japan had no military aims toward the Soviet Union. In this way, Hirohito allegedly kept Japan out of war with Russia and was thus able to concentrate his military resources for his strike through China and later across the Pacific.

Sorge, for his part, played down Lyushkov's defection, minimizing the worth of his information regarding Soviet military installations, likening the general's information to that of émigrés leaving Germany and then writing books condemning the Nazi regime. His German Embassy contacts seemed to agree with him but Japanese officials showed no response to Sorge's remarks. The Japanese, through a special envoy, Yosuke Matsuoka, conducted secret meetings with the Soviets and, to the surprise of all, signed a neutrality pact with Russia on April 13, 1939. The agreement, drafted within twenty-four hours, guaranteed the frontiers and borders of the two powers.

The Germans, Sorge quickly learned, were in shock, particularly since Hitler had been planning an attack on Russia and expected Japan to attack the Soviets in the east. Because of his special standing with the German Embassy in Tokyo, Sorge was privy to top-secret German plans and all that the Germans knew about Japan's military and political movements. Also, through Ozaki, who had a link to Japan's Prime Minister, Prince Konoye, almost all top-secret plans of the Japanese fell into Sorge's hands. Sorge himself was used by his close friend, Ambassador Ott, as a special envoy to China to confer with German and Japanese officials there, learning the aims of both.

Sorge was then in a position to supply Moscow with advance notice of impending events of great importance to the Soviets. He obtained a clause-by-clause copy of what was later known as the Anti-Comintern Pact between Germany, Italy, and Japan, sent by Sorge to Moscow six weeks before the pact was signed. Sorge notified Moscow of Japan's full-scale attack on China five weeks before the attack. Sorge, through his contacts in the German Embassy, learned several weeks in advance of Hitler's impending attack on the Soviet Union in 1941 and warned the Fourth Bureau of this plan. In this instance, Joseph Stalin, much to Sorge's surprise, shock, and anger, remained passive, taking no precaution.

The Soviets had signed a nonaggression pact with Germany two years earlier and it may have been that Stalin simply did not believe Sorge's report. He had received a similar warning from British intelligence but also ignored this report.

Sorge was furious at Stalin, asking associates: "Why does he not react?" When German Panzer divisions roared into Russia, conquering hundreds of miles of territory within days, Sorge sank into deep depression. His mistress, Miyake, found him weeping in his study, which was crammed with thousands of books on Japan and the Far East. He was inconsolable and wept uncontrollably for hours on end. When she asked him why he was weeping, Sorge replied: "Because I am lonely. I have no real friends."

"But surely you have Ambassador Ott and other good German friends."

"No, no," sobbed Sorge. "They are not my real friends."

In this rare view of Richard Sorge, his utter desolation and seemingly intolerable loneliness symbolized the empty lifestyle of even the most accomplished of spymasters. Sorge, nevertheless, continued to supply Moscow with priceless espionage intelligence. His reports allayed the worst Soviet fears that Japan would strike in the east and Russia would be compelled to fight on two fronts, the possibility of which would surely cause the collapse of its Communist state. Sorge emphasized to Moscow that the Japanese had no intention of attacking Russia, that its armies were preoccupied with China, and its fleet was in the south, intent on overrunning the Pacific. He notified Moscow some time in advance of Japan's move against French Indo-China and pointed out that relations between the U.S. and Japan were worsening, ever since the U.S. attempted to mediate a peace settlement between China and Japan.

Sorge also emphasized that the U.S., not the Soviet Union, would be Japan's next major target. He followed this report with a message in which he stated that though millions of troops had been mobilized, the Japanese Army had sent only fifteen divisions to the north to protect the borders, certainly far from the invasion force the Soviets expected. Of equal importance was information Ozaki obtained for Sorge regarding the true aims of the Japanese in the Pacific. Its largest fleet, including four of its first-line aircraft carriers, was preparing in the fall of 1941 a circuitous route that would undoubtedly take it through northern waters and within several hundred miles of Hawaii.

This was, as Sorge knew, the hub of U.S. naval operations, headquartered in Pearl Harbor. Sorge wrote a lengthy memo for Moscow in which he described the Japanese Navy preparations, and, although he did not have evidence which specified the exact target of the fleet, Sorge himself reasoned that the attack by the Japanese would be made in the early part of December 1941 and that it would be against Honolulu and Pearl Harbor. He sent this message to Moscow but, as was the case with his warning of Hitler's impending attack against Russia, the Pearl Harbor warning was not acted upon. Stalin did not take the trouble to inform the U.S., his ally.

A short time later the most effective spy ring in the Far East was dismantled because of a routine police sweep of Japanese Communists. On September 28, 1941, an elderly seamstress named Tomo Kitabayashi was picked up by local police checking members of the disorganized Communist Party. She was grilled about those who had rented rooms from her and the old woman blurted every name she could remember, including that of a young man born in Okinawa and studying in the U.S., Yotoku Miyagi.

Richard Sorge in Japan, shortly before he was arrested in 1941 and charged with espionage; he was hanged in 1944.

It took the police more than a week to locate Miyagi. They burst into his home on October 11, 1941, and began a thorough search. Detectives found a confidential memo written on the stationery of the South Manchurian Railway, one which bore the signature of Hotsumi Ozaki. What was a painter doing with such a memo, police asked Miyagi. He refused to answer any questions. Miyagi was interrogated and beaten but he kept silent. At one point, in an effort to commit suicide, Miyagi leaped from a chair and dashed to a second-story window, hurling himself through it. A tree beneath the window, however, softened his fall and he only succeeded in breaking his leg.

Questioning of Miyagi began again the next day and this time he broke, offering a "voluntary statement." He said he belonged to a Communist spy ring controlled by Richard Sorge and other members, including Kawai, Ozaki, Vukelic, and Klausen. Realizing that important people were involved in Miyagi's confession, the police took the matter to the Foreign Section of the Higher Police (or Kempei Tai) in Tokyo. Officials there, however, refused at first to accept Miyagi's statements. Sorge was a high-level adviser to none other than the German Ambassador, General Ott. If he was arrested, they concluded, even for routine questioning, German-Japanese relations might be severely endangered.

It was decided to leave the Europeans in the so-called ring alone for the time being. The Japanese were another matter. Ozaki was arrested on October 14, 1941. Despite his high standing with Prime Minister Konoye, Ozaki was severely beaten and questioned. He eventually affirmed all of Miyagi's

statements, implicating Sorge, Vukelic, Klausen, and Kawai. It was then decided that the Europeans would be arrested. Before police closed in, Sorge met with Vukelic and Klausen. He told them that Miyagi and Ozaki had failed to appear several times at pre-arranged rendezvous. They called the homes and offices of Miyagi and Ozaki and got no answers. Sorge properly concluded in a despondent voice: "They must have been arrested by the police."

A few days later Sorge sent his last message to Moscow, one which Sorge thought to be the exact date of the Japanese attack against Hawaii. The last coded message was deciphered in Moscow and read: "Japanese carrier force attacking United States Navy at Pearl Harbor, probably dawn, 6th November." He also added in the same message that his ring had been compromised and that he was disbanding the group, advising them to save themselves as best they could.

Sorge did not make preparations to flee Japan. He adopted a fatalistic attitude and went about his usual routine, having breakfast with Ambassador Ott, working on a few stories during the day, and then, after a nap, enjoying Tokyo's nightlife. His home became an eyesore. Inside his small house books and papers were scattered about on the floor. Spilled whiskey was everywhere and gave a strong stench to the rooms. Outside, the debris piled up so that the neighbors took to complaining. Sorge was physically and mentally deteriorating as he awaited his own arrest.

It came a little before dawn on October 18, 1941. After enjoying another night on the town, Sorge was driven home in a German Embassy car. Outside his house lurked Detective Hideo Ohashi and several policemen and Kempei Tai officials. Ohashi waited patiently for the car to drive away, not wishing to embarrass German officials. As soon as the car disappeared, Ohashi and others broke down the door to Sorge's house. They found the master spy in his living room. He was wearing pajamas and had just taken a stiff drink of whiskey.

Two policemen shoved him, still pajama-clad, into a police car waiting outside. He was first driven to the local police station but then moved within minutes to Sugamo Prison. Klausen and Vukelic were picked up within an hour and also taken to the prison. Klausen had apparently absorbed Sorge's fatalism. He had become sloppy, leaving no less than ten uncoded messages for Moscow in plain sight on his desk. He had also made no attempt to conceal his equipment. Vukelic, along with Sorge, had also left incriminating evidence everywhere in his home and office.

Upon hearing the news of Sorge's arrest, none of his Japanese and German friends believed for a minute that he was a spy. General Ott, though shocked, told Japanese officials that Sorge was certainly the victim of some anti-German plot on the part of "ill-tempered Japanese." He emphasized that Sorge was a trusted member of the Nazi Party and one who was entrusted with "the most sensitive" documents in the German Embassy.

Klausen was adamant in his denials until he was tortured. He broke down and fully implicated Sorge, Ozaki, and the others. Vukelic, however, who had been a Russian officer, refused to admit anything. He was brutally tortured and still he resisted implicating anyone. Vukelic, after a brief trial, was given a life sentence. Klausen, who cooperated, was also given a life term. His wife, Ann Klausen, who had served the ring as a courier, received a three-year prison term.

Historically, criminal and state trials in Japan were held in secret and this was the case with Sorge and his accomplices. Little was heard of the case by outsiders, except that Sorge and his associates had been compelled to write out their confessions in autobiographical form. Sorge had actually resisted the tortures of his Japanese interrogators for six days until he confessed. His detailed confession was in excess of 50,000 words, the size of a small book, which he took pains to write over several years.

On November 7, 1944, the Governor of Sugamo Prison entered Sorge's cell. Both men ceremoniously bowed to each other. The Governor then told Sorge that he would be executed within the hour. Sorge said nothing. He changed into new, clean clothing provided for him. He was then handcuffed and a tall straw hat, which covered his entire head, was placed on his head. He was then led out of his cell, down a corridor, and out into a prison courtyard, taken to a tall concrete building. Here a prison chaplain offered Sorge tea and cakes and asked if he had any last requests. He had none. The chaplain then asked if Sorge had any last statements to make.

"No, none," Sorge replied in a low voice. Thanking the prison officials and chaplain for their kindness to him, Sorge was then led into another room, where a gallows waited. A half hour earlier, Sorge knew, Ozaki had been hanged from these very gallows. Sorge was placed on the trapdoor and a noose was tightened about his neck. At 10:20 A.M. the trapdoor slammed open and Sorge dropped into space. At 10:36 A.M., a prison doctor examined the swinging corpse and pronounced Dr. Richard Sorge dead.

Moscow showed its gratitude for Sorge's service with utter silence. It refused to admit that he had ever worked for the Soviet Union, let alone had served as its most spectacular spymaster and a large contributor to their victory over Germany. In 1964, however, the Kremlin suddenly announced that Richard Sorge had been declared a Hero of the Soviet Union. In the following year, the Soviets placed Sorge's image on a postage stamp, which is now a much sought-after item of philately.

[ALSO SEE: *Abwehr; Morris Cohen; Eastern Jewel; Gestapo; GRU; Vernon Kell; Kempei Tai; Isaac Trebitsch Lincoln; Ruth Kuczynski; MI5; Walther Nicolai; NKVD; Red Orchestra; Special Branch*]

SOUSTELLE, JACQUES
Free French Spymaster in World War II ▪ (1912–)

SOUSTELLE WAS AN INTELLECTUAL AND AN ARCHEOLOgist who went to London to join Charles de Gaulle and his Free French forces during World War II. In 1944, he assumed command of de Gaulle's intelligence operations in Algiers. He remained in Algeria following the war and rose to the rank of Governor-General.

Resistance to Algeria's becoming independent was widespread among French settlers and army officers and Soustelle joined the conspiracy to prevent Algeria's separation from France. Largely because of this conspiracy, de Gaulle returned to power in France in 1958. Soustelle, who went underground in Paris, was sought by French intelligence as one of the ringleaders opposing Algerian independence (employing the motto "Algérie Française").

When French agents closed in on an apartment where Soustelle was hiding, he made a spectacular escape down a fire escape; he jumped into the trunk of a waiting car, which sped off as agents pursued in other cars. He managed to return to Algeria but his conspiracy was crushed when de Gaulle announced Algeria's independence. Soustelle returned to archeology and the academic life.

SOUTHER, GLEN MICHAEL (MIKHAIL YEVGENYEVICH ORLOV)
U.S. Spy for Soviets ▪ (1957–1989)

SOUTHER SERVED ON THE CARRIER *NIMITZ* BASED IN Norfolk, Virginia, from July 1976 to November 1978. He moved to the staff of the Sixth Fleet in Italy in 1979, and, in 1982, he transferred to the Naval Air Training Command on the Patuxent River in Maryland. In that year, Souther was honorably discharged with the rank of petty officer first class. He served in the Naval Reserve until May 1986, then vanished.

In late 1985, the Navy was rocked by an espionage ring conducted by John A. Walker, whose wife had informed on him. Hearing of this, Souther's brother-in-law remembered the 1981 incident where Souther's ex-wife had informed on him and felt that the woman's statements should be reconsidered by Navy investigators. The FBI suspected Souther of feeding KGB handlers information on satellite-surveillance programs while working in the Naval Reserve at Norfolk, Virginia.

He apparently knew that FBI agents were tailing him and had seen him rendezvous with KGB field agents. Exactly when Souther was recruited to the KGB is unknown but it was reported that he agreed to spy against the U.S. while on his Italian tour of duty.

Souther did not resurface until July 20, 1988, when he was profiled in a television program, "Camera on the World," which portrayed Souther living in Russia. During the fifty-minute program, Souther stated that he had defected to the Soviet Union because of the negative attitude toward Russia that had been drummed into him in the U.S. from childhood. He was disillusioned with American nuclear arms policies, he said, and added that he had discovered at an early age the works of revolutionary Russian poet Vladimir Mayakovsky, which inspired his admiration for the Soviet Union.

The defecting American was critical of American intelligence, condemning the many espionage missions in which he was involved, including the 1986 bombing raid on Libya, an attack aimed at the sponsor of international terrorism, Muammar Qaddafi. Souther inferred (rather naively) that the CIA had something to do with the Chernobyl nuclear accident in April 1986.

U.S. Naval intelligence minimized the damage that Souther had done through his spying activities. Precisely what information on spy satelllites he was able to turn over to his KGB handlers is not known. When his suicide was announced by Moscow in June 1989 in an obituary appearing in the Defense Ministry newspaper *Krasnaya Zveda*, Souther was referred to as Mikhail Orlov. The paper reported that "he had a short but full and brilliant life totally devoted to the struggle for removing the threat of nuclear war hanging over mankind and for a better life for ordinary people." The report added: "Over a long period he performed important special missions and made a major contribution to ensuring state security." The paper identified Souther as "a Soviet agent and KGB officer."

What makes the Soviet statements suspect is the fact that the KGB seldom if ever admits to any American spy being a Soviet agent, let alone "a KGB officer." It is quite possible that the hapless Souther was not a double agent but a triple agent, one who posed as a defector to gain access to Soviet intelligence, and, when the KGB learned of this, it simply arranged for Souther's mysterious death, then publicly claimed the defector as one of their own as a taunt to the CIA, as well as a hidden message stating that they, the Soviets, knew Souther was a plant all along. These are the deadly games played in espionage.

[ALSO SEE: *FBI; KGB; Muammar Qaddafi; John A. Walker*]

SPECIAL BRANCH
Counterespionage Division of Scotland Yard ▪ (1883–)

SCOTLAND YARD'S SPECIAL BRANCH CAME INTO EXIStence in 1883, when a detail of about a dozen men were assigned to combat an outbreak of Irish terrorism in London. The division was originally called the Irish Special Branch. Since that time, Special Branch has enlarged to a substantial force of detectives and security personnel (about 1,600 employees) who protect foreign dignitaries against would-be assassins and, most often, work with agents of British counterintelligence, MI5.

Since MI5 has no authority to make arrests, Special Branch agents accompany British counterintelligence agents in such matters, arresting suspects and appearing in court in support of espionage charges. (Only rarely do representatives of MI5 make court appearances in such trials.) In this way, Special Branch serves as a shield or screen against media probes into MI5 activities.

In addition to working with MI5, Special Branch works closely with MI6 (SIS) in Europe, often having its agents infiltrate Irish terrorist organizations. In 1910–1911, Special Branch, as well as the Metropolitan Police and the then Home Secretary, Winston Churchill, were severely criticized for the way they handled a small group of lethal anarchists, led by the notorious Peter the Painter. This group of mostly Russian refugees had fled the clutches of the czar's secret police, the Okhrana, going to London, where they committed a series of burglaries.

Several of the anarchists were captured but two of them, Fritz Svaars and Jacob Vogel, were trapped on January 1, 1911, by Special Branch officers at 100 Sidney Street, a London tenement building. The fierce shootout resulted in Churchill ordering more than 200 officers and a Scots Guard troop to the scene. Churchill himself could not resist the impulse to slip into the area to witness the gunfight, a rarity in the annals of British crime, and one that became famous as "The Siege of Sidney Street." The two anarchists battled the British host to a standstill until the building caught fire and burned down. Svaars committed suicide in the flames and Vogel, wounded, was finally captured.

During World War I, Special Branch became famous for its close cooperation with Vernon Kell's MI5 and its prompt and widespread arrests of virtually all of the German spy networks that had been been secretly established in England by Gustav Steinhauer and Walther Nicolai and his deputies at the German Abwehr. Thus erstwhile agents such as Karl Ernst and Karl Lody fell into its hands. So, too, did the German spymaster Franz Rintelen, who had sabotaged shipping in the U.S. and was hauled off a liner bound for

Holland after he had been identified by codebreakers working under the direction of William Reginald Hall at British naval intelligence in the famous Room 40.

During these years, Special Branch was headed by Basil Thomson, one of the greatest spy catchers of them all. It was to Thomson that the scheming Mata Hari went for an interview to see if she was suspected of being a German agent. He advised her to quit espionage and save her life, but Mata Hari ignored him and went on her adventurous way to more spying and a date with a French firing squad in 1917.

The detection of German agents by MI5 and their surveillance and arrests in World War I, led by Special Branch's chief, the indefatigable Basil Thomson, eliminated dozens of dangerous German spies from sending vital information to Germany and occurred just after World War I began, although one celebrated German agent, Julius Silber, operated freely as an independent Abwehr spy in the British Postal Censorship Office throughout the war and was never detected.

Special Branch repeated its astounding achievements of World War I during World War II when it worked hand-in-glove with MI5 to capture and "turn" almost every German spy planted in England. Agents from Special Branch tracked down and arrested the Abwehr spies of Admiral Canaris and Walter Schellenberg throughout the British Isles, nabbing the ubiquitous Arthur Owens, a mean-minded Welshman whose Abwehr cover name was "Johnny," and the misguided German saboteur Karel Richard Richter. It also caught an American named Tyler Kent who worked in the American Embassy and who stole the top-secret correspondence between Roosevelt and Churchill, turning this over to the Nazis at the beginning of World War II.

In more recent times, Special Branch, led by such strong-willed men as Leonard Burt and Guy Liddell, has played a vital role with MI5 in arresting scores of Soviet agents during the Cold War, including A-bomb scientists Klaus Fuchs and Allan Nunn May, Gordon Lonsdale, Peter and Helen Kroger, Harry Houghton and Ethel Gee, Frank Clifton Bossard, and William Martin Marshall.

It has also pursued and captured agents who spied for Iraq (Percy Allen), for South Africa (Helen Keenan), and other nations, friendly and unfriendly toward England. Its agents also labored through the mire of what became known as the Profumo Affair. One of Special Branch's greatest assets is its ability to identify suspected spies from its research files which are kept up-to-date and supplemented by information shared between the FBI, Interpol, and other criminal justice and intelligence agencies.

Any person suspected of espionage is checked through Special Branch's files, as well as that of MI5, before the person is politely interviewed by Special Branch agents. This was the procedure in 1929 when the greatest spy of the twentieth century, Richard Sorge, was interviewed by agents of Special Branch. This was at a time long before Sorge had established his Soviet spy network in Japan. The experience so unnerved this most secretive of men that he blurted to a friend: "England knows more about spying than any other country," a singular tribute, no doubt to MI5 and its brother agency, Special Branch.

[ALSO SEE: *Abwehr; Wilhelm Canaris; Karl Ernst; Klaus Fuchs; William Reginald Hall; Harry Houghton; Helen Keenan; Vernon Kell; Tyler Kent; Peter and Helen Kroger; Guy Liddell; Karl Lody; Gordon Lonsdale; Mata Hari; Allan Nunn May; MI5; MI6; Walther Nicolai; Arthur Owens; Karel Richard Richter; Franz Rintelen; Room 40; Walter Schellenberg; Julius Silber; SIS; Richard Sorge; Basil Thomson*]

STANDEN, ANTHONY
English Agent in Elizabethan Era ▪ (1548?–1601?)

STANDEN WAS A MEMBER OF THE COURT OF THE duke of Tuscany, from which he sent secret reports to Francis Walsingham, spymaster for Queen Elizabeth I. The reports from Tuscany were so detailed and informative that Walsingham asked Standen to establish spy networks in Spain and France. This he did, employing spies in the French and Spanish courts and gathering information about those who were conspiring to replace Elizabeth with her sister, Mary, Queen of Scots.

Elizabeth plotted with Walsingham to forge documents that made Mary, then her prisoner, guilty of conspiring to dethrone her, using this as an excuse to have Mary executed. Philip II of Spain, Standen learned, was so incensed by the execution that he vowed to avenge Mary's death by sending an armada against England. In 1587, Standen learned from his spy in the Spanish court the exact plans for the armada and sent this on to Walsingham.

In the following year, Standen went to Spain and organized a network of spies along the Spanish and French coasts that reported on the sailing of the armada, its number of ships, and troop transports. Though a fierce storm destroyed a number of the Spanish ships, much of the armada was intact when the British fleet met it and, using the information Standen and his agents had supplied, defeated the Spanish fleet.

[ALSO SEE: *Francis Walsingham*]

STASHINSKY, BOGDAN
Soviet Spy & SMERSH Assassin ■ (1931–)

BORN ON NOVEMBER 4, 1931, IN BORSHTSHEVICE, near Lvov in the Polish Ukraine, Stashinsky grew up in turmoil. Following the non-aggression pact signed by Hitler and Stalin in 1939, Stashinky's province was absorbed by Russia and the Soviets began to indoctrinate inhabitants with communism. Then the Nazis overran the province in 1941 and imposed their own dreaded policies. In 1944, the Russians battled the Germans out of the region and reimposed their own savage regime.

Stashinsky was a student-teacher in 1950 when he was arrested for traveling on a train without a ticket in the Ukraine. He was taken to the offices of the Transport Police. There, a KGB officer, Konstantine Sitnikovsky, told him that he would not be prosecuted if he turned informant on those Ukrainians who expressed anti-Communist opinions.

The KGB officer, for some time, had had agents observing Stashinsky and his family and knew that his relatives were members of the Organization of Ukrainian Nationalists, which was staunchly anti-Soviet. Sitnikovsky proposed that Stashinsky spy on OUN members and report their activities. In return, the KGB officer promised that Stashinsky's family would be protected. Stashinsky complied, performing so well that he was recruited into the KGB as an agent (he later said he was ordered to become a Soviet spy).

In 1953, Stashinsky was sent to Kiev for extensive KGB espionage training, including language courses in German. He was then sent to East Germany in 1954, where he served the Soviets as a counterspy (informant) in East Berlin and a courier, carrying documents and photos stolen in West Berlin. Using the cover name of Josef Lehmann (his false passport indentified his background as Polish/German), he carried money and coded messages to KGB agents in West and East Berlin, as well as seeking out and identifying to his KGB handlers all OUN émigrés who were living in West Germany.

So effective was Stashinsky that he was recalled to Moscow and inducted into the special KGB division called SMERSH ("Death to All Spies!"). He accepted his new role of professional assassin without reservations. His first assignment was to assassinate Dr. Lev Rebet, leader of the OUN in West Germany.

By September 1957, Stashinsky went to Karlshorst, where SMERSH maintained headquarters, and was told how to murder Rebet. SMERSH had developed a special weapon for the job, a metal tube as thick as a finger, about seven inches in length, divided into three sections that screwed together. At one end was a fixed firing pin that released when a spring was pressed. Once released, the pin detonated a tiny percussion cap that moved a metal lever in the middle section, crushing a glass ampoule in the upper section, which contained cyanide gas. The poison shot from the mouth of the tube in the form of vapor. The released gas, fired into a victim's face from a distance of one and a half feet, caused the victim's arteries to contract, and brought death within minutes. In a few more minutes the arteries would expand to normal size so that there would be no trace of the cyanide. Any physician examining the victim would conclude that he had died from heart failure.

There was a small problem in using the newly developed murder weapon, Stashinsky was told. It might also kill the user. The gas might blow back upon the killer and most likely cause a fatal cardiac arrest. To prevent his own death, Stashinsky was given nerve pills, anti-gas pills, and a poison antidote. He was told to take one of each of the pills and the antidote immediately after pulling the trigger on the tube. The anti-gas pill contained sodium thiosulphate and amyl nitrate.

A SMERSH handler then cautioned Stashinsky to kill his victim in a lonely place but "if a third person appears immediately after the attack, you must pretend to go to the victim's aid. On no account try to run for it. Nobody will recognize it as murder. After pretending to help, disappear from the scene as unobtrusively as possible." Since SMERSH researchers diligently studied murder methods the world over it is not coincidental that its instructions on the methods of murder and the conduct of killers was almost identical to that practiced by the Sicilian Mafia or the Neopolitan Camorra. These secret criminal societies

Ukrainian leader-in-exile Lev Rebet, executed by SMERSH assassin Bogdan Stashinsky with an insidious gas pellet gun.

Stefan Bandera, another murder victim who died at the hands of Bogdan Stashinsky.

invariably sent motiveless strangers to kill victims and their sinister chiefs always cautioned them, if others came upon the murder scene, to "pretend to be shocked at discovering the body, and never run because if you run, someone runs after you."

On October 9, 1957, Stashinsky was given £200 in expense money and a tin of frankfurter sausages. The weapon was packed inside the tin. He then flew to Munich, where he took a room in the Stachus Hotel. He removed the gas weapon from the tin of frankfurters, assembled it, and rolled it into a newspaper. He then began haunting Rebet's offices at 8 Karlplatz. On the morning of October 12, 1957, Stashinsky, knowning Rebet's punctual habits, went to the office building where Rebet arrived every morning precisely at 9:30 A.M. and positioned himself on a landing above a flight of stairs in the building. He took his protective pills and waited.

A few seconds later, Rebet arrived on time and began walking up the stairs to his office. Stashinsky began walking down. As they passed, the assassin lifted the rolled-up newspaper to an angle where its opening was level with the victim's face. He fired the gas weapon. The vapor caught Rebet square in the face but he seemed not to notice it and continued up the stairs. Within a few more steps, Rebet stoppped, slumped against the wall, clawed at the air, then fell dead.

Stashinsky walked down the stairs, slipping the rolled-up newspaper into his pocket. He walked to a bridge and dropped the weapon into the water. He waited for about a half hour, then returned to 8 Karlplatz, where a group of people were standing,

along with police officers. He confirmed that Rebet was dead, then checked out of his hotel, and boarded a Pan Am flight back to Berlin. Rebet's body underwent a post-mortem examination, where physicians determined his death was from "natural causes."

OUN leader Stefan Bandera was then selected as the next victim of Stashinsky's gas gun. In January 1959, the assassin returned to Munich under the alias of Hans Budeit. He scouted about the city for Bandera, who was known to the Soviets to be in hiding, using the cover name Stefan Popel.

The killer found his victim simply by looking through the telephone book. Bandera's phone and address was listed under the name Stefan Popel. Stashinsky then went to Bandera's home and kept him under surveillance, marking down his daily routines, before returning to Moscow, where he reported his findings to SMERSH chief Gregory Aksentyevich. Stashinsky was taken into an office by Aksentyevich and shown a "murder kit" which SMERSH had assembled for him. It contained a skeleton key with four interchangeable parts, ten anti-poison tablets, ten gas ampoules and an improved gas weapon which was double-barreled.

Returning to Munich, Stashinsky stayed at the Hotel Schottenhamel, dogging Bandera's steps. He prepared to attack his next victim as Bandera parked his car, but lost his will to murder. He went to a woods where he fired off both barrels of the gas gun, then threw it into a river. Stashinsky later stated: "When I saw Bandera standing in the garage I became conscious of the fact that in a few minutes he would no longer be alive, and that he had done nothing against me personally. My assignment was obscured by purely humane considerations."

Stashinsky returned to Moscow, saying that he had lost the gas gun in transit. His SMERSH handlers merely gave him another and ordered him back to Munich, telling him that while he was there he was not only to murder Bandera but also kill Yaroslav Stetsko, another OUN leader. When he dutifully returned to Munich, Stashinsky waited for Bandera to return home on the afternoon of October 15, 1957. He used one of the skeleton keys to let himself into Bandera's apartment building and waited for him at the head of the stairs, timing his entry with Bandera's arrival.

While his victim was parking his car, Stashinsky heard footsteps on the landing above and he went down the stairs to the main lobby, where he pushed the button for the elevator, pretending to wait for it. He turned his back to the woman who passed him on her way out. Bandera then entered the small lobby and Stashinsky was pleased to see that his arms were loaded with groceries, making him defenseless. He knew that Bandera carried a gun in a shoulder holster. There was no chance of his victim reaching for the gun with his arms full of grocery bags.

Bandera's key was still in the lock, stuck, as the victim struggled with his groceries and tried to pull it out. Boldly, Stashinsky walked up to him and said: "Isn't it working?"

Without looking at Stashinsky, Bandera pulled the key free, saying: "Yes, I think it's all right."

With that Stashinsky held up a rolled-up newspaper and fired the two barrels of the gas gun into Bandera's face. In seconds the victim gasped, dropped the groceries, and then fell to the floor dead. Stashinsky left the building and made his escape but inhabitants entering the building saw him leaving just before discovering the body in the lobby. Stashinsky then sent a coded message to Moscow which read: "I have met the person in question and the greeting was satisfactory."

This time, however, a post-mortem examination, which was quickly conducted after the discovery of Bandera's body, revealed the presence of cyanide in the stomach. Still, his death was attributed to "causes unknown." By then Stashinsky was en route to Russia and, once he arrived in Moscow, he was again hailed as a hero by his SMERSH bosses. On December 4, 1959, KGB director Alexander Shelepin awarded him the Order of the Red Banner "for successfully contributing to the solution of an important problem."

SMERSH then began planning the next assignment for its top assassin. Stashinsky, however, had other plans. After killing Rebet, he had met and married an East German woman, Inge Pohl. To her he confided his real work for the KGB. He told her that the murders he had committed sickened him and, encouraged by her, he began to make plans to defect in 1960. Pregnant, she personally pleaded with her husband's SMERSH bosses to allow her to return to her parents' home in East Berlin, where she would have her child. She was allowed to leave Moscow and a son was born to her in March 1961. The child died on August 9, 1961, and Stashinsky asked for leave to visit his grief-stricken wife in East Berlin.

The assassin was permitted to go to East Berlin but he was shadowed constantly and even his bedroom was bugged. However, during the baby's funeral on August 12, 1961, in a cemetery close to West Berlin, Stashinsky and his wife, along with his wife's 16-year-old brother, managed to slip away from the funeral services and make good their escape. First they ran on foot to Falkensee, a few miles outside of Berlin. Then they took an East Berlin taxi into the American Zone of West Berlin, where Stashinsky immediately surrendered to American officials. Ironically, had the Stashinskys delayed their escape by one day, they would most likely have been cut off from the West. About twenty-four hours after they arrived in West Berlin, the Berlin Wall went up (on the night of August 13–14, 1961).

Stashinsky was placed on trial for the murders of Rebet and others and helped to convict himself by supplying incontrovertible evidence that he had been the assassin. He was sentenced to eight years hard labor. His revelations in a Karlsruhe courtroom in December 1961 shocked the world, which had come to believe that SMERSH had long ago been dismantled by the Soviets.

Stashinsky served only a few years before being released, reportedly to aid the CIA and other intelligence agencies in solving other SMERSH killings and to blueprint the methods and operations of the murder division of the KGB. He was given an alias and a job and settled down in West Germany. The Soviets said nothing. A KGB officer later told a visiting Western diplomat: "We shall get Stashinsky sooner or later." To this date, they have not found their favorite assassin.

[ALSO SEE: CIA; KGB; SMERSH]

STEPHENSON, WILLIAM SAMUEL
British Spymaster in World War II ■ (1896–1989)

ONE OF ENGLAND'S MOST ASTUTE SPYMASTERS, William Stephenson was many times a hero before he became the U.S. coordinator of SIS-OSS operations in New York in World War II.

Born January 11, 1896, in Point Douglas, Manitoba, near Winnipeg, Stephenson, as a youth, was fascinated by inventions and experimented with electricity, steam engines, crude airplanes, and wireless sets. He was a student of Morse code and learned to send like an expert before he graduated high school in 1914, the year in which England went to war. Stephenson joined the Royal Canadian Engineers and was sent to France. In 1915 he was commissioned a lieutenant and, in another year of war, he was promoted to captain. Gassed twice, Stephenson was sent to England to recuperate.

Stephenson instead volunteered for the Royal Flying Corps, took a demotion to lieutenant, and joined the 73 Squadron. He took several "suicide" missions, flying low over German territory to observe heavy concentrations of troops. He also attacked large forces of German ground troops and transports, winning the Distinguished Flying Cross. He later won the Military Cross for similar action. In all, Stephenson was credited with shooting down twenty-six German aircraft and added the French Legion of Honor and Croix de Guerre with Palm to his collection of medals.

In one action in 1918, Stephenson was shot down and captured behind enemy lines. He escaped within a few months, turning in a detailed report on the prison camp where he had been held. This report reached William Reginald Hall, head of British naval intelligence, who kept in contact with Stephenson during the 1920s and 1930s. During the time, Stephenson built up his father's business and invested in other enterprises that made him a multimillionaire. Ironically, he made most of his money on an ingenious can-opener he filched in the German prison camp, one which he took with him when he escaped. He learned that the can-opener had been patented only in Germany. In 1920, he adapted the can-opener, taking out worldwide patents on it, and it reaped him a fortune. He also began manufacturing radios, phonographs, cars, and airplanes, as well as investing in steel manufacturing.

He married Mary Simmons and traveled throughout Europe in the 1920s and 1930s, watching closely the rise of the Nazis and Adolf Hitler. He shared his findings with the British intelligence community. Offering his services to British intelligence, Stephenson became involved in espionage as a private citizen and was instrumental in learning about the German intentions to develop heavy water in Norway as part of creating atomic bombs.

At the beginning of World War II, Stephenson was named head of SIS (MI6) operations in the U.S., his job being to work closely with the newly formed American intelligence service, OSS, which was headed by William J. Donovan.

Establishing his headquarters in New York under the guise of a British business, Stephenson actually headed the BSC, British Security Coordination, which was located in Room 3603 in the RCA Building. He worked with Allen Dulles and with Donovan, who was headquartered in Washington, D.C., cementing American and British intelligence operations. Several SIS agents in the U.S. operated under Stephenson's direction, including the attractive and enterprising Amy Thorpe Pack, who successfully infiltrated the Vichy French Embassy in Washington to secure vital information for the Allies.

When America entered the war, Stephenson continued his coordinating work with the OSS but he also worked closely with its British counterpart, SOE (Special Operations Executive), which, like the OSS, sent agents, supplies, and weapons to underground resistance groups in Nazi-occupied Europe. Stephenson was knighted in 1946 for his work for British intelligence and, following World War II, he went into business with Donovan.

Stephenson bought a luxurious retreat in Jamaica and became an adviser on industrial development for Canada and other governments. He died in Paget, Bermuda, on January 31, 1989, at the age of ninety-three. Upon his death, the London *Times* reported that although Stephenson had been a genuine intelligence hero, much in his background had been that of his own invention. For instance, Stephenson claimed to have discovered and reported on Enigma, the encoding machine created by the Germans. There is no record of this in the annals of British intelligence.

Moreover, Stephenson claimed to have had close, secret associations with Winston Churchill and President Roosevelt during World War II and this also proved to be Stephenson's own invention. Churchill's private secretary, John Colville, stated that Stephenson's stories about his meetings with

British spymaster William Stephenson, a Canadian millionaire, shown in 1940 when he secretly established SIS offices in New York to work with American intelligence.

Churchill were "completely untrue, absolute nonsense." Stephenson's biographies, including the best-selling *A Man Called Intrepid*, were edited by him and he obviously and considerably tailored his own personal history.

[ALSO SEE: *William J. Donovan; Allen Dulles; OSS; MI6; Amy Thorpe Pack; SIS*]

STIEBER, WILHELM
German Spymaster ▪ (1818–1882)

ONE OF GERMANY'S MOST EFFICIENT AND SUCCESSFUL spymasters, Stieber was born in Meresburg, Saxony, on May 3, 1818. He entered Berlin University, studying theology in preparation for entering the Lutheran ministry, which was his father's wish. This ambition was not shared by Stieber, who abandoned theology for the study of law. He graduated with a law degree in 1841, at which time his father disowned him.

Undaunted, Stieber opened his own law practice as a criminal lawyer. He had, by then, learned much about criminals and criminal law. To finance his legal education he had worked endless hours as a clerk in

Germany's first great spymaster, Wilhelm Stieber, who began his career by "arranging" to save the life of Prussian King William Frederick.

criminal courts and police stations. Stieber's clients came from the lowest elements of German society—rapists, thieves, and killers. All were anti-government in attitude and they believed that Stieber shared their political views, never knowing that he was a monarchist to the marrow.

Stieber enjoyed fantastic success as a criminal lawyer, successfully defending more than 3,000 clients from 1845 to 1850. Most of his success was due to the fact that during these years Stieber worked secretly for the police as an *agent provocateur*. Through his clients he was able to identify scores of political radicals conspiring against the monarchy. He also edited the *Police Journal* in Berlin and through his contacts in law enforcement he was able to learn what kind of evidence would be brought against his clients and was expertly prepared to rebuff the arguments of prosecutors.

In 1848, King Frederick William of Prussia was suddenly surrounded by a hostile socialist crowd shouting threats against him. His guards were nowhere to be found. A man stepped from the crowd, approaching the petrified king, taking him by the arm and into a building where he bolted the door against the crowd. He introduced himself as Wilhelm Stieber.

The grateful king rewarded Stieber by appointing him chief of the Berlin criminal police, a position that he may have engineered for himself, for it was later claimed that the calculating Stieber had hired police informants to threaten the king so that he could appear his saviour. Two years later, the king asked Stieber to undertake a secret mission to London, where he was to spy on the activities of Karl Marx and other radical Germans living in England.

Using the cover name of Schmidt, Stieber posed as an editor of a radical publication, collecting the works of Marxists. He met many Communists and reportedly Marx himself and his secret report on their activities was later used in the first international Communist trials in Cologne in 1852. In that year, Stieber went to Paris, where he infiltrated radical circles and was able to learn the identities of radicals living in Germany. They were subsequently arrested.

Stieber's authority in Germany increased to the point where, next to the Kaiser, he was the most powerful man in the land. All that changed in 1858 when Frederick Willliam was pronounced insane and sent to an institution, his brother Wilhelm I assuming the throne. Kaiser Wilhelm disliked and distrusted Stieber. He accused him of abusing his powers and exercising extremely brutal interrogation methods in handling suspects. He was brought to trial but turned the tables on his enemies by utilizing an excuse that would later be uttered myriad times by Germans in World War I and World War II for endless offenses and atrocities: that he was only following orders, in this case, the direct orders of King Frederick William.

He was released and briefly resumed his post, immediately ordering the arrests of dozens of those involved in his trial. Kaiser Wilhelm then dismissed him from his post and ordered him to leave Berlin. Stieber went to St. Petersburg, where he was hired by the Russian Foreign Branch, which was in charge of all counterintelligence. The one-time German policeman instituted rigid systems that overhauled the service, as well as introduced the widespread use of informants, as well as double and even triple spies to ferret out anti-czarist radicals, a practice that the Okhrana would hone to perfection in the next forty years, developing such outrageous police spies as Yevno Azev and political malcontents as George Gapon.

In 1863, Stieber's fortunes again rose in Germany. In that year he met and befriended Otto von Bismarck, who was then German ambassador to Russia and who already appreciated the work of the spymaster. While Stieber worked for the Russians, he collected an enormous amount of secret information on Russia and sent this on to Berlin, in hopes that he might be reinstated by the Kaiser. Stieber warned Bismarck that an attempt would be made on his life and, after that abortive attempt was made, Bismarck, like William Frederick, became eternally grateful to the spymaster.

When Bismarck became chancellor, he named Stieber to head the Secret Security Police. The spymaster quickly and tirelessly worked to establish what he called the Central Intelligence Bureau, one that gathered mountains of information on radicals through a massive informant system. Bismarck then asked Stieber to obtain secret information in Austria, a country against whom the "Iron Chancellor" was plotting war. Stieber undertook the mission

Above, the battle of Sadowa on July 3, 1866, resulted in
an overwhelming victory of Prussia over Austria, thanks
to vital information provided by superspy Stieber.

Napoleon III of France (right), shown listening to the
humiliating terms dictated by Prussian Chancellor
Otto von Bismarck after the French defeat in the
Franco-Prussian War of 1870; Stieber's espionage
networks contributed greatly to the Prussian victory.

himself, driving a cart into Austria while disguised as
a peddler. He sold religious objects as well as porno-
graphic drawings. Many months later he returned to
Berlin to present Bismarck with detailed maps of all
Austrian fortifications and defenses, disposition and
supply lines of its armies, and a complete set of its
battle plans.

In 1866, Bismarck's legions, following Stieber's
maps and information, quickly defeated Austria's
forces. Stieber himself accompanied the invading
Germans as head of a new organization, the Field
Security Police, the first counterintelligence unit to
go into an enemy country. As such, it recorded the
identities of all those radicals who might later prove
military enemies of Germany.

When recalled to Berlin, Stieber became
Bismarck's right arm. He regained the Kaiser's favor
and became the chief of German counterintelligence,
a new area of intelligence. Stieber was the first to
inaugurate military censorship and disinformation,
spreading false propaganda that gave good news to
the homefront to bolster morale and news of disaster

through the camps of the enemy to demoralize its
fighting spirit.

Then there was a newly designated enemy.
Bismarck pointed to France and Stieber went diligently into that country, establishing the most
widespread spy network in espionage history. His
agents were disguised as businessmen, salesmen,
peddlers, priests, and tourists. They traveled through-

out France for several years, recording the populations of every town, and the military installations and defenses for each. They marked the placement of every farmhouse and counted the cattle in each pasture so that German officers later leading their troops through these areas would know exactly how many steers could be butchered to feed their men and how many houses were available to billet their troops.

More than 20,000 spies were on Stieber's payroll when Bismarck launched the Franco-Prussian War of 1870. Thanks to information provided by his spymaster, the troops of the Iron Chancellor took every key objective swiftly. More than 10,000 German spies were at Versailles when the French signed a humiliating peace treaty in January 1871.

Following the war, Stieber remained as chief of the Central Intelligence Bureau, continuing to support a small army of spies who reported on German aristocrats, bureaucrats, businessmen, and industrial leaders, many of whom being his personal enemies. He kept records on all of them and used these files to blackmail his foes into silence. He established the notorious Green House in Berlin, a fabulous bordello where all the women inmates were Stieber's agents, collecting information on important clients that they turned over to the spymaster.

Stieber was nevertheless a social pariah among the Junker class, the German high command, and the financial elite of Germany. Though despised, his influence was to be felt for a century to come in every espionage agency throughout the world. It was Stieber who employed spies by which he controlled the press, the banks, industry, and business. It was Stieber who invented sophisticated terrorism and blackmail for espionage use. It was Stieber who created psychological warfare, censorship, and women as bait to gain intelligence, an espionage game that he taught everyone to play unfairly.

[ALSO SEE: *Yevno Azev; George Gapon; Okhrana*]

SÛRETÉ-NATIONALE
French State Police • (1800s–)

SIMILAR TO THE SPECIAL BRANCH OF SCOTLAND YARD, the Sûreté is a state police agency which concentrates upon criminal investigation and arrest but it also works in close cooperation with French intelligence agencies in detecting terrorists and espionage agents operating in France. Sûreté agents have worked with DST (French counter-intelligence) in identifying terrorists, as well as SDECE, now DGSE, (French intelligence) in pinpointing foreign secret agents.

[ALSO SEE: *DST; SDECE; Special Branch*]

SZABO, VIOLETTE
British Agent in World War II • (1922–1944)

VIOLETTE BUSHELL WAS BORN AND RAISED IN PARIS, France, where her father, a British citizen, earned his living as a taxi driver. When her huband was killed fighting with the British at El Alamein, Violette Szabo volunteered for service with the SOE (Special Operations Executive), despite the fact that she had had a child, a little girl. Her qualifications were exceptional. Szabo spoke French fluently and she was a crack shot, so much so that she had been barred from every shooting gallery in London because she had won so many prizes.

SOE chief Maurice Buckminster remembered Szabo later as "really beautiful with a porcelain clarity of face." Black-haired with large, expressive dark eyes and high cheekbones, she looked very much like the latter-day actress Marta Toren. Selwyn Jepson, the SOE official who recruited Szabo, felt she would work well in France with the underground although he felt that the eagerness Szabo displayed in wanting to risk her life as an SOE agent might be symptomatic of many another spy with a suicidal urge, a psychological characteristic that often fit those who had just lost a loved one to the enemy.

Szabo nevertheless proved to be an excellent trainee, passing all of her espionage courses with flying colors. For her first mission, she was assigned to Philippe Liewer, a one-time correspondent for Havas news agency. She parachuted near Rouen with the specific assignment of determining the exact underground forces in that area. Szabo managed to locate the local resistance leaders in Rouen and set up communications between them and SOE in England. Her mission completed, she made her way to a secret airfield where she was to be picked up. En route she was twice arrested by rural French gendarmes but talked her way out and was released.

Picked up by a small British plane, Szabo returned to England, persistently requesting another mission. Her handlers were reluctant to send her back to France but relented when they were faced with a shortage of agents following the Normandy invasion. Szabo again parachuted behind German lines to make contact with a local *maquis* group. This she did, meeting with a resistance leader and giving him information he had to relay to other underground leaders in Paris. At that moment, however, a German patrol surrounded the farmhouse in which Szabo and the others were meeting.

As the *maquis* leader made his escape, Szabo gave him covering fire with a Sten gun, shooting several German soldiers who rushed the house. She was captured when her ammunition ran out and she was taken to Gestapo headquarters, where she was tortured, raped repeatedly, and kept naked and shivering in a damp cell. She told her interrogators nothing. She was finally ordered to be sent to Ravensbrück concentration camp. En route, according to F. F. E. Yeo-Thomas, another SOE agent who had been captured and was on the same train, Szabo, weak from torture and with another girl chained to her wrist, crawled the length of a train corridor to get water for other parched prisoners.

More torture followed at Ravensbrück but Szabo remained heroically silent and in the memories of those females who survived that camp, she proved to be the most courageous of them all. Her brutish German guards finally tired of getting no response to their exhaustive beatings and killed her. These savage guards were later tried and executed for the murder of Szabo and others.

On New Year's Day, 1947, a small, dark-haired little orphan girl, Tania Szabo, was escorted into a large office where several generals stood to attention. She was handed England's George Cross, awarded posthumously to her mother, for valor of the highest order. Violette Szabo's story was later told in the film *Carve Her Name with Pride*.

[ALSO SEE: *SOE; F. F. E. Yeo-Thomas*]

SZEK, ALEXANDER
British Spy in World War I ▪ (1886–1915)

AT THE BEGINNING OF WORLD WAR I, REGINALD Hall, head of British cryptoanalysis of naval intelligence, was told by his top code people in the Admiralty's Room 40 that strange signals were coming from a transmitter in German-occupied Brussels. Alfred Ewing, who headed the cryptography section in Room 40, worked on the coded signals for weeks but could not decipher the code.

The wireless transmitting station, another British agent reported a short time later, was operated by a young radio expert named Alexander Szek. When Hall heard the name he mumbled: "Szek, Szek, that doesn't sound like a German name."

Working with Vernon Kell's MI5, Hall was able to learn that Szek was an Austrian but had been born in Croydon, in south London, a fact unknown to the Germans. Many of his relatives were still living in England, including the radio operator's father. Hall begged the old man to write his son a letter, asking him to work for his native land, England. The letter was taken to Holland and from there a British agent smuggled it into Belgium and delivered it to Szek.

Szek was nervous about stealing the German code book as the agent requested. The agent told him that if he refused, his family members might be imprisoned in England. He agreed.

Getting the diplomatic code book was impossible, or even a copy of it. The book was kept by a German intelligence officer who used the book only when sending messages and, at such time, Szek had brief access to it. The British agent in Brussels suggested that the radio operator memorize the book a few lines at a time, write down the lines, and deliver these to him.

In early 1915 Szek began writing down a page of symbols from the book, delivering these by hand to his contact. As the weeks went by the young man appeared more and more nervous. The agent reported to Hall and his subordinate Henry Oliver that he believed Szek was about to have a nervous breakdown, so terrified was he of being detected. Szek begged the agent to have him smuggled to England but he was told that if this occurred the Germans might change the code, making their effort useless. Szek was insistent. On Oliver's orders, he was promised a safe passage to England after he delivered the last pages of the code book.

This was done, with Szek personally crossing the border into Holland to hand the final pages to Major Laurie Oppenheim, the British military attaché at The Hague, who, in turn, sent them on to Hall and Oliver. Szek was not taken to England, however, but asked to return to Brussels with the promise that he would be smuggled out a short time later.

Some weeks later Alexander Szek made a passage, not to England, but into death. He was found murdered in his Brussels room. One report had it that he had been killed by a burglar but there was little to steal from the young man. Then the British reported that the Germans had killed him. The truth was that Reginald Hall ordered that Szek be killed by British agents to prevent him from fleeing and thereby alerting the Germans to the possibility that he had stolen the only thing of value in his drab existence, the precious code book.

Henry Oliver supported this execution by later stating that he had paid £1,000 for a contract killing. In his declining years, Oliver, who reached the rank of rear admiral, confided to British Navy Captain Stephen Roskill that "I paid £1,000 to have that man shot." To British naval intelligence at the time it was a small price to pay for such valuable information.

As events proved only a few months later in 1915, however, the British obtained the same diplomatic code and much more. Wilhelm Wassmuss, an Arabian adventurer who served as the German vice-consul in Bushire, learning that British troops were almost at his doorstep, raced from his residence in his pyjamas, jumped onto a horse, and fled madly into the desert. He left behind all of the German diplomatic codes in a trunk, priceless information that found its way to Room 40 at the Admiralty office.

[ALSO SEE: *Reginald Hall; Vernon Kell; MI5; Room 40; Wilhelm Wassmuss*]

TAI LI
Nationalist Chinese Spymaster • (1895–1945)

THE BACKGROUND OF CHINESE SPYMASTER TAI LI IS uncertain, but he surfaced about 1925 as an ardent supporter of Nationalist leader Chiang Kai-shek. He was made head of Chiang's military police in Shanghai in 1927, where he quickly established a large network of spies, especially among the Chinese criminal element. By the early 1930s, he was able to identify many international spies operating in Shanghai, including the Japanese siren spy Eastern Jewel, Isaac Trebitsch Lincoln, an international spy who was then selling his information to the Japanese, and Richard Sorge (then using the name "Johnson"), whom Tai Li suspected of being a German agent when, in reality, he was a Soviet spy.

At the same time Tai Li was establishing his spy network, Mao Tse-tung's spymaster, K'ang Sheng, was creating a Communist espionage network in Shanghai. Tai Li knew of this organization but had difficulty penetrating its cells, let alone finding its leader. Tai Li's information on the Japanese, however, proved useful to Chiang Kai-shek, who promoted him as head of his intelligence service after Morris "Two-Gun" Cohen was captured and imprisoned by the Japanese in 1942.

During World War II, Tai Li worked closely with the American OSS and its chief, William J. Donovan. Both Chinese and American intelligence exchanged information that, by 1944, allowed Chiang to take the initiative. Because of Tai Li's information on the location of Japanese troops, as well as their shattered supply lines, he was able to strike effectively at the invaders and drive them out of southern China.

Following World War II, Donovan conferred with Tai Li about the threat of the Chinese Communists. Tai Li reported that his network knew everything about Mao's depleted forces and that they posed no threat to Chiang. In this he was completely wrong. A short time later, Tai Li was killed when his plane exploded in mid-flight, undoubtedly from a bomb planted by one of K'ang Sheng's agents.

[ALSO SEE: *Morris Cohen; William J. Donovan; Eastern Jewel; K'ang Sheng; Isaac Trebitsch Lincoln; OSS; Richard Sorge*]

TALLMADGE, BENJAMIN
American Spymaster in American Revolution • (1754–1835)

A NEW YORKER, TALLMADGE GRADUATED FROM YALE in 1773, and went to work for the Connecticut school system. When the Revolution broke out in 1775, he immediately volunteered as a member of that state's militia and was commissioned with the rank of lieutenant. He was promoted to the rank of captain in 1776 and a major the following year, distinguishing himself in the battles of White Plains, Long Island, Brandywine, Germantown, and Monmouth.

By 1778, Washington resolved to have an effective spy network. All of his secret agents before that time had proved brave but ineffectual like the unfortunate Nathan Hale, who had been hanged for his espionage by the British in 1776. He had had bad luck with those spies he had developed on his own, such as George Higday, who lived in British-occupied territory and who had offered to take messages from spies to Washington and even serve as a spy himself. Washington wrote to Tallmadge about this spy, but the letter was intercepted by the British, who were thus able to identify and arrest Higday on July 13, 1778.

The hapless Higday, a well-intentioned amateur, was typical of the agents working for Washington until he ordered Major Tallmadge to establish a reliable spy ring in New York City, which was then occupied by British forces under the command of General Clinton. Washington wanted intelligent, well-placed agents who knew what information would be of value to him.

Tallmadge knew just the right people to contact, his good friends Robert Townsend and Enoch Hale (Nathan Hale's brother), who had graduated from Yale with him in 1773, along with Austin Roe, Abraham Woodhull, and Caleb Brewster. This network of New York spies was known as the Culper Ring and Tallmadge directed it under the alias of John Bolton.

Almost at the same time, his opposite number in Clinton's army, John Andre (using the alias of John Anderson), was attempting to establish a network of spies inside the territory occupied by Washington's army at White Plains. It was really no match for the

Culper Ring, which quickly established the polished methods of professional spies. All of its members in New York operated with tight secrecy, each agent using an alias which was only known to Tallmadge. Woodhull used the alias Samuel Culper Sr., Townsend employed the name Samuel Culper Jr.

Townsend was the real leader of the Culper Ring, a successful businessman in New York who was thought by the British to be a loyalist. His mercantile business was ideally suited to conveying messages to Washington. His employees brought foodstuffs from Long Island farms into New York, pack trains operated by Austin Roe, who served as a courier for the network. Roe took Townsend's coded reports to Woodhull, who lived in Setauket, Long Island, on the shores of Long Island Sound.

After receiving Townsend's messages, Woodhull would hang a black petticoat on a clothesline. Brewster, a boatman, knew this signal meant Woodhull was safe to approach and had information to be picked up. The boatman would retrieve the message and take it to Enoch Hale or Tallmadge, who, in turn, presented the information to Washington. The group invented its own code, which became so complicated that they had to provide members with a "pocket dictionary" defining the espionage terms they employed.

Through the enterprising Townsend, Tallmadge was able to present Washington with an accurate, almost day-to-day report on British military operations and positions in New York, as well as Clinton's stores and military supplies, including information on all British shipping and the arrival of reinforcements.

In the fall of 1780, Tallmadge inadvertently became involved with Benedict Arnold's traitorous scheme to deliver West Point to the British. Arnold had been in communication with British intelligence chief Major John Andre and he had arranged to meet Andre behind American lines to prepare for the seizure of the American bastion. Knowing Tallmadge might intercept Andre, he boldly wrote to Washington's spymaster: "If Mr. John Anderson, a person I expect from New York, should come to your quarters, I have to request that you will give him an escort of two horsemen to bring him on his way to this place, and send an express to me, that I may meet him. If your business will permit, I wish you to come with him."

John Anderson was the alias used by Andre as he made his way through the American lines. Andre went up the Hudson in an armed British sloop, met with Arnold, and then, when attempting to return to the British lines, foolishly changed from his military uniform into civilian clothes. He was stopped while riding alone by three American soldiers, who took him to their commanding officer. He was turned over to Tallmadge on September 26, 1780. Instead of sending Anderson on to Arnold, Tallmadge had the prisoner searched and the plans for West Point were found in Andre's boots. Almost at the same time, Tallmadge received a coded message from Townsend through the Cupler Ring courier system that he should be on the lookout for a "John Anderson," who was none other than the British spymaster John Andre.

Concluding that Arnold had turned traitor, Tallmadge escorted Andre to Washington, who refused to see the British officer. Andre was imprisoned, charged with being a spy. A military tribunal sentenced him to death and he was hanged on October 2, 1780. Tallmadge accompanied Andre to the gallows, full of admiration for the brave British soldier who fearlessly accepted his fate.

Tallmadge attempted to overtake Arnold, but Arnold had learned of Andre's capture and had successfully escaped to the British lines to live out his life in misery.

When Tallmadge's master spy Townsend heard of Andre's death, he closed his store for several weeks, telling his agents to cease their operations. He feared that the British might somehow, through Arnold, expose the Culper Ring. His fears were groundless and he was soon back in operation, sending Tallmadge vital information.

Arnold, however, was not finished with his deviltry. As part of his bargain with General Clinton, he was made a brigadier in the British army with specific instructions to convince revolutionary leaders and their men to desert Washington and come over to the British side. He did manage to persuade some turncoats to join him but these were ragtag opportunists and mercenaries. Cleverly, Arnold then wrote a letter to Tallmadge, a man he did not know well, asking him to abandon the American cause and join him and the British.

On October 25, 1780, Arnold wrote to Tallmadge: "As I know you to be a man of sense, I am convinced you are by this time fully of the opinion that the real interest and happiness of America consists of a reunion with Great Britain. To effect which happy purpose I have taken a commision in the British army and invite you to join me with as many men as you can bring over with you. If you think proper to embrace my offer, you shall have the same rank you now hold, in the cavalry I am about to raise. I shall make use of no arguments to convince you or to induce you to take a step which I think right. Your own good sense will suggest everything I can say on the subject."

This letter was sent by a secret agent to the American lines but the agent did not deliver it at that time since Tallmadge had just succeeded in leading a victorious raid against a British position in Oyster Bay. The agent thought it imprudent to deliver such a message to a man who was then tasting the fruits of triumph, believing that Tallmadge would be more susceptible to Arnold's offer after Washington suffered some military setbacks. The letter was not delivered for several months and when Tallmadge finally read it, he was shocked. He also immediately realized that Arnold had somehow learned that he was

Washington's spymaster and suspected that the letter was nothing more than a device to compromise his image and reputation as a fierce and loyal patriot.

Arnold was not the only former patriot to entreat Tallmadge to return to the British fold. He, along with many other revolutionary leaders, received an undated missive from Silas Deane, the one-time American representative in Paris who had helped Benjamin Franklin to persuade the French to enter the war on the American side. Deane had reportedly become disillusioned with the American cause and had gone over to the British. He wrote to Tallmadge, asking him to help effect a reunion with Great Britain. This was another letter Tallmadge did not answer. The enigmatic Deane finally went to live in England, aided by the British spy Paul Wentworth, but his one-time services to America were posthumously recognized by the U.S. Congress.

Tallmadge increasingly doubled his duties as spymaster with those of a military commander, leading raids against British strongholds such as Fort George, where he destroyed great quantities of British supplies. He continued to serve Washington faithfully until the end of the war. In 1783 he was promoted to the rank of breveted lieutenant general, a strictly titular position.

Following the war, Tallmadge became a successful merchant in Litchfield, Connecticut. In 1801 he was elected to Congress and served there until 1817 as a staunch Federalist and supporter of the policies advocated by his old commander, George Washington. He and Washington remained close friends until the commander-in-chief's death. Until that time, Washington, whose ledgers revealed that he had spent $17,617 to support his spy networks throughout the Revolutionary War, remained in contact with all of the Culper Ring spies, visiting Tallmadge, Townsend, Woodhull, and others regularly.

Washington frequently expressed his gratitude to them for the risks they had run. He was also determined that no retaliatory harm would ever come to them for their services and, to that end, ordered that the records involving the Culper Ring be sealed. For more than a century, no one knew, except Tallmadge and Washington, the actual identities of the New York spies.

[ALSO SEE: *John Andre; Benedict Arnold; Caleb Brewster; Culper Ring; Silas Deane; Nathan Hale; Robert Townsend; Paul Wentworth; Abraham Woodhull*]

THOMPSON, BENJAMIN
British Spy in American Revolution ▪ (1753–1814)

A SELF-TAUGHT SCIENTIST AND NATIVE OF MASSAchusetts, Thompson worked in Salem and Boston as a youth. He was fascinated by gunpowder and other forms of explosives and religiously studied these compounds. He apprenticed to a physician in his hometown of Woburn, Massachusetts, in 1770, taking an equally passionate interest in medicine but he never pursued a medical degree.

Becoming a schoolteacher, Thompson married a rich widow in Rumford (later Concord), New Hampshire. His wife was a dedicated loyalist who brought him into high British social circles. He befriended the British state governor, who gave him a commission in the local militia. Though never outwardly a loyalist, Thompson's secretly supported the British throughout the early stages of the American Revolution, spying on Patriots and identifying them to British authorities. In 1774, he was suspected of being a loyalist and was brought before New Hampshire's patriotic Committee of Safety, which accused him of being a spy for the British. He was acquitted for lack of evidence but soon fled to the protection of General Thomas Gage, commander of British forces in Massachusetts.

Thompson was persuaded by Gage to return to Rumford and resume his espionage work on behalf of King George. This he did, using his scientific knowledge to create an invisible ink made from tannic acid, writing that became visible only when washed with ferrous sulphate. He wrote his secret messages with this invisible ink, between the visible lines of apparently innocent letters.

Following the outbreak of the Revolution in 1775, and almost immediately after the battle of Lexington, Thompson sent a secret report to Gage, then besieged in Boston, that Washington was raising an army of more than 30,000 to oppose him. Again suspected of being a British spy, Thompson was once more hauled before the Committee of Safety but he was again released for lack of evidence. This last experience so frightened Thompson that he fled to Boston, where he sought Gage's permanent protection. Once there, the turncoat wrote a definitive report for Gage which he titled *State of the Rebel Army*. This report was so encompassing that it was used as a guide by British commanders for years to come.

When General William Howe, who had replaced Gage, decided to quit Boston and concentrate his forces in New York, Thompson sailed for London, fearing that he would be executed by the Patriots if found in Boston. He suspected that Patriot spy Paul Revere, who had remained in Boston throughout

Benjamin Thompson, the celebrated physicist from New Hampshire, served as a spy for the British during the American Revolution.

the British occupation and had been sending the Patriots information, knew that he was a spy and would expose him to Washington once Boston was reoccupied by the Americans.

There was good reason for Thompson's apprehensions. Another British spy, Benjamin Church, had been exposed as an enemy agent and it was strongly suspected that his chief confederate had been Benjamin Thompson, who, before they were seized by revolutionaries, went through Church's confidential letters and removed all of those that might incriminate him.

Thompson did not return to America until 1781, when he arrived as a member of a British military commission. He achieved very little and, after the surrender of Cornwallis at Yorktown, he returned to England, where he remained until he died. He became one of that country's greatest scientists, researching heat and light and advancing scientific theories still held today. His accomplishments in the field of physics led to his being elected to the Royal British Society and to his being elevated to the nobility by the Holy Roman Emperor, who bestowed upon Thompson the title of Count Rumford.

[ALSO SEE: *Benjamin Church; Paul Revere*]

THOMPSON, HARRY
American Spy for Japan ▪ (1910–)

ADMIRAL JOSEPH M. REEVES, A STERN DISCIPLINARIAN with a no-nonsense attitude toward all things military, was persistently bothered by his secretary one day in January 1935. A 19-year-old youth was in his outer office located in the San Diego Navy Station and kept demanding to see Reeves "on an urgent matter." Instead of calling for security guards, Reeves broke his own rules and told his secretary to send the boy in to see him.

Emaciated and nervous, Willard Turntine was ushered into Reeves' presence. He sat down silently, waiting until the secretary left the room. Then he blurted out a fantastic story that amazed and fascinated the admiral. A year earlier, in Los Angeles, Turntine said, he was homeless and with a single nickel in his pocket. He had bummed a cigarette from a 24-year-old man named Harry Thompson, an ex-yeoman of the U.S. Navy.

Turntine had told Thompson that he had had nothing to eat for days and the kindly ex-Navy man had taken him to his Long Beach apartment and fed him. Turntine, then on the bum from his hometown of St. Louis, was invited to stay with Thompson, who, he said, "just wanted some company." Turntine was careful to tell Admiral Reeves that his relationship with Thompson was not based on homosexuality, that Thompson "never laid a hand on me." They were just friends. Thompson kept him around, Turntine said, to "clean up and run errands for him."

Though Thompson never worked, he always had money, the youth emphasized. When Turntine asked him how he got his money, Thompson grinned and said: "Some day I might tell you . . . maybe." Though he was no longer in the Navy, Thompson constantly talked about his former life as a seaman serving on board the great battleships the *Colorado*, the *Mississippi*, and the *Texas*. Also, whenever he learned that these ships were anchored at San Diego or San Pedro, especially when accompanied by the radio-control ship *Utah* (later sunk at Pearl Harbor), he would travel to those harbors to meet old friends still serving on those ships, buying them drinks over long weekends.

"I just like to keep in touch with what's going on," Thompson replied to Turntine's questions. Then he would clam up. He was also tight-lipped about a visitor who came to see Thompson a few times a month, a young Japanese student who furtively entered Thompson's apartment, looking about carefully before he sat down. He had been introduced to Turntine by Thompson simply as "Tanni." Before Tanni began any conversation with Thompson, the ex-Navy man invariably fished a few dollars from his pocket and tossed these to Turntine,

Ex-American sailor Harry Thompson, who spied for the Japanese during the 1930s.

telling him to go out and "see a movie or get a sandwich."

Returning after Tanni left, Turntine noticed that Thompson seemed more cheeful and that his pockets bulged with cash. After Tanni had made several trips to the Long Beach apartment, Turntine finally worked up his nerve to inquire about the visitor: "Who is this Japanese guy anyway?" he asked Thompson. "Do you have some kind of business with him?"

Thompson merely shrugged, then said: "The world owes me a living, Okay? If my country won't give me a living, some other country will." This slip of the tongue was nothing compared to what Thompson began leaving about the apartment in plain sight, strange notes from Tanni that appeared to be written in some sort of code. When Thompson found Turntine studying one of these sheets of paper, he snatched it from his grasp. Later, Thompson told Turntine that maybe he could fix it so that Turntine went to work for Tanni, too. He later said that he had spoken to his Japanese friend but that Tanni could not make up his mind about giving Turntine a job.

By Christmas 1934, when Tanni gave Thompson a great deal of money in return for a briefcase full of documents, Turntine was convinced that his friend and benefactor was a spy. His conscience told him to go to the authorities but he waited until Thompson left on another trip before he traveled to see Admiral Reeves in San Diego.

Reeves had patiently listened to this incredible tale, taking notes. When Turntine finished, Reeves told him that he had "done the right thing." The admiral then told him return to Thompson's apartment in Long Beach. "Carry on as usual, but do not, under any circumstances, let Harry Thompson know that you came to see me."

Turntine did return to Thompson's apartment while Admiral Reeves contacted ONI. Agents of the Office of Naval Intelligence quickly put Thompson and his Long Beach apartment under surveillance while other agents began looking into the background of the mysterious Tanni. He suddenly showed up to meet briefly with Thompson and was followed back to his home in Palo Alto. ONI soon learned that Tanni was 30-year-old Toshio Miyazaki, a Japanese student attending Stanford University. He had entered the U.S. on August 24, 1933, and had immediately enrolled at Stanford. He was much more than a student, however; he was also a lieutenant commander in the Japanese Navy.

ONI agents tailed Miyazaki everywhere, even on a trip to San Francisco, where he went to an expensive restaurant and then on to one of the city's most expensive whorehouses. Two hours later he caught the train for Los Angeles and, immediately after leaving Union Station, took a taxi to 117½ Weller Street, the address of a clinic operated by a Japanese physician, Dr. Takashi Furusawa, which proved to be a meeting place for many known Japanese and even German espionage agents.

Miyazaki, after visiting for about an hour with Dr. Furusawa and others, then took a taxi to Thompson's Linden Street apartment in Long Beach. Turntine was not present, Thompson having given him money to "lose" himself for a few hours. ONI agents, however, had taken a room in the building opposite Thompson's apartment building and they had a clear view through binoculars and recording telescopes of Thompson's front room. They observed Miyazaki handing Thompson a thick wad of bills and then Thompson and Miyazaki conferring over a large sheet of paper, which appeared to be a map, for some time. Thompson then went into the bedroom and returned with several sheets of paper, each being carefully examined by both men.

Miyazaki left at 10 P.M., taking Thompson's papers and notes with him. He took a taxi to Los Angeles and to the Red Mill, another notorious brothel where he stayed for three-quarters of an hour. He then caught the night train for San Francisco. On the following morning he was attending lectures at Stanford. A few days later, ONI agents learned that Miyazaki kept considerable sums at the Yokohama Specie Bank in San Francisco, an account that was always replenished each month from an unknown source. ONI agents learned that the Japanese spy paid Thompson two hundred dollars a month cash from this account without variation.

The day following Miyazaki's visit, Turntine was surprised to see Thompson return home wearing a brand-new Navy uniform, that of a petty officer. "I'm reenlisting," Thompson told him.

"If that's so," Turntine boldly stated, "then how about fixing me up with your job."

"What job?"

"The one with the Japanese guy."

Thompson's face froze. He said solemnly: "If you ever tell anyone about what's going on, you won't live long."

ONI felt that it had assembled enough evidence to convict Miyazaki, Thompson, and even the nest of Japanese spies congregating at Dr. Furusawa's Los Angeles clinic, but the U.S. State Department, then attempting to appease the Japanese and persuade their Washington envoys to cease their aggression in China, ordered ONI to take no action. ONI did the next best thing and warned all sailors on shore leave in southern California not to talk to Harry Thompson.

The spy continued courting information from his old Navy friends but found they were unwilling to give him any news about Navy operations. Thompson nevertheless reported what he did discover to Miyazaki, meeting with him in his Linden Street apartment, and, on a few occasions, at the St. Francis Hotel in San Francisco. Thompson realized that his sources were drying up and, with little to report, told Miyazaki that he suspected Turntine had reported them. The Japanese spymaster, though not directly ordering Thompson to kill Turntine, suggested that "he be taken care of."

Anticipating such a move, ONI had gotten Turntine a job as a salesman in a San Francisco department store. He had moved into an apartment of his own, also provided by the ONI. A few days after Turntine departed, Thompson began to drink heavily. He went on benders that lasted for several days, remaining in his apartment. Miyazaki showed up and did not like what he saw. ONI agents watched as the Japanese spy sternly rebuked his tipsy agent for drinking. After Miyazaki left that night, Thompson was seen to sit down at a table and labor over a letter which he did not complete. He crumpled the paper and tossed it into the waste can, a letter later retrieved by ONI. It was his resignation from the Japanese intelligence service, addressed to Miyazaki.

Then Thompson did manage to formally quit and Miyazaki accepted his resignation. At that point, Japanese intelligence felt Miyazaki was about to be exposed and ordered him home to Japan. Once the spymaster was gone, ONI got permission from the State Department to arrest Thompson on March 5, 1936. He was placed on trial for espionage and it was quickly proved that he had been spying for Japan as a hired agent since 1933. Turntine testified against Thompson, who, in July 1936, was convicted and sent to the federal prison at McNeil Island to serve fifteen years behind bars.

When reading about Thompson's conviction, John S. Farnsworth, one-time lieutenant commander in the Navy and a spy for the Japanese since 1934, turned himself in to the Universal News Service.

[ALSO SEE: John S. Farnsworth; Takashi Furusawa]

THOMSON, BASIL
Director of Scotland Yard's Special Branch
■ (1861–1939)

THE SON OF ARCHBISHOP WILLIAM THOMSON OF York, England, Thomson was educated at Eton and Oxford, becoming a lawyer before joining the colonial service. He served in Fiji and Tonga, where he was briefly the prime minister. After returning to England, in 1896, Thomson was appointed governor of Dartmoor and Wormwood Scrubs prisons, where some of England's most infamous prisoners were jailed.

In 1913, Thomson was named chief of the Criminal Investigation Department at Scotland Yard. At that time the Yard's Special Branch also fell under his supervision. During World War I, he worked with Vernon Kell's MI5, as Special Branch had the only authority to arrest spies on behalf of British counter-intelligence. He was responsible for the arrest and jailing of German spies rooted out by MI5, including Karl Ernst and Karl Hans Lody.

It was Thomson who boarded the Dutch liner carrying German spymaster Franz von Rintelen,

Sir Basil Thomson, head of Scotland Yard's Special Branch, who worked with MI5 for decades to seize scores of spies in England.

arresting him and removing him to prison, on a tip from Reginald Hall's naval intelligence, which had intercepted an Abwehr coded message and determined the spy would be on the vessel. Thomson's reputation as a spycatcher was such that Mata Hari came to see him when passing through London to learn if Special Branch really knew that she was a German spy. Thomson, in his interview with her, guessed as much and warned her to "quit the dangerous business" in which she was involved, advice she never took. Had she, Mata Hari might not have faced a French firing squad a short time later.

Because of his superlative work with Special Branch in World War I, Thomson was knighted in 1918. He retired in 1921, and died in March 1939, not living to see Special Branch perform its outstanding counterintelligence work in World War II and throughout the Cold War.

[ALSO SEE: *Abwehr; Karl Ernst; William Reginald Hall; Vernon Kell; Karl Hans Lody; Mata Hari; MI6; Franz von Rintelen; Special Branch*]

THURLOE, JOHN
Spymaster for Oliver Cromwell ▪ (1616–1668)

LIKE HIS MASTER OLIVER CROMWELL, THURLOE WAS A maverick politician with independent religious beliefs. The son of a clergyman in the Church of England, he joined Cromwell in the Great Rebellion against Charles I in 1642. He studied for the law and took his degree in 1645. In 1651 he was sent to the Netherlands on a special diplomatic mission and was named secretary to the council of state by Cromwell the following year.

Next to Cromwell, Thurloe was the the most powerful man in England, his real position being that of a viceroy. After Cromwell engineered the execution of Charles I, he was beset by plots and conspiracies by monarchists seeking to place Charles II on the throne. To combat these royalists, Cromwell ordered Thurloe to establish a spy system to identify the plotters.

A master at organization, Thurloe put together the most effective espionage network since the days of Francis Walsingham, spymaster for Queen Elizabeth I. He began a postal censorship program and hired Oxford mathematician John Wallis to establish a cryptology department, which could break any known code of that day. Within months, Thurloe was actually directing three separate spy networks: a counterintelligence organization in England, a spy network throughout Europe, and even an espionage ring in the new colonies of America. Thurloe culled his spies from all ranks—scholars and renegades, impoverished aristocrats eager to earn money, archcriminals

Oliver Cromwell's powerful Secretary of State and spymaster John Thurloe, whose vast espionage networks worked against the restoration of the British monarchy.

whom he reprieved in the shadow of the gallows on the promise they would spy for him.

His spies were able to inform him of the sailing schedules of Spanish treasure ships, which allowed British warships to intercept them. Other Thurloe agents bribed royalists to betray their plots and fellow conspirators, as was the case when he dismantled the royalist secret society known as the Sealed Knot. (In that case, Thurloe paid Sir Richard Willis a fortune to identify his fellow conspirators.) Charles II was almost kidnapped in one Thurloe-inspired scheme that was upset at the last minute when one of his own men betrayed the plan, a rare exception among Thurloe's legions of spies. The traitor was Sir George Downing, British Resident in Holland.

After Cromwell's death, Thurloe served Richard Cromwell but he was imprisoned when Charles II regained the throne in 1660. On the promise that he would obediently serve the king, he was released. Thurloe spent the remainder of his life writing in-depth essays on political problems, although Charles II realized Thurloe's worth as one of the world's greatest spymasters and often consulted with him, almost to the day of Thurloe's death on February 21, 1668.

[ALSO SEE: *Francis Walsingham*]

THYRAUD DE VOSJOLI, PHILIPPE
French Spymaster ▪ (1921–)

AFTER SPENDING TWENTY-FIVE YEARS CEMENTING relationships with his own French intelligence service (SDECE) and that of the British MI6 and the American CIA, Thyraud was confronted with an almost insurmountable problem. Charles de Gualle, once he resumed power, had decreed that France would distance itself from all other nations and this meant that its intelligence chiefs would no longer work closely with its Allies.

Aggravating the strained relations between the SDECE and the CIA was the publicly known fact that Richard Helms of the CIA had forged a strong link to French intelligence chief Jacques Soustelle. The French spymaster was closely associated with French generals in Algiers who were in open revolt against de Gaulle. Further trouble came in the form of KGB defector Colonel Anatoli Golytsin, who in 1962 was sheltered by the CIA and who quickly identified Georges Paques, a senior French NATO official, as a KGB spy who had been turning over secrets to the Soviets. Golytsin also told Washington intelligence officials that within SDECE itself was a secret Soviet network operating under the code name Sapphine. The defector then insisted that within de Gaulle's personal staff was a Soviet mole handing over every French state secret.

Meanwhile, newspapers in France, England, and America conducted a spy hunt through their pages, naming names and being sued in the process. Thyraud returned to France and resigned his position, giving as his reason the widespread corruption within SDECE and the infiltration of the French intelligence service by agents of a "foreign service." He was, in turn, accused of being a defector himself, that his loyalties lay with the U.S. and its CIA, not with his homeland, France.

Thyraud had to deal with these vexing accusations. Complicating matters was an author, Leon Uris, who developed a story from a manuscript Thyraud wrote after his resignation, one which employed the Golytsin defection as the hub for a novel which Uris later titled *Topaz*, which also profiled a handsome, daring French intelligence officer and his close friendship with the CIA, a character undoubtedly based upon Thyraud. *Topaz* would later be made into a film directed by Alfred Hitchcock.

To escape criticism in France, Thyraud left France and resettled in Miami, Florida. He sued Uris for damages relating to the profits of *Topaz* and was awarded a large sum by a Los Angeles court in 1972.

[ALSO SEE: *CIA; Anatoli Golytsin; Richard Helms; KGB; Georges Paques; SDECE; Jacques Soustelle*]

TOWNSEND, ROBERT
American Spy in Revolution ▪ (1754–1838)

A QUAKER AND A SUCCESSFUL MERCHANT IN NEW York, Townsend was recruited into George Washington's intelligence service by its top spymaster, Benjamin Tallmadge, his old classmate at Yale. So, too, was Townsend's friend Enoch Hale, another Yale graduate and the brother of executed hero and spy Nathan Hale. Townsend, along with other Tallmadge recruits—Abraham Woodhull, Austin Roe, and Caleb Brewster—established the redoubtable Culper Ring inside British-occupied New York during the American Revolution.

Townsend had the perfect cover in that his business involved selling the foodstuffs and wares produced in the farms and villages outside of Manhattan, wholesaling these foods and supplies to the retail shops in Manhattan. He therefore had the perfect excuse to send his pack trains, under the supervision of Austin Roe, another astute spy in his ring, back and forth between the British and American lines. In this way, Townsend sent information to Tallmadge via Roe, who passed it on to Woodhull, who lived at Setauket on Long Island, who gave the messages to a boatman, Caleb Brewster, who rowed across the sound to deliver the information to Tallmadge, who then passed it on to Washington.

The ring operated successfully from 1778 to 1783 without one of its agents ever being exposed or compromised. This was due to the strict secrecy practiced by the Culper Ring. Only a few of the members knew the others. Woodhull used the alias of Samuel Culper Sr., and Townsend was Samuel Culper Jr. To assure his image as a staunch Tory, Townsend joined a volunteer regiment of loyalists in New York and wrote anti-American articles for the *Royal Gazette*, edited by double agent James Rivington. In 1779, Townsend went into partnership with the shifty Rivington, opening a coffeehouse. Townsend never knew that Rivington later changed sides and became a secret agent for Washington. Rivington never knew Townsend was the leader of the celebrated Culper Ring.

A few others aided Townsend but these were mostly relatives, including a mysterious woman who is referred to simply as "355." She was later identified as Townsend's mistress, who gave birth to their son. Apparently Benedict Arnold, after he had deserted the American cause and had joined the British, learned of "355"'s identity and betrayed her to the British. She reportedly died on a British prison ship in 1781.

Townsend believed that Arnold might also identify him but, after some time, he realized that the traitor had little insight into American espionage in New York.

Townsend confided to Tallmadge in a brief, coded note that "I am happy to think that Arnold does not know my name." Though Townsend hated Arnold, he had considerable respect for the man Arnold sacrificed to the gallows in his attempted betrayal of West Point, Major John Andre, head of British intelligence for General Clinton.

The information Robert Townsend supplied through the Culper Ring proved invaluable to Washington. He received weekly reports on Clinton's military strength, amount of supplies, artillery, ammunition, new stores arriving in British ships, and reinforcements coming by sea, as well as Clinton's battle plans. Throughout the war Washington never knew the real identity of Robert Townsend. Only Tallmadge (and Washington *after* the war) knew his name and that secret was kept in sealed records for more than one hundred years following the Revolution. Following the war, Townsend continued his successful merchant business, then retired to Oyster Bay. He never talked of his role as Washington's greatest spy, taking that secret with him to the grave.

[ALSO SEE: *John Andre; Benedict Arnold; Caleb Brewster, Nathan Hale; James Rivington; Benjamin Tallmadge; Abraham Woodhull*]

TOYAMA, MITSURU
Japanese Secret Society Leader and Spymaster ▪ (1855–1944)

BORN TO A SAMURAI FAMILY IN REMOTE FUKUOKA, Japan, Toyama was a rabid nationalist advocating world conquest by the time he reached his twenties. He was arrested several times for leading samurai uprisings and was eventually sent to prison for three years. When released he joined the jingoistic nationalist secret society Kyoshisha, and soon rose in its ranks.

A stickler for organization and discipline, Toyama soon attracted his own large following, mostly those who were part of Japan's widespread street gangs. He employed this force to put down workers' strikes, particularly in the coal mine regions, taking the pay of the mine owners.

In 1881, Toyama established his own secret society, Genoyosha (Black Dragon Society or Dark Ocean Society), which soon grew to enormous proportions, having tens of thousands of diehard members who enforced the edicts of business tycoons and, especially, the militarists. Toyama early on cemented relationships with Army officers advocating military expansion and naked aggression. On behalf of these militarists, Toyama sent out his secret agents to spy on moderate and liberal Japanese politicians whom his agents also assassinated at the behest of Army commanders.

Toyama eventually became so powerful that he himself gave orders to have political opponents murdered, including the queen of Korea in 1894, a murder that led to the long Japanese occupation of Korea. It was also Toyama who lobbied for the military confrontation with Russia. To that end, he provided an army of spies in Manchuria to gather information on the czar's land forces and the Russian fleet at Port Arthur. Information gathered by Black Dragon spies aided the Japanese fleet that vanquished the Russian fleet in the Russo-Japanese War of 1904–1905.

The power Toyama wielded in Japan was enormous, although he was ever submissive to Emperor Hirohito, especially when the monarch decided on world conquest in the late 1920s. Toyama's society had at its command more than 60,000 gangsters who acted as strike breakers and civilian supporters of the Japanese militarists, as well as supplying secret information on internal and external enemies, working closely with Kempei Tai (Japan's internal secret police) and Special Service Organ (foreign intelligence).

Throughout World War II, Toyama continued to loudly advocate a suicidal war of devastation against those nations Japan had made its enemies. He lived to the age of eighty-nine, dying in 1944, but not before he witnessed the collapse of the Japanese military empire he had worked so fanatically to establish.

[ALSO SEE: *Black Dragon Society; Kempei Tai*]

TREPPER, LEOPOLD (AKA: GRAND CHEF)
Polish Spymaster for Soviets ▪ (1904–1982)

DURING THE DAYS OF THE RED ORCHESTRA (ROTE Kapelle), the Communist underground in Nazi-occupied Europe in World War II, Leopold Trepper emerged as an extraordinary spymaster known for his unerring, swift judgments, daring schemes, and his ability to take the initiative without waiting for directives from the Center in Moscow. He was known as the "Grand Chef," and his ability to escape the clutches of the Nazis, as well as his own Communist Party inquisitors, was nothing less than phenomenal.

Born in Neumark, Poland, Trepper went to work in the Galician mines, where he witnessed the incredible hardships of the workers who were kept at slave wages by mine owners. The experience convinced him to join the Communist Party and, in 1925, he organized a massive and illegal strike at Dombrova, which caused his arrest and an eight-month prison sentence.

To escape the poverty and misery of Poland, Trepper migrated to Palestine in 1926, working on a kibbutz, a communal farm, but this satisfied him less than Communist plotting and intrigues. He worked against the British, then controlling Palestine, and was expelled after being identified as a Communist agent in 1928. Going to France, Trepper worked for Rabcors, an illegal political organization that was broken up by French intelligence in 1932. Trepper escaped to Moscow, where he became a full-fledged NKVD/KGB spy, moving between Paris and Moscow for the next six years.

Trepper survived the Stalinist purges of 1937 and 1938 by convincing the Center of his loyalty to the Soviets. He returned to France in 1939 to become the Resident Director of all Soviet espionage in western Europe, replacing Walter Krivitsky, who had defected to the West. At this time he was dubbed the Grand Chef (Big Chief). Operating mainly in France and Belgium, Trepper established Red Orchestra underground operations in Germany, Holland, and Switzerland.

In Germany, Trepper set up several espionage networks through KGB spymasters Alexander Erdberg and Bogdan Kobolov. One of these was headed by Harro Schulze-Boysen, a Junker and one of the few Red Orchestra spymasters who was not a Communist but who hated Hitler's regime and worked with existing Communist spy rings led by Arvid Harnack and Adam Kuckhoff. Schulze-Boysen, like many working for the Red Orchestra in Germany, was well placed to obtain high-level military and political information, being a press officer in the German Air Ministry.

Trepper's networks in France were widespread, the most effective spy ring headed by Vasili Maximovich and his sister Anna. When the Germans overran France, Vasili became an interpreter for a German general and soon had access to German Headquarters documents in Paris, especially after he married a German woman who worked for the German military administration.

Through these sources, along with Anna Maximovich, who used her mental clinic as a letter-box operation, Trepper was able to learn the true French attitude toward the occupying Germans, the Nazi military strength and troop positions throughout France, and the location of secret internment camps, as well as a constantly updated list of Nazi prisoners. Trepper was also able to keep track of all forced labor projects secretly undertaken by the Germans in northern France.

In Switzerland, Trepper's main spy ring was led by rotund, buck-toothed Sandor Rado, who controlled a number of gifted agents and had a radio network that beamed information collected by Trepper's agents throughout Europe directly to the Center in Moscow. The source of most of the important information Rado's network acquired was from an agent code-named Lucy, who was really Rudolf Roessler, one of the most astute and successful Allied agents of World War II.

In Belgium, the Big Chief's lieutenant was Victor Sukulov, a Latvian and former Red Army officer who used the cover name of Edward Kent. Sukulov had originally been instructed to establish a Communist spy ring in Copenhagen but when war broke out in 1939, he was sent, instead, to Brussels, which is where Trepper made his headquarters. This operation was vast, supported by a network of hundreds of spies matching wits with Gestapo agents.

A large radio operation was established by Sukulov in a villa in Etterbeck, a suburb of Brussels. Trepper at that time used the cover name Jean Gilbert, posing as a Belgian manufacturer of raincoats, a cover that allowed him to freely move from country to country. Through his high-positioned spies, Trepper was able to learn not only of Hitler's Operation Barbarossa, the invasion of Russia in 1941, but the exact strength of German armored and infantry forces to be used, down to the regiment level. His radio message to Moscow concerning the impending attack went unheeded by Stalin, who refused to believe Hitler would invade. A similar message arrived from Stalin's top spy in Tokyo, Richard Sorge, but the Russian dictator refused to believe that report, too, one of many near-fatal errors committed by Stalin in World War II.

So effective were Trepper's Red Orchestra networks that Moscow received in the first few days of the invasion no less than 500 messages from Communist agents, each detailing every tactical and strategic move anticipated by the German high command. All of this shortwave activity had not gone unnoticed by the Gestapo and the German security department, the RSHA.

German direction-finding units (known as *Peilung*) worked frantically by the hundreds to pinpoint Trepper's radio sites but his operators were experienced enough to regularly move the locations of their radios and to broadcast such short transmissions that there was not enough time for DF units to intersect and locate the stations. Further, the codes employed by Trepper's agents were impossible to decipher.

Moscow was really the undoing of its own networks. It demanded of Trepper so much information that his wireless stations worked five hours at a stretch, midnight until 5 A.M. through late 1941, allowing the German direction-finding units more than enough time to pinpoint network locations. Finally, the Abwehr and the Gestapo, working in unison (a rare occasion), identified Trepper's main headquarters at the Etterbeck villa.

On the night of December 14, 1941, heavily armed German soldiers and Gestapo and Abwehr agents, wearing socks over their boots to muffle their movements, surrounded the place, as well as three adjacent houses used by Trepper's agents. The Germans went into the houses, finding the radio equipment on the second floor of the villa and inside the other houses a great deal of documents, rubber stamps, high-quality invisible ink—all the apparatus of espionage. They also found on the premises three groggy spies, Mikhail Makarov, Rita Arnould, and Sophie Pozanska, who gave her name as Ann Verlinden.

Just as the Germans were ransacking the houses, Trepper himself appeared. Seized by German soldiers, the ever cool-headed spymaster pretended shock, saying that he was only a poor seller of rabbits who had knocked on the door to make a sale. A German officer looked Trepper over carefully. He was wearing a suit so threadbare that it was almost in rags. The old boots on his feet were those of a man used to trudging down roads. Outside in a cart were small wire-mesh cages containing some live rabbits.

The impersonation was too good to be disbelieved. "You and your rabbits get out of here," ordered the German officer. "Next time sell your rabbits during the day, or you may get a bullet in the head!" He pointed to the three agents who were struggling with their captors and joked: "These are the only rabbits we want." For a few seconds, Trepper's own trapped agents stared back at him with large, frightened eyes but they said nothing. The spymaster was shoved out the door and went on his way quickly, heading for France.

A few minutes later, Pozanska broke free, tore a small leather strap from her neck and opened the little container dangling at its end to produce and swallow a cyanide tablet. She crashed dead to the floor in seconds. The Germans found the poison pills Makarov and Arnould had hidden and destroyed them before the spies could follow Pozanska's lead. An Abwehr officer grinned at the pair, pointing to the floor where Pozanska's body lay: "In time to come, you will think back on her and know that she was the fortunate one."

Makarov and Arnould were taken to Gestapo headquarters and tortured immediately, their brutal interrogators demanding that they tell them everything about their Red Orchestra network. Makarov was tough, shouting obscenities at the Gestapo thugs until they became so enraged that they killed him, undoubtedly Makarov's goal. Arnould, however, was different. She shook with fear as the Germans talked to her. Unlike the strapping Makarov, they applied no torture to her, but they did leave the door of the interrogation room open so that she could hear the dying screams of her fellow agent.

Quaking in terror, the woman agreed to tell the Germans everything she knew. Her subtle inquisitors brought her food and coffee and cigarettes. They assured Arnould that no harm would come to her. Then she began to talk, identifying Johann Wenzel as the chief radio operator for the network in Belgium. She identified Sukulov as the Petit Chef (Little Chief) and Trepper as the Grand Chef (Big Chief). She described in detail the appearance of Sukulov, and even provided a photo of Trepper.

Playing the role of considerate jailors, Gestapo officials then took Arnould to a small hotel, where she was given a comfortable room and kept under guard. She was told that as long as she cooperated, she would not be imprisoned and would be released a short time later. She was systematically pumped for information for weeks. When the Gestapo realized Arnould had nothing more to reveal, a group of its agents burst into her room, raped her until she fell unconscious, then dragged her naked to the backyard of the hotel, where she was beheaded, her decapitated corpse left to rot.

Meanwhile, Sukulov had abandoned his small firm in Brussels, telling his staff that as a citizen of Uruguay, which had just declared war on Germany, he could no longer remain in Belgium. He fled to Paris with Trepper, where they immediately set up headquarters, working closely with the Maximovich ring. Belgium as a base for the Red Orchestra, however, was not abandoned. A handsome and dashing blonde Russian KGB officer named Konstantin Yefremov, assisted by the radio man Wenzel, opened another station in Brussels and, within a week, was sending out messages to the Center.

Abwehr agents just as doggedly used direction-finding equipment to pinpoint Wenzel's station. On June 30, 1942, German agents smashed down the door of Wenzel's room, finding his radio, several coded messages, and two messages in clear German. Wenzel was arrested but he proved to be uncooperative. He was then told that he could choose between collaboration or death. One of the Gestapo agents then showed Wenzel a photograph of Rita Arnould's decapitated body. Wenzel nodded, agreeing to work with the Germans. He proved to be the greatest spy catch of the Abwehr at that time.

Wenzel not only confirmed the identities of Sukulov and Trepper as the leaders of the Red Orchestra, he identified the Soviet networks in Berlin, which led to the arrest of the rings headed by Schulze-Boysen and Harnack. Moreover, he presented the Nazis with information on how to break the Russian codes. Within a few weeks, the Abwehr had complete information on the Red Orchestra and it got busy arresting hundreds of Soviet agents.

Though Wenzel identified his nominal superior, Yefremov, he did not know the whereabouts of the wiley 28-year-old spymaster. He believed that Abraham Raichman, who functioned as his network's false document expert, might be able to locate Yefremov.

Abraham Raichman, following torture, agreed to go to Paris under guard and seek out the Big Chief, Trepper. He arrived in Paris under guard in October 1942. Contacting a number of Soviet agents, Raichman betrayed them to his Gestapo escort but he was unable to locate Trepper. By that time Trepper had learned that Raichman was being used as bait by the Nazis and went underground. Raichman identified Germaine Schneider as one of the French network's most important couriers but she fled before she could be arrested. She was later tracked down and imprisoned.

Raichman led Abwehr and Gestapo agents to the offices of Simex, a firm specializing in the purchase and sale of industrial diamonds that Trepper used as a cover and for which he was the manager in Paris. German agents learned from Simex employees, chiefly Maria Kalinina, Trepper's secretary, and her son Evegeny, a company chauffeur, that Trepper was somewhere in Paris but had disappeared. Then the Germans tried to lure the spymaster from hiding by leaving a message at his firm that a German firm wanted to purchase $1,500,000 worth of industrial diamonds but that it would deal only with the manager, Jean Gilbert (Trepper's alias). This bait did not work. Trepper failed to appear.

Then an Abwehr agent found a small diary in Trepper's office desk at Simex, one which listed all of his appointments with a Parisian dentist. German agents went to the dentist and found that Trepper was scheduled for another visit on November 16, 1942.

Dozens of heavily-armed German agents waited for the Big Chief on that date, at the entrance to the building, on the staircases, inside the elevator, on all floors. Trepper did not appear. Then some of the agents heard noise inside the dentist's office and walked inside. Trepper was in the chair, the dentist about to drill into a cavity. Somehow the spymaster had gotten into the building without being seen.

A half dozen Abwehr agents pointed guns at the spymaster. "You are under arrest," one of them said. Trepper looked dejected, then said in perfect German: "You did a fine job." Trepper was first questioned by the Abwehr. When he refused to talk, he was told that, unfortunately, he would have to be turned over to the Gestapo and he was reminded how that organization interrogated prisoners. Suddenly the iron-willed Big Chief gave in, agreeing to cooperate with German intelligence. He collaborated by first betraying several of his own agents. Then he played the "radio game," sending false information to the Center in Moscow. The Germans told him that they wanted Trepper to keep this avenue of communciation open for possible peace negotiations.

Trepper knew that Moscow would see through his "playback" information. When Moscow demanded that Trepper send them some specific top-secret information, the Germans refused. Moscow then realized that Trepper had been turned. By June 1943, Trepper was living in a private house in Paris. At that time he managed to slip away from his guards and escape.

The one man not betrayed by Trepper was Victor Sukulov, who had established a Red Orchestra network in Marseilles. Sukulov was nevertheless tracked down and arrested. Unlike his chief, he utterly refused to cooperate with the Germans. Then a friend, Margarete Barcza, was brought into a room where Sukulov waited. The Petit Chef snapped, racing to the young woman and embracing her, shouting to his captors that if she were released he would tell everything he knew. Sukulov, like Trepper, exposed what was left of the Red Orchestra in France, and he, too, sent false messages to Moscow.

Sukulov also attempted on behalf of the Abwehr to expose the strong Soviet network in Switzerland operated by Sandor Rado but he was unable to penetrate its security. He was, however, able to contact Rado's top radio operator, Alexander Foote, but Foote became suspicious when Sukulov began asking for identities and addresses of the agents in Switzerland. Foote wired his suspicions to the Center, which then officially shut down contact with all of Trepper's networks, realizing that they had been compromised and turned.

At the end of World War II, Sukulov, fearful of revenge from the Allies, especially the Soviets, retreated with the Werhmacht into Germany. He later fled to the Balkans, where he was reportedly murdered by SMERSH agents.

Leopold Trepper's end was much different. Still the bold and daring spymaster, Trepper emerged from hiding with the French resistance after the liberation of Paris. He flew to Moscow in Stalin's personal plane but instead of receiving a hero's welcome, he was thrown into a cell at Lubianka Prison. Instead of admitting to his KGB interrogators that he had turned collaborator, he staunchly defended himself, saying that he misled his German captors all the while he was a captive and that he had gotten word to the Communist underground in Paris that he was a prisoner and that he was sending misinformation to the Center at the direction of the Abwehr.

At first KGB officers scoffed at the claim but the ever resourceful Trepper had evidence to prove his statements. Before leaving Paris for Moscow, Trepper had taken pains to collect a number of signed statements from French Communists that he had, indeed, made contact with them while a prisoner and had told them of his double agent's role. Trepper turned over the documents and Stalin, who mistrusted his once great spymaster, was taken aback. He had originally planned to have Trepper thoroughly interrogated and then shot. Now, he was not so sure. Trepper, as he had done so many times earlier in his fabulous spy career, had planted a nagging doubt in the minds of his accusers.

Trepper was kept in prison and would have been released had he not complained that Stalin had not appreciated his efforts while directing the Red Orchestra and that his warning of Hitler's impending invasion of Russia had gone unheeded by Stalin. The dictator rankled at the reminder and ordered Trepper imprisoned indefinitely. It was not until four years after Stalin's death, in 1957, that Trepper was released.

The spymaster returned to Poland, where he rejoined his wife and three sons. When he sought recognition from Moscow for his espionage service to the Soviets, he was written out of the official Soviet history of the Red Orchestra. Following the Six-Day War, Trepper and his family suffered, as did all Jews in Poland, from a violent outbreak of anti-Semitism. Trepper decided to quit his native land and applied for a visa to migrate to Israel. The Polish government, at the instigation of the KGB in Moscow, refused.

Trepper defied the government, contacting members of the Western press he knew to explain the persecution he and other Polish Jews were experiencing. An international storm of protest then enveloped the Polish government, which finally relented and let Trepper and other Jews leave for Israel. Trepper and his family settled in Jerusalem in 1974. He died there eight years later at the age of seventy-seven, an ancient spymaster who had been clever enough to survive the evils of his own era, many of them of his own making.

[ALSO SEE: *Abwehr; Gestapo; KGB; Walter Krivitsky; NKVD; Sandor Rado; Red Orchestra; Rudolf Roessler; Harro Schulze-Boysen; Richard Sorge; RSHA*]

TURING, ALAN
British Cryptologist in World War II ▪ (1912-1954)

BORN IN LONDON TO A CIVIL SERVANT, TURING graduated from Cambridge in 1934. A mathematical genius, Turing was fascinated by computers and wrote reports on their capabilities as early as 1936. In World War II, Turing worked at the Government Code and Cypher School at Bletchley Park, outside of London. He, Gordon Welchman, and their gifted superior Dillwyn Knox studied a captured Enigma machine used by the Germans to encrypt their unbreakable codes. They built a duplicate machine which allowed them to crack the German codes and were thus able to supply the Allies with decoded messages passing between members of the German high command, an incredible intellectual achievement that helped to bring the war to a speedier end.

When German cryptographers constructed a machine even more sophisticated and advanced than Enigma, Knox, Turing, Welchman and others were able to duplicate it and then respond with their own creation, Colossus, the first programmed electronic digital computer in the world, one which instantly analyzed and deciphered almost every German code.

Unfortunately, Turing never lived to see the blossoming of the computer age, much of it due to his own invention and creativity. He died of poison, apparently self administered, in 1954.

[ALSO SEE: *Ultra*]

ULTRA
British Communications Intelligence in World War II ▪ (1939–1945)

AT THE BEGINNING OF WORLD WAR II IN 1939, British communications intelligence found it impossible to decipher the coded messages being sent by the German military, which was then using what it called the Enigma machine. This was an extremely complicated electronic-mechanical device consisting of a series of drums and wheels that first appeared on the commercial market in 1926.

German cryptographers perfected this machine by combining the work of two electric typewriters connected jointly to the independently turning wheels, each wheel bearing twenty-six cryptographic signs. The operator encrypted codes by typing in plain language a message on the first machine, which the second machine would, as designated by the operator, immediately place into code. The Germans had modified the machine by placing obstacles inside of its mechanical operation to thwart codebreakers who might obtain a copy of the machine. As part of their Axis treaty with Japan, the Germans gave Japanese intelligence a copy of the machine, which the Japanese modified and was dubbed Purple; this machine duplicated by American cryptologist William Friedman, who was thus able to break the top Japanese diplomatic and military codes at the beginning of America's war with Japan. American Signal Intelligence, like its counterpart in Bletchley, England, also referred to Purple as part of its own Ultra Code department.

British cryptographers working at the Govenment Code and Cypher School in Bletchley Park, fifty miles north of London in Buckinghamshire, were fortunate enough to obtain a captured Enigma machine which they duplicated, and were able to break the secret German codes. The Germans, for their part,

went through the entire war operating Enigma and believing that their codes sent through this machine remained sacrosanct.

The British Ultra department swelled from a small staff at Bletchley to a huge and sprawling operation to which were added cryptographers from the American OSS and Signal Intelligence, as well as Free French intelligence experts. Thousands of Ultra workers, decoding hundreds of German messages each day, worked four shifts. Copies of all messages were photographed and the photographic copies placed in the Bodleian Library at Oxford in case German bombers located and destroyed the mansion and adjoining buildings at Bletchley. Security was rigid at Bletchley and it is a wonder that, out of the many thousands of Allied intelligence agents exposed to Enigma, the secret that the British had broken Enigma was never exposed to the Germans.

In 1942, Ultra endured a temporary setback when German naval intelligence developed a new Enigma machine for communications to its U-boats. Again, the British were lucky enough to obtain a copy of the new Enigma machine from a German U-boat and were able to update their own version of the new Enigma. This allowed Ultra to provide the British Admiralty Office with precise information on the location of the the German submarines, which were then sought out and destroyed.

SIS and OSS worked closely with Ultra to plant captured German agents who had turned and spread disinformation to Abwehr spymasters. Several of these double agents informed the Abwehr that the Allies would be invading Greece and the Balkans, not Sicily as the Germans expected. The Germans weakened their garrisons on Sicily and strengthened the Balkan area defenses. Once Ultra confirmed these new German battle plans, the invasion of Sicily went forward as planned.

Ultra also monitored disinformation about the invasion of France in fantastic schemes called Operation Bodyguard and the planting of a body of a British officer in Spain carrying misleading information on the invasion. Ultra was able to confirm that the Germans accepted the false information as real, and, as in the case of the Sicilian invasion, moved troops and armor away from the actual invasion site.

Though the British shared Ultra secrets with the Americans and, to a lesser degree, the French, it kept its operations and the fact that it had broken Enigma from the Russians, finding ways to provide the Soviets with information it had acquired but without revealing the source of that information. All information concerning German operations in Russia were sent from Ultra through several channels until it reached a British agent working with the Communist spy network of Sandor Rado in Switzerland. This agent, Alexander Foote, in turn, sent on the information to Moscow in such a way as to make the Center believe it was originating with the Rado ring, not the Bletchley operation in England.

The decoding breakthroughs developed at Bletchley led to the creation of more sophisticated digital computer systems such as Colossus, created by British cryptographer Alan Turing. More advanced versions of such analytical computer systems allowed British intelligence to enter the Cold War with a decided edge over the KGB and other intelligence agencies hostile to the West in signals and communications intelligence, as did the American CIA.

[ALSO SEE: *Jack Berg; CIA; William J. Donovan; Double-Cross System; Johannues Marinus Dronkers; Allen Dulles; Alexander Foote; Elizabeth and William Friedman; KGB; The Man Who Never Was; Stewart Graham Menzies; OSS; Purple Machine; Sandor Rado; SIS; William Samuel Stephenson; Alan Turing*]

UNITED NATIONS
Spy Center for Soviets ▪ (1946–   )

THE UNITED NATIONS, CREATED AFTER WORLD WAR II and located in New York, has, since its inception, been a hub of Soviet spying activities, in violation of UN charter regulations. Article 100 stipulates that that members "shall not seek or receive instructions from any government or from any external authority." The Soviets flagrantly violated regulations; of its standard 700 officials at the UN, at least one third of these are KGB or GRU agents.

Their aim is to obtain secret UN records and files and recruit new KGB spies from other attending countries, especially those in the U.S. Soviet agents at the UN have traditionally operated with immunity—the FBI is forbidden to enter the UN building—traveling with unrestricted movement throughout the U.S., to collect scientific, technical, military, political, and industrial intelligence.

The most important defector to the U.S. in 1978 was Arkady Shevchenko, the under secretary general at the UN who later stated that the UN was "the most important base of all Soviet intelligence operations in the world." Of similar worth to Soviet espionage are the many UN agencies around the world, particularly the Atomic Energy Commission in Vienna and UNESCO in Paris.

VAN LEW, ELIZABETH
Union Spy in Civil War ▪ (1817–1900)

ON TOP OF THE HIGHEST OF SEVEN HILLS IN Richmond, Virginia, towered the resplendent mansion of Elizabeth Van Lew, Southern spinster and Union spy, who became the most hated woman in the Confederacy and one of the most adored in the ranks of Union soldiers. The Van Lew mansion on Church Hill, built in 1799, boasted three stories, huge rooms, a library where Van Lew kept her horse and, on the third floor, beneath the attic and over the front portico, a hidden room where Van Lew hid as many as twenty to fifty escaping Union soldiers at a time.

Born on October 17, 1817, Elizabeth Van Lew grew up the pampered daughter of a wealthy hardware store owner. She received a good education and was well read. By the time the American Civil War broke out in 1861, she was already a staunch Abolitionist who had, in the words of one account, "contracted a fevered hatred for slavery." After Fort Sumter fell in 1861 and the South prepared for war, Van Lew, wearing black and accompanied by servants, openly declared herself an Abolitionist.

Polite Richmond society did not allow Van Lew to be attacked but she was sorely criticized wherever she went. Women sneered at her and men shook their fists in her direction, calling her "witch" and "traitor." Of course, these epithets were hurled because of Van Lew's publicly voiced political opinions. Had her neighbors known that she was actually abetting escaped Union prisoners, her fate would most certainly have been death.

Shunned as a social pariah and branded an eccentric instead of a traitor (it was too ungentlemanly in the South to conceive of a female as a dangerous sympathizer), Van Lew collected fruit in baskets and took them to Libby Prison to hand out to starving Union prisoners. This she did after wangling a pass from the Treasury Department and flattering the Confederate secret police chief, General John H. Winder. She was allowed to "visit the prisoners and send them books, luxuries, delicacies, and what she may please."

Van Lew won over the wardens of the prisons by having their favorite foods prepared for them. While distributing food and books from her amply stocked library, Van Lew won the affection and gratitude of countless Union soldiers but, early in the war, she was also asked to spy for the Yankees, a task she readily agreed to perform. Shortly after the disastrous Union defeat at Bull Run in 1861, she received from an unknown courier a cipher from Union General George Henry Sharpe which she was to use in her coded messages. She kept this cipher, written on a two-inch scrap of green paper, inside a watch she kept on her person at all times.

To achieve her ends, Van Lew summoned an ex-slave and one-time servant, Mary Elizabeth Bowser, asking her to work as an agent. The black woman agreed and Van Lew managed to get her hired as a servant in the household of Jefferson Davis, the President of the Confederacy. Within months, Bowser, an intelligent woman with a good education (provided by Van Lew), began providing her spymaster with abstracts of military orders and battle plans she brought from the office Davis maintained in his home.

When a Confederate doctor refused to allow Van Lew's foodstuffs to be distributed to Union prisoners in Libby's hospital, Van Lew went back to General Winder, flattering him into cooperation. Winder rebuked the physician and the men in the hospital received Van Lew's custards and homemade bread. When distributing these foods, Van Lew would take messages from prisoners. Some of these were merely letters to their loved ones, others contained information on Confederate defense positions, troop movements, supply lines. All of these messages Van Lew collected and slipped into the false bottom of an antique French plate warmer.

Van Lew's servants then took the messages to others at relay stations the spymaster had established. She had set up a network of small homes where her servants lived and these ex-slaves passed on her missives to Union spymasters such as Allan Pinkerton and, later, Lafayette Baker, head of the Union's intelligence service.

Though most southern officials believed Van Lew was a well-meaning middle-aged woman whose loyalties were askew, others, including Winder himself, suspected that she might also be a spy. While visiting prisoners at Castle Thunder in 1862, Van Lew was approached by a Confederate captain to whom she had ingratiated herself. "You have been reported several times," he whispered to her. A few days later a young man in tattered clothes called at her mansion, asking to board there.

Van Lew felt a sudden sense of dread and told the man that she had no available rooms. He begged to sleep anywhere, even in the library. She refused. As she suspected, he was a spy sent by the benign but clever Winder. Confederate agents watched the Van Lew mansion night and day but eventually reported that nothing unusual occurred. Still, hatred for Van Lew was so strong in Richmond, especially among Southern females, that it was urged she be arrested and confined to her home.

Seeing her peril, Van Lew cleverly chose a new role, that of an unbalanced but harmless woman. She began to appear at the prisons in food-stained dresses, her hair unkempt, muttering to herself. "Old Bet's gone crazy," the Confederate guards jeered. The label was picked up throughout Richmond until children seeing Van Lew on the street would chant: "Crazy Bet, crazy Bet, lives in a mansion with no rooms to let."

Her impersonation of a loony was emphasized when, in 1863, General Robert E. Lee ordered all horses in the Confederacy confiscated for his cavalry. Three of Van Lew's handsome white coach horses were confiscated but she was determined to keep the last animal, hiding him in the smoke house, the storage shack, and other places when Southern searchers appeared. Finally, she had her servants spread straw on the floor of her magnificent library and then she personally led the horse up the stairs of her mansion, through the door, and down the large foyer, taking it to the library, where it made itself at home while all the while her neighbors hooted at another eccentric gesture by "Crazy Bet."

The horse remained in Van Lew's possession throughout the war and, often as not, it pulled a cart full of straw under which escaped Union soldiers hid, Van Lew driving it through graveyards and down dark lanes to a relay station where the fugitives would be deposited before moving on toward the Union lines and freedom. Prison escapes from Libby and other Richmond prisons increased in 1863. Confederate jailers were not that concerned if a starving, weak-legged prisoner escaped since the whole of the Confederacy was a sort of prison.

Escapes were frequent, often imaginative. A Union soldier who had been a master tailor was asked to make a new Confederate uniform for a Southern officer. Once he was given the proper cloth he made several, the extra Confederate uniforms donned by Union soldiers who simply walked out of prison wearing them. Many of the escapees knew to go to Van Lew's home, slipping into her house through a prearranged route. Once inside, Van Lew would shelter them in the huge hidden room on the third floor until she could arrange to have them sent on to another home.

In Febuary 1864, a Union cavalry raid led by Judson Kilpatrick and Ulric Dahlgren ended in disaster when Kilpatrick was turned back by strong Southern forces, Dahlgren was shot, and ninety-two of his men taken prisoner. On Dahlgren's body papers were found which showed that his orders were to burn Richmond and assassinate President Davis. When this was made public the Southern outcry was tremendous and Davis himself, incensed at such barbaric warfare, ordered Dahlgren to be buried "in the cemetery of a thousand grassless graves," the final resting place for dead Union soldiers.

In a secret ceremony conducted in the middle of the night by Major John Wilder Atkinson and his hand-picked Confederate troops, Dahlgren's corpse, confined to a plain pine box, was buried in an unmarked grave. A witness hiding in the cemetery, a Negro woman sent there on Van Lew's orders, witnessed the burial spot and reported its location to the spymaster the next day. That night, Crazy Bet went to the cemetary and jammed a stick in the earth to mark the spot.

Later, Van Lew had several German farmers in her employ secretly go to the cemetery at night, dig up the body (which was easily identified since Colonel Dahlgren had lost a leg at Gettysburg), and place it in a metal coffin. The coffin was then put into a wagon and a layer of earth over it and on this a number of small, bundled peach trees ready for planting. The cart was driven past Confederate pickets to Yellow Tavern, where the body was reburied, the spot marked by the planted peach trees. Van Lew then sent a message to General Ben Butler, requesting that he notify Dahlgren's father, Admiral John Adolph Dahlgren, that his son's body was safe and would be returned to him after "this unhappy war is over."

Though she had saved Dahlgren's body (which was returned to Washington after the war), Van Lew was not able to save the life of another Union spy, Timothy Webster, one of the most courageous of northern agents who was executed in Richmond for espionage.

The Union spymaster went on planning escapes for Union prisoners, the most spectacular of which occurred in the winter of 1864 when 109 men, led by Colonel Thomas E. Rose and Colonel Abel Streight, dug a fifty-eight-foot tunnel beneath Libby Prison, struggling against huge water rats and sewer gas, and caused the greatest escape of Federal prisoners in the history of the war. Of those fleeing, forty-nine men, including Streight, managed to cram themselves into Van Lew's hidden room and were later smuggled back to the Union lines. There was no doubt that Van Lew planned the escape and told the Union soldiers where to dig.

Throughout 1864 and into 1865, Van Lew, through five relay stations, sent daily coded messages to General U.S. Grant, telling him of Confederate morale in Richmond, as well as its defenses and troop strength. An old Negro who was never questioned by Confederate pickets trudged past Southern lines and into Grant's quarters with Van Lew's dispatches hidden between the soles of his huge brogans. He carried flowers, his cover, which Van Lew picked from her gardens each morning, and these adorned Grant's table at breakfast. The Negro courier was never stopped by Confederate guards "because of his humble station in life."

General Winder knew that Van Lew was smuggling fugitives and information to the Union but he could not prove it. At one point, frustrated, he ordered his men to search the Van Lew mansion. Dozens of Confederate soldiers and officers, sabres rattling, boots thumping on the stairs and throughout the rooms of the mansion, failed to find anything. They missed, of course, the hidden panel on the attic staircase and the room behind it where dozens of escaped Union soldiers sat breathlessly waiting for the searchers to leave.

A few hours later, Van Lew, dressed in a filthy frock and carrying a moth-eaten parasol, marched into General Winder's office. She spun the parasol crazily while acting the lunatic and said: "Sir! Your ordering underling officers to search my home for evidence to convict me in league with the enemy is beneath the conduct of an officer and a gentleman!"

Winder fumed and fussed, then, as always, apologized.

A few months later Lee abandoned Richmond to Grant, retreating toward Appomattox and surrender. When Richmond fell, mobs of gamblers, whores, thugs, and thieves ran amok through the city, torching everything. Van Lew, driving her carriage through the chaotic streets, was hailed, as usual, as "Crazy Bet!" She witnessed the death throes of the Confederacy. Police were helpless against the looters and arsonists. General Richard Ewell rode frantically through the streets with his staff trying to quell the rioters but it was a useless gesture.

Van Lew rode home and sat on her front porch, flanked by six great pillars, looking down from Church Hill to see Richmond in flames. Then she retrieved a large Union flag which had been smuggled to her some months earlier and climbed to the attic, stepping out to the roof and running up the flag. Below in the city, hundreds stared upward at the flag of the hated enemy. Suddenly the mob raced up the hill, trampling through the Van Lew gardens, vowing to tear down the despised banner.

As they approached the house, a small woman dressed in black stepped onto the porch and valiantly faced the mob. She held up her hands to quiet the throng and said: "Lower this flag or hurt one bit of my house and I will see that General Butler pays you back in kind. . . . Every one of you!" She began to point to members in the mob, saying "I know you! . . . And you! . . . And you!" The crowd retreated, then collapsed into tiny groups that wordlessly slipped back down the hill.

General Grant, hearing that Lee had evacuated Richmond, sent a troop of Union cavalry into the city to immediately protect his most valuable agent, Elizabeth "Crazy Bet" Van Lew. The Union soldiers found her inside the Confederate War Department offices, carefully sorting papers left by the fleeing Southerners, saying that she had gone to these offices to collect documents "General Grant might find . . . valuable." She was a spymaster to the last.

Grant later visited Van Lew, sat drinking tea on the rear piazza of her mansion, and thanked her for her extraordinary espionage services. So did General Butler and other Union officers and officials. When the citizens of Richmond learned that Van Lew had been a secret agent for the Union all along, she was ostracized and the hardware store her brother ran was boycotted. Her fortune gone, Van Lew was reduced to living in poverty but she was rescued in 1869 when U.S. Grant became President.

One of his first acts as President was to appoint Elizabeth Van Lew the Postmistress of Richmond with an annual salary of $4,000 a year. She lost the post later and was impoverished to the point of selling her silverware and antiques to survive. Then the son of Captain Paul Revere, grandson of the revolutionary hero, arrived to provide a yearly annuity for Van Lew. She had helped Captain Revere escape Libby Prison (he was later killed at Gettysburg). On September 25, 1900, after a long illness, the spymaster of Richmond died in her home atop Church Hill. Some time later all her furniture, heirlooms, beloved books, and personal letters were sold off in a Boston auction to pay her long-standing debts. Her personal correspondence with Oliver Wendell Holmes, President Grant, President Garfield, President Hayes, and dozens of Union generals, was sold for $10. The large American flag she had raised over burning Richmond was purchased for $75.

The spymaster was buried in Shockhoe Cemetery with only a few relatives in attendance. A simple marker was replaced two years later when a 2,000-pound stone arrived from Massachussets from the Revere family. It was placed at the head of the grave. A bronze plaque in the center bore an inscription, which read:

ELIZEBETH VAN LEW
1818 1900

She risked everything that is dear to man—friends fortune, comfort, health, life itself, all for the one absorbing desire of her heart, that slavery be abolished and the Union be preserved.

Long into the twentieth century the classic old houses of Richmond were preserved, including the residence of Jefferson Davis. Not so, the most resplendent Van Lew home on Church Hill. The local school board decreed that it had to be taken down so that a school could be erected in its place. In 1911, wreckers climbed Church Hill and hammered away at the old mansion until it was nothing but rubble. Richmond had taken its final revenge on its most treasonable child.

[ALSO SEE: *Lafayette Baker; Allan Pinkerton; Timothy Webster*]

British official John Vassall, shown in his luxury London apartment, was blackmailed into spying for the KGB in the 1950s after Soviet agents learned of his homosexuality.

VASSALL, WILLIAM JOHN
British Spy for Soviets ▪ (1924–   )

LONDON-BORN VASSALL WAS THE SON OF A CHURCH of England clergyman. He left school at the age of sixteen to work at a bank. He then worked as a clerk in the Admiralty offices and was sent as an assistant to the naval attaché at the British Embassy in Moscow in 1954.

KGB agents learned that Vassall was a homosexual and quickly compromised him, showing him photos they had taken of him and other homosexuals they had sent to seduce him. Vassall quickly became a KGB spy, stealing classified information from the Embassy and passing it to his Soviet handlers.

Returning to London in 1956, Vassall was assigned to the Admiralty, where he continued his spying for the KGB. He was paid so well that he was able to rent an apartment in the exclusive Dolphin Square district, one which he furnished with expensive antiques.

Vassall was promoted in 1959 to a position of greater security, one which allowed him to steal Admiralty secrets concerning radar, newly invented torpedoes, anti-submarine devices, and sophisticated new armaments. Further, he provided the Soviets with fleet operational orders and communications, as well as classified publications.

When the Portland Spy Case broke and such spies as Gordon Lonsdale, Helen and Peter Kroger, and Harry Houghton were exposed as spies stealing Admiralty secrets, Soviet spymasters ordered Vassall to cease operations. He resumed his espionage some months later when it was felt that he would not be detected. He was able to secure details of the new *Invincible* class carriers being built by the British and

this information greatly aided the Soviets in the development of their helicopter carriers, *Moskva* and *Leningrad*.

In 1962, MI5 finally caught onto Vassall when the British Embassy in Moscow reported that the Soviets were in possession of information that could only have come from the British Admiralty Office in London. Several persons in the office were investigated and the hunt narrowed down to Vassall, who was arrested by Special Branch. Classified documents were found in his apartment. He was sentenced to serve eighteen years in prison but was paroled in 1973. It was later theorized that Vassall had been exposed by the Soviets themselves to divert attention from other, more important agents they had planted at the Admiralty offices.

[ALSO SEE: *Harry Houghton; KGB; Helen and Peter Kroger; Gordon Lonsdale; MI5; Special Branch*]

VENLO INCIDENT
Capture of British Agents by SD Agents in World War II ▪ (1939)

NO OTHER ESPIONAGE ADVENTURE IN WORLD WAR II proved to be as embarrassing for British intelligence as the Venlo Incident in 1939. Not only were two top British spymasters snared by German intelligence but their superiors, such as the much overrated Claude Dansey, deputy chief of SIS under Graham Stewart Menzies, were shown to be what they were—gentlemen amateurs playing at espionage and in their aloof attitudes and naive spying grossly incompetent amateurs at that.

SIS (MI6) had long searched for a German underground that might be able to overthrow the maniacal dictatorship of Adolf Hitler. Two of Dansey's top SIS officers, Captain Sigismund Payne Best and Major R. H. Stevens, attempted to infiltrate what they thought to be a genuine German resistance movement. At the same time, Reinhard Heydrich, the sinister and calculating chief of the SD (security police), along with his boss, Heinrich Himmler, chief of the Gestapo and the SS, drew up plans to infiltrate British intelligence.

They began by having an SD informer, Dr. Franz Fischer, who operated in the Netherlands as a Catholic refugee, contact Dr. Klaus Sprieker, a leader of Catholic refugees in Paris. Sprieker worked for Dansey as an informant. After conferring with Fischer, Sprieker was convinced that he might prove to be the perfect conduit by which SIS could contact the German underground and he told this to Dansey. Without checking Fisher's background, Dansey, in turn, in the fall of 1939, recommended Fischer to Best and Stevens, saying that Fischer was "in a position to obtain information of vital importance through his contacts with airforce officers." Had Dansey or anyone else at SIS checked, they would have learned that Fischer had been a wanted felon and a fugitive from the criminal police in Frankfurt, where, in 1933, he had misappropriated 350,000 marks from a fuel distribution center where he was the manager. He had fled to Switzerland and then to Paris, until he agreed to spy for Heydrich and the SD.

Best had Fischer travel to London, where he interrogated him. He then wrote to Dansey, saying that he was suspicious of the man. Dansey wrote back, telling Best that "Dr. Sprieker knew Fischer well and that he was quite trustworthy." Fischer told Best that his top underground contact was an officer in the Luftwaffe, a Major Solms, who possessed details of a military conspiracy against Hitler, a resistance fighter who had also been in contact with Dr. Sprieker. Best was told to meet with Solms and traveled to Venlo, Holland, on the German-Dutch border.

Solms was really an SD agent named Johannes Traviglio, a failed opera singer. Meeting in the Hotel Wilhelmina in Venlo, Best and Solms had little to say to each other. The strapping German admitted that he was little more than an errand boy and that he would have to get approval from his "chief" before he could tell Best anything of consequence about the German underground. He did say that the highest-ranking German generals were involved in a conspiracy to remove Hitler but he could provide no details. That would be done by his "chief," who would only meet directly with Best.

Stevens accepted the conspiracy story as real and never expressed any doubts about Solms or Fischer. His friend, Captain B. B. Scholfield, a naval attaché in The Hague, cautioned him that the whole thing might be a ruse, "but he refuted any suggestion that it might be a trap, so I could do nothing but wish him luck." By this time, Germany was at war with England and France after having invaded Poland on September 1, 1939. When the war was only a few days old, Best and Stevens confided their mission to Dutch General van Oorschot, who assigned to them his aide, Lieutenant Klop.

The 29-year-old Walter Schellenberg, who was then directing the German operation, then decided to meet the SIS officers himself, driving to The Hague with two aides. He introduced himself as Major Schaemmel and proceeded to ask Best if England would consider a peace "which was both just and honorable." Best said he would find out what the government position might be. The Germans then said they would meet with Best and his men on November 9, 1939, in a café in Venlo.

It was at this time, apparently convinced that they could not penetrate SIS beyond Best and Stevens, that Heydrich decided to spring the trap. Schellenberg arrived at the Venlo cafe first and sat outside at a table alone sipping a brandy. A car packed with SD agents, led by agent provocateur Alfred Naujocks, was parked nearby, hidden from view. At about 3:30 P.M., the British arrived in a large Buick.

At that moment the SD car suddenly roared into sight, its occupants firing shots "to add to the surprise," according to Schellenberg. The Dutch frontier guards were thoroughly disoriented and ran about without drawing their own guns. As Schellenberg approached the Buick, Klop, at the sound of the firing, jumped from the passenger seat and drew a large service revolver. He aimed it at Schellenberg but at that moment the SD car screeched around the corner and came to a halt in front of Klop. The brave Dutch officer, realizing the trap, began to fire at the SD car, his bullets smacking into the windshield, crystalline threads spreading from the bullet holes.

Naujocks, a cold-blooded SD killer, jumped from the car and he and Klop advanced on each other in a duel, both firing pistols. Suddenly, Klop lowered his weapon and sank mortally wounded to the pavement. Naujocks turned to Schellenberg and shouted: "Will you get the hell out of this! God knows why you haven't been hit!"

Schellenberg ran to his car, looking over his shoulder to see Best and Stevens dragged from the Buick and shoved into the SD car "like bundles of hay" by Naujocks and his men. When the SD chief ran around a corner he bumped into a gigantic SD officer, one who had been added to the SD contingent at the last minute and did not know Schellenberg. He jammed a pistol into Schellenberg's face, apparently thinking he was Captain Best.

"Don't be stupid!" Schellenberg said, shoving the pistol from his face. "Put that gun away!" The SD man struggled with Schellenberg and fired the weapon, a bullet whizzing past the SD chief's head. Naujocks ran over and intervened, explaining to his fellow SD guard that Schellenberg was in charge of the German operation. As the giant blathered his apologies, Schellenberg dashed for his car and drove off toward the German border. The SD men dragged the wounded Klop into their car, which then raced after Schellenberg's fleeing auto.

The British spymasters and Klop were taken to Dusseldorf, where Klop later died of his wounds. Best and Stevens were grilled mercilessly until they confessed to all sorts of crimes, including the sabotaging of German, Italian, and Japanese ships. They were then sent to a concentration camp, where they remained until freed by Allied troops in 1945. Oddly, the day before the Venlo incident occurred, George Elser, a nondescript 36-year-old mechanic from Württemberg, was arrested for planting a bomb in the Burgerbrau Keller in Munich, which blew up on November 8, 1939 at 9:21 P.M., eleven minutes after Adolf Hitler had left the place after celebrating the anniversary of his failed 1923 putsch. Eight people were killed and sixty-two injured.

Best and Stevens were tied by Himmler and Heydrich to the Elser assassination attempt against Adolf Hitler, although it appears that this was just more Nazi subterfuge, that Elser may have been yanked from a concentration camp and made to appear an assassin when the bombing had been the evil work of the Nazis themselves.

The Venlo incident was a tactical victory for German intelligence, one which exposed the SIS as a doddering and inept intelligence organization. Dansey, of course, was the real villain; he had used his top agents like pawns, throwing them away on a madcap scheme. His superior, Menzies, who became chief of SIS a short time later when Hugh Sinclair died, took the responsibility for the fiasco at Venlo. He was to regret the botched mission for the rest of his life. In 1947, Best came to him to state that his life had been ruined at Venlo. The Germans had confiscated his business and property and he had been reduced to living in near poverty in Devon.

Best asked for compensation, about £15,000. Menzies told him that SIS funds were depleted and no such sum could be awarded. Then Best more or less threatened Menzies that if he were not compensated for his ordeal (Dansey was by then dead), he would expose Menzies as the man who was responsible for the debacle in Holland. The two crusty intelligence officers haggled for months until about £6,000 was given to Best. It was a shoddy end to what was, at best, a slapdash intelligence mission.

[ALSO SEE; *Claude Dansey; Gestapo; Reinhard Heydrich; Heinrich Himmler; Graham Stewart Menzies; MI6; Alfred Helmut Navjocks; Walter Schellenberg; SD; SIS*]

VIDOCQ, EUGENE-FRANCIS
French Agent ▪ (1775–1857)

BORN TO A BAKER IN ARRAS, VIDOCQ WAS EDUCATED by the Franciscans. At the outbreak of the French Revolution, he joined the French army, fighting under the banner of a rising young general named Napoleon Bonaparte. A ladies' man, Vidocq became incensed when hearing that one of his mistresses had been seduced and abused by another man. The large, big-boned Vidocq beat the seducer senseless, was arrested, convicted of assault, and sent to prison in 1797.

Vidocq made many escape attempts, which added years to his otherwise short sentence. Finally, in 1799, he made good his escape, going to Paris, where he established a small shop and sold used clothes. The denizens of the underworld Vidocq knew so well, however, blackmailed him, saying that unless he paid them they would go to the police. The fugitive paid the blackmail for many years but by 1809 he had had enough. He went to the police, offering a clever proposal.

If the charges were dropped against him, the bold Vidocq suggested, he would inform on the most vicious criminals in Paris. He promised to provide enough evidence to send these felons to prison for life. The offer appealed to the calculating Joseph Fouché, Napoleon's minister of police and spymaster. He accepted Vidocq's proposal and within a year Vidocq had sent more than 800 killers and thieves to prison on evidence he provided to Fouché.

Vidocq was so treasured by Fouché that he appointed him head of the Sûreté, the newly organized Criminal Investigation Department. Approaching his task with the philosophy that "it takes a thief to catch a thief," Vidocq hired about twenty of the toughest ex-convicts he had met in prison, employing them as his agents. He promptly arrested his own men on bogus charges and sent them back to prison. This was a ruse to plant them among criminals who told them of various crimes and criminals working outside of prison.

For twenty years Vidocq worked to clear Paris and other major cities of the worst criminal element. In the process he became known as the greatest detective in France. He resigned his post in 1827, saying that old wounds received in prison and in the many escapades as head of the Sûreté had enfeebled him. He was recalled in 1832 to crush a political revolt, then resigned once more.

In 1833, Vidocq, though rich, could not resist working in law enforcement of some kind. He established a detective agency, the first of its kind in the world, providing agents to combat the myriad swindlers who bilked merchants and tradesmen. Vidocq also took private cases and met with great success in solving sensational crimes, from robbery to murder.

When King Louis Philippe was overthrown in 1848, Alphonse Lamartine, head of the provisional government, asked Vidocq to undertake a secret mission on behalf of France. He accepted, going to London to confer with Prince Louis Napoleon, nephew of Bonaparte the emperor. Lamartine wanted to know Napoleon's intentions, Vidocq asked the prince. Napoleon told him he would wait and see, that he had no plans for a military coup.

Vidocq returned to Lamartine with the news that Napoleon would not cause a civil war in France to assert his right to his uncle's throne. This moderate position proved wise; Napoleon was elected to the National Assembly and within a year was elected president of France. Subtly, he gathered overwhelming political strength until he was made Napoleon III, emperor of the Second Empire.

Napoleon had been so impressed with Vidocq that he often engaged the great detective to undertake secret missions on behalf of the French military and the ministry of the interior. Vidocq remained active as a secret French agent almost to the time of his death.

[ALSO SEE: *Joseph Fouché*]

VOSS, OTTO HERMAN
German Spy in America ▪ (1899– ?)

ONE OF THE FIRST NAZI AGENTS TO OPERATE IN America, Voss was part of a serious network of German spies bent on stealing U.S. aviation secrets to aide the Luftwaffe in secretly building up a modern air force. Colonel Erich Fritz Gempp, then the director of the understaffed Abwehr, selected William Lonkowski (an alias) to establish a spy network in the U.S. Lonkowski arrived in New York in 1927. He immediately went to see Otto Hermann Voss, whom the Abwehr listed as an "available agent."

Voss had been born and educated in Hamburg and was a naturalized American citizen but his loyalties belonged to Germany. He had written German authorities of his willingness to help the Fatherland in any way. At the time Lonkowski took him up on his offer, Voss was an above average aviation mechanic at the Sikorsky aircraft plant in Farmingdale, Long Island, where U.S. Army fighter planes were manufactured.

Through Voss, Lonkowski met and also recruited a younger man, Werner Georg Gudenberg, also a native of Hamburg and an engineering draftsman who had a basic understanding of electronics and who also worked in an aircraft manufacturing plant where army bombers were made. Both men, at Lonkowski's direction, began stealing secrets from their employers and turning them over to the German spymaster, who passed them on to Johanna Hofmann, a 26-year-old hairdresser who worked on the German liner *Europa*. Hofmann, who died her hair a bright orange, spoke no English but dutifully delivered Voss's stolen documents to Luftwaffe officials in Germany.

Voss was active at his job, making copies of blueprints and plans for fighter planes. Security at the Sikorsky plant was so lax that he found the complete blueprints for a new, experimental sea plane being developed for the U.S. Navy in a garbage can and he delivered the plans to Lonkowski that night. Seven days later the plans were on the desks of Luftwaffe generals in Berlin.

Lonkowski had by then established a widespread German spy network throughout the U.S., his spies filching secrets from almost every aircraft plant in the country. Content that his ring was operating smoothly, Lonkowski returned to Germany to brief his Abwehr superiors. While gone, he left his network in charge of slick Dr. Ignatz Griebl.

All of Lonkowski's long-labored organization came crashing to ruins after Griebl enlisted the aid of a flamboyant, unpredictable, and outlandish agent, Guenther Gustave Rumrich, who boldly posed as the "Under Secretary of State," to secure blank passport applications, which led to his arrest. Rumrich quickly turned informant, which led to the arrest of Voss, Gudenberg, Griebl, and others. Lonkowski escaped since he was out of the country at the time.

Voss' conviction hinged on two documents FBI agent Leon G. Turrou had unearthed, both signed by Voss and addressed to Captain Erich Pheiffer of German naval intelligence. The documents detailed a fuel tank design Voss had stolen at the Sikorsky plant. In the end, the German-American mechanic stood before Judge John C. Knox and received the stiffest sentence meted out to the German spies, six years in prison. The others drew lesser sentences. All would probably have been executed, Judge Knox pointed out, in time of war. "But in this country we spread no sawdust on our prison yards," intoned Knox, referring to the manner in which Germany dealt with spies in peacetime, execution by ax. The next day, in Berlin, as if to prove his point, a Nazi headsman decapitated two spies "for unnamed foreign powers."

[ALSO SEE: *Abwehr; Wilhelm Canaris; FBI*]

WALKER, JOHN ANTHONY, JR.
U.S. Spy for Soviets ▪ (1938–   )

THE FBI OFFICE IN HYANNIS RECEIVED FEW CALLS, certainly nothing like the phone traffic handled in the Boston office or other Bureau offices in major American cities. Moreover, the existence of the Hyannis office itself might present a puzzle to anyone asking why the FBI would want to have an office in the Massachusetts heartland of wealthy landowners and rich vacationers, an area absent of serious crime, let alone spies. The office in Hyannis, of course, had been established by J. Edgar Hoover at the time John Fitzgerald Kennedy was president, mostly to provide on-hand agents to serve the Kennedy clan.

Hoover had not opened the FBI satellite office out of goodwill and concern for the Kennedys, whom he despised. It was the expedient thing to do, just as transferring Barbara Walker's call to Hyannis was the expedient thing to do—it gave the Hyannis agents some work.

On November 29, 1984, an FBI agent appeared at Barbara Walker's home and listened to her describe her ex-husband, John Anthony Walker, Jr., as a dangerous spy. The FBI man patiently heard her out, then went back to his office and filed his report, which he labeled "65-0," sixty-five meaning the subject was espionage, zero meaning that Barbara Walker's information was useless and should not be investigated. The Boston office filed the report in the inactive files and nothing was done. Laura Walker, Walker's daughter, whom her father had attempted to inveigle into espionage and who had encouraged her mother to call the FBI, then called the Bureau in Boston herself on January 24, 1985. She wanted to know what the FBI was doing about her treasonable father. Still nothing was done.

Then, in February, an FBI supervisor reviewing the Zero file read the contents of the interview

with Barbara Walker closely. He decided it had some merit after all and sent a confidential memo to the Washington, D.C., FBI headquarters via AIR-TEL. He did not include the original date of the interview with Barbara Walker. Whoever received the AIRTEL message did nothing about it, buried the report, and forgot it.

Somehow, Jospeh Wolfinger, assigned to the FBI's counterintelligence division in its Norfolk, Virginia, offices, received a copy of the AIRTEL message. He sought and got approval for a full-scale investigation.

It began with an interview with Laura Walker, who lived in Buffalo, New York. Two agents heard the woman say that her father had many times asked her to sell secret military information while she was in the army and stationed at Fort Gordon, Georgia. She went on to explain that her father, a career Navy man, never had any money and that the family had been poor for some years. Suddenly, cash was plentiful but her father became furtive.

The FBI began to build its case against Walker, learning that in 1968, when a café he owned in South Carolina failed, he came into substantial ready cash. He apparently contacted the Soviets in that year and began to sell them secrets from the submarine base at Norfolk where he was then stationed. In that year he moved his family into an expensive apartment and bought two sailboats, one costing $5,500. He spent that much on new furniture. A short time later Barbara Walker found a Minox camera in her husband's desk at home, along with a metal box, which contained maps for drop sites and a note apparently from his Soviet handler saying "Information not what we wanted, want information on rotor." This was a reference to the rotor used in the Navy cipher machines then employed for coding secret messages.

Though Walker was no longer in the Navy in 1985, his wife believed that he was still obtaining secrets for the Soviets from his older brother Arthur, a retired lieutenant commander in the navy. She did not suspect that her son Michael, then serving as a seaman on board the aircraft carrier *Nimitz*, was involved. She also knew that her husband was in regular contact with someone named "Wentworth," a petty officer serving at a U.S. naval station somewhere along the California coast. (This was Jerry Alfred Whitworth, who worked in collusion with Walker in filching secrets and selling them for hefty Soviet cash rewards.)

Walker had begun selling secrets to the Soviets while at Norfolk in 1962, or "yellow" as he later called it, a term relating to the yellow sheets feeding through a monitor roll, a continuous printout of teletype traffic that contained all sorts of information, from birthday greetings to enlisted men from relatives to top-secret information on ships, armaments, listening and tracking devices, jet fighters on aircraft, and contingency battle plans.

Reassigned to San Diego in 1969, Walker was put in charge of the radioman school, training recruits in using communications equipment. Since he had less access to secrets, he was able to supply his Soviet handlers with less substantial secrets and his monthly stipend from the KGB dropped from $4,000 a month to $2,000 a month. He nevertheless passed naval orders and other intelligence information to the Soviets. It was while in San Diego that Walker recruited Whitworth into his spy ring.

Knowing he would retire in 1975 after twenty years in the navy, Walker planned to use Whitworth as his conduit for information after he left the service. Though Whitworth would be assigned sea duty, he would simply steal secrets and funnel them to Walker whenever his ship docked. Wherever that ship docked, Walker would be waiting for him to receive the secrets and dole out the cash. Walker enacted this plan with Whitworth without ever consulting his KGB handlers or control.

First, however, he went to sea himself on the *Niagara Falls*, as its chief radioman. He photographed each day the ship's cryptographic material churning from its code machines. In about a year and a half he made two deliveries to his Soviets spymasters in Washington, D.C., but his material was so good that he was again being paid $4,000 a month in cash by the Russians.

By the time he was reassigned to Norfolk, Walker was making regular weekly drops in the Maryland and Virginia countryside. He would drop his microfilm at the bottom of a trash bag—the trash would never contain food or anything with strong odors which might attract animals. He would then proceed to a prearranged letter drop area to retrieve his Soviet cash payments and instructions or "wish lists" of secrets wanted by the KGB. He would also be told at times on how to improve his espionage techniques. At one point, his Soviet handler suggested he read the novel *The French Connection* so that he could better learn the art of surveillance, a procedure that the FBI might practice against him.

By the time Walker had retired in 1975, Whitworth had gone on to become an officer involved with Navy satellite communications, information he passed to Walker, who, in turn, sent it on to the Soviets. Whitworth's information was so valuable to the Soviets that Walker convinced his KGB bosses to pay him a lump sum, $200,000, which he would split with Whitworth as an inducement for Whitworth to reenlist in 1980, even though Whitworth had earlier told Walker that he intended to retire at that time. The Soviets paid and Whitworth reenlisted and went on supplying Walker with top secrets, stealing from the Navy offices in Alameda where, as traffic manager, he had access to every communications report.

Whitworth found it next to impossible to photograph the cryptographic material in his offices and thought it too dangerous to take material out overnight. Walker solved that problem by having the Soviets buy Whitworth a van with tinted windows. Whitworth parked the van next to his office and, when he stepped out for lunch, he brought with him the day's "yellow," stepping into the van to photograph the secrets, then returning the reports within a few minutes to his office.

In December 1981, however, Whitworth was routinely transferred to other duties that cut off his access to secret information. Walker attempted to enlist his daughter in his espionage ring but she refused. Walker's sources were drying up and he delivered less and less material to his Soviet bosses, who were growing less and less interested in paying large sums of money for mediocre material. They had, by then, a number of other American spies funneling military secrets to them, including Ronald Pelton, an NSA analyst who simply walked into the Soviet Embassy in Washington and offered his services, working with KGB spymaster Vitaly Yurchenko. By 1983, Pelton had delivered top secrets to his Soviet bosses in several trips to Vienna.

With his sources drying up, Walker sold the Soviets his own son, Michael Lance Walker, as a spy. Michael Walker was then an ordinary seaman, having joined the Navy in 1982 at age twenty. He had joined to be a spy and make money the way his father had done, a father who had weened him on adopting a conscienceless attitude toward treason, that making big money was all that mattered.

Walker encouraged his son to steal classified documents, which he began to do in 1983. Walker then showed his son how to use a Minox camera to photograph a series of secret documents and began paying him money, congratulating him for every secret stolen. As a yeoman striker working in the operations office of the carrier *Nimitz*, Michael Walker had access to secrets and stole them regularly, delivering these to his father whenever the ship docked and receiving $1,000 payments a short time later.

In 1984, Whitworth then resurfaced, attempting to sell Walker more information but he was rebuffed, told that his information was low grade and worthless to the Soviets, adding that "lower-cost replacements" (meaning his own son) were available. In short, Whitworth was told he was no longer wanted by the Soviets, an arbitrary move on Walker's part. Whitworth returned to the West Coast, where he brooded about no longer having the handsome profits from espionage. He also believed that Walker was holding out money due him. Bitter and seeking revenge, he wrote an anonymous letter to the FBI office in San Francisco, hinting that a major American spymaster had been stealing Navy secrets for years.

This led to more anonymous letters from Whitworth and communications from the FBI. Before Whitworth could expose Walker, Laura Walker, at the FBI's request, phoned her father several times, her conversations tapped by the Bureau. Walker's statements were enough to prompt the FBI into arresting him, his son Michael, his brother Arthur, and Jerry Whitworth. It was the end of a financial bonanza for Walker, who had made an estimated $1 million from the Soviets for selling secrets for about seventeen years. He was convicted and sent to prison for life. His son Michael received a twenty-year sentence, Arthur Walker got three life terms and Whitworth received 365 years in prison. None of them, except Michael, the most pathetic of them all, expressed any regret for selling out their country.

[ALSO SEE: *FBI; KGB*]

WALLENBERG, RAOUL
Swedish Diplomat and Secret Agent ▪ (1913–1965?)

THE SON OF A WEALTHY SWEDISH BANKER, Wallenberg was educated to become an architect or go into the family banking business. He did neither, spending his youth as a European playboy. Almost as an afterthought, when World War II broke out, he entered the Swedish diplomatic service.

In 1944, however, he suddenly thrust himself into one of the most dangerous assignments any diplomat ever undertook. He volunteered, for inexplicable reasons, to go to the Swedish Embassy in Budapest with the special purpose of trying to save as many Jews as he could. Adolf Eichmann, a fanatical Nazi carrying out the orders of Heinrich Himmler, was then busy attempting to round up what remained of the Jewish population in Hungary—about 225,000 people—and ship them as soon as possible to concentration camps where they would be exterminated.

When Wallenberg arrived at the Swedish Embassy as a special attaché, he immediately began to find ways to protect the Jews from Eichmann's fatal deportation to Germany or Poland. At his disposal was more than $1 million with another $1 million available from U.S. sources. He would buy the Jews from the Nazis if need be.

Wallenberg first announced that Swedish passports would be given to all Jews who could prove family or business connections with Sweden. Swarms of Hungarian Jews mobbed the Swedish Embassy and hundreds of passports were issued, many to those for whom Wallenberg "invented" business connections in Sweden. These Jews were exempt from wearing the telltale Star of David on their clothes and were entitled to immigrate to Sweden immediately.

Admiral Miklos Horthy, the fascist regent of Hungary and Hitler's puppet dictator, was an anti-Semite of the first order and he encouraged his wife and children to adopt a similar attitude. The Arrow Cross, the Hungarian fascist party, encouraged its brutal members to attack Jews in the streets, drive them from their homes and apartments, and confiscate their belongings.

The heroic Raoul Wallenberg, Swedish vice consul in Budapest during World War II, who operated an espionage network to save tens of thousands of condemned Jews.

Wallenberg played on the fear of the Hungarian police and officials, telling them that unless he was allowed to distribute thousands of passports which made Hungarian Jews automatic Swedish citizens, they would undoubtedly be considered war criminals after the Allies won the war and be brought to trial. He boldly lied by saying that he had the power to designate exemptions for those who cooperated with him. He was allowed to initially distribute 4,500 passes and place these Jews in "safe" houses under Swedish protection from Eichmann's roving squads of SS men.

As the German war machine began to collapse, many rabid anti-Semitic Hungarian officials adopted a more moderate approach to the "Jewish problem." As the war dragged on to a close, Horthy himself saw that the Nazis were fanatics who would fight to the last but that their regime was doomed. He replaced all of the fascists in his dictatorship with moderate or anti-Nazi officials, placing General Géza Lakatos at the head of the government, telling him to make a separate peace with the Allies and "put an end to the inhuman, foolish, cruel persecution of the Jews." This, of course, was a self-serving move to protect himself against being branded a war criminal.

None of this meant anything to the German troops and the SS forces occupying Hungary. Eichmann went on rounding up Jews, packing them onto trains and sending them to concentration camps. Wallenberg made an effort to persuade Eichmann to cooperate. He told Wallenberg "I plan to do everything to keep you from saving your Jews. Your diplomatic passport won't protect you from everything. Even a neutral diplomat can meet with an accident."

Ignoring Eichmann's death threat, Wallenberg worked feverishly to save more and more Jews, hiring them by the hundreds, buying them literally from Nazi captors who allowed him to hand out Swedish passports to as many Jews as he could while they were being herded into the cattle cars of death trains. The SS also protected and encouraged the Arrow sadists to attack and murder any Jews they could locate, particularly in Buda, across the Danube from Pest.

Wallenberg resolved to stop these killings and filed many official protests against the atrocities. He threatened Allied reprisal and then became a spymaster, leading a guerrilla movement where groups of underground fighters combated the Arrow squads and even the SS in saving Jews randomly picked up on the street. His spies infiltrated Arrow groups and informed him of their planned raids so that Wallenberg could evacuate apartments and houses on the "strike" list.

Using a great deal of money, Wallenberg bribed Hungarian police to allow Jews to escape from the Central and International ghettos. He collaborated with an underground Zionist group that dressed its most Aryan-looking members in Arrow Cross uniforms. These impersonators rescued many Jews from fascist captors. Wallenberg drove about the city of Pest day and night for months, handing out Swedish

Efim Moshinsky, a former KGB agent who claimed to have seen Wallenberg as late as 1961, when the forgotten Swede was a prisoner on Wrangell's Island.

passports and forged baptismal certificates so that Jews could prove they were Christians if caught.

When Hungarian officials reduced the food rations sent to the Jewish ghettos to a starvation level, Wallenberg stormed into the offices of Sedey, chief of police. He shouted at Sedey that if the Jews died, he would be later held responsible for their deaths. Sedey said that the Jews were no worse off than the other inhabitants of Budapest, who were by then all on meager rations.

"You have a special obligation to the Jews because you have imprisoned them in a ghetto. Jailers have a moral responsibility to feed their prisoners!"

Sedey was dumbfounded at the shouting Wallenberg. When he began to stammer, Wallenberg knew he had thoroughly intimidated the police chief. He pulled a young officer from his desk chair, sat down, and typed out an order that instructed officials to immediately distribute food to the Jews in the ghetto. Whipping this paper from the typewriter, he placed it in front of Sedey and shouted: "Sign it!" The thoroughly cowed Sedey signed the order and Wallenberg raced off to have it enacted.

Wallenberg, as all of his aides knew, was alone. He was patient but bold. He was the diplomat of a neutral country but acted as if he commanded the Allied armies. To the dozens of men and women who worked with him he was "a modest, unassuming boy with an iron will."

One of countless Jews Wallenberg saved later recalled: "Wallenberg was very elegant yet so very natural. I thought that it was fantastic that such a man would suddenly appear in the middle of the night to save Jews, as if he had done it all his life."

The playboy who had dissipated his youth in the nightclubs of Europe had been transformed to a hero, an idol, a hope. He had been given a great purpose in life and he embraced that ambition with passion and dedication. When a friend asked if he was afraid, Wallenberg replied softly with a smile: "I like this dangerous game. I love this dangerous game." He knew that only the strong image he projected was his true protection. His authority was the image of a shuddering future where Allied tribunals would send war criminals to the scaffold.

This posture undoubtedly saved more than 30,000 Jews in war-torn Budapest. When the Russians finally drove into Budapest, Wallenberg went off to meet with Russian generals, seeking their aid in protecting what was left of Hungarian Jewry. He was, however, taken by NKVD officials to Moscow, kept under guard, and treated like a prisoner. He was imprisoned in Lubianka Prison and interrogated repeatedly. Wallenberg protested, saying that he was a Swedish diplomat. One of his interrogators said: "We know all about you, that you come from a big capitalist family in Sweden." He was then accused of being a German spy. He was moved to another prison in Lefortovskaya, and kept there from April 1945 until the spring of 1947.

From that point on, no one could report the whereabouts of Raoul Wallenberg. He tapped out a message to a fellow prisoner on the wall of his cell: "They are taking us away." It was speculated that he was taken to Siberia but that report was never substantiated. Wallenberg simply vanished into the political maelstrom that was Stalin's Russia. Swedish authorities who had been searching for the heroic diplomat were told by Russian officials in mid-1947 that "Wallenberg is not in the Soviet Union and is unknown to us."

Reports came over the years from inmates released from Russian prisons that they had seen Wallenberg in 1951, in 1959, and as late as 1964 or 1965, when it was reported that he died in Vladimir prison. Swedish authorities did not accept the report of his death until the early 1980s. The consistent reluctance of the Russians to even admit that Wallenberg was their prisoner may have stemmed from the fact that they had made a mistake in first arresting, detaining, and prolonging his imprisonment and, by 1946 or 1947 it was too late to admit that mistake so they merely kept Wallenberg in prison until he died.

Another theory has it that Wallenberg had become so "damaged" or "injured" while being held by the Russians that even if they wanted to return him to the West they could not without revealing their inhuman treatment of a diplomat from a neutral country. Wolfgang Vogel, a successful East German lawyer who negotiated many exchanges of spies between Russia and the West, reported in 1980 that Wallenberg was "long dead." When Vogel was pressed for authentication, the Communist attorney snorted: "What do you want me to do—bring the bones?"

[ALSO SEE: *Heinrich Himmler; NKVD; KGB*]

Sir Francis Walsingham was England's first great spymaster; he mercilessly protected the throne of his sovereign, Queen Elizabeth I, using his vast espionage network to uncover plots, conspiracies, and assassins, and employing forgery and treachery to achieve his calculated goals.

WALSINGHAM, FRANCIS
Spymaster for Elizabeth I ▪
(c.1532–1590)

THE SON OF A NORFOLK LAWYER IN THE COURT OF Henry VIII, Walsingham graduated from Cambridge with a law degree in 1552, spending the next six years on the Continent in protest against the Catholic reign of Queen Mary. While living in Italy he befriended several aristocrats who were furthering the espionage arts of secret writing that had come into existence during the Renaissance. He went on to study and master codes and ciphers.

When Queen Elizabeth I assumed the throne, Walsingham returned to England in 1558. He took an active part in the persecution of Catholics and, with the backing of William Cecil, entered Parliament in 1663. Joining the Privy Council in 1573, he was knighted in 1577. Throughout this period Walsing-ham proved a staunch supporter of Elizabeth and her rigid anti-Catholic policies.

The ousted Catholics championed Mary Stuart, Queen of Scotland, in that she promoted the Catholic faith and had an equal claim to the British throne. In jeopardy, Elizabeth offered Mary sanctuary against the Scottish reformers and then betrayed her, imprisoning her. She then plotted with Walsingham, whom she had made her spymaster, to compromise Mary.

Long earlier, Walsingham had established the most extensive spy network the world had ever seen, placing secret agents throughout Europe, especially in the Catholic courts of Spain, Italy, and France, to ferret out Catholic plots against Elizabeth. To that end, he sent the poet Christopher Marlowe to study at a Catholic seminary in Rheims where anti-Elizabeth plots were being hatched.

Marlowe later became a celebrated playwright and Walsingham's homosexual lover, but he was mysteriously murdered in a tavern brawl, which may have been staged to effect his permanent disappearance. Walsingham had a penchant for using writers as spies. William Fowler, the Scots poet, worked for him at one time or another, as did Matthew Royston.

Queen Elizabeth I, who most probably conspired with Walsingham to forge a document which would allow her to execute her half-sister, Mary, Queen of Scots.

The hapless Mary Stuart, Queen of Scots, a Catholic monarch sent to the headsman by her half-sister Queen Elizabeth I, after being compromised by a forged letter produced by Walsingham.

Many of the so-called plots against Elizabeth were probably invented by the insidious Walsingham. He jailed many innocent persons whom he accused of espionage in order to enhance his image of spy-catcher with his sovereign. One real plot, however, involved Anthony Babington, who planned to release Queen Mary from the Tower of London and remove Elizabeth in 1586. Walsingham's spies unearthed the plot and Babington and others paid the price of their lives.

One of Walsingham's most astute and assiduous spies was Anthony Munday, who lived in Rome and infiltrated the English College there, exposing many Catholic plots and identifying many anti-Elizabethan spies for his spymaster in London. At home he relied upon John Dee and Thomas Phelippes, both scholars of ancient ciphers and codes, to decode all of Queen Mary's mail, which was intercepted by another Walsingham spy, Gilbert Gifford, who posed as an ardent Catholic and gained Mary's confidence.

Through these men Walsingham built a case against Mary, one which eventually spelled her doom. Mary's correspondence, according to Dee and Gifford, also a cryptographer of sorts, contained secret treasonable statements. One letter of Mary's in particular was used by Walsingham to prove that Mary had been part of the Babington plot and it brought about a death warrant from Elizabeth. It is likely, however, that Walsingham himself, or Dee or Gifford acting under his direction, concocted this forgery, perhaps with Elizabeth's collusion, in order to eliminate Mary.

When Elizabeth sent Mary to the block in 1587, King Philip of Spain became enraged, branding Elizabeth a regicide. The Catholic monarch sought revenge against Elizabeth and began to build a huge armada that would sail to England, invade the island, and sweep the English Protestant queen from her throne. Walsingham, however, sent one of his best spymasters, Anthony Standen, to organize a spy network along the coasts of Spain and France. Standen was able to learn the exact time of sailing and route taken by the armada and sent this information to Walsingham.

One of Standen's agents was on the staff of the Marquis of Santa Cruz, who had been appointed by Philip as the grand admiral of the armada. This agent was able to learn the exact number of vessels in the armada, their captains and crews, the number of troops being conveyed, along with all stores, ammunition, and armor to be employed in the invasion. Acting on Standen's information, Elizabeth's fleet intercepted the armada and destroyed what was left of it after it had been decimated by a powerful hurricane.

Though he had given great service to Elizabeth, Walsingham did not find his queen a grateful monarch. After her triumph over Spain and its vanquished armada, Elizabeth all but ignored her spymaster. Walsingham, whom Elizabeth obviously distrusted as being too powerful and having information that might implicate her in Mary's official "murder." She removed him from office. He died penniless two years later. The many petitions he sent to Elizabeth were returned to him unanswered.

Walsingham's espionage procedures and systems, however, outlived him and were employed by John Thurloe, Oliver Cromwell's exacting spymaster. Walsingham's code expert Thomas Phelippes, upon his spymaster's death, founded and became the proprietor of the first private espionage agency, one that successfully catered to the English gentry. Like Thurloe and Phelippes, countless spymasters to come the world over would owe a debt to the clever, immoral Walsingham.

[ALSO SEE: *Anthony Babington; John Dee; Christopher Marlowe; Anthony Munday; Anthony Standen; John Thurloe*]

WALTERS, ANNE-MARIE
British Spy in World War II ▪ (1924–)

BORN IN ENGLAND, WALTERS' FATHER WAS BRITISH, her mother French. She was raised in France but was in England when World War II broke out in 1939. Speaking fluent French and English she was recruited at age nineteen by the French section of the SOE. In the summer of 1943 she underwent espionage training and was scheduled to parachute into southwestern France in November, accompanying a 20-year-old medical student named Jean-Claude Arnault.

On the night of January 3, 1944, both were parachuted into Gascony. Walters was assigned as the personal courier and liaison SOE officer to French underground leader Lieutenant-Colonel George Starr, codenamed Patron. Starr had worked in the Belgian mining industry and had fled to France when the Germans invaded. In 1944, he would lead 1,000 resistance fighters into Toulouse to recapture the government with the Allies. Starr's SOE underground unit was one of the most efficient during the war; his radio operator, Yvonne Cormeau, transmitted and

received messages uninterruptedly for thirteen months without ever being detected by the direction-finding units of the Gestapo.

Walters had a similar record as a courier, taking many risks over several months to carry information back and forth from Starr to his many other resistance groups throughout southwestern France. In many instances, she was stopped, sometimes searched, by Vichy French police and Gestapo agents but she always managed to talk her way out of a trap. While staying with a small resistance group, she and others were identified by an informer and she fled, escaping in a perilous journey over the Pyrenees to Spain in August 1944, eventually returning to England, where she was awarded medals for gallantry.

[ALSO SEE: *SOE*]

WASHINGTON, GEORGE
Commander of Continental Army in American Revolution ▪ (1732–1799)

SHORTLY AFTER WASHINGTON ASSUMED COMMAND OF the Continental Army in 1775 he lay siege to Boston, where British forces occupied the city. The British, it appeared, anticipated his every move but this dilemma was solved when Washington learned that he had a spy in his midst. Benjamin Church, Washington's surgeon general, had been sending the British information on the American forces. Washington learned of this through some of Church's letters that had been intecepted. Church was dismissed and Washington suffered another setback in 1776 when his top spy, Nathan Hale, was caught and hanged.

From that time through 1778, Washington served as his own spymaster. He personally dealt with Patriot spies who informed him that the Hessian mercenaries camped at Trenton, New Jersey, had taken no preparations for defense of their position. Relying on this information, Washington's small army crossed the Delaware River on Christmas Eve, 1776, and attacked the sleeping Hessian troops by surprise, winning an important victory.

When Sir Henry Clinton replaced Howe in 1778, Washington again lay siege to New York. At this time, he employed a well-meaning but inept spy named George Higday; one of Washington's letters to Higday was intercepted due to the spy's bungling. Higday was arrested on July 13, 1778, an espionage setback that embarrassed Washington and caused him to establish a secure espionage service and place Major Benjamin Tallmadge at its head. Tallmadge enlisted the aid of many of his fellow Yale graduates, who established the Culper Ring inside New York City. This tightly operated espionage network was headed by Robert Townsend, who supplied Tallmadge and Washington exact information on Clinton's army.

Washington had become an excellent director of espionage for the American cause. He met with many of his spymasters, urging them to use invisible inks, ciphers, and codes in their communications with him. In some instances, such as the sensitive Culper Ring members, he refused to even know their names lest he ever mention them and inadvertently compromise them.

One of Washington's great disappointments involved his protégé and one of the most fiercely courageous American generals, Benedict Arnold, who met with Clinton's spymaster, Major John Andre, in an effort to deliver West Point into British hands. Andre was accidentally captured by three American soldiers and taken to Tallmadge, which led to Arnold's flight to the British lines. Since Andre had been captured wearing civilian clothes, he was deemed a common spy and was condemned to death by a military tribunal. Washington refused to reprieve Andre from the gallows, a decision which his top spy in New York, Robert Townsend, could not understand. Washington's harsh attitude at that time may have been prompted by the memory of the execution of *his* spy, Nathan Hale, in 1776 by the British, although it was never determined that Washington acted out of vengeful retaliation.

The commander-in-chief was also a master of disinformation. On many occasions he planted false information that misled the British. His most successful ploy in this area was convincing Clinton not to attack newly landed French forces at Newport, Rhode Island, under the command of Jean Baptiste de Vimeur, Comte de Rochambeau. Washington planned to link up with these forces but he had to make sure that Clinton did not move his troops out of New York, which Washington was then besieging.

The ruse Washington planted went through a rabid Tory named James Rivington, who was a genuine British spy until the tide of war began to turn in favor of the Americans. At that point Rivington secretly became a double agent, working really for Washington. Rivington reported to Clinton that he had obtained information that Washington, instead of joining with the French, was about to attack New York.

So convincing was Rivington (he actually published this news in his Tory newspaper) that Clinton dug in, preparing to fight a defensive battle. Meanwhile, Washington left a token force before New York, which made it appear that he was mounting an attack and took his main force to meet the French and then march to Yorktown, Virginia, where he achieved an overwhelming victory over British forces under General Cornwallis and brought an end to the American Revolution.

[ALSO SEE: *John Andre; Benedict Arnold; Benjamin Church; Culper Ring; Nathan Hale; James Rivington; Benjamin Tallmadge; Robert Townsend*]

WASSMUSS, WILHELM
German Agent in World War I ■
(1880–1931)

THOUGH A DIPLOMAT IN THE GERMAN FOREIGN OFFICE, Wassmuss was by nature a wild adventurer, an eager spymaster, and one of the greatest liars in the world. For several years during World War I, he effectively wielded the tribes of southern Persia against whole British armies through payments of gold, promises of more gold, and the most fantastic tales ever uttered in that part of the world. Wassmuss was rightly known at that time as the "T. E. Lawrence of Persia."

Born in Hanover, Wassmuss early on dreamed of traveling to exotic lands and experiencing great adventures. Upon his university graduation, he applied and was accepted into the Kaiser's foreign service. He was first sent to Madagascar, then, promoted to the rank of vice consul, he was assigned to the German consulate in Bushire, Persia, in 1909. The following year he returned to Madagascar and remained there until 1913.

When World War I broke out in 1914, Wassmuss was already relocated in Bushire. He quickly realized that southern Persia would be a plum the British would want to pick since it was rich with oil reserves. When all of the other German diplomats accepted their passports at the opening of hostilities and departed for Germany, Wassmuss saw his opportunity to lead the Persians in a great crusade. He alone decided to stay behind and face the wrath of England. Like Lawrence in Arabia, Wassmuss had a great affinity toward the Persian tribes. He spoke their languages fluently and he had learned, as he had in Madagascar, the traditions and customs of these nomads.

He met with superiors in Constantinople and proposed leading the Persian tribes in a guerrilla war against the British. His plan was approved. Amply supplied by the foreign office with gold—in fact, his supply was almost limitless, thanks to the Kaiser's personal instructions to the foreign office to give the vice-consul all the gold he demanded—Wassmuss began a propaganda campaign to turn the Persians against the British, telling them that their true friend and the eventual victor of World War I would be Germany.

Persia, at the time the war started, was, by international agreement, under the protection of a neutral force that was made up entirely by Swedes, although Turkey, which had declared on the side of Germany, was the nominal ruler of the Persian lands. The neutral Swedish government, which England knew full well, was very much pro-German.

British SIS agents soon reported that the Persian oil lands would most likely fall into German hands

The German adventurer and spymaster Wilhelm Wassmuss, who led the tribes of Persia against the British as effectively as Lawrence of Arabia vexed the Turks in World War I; his great error was leaving his diplomatic code book behind when fleeing British troops in 1915.

with the aid of the local Swedish military forces and through the schemes of a stubborn German diplomat, Wilhelm Wassmuss, who appeared to be buying the loyalty of all the tribes. Leading the Bakhitiari tribe, Wassmuss also cut the Anglo-Persian pipeline on February 5, 1915.

Wassmuss distributed anti-British leaflets to the tribes in Dizful and Shushtar, convincing the local chieftains that the British were the sworn enemy of the Sultan of Turkey, who was the Caliph of Islam. He urged a *jihad,* or holy war, be fought against the British.

A British expeditionary force was sent to capture Bushire in the summer of 1915. Wassmuss first learned of its approach when it was only a few miles from the town.

As Wassmuss rubbed the sleep from his eyes, he heard the rattle of machine gun fire in the distance. Then a servant brought the news that a British armored column was already at the outskirts of the city. Wassmuss leaped from his bed and ordered his treasure chests of gold to be carried to the one automobile at his disposal. He stood in the street outside the consulate in his pajamas, directing the loading of the chests. With his valet behind the wheel, he soon realized that the chests left no room for him.

"Drive on!" he ordered the valet, telling him to go to a village in the nearby mountains where the tribal chief was his close friend.

"But how will you escape, excellency?" the valet nervously inquired.

"By the fastest possible means—now, go on!"

The auto sputtered through the narrow streets and was soon laboring up a narrow mountain road toward the distant village. Wassmuss was not far behind. He found a horse-drawn cart and paid the owner a princely sum for the animal. Detaching it from the cart, Wassmuss mounted the horse and, his silk pajamas flapping in the wind, rode pell-mell after his valet and gold-packed car.

Hours later British officers were sipping rare wines retrieved from the German consulate basement, laughing at the description given to them of Wassmuss' wild flight. A short time later, William Reginald Hall, chief of British naval intelligence, met a Navy officer who had been invalided from the Persian Gulf and who regaled him with the same hilarious story. Hall, however, did not laugh.

"The man escaped while clad only in his pajamas? Then where is his baggage containing his clothes and personal effects?" The Navy officer told Hall that all of Wassmuss' belongings had been transported to England and were at that moment stored in the basement of the India House in London. Hall lost no time in sending one of his top aides to conduct a thorough search of Wassmuss' belongings. The aide returned with one of the greatest espionage treasures of the war, the German diplomatic codebook that Wassmuss, in his haste, had left behind.

Through the codebook retrieved from Bushire, British intelligence was able to read almost every top-level diplomatic message sent from Berlin for the remainder of the war. The diplomatic code being sent to America was cut off when the transatlantic cable to Germany was severed by the British. The Germans simply borrowed the use of the Swedish access to the cable. When England warned Sweden to halt this practice, the pro-German Swedes sent their own messages for the Germans, a practice identified by British intelligence but one that was permitted to continue since all of the diplomatic Swedish/German messages were being then intercepted by Hall and his cryptographers in Room 40 and were being quickly decoded thanks to Wassmuss' codebook. That codebook became much more important when its contents allowed Hall's cryptographers to decode the infamous "Zimmermann Telegram," sent to the Mexican government in 1917.

Meanwhile, Wassmuss was not inactive in Persia. He reached the provincial capital of Shiraz, where he led a raid against the British, one in which the British vice-consul was killed. Wassmuss had in his possession at that time an estimated 200,000 gold marks and he used some of this sum to bribe the governor of Shiraz into ousting the British diplomats there. The entire British colony was driven out of the area and sent back to the coastal towns.

So effective were Wassmuss' desert forces that the British placed a reward of £20,000 pounds for Wassmuss dead or alive. The spymaster gained even greater notoriety in the London offices of the British Foreign Office. In its main conference room maps of the world were displayed on the walls. Each map listed the present British positions and enemy dispositions. A huge map of Persia bore only one name in gigantic letters: "WASSMUSS."

As the war progressed the British made little headway in Persia. In fact, British troops lost ground, met everywhere by increased military pressure from the Persian tribes. Whatever Wassmuss wanted, he got from the tribes and he generously paid them for their military achievements. At one point, these tribes were holding down three British divisions, troops that could have been used on the Western Front, a situation that prompted a British general to remark: "That man Wassmuss is worth a whole corps."

When Persian leaders heard that the British had achieved a victory at the battle of the Somme, they began to waver in their loyalty to Germany. Wassmuss boldly dismissed such news, saying it was nothing but British propaganda. He then went on to deliver the most fantastic lies in order to keep the Persians as allies, saying that a mighty German army had not only invaded England but had taken King George V prisoner. A few weeks later he told the tribesmen, who were shut off from the rest of the world, that his wireless operator had given him the news that King George had been executed in a public square in London. The more bad news Wassmuss learned of Germany's fate, the more he lied, announcing to naive tribal chieftains that Russia had surrendered to the German army, and that France was about to capitulate.

By 1918 even the most cleverly positioned fabrications could not prevent the Persian chiefs from learning the truth. By then Wassmuss had all but depleted his once vast holdings of gold and he began giving the chieftains promissory notes. When his "creditors" demanded payment in gold, Wassmuss admitted that he had none to give, that he was waiting for the Kaiser to send more gold to him, gold that never arrived. When the war ended, Wassmuss was threatened with death but he managed to escape Persia and return to Germany in 1919.

Wassmuss attempted to persuade the Foreign Office to honor his pledges to the Persian tribesmen but he was told that Germany was bankrupt. He returned to Bushire in 1924 and tried to make amends by cheaply buying up farmlands, promising to repay German war debts from the profits the crops would bring. The crops failed and Wassmuss returned to Berlin, where he died in 1931 without money, friends, or even recognition of his brilliant wartime service. Four years later, his counterpart, T. E. Lawrence, died in England and was celebrated the world over as a spectacular World War I hero, accomplishing in Arabia the same thing as Wassmuss had achieved in southern Persia, except for one difference. Lawrence had been on the winning side.

[ALSO SEE: *William Reginald Hall; T. E. Lawrence; Room 40; SIS; Alexander Szek; Zimmermann Telegram*]

WATERGATE SCANDAL
U.S. Political Espionage Operation ▪ (1972–1974)

ON JUNE 17, 1972, DURING THE U.S. PRESIDENTIAL campaign, five men broke into the Watergate apartment-office complex in Washington, D.C. The aim of these burglars was to obtain operations information from the offices of the Democrat headquarters in the building. The five men, known as the "White House Plumbers," were arrested. These included Eugenio Martinez, Virgilio Gonzalez, Frank Sturgis, Bernard Barker, and James McCord.

It was soon revealed that the burglar squad was operating under the direction of E. (Everette) Howard Hunt and G. (George) Gordon Liddy, who were also arrested. Hunt, Liddy, and McCord had all been former members of the CIA. The burglars had carried with them sophisticated espionage equipment used by the CIA, including cameras, lockpicks, miniature tear-gas devices, bugging equipment, and walkie-talkies, over which they communicated with Hunt and Liddy.

The CIA, though suspected of being involved with the break-in at the President's behest, was subsequently cleared of any affiliation with the Watergate burglars. This was not the case with the FBI, which was later found to have suppressed evidence in the Watergate hearings following the break-in. When all seven men were sent to prison, McCord became angry when he did not receive a pardon from President Richard M. Nixon. He wrote a letter to Judge John Sirica, who had presided over the trial of the burglars. McCord implicated White House staff members in Watergate, pointing to President Nixon's culpability.

Nixon was already implicated, however, since Liddy and McCord were members of the Committee to Re-Elect the President. A senate investigating committee, with Senator Sam Ervin of South Carolina at its head, was then established to look into the matter. It discovered that White House staffers Egil "Bud" Krogh and Jeb Stuart Magruder had hired Liddy and Hunt to supervise the break-in. Magruder headed a dirty tricks division of the committee to reelect the president, which was aptly called CREEP.

Much of what had been uncovered in the trial of the seven White House Plumbers had pointed to Nixon and his White House staff as being directly involved in the Watergate break-in. The burglars had photographed Democrat documents, installed listening devices in the Democrat headquarters, laundered money to prevent identification of its source, had used secret couriers to deliver payoffs and even used letter drops for the pickup and delivery of information and cash, all strong evidence of tried-and-true espionage practices and all of it managed on a sophisticated level that could only have involved professional agents acting under the direction of the White House.

Then John Dean, White House counsel to President Nixon, implicated the president and almost all of his top aides, including Attorney General John Mitchell, H. R. (Harry Robbins) Haldeman and John D. (Daniel) Erlichman, Robert C. Mardian, Dwight L. Chapin, Richard Colson, and others. Tapes made in the Oval Office of the White House reinforced Dean's statements. The House Judiciary Committee then began to prepare articles of impeachment.

Shortly after releasing the White House transcripts (tapes), Nixon, on August 5, 1974, resigned his position, the first U.S. president to ever do so. Vice President Gerald R. Ford replaced him. Dozens of Nixon aides went to prison for perjury and other offenses in the massive attempted cover-up, including Mitchell, Haldeman, Erlichman, Mardian, Chapin, Colson, and others. Nixon was pardoned by his successor Ford and thus evaded serving a jail term.

WEBSTER, TIMOTHY
Union Spy in Civil War ▪ (1821–1862)

AFTER LINCOLN'S INAUGURATION AND THE OUTBREAK of the Civil War in 1861, the new president realized that the Union was hopelessly uninformed about Confederate activities. In fact, Confederate spies were everywhere and contributed greatly—as did Mrs. Rose Greenhow, the southern belle in Washington—to the early victories of the South. It was Greenhow who sent information to General P. G. T. Beauregard that enabled the Confederates to sweep the field at the first battle of Bull Run.

To establish an effective Union counterintelligence and espionage, Lincoln sent for the celebrated detective Allan Pinkerton, making him chief of Union intelligence. Pinkerton selected the best detectives in his service to work with him, especially those who had helped him smuggle Lincoln to Washington for his inauguration after an assassination plot against him was uncovered.

The most conscientious and dedicated agent Pinkerton had was Timothy Webster, who had been born in London and immigrated to America with his family when he was a small boy. He grew up in Princeton, New Jersey, receiving scant education. He

became a laborer before joining the New York police department. He was assigned to handle security at the World's Fair of 1853 and it was here that he met a visitor, Allan Pinkerton, who had a year earlier established the Pinkerton National Dectective Agency in Chicago. The following year, Webster was hired by Pinkerton and became one of his top agents.

When Pinkerton began the Union's secret service he kept Webster and his other best agents busy with tracking down draft dodgers (a hopeless task in that there were literally tens of thousands of these shirkers in the North), and exposing corrupt suppliers of military goods and foodstuffs. The Pinkertons exposed and brought to trial meat packers who had shipped tainted or rotten meats to General McClellan's troops. They unearthed short-changing cotton brokers and robbery rings that looted military storehouses. Much of the time, the federal government did not honor Pinkerton's operating expenses, causing him to send for money from his own lucrative detective agency in Chicago to support his newly formed secret service.

Not until late 1861 did Pinkerton energetically begin to send his men into Confederate territory to learn the enemy's positions, strengths, and plans. Webster was one of the first of these, going into Maryland and Virginia, where he passed himself off as a Southern sympathizer who lived in Washington. He offered his services to Southern military commanders and was sent on missions to Washington, returning with what these commanders believed to be valuable information. The information Webster provided, however, was misleading and doctored by Pinkerton himself.

Thus, as a convincing double agent, Webster first installed himself in Miller's Hotel in Baltimore, passing himself off "as a gentleman of means and leisure." Pinkerton provided Webster with a handsome team of horses and a resplendent carriage, as well as considerable cash to give small fetes and buy all the drinks necessary in the Baltimore bars while cadging information from secessionists.

John Scully, another Union spy, served as Webster's courier, taking his messages to Pinkerton in Washington. Webster made sure that Scully could always get past Southern sentries with a simple trick. He and Scully went to a Baltimore photographic gallery where they posed smiling, holding a Confederate flag between them. Both men kept this photo in their wallets at all times and when Confederate soldiers or agents searched them and found the photo they immediately released them, believing them to be staunch Southern sympathizers.

Webster then shifted his operations to Richmond where he again was welcome as a Southern sympathizer. He sent on his messages to Baltimore and from there the coded letters went to Pinkerton in Washington. On one occasion, Webster personally took important messages to Pinkerton, leaving Richmond for Baltimore and from there going on to Richmond. He was stopped by a Northern agent in Baltimore who held him captive in a hotel room until Pinkerton arrived. Rather than expose his double agent, Pinkerton arranged for Webster to escape from the two guards Pinkerton assigned to escort Webster to Fort McHenry for internment.

When news of this spectacular escape was learned in the South, Webster became a hero in Richmond. He was lionized and feted by important Southern leaders. Judah P. Benjamin, Confederate Secretary of War, was so impressed by Webster that he made him his personal courier. As such, he could freely move between Confederate and Union lines, delivering Benjamin's personal mail (making copies, which were given to Pinkerton), as well as scouting through the Southern military installations and forces.

When returning to Baltimore in late 1861, Webster learned of a secret Southern organization called the Knights of Liberty, a Southern fifth column whose leaders boasted that they could muster 7,000 armed men to attack and seize Washington. Webster not only joined this group but became a leader, addressing its members at secret meetings. Pinkerton was appraised of the group's activities and even added two more of his agents to the secret Knights society. Both of these Union agents were unknown to Webster and he to them to avoid any compromise.

Pinkerton then arranged for a large-scale raid in Baltimore against the Knights. Union forces battered down the door of the meeting place while Webster himself was thundering threats against Lincoln on the platform. As the Southern sympathizers scurried about in panic, Webster escaped through a window and fled to Richmond. Almost all of the secret society members were arrested and imprisoned. Two of those caught in the raid were leading newspapermen, Frank Key Howard, editor for the Baltimore *Exchange*, and T. W. Hall, editor for *The South*. Both men, along with about two dozen others, were imprisoned and held without bail. A large cache of rifles and ammunition was also discovered and confiscated. These weapons were later distributed to McClellan's troops.

Webster, meanwhile, took up permanent residence at the Spotswood Hotel in Richmond, where he worked with a courier, Hattie Lawton. He continued to carry Benjamin's mail and befriended many Confederate dignitaries and leaders such as John Beauchamp Jones, whose Civil War diary later became a literary classic. Webster wrote some of his own espionage classics, reports so detailed that it took Pinkerton and his aides several days to decode the lengthy messages. One report was thirty-seven pages long and contained the smallest details on Richmond's defense works, its seventeen Enfield guns, the height of its breastworks and that they were constructed of "split pine logs." It reported on the illnesses spreading through the Confederate army, the percentage of soldiers who were without shoes, the price of corn and hay.

In February 1862, however, Webster's messages stopped altogether. He was by then very ill, suffering

The valiant Union spy and Pinkerton agent Timothy Webster, who was hanged for spying in Richmond in 1862.

from inflammatory rheumatism, an affliction he had endured for some years. Hattie Lawton was nursing him and this left Pinkerton without a spymaster in Richmond or any flow of vital information from the Southern capital. To correct that problem he sent two men, Pryce Lewis and John Scully, to Richmond.

The mission to Richmond began badly. Lewis and Scully found it difficult dodging their own Union patrols and the skiff in which they were rowing across the Potomac was overturned in a fierce storm. They had to swim to the Virginia shore. They somehow managed to avoid the many Confederate cavalry patrols around Richmond and enter the capital, where they made their way to the ailing Webster. Both men then took rooms at the Ballard House on February 26, 1862. They waited for Webster to painfully complete his final report.

The next afternoon they went to visit Webster and were suddenly surprised to see a Confederate officer and several soldiers enter Webster's rooms. The officer was Captain Sam McGubbin, who headed the counter-intelligence department of General John H. Winder's intelligence service. Both Scully and Lewis froze but soon relaxed when McGubbin appeared to be making a social call on Webster, inquiring after his health. At that moment, ironic fate entered the room in the form of the son of former Senator Jackson Morton.

The youth looked at Scully and Lewis closely. Both agents lowered their heads, knowing they had been recognized as the two guards Pinkerton had placed on the Morton family when they had been detained as Southern sympathizers. Both Lewis and Scully mumbled their goodbyes and left the room but they were seized and arrested before they left the hotel.

Both Scully and Lewis were tried separately and found guilty of espionage, both refusing to admit anything. They were sentenced to be hanged on April 4, 1862. A priest came to take Scully's confession before execution and at that time Lewis desperately wrote a note to the British consul in Richmond, demanding the protection of the British government and stating that both he and Scully were English subjects (this was true). He gave the note to the priest, who promised to deliver it.

Judge Crump, the magistrate who had presided at the trials of Lewis and Scully, then visited the spies and asked them some routine questions, then left, mumbling: "I wish you were Yankees!"

That night Lewis huddled in a blanket, expecting death. He would later write: "I had no fear of dying. I felt sure the physical pain would not be greater than an instant's toothache, as to hereafter, I believed in a just God. I was in his power. If he was not just I could not help it. I was 27, strong as a lion, and physically without nervousness."

Then a "fussy little man" named John Frederick Cridland entered Lewis' cell. He was the British consul in Richmond. He said that he had gotten Lewis' note but felt that he had little ability to save him even though he admitted that he had not seen the evidence presented against him and Scully in their trials. At the time, however, the intervention of Cridland on behalf of England would mean much, as Lewis knew. The Confederacy had desperately courted England to intervene in the war on the Southern side and, Lewis reasoned, the execution of two British-born Union spies would not sit well with English politicians and public alike.

Cridland said he would demand to see the evidence in the trials and departed. Lewis began to have hope that his ploy might bring about a reprieve. Then he noticed Scully weeping and told him to have courage. Scully sobbed that he had sent a message with the priest, too, one to General Winder saying that he would confess everything. Lewis flew into a rage but before he could vent his anger on his fellow spy, he was dragged to another cell and watched as Winder and Randolph Tucker, Virginia's state attorney, entered Scully's cell to hear his confession.

The next morning, while Lewis peered from the window of his cell to the street below, he saw a carriage draw up in front of the prison. Out of it stepped two of Winder's agents and following them was a well-dressed but enfeebled man. He was Timothy Webster, who was followed by Hattie Lawton. Lewis now knew that John Scully had betrayed the great Union spy in Richmond to save his own life.

Though Winder and others urged Lewis to confess, he remained silent. Meanwhile, Cridland had examined the trial transcripts and then confronted Secretary of War Benjamin with the fact that Scully and Lewis had been tried and convicted before they could obtain evidence for their defense, which, Cridland pointed out, caused the trial to be tainted with a "reversible error." This argument carried great weight with the keen legal mind of Benjamin, who prided himself on upholding justice and adhering to the law. He overruled the court-martials of both Lewis and Scully and postponed their executions.

Timothy Webster by then had been charged with espionage and was tried at the Richmond courthouse. Lewis was brought to testify against him but he refused to implicate him, saying that he had learned from a gossip that Webster sometimes carried mail beyond the Yankee lines and that he had gone to see Webster simply to have him take a letter to a friend in Baltimore. Scully testified separately and later admitted to Lewis in their cell that he had compromised Webster.

Webster was condemned to be hanged; Hattie Lawton, his faithful courier and nurse, was sentenced to serve a prison term of one year and one day. Allan Pinkerton begged McClellan to send a messenger under a flag of truce to Richmond, asking that the three men be exchanged.

McClellan shook his head, saying that such an act was impossible, that it would appear to be a tacit admission that the three men were spies and seal the deaths of all of them, instead of merely Webster. Next, Pinkerton went to Lincoln, who convened a special cabinet meeting. Iron-fisted Edwin McMasters Stanton, the Union Secretary of War, promised he would do all he could to save Webster's life but that he would do nothing for Lewis and Scully "who betrayed their companion to save their own lives."

Stanton sent an envoy under a flag of truce to Richmond to see President Jefferson Davis. His message to Davis was that Washington had not mistreated Confederate spies and had hanged none of them. It asked that Webster be spared. But typical of the rigid Stanton, the note also cautioned that if the South hanged Union spies, the North could do the same.

This was just enough of a threat to the proud Davis for him to refuse clemency to Webster. The death sentence would be carried out. Webster begged General Winder from his deathbed that he be shot, not hanged. He felt that he deserved an honorable end.

Winder refused. Hattie Lawton then begged for Webster's life but her pleas were ignored. On April 29, 1862, Webster was helped to a carriage, with Lawton at his side. He was driven through the streets to the fairgrounds at Camp Lee, where thousands milled about a high scaffold.

Webster and Lawton were shocked to learn that it was to be a public execution, such was the wrath President Davis felt for Stanton's undiplomatic threat. Among the crowd were many Richmond belles, their dresses flaring over delicate hoops. They wore black gloves for the occasion, tightly buttoned about small wrists, and finely woven shawls over their shoulders to ward off the crisp spring morning wind. Webster was helped from his carriage and up the scaffold stairs to face an executioner named Kapard, the jailer at Castle Thunder, a man not well experienced in hanging. Actually, Timothy Webster would be the first American spy to be hanged on his own native soil since Nathan Hale was similarly executed in 1776.

When the trap was sprung, however, he fell to the ground, since Kapard had placed the hangman's noose too loosely about Webster's neck. In great pain, Webster lay on the ground for some minutes until two guards picked him up and carried him back up the gallows stairs to stand him once more on the trapdoor. This time the nervous Kapard adjusted the noose so tightly that Webster's face turned dark red. He gasped: "Strangled! I suffer a double death!"

Again the body shot downward through the open trapdoor but this time the rope held.

Hattie Lawton was allowed to accompany the corpse to a Richmond funeral parlor, where the body was placed in a metal coffin. That night the body was buried in the paupers' section of Richmond cemetery. His grave was unmarked and the earth trampled flat by slaves at the order of Confederate jailers. When Pinkerton heard that his finest agent had been buried in an unmarked grave he vowed to find it and return the body "to Northern soil" following the war. He was able to do this thanks to another courageous Union spy, a woman named Elizabeth Van Lew.

[ALSO SEE: *Rose Greenhow; Nathan Hale; Allan Pinkerton; Elizabeth Van Lew*]

WELLINGTON, DUKE OF (ARTHUR WELLESLEY)
British General and Spymaster ▪ **(1769–1852)**

BORN IN IRELAND AS ARTHUR WELLESLEY, Wellington was the son of Garret Wesley, 1st Earl of Mornington. He entered the British army in 1787, slowly rising in the grades until, in 1799, he commanded a division in the war against the Sultan of Tipu in India. He was appointed to supreme commander of the Deccan by his brother, Richard Colley Wellesley, who was then governor-general of India, a post he held until 1805.

Wellington made his name in the Napoleonic wars, beginning in Spain in 1805, when he was placed in charge of the British Peninsular War in Spain with the rank of lieutenant general. It was during this campaign that Wellington established his first espionage service, one which infiltrated the French forces with Spanish volunteers. These agents reported back to Wellington the strength and disposition of Napoleon's troops, as well as their battle plans.

Shortly before that time, Napoleon had shrewdly manipulated the Spanish into sending their best forces, troops that would have otherwise sided

England's famous military leader, the Duke of Wellington, who adroitly used espionage to win his battles against the armies of Napoleon Bonaparte.

with Wellington, to remote Danish islands where they were to protect against an English invasion, a myth created in the mind of the Spanish general by Bonaparte. Wellington sent his agent, James Robertson, a Scottish cleric, to the Danish islands and, once making his way past the French patrols, reached the Spanish commander and persuaded him to sail back to Spain and join with Wellington against the French.

Captain Henry Hardinge served as Wellington's espionage chief during the campaign and much of the information Hardinge provide proved instrumental in the many British victories in Spain. After Wellington received his title in 1814, he was placed in supreme command of Allied troops fighting and beating Napoleon's army at Waterloo, a resounding defeat that ended Bonaparte's reign as the French emperor and sent him into permanent exile on the barren island of St. Helena. At Waterloo, Hardinge's vast and efficient spy network proved more than a match for French agents, spreading misinformation regarding Wellington's position and battle plans and completely misleading Bonaparte as to the whereabouts of German General Blucher, whose surprise attack on Napoleon's flank utterly crushed the Old Guard.

WENNERSTROM, STIG
Swedish Spy for Soviets ▪ (1906– ?)

THE SON OF A SWEDISH NAVAL OFFICER, WENNERstrom was born and raised in Stockholm. He entered the Swedish Navy in 1929 as a cadet. In 1940, he was sent as an air attaché to the Swedish Embassy in Moscow, where he cemented liaisons with KGB spymasters. He also had created strong ties with members of the Abwehr and while in Moscow, he smuggled information to German intelligence. He was thus a double spy.

Returning to Sweden in 1941, Wennerstrom became a lieutenant-colonel. He was then, as he had been for many years earlier, a member of Swedish intelligence. His real job was to report on activities of the Russian military but by the time he returned to the Swedish Embassy in Moscow in 1949, he was already a double agent working for the KGB. His good friend, Colonel Nikolai Nikitushev, a ranking member of the KGB, had recruited him into the Russian spy service as early as 1941.

When Wennerstrom served in the Swedish Embassy in Washington, 1952–1957, he reported to Moscow all he could learn about the U.S. military and NATO (North Atlantic Treaty Organization). Oddly, he also sent information to Reinhard Gehlen, who headed West German intelligence, which had a strong liaison with the American CIA. Thus, Wennerstrom supplied information indirectly to the U.S. He was by then a master spy supplying information to many nations. His incentives were many—he received enormous payments for this information, as well as information from these agencies, which he used as barter to enemy intelligence agencies.

When returning to Sweden, Wennerstrom promptly turned over to his KGB spymasters the complete plans of the Swedish defense system established against Russia. Wennerstrom was identified as the source of the leaked information but Swedish authorities refused to believe that one of their most trusted officers could be a traitor and double agent.

Then, in 1963, Mrs. Carin Rosen, a maid working in the Wennerstrom home, provided the proof in the form of films of secret Swedish documents which she had found hidden in an urn in her employer's lavish mansion.

Wennerstrom was arrested on June 20, 1963 and, after interrogation, confessed that he had been a double agent for Moscow for many years, as well as other nations. He explained that he had served as a double spy "in the cause of peace," a rationale which was dismissed as nonsense. Wennerstrom was sent to prison for life in February 1964. Since Wennerstrom had access to the complete military plans of Sweden, those plans and operations had to be completely revamped at a staggering expense.

WENTWORTH, PAUL
American Agent for the British ▪ (1740?–1793)

WENTWORTH CAME FROM A WELL-ESTABLISHED New Hampshire family. He relocated to London around 1760, where he made a fortune in stocks. Purchasing inexpensive lands in Guyana, he then doubled his fortune from sugar and rice plantations. Working as an accountant for Wentworth from 1763 to 1766 was Edward Bancroft, who would later figure largely in Wentworth's espionage operations during the American Revolution.

When trouble began in the colonies, Wentworth was already back in London representing New Hampshire interests. He opposed any break with England and when the Revolution broke out he offered to spy on his fellow Americans. He established an espionage network in America and in Europe. In France he was fortunate enough to have as his top agent his former employee, Bancroft, who was then secretary to Silas Deane, one of the American envoys to the French court, the other two being Benjamin Franklin and Arthur Lee.

It was Deane's job to persuade the French to intervene in the Revolution on the American side. All of Deane's secret meetings and correspondence regarding that mission were recorded by Bancroft and passed on to Wentworth, who turned the information over to William Eden, the British under secretary of state and head of England's secret service. Deane would later sour on the Revolution after he was wrongly accused by the Continental Congress of misappropriating funds and migrate to London, where he urged Americans to reunite with England.

Wentworth made a special effort to persuade Franklin to cooperate with the British. The wise old Franklin agreed to meet with Wentworth on the condition that the British spymaster make no mention of rewards "in any part of the conversation." Wentworth took an overbearing approach at this meeting, telling Franklin that the British government was willing to go on fighting for ten years to prevent independence. Franklin responded calmly by saying that the Americans were prepared to go on fighting for fifty years.

The wily Franklin then used this meeting to hint to the French that there might be a reconciliation between the Americans and the British. France wanted an independent America in the new world, not a powerful British colony that might expand the New World domain of the English king. This was one of the primary reasons why France decided at that time to side with the Americans, sending its fleets and armies to aid Washington in eventually winning the war against England.

Following the war there were little spoils for Wentworth. He lost his lands in New Hampshire but was awarded a title in England and became a member of Parliament for six weeks. In 1790, he returned to his sugar plantations in Guyana, where he died three years later.

[ALSO SEE: *Edward Bancroft; Silas Deane*]

WICKHAM, WILLIAM
British Spymaster During French Revolution ▪ (1761–1840)

BORN INTO WEALTH IN YORKSHIRE, ENGLAND, Wickham attended Harrow and Oxford before taking a law degree in Geneva, Switzerland, in 1786. He married a Swiss woman in 1788. He then entered the diplomatic service. Because of his knowledge of Switzerland, Wickham was sent to that country in 1794 as assistant to the British ambassador. A year later he himself was named ambassador. His duties were chiefly that of a spymaster.

By 1795, England was openly combating the French revolutionaries who had usurped and beheaded King Louis XVI and his queen, Marie Antoinette. Wickham established a spy network in Switzerland and in France, and directed his agents to plan invasions of France by royalists for any foreign powers who might be able to restore the French monarchy of King Louis XVIII, who was then living in exile.

Wickham's agents at every turn attempted to discredit French revolutionaries, foment rebellion against their rule, and disable the workings of an already shattered government. To accomplish those goals, the British government secretly endowed Wickham with an enormous amount of money. A good deal of that money was spent in a complex plot to bring French General Charles Pichegru, then a revolutionary general, into the royalist camp with all of his troops.

Pichegru had become disenchanted with the revolution because of its excessive violence and had indicated that he was willing to abandon its cause, going over to the ranks of Louis Joseph de Bourbon, Prince Condé, who maintained an army on the Rhine. Condé's agent was Comte de Montgaillard, who used a Swiss printer named Louis Fauche-Borel as the contact with Pichegru. Fauche-Borel, a born intriguer, gave Pichegru £8,000 which Wickham advanced to feed and supply Pichegru's troops.

Once the French general received this payment, however, he vacillated, then reported that the time was not right for him to make his move. Pichegru would make his move in 1804, but his revolt against Bonaparte was short-lived. His plot was quickly detected by Joseph Fouché's agents and he was arrested and imprisoned, found mysterialy murdered in his cell a short time later.

Wickham nevertheless went on spying against the French, successfully reporting their troop positions, armaments, and operations. French spies, however, learned of his network. France pressured Swiss authorities to oust the British spymaster and he resigned, returning to England. He returned to Switzerland in 1799, where he again directed his spy network for another three years, this time applying his espionage against Napoleon. Again the French caused his ouster from Switzerland and this time Wickham remained at home. In 1802 he was named chief secretary for Ireland, a post he held for five years until retiring.

[ALSO SEE: *Louis Fauche-Borel; Joseph Fouché*]

WILMOTH, JAMES R.
U.S. Spy for Soviets ▪ (1968–)

A NATIVE OF OMAHA, NEBRASKA, WILMOTH JOINED the U.S. Navy in 1987, becoming an airman recruit and, in May 1988, was assigned to duty on board the aircraft carrier *Midway*, working in the food service. For several months in 1989, Wilmoth was kept under surveillance when the ship docked at the U.S. Navy base in Yokosuka, Japan. Though not cleared to handle any classified information, Wilmoth obtained printouts from the traffic sent from the carrier regarding fleet operations and apparently sold or attempted to sell this information to a Soviet agent in Japan.

On July 25, 1989, Wilmoth was arrested and a court-martial convened by Vice Admiral Henry Mauz, commander of the 7th Fleet in Japan, which found him guilty on September 24, 1989. He was sent to prison for thirty-five years, one of the longest sentences ever handed down by a U.S. military court.

WILSON, EDWIN
Renegade CIA Agent ▪ (1928–)

A ONE-TIME OPERATIVE FOR U.S. NAVY INTELLIGENCE, Wilson went on to spend sixteen years working for the CIA. As a so-called expert on the Middle East, Wilson, by the early 1970s, began to collect data that would serve his own interest. In 1971, he met and befriended one of the brain-trust members of the CIA, the brilliant Waldo "Doobie" Dubberstein, a CIA analyst who was entrusted with America's top secrets, ranging from the design of nuclear missiles to the Pentagon's contingency atomic war plans.

Wilson, who had planned to leave the CIA and establish a private intelligence agency of his own, cultivated Dubberstein, who, in addition to his top intelligence position with the CIA and the Pentagon, was one of the world's leading archeologists and bilblical scholars.

In 1978, the hulking Wilson met with Dubberstein, telling him that he was on a hush-hush mission concerning Libya, or so Dubberstein later claimed. Dubberstein was then senior officer in charge of analysis of the Middle East, South Asia, and North Africa for the Pentagon's Defense Intelligence Agency (DIA), and could give him considerable help. He was also chief adviser to the Joint Chiefs of Staff on intelligence concerning Egypt, Israel, Iran, Iraq, Syria, Jordan, Libya, the Sudan, and other politically explosive countries. Dubberstein had advised the Joint Chiefs on such sensitive subjects as Israel's capability of building and testing a nuclear weapon and whether or not Hafez Assad, Syria's unpredictable leader, would attack Israel.

Dubberstein not only lectured scores of high-ranking military officers about the Middle East as a CIA consultant, but he also directed the Justice Department's Office of National Narcotics Intelligence Estimate. He also headed international studies for the American Enterprise Institute, a conservative American think tank. "He was the absolute cream of

Maverick spy and former CIA agent Edwin Wilson (center, holding files), shown on December 20, 1982, after being sentenced to fifteen years in prison for illegally selling arms to Libya.

the [intelligence] crop," an FBI spokesman later stated. "You know, the CIA used to have Mr. Dubberstein brief the press."

Though lionized as one of America's most astute intelligence analysts and a preeminent scholar, Dubberstein, as Wilson, knew, craved money, a good deal of money. In addition to supporting his elderly wife in a comfortable home, he had an East German girlfriend less than half his age. Wilson promised him money, a lot of money, if he would provide CIA and Pentagon secrets, according to those who later prosecuted Wilson. Dubberstein would later state that he provided intelligence information which he purposely altered in a scheme to aid American intelligence, false information that Wilson fed to Libyan strongman Muammar Qaddafi, for which Wilson received millions in return.

Wilson, meanwhile, had made millions through his private espionage agency, which was a front for the illegal purchase and selling of arms to Qaddafi and other Middle East dictators. He marketed his military wares from an opulent London headquarters and set up safe houses throughout the city, where he held secret meetings with furtive buyers. Through Dubberstein, he was also able to sell to Qaddafi and others top Pentagon and CIA secrets, including the contents of Dubberstein's classified daily publication, *Defense Intelligence Commentary*, which was distributed to the American intelligence community.

In addition to Dubberstein, Wilson continued to maintain his contacts with former CIA associates, who later claimed that they believed Wilson was operating (and apparently getting secrets from them) with the CIA blessing. One of Wilson's operations was directing hit squads assigned to murdering enemies of Qaddafi. One of those working for Wilson in that capacity was Eugene Tafoya, a one-time American special forces soldier who served as one of Wilson's couriers. In January 1982, Tafoya was imprisoned for two years for assault and conspiracy in the shooting of one of Qaddafi's opponents.

Five months later, Wilson himself came under heavy CIA scrutiny. Qaddafi, an expert at double-dealing, apparently came to distrust Wilson and the genuineness of the information he was buying from the renegade intelligence agent. The shifty dictator may have leaked information to the CIA about Wilson, who was making demands on Qaddafi for more and more cash, apparently threatening to reveal their illegal association.

Wilson was lured back to the U.S. via Santa Domingo on the promise of an undercover CIA agent that he could purchase an enormous shipment of sophisticated arms, perhaps even nuclear weapons, if he could attend a secret meeting in New York. When Wilson got off the plane at Kennedy Airport to attend that meeting, he was immediately seized by FBI agents and jailed. The following December he was convicted of illegal arms sales, espionage and treason in Alexandria, Virginia.

Sent to prison for thirty years, Wilson immediately began planning revenge. He tried to persuade two fellow prisoners to murder two federal prosecutors who had sent him behind bars. When released, the prisoners were to kill these two men in their homes. He also gave the prisoners a list of others he wanted murdered, including a former business associate and five of the jurors who had convicted him. The prisoners went to prison officials and Wilson was again tried in November 1983, receiving another twenty-five-year sentence for attempted murder.

By then, several others who had been associated with the terrifying Wilson had met untimely deaths. The venerable Dubberstein had been indicted for selling Wilson America's top secrets. The 75-year-old intelligence analyst and scholar did not wait to come to trial. On April 30, 1983, he put on his best three-piece suit and hat and visited his 32-year-old East German mistress in her expensive Arlington, Virginia, apartment, for which he paid the rent. After chatting with her briefly, he went to the basement of that building, sat in the middle of the cement floor on a plain chair, and unwrapped a shotgun he had recently purchased. He placed two shells into it, then stuck the two barrels into his mouth and pulled both triggers, blowing the top of his head, hat and all, into the basement wall. On the floor next to his bloody corpse investigators later found a note reading: "I am not guilty!"

Before Dubberstein's suicide came the death of Kevin Mulcahy, who died in the fall of 1982. This former CIA contract employee, who had been closely associated with Wilson, was found dead of exposure on the porch of a small motel in rural Virginia. His death was ruled accidental and attributed to alcoholism. Two years earlier, Cuban-American Raphael Villaverde, who reportedly worked for Wilson as one of his hit men, was blown to bits as he guzzled Tequila, waved to friends, and roared through the waters of Vero Beach, Florida, just before his expensive speedboat exploded. Friendship with Edwin Wilson, self-styled spymaster, was a lethal proposition, as many discovered too late.

[ALSO SEE: CIA; FBI; Muammar Qaddafi]

WISNER, FRANK G.
CIA Deputy Director ▪ (1909–1965)

A NATIVE OF MISSISSIPPI, WISNER WAS A WALL Street lawyer and friend of William J. Donovan, head of OSS, who recruited him for espionage work in World War II. John Toulmin, a deputy chief of OSS, appointed him station director in Istanbul in early 1944, where he quickly established a reliable espionage organization whose tentacles curled into Nazi-occupied countries of southeastern Europe. Through Wisner's spy network, he was able to provide invaluable information to the U.S. Air Force regarding the Ploesti oil fields in Rumania, which were successfully bombed out of operation a short time later.

In September 1944, Wisner went to Bucharest to further direct OSS operations, but when the Russians "liberated" the Rumanian capital it summarily ousted Wisner and his OSS command from the city. Incensed, Wisner got a first-hand view of Soviet dictatorship, and, following the end of World War II, he was extremely vocal in pointing to the Soviet Union as the world's next menace.

Returning to his legal practice, Wisner found his old way of life without purpose. He felt the threat of communism so deeply that he volunteered to combat it in any way he could. He went back to Washington, where, in 1945, he became Deputy Assistant Secretary of State of Occupied Areas. His real job was to gather intelligence in war-ruined Europe, particularly in Berlin, which had been divided into four separate military zones following the collapse of Hitler's regime—American, British, French, and Soviet.

This was the fertile espionage ground where the seeds of the Cold War were planted. Working with Wisner were such gifted men as Arthur Schlesinger Jr. and Harry Rositzke, who worked in the Paris offices, and Richard Helms, who worked with Wisner in his Wiesbaden offices. These men—Cold Warriors they were labeled—early on learned first-hand how their former Russian allies planned to subvert democracy in Germany.

One of Wisner's men in Berlin was Peter Tompkins, who had been an OSS agent in North Africa, and who had landed with U.S. troops at Salerno. He was the agent who guided OSS director William Donovan to meet the most distinguished anti-fascist in Italy, the aged historian and philosopher Benedetto Croce. He would go on to become the only OSS agent in German-occupied Rome, sending out priceless information on German military movements to American commanders at the Anzio beachhead.

After the OSS was disbanded and the CIA was established by President Truman, Wisner assumed the post of Assistant Director of Policy Coordination with the specific mission of combating covert activities of the KGB. The Soviets at that time were spending about $250 million each year to establish Communist front organizations throughout the free world.

In 1949, Wisner conceived of a propaganda tool that would forever vex the Soviets: Radio Free Europe, which consistently beamed its broadcasts about democracy to the Soviet-controlled nations throughout eastern Europe. At about the same time, Wisner realized that the CIA could not combat the tens of thousands of Soviet agents flowing from East Germany to the West and proposed that former Wehrmacht general and German spymaster Reinhard

Gehlen head a West German intelligence agency. The Gehlen organization proved to be extremely effective in countering Soviet espionage.

An expert at disinformation, it was Wisner, with the collusion of Allen Dulles, who apparently planted the idea with Joseph Stalin that KGB agent Noel Field was really a CIA plant (Field had been a former OSS courier for Allen Dulles in World War II). Field, who had gone to live in Prague after the war, was arrested and held as a CIA spy, as were many of his friends and Eastern Bloc country leaders. It would be some time before the KGB determined that Field was not a spy and released him.

Wisner reveled in his ability to mastermind such hoaxes and bragged about his ability to conduct covert operations. During the CIA attempt to take over Communist-held Albania, the CIA used the British-held island of Malta as a training and staging area for anti-Communist Albanian emigres. About that time, Wisner told British spy and traitor Kim Philby: "Whenever we want to subvert any place we find that the British own an island within easy reach." By telling Philby about the Albanian operation, the CIA spymaster did not realize that he was really telling the Russians. Philby passed on the information of the covert Albanian operation and the Soviets met the challenge by arresting all of the Albanian agents sent into the country.

As head of special CIA operations, Wisner initiated the Berlin Tunnel operation wherein a tunnel was dug into East Berlin and there CIA electronics experts monitored all military and diplomatic phone calls in East Berlin. He was also responsible for obtaining the 1956 secret speech Nikita Khrushchev gave in the Kremlin in which he denounced Joseph Stalin. Wisner was one of the CIA chiefs responsible for the successful coup in Guatemala and the failed coup in Indonesia.

From 1953 to 1958, Wisner was Deputy Director for Plans at the CIA, handling all covert operations and dirty tricks. He worked closely with CIA consultant Dr. Sidney Gottlieb, a strange little scientist (not unlike the Hollywood character Dr. Strangelove) who concocted bizarre schemes to assassinate Cuban dictator Fidel Castro, such as slipping him poisoned cigars or shooting poison darts into a wet suit Castro was expected to wear when scuba diving (which Castro never did).

Wisner helped direct radio propaganda into Soviet-occupied Hungary in 1956, causing the Hungarians to revolt against their oppressors, driving them briefly out of power. At the time, Hungarian anti-Communist leaders had been promised that American forces would come to their aid once they revolted. When this did not happen, the Russians returned in force and crushed the Hungarian revolution. Wisner had envisioned a widespread anti-Communist revolt that would unseat the Soviets from all of the Eastern Bloc countries. When the Hungarians were defeated, he went to pieces, suffering the first of many nervous breakdowns, brought on by a severe attack of hepatitis.

After returning to work, Wisner became the station chief in London but he suffered several more nervous breakdowns and, after long periods in the hospital, he resigned from the CIA in 1962. In 1965, tormented by what was described as "his own inner demons," Wisner used a shotgun to kill himself.

[ALSO SEE: *Berlin Tunnel; CIA; Allen Dulles; William Donovan; Noel Field; Reinhard Gehlen; Sidney Gottlieb; Richard Helms; KGB; OSS; Kim Philby*]

WOLF, MARKUS JOHANNES
East German Spymaster ▪ (1923–)

A GRADUATE OF THE LIEBKNECHT ACADEMY (NAMED after the German Communist Karl Liebknecht, murdered with Rosa Luxemberg in 1919), German-born Wolf was taken to Moscow in 1933 when his family fled the Nazi regime of Adolf Hitler. He was trained in espionage from an early age, and, as a protege of Yuri Andropov, was sent in disguise to report on the Nuremberg Trials in 1945, under the cover of a newsman with the alias of Michael Storm. He gathered information on the Western allies which the KGB found so useful they next sent him as a cultural or military attaché to several Soviet embassies around the world to secretly gather information.

When stationed at the Soviet Embassy in Helsinki he used the alias Kurt Werner. He also served in the Embassy in Aden, South Yemen, then controlled by the East German Communists. Through his efforts, Wolf was able to destabilize the Saudi Arabian monarchy before being permanently assigned in East Germany.

By the time he was 28 in 1951, the remarkable Wolfe had been made a major general and was placed in command of foreign intelligence in the East German Ministry of State, answerable only to Ernst Wollweber, who headed all intelligence, counter-intelligence, and sabotage. Wolf built up an espionage network that rivaled that of Reinhard Gehlen, his counterpart in West Germany. He flooded West Germany with spies, including more females than any single agency had ever employed.

Wolfe was particularly adept in working his top agents into high-level West German positions. One, Gunther Guillaume, became the personal aide to West German Chancellor Willy Brandt, and when this was exposed in 1974, Brandt's administration collapsed.

Unlike Brandt, Wolf proved himself to be the consummate survivor. He retired from service in 1989, just as communism was collapsing throughout eastern Europe. Some time earlier, Wolf had written a book, *Troika*, in which he became critical of the

Communist Party's inability to change, a rather courageous thing to do when such criticism was not in vogue. Also, unlike the chiefs of the hated East German secret police, the Staasi, who were hunted down and imprisoned, even killed, after the fall of the Communist state, spymaster Wolf was permitted to enjoy his retirement unmolested.

[ALSO SEE: *Reinhard Gehlen; Gunther Guillaume; KGB; Ernst Wollweber*]

WOLLWEBER, ERNST
East German Spymaster ▪ (1898–1967)

BORN TO A MINER IN THE RUHR, WOLLWEBER HAD little formal schooling before going to work as a stevedore on the docks at Kiel, Hamburg, and other ports. He became a Communist at this time and, in 1917, joined the Kaiser's Navy. Following the collapse of the German military machine in 1918, he helped to lead the German sailors' revolt in Kiel.

When German troops broke the Navy revolt, Wollweber and others commandeered a trawler and sailed to Russia, where they joined the Bolsheviks. Trained by the GPU in espionage, Wollweber returned to Germany to organize the International Seaman's Union, which was dominated by Communists such as himself. Through this organization, Wollweber spied on government officials of the Weimar Republic and on the Nazis when Hitler came to power in 1933.

Between World War I and World War II, Wollweber traveled around the world, converting the many chapters of the World Federation of Trade Unions to communism and using its members as Soviet spies. He and his agents also sabotaged countless British and French freighters so that they "accidentally" blew up during ocean crossings, as a way of combating capitalism. Before Hitler came to power, Wollweber was elected to the Reichstag as a member of the Communist Party. When the Nazis took over, he fled to Denmark, where he became head of the Comintern and continued to direct his spy network in Germany.

In 1940, as the Germans invaded Denmark, the spymaster fled once again, this time going to neutral Sweden, reestablishing his espionage headquarters in Stockholm. He had about forty Scandinavian agents at this time whom he kept busy with lethal acts of sabotage. These saboteurs blew up power stations operating in the Swedish iron-ore fields, which reportedly fed the German war machine.

Swedish counterespionage, however, smashed Wollweber's ring and sent the spymaster to prison for three years. Released in 1945, he returned to Germany, going to the Russian zone of East Berlin. He was appointed minister of state security for the East German government in 1953 by his old friend Walter

Ulbricht, Communist dictator of East Germany, who had sacked the ineffective Wilhelm Zaisser. Using a vast network of spies and saboteurs, Wollweber ordered bombs to be placed on board the great liners *Queen Elizabeth, Queen Mary, Empress of Canada,* and the British aircraft carrier *Indomitable,* explosions that were later explained as "accidents." The agents responsible for this sabotage had been trained in the Maritime School at Wustrow, their instructors being Wollweber's old sabotage agents from the 1930s.

Wollweber's brilliant director of foreign espionage, General Markus Wolf, was able to place several spies into high-level West German positions, despite the energetic counterintelligence activities of Reinhard Gehlen's West German organization. Gehlen, also a brilliant spymaster, did the same, placing Walter Gramisch into Wollweber's own office, a position from which he fed top secret East German information to Gehlen for seven years.

In the mid-1950s, the uncouth dockworker wallowed in the luxuries of his office. He became so obese that he required help getting into his chauffeur-driven limousine. While East Germans were starving, Wollweber spent three hours each night dining in the few quality restaurants in East Germany—those reserved for high-ranking Communists. The bloated Wollweber earned the nickname "the walking pancake."

So powerful did he believe himself to be that Wollweber began scheming against his own first minister, Otto Grotewohl, then Ulbricht himself. When Ulbricht learned of Wollweber's intrigues he ordered him dismissed from the Central Committee and his espionage post. By that time, there was little left of Wollweber's intelligence organization, one which Markus Wolf had to rebuild at great expense. Wollweber remained a political pariah for ten years until he died in obscurity.

[ALSO SEE: *Reinhard Gehlen; Markus Wolf*]

WOODHULL, ABRAHAM
American Spy in Revolution ▪ (1750–1826)

A NATIVE OF LONG ISLAND, WOODHULL'S FAMILY farm was located in Setauket, property that ran to the shores of the Sound, across from Connecticut. When the American Revolution broke out, Woodhull joined the Patriots. When Washington ordered Major Benjamin Tallmadge to establish an American espionage network, Woodhull not only volunteered but helped Tallmadge recruit Robert Townsend, a successful merchant in New York City, which was then occupied by the British.

Using the name Samuel Culper Sr., Woodhull received messages from Townsend, who used the alias Samuel Culper Jr., their network being known as the Culper Ring. Austin Roe, supervisor for Townsend's mule pack trains, which carried goods in and out of New York, served as a courier, bringing coded messages from Townsend to Woodhull. He, in turn, would pass the messages to Caleb Brewster, a sailor who rowed back and forth across the Sound, taking the information to Tallmadge on the Connecticut side.

Timid and always fearful of detection, Woodhull never accepted any messages directly from Roe but had the courier place Townsend's messages in small wooden boxes Woodhull placed at various sites on his farm. He would then retrieve the messages and signal Brewster to row across the Sound for them by placing a black petticoat on the wash line, which could be seen from across the waters.

The Culper Ring operated a great spy service for Washington, one that was never penetrated or detected by the British throughout the war. In 1783, when the American victory was complete, Woodhull went on operating his successful farm. He became active in politics and later became a judge. No one in his lifetime, outside of Washington, Tallmadge, and those inside the Culper Ring, ever knew that Woodhull had been one of America's most successful spies.

[ALSO SEE: *Caleb Brewster: Culper Ring; Benjamin Tallmadge; Robert Townsend; George Washington*]

WRIGHT, PATIENCE
American Spy During American Revolution ▪ (1726?–1786)

A QUAKER, WRIGHT WAS ONE OF FIVE DAUGHTERS born to a farmer in Oyster Bay, Long Island. She moved with her family to Bordertown, New Jersey, in 1729 and married Joseph Wright in 1749. When her husband died in 1769, Wright had had four children and was about to give birth to another. Widowed and in her forties, she moved with her children and sister to Philadelphia, where she opened up a studio. There she made wax busts of prominent people and flourished, especially under the sponsorship of Benjamin Franklin.

Wright was a gifted sculptor and became so successful that she moved to London with letters of introduction from Franklin in 1772. There she opened another shop and was soon patronized by the rich and powerful, including William Pitt, Prime Minister Lord North, even King George III and Queen Caroline. (Her life-size figure of William Pitt, completed in the year of his death in 1778, still stands today in Westminster Abbey.)

When the American Revolution broke out, Wright, a fierce Patriot, began to milk important information from her patrons, sending this to America. As she sculpted, she encouraged her models to gossip and chat and thus learned about British troop and fleet movements, political views about America of prominent Englishmen, supplies and ammunitions flowing to British armies in the colonies. All of this Wright passed on to her American friends. When she learned that British agents suspected her and were reading her mail, Wright sent her information inside of wax heads being shipped to her sister's studio in Philadelphia.

Wright also sent information to Franklin when he went to Paris as a special envoy to plead the American cause before the French court. Wright's secret messages were sent to Edward Bancroft, secretary to Silas Deane and Franklin. Bancroft was, in reality, a double agent serving the British so there is no doubt that William Eden, chief of the British secret service, and Paul Wentworth, his top spymaster in England, knew of Wright's espionage, but they did not order her arrest. Instead, the British merely read her messages to Franklin and took appropriate actions to countermeasure her information. This may have even meant rerouting troop and supply shipments to America.

By 1781, Wright traveled to Paris, where she was again sponsored by Franklin. Her studio there, however, did not meet with the success she anticipated and she returned to London in the following year. With the American Revolution won, Wright planned to returned to the land of her birth but she died before sailing in 1786.

[ALSO SEE: *Edward Bancroft; Silas Deane; William Eden; Paul Wentworth*]

WRIGHT, PETER
MI5 Deputy Director ▪ (1916–   )

T HE SON OF MAURICE G. M. WRIGHT, HEAD of research for the Marconi Company who had worked as an electronics expert and who had been recruited as an agent for MI6 by Reginald Hall during World War I, Peter Wright attended Oxford and worked in the Admiralty Research Office during World War II. He was head of scientific research for a private firm before he was recruited to MI5 by Sir Frederick Brundrett in 1949 as a scientific adviser. He joined MI5 full-time in 1955.

Until his retirement as deputy director of MI5, Wright worked through the Cold War years handling the technical end of British counterintelligence, including its sophisticated wiretapping devices, direction-finding units (in detecting rogue transmitters), and other espionage devices. He was exposed to the traitorous work by Soviet double agents Guy Burgess, Donald Maclean, Kim Philby, and Anthony Blunt, and in his book *Spycatcher*, Wright went on to name the very head of MI5, Sir Roger Hollis, as the notorious and much sought-after "fifth man" in that celebrated spy conspiracy.

Wright's position also put him in contact with J. Edgar Hoover, head of the FBI, a man whom he came to distrust and dislike. When visiting the Bureau's Washington headquarters he noticed that "antiseptic white tiles shone everywhere. Workmen were always busy, constantly repainting, cleaning and polishing. The obsession with hygiene reeked of an unclean mind." He also noticed that MI5 chief Hollis played a slavish role whenever he dealt with Hoover: "Hollis had an essential weakness of character which enabled him to play the earnest supplicant to Hoover's blustering bully."

At the CIA, Wright had developed a strong friendship with James Jesus Angleton, head of counterintelligence, a man obsessed with the idea that there were deep moles planted in the agency and who spent most of his time looking for them without success. After William Colby pressured Angleton into resigning, which caused the entire senior staff to leave the CIA, the counterintelligence chief met with Wright to curse Colby, saying: "two hundred years of counterintelligence thrown away!"

Wright's book, written after his retirement from MI5, raised more than one eyebrow. He confirmed, for instance, that an MI5 cabal had plotted to discredit then Prime Minister Harold Wilson by labeling him a Communist.

The publication of Wright's revealing autobiography and its exposure of MI5 operations so rattled Prime Minister Margaret Thatcher that she conducted a two-year campaign to ban the book everywhere Britons might read it. In Australia, where Wright had taken up residence as a farmer, the British government filed a suit to prevent the publication of an Australian edition. Thatcher's efforts succeeded in making it a runaway best-seller in the U.S. and elsewhere, with more than a quarter of a million copies sold. The book was not only banned in England but newspapers were ordered not to review it.

(This author has experienced similar treatment when my book *Dillinger: Dead or Alive?* was published in 1970; J. Edgar Hoover personally went on the attack against this author, writing letters to such publications as the *National Observer*, asking its editors how they dared to review a book which dissected the FBI's cornerstone case, a letter which the *Observer* boldly printed. Next, Hoover sent FBI agents to visit the publisher of *ChicagoLand Magazine*, for which I was then editor-in-chief. Following that visit, I was given the option of either refusing to promote the Dillinger book or quit the magazine; I chose the latter course. Hoover became one of my devoted readers thereafter, not out of fondness, I realize. When this author's critical portrait of

him, *Citizen Hoover*, was about to be published in 1972, he demanded and got galley proofs of the book, which were reportedly on his bedstand on the day of his death.)

Wright's book led to a confrontation between the Thatcher government and the press, which saw its freedom threatened, if not bullied into silence. Seven of Britain's twenty newspapers violated the ban in reporting Wright's allegations, all of which had by then become public knowledge.

[ALSO SEE: *James Jesus Angleton; Anthony Blunt; Guy Burgess; CIA; William Colby; FBI; William Reginald Hall; Roger Hollis; J. Edgar Hoover; Donald Maclean; MI5; MI6; Kim Philby*]

WYNNE, GREVILLE
British Agent ▪ (1919–   )

A 1938 GRADUATE OF NOTTINGHAM UNIVERSITY AND an electrical engineer, Wynne served in British intelligence during World War II, and during the Cold War he became a businessman, moving throughout eastern Europe with a traveling trade show. In 1960, Wynne went to Moscow to arrange for a Russian trade delegation to visit London. The head of this trade delegation was high-ranking KGB spymaster Oleg Penkovsky.

The KGB spymaster had long earlier become disillusioned with communism and the brutal tactics of the KGB. He offered his services to the West as a double agent and Wynne became his cutout, or contact man, in London and also in Moscow. They met secretly in restaurants and public places, exchanging information. Penkovsky was arrested in 1962 and Wynne was also arrested when he arrived in Buda-pest on a flight from Moscow just after having seen Penkovsky. Both were tried in Moscow on May 7, 1963. Following their convictions, Penkovsky was sentenced to death (his secret execution following a short time later). Wynne was given eight years in prison and was later exchanged for Soviet agent Gordon Lonsdale.

[ALSO SEE: *Gordon Lonsdale; KGB; Oleg Penkovsky*]

YAGODA, GENRIKH GREGOREVICH
OGPU/NKVD Director ▪ (1891–1938)

JOSEPH STALIN'S SELECTION OF GENRIKH (HENRY) Yagoda as the replacement of Vyacheslav Menzhinsky to head the OGPU was one of genocidal expediency. The Russian dictator had long known Yagoda, who had been born in Lodz, the son of a chemist. Coarse, uneducated, and reveling in his illiteracy, Yagoda was nevertheless ruthlessly energetic in carrying out Stalin's orders.

A Polish Jew, he had joined the Revolution of 1917 and had served in the Red Army during the Russian civil war. In 1920, he worked for the Cheka, the successor to the Okhrana, the czarist secret police. His role model was Felix Dzerzhinsky, the brutal and uncompromising Cheka chief.

Throughout the early 1920s, Yagoda busied himself with directing slave labor in Russia, compelling hundreds of thousands of prisoners to complete public works programs, many at the expense of their lives. In 1926, Dzerzhinsky died of overwork, and was replaced by Menzhinsky, who appointed Yagoda as an officer-agent in SMERSH, the Ninth Division of the OGPU, its liquidation arm that sought out dissident Communists and murdered them.

When Menzhinsky introduced Yagoda to his fellow OGPU officers in 1926, he smilingly stated: "This young man enjoys the full confidence of Comrade Stalin." He also enjoyed secret orders from his mentor Stalin to murder anyone who appeared to challenge the dictator's authority. He surrounded himself with first hundreds, then thousands of officers loyal to himself while taking over all foreign espionage from Menzhinsky. He also became the director of SMERSH, training and assigning OGPU assassins to murder fallen-away troublesome Communists throughout Europe, chiefly those who dared to criticize Joseph Stalin.

Greedy and hedonistic, Yagoda plundered the bank accounts and homes of his wealthiest victims to enrich himself. By the early 1930s, he lived in regal style, having a lavish mansion in Spiridonovka Street in Moscow, one which was decorated in the Asiatic style, with carpets on the walls, thick rugs on the floor, and large divans. There was also a large private indoor pool where Yagoda would organize sex orgies for high-ranking Party officials. These revels would last for several days as Yagoda brought forth dozens of young Russian girls who were raped repeatedly before being sent to Red Army brothels.

The OGPU operated the Moscow Casino in the late 1920s and early 1930s, and here Yagoda could be found almost every night gambling away fortunes he had looted from others. He would then go on to the Hotel Metropole to indulge in its rich cuisine and listen to jazz musicians, voluptuous women wearing sable at his side. He maintained country villas and was driven about in limousines.

While indulging the extravagant life, Yagoda took time to persecute Stalin's enemies, many of whom he dispatched with poison. Developing new, quick-acting poisons was Yagoda's hobby and he maintained a laboratory for that purpose. One of those poisons Yagoda used to murder his chief, Menzhinsky, in May 1934, probably on Stalin's orders, since Stalin needed a security chief in power who would do his bidding without question. One of Stalin's first directives to Yagoda was to assassinate S. M. Kirov, a member of the Politburo, Stalin's chief lieutenant in Leningrad and one of the founding fathers of Communist Russia.

On December 1, 1934, Kirov was shot and killed as he walked down a corridor on the sixth floor of the Smolny Institute. His killer was a young Communist named Leonid V. Nikolaev, who, along with thirteen accomplices, was executed by firing squad on December 29, 1934. Yagoda had been behind the assassination, of course, inducing the naive Nikolaev to murder Kirov, a man Stalin distrusted and feared might usurp him. The assassin was executed before he could reveal Yagoda's involvement or, more important, Stalin's duplicity. (This was the plot revealed by Nikita Khrushchev in his famous 1956 Kremlin speech in which he denounced Joseph Stalin.)

Stalin blamed Kirov's murder on all of those old Bolsheviks he sought to eliminate, especially Zinoviev and Kamenev, who had been critical of his oppressive dictatorship. Yagoda provided the "evidence" against these elder Communists, who were brought to Moscow show trials in 1935 and 1936. Yagoda then carried out mass arrests and executions on a scale never before seen. Thousands of old Party members were murdered, as well as high-ranking military officers Stalin feared might have too much power.

Stalin then turned on Yagoda, having Yagoda's own deputy, Nicolai Yezhov, arrest the spymaster and mass murderer, accusing him of engineering Kirov's death. Yagoda and others went on trial in March 1938 and, at first, the spymaster denied his guilt. During a recess he was taken from court and to the basement torture chambers of his own Lubianka Prison, where his shoulders were promptly dislocated.

Yagoda was back in court a few hours later confessing to every charged hurled at him by the prosecution. Much of it was true, much absurd. He admitted to poisoning Menzhinsky, plotting Kirov's murder on behalf of others (but not Stalin, of course), poisoning Maxim Gorky and his son to death, as well as wiping out thousands of political victims, all as part of a conspiracy he hatched with the Western powers.

Yagoda was sent to prison while Yezhov took over the OGPU, which had been name-changed to the NKVD. There the mass murderer pondered his fate, realizing, no doubt, that Stalin had to get rid of him in order to cover up the trail that led directly to him for the Kirov killing. Sometime in 1938, Yezhov, following Stalin's orders, had Yagoda dragged from his cell, shoved against a wall in Lubianka Prison, and shot to death.

[ALSO SEE: *Cheka; Felix Dzerzhinsky; GPU; NKVD; OGPU; SMERSH; Nicolai Yezhov*]

Herbert Osborne Yardley, America's first great cryptologist, who cracked the Japanese codes in the early 1920s.

YARDLEY, HERBERT OSBORNE
American Cryptologist in World War I ■ (1889–1958)

BORN IN APRIL 1889 IN WORTHINGTON, INDIANA, Yardley dreamed of becoming a criminal lawyer but, following his high school graduation in 1907, he hit the road, bumming about the U.S.

In 1912 he obtained a job in Washington, working for the State Department as a telegraph operator. He found the work fascinating and played a little game by decoding messages to President Woodrow Wilson.

For four years, Yardley toyed with messages sent to President Wilson, arguing with his superiors that American codes were hopelessly outdated. He proved this by decoding a highly sensitive message to Wilson from the American ambassador in Berlin. He then pointed out to his superiors that the British, then controllers of the Atlantic Cable, could obviously do the same and were privy to all of America's most secret diplomatic messages. To more than prove his point, Yardley authored a 100-page report titled *Exposition on the Solution of American Diplomatic Codes*. He submitted this to his superior, who became incensed since it was he who had developed most of these top codes.

Yardley then told his superior that his codes were predictable, and, to painfully prove his point, he opened the man's locked office safe within a few minutes, rightly figuring out that the combination was based on the telephone number of President Wilson's fiancée. Such brazen tactics almost lost Yardley his job but when America entered World War I in 1917, he was sent to the War Department and then on to the U.S. Signal Corps, where he was given the rank of lieutenant and named the head of a special bureau dealing with cryptology called MI8 (Military Intelligence, Section 8).

Within months, Yardley's small bureau had broken almost all of the German diplomatic and Abwehr codes. One of his many cryptological coups was deciphering a letter found on Lothar Witzke, a German saboteur who was picked up by American agents after he entered the U.S. from Mexico. Witzke was one of those responsible for the Mare Island sabotage (and most probably the Black Tom explosion). The letter found on Witzke proved that he was a saboteur for Germany and caused him to be tried and convicted, then condemned, the only German agent in World War I to receive a death sentence. Witzke was not executed, however, but received a reprieve at the last minute from President Wilson. For this exploit, Yardley was promoted to the rank of major. His achievement firmly entrenched cryptology inside the American intelligence community.

In August 1918, while battles still raged along the Western Front, Yardley went to Europe to learn more about cryptology from the British and French intelligence agencies. In England, he met Vernon Kell, head of MI5, and Admiral William Reginald Hall, head of British naval intelligence, whose celebrated Room 40 operation had broken the coded contents of the notorious Zimmermann Telegram, a deciding factor for the America's entry into the war against Germany. He also went to France, where he studied the operations of French cryptology.

After attending the Paris Peace Conference in 1919 as chief cryptologist of the American delegation, Yardley was told that his job was at an end. He disagreed, pointing out that America had enemies around the world and the codes of these nations would have to be deciphered so that the U.S. could realize any future threat to its security. He prepared a comprehensive plan to establish a peacetime cryptological bureau and submitted this to the State Department and the Chief of Staff, a report titled *Code and Cipher Investigation and Attack.*

General Marlborough Churchill, head of Army Intelligence, was so impressed with Yardley's report that he was determined not to let MI8 go out of existence. He persuaded officials in the State Department to fund an "unofficial" code-breaking operation. Because of legalities, the State Department insisted that this operation not be located in Washington. Instead, in 1919, Yardley opened up his cryptology bureau in a four-story New York City brownstone at 141 East 37th Street, just east of Lexington Avenue.

Yardley quickly organized a staff of twenty top cryptologists, mostly those who had worked under him at MI8, including Dr. Charles Mendelsohn and Victor Weiskopf. One of his most brilliant codebreakers was F. Livesey, who became his assistant. Yardley dubbed the operation the American Black Chamber (after the French Black Chamber, the cryptology division of French intelligence in World War I that he so admired), a name that soon became world famous.

Yardley's group proved to be successful in breaking the difficult codes of the newly formed Cheka, the Bolshevik secret police in Russia which had supplanted the czarist secret police, the Okhrana. Further, the American Black Chamber was then ordered to break the Japanese diplomatic codes so that the U.S. would better be able to negotiate with Japan at the 1921 Washington Naval Conference. This conference involved decisive negotiations involving the tonnage of warships of all major nations at that time.

The formula then being argued would limit warship tonnage to each nation. The U.S. was deeply concerned about Japan, an aggressive nation since its naval victories over Russia in 1904–1905 in the Russo-Japanese War. Knowing that Japan had set itself on a war footing and was eager to build up its war fleet, the U.S. wanted to curb that warship escalation and insisted that Japan's ratio to U.S. warships be 10:6 (one million tons of U.S. naval strength for each 600,000 tons of Japanese naval strength).

Japanese negotiators insisted upon a 10:7 ratio and stubbornly clung to that argument for months. Yardley's code-breaking operation, however, was able to break the then top Japanese diplomatic code and deciphered messages between its delegation to the U.S. and Tokyo that clearly showed that the Japanese, to "avoid a clash," were to compromise at 10:6. When U.S. negotiators learned of this, they stiffened their resolve and the Japanese finally accepted the compromise.

In 1924, Yardley's funds were considerably reduced by the State Department, which was then undergoing budget cuts under direct orders from President Calvin Coolidge. In 1929, Henry L. Stimson became Secretary of State. In reviewing the American Black Chamber operation, Stimson dismissed the organization as non-essential. Stimson, an old-school diplomat, was repelled by espionage and covert operations of any kind. He reportedly told Yardley in a reproachful, stuffy manner: "Gentlemen do not read each other's mail." He then ordered the State Department to cease funding Yardley's operation. It simply went out of business because the crusty, naive Stimson was unable to grasp the vital importance of intelligence information.

Yardley suffered greatly. He found himself unemployable, having earned a reputation as a man who had alienated heads of state. After using up his savings, he wrote an enormously successful book titled *The American Black Chamber*, which was first serialized in the *Saturday Evening Post*. Though the book earned Yardley a great deal of money, it also earned him the enmity of Congress, where he and the book were denounced as having given away America's secrets.

Other cryptologists, including the greatest American cryptologist of them all, William F. Friedman, chief of the U.S. Army Signal Corps Code and Cipher Section, took exception to the book, saying that Yardley had cast a slur on American cryptographic work. Congress then passed a bill, "For the Protection of Government Records," which prohibited the public revelation of government secrets by federal emloyees or former employees. In 1933, the newly elected President Franklin D. Roosevelt signed this bill, creating Public Law 37, making it a crime for anyone to use material in official codes for personal reasons.

Yardley's book sales were stopped but by then he had already captured a huge audience and earned considerable profits. He next busied himself with developing invisible inks, which he attempted to sell to the government without success. To earn a living, Yardley continued writing, going after what he properly considered the most menacing nation at that time, Japan. He wrote a manuscript entitled *Japanese Diplomatic Secrets*, but this book was seized before publication and did not see print, the government upholding Public Law 37. He next churned out a spy-comedy called *The Blonde Countess*, which, combined with code-breaking elements from *The American Black Chamber*, made up the script for a 1935 MGM movie, *Rendezvous*, starring William Powell and Rosalind Russell.

Though he reapplied for cryptographic work with the government, Yardley, because of his exposé, found himself *persona non grata*, so he went to China in 1938, where he worked with Chiang Kai-shek's intelligence bureau, working under the spectacular Morris "Two-Gun" Cohen. By 1941, Yardley had moved to Canada to help establish a code-breaking bureau but he returned to the U.S. after World War II began and was finally given a government job, but not one in the area of cryptology.

Yardley was given a paper-shuffling job with the Office of Price Administration. By that time, William F. Friedman and others had preempted Yardley's place in American cryptology to the point where they were able to break the so-called "unbreakable" Japanese codes transmitted through what was called the Purple Machine, predicting Japanese military movements and battle plans throughout World War II.

Following the war, Yardley pursued his old hobby, poker, writing articles about the game and, in 1957, producing another book, *The Education of a Poker Player*. Sales were brisk but Yardley did not live to enjoy his newfound success; he died the following year, all but forgotten as America's founding father of modern cryptology. It should also be said that without Yardley's considerable contribution, including his unpublished manuscript concerning Japanese diplomatic codes (perused by cryptographers in the U.S. Signals Intelligence Service), the successes enjoyed by others coming after him may not have been possible.

[ALSO SEE: *Abwehr; Cheka; Morris Cohen; William F. Friedman; William Reginald Hall; Vernon Kell; Mare Island Sabotage; MI5; Okhrana; Purple Machine; Zimmermann Telegram*]

YEO-THOMAS, F. F. E.
British Spy in World War II ▪ (1901–1964)

L ONDON-BORN YEO-THOMAS SPENT MOST OF HIS LIFE in France, his father having a lucrative business in Paris. He was educated in England and France and fought with the French Army in World War I. A born adventurer, he then went to Poland and fought with the Poles against the Bolshevik invaders in the Polish-Russian War of 1919–1920. He was captured at Zitomir by the Soviets but managed to escape before being executed.

Making his way back to Paris, Yeo-Thomas opened a fashion house called Molyneux, which proved to

F. F. E. Yeo-Thomas, one of England's greatest and most heroic spies in World War II, an SOE agent who parachuted three times into Nazi-occupied France and would survive unspeakable tortures at the hands of the Gestapo.

be successful. At the outbreak of World War II, he joined the RAF and, speaking flawless French, served as an interpreter. When France collapsed in 1940 and the British evacuated Dunkirk, Yeo-Thomas went with them. He worked as an interpreter with General de Gaulle's Free French forces in England in 1941 and the following year joined the ranks of SOE (Special Operations Executive), the British-controlled espionage organization that worked with the underground movements in Nazi-occupied European countries.

Yeo-Thomas' role was that of a liaison officer between SOE and BCRA (de Gaulle's Free French Intelligence Bureau), working with Andre Dewavrin, who used the code name Colonel Passy. He accompanied Dewavrin on his first clandestine visit to France in 1943, using the code name the "White Rabbit." (Yeo-Thomas used many other names during his missions to France, including the name of one of England's greatest poets, Shelley.) Their job was to organize the many underground groups in France and to plan strategy with their leaders. Also joining them was Dewavrin's top BCRA agent, Major Pierre Brosselette.

Dewavrin's admiration for Yeo-Thomas was to grow to the point where he later called him "one of the most magnificent heroes of the war, a valued comrade, a dear friend, with intelligence and quiet and determined courage." The SOE agent spent several months in occupied France with Dewavrin, bringing together the arguing factions of the underground into one unified force acting under directions from London. All agreed to place more emphasis on the gathering of intelligence than the committing of sabotage.

It was at this time that Yeo-Thomas, as an SOE observer, noted that de Gaulle's reputation in France was by then enormous with the underground resistance fighters and the young men who had gone to the hills to avoid Nazi labor conscription, the groups known as the *maquis*. When he returned to London, de Gaulle, whose relationship with the SOE had always been strained on competitive grounds, welcomed Yeo-Thomas with open arms, awarding him the Croix de Guerre with palms. The Air Ministry forbade Yeo-Thomas (still nominally a member of the RAF) to wear this medal since de Gaulle was not yet the recognized head of France.

Later in 1943, BCRA was dealt a heavy blow when their top and most valiant agent, Jean Moulin, was captured along with General Delestraint. Brosselette was sent to replace Moulin and Yeo-Thomas went with him. Both men parachuted into France to learn that the Gestapo had decimated the ranks of the resistance through intelligence learned by Abwehr spies. Yeo-Thomas also learned firsthand how poorly equipped the underground groups were, especially the nomadic *maquis* groups.

After eight weeks, he was picked up by plane and taken back to London, where he went directly to Winston Churchill, asking to meet him. The Prime Minister said he would give the spy five minutes of his time but wound up listening in fascination to Yeo-Thomas' description of the French resistance fighters, explaining the desperate need for arms and ammunition for the resistance groups in France. The Prime Minister promised that arms and supplies would be forthcoming in increased parachute drops, also promising that more British planes would be used to make these vital drops, a promise subsequently kept.

Meanwhile, Yeo-Thomas learned that Brosselette, who had remained in France, had been captured by the Gestapo. He was determined to rescue his friend. He parachuted into France for a third time.

Once he arrived in France, Yeo-Thomas contacted underground leaders and arranged for a small group to slip into Rennes Prison, where Brosselette was being held prisoner. They would overpower the guards and free the BCRA leader, then escape into the countryside, where a Lysander plane would pick them up and fly back to England.

The day before the planned rescue, however, Yeo-Thomas was betrayed by his courier, a young man who had earlier been arrested by the Gestapo and agreed to work with the Germans rather than be executed.

Waiting for the courier to arrive at a Métro station in Paris to give him the final reports from the agents involved in the rescue attempt, the SOE spy was seized by Gestapo agents. He attempted to swallow his L-tablet, which contained cyanide and would bring death within five seconds, but he was restrained. Even before he arrived at Gestapo headquarters, the agent's tortures began as Gestapo thugs beat and punched him in the back seat of the car.

Once at headquarters, Yeo-Thomas was stripped naked, his hands handcuffed behind him, and he was forced to stand on a telephone book while vicious German interrogators kicked and punched him into unconsciousness. He refused to say anything. He was then beaten with an oxgut whip with a flexible steel rod inside of it but he would say nothing. His feet were then chained and he was thrown into a large bath brimming with ice-cold water.

Revived, he was again grilled. Saying nothing, Yeo-Thomas was thrown back into the bath. This barbarous activity was repeated time and time again. When the stubborn agent still refused to talk, Gestapo interrogators beat him senseless with rubber coshes about the head and testicles. All these tortures were repeated nonstop for twelve hours. Still, the courageous spy refused to talk.

Finally, the Nazis gave up and threw him into a cell. Brosselette, he learned, was already dead, having committed suicide by hurling himself from a prison window. Yeo-Thomas spent several months in Fresnes Prison and was then removed to Buchenwald concentration camp. On the train trip, he was crammed into a car with many other beaten prisoners, including the beautiful SOE agent Violette Szabo.

In Buchenwald, Yeo-Thomas underwent more horrors, beatings, and starvation. Though a slightly built man, he nevertheless possessed an iron will to survive. He managed to escape but was recaptured and was so severely beaten that he was expected to die. He survived, then, with the connivance of a German guard, exchanging identities with an inmate who had died of typhus. He then slipped from the camp and made his torturous way to the lines of the advancing Americans, found by GIs more dead than alive. For his bravery, Yeo-Thomas was awarded the George Cross, one of England's highest honors. Following the war, he testified against the war criminals at Buchenwald and then went back to his quiet business of women's fashions.

[ALSO SEE: *Abwehr; BCRA; Pierre Brosselette; Andre Dewavrin; Gestapo; Jean Moulin; SOE; Violette Szabo*]

YEZHOV, NICOLAI
NKVD Director ▪ (c.1895–1938?)

LIKE HIS PREDECESSOR, GENRIKH G. YAGODA, YEZHOV was a cold-blooded killer who murdered on Stalin's orders. He had been a zealous Bolshevik who followed Stalin's orders from 1918 onward. After serving in various capacities of the Cheka, GPU, and OGPU, he became, at Stalin's insistence, Yagoda's deputy. After Yagoda had served the dictator's purposes, he summarily dismissed him, sending a telegram to the Politburo on September 25, 1936, which stated: "The immediate appointment of Comrade Yezhov as People's Commissar of Internal Affairs [the NKVD] is unquestionably necessary. Yagoda is proving incapable of dealing with the Trotsky-Zinoviev Bloc."

Thus Yezhov received his orders to eliminate his chief, Yagoda, and promptly threw him into a cell to await a mock trial and summary execution. This Stalin had planned as early as 1936 when he took Yezhov into his confidence, grooming him as a hired assassin to replace another hired assassin, Yagoda. By late 1936, Yezhov, not Yagoda, was invited to celebrate in drunken revels with Stalin. On the anniversary of the Cheka's establishment, Stalin invited several of his secret police cronies to a drunken bash. Yezhov brought along K. V. Pauker, head of the Operations Department of the NKVD, which was responsible for the safety of Stalin and other Party leaders.

Pauker was known for his buffoonery and, on that night, was urged by Yezhov to perform for Stalin. He did so by drunkenly impersonating Zinoviev in his last moments of life, just as he was being dragged from his cell to be shot. Pauker, pretending to be Zinoviev (he had aided Yezhov in the condemned man's execution), fell to his knees in front of Stalin, wailing, "For God's sake, Comrade, call up Joseph Vissaronovich!" Pauker, a Jew like Zinoviev, then repeated the scene, this time putting into Zinoviev's mouth the words: "Hear, Israel, our God is the only God!"

The drunken Stalin laughed so long and hard that he fell to the floor clutching his girthsome belly with both hands, waving for Pauker to stop. This brand of ghoulish display was the only kind of humor Stalin appreciated, especially when it came from men exactly like himself, barbarians who sadistically thrilled to the deaths of others. Pauker himself would be sent to prison on orders from Stalin and would also be dragged from his cell before a firing squad, screaming, just as Zinoviev had, and one wonders if Pauker thought back at that moment on the drunken revel where he had mocked his own victim years earlier for behaving in the same manner.

Yezhov, with Stalin personally writing out the death lists, began to liquidate Yagoda's senior officers in the NKVD in March 1937. He barricaded himself in a wing the Lubianka Prison, then ordered his henchmen to commence their bloodbaths. Yagoda's top espionage and assassination experts were separately ordered on missions outside Moscow. They left individually by train and when reaching their destination, each man was arrested and bundled back secretly to Lubianka, a prison cell, and eventual execution. Since all left on undisclosed missions, their disappearances were not noticed for weeks or months.

A general purge was then conducted by Yezhov inside the NKVD. More than 3,000 officers were summarily executed in 1937. One of the worst of Yagoda's officers, an interrogator named Chertok (Little Devil), did not wait for arrest. He threw himself from the 12th floor balcony of his Lubianka office, smashing himself to pieces in full view of passersby. Many others simply ran screaming into the streets, where they blew out their brains. Some burned themselves to death.

Before the final purge came to an end, more than two million Russians—political foes of Stalin's, the military of all ranks, peasants and gypsies who had resisted agrarian reform and collectivism—were killed by Yezhov's roving murder squads. Aiding Yezhov's reign of terror was Lavrenti Beria, a brutal, sadistic policeman from Stalin's own province of Georgia, and roly-poly Nikita Khrushchev, the First Party Secretary in Moscow.

The slaughter became exhausting work, and Stalin sympathetically told Yezhov that he needed some help, a really reliable deputy to aid him in his heavy burdens. Stalin asked Yezhov who he might like to have as his deputy. Yezhov suggested Georgi Malenkov, who had earlier served as his deputy. "No," Stalin responded, "it looks like we'd better not reassign Malenkov to you." He suggested his old Bolshevik comrade, Lavrenti Beria.

The cunning Yezhov certainly knew what that meant. He, like his predecessor Yagoda, had fallen from Stalin's favor and he was being groomed for a jail cell. Beria, Yezhov knew full well, was a bloodthirsty assassin like himself. Having no choice, Yezhov appointed Beria his deputy and went forth with him in a massive purge of the Red Army in which more than 35,000 top-ranking officers were seized and executed on the bogus charge of being collaborators with the Nazis in Germany.

Yezhov was arrested by Beria a short time later and he was thrown into a cell in his own prison. His deputies and officers were also arrested. All were murdered, including Yezhov, probably about 1938. One report had it that Beria himself entered his chief's cell and placed chicken wire about Yezhov's neck, then strangled him and strung him up from a window bar, leaving his carcass to rot for months, showing the decaying corpse to other prisoners in order to intimidate them into making confessions.

Beria was to rule the NKVD/KGB for decades to come, proving himself to be the very worst of the death-loving maniacs who headed Soviet intelligence. He thrived on sadistic punishments, weird tortures, sexual abuse, and constant exercising of his power. He thrilled to the idea that he could instill fear in any of his cronies with offhand remarks. He, too, would be assassinated, but not before he persecuted millions of helpless Russians.

Beria was the special invention of Joseph Stalin, and, like all of his predecessors, had been chosen as one who could oppress the Russian people without any national reservations or ethnic conscience, since he himself was ostensibly a "foreigner," coming, as did Stalin, from the remote province of Georgia. Dzerzhinsky and Menzhinsky had been Poles who bore deep-rooted hatreds for the Russians. So did the Latvian Yagoda and the Jew Yezhov. All of these men had been dehumanized and bloodied during the Russian Revolution, the Russian civil war, and the terrors that followed.

None owed their allegiance to anyone but the man who installed them in their dreaded office, Joseph Stalin. They were his creatures, concocted in a political laboratory not unlike the horrid monster madly pieced together by the mythical Dr. Frankenstein. And like that nocturnally prowling creature their cherished home was the churned earth of the graveyard.

[ALSO SEE: *Lavrenti Beria; Cheka; GPU; NKVD; OGPU; Leon Trotsky; Genrikh Yagoda*]

YOSHIKAWA, TAKEO
Japanese Spy in World War II ▪ (1916– ?)

AN ENSIGN OSTENSIBLY ASSIGNED TO THE JAPANESE consulate in Hawaii as a secretary, Yoshikawa was, in reality, the leading spymaster who was to collect all information he could about the U.S. fleet at Pearl Harbor. He had this specific assignment when he arrived in Honolulu on March 27, 1941, on board the *Nita Maru*, using the cover name of Tadasi Morimura. At that very moment, Japanese warlords in Tokyo were planning their sneak attack on the U.S. naval base, which was to take place eight months later.

Taken before Nagao Kita, who had himself newly arrived in Honolulu on March 14 to assume the duties of consul general, Yoshikawa presented a letter from Captain Bunjiro Yamaguchi, who was in the intelligence section of the Naval General Staff. The letter also contained six crisp, new $100 bills, which were to be used for Yoshikawa's spy mission. A graduate of the espionage school in Eta Jima, Yoshikawa had been released from the Japanese Navy because of stomach ailments but had later joined its espionage service,

learning English and becoming an expert on the U.S. fleet in the Pacific.

Yoshikawa did nothing in the line of secretarial work for his consulate. He spent his time taking sight-seeing tours around Oahu, gathering information on the U.S. warships anchored at Pearl Harbor. Next he hired a Japanese taxi driver, John Yoshige Mikami, who drove him about the island. The spy also spent considerable time at a Japanese teahouse, the Shunchoro, located on Alewa Heights, which gave a commanding view of Pearl Harbor. From the second story of this building Yoshikawa studied the American fleet movements through a powerful telescope.

The spy attempted to scout the mouth of the channel leading into Pearl Harbor but found the area around this spot so closely guarded that he never got close enough to make precise observations. He naturally assumed that the channel entrance was protected with a submarine net, which was lowered and raised when the warships passed through. At other locations, Yoshikawa would spend entire days, from early dawn to dusk, sitting atop hills where he could observe the Army Air Corps scout planes that patrolled the island, their morning flights, direction of flight, and time of return. Within a few months, he knew for a certainty that the patrol planes scarcely if ever scouted the area north of Oahu.

Yoshikawa did not act alone. He was aided by Richard Kotoshshirodo, who worked in the consulate and had an encyclopedic recall regarding the warships of the U.S. Navy; Kohichi Seki, who had been the spy in residence before Yoshikawa's arrival; Otojiro Okuda, another consulate official; and Kita himself. What the spy and his aides did not investigate was the U.S. radar installations in Oahu. Inadequate as they were, operating on a piecemeal basis, radar posed a serious detection threat to the Japanese fleet which would be steaming from the northwest toward Oahu.

The reason for this lay in the Japanese tactical approach to the attack on Pearl Harbor and the fact that its warships operated without radar. In fact, Japan's military leaders had very little knowledge or even interest in radar in 1941. The planes from Japanese carriers flew at high altitudes to best coordinate their flight and attack patterns as well as take advantage of any available cloud cover. Also, even though Yoshikawa thoroughly scouted the oil tank reserves and pinpointed the locations of the oil tanks, these were logistical, not tactical, targets. The attacking planes would concentrate on the destruction of the airfields on Oahu and, chiefly, the obliteration of the battleships. This was the battle plan of Admiral Yamamoto and his espionage network in Hawaii headed by Yoshikawa, who concentrated on gathering information mostly on those targets.

Yoshikawa, despite all of his precautions, impersonations, and careful movements, did not go unobserved. The FBI headquarters in Oahu, directed by Robert L. Shivers, long knew of Japanese espionage activities in Hawaii and agents often trailed Yoshikawa about the island during his sightseeing and picnicking. There was, however, nothing they could do since it was not illegal to observe Navy warships, fleet operations, Air Force fields, and warplanes from public locations. Since the spy never slipped inside or forced his way onto an American military installation, he was free to go on observing.

The spy also worked closely in the late months of 1941 with a Nazi Party member and longtime resident of Hawaii, Bernard Julius Otto Kuhn, who, along with his wife and grown daughter, was in the pay of the Japanese secret service. Mrs. Kuhn operated a beauty parlor in Honolulu which was patronized by the wives of high-ranking U.S. Navy officers and through their gossip she was an invaluable source of information for Yoshikawa, as was Kuhn's attractive daughter Ruth, who dated many young American naval officers, toured the battleships with them and reported what she saw in detail to her father who passed this information on to Yoshikawa.

Right up till the night before the attack the diligent Yoshikawa kept collecting information. A week earlier he was seen in bars buying drinks for American servicemen, engaging them in conversation and pumping them for infomation on the fleet. He took a different girlfriend to the beach twice, sometimes three times a day, where he frolicked in the waves but he was really measuring tide heights and beach gradients. He played the drunken bum at night, staggering down alleyways to rummage through garbage cans outside military installations in hopes of finding discarded information that might be useful.

Yoshikawa was an astute spy. He knew that his phone was tapped so he called girlfriends and wearied American monitoring agents with endless chatter. He also knew that those messages not sent via cable and transmitted directly from the Japanese consulate to submarines lurking outside of Pearl Harbor, for relay to the Japanese fleet steaming toward Hawaii, were being monitored by American intercept agents. For this reason, and at the instruction of Tokyo, he destroyed all of his top-level codes a week before the attack and used only a low-level and uncommon code not easily identified for the remainder of that crucial week.

Japanese spymaster Takeo Yoshikawa (shown after World War II), who scouted the U.S. Pacific fleet at Pearl Harbor, reporting to the Japanese fleet only hours before the sneak attack of December 7, 1941.

The last message sent from Yoshikawa to the attacking fleet, on the night of December 6, 1941, reported that the U.S. carriers had left Pearl Harbor but he did specify that the battleships and other war vessels were at anchor and awaiting destruction.

Following the horrific attack the next morning, Yoshikawa was inside the Japanese consulate destroying codes and incriminating documents. Following the U.S. declaration of war with Japan, he and the entire consulate staff were detained. Because all possessed diplomatic immunity, they were shipped back to Japan. Yoshikawa had done his job well. Most of the U.S. fleet in the Pacific had been dismantled. Pearl Harbor was a smoking wreck of a base and the thousands of U.S. servicemen killed were still being buried when the spy sailed out of the harbor to return to his homeland, where praise and medals awaited him.

[ALSO SEE: *Bernard Julius Otto Kuhn*]

ZABOTIN, NIKOLAI
Soviet Spymaster ▪ (? –1945)

POSTED TO THE SOVIET EMBASSY IN OTTAWA AS A military attaché during World War II, Zabotin's true mission to Canada as a GRU spymaster was to establish a spy network to steal atomic secrets. This he accomplished in a good part through Dr. Allan Nunn May, a British nuclear scientist. Zabotin's network began to include members of the British High Commission and officials in the Canadian Ministries of Defense and External Affairs.

Communist Fred Rose, a member of the Canadian parliament, worked with Zabotin to steal secrets and transmit them to Moscow. When Zabotin's network seemed to be at its most productive, disaster struck in the form of Igor Gouzenko, a cipher clerk in the Soviet Embassy. Gouzenko defected and took voluminous materials with him to prove the existence of Zabotin's widespread espionage.

Gouzenko's revelations led to the speedy dismantling of Zabotin's network. He and others from the Soviet Embassy fled Canada on the Soviet ship *Alexandrov*. When this ship sailed out of New York harbor in 1945 without going through normal customs procedures, it listed Zabotin as a passenger but he vanished at that point.

One report later had it that he leaped into the sea rather than face the wrath of Joseph Stalin for his failure to prevent Gouzenko's defection. Another tale had him dying of a heart attack only a few days after his arrival in Moscow. Apparently, Zabotin's cynical attitude had prompted Gouzenko's defection. Zabotin, according to the most reliable report, did return to Moscow, where he was tried and convicted of allowing Gouzenko to defect and was sent to prison at hard labor for four years.

[ALSO SEE: *Igor Gouzenko; GRU; Allan Nunn May*]

ZIMMERMANN TELEGRAM
Secret German Communication in World War I ▪ (1917)

THE GREATEST CRYPTOGRAPHY COUP OF WORLD War I occurred at 10:30 A.M. on January 17, 1917, inside Room 40 of the old Admiralty Building in London. At that moment, a telegram from German Foreign Minister Arthur Zimmermann to the German ambassador in Washington, Count Johann von Bernstorff, was intercepted and handed over to two British cryptographers. Reverend William Montgomery, a church historian turned cryptographer, along with his colleague, Nigel de Grey. They immediately went to work on the coded message.

The Zimmermann Telegram had been sent via the Atlantic Cable which British naval intelligence under the direction of Admiral William Reginald Hall had long earlier accessed. The message, dated Berlin, January 16, 1917, was comprised of a thousand numerical code groups. Montgomery and de Gray were able to decipher only part of the message, using the German diplomatic code book which had been retrieved from the confiscated belongings of Wilhelm Wassmuss, the German vice consul in Persia, who had hastily fled his offices in 1915 as British forces advanced. The cryptographers learned enough from the telegram to know that they were dealing with one of the most important secret messages of the war, one which could bring the U.S. into the conflict.

A copy of the coded Zimmermann Telegram of 1917, one of the great German communications blunders of World War I.

By that time World War I had been raging for three years with little prospect that it would soon be over. The unbreached Hindenburg line was intact and the Allies had suffered stupendous losses. Worse, Russia was on the verge of military collapse and revolution. Once that country was out of the war, Germany would be able to abandon the Eastern Front and be able to move more than one million veteran troops to the West, a force that would most certainly decide the war in Germany's favor unless it was countered by a strong, new ally with fresh armies, the U.S.

The U.S., though it had shown sympathy and demonstrated support for the Allied cause, had struggled to remain neutral for three years. President Woodrow Wilson had been reelected to office in 1916 on the slogan: "He kept us out of war!" The Zimmermann Telegram, the British knew, would change all that. Foreign Minister Zimmermann, however, believed that what he proposed in the telegram would quickly bring England to its knees before America joined with the Allies.

Addressed to Bernstorff, it read:

Foreign Office Telegraphs January 16: Number 1. Strictly Secret. Yourself to decipher.

We intend to begin unrestricted U-Boat warfare on the first of February. We shall endeavor in spite of this to keep the United States neutral. In the event of this not succeeding, we offer Mexico an alliance on the following basis: Make war together, make peace together. Generous financial support and an understanding on our part that Mexico is to reconquer the lost territories in Texas, New Mexico and Arizona. The settlement in detail is left to you.

You will inform the president [of Mexico] of the above in the strictest secrecy as soon as the outbreak of war with the United States is certain and add the suggestion that he should, on his own initiative, invite Japan to join immediately and at the same time mediate between Japan and ourselves.

Please call the President's attention to the fact that the ruthless employment of our submarines now offers the prospect of compelling England to make peace within a few months.

Acknowledge Receipt.

Zimmermann.

When Admiral Hall received the fully deciphered message, he hurried it along to Foreign Secretary Arthur Balfour. Delighted at having evidence that would convince President Wilson of Germany's true aims in arranging U.S. territory to be seized, Balfour had to be restrained from sending a copy of the decoded message to the U.S. by Hall, who first wanted to provide a proper cover story as to how the British obtained the information.

Hall and the SIS did not want it known by any parties that Room 40 had long held the key to the German high diplomatic codes. The British waited for thirty-five days until one of their agents, later identified

Nigel de Grey, one of the two cryptographers in the Admiralty's famous Room 40, which intercepted the Zimmermann Telegram and decoded its ominous message, which, more than any other act, provoked America into entering the war on the side of the Allies in 1917.

only as "Mr. H.," had stolen a copy of the Zimmermann Telegram from the German ambassador to Mexico, von Eckhardt, after it had been delivered to the President of Mexico. At the time, Mexico and the U.S. were at loggerheads, a U.S. expeditionary force under the command of General John J. Pershing having chased Pancho Villa throughout the northern provinces of Mexico after the bandit-revolutionary had led a bloody raid into the U.S.

With all these facts at hand, Balfour, armed with the copy of the Zimmermann Telegram as it was received in Mexico (slightly reworded in the decoding), visited American Ambassador William Hines Page in London. The effect was explosive. The anti-British lobby in America cried "forgery!" until Zimmermann himself made the most incredible mistake of admitting the telegram was genuine. President Wilson frantically tried to find an alternate solution to declaring war for three weeks. However, in that time, the Germans made good on their resolve to conduct unrestricted submarine warfare in the Atlantic and sunk three American merchant ships in March 1917. On April 2, Wilson asked Congress for a declaration of war and got it on April 6, 1917.

The Zimmermann Telegram undid the German strategy. America entered the war, sending armies to France that would eventually provide an overwhelming victory for the Allies. Mexico did not move against the U.S. and had it been so inclined its forces were in such disarray that it could not have been effective. It was never learned if Japan had been approached to quit its neutrality in favor of attacking the U.S. That decision would come from Tokyo twenty-four years later when Japan launched its sneak attack against the U.S. naval forces anchored in the peaceful waters of Pearl Harbor.

Arthur Zimmermann's gigantic *faux pas* led to his dismissal in 1917 and he was never again given a government post in Germany. He lived as a recluse to the end of his life, long enough to see Germany once more launch another world war. The interception and decoding of his ill-advised telegram proved to be the greatest triumph for cryptography in the twentieth century, a victory long savored by the obscure and unheralded analysts working inside of the now legendary Room 40.

[ALSO SEE: *William Reginald Hall; Room 40; SIS; Wilhelm Wassmuss*]

ZUBATOV, S. V.
Police Spymaster in Czarist Russia ▪ (1868–1917)

To COUNTER THE REVOLUTIONARY TIDE THAT WAS beginning to sweep over czarist Russia at the turn of the century, S. V. Zubatov, police chief of the Okhrana, the czarist secret police, invented what came to be known as "police socialism," or "Zubatovism," according to Nicolai Lenin and his Bolsheviks. Zubatov's scheme was spectacular in that it was designed to steal the thunder from Lenin and other revolutionary leaders. The Okhrana, Zubatov cleverly insisted, would preempt the Bolsheviks by organizing the Russian workers on a large scale, and keep them under control while appearing to work toward the goals they desired.

A police official all his life, Zubatov did not devise his plan as a cynical method of manipulating Russian workers. He was, quite the contrary, a radical who truly believed in a sort of Populist autocracy. He felt that by secretly controlling revolutionaries, he could ease reform into existence without disturbing the middleclass, the nobles and, most importantly, the autocratic power of the czar.

Using scores of police spies, Zubatov, in 1901, organized the Society for Mutual Aid for Working Men in the Mechanical Industries. In all major cities, tens of thousands of workers joined the union, not knowing, of course, that it was secretly sponsored by the Okhrana. One of Zubatov's chief organizers of this union was Yevno Azev, the most spectacular police spy in history. Meetings were regularly held without incident. Those elected to the union leadership were Okhrana spies who made sure that the attitude at these meetings always reflected reverence and loyalty to the czar.

To show that the national union was effective, Zubatov pressured employers to grant small concessions to the workers. Though Zubatov eschewed the support of intellectuals, he was practical enough to realize that without some sort of intellectual representation, his union movement would be suspect. He recruited professors and journalists to support the movement and they dutifully delivered lectures laced with unwavering allegiance to the czar.

Zubatov's successes throughout Russia were phenominal. He even organized the most proletarian class of Russia, the Jewish workers of the Ukraine. When jittery Bolsheviks ran to Lenin to complain about Zubatov, the revolutionary leader simply smiled and waved them away, saying that Zubatov was but a passing notion, that the workers would eventually see through his ruse and benefit from learning about organizing and pressuring employers. This began to happen but what undid Zubatov were the very people he sought to protect, the industrialists.

The Ministry of Finance was inundated with demands from industry leaders, both Russian and foreign businessmen financing industries in Russia. They demanded that such government-backed unionism cease, stating that industrial growth could not be promoted by a government that also promoted agitation against industry. A coalition of French industrialists then openly complained to the Ministry of Foreign Affairs, stating that since Russia was a member of the Allied Powers, it was its duty to protect the interests of Allied industrialists doing business in Russia, not to whip up union attacks against them.

Right-wing elements began to attack Zubatov in the press for, by then, he was directly associated with the union movement. He was portrayed as "a servant of the Jews." Then, some of his unions went further than he envisioned and beyond the control of his secret agents. In the summer of 1903, a number of police unions went on strike.

This led to Zubatov's dismissal. He was advised to leave Russia since both the revolutionaries now knew that he was an Okhrana spymaster and would seek revenge. He was also hated by the aristocracy and industrialists for creating a revolutionary state of mind in Russia. Oddly, a year after Zubatov was dismissed, he was replaced by an Okhrana-employed priest, Father George Gapon, who attempted to put "Zubatovism" into effect all over again with bloody results.

Given a large sum of money, Zubatov went into exile but he remained a fervent czarist. He wrote letters to the Russian press, stating that without taking his advice, Russia was doomed. In 1917, Zubatov heard that the czar had abdicated. To prove his utter allegiance to the Russian autocrat, he placed a revolver to his temple and blew out his brains.

[ALSO SEE: *Yevno Azev; George Gapon; Okhrana*]

GLOSSARY

ACRONYMS

ABN: Anti-Bolshevik Bloc of Nations.

ABWEHR: German intelligence, 1866–1945.

ACOUSTINT: Acoustic intelligence.

AEC: Atomic Energy Commission.

AGI: U.S. and British intelligence classification for a naval intelligence vessel electronically monitoring signals, such as the U.S.S. *Pueblo*.

AMT BLANK: A West German intelligence network which began operating in the 1950s.

ASA: U.S. Army Security Agency which deals with communications intelligence and works closely with the NSA.

ASIO: Australian Security and Intelligence Organization, established in 1946.

A-2: U.S. Air Force Intelligence.

BBC: British Broadcasting Corporation.

BCRA: Free French intelligence service during World War II, established by Charles de Gaulle, 1940–1945.

BEF: British Expeditionary Force (in France, World War II).

BfV: (*Bundesamt für Verfassungsshutz*) West German counterintelligence, established in 1950.

BND: (*Bundesnachrichtendienst*) West German intelligence, established in 1956.

BOSS: Counterintelligence branch of New York Police Department, established in 1960s.

BOSS: South African intelligence agency, 1950–1978.

BSC: British Security Coordination, a division of SIS/MI6, located in New York and Washington, D.C., before and during World War II, and headed by Canadian millionaire William Stephenson (code name Intrepid), who worked with William Donovan and Allen Dulles of OSS to establish Allied espionage operations, as well as bring the U.S. into the war on the side of the British.

C: Designation of chief of British intelligence.

C&D: Censorship and Documents division in OSS.

CAT: Civil Air Transport.

CDA: Combined Development Agency (of the U.S., Great Britain, and Canada)

CELD: Central External Liaison Department, China's intelligence service.

CENTER: KGB intelligence headquarters in Moscow at No. 2 Dzerzhinsky Square, established in 1924.

CESID: Spanish intelligence service, responsible for Spain's intelligence and counterintelligence, established in 1977.

CHAOS: CIA domestic security files and operations in U.S.

Cheka: (*Chrezvychanaya Kommissya po Borbe s Kontr-revolutsyey*) Soviet secret state police and intelligence organization, 1917–1922.

CI: Counterintelligence.

CIA: U.S. Central Intelligence Agency, established in 1947 by President Harry S. Truman.

CIC: U.S. Counterintelligence Corps.

CIG: U.S. Central Intelligence Group, predecessor to CIA.

CIPA: U.S. Classified Information Procedures Act.

CMS: U.S. Classified Materials System.

COI: U.S. Office of the Coordinator of Information, predecessor of the OSS.

COMINT: Communications intelligence, used by U.S. intelligence agencies, pertaining to any electronic intelligence gathered from enemy or even friendly governments through intercepts, or sent electronically as ciphers or codes or a combination of both.

COMIREX: U.S. Committee on Imagery Requirements and Exploitation.

COMSEC: Communications security whereby cryptology methods, including transmissions, electronic emissions, and physical security for equipment, documents, and materials are protected from intercept, intrusion, and capture.

COPS: Chief of Operations in the CIA's DDP.

CPC: Combined Policy Committee for the Development of Atomic Energy (of the U.S., Great Britain, and Canada).

CPGB: Communist Party of Great Britain.

CPUSA: Communist Party of the U.S.A.

CSIS: Canadian Security Intelligence Service, established in 1983.

CUKR: Present-day acronym for SMERSH, the one-time liquidation arm of the KGB, which is now hidden as a secret department of the Russian Army.

DCI: Director of U.S. Central Intelligence.

DDA: Director of Administration at the CIA.

DDCI: Deputy Director of Central Intelligence at CIA.

DDI: Directorate of Intelligence (analysis) at CIA.

DDP: Directorate of Plans at CIA.

DDS: Directorate of Support at CIA.

DDS&T: Directorate of Science and Technology at CIA.

DGI: Cuban secret service, established in 1960 with the aid, supervision, and direction of the KGB.

DGSE: French intelligence, which, before 1982, was known as SDECE.

DIA: U.S. Defense Intelligence Agency (of the Pentagon), established in 1961.

DIE: Rumanian intelligence service during the Cold War.

DIS: U.S. Defense Investigative Service.

DISCO: U.S. Defense Industrial Security Clearance Office.

DMI: Director of military intelligence (Great Britain).

DNI: Director of Naval Intelligence (U.S.)

DORA: Code name for the GRU espionage network operated by Alexander Sandor Rado (an anagram of his real name) in Switzerland during World War II.

DS: (*Darjavna Sugurnost*) Bulgarian secret service.

DST: French counterespionage and counterterrorist agency, established in 1910.

EH: Electra House (British secret propaganda committee, later PWE).

ELINT: Electronic intelligence, which came into existence with the invention of the radio.

FBI: U.S. Federal Bureau of Investigation, responsible for all U.S. counterintelligence within the Western Hemisphere, established in 1924.

FBIS: U.S. Foreign Broadcast Information Service.

FEA: U.S. Foreign Economics Administration.

FI: Foreign Intelligence, collection of intelligence in the DDP of the CIA.

FIS: U.S. Foreign Information Service, propaganda arm of OSS operating during World War II.

FUSAG: U.S. First Army Group, a mythical military force in World War II, ostensibly commanded by General George S. Patton, which was designed in Operation Fortitude South to hoodwink the Germans into believing that the 1944 invasion of France would be at Pas de Calais (instead of Normandy, the actual intended landing site). To that end dummy landing craft were assembled in the ports opposite Calais, along with wooden guns, and canvas tanks and trucks. German aerial reconnaissance reported this military buildup, which convinced Hitler that, indeed, the attack would be at Pas de Calais and he, in turn, concentrated his heavy armored forces in that area, away from Normandy, which had (with the exception of the Omaha beach area) only comparably light defenses at the time of the invasion.

GCHQ: British signals intelligence service, established in 1914.

GC&CS: British Government Code & Cipher School, controlled by the Foreign Office.

GIA: Egyptian intelligence service, also known as Mukhabarat El-Aam, established in 1951.

GPU: (*Gosudarstvennoye Politsheskoye Upravlenye*) Soviet secret police and intelligence service, 1922–1923.

GRU: (*Glavnoye Razvedyvatelnoye Upravlenye*) Soviet intelligence HQ for Red Army, established in 1920.

G-2: U.S. Army Intelligence.

G-3: U.S. Army Operations.

HUMINT: Human intelligence or information gathered by field agents by traditional espionage methods.

HVA: (*Haupt-Verwaltung Aufklärung*) East German intelligence service, 1956–1989.

IAC: U.S. Intelligence Advisory Committee.

IC: Intelligence community.

IMINT: Image intelligence (photos obtained from aircraft or satellites).

IMRO: Macedonian terrorist and intelligence organization, 1893–1934.

INR: Bureau of Intelligence and Research in the U.S. Department of State.

INU: The section of the NKVD which directed all Soviet agents operating in foreign lands, known as the Foreign Section.

IOB: U.S. Intelligence Oversight Board, a subcommittee of the PFIAB.

IPC: U.S. Intelligence Priorities Committee.

IPR: Institute of Pacific Relations.

JANIS: U.S. Joint Army-Navy Intelligence Surveys.

JBC: Joint Broadcasting Committee, a World War II British propaganda tool which made broadcasts to Europe, chiefly Germany, designed to expose the evils of the Nazi dictatorship.

JEDBURGH: Allied paramilitary teams in World War II, also known as "Jeds."

JIC: U.S. Joint Intelligence Committee for the Joint Chiefs of Staff.

KGB: (*Komitat Gosudarstvennoy Bezopastnosti*) Soviet secret police and intelligence organization, established in 1954, the successor to the MVD.

KISS: South Korean intelligence and security service.

KPD: Communist Party of Germany (*Kommunistiche Partei Deutschlands*).

KS: (*Kundschaftsstelle*) Austro-Hungarian intelligence service up to and including World War I.

MAD: (*Militärischer Abschirm-Dienst*) Military counterintelligence for the *Bundeswehr*, Federal German Armed Forces.

MAUD: British committee of scientists who endorsed the efforts of England in developing a nuclear bomb during World War II.

MfS: (*Ministerium fur Staatssicherheit*) Ministry of State Security, East German intelligence, 1950–1989.

MGB: (*Ministerstvo Gosudarstvennoy Bezopasnosti*) Ministry of State Security for the Soviet Union, 1946–1953, its successor being the KGB.

MI: Military intelligence (Great Britain).

MI3: A branch of British intelligence prior to World War II which was responsible for monitoring the growth of German militarism, later called MI14.

MI5: British counterintelligence, established in 1909.

MI6: British intelligence, established in 1911, also known as SIS.

MI7: A branch of British intelligence dealing with Russia in World War I and the following revolution and civil war.

MI8: (Military Intelligence, Section 8), a bureau of the U.S. Signal Corps during World War I which dealt with codes and ciphers and which was headed by cryptology genius Herbert O. Yardley.

MI8: A branch of British intelligence in World War II which was responsible for monitoring broadcasts having to do with German bombers during the Blitz; also called the Radio Security Service.

MI9: A branch of British intelligence dealing with escape and evasion in World War II.

MI11: A branch of British intelligence dealing with field security.

MI14: A branch of British intelligence prior to World War II which was responsible for monitoring the growth of German militarism, originally called MI3.

MI19: A branch of British intelligence dealing with interrogation of military prisoners, political émigrés, defectors, and misplaced persons in World War II.

MICE: An acronym for Money, Ideology, Compromise, and Ego, the four basic motivations involved, separately or collectively, in entrapping and blackmailing persons with secrets to impart.

MS: Most Secret, a term chiefly used by British intelligence and used interchangeably with Top Secret.

MUCR: Monarchists Union of Central Russia, ostensibly an anti-Bolshevik organization of the early 1920s which plotted the overthrow of the Russian Revolution but was, in reality, a Cheka front used to lure anti-Communists into Russia, such as the noted British spy Sidney Reilly, where they could be summarily executed.

MVD: (*Ministerstvo Vnyutrennikh Dyel*) Soviet secret police and intelligence organization, 1946–1954.

NAC: National Agency Check.

NAICHO: Japanese intelligence responsible for national security, established in 1960.

NATO: North Atlantic Treaty Organization, signed into existence in 1949, and made up of Western Powers.

NCNA: New China News Agency, recruiting and intelligence gathering arm of China's CELD.

NIA: U.S. National Intelligence Authority, the supervising group on policy of the CIG.

NID: British Naval Intelligence Department.

NIE: U.S. National Intelligence Estimate.

NIPE: U.S. National Intelligence Programs Evaluations.

NIS: U.S. Naval Investigative Service, which deals with espionage and counterespionage within the U.S. Navy.

NIS: National Intelligence Service, South Africa.

NISC: U.S. National Intelligence Support Center, an agency of the U.S. Navy responsible for technical intelligence, research, and other support operations.

NKGB: (*Narodniy Kommissariat Goudarstvennoy*) A subdepartment of the NKVD which was made into a separate commissariat in 1941 and again in 1943.

NKVD: (*Narodniy Kommissariat Vnyutrennikh Dyel*) Soviet secret police and intelligence organization, 1934–1946.

NKVT: U.S.S.R. Commissariat for Foreign Trade, which, in the 1920s and 1930s, established trading organizations such as Amtorg in the U.S. and Arcos in England and similar trade operations in every major European capital and in the U.S. as covers for massive espionage operations and countless Soviet networks employing thousands of Soviet agents.

NSA: U.S. National Security Agency, a signals intelligence organization, established in 1952.

NSC: U.S. National Security Council, established in 1947.

NTS: (*Nationalniy Trudovoy Soyuz*) National Labor Union, an anti-Communist Russian exile organization headquartering in West Germany; also called National Solidarists Alliance.

OAG: U.S. Operations Advisory Group, a subcommittee of NSC which reviews proposals for foreign covert operations.

OCI: Office of Current Intelligence at the CIA.

OEEC: Organization for European Economic Cooperation.

OG: Operational Group Command of the OSS.

OGPU: (*Obyedinyonnoye Golsudarstvennoy Politicheskoye*) Soviet secret police and intelligence organization, 1923–1934.

OKW: (*Ober-Kommando Wehrmacht*) High Command of German armed forces during the Nazi regime, 1933–1945.

OMS: A section of the Organization Bureau (*Orgburo*) of the OGPU, responsible for gathering all intelligence outside of the Soviet Union.

ONE: Office of National Estimates at the CIA.

ONI: U.S. Office of Naval Intelligence.

OO: Office of Operations at the CIA, one which overtly collects information.

OPC: Office of Policy Coordination, established by the National Security Council in 1948 to conduct covert operations; dismantled in 1952 since its operations often duplicated the CIA's OPO (Office of Special Operations).

OPO: The CIA's Office of Special Operations, responsible for conducting covert operations throughout the world.

ORE: Office of Reports and Estimates at the CIG and later the CIA.

ORGBURO: Organization Bureau of the OGPU, which, through its OMS Section, was responsible for gathering all intelligence outside of the Soviet Union.

ORR: Office of Research and Reports at the CIA.

OSI: Office of Scientific Intelligence at the CIA.

OSS: U.S. Office of Strategic Services, American Intelligence during World War II, 1940–1946.

OUNR: Organizations of Ukrainian Nationalists Revolutionaries, an anti-Communist Ukrainian exile organization headquartering in West Germany.

OWI: Office of War Information (during World War II).

PFIAB: U.S. President's Foreign Intelligence Advisory Board.

PLO: Palestine Liberation Organization, organized from many Palestinian factions in 1964 and later headed by Yasir Arafat, who first advocated and directed terrorist operations from bases in Jordan; later postured itself as a political organization of a benign nature. Early operations were supported by left-wing groups aligned with the KGB.

POTUS: Acronym used by Winston Churchill in his ciphonic messages to President Franklin D. Roosevelt during World War II.

POUM: Trotskyite workers' organization in Spain, influential during the Spanish Civil War, 1936–1939.

PWE: Political Warfare Executive. England's propaganda department in World War II.

Q: Clearance classification assigned by the Department of Energy for access to nuclear information.

R&A: Research and Analysis unit in OSS.

RB-47: U.S. spy plane, 1960.

RCMP: Royal Canadian Mounted Police.

RD: Restricted data.

RDF: Radio Direction Finding equipment. Though used in a cursory fashion with primitive equipment during World War I, sophisticated RDF equipment was not fully developed and employed until World War II, with the Germans and British having the most advanced technology. To be effective RDF equipment required several beamed signals (usually from two or more mobile RDF units) to intersect a radio signal and thus pinpoint its location. It invariably took time to move RDF mobile units into the right positions, which clandestine radio operators knew, which is the reason why they kept their messages short and moved their transmitters frequently to different locations.

RIAS: (*Rundfunk Im Amerikanischen*) American radio stations transmitting from West Berlin during the Cold War.

RSHA: (*Reichssicherheits-Hauptamt*) Central security department of Hitler's Third Reich, 1939–1945, which was headed by Heinrich Himmler and included the Gestapo and the SD.

RVPS: Royal Victoria Patriotic School, located in Wandsworth, England, and operated by MI9 of British Intelligence during World War II, which screened refugees from Europe.

SACO: Sino-American Cooperative Organization.

SATCOM: Satellite communications.

SATNAV: Satellite navigation.

SAVAK: (*Sazamane Etelaat va Amniate Kechvar*) Iranian Security and Intelligence Service.

SB: Polish intelligence service.

SBI: Special background information.

SCI: Special compartmented information (CIA).

SCR: Society for Cultural Relations, a Communist front in the 1920s and 1930s which was established by the KGB in western universities where future Soviet spies were nurtured and recruited; particularly effective in British academies such as Trinity College and Cambridge, from which came such traitors and Soviet agents as Anthony Blunt, Guy Burgess, Donald Maclean, and Kim Philby; also known as VOKS.

SD: (*Sicherheitsdienst*) Nazi Party intelligence department, 1931–1945.

SDECE: (*Service de Documentation Extérieure et de Contre-espionage*) French intelligence, established in 1958; retitled DGSE in 1982.

SDF: Social Democratic Federation, a hardcore Marxist organization founded in England in 1881 by millionaire political eccentric Henry Hyndman.

SE: Soviet East European Division of the CIA, from the 1970s.

SEALS: Sea Air and Land service (U.S. Navy special forces).

SHAEF: Supreme Headquarters Allied Expeditionary Force (in World War II).

SIGENT: Signals intelligence, used by U.S. intelligence agencies, pertaining to any electronic intelligence gathered from enemy or even friendly governments.

SIGINT: Signals intelligence, used by British intelligence, pertaining to any electronic intelligence gathered from enemy or even friendly governments.

SIS: New Zealand's intelligence and counterintelligence service, established in 1947.

SIS: British Secret Intelligence Service, established in 1909, also MI6 by 1911.

SIS: U.S. Signal Intelligence Service, established in 1929.

SMERSH: Soviet assassination division of KGB, established in 1917; now called CUKR.

SMOTH: British intelligence in Washington, D.C., through which the FBI exchanges communications intelligence with MI5 and MI6 under the 1943 and 1947 UKUSA agreements.

SMUN: CIA acronym for the Soviet mission to the United Nations in New York.

SNB: (*Spava Narodni Bespecnosti*) Department of National Security, the Czechoslovakian intelligence service.

SNIE: U.S. Special National Intelligence Estimate.

SO: Special Operations of OSS.

SOE: Special Operations Executive, British-directed espionage/sabotage organization working with underground resistance fighters in Nazi-occupied countries during World War II, 1940–1945.

SR: (*Service des Renseignements*), Free French intelligence during World War II.

SS: (*Schutz Staffl*) Defense Units, conducting special security and political services as a security police of the Gestapo and SD, established in 1933.

SSA: U.S. Signals Security Agency.

SSD: (*Staats Sicherheitsdienst*) East German counterintelligence during the Cold War.

SSU: Strategic Services Unit of OSS, responisble for espionage and counterespionage in World War II, moved to the U.S. War Department in 1945.

STASI: (*Ministerium für Staatssicherheit*) East German security and intelligence service during the Cold War.

TASS: (*Telegravnoye-Agenstvo Sovietskovo Soyuza*) Ostensibly a telegraphic news service similar to the AP and UPI in the U.S., but one which was used as a propaganda tool for the Communist Party in Russia, as well as a cover for KGB agents operating throughout the world.

TELINT: Telemetry intelligence.

TK: Acronym for Talent Keyhole, a code name for satellite photography, or KH (Keyhole) photo-reconnaissance satellites.

TS: Top secret.

UDT: Underwater demolition team.

UKUSA: United Kingdom–United States Security Agreement, a secret 1943 pact, extended in 1947, and still unacknowledged by either government, wherein cryptographic systems, cryptanalytical techniques, radio interception, direction finding, and other technical communications information are fully exchanged, particularly as it applies to Communist communications intelligence.

USIB: U.S. Intelligence Board.

USIS: U.S. Information Service.

VOKS: Another acronym for the Society for Cultural Relations (SCR), a Communist front used to recruit KGB agents from western universities.

VOPO: (*Volks-Polizei*) People's Police in Soviet-controlled East Germany during the Cold War.

WIN: Polish Freedom and Independence Movement in late 1940s.

WPB: U.S. War Production Board during World War II.

X-2: Counterintelligence unit at OSS in World War II.

TERMS

Accommodation Address: An address, such as as a post office box, used by cut-outs or go-betweens to pick up and receive messages.

Acoustic intelligence: Information taken from audio sources which can be electronically enhanced.

Agent: A person, usually foreign, obtaining information for and under the supervision of an intelligence organization.

Agent, notional: An agent who does not exist, a fiction created by an intelligence agency to deceive and misdirect the enemy, such as the corpse employed in Operation Mincemeat by British intelligence during World War II.

Agent, secret: An undercover agent or any person acting as a clandestine spy or saboteur and under the direction of an intelligence organization.

Agent of influence: An agent who attempts to wield opinion rather than to spy as a clandestine agent; such agents are usually politicians, academics, journalists, social leaders, scientists, or editors.

Agent provocateur: An agent who provokes illegal acts such as riots, rebellion, mutiny, or acts of espionage or sabotage by those under suspicion.

Al Mukharabat: Iraq secret service, established in 1968.

Alliance International Service: One of the most effective French underground espionage networks in World War II, headed and generally peopled by female French spies.

Approach: The method employed in recruiting a new foreign agent to an intelligence service, or luring an in-place agent from the other side to become a double agent.

Archives: Central files or central index, used by the KGB.

Artichoke: Jargon for using drugs, hypnotism, or brainwashing techniques in testing the loyalty of in-place agents or defecting agents.

Assessment: Evaluating the worth of a potential spy.

Asset: Agents, sympathizers, or supporters positioned in target countries or areas.

Background Investigation: Investigation of those who require a security clearance in working with classified documents. Such investigations in the U.S. are conducted by the FBI.

Bagman: An agent who acts as a paymaster to spies or makes bribes to those in authority.

Black bag job: Act of bribery or burglary by an agent or agents, such as the Watergate burglary.

Black Cabinet: Postal censorship offices in any country.

Black Chamber: Postal censorship offices, or secret cryptology/code-breaking operations, in any country.

Black Dragon Society: Japanese nationalist society and espionage organization, 1901–1945, established by Mitsuru Toyama.

Black Hand Society: Serbian nationalist society and espionage organization, 1903–1917, established by Dragutin Dimitrijevic.

Blackmail: The act of blackmailing someone into imparting secrets after having caught that person in an illegal or immoral act which invariably has been staged by the blackmailing agents. The most often used ploy in such entrapments is providing a male or female prostitute to compromise the blackmail victim.

Black operator: Soviet jargon for foreign agents working for the KGB or GRU.

Black Orchestra: The German underground working to overthrow the Nazis and Hitler's Third Reich, 1933–1944.

Blown: The discovery of an agent's true identity or the penetration of an agent's cover story or cover operation.

Bona fides: An agent's credentials.

Boxed: An agent being examined by a polygraph (lie detector). Few agents are able to deceive lie detectors, although a few, such as Aldridge Ames, have claimed that certain tactics can overcome the average nervousness produced by such tests.

Brainwashing: Psychological techniques employed in altering the thought processes of persons from whom information or services are sought. The term suggests a "scrubbing of the mind," wherein all ideas deemed "dirty" by the brainwasher are given up (secrets) and "clean" ideas substituted. Brainwashing is achieved through logical arguments, or incessant arguments (the Chinese method), one where a prisoner is kept isolated in a small cell and is addressed ceaselessly by interrogators who point out the virtues of Marxism and the evils of democracies, denying, if necessary, basic comforts of food, sleep, and warmth to inmates until their will to resist is demolished and they embrace communism wholeheartedly as their only salvation, physically and spiritually. Constant indoctrination follows to maintain the "brainwashed" state of mind.

Brandenburgers: An elite corps of Abwehr commandos created by German spymaster Admiral Wilhelm Canaris and employed in World War II for special operations, particularly the sham attack on a Gleiwitz radio station in 1939, which was used to give cause to Hitler's invasion of Poland and the beginning of World War II.

Bugging: The use of electronic devices to eavesdrop or monitor audible and phone conversations.

Bureau Ha: Private Swiss intelligence organization, 1939–1945, established to spy on Nazi Germany.

Burned: Compromised or caught in the act red-handed.

Bury: To conceal information by inserting such information into innocuous-appearing documents.

Case officer: Spymaster in charge of an espionage network or networks, or an agent in charge of several separate field agents and one who is required to recruit new agents.

Cell: Basic and most expendable unit of an espionage network.

Central External Liaison Department: China's intelligence and counterintelligence services, established circa 1950.

Central Intelligence Bureau: Germany's intelligence service, established by spymaster Wilhelm Stieber in the 1860s.

Chekist: A member or former member of the Cheka, the first Soviet secret police, which replaced the czarist Okhrana.

Cipher: Secret message writing which manipulates symbols representing various letters of the alphabet. Ciphers and codes are sometimes combined for top secret messages to further assure security, codes containing symbols which can signify entire words, phrases, or even sentences. Cryptology is the science of ciphers. Master cryptologists in the past have designed elaborate ciphers. Blaise de Vigenere, of sixteenth-century France, created the Vigenere table, one in which the alphabet is written out on each line of a square, with each new line begining one letter behind the one above it, the first beginning A, B, C, the second beginning B, C, D, and so on. The square is deciphered by the recepient only if he possesses a key which tells him in which line a letter is in and how far across the line to proceed to locate that letter. The German Enigma cipher was created through a mechanical device consisting of rotors that involved concentric circles, each bearing the letters of the alphabet, and, when the interior circle was spun in such a fashion as to bring its letters into alignment with those circles on the outside, the true message was revealed. Today's ciphers are much advanced via computers, such as those created by NSA (National Security Agency), which has established a "data encryption standard" involving keys that are dozens of numbers long, providing myriad complexities that offer so-called "unbreakable" codes; however, sophisticated computers can be devised to read such complex ciphers.

Ciphony: The scrambling through technology of the spoken word via telephone. Phone conversations are altered to mere squeaks and shrill noises by simply altering the electronic current of the conversations with special equipment attached to secure phone lines. Descramblers restore the current to normal receivership so that the conversations are intelligible. The phone conversations between British Prime Minister Winston Churchill and U.S. President Franklin D. Roosevelt during World War II were supposedly scrambled through sophisticated ciphony equipment. These two world leaders conversed freely about top secret matters, thinking their every word was being distorted to total unintelligibility via transatlantic telephone. This was not the case. German engineer Kurt Vetterlein had devised a descrambler in 1942 which allowed the Abwehr to listen to these conversations and learn, for instance, of plans to take Italy out of the war in 1943. The ciphony system was drastically updated in 1944 and was thereafter unbreakable.

Clandestine mentality: Paranoid behavior, usually displayed by spymasters such as the CIA's deputy director, James Jesus Angleton

Clandestine operation: A covert or secret operation conducted by an intelligence organization against an enemy or even friendly government.

Cobbler: An espionage craftsman whose expertise is forging false documents such as passports, visas, birth certificates, diplomas, government documents, and even currency.

Code: Secret messages made up of symbols representing words, phrases, or sentences, unlike ciphers, which represent letters of the alphabet. Codes can be encyrpted or put into cipher to provide additional security. Codes can be combined with ciphony, which makes use of sound only, as in the transmission of Morse code via transmitters and receivers. Codes can also be transmitted visually, such as the use of flags or light signals. Codes, like ciphers, are based upon transposition or substitution. Transposition is usually no more than distortion of word patterns, where substitution is invariably the option employed for the most secure codes. Keys to the substitution of words are usually contained in code books possessed by the sender and recepient. The code book, in case an agent is seized, may be any kind of book, including a novel, a dictionary, or the Bible, so as not to be recognized as the code book. Code references for each word of a message will relate to a page, a line on that page, and a numbered position of the line on that page. To add more security, the key is shifted routinely so that page six may later mean page eight. Military or diplomatic code books offer a secret glossary of terms and definitions which are used in decoding secret coded messages. Cryptanalysts discovering the meaning of sets of symbols might be able to break a cipher but such discoveries may only reveal a portion of a code. Once a code book is acquired by the enemy, however, the entire code is readable, as was the case when the British Admiralty's Room 40 obtained the German diplomatic code book in 1915 and were thus able to decode the notorious Zimmermann Telegram, which subsequently brought America into the war on the side of the Allies in 1917.

Code name: A proper name alias or a nickname or even a combination of letters or numbers which has been assigned to an agent by a spymaster for a network or a national intelligence agency by which he is carried on a secret roster, which, if obtained by the enemy, will not supposedly yield the true identity of the agent. Code names are traditionally used by radio operators of clandestine transmitters. The code name for the infamous German spy Mata Hari was H.21.

Code word: Word or term given to a secret operation or project to conceal meaning, intention, or objective. The code name "Overlord" was the term used for the intended Allied invasion of France in 1944.

Collection: Obtaining, assembling, and organizing information for further intelligence use.

Colossus: British communications intelligence computer developed toward the end of World War II that superbly decoded and deciphered Axis communications.

Communications security: Protecting intelligence information transmitted by any kind of electronic methods.

Company, The: The CIA (U.S.) Central Intelligence Agency.

Compartmentation: Establishing separate procedures in the handling of intelligence data; restricting on a "need-to-know" basis those involved in the same procedures or operations so that each person works in a "compartment" where other areas and personnel of an operation remain unknown to him or her.

Concealment devices: Secret tools of spycraft such as invisible ink, film, microdots, ciphers, codes, or poisons.

Confidential: The lowest U.S. security classification regarding national security information held by someone working in the intelligence community.

Contact: An agent who serves as a liaison person or cut-out between field spies and the spymaster or control who supervises the activities of field agents.

Control: The supervising agent or spymaster who directs, usually in an administrative capacity and often without revealing his true identity to his agents, the activities of one or more spies working in the field.

Co-option: The taking over and controlling of a spy from one intelligence service by an agent or agents of an opposing intelligence organization.

Counterespionage: The science of spying on spies, or a national agency practicing counter-intelligence. Most countries have counter-espionage organizations that must not only combat foreign agents in their lands but also saboteurs and their own nationals who may be working for enemy nations. Such agencies usually compete for budgets and inner agency recognition with their own country's espionage organization. The FBI, for instance, is not only one of the U.S. federal law enforcement agencies, it is also responsible for counter-espionage, thus becoming involved in a field where it competes with the CIA. In England MI5 and MI6 are on similar footing and in West Germany it is the BfV and the BND.

Counterintelligence: The science of spying on spies, or a national organization practicing counter-espionage, and the methods and safeguards taken in such activities.

Counterspy: Where the spy is the sword, the counterspy is the shield; counterspies are those agents working with counterespionage or counterintelligence agencies. Their job is to quickly expose the spy or forestall the spy's ability to obtain vital information, usually through disinformation. Counterspies at head-quarters may simply clip newspapers, censor mail, or analyze reports from informers in order to determine the plans of the enemy. Other counterspies may install listening devices or bugs in offices maintained by hostile countries, or act as *agents provocateurs* by infiltrating espionage networks and urging those enemy agents to commit illegal acts for which they can be arrested and imprisoned, as was the case of the notorious Yevno Azev, the spectacular Okhrana master spy, counterspy, and *agent provocateur.* The most successful counterspies are double agents, those who become agents for an espionage organization while already being an agent for another; these spies are called "moles," a word coined by spy writer John Le Carré. (Such counterspies were typified by the British traitor-agents Anthony Blunt, Guy Burgess, David Maclean, Kim Philby, and, perhaps, Roger Hollis, who was himself head of MI5.) Other counterspies are sometimes recruited from enemy espionage agencies where they are already in place, such as GRU spymaster Oleg Penkovsky. Some counterspies are "turned" so that they appear to be conducting espionage for their nation but, in fact, are working on behalf of the enemy, sending disinformation to their headquarters. This was the case with almost all of the Abwehr spies sent to England during World War II.

Countersurveillance: The detection of surveillance by an opposing counterespionage organization.

Country team: The chiefs of all intelligence agencies of a single government operating in a foreign country.

Courier: An agent belonging to a spy network who retrieves and delivers messages, documents, film, microdots, or any other form of secret information. Most often, couriers have no idea what information they are carrying, nor the true identities of those spies they may contact in their normal routine. Often such couriers never make contact but simply conduct pickups and deliveries to "letter drops." The role of the courier, which requires no special skill, is nevertheless one of the most difficult of jobs in that total security must be practiced at all times. Couriers are the main targets for counterespionage organizations and their alertness and safeguarding tactics may spell success or failure for an entire spy network.

Cousins: The name for the CIA used by British intelligence, MI6/SIS.

Cover: A business/trade front which covers actual espionage operations and activities.

Cover name: An alias used by an agent which conceals his or her true name. Many intelligence agencies, especially those of Russia, draw their aliases from the names of dead children, whose birth certificates are easily obtained and verified by "ghouls," agents haunting graveyards to verify obituary notices.

Cover story: A false story, background, or biography which covers the espionage activities of a spy and explains the reasons for his presence in enemy country. The best cover stories are those that appear to be true when the real reason is to achieve a covert mission. Those traveling on vacation present plausible cover stories. In fact, the founder of a famous publishing firm that deals with vacations and travels served in the OSS during World War II. Traveling salesmen and writers who travel from country to country have built-in cover stories wherein their occupations normally take them into areas where they will also involve themselves in espionage, which was the case of Somerset Maugham, who worked for British intelligence in Switzerland during World War I while ostensibly working on a play.

Covert operation: A clandestine mission. In wartime this invariably means a mission of sabotage but in peacetime such an operation may mean anything from dirty tricks, propaganda campaigns in foreign countries, or illegal acts such as counterfeiting or kidnapping, even assassination.

Cryptology: The science of ciphers involving cryptography, the enciphering of messages; cryptograms, the enciphered messages themselves; and cryptanalysis, the deciphering of messages. Cryptographers employ transposition and substitution when enciphering messages. Transposition uses all the letters of the alphabet, which are shifted to different positions. Substitution employs the use of letters to represent other letters or symbols.

Cut-out (or Cutout): An agent who serves as a liaison or go-between person or contact person between field spies and the spymaster or control who supervises the activities of field agents; cut-outs often impart instructions and make low-level decisions.

Damage report: The assessment and evaluation of damage to an agent, station, network, espionage operation, or organization brought about by exposure and identification.

Dead drop: A place where messages and other items such as cash or equipment are left for other agents to retrieve. Also known as a dead letter box or drop. (A "live drop" is where people meet to pass information and material.)

Dead letter box: A secret site where field agents leave information and retrieve money, equipment, and instructions from spymasters, handlers, or caseworkers.

Debriefing: The process of obtaining all the information available from an agent or a group of agents following a specific mission or a period of service; imparted information from organization chiefs of a cautionary nature invariably accompanies such debriefings.

D-Department: Department of British Secret Intelligence Service.

Deep cover: A sleeper spy who operates under many layers of legends or false backgrounds, waiting to be activated; also applies to long-range operations planned far in advance of wars.

Defector: A spy who voluntarily changes sides, deserting to the camp of the enemy, especially during the Cold War.

Defector-in-place: Any agent who defects to the opposing side but who remains in his position to act as a double agent for that opposing side.

Desk man: Control (controller) at headquarters or one who directs espionage or counterespionage operations against a certain country. The CIA traitor Aldridge Ames was for some time head of the Soviet desk in Italy, and later held the same position at CIA headquarters in Langley, Virginia.

Deuxième Bureau: French intelligence service for the High Command.

Diplomatic cover: Any agent who has diplomatic immunity from arrest and prosecution in a foreign country, particularly those who are official representatives of their countries, such as embassy personnel.

Directorate of Security: British counterintelligence.

Disinformation: Secret information cleverly and convincingly doctored in such a way as to make that information appear to be genuine. For instance, a double agent wishing to convince the recipient of his report as to its veracity might stipulate that a certain act of sabotage had been accomplished by merely reciting the details of some destruction later reported in the press as a fire or explosion of undetermined origin. Though the mishap, in truth, is one of an accidental nature, the double agent claims it as his own work of sabotage.

D Notice Committee: British censorship committee, established 1912.

Double agent: A spy who works for both sides but whose loyalty is to only one and whose real service to the other is betrayal.

Double-Cross System: Using captured agents who have been turned to work as double agents by sending disinformation to their former spymasters. Also known as the Playback System.

Doubling: Turning an enemy agent so that he works as a double agent for the organization he originally opposed.

Drop: A place where messages and other items such as cash or equipment are left for other agents to retrieve. Also known as a dead letter box or dead drop. (A "live drop" is where people meet to pass information and material.)

Enciphered telephony: The scrambling of telephone conversations making such conversations unintelligible to anyone except those employing the technique when assisted with deciphering telephone equipment, which instantly unscrambles the conversations as they occur between and for the participating parties.

Encryption: Converting clear text into cipher or code or both.

Enigma: German cipher equipment in World War II, 1937–1945: The Enigma Machine created by German cryptologists before World War II transmitted the bulk of all top secret diplomatic and most military messages throughout the war. The plaintext was enciphered by a rotor system, one for the plaintext, a twin rotor system automatically translating to an encoded/enciphered message. As the plaintext was entered on a typewriter keyboard, the rotors would advance each letter, each position representing a letter of the alphabet and encoding each letter by routing through a wiring system of contacts on the wheels an electrical current which illuminated a small bulb indicating the encoded letter. The twin rotors advanced in relation to each other. The Enigma Key was the initial position of the rotors set with a plugboard. The British obtained Enigma Machines from the Polish and French underground at the beginning of the war and British cryptologists at Bletchley, known as Ultra, were able to reconstruct an identical machine, and a primitive computer machine (called Bombe) developed by Alan Turing accelerated the decrypting process by automatically sifting through the hundreds of thousands of mathematical combinations to define which rotor setting determined the Enigma Key for each day's messages. When the settings of the plugboard and rotors could be established, the German messages were automatically decrypted into plaintext. The Germans never knew that the British had broken their "unbreakable" code/cipher system.

Espionage: The craft of spying or, when used as a noun, an organization or agency that practices spying.

Espionage Abteilung: Swiss counterintelligence, established in World War II.

Exchange: The act of exchanging one or more captured or imprisoned spies for one or more spies from the other side. This practice really began in the American revolution but it came into full use during the Cold War with the exchange of Soviet agent Rudolf Abel and U-2 pilot Gary Francis Powers in 1962.

Executive action: Assassination or murder performed with the approval and direction of an intelligence organization.

Farm, The: The training school for CIA recruits in Virginia.

Field agent: An agent who works literally in the field of operations, securing by one means or another the secrets desired by his case officer or spymaster.

Field man: The same as field agent.

Fifth Man: The man who warned the fourth man, Anthony Blunt, to warn Burgess, Maclean, and Philby that they were suspected of being Soviet double agents. Some reports have it that this man was Roger Hollis, head of MI5.

Fourth Man: Soviet agent and British art historian Anthony Blunt, the man who warned the three Soviet double agents Burgess, Maclean, and Philby of their impending arrests.

Friends: MI5 term for MI6, often a misnomer since there was a considerable reluctance on the part of British counterintelligence to fully trust MI6 after the many double agents found in MI6 ranks such as Guy Burgess, David Maclean, and Kim Philby.

Gestapo: (*Geheime Staats Polizei*) German secret state police within RSHA for Hitler's Third Reich, 1933–1944.

Ghoul: An agent whose job it is to haunt graveyards, verifying the obituaries of dead children by checking grave registration and tombstone inscriptions, the names for which will be used as cover names by field agents. This was the lonely job of Victor Spencer, a Soviet agent in Canada.

Go-between: A cut-out or liaison agent who works with field agents and represents the spymaster of a network or ring; this agent is not merely a courier but imparts instructions and makes low-level decisions.

Gold: Code name for the Berlin Tunnel, which was secretly dug by the CIA and SIS as a listening post inside East Berlin in 1955.

Handler: One or more (handlers) agents who convey to spies their missions and assignments as ordered by control. Handlers usually work in the field, rather than in administrative capacities.

Hard target: An enemy country which spies find difficult to penetrate or in which to successfully operate or obtain information. In World War II, Japan was a "hard target."

Honey trap: An operation wherein someone is sexually compromised by a raven or swallow, and then forced into committing espionage; also called honey pot.

Illegal: Any spy who is not covered by diplomatic immunity, and who therefore cannot escape being tried for espionage.

Illegal operation: An espionage operation which is illlegal in the country where it is conducted.

Illness: The exposure or arrest of an agent; KGB use.

Indicator: A cryptonym indicating the sensitive nature of a message's contents.

Industrial espionage: The collection of secret information in business to increase the share of a given market. Spies in this field operate with the same procedures and equipment as in international espionage except that they rarely face criminal charges, their greatest risk being the loss of a job. Most governments routinely practice industrial espionage in fields involving international business and industry, particularly in highly competitive fields. In the mid-1960s, a KGB industrial spy network in France, headed by Herbert Steinbrecher, stole the plans for the Concorde.

In place: A field agent who is already established and working in a given area.

Intelligence: Information of a secret nature from a foreign power; an organization that gathers information of a secret nature from a foreign power.

Intercepts: Intelligence gathered through electronic eavesdropping of radio messages which, in the U.S., is almost the exclusive province of the NSA (National Security Agency). The NSA employs spy satellites and other means of intercepting classified messages.

Interrogation: The craft of compelling someone to reveal information which he or she is trying desperately to conceal. In the crudest form, this involves violence and torture. Historically, the Inquisition employed the rack, the Chinese their water torture, and, in modern times, the fixing of electrodes to sensitive body areas. The KGB and Chinese intelligence for years adopted an interrogation which simply wore out the subject, keeping a person without sleep for days until his will was worn down and exhaustion forced the desired answers, a system termed "brainwashing." As in police work, interrogation teams often use the "good man"–"bad man" technique, where one interrogator is brutal and offensive, the other sympathetic and kind, until the subject turns in gratitude to the latter to tell all. When IRA terrorism was at its height in northern Ireland the British Army placed hoods over suspects and made them lean against walls with only their fingertips while dinning into their ears "white noise," a piercing high-pitch screech. After several hours of this torture, subjects invariably told all. When released, the subjects bore no telltale signs of torture. (This kind of interrogation was discarded after the press described its use and a public outcry ensued.) Drugs and truth serums are also employed by interrogators, as well as hypnosis. The most sophisticated and effective interrogators are those who assemble an overwhelming amount of evidence and then patiently, systematically present this to the subject, probing until a weakness is found and then exploiting that weakness until the subject breaks and confesses. One of the most skillful MI5 interrogators was William Skardon, who induced Soviet agents Klaus Fuchs and Anthony Blunt to admit their espionage.

Invisible ink: Writing fluids used to conceal messages inside of other typed or hand-written messages. The use of invisible inks by spies is ancient. Milk, sugar-water, and lemon and lime juice have all been used for such writings, which, when heated, become visible. In more modern times lead nitrate, cobalt chloride, and copper sulphate (blue vitriol) have been used. While some chemicals react to heat, others require a reagent before invisible inks become apparent. Invisible inks are almost never used anymore since they are so easily detected.

Jib, The: A CIA inflatable dummy issued to agents and used from the early 1980s onward to replace an escaping agent inside of a car after the escapee rolls from the passenger side of the car as it is traveling at slow speeds.

Kempei Tai: Japanese secret police, sometimes called the "Thought Police," 1936–1945, which served as Japanese counterintelligence in World War II.

King's Secret: French intelligence service under Louis XV, 1740s–1760s.

Kundschaftsstelle: Austrian-Hungarian counterintelligence.

Legal: Any spy or oganization having diplomatic immunity from prosecution for crimes and espionage.

Legend: A false background or biography for a spy.

Letter box: The address of an agent who acts as a secret postal clerk, receiving information and handing this over to other agents. The most infamous letter box in pre–World War I England was a barbershop operated by German agent Karl Ernst.

Letter drop: An address or hiding place where information in the form of letters (in code or written in invisible ink), documents, microfilm, microdots, or other materials are hidden and which are visited by field agents who leave the information, and their handlers or cut-outs who leave instructions, cash, and sometimes equipment and supplies.

Liaison: A cut-out or go-between who acts as a contact agent between a spymaster and field agents.

Live drop: A site for a secret rendezvous between spies who meet and exchange information and materials.

Magic: U.S. cryptological system which broke the principal Japanese cipher (produced by Japan's Purple Machine) of World War II.

Maquis: French resistance organization during World War II.

Microdot: A photograph of a secret message reduced to microscopic size for easy concealment. So small are microdots that they can appear to be a period at the end of a sentence in a typed letter and are only visible under powerful microscopes. Though miniature photography was employed by espionage agents as early as the Franco-Prussian War of 1870–1871, the microdot did not come into widespread espionage use until the Cold War.

Mixed Bureau: Allied counterintelligence in World War I, 1914–1918.

Mole: A counterspy who joins an enemy espionage agency to report on that organization's operations. Deputy director of the CIA James Jesus Angleton was obsessed with the idea that the agency had been infiltrated with one or more KGB moles and searched vainly for years to uncover these traitors. A mole may also be an in-place agent who is "turned" by a rival espionage agency so that he secretly acts on behalf of the enemy. This term was invented by spy novelist John Le Carré and has since been used by members of the intelligence community.

Monitors: A technique of intercepting radio or telephone conversations when they are scrambled. The sophisticated Abwehr monitoring station at Brest, France, was able to intercept and unscramble almost all of the Roosevelt-Churchill conversations during World War II.

Mossad: Israeli intelligence, established 1951.

Mukhabarat: Libyan intelligence service.

Mukhabarat El-Aam: Egyptian intelligence, established in 1951. Also known as GIA.

Music box: A radio transmitter.

Musician: A radio operator.

Naked: A spy operating without cover or back-up.

National Center: White Russian émigré society which secretly funded anti-Bolshevik forces during the Russian Civil War and to which British intelligence was closely associated.

Neighbor: Another branch of an intelligence service or another friendly intelligence service.

Network: A group of spies (not necessarily known to each other) that has been organized under the direction of a single control or spymaster. Usually each network has a number of cells, each cell consisting of three or more agents with each agent ideally knowing no more than one other agent. Each cell has a chief who issues orders from the network spymaster, those orders delivered by cut-outs and couriers. Agents who serve as specialists in photography, documents, or bugging devices operate inside a single cell with only one or two agents known to them and vice versa. Since these specialists are most vulnerable to detection they are purposely limited as to knowing the identities of other agents and other cells and seldom, if ever, the identity of the network spymaster.

No-beef: Code name for CIA payments to King Hussein of Jordan, payments that amounted to untold millions of dollars over a 20-year period, which were delivered to the monarch by the CIA station chief in Amman. In return, Hussein reportedly allowed the CIA to freely operate in Jordan. When these governmental bribes were made known in the American press, all payments were ostensibly stopped. Hussein admitted to receiving the payments, claiming they were not personal payoffs but funds used to advance Jordanian security and intelligence.

Okhrana (or Ochrana): Czarist secret police and intelligence organization, 1881–1917.

Onetime pad: Simple encoding system using five letter groups and employed only once.

Open code: Communicating by telephone or written messages in which arcane or esoteric references are made and known to have another significant meaning to the recipient.

Operation Barbarossa: The German invasion of Soviet Russia in 1941.

Operation Bernhard: A fantastic scheme developed by Alfred Naujocks of SD intelligence to print billions of forged British bank notes and drop these by plane over England in 1940 in an attempt to ruin the British economy, a plan which was not adopted by Hitler.

Operation Big Ben: An SOE operation in 1944 involving Polish underground fighters who had recovered an errant V-2 rocket, which was dismantled; parts of the rocket, along with blueprints of the overall rocket drawn by a Polish engineer, were picked up by a British bomber and flown to England for examination.

Operation Bodyguard: An MI5 operation wherein German intelligence was hoodwinked into believing that the Allied invasion of Europe would take place at Pas de Calais, instead of the actual landing site, Normandy.

Operation Bride: The initial operations launched just after World War II by the combined communications intelligence agencies of the U.S., Britain, Canada, and Australia to collect and decode and decipher all Soviet traffic.

Operation Chaos: A CIA operation enacted in July 1968 which was aimed at disrupting U.S. student protests against the Vietnam War. This was a legal operation insofar as the CIA's investigation outside of the U.S. of such movements in conformance to its charter, which prohibited CIA involvement in the Western Hemisphere, which is exclusively the chartered domain of the FBI. The CIA, however, monitored anti-war demonstrators and demonstrations within the U.S., even though such illegal activities caused bitter feuds within the agency at the time. CIA chief Richard Helms continued these illegal operation at the insistence of President Lyndon B. Johnson, the architect of America's involvement in the Vietnam War, and, later, President Richard M. Nixon, all of which was later revealed in the aftermath of Watergate.

Operation Damocles: An Israeli covert operation in 1962 mounted by the Mossad in Egypt, the purpose being to intimidate and even kidnap German scientists (some being former Nazis) working with Nasser's Egyptian government.

Operation Felix: The planned and later abandoned German invasion of Gibraltar in World War II which was masterminded by Abwehr chief Admiral Wilhelm Canaris.

Operation Fortitude South: A grand deception involving the mythical U.S. First Army Group (FUSAG), reportedly headed by American General George S. Patton, in which dummy landing craft were amassed at ports opposite Pas de Calais and canvas planes, trucks, and tanks assembled in staging areas to support the ruse that the Allied invasion would be made at Pas de Calais, an operation that convinced Hitler to concentrate most of his armored divisions in that area, thus leaving Normandy, the real intended landing site, relatively free of heavy defenses.

Operation Gold: The joint CIA-MI6 operation involving the building and maintenance of the Berlin Tunnel, which clandestinely monitored Communist communications in East Berlin during the mid-1950s.

Operation Heinrich: Abwehr operation during World War II, in the 1944 Battle of the Bulge, wherein German slave laborers were allowed to escape to American lines, unwittingly carrying false intelligence in their belongings, which had been planted by German agents and designed to mislead the Allies as to the strength and positions of German forces.

Operation Mincemeat: British SIS operation in World War II involving the planting of a body on Spanish shores which indicated an Allied attack through Greece in 1943, a bogus plan which was accepted by the Germans and caused them to move reinforcements to Greece and away from the intended invasion of Italy; also known as The Man Who Never Was.

Operation Mongoose: A failed CIA operation in the early 1960s to assassinate Cuban Communist dictator Fidel Castro.

Operation Noah's Ark (1943–1944): A French underground espionage operation conducted by the Alliance International Service in World War II which located the manufacturing and launch sites for Germany's V-1 and V-2 rockets.

Operation Noah's Ark (1969): A Mossad operation which involved smuggling five gunboats out of Cherbourg harbor on December 25, 1969. The Israeli-designed and paid-for boats were prohibited from being delivered to Israel by an arms ban imposed by President Charles de Gaulle after the raid on Beirut Airport on December 28, 1968, by Israeli commandos. A year later, Mossad agents smuggled Israeli sailors on board the gunboats, which were secretly stored with supplies and fueled for "sea trials." Before French authorities could act, the gunboats started up their engines and sped out of the port, arriving later in Israel. Other than the Arab nations, the world applauded the daring coup. France, however, felt humiliated, President Pompidou stating: "We have been made to look complete fools."

Operation North Pole: The system employed by the Abwehr wherein captured British spies in Holland during World War II were turned to transmit disinformation to England on behalf of the Germans.

Operation Overlord: The Allied invasion of Normandy on June 6, 1944.

Operation Pastorius (German sabotage mission in U.S., 1942): Following a plan envisioned by Adolf Hitler, Abwehr chief Wilhelm Canaris and his subordinate Erwin von Lahousen dispatched eight poorly trained saboteurs in two submarines to the U.S. In June 1942, four of the saboteurs were landed near St. Augustine, Florida, four others at Amagansett Beach, Long Island, N.Y. The German agents were to destroy a cryolite factory outside of Philadelphia where materials were manufactured to create aluminum and plants owned by the Aluminum Company of America in Alcoa, Tennessee; Massena, New York; and East St. Louis, Missouri. The aim was to cripple the U.S. airplane industry. Leaders of the mission were George John Dasch (1903-1970), a one-time U.S. Army Air Corps mechanic, and Ernest Peter Burger. Both leaders were spotted by Coast Guardsman Jack Culley, when landing and they were later tracked to New York City where they were arrested. They turned informants on the other six to save themselves (a deal they cut with J. Edgar Hoover). All eight were found guilty of espionage and sabotage by a military tribunal. Werner Thiel, Edward Kerling, Heinrich Heinck, Richard Quirin, Hermann Neubauer, and Herbert Hans Haupt were executed in the electric chair in the Washington, D.C. jail in August 1942; Dasch and Burger, who also testified against eight men and six women who aided the saboteurs, were given 30-year prison terms. Lahousen was not surprised at the outcome of Hitler's ill-conceived operation, saying later that "it turned out to be the biggest blunder that ever occured in Abwehr II." Hitler blamed Dasch for the failure, calling him "an incompetent swine!"

Operation Plumbat: A Mossad mission in 1968 wherein the German vessel *Scheerbergs*, loaded with 200 tons of uranium oxide which could be used in producing nuclear weapons, sailed from Antwerp and then vanished, later reappearing under a different name and with different papers. The cargo, which was apparently used for Israel's nuclear reactor, had been purchased through a series of dummy companies which had been set up by the Mossad. The operation was revealed in 1978 by Haakon Wiker, former chief prosecutor of Norway, who claimed to have gotten the information from captured Mossad agent Dan Aerbel, a participant in Plumbat.

Operation Red Pepper: A joint FBI-RCMP operation which consisted of keeping Soviet agent Hugh Hambleton under surveillance in Canada, filming him with Soviet bloc agents and then raiding his home and that of his mother in 1979 to discover a transmitter and other incriminating evidence. Hambleton confessed his guilt but was not prosecuted.

Operation Rice Bowl: The failed attempt by the CIA and the DIA to rescue the fifty-three U.S. hostages taken during the Iranian revolution led by Ayatollah Khomeini. Dozens of agents in disguise moved in and out of Teheran to provide information for the raid that was to rescue the hostages, but the attempt collapsed when a helicopter crash left eight dead. The CIA and DIA agents fled Iran, which was then in the fanatical grip of Khomeini's followers.

Operation Sea Lion: Hitler's abortive plan to invade England in 1940.

Operation Sunrise: OSS operation in World War II which was headed by Allen Dulles wherein a separate surrender of German troops in Italy under the command of SS General Karl Wolf was negotiated but did not occur.

Operation Sussex: Code name for the dropping of saboteurs behind German lines prior to the D-Day invasion of Normandy on June 6, 1944, an operation conducted by MI6 and supervised by Claude Dansey.

Operation Suzanna: Code name for the disastrous Israeli military intelligence operation in Egypt in 1954 in which American and British property was attacked in order to discredit the Nasser regime with Western powers.

Operation Torch: The Allied invasion of North Africa in 1942.

Operation Valkyrie: The abortive attempt by members of Germany's Black Orchestra to assassinate Adolf Hitler on July 20, 1944, by planting a bomb in the dictator's East Prussia military retreat. The bomb did kill a number of Nazis but Hitler received only a slight wound in the arm. The ringleaders of Operation Valkyrie were quickly rounded up and either executed immediately or tried by kangaroo courts and then murdered. More than 5,000 persons were executed as the result of this failed operation.

Operation White: Hitler's sneak invasion of Poland on September 1, 1939.

Overt information: Legally gathered information from published sources.

Paris Agency: Monarchist espionage network during the French Revolution, 1791–1797.

Paroles: Key words between agents to establish mutual identification.

Playback System: Using captured agents who have been turned to work as double agents by sending disinformation to their former spymasters. This system came into widespread use during World War II when German intelligence employed captured British spies in Holland in what was called Operation

North Pole. Captured members of the Red Orchestra were also used the same way by the Germans. The British did the same in what they called the Double-Cross System, compelling or persuading captured German agents to send disinformation to the Abwehr almost throughout the war. In America, double agent William Sebold performed the same service for the FBI.

Plumber: Anyone responsible for breaking into and burglarizing a secure area during a covert operation. The Watergate burglars were called Plumbers.

Plumbing: The structuring of participants and responsibilities involved in a covert operation.

Polygraph: A lie detector; a machine which electronically measures nervous reflexes to a series of questions. This is done by placing a pneumograph around the chest to monitor the subject's breathing and a rubber cuff around the upper arm to measure any drastic rise or fall in blood pressure and pulse rate. Electrodes are also placed on the subject's hands to record any excessive sweating. Wires from these instruments feed to a needle which marks a continuous roll of paper. If the needle records a steady pattern in response to questions asked, the subject is then deemed to be telling the truth. Any needle marks that are at wide variance with the norm indicate the subject is lying in response to certain questions. The CIA traitor Aldrich Ames was given regular polygraph tests and claimed to be able to overcome anxiety by simply staying up all night and taking the test in a state of utter exhaustion and relaxation.

Positive Vetting: British security checks for intelligence service recruits which involves the subject providing detailed information about his grandparents, parents, relatives, spouses, education, employment history, and political affiliation, as well as two character references. This allows agents to check on someone's entire personal, educational, employment and political history. Prior to the time British intelligence was shown to be rife with traitors such as Burgess, Maclean, and Philby, its custom was to merely check on two character references and then trust the subject's honorable word. Since recruitment in that era was restricted to uppercrust schools such as Trinity College, it was believed that old school traditions and ties bound recruits by unflagging loyalty to their country. This the British learned was naive in the extreme. The spies in the heart of British intelligence had no honor and knew no loyalty except to Moscow. American intelligence services, particularly the FBI and CIA, pressured the British into adopting a Positive Vetting system of background checks, one employed in the U.S. for anyone requiring a clearance to view or handle classified materials.

Princes, The: Danish resistance organization during World War II.

Purple Machine: Japanese cipher equipment, 1937–1945, similar to that of the German Enigma encoding-enciphering machine duplicated by U.S. Signals Intelligence just prior to World War II, enabling U.S. intelligence agencies to read Japan's top diplomatic and military codes and ciphers throughout the war.

Radio: A short-wave radio transmitter used to send and receive messages in code or cipher or both.

Radio Liberty: American-controlled broadcasting system in West Germany that transmitted propaganda to the Soviet Union during the Cold War.

Radio Free Europe: American-controlled broadcasting system in western Europe that transmitted propaganda to the Warsaw Pact countries dominated by Soviet Russia during the Cold War.

Radio operator: The operator of a short-wave transmitter used in sending and receiving coded or enciphered messages.

Raven: A male prostitute working in collusion with spies to compromise someone with secrets to impart and provide, usually through secretly taken photographs, evidence which will compel the victim into providing information.

Recognition signal: A secret sign or password used by agents to recognize each other in a first-time rendezvous. When atom spy Klaus Fuchs met Harry Gold, his Soviet contact in New York, for the first time his recognition signal was to carry a tennis ball in his hand. Fuchs was told that his contact would be wearing gloves and carrying another pair of gloves and a book with a green binding.

Red Brigades: Left-wing Italian radical terrorist organization founded in 1969 at the Trento University by student Renato Curcio and suspected of being KGB-financed and armed. The Brigades specialized throughout the 1970s and mid-1980s in political kidnappings and assassinations until more than 500 of its members were finally apprehended and imprisoned.

Red Orchestra: The many Soviet spy networks operating in Germany and Nazi-occupied Europe during World War II, 1939–1943.

Resident director: A spymaster or control whose authority covers a network in a city, district, state, province, or even an entire country. This term has almost been exclusively used by the Soviets.

Ring: A group or network of spies.

Room 40: Cryptology office in British Admiralty Building in London in World War I where German codes and ciphers were broken.

Rote Kapelle: Red Orchestra, the Soviet underground in World War II.

Sabotage: The destruction of any physical object through clandestine means which damages essential enemy targets.

Safe house: Any building where agents can safely meet or hide for a lengthy period of time without fear of detection. Also applied to defectors.

Sanitize: Preparing a document before its release by doctoring or censoring part of its contents.

Scientific intelligence: Technical applications to espionage and counterespionage. These include a myriad of fields: biology in detecting subtle poisons; chemistry, which employs sensitive acids to examine documents (to make invisible writings apparent); electronics, which employs bugging devices and, for military intelligence, the use of radar, sonar, and direction-finding equipment; medicine, where the polygraph is used or truth serums and mind-altering drugs are employed; photography, which has produced microfilm and the microdot to contain infinitesimal messages; physics, which might involve laser beams.

Secret: The second highest U.S. security classification regarding national security information held by someone working in the intelligence community.

Secret writing: Writing that is put into coded or enciphered form by cryptographers. Also writing that is made with invisible ink.

Security: The steps spies or spy networks take to secure themselves from penetration and exposure. During World War II, Norwegian Resistance issued a table of security instructions which have since proven to be the hallmark of espionage security: 1) Don't gossip, especially in public places; 2) Never commit secret information to paper unless absolutely necessary; 3) Do not call on an associate agent you have not seen in some time unless first phoning to make sure he or she is not under suspicion or surveillance; 4) Never use your own phone to contact a fellow agent; 5) Be prepared for security police or counterintelligence to call for you at your work or home at any time, even on an innocent inquiry. If so, attempt to escape. If no escape can be made, confront police with dignified silence and indignation but do not display defiance. Take warm clothing with you. This advice was nothing more than common sense but good security is made up of common sense.

Security check: In radio transmissions of coded or enciphered messages, these checks consist of inserting secret signs—a purposely garbled or mutilated letter at set intervals—which conveys to the receiver that the message is genuine and not being sent under duress, or, conversely, meaning that the message is bogus and is being sent under duress. In regard to recruits applying for intelligence service, a thorough background check (in the U.S. always conducted by the FBI) into that recruit's family history, education, friends, relatives, employment, and political affiliation.

Shabak: The counterintelligence department of Israel's Shin Beth, officially known as Sharuth Bitakhon Klali.

Shadow: An agent following another, a tail, a form of street surveillance where one agent follows another on foot.

Shin Beth: Israel's counterintelligence service.

Shoe: A false passport or visa.

Shopping list: Types of information desired by an intelligence organization, or technological items or weapons required for a specific espionage operation.

Sleeper: An agent who is assigned to an area which may in the future be operational and one who waits to be activated. Usually such agents operate outside of established networks and are known only to spymasters at headquarters. One of the most successful sleeper agents of World War II was German spy Simon Emil Koedel, who operated in the U.S., gaining access to almost every important defense plant in America and delivering invaluable information to his Abwehr spymasters in Germany.

Soft target: A country or geographical area where espionage goals are easily achieved. In World War II, Spain and Portugal were "soft targets."

Soviet secret police: Since the Russian Revolution of 1917, Soviet Russia was ruled by a secret state police and intelligence organization operating on a global basis. This organization has had many names but remains the same organization. Names for this organization over the years have been: Cheka, 1917–1922; GPU, 1922–1923; OGPU, 1923–1934; NKVD, 1934–1946; MVD, 1946–1954; KGB, 1954–.

Special Committee: A committee (established in 1955) of the U.S. National Security Council, which is made up of the President and members of the CIA, State Department, and Defense Department and which approves all U.S. covert operations.

Special Service Organ: Japanese military intelligence from 1900 to 1945, headed in China during World War II by Kenji Doihara who was later hanged as a war criminal.

Spook: American term for a spy or secret agent.

Spy: An agent who obtains classified information about one country or side which benefits another country or side. The Hague Convention of 1899 defined a spy as "one who, acting clandestinely, or on false pretenses, obtains, or seeks to obtain, information in the zone of operations of a belligerent, with the intention of communicating it to the hostile party."

Spy Aircraft (Aerial Espionage, from 1862): Aircraft in one form or another used for reconnaissance since the American Civil War when tethered balloons were raised to allow observers to peer across enemy lines and evaluate troop positions and strengths. French intelligence used balloons for aerial reconnaissance in the Franco-Prussian War of 1870. In World War I, low-flying primitive planes, observation balloons and derigibles were used to photograph enemy positions along the Western and Eastern fronts. Lawrence of Arabia used planes to scout the enemy and take photographs of Turkish military positions during World War I, and, Pancho Villa employed planes for the same purpose during the Mexican civil wars. From 1939 to the end of World War II, aerial espionage increased, with all major powers involved establishing vast aerial intelligence services within their air forces. At the end of that global conflict more than thirty million negatives were held in the film repository of the U.S. Department of Defense (from American, British, and captured German and Japanese intelligence film archives). Aerial intelligence photography during World War II concentrated on potential bombing sites, as well as targets that had been repeatedly bombed so that military experts could properly analyze the effectiveness of such bombing. Thus, those in aerial military intelligence could study and assess the results of Japanese dive bombers at Pearl Harbor on December 7, 1941 (through captured Japanese aerial negatives), skip-bombing off New Guinea, cluster bombing at the siege of Stalingrad and the celebrated bombing raid against the oilfields in Ploesti, Rumania. Through such aerial photographic intelligence, bombing targets were selected, accuracy of bombing determined, enemy orders of battle realized, defense positions pinpointed, and new terrain for potential operations more easily analyzed. Sophisticated aerial intelligence enabled Allied forces to become more effective in their air war and more quickly bring World War II to an end. Spy aircraft became extremely advanced during the Cold War and by the mid-1950s, the U.S. employed the U-2 spy plane, also called the Black Lady. Two dozen U-2 planes, at a cost of $1 million each, were used to fly over the Soviet Union to gather aerial photographic intelligence, taking hundreds of rolls of film by specially-developed cameras that provided photos offering pinpoint detail. The U-2s traveled at such high altitudes and moved at such supersonic speeds that they were thought to be invulnerable to ground or air attack by the Soviets. This was disproved when U-2 pilot Gary Francis Powers was shot down near Sverdlovsk in 1960. Two years later, U-2 planes flying over Cuba were able to pinpoint Russian offensive missiles which led to the Cuban Missile Crisis where Nikita Khrushchev, when confronted with the aerial photographic evidence, withdrew Soviet missiles from Cuba. The CIA continued to use an even more advanced version of the U-2 thereafter, the TR-1A which could carry nearly two tons of sensors and equipment and operated in all types of weather in accomplishing its photo intelligence operations. The U.S. next employed the super sophisticated SR 71, the Blackbird, the fastest aircraft in the world, traveling at three times the speed of sound, capable of reaching an altitude above 80,000 feet and having a 2,675-mile range. These spy aircraft spot check the world's trouble areas daily. They photographed almost every stage of the 1973 Yom Kippur War and recorded events in China, Yemen, and Afghanistan. U.S. spy aircraft contributed greatly to the Allied victory in the Gulf War against Iraq. Almost every key target blasted by Allied bombers was pinpointed by spy aircraft. Supplementing such spycraft as the Blackbird is the RC-135, the size of a Boeing liner which is packed with sophisticated sensors and monitoring equipment capable of intercepting radio signals with perfect accuracy at a distance of 1,000 miles which precludes these planes having to fly directly over enemy territory. (The Korean airliner shot down by the Russians in 1983 was mistaken for an RC-135.) Crews for these planes are manned by U.S. National Defense Agency experts, along with USAF personnel. Awacs planes made by Boeing and Nimrod having gigantic radar dishes which can peer 200 or more miles into enemy territory and are used by American, British, and NATO air forces. Strategic aerial reconnaissance is achieved by satellites (called Spy-in-the-Sky) which hover at between 100 and 200 miles above photographic targets.

Spy-in-the-Sky (Espionage Satellites, from 1980s): As aerial intelligence technology improved, so did the use of outer space spy satellites; the U.S. and the Soviet Union, have raced since 1957 (when Russia's Sputnik was launched and the U.S.'s Vanguard the following year) to place more and more sophisticated orbiting satellites in space in order to electronically record intelligence data on earth. While rocketry and space-age technology expanded from that time to this, more refined satellites were placed into orbit with radar and camera equipment sensitive enough to survey large geographical areas or focus upon objects no more than two-feet long from an altitude of more than 100 miles, producing clear television images to monitoring stations almost anywhere in the world, these satellites recording sounds and impulses, written and spoken to the level of telephone calls. In 1961, the U.S. launched its first Samos (Satellite and Missile Observer) satellite and since that time it has put into space hundreds of Spy-in-the-Sky satellites that move at 18,000 m.p.h., criss-crossing the Soviet Union, China and other problem areas. Through these satellites U.S. intelligence is able to record nuclear test explosions, rocket-launchings, troop and armored movements, as well as military commands via telephone. When the Samos satellites eventually fall from space to earth, programmed to invariably land in "safe" Pacific waters, their ejected information capsules are retrieved from the sea by rescue helicopters and planes. In the war of space espionage, the U.S. placed the super sophisticated Rhyolite and subsequent advanced versions of this spy satellite (Big Bird and Keyhole) into space. Information on Rhyolite was sold to KGB agents in Mexico City by two drug-taking Californians, Christopher John Boyce and Andrew Daulton Lee in 1975–1976. The Soviets mustered their last great Spy in the Sky operations during the early 1970s. In 1973, it was able to startle Egyptian premier Anwar Sadat by showing him photos of Israeli advances in the Arab-Israeli war which had been taken from deep space, photos taken by Russian space satellites which accurately depicted Israeli armored columns racing toward Ismailia and Cairo. In Star Wars scenarios, the Soviets fell drastically behind the espionage space race in the 1980s and, instead of putting competing spy satellites into space, concentrated on launching killer satellites that would seek out U.S. spy satellites and, by merely programming collisions between its own satellites and that of the U.S., cause the destruction of both. U.S. counterespionage in space improved, however, to the point where it developed satellites lurking in deep space that were programmed to seek out and collide with and thus destroy Soviet killer satellites. Moreover, as the Russian satellite program collapsed from financial bankruptcy, U.S. intelligence stepped up its Spy-in-the-Sky intelligence by employing the space shuttle to plant additional, even more sophisticated spy satellites in space, as well as maintain those launched years earlier. Since the collapse of communism in Russia in 1989-1991, the U.S. is now the only nation controlling Spy-in-the-Sky intelligence and its accuracy and importance was demonstrated in the overwhelming victory by Allied forces in the Gulf War against the antiquated war machine of Iraq's dictator, Saddam Hussein.

Spy Ships (Espionage Vessels from 1950s): Ships of all nations have been employed as espionage vessels, lurking off the shores of enemy nations to monitor troop positions and movements, defensive gun emplacements, locations of munitions and manufacturing centers of war goods, intended tactics and strategy. During the Napoleonic wars, ships sailed close to the shores of England and France to pick up the lantern or flag signals of shore-based spies relaying information on the enemy. In a scene from Alexander Dumas' *The Count of Monte Cristo*, spies are depicted sending lantern signals from shore to a French ship to announce in code the escape of Napoleon from his exile on the island of Elba. In World War I, warships were used to gather intelligence by landing and picking up spies who operated ship-to-shore communications systems. The same methods were improved in World War II when vessels, particularly submarines, were used to smuggle spies onto enemy shores. In this way the German Abwehr, the British SIS and SOE, and the American OSS were able to land their agents. SIS used a submarine to plant the body of a dead officer which decoyed German intelligence away from the intended Allied invasion of Europe in Normandy in a fantastic espionage scheme known as The Man Who Never Was (or Operation Mincemeat).The Germans used submarines as spy vessels off the coast of England and the U.S. and landed Nazi saboteurs off the coasts of New York and Florida in a sabotage scheme called Operation Pastorius. Japanese submarines were used as spy vessels before the attack on Pearl Harbor, laying off the Hawaiian coast to pick up signals from its land-based spies, particularly the Kuhn family which reported by signals from their home the accuracy of Japanese bombs being dropped on American battleships during the Pearl Harbor attack, the signals being picked up by the Japanese consulate, then relayed to an offshore Japanese submarine which, in turn, passed those messages on to the Japanese fleet north of Hawaii. U.S. submarines penetrated Japanese waters to make observations prior to land invasions or bombing missions against Japanese-held islands in the Pacific. One U.S. submarine actually slipped past the protective nets guarding Tokyo Bay, lay submerged by day and, by night, landed a group of agents who meticulously recorded Japanese antiaircraft installations and manufacturing centers, as well as weather conditions before returning by rubby dinghy to the sub. The submarine then escaped into the open sea to radio in code the information which was used to devastating effect by two dozen bombers launched from the aircraft carrier *Hornet*. James H. Doolittle led the celebrated bombing raid over Tokyo in 1942, the first offensive action taken by the U.S. following Pearl Harbor and the targets hit were those pinpointed by the naval intelligence team that had landed from the submarine inside Tokyo Bay (as depicted in the film *Destination Tokyo*). In the Cold War, the Russians employed ancient trawlers which passed themselves off as fishing vessels, sailing close to the shores of Western nations. These ships were packed with electronic equipment used to monitor the location and movements of warships, particularly aircraft carriers. At one point, the Soviets had more than fifty of these vessels probing U.S. waters. The U.S. has used a few similar spy ships as listening posts but these vessels met with little success and considerable tragedy. The USS *Liberty*, an ancient 10,000-ton freighter, was converted into a floating platform used for electronic surveillance of the Six Day War. Achored off the coast of the Sinai Peninsula, the ship was staffed by language and code experts. During the fighting, the Hebrew and Arabic language experts were able to monitor battle orders in both languages and relay this information to U.S. intelligence centers. Israeli intelligence, the Mossad, identified the *Liberty* as an NSA spy ship and Mirage jets were sent to bomb and stafe it mercilessly, even though the American flag was flying from its masthead. During the Israeli attack, thirty-four aboard the spy ship were killed and seventy-five wounded. The Israelis later apologized, saying that it mistook the vessel for one of the enemy's. No flag was flying from the vessel, Israeli spokesmen pointed out but they made no response to the retort that their own planes had shot the American flag to pieces. The Israelis attacked the Liberty in the belief that if they prevented the spy ship's information from reaching Washington, the U.S. would not insist upon a cease fire until all their strategic goals had been achieved. Another U.S. spy ship, the USS *Pueblo*, encountered an even worse fate. The NSA vessel, staffed with naval intelligence personnel, was laying in North Korean waters, monitoring Communist military and diplomatic nets. On January 23, 1968, a North Korean submarine chaser attacked the helpless *Pueblo*, injuring several crewmen before the ship was captured. Commander Lloyd M. Bucher and his men attempted to destroy the electronic equipment, codes and ciphers but the ship was boarded so quickly that the Americans were caught red-handed. The crew was interned in a camp near Pyongyang for eleven months, physically and pyschologically tortured into making confessions that they were spies. On December 22, 1968, Major General Gilbert H. Woodward

signed a statement at Panmunjom which was addressed to the Government of the Democratic People's Republic of Korea which stated: "The Government of the United States of America, acknowledging the validity of the confessions of the crew of the USS *Pueblo* and of the documents of evidence produced by the represenative of the Government of the Democratic People's Republic of Korea to the effect that the ship, which was seized by the self-defense measures of the vessels of the Korean People's Army in the territorial waters...shoulders full responsibility. Simultaneously, with the signing of the document, the undersigned acknowledges receipt of 82 former crew members of the *Pueblo* and one corpse [Fireman Duane Hodges, killed during the attack on the ship]." Woodward handed this document to North Korean General Chung Kuk Pak and then immediately repudiated the document. Pak ignored the verbal repudiation, then ordered the *Pueblo*'s crew released. Bucher was severely criticized for mishandling the affair; his superiors believed that he and his men should have been able to get rid of the eavesdropping equipment, codebooks, ciphers and other intelligence paraphenalia before the capture. Though Russian trawlers still sail dangerously close to U.S territorial waters in an effort to conduct electronic surveillance, the use of spy ships is considered outmoded, particularly with the overwhelming success of the U.S. Spy-in-the-Sky system.

Spymaster: The supervising agent in charge of a network of spies, usually in an administrative capacity, or the chief of national intelligence or military intelligence.

Station: A post where espionage operations are conducted, usually an embassy.

Strategic intelligence: The collecting and analyzing of information involving the political intentions and military strengths of foreign nations.

Stringer: A freelance agent who works periodically or occasionally for an intelligence agency. This agent is a part-time spy who usually works for set rewards and takes only specific missions and is not permanently on call. Some stringers are specialists in accomplishing specific missions (such as break-ins, burglaries, photographing documents) but stringers are invariably used as decoys or cut-outs. It was said that Mata Hari was a stringer for the German Abwehr who served as an unwitting decoy and was sacrificed to a firing squad to put Allied counterintelligence off the track of more important German agents. The stringer is almost always motivated by money and is considered the least reliable of agents.

Sûreté-Nationale: French police and counterespionage organization, established in 1800s.

Swallow: A female prostitute working in collusion with spies to compromise someone with secrets to impart and provide, usually through secretly taken photographs, evidence which will compel the victim into providing information.

Swallow's nest. The residence of a swallow or female prostitute whose job it is to sexually engage a spy to compromise him; such apartments or homes are equipped with hidden cameras and recorders to film and record the sexual actions of victims in order to compromise and turn them to working for the opposing intelligence organization.

Swim: To travel.

Take, the: The information gathered from espionage.

Tapping: Intercepting telephone conversations and messages.

Treff: German word meaning a clandestine meeting between a handler and a field agent, usually for the purpose of determining whether or not the handler will accept the services of a new or apprentice spy.

Terminated: Murdered. Sometimes used as "Terminated with extreme prejudice."

Throwaway: A cover story or legend which can be discarded when it does not withstand interrogation and another cover story or legend, layered beneath the original, is then offered; also an agent who is considered expendable, as was the case with Mata Hari, the German spy of World War I.

Top Secret: The highest U.S. security classification regarding national security information held by someone working in the intelligence community.

Triangulation: Used in direction finding wherein three radio receivers with revolving antennae (often on vehicles) representing the angles of a triangle take bearings on a radio signal transmitted within the triangle. The courses of the bearings are plotted on a map of the area within the triangle and, where the courses intersect the secret radio is pinpointed. The Germans first developed this effective radio direction finding technique in World War II.

Triple agent: A spy who is recruited again by his original intelligence agency after having gone over to an enemy intelligence organization; or he or she may be an agent working for three separate intelligence agencies, showing loyalty to all, even though they may be adversarial, which was often the case with Isaac Trebitsch Lincoln.

Truth drugs: Anaesthetics employed in interrogation which reportedly act as truth serums, compelling the subject to make admissions he or she would not otherwise make. This is arguable by most physicians who do not recognize the drugs as causing the subject to tell the truth when he is determined not to do so. Such drugs can produce admissions only if the subject secretly wishes to confess. The most commonly used truth drug of World War II was Scopolamine (hyoscine), which was employed by the counterintelligence division of the Abwehr. This drug is one of the belladonna alkaloids and is considered very dangerous when not given in extremely controlled doses. The drug affects the nervous system, releasing control of essential functions such as heart, bowel, and bladder. This highly toxic drug is extremely risky, even though it was at one time popularly used to ease the pain of childbirth. When used on captured agents, this drug was combined with morphine to produce a "twilight sleep," where victims would respond to questions in a semi-conscious state. Sodium thiopental (Pentathal), a short-acting barbiturate, was also used by Soviet interrogators, another dangerous drug which is administered intravenously in strictly controlled doses. Subjects given this drug are conscious for a very short time before becoming unconscious and unresponsive to interrogation. Amobarbital, another barbiturate, induces a semi-conscious state in the subject. It is believed that all interrogators in all intelligence agencies have used or still use these drugs to induce subjects into providing information.

Turn: To convert a spy by threat or persuasion into being a double agent, working for the very country he or she has been assigned to spy upon. In such instances, the "turned" spy invariably sends back disinformation which is skillfully concocted to appear genuine.

Ultra: British communications intelligence during World War II, 1939–1945, especially as applied to intercepted and deciphered German messages.

Uncle: Reference to any headquarters of an espionage service.

Unwitting agent: A spy who thinks he is working for one side when he is really working for another.

V-Man: (*Vertrauens-Mann*) An informer who can be trusted, usually a citizen of the country in which agents are operating.

Walk-in: The act of someone literally walking into a meeting or a meeting place from the street with an offer to act as a spy or with secrets to impart.

Watchers: Agents who keep persons under surveillance.

Wet job: Any operation in which blood is shed.

Wire tapping: Intercepting telephone conversations or messages.

FILMOGRAPHY

THE FOLLOWING FILMOGRAPHY LISTS THEATRICALLY-released films that are based, in whole or in part, on actual espionage cases or spies, many of which are cross-referenced to text entries as signified by *q.v.* (ABBREVIATIONS: b/w= black and white; c= color; d= director; lp= leading players; m= minutes/runing time)

ABRAHAM LINCOLN (1930), 97m, Griffith/UA, b/w, d, D.W. Griffith, lp, *Walter Huston, Una Merkel, Kay Hammond, E. Alyn Warren, Hobart Bosworth, Henry B. Walthal, Ian Keith, Frank Campeau, Francis Ford*

In this, one of the better Lincoln biopics, Lincoln's assassination (*q.v.*, under Lafayette Baker) is handled in detail with Huston as Lincoln and Keith as his killer, John Wilkes Booth. (Avail. on cas.)

ACROSS THE PACIFIC (1942), 97m, WB/FN, b/w, d, John Huston, lp, *Humphrey Bogart, Mary Astor, Sydney Greenstreet, Charles Halton, Victor Sun-Yen, Roland Got, Lee Tung Foo, Frank Wilcox, Monte Blue*

Humphrey Bogart and Mary Astor battle Japanese spies in Across the Pacific.

A taut spy yarn. Bogart is a cashiered American army officer seeking employment, traveling on a Japanese ship to Panama, wooing Astor and agreeing en route to sell U.S. secrets about the Panama Canal to Greenstreet. It's a ruse. Bogart is true-blue, a counterintelligence agent pinpointing enemy agents; he rounds up them singlehandedly in Panama before they can bomb the canal out of existence. Greenstreet's role of Dr. Lorenz, the Nazi spymaster working with Japanese agents in Panama, is based upon Dr. Bernard Kuhn (*q.v.*), the Nazi spy working with Japanese intelligence in Hawaii. (Avail. on cas.)

ACTION IN ARABIA (1944), 75m, RKO, b/w, d, Leonide Moguy, lp, *George Sanders, Virginia Bruce, Lenore Auburt, Gene Lockhart, Robert Armstrong, H. B. Warner, Alan Napier, Andre Charlot, Marcel Dalio, Robert Anderson, Jamiel Hasson, John Hamilton*

Sanders is an American newsman in Damascus in 1941 who learns that Nazi agents are enlisting Arab tribes to fight for their cause and exposes the spy ring on behalf of the Allies. The story line for this fairly rousing film stems from the activities of Wilhelm Wassmus (*q.v.*), who united the tribes of Persia under the German banner in WW I, much the same way T. E. Lawrence (*q.v.*), organized the Arab tribes to fight for the British. (Avail. on cas.)

ADVENTURES OF CASANOVA (1948), 83m, EL, b/w, d, Roberto Galvadon, lp, *Arturo de Cordova, Lucille Bremer, Turhan Bey, John Sutton*

De Cordova is convincing in the role of the lover-spy Casanova (*q.v.*), who spied upon the British for French King Louis XV.

ADVISE AND CONSENT (1962), 140m, COL, c, d, Otto Preminger, lp, *Henry Fonda, Charles Laughton, Don Murray, Walter Pidgeon, Peter Lawford, Gene Tierney, Franchot Tone, Lew Ayres, Burgess Meredith*

Preminger provides a taut and intriguing film about a senatorial confirmation procedure in which Fonda is to be affirmed as Secretary of State. The political wheeling and dealing of senators Laughton, Pidgeon, Lawford and others is incisively revealing. Then Meredith comes forward to accuse Fonda of being a one-time Communist, setting up a fierce confrontation indentical to that of Whittaker Chambers (*q.v.*) and Alger Hiss (*q.v.*), and a shocking outcome. (Avail. on cas.)

AGAINST THE WIND (1948, Brit.), 96m, Ealing/GFD, b/w, d, Charles Crichton, lp, *Robert Beatty, Jack Warner, Simone Signoret, Gordon Jackson, Paul Dupuis, Gisele Preville, John Slater, Peter Illing*

Trainees for SOE (Special Operations Executive), a British spy service in WW II, in Against the Wind, *with Simone Signoret at right in her first film appearance.*

Based on SOE (*q.v.*), Special Operations Executive, the British espionage arm that worked with underground units during WW II, this film introduced the fine actress Signoret who plays a role based on two heroic British spies, Odette Sansom (*q.v.*) and Violette Szabo (*q.v.*). Much of the film demonstrates in fascinating detail the preparation and education of SOE spies before they were sent into occupied France. (Avail. on cas.)

ASSASSINATION OF TROTSKY, THE (1972/Fr./Ital.), 105m, Cinerama, c, d, Joseph Losey, lp, *Richard Burton, Alain Delon, Romy Schneider, Valentina Cortese, Enrico Maria Salerno, Luigi Vannucchi*

An interesting spy yarn showing how Trotsky was killed by Soviet assassin Jacson (Jaime Mercader, *q.v.*, under SMERSH), played by Delon. The planned liquidation is presented in a documentary style and, much to director Losey's credit, is accurate in detail. (Avail. on cas.)

BACKGROUND TO DANGER (1943), 80m, WB, b/w, d, Raoul Walsh, lp, *George Raft, Brenda Marshall, Sydney Greenstreet, Peter Lorre, Osa Massen, Turhan Bey, Kurt Katch, Frank Puglia, Curt Furberg*

OSS agent George Raft, at right, looks for Nazi spies in an Ankara cabret in Background to Danger.

Raft is a tough American OSS (*q.v.*) agent attempting to foil Nazi spies led by Greenstreet in Ankara, Turkey. The film depicts Franz von Papen (*q.v.*), the German spymaster, played by Furberg, and his attempted assassination, although here it is shown that the botched murder attempt is conducted by the Nazis themselves, when, in truth, the assassins were SMERSH (*q.v.*) agents. (Avail. on cas.)

BAD COMPANY (1994), 118m, c, d, Damian Harris, lp, *Ellen Barkin, Laurence Fishburne, Frank Langella, Michael Beach, Gia Carides, David Ogden Stiers, Spalding Gray, James Hong, Daniel Hugh-Kelly*

A company of ex-spies serves corporate clients with dirty tricks and espionage. Fishburne is not unlike the rogue CIA-agent Edwin Wilson (*q.v.*), willing to sell out anyone and everyone while gathering power to himself. (Avail. on cas.)

BEASTS OF BERLIN (1939), (AKA: HITLER, BEAST OF BERLIN), 87m, PDC, b/w, d, Sherman Scott, lp, *Roland Drew, Steffi Duna, Greta Granstedt, Alan Ladd, Lucien Prival, Vernon Dent, John Ellis*

Because of its staunch anti-Hitler stand, this film was not released until after America went to war with Germany. It shows the courageously few "good Germans" who organized resistance to the barbaric Third Reich, an organization known as the Black Orchestra (*q.v.*). This was one of Ladd's first appearances on screen.

BETRAYAL FROM THE EAST (1945), 82m, RKO, b/w, d, William Berke, lp, *Lee Tracy, Nancy Kelly, Richard Loo, Abner Biberman, Regis Toomey, Philip Ahn, Addison Richards, Louis Jean Heydt, Jason Robards, Sr*

Tracy, an ex-GI thought to be out for money, is contacted by Japanese agents led by Richard Loo and asked to steal

military secrets. This film, narrated by Drew Pearson, is based on the exploits of Torchichi Kono (*q.v.*), played by Loo, and carnival barker and one-time sailor Al Blake, as well as former American seaman Harry Thompson (*q.v.*), who sold secrets to the Japanese. (Avail. on cas.)

BLOOD ON THE SUN (1945), 98m, UA, b/w, d, Frank Lloyd, lp, *James Cagney, Sylvia Sidney, Wallace Ford, Rosemary De Camp, Robert Armstrong, John Emery, Leonard Strong, Frank Puglia, Jack Halloran*

Newspaperman Cagney and Allied spy Sidney risk their lives in obtaining and smuggling out of Japan the secret Japanese plan of world conquest known at the Tanaka Plan, prepared for Emperor Hirohito by Baron Giichi Tanaka (*q.v.*, under Yoshitaro Amana and John S. Farnsworth). Tanaka is played by John Emery. Cagney's role as a newspaper editor closely resembles the career and espionage activities of Richard Sorge (*q.v.*) and his Tokyo spy ring. (Avail. on cas.)

CANARIS (1955, Ger.), 113m, Europa/Fama, b/w, d, Alfred Weldenmann, lp, *O. E. Hasse, Adrian Hovan, Barbara Ruetting, Martin Held, Wolfgang Preiss, Peter Masbacher, Arthur Schroeder, Charles Regnier*

Veteran character actor Hasse is riveting as Admiral Carnaris (*q.v.*) as he uses the power of the Abwehr (*q.v.*) against Hitler and his murderous RSHA chief, Reinhard Heydrich (*q.v.*), chillingly played by Martin Held.

CARDINAL RICHELIEU (1935), 83m, FOX/UA, b/w, d, Rowland V. Lee, lp, *George Arliss, Edward Arnold, Halliwell Hobbes, Maureen O'Sullivan, Cesar Romero, Douglas Dumbrille, Violet Kemble-Cooper*

The scheming French prelate and spymaster Richelieu (*q.v.*) is adroitly essayed by Arliss, as he manipulates his agents in the building of his power base.

CARVE HER NAME WITH PRIDE (1958, Brit.), 119m, Rank, b/w, d, Lewis Gilbert, lp, *Virginia McKenna, Paul Scofield, Jack Warner, Denise Grey, Alain Saury, Maurice Ronet, Anne Leon, Sydney Tafler, William Mervyn*

Virginia McKenna gives a stirring performance as the SOE (*q.v.*) spy Violette Szabo (*q.v.*), who was captured and later murdered in Ravensbruck concentration camp. Her SOE spymaster, Col. Maurice Buckmaster (*q.v.*, under Violette Szabo) is played by stalwart veteran actor Mervyn. (Avail. on cas.)

CHE! (1969), 96m, FOX, c, d, Richard Fleischer, lp, *Omar Sharif, Jack Palance, Cesare Danova, Robert Loggia, Woody Strode, Barbara Luna, Frank Silvera, Albet Paulsen, Linda Marsh, Tom Troupe, Rudy Diaz*

This film chronicles the involvement of KGB spy Tamara Bunke/Tania (*q.v.*), played by Marsh, with Cuban revolutionary Che Guevara, essayed by Omar Sharif.

CLOAK AND DAGGER (1946), 106m, United States Pictures/WB, b/w, d, Fritz Lang, lp, *Gary Cooper, Lilli Palmer, Robert Alda, Vladimir Sokoloff, J. Edward Bromberg, Marjorie Hoshelle, Ludwig Stossel, Helene Thimig, Dan Seymour, Marc Lawrence, James Flavin*

Gary Cooper is a scientist who works with Lilli Palmer and the underground to smuggle a scientist out of Italy in WW II, an exciting, well-directed film based on a mission accomplished by OSS agent and former Brooklyn

Dodgers player, Morris Berg (q.v.). Flavin essays a role which is based on OSS chief William "Wild Bill" Donovan (q.v.). (Avail. on cas.)

COCKLESHELL HEROES (1955), 97m, Warwick/COL, c, d, Jose Ferrer, lp, *Ferrer, Trevor Howard, Victor Maddern, Anthony Newley, David Lodge, Peter Arne, Percey Herbert, Graham Stewart, John Fabian*

This WW II action film is based on British sabotage of German warships by British Royal Marines led by Ferrer. The technical adviser on the film was British frogman spy Lionel Phillip Kenneth Crabb (q.v.), who was killed while attempting to investigate sonar devices on Russian warships visiting England.

CONFESSIONS OF A NAZI SPY (1939), 110m, WB/FN, b/w, d, Anatole Litvak, lp, *Edward G. Robinson, Francis Lederer, George Sanders, Paul Lukas, Henry O'Neill, Lya Lys, Grace Stafford, James Stephenson, Sig Ruman, Fred Tozere, Dorothy Tree, Joseph Sawyer, Eily Malyon, Celia Sibelius, Hans von Twardowsky, Lionel Royce*

Drawn from the headlines of the day, this thunderously anti-Nazi film, courageously made by Warner Brothers/First National shortly before World War II, dealt with the anti-Semitic Nazi American Bund and the host of spies that flourished under its racist banner. (The film was banned in Germany after Hitler viewed it and went into a mouth-foaming tirade against "those dirty Hollywood Jews." Paul Joseph Goebbels, Nazi Propaganda Minister, however, secretly admired the film for detailing the intricate Nazi spy network then pilfering U.S. secrets.) Lederer's role is based on Guenther Gustav Rumrich (q.v. under Guy Liddell and Otto Herman Voss), a German-American who obtains U.S. military secrets by impersonating army and State Department officials. His spymasters, Lukas and Sanders, sharply essay the shrewd real-life Nazi spy chiefs Dr. Ignatz Griebl (q.v., under Wilhelm Canaris and Otto Herman Voss), and William Lonkowski (q.v., under Canaris and Voss). British intelligence is shown detecting this network by unearthing a Nazi mole in Scotland who is using her home as a letter-drop for the spies in the U.S. Malyon plays a role based on the real-life spy Jennie Wallace Jordan (q.v., under Guy Liddell) operating the letter-drop in Dundee, Scotland. The role of the FBI bureau chief in New York, marvelously played by Edward G. Robinson, is based upon FBI Special Agent Leon G. Turrou (q.v., under Voss) who gathered evidence and confessions that brought about the wholesale arrests of all the Nazi spies in this network

CONSPIRATOR (1949, Brit.), 87m, MGM, b/w, d, Victor Saville, lp, *Robert Taylor, Elizabeth Taylor, Robert Flemyng, Harold Warrender, Honor Blackman, Marjorie Fielding, Thora Hird, Wilfrid Hyde-White*

Robert Taylor, a British officer selling secrets to the Soviets in Conspirator, *knows his wife, Elizabeth Taylor, suspects him of espionage.*

Robert Taylor plays a British officer feeding the Soviets military secrets while his wife, Elizabeth Taylor, comes to suspect him. Taylor's role is modeled after the espionage career of Captain John Herbert King (q.v., under Walter Krivitsky), who worked in the Foreign Office and funneled top secret codes and ciphers to OGPU (q.v.) agents before his conscience got the better of him and he confessed to two MI5 (q.v.) agents. Taylor commits suicide in the film where King went to prison for ten years. (Avail. on cas.)

COUNTERFEIT TRAITOR, THE (1962), 140m, PAR, c, d, George Seaton, lp, *William Holden, Lilli Palmer, Hugh Griffith, Ernst Schroder, Eva Dahlbeck, Eulf Palme, Carl Raddatz, Wolfgang Preiss, Klaus Kinski, Helo Gutschwager, Erica Beer, Charles Regnier*

Holden plays the Swedish businessman, Eric Erickson (q.v.), who ostensibly worked for the Nazi war machine but who really spied for the Allies in WW II. This is a taut spy drama with Lilli Palmer essaying a role that almost duplicates her part in *Cloak and Dagger*, made sixteen years earlier. (Avail. on cas.)

DARK JOURNEY (1937, Brit.), (AKA: THE ANXIOUS YEARS), 77m, Korda/LF/UA, b/w, d, Victor Saville, lp, *Conrad Veidt, Vivien Leigh, Joan Gardner, Anthony Bushell, Ursula Jeans, Eliot Makeham*

Leigh operates a designer dress shop in neutral Stockholm during WW I and gathers information for the Allies while falling in love with Veidt, a German counterintellingence officer out to trap her. A superb cat-and-mouse espionage film, the story is based on French double agent Marthe Richer (q.v.) who owned a dress shop in Paris and went to Spain, then South America, stealing secrets from Germany while falling in love with her Abwehr (q.v.) spymaster Hans Kron. (Avail. on cas.)

DARLING LILI (1970), 136m, Geoffrey Prod/PAR, c, d, Blake Edwards, lp, *Julie Andrews, Rock Hudson, Jeremy Kemp, Lance Percival, Jacques Marin, Michael Whitney, Mimi Monte*

Julie Andrews plays a musical hall singer who spies for the Germans in WW I, a role based on Mata Hari (q.v.). This is not a serious film, only an expensive showcase for Andrews, created by her husband producer-director Edwards. Kemp is, however, effective in playing Andrews' spymaster, a role rooted to the real life Traugott von Jagow, who was Mata Hari's espionage chief. (Avail. on cas.)

DAWN (1928, Brit.), silent, 64m, British and Dominions/Woolf and Freedman, b/w, d, Herbert Wilcox, lp, *Sybil Thorndike, Marie Ault, Mary Brough, Ada Brodart, Dacia Deane, Haddon Mason, Mickey Brandford*

This silent film is faithful to the tale of British agent and heroic nurse Edith Cavell (q.v.), who is well essayed by Thorndike.

DECISION BEFORE DAWN (1951), 119m, FOX, b/w, d, Anatole Litvak, lp, *Richard Basehart, Gary Merrill, Oker Werner, Hildegarde Neff, Dominique Blanchar, O. E. Hasse, Wilfried Seyfert, Hans Christian Blech, Helene Themig, Robert Freytag, George Tyne, Adolph Lodel*

A classic WW II espionage film. Director Litvak deals with the training of German POWs as spies by Army G-2, including Werner and Blech, who are sent on separate missions to collect information behind German lines. Basehart joins Blech, attempting to secretly negotiate the surrender of a German panzer division through members of the Black Orchestra (q.v.). This operation was based upon OSS (q.v.) agents of Allen Dulles attempting to persuade German General Kurt Wolff (q.v., under Dulles) to surrender all German units fighting in Italy. Werner is a standout as a conscientious young German soldier who spies on his own people in order to bring the war to an end, sacrificing his life while saving Basehart.

DESERT FOX, THE (1951), 88m, FOX, b/w, d, Henry Hathaway, lp, *James Mason, Cedric Hardwicke, Jessica Tandy, Luther Adler, Everett Sloane, Leo G. Carroll, George Macready, Richard Boone, Edward Franz, Desmond Young, William Reynolds, Charles Evans*

Eduard Franz is Count von Stauffenberg in The Desert Fox, *a member of the German Black Orchestra out to assassinate Hitler.*

Mason is superb as Field Marshal Erwin Rommel, the celebrated "Desert Fox" who outfought and out-generaled the British army in North Africa. Much of the film is devoted to Mason's disaffection with Hitler and his participation in the Black Orchestra (q.v.) which made an attempt on the dictator's life in 1944, one which exposed Rommel and brought about his death by suicide. (Avail. on cas.)

DESPERATE JOURNEY (1942), 107m, WB, b/w, d, Raoul Walsh, lp, *Errol Flynn, Ronald Reagan, Raymond Massey, Nancy Coleman, Alan Hale, Arthur Kennedy, Sig Ruman, Patrick O'Moore, Ronald Sinclair*

A derring-do war yarn has Flynn, Reagan, Kennedy and Hale surving the crash of their bomber behind German lines and their journey back to England, committing sabotage and espionage along the way, with the considerable help of members of the Black Orchestra (q.v.), as personified by Coleman. (Avail. on cas.)

DESTINATION TOKYO (1944), 135m, WB, b/w, d, Delmer Daves, lp, *Cary Grant, John Garfield, Alan Hale, John Ridgely, Dane Clark, Warner Anderson, William Prince, Bob Hutton, Tom Tully, Faye Emerson, John Forsythe, Peter Whitney, Warren Douglas, Whit Bissell*

An American intelligence agent, John Ridgely, on ladder, is taken aboard a submarine in Destination Tokyo.

Exciting tale of an American submarine (q.v., under Spy Ships, Glossary) skippered by Grant that picks its dangerous way into Tokyo Bay, then lands an intelligence unit led by Japanese-speaking Ridgely on a remote coastal spot to gather information on Tokyo military and industrial targets which are later to be bombed by Doolittle's raiders. Grant, Garfield and the rest of the cast are terrific, and the detail shown in collecting and communicating intelligence information is impressive. (Avail on cas.)

DISHONORED (1931), 91m, PAR, b/w, d, Josef von Sternberg, lp, *Marlene Dietrich, Victor McLaglen, Lew Cody, Gustav von Seyffertitz, Warner Oland, Barry Norton, Davison Clark*

Marlene Dietrich plays agent X-27 for the Austrian secret service in WW I, a role wholly based upon Mata Hari (q.v.), whose German code designation was H.21. The character of her spymaster, Seyffertitz, is undoubtedly role modeled by Abwehr spymaster Walter Nicolai (q.v.). Dietrich, like her role model, is captured and sentenced to death, choosing to "die in the uniform in which I served not my country but my countrymen." She faces a firing squad dressed as a common streetwalker, the profession she practiced before becoming a spy. In a bizarre last scene before the firing squad, Dietrich applies makeup and lipstick, as if ready to solicit her final customer, Death. (Avail. on cas.)

DREYFUS CASE, THE (1931, Brit.), 90m, British International/COL, b/w, d, F. W. Kraemer, lp, *Cedric Hardwicke, Charles Carson, George Merritt, Sam Livesey, Beatrix Thomson, Garry Marsh, Randle Ayrton, Henry Caine, Reginald Dance, George Skillan*

Hardwicke is brilliant and moving as the French officer on the General Staff, Alfred Dreyfus (q.v.), who is wrongly accused of espionage committed by his fellow officer, Ferdinand Esterhazy (q.v.), who is sharply essayed by Marsh.

DREYFUS CASE, THE (1940, Ger.), (AKA: DREYFUS), 80m, International Road Shows, b/w, d, Richard Oswald, lp, *Fritz Kortner, Greta Moshelm, Albert Basserman, Oscar Homolka, Ferdinand Hart, Heinrich George*

The technical and directorial elements of this film are less impressive than the 1931 British production by the same name and Warner Brothers' great *Life of Emil Zola*, which covers the same ground. Kortner, however, does a fairly good job as the persecuted Alfred Dreyfus (q.v.), who is the wrongly accused spy, as does Homolka as the real spy Esterhazy (q.v.). This film was made in the early 1930s before the anti-Semitic Nazis took over film production in Germany (they would never have allowed the production) and not released abroad until 1940 when Hitler was in power. By then, director Oswald, and many in the cast—Basserman, Holmolka and others—had fled to England and then to Hollywood.

EDGE OF DARKNESS (1943), 120m, WB, b/w, d, Lewis Mileston, lp, *Errol Flynn, Ann Sheridan, Walter Huston, Nancy Coleman, Helmut Dantine, Judith Anderson, Ruth Gordon, John Beal, Morris Carnovsky, Charles Dingle, Roman Bohnen, Richard Fraser, Art Smith, Kurt Katch*

A stirring portrait of the Norwegian underground during WW II, uses as its story base the resistance of the Home Front (q.v., under Oslo Squad and Henry Oliver Rinnan). Flynn is the resistance leader in a small Norwegian village occupied by brutal Nazi troops commanded by Dantine, its oppressed residents finally revolting to wipe out the German invaders. (Avail. on cas.)

FALCON AND THE SNOWMAN, THE (1985), 131m, Orion c, d, John Schlesinger, lp, *Timothy Hutton, Sean Penn, Pat Hingle, Richard Dysart, Lori Singer, David Suchet, Dorian Harewood*

American spies Christopher John Boyce (q.v.) and Andrew Daulton Lee (q.v.), are profiled in this rather turgid espionage film which, like the book from which it is drawn, attempts to shift all the blame for the actions of the spying pair on Boyce's rigid FBI-man father (Hingle) and Lee's totally permissive parents, a thoroughly wrong interpretation. Boyce and Lee used their disaffection with the Vietnam War to take drugs and then sell out spy-in-the-sky secrets from TRW (where Boyce worked) to a KGB (q.v.) officer (Suchet) in the Russian Embassy in Mexico City. They knew exactly what they were doing and it was not out of principle but for cold, hard cash, which they lavished on themselves until they were caught, tried, and sent to prison. (Avail. on cas.)

FATHER GOOSE (1964), 115m, UNIV, c, d, Ralph Nelson, lp, *Cary Grant, Leslie Caron, Trevor Howard, Jack Good, Verina Greenlaw, Pip Sparke, Jennifer Berrington, Stephanie Berrington, Laurelle Fesette*

Grant is often hilarious as a boozy Coast Watcher (q.v., under Allied Intelligence Bureau and ASIO) on a small Pacific island during WW II, passing information to Howard concerning Japanese plane and ship movements and schedules. His troubles are increased after he rescues Caron and a bevy of young girls who try to reform him. A light-hearted comedy which details the duties of Coast Watchers, those indefatigable behind-the-lines spies who so greatly added to the U.S. victory in the Pacific. (Avail. on cas.)

FIVE FINGERS (1952), (AKA: OPERATION CICERO), 108m, FOX, b/w, d, Joseph L. Maniewicz, lp, *James Mason, Danielle Darrieux, Michael Rennie, Walter Hampden, Oscar Karlweis, Herbert Berghof, John Wengraf, A. Ben Astar, Roger Plowden, Michael Pate, Ivan Triesault*

Intriguing spy film based on the spectacular espionage career of Elyeza Bazna (q.v.), the celebrated secret agent who became known as "Cicero," captivatingly played by the sauve Mason in one of his best performances. Mason, like his real life role model, is a valet to the British Ambassador (Hampden) in Ankara who steals British top secrets and sells same to the Germans for huge sums, escaping to South America at the last minute to ostensibly live out a life of ease. Wengraf gives a taut little performance as Franz von Papen (q.v.), the German spymaster of two wars. The methodology of spies is handled with careful detail by director Mankiewicz. (Avail. on cas.)

FLIGHT FOR FREEDOM (1943), 101m, RKO, b/w, d, Lothar Mendes, lp, *Rosalind Russell, Fred MacMurray, Herbert Marshall, Eduardo Ciannelli, Walter Kingsford, Damian O'Flynn, Jack Carr, Richard Loo*

Russell plays a daring aviatrix who is undoubtedly based upon Amelia Earhart. After becoming world famous, she undertakes a dangerous aerial reconnaisance mission over Pacific islands where Japanese are reportedly building airstrips from which to launch air strikes against the U.S. prior to WW II. Russell is shot down by Japanese warplanes, which was the prevalent report later applied to Earhart, who disappeared in an around-the-world flight in 1937. Interesting if not convincing.

FOREIGN CORRESPONDENT (1940), 120m, UA, b/w, d, Alfred Hitchcock, lp, *Joel McCrea, Laraine Day, Herbert Marshall, George Sanders, Albert Basserman, Robert Benchley, Edmund Gwen, Eduardo Ciannelli, Martin Kosleck, Harry Davenport, Barbara Pepper, Eddy Conrad*

Kidnapped political leader Albert Basserman, center, has been drugged by spymaster Eduardo Ciannelli, left, in Hitchcock's Foreign Correspondent.

This film is based on Lord Robert Cecil's World Peace Congress (q.v., under Harold "Kim" Philby), which ostensibly sought to prevent WW II, an organization actually set up by NKVD (q.v.) spymasters Willi Muzenberg and Kim Philby, with the gullible and duped Cecil as its head. It functioned as a front for espionage activities in the late 1930s, not for the Germans, as the film profiles, but for Soviet espionage. Hitchcock told this author in 1969 that he "got the idea from [a] Dr. Buchman [one of Cecil's representatives]—you know—'peace, peace, and everybody love each other,' and all the time he was an agent." The smooth Marshall is the cunning peace advocate and secret German agent, Day is his naive daughter, and McCrea and Sanders are suspicious journalists who, after a series of fantastic adventures, rescue kidnapped politician Basserman and expose the spy ring. A masterful espionage film by a masterful film director. (Avail. on cas.)

FOUR FEATHERS, THE (1939, Brit.), 130m, Korda–London Film/UA, c, d, Zoltan Korda, lp, *John Clements, Ralph Richardson, C. Aubrey Smith, June Duprez, Allan Jeayes, Jack Allen, Donald Gray, Frederick Culley, Amid Teftazani, Henry Oscar, John Laurie, Robert Rendel*

One of the great adventure films, the story is loosely based on the exploits of British spy and linguist Richard Burton (q.v.), who disguised himself as an Arab to go among the tribes hostile to British rule in North Africa, although the time and locale have been changed to Kitchener's 1898 Sudan campaign. Clements is the one-time British officer who impersonates a mute tribesman in order to save captured British officers who have earlier branded him a coward by giving him white feathers, thus the title of the film. (Avail. on cas.)

FRAULEIN DOKTOR (1969, Ital./Yugo.), 102m, Cinematografica–Avala/PAR, c, d, Alberto Lattuado, lp, *Suzy Kendall, Kenneth More, Capucine, James Booth, Alexander Knox, Nigel Green*

This bizarre film has little to do with the real "Fraulein Doktor,"Elsbeth Schragmüller (q.v.), who is played as a sizzling, enigmatic sex siren by Kendall. She sabotages trains, commits wholesale murder and even enters into a lesbian affair with Capucine to achieve her espionage ends. In truth, Schragmüller was one of the Abwehr's spymasters who taught the fine and deadly arts of espionage but did not operate behind enemy lines.

GENERAL DIED AT DAWN, THE (1936), 97m, PAR, b/w, d, Lewis Milestone, lp, *Gary Cooper, Madeleine Carroll, Akim Tamiroff, Dudley Digges, Porter Hall, William Frawley, J. M. Kerrigan, Philip Ahn*

An eerie film dealing with a Chinese warlord and Cooper, a gunrunning agent for Chiang Kai-shek. Tamiroff is scary as the bloodthirsty Chinese general from whose clutches the lovely Carroll is rescued by Cooper, his role being based upon the daring exploits of Morris "Two-Gun" Cohen (*q.v.*), Chiang's intelligence chief. (Avail. on cas.)

HANGMEN ALSO DIE (1943), (AKA: LEST WE FORGET), 131m, UA, b/w, d, Fritz Lang, lp, *Brian Donlevy, Walter Brennan, Anna Lee, Gene Lockhart, Dennis O'Keefe, Alexander Granach, Margaret Wycherly, Nana Bryant, Billy Roy, Hans von Twardowski, Tonio Selwart*

A strong anti-Nazi propaganda film. Lang devastatingly portrays Reinhard Heydrich (*q.v.*), played by Twardowski, as the oppressive RSHA (*q.v.*) and SD (*q.v.*) chief of the Nazi regime in Czechoslovakia, where he is killed by Donlevy and other partisans.

HEROES OF TELEMARK, THE (1965, Brit.), 131m, Benton/Rank, c, d, Anthony Mann, lp, *Kirk Douglas, Richard Harris, Ulla Jacobsson, Michael Redgrave, David Weston, Sebastian Breaks, John Golightly*

Douglas is the leader of a Norwegian underground unit attempting to destroy a plant in Norway where the Germans are producing heavy water for the creation of an atomic bomb. After several failed attempts to demolish the plant, Douglas and Harris place a bomb on a ferry carrying the heavy water and sink it in a lake. An exciting and realistic spy yarn, Douglas is outstanding in a role that is based on Norwegian spymaster and saboteur Knut Haukelid (*q.v.*).

HITLER (1962), 107m, Three Crown/AA, b/w, d, Stuart Heisler, lp, *Richard Basehart, Cordula Trantow, Maria Emo, Martin Kosleck, John Banner, Martin Brandt, John Wengraf, William Sargent, Gregory Gay*

A manic biopic on the dictator, overplayed by Basehart, which focuses upon his warped lovelife; but the activities of the very real Black Orchestra (*q.v.*) is also chronicled, particularly the abortive 1944 attempt to assassinate Hitler by members of the German high command. (Avail. on cas.)

HITLER GANG, THE (1944), 101m, PAR, b/w, d, John Farrow, lp, *Robert Watson, Roman Bohnen, Martin Kosleck, Victor Varconi, Louis Van Rooten, Alexander Pope, Ivan Triesault, Poldy Dur, Helen Thimig, Reinhold Schunzel, Sig Rumann, Alexander Granach, Walter Kingsford*

A straightforward profile of Hitler, played convincingly by Watson, and his henchmen, including Van Rooten as Himmler (*q.v.*), head of the dreaded Gestapo (*q.v.*), SS, and RSHA (*q.v.*).

HITLER'S MADMAN (1943), (AKA: HITLER'S HANGMAN), 84m, PRC/MGM, b/w, d, Douglas Sirk, lp, *John Carradine, Patricia Morison, Alan Curtis, Ralph Morgan, Howard Freeman, Ludwig Stossel, Edgar Kennedy*

Director Sirk was himself a fugitive from the Gestapo (*q.v.*) and SD (*q.v.*) when he fled Germany for Hollywood, and one of his first films was to depict Reinhard Heydrich (*q.v.*) and Heinrich Himmler (*q.v.*), respectively played by Carradine and Freeman. When RSHA (*q.v.*) head Heydrich/Carradine is killed by partisans, Sirk accurately shows how Himmler/Freeman takes revenge by systematically destroying the Czechoslovakian town of Lidice.

HORSE SOLDIERS, THE (1959), 119m, Mirsch/UA, c, d, John Ford, lp, *John Wayne, William Holden, Constance Towers, Althea Gibson, Hoot Gibson, Anna Lee, Russell Simpson, Stan Jones, Carleton Young*

This rousing Civil War film, which depicts a daring Union cavalry raid led by Wayne deep into Confederate territory, has Holden as his contentious brigade doctor, who exposes Towers as a Rebel spy (she has overheard Wayne's plans through an air vent in her mansion where the Union troops are billeted). Wayne takes Holden with him and his troops as they strike southward in a series of skirmishes and escapes. Towers' character is loosely based on the daring Confederate spy Belle Boyd (*q.v.*), who used the air vents in her aunt's boarding house to learn the plans of visiting Yankees, information that she then delivered to Confederate commanders such as Gen. Thomas Jonathan Jackson (*q.v.*). (Avail. on cas.)

HOUSE ON 92ND STREET, THE (1945), 88m, FOX, b/w, d, Henry Hathaway, lp, *William Eythe, Lloyd Nolan, Signe Hasso, Leo G. Carroll, Lydia St. Clair, William Post, Jr., Harry Bellaver, Bruno Wick, Harro Meller, Charles Wagenheim, Alfred Linder, Renee Carson, John McKee*

Employing a semi-documentary approach, Hathaway presents a stark story of Nazi espionage in the U.S. prior to WW II, with Eythe serving as a German double agent. Eythe's role is based on William G. Sebold (*q.v.*), who reluctantly trained in Germany as an Abwehr (*q.v.*) spy, but, when arriving in the U.S., volunteered to work with the FBI (*q.v.*) to expose the Nazi spy ring. Carroll is superb as the cunning German spymaster whose role model was most certainly Frederick Joubert Duquesne (*q.v.*, under Sebold). Nolan as a hard-hitting FBI chief gives a riveting performance, and Hasso, who operates a designer dress shop at 92nd Street in New York (hence the film's title) as a cover for Nazi spy operations, provides one of the most astounding finales in any film. (Avail. on cas.)

I ACCUSE (1958, Brit.), 99m, MGM, b/w, d, Jose Ferrer, lp, *Ferrer, Anton Walbrook, Viveca Lindfors, Leo Genn, Emlyn Williams, Donald Wolfit, Herbert Lom, Harry Andrews, Felix Aylmer, Peter Illing*

This version of France's most sensational spy case, that of the much persecuted and wrongly-accused Alfred Dreyfus (*q.v.*), sensitively played by Ferrer, sees Walbrook render a shuddering performance as the real arch spy, Ferdinand Esterhazy (*q.v.*). The great cast lends magnificent support to a film high on production values.

I WAS A SPY (1934, Brit.), 83m, GAU-British/FOX, b/w, d, Victor Saville, lp, *Madeleine Carroll, Conrad Veidt, Herbert Marshall, Gerald du Maurier, Edmund Gwen, Donald Calthrop, Anthony Bushell*

In an above average spy drama, Madeleine Carroll plays Belgian nurse and Allied spy Marthe Cnockhaert McKenna in WW I, who is shown infiltrating the German high command and passing secrets to the British, only to be caught and saved from a firing squad at the last moment. Much of the background material used stems from the spectacular espionage career of the heroic Belgian school teacher, Louise de Bettignies (q.v.).

I WAS AN AMERICAN SPY (1951), 84m, MON-AA, b/w, d, Lesley Selander, lp, *Ann Dvorak, Gene Evans, Douglas Kennedy, Richard Loo, Leon Lontoc, Chabing, Philip Ahn, Marya Marco, Nadene Ashdown*

Gene Evans and Ann Dvorak in I Was an American Spy.

Dvorak plays real-life Claire Phillips, who spied for America during the Japanese occupation of the Philippines in WW II. General Mark W. Clark provides an opening narrative for this film.

IN HARM'S WAY (1965), 165m, Sigma Productions/PAR, b/w, d, Otto Preminger, lp, *John Wayne, Kirk Douglas, Patricia Neal, Tom Tryon, Paula Prentiss, Brandon de Wilde, Jill Haworth, Dana Andrews, Stanley Holloway, Burgess Meredith, Franchot Tone, Slim Pickens, Henry Fonda, James Mitchum, George Kennedy, Bruce Cabot*

Preminger's epic film of the Pacific sea war (fought with minature boats) sees Wayne and Douglas battle the Japanese and their own considerable personal problems. A good deal of fascinating time is given to Holloway, one of the innumerable Coast Watchers (q.v., under Allied Intelligence Bureau and ASIO) who gathered information behind enemy lines at great personal risk. (Avail. on cas.)

INVADERS, THE (1941), (AKA: 49TH PARALLEL), 105m, GFD/ORTUS/COL, b/w, d, Michael Powell, lp, *Leslie Howard, Raymond Massey, Laurence Olivier, Anton Walbrook, Eric Portman, Glynis Johns, Nial MacGinnis, Finlay Currie, Raymond Lovell, John Chandos*

Laurence Olivier, who defies the Nazis in The Invaders (49th Parallel).

A terrific cast and script makes this escape/espionage tale a first rate production, one which shows a strutting German naval officer, Portman, and some of his men from a Nazi submarine fleeing across Canada, attempting to enter the U.S. and safety (this was just before America entered WW II). The Nazis encounter one form of resistance or another from Howard, Olivier, Walbrook (in one of his finest performances as the leader of an agrarian religious sect), and Massey, until Portman, alone, almost escapes. The tale is based upon Lt. Franz von Werra, who escaped from a Canadian prisoner-of-war camp, who attempted to gather secrets in Canada and

communicate same to Berlin. (Avail. on cas under the title, 49TH PARALLEL)

IRON CURTAIN, THE (1948), (AKA: BEHIND THE IRON CURTAIN), 87m, FOX, b/w, d, William A. Wellman, lp, *Dana Andrews, Gene Tierney, June Havoc, Berry Kroeger, Edna Best, Stefan Schnabel, Nicholas Joy, Edward Franz, Frederic Tozere, Noel Cravat, Christopher Robin*

Shot on location in Canada, where the actual events occured, Wellman's film faithfully recreates the defection of KGB (q.v.) spy Igor Gouzenko (q.v.), expertly played by Andrews. Tierney is excellent as Gouzenko's wife, urging him to abandon the Soviets and his position in the Soviet Embassy in Ottawa so that their small child can grow up in a free country.

JACK LONDON (1943), 94m, UA, b/w, d, Alfred Santell, lp, *Michael O'Shea, Susan Hayward, Osa Massen, Harry Davenport, Frank Craven, Virginia Mayo, Ralph Morgan, Louise Beavers, Jonathan Hale, Leonard Strong, Paul Hurst, Regis Toomey, Hobart Cavanaugh, Morgan Conway*

In a disappointing biopic of the great adventurer-writer London, played by O'Shea, the plot goes from one adventure to another as London's wife Hayward copes with his long absences. Much of the latter part of the film deals with London's experiences as a foreign correspondent in the Russo-Japanese war, where he meets and befriends Strong, essaying Giichi Tanaka, then a captain in the Japanese Army, head of a secret service preparing for world conquest, a scheme which Strong boldly outlines to O'Shea, the so-called Tanaka Plan (q.v., under Yoshitaro Amana and John S. Farnsworth). (Avail. on cas.)

KNIGHT WITHOUT ARMOR (1937, Brit.), 107m, Korda–London Film/UA, b/w, d, Jacques Feyder, lp, *Marlene Dietrich, Robert Donat, Irene Vanbrugh, Herbert Lomas, Austin Trevor, Basil Gill, John Clements, Miles Malleson, Hay Petrie*

An exciting, lavishly-mounted spy film, which begins in czarist Russia where Donat becomes a British agent inside a revolutionary party and is sent to Siberia for aiding a wounded assassin. He befriends revolutionary leader Gill who, following their release after the revolution of 1917, makes him a commissar. Donat is assigned to take Dietrich, an aristocrat, to Petrograd for trial, but after a series of escapes and fantastic adventures, he rescues her while gathering information on the Red Army. The role superbly enacted by Donat is based upon the spectacular British spy Paul Dukes (q.v.), the only secret agent ever to be knighted in England as a direct reward for espionage. (Avail. on cas.)

LAST EMPEROR, THE (1987), 160m, COL, c, d, Bernardo Bertolucci, lp, *John Lone, Joan Chen, Peter O'Toole, Ying Ruocheng, Victor Wong, Dennis Dun, Ryuichi Sakamoto, Maggie Han, Wu Jun Mei*

In a overlong, often confusing biopic of China's last emperor, Henry Pu-Yi (q.v., under Kenji Doiharia and Eastern Jewel), a Japanese puppet during the 1930s and in WW II, flamboyant director Bertolucci employs so many flashbacks and flash forwards that the story line is hard to follow. He does, however, present the fabulous Japanese spy Eastern Jewel (q.v.), played to the hilt by Han, in all her sinister glory as she manipulates the gullible Pu-Yi, pensively essayed by Lone, into the hands of Japanese militarists. (Avail. on cas.)

LAWRENCE OF ARABIA (1962, Brit.), 220m, Horizon/
COL, c, d, David Lean, lp, *Peter O'Toole, Alec Guinness,
Anthony Quinn, Jack Hawkins, Jose Ferrer, Anthony Quayle,
Claude Rains, Arthur Kennedy*

A magnificent adventure film, O'Toole accurately presents the enigmatic T. E. Lawrence (*q.v.*), the mystic
leader of the Arabian tribes against the Turks in WW I.
Equally fascinating are the performances of Guinness,
Quinn, Hawkins, and Kennedy, playing an American
newsman who is based on Lowell Thomas, the writer
who made Lawrence famous through his articles and
books. At one point, O'Toole scouts a Turkish town
(Lawrence acted as his own spymaster), and is captured,
then tortured and sexually attacked by a sadistic Turkish
commander played by Ferrer, a brutal act which
Lawrence himself suffered and one that ruined his life.
(Avail. on cas.)

LIFE OF EMILE ZOLA, THE (1937), 123m, WB, b/w, d,
William Dieterle, lp, *Paul Muni, Gale Sondergaard, Joseph
Schildkraut, Gloria Holden, Donald Crisp, Erin O'Brien-Moore,
John Litel, Henry O'Neill, Morris Carnovsky, Louis Calhern,
Ralph Morgan, Robert Barratt, Vladimir Sokoloff, Harry
Davenport, Robert Warwick, Charles Richman*

A great film about the great writer, Emile Zola, wonder-
fully enacted by Muni, the powerhouse actor of the
1930s, a tale which is mostly devoted to the wrongly-
imprisoned Alfred Dreyfus (*q.v.*), the Jewish French officer falsely accused of espionage by the French High
Command. Schildkraut is marvelous as the innocent
Dreyfus (and won an Academy Award for best supporting actor for his part), as is the rest of the superb cast,
especially Barrat, as the real spy, Ferdinand Esterhazy
(*q.v.*). (Avail. on cas.)

LINCOLN CONSPIRACY, THE (1977), 90m, Sunn Classics,
c, d, James L. Conway, lp, *Bradford Dillman, John Dehner, John
Anderson, Robert Middleton, James Greene, Whit Bissell, Dick
Callinan, E. J. Andre*

A "re-creation" film concerned with the assassination of
Abraham Lincoln, who is played by Anderson. John
Wilkes Booth, enacted by Dillman, performs the murder
with the connivance of Secretary of State Edwin Stanton,
Middleton, and Union espionage chief, Lafayette Baker
(*q.v.*), essayed by Dehner. A rather muddled film that
raises some of the serious questions stemming from
Lincoln's murder.

MAN IN THE GLASS BOOTH, THE (1975), 117m,
American Film Theatre, c, d, Arthur Hiller, lp, *Maximilian
Schell, Lois Nettleton, Luther Adler, Lawrence Pressman, Henry
Brown, Richard Rasof, David Nash*

Schell is riveting as the man captured by the Mossad
(*q.v.*; also see Isser Harel) and placed on trial, his role
model being Adolf Eichmann (*q.v.*, under Raoul
Wallenberg). When captured in South America,
Eichmann was spirited to Israel, where he was placed on
trial in a glass booth. Convicted of helping to murder
countless Jews in WW II, he was executed.

MAN ON A STRING (1960), (AKA: CONFESSIONS OF A
COUNTERSPY), 92m, COL, b/w, d, Andre de Toth, lp, *Ernest
Borgnine, Kerwin Mathews, Colleen Dewhurst, Alexander
Scorby, Glenn Corbett, Vladimir Sokoloff, Friedrich Joloff,
Richard kendrick, Ed Prentiss*

Borgnine is spying for the KGB (*q.v.*) when CIA (*q.v.*)
agents turn him into an American double agent. His role
model is Boris Morros (*q.v.*), the Hollywood musical
composer who had been forced to spy for Russia for
years before exposing the Soviet rings in the U.S. for
which he labored.

MAN WHO NEVER WAS, THE (1956, Brit.), 103m,
Sumar/FOX, c, d, Ronald Neame, lp, *Clifton Webb, Gloria
Graham, Robert Flemying, Laurence Naismith, Geoffrey Keen,
Michael Hordern, Moutrie Kelsall*

*Clifton Webb plays
Ewen Montagu, the
British intelligence
officer who created
the greatest espi-
onage hoax of WW
II in The Man Who
Never Was.*

Webb plays Commander Ewen Montagu, who brain-
storms the British espionage operation known as The
Man Who Never Was (*q.v.*), also code-named Operation
Mincemeat. He and SIS (*q.v.*) agents plant a body on the
shores of Spain, a corpse carrying information which
convinces the Abwehr (*q.v.*) that the Allies will invade
Greece, and German divisions are moved to fend off an
attack that never occurs; instead the Allies land in Sicily
where they successfully capture the island. This clever
espionage coup was a decisive contribution to Allied
victory, one which director Neame handles with style,
providing no little suspense. (Avail. on cas.)

MANCHURIAN CANDIDATE, THE (1962), 126m, M.C.–
Essex/UA, b/w, d, John Frankenheimer, lp, *Frank Sinatra,
Laurence Harvey, Janet Leigh, Angela Lansbury, Henry Silva,
James Gregory, Leslie Parrish, John McGiver, Khigh Dhiegh,
James Edwards, Douglas Henderson*

*Frank Sinatra
discovering the
secret code in
The Manchurian
Candidate.*

This chilling film depicts brainwashing as practiced by
the Chinese Communists on captured American POWs
in the Korean War, one where Harvey is programmed to
kill as would a robot once his control activates a prearranged code. Though returned to the U.S., Harvey is
still a pawn in the hands of his Communist control, who
is his own mother, Lansbury, a fanatical Soviet spymaster planning the murder of a presidential contender,
using her own son as the instrument of assassination.
She also dominates her husband, Gregory, a witch-hunting senator whose role is based on the notorious
Communist hunter, Senator Joseph McCarthy (*q.v.*).
Sinatra, an army pal of Harvey's, overcomes his own

brainwashing to realize the plot and moves to prevent the assassination. Harvey, Lansbury, Gregory and Sinatra give stellar performances in this still fascinating production. (Avail. on cas.)

MARY OF SCOTLAND (1936), 123m, RKO, b/w, d, John Ford, lp, *Katharine Hepburn, Fredric March, Florence Eldridge, Douglas Walton, John Carradine, Robert Barrat, Gavin Muir, Ian Keith, Walter Bryon*

Hepburn is a spirited Mary, Queen of Scots, tempestuously defying the nobles of Scotland, betrayed by her husband Darnley, played by Walton and giving up all for her true love, Bothwell, essayed by March. Jailed, Hepburn escapes to England, asking her sister Elizabeth I, Eldridge, to aid her in retrieving her throne from the Scottish nobles, not knowning that Eldridge has secretly backed the nobles. Instead of help, Hepburn is imprisoned while Elizabeth's intelligence chief, Walsingham (q.v.), played by Bryon, makes it appear that Hepburn has committed treason against Eldridge/Elizabeth, who then sends her sister to the headsman and seizes the throne of Scotland. (Avail. on cas.)

MARY, QUEEN OF SCOTS (1971, Brit.), 128m, UNIV, c, d, Charles Jarrott, lp, *Vanessa Redgrave, Glenda Jackson, Patrick McGoohan, Timothy Dalton, Nigel Davenport, Trevor Howard, Richard Warner*

A poor remake of the 1936 John Ford film, with Redgrave as Mary, Jackson as the scheming Elizabeth, and Warner as her intelligence chief, Walsingham (q.v.) who connives to compromise Mary so that she can be executed for treason and Jackson can take her throne.

MASK OF DIMITRIOS, THE (1944), 95m, WB, b/w, d, Jean Negulesco, lp, *Sydney Greenstreet, Zachary Scott, Peter Lorre, Faye Emerson, George Tobias, Victor Franchen, Steven Garay, Florence Bates, Eduardo Ciannelli, Kurth Katch, Marjorie Hoshelle, Georges Metaxa*

Faye Emerson, consort of spies, in The Mask of Dimitrios.

A wonderful cast, taut script, and sharp direction provides a great espionage film where Scott is a master spy for many nations, a role which author Eric Ambler (who wrote the novel by the same name) undoubtedly based on Isaac Trebitsch Lincoln (q.v.), and the covert operations of IMRO (q.v.), a Macedonian terrorist group that fomented revolutions and wars in Greece and Turkey. Scott is superb as the shifty Dimitrios, Greenstreet fascinating as his equally cunning confederate, and Lorre marvelous as the detective writer investigating the spy's incredible career.

MATA HARI (1931), 91m, MGM, b/w, d, George Fitzmaurice, lp, *Greta Garbo, Ramon Novarro, Lionel Barrymore, Lewis Stone, C. Henry Gordon, Karen Morley, Alec B. Francis, Blanche Frederici*

The great Garbo is Mata Hari (q.v.), the dancer who spied for Germany in WW I, mostly in name only. Few real facts are presented, with director Fitzmaurice stylishly concentrating on the spy's exotic dancing and her love affair with a Russian pilot, Navarro. The many affairs the spy conducted in which she seduced secrets from her high-placed lovers are treated as ambiguous trysts, nothing explicit, and Garbo finally goes to the firing squad, remaining beautiful, brave, and enigmatic. (Avail. on cas.)

MATA HARI (1965, Fr./Ital.), (AKA: MATA HARI, AGENT H.21), 95m, Filmel Films Du Carrose–Simar Fida Cinematografica Magna Pictures, b/w, d, Jean-Louis Richard, lp, *Jeanne Moreau, Jean-Louis Trintignant, Claude Rich, Frank Villard, Albert Remy*

Moreau presents a sensuous and fairly accurate portrait of the dancer Mata Hari (q.v.), who steals secrets in the bedroom and wows audiences with her fleshy performances, falling in love with Trintignant before going the firing squad.

MATA HARI (1985), 108m, Cannon, d, Curtis Harrington, lp, *Sylvia Kristel, Christopher Cazenove, Tobias Rolt, Gaye Brown, Gottfired John, William Fox, Michael Anthony, Vernon Dobtcheff*

In this version, Kristel plays Mata Hari (q.v.) as a sluttish harlot and dances almost naked, oddly exposing her breasts when the real spy hid her underdeveloped breasts beneath breastplates and wore nothing else. A poor production that has little to do with the real facts, this film was simply an R-rated sex film posing as an espionage movie. (Avail. on cas.)

MOLLY MAGUIRES, THE (1970), 124m, Tamm Productions/PAR c, d, Martin Ritt, lp, *Richard Harris, Sean Connery, Samantha Eggar, Frank Finlay, Anthony Zerbe, Bethel Leslie, Art Lund, Anthony Costello*

In a grim and fascinating portrait of early-day American labor struggles, Ritt portrays the secret Irish society, the Molly Maguires, in all its ruthlessness—blowing up mines and coal trains and shooting down mine bosses and their hired guards—as they strive to improve their miserable wages and living conditions. Harris is outstanding as the Pinkerton labor spy, James McParland (q.v.), and even more riveting is Connery as the Molly leader, John "Black Jack" Kehoe, who, along with others, went to the gallows on the testimony of McParland. (Avail. on cas.)

NORTHERN PURSUIT (1943), 94m, WB, b/w, d, Raoul Walsh, lp, *Errol Flynn, Julie Bishop, Helmut Dantine, John Ridgely, Gene Lockhart, Tom Tully, Bernard Nedell, Warren Douglas, Monte Blue, Alec Craig*

Like *The Invaders*, this film is based upon the escape and espionage operations of Franz von Werra, a German officer who fled a Canadian POW camp early in WW II, an exciting if not implausible Flynn action movie where Flynn plays a discredited Mountie in order to join a Nazi spy ring, a ploy used a year earlier by Warner Brothers in its production of *Across the Pacific*. (Avail. on cas.)

NOTORIOUS (1946), 101m, RKO, b/w, d, Alfred Hitchcock, lp, *Cary Grant, Ingrid Bergman, Claude Rains, Louis Calhern, Mme, Konstantin, Reinhold Schunzel, Moroni Olsen, Ivan Triesault*

FBI man Cary Grant and spy Ingrid Bergman in Hitchcock's Notorious.

In this subtle spy film, Hitchcock profiles Bergman as the daughter of a convicted Nazi espionage agent. She goes to work with the FBI (*q.v.*) in South America to expose some wealthy German agents who are developing the atomic bomb. Her control is suave Grant, who falls in love with her, rescuing Bergman before her husband, Rains, leader of the spy nest, can slowly poison her to death. Bergman's role is based upon Ruth Kuhn, the daughter of Bernard Julius Otto Kuhn (*q.v.*), who spied on naval installations at Pearl Harbor for the Japanese before the 1941 sneak attack, although Ms. Kuhn went to jail, not to South America to work with the FBI. The film is nevertheless a suspenseful spy movie, as well as presenting a great love story. Its screenwriter, Ben Hecht, introduced uranium as the "MacGuffin," in the film, knowing this was an ore used in the making of the atomic bomb, information he had gotten from science magazines. The FBI, alerted by a Cal Tech scientists Hecht and Hitchcock had interviewed, kept the production under surveillance and later warned RKO not to use the uranium angle, but it was kept in the film. (Avail. on cas.)

NURSE EDITH CAVELL (1939), 95m, Imperadio/RKO, b/w, d, Herbert Wilcox, lp, *Anna Neagle, Edna May Oliver, George Sanders, May Robson, ZaSu Pitts, H. B. Warner, Sophie Stewart, Mary Howard*

Neagle is terrific as the heroic Edith Cavell (*q.v.*), who rescued hundreds of Allied soldiers in German-occupied Belgium during WW I, sending them along an escape route to safety before German agents arrested her and stood her before a firing squad. (Avail. on cas.)

O.S.S. (1946), 107m, PAR, b/w, d, Irving Pichel, lp, *Alan Ladd, Geraldine Fitzgerald, Patric Knowles, John Hoyt, Gloria Saunders, Richard Benedict, Harold Vermilyea, Don Beddoe, Onslow Stevens*

This solid spy film dramatizes the training of several new recruits—Ladd, Fitzgerald, and Beddoe—to the Office of Strategic Services, better known as OSS (*q.v.*), America's intelligence service in WW II. All are parachuted into occupied France to get important information while working with the underground. They have been trained to know that the slightest detail might give them away, and this happens when Beddoe employs a fork in the wrong manner in a French restaurant. Ladd and Fitzgerald fall in love but Fitzgerald, who has compromised a German officer, later falls victim to his vengeance. Only Ladd survives to see American troops pouring into France for a smashing finale. The film, like its FOX counterpart, *13 Rue Madeleine*, details the methods and art of espionage. OSS director William "Wild Bill" Donovan (*q.v.*), allowed Paramount executives three weeks to go through OSS files to cull stories for the production, and more than thirty ex-OSS agents worked on the film either as technical advisers or in bit parts.

ODETTE (1951, Brit.), 123m, Wilcox/Neagle/Imperadio/Lopert–Dowling/UA, b/w, d, Herbert Wilcox, lp, *Anna Neagle, Trevor Howard, Marius Goring, Peter Ustinov, Bernard Lee, Maurice Buckmaster*

Neagle is a convincing Odette Sansom (*q.v.*), and Howard is intrepid as her espionage chief, Peter Churchill (*q.v.*), in this true-to-life portrait of SOE (*q.v.*) spies in WW II. Goring gives a chilling performance as the clever Abwehr (*q.v.*) counterintelligence agent, Hugo Bleicher. Maurice Buckmaster, an SOE chief, plays himself.

OPERATION DAYBREAK (1976, U.S./Brit./Czech.), (AKA: PRICE OF FREEDOM), 118m, Vista–Schuster–American Allied–Ceskoslovensky–Barrandov/ WB, c, d, Lewis Gilbert, lp, *Timothy Bottoms, Martin Shaw, Joss Ackland, Nicola Pagett, Anthony Andrews, Anton Diffring*

An excellent recreation of the partisan attack on RSHA (*q.v.*) and SD (*q.v.*) leader Reinhard Heydrich (*q.v.*), brilliantly played by Diffring. Bottoms, Shaw, and Andrews are the valiant Czech paratroopers who perform the assassination, which brought down the wrath of Heinrich Himmler (*q.v.*) on the Czech town of Lidice, which he ordered destroyed in retaliation for Heydrich's death.

OPERATION EICHMANN (1962), 92m, Bischoff–Diamond/ AA, b/w, d, R. G. Springsteen, lp, *Werner Klemperer, Ruta Lee, Donald Buka, Barbara Turner, John Banner, Hanna Landy, Lester Fletcher, Steve Gravers.*

This film was quickly churned out from the headlines of the day, which profiled the capture of escaped Nazi war criminal Adolf Eichmann (*q.v.*, under Raoul Wallenberg), by Mossad (*q.v.*) leader Isser Harel (*q.v.*). Klemperer is impressive as the arrogant Eichmann and Buka convincing in a role based upon Harel.

OPERATION MANHUNT (1954), 77m, UA, b/w, d, Jack Alexander, lp, *Harry Townes, Irja Jensen, Jacques Aubuchon, Robert Goudier, Albert Miller, Karen Shaffer, Kenneth Wolfe, Will Kuluva*

A tense spy drama profiles the defection of Russian code clerk Igor Gouzenko (*q.v.*), from the Russian Embassy in Ottowa, Canada, and the lengths KGB (*q.v.*) and assassins from SMERSH (*q.v.*) go to in order to recapture the one-time spy. Townes is convincing as Gouzenko in an accurate and telling film which offers Gouzenko himself in an epilog.

OPERATOR 13 (1934), (AKA: SPY 13), 86m, MGM, b/w, d, Richard Boleslavsky, lp, *Marion Davies, Gary Cooper, Jean Parker, Katharine Alexander, Ted Healy, Russell Hardie, Henry Wadsworth, Douglas Dumbrille, Willard Robertson, Fuzzy Knight, Sidney Toler*

Davies is a stage actress who agrees to spy for the North in the Civil War, her role wholly taken from the life of Union spy Pauline Cushman (*q.v.*). Cooper is a Confederate officer and spycatcher, who, after many adventures, captures Davies but, having fallen in love with her, allows her to return to Union lines. A good spy drama that details Civil War espionage.

PRINCE OF PLAYERS (1955), 102m, FOX, b/w, d, Philip Dunne, lp, *Richard Burton, Maggie MacNamara, John Derek, Raymond Massey, Charles Bickford, Elizabeth Sellars, Eva Le Gallienne*

Though this film focuses on Burton as master actor Edwin Booth, much attention is given to his younger brother, John Wilkes Booth (q.v., under Lafayette Baker), played by Derek, and his mad scheme to kill Abraham Lincoln. Ironically, Ian Keith, who played John Wilkes Booth twenty-five years earlier in Griffith's *Abraham Lincoln*, appears as a bit player.

PRISONER OF SHARK ISLAND, THE (1936), 95m, FOX, b/w, d, John Ford, lp, *Warner Baxter, Gloria Stewart, Joyce Kay, Claude Gillingwater, Douglas Wood, Harry Carey Sr., Fred Kohler Jr., John Carradine, Paul Fix, Francis McDonald, Arthur Byron, O. P. Heggie*

Warner Baxter in John Ford's The Prisoner of Shark Island.

Ford offers a gripping tale, that of Dr. Samuel A. Mudd, the physician who treated John Wilkes Booth's broken leg after he had killed President Lincoln. Baxter is magnificent as Mudd, who is convicted by a secret court martial and sent to rot in the Dry Tortugas on "Shark Island" (Fort Jefferson), where he eventually earns his freedom by stemming a yellow fever epidemic. McDonald plays a furtive Booth who, this film presumes, did not really know Mudd (q.v., under Lafayette Baker) when just the opposite was the case. An outstanding historical drama from a master filmmaker.

PURPLE HEART, THE (1944), 99m, FOX, b/w, d, Lewis Milestone, lp, *Dana Andrews, Richard Conte, Farley Granger, Kevin O'Shea, Donald Barry, Trudy Marshall, Sam Levene, Charles Russell, Richard Loo, Philip Ahn, Kurt Katch, Allen Yung, Tala Birell, John Craven, Gregory Gaye*

Milestone provides a rousing WW II propaganda film which portrays two American bomber crews captured from Doolittle's 1942 Tokyo raid who are tried by a Japanese kangaroo court for mass murder. Yung plays Mitusru Toyama (q.v.), head of the Black Dragon Society (q.v.), who sits in judgment of the doomed Americans. Excellent performances from Andrews, Levene, Conte, Granger, and Loo, a sadistic Japanese interrogator who orders the torture and maiming of his prisoners without getting a single confession. (Avail. on cas.)

RENDEZVOUS (1935), 91m, MGM, b/w, d, William K. Howard, lp, *William Powell, Rosalind Russell, Binnie Barnes, Lionel Atwill, Cesar Romero, Samuel S. Hinds, Henry Stephenson, Frank Richer, Charles Grapewin, Leonard Mudie, Howard Hickman, Charles Trowbridge*

Powell is a puzzle editor for a newspaper when he joins up to fight in WW I. Before shipping out, he meets Russell and falls in love. She pulls strings through her father's Washington connections and has Powell brought back and placed in charge of a code-breaking unit service, which deciphers the top German code. This spy comedy is based upon two books written by America's foremost cryptographer of the day, Herbert O. Yardley (q.v.),

American Black Chamber and *The Blonde Countess*. Yardley and MGM were severely criticized by the U.S. Signal Corps for showing precise methods used by American agents in deciphering codes, but this fascinating information remains in the film.

RING OF SPIES (1964, Brit.), (AKA: RING OF TREASON), 90m, BL, b/w, d, Robert Tronson, lp, *Bernard Lee, William Sylvester, Margaret Tyzack, David Kossoff, Nancy Nevinson, Thorley Walters*

This film depicts the real-life espionage activities of England's Portland spy ring, which stole Admiralty secrets, with Lee playing Harry Houghton (q.v.), Sylvester essaying Soviet spymaster Gordon Lonsdale (q.v.), and Kossoff and Nevinson playing the KGB (q.v.) spy couple Peter and Helen Kroger (q.v.). Director Tronson rightly took a documentary approach in portraying this actual and deadly nest of spies.

SABOTEUR (1942), 108m, UNIV, b/w, d, Alfred Hitchcock, lp, *Robert Cummings, Priscilla Lane, Otto Kruger, Alan Baxter, Clem Bevans, Norman Lloyd, Alma Kruger, Vaughan Glaser, Dorothy Peterson, Ian Wolfe, Frances Carson, Murray Alper, Kathryn Adams*

German spy Norman Lloyd at the top of Statue of Liberty with Priscilla Lane in Hitchcock's Saboteur.

Hitchcock profiles Abwehr (q.v.) spy and sabotage operations in the U.S., beginning with a West Coast aircraft plant fire which Cummings is wrongly accused of setting, causing him to flee with Lane in tow, seeking Lloyd, the man who actually set the fire. He goes first to a western ranch where he encounters spymaster Kruger, then to New York with spy Baxter, where he and Lane finally expose the Nazi spy ring and pursue Lloyd to the Statue of Liberty, from which Lloyd spectacularly falls to his death. A great action film, Hitchcock employed some newsreel footage of the liner *Normandie* which, after a mysterious fire, had capsized at its berth, a scene to which naval intelligence, ONI (q.v.), objected, saying that, by cutting from that scene to a smugly smiling Lloyd, Hitchcock was implying that the liner had been sabotaged. ONI insisted the scene be cut. Hitchcock kept it in and it can be seen in today's prints of the film. (Avail. on cas.)

SECRET AGENT, THE (1936, Brit.), 83m, GAU, b/w, d, Alfred Hitchcock, lp, *Madeleine Carroll, John Gielgud, Peter Lorre, Robert Young, Percy Marmont, Florence Kahn, Lilli Palmer, Charles Carson*

Hitchcock's tale of intrigue has Gielgud playing Richard Ashenden, a British spy character created by Somerset Maugham (q.v.), who served as a British agent in Switzerland in WW I, which is the locale and time frame of this movie. Gielgud, with Carroll impersonating his wife, go to Switzerland, where Gielgud, with Lorre's help, liquidates a German double agent, Marmont.

Young, who pretends to be in love with Carroll, is the real German agent, who almost kills the Allied spies but is interrupted by a train crash. Lorre's role was no doubt inspired by the exploits of Isaac Trebitsch Lincoln (q.v.), a spy for many nations. (Avail. on cas.)

SINK THE BISMARCK! (1960, Brit.), 97m, FOX, b/w, d, Lewis Gilbert, lp, *Kenneth More, Dana Wynter, Carl Mohner, Laurence Naismith, Geoffrey Keen, Karel Stepanek, Michael Hordern, Maurice Denham*

Using a documentary approach, Gilbert shows how the dreaded German pocket battleship *Bismarck* sailed into the high seas to take on the British fleet, sank the *Hood* in one salvo, and was then tracked down and destroyed in a wild surface battle. The film opens with the scene of a spy reporting on the departure of the *Bismarck* from a Scandinavian fjord, this agent being part of a network answering to British spymaster Captain Henry Mangles Denham, who was stationed in Stockholm. (Avail. on cas.)

TALL TARGET, THE (1951), 78m, MGM, b/w, d, Anthony Mann, lp, *Dick Powell, Paula Raymond, Adolphe Menjou, Marshall Thompson, Ruby Dee, Will Geer, Richard Rober, Florence Bates, Victor Kilian, Katherine Warren, Leif Erickson, Peter Brocco, Barbara Billingsley, Will Wright, Regis Toomey, Jeff Richards, Tom Powers*

Powell plays the role of New York police detective John Kennedy (q.v., under Allan Pinkerton), who learns of a plot in Baltimore to kill President-elect Abraham Lincoln in 1860 as he travels by train toward Baltimore and Washington to his inauguration. Powell is excellent as the dogged detective who learns that Southern spies and assassins are on board the train carrying Lincoln. He tracks down the suspects one by one, including the smooth-talking Menjou, a commander of a militia force. A superbly crafted film full of tense moments heightened by Powell's superior performance as the dedicated detective. All of the story is based upon the actual facts surrounding the Baltimore Plot unearthed by Pinkerton and Kennedy.

THEY CAME TO BLOW UP AMERICA (1943), 73m, FOX, b/w, d, Edward Ludwig, lp, *George Sanders, Anna Sten, Ward Bond, Dennis Hoey, Sig Ruman, Ludwig Stossel, Robert Barratt, Poldy Dur, Ralph Byrd, Elsa Janssen, Rex Williams, Charles McGraw, Sven Hugo Borg, Kurt Katch*

Based on the Abwehr's (q.v.), abortive Operation Pastorius (q.v., under FBI, J. Edgar Hoover, and Erwin von Lahousen), wherein eight German agents were landed on American shores to commit widespread sabotage, the film centers about German-born FBI mole George Sanders, who infiltrates German intelligence, being sent with the saboteurs to America, where he exposes them before they can do any damage. Courtroom scenes showing the Nazis on trial consume most of the film, background of their sabotage mission shown in flashback. Though there is considerable suspense while the suave Sanders plays his double-agent game, the producers played fast and loose with the facts. None of the real eight German agents were FBI moles, six of them were executed and two were given prison terms for cooperating with the prosecution. This production was closely scrutinized by J. Edgar Hoover of the FBI, who was present during the actual trial of the saboteurs and who insisted, in his typical high-handed fashion, that the film's story be told according to his own myth-making dictates.

THIEF, THE (1952), 85m, UA, b/w, d, Russell Rouse, lp, *Ray Milland, Martin Gabel, Rita Gam, Harry Bronson, John McKutcheon, Rita Vale, Rex O'Malley, Joe Conlin*

Ray Milland, in an unusual talkie that has no dialog (although sound effects, music and some narration are present), is a nuclear scientist who appears to be based upon Dr. Frank Oppenheimer, younger brother of J. Robert Oppenheimer, chief architect of the atom bomb. The younger Oppenheimer was a member of the Communist party and in contact with KGB spymaster Steve Nelson (q.v.) in the early 1940s. Milland is shown stealing nuclear secrets and attempting to deliver these on film to a Russian agent before he realizes that he is being tailed by the FBI (q.v.) and flees to New York, where he makes plans to defect to the Soviet Union until his merciless conscience overwhelms him and directs him down another path. A taut, tense espionage drama with Milland giving a superb performance. (Avail. on cas.)

13 RUE MADELEINE (1946), 95m, FOX, b/w, d, Henry Hathaway, lp, *James Cagney; Annabella, Richard Conte, Frank Latimore, Walter Abel, Melville Cooper, Sam Jaffe, Marcel Rousseau, Everett G. [E. G.] Marshall, Blanche Yurka, Peter von Zerneck, Alfred Linder, Judith Lowry, Richard Gordon, Walter Greaza, Ben Low, Roland Belanger, James Craven, Edward Cooper, Alexander Kirkland, Karl Malden*

A taut semi-documentary, this film was in keeping with director Hathaway's earlier spy drama, *The House on 92nd Street* which dealt with German spies operating in America. In this movie Hathaway profiles a small group of American agents as they go through OSS (q.v.) training under the leadership of Cagney, who gives a standout performance. The mission undertaken by new agents Annabella, Conte, and Latimore is to drop by parachute into France and kidnap a French engineer, Rousseau, but Conte, an Abwehr (q.v.) mole, kills Latimore by severing his rip cord before the drop. Cagney then goes into occupied France to contact resistance fighters led by Jaffe and accomplishes the mission but is captured by Conte and Gestapo agents. He is taken to 13 Rue Madeleine, Gestapo (q.v.) headquarters, where he is tortured and beaten, but, before he is compelled to talk, Allied planes bomb the building and kill all inside, including Cagney and the insidious Conte. Much of the film details the training undergone by OSS agents with the hair-raising events of the mission shown in the final half of the film, one which realistically depicts American spies working with the French underground. The OSS initially lent its support to this production, but William "Wild Bill" Donovan (q.v.), chief of OSS, objected to the introduction of Conte as a Nazi spy who could penetrate American intelligence. When the producers refused to eliminate Conte's role, Donovan withdrew OSS endorsement. (Avail. on cas.)

39 STEPS, THE (1935/Brit.), 85m, Gaumont/General Films Dist., b/w, d, Alfred Hitchcock, lp, *Madeleine Carroll, Robert Donat, Lucie Mannheim, Godfrey Tearle, Peggy Ashcroft, John Laurie, Helen Haye, Wylie Watson, Frank Cellier, Peggy Simpson, Gus McNaughton, Jerry Vernon, Miles Malleson*

Donat is an innocent man who rescues Mannheim from strange killers stalking her, allowing her to stay at his London flat. In the middle of the night, she staggers into his room, sprawling over him with a knife in her back. Donat, rather than be blamed for her murder, sets out for Scotland, where Mannheim has earlier told him the head of a spy ring is operating. He meets Carroll on a train,

Madeleine Carroll and Robert Donat in Hitchcock's classic spy film, The 39 Steps.

asking for her help, but she betrays him to detectives. Donat, chased by police, leaps from the train and makes his way across the moors. He is welcomed as a guest at a grand manor house; here he meets Tearle who is missing his index finger; Mannheim has told him that the spymaster is missing just that finger. Arrested, Donat escapes, only to meet Carroll once more and, after several adventures, the couple return to London, where, while sitting in the audience at the Palladium, Donat prompts a musical hall entertainer, Watson (playing Mr. Memory, a man with a photographic memory and total recall) to expose the spy ring from the stage, causing spymaster Tearle to shoot Watson from his box seat. Tearle is captured by police who have been following Donat as Watson, with his dying gasps, relates detailed information on top secret equipment to Donat, Carroll, and the police, thus vindicating the hunted Donat. The film is crammed with exciting chases and hair-raising escapes and remains a Hitchcockian classic. Though the "foreign power" behind the spy ring is never identified, there is little doubt that it was Germany, which had by the mid-1930s established several spy networks in England. Tearle's spymaster role was based upon Lord Runciman, one of the directors of the pro-Nazi Anglo-German Fellowship League (*q.v.*, under Guy Burgess and Harold "Kim" Philby). (Avail. on cas.)

TOPAZ (1969, Brit.), 126m, UNIV, c, d, Alfred Hitchcock, lp, John Forsythe, Frederick Stafford, Dany Robin, John Vernon, Karin Dor, Michael Piccoli, Phillipe Noiret, Claude Jade, Michel Subor

Spies at work—Roscoe Lee Browne and Don Randolph photograph Castro's secrets in Topaz.

In this Hitchcock spy film, CIA (*q.v.*) agent Forsyth, through a Russian defector, uncovers a KGB (*q.v.*) spy ring inside French intelligence, one code-named Topaz. (The real name of the actual Soviet ring that had pene-

trated the French high command was Sapphine, *q.v.*, under Deuxième Bureau and Philippe Thyraud de Vosjoli.) In providing French agent Stafford with this information, Forsyth gets Stafford to undertake a perilous mission to Cuba, where he confirms the presence of Russian missiles, returning with photos of same, which allows the U.S. to confront Russia and become victorious in the Cuban Missile Crisis (*q.v.*). Only the existence of the KGB moles in French intellingence was based on real fact; American U-2 spy planes, not the French, provided the proof of the Soviet missiles in Cuba. (Avail. on cas.)

TRIPLE CROSS (1967, Fr./Brit.), 126m, Cineurop/WB, c, d, Terence Young, lp, *Christopher Plummer, Romy Schneider, Trevor Howard, Gert Frobe, Yul Brynner, Claudine Auger, Georges Lycan, Jess Hahn*

Christopher Plummer plays Eddie Chapman (*q.v.*), a British safecracker who is in jail in Jersey, one of the Channel Islands occupied by the Germans when WW II breaks out. He offers to spy against England, a country that has wronged him. Plummer goes on to perform amazing and devastating sabotage, as well as securing England's greatest secrets for the Abwehr (*q.v.*), only to survive the war as a British double agent who had mislead his German spymasters all along. (Avail. on cas.)

WALK EAST ON BEACON (1952), 98m, COL, b/w, d, Alfred Werker, lp, *George Murphy, Finlay Currie, Virginia Gilmore, Karel Stepanek, Louisa Horton, Peter Capell, Bruno Wick, Karl Weber, Ernest Graves*

FBI man George Murphy, left, leads the hunt for Soviet spies in Walk East on Beacon.

This film was the creation of J. Edgar Hoover (*q.v.*), or rather stemmed from an article he penned entitled "The Crime of the Century," one in which he depicted the operations of vast Soviet spy networks in the U.S., particularly those stealing atomic secrets. Hoover drew upon a bevy of real spies—Judith Coplon (*q.v.*), loosely essayed by Gilmore, Soviet spy Rudy Baker (*q.v.*), played by Graves, shipped back to Russia after failing in his mission, NKVD/KGB (*q.v.*) spymaster Arthur Adams (*q.v.*), portrayed by Stepanek—who had been stealing American secrets for years. Murphy is the FBI agent who leads the investigation into exposing the spy ring in a surprisingly exciting and informative film where dead letter drops, codes, ciphers, microdots, and all the methods and tools of espionage agents are carefully demonstratred. Hoover supervised the entire production to give it his stamp of approval.

BIBLIOGRAPHY

ENS OF THOUSANDS OF SOURCES HAVE BEEN EMPLOYED by the author in researching this work over the last three decades, including books, periodicals, reports, and newspapers (articles for the latter too numerous to cite herein), as well as personal interviews and extensive correspondence with those involved with intelligence. What follows are the basic published reference sources used in the compiling, writing, and overall preparation of this work.

BOOKS

Aaron, Daniel (ed.). *America in Crisis.* New York: Knopf, 1953.

Abbait, A. H. *Italy and the Abyssinian War.* London: General Press, 1936.

Abbott, Wilbur C. *New York in the American Revolution.* New York: Scribner's, 1929.

Abel, Ellie. *The Missile Crisis.* Philadelphia: Lippincott, 1966.

Abell, L. E. *Recollections of the Emperor Napoleon.* London: John Murray, 1848.

Abend, Hallett, and Billingham, Anthony J. *Can China Survive?* New York: Ives Washburn, 1936.

————. *Chaos in Asia.* New York: Ives Washburn, 1939.

————. *My Life in China, 1926–1941.* New York: Harcourt, Brace, 1943.

Abernethy, Thomas Perkins. *The Burr Conspiracy.* New York: Oxford, 1954.

Abott, A. *The Assassination and Death of Abraham Lincoln.* New York: American News, 1865.

Abramovitch, Raphael R. *The Soviet Revolution.* New York: International Universities Press, 1962.

Abrikossow, Dimitri I. *Revelations of a Russian Diplomat.* Seattle: University of Washington Press, 1964.

Abshagan, Karl Heinz. *Canaris: Patriot und Weltbürger.* Stuttgart: Union Deutsche Verlagsantalt, 1950.

Accoce, Pierre, and Quet, Pierre. *A Man Called Lucy.* New York: Coward-McCann, 1967.

Acerbo, Giacomo. *Fascism in the First Year of Government.* Rome: Giorgio Berlutti, 1923.

Acheson, Dean. *Present at the Creation.* New York: W. W. Norton, 1969.

Adamic, Louis. *Dinner at the White House.* New York: Harper, 1946.

Adams, Andrew. *Ninja: The Invisible Assassins.* Burbank, Calif.: Ohara, 1976.

Adams, Arthur E. *Bosheviks in the Ukraine: The Second Campaign, 1918–1919.* New Haven, Conn.: Yale University Press, 1963.

Adams, James. *The Funding of Terror.* New York: Simon & Schuster, 1986.

Adamson, Ian. *The Forgotten Men.* London: G. Bell, 1965.

Adcock, F. E. *The Roman Art of War Under the Republic.* Cambridge, Mass.: Harvard University Press, 1940.

Adleman, Robert, and Walton, George. *Rome Fell Today.* Boston: Little, Brown, 1968.

————. *The Champagne Campaign.* Boston: Little, Brown, 1969.

Adshagen, Karl-Heinz. *Canaris.* London: Hutchinson, 1956.

Africa, Thomas. *Rome of the Caesars.* New York: John Wiley & Sons, 1965.

Agabekov, Georges. *OGUP: The Russian Secret Terror.* New York: Brentano's, 1931.

Agar, Augustus W. S. *Baltic Episode: A Classic of Secret Service in Russian Waters.* London: Hodder & Stoughton, 1963.

Agawa, Hiroshi. *Yamamoto Isoroku.* Tokyo: Shincho Shahan, 1965.

Agee, Philip. *Inside the Company: CIA Diary.* New York: Stonehill, 1975.

————, and Wolf, Louis (eds.). *Dirty Work: The CIA in Western Europe.* Secaucus, N.J.: Lyle Stuart, 1978.

Aglion, Raoul. *War in the Desert.* New York: Henry Holt, 1941.

Agoncillo, Teodoro A. *The Fateful Years: Japan's Adventure in the Philippines, 1941–1945.* (2 vols.). Quezon City, Philippines: R. P. Garcia, 1965.

Agourtine, Leon. *Le General Soukhomlinov.* Clichy, France: l'Auteur, 1951.

Aida, Yuji. *Prisoner of the British.* London: Cresset, 1966.

Akhmedov, Ismail. *In and Out of Stalin's KGB.* Frederick, Md.: University Publications, 1984.

Albertini, Luigi. *Origins of the War of 1914.* London: Oxford, 1952–1957.

Albrecht-Carrié, René. *Italy from Napoleon to Mussolini.* New York: Columbia University Press, 1960.

Alcorn, Robert. *No Bugles for Spies.* New York: David McKay, 1962.

————. *No Banners, No Bands.* New York: David McKay, 1965.

Alden, John Richard. *The American Revolution, 1775–1783.* New York: Harper, 1962.

Alexander, C. W. *Career and Adventures of John H. Surratt.* Philadelphia: Published by author, 1866.

Alexander, Grand Duke. *Once a Grand Duke.* New York: Garden City, 1932.

Alexander, Holmes. *Aaron Burr: The Proud Pretender.* New York: Harper, 1937.

Alexander, Robert J. *Communism in Latin America.* New Brunswick, N.J.: Rutgers University Press, 1960.

Alexander, Yonah (ed.). *International Terrorism: National, Regional and Global Perspectives.* New York: AMS Press, 1976.

Alexandrov, Vistor. *Journey Through Chaos.* New York: Crown, 1945.

Alger, John Goldworth. *Paris in 1789–94.* London: G. Allen, 1902.

Alioshin, Dimitri. *Asian Odyssey.* New York: Henry Holt, 1940.

Allbury, A. G. *Bamboo and Bushido.* London: Robert Hale, 1955.

Allen, G. C. *A Short Economic History of Modern Japan.* London: Allen & Unwin, 1962.

Allen, Louis. *Japan: The Years of Triumph.* London: Purnell, 1971.

Allen, Peter. *The Crown and the Swastika.* London: Hale, 1983.

Allen, Robert S. *Lucky Forward.* New York: Vanguard, 1947.

Allen, Thomas B., and Polmar, Norman. *Merchants of Treason: America's Secrets for Sale.* New York: Delacorte, 1988.

Alliluyeva, Svetlana. (trans. Priscilla Johnson,) *Twenty Letters to a Friend.* New York: Harper, 1967.

————. *Only One Year.* New York: Harper, 1969.

Allison, John M. *Ambassador from the Prairie.* Boston: Houghton Mifflin, 1973.

Allon, Yigal. *Shield of David.* London: Weidenfeld & Nicolson, 1970.

————. *The Making of Israel's Army.* London: Valentine Mitchell, 1970.

Almedingen, E. M. *The Romanovs: Three Centuries of an Ill-Fated Dynasty.* New York: Holt, Rinehart & Winston, 1966.

Alsop, Stewart, and Braden, Thomas. *Sub Rosa: The OSS and American Espionage.* New York: Harcourt, Brace & World, 1964.

————. *The Center.* New York: Harper, 1968.

Altavilla, Enrico. *The Art of Spying.* Englewood Cliffs, N.J.: Prentice-Hall, 1967.

Amalrik, Andrei. *Will the Soviet Union Survive Until 1984?* New York: Harper, 1969.

Amery, Julien. *Sons of the Eagle: A Study in Guerrilla War.* London: Macmillan, 1948.

Amies, Hardy. *Just So Far.* London: Collins, 1954.

Amort, R., and Jedlicka, M. *The Canaris File.* London: Wingate, 1970.

Amrine, Michael. *The Great Decision: The Secret History of the Atomic Bomb.* New York: Putnam's, 1959.

Amster, Gerald, and Asbell, Bernard. *Transit Point Moscow.* New York: Holt, Rinehart and Winston, 1984.

Anders, Karl. *Murder to Order.* New York: Devin, 1967.

Anders, Wladyslaw. *Hitler's Defeat in Russia.* Chicago: Regnery, 1953.

Andersen, Hartvig. *The Dark City.* New York: Rinehart, 1954.

Andics, Hellmut. *Rule of Terror: Russia Under Lenin and Stalin.* New York: Holt, Rinehart and Winston, 1969.

Andreas-Friedrich, Ruth. *Berlin Underground, 1939–1945.* London: Latimer House, 1948.

Andregg, Charles H. *Management of Defense Intelligence.* Washington, D.C.: Industrial College of the Armed Forces, 1968.

Andrew, Christopher. *Her Majesty's Secret Service: The Making of the British Intelligence Community.* New York: Penguin, 1987.

————, and Gordievsky, Oleg. *KGB: The Inside Story.* New York: HarperCollins, 1990.

Andrew, Roland G. *Through Fascist Italy.* London: Harrap, 1935.

Anker, Kurt. *Kronprinz Wilhelm.* Berlin: E. S. Mittler, 1919.

Anstruther, Ian. *Oscar Browning: A Biography.* London: John Murray, 1983.

Anthony, K. S. *Catherine the Great.* New York: Knopf, 1925.

Antonius, George. *The Arab Awakening.* London: Hamish Hamilton, 1938.

Aoko, Tokuzo. *The Pacific War.* Tokyo: Gatujutsu Bunken Fukyukai, 1953.

Apenszlak, Jacob (ed.). *The Black Book of Polish Jewry: An Account of the Martyrdom of Polish Jewry Under the Nazi Occupation.* New York: Roy Publishers, 1943.

Aptheker, Herbert. *History and Reality.* New York: Cameron, 1955.

Archer, Jules. *Treason in America.* New York: Hawthorn, 1971.

————. *They Made a Revolution: 1776.* New York: Scholastic, 1973.

Arct, Bohdan. *Poles Against the "V" Weapon.* Warsaw: Interpress, 1972.

Arendt, Hannah. *The Origins of Totalitarianism.* London: Allen & Unwin, 1958.

————. *Eichmann in Jerusalem: A Report on the Banality of Evil.* New York: Viking Press, 1963.

Argall, Phyllis. *Prisoner in Japan.* London: Geoffrey Bles, 1945.

Armstrong, Hamilton Fish. *Tito and Goliath.* New York: Macmillan, 1951.

Armstrong, John A. *Ukrainian Nationalism, 1939–1945.* New York: Columbia University Press, 1955.

————. *The Politics of Totalitarianism.* New York: Random House, 1961.

Army Security Agency. *Historical Background of the Signal Security Agency.* Washington, D.C.: ASA, 1946.

Army Times (eds.). *The Tangled Web.* Washington, D.C.: Robert B. Luce, Inc., 1963.

————. *Heroes of the Resistance.* New York: Dodd, Mead, 1975.

Arnold, H. H. *Global Mission.* New York: Harper, 1945.

Aron, Raymond. *The Opium of the Intellectuals.* Garden City, N.Y.: Doubleday, 1957.

Aron, Robert. *De Gaulle Before Paris.* London: Putnam's, 1962.

————. *De Gaulle Triumphant.* London: Putnam's, 1964.

————. *France Reborn.* New York: Scribner's, 1964.

————. *The Vichy Regime, 1940–1944.* Boston: Beacon Press, 1969.

Arthur, George. *Life of Lord Kitchener.* New York: Macmillan, 1920.

————. *George V.* New York: Cape, 1930.

Ashman, Charles. *The CIA-Mafia Link: The Inside Secrets of Assassination.* New York: Manor Books, 1975.

Ashman, Chuck, and Trescott, Pamela. *Diplomatic Crime.* Washington, D.C.: Acropolis Books, 1987.

Asprey, Robert B. *The German High Command at War: Hindenburg and Ludendorff Conduct World War I.* New York: Morrow, 1991.

Aster, S. *The Making of the Second World War.* London: André Deutsch, 1973.

———— (ed.). *The "X" Documents.* London: André Deutsch, 1974.

Astley, John Bright. *The Inner Circle.* London: Hutchinson, 1971.

Aten, Marion, and Orrmont, Arthur. *Last Train Over Rostov Bridge.* New York: Messner, 1961.

Attiwill, Kenneth. *The Singapore Story.* London: Fredrich Muller, 1959.

Aviel, Ehud. *Open the Gates.* New York: Atheneum, 1975.

Avrich, Paul. *The Russian Anarchists.* Princeton, N.J.: Princeton University Press, 1967.

————. *Kronstadt: 1921.* Princeton, N.J.: Princeton University Press, 1970.

Aydelotte, Frank. *Elizabethan Rogues and Vagabonds.* Oxford, England: Clarendon Press, 1913.

Ayers, Bradley Earl. *The War That Never Was: An Insider's Account of CIA Covert Operations Against Cuba.* Indianapolis: Bobbs-Merrill, 1976.

Babington-Smith, Constance. *Air Spy: The Story of Photo Intelligence in World War II.* New York: Harper & Row, 1957.

Badash, Lawrence. *Kapitza, Rutherford and the Kremlin.* New Haven, Conn.: Yale University Press, 1985.

Baehr, Harry W., Jr. *The New York Tribune Since the Civil War.* New York: Dodd, Mead, 1936.

Bailey, Geoffrey. *The Conspirators.* New York: Harper, 1960.

Bakeless, John. *Turncoats, Traitors and Heroes.* Philadelphia: Lippincott, 1959.

Baldwin, Hanson W. *Battles Lost and Won.* New York: Harper & Row, 1966.

Balfour, Michael. *The Kaiser and His Times.* Boston: Houghton Mifflin, 1964.

Ballou, Robert O. Shinto: *The Unconquered Enemy.* New York: Viking,   1945.

Baker, Carlos. *Ernest Hemingway.* New York: Scribner's, 1969.

Baker, W. J. *A History of the Marconi Company.* New York: St. Martin's Press, 1971.

Balabanoff, Angelica. *My Life as a Rebel.* New York: Harper, 1938.

Balchen, Bernt. *Come North With Me.* New York: E. P. Dutton, 1958.

Ball, Desmond. *Pine Gap: Australia and the U.S. Geostationary Signals Intelligence Satellite Program.* Sydney, Aus.: Allen & Unwin, 1988.

————. *Australia's Secret Space Program.* Canberra, Aus.: Australian National University, 1988.

————. *Soviet Signals Intelligence (SIGENT): Intercepting Satellite Communications.* Canberra, Aus.: Australian National University, 1989.

————. *Intelligence in the Gulf War.* Canberra, Aus: Australian National University, 1991.

Bamford, James. *The Puzzle Palace: A Report on NSA, America's Most Secret Agency.* Boston: Houghton Mifflin, 1982.

Bank, Aaron. *From OSS to Green Berets.* Novato, Calif.: Presidio, 1986.

Barghoorn, Frederick C. *"The Security Police," Interest Groups in Soviet Politics.* Princeton, N.J.: Princeton University Press, 1971.

Barker, Ralph. *One Man's Jungle.* London: Chatto & Windus, 1975.

Barker, Wayne (ed.) *The History of Codes and Ciphers in the United States During the Period Between the World Wars, Part II, 1930–1939.* Laguna Hills, Calif.: Aegean Park Press, 1989.

Barrett, David. *Dixie Mission: The United States Army Observer Group in Yenan.* Berkeley: Center for Chinese Studies, 1970.

Barrett, Neil. *Chinghpaw.* New York: Vintage, 1962.

Barron, John. *KGB: The Secret Work of Soviet Secret Agents.* New York: Reader's Digest Association, 1974.

————. *MiG Pilot.* New York: Avon, 1981.

————. *KGB Today: The Hidden Hand.* New York: Reader's Digest Association, 1983.

————. *Breaking the Ring: The Bizarre Case of the Walker Family Spy Ring.* Boston: Houghton Mifflin, 1987.

Barros, James. *No Sense of Evil: The Espionage Case of E. Herbert Norman.* New York: Ivy Books, 1987.

Barth, Alan. *Government by Investigation.* New York: Viking, 1955.

Bartz, Karl. *The Downfall of the German Secret Service.* London: Kimber, 1956.

Bar-Zohar, Michael. *Spies in the Promised Land.* London: Davis-Poynter, 1972.

————. *Ben-Gurion.* London: Weidenfeld & Nicoloson, 1977.

————, and Haber, Eitan. *The Quest for the Red Prince.* New York: Morrow, 1983.

Bassett, Margaret. *Profiles and Portraits of American Presidents.* New York: McKay, 1964.

Basso, Hamilton. *Beauregard the Great Creole.* New York: Scribner's, 1933.

Bates, David Homer. *Lincoln in the Telegraph Office.* New York: Century, 1907.

Batsell, Walter R. *Soviet Rule in Russia.* New York: Macmillan, 1929.

Battaglia, Roberto. *The Story of the Italian Resistance.* London: Oldhams Press, 1957.

Bauer, Yehuda. *Flight and Rescue: Brichah.* New York: Random House, 1970.

————. (trans. Alton M. Winters) *From Diplomacy to Resistance: A History of Jewish Palestine, 1939–1945.* New York: Atheneum, 1973.

Bazeries, Etienne. *Les chiffres secrets dévoilés.* Paris: Librarie Charpentier et Fasquelle, 1901.

Bazna, Eleyza. *I Was Cicero.* New York: Harper, 1962.

Beamish, John. *Burma Drop.* London: Elek Books, 1958.

Beachhofer-Roberts, Carl Eric. *In Deniken's Russia and the Caucasus, 1919–1920.* London: Collins, 1921.

Beard, Charles A. *President Roosevelt and the Coming of the War.* New Haven, Conn.: Yale University Press, 1941.

Beasley, W. G. *The Modern History of Japan.* New York: Praeger, 1963.

Beatty, Bessie. *The Red Heart of Russia.* New York: The Century Co., 1918.

Bechvar, Gustav. *The Lost Legion: A Czechoslovakian Epic.* London: Stanley Paul, 1939.

Becker, Jillian. *The PLO: The Rise and Fall of the Palestine Liberation Organization.* New York: St. Martin's, 1984.

Beesley, Patrick. *Very Special Intelligence.* London: Hamish Hamilton, 1977.

————. *Room 40: British Naval Intelligence, 1914–1918.* New York: Harcourt Brace Jovanovich, 1982.

Beevor, J. G. *SOE, Recollections and Reflections, 1940–45.* London: Bodley Head, 1981.

Begin, Menachem. *The Revolt: Story of the Irgun.* New York: Henry Schuman, 1951.

Beirne, Francis F. *Shout Treason: The Trial of Aaron Burr.* New York: Hastings House, 1959.

Beker, Henry, and Piper, Fred. *Cipher Systems.* New York: John Wiley, 1982.

Belden, Jack. *China Shakes the World.* New York: Harper, 1949.

Belfrage, Cedric, and Aronson, James. *Something to Guard: The Stormy Life of the National Guardian, 1948–1967.* New York: Columbia University Press, 1979.

Bell, Griffin B., and Ostrow, Ronald J. *Taking Care of the Law.* New York: Morrow, 1982.

Belloc, Hillaire. *Richelieu.* Philadelphia: Lippincott, 1929.

————. *The French Revolution.* New York: Oxford, 1966.

Beloff, Max. *The Foreign Policy of Soviet Russia, 1929–1941.* (2 vols.) London: Oxford, 1947-1949.

————. *Soviet Policy in the Far East, 1944-1951.* New York: Oxford, 1953.

Bemis, Samuel Flagg. *The Diplomacy of the American Revolution.* New York: Appleton-Century, 1935.

Benckendorff, Count Paul. *Last Days at Tsarskoe Selo.* London: Heinemann, 1927.

Benda, Harry J. *The Crescent and the Rising Sun: Indonesian Islam Under the Japanese Occupation, 1942–1945.* The Hague: W. van Hoeve, Ltd, 1958.

Ben Dan, E. *L'Espion qui venait d'Israel.* Paris: Librairie Artheme Fayard, 1967,

Benedict, Ruth. *The Chrysanthemum and the Sword.* Boston: Houghton Mifflin, 1946.

Ben-Gurion, David. *Israel, A Personal History.* Tel Aviv: Sabra Books, 1972.

Ben-Hanan, Elie. *Our Man in Damascus.* Tel Aviv: A.D.M., 1969.

Bennecke, Heinrich. *Hitler und die SA.* Munich: Olzag Verlag, 1962.

————. *Die Reichswehr und der "Röm-Putsch."* Munich: Olzag Verlag, 1964.

Bennett, H. Gordon. *Why Singapore Fell.* Sydney, Australia: Angus and Robertson, 1944.

Bennett, J. W., and Hobart, W. A., and Spitzer, J. B. *Intelligence and Cryptanalytic Activities of the Japanese During World War.* Laguna Hills, Calif.: Aegean Park Press, 1986.

Benouville, Guillain de. *The Unknown Warriors.* New York: Simon & Schuster, 1949.

Ben-Porat, Yeshayahu, et al. *Entebbe Rescue.* New York: Delacorte, 1977.

Ben Shaul, Moshe. *Generals of Israel.* Tel Aviv: Hadar, 1968.

Bentley, Elizabeth. *Out of Bondage.* New York: Devin-Adair, 1951.

Benvenisti, Meron. *The Sling and the Club.* Jerusalem: Keter Publishing House, 1988.

Bergamini, David. *Japan's Imperial Conspiracy.* New York: Morrow, 1971.

Berier, Jacques. *Secret Weapons—Secret Agents.* (trans. Edward Fitzgerald) London: Hurst & Blackett, 1956.

Bernadotte, Count Folke. *The Fall of the Curtain.* London: Cassell, 1945.

Bernard, Henri. *La Résistance 1940–1945.* Brussels: La Renaissance du Livre, 1968.

Bernikow, Louise. *Abel.* New York: Trident Press, 1970.

Bernstorff, Count Johann von. *My Three Years in America.* New York: Scribner's, 1920.

Beschloss, Michael R. *Mayday: Eisenhower, Khrushchev and the U-2 Affair.* New York: Harper, 1986.

————. *The Crisis Years: Kennedy and Khrushchev, 1960–1963.* New York: HarperCollins, 1991.

Best, S. Payne. *The Venlo Incident.* London: Hutchinson, 1951.

Best, Werner. *Die Deutsche Polizei.* Darmstadt: L.C. Wittich, 1941.

Bethell, Nicholas. *The Last Secret.* New York: Basic Books, 1974.

————. *Betrayed.* New York: Times Books, 1984.

Bezymenski, Lev. *Martin Bormann.* Zurich: Aurora Verlag, 1965.

Bialoguski, Michael. *The Case of Colonel Petrov.* New York: McGraw-Hill, 1955.

Biew, A. M. *Kapitza: The Story of the British-Trained Scientist Who Invented the Russian Hydrogen Bomb.* London: Frederick Muller, 1956.

Billington, James H. *The Icon and the Axe.* New York: Knopf, 1966.

Birmingham, Stephen. *Real Lace.* London: Hamish Hamilton, 1974.

Bingham, John. *The Double Agent.* New York: Dutton, 1967.

Bisson, T. A. *Japan in China.* New York: Macmillan, 1938.

Bittman, Ladislav. *The Deception Game: Czechoslovak Intelligence in Soviet Political Warfare.* Syracuse, N.Y.: Syracuse University Press, 1972.

Black, Ian, and Morris, Benny. *Israel's Secret Wars: A History of Israel's Intelligence Service.* New York: Grove, 1991.

Blackburn, Douglas. *Secret Service in South Africa.* London: Cassell, 1911.

Blackstock, Paul. *The Strategy of Subversion.* Chicago: Quadrangle, 1964.

————. *Agents of Deceit.* Chicago: Quadrangle, 1966.

Blair, Bruce. *The Logic of Accidental War.* Washington, D.C.: Brookings Institution, 1993.

Blake, George. *No Other Choice.* New York: Simon & Schuster, 1990.

Blank, A. S., and Mader, Julius. *Rote Kapelle gegen Hitler.* East Berlin: Verlag der Nation, 1979.

Blaufarb, Douglas. *The Counter-Insurgency Era.* New York: Free Press, 1977.

Bleicher, Hugo. *Colonel Henri's Story.* London: William Kimber, 1968.

Blitzer, Wolf. *Territory of Lies: The Exclusive Story of Jonathan Jay Pollard: The American Who Spied on His Country for Israel and How He Was Betrayed.* New York: Harper, 1989.

Bliven, Bruce, Jr. *The Wonderful Writing Machine.* New York: Random House, 1954.

Blum, Howard. *I Pledge Allegiance: The True Story of the Walkers: An American Spy Family.* New York: Simon & Schuster, 1987.

Blum, Richard H. *Surveillance and Espionage in a Free Society.* New York: Praeger, 1972.

Blum, William. *The CIA, A Forgotten History: U.S. Global Interventions Since World War 2.* Atlantic Highlands, N.J.: Zed Books, 1986.

Blumberg, Stanley A. and Owens, Gwinn. *The Survival Factor: Israeli Intelligence from World War I to the Present.* New York: Putnam's, 1981.

Blunt, Wilfrid. *Married to a Single Life.* Salisbury, Eng.: Chantry Press, 1984.

Blythe, Ronald. *The Age of Illusions, 1914–1940.* London: Hamish Hamilton, 1963.

Bombaugh, C. C. *Oddities and Curiosities.* New York: Dover, 1957.

Bond, Raymond T. *Famous Stories of Code and Cipher.* New York: Rinehart, 1947.

Booker, Edna Lee. *News Is My Job*. New York: Macmillan, 1940.

Borg, Dorothy. *The United States and the Far Eastern Crisis of 1933–1938*. Cambridge, Mass.: Harvard University Press, 1964.

Borkin, Joseph. *The Crime and Punishment of I. G. Farben*. New York: Free Press, 1978.

Borton, Hugh. *Japan's Modern Century*. New York: Ronald Press, 1955.

Bothwell, Robert, and Granatstein, J. L. *The Gouzenko Transcripts*. Ottawa: Deneau, 1982.

Botkin, Gleb. *The Real Romanovs*. New York: Revell, 1931.

Boucard, Robert. *Les Dessous de l'Espionnage, 1939–1945*. Paris: Editions Descamps, 1958.

Boule, Pierre. (trans. Xan Fielding.) *The Source of the River Kwai*. London: Secker & Warburg, 1967.

Bourdeaux, Michael. *Religious Ferment in Russia*. New York: St. Martin's, 1968.

Bourke, Sean. *The Springing of George Blake*. London: Cassell, 1970.

Boveri, Margaret. *Treason in the Twentieth Century*. New York: Putnam, 1963.

Bowen, Elizabeth. *Death of the Heart*. London: Jonathan Cape, 1938.

Bowen, John. *Undercover in the Jungle*. London: William Kimber, 1978.

Bowie, Beverly. *Operation Bughouse*. New York: Dodd, Mead, 1947.

Boyle, Andrew. *The Climate of Treason*. London: Coronet, 1980.

Bozell, L. Brent, and Buckley, William. *McCarthy and His Enemies*. Chicago: Regnery, 1954.

Bracher, Karl Dietrich. *The German Dictatorship: The Origins, Structure and Effects of National Socialism*. (trans. Jean Steinberg) New York: Praeger, 1970.

Braddon, Russell. *The White Mouse*. New York: W. W. Norton, 1956.

Bradlee, Ben C. *Conversations with Kennedy*. New York: W. W. Norton, 1975.

Bradsher, Henry. *Afghanistan and the Soviet Union*. Durham, N.C.: Duke University Press, 1985.

Branch, Taylor, and Propper, Eugene M. *Labyrinth*. Viking, 1982.

Brandt, Ed. *The Last Voyage of the USS* Pueblo. New York: W. W. Norton, 1969.

Brant, Irving. *James Madison*. Indianapolis, Ind.: Bobbs-Merrill, 1941.

Brelis, Dean. *The Mission*. New York: Random House, 1958.

Breuer, William B. *The Secret War With Germany: Deception, Espionage and Dirty Tricks, 1939–1945*. Novato, Calif.: Presidio, 1988.

Brines, Russell. *MacArthur's Japan*. New York: Lippincott, 1948.

Brinkley, George A. *The Volunteer Army and Allied Intervention in South Russia, 1917–1921: A Study in the Politics and Diplomacy of the Russian Civil War*. University of Notre Dame Press, 1966.

Broglie, Duc de. *Le Secret du roi: Correspondance secrete de Louis XV avec ses agents diplomatiques, 1752–1774*. Paris: Calmann Levy, 1879.

Brome, Vicent. *The Spy*. New York: W. W. Norton, 1957.

———. *The International Brigades*. London: Heinemann, 1965.

Brook-Shepherd, Gordon. *The Storm Petrels*. New York: Ballantine, 1982.

Brooks, Lester. *Behind Japan's Surrender*. New York: McGraw-Hill, 1968.

Brown, Anthony Cave. *Bodyguard of Lies*. London: W. H. Allen, 1976.

———, and MacDonald, Charles B. *On a Field of Red: The Communist International and the Coming of World War II*. New York: Putnam's, 1981.

———. *The Last Hero: Wild Bill Donovan*. New York: Vintage Books, 1984.

———. *"C": The Secret Life of Sir Stewart Menzies, Spymaster to Winston Churchill*. New York: Macmillan, 1987.

Brown, Delmer M. *Nationalism in Japan*. Los Angeles: University of California Press, 1955.

Brown, J. A. C. *Techniques of Persuasion*. London: Pelican, 1963.

Brown, Ralph. *Loyalty and Security*. New Haven, Conn.: Yale University Press, 1958.

Browne, Courtney. *Tojo: The Last Banzai*. New York: Holt, Rinehart & Winston, 1967.

Bruce, George. *The Warsaw Rising*. London: Rupert Hart-Davis, 1972.

Brugioni, Dino. *Eyeball to Eyeball: The Inside Story of the Cuban Missile Crisis*. New York: Random House, 1991.

Bryant, Louise. *Mirrors of Moscow*. New York: Thomas Seltzer, 1923.

Brzezinski, Zbigniew. *Ideology and Power in Soviet Politics*. New York: Praeger, 1962.

———. *Power and Principle: Memoirs of the National Security Adviser, 1977–1981*. New York: Farrar, Straus and Giroux, 1983.

Buchan, John. *A History of the Great War*. Boston: Houghton Mifflin, 1922.

Buchanan, George. *My Mission to Russia* (2 vols.). New York: Cassell, 1923.

Buchanan, Meriel. *The Dissolution of an Empire*. London: Murray, 1932.

Bucher, Lloyd. *Bucher: My Story*. Garden City, N. Y.: Doubleday, 1970.

Buchheim, Hans, et al. (trans. R. H. Barry and others.) *The Anatomy of the SS State*. London: Collins, 1968.

Buckmaster, Maurice. *They Fought Alone*. New York: W. W. Norton, 1958.

Budenz, Louis Francis. *This Is My Story*. New York: McGraw-Hill, 1947.

———. *Men Without Faces*. New York: Harper, 1950.

Bulloch, James D. *The Secret Service of the Confederate States in Europe*. New York: Thomas Yoseloff, 1959.

Bulloch, John, and Miller, Henry. *Spy Ring*. London: Secker & Warburg, 1961.

———. *M.I.5*. London: Arthur Barker, 1963.

———. *Akin to Treason*. London: Arthur Barker, 1966.

Bullock, Alan. *Hitler: A Study in Tyranny*. London: Oldhams Press, 1964.

Bullock, Cecil. *Etajima: The Dartmouth of Japan*. London: Sampson Low, Marston & Co., 1942.

Bulygin, Paul, and Kerensky, Alexander. *The Murder of the Romanovs*. London: Hutchinson, 1935.

Bunyon, James, and Fisher, H. H. *The Bolshevik Revolution, 1917–1918*. London: Oxford University Press, 1934.

Bunyon, James (ed.). *Intervention, Civil War, and Communism in Russia: April–December 1918, Documents and Materials*. Baltimore: Johns Hopkins University Press, 1936.

Buranelli, Prosper, et al. *The Cryptogram Book*. New York: Simon & Schuster, 1928.

Burchett, Wilfrid. *At the Barricades*. London: Quartet, 1980.

Burke, Michael. *Outrageous Good Fortune*. Boston: Little, Brown, 1984.

Burleson, Clyde W. *The Jennifer Project*. New York: Prentice-Hall, 1977.

Burn, Michael. *The Debatable Land*. London: Hamish Hamilton, 1970.

Burnett, Edmund C. (ed.). *Letters of Members of the Continental Congress*. Washington, D.C.: Carnegie Institution of Washington, 1921–1936.

Burney, Christopher. *The Dungeon Democracy*. London: Heinemann, 1945.

Burnham, James. *The Web of Subversion*. New York: John Day, 1959.

Burrows, William E. *Deep Black: Space Espionage and National Security*. New York: Random House, 1986.

————. and Windrem, Robert. *Critical Mass: The Dangerous Race for Superweapons in a Fragmenting World*. New York: Simon & Schuster, 1994.

Burt, Harry Kendal, and Leasor, Thomas James. *The One That Got Away*. New York: Random House, 1956.

Burton, Hugh. *Japan's Modern Century*. New York: The Ronald Press, 1955.

Busch, Francis X. *Guilty or Not Guilty?* Indianapolis, Ind.: Bobbs-Merrill, 1952.

Bush, Lewis. *Land of the Dragonfly*. London: Robert Hale, 1959.

————. *The Road to Inamura*. London: Robert Hale, 1961.

Buss, Claude A. *Asia in the Modern World*. New York: Macmillan, 1964.

Butcher, Harry C. *My Three Years with Eisenhower*. New York: Simon & Schuster, 1946.

Butler, Ewan. *Amateur Agent*. New York: W. W. Norton, 1963.

Butler, J. R. M. *Lord Lothian*. New York: St. Martin's, 1960.

Butow, Robert J. C. *Japan's Decision to Surrender*. Stanford, Calif.: Stanford University Press, 1954.

————. *Tojo and the Coming of the War*. Princeton, N.J.: Princeton University Press, 1961.

Buttinger, Joseph. *Vietnam: A Dragon Embattled*. New York: Praeger, 1967.

Byas, Hugh. *Government by Assassination*. New York: Knopf, 1942.

————. *The Japanese Enemy: His Power and His Vulnerability*. New York: Knopf, 1942.

Bykov, P. M. *The Last Days of Tsardom*. London: Martin Lawrence, 1935.

Byrnes, James F. *Speaking Frankly*. New York: Harper, 1947.

————. *All in One Lifetime*. New York: Harper, 1958.

Brynes, Robert E. *Pobedonostsev: His Life and Thought*. Bloomington, Ind.: University of Indiana Press, 1968.

Byron, John, and Pack, Robert. *The Claws of the Dragon: Kang Sheng*. New York: Simon & Schuster, 1992.

Byron, Robert. *The Byzantine Achievement*. New York: Knopf, 1929.

Cadogan, Sir Alexander. *Diaries, 1938–1945*. London: Cassell, 1971.

Callaghan, Daniel. *Dangerous Capabilities: Paul Nitze and the Cold War*. New York: HarperCollins, 1990.

Callwood, June. *Emma*. New York: Beaufort Books, 1984.

Calvocoressi, Peter, and Wint, Guy. *Total War: Causes and Courses of the Second World War*. London: Allen Lane, 1972.

————. *Top Secret Ultra*. New York: Pantheon, 1980.

Campbell, Duncan. *The Unsinkable Aircraft Carrier: American Military Power in Britain*. London: Michael Joseph, 1984.

Campbell, Helen Jones. *Confederate Courier*. New York: St. Martin's, 1964.

Candela, Rosario. *The Military Cipher of Commandant Bazaries*. New York: Cardanus Press, 1938.

Capley, Michel. *Guerrilla au Laos*. Paris: Presses de la Cité, 1966.

Carell, Paul. (trans. Ewald Osers.) *Hitler's War on Russia*. London: Harrap, 1940.

————. *The Foxes of the Desert*. London: Macdonald, 1960.

Carlson, John Roy (Arthur Derounian). *Under Cover: My Four Years in the Nazi Underworld of America*. New York: Dutton, 1943.

Carpenter, T. *The Trial of Col. Aaron Burr*. Washington, D.C.: n.p., 1808.

Carpozi, George, Jr. *Red Spies in the U.S.* New Rochelle, N.Y.: Arlington House, 1973.

Carr, E. H. *Studies in Revolution*. London: Macmillan, 1950.

————. *A History of Social Russia*. New York: Macmillan, 1951.

Carr, Harry. *Riding the Tiger: An American Newspaperman in the Orient*. Boston: Houghton Mifflin, 1934.

Carr, Robert Kenneth. T*he House Committee on Un-American Activities, 1945–1950*. Ithaca, N.Y.: Cornell University Press, 1952.

Carroll, John M. *Secrets of Electronic Espionage*. New York: Dutton, 1966.

Carroll, Wallace. *Persuade or Perish*. Boston: Houghton Mifflin, 1948.

Carston, F. L. *The Reichswehr and Politics, 1918 to 1933*. Oxford, Eng.: Clarendon Press, 1966.

Castro, Orlando Hidalgo. *Spy for Fidel*. Miami, Fla.: E. A. Seemann, 1971.

Cate, Curtis. *Antoine de Saint-Exupéry*. New York: Putnam's, 1970.

Causton, E. E. N. *Militarism and Foreign Policy in Japan*. London: Allen & Unwin, 1936.

Caute, David. *The Fellow-Travellers*. New York: Macmillan, 1973.

Cecil, Robert. *A Divided Life: A Personal Portrait of the Spy Donald Maclean*. New York: Morrow, 1989.

Central Intelligence Agency. *Foreign Intelligence and Security Services: USSR*. Washington, D.C.: CIA, 1975.

————. *Elites and the Distribution of Power in Iran*. Washington, D.C.: CIA, 1976.

————. *Foreign Intelligence and Security Services: Israel*. Washington, D.C.: CIA, 1977.

————. *The Rote Kapelle: The CIA's History of Soviet Intelligence and Espionage Networks in Western Europe, 1936–1945*. Frederick, Md.: University Publications, 1982.

————. *KGB and GRU*. Washington, D.C.: CIA, 1984.

Ceplair, Larry, and Englund, Steven. *The Inquisition in Hollywood*. New York: Anchor, 1980.

Chacornac, Paul. *Grandeur et adversité de Jean Tritheme*. Paris: Editions Traditionelles, 1963.

Chamberlain, William Henry. *The Russian Revolution 1917–1921*. (2 vols.) New York: Macmillan, 1935.

————. *Japan Over Asia*. Boston: Little, Brown, 1938.

Chambers, Robert W. *The Tracer of Lost Persons*. New York: Appleton, 1906.

Chambers, Whittaker. *Witness*. New York: Random House, 1952.

———. *Cold Friday.* New York: Random House, 1964.

Chapman, Colin. *August 21st: The Rape of Czechoslo-vakia.* Philadelphia: Lippincott, 1968.

Chapman, Guy. *The Dreyfus Case.* New York: Reynal, 1955.

Chapman, F. Spencer. *The Jungle is Neutral.* London: Chatto & Windus, 1949.

Charques, Richard. *The Twilight of Imperial Russia.* Fair Lawn, N.J.: Essential Books, 1959.

Chastellain, J. *L'Espionage Soviétique aux Esats Unis: L'Affaire Alger Hiss.* Lausanne, Switz.: Jaunin, 1950.

Chatel, Nicole, and Guérin, Alain. *Camarade Sorge.* Paris: Julliard, 1965.

Chennault, Claire. *Way of a Fighter.* New York: Putnam's, 1949.

Cherry, Colin. *Of Human Communication.* New York: Wiley, 1957.

Chester, Lewis, Fay, Stephen, and Young, Hugo. *The Zinoviev Letter.* Philadelphia: Lippincott, 1968.

Chiba, Reiko. The *Japanese Fortune Calendar.* Rutland, Vt.: Charles E. Tuttle Co., 1965.

Childs, J. Rives. *Before the Curtain Falls.* Indianapolis, Ind.: Bobbs-Merrill, 1932.

———. *German Military Ciphers from February to November, 1918.* Washington, D.C.: Government Printing Office, 1935.

Chornovil, Vyacheslav (ed.). *The Chornovil Papers.* New York: McGraw-Hill, 1968.

Christensen, Synnöve. *Norway Is My Country.* London: Collins, 1943.

Christian, George. *The President Steps Down.* New York: Macmillan, 1970.

Churchill, Peter. *Of Their Own Choice.* London: Hodder & Stoughton, 1952.

———. *Duel of Wits.* London: Hodder & Stoughton, 1953.

———. *The Spirit in the Cage.* London: Hodder & Stoughton, 1954.

Churchill, Winston S. *London to Ladysmith.* London: Longman, 1900.

———. *The World Crisis: The Aftermath.* London: Thornton Butterworth, 1929.

———. *The World Crisis.* London: Thornton Butter-worth, 1930.

———. *My Early Life.* London: Thornton Butter-worth, 1930.

———. *The Second World War.* (6 vols.) Boston: Houghton Mifflin, 1950-1953.

Ciano, Count Galeazzo. *Ciano's Diary.* London: Heinemann, 1947.

Clark, Eleanor. *The Bitter Box.* Garden City, N.Y.: Doubleday, 1946.

Clark, Leonard. *The Marching Wind.* New York: Funk, 1954.

Clark, Mark. *Calculated Risk.* New York: Harper, 1950.

Clark, Ronald. *The Man Who Broke Purple: The Life of Colonel William F. Friedman, Who Deciphered the Japanese Code in World War II.* Boston: Little, Brown, 1977.

Clarke, Comer. *Eichmann: The Man and His Crimes.* New York: Ballantine, 1960.

———. *The War Within.* London: World, 1961.

Cline, Ray S. *Secrets, Spies and Scholars: Blueprint of the Essential CIA.* Washington, D.C.: Acropolis Books, 1976.

———. *The CIA Under Reagan, Bush & Casey.* Washington, D.C.: Acropolis Books, 1981.

———, and Alexander, Yonah. *Terrorism: The Soviet Connection.* New York: Crane Russak, 1984.

Clissold, Stephen. *Whirlwind.* New York: Philosoph-ical Library, 1949.

Clubb, O. Edmund. *20th Century China.* New York: Columbia University Press, 1946.

———. *The Witness and I.* New York: Columbia University Press, 1974.

Cohen, E. (trans. M. H. Braaksma.) *Human Behavior in the Concentration Camps.* New York: W. W. Norton, 1953.

Cohen, Jerome B. *Japan's Economy in War and Recon-struction.* Minneapolis: University of Minnesota Press, 1949.

Coit, Margaret L. *Mr. Baruch.* London: Gollancz, 1958.

Colby, William. *Honorable Men: My Life in the CIA.* New York: Simon & Schuster, 1978.

Cole, Hubert. *Laval.* London: Heinemann, 1963.

Cole, J. A. *Prince of Spies: Henri Le Caron.* London: Faber & Faber, 1984.

Cole, Wayne S. *Senator Gerald P. Nye and American Foreign Relations.* Minneapolis: University of Minnesota Press, 1962.

Collier, Basil. *The War in the Far East, 1941–1945: A Military History.* New York: Morrow, 1969.

———. T*he Battle of the V Weapons.* London: Hodder & Stoughton, 1964.

Collier, Richard. *Ten Thousand Eyes.* New York: E. P. Dutton & Co., 1958.

Collins, Larry, and Lapierre, Dominique. *Is Paris Burning?* New York: Simon & Schuster, 1969.

———. *O Jerusalem.* New York: Simon & Schuster, 1971.

Colvin, Ian. *Master Spy.* New York: McGraw-Hill, 1951.

———. *Vansittart in Office.* London: Gollancz, 1965.

Compton, James V. *The Swastika and the Eagle: The United States and the Origins of World War II.* Boston: Houghton Mifflin, 1967.

Connolly, Cyril. *The Missing Diplomats.* London: Queen Anne Press, 1952.

Conquest, Robert. *The Great Terror: Stalin's Purge of the Thirties.* New York: Macmillan, 1968.

———. *The Soviet Police System.* New York: Praeger, 1968.

——— (ed.). *Justice and the Legal System in the USSR.* London: The Bodley Head, 1968.

———. *The Great Terror: A Reassessment.* New York: Oxford, 1990.

Cook, Blanche Wiesen. *The Declassified Eisenhower: A Divided Legacy.* Garden City, N.Y.: Doubleday, 1981.

Cook, Fred J. *The Unfinished Story of Alger Hiss.* New York: Morrow, 1958.

———. *The FBI Nobody Knows.* New York: Pyramid, 1965.

Cookridge, E. H. (pseud.). *Soviet Spy Net.* London: Muller, 1955.

———. *Inside SOE.* London: A. Barker, 1966.

———. *The Third Man: The Full Story of Kim Philby.* New York: Putnam's, 1968.

———. *Gehlen, Spy of the Century.* New York: Random House, 1971.

———. *Spy Trade.* New York: Walker, 1971.

Cooley, John K. *Libyan Sandstorm.* New York: Holt, Rinehart and Winston, 1982.

Coon, Carleton. *A North Africa Story.* Ipswich, Mass.: Gambit, 1980.

Cooper, A.R. *Born to Fight.* London: Blackwood, 1969.

Cooper, Bert. *Case Studies in Insurgency and Revo-lutionary Warfare: Vietnam, 1941–54.* Washington, D.C.: Special Operations Research Office, 1964.

Cooper, Dick. *Adventures of a Secret Agent*. London: Muller, 1957.

Copeland, Miles. *The Game of Nations*. New York: Simon & Schuster, 1969.

———. *Without Cloak or Dagger*. New York: Simon & Schuster, 1974.

Corson, William R. *The Armies of Ignorance: The Rise of the American Intelligence Empire*. New York: Dial, 1977.

Costello, John, and Crowley, Robert T. *The New KGB: Engine of Soviet Power*. New York: Morrow, 1985.

———. *Mask of Treachery*. New York: Morrow, 1988.

———. and Tsarev, Oleg. *Deadly Illusions*. New York: Crown, 1993.

Courtney, Anthony. *Sailor in a Russian Frame*. London: Johnson, 1968.

Coward, Noel. *Future Indefinite*. Garden City, N.Y.: Doubleday, 1954.

Cowles, Virginia. *The Rothschilds: A Family Fortune*. London: Weidenfeld & Nicolson, 1979.

Cox, Arthur Macy. *The Myths of National Security: The Peril of Secret Government*. Boston: Beacon Press, 1975.

Craft, James (ed.). *The Soviet Union Today*. Chicago: University of Chicago Press, 1983.

Craig, Gorgon A., and Gilbert, Felix (eds.). *The Diplomats, 1919–1939*. Princeton, N.J.: Princeton University Press, 1953.

———. *The Politics of the Prussian Army, 1640–1945*. Oxford: Oxford University Press, 1955.

Craig, William. *The Fall of Japan*. New York: Dial Press, 1967.

Craigie, Sir Robert. *Behind the Japanese Mask*. London: Hutchinson, 1945.

Crankshaw, Edward. *The Gestapo*. London: Putnam's, 1956.

Crickmore, Paul. *Lockheed SR-71 Blackbird*. London: Osprey, 1986.

Croce, Benedetto. *Croce, the King, and the Allies*. London: Muller, 1957.

Crow, Carl. *400 Million Customers*. New York: Harper, 1937.

———. *Foreign Devils in the Flowery Kingdom*. New York: Harper, 1940.

——— (ed.). *Japan's Dream of World Empire: The Tanaka Memorial*. New York: Harper, 1942.

Crowley, James B. *Japan's Quest for Autonomy: National Security and Foreign Policy, 1930–1938*. Princeton, N.J.: Princeton University Press, 1966.

Crozier, Brian. *Franco*. Boston: Little, Brown, 1967.

Crozier, J. *In the Enemy's Country*. New York: Knopf, 1931.

Cruickshank, Charles. *The Fourth Arm: Psychological Warfare, 1938–1945*. London: Davis-Poynter, 1947.

———. *SOE in Scandinavia*. New York: Oxford, 1986.

Cyprian, T., and Sawicki, J. *Nazi Rule in Poland 1939-1945*. Warsaw: Polonia, 1961.

Cunningham, W. Scott. *Wake Island Command*. Boston: Little, Brown, 1961.

Dahlerus, Birger. *The Last Attempt*. London: Hutchinson, 1948.

Dallin, Alexander. *German Rule in Russia, 1941–1945*. New York: Macmillan, 1957.

———. *The Soviet Union and the United Nations*. New York: Praeger, 1962.

Dallin, David J. *Soviet Espionage*. New Haven, Conn.: Yale University Press, 1955.

———. *The Changing World of Soviet Russia*. New Haven, Conn.: Yale University Press, 1956.

Dalton, Hugh. *The Fateful Years: Memoirs, 1931–1945*. London: Frederick Muller, 1957.

Daniels, Robert V. *Red October: The Bolshevik Revolution of 1917*. New York: Scribner's, 1967.

Dank, Milton. *The French Against the French: Collaboration and Resistance*. London: Cassell, 1978.

Darling, Donald. *Secret Sunday*. London: Kimber, 1975.

———. *Sunday at Large*. London: Kimber, 1977.

Davidson, Basil. *Partisan Picture*. London: Bedford Books, 1946.

Davidson, Eugene. *The Trial of the Germans*. New York: Macmillan, 1966.

Davies, D. W., and Price, W. L. *Security for Computer Networks*. New York: John Wiley, 1984.

Davies, Merton E., and Harris, William R., *RAND's Role in the Evolution of Balloon and Satellite Observation Systems and Related U.S. Space Technology*. Santa Monica, Calif.: RAND, 1988.

Davis, Burke. *Get Yamamoto*. New York: Random House, 1969.

Davis, Forrest, and Lindley, Ernest K. *How War Came: An American White Paper from the Fall of France to Pearl Harbor*. New York: Simon & Schuster, 1942.

Davis, John H. *The Guggenheims*. New York: Morrow, 1970.

Davis, Richard. *The English Rothschilds*. London: Collins, 1968.

Dawidowicz, Lucy S. *The War Against the Jews, 1939–1945*. New York: Holt, Rinehart & Winston, 1975.

Dawisha, Karen. *The Kremlin and the Prague Spring*. Berkeley, Calif.: University of California Press, 1984.

Dawson, Raymond. *The Chinese Chameleon*. London: Oxford University Press, 1967.

Dayan, Moshe. *The Story of My Life*. London: Weidenfeld & Nicolson, 1976.

Deacon, Richard. *A History of the Russian Secret Service*. New York: Taplinger, 1972.

———. *The Chinese Secret Service*. New York: Taplinger, 1974.

———. *The British Connection*. London: Hamish Hamilton, 1979.

———. *A History of the British Secret Service*. London: Granada, 1980.

———. *The Cambridge Apostles*. London: Robert Royce, 1985.

———. *The Israeli Secret Service*. New York: Taplinger, 1985.

———. *The French Secret Service*. London: Grafton, 1990.

Deakin, F. W. D. *The Brutal Friendship*. New Yorker: Harper, 1957.

———. *The Last Days of Mussolini*. New York: Pelican, 1962.

———, and Storry, G. R. *The Case of Richard Sorge*. New York: Harper, 1966.

Dean, J. R. *The Strange Alliance*. New York: Viking, 1947.

Dean, Sir Maurice. *The Royal Air Force in Two World Wars*. London: Cassell, 1979.

Deane, John R. *The Strange Alliance: The Story of Our Efforts at Wartime Cooperation with Russia*. New York: Viking Press, 1947.

Deavours, Cipher A., and Kruh, Louis. *Machine Cryptography and Modern Cryptanalysis*. Dedham, Mass.: Artech House, 1985.

Decker, Malcolm. *Benedict Arnold: Son of the Havens.* New York: Antiquarian Press, Ltd., 1961.

Dedijer, Vladimir. (trans. Alex Brown) *With Tito Through the War: Partisan Diary, 1941–1944.* London: Alexander Hamilton, 1951.

DeForest, Orrin, and Chanoff, David. *Slow Burn: The Rise and Bitter Fall of American Intelligence in Vietnam.* New York: Simon & Schuster, 1990.

De Gaulle, Charles. *War Memoirs.* (3 vols.) New York: Simon & Schuster, 1955–1960.

de Gramont, Sache. *The Secret War.* New York: Putnam's, 1962.

Degras, Jane. *The Communist International: Selected Documents, 1919–1928.* (2 vols.) London: Oxford University Press, 1960.

De Guingand, Francis W. *Operation Victory.* New York: Scribner's, 1947.

Deindorfer, Robert G. (ed.). *The Spies: Great True Stories of Espionage.* New York: Fawcett, 1949.

De Jong, Louis. *The German Fifth Column in the Second World War.* Chicago: University of Chicago Press, 1956.

de Jonge, Alex. *The Life and Times of Gregori Rasputin.* New York: Coward, McCann & Geoghegan, 1982.

Dekel, Efraim. *Shai: The Exploits of Hagana Intelligence.* Tel Aviv: Yoseleff, 1959.

Delaney, Paul. *The Neo-Pagans.* London: Macmillan, 1987.

Delarue, Jacques. (trans. Mervyn Savill.) *The History of the Gestapo.* London: Macdonald, 1964.

Delmer, Sefton. *The Black Boomerang.* London: Secker & Warburg, 1962.

———. *The Counterfeit Spy.* London: Hutchinson, 1971.

Delzell, C. L. *Mussolini's Enemies.* Princeton, N.J.: Princeton University Press, 1961.

Demeter, Karl. (trans. Angus Malcolm.) *The German Officer Corps.* London: Weidenfeld & Nicolson, 1965.

Deniken, Anton I. *The White Army.* London: Jonathan Cape, 1930.

Dennett, Tyler. *Americans in Eastern Asia.* New York: Macmillan, 1922.

Deriabin, Peter, and Gibney, Frank. *The Secret World.* New York: Doubleday, 1959.

———. *Watchdogs of Terror.* New Rochelle, N.Y.: Arlington House, 1972.

Derogy, Jacques, and Carmel, Henri. *The Untold Story of Israel.* New York: Grove, 1979.

Dershowitz, Alan M. *The Best Defense.* New York: Random House, 1982.

de Silva, Peer. *Sub Rosa: The CIA and the Uses of Intelligence.* New York: Times Books, 1978.

De Toledano, Ralph, and Lasky, Victor. *Seeds of Treason.* New York: Funk & Wagnalls, 1950.

———. *Spies, Dupes and Diplomats.* New York: Duell, Sloan & Pearce, 1952.

———. *Lament for a Generation.* New York: Farrar, Strauss & Giroux, 1960.

———. *The Greatest Plot in History.* New York: Duell, Sloan and Pearce, 1963.

Deutscher, Isaac. *The Prophet Armed: Trotsky, 1879–1921.* London: Oxford Unversity Press, 1954.

———. *The Prophet Unarmed.* New York: Oxford University Press, 1959.

de Villemarest, Pierre. *Le Coup d'Etat de Markus Wolf: La guerre secrete des deux Allemagnes.* Paris: Stock, 1991.

Devillers, Philippe. *Histoire du Vietnam.* Paris: Editions du Sueil, 1952.

de Vosjoli, Thyraud. *Lamia.* Boston: Little, Brown, 1970.

Dewar, Hugo. *Assassins at Large.* London: Wingate, 1951.

Dewavrin, André (Col. Passy). *Souvenirs.* (3 vols.) Monte Carlo: R. Solar, 1947–1951.

Diamond, Sandor A. *The Nazi Movement in the United States, 1924–1941.* Ithaca, N.Y.: Cornell University Press, 1974.

Dickson, Paul. *The Electronic Battlefield.* Blooming-ton, Ind.: Indiana University Press, 1976.

Dies, Martin. *Trojan Horse in America.* New York: Dodd, Mead, 1940.

Dille, John. *Spy in the U.S.* New York: Harper, 1961.

Dilkes, David. *The Diaries of Sir Alexander Cadogan.* London: Cassell, 1971.

Dinnerstein, Herbert S. *The Making of a Missile Crisis.* Baltimore: Johns Hopkins University Press, 1976.

Dirksen, Herbert von. *Moscow, Tokyo, London.* London: Hutchinson, 1951.

Dixon, C. Aubrey, and Heilbrunn, Otto. *Communist Guerrilla Warfare.* London: Allen & Unwin, 1954.

Djilas, Milovan. *The New Class.* New York: Praeger, 1957.

———. *Conversations with Stalin.* New York: Harper, 1962.

———. (trans. Michael Petrovich) *Wartime.* London: Secker & Warburg, 1977.

Dmytryshyn, Basil. *USSR: A Concise History.* New York: Scribner's, 1965.

Dobson, Christopher. *Black September: Its Short, Violent History.* New York: Macmillan, 1974.

Dollmann, Eugen. *Call Me Coward.* London: William Kimber, 1956.

Dönitz, Karl. (trans. R. H. Stevens.) *Memoirs: Ten Years and Twenty Days.* London: Weidenfeld & Nicolson, 1959.

Donner, Frank. *The Age of Surveillance.* New York: Knopf, 1980.

Donovan, James B. *Strangers on a Bridge: The Case of Colonel Abel.* New York: Atheneum, 1967.

Donovan, Robert J. *Conflict and Crises: The Presidency of Harry S. Truman, 1945–1948.* New York: W. W. Norton, 1977.

———. *The Tumultuous Years: The Presidency of Harry S. Truman.* New York: W. W. Norton, 1982.

Donovan, William J., and Mowrer, Edgar. *Fifth Column Lessons for America.* Washington, D.C.: American Council on Public Affairs, 1941.

Dorling, H. Taprell. *Ribbons and Medals.* London: Phillip, 1960.

Dormer, Hugh. *Diaries.* London: Jonathan Cape, 1947.

Dornberger, Walter. *V-2.* New York: Viking, 1958.

Dorwart, Jeffrey M. *The Office of Naval Intelligence: The Birth of America's First Intelligence Agency, 1865–1918.* Annapolis, Md.: Naval Institute Press, 1979.

———. *Conflict of Duty: The U.S. Navy's Intelli-gence Dilemma, 1919–1945.* Annapolis, Md.: Naval Institute Press, 1983.

Dourlein, Peter. *Inside North Pole.* London: Kimber, 1953.

Downes, Donald. *The Scarlet Thread: Adventures in Wartime Espionage.* London: Verschoyle, 1953.

Downton, Eric. *War Without End.* Toronto: Stoddart, 1987.

Draper, Theodore. *The Roots of American Communism.* New York: Viking, 1957.

———. *American Communism and Soviet Russia.* New York: Viking, 1960.

Driberg, Tom. *Guy Burgess: A Portrait with Background.* London: Weidenfeld and Nicolson, 1956.

————. *Ruling Passions.* London: Jonathan Cape, 1977.

Du Berrier, Hillaire. *Tragedy of a Betrayed.* Boston: Western Islands, 1965.

Dubois, Josiah E. and Johnson, Edward. *Generals in Gray Suits.* London: Bodley Head, 1953.

Dugan, James, and Stewart, Carroll. *Ploesti.* New York: Random House, 1962.

Duke, Florimond. *Name, Rank, and Serial Number.* New York: Meredith Press, 1969.

Dull, Paul S., and Umemura, Michael Takaaki. *The Tokyo Trials: A Functional Index to the Proceedings of the International Military Tribunal for the Far East.* Ann Arbor, Mich.: University of Michigan Press, 1957.

Dulles, Allen W. *Germany's Underground.* New York: Macmillan, 1947.

————. *The Craft of Intelligence.* New York: Harper, 1963.

————. *The Secret Surrender.* New York: Harper, 1966.

Dulles, Foster Rhea. *China and America: The Story of Their Relations Since 1784.* Princeton, N.J.: Princeton University Press, 1946.

Dunlop, Richard. *Behind Japanese Lines.* Chicago: Rand-McNally, 1979.

————. *Donovan, America's Master Spy.* Chicago: Rand-McNally, 1982.

Dvornik, Francis. *Origins of Intelligence Services.* New Brunswick, N.J.: Rutgers University Press, 1974.

Dyson, John. *Sink the Rainbow.* London: Gollancz, 1986.

Dzhirvelov, Ilya. *Secret Servant: My Life with the KGB and the Soviet Elite.* New York: Harper, 1987.

Dziak, John J. Chekisty: *A History of the KGB.* Lexington, Mass.: Lexington Books, 1988.

Dzyuba, Ivan. *Internationalism or Russification?: A Study in the Soviet Nationalties Problem.* London: Camelot Press, 1968.

Ebon, Martin. *The Soviet Propaganda Machine.* New York: McGraw-Hill, 1987.

Eden, Anthony. *The Reckoning.* London: Cassell, 1965.

Edinger, Lewis. *German Exile Politics.* Berkeley, Calif.: University of California Press, 1956.

Edwards, Bob, and Dunne, Kenneth. *Study of a Master Spy.* London: Housemans, 1961.

Egremont, Max. *Balfour.* London: Collins, 1980.

Ehrlich, Blake. *The Resistance: France, 1940–1945.* Boston: Little, Brown, 1965.

Eichelberger, Robert L. *Our Jungle Road to Tokyo.* New York: Viking, 1950.

Eisenberg, Dennis, and Landau, Eli. *Carlos: Terror International.* London: Corgi Books, 1976.

————, and Dan, Uri. *The Mossad: Israel's Secret Intelligence Service.* New York: Signet, 1978.

Eisenhower, Dwight D. *Crusade in Europe.* Garden City, N.Y.: Doubleday, 1948.

————. *Waging Peace, 1956–1961.* Garden City, N. Y.: Doubleday, 1965.

Ekins, H. R., and Wright, Theon. *China Fights for Her Life.* New York: McGraw-Hill, 1938.

El-Ad, Avri. *Decline of Honour.* Chicago: Henry Regnery, 1976.

Eldridge, Fred. *Wrath in Burma.* New York: Doubleday, 1946.

Elliot-Bateman, Michael. *The Fourth Dimension of Warfare: Intelligence/Subversion/Resistance.* Manchester, Eng.: Manchester University Press, 1970.

Ellis, Kenneth. *The Post Office in the Eighteenth Century: A Study in Administrative History.* London: Oxford University Press, 1958.

Elsbree, Willard S. *Japan's Role in Southeast Asian Nationalist Movements, 1940–1945.* Cambridge, Mass.: Harvard University Press, 1953.

Engle, Anita. *The Nili Spies.* London: Hogarth, 1959.

Enright, D. J. *The World of Dew.* London: Secker & Warburg, 1955.

Epstein, Edward Jay. *Legend: The Secret World of Lee Harvey Oswald.* New York: Reader's Digest Press, 1978.

Erdstein, Erich, and Bean, Barbara. *Inside the Fourth Reich.* New York: St. Martin's, 1977.

Erickson, John. *The Soviet High Command: A Military Political History, 1918-1941.* London: St. Martins, 1962.

Ernst, Morris L. *Report on the American Communist.* New York: Henry Holt, 1952.

Evans, Rowland, and Novak, Robert. *Nixon in the White House.* New York: Random House, 1971.

Ewing, A. W. *The Man of Room 40: The Life of Sir Alfred Ewing.* London: Hutchinson, 1939.

Fainberg, Anthony. *Strengthening IAEA Safeguards: Lessons from Iraq.* Stanford, Calif.: Stanford University Press, 1993.

Fairservis, Walter A. *The Origins of Oriental Civilization.* New York: New American Library, 1959.

Faligot, Roger, and Krop, Pascal. *La Piscine: The French Secret Service Since 1984.* London: Basil Blackwell, 1989.

Falk, Stanley L. *The National Security Structure.* Washington, D.C.: Industrial College of the Armed Forces, 1967.

Falkner, Leonard. *A Spy for Washington.* New York: Reader's Digest Association, 1957.

Fall, Bernard. *The Two Vietnams.* New York: Praeger, 1964.

Farago, Ladislas. *Burn After Reading.* New York: Walker, 1961.

————. *The Broken Seal: The Story of "Operation Magic" and the Pearl Harbor Disaster.* New York: Random House, 1967.

————. *The Game of the Foxes.* New York: David McKay, 1971.

————. *Aftermath.* New York: Simon & Schuster, 1974.

Farran, Roy. *Winged Dagger.* London: Collins, 1948.

————. *Operation Tombola.* London: Collins, 1960.

Fea, Allan. *Secret Chambers and Hiding-Places.* London: S. H. Bousfield, 1901.

Fehrenbach, T. R. *This Kind of War: A Study in Unpreparedness.* New York: Macmillan, 1963.

Feillet, A., and Gourdault, J. (eds.) *Oeuvres.* Paris: Librairie Hachette & Cie, 1876.

Feis, Herbert. *The Road to Pearl Harbor: The Coming of the War Between the United States and Japan.* Princeton, N.J.: Princeton University Press, 1950.

————. *The China Tangle: The American Effort in China from Pearl Harbor to the China Mission.* Princeton, N.J.: Princeton University Press, 1953.

————. *Churchill, Roosevelt and Stalin.* Princeton N.J.: Princeton University Press, 1957.

————. *Japan Subdued: The Atomic Bomb and the End of the War in the Pacific.* Princeton, N. J.: Princeton University Press, 1961.

Felix, Christopher (pseud.). *A Short Course in the Secret War.* New York: Dutton, 1963.

Ferguson, Bernard. *The Watery Maze.* New York: Holt, Rinehart & Winston, 1961.

Fergusson, Thomas G. *British Military Intelligence, 1870–1914: The Development of a Modern Intelligence Organization.* Frederick, Md.: University Publications, 1984.

Ferns, Harry S. *Reading from Left to Right: One Man's Political History.* Toronto: University of Toronto Press, 1983.

Fiedler, Leslie. *An End to Innocence.* Boston: Beacon Press, 1955.

Fielding, Daphne. *The Nearest Way Home.* London: Eyre & Spottiswoode, 1970.

Fielding, Xan. *Hide and Seek.* London: Secker & Warburg, 1954.

————. *The Stronghold, An Account of the Four Seasons in the White Mountains of Crete.* London: Secker & Warburg, 1955.

Finder, Joseph. *Red Carpet.* New York: Holt, Rinehart & Winston, 1983.

Fineberg, S. Andhill. *The Rosenberg Case.* New York: Oceana, 1952.

Finney, Charles G. *The Old China Hands.* New York: Doubleday, 1961.

Firmin, Stanley. *They Came to Spy.* London: Hutchinson, n.d.

Fischer, Louis. *The Life of Lenin.* New York: Harper, 1964.

Fitzgibbon, Constantine. *The Shirt of Nessus.* London: Cassell, 1956.

————. *Secret Intelligence in the 20th Century.* London: Hart-Davis MacGibbon, 1976.

Fleisher, Wilfrid. *Volcanic Isle.* Garden City, N.Y.: Doubleday, Doran & Co., 1941.

Fleming, Peter. *Operation Sea Lion.* New York: Simon & Schuster, 1957.

————. *The Fate of Admiral Kolchak.* London: Rupert Hart-Davis, 1963.

Fletcher, William C. *Nikolai.* New York: Macmillan, 1968.

————. *Religion and Soviet Foreign Policy, 1945–1970.* London: Oxford University Press, 1973.

Flicke, Wilhelm F. *War Secrets in the Ether.* Laguna Park, Calif.: Aegean Park Press, 1977.

Florinsky, Michael T. *The End of the Russian Empire.* New York: Collier Books, 1961.

Foner, Philip S. *The Bolshevik Revolution.* New York: International, 1967.

Fontaine, Roger. *Terrorism: The Cuban Connection.* New York: Crane Russak, 1988.

Foot, Michael R. D. *SOE in France.* London: HMSO, 1966.

————. *Resistance: An Analysis of European Resistance to Nazism, 1940–1945.* London: Eyre Methuen, 1976.

————. *Six Faces of Courage.* London: Eyre Methuen, 1978.

————, and Langley, J. M. *MI19: Escape and Evasion, 1939–1945.* London: Bodley Head, 1979.

Foote, Alexander. *Handbook for Spies.* New York: Museum Press, 1964.

Footman, David. *Civil War in Russia.* London: Faber and Faber, 1961.

Ford, Corey, and McBain, Alistair. *Cloak and Dagger.* New York: Random House, 1945.

————. *A Peculiar Service.* Boston: Little, Brown & Co., 1965.

————. *Donovan of O.S.S.* Boston: Little, Brown, 1970.

Forman, Harrison. *Horizon Hunter.* New York: McBride, 1940.

Fotic, Constantin. *The War We Lost.* New York: Viking, 1948.

Fourcade, Marie-Madeleine. *Noah's Ark.* London: Allen & Unwin, 1973.

Fox, Ralph. *Lenin: A Biography.* New York: Harcourt, Brace, 1934.

Franck, Thomas M., and Weisband, Edward (eds.) *Secrecy and Foreign Policy.* New York: Oxford, 1974.

François-Poncet, André. (trans. Jacques Le Clerq.) *The Fateful Years.* London: Gollancz, 1948.

Franklin, Noble. *Imperial Tragedy.* New York: Coward-McCann, 1961.

Freedman, Lawrence. *U.S. Intelligence and the Soviet Strategic Threat.* Princeton, N.J.: Princeton University Press, 1986.

Freeland, Richard M. *The Truman Doctrine and the Origins of McCarthyism.* New York: Knopf, 1972.

Freeman, Douglas Southall. *George Washington.* New York: Scribner's, 1951.

Frenay, Henri. (trans. Dan Hofstadter.) *The Night Will End: Memoirs of the Resistance.* London: Abelard, 1976.

Friedman, Irving S. *British Relations with China, 1931–1939.* New York: Institute of Pacific Relns., 1940

Friedman, Tuvia. *The Hunter.* London: Gibbs & Phillips, 1961.

Friedman, William F., and Mendelsohn, Charles J. *The Zimmermann Telegram of January 16, 1917, and Its Cryptographic Background.* Washington, D.C.: U. S. War Department, 1938.

————, and Friedman, Elizabeth S. *The Shakespearean Ciphers Examined.* Cambridge, Mass.: Harvard University Press, 1957.

Friedrich, Carl (ed.). *American Experiences in Military Government in World War II.* New York: Rinehart, 1948.

Frillmann, Paul, and Peck, Graham. *China: The Remembered Life.* Boston: Houghton Mifflin, 1968.

Frischauer, Willi. *Himmler.* London: Oldhams, 1953.

Frolick, Josef. *The Frolick Defection.* London: Leo Cooper, 1975.

Fry, Varian. *Surrender on Demand.* New York: Random House, 1945.

Fuchida, Mitsuo, and Okumiya, Masatake. *Midway, The Battle that Doomed Japan: The Japanese Navy's Story.* Annapolis, Md.: U.S. Naval Institute, 1955.

Fuller, J. F. C. *The Last of the Gentleman's Wars.* London: Faber & Faber, 1937.

Fuller, Jean Overton. *Double Webs.* New York: Putnam's, 1958.

————. *The German Penetration of SOE.* London: William Kimber, 1975.

Fülöp-Miller, René. *Rasputin: The Holy Devil.* New York: Garden City, 1928.

Funk, Arthur. *Charles de Gaulle: The Crucial Years.* Norman, Okla.: University of Oklahoma Press, 1959.

————. *The Politics of Torch.* Lawrence, Kan.: University of Kansas, 1976.

Futrell, R. F. *The United States Air Force in Korea.* New York: Arno, 1971.

Furze, G. A. *Information in War.* London: W. Clowes & Sons, 1895.

Fyfe, David Maxwell (ed.). *War Crime Trials.* (9 vols.) London: William Hodge & Co. Ltd., 1948-1952.

Gaddis, John Lewis. *The United States and the Origins of the Cold War.* New York: Columbia University Press, 1972.

Gaevernitz, Gero V. S. *They Almost Killed Hitler.* New York: Macmillan, 1947.

Gage, Jack. Greek Adventure: *Six Months in the Life of a South African Officer in Occupied Greece.* Capetown, South Africa: Unie-Volkspers Beperk, 1950.

Gale, Esson. *Salt for the Dragon.* East Lansing, Mich.: Michigan State College Press, 1953.

Gallegos, Adrian. *From Capri to Oblivion.* London: Hodder & Stoughton, 1959.

Gallery, Daniel V. *Clear the Decks!* New York: Morrow, 1951.

Gallin, Mother Mary Alice. *Ethical and Religious Factors in the German Resistance to Hitler.* Washington, D.C.: Catholic University of America, 1955.

Gamow, George. *My World Line.* New York: Viking, 1970.

Ganier-Raymond. Philippe. *The Tangled Web.* New York: Pantheon, 1968.

Gann, L. H. *A History of Southern Rhodesia.* London: Chatto & Windus, 1965.

Garder, Michel. La Guerre *Secréte des Services Spéciaux Français.* Paris: Plon, 1967.

Gardner, B. Mafeking: *A Victorian Legend.* London: Cassell, 1966.

Gardner, Virginia. *The Rosenberg Story.* New York: Masses and Mainstream, 1954.

Garlinski, Josef. (trans. Paul Stevenson.) *Poland, SOE and the Allies.* London: Allen & Unwin, 1969.

————. *The Enigma War.* New York: Scribner's, 1979.

Garrow, David J. *The FBI and Martin Luther King, Jr.* New York: W. W. Norton, 1981.

Garthoff, R. L. *Soviet Military Doctrine.* Glencoe, Ill.: Free Press, 1953.

————. *The Soviet Image of Future War.* Washington, D.C.: Public Affairs Press, 1959.

Gauche, Maurice. *Le deuxième bureau au travail, 1935–1940.* Paris: Dumont, 1955.

de Gaulle, Charles. (trans. Jonathan Griffin.) *War Memoirs, Volume I, The Call to Honor, 1940–1942.* London: Collins, 1955.

————. (trans. Joyce Murchie and Hamish Erskine.) *Memoirs, Volume II, Unity, 1942–1944.* London: Weidenfeld & Nicolson, 1959.

Gayne, Mark J. *Japan Diary.* New York: William Sloane, 1948.

Gehlen, Reinhard. *The Service: The Memoirs of Reinhard Gehlen.* New York: World, 1972.

Gelb, Norman. *Enemy in the Shadows: The World of Spies and Spying.* New York: Hippocrene, 1976.

George, Willis. *Surreptitious Entry.* New York: Appleton-Century, 1946.

Gerson, Leonard D. *The Secret Police in Lenin's Russia.* Philadelphia: Temple University Press, 1976.

Gilber, Felix. *Hitler Directs His War.* New York: Oxford, 1950.

Gilbert, G. M. *Nuremberg Diary.* New York: New American Library, 1947.

————. *The Psychology of Dictatorship.* New York: Ronald Press, 1950.

Gilbert, Martin. *The Arab-Israeli Conflict.* London: Weidenfeld & Nicolson, 1974.

Gilchrist, Andrew. *Bangkok Top Secret.* London: Hutchinson, 1970.

Gill, William J. *The Ordeal of Otto Otepka.* New Rochelle, N.Y.: Arlington House, 1969.

Gillman, Peter, and Gillman, Leni. *Collar the Lot.* London: Quartet, 1980.

Ginzburg, Evegenia Semyonovna. *Into the Whirlwind.* New York: Harcourt, 1967.

Giradet, Edward R. *Afghanistan: The Soviet War.* New York: St. Martin's, 1985.

Gisevius, Hans Bernd. *To the Bitter End.* Boston: Riverside Press, 1947.

————. *Wo ist Nebe?* Zurich: Droemersche, 1966.

Giskes, H. J. *London Calling North Pole.* London: William Kimber, 1953.

Gitlow, Benjamin. *I Confess.* New York: Dutton, 1940.

Glantz, David. *Soviet Military Intelligence in War.* London: Cassell, 1990.

Glees, Anthony. T*he Secrets of the Service: British Intelligence and Communist Subversion, 1939–1951.* London: Jonathan Cape, 1987.

Glen, Alexander. *Footholds Against a Whirlwind.* London: Hutchinson, 1975.

Glines, Carroll V. *The Doolittle Raid.* New York: Orion, 1988.

Glyden, Yves. *The Contributions of the Cryptographic Bureaus in the World War.* Laguna Hills, Calif.: Aegean Park Press, 1978.

Godley, A. D., trans. *Herodotus.* London: William Heinemann Ltd., 1963.

Goebbels, Josef. *Diaries, 1939–41.* London: André Deutsch, 1982.

Golan, Aviezer, and Pinkas, Danny. *Shula: Code Name the Pearl.* New York: Delacorte, 1980.

Goldsmith, John. *Accidental Agent.* London: Leo Cooper, 1971.

Goldstein, Alvin H. *The Unquiet Death of Julius and Ethel Rosenberg.* New York: Lawrence Hill, 1975.

Gollomb, Joseph. *Armies of Spies.* New York: Macmillan, 1939.

Golytsin, Anatoli. *New Lies for Old.* London: Bodley Head, 1984.

Goodman, Walter. *The Committee.* New York: Knopf, 1978.

Gorbatov, A. V. (trans. Gordon Clough and Anthony Cash.) *Years Off My Life.* London: Constable, 1964.

Gordon, Harold J. *The Reichswehr and the German Republic.* London: OUP, 1947.

Gordon-Smith, Alan. *The Babington Plot.* London: Macmillan, 1936.

Görlitz, Walter, and Quint, Herbert A. *Adolf Hitler.* Stuttgart: Steingruben, 1952.

————. *History of the German General Staff, 1657–1945.* New York: Praeger, 1957.

————. *Die Waffen-SS.* Berlin: Arani, 1960.

Gorkin, Julian. *L'Assassinat de Trotsky.* Paris: Julliard, 1970.

Gould, Randall. *China in the Sun.* New York: Doubleday, 1946.

Goulden, Joseph C. The *Death Merchant: The Rise and Fall of Edwin P. Newman.* New York: Simon & Schuster, 1984.

Gouzenko, Igor. *The Iron Curtain.* New York: E.P. Dutton & Co., 1948.

————. *This Was My Choice.* Montreal: Palm, 1968.

Grabo, Carl. *Crows Are Black Everywhere.* New York: Putnam's, 1945.

Graham, Stephen. *Alexander of Yugoslavia.* New Haven, Conn.: Yale University Press, 1939.

Graham-Murray, J. *The Sword and the Umbrella.* New York: Times Press, 1965.

Gramont, Sacho de. *The Secret War.* New York: Putnam's, 1962.

Granatstein, J. L. *A Man of Influence.* London: Deneau, 1981.

————, and Stafford, David. *Spy Wars: Espionage and Canada from Gouzenko to Glasnost.* Toronto: Key Porter, 1990.

Graves, William S. *America's Siberian Adventure, 1918–1920.* New York: Jonathan Cape and Harrison Smith, 1931.

Gregory, J. F. (comp.). *Telegraphic Code to Insure Secrecy in the Transmission of Telegrams.* Washington, D.C.: Government Printing Office, 1886.

Grew, Joseph C. *Ten Years in Japan.* New York: Simon & Schuster, 1944.

—————. *Turbulent Era: A Diplomatic Record of Forty Years, 1904–1945.* (2 vols.) Boston: Houghton Mifflin, 1952.

Griffis, Stanton. *Lying in State.* Garden City, N.Y.: Doubleday, 1957.

Griffith, Robert. *The Politics of Fear: Joseph McCarthy and the Senate.* Lexington, Ky.: University of Kentucky Press, 1970.

Griffiths, Richard. *Fellow Travellers of the Right: British Enthusiasts for Nazi Germany, 1933–1939.* London: Constable, 1980.

Gross, Babette. (trans. Marian Jackson.) *Willi Müzzenberg: A Political Biography.* East Lansing, Mich.: Michigan State University Press, 1974.

Groussard, Serge. *The Blood of Israel.* New York: Morrow, 1973.

Groves, Leslie M. *Now It Can Be Told: The Story of the Manhattan Project.* New York: Harper, 1962.

Guderian, Heinz. (trans. Constantine Fitzgibbon.) *Panzer Leader.* London: Michael Joseph, 1952.

Gudgin, Peter. *Military Intelligence: The British Story.* London: Arms and Armour, 1989.

Guérin, Alain, and Chatel, Nicole. *Comrade Sorge.* Paris: Julliard, 1965.

Gulbenkian, N. S. *Pantaraxia.* London: Hutchinson, 1971.

Gunther, John. *Roosevelt in Retrospect.* New York: Harper, 1950.

—————. *Riddle of MacArthur: Japan, Korea and the Far East.* New York: Harper, 1951.

Guthrie, Duncan. *Jungle Diary.* London: Macmillan, 1946.

Guttmann, Allen. *The Wound in the Heart.* New York: Free Press, 1962.

Haas, Albert. *The Doctor and the Damned.* New York: St. Martin's, 1984.

Habas, Bracha. *The Gate Breakers.* New York: Thomas Yoseloff, 1963.

Hadawi, Sami. *Bitter Harvest: Palestine Between 1914–1979.* Delmar, N. Y.: Caravan, 1979.

Hagen, Louis. *The Secret War for Europe.* New York: Stein and Day, 1969.

Hahn, Emily. *China to Me.* Garden City, N.Y.: Doubleday, 1944.

Halasz, Nicholas. *Captain Dreyfus.* New York: Simon & Schuster, 1955.

Haldane, Charlotte. *The Truth Will Out.* London: Weidenfeld & Nicolson, 1949.

Haldeman, H. R. *The Ends of Power.* New York: Times Books, 1978.

Hall, H. Duncan. *North American Supply.* London: Her Majesty's Stationery Office, 1955.

Hall, Richard. *The Rhodes Scholar Spy.* New York: Random House, 1991.

Hall, Roger. *You're Stepping on My Cloak and Dagger.* New York: W. W. Norton, 1957.

Halle, Louis. *The Cold War as History.* London: Chatto & Windus, 1967.

Halliday, E. M. *The Ignorant Armies.* New York: Harper, 1960.

Hamilton-Hill, Donald. *SOE Assignment.* London: William Kimber, 1973.

Hamm, Harry. *Albania: China's Beachhead in Europe.* New York: Praeger, 1963.

Hammer, Armand. *Hammer.* New York: Putnam's, 1987.

Hammer, Ellen. *The Struggle for Indochina.* Stanford, Calif.: Stanford University Press, 1953.

Hamming, Richard W. *Coding and Information Theory.* New York: Prentice-Hall, 1986.

Hamson, Denys. *We Fell Among Greeks.* London: Jonathan Cape, 1946.

Hanayama, Shinsho. *The Way of Deliverance: Three Years with the Condemned Japanese War Criminals.* New York: Scribner's, 1950.

Hanson, Philip. *Soviet Industrial Espionage.* London: Royal Institute of International Affairs, 1987.

Hansson, Per. (Trans. Maurice Michael.) *The Greatest Gamble.* London: Allen & Unwin, 1967.

Harcave, Sidney. *First Blood: The Russian Revolution of 1905.* New York: Macmillan, 1964.

Hardy, Jonathan Gathorne. *The Public School Phenomenon.* London: Hodder & Stoughton, 1977.

Harel, Isser. *The House on Garibaldi Street.* London: André Deutsch, 1975.

Hargreaves, Reginald. *Red Sun Rising: The Siege of Port Arthur.* Philadelphia: J. B. Lippincott, 1962.

Harkabi, Yehoshafat. *Fatah in the Arab Strategy.* Tel Aviv: Marachot Publishers, 1969.

—————. *The Palestinians from Quiescence to Awakening.* Jerusalem: Magnes Press, 1979.

Harney, Malachi L. and Cross, John C. *The Informer in Law Enforcement.* Springfield, Ill.: Charles C. Thomas, 1960.

Harriman, W. Averell, and Abel, Elie. *Special Envoy to Churchill and Stalin.* New York: Random House, 1975.

Harris, Kenneth. *Attlee.* London: Weidenfeld & Nicolson, 1962.

Harrison, Gordon A. *Cross-Channel Attack.* Washington, D.C.: Government Printing Office, 1951.

Harrison, J. P. *The Long March to Power.* London: Macmillan, 1973.

Harrison, Tom. *World Within: A Borneo Story.* London: Cresset Press, 1959.

Hart, Alan. *Arafat: Terrorist or Peacemaker?* London: Sidgwick & Jackson, 1984.

Hart, B. H. Liddell. *The German Generals Talk.* New York: Morrow, 1948.

————— (ed.). *The Red Army.* New York: Harcourt, Brace, 1956.

Hart, Walter Louis D'Arcy, and Frost, Oliver Harry. *The Man Who Never Was.* Philadelphia: J. B. Lippincott Company, 1953.

Harwell, Jock. *Spies and Spymasters.* London: Thames & Hudson, 1977.

Hassell, Ulrich von. *The Von Hassell Diaries.* New York: Doubleday, 1947.

Haswell, Jock. *British Military Intelligence.* London: Weidenfeld & Nicolson, 1973.

Hauge, E. O. (trans. Malcolm Munthe.) *Salt-Water Thief.* London: Duckworth, 1958.

Haukelid, Knut. (trans. F. H. Lyon.) *Skis Against the Atom.* London: William Kimber, 1954.

Hayden, Sterling. *Wanderer.* New York: Knopf, 1963.

Hayes, Carlton. *Wartime Mission in Spain.* New York: Macmillan, 1945.

Hayes, Paul M. *Quisling.* London: David & Charles, 1971.

Headrick, Daniel R. *The Invisible Weapon: Telecommunications and International Politics, 1851–1945.* New York: Oxford, 1991.

Heaps, Leo. *Hugh Hambleton, Spy*. London: Methuen, 1983.

Heckscher, August. *A Pattern of Politics*. New York: Reynal, 1947.

Heckstall-Smith, Anthony. *Sacred Cowes*. London: Anthony Blond, 1965.

Heiber, Helmut. *Adolf Hitler*. Berlin: Colloquium, 1960.

Heikal, Mohamed. *The Road to Ramadan*. London: Collins, 1975.

Hellman, Geoffrey. *How to Disappear for an Hour*. New York: Dodd, Mead, 1947.

Henderson, David. *Field Intelligence: Its Principles and Practice*. London: HMSO, 1904.

Hendrick, Burton J. *The Age of Big Business*. New Haven, Conn.: Yale University Press, 1921.

————. *The Life and Letters of Walter H. Page*. Garden City, N.Y.: Doubleday, 1925.

Herken, Gregg. *The Winning Weapon: The Atomic Bomb in the Cold War, 1945–1950*. New York: Knopf, 1980.

Hersh, Seymour M. *The Price of Power: Kissinger in the Nixon White House*. New York: Summit Books, 1983.

————. *"The Target Is Destroyed": What Really Happened to Flight 007 and What America Knew About It*. New York: Random House, 1986.

————. *The Samson Option: Israel's Nuclear Threat and American Foreign Policy*. New York: Random House, 1991.

Herzog, Chaim. *The War of Atonement*. London: Weidenfeld & Nicolson, 1975.

Herzog, Wilhelm. *From Dreyfus to Pétain*. New York: Creative Age, 1947.

Heslop, Richard. *Xavier*. London: Rupert Hart-Davis, 1970.

Hewins, Ralph. *Quisling: Prophet Without Honour*. London: W. H. Allen, 1965.

Hewitt, Malyn. *Portugal in Africa*. New York: Hurst, 1981.

Heymont, Irving. *Combat Intelligence in Modern Warfare*. Harrisburg: Stackpole, 1960.

Higgins, Trumbull. *Korea and the Fall of MacArthur*. London: Oxford University Press, 1960.

Hilburg, Raul, *The Destruction of the European Jews*. Chicago: Quadrangle Books, 1961.

Hill, Christopher. *Lenin and the Russian Revolution*. London: English Universities Press, 1957.

Hill, Elizabeth, and Mudie, Doris (eds.). *The Letters of Lenin*. New York: Harcourt, Brace, 1937.

Hillcourt, W. *Baden-Powell: The Two Lives of a Hero*. London: Heinemann, 1964.

Hilsman, Roger. *To Move a Nation*. Garden City, N.Y.: Doubleday, 1967.

Hinchley, Vernon. *Spies Who Never Were*. New York: Dodd, Mead, 1965.

Hingley, Ronald. *The Russian Secret Police: Muscovite, Imperial Russian and Soviet Political Security Operations, 1556–1970*. New York: Simon & Schuster, 1970.

Hinsley, F. H. British Intelligence in the Second World War. London: HMSO, 1981.

————, and Strip, Alan (eds.). *Codebreakers: The Inside Story of Bletchley Park*. New York: Oxford, 1993.

Hirsch, Richard. *The Soviet Spies*. New York: Duell, Sloan and Pearce, 1974.

Hirszowicz, Lukasz. *The Third Reich and the Arab East*. London: Routledge & Kegan Paul, 1966.

Hiss, Alger. *In the Court of Public Opinion*. New York: Knopf, 1957.

Hitchcock, Walter T. (ed.). *The Intelligence Revolu-tion: A Historical Perspective*. Washington, D.C.: Office of Air Force History, 1991.

Hitler, Adolf. (trans. Ralph Manheim.) *Mein Kampf*. Boston: Houghton Mifflin, 1943.

————. *Hitler's Secret Conversations*. New York: Farrar, Straus & Young, 1953.

Hoare, Geoffrey. *The Missing Macleans*. London: Cassell, 1955.

Hoare, Samuel. *The Fourth Seal*. London: Heine-mann, 1930.

————. *Complacent Dictator*. New York: Knopf, 1947.

Hobson, J. A. *Imperialism: A Study*. London: Allen and Unwin, 1948.

Hodges, Andrew. *Alan Turing: An Enigma*. New York: Simon & Schuster, 1983.

Hodgson, Godfrey. *America in Our Times*. Garden City, N.Y.:   Doubleday, 1976.

Hoegner, Wilhelm. *Der Schwierige Aussenseiter*. Munich: Isar Verlag, 1959.

Hoehling, H. A. *Edith Cavell*. London: Cassell, 1958.

Hoettl, Wilhelm. *The Secret Front: The Story of Nazi Political Espionage*. New York: Praeger, 1954.

Hoffman, Robert L. *More Than A Trial: The Struggle over Captain Dreyfus*. New York: The Free Press, 1980.

Hoffmann, Max von. *War Diaries and Other Papers*. (trans. Eric Sutton) London: Martin Secker, 1929.

————. *The War of Lost Opportunities*. London: Kegan Paul, Trench, Trubner & Co., 1924.

Höhne, Heinz. (trans. Richard Barry.) *The Order of the Death's Head: The Story of Hitler's SS*. New York: Coward-McCann, 1970.

————. and Zolling, Hermann. *The General Was a Spy: The Truth About General Gehlen and His Spy Network*. New York: Coward, McCann & Geohegan, 1972.

————. *Canaris: Hitler's Master Spy*. Garden City, N.Y.: Doubleday, 1979.

Holcombe, Arthur N. T*he Spirit of the Chinese Revolution*. New York: Knopf, 1930.

Hollins, Christopher. *The American Heresy*. New York: Sheed & Ward, 1927.

Holmes, W. J. *Double-Edged Secrets: U.S. Naval Intelli-gence Operations in the Pacific During World War II*. Annapolis, Md.: Naval Institute Press, 1979.

Holtom, D. C. *Modern Japan and Shinto Nationalism*. Chicago: University of Chicago Press, 1947.

Hood, William. *Mole*. London: Weidenfeld and Nicolson, 1982.

Hoover, Calvin. *Memoirs of Capitalism, Communism and Nazism*. Durham, N.C.: Duke University Press, 1965.

Hoover, J. Edgar (written by Fern Stukenbroeker.) *Masters of Deceit*. New York: Henry Holt, 1958.

Horan, James D., and Swiggett, Howard. *The Pinkerton Story*. New York: Putnam's, 1951.

————. *Desperate Women*. New York: Putnam's, 1952.

————. *Confederate Agent*. New York: Crown, 1954.

————. *The Pinkertons: The Detective Dynasty That Made History*. New York: Crown, 1967.

Horthy, Nicholas von. *Ein Leben für Ungarn*. Bonn: Athenaum, 1953.

Hougan, Jim. *Spooks: The Haunting of America—The Private Use of Secret Agents*. New York: Morrow, 1978.

Houghton, Harry. *Operation Portland*. London: Hart-Davis, 1972.

Howard, Michael. *British Intelligence in the Second World War*. London: Her Majesty's Stationery Office, 1990,

Howarth, David. *The Shetland Bus.* London: Nelson, 1951.
————. *We Die Alone.* London: Collins, 1955.
————. *D Day: The Sixth of June, 1944.* New York: McGraw-Hill, 1959.
Howarth, Patrick (ed.). *Special Operations.* London: Routledge & Kegan Paul, 1955.
————. *Undercover: The Men and Women of the Special Operations Executive.* London: Rout-ledge & Kegan Paul, 1980.
————. *Intelligence Chief Extraordinary.* London: The Bodley Head, 1986.
Howarth, T. E. B. *Cambridge Between Two Wars.* London: Collins, 1978.
Howe, Ellic. *The Black Game.* London: Michael Joseph, 1982.
Howe, Irving, and Coser, Lewis. *The American Communist Party: A Critical History.* New York: Praeger, 1962.
Howe, Russell W. *Mata Hari.* New York: Dodd, Mead, 1986.
Howeth, Capt. L. S. *History of Communications-Electronics in the United States Navy.* Washington, D.C.: Government Printing Office, 1963.
Hoy, Hugh Cleland. *40 Q.B., or How the War Was Won.* London: Hutchinson, 1932.
Hsiung, S. I. *The Life of Chiang Kai-shek.* London: Davies, 1948.
Hsu Shu-hsi. *The War Conduct of the Japanese.* Hangkow: Kelly and Walsh, 1938.
Hudson, G. F. *The Far East in World Politics.* London: Oxford, 1937.
Hughes, H. Stuart. *The United States and Italy.* Cambridge, Mass.: Harvard University Press, 1953.
Hughes, Richard. *Foreign Devil: Thirty Years of Reporting from the Far East.* London: Century, 1984.
Hughes, Quentin. *Britain in the Mediterranean and the Defense of Her Naval Stations.* Liverpool: Penpaled Books, 1981.
Hughes, Thomas B. *American Genesis: A Century of Invention and Technological Enthusiasm, 1870–1970.* New York: Penguin, 1990.
Hull, Cordell. *The Memoirs of Cordell Hull.* New York: Macmillan, 1950.
Hunt, E. Howard. *Give Us This Day.* New Rochelle, N.Y.: Arlington House, 1973.
————. *Undercover.* New York: Putnam's, 1974.
Hunt, Linda. *Secret Agenda: The United States Government, Nazi Scientists, and Project Paperclip, 1945 to 1990.* New York: St. Martin's Press, 1991.
Huot, Louis. *Guns for Tito.* New York: L. B. Fischer, 1945.
Hurt, Henry. *Shadrin: The Spy Who Never Came Back.* New York: McGraw-Hill, 1981.
Hutton, Bernard. *School for Spies.* London: Neville Spearman, 1961.
Hutton, Bernard. *Commander Crabb Is Alive.* London: Tandem, 1968.
Hyde, Douglas. *I Believed.* London: Heinemann, 1951.
Hyde, H. Montgomery. *Room 3603.* New York: Farrar, Straus, 1962.
————. *The Quiet Canadian: The Secret Service Story of Sir William Stephenson.* London: Hamish Hamilton, 1964.
————. *Cynthia: The Spy Who Changed the Course of the War.* London: Hamish Hamilton, 1966.
————. *The Atom Bomb Spies.* New York: Atheneum, 1980.

————. *Secret Intelligence Agent.* New York: St. Martin's, 1982.
Hymoff, Edward. *The OSS in World War II.* New York: Ballantine, 1972.
Hynd, Alan. *Passport to Treason: The Inside Story of Spies in America.* New York: McBride, 1943.
Hynes, Stanley. *The Auden Generation.* Princeton, N.J.: Princeton University Press, 1982.

Icardi, Aldo. *American Master Spy.* New York: University Books, 1956.
Ind, Allison. *Short History of Espionage.* New York: McKay, 1963.
Iklé, Frank William. *German-Japanese Relations, 1936-1940.* New York: Bookman Associates, 1956.
Immerman, Richard H. *Ike's Spies.* Garden City, N.Y.: Doubleday, 1981.
Ind, Allison. *Allied Intelligence Bureau.* New York: David McKay, 1958.
————. *A Short History of Espionage.* New York: McKay, 1963.
————. *A History of Modern Espionage.* London: Hodder & Stoughton, 1965.
Infield, Glenn B. *Skorzeny.* New York: St. Martin's, 1981.
Ingersoll, Ralph. *Top Secret.* New York: Harcourt, Brace, 1946.
Inglis, Brian. *Roger Casement.* London: Hodder & Stoughton, 1973.
International Conference on the History of the Resistance. *European Resistance Movements, 1939–1945.* London: Pergammon, 1964.
Irving, David. *The Mare's Nest.* London: William Kimber, 1964.
————— (ed.). *Breach of Security: The German Secret Intelligence File on Events Leading to the Second World War.* London: Kimber, 1968.
Irwin, Anthony. *Burmese Outpost.* London: Collins, 1945.
Iriye, Akira. *Across the Pacific.* New York: Harcourt, 1967.
Isaacs, Harold R. *The Tragedy of the Chinese Revolution.* Stanford, Calif.: Stanford University Press, 1938.
Israel, Fred (ed.). *The War Diary of Breckinridge Long.* Lincoln, Neb.: University of Nebraska Press, 1966.
Isserman, Maurice. *Which Side Were You On? The American Communist Party During the Second World War.* Middletown, Conn.: Wesleyan University Press, 1982.

Jaffe, Philip J. *The Rise and Fall of American Communism.* New York: Horizon, 1975.
James, David H. *The Rise and Fall of the Japanese Empire.* London: Allen & Unwin, 1951.
James, Robert Rhodes. *Memoirs of a Conservative.* London: Macmillan, 1970.
James, Sir William. *The Sky Was Always Blue.* London: Methuen, 1951.
————. *The Eyes of the Navy: A Biographical Study of Admiral Sir William Hall.* London: Metheun, 1956.
Janin, Pierre T. C. *Ma Mission en Sibérie, 1918-1920.* Paris: Pavot, 1933.
Jansen, Marius B. *The Japanese and Sun Yat-sen.* Cambridge, Mass.: Harvard University Press, 1954.
Jardine, Douglas. *The Mad Mullah of Somaliland.* London: Herbert Jenkins, 1923.
Jaworski, Leon. *The Right and the Power.* New York: Reader's Digest Press, 1977.

Jeantet, Gabriel. *Pétain contre Hitler.* Paris: Le Table Ronde, 1966.

Jedlicka, Ludwig. *Der 20 Juli 1944 in Osterreich.* Vienna: Verlag Herold, 1965.

Jefferys-Jones, Rhodi. *American Espionage.* New York: The Free Press, 1977.

Jensen, Merrill. *The Founding of a Nation: A History of the American Revolution, 1763–1776.* New York: Oxford, 1968.

Jewish Black Book Committee (compilers). *The Black Book: The Nazi Crimes Against the Jewish People.* New York: Duell, Sloan & Pearce, 1946.

Joesten, Joachim. *Stalwart Sweden.* Garden City, N.Y.: Doubleday and Doran, 1943.

John, Otto. *Twice Through the Lines.* New York: Harper, 1972.

Johns, Philip. *With Two Cloaks.* London: Kimber, 1979.

Johnson, Brian. *The Secret War.* New York: Methuen, 1978.

Johnson, Chalmers. *An Instance of Treason: Ozaki Hotsumi and the Sorge Spy Ring.* Stanford, Calif.: Stanford University Press, 1964.

Johnson, Haynes. *The Bay of Pigs.* New York: W. W. Norton, 1964.

Johnson, Nicholas L. *Soviet Military Strategy in Space.* London: Jane's, 1987.

———. *The Soviet Year in Space, 1989.* Colorado Springs: Teledyne Brown Engineering, 1990.

Johnson, R. W. *Shoot-Down: Flight 007 and the American Connection.* New York: Viking, 1986.

Johnson, Stowers. *Agents Extraordinary.* London: Robert Hale, 1975.

Johnston, Reginald F. *Twilight in the Forbidden City.* London: Gollancz, 1934.

Jolly, Cyril. *The Vengeance of Private Pooley.* London: Heinemann, 1956.

Jones, F. C. *Japan's New Order in East Asia: Its Rise and Fall, 1937–1945.* London: Oxford University Press, 1954.

Jones, Reginald V. *The Wizard War: British Scientific Intelligence in the Second World War.* New York: Coward, McCann & Geohegan, 1978.

———. *Reflections on Intelligence.* London: Mandarin, 1990.

Jones, William. *Twelve Months with Tito's Partisans.* London: Bedford, 1946.

Jordan, William. *Conquest without Victory.* London: Hodder & Stoughton, 1969.

Joshua, Wynfred. *Soviet Penetration into the Middle East.* New York: National Strategy Information Center, 1970.

Jowitt, William Allen. *The Strange Case of Alger Hiss.* Garden City, N.Y.: Doubleday, 1953.

Judd, Sylvester. *History of Hadley.* Northampton, Mass.: Metcalf & Co., 1863.

Jungk, Robert. *Brighter Than a Thousand Suns.* New York: Harcourt Brace Jovanovich, 1958.

Kahn, Albert E. *Sabotage! The Secret War Against America.* New York: Harper, 1942.

———., and Sayers, Michael. *The Great Conspiracy: The Secret War Against Soviet Russia.* Boston: Little, Brown, 1946.

Kahn, David. *The Code Breakers: The Story of Secret Writing.* New York: Macmillan, 1967.

———. *Hitler's Spies: German Military Intelligence in World War II.* New York: Macmillan, 1978.

———. *Kahn on Codes: Secrets of the New Cryptology.* New York: Macmillan, 1983.

———. *Seizing the Enigma: The Race to Break the German U-Boat Codes, 1939–1943.* Boston: Houghton Mifflin, 1991.

Kahn, E. J., Jr. *The China Hands.* New York: Viking, 1975.

Kallay, Miklos. *Hungarian Premier.* New York: Columbia University Press, 1954.

Kalugin, Oleg. *The First Directorate: My 32 Years in Intelligence and Espionage Against the West.* New York: St. Martin's, 1994.

Kaplan, Fred. *The Wizards of Armageddon.* New York: Simon & Schuster, 1983.

Karpovich, Michael T. *Imperial Russia, 1801–1917.* New York: Holt, 1932.

Karski, Jan. *Story of a Secret State.* London: Hodder & Stoughton, 1945.

Kase, Toshikazu. *Journey to the Missouri.* New Haven, Conn.: Yale University Press, 1952.

Kates, George N. *The Years That Were Fat: Peking, 1933–1940.* New York: Harper, 1952.

Katz, Barry M. *Foreign Intelligence: Research and Analysis of the Office of Strategic Services, 1942–1945.* Cambridge, Mass.: Harvard University Press, 1989.

Katz, Samuel M. *Soldier Spies: Israeli Military Intelligence.* Novato, Calif.: Presidio, 1992.

Kaznacheev, Aleksandr. *Inside a Soviet Embassy.* Philadelphia: Lippincott, 1962.

Keats, John. *They Fought Alone.* Philadelphia: Lippincott, 1963.

Kedward, H. Roderick. *The Dreyfus Affair.* New York: Harper, 1965.

Keegan, John. *Six Armies in Normandy.* New York: Viking, 1982.

Kemp, Peter. *Mine Were of Trouble.* London: Cassell, 1957.

———. *No Colours or Crest.* London: Cassell, 1958.

———. *Alms for Oblivion.* London: Cassell, 1961.

Kempner, Robert M. W. *Eichmann und Komplizen.* Zurich: Europa Verlag, 1961.

———. *SS im Kreuzvehör.* Munich: Rütten & Loening, 1964.

Kempton, Murray. *Part of Our Time: Some Momuments and Ruins of the Thirties.* New York: Simon & Schuster, 1955.

Kendall, W. *The Revolutionary Movement in Britain, 1900–1921.* London: Weidenfeld & Nicolson, 1964.

Kennan, George F. *Russia Leaves the War.* Princeton, N.J.: Princeton University Press, 1956.

———. *Russia and the West under Lenin and Stalin.* Boston: Little, Brown, 1961.

Kennedy, Malcolm. *Some Aspects of Japan and Her Defense Forces.* Kobe, Japan: J. L. Thompson, 1928.

———. *The Problem of Japan.* London: Nesbit & Co., 1935.

———. *A History of Japan.* London: Weidenfeld & Nicolson, 1963.

Kennedy, Robert F. *Thirteen Days.* New York: W. W. Norton, 1969.

Kennett, Lee. *The First Air War, 1914–1918.* New York: Free Press, 1991.

Kent, Sherman. *Strategic Intelligence for American World Policy.* Princeton, N.J.: Princeton University Press, 1951.

Kerensky, Alexander F. *The Catastrophe.* New York: Appleton, 1927.

———. *The Crucifixion of Liberty.* New York: John Day, 1934.

———. *Russia and History's Turning Point.* New York: Duell, Sloan and Pearce, 1965.

Kerry, Earl of. *The Secret of the Coup D'Etat: Unpublished Correspondence of Prince Louis Napoleon, MM. De Morny, De Flahault, and Others, 1848 to 1852.* New York: Putnam's, 1924.

Kersaudy, Francois. *Churchill and De Gaulle.* New York: Atheneum, 1982.

Kersten, Felix. *The Kersten Memoirs.* New York: Macmillan, 1957.

Kerzhentsev, P. *Life of Lenin.* New York: International Publishers, 1939.

Kessel, Joseph. (trans. Helen Weaver, Leo Raditsa.) *The Man with the Miraculous Hands.* New York: Farrar, Straus & Cudahy, 1961.

Kessler, Ronald. *Moscow Station: How the KGB Penetrated the American Embassy.* New York: Scribner's, 1989.

————. *The Spy in the Russian Club.* New York: Scribner's, 1990.

————. *Escape from the CIA.* New York: Pocket Books, 1991.

Khokhlov, Nikolai. (trans. Emily Kingsbery.) *In the Name of Conscience.* New York: McKay, 1959.

Khrushchev, Nikita. (trans. Strove Talbott.) *Khrushchev Remembers.* Boston: Little, Brown, 1970.

Kimmche, Jon and David. *The Secret Roads.* London: Secker & Warburg, 1955.

————. *Spying for Peace.* London: Weidenfeld & Nicolson, 1961.

Kimmel, Husband E. *Admiral Kimmel's Story.* Chicago: Regnery, 1955.

King, Michael. T*he Death of the Rainbow Warrior.* London: Penguin, 1986.

Kipling, Rudyard. *Kim.* London: Macmillan, 1901.

Kirkpatrick, Lyman B. *The Real CIA.* New York: Macmillan, 1968.

Kissinger, Henry. *Years Of Upheaval.* Boston: Little, Brown, 1982.

Klass, Philip. *Secret Sentries in Space.* New York: Random House, 1971.

Klehr, Harvey, and Radosh, Ronald. *Amerasia.* New York: W. W. Norton, 1988.

Klein, Alexander. *The Counterfeit Traitor.* New York: Holt, Rinehart, 1958.

Klyuchevsky, Vassily O. *Peter the Great.* New York: Dutton, 1963.

Knebel, Fletcher, and Bailey, Charles W. II. *No High Ground.* New York: Harper, 1960.

Knight, Frida. *The French Resistance 1940–1944.* London: Lawrence & Wisehart, 1975.

Knightley, Phillip. *The Second Oldest Profession: Spies and Spying in the Twentieth Century.* New York: W. W. Norton, 1986.

Koch, Edward. *Cryptography and Cipher Writing.* Belleville, Ill.: Buechler Publishing Co., 1936.

Koen, Ross Y. *The China Lobby in American Politics.* New York: Macmillan, 1960.

Kogan, Norman. *Italy and the Allies.* Cambridge, Mass.: Harvard University Press, 1956.

Kogon, Eugun. *The Theory and Practice of Hell.* London: Secker & Warburg, 1951.

Kohl, Robert L. *RKFVD: German Resettlement and Population Policy. 1939–1945.* Cambridge, Mass.: Harvard University Press, 1957.

Kolko, Gabriel. *The Politics of War.* New York: Random House, 1968.

Koop, Theodore F. *Weapon of Silence.* Chicago: University of Chicago Press, 1946.

Kordt, Erich. *Nicht aus den Akten.* Stuttgart: Deutsch Verlag, 1950.

Kossmann, E. H. *The Low Countries, 1780–1940.* London: Oxford University Press, 1978.

Kovpak, G. A. (trans. Ernst and Mira Lesser.) *Our Partisan Course.* London: Hutchinson, 1947.

Kramarz, Joachim. (trans. R. H. Barry.) *Stauffenberg: The Life and Death of an Officer.* London: André Deutsch, 1967.

Kramish, Arnold. *The Griffin.* Boston: Houghton Mifflin, 1986.

Kranzler, David. *Japanese, Nazis and Jews: The Jewish Refugee Community of Shanghai, 1938–1945.* New York: Yeshiva University Press, 1976.

Kravchenko, Victor. *I Chose Freedom.* New York: Scribner's, 1946.

Krivitsky, Walter G. *In Stalin's Secret Service.* New York: Harper, 1939.

Krotov, Yuri. *I Am from Moscow.* New York: Dutton, 1967.

Kublin, Hyman. *Sun Yat-sen: Asian Revolutionary.* Princeton, N.J.: Princeton University Press, 1964

Kulik, K. *Alexander Korda.* London: W. H. Allen, 1975.

Kussinen, Aino. *Before and After Stalin.* London: Michael Joseph, 1974.

Ladd, David. *Commandos and Rangers.* New York: St. Martin's, 1978.

Ladd, James, Melton, Keith, and Mason, Peter. *Clandestine Warfare.* London: Blandford, 1988.

LaFeber, Walter. *America, Russia and the Cold War, 1945–1971.* New York: Wiley, 1972.

Laffin, John. *Codes and Ciphers.* New York: Abelard-Schuman, 1964.

Lamb, Donald. *The Drift to War, 1922–1939.* New York: St. Martin's, 1991.

Lamont, Lansing. *Day of Trinity.* New York: Atheneum, 1965.

Lampe, David. *The Savage Canary: The Story of Resistance in Denmark.* London: Cassell, 1957.

————. *The Last Ditch.* London: Cassell, 1968.

Lamphere, Robert J., and Shachtman, Tom. *The FBI-KGB War: A Special Agent's Story.* New York: Random House, 1986.

Lancaster, Donald. *The Emancipation of French Indochina.* London: Oxford University Press, 1961.

Landau, Henry. *The Enemy Within: The Inside Story of German Sabotage in America.* New York: Putnam's, 1937.

Landon, Kenneth. *Siam in Transition.* Chicago: University of Chicago Press, 1939.

Lane, Arthur Bliss. *I Saw Poland Betrayed.* Indianapolis: Bobbs-Merrill, 1948.

Langelaan, George. *Knights of the Floating Silk.* London: Hutchinson, 1959.

Langer, William. *Our Vichy Gamble.* New York: W. W. Norton, 1947.

————, and Gleason, S. Everett. *The Challenge to Isolation, 1937–1940.* New York: Harper, 1952.

————. *The Undeclared War.* New York: Harper, 1953.

Langley, J. M. *Fight Another Day.* London: Collins, 1974.

Lansdale, Edward G. *In the Midst of Wars.* New York: Harper, 1972.

Laqueur, Walter Z. *Young Germany.* London: Routledge & Kegan Paul, 1962.

————. *Russia and Germany.* London: Weidenfeld & Nicolson, 1965.

————. *The Struggle for the Middle East: The Soviet Union and the Middle East, 1948–1968.* London: Routledge & Kegan Paul, 1969.

————. *Guerrilla: A Historical and Critical Study.* London: Weidenfeld & Nicolson, 1977.

————. *A World of Secrets.* New York: Basic Books, 1985.

Larteguy, Jean. *The Walls of Israel.* New York. M. Evans, 1969.

Lasky, Victor. Arthur J. Goldberg: *The Old and the New.* New Rochelle, N.Y.: Arlington House, 1970.

Latham, Earl. *The Communist Controversy in Washington.* New York: Atheneum, 1966.

———— (ed.). *The Meaning of McCarthyism.* Lexington, Mass.: Heath, 1973.

Lattimore, Owen. *Manchuria: Cradle of Conflict.* New York: Macmillan, 1932.

Launay, J. De. *European Resistance Movements.* London: Pergamon, 1960.

Lavine, Harold. *Fifth Column in America.* New York: Doubleday, Doran, 1940.

Lawrence, T. E. *Seven Pillars of Wisdom.* London: Jonathan Cape, 1935.

Lawson, Don. *The French Resistance: The True Story of the Underground War Against the Nazis!* New York: Wanderer Books, 1984.

Lawton, Lancelot. *The Russian Revolution (1917–1926).* London: Macmillan, 1927.

Layton, Edward T., with Pineau, Roger, and Costello, John. *"And I Was There": Pearl Harbor and Midway—Breaking the Secrets.* New York: Morrow, 1985.

Leahy, William. *I Was There.* New York: McGraw-Hill, 1950.

Leasor, James. *War at the Top.* London: Michael Joseph, 1950.

Leber, Annedore. (trans. Rosemary O'Neill.) *Conscience in Revolt: Sixty-Four Studies of Resistance in Germany 1933–1945.* London: Mitchell, 1957.

LeChéne, Evelyn. *Watch for Me by Moonlight: A British Agent with the French Resistance.* London: Eyre Methuen, 1973.

Lee, Clark. *Douglas MacArthur: An Informal Biography.* New York: Holt, 1952.

Leggett, George. *The Cheka: Lenin's Political Police.* Philadelphia: Temple University Press, 1976.

Lehmann, John. *The Whispering Gallery.* Philadelphia: West, 1954.

————. *In the Purely Pagan Sense.* London: GMP, 1985.

Lehovich, Dimitry V. *White Against Red.* New York: Norton, 1974.

Leigh, David. *The Frontiers of Secrecy.* London: Junction Books, 1980.

LeMay, Curtis. *Mission with LeMay.* New York: Doubleday, 1965.

Lenczowski, George. *Soviet Advances in the Middle East.* Washington, D.C.: American Enterprise Institute, 1972.

Lensen, George Alexander. *The Damned Inheritance: The Soviet Union and the Manchurian Crises, 1924–1935.* Tallahassee, Fla.: The Diplomatic Press, 1974.

Leonard, Royal. *I Fly for China: Chiang Kai-shek's Personal Pilot.* New York: Doubleday, 1942.

Lerner, Daniel, with Pool, Ithielde Sola, and Schueller, George K. *The Nazi Elite.* Stanford, Calif.: Stanford University Press, 1951.

Leroy-Beaulieu, Anatole. (trans. Z. Ragozin) *The Empire of the Tsars.* (2 vols.) New York: Putnam's, 1898.

Leslie, Peter. *The Liberation of the Riviera.* New York: Wyndham Books, 1980.

Lester, Elenore. Wallenberg: *The Man in the Iron Web.* Englewood Cliffs, N.J.: Prentice-Hall, 1982.

Lett, Gordon. Rossano: *An Adventure of the Italian Resistance.* London: Hodder & Stoughton, 1955.

Levchenko, Stanislav. *On the Wrong Side: My Life in the KGB.* New York: Pergamon-Brassey, 1988.

Leverkuehn, Paul. *German Military Intelligence.* New York: Praeger, 1954.

Levine, Isaac Don. *The Man Lenin.* New York: Thomas Seltzer, 1924.

————. *Stalin's Great Secret.* New York: Coward-McCann, 1956.

————. *The Mind of an Assassin.* New York: Farrar, Straus & Cudahy, 1959.

Levitt, Morton, and Levitt, Michael. *A Tissue of Lies: Nixon vs. Hiss.* New York: McGraw-Hill, 1979.

Lewin, Ronald. *Ultra Goes to War.* London: Hutchinson, 1978.

————. *The American Magic.* New York: Farrar, Straus & Giroux, 1982.

Lewis, David. *Prisoners of Honor: The Dreyfus Affair.* New York: Morrow, 1973.

Lewis, Flora. Red Pawn: *The Story of Noel Field.* Garden City, N.Y.: Doubleday, 1965.

Lewis, I. M. T*he Modern History of Somaliland, From Nation to State.* London: Weidenfeld & Nicol-son, 1965.

Lewis, Wilmarth. *One Man's Education.* New York: Knopf, 1967.

Ley, Ronald. *A Whisper of Espionage.* Garden City Park, N.Y.: Avery, 1990.

L'Herminier, J. *Casablanca.* London: Muller, 1953.

Liddell Hart, Basil Henry. *The Remaking of Modern Armies.* Boston: Little, Brown, 1928.

————. *The German Generals Talk.* New York: William Morrow, 1948.

————. *A History of World War I.* London: Cassell, 1970.

Lieu, F. F. *A Military History of Modern China, 1924–1949.* Princeton, N.J.: Princeton University Press, 1956.

Lincoln, W. Bruce. *Passage Through Armageddon: The Russians in War and Revolution, 1914–1918.* New York: Simon & Schuster, 1986.

————. *Red Victory: A History of the Russian Civil War.* New York: Touchstone, 1989.

Lindsey, Robert. *The Falcon and the Snowman: A True Story of Friendship and Espionage.* New York: Simon & Schuster, 1979.

Linebarger, Paul. *The China of Chiang Kai-shek.* Boston: World Peace Foundation, 1941.

Linklater, Eric. *Juan in China.* London: Jonathan Cape, 1937.

Lipper, Elinor. *Eleven Years in Soviet Prison Camps.* Chicago: Regnery, 1951.

Littlejohn, D. *The Patriotic Traitors.* London: Heinemann, 1965.

Litvinov, Pavel. (trans. Manya Harari.) *The Demonstration in Pushkin Square.* Boston: Gambit, 1969.

Livingstone, Neil C., and Halevy, David. *Inside the PLO.* New York: William Morrow, 1990.

Lobanov-Rostovsky, Prince Andrei. *The Grinding Mill: Reminiscences of War and Revolution in Russia, 1913–1920.* New York: Macmillan, 1935.

Lockhart, J. G., and Woodhouse, C. M. *Rhodes.* London: Hodder & Stoughton, 1963.

Lockhart, Robert H. Bruce. *British Agent.* London: Putnam's, 1933.

————. *Comes the Reckoning*. London: Putnam's, 1947.

————. *Friends, Foes and Foreigners*. London: Putnam's, 1957.

Lockhart, Robin Bruce. *Reilly: Ace of Spies*. London: Hodder & Stoughton, 1967.

————, *Reilly: The First Man*. New York: Penguin, 1987.

Loftus, John. *The Belarus Secret*. New York: Knopf, 1982.

Logoreci, Anton. *The Albanians: Europe's Forgotten Survivors*. London: Gollancz, 1977.

Lohbeck, Don. *Patrick H. Hurley*. Chicago: Regnery, 1956.

Longford, Elizabeth. *Queen Victoria: Born to Succeed*. New York: Harper, 1964.

Longworth, Philip. *The Cossacks: Five Centuries of Turbulent Life on the Russian Steppes*. New York: Holt, Rinehart and Winston, 1969.

Lonsdale, Gordon. *Spy: Twenty Years in Soviet Secret Service*. New York: Hawthorn, 1965.

Lord, Walter. *Day of Infamy*. New York: Holt, Rinehart & Winston, 1957.

————. *Incredible Victory*. New York: Harper, 1967.

Lory, Hillis. *Japan's Military Masters*. New York: Viking, 1943.

Lotz, Wolfgang. *The Champagne Spy*. London: Valentine Mitchell, 1972.

Love, Kennett. *Suez, the Twice Fought War*. London: Longman, 1970.

Lovell, Stanley. *Of Spies and Strategems*. New York: Prentice-Hall, 1963.

Lowenheim, Francis L. (ed.) *Roosevelt and Churchill: Their Secret Wartime Correspondence*. New York: Saturday Review Press/Dutton, 1975.

Lowenthal, Max. *The Federal Bureau of Investigation*. New York: Harcourt, Brace, 1950.

Lucas, Norman. *The Great Spy Ring*. London: Arthur Barker, 1966.

Lüdecke, Winfried. *The Secrets of Espionage: Tales of the Secret Service*. Philadelphia: J. B. Lippincott Company, 1929.

Ludendorff, Erich. *Ludendorff's Own Story*. New York: Harper, 1919.

Lukas, J. Anthony. *Nightmare: The Underside of the Nixon Years*. New York: Viking, 1976.

Lussu, Joyce. *Freedom Has No Frontier*. London: M. Joseph, 1969

Luxemburg, Rosa. *The Russian Revolution*. Ann Arbor, Mich.: University of Michigan Press, 1961.

Maanen, Gert Van. *The International Student Movement & Background*. The Hague: Interdoc, 1966.

McAleavy, Henry. *A Dream of Tartary: The Origins and Misfortunes of Henry Pu-Yi*. London: Allen & Unwin, 1963.

MacArthur, Douglas. *Reminiscences*. New York: McGraw-Hill, 1954.

McAuliffe, Mary Sperling. *Crisis on the Left: Cold War Politics and American Liberals, 1947–1954*. Amherst, Mass.: University of Massachusetts Press, 1978.

McCaleb, Falvius. *The Aaron Burr Conspiracy*. New York: Dodd, Mead, 1903.

McCullagh, Francis. *A Prisoner of the Reds*. London: John Murray, 1921.

MacDonald, Alexander. *Bangkok Editor*. New York: Macmillan, 1945.

Macdonald, Bruce J. S. *The Trial of Kurt Meyer*. Toronto: Clarke Irwin, 1954.

MacDonald, Callum. *The Killing of SS Obergruppen-fuhrer Richard Heydrich*. New York: Free Press, 1989.

MacDonald, Elizabeth. *Undercover Girl*. New York: Macmillan, 1947.

MacDonald, Malcolm. *People and Places*. London: Collins, 1969.

MacFarlane, L. J. *The British Communist Party: Its Origins and Development*. London: MacGibbon & Kee, 1966.

McGarvey, Patrick J. *CIA: The Myth and the Madness*. New York: Dutton, 1972.

McGovern, James. *Crossbow and Overcast*. New York: Morrow & Co. Inc., 1964.

Mackenzie, Compton. *Greek Memories*. London: Chatto & Windus, 1932.

MacKinnon, Janice R., and MacKinnon, Stephen R. *Agnes Smedley: The Life and Times of an American Radical*. Berkeley, Calif.: University of California Press, 1988.

Macksey, Kenneth. *The Partisans of Europe in World War II*. London: Hart-Davis, MacGibbon, 1975.

McLachlin, Donald. *Room 39*. New York: Atheneum, 1968.

Maclean, Fitzroy. *Escape to Adventure*. Boston: Little, Brown, 1951.

————. *Disputed Barricade: The Life and Times of Josip Broz-Tito, Marshal of Yugoslavia*. London: Jonathan Cape, 1957.

————. *Take Nine Spies*. New York: Atheneum, 1978.

MacMillan, Gerald. *Honours for Sale*. London: Richard Press, 1954.

Macmillan, Harold. *The Blast of War*. London: Macmillan, 1947.

————. *At the End of the Day*. London: Macmillan, 1973.

MacNeice, Louis. *The Strings Are False*. London: Faber & Faber, 1982

Macrae, R. Stuart. *Winston Churchill's Toyshop*. London: Roundwood Press, 1971.

MacVane, John. *Journey Into War*. New York: Appleton-Century, 1943.

Magnus, Philip. *King Edward the Seventh*. New York: Dutton, 1964.

Maisky, Ivan. *Who Helped Hitler?* London: Hutchinson, 1964.

Maki, John M. *Conflict and Tension in the Far East: Key Documents, 1894–1960*. Seattle: University of Washington Press, 1961.

Manchester, William. *The Arms of Krupp, 1587–1968*. Boston: Little, Brown, 1968.

————. *The Glory and the Dream*. Boston: Little, Brown, 1973,

Mangold, Tom. *Cold Warrior: James Jesus Angleton: The CIA's Master Spy Hunter*. New York: Simon & Schuster, 1991.

Mann, Wilfrid Basil. *Was There a Fifth Man?* London: Pergamon Press, 1982.

Mansergh, Nicholas. *The Coming of the First World War*. New York: Longmans, Green, 1949.

Manvell, Roger, and Fraenkel, Heinrich. *The Men Who Tried to Kill Hitler*. New York: Coward-McCann, 1964.

————. *Himmler*. New York: Putnam's, 1965.

————. *The Canaris Conspiracy*. New York: McKay, 1969.

Maraini, Fosco. *Meeting with Japan*. New York: Viking, 1960.

Marchenko, Anatoly. (trans. Michael Scammell.) *My Testimony.* New York: Dutton, 1969.

Marchetti, Victor, and Marks, John D. *The CIA and the Cult of Intelligence.* New York: Knopf, 1974.

March-Phillipps, G. *Ace High.* London: Macmillan, 1938.

Marcu, Valeriu. *Lenin.* London: Gollancz, 1928.

Marder, Munya. *Strictly Illegal.* London: Robert Hale, 1964.

Marion, Pierre. *La Mission impossible: A la tête des Services Secrets.* Paris: Calmann, 1991.

Marks, John. *The Search for the "Manchurian Candidate"—The CIA and Mind Control: The Story of the Agency's Secret Efforts to Control Human Behavior.* New York: Times Books, 1979.

Marshall, Bruce. *The White Rabbit: From the Story Told to Him by Wing Commander F. F. E. Yeo-Thomas.* London: Evans, 1952.

Martelli, George. *Agent Extraordinary: The Story of Michel Hollard.* London: Collins, 1960.

————. *Leopold to Lumumba.* London: Champman & Hall, 1962.

Martin, David. *Ally Betrayed.* New York: Prentice-Hall, 1946.

————. *Patriot or Traitor.* Stanford, Calif.: Stanford University Press, 1978.

Martin, David. *Screening Federal Employees.* Washington, D.C.: Heritage Foundation, 1983.

Martin, David C. *Wilderness of Mirrors.* New York: Harper, 1980.

Martin, Edward M. *The Allied Occupation of Japan.* New York: The American Institute of Pacific Relations, 1948.

Martin, George. *Madam Secretary: Frances Perkins.* Boston: Houghton Mifflin, 1976.

Martin, Ralph G. *The Woman He Loved.* New York: Simon & Schuster, 1974.

Martines, Lauro. *The Social World of the Florentine Humanists, 1390–1460.* Princeton, N.J.: Princeton University Press, 1963.

Maruyama, Masao. *Thought and Behavior in Modern Japanese Politics.* London: Oxford University Press, 1963.

Maschwitz, Eric. *No Chip on My Shoulder.* London: Herbert Jenkins, 1957.

Mashbir, Sidney. *I Was an American Spy.* New York: Vantage, 1953.

Massie, Robert K. *Nicholas and Alexandra: An Intimate Account of the Last of the Romanovs and the Fall of Imperial Russia.* New York: Atheneum, 1967.

————. *Dreadnought: Britain, Germany and the Coming of the Great War.* New York: Random House, 1991.

Massing, Hede. *This Deception.* New York: Duell, Sloan and Pearce, 1951.

Masson, Madeleine. *Christine: A Search for Christine Granville.* London: Hamish Hamilton, 1975.

Masters, Anthony. *The Summer That Bled.* New York: St. Martin's, 1973.

————. *The Man Who Was M.: The Life of Maxwell Knight.* London: Basil Blackwell, 1984.

Masterman, Sir John C. *The Double-Cross System in the War of 1939–1945.* New Haven, Conn.: Yale University Press, 1972.

————. *On the Chariot Wheel.* London: Oxford University Press, 1975.

Mastny, Vojtech. *The Czechs Under Nazi Rule: The Failure of Nazi Rule, 1939–1942.* New York: Columbia University Press, 1971.

Matthews, T. S. *Name and Address.* New York: Simon & Schuster, 1960.

Mauborgne, J. O. *An Advanced Problem in Cryptography.* Fort Leavenworth, Kan.: Press of the Army Service Schools, 1914.

Maugeri, Franco. *From the Ashes of Disgrace.* New York: Reynal and Hitchcock, 1948.

Maugham, W. Somerset. *Ashenden.* London: Heinemann, 1928.

————. *The Summing Up.* London: Heinemann, 1938.

Max, Alphonse. *Guerrillas in Latin America.* The Hague: Interdoc, 1967.

Maxton, James. *Lenin.* London: Peter Davies, 1932.

Maxwell, Gavin. *The House of Elrig.* London: Longmans, 1965.

May, Ernest (ed.). *Knowing One's Enemies: Intelli-gence Assessment Before the Two World Wars.* Princeton, N. J.: Princeton University Press, 1984.

May, Thomas E. *The Constitutional History of England.* London: Longmans, Green, 1912.

Mayer, Martin. *Emory Buckner.* New York: Harper, 1968.

Mayhew, Christopher. *Time to Explain.* London: Hutchinson, 1987.

Mazour, Anatole G. *Russia Past and Present.* New York: Van Nostrand, 1951.

————. *The Rise and Fall of the Romanovs.* New York: Van Nostrand, 1960.

Mead, Peter. *The Eye in the Air: History of Air Observation and Reconnaissance, 1785–1945.* London: Her Majesty's Stationary Office, 1983.

Mecklin, John. *Mission in Torment.* New York: Doubleday, 1965.

Medlicott, W. N. *The Economic Blockade.* (2 vols.) London: H. M. Stationary Office, 1952–1959.

Medvedev, Zhores, and Medvedev, Roy. *A Question of Madness.* New York: Knopf, 1961.

Meeropol, Robert, and Meeropol, Michael. *We Are Your Sons.* Boston: Houghton Mifflin, 1975.

Meir, Golda. *My Life.* London: Weidenfeld & Nicolson, 1975.

Meissner, Hans Otto. *The Man with Three Faces.* New York: Reinhart, 1955.

Mellenthin, F. W. *Panzer Battles.* Norman, Okla.: University of Oklahoma Press, 1958.

Melman, Yossi, and Raviv, Dan. *The Imperfect Spies: The History of Israeli Intelligence.* London: Sidgwick & Jackson, 1989.

Melvern, Linda, Hebditch, David, and Anning, Nick. *Techno-Bandits: How the Soviets Are Stealing America's High-Tech Future.* Boston: Houghton Mifflin, 1984.

Mendelssohn, Peter de. *Japan's Political Warfare.* London: Allen & Unwin, 1944.

Meskill, Johanna Menzel. *Hitler and Japan: The Hollow Alliance.* New York: Atherton, 1966.

Meyer, Herbert E. *Real-World Intelligence.* New York: Weidenfeld & Nicholson, 1987.

Michel, Henri. (trans. Richard Barry.) *The Shadow War: Resistance in Europe 1939–1945.* London: André Deutsch, 1972.

Milazzo, Matteo J. *The Chetnik Movement and the Yugoslav Resistance.* Baltimore: Johns Hopkins University Press, 1975.

Miles, Milton. *A Different Kind of War.* New York: Doubleday, 1967.

Miliukov, Paul, et al. (trans. Charles Lam Markmann.) *History of Russia.* New York: Funk & Wagnalls, 1969.

Millar, George. *Maquis.* London: Heinemann, 1945.

————. *Horned Pigeon.* London: Heinemann, 1946.

Miller, Douglas T., and Nowak, Marion. *The Fifties: The Way We Really Were.* Garden City, N.Y.: Doubleday, 1977.

Miller, Francis P. *Man from the Valley.* Chapel Hill, N.C.: University of North Carolina, 1971.

Miller, George A. *Language and Communication.* New York: McGraw-Hill, 1951.

Miller, Jay. *Lockheed U-2.* Austin, Tex.: Aerofax, 1983.

Miller, Joan. *One Woman's War: Personal Exploits in MI5's Most Secret Station.* Dublin: Brandon, 1986.

Miller, Nathan. *Spying for America.* New York: Paragon, 1989.

Millin, S. G. *Rhodes.* London: Chatto & Windus, 1952.

Millis, Walter. *This Is Pearl! The United States and Japan—1941.* New York: Morrow, 1947.

————. *The Forrestal Diaries.* New York: Viking, 1951.

Minney, R. J. *Carve Her Name with Pride: The Story of Violette Szabo.* London: Collins, 1964.

Mitchell, Broadus. *Depression Decade.* New York: Harper, 1957.

Miyatovitch, Cheddo. *Serbia of the Serbians.* London: Pitman, 1915.

Mockler, Anthony. *The Mercenaries.* New York: Macmillan, 1969.

Moen, Lars. *Under the Iron Heel.* London: Robert Hale, 1941.

Monat, Pawel, with Dille, John. *Spy in the U.S.* New York: Berkley, 1961.

Montagu, Ewan. *The Man Who Never Was.* New York: Lippincott, 1954.

————. *Beyond Top Secret Ultra.* London: Davies, 1977.

Montross, Lynn. *War Through the Ages.* New York: Harper, 1960.

Moorad, George. *Lost Peace in China.* New York: Dutton, 1949.

Moore, Dan, and Waller, Martha. *Cloak and Cipher.* New York: Bobbs-Merrill, 1962.

Moore, Frederick. *With Japan's Leaders.* New York: Scribner's, 1942.

Moore, Harriet L. *Soviet Far Eastern Policy, 1931–1945.* Princeton, N.J.: Princeton University Press, 1945.

Moorehead, Alan. *The Traitors.* New York: Harper & Row, 1952.

————. *The Russian Revolution.* New York: Harper, 1958.

Moravec, Frantisek. *Master of Spies.* London: Bodley Head, 1975.

Morgan, Frederick. *Overture to Overlord.* New York: Doubleday, 1950.

Morgan, William. *The O.S.S. and I.* New York: W. W. Norton, 1957.

Morgenstern, George. *Pearl Harbor: The Story of the Secret War.* New York: Devin-Adair, 1947.

Morin, Henri. *Secret Service.* Paris: G. Durassie & Cie, 1959.

Morin, Relman. *Circuit of Conquest.* New York: Knopf, 1943.

————. *East Wind Rising.* New York: Knopf, 1960.

Morison, Samuel E. *Two-Ocean War.* Boston: Little, Brown, 1963.

Morley, James W. *The Japanese Thrust into Siberia, 1918.* New York: Columbia University Press, 1957.

Morris, Roger. *Uncertain Greatness.* New York: Harper, 1977.

Morrison, Elting E. *Turmoil and Tradition: A Study of the Life and Times of Henry L. Stimson.* Boston: Houghton Mifflin, 1960.

Morrison, Ian. *Malaya Postscript.* Sydney, Aus.: Angus and Robertson, 1943.

————. *Grandfather Longlegs.* London: Faber & Faber, 1947.

Morrison, Philip, and Morrison, Emily (eds.). *Charles Babbage and His Calculating Engines.* New York: Dover, 1961.

Morros, Boris. *My Ten Years as a Counterspy.* New York: Viking, 1959.

Mosley, Diana. *The Duchess of Windsor.* London: Sidgwick & Jackson, 1980.

Mosley, Leonard. *The Cat and the Mouse.* New York: Harper, 1959.

————. *Hirohito, Emperor of Japan.* New York: McGraw-Hill, 1966.

————. *The Reich Marshal.* London: Weidenfeld & Nicolson, 1974.

————. *Dulles.* New York: Dial, 1978.

Mosley, Oswald. *My Life.* London: Nelson, 1968.

Moss, Robert. *Urban Guerrilla.* London: Temple Smith, 1972.

Moss, W. Stanley. *Ill Met by Moonlight.* London: Harrap, 1950.

Mountbatten, Louis. *Report to the Combined Chiefs of Staff from the Supreme Commander, Southeast Asia.* New York: Philosophical Library, 1951.

Mowat, Charles Loch. *Britain Between the Wars, 1918–1940.* London: Methuen, 1955.

Mowrer, Edgar. *Triumph and Turmoil.* New York: Weybright, 1968.

Moyzisch, L.C. *Operation Cicero.* New York: Coward-McCann, 1950.

Mulgan, John. *Report on Experience.* New York: Oxford University Press, 1947.

Munthe, Malcolm. *Sweet Is War.* London: Duckworth, 1954.

Mure, David. *Master of Deception: Tangled Webs in London and the Middle East.* London: William Kimber, 1980.

Murphy, Brendan M. *Turncoat.* New York: Harcourt Brace Jovanovich, 1987.

Murphy, Edward R., with Gentry, Curt. *Second in Command: The Uncensored Account of the Capture of the Spy Ship* Pueblo. New York: Holt, Rinehart and Winston, 1971.

Murphy, Rhoads. *Shanghai: Key to Modern China.* Cambridge, Mass.: Harvard University Press, 1953.

Murphy, Robert. *Diplomat Among Warriors.* New York: Doubleday, 1954.

Musard, Francois. *Les Glières.* Paris: Laffont, 1965.

Mydans, Carl. *More Than Meets the Eye.* New York: Harper, 1959.

Myers, E. W. C. *Greek Entanglements.* London: Rupert Hart-Davis, 1955.

Myers, Gustavus. *History of Great American Fortunes.* New York: Random House, 1936.

Nash, Jay Robert. *Citizen Hoover: A Critical Study of the Life and Times of J. Edgar Hoover and His FBI.* Chicago: Nelson-Hall, 1972.

————. *Bloodletters and Badmen: A Narrative Encyclopedia of American Criminals from the Pilgrims to the Present.* New York: M. Evans & Co., 1973, 1983, 1991, 1995.

————. *Hustlers and Con Men: An Anecdotal History of the Confidence Man and His Games.* New York: M. Evans & Co., 1976.

————. *Among the Missing, An Anecdotal History of Missing Persons from 1800 to the Present.* New York: Simon & Schuster, 1978.

————. *Almanac of World Crime.* Garden City, N.Y.: Doubleday, 1981.

————. *Look for the Woman: A Narrative Encyclopedia of Female Criminals from Elizabethan Times to the Present.* New York: M. Evans & Co., 1981.

————. *The Motion Picture Guide.* (16 vols.) Chicago: CineBooks, Inc., 1986–1990.

————. *Encyclopedia of World Crime.* (6 vols.) Wilmette, Ill.: CrimeBooks, Inc., 1990.

National Cryptologic School. *On Watch: Profiles from the National Security Agency's Past 40 Years.* Fort Meade, Md.: NCS, 1986.

Naval Security Group Command. *Naval Cryptology in National Security.* Washington, D.C.: NSGC, 1985.

Navarre, Henri. *Le Service de Reseignement, 1871–1944.* Paris: Plon, 1978.

Navasky, Victor. *Naming Names.* New York: Viking, 1980.

Neave, Airey. *Saturday at MI9.* London: Hodder & Stoughton, 1969.

Neff, Donald. *Warriors for Jerusalem: The Six Days That Changed the Middle East.* New York: Simon & Schuster, 1984.

Nelson, Steve, Barrett, James R., and Ruck, Rob. *Steve Nelson: American Radical.* Pittsburgh: University of Pittsburgh Press, 1981.

Nelson, Otto L., Jr. *National Security and the General Staff.* Washington, D.C.: Infantry Journal Press, 1946.

Neumann, Franz. *Behemoth: The Structure and Practice of National Socialism.* London: Gollancz, 1943.

Neusüss-Hunkel, Ermenhild. *Die SS.* Hanover: Norddeutsche Verlag, 1956.

Nevins, Allan. *The United States in a Chaotic World, 1918–1933.* New Haven, Conn.: Yale University Press, 1950.

Newhall, Beaumont. *Airborne Camera: The World from the Air and Outer Space.* New York: Hastings House, 1969.

Newhouse, John. *Cold Dawn.* New York: Holt, Rinehart & Winston, 1973.

————. *War and Peace in the Nuclear Age.* New York: Knopf, 1989.

Newman, Bernard. *Epics of Espionage.* New York: Philosophical Library, 1951.

Newman, Joseph. *Goodbye Japan.* New York: L. B. Fischer, 1942.

————. *How I Got That Story.* New York: Dutton, 1967.

Newton, Verne W. *The Cambridge Spies: The Untold Story of Maclean, Philby and Burgess in America.* Lanham, Md.: Madison Books, 1991.

Nicholaevsky, Boris I. *The Crimes of the Stalin Era.* New York: New York Leader, 1932.

Nicolai, Walther. *The German Secret Service.* London: Stanley Paul, 1924.

Nicholas, Elizabeth. *Death Be Not Proud.* London: Cresset Press, 1958.

Nicolson, Harold. *King George the Fifth.* London: Constable, 1952.

————. *Diaries and Letters, 1930–1964.* London: Penguin, 1984.

Nicolson, Nigel. *Portrait of a Marriage.* New York: Atheneum, 1980.

Nikolajewsky, Boris. *Aseff the Spy.* Garden City, N.Y.: Doubleday & Co., 1934.

Nimitz, Chester W., and Potter, E. B. *The Great Sea War.* Englewood Cliffs, N.J.: Prentice-Hall, 1960.

Ninio, Marcelle, et al. *Operation Susannah.* New York: Harper, 1978.

Nitobe, Inazo. *Bushido: The Soul of Japan.* New York: Putnam's, 1905.

Nitze, Paul. *From Hiroshima to Glasnost.* New York: Grove, 1989.

Nizer, Louis. *The Implosion Conspiracy.* Garden City, N.Y.: Doubleday, 1973.

Nogueres, Henri. *Histoire de la Résistance en France.* Paris: Laffont, 1969.

Nollau, Gunther. *International Communism and World Revolution.* London: Hollis and Carter, 1961.

Norman, Bruce. *Secret Warfare: The Battle of Codes & Ciphers.* New York: Dorset Press, 1973.

North, R. C. *Kuomintang and the Chinese Communist Elites.* Stanford: Stanford University Press, 1952.

Nutting, Anthony. *The Scramble for Africa.* London: Constable, 1970.

Oberdorfer, Don. *The Turn: From the Cold War to a New Era.* New York: Touchstone, 1991.

Obolensky, Serge. *One Man in His Time.* New York: McDowell-Obolensky, 1958.

Occleshaw, Michael. *Armour Against Fate: British Military Intelligence in the First World War.* London: Columbus, 1989.

Offer, Yehuda. *Operation Thunder.* Harmondsworth, England: Penguin, 1976.

Ogata, Sadako N. *Defiance in Manchuria: The Making of Japanese Policy, 1931–1932.* Berkeley, Calif.: University of California Press, 1964.

Oliver, Robert. *Syngman Rhee.* New York: Dodd, Mead, 1954.

Olsen, Oluf Reed. (trans. F. H. Lyon.) *Two Eggs on My Plate.* London: Allen & Unwin.

O'Neill, Robert J. *The German Army and the Nazi Party, 1933-1939.* London: Cassell, 1966.

Ore, Oystein. *Cardano: The Gambling Scholar.* Princeton, N.J.: Princeton University Press, 1953.

Orloff, Vladimir. (trans. Mona Heath.) *My Memoirs of Russia's Political Underworld.* London: Harrap, 1932.

Orlov, Alexander (Leon Lazerevik Feldbin). *The Secret History of Stalin's Crimes.* New York: Random House, 1953.

————. *Handbook of Intelligence and Guerrilla Warfare.* Ann Arbor, Mich.: University of Michigan Press, 1965.

Orlow, Dietrich. *The History of the Nazi Party, 1919–1933.* (2 vols.) Pittsburgh, Pa.: University of Pittsburgh, 1969–1973.

Oshinsky, David M. *A Conspiracy So Immense: The World of Joe McCarthy.* New York: Macmillan, 1983.

Ossendowski, Ferdinand. *Beasts, Men and Gods.* New York: Dutton, 1922.

Ostrovsky, Victor, and Hoy, Claire. *By Way of Deception: The Making and the Unmaking of a Mossad Officer.* New York: St. Martin's, 1990.

O'Toole, George. *Honorable Treachery: A History of U.S. Intelligence, Espionage, Covert Action from the American Revolution to the CIA.* New York: Atlantic Monthly Press, 1991.

Owen, Frank. *Tempestuous Journey: Lloyd George, His Life and Times.* London: Hutchinson, 1954.

————. *The Eddie Chapman Story.* New York: Messmer, 1954.

Pacepa, Ion Mihai. *Red Horizons: Chronicles of a Communist Spy Chief.* Washington, D.C.: Regnery-Gateway, 1987.

Packer, Herbert L. *Ex-Communist Witnesses: Four Studies in Fact-Finding.* Stanford, Calif.: Stanford University Press, 1962.

Padfield, Peter. *Dönitz: The Last Führer.* New York: Harper, 1984.

Paetel, Karl O., et al. *"The SS" in the Third Reich.* London: Weidenfeld & Nicolson, 1955.

Page, Bruce, Leitch, David and Knightley, Phillip. *The Philby Conspiracy.* New York: Doubleday, 1969.

Paige, Glenn D. *The Korean Decision.* New York: The Free Press, 1968.

Paine, Lauran. *German Military Intelligence in World War II: The Abwehr.* New York: Military Heritage Press, 1984.

Pakenham, Thomas. *The Boer War.* London: Weidenfeld & Nicolson, 1979.

Paléologue, Maurice. (trans. Eric Mosbacher.) *An Intimate Journal of the Dreyfus Case.* New York: Criterion, 1957.

Paloczi-Horvath, George. *The Undefeated.* Boston: Little, Brown, 1959.

Papen, Franz von. *Memoirs.* London: André Deutsch, 1952.

Pash, Boris. *The Alsos Mission.* New York: Award House, 1969.

Papen, Franz von. *Memoirs.* London: André Deutsch, 1952.

Pares, Bernard. *The Fall of the Russian Monarchy.* New York: Knopf, 1939.

———. *A History of Russia.* (5th ed., revised). New York: Knopf, 1951.

Parrish, Thomas. *The American Codebreakers: The U.S. Role in Ultra.* Chelsea, Mich.: Scarborough House, 1991.

Parry, Albert. *The New Class Divided.* New York: Macmillan, 1966.

Passy, Colonel (André Dewavrin). *Missions Secrétes en France.* Paris: Plon, 1951.

Paterson, Thomas G. *The Origins of the Cold War.* Lexington, Mass.: Heath, 1974.

Patmore, Derek. *Balkan Correspondent.* New York: Harper, 1941.

Patton, George. *War as I Knew It.* Boston: Houghton Mifflin, 1947.

Pawle, Gerald. *The Secret War.* New York: Sloane, 1957.

Payne, Robert. *Lenin.* New York: Simon & Schuster, 1964.

———. *The Life and Death of Adolf Hitler.* New York: Popular Library, 1974.

Pean, Pierre. *Secret d'Etat: La France du Secret, Les Secrets de la France.* Paris: Fayard, 1986.

Pearlman, Moshe. *The Capture of Adolf Eichmann.* London: Weidenfeld & Nicolson, 1961.

Pearlstien, Edward W. (ed.). *Revolution in Russia!* New York: Viking, 1967.

Pearson, John. *The Life of Ian Fleming.* New York: McGraw-Hill, 1966.

Peck, Graham. *Two Kinds of Time.* Boston: Houghton Mifflin, 1950.

Peebles, Curtis. *Guardians: Strategic Reconnaissance Satellites.* Novato, Calif.: Presidio, 1987.

Peers, William R., and Brelis, Dean. *Behind the Burma Road.* London: Robert Hale, 1964.

Peierls, Rudolf. *Bird of Passage: Recollections of a Nuclear Physicist.* Princeton, N.J.: Princeton University Press, 1985.

Peis, Gunter. *The Man Who Started the War.* London: Oldhams, 1960.

Pells, Richard H. *Radical Visions and American Dreams.* New York: Harper, 1973.

Pendar, Kenneth. *Adventure in Diplomacy.* New York: Dodd, Mead, 1945

Penkovskiy, Oleg. *The Penkovskiy Papers.* Garden City, N.Y.: Doubleday & Company, 1965.

Pennypacker, Morton. *General Washington's Spies on Long Island and in New York.* Brooklyn, N.Y.: Long Island Historical Society, 1939.

Penrose, Barrie, and Courtiour, Roger. *The Pencourt File.* London: Secker and Warburg, 1978.

———, and Freeman, Simon. *Conspiracy of Silence: The Secret Life of Anthony Blunt.* New York: Vintage, 1988.

Pernikoff, Alexandre. Bushido: *The Anatomy of Terror.* New York: Liveright, 1943.

Perrault, Giles. *The Red Orchestra.* New York: Simon & Schuster, 1969.

Perry, Robert L. *Origins of the USAF Space Program, 1945–1956.* Washington, D.C.: U.S. Air Force Systems Command, 1962.

Persico, Joseph E. *Piercing the Reich.* London: Michael Joseph, 1979.

———. *Casey: From the OSS to the CIA.* New York: Viking, 1990.

"Pertinax" (André Géraud). *The Gravediggers of France.* New York: Doubleday, Doran, 1944.

Peterzell, Jay. *Reagan's Secret Wars.* Washington, D.C.: Center for National Security Studies, 1984.

Petrov, Vladimir. *Empire of Fear.* New York: Praeger, 1956.

Philbrick, Herbert A. *I Led Three Lives.* Washington, D.C.: The Capitol Hill Press, 1973.

Philby, Eleanor. *Kim Philby, the Spy I Loved.* London: Hamish Hamilton, 1968.

Philby, Kim. *My Silent War.* London: MacGibbon & Kee, 1962.

Phillips, Cable. *From the Crash to the Blitz, 1929–1939.* New York: Macmillan, 1969.

Phillips, C. E. *The Raiders of Arakan.* London: Heinemann, 1971.

Phillips, David Atlee. *The Night Watch.* New York: Atheneum, 1976.

Phillips, William. *Ventures in Diplomacy.* Boston: Beacon, 1953.

Piekalkiewicz, Janusz. *Secret Agents, Spies and Saboteurs.* New York: Morrow, 1973.

Pierce, J. R. *Symbols, Signals and Noise: The Nature and Process of Communication.* New York: Harper, 1961.

Pierre-Gosset, René. *Conspiracy in Algiers.* New York: The Nation, 1945.

Pierrepoint, Albert. *Executioner Pierrepoint.* London: Harrap, 1968.

Piggott, Francis. *Broken Thread.* Aldershot, Eng.: Gale and Polden, 1950.

Pilat, Oliver. *The Atom Spies.* New York: G.P. Putnam's Sons, 1952.

Pimlott, Ben. *Hugh Dalton.* London: Macmillan, 1985.

Pincher, Chapman. *Inside Story: A Documentary of the Pursuit of Power.* New York: Stein & Day, 1979.

———. *Their Trade Is Treachery.* London: Sidgwick & Jackson, 1981.

———. *Too Secret Too Long.* New York: St. Martin's Press, 1984.

———. *A Web of Deception: The Spycatcher Affair.* London: Sidgwick & Jackson, 1987.

Pinto, Oreste. *Spy Catcher.* New York: Harper, 1952.
———. *Friend or Foe?* New York: G.P. Putnam's Sons, 1953.
Piquet-Wicks, Eric. *Four in the Shadows.* London: Jarrolds, Norwich, 1957.
Pistrak, Lazar. *The Grand Tactician: Khrushchev's Rise to Power.* New York: Praeger, 1961.
Pitman, Ben. *The Assassination of President Lincoln and the Trial of the Conspirators.* (facsimile ed.) New York: Funk & Wagnalls, 1954.
Platt, Washington. *Strategic Intelligence Production.* New York: Praeger, 1962.
Playfair, Giles, and Sington, Derrick. *The Offenders.* London: Secker & Warburg, 1957.
Plum, William R. *The Military Telegraph During the Civil War in the United States.* Chicago: Jansen, McClurg & Co., 1882.
Pocock, Chris. *Dragon Lady: The History of the U-2 Spyplane.* Shrewsbury, Eng.: Airlife, 1989.
Poincaré, Raymond. (trans. Sir George Arthur.) *Memoirs.* New York: Doubleday, 1928.
Polish Ministry of Information (in England during World War II). *The Black Book of Poland.* New York: Putnam's, 1942.
Pollack, Emanuel. *The Kronstadt Rebellion.* New York: Philosophical Publishers Library, 1959.
Pollen, John Hungerford. *Mary Queen of Scots and the Babington Plot.* Edinburgh: University of Edinburgh, 1922.
Pope, Arthur Lipham. *Maxim Litvinoff.* London: Secker & Warburg, 1943.
Pope-Hennessey, James. *Queen Mary.* New York: Knopf, 1960.
Popov, Dusko. *Spy-Counterspy.* New York: Grosset & Dunlap, 1974.
Poretsky, Elisabeth. *Our Own People: A Memoir of Ignace Reiss and His Friends.* London: Oxford University Press, 1969.
Potter, John Deane. *A Soldier Must Hang: The Biography of an Oriental General.* London: Frederick Miller, 1953.
———. *Admiral of the Pacific.* London: Heinemann, 1965.
Powell, John B. *My 25 Years in China.* New York: Macmillan, 1945.
Powell, William H. (comp.). *List of Officers of the Army of the United States from 1779 to 1900.* New York: L. R. Hamersley & Co., 1900.
Powers, Gary Francis, and Gentry, Curt. *Operation Overflight: The U-2 Spy Pilot Tells His Story for the First Time.* New York: Holt, Rinehart & Winston, 1970.
Powers, Richard. *Secrecy and Power: The Life of J. Edgar Hoover.* New York: Free Press, 1987.
Powers, Thomas. *The Man Who Kept the Secrets: Richard Helms and the CIA.* New York: Knopf, 1979.
Pozner, Vladmir. *Bloody Baron: The Story of Ungern-Sternberg.* New York: Random House, 1938.
Prados, John. *The Soviet Estimate: U.S. Intelligence Analysis and Russian Military Strength.* New York: Dial, 1982.
———. *Presidents' Secret Wars: CIA and Pentagon Covert Operations from World War II Through Iranscam.* New York: Quill, 1988.
Prange, Gordon W. *At Dawn We Slept: The Untold Story of Pearl Harbor.* New York: McGraw-Hill, 1981.
———. *Miracle at Midway.* New York: McGraw-Hill, 1982.
———. *Target Tokyo: The Story of the Sorge Spy Ring.* New York: McGraw-Hill, 1984.
———, with Goldstein, Donald M., and Dillon, Katherine V. *Pearl Harbor: The Verdict of History.* New York: McGraw-Hill, 1986.
Pratt, Fletcher. *Secret and Urgent.* Indianapolis, Ind.: Bobbs-Merrill, 1939.
Press, Sylvia. *The Care of Devils.* Boston: Beacon, 1958.
Price, G. Ward. *Giraud and the North African Scene.* New York: Macmillan, 1944.
Price, Willard. *Japan and the Son of Heaven.* New York: Duell, Sloan & Pearce, 1945.
Pridham, Francis. *Close of a Dynasty.* London: Wingate, 1956.
Priesseisen, Ernst L. *Germany and Japan: A Study in Totalitarian Diplomacy, 1933–1941.* The Hague: Martinus Nijhoff, 1958.
Priestley, R. E. *The Signal Service in the European War of 1914 to 1918.* London: Institute of Royal Engineers, 1921.
Pritt, D. N. *Spies and Informers in the Witness Box.* London: Bernard Hanison, 1958.
Prouty, L. Fletcher. *The Secret Team.* New York: Prentice-Hall, 1973.
Pryce-Jones, David. *Paris in the Third Reich.* New York: Holt, Rinehart and Winston, 1981.
Pujol, Juan. *Operation Garbo.* New York: Random House, 1985.
Putlitz, Wolfgang von und zu. *The Putlitz Dossier.* London: Wingate, 1957.

Quayle, Anthony. *Eight Hours from England.* London: Heinemann, 1945.

Rabin, Yitzhak. *The Rabin Memoirs.* London: Weidenfeld & Nicolson, 1979.
Rabinowitch, Alexander. *Prelude to Revolution: The Petrograd Bolsheviks and the July 1917 Uprising.* Bloomington, Ind.: Indiana University Press, 1968.
Raczynski, Count Edward. *In Allied London.* London: Weidenfeld & Nicolson, 1962.
Radkey, Oliver Henry. *The History of the Russian Revolution.* Ann Arbor, Mich.: University of Michigan Press, 1957.
———. *The Sickle Under the Hammer.* New York: Columbia University Press, 1963.
Rado, Sandor. *Code-name Dora.* New York: Abelard, 1977.
Radosh, Ronald, and Milton, Joyce. *The Rosenberg File.* New York: Vintage Books, 1984.
Radziwill, Catherine. *Nicholas II: The Last of the Tsars.* London: Cassell, 1931.
Raeder, Erich. (trans. Harry W. Drexl.) *My Life.* Annapolis, Md.: U.S. Naval Institute, 1960.
Rake, Dennis. *Rake's Progress.* London: Frewin, 1968.
Randall, Brian. *Report on Colossus.* Newcastle, Eng.: Newcastle University, 1976.
Randall, Willard Sterne. *Benedict Arnold: Patriot and Traitor.* New York: Morrow, 1990.
Ranelagh, John. *The Agency: The Rise and Decline of the CIA.* New York: Simon & Schuster, 1986.
Ransom, Harry Howe. *Central Intelligence and National Security.* Cambridge, Mass.: Harvard University Press, 1958.
———. *The Intelligence Establishment.* Cambridge, Mass.: Harvard University Press, 1970.
Ransome, Arthur. *Russia in 1919.* New York: B. W. Huebsch, 1919.
Rasputin, Maria. *My Father.* London: Cassell, 1934.

Rauch, Georg von. *A History of Soviet Russia.* New York: Praeger, 1957.

Rauschning, Hermann. *Hitler Speaks.* London: Thornton Butterworth, 1939.

Rayne, J. *Sun, Sand and Somalis.* London: H. F. G. Witherby, 1921.

Read, Anthony. and Fisher, David. *Operation Lucy: Most Secret Spy Ring of the Second World War.* London: Hodder & Stoughton, 1980.

————. *Colonel Z: The Life and Times of a Master of Spies.* London: Hodder & Stoughton, 1984.

————. *The Deadly Embrace: Hitler, Stalin, and the Nazi Soviet Pact 1939–1941.* New York: W. W. Norton, 1988.

Read, Conyers. *Mr. Secretary Walsingham and the Policy of Queen Elizabeth.* Cambridge, Mass.: Harvard University Press, 1925.

Reddaway, Peter. *Uncensored Russia.* New York: American Heritage, 1972.

Redman, H. Vere. *Japan in Crisis.* London: Allen & Unwin, 1935.

Reed, John. *Ten Days That Shook the World.* New York: Random House, 1960.

Rees, David. *Harry Dexter White: A Study in Paradox.* New York: Coward, McCann & Geohegan, 1973.

Rees, Goronwy. *A Chapter of Accidents.* London: Chatto & Windus, 1972.

Reese, Mary Ellen. *General Reinhard Gehlen: The CIA Connection.* Fairfax, Va.: George Mason University Press, 1990.

Reeves, John. *The House of Rothschild: The Financial Rulers of Nations.* New York: Gordon Press, 1975.

Reilly, Sidney. *Britain's Master Spy: His Own Story.* New York: Dorset Press, 1985.

Reinach, Joseph. *Historie de l'affaire Dreyfus.* (7 vols.) Paris: La Revue Blanché, 1901–1911.

Reinhardt, Gunther. *Crime Without Punishment.* New York: Hermitage House, 1952.

Reinsch, Paul S. *An American Diplomat in China, 1913–1919.* New York: Doubleday Page, 1922.

Reischauer, Edwin O. *United States and Japan.* Cambridge, Mass.: Harvard University Press, 1957.

————. *Japan Past and Present.* New York: Knopf, 1964.

————. *The Japanese.* London: Belknap, 1977.

Reit, Seymour. *Masquerade.* New York: Hawthorne, 1978.

Reitlinger, Gerald. *The Final Solution.* London: Valentine Mitchell, 1953.

————. *The SS: Alibi of a Nation.* London: Heinemann, 1956.

————. *The House Built on Sand.* London: Weidenfeld & Nicolson, 1960.

Rémy, Colonel (Gilbert Renault). *Mes Grands Hommes et Quelques Autres.* Paris: Bernard Grosset, 1982.

Renault-Roulier, Gilbert. *Mémoires d'un Agent Secret de la France Libre.* Paris: Editions France Empire, 1961.

Rendel, A. M. *Appointment in Crete: The Story of a British Agent.* London: Allen Wingate, 1953.

Repington, Charles à Court. *Vestigia.* London: Constable, 1919.

Reuben, William A. *The Atom Spy Hoax.* New York: Action Books, 1955.

Revel, Jean-François. *How Democracies Perish.* Garden City, N.Y.: Doubleday, 1983.

Reynolds, Nicholas. *Treason Was No Crime: Ludwig Beck, Chief of the German General Staff.* London: Kimber, 1976.

Reynolds, Quentin. *The Man Who Wouldn't Talk.* New York: Random House, 1953.

————. *Minister of Death: The Eichmann Story.* New York: Viking Press, 1960.

Riasanovsky, Nicholas. *A History of Russia.* New York: Oxford University Press, 1963.

Ribbentrop, Joachim von. (trans. Oliver Watson.) *The Ribbentrop Memoirs.* London: Weidenfeld & Nicolson, 1954.

Richardson, Stewart. *The Secret History of World War II.* New York: Berkley, 1987.

Richardson, William and Freidin, Seymour (eds.). (trans. Constantine Fitzgibbon.) *The Fatal Decisions.* London: Michael Joseph, 1956.

Richelson, Jeffrey T. *The U.S. Intelligence Commun-ity.* Cambridge, Mass.: Ballinger, 1985.

————. *Sword and Shield: Soviet Intelligence and Security Apparatus.* Cambridge, Mass.: Ballinger, 1986.

————. *American Espionage and the Soviet Target.* New York: Quill, 1988.

————. *America's Secret Eyes in Space: The U.S. Key-hole Spy Satellite Program.* New York: Harper, 1990.

————. *A Century of Spies.* New York: Oxford, 1995.

Ridgway, Matthew B. *The Korean War.* Garden City, N.Y.: Doubleday, 1967.

Riess, Curt, *Total Espionage.* New York: Putnam's, 1941.

————. *They Were There.* New York: Putnam's, 1944.

Rieul, Roland. *Escape into Espionage.* New York: Walker, 1987.

Rintelin, Franz von. *Memoirs.* London: André Deutsch, 1952.

Ritter, Gerhard. *Carl Goerdeler und die deutsch Widerstandsbewegung.* Stuttgart: Deutsche Verlag, 1956.

Roberts. J. M. *The Penguin History of the World.* New York: Penguin, 1990.

Robinson, Howard. *The British Post Office: A History.* Princeton, N.J.: Princeton University Press, 1948.

Rodzianko, M. V. *The Reign of Rasputin.* London: Philpot, 1927.

Rohwer, Jurgen. *The Critical Convoy Battles of March 1943.* Annapolis, Md.: Naval Institute Press, 1977.

Röling, Dr. B. V. A., and Rütter, Dr. C. F. *The Tokyo Judg-ments: The International Military Tribunal of the Far East.* Amsterdam: APA University Press, 1977.

Romanones, Aline. *The Spy Wore Red.* New York: Random House, 1987.

Romans-Petit, Colonel Henri. *Les Maquis de l'Ain.* Paris: Hachette, 1974.

Romualdi, Serafino. *Presidents and Peons.* New York: Funk & Wagnalls, 1967.

Ronge, Maximilian. *Kriegs und Industri-espionage.* Zurich: Amalthea Verlag, 1930.

Roosevelt, Archie. *For Lust of Knowing: Memoirs of an Intelligence Officer.* Boston: Little, Brown, 1988.

Roosevelt, Elliott. *As He Saw It.* New York: Duell, Sloan and Parce, 1946.

————. *F.D.R.: His Personal Letters.* (vol. III, 1938–1945) New York: Duell, Sloan & Pearce, 1950.

Roosevelt, Kermit. *War Report of the OSS.* New York: Walker, 1976.

Root, Jonathan. *The Betrayers.* New York: Coward-McCann, 1963.

Root, Waverly. *Secret History of the War.* New York: Scribner's, 1945.

Rootham, Jasper. *Misfire: The Chronicle of a British Mission to Mihailovich, 1943–1944.* London: Chatto & Windus, 1946.

Ropp, Theodore. *War in the Modern World.* Durham, N.C.: Duke University Press, 1959.

Rorty, James, and Decter, Moshe. *McCarthy and the Communists.* Boston: Beacon, 1954.

Roscoe, Theodore. *The Web of Conspiracy.* Englewood Cliffs, N. J.: Prentice-Hall, 1959.

Rose, Norman. *Vansittart, Study of a Diplomat.* London: Heinemann, 1958.

Rosenman, S. I. *Working with Roosevelt.* New York: De Capo Press, 1972.

Rosinski, Herbert. *The German Army.* New York: Praeger, 1966.

Rositzke, Harry. *The CIA's Secret Operations.* New York: Reader's Digest Press, 1970.

———. *The KGB: The Eyes of Russia.* Garden City, N.Y.: Doubleday, 1981.

Roskill, Stephen. *Hankey: Man of Secrets.* London: Collins, 1972.

Rothfels, Hans. *The German Opposition to Hitler.* New York: Henry Regnery, 1948.

Rothschild, Victor. *Random Variables.* London: Collins, 1981.

Roussey, de Sales, Raoul. *The Making of Yesterday.* New York: Reynal and Hitchcock, 1947.

Rout, Leslie B. and Bratzel, John F. *The Shadow War: German Espionage and the United States Counterespionage in Latin America During World War II.* Frederick, Md.: University Publications, 1986.

Rovere, Richard H. *Senator Joe McCarthy.* Cleveland: World, 1960.

———. *The American Establishment and Other Reports, Opinions and Speculations.* New York: Harcourt, Brace & World, 1962.

Rowan, Ford. *Techno Spies.* New York: Putnam's, 1978.

Rowan, Richard Wilmer. *Spy and Counter-Spy.* London: John Hamilton, 1929.

———. *The Pinkertons: A Detective Dynasty.* Boston: Little, Brown, 1931.

———, with Deindorfer, Robert. *Secret Service: 33 Centuries of Espionage.* New York: Hawthorn Books, 1967.

Rowse, A. L. *Homosexuals in History.* London: Weidenfeld & Nicolson, 1977.

Ruby, Marcel. *F Section, SOE: The Story of the Buckmaster Network.* London: Leo Cooper, 1988.

Runciman, Steven. *Byzantine Civilization.* London: Longmans, 1933.

Rutter, O. *British North Borneo.* London: Constable, 1922.

Russell, Lord of Liverpool. *The Knights of Bushido: The Shocking History of Japanese War Atrocities.* New York: Dutton, 1958.

Russell, William. *Berlin Embassy.* New York: E. P. Dutton, 1941.

Ryan, Cornelius. *The Longest Day.* New York: Simon & Schuster, 1959.

———. *The Last Battle.* New York: Simon & Schuster, 1966.

Ryan, Paul B. *The Iranian Rescue Mission: Why It Failed.* Annapolis, Md.: Naval Institute Press, 1985.

Sabattier, G. *Le Destin de l'Indochine.* Paris: Plon, 1952.

Sacher, Howard. M. *The Course of Modern Jewish History.* Cleveland: World, 1958.

Sainteny, Jean. *Histoire d'une Paix Manquée.* Paris: Amiot Dumont, 1953.

Sakai, Saburo, with Caidin, Martin. *Samurai!* New York: Dutton, 1957.

Salinger, Pierre. *With Kennedy.* New York: Doubleday, 1966.

Salisbury, Harrison (ed.). *The Soviet Union: The Fifty Years.* New York: Harcourt, Brace & World, 1967.

Salvadori, Massimo. *The Labour and the Wounds: A Personal Chronicle of One Man's Fight for Freedom.* London: Pall Mall, 1958.

Sansom, Sir George Bailey. *A History of Japan.* (3 vols.) Stanford, Calif.: Stanford University Press, 1958.

Saposs, David Joseph. *Communism in American Politics.* Washington, D. C.: Public Affairs Press, 1960.

Saraphis, S. (trans. Marian Pascoe.) *Greek Resistance Army: The Story of E. L. A. S.* London: Birch Books, 1951.

Sargant, William. *Battle for the Mind.* London: Heinemann, 1957.

Sarton, George. *Six Wings: Men of Science in the Renaissance.* Bloomington, Ind.: Indiana University Press, 1957.

Saunders, Hilary St. George. *Combined Operations.* New York: Macmillan, 1943.

Sawatsky, John. *Men in the Shadows: The RCMP Security Service.* Garden City, N.Y.: Doubleday, 1980.

———. *For Services Rendered.* Garden City, N.Y.: Doubleday, 1982.

Sawyer, Roger. *Casement: The Flawed Hero.* London: Routledge & Kegan Paul, 1985.

Sayer, Ian, and Botting, Douglas. *America's Secret Army: The Untold Story of the Counterintelli-gence Corps.* New York: Watts, 1989.

Sayers, Michael, and Kahn, Albert E. *Sabotage! The Secret War Against America.* New York: Harper, 1942.

Schachner, Nathan. *Aaron Burr: A Biography.* New York: Frederick A. Stokes, 1937.

Schama, Simon. *Two Rothschilds and the House of Israel.* New York: Knopf, 1982.

Schaar, John H. *Loyalty in America.* Berkeley, Calif.: University of California Press, 1957.

Schechter, Betty. *The Dreyfus Affair: A National Scandal.* Boston: Houghton Mifflin, 1965.

Schechter, Jerrold L., and Deriabin, Peter S. *The Spy Who Saved the World: How a Soviet Colonel Changed the Course of the Cold War.* New York: Scribner's, 1992.

Schellenberg, Walter. *The Labyrinth: The Memoirs of Walter Schellenberg.* New York: Harper & Row, 1956.

Schemmer, Ben. *The Raid.* New York: Harper, 1976.

Scheutz, Arthur (Tristan Busch). (trans. Anthony V. Ireland.) *Secret Service Unmasked.* London: Hutchinson, 1948.

Schiff, Ze'ev. *A History of the Israeli Army, 1874 to the Present.* New York: Macmillan, 1985.

Schlabrendorff, Fabian von. *The Secret War Against Hitler.* New York: Pitman, 1965.

Schlesinger, Arthur M., Jr. *Crisis of the Old Order.* Boston: Houghton Mifflin, 1956.

———. *The Coming of the New Deal.* Boston: Houghton Mifflin, 1959.

———. *The Politics of Upheaval.* Boston: Houghton Mifflin, 1960.

———. *A Thousand Days.* Boston: Houghton Mifflin, 1965.

———. *The Age of Roosevelt.* Boston: Houghton Mifflin, 1969.

———. *Robert Kennedy and His Times.* Boston: Houghton Mifflin 1978.

Schlesinger, Robert J. *Principles of Electronic Warfare.* Englewood Cliffs, N.J.: Prentice-Hall, 1961.

Schmidt, Paul. *Hitler's Interpreter.* London: Heine-mann, 1951.

Schneir, Walter, and Schneir, Miriam. *Invitation to an Inquest.* Garden City, N.Y.: Doubleday, 1965.

Schoenbrun, David. *Soldiers of the Night: The Story of the French Resistance.* New York: E. P. Dutton, 1980.

Schorr, Daniel. *Clearing the Air.* Boston: Houghton Mifflin, 1977.

Schramm, Wilhelm von. (trans. R. T. Clark.) *Conspiracy Among Generals.* London: Allen & Unwin, 1956.

Schuman, Frederick L. *Russia Since 1917.* New York: Knopf, 1957.

Schwartz, Harry. *Prague's 200 Days.* New York: Praeger, 1969.

Schwarzwalder, John. *We Caught Spies.* New York: Duell, Sloan & Pearce, 1946.

Schweitzer, Peter. *Friendly Spies: How America's Allies Are Using Economic Espionage to Steal Our Secrets.* New York: Atlantic Monthly Press, 1993.

Scott, Peter Dale, Hoch, Paul L., and Stetler, Russell (eds.). *The Assassinations.* New York: Vintage, 1976.

Scott, Robert L. *Damned to Glory.* New York: Scribner's, 1944.

Seabury, Paul. *The Wilhelmstrasse: A Study of German Diplomats Under the Nazi Regime.* Berkeley, Calif.: University of California Press, 1954.

Seale, Patrick, and McConville, Maureen. *Philby: The Long Road to Moscow.* New York: Simon & Schuster, 1973.

———. *Assad of Syria: The Struggle for the Middle East.* London: L. B. Tauris, 1988.

Seaton, Albert. *The Russo-German War, 1941–1945.* London: Barker, 1971.

———. *The German Army, 1933–45.* London: Weidenfeld & Nicolson, 1982.

Seitz, Albert. *Mihailovic: Hoax or Hero?* Columbus, Ohio: Leigh House, 1953.

Sejna, Jan. *We Will Bury You.* London: Sidgwick and Jackson, 1982.

———, and Douglass, Joseph D. *Decision-Making in Communist Countries: An Inside View.* London: Pergamon, 1986.

Seldes, George. *You Can't Print That.* New York: Payson and Clarke, 1929.

Service, John. *The Amerasia Papers: Some Problems in the History of U.S.-China Relations.* Berkeley, Calif.: Center for Chinese Studies, 1971.

Seth, Ronald. *Secret Servants: A History of Japanese Espionage.* New York: Farrar, Straus & Giroux, 1957.

———. *Anatomy of Spying.* London: Arthur Barker, 1961.

———. *Unmasked: The Story of Soviet Espionage.* New York: Hawthorn, 1965.

———. *The Spy Who Wasn't Caught.* London: Hale, 1966.

———. *The Sleeping Truth.* New York: Hart, 1968.

Seton-Watson, Hugh. *The East European Revolution.* London: Methuen, 1950.

Seton-Watson, R. W. *Sarajevo.* London: Hutchinson, 1927.

Shannon, David A. *The Decline of American Communism.* New York: Harcourt Brace, 1959.

Shaplen, Robert. *The Lost Revolution.* New York: Harper, 1965.

Sharp, Malcolm P. *Was Justice Done?: The Rosenberg-Sobell Case.* New York: Monthly Review Press, 1956.

Sheba, Kimpel. *I Cover Japan.* Tokyo: Tokyo News Service, 1952.

Sheean, Vincent. *Personal History.* New York: Doubleday, 1935.

———. *Between the Thunder and the Sun.* New York: Random House, 1943.

———. *This House Against This House.* New York: Random House, 1946.

Shepherd, Gordon. *Dollfuss.* New York: Macmillan, 1961.

Sheridan, James E. *Chinese Warlords: The Career of Feng Yu-hsiang.* Stanford, Calif.: Stanford University Press, 1966.

Sherwin, Martin J. *A World Destroyed.* New York: Knopf, 1975.

Sherwood, Robert E. *Roosevelt and Hopkins.* New York: Harper, 1950.

Shevchenko, Arkady N. *Breaking with Moscow.* New York: Knopf, 1985.

Shiber, Etta. *Paris Underground.* New York: Scribner's, 1943.

Shigemitsu, Mamoru. *Japan and Her Destiny.* New York: Dutton, 1958.

Shils, Edward Albert. *The Torment of Secrecy: The Background and Consequences of American Security Policies.* Glencoe, Ill.: Free Press, 1956.

Shirer, William. *Berlin Diary.* New York: Knopf, 1941.

———. *End of a Berlin Diary.* New York: Knopf, 1947.

———. *Stranger, Come Home.* Boston: Little, Brown, 1954.

———. *The Rise and Fall of the Third Reich.* New York: Simon & Schuster, 1960.

———. *The Collapse of the Third Republic.* New York: Simon & Schuster, 1979.

Shub, David. *Lenin.* New York: Doubleday, 1950.

Shultz, George. *Turmoil and Triumph: My Years as Secretary of State.* New York: Scribner's, 1993.

Signal Security Agency. *French Codes Studied by MI8 in 1921–1923.* Washington, D.C.: SSA, 1945.

Silber, Julius C. *Invisible Weapons.* London: Hutchinson, 1932.

Simpson, Christopher. *Blowback.* London: Weiden-feld & Nicolson, 1987.

Sinclair, Andrew. *The Red and the Blue: Cambridge, Treason and Intelligence.* Boston: Little, Brown, 1986.

Singer, Kurt. *Spies and Traitors of World War II.* New York: Prentice-Hall, 1945.

———. *Spies Who Changed History.* New York: Ace-Star, 1960.

———. *Mata Hari.* New York: Universal, 1967.

Skeat, W. W. *Malay Magic.* London: Macmillan, 1900.

Skendi, Stavro. *The Albanian National Awakening, 1878–1912.* Princeton, N. J.: Princeton Univers-ity Press, 1967.

Skidelsky, Robert. *Oswald Mosley.* London: Macmillan, 1975.

Skorzeny, Otto. *Skorzeny's Special Missions.* London: Robert Hale, 1957.

Slater, Leonard. *The Pledge.* New York: Simon & Schuster, 1970.

Slessor, Sir John. *The Central Blue.* London: Cassell, 1956.

Smedley, Agnes. *Daughter of Earth.* New York: Coward-McCann, 1935.

Smiley, David. *Albanian Assignment.* London: Chatto & Windus, 1984.

Smith, B. *The History of the Lancashire Fusiliers.* London: Sackville Press, 1901.

Smith, Bradley F. *The Shadow Warriors.* London: André Deutsch, 1983.

———. *The Ultra Magic Deals, and the Most Secret Special Relationship, 1940–1946.* Novato, Calif.: Presidio, 1993.

Smith, Clarence Jay, Jr. *Finland and the Russian Revolution, 1917–1922.* Atlanta: University of Georgia Press, 1958.

Smith, Colin. Carlos: *Portrait of a Terrorist.* New York: Holt, Rinehart & Winston, 1976.

Smith, John Chabot. *Alger Hiss: The True Story.* New York: Holt, Rinehart and Winston, 1976.

Smith, Joseph Burckholder. *Portrait of a Cold Warrior.* New York: Putnam's 1976.

Smith, Lawrence Dwight. *Cryptography: The Science of Secret Writings.* New York: Dover, 1955.

Smith, Lou. *The Secrets of MI6.* New York: St. Martin's, 1975.

Smith, Nicol, and Clark, Blake. *Into Siam: Underground Kingdom.* Indianapolis, Ind.: Bobbs-Merrill, 1946.

Smith, R. Jack. *The Unknown CIA: My Three Decades with the Agency.* New York: Berkley, 1992.

Smith, R. Harris. *OSS, The Secret History of America's First Central Intelligence Agency.* Berkeley: University of California Press, 1972.

Smith, Tommy J. *Ultra in the Battle of Britain: The Key to Success.* Carlisle Barracks, Penn.: U.S. Army War College, 1980.

Smith, Walter Bedell. *My Three Years in Moscow.* Philadelphia: Lippincott, 1950.

Smyth, Howard McGaw. *Secrets of the Fascist Era.* Carbondale, Ill.: Southern Illinois University Press, 1975.

Snepp, Frank. *Decent Interval.* New York: Random House, 1977.

Snow, Edgar. *Red Star over China.* London: Gollancz, 1937.

Snyder, Louis (ed.). *The Dreyfus Case: A Documen-tary History.* New Brunswick, N.J.: Rutgers University Press, 1973.

Sobell, Morton. *On Doing Time.* New York: Scribner's, 1974.

Solomon, Flora, and Litvinoff, Barnet. *Baku to Baker Street.* London: Collins, 1984.

Somerville, John. *The Communist Trials and the American Tradition.* New York: Cameron, 1956.

Sorensen, Theodore C. *Kennedy.* New York: Harper & Row, 1965.

Sorokim, Pitrim. *Leaves from a Russian Diary.* New York: Dutton, 1924.

Soustelle, Jacques. *Envers et contre Tout.* Paris: Laffont, 1950.

Spector, Ronald H. *Eagle Against the Sun: The American War with Japan.* New York: Vintage, 1985.

Speer, Albert. *Inside the Third Reich.* New York: Macmillan, 1962.

Speidel, Hans. (trans. Theo R. Crevenna.) *Invasion 1944: Rommel and the Normandy Campaign.* Chicago: Regnery, 1950.

Spencer Chapman, F. *The Jungle Is Neutral.* London: Chatto & Windus, 1949.

Spiro, Edward (E. H. Cookridge). *The Net That Covers the World.* New York: Henry Holt, 1955.

Spivak, J. L. *Europe Under Terror.* London: Gollancz, 1936.

Stafford, David. *Camp X.* New York: Dodd, Mead, 1987.

Stanley, Roy M. *World War II Photo Intelligence.* New York: Scribner's, 1981.

Stansky, Peter, and Abraham, W. *Journey to the Frontier: A Biography of Julian Bell and John Cornford.* London: Constable, 1970.

Stares, Paul. *The Militarization of Space: U.S. Policy, 1945–1984.* Ithaca, N.Y.: Cornell University Press, 1985.

Starobin, Joseph. *American Communism in Crisis, 1943–1957.* Cambridge, Mass.: Harvard University Press, 1972.

Stead, Philip John. *The Second Bureau.* London: Evans, 1959.

Steed, H. Wickham. *The Hapsburg Monarchy.* London: Constable, 1913.

Steevens, George Warrington. *The Tragedy of Dreyfus.* New York: Harper, 1899.

Steinberg, I. N. *In the Workshop of the Revolution.* New York: Rinehart, 1953.

Steinhauer, Gustav. *Steinhauer: The Kaiser's Master Spy.* New York: D. Appleton and Company, 1931.

Stephan, John J. *The Russian Fascists: Tragedy and Farce in Exile, 1924–1945.* New York: Harper, 1978.

Sterling, Claire. *The Terror Network.* New York: Berkley, 1982.

Stern, Lawrence. *The Wrong Horse.* New York: Times Books, 1977.

Stern, Philip Van Dorn. *Secret Missions of the Civil War.* Chicago: Rand McNally, 1959.

Stettinius, Edward R., Jr. *Roosevelt and the Russians.* Garden City, N.Y.: Doubleday, 1949.

Steven, Stewart. *Operation Splinter Factor.* Philadelphia: Lippincott, 1974.

Steven, Stewart. *The Spymasters of Israel.* New York: Macmillan, 1977.

Stevens, G. W. W. *Microphotography: Photography at Extreme Resolution.* New York: John Wiley, 1957.

Stevenson, William. *A Man Called Intrepid: The Secret War, 1939–1945.* London: Macmillan, 1976.

———. *90 Minutes at Entebbe.* London: Bantam, 1976.

———. *Intrepid's Last Case.* New York: Random House, 1983.

Stewart, George. *The White Armies of Russia: A Chronicle of Counter-Revolution and Allied Intervention.* New York: Macmillan, 1933.

Stieber, Wilhelm J.C.E. *The Chancellor's Spy: The Revelations of the Chief of Bismarck's Secret Service.* New York: Grove Press, 1979.

Stiller, Werner, and Adams, Jefferson. *Beyond the Wall: Memoirs of an East and West German Spy.* New York: Brassey's, 1992.

Stilwell, Joseph. *The Stilwell Papers.* New York: William Sloane, 1948.

Stimson, H. L., and Bundy, MacGeorge. *On Active Service in Peace and War.* New York: Harper, 1949.

Stirling, J. *The Colonials in South Africa.* London: Blackwood, 1967.

Stockwell, John. *In Search of Enemies: A CIA Story.* New York: W. W. Norton, 1978.

Stone, I. F. *The Truman Era.* New York: Vintage, 1973.

Storrs, Sir Ronald. *Memoirs.* New York: Putnam's, 1937.

Storry, Richard. *Double Patriots: A Study of Japanese Nationalism.* Boston: Houghton Mifflin, 1957.

Stott, William. *Documentary Expression and Thirties America.* New York: Oxford University Press, 1973.

Straight, Michael. *After Long Silence.* London: Collins, 1983.

Stratton, Roy. *SACO, The Rice Paddy Navy.* New York: C. S. Palmer, 1950.

Strauss, Lewis L. *Men and Decisions.* Garden City, N.Y.: Doubleday & Co., 1962.

Strickland, Alice. *Life of Mary Queen of Scots*. London: George Bell, 1907.

Strik-Strikfeldt, Wilfried. *Against Hitler and Japan*. New York: John Day, 1973.

Stripling, Robert. *The Red Plot Against America*. Drexel Hill, Pa.: Bell, 1949.

Strong, Kenneth. *Intelligence at the Top*. New York: Doubleday, 1969.

Stuart, Gilbert. *Kind-hearted Tiger*. London: Adolf Deutsch, 1965.

Stuart, Graham H. *The Department of State*. New York: Macmillan, 1949.

Stuart, John Leighton. *Fifty Years in China*. New York: Random House, 1954.

Sullivan, Mark. *Our Times*. (Six Volumes) New York: Scribner's, 1930.

Sulzberger, C. L. *A. Long Row of Candles*. New York: Macmillan, 1969.

Summers, Anthony, and Dorril, Stephen. *Honeytrap: The Secret Worlds of Stephen Ward*. London: Weidenfeld & Nicolson, 1982.

Sutherland, Douglas. *The Fourth Man*. London: Secker & Warburg, 1980.

Suvorov, Viktor. *Inside Soviet Military Intelligence*. New York: Macmillan, 1984.

Swanberg, W. A. *Luce and His Empire*. New York: Scribner's, 1972.

Swearingen, Rodgers, and Langer, Paul. *Red Flag in Japan*. Cambridge, Mass.: Harvard University Press, 1951.

Sweet-Escott, Bickham. *Baker Street Irregular*. London: Methuen, 1965.

Sweezy, Paul (ed.). *Paul Baran, A Collective Portrait*. New York: Monthly Review Press, 1965.

Sykes, Christopher. *Troubled Loyalty: A Biography of Adam von Trott zu Stolz*. London: Collins, 1968.

Talbott, Strobe. *The Master of the Game*. New York: Knopf, 1988.

Tammes, Rudolf. *The United States and the Cold War in the High North*. Oslo, Norway: Notam, 1991.

Tangye, Derek. *The Ambrose Rock*. London: Michael Joseph, 1982.

Tanin, O., and Yohan, E. *When Japan Goes to War*. New York: International Publishers, 1936.

Tannenbaum, Joseph. *Race and Reich*. New York: Twayne Publishers, 1956.

Tarling, N. *Britain, the Brookes and Brunei*. London: Oxford University Press, 1971.

Tasaki, Hanama. *Long the Imperial Way*. Boston: Houghton Mifflin, 1950.

Tauras, K. V. *Guerrilla Warfare on the Amber Coast*. New York: Voyages Press, 1962.

————. *Richer by Asia*. Boston: Houghton Mifflin, 1947.

————. *Awakening from History*. Boston: Gambit, 1969.

Taylor, Henry J. *Men of Power*. New York: Dodd, Mead, 1946.

Taylor, Maxwell. *Swords and Plowshares*. New York: W. W. Norton, 1972.

Taylor, Telford. *Sword and Swastika: Generals and Nazis in the Third Reich*. New York: Simon & Schuster, 1952.

————. *Grand Inquest—The Story of Congressional Investigations*. New York: Simon & Schuster, 1955.

————. *Munich: The Price of Peace*. Garden City, N.Y.: Doubleday, 1979.

Taylor von Mehren, Arthur (ed.). *Law in Japan*. Cambridge, Mass.: Harvard University Press, 1963.

Temperley, H. W. *History of Serbia*. London: Bell, 1917.

Terraine, John. *White Heat: The New Warfare, 1914–1918*. London: Leo Cooper, 1992.

Tevet, Shabati. *Moshe Dayan: The Soldier, the Man, the Legend*. London: Weidenfeld & Nicolson, 1972.

Thayer, Charles. *Hands Across the Cavier*. New York: Lippincott, 1953.

Thayer, George. *The War Business*. New York: Simon & Shuster, 1969.

Thierry, Wolton. *Le KGB en France*. Paris: Bernard Grasset, 1986.

Theobald, Robert A. *The Final Secret of Pearl Harbor*. New York: Devin-Adair, 1954.

Theoharis, Arthan (ed.). *Beyond the Hiss Case*. Philadelphia: Temple University, 1982.

Thomas, Hugh. *The Murder of Rudolf Hess*. London: Hodder & Stoughton, 1978.

Thomas, John Oram. *The Giant-Killers: The Danish Resistance Movement, 1940–1945*. London: Michael Joseph, 1975.

Thomas, Lowell. *Old Gimlet Eye: The Adventures of Smedley D. Butler*. New York: Farrar and Rinehart, 1933.

Thomas, Marcel. *L'Affaire sans Dreyfus*. Paris: Fayard, 1961.

Thomson, Sir Basil. *The Scene Changes*. London: Collins, 1938.

Thompson, James W., and Padover, Saul K. *Secret Diplomacy: A Record of Espionage and Double-Dealing, 1500–1815*. London: Jarrolds, 1937.

Thompson, Victor A. *Modern Organizations*. New York: Knopf, 1961.

Thorne, Christopher. *Allies of a Kind*. New York: Oxford, 1978.

Thwaites, Norman. *Velvet and Vinegar*. London: Grayson & Grayson, 1932.

Thwaites, Michael. *Truth Will Out*. London: Collins, 1980.

Tickell, Jerrard. *Odette: The Story of a British Agent*. London: Chapman & Hall, 1949.

————. *Moon Squadron*. London: Mann, 1956.

Tilman, H. W. *When Men and Mountains Meet*. Cambridge, Eng.: Cambridge University Press, 1946.

Timperley, H. J. *Japanese Terror in China*. New York: Modern Age Books, 1958.

Tinnin, David B., and Christensen, Dag. *The Hit Team*. Boston: Little, Brown, 1976.

Todd, Judith. *Rhodesia*. London: MacGibbon & Kee, 1966.

Togo, Shigenori. *The Cause of Japan*. New York: Simon & Schuster, 1956.

Toland, John. *Tokyo Record*. New York: Reynal & Hitchcock, 1943.

————. *But Not in Shame: The Six Months After Pearl Harbor*. New York: Random House, 1961.

————. *The Last 100 Days*. New York: Random House, 1965.

————. *The Rising Sun*. New York: Random House, 1970.

Tolischus, Otto. *Tokyo Record*. London: Hamish Hamilton, 1943.

Tolstoy, Nikolai. *Victims of Yalta*. London: Hodder & Stoughton, 1977.

————. *Stalin's Secret War*. New York: Holt, Rinehart and Winston, 1981.

Tompkins, Peter. *A Spy in Rome*. New York: Avon, 1962.

————. *The Murder of Admiral Darlan.* New York: Simon & Schuster, 1965.

————. *Italy Betrayed.* New York: Simon & Schuster, 1966.

Toye, Francis. *For What We Have Received: An Autobiography.* New York: Knopf, 1948.

Treadgold, Donald W. *Lenin and His Rivals.* New York: Praeger, 1955.

Trefousse, Hans Louis (ed.). *What Happened at Pearl Harbor: Documents Pertaining to the Japanese Attack of December 7, 1941, and Its Background.* New York: Twayne, 1958.

Tregonning, K. G. *Under Chartered Company Rule, Borneo, 1881–1963.* Kuala Lumpur: University of Malaya Press, 1965.

Trenowden, Ian. *Operations Most Secret: SOE, The Malayan Theatre.* London: William Kimber, 1978.

Trepper, Leopold. *The Great Game.* London: Michael Joseph, 1977.

Treverton, Gregory F. *Covert Action: The Limits of Intervention in the Postwar World.* New York: Basic Books, 1987.

Trevor-Roper, H. R. *The Bormann Letters.* London: Weidenfeld & Nicolson, 1954.

————. *The Last Days of Hitler.* New York: Macmillan, 1956.

————. *The Philby Affair.* London: William Kimber, 1968.

————. *Blitzkrieg in Defeat.* New York: Rinehart & Winston, 1971.

————. *Hermit of Peking.* New York: Knopf, 1977.

Trotsky, Leon. *My Life.* New York: Scribner's, 1930.

————. *Stalin.* New York: Harper, 1941.

————. *Trotsky's Diary in Exile.* Cambridge, Mass.: Harvard University Press, 1958.

————. *Lenin.* New York: Grosset & Dunlap, 1960.

————. *Terrorism and Communism.* Ann Arbor, Mich.: University of Michigan Press, 1961.

Troy, Thomas F. *Donovan and the CIA: A History of the Establishment of the Central Intelligence Agency.* Frederick, Md.: University Publications, 1981.

Trufanov, Sergei (Iliodor). *The Mad Monk of Russia.* New York: Century, 1918.

Truman, Harry S. *Memoirs.* New York: Doubleday, 1956.

Trythall, Anthony J. *Boney Fuller, The Intellectual General.* London: Cassell, 1977.

Tsipis, Kosta (ed.). *Arms Control Verification: The Technologies That Make It Possible.* London: Pergamon, 1985.

Tucker, Robert C., and Cohen, Stephen F. (eds.). *The Great Purge Trial.* New York: Grosset, 1965.

Tuchman, Barbara. *The Zimmermann Telegram.* New York: Viking Press, 1958.

————. *The Guns of August.* New York: Macmillan, 1962.

————. *The Proud Tower.* New York: Macmillan, 1966.

————. *Stilwell and the American Experience in China, 1911–1945.* New York: Macmillan, 1971.

Tuleja, Thaddeus. *Climax at Midway.* New York: Norton, 1960.

Tully, Andrew. *CIA: The Inside Story.* New York: Morrow, 1962.

————. *Inside Interpol.* New York: Walker, 1965.

————. *White Tie and Dagger, Inside Embassy Row: The Story of How Foreign Embassies Spy on the U.S. and Influence American Opinion, Policy and Laws.* New York: Morrow, 1967.

————. *The Super Spies.* New York: Morrow, 1969.

————. *Inside the FBI.* New York: McGraw-Hill, 1980.

Tunney, Thomas J. *Throttled! The Detection of the German and Anarchist Bomb Plotters.* Boston: Small, Maynard & Co., 1919.

Tupper, Harmon. *To the Great Ocean.* Boston: Little, Brown, 1965.

Turing, Sara. *Alan M. Turing.* Cambridge: Hefer, 1959.

Turner, Stansfield. *Secrecy and Democracy: The CIA in Transition.* Boston: Houghton Mifflin, 1985.

Turney-High, Harry Holbert. *Primitive War: Its Practices and Concepts.* Columbia, S.C.: University of South Carolina Press, 1949.

Ulam, Adam B. *The Bolsheviks: The Intellectual, Personal, and Political History of the Origins of Russian Communism.* New York: Macmillan, 1965.

————. *Stalin.* New York: Viking, 1973.

Ullman, Richard H. *Anglo-Soviet Relations, 1917–1921.* Princeton, N.J.: Princeton University Press, 1961.

————. *Britain and the Russian Civil War, November 1918–February 1920.* Princeton, N.J.: Princeton University Press, 1968.

Urquhart, Brian. *A Life in Peace and War.* New York: Harper, 1987.

U.S. Office of Strategic Services, Psychological Assessment Staff. *Assessment of Men.* New York: Rinehart, 1948.

Usborne, Richard. *Clubland Heroes.* London: Barrie & Jenkins, 1953.

Utley, Freda. *The China Story.* Chicago: Regnery, 1951.

————. *The Odyssey of a Liberal.* Washington, D.C.: Washington National Press, 1970.

Vagts, Alfred. *Defense and Diplomacy.* New York: King's Crown, 1958.

Vaillé, Eugene. *Le Cabinet Noir.* Paris: Presses Universitaires de France, 1950.

Valenta, Jiri. *Soviet Intervention in Czechoslovakia, 1968: Anatomy of a Decision.* Baltimore: Johns Hopkins University Press, 1979.

————, and Potter, William (eds.). *Soviet Decision-making for National Security.* London: Allen & Unwin, 1984.

Valtin, Jan (Richard Krebs). *Out of the Night.* New York: Alliance, 1941.

Van der Vat, Dan. *The Atlantic Campaign: World War II's Great Struggle at Sea.* New York: Harper, 1988.

————. *The Pacific Campaign: World War II, The U.S. Japanese Naval War, 1941–1945.* New York: Simon & Schuster, 1991.

Van Doren, Carl. *Secret History of the American Revolution.* New York: Viking Press, 1941.

Vance, Cyrus. *Hard Choices: Critical Years in America's Foreign Policy.* New York: Simon & Schuster, 1983.

Vandenbosch, Amry. *The Neutrality of the Nether-lands During the World War.* Amsterdam: Eerdmans, 1927.

Vansittart, Lord. *The Mist Profession.* London: Hutchinson, 1958.

Varner, Roy, and Collier, Wayne. *A Matter of Risk.* New York: Random House, 1977.

Vasari, Giorgio. (trans. Gaston du C. de Vere.) *Lives of the Most Eminent Painters, Sculptors and Architects.* London: Medici Society, 1912–1915.

Vassall, John. *Vassall.* London: Sidgwick & Jackson, 1975.

Vassilyev, A. T. *The Okhrana: The Russian Secret Police.* London: Harrap, 1930.

Vaughn, Miles W. *Under the Japanese Mask*. London: Lovat Dickson, 1937.

Verbitzky, Anatole, and Adler, Dick. *Sleeping with Moscow*. New York: Shapolsky Publishers, 1987.

Vercors (Jean Bruller). (trans. Rita Barisse.) *The Battle of Silence*. London: Collins, 1968.

Verity, Hugh. *We Landed by Moonlight*. London: W. H. Allen, 1978.

Vermpm. Betty D. *Ellen Wilkinson, 1891–1947*. London: Croom Helm, 1979.

Verrier, Anthony. *Through the Looking Glass: British Foreign Policy in an Age of Illusion*. London: Jonathan Cape, 1983.

Vespa, Amleto. *Secret Agent of Japan*. Boston: Little, Brown, 1938.

Vining, L. E. *Held by the Bolsheviks*. London: St. Catherine's Press, 1924.

Vladimirov, Leonid. *The Russian Space Bluff*. New York: Dial, 1973.

Volkman, Ernest. *Warriors of the Night*. New York: Morrow, 1985.

Vomécourt, Philippe de. *Who Lived to See the Day: France in Arms, 1940–1945*. London: Hutchinson, 1961.

Waagenaar, Sam. *Mata Hari*. Paris: Fayard, 1965.

Waite, Robert G. L. *Vanguard of Nazism: The Free-Corps Movement in Postwar Germany, 1918–1923*. Cambridge, Mass.: Harvard University Press, 1952.

Walker, David E. *Adventure in Diamonds*. London: Evans, 1955.

———. *Lunch with a Stranger*. London: Allen Wingate, 1957.

Wall, Bernard. *Headlong into Change*. London: Harvill Press, 1969.

Wallace, Henry A. *Soviet Asia Mission*. New York: Reynal, 1946.

Walpole, Spencer. *The Life of the Rt. Hon. Spencer Perceval*. London: Hurst & Blackett, 1874.

Walters, Vernon. *Silent Missions*. Garden City, N. Y.: Doubleday, 1978.

Walworth, Arthur. *Woodrow Wilson*. Boston: Houghton Mifflin, 1965.

Warburg, James. *The Long Road Home*. Garden City, N.Y.: Doubleday, 1964.

Ward, Estolv E. *Harry Bridges on Trial*. New York: Modern Age, 1940.

Warlimont, Walter. *Inside Hitler's Headquarters*. New York: Praeger, 1966.

Wark, Wesley K. *The Ultimate Enemy: British Intelligence and Nazi Germany, 1933–1939*. Ithaca, N.Y.: Cornell University Press, 1985.

Warshow, Robert. *The Immediate Experience*. Garden City, N.Y.: Doubleday, 1962.

Warren, William. *The Legendary American*. Boston: Houghton Mifflin, 1970.

Watson-Watt, Robert. *The Pulse of Radar*. New York: Dial, 1959.

Way, Peter. *Codes and Ciphers*. New York: Crown, 1977.

Wechsler, James A. *The Age of Suspicion*. New York: Random House, 1960.

Wedemeyer, Albert. *Wedemeyer Reports*. New York: Henry Holt, 1958.

Weinstein, Allen. *Perjury: The Hiss-Chambers Case*. New York: Knopf, 1978.

Weintraub, Stanley, and Weintraub, Rodeele (eds.). *Evolution of a Revolt: Early Postwar Writings of T. E. Lawrence*. University Park, Penn.: Pennsylvania State University Press, 1968.

Welch, Robert, Jr. *The Life of John Birch*. Boston: Western Islands, 1967.

Welchman, Gordon. *The Hut Six Story: Breaking the Enigma Codes*. New York: McGraw-Hill, 1986.

Welles, Sumner. *Seven Major Decisions*. New York: Harper, 1951.

Werbell, Frederick E., and Clarke, Thurston. *Lost Hero: The Mystery of Raoul Wallenberg*. New York: McGraw-Hill, 1982.

Werner, Ruth (Ruth Kuczynski). *Olga Benario*. Berlin: Verlag Neues Leben, 1962.

———. *Sonja's Rapport*. Berlin: Verlag Neues Leben, 1982.

Werth, Alexander. *Russia at War, 1941–1945*. New York: Caroll & Graf, 1984.

West, Nigel. *MI5: British Security Operations, 1909–1945*. London: Bodley Head, 1981.

———. *A Matter of Trust*. London: Weidenfeld & Nicolson, 1982.

———. *The Circus: MI5 Operations, 1945–1972*. New York: Stein & Day, 1983.

———. *A Thread of Deceit: Espionage Myths of World War II*. New York: Random House, 1985.

———. *GCHQ: The Secret Wireless War, 1900–1986*. London: Weidenfeld and Nicolson, 1986.

———. *Molehunt*. London: Weidenfeld & Nicolson, 1988.

———. *Secret War: The Story of SOE, Britain's Wartime Sabotage Organization*. London: Hodder & Stoughton, 1992.

West, Rebecca. *Black Lamb and Grey Falcon*. New York: Viking Press, 1943.

———. *The Meaning of Treason*. London: Macmillan, 1949.

———. *A Train of Powder*. New York: Viking Press, 1953.

———. *The New Meaning of Treason*. New York: Viking, 1967.

West, W. J. *Truth Betrayed*. London: Duckworth, 1987.

Wexley, John. *The Judgment of Julius and Ethel Rosenberg*. New York: Ballantine Books, 1977.

Weyl, Nathaniel. *Treason: The Story of Disloyalty and Betrayal in American History*. Washington, D.C.: Public Affairs Press, 1950.

———. *The Battle Against Disloyalty*. New York: Crowell, 1951.

Whaley, Barton. *Codeword Barbarossa*. Cambridge, Mass.: MIT Press, 1973.

Wheatley, Ronald. *Operation Sea Lion*. London: Cassell, 1958.

Wheeler-Bennett, John W. *The Nemesis of Power*. New York: St. Martin's, 1953.

———. *King George VI*. New York: St. Martin's, 1958.

White, Dorothy Shipley. *Seeds of Discord*. Syracuse, N.Y.: Syracuse University Press, 1964.

White, Theodore H., and Jacoby, Annalee. *Thunder Out of China*. New York: William Sloane, 1946.

———. *Fire in the Ashes*. New York: William Sloan Associates, 1953.

———. *In Search of History*. New York: Harper, 1978.

White, William C. *Lenin*. New York: Harrison Smith, 1936.

White, William L. *The Little Toy Dog*. New York: Dutton, 1962.

Whitehead, Don. *The F.B.I. Story*. New York: Random House, 1956.

———. *Journey Into Crime*. New York: Random House, 1960.

———. *Attack on Terror*. New York: Funk & Wagnalls, 1970.

Whitehouse, Arch. *Espionage and Counterespionage.* Garden City, N.Y.: Doubleday & Co., 1964.

Whiteside, Thomas. *An Agent in Place.* New York: Viking Press, 1966.

Whiting, Charles. *The Battle for Twelveland.* London: Leo Cooper, 1975.

Whitwell, John (pseud.). *British Agent.* London: William Kimber, 1966.

Wiesenthal, Simon. *The Murderers Among Us.* London: Heinemann, 1967.

Wighton, Charles. *Heydrich.* London: Oldhams Press, 1962.

————. *World's Greatest Spies.* London: Oldhams Press, 1962.

Willert, Sir Arthur. *The Road to Safety.* London: Derek Verschoyle, 1952.

Williams, Basil. Stanhope: *A Study in Eighteenth Century War and Diplomacy.* Oxford, Eng.: Clarendon Press, 1932.

Williams, J. H. *Elephant Bill.* London: Rupert Hart-Davis, 1950.

Williams, Robert Chadwell. *Klaus Fuchs: Atom Spy.* Cambridge, Mass.: Harvard University Press, 1987.

Willoughby, Charles A. *Shanghai Conspiracy: The Sorge Spy Ring.* New York: Dutton, 1952.

Wills, Garry. *Nixon Agonistes.* New York: New American Library, 1970.

Wilkinson, James D. *The Intellectual Resistance in Europe.* Cambridge, Mass.: Harvard University Press, 1981.

Wilmot, Chester. *The Struggle for Europe.* New York: Harper, 1952.

Wilson, Colin. *Rasputin and the Fall of the Romanovs.* New York: Farrar, Straus, 1964.

Wilson, Edmund. *To the Finland Station.* New York: Doubleday, 1953.

Wilson, Harold. *Labour Government, 1964–1970.* London: Weidenfeld and Nicolson, 1971.

Wilson, Hugh. *Diplomat Between Wars.* New York: Longmans, Green, 1941.

Wilson, Hugh, Jr., *Disarmament and Cold War in the Thirties.* New York: Vantage, 1963.

Wilson, John S. *Scouting 'Round the World.* London: Blandford, 1959.

Wilton, Robert. *The Last Days of the Romanovs.* London: Thornton Butterworth, 1920.

Winks, Robin. *Cloak and Gown.* New York: Morrow, 1987.

Winterbotham, Frederick W. *Secret and Personal.* London: William Kimber, 1969.

————. *The Ultra Secret.* London: Weidenfeld & Nicolson, 1974.

————. *The Nazi Connection.* London: Weidenfeld & Nicolson, 1978.

Winton, John. *Ultra at Sea: How Breaking the Nazi Code Affected Allied Naval Strategy During World War II.* New York: Morrow, 1988.

Wintringham, T. H. *Mutiny: Being a Survey of Mutinies from Spartacus to Invergordan.* London: Stanley Nott, 1936.

Wise, David, and Ross, Thomas. *The Invisible Government.* New York: Random House, 1964.

————. *The Espionage Establishment.* New York: Random House, 1967.

————. *The Spy Who Got Away.* New York: Random House, 1988.

————. *Molehunt: The Secret Search for Traitors That Shattered the CIA.* New York: Random House, 1992.

Wiskemann, Elizabeth. *The Europe I Saw.* London: Collins, 1968.

Witcover, Jules. *Sabotage at Black Tom: Imperial Germany's Secret War in America, 1914–1917.* Chapel Hill, N.C.: Algonquin Books, 1989.

Wittlin, Thaddeus. Commissar: *The Life and Death of Lavrenti Pavlovic Beria.* New York: Macmillan, 1972.

Wohlstetter, Roberta. *Pearl Harbor: Warning and Decision.* Stanford, Calif.: Stanford University Press, 1962.

Wolfe, Bertram D. *Three Who Made a Revolution.* New York: Dial, 1948.

————. *Khrushchev and Stalin's Ghost.* New York: Praeger, 1957.

Wolin, Simon, and Slusser, Robert M. *The Soviet Secret Police.* New York: Praeger, 1967.

Woltin, Thierry. *Le KGB en France.* Paris: Bernard Grasset, 1986.

Wood, Neil. *Communism and the British Intellectuals.* London: Gollancz, 1959.

Woods, David L. *A History of Tactical Communications Techniques.* Orlando, Fla.: Martin Co., 1965.

Woodhouse, C. M. *Apple of Discord: A Survey of Greek Politics in Their International Setting.* London: Hutchinson, 1948.

————. *The Struggle for Greece, 1941–1949.* London: Hart-Davis, McGibbon, 1976.

Woodward, Bob. *Veil: The Secret Wars of the CIA, 1981–1987.* New York: Simon & Schuster, 1987.

————. *The Commanders.* New York: Simon & Schuster, 1991.

Woodward, Sir Llewellyn. *British Foreign Policy in the Second World War.* London: Her Majesty's Stationery Office, 1962.

Woolf, Leonard. *Downhill All the Way.* London: Hogarth Press, 1967.

Worsley, T. C. *Flannelled Fool.* London: Hogarth Press, 1985.

Wright, Ernest Vincent. *Gadsby: The Story of Over 50,000 Words Without Using the Letter E.* Los Angeles: Wetzel Publishing, 1939.

Wright, Peter. *Spycatcher.* New York: Viking, 1987.

Wrixon, Fred B. *Codes and Ciphers.* New York: Prentice-Hall, 1992.

Wulf, Josef. *Heinrich Himmler.* Berlin: Arani, 1960.

Wynne, Greville. *The Man from Odessa: The Secret Career of a British Agent.* London: Granada, 1983.

Yardley, Herbert O. *The American Black Chamber.* Indianapolis, Ind.: Bobbs-Merrill, 1931.

————. *The Education of a Poker Player.* New York: Simon & Schuster, 1957.

————. *The Chinese Black Chamber.* Boston: Houghton Mifflin, 1983.

Yates, Frances A. *Giordano Bruno and the Hermetic Tradition.* London: Routledge and Kegan Paul, 1964.

Yergin, Daniel. *Shattered Peace.* Boston: Houghton Mifflin, 1977.

"Yipsilon" (pseud.). *Pattern of World Revolution.* New York: Ziff Davis, 1947.

Yoshihashi, Takehiko. *Conspiracy at Mukden.* New Haven, Conn.: Yale University Press, 1963.

Young, A. Morgan. *Japan in Recent Times, 1912–1926.* New York: Morrow, 1929.

————. *Imperial Japan, 1926–1938.* New York: Morrow, 1938.

Young, Desmond. *The Desert Fox.* New York: Harper, 1950.

Young, Filson. *With the Battle Cruisers.* London: Cassell, 1921.

Young, John. *The Research Activities of the South Manchurian Railway Company, 1907–1945: A History and Bibliography.* New York: Columbia University, 1966.

Young, Kenneth. *Balfour.* Edinburgh: G. Bell, 1963.

Youssaf, Mohammad. *The Bear Trap.* London: Leo Cooper, 1992.

Yussoupov, Felix. *Rasputin.* New York: Dial, 1927.

Zacharias, Ellis M. *Secret Missions.* New York: Putnam's, 1946.

————. with Farago, Ladislas. *Behind Closed Doors.* New York: Putnam's, 1950.

Zarudnaya, Elena (trans.). *Trotsky's Diary in Exile.* Cambridge, Mass.: Harvard University Press, 1958.

Zavarzine, P. (trans. J. Jeanson.) *Souvenirs d'un chef de l'Okhrana, 1900–1917.* Paris: Payot, 1930.

Zawodny, J. H. *Nothing But Honor: The Story of the Warsaw Rising, 1944.* London: Macmillan, 1978.

Zeiger, Henry A. *The Case Against Adolf Eichmann.* New York: Signet, 1960.

Zeligs, Meyer A. *Friendship & Fratricide: An Analysis of Whittaker Chambers and Alger Hiss.* New York: Viking, 1967.

Zeller, Eberhard. *The Flame of Freedom.* London: Woolf, 1967.

Zeman, Z. A. B. *Germany and the Revolution in Russia, 1915–1918.* London: Oxford University Press, 1958.

Zhukov, G. K. *The Memoirs of Marshal Zhukov.* New York: Delacorte, 1971.

Zink, Harold. *The United States in Germany.* Princeton, N.J.: Van Nostrand, 1957.

Zipfel, Friedrich. *Gestapo und Sicherheitsdienst.* Berlin: Arani, 1960.

Zobel, Hiller B. *The Boston Massacre.* New York: W. W. Norton, 1970.

Zuckerman, Solly. *From Apes to Warlords.* London: Hamish Hamilton, 1978.

Zumwalt, Elmo R., Jr. *On Watch.* New York: Quadrangle, 1976.

PERIODICALS

"Abel for Powers," *Time*, February 16, 1962.

"Ace Reporter Bob Woodward Lifts the Veil on the Secrets of CIA Chief William Casey," *People*, October 12, 1987.

Alpern, David M. "The Man Who Wasn't There: Bill Casey's Off-The-Books CIA," *Newsweek*, October 5, 1987.

Alsop, Joseph. "Miss Bentley's Bondage," *Commonweal*, November 9, 1951.

————. "The Strange Case of Louis Budenz," *Atlantic Monthly*, April 1952.

Anders, Roger M. "The Rosenberg Case Revisited: The Greenglass Testimony and the Protection of Atomic Secrets," *The American Historical Review*, April 1978.

Andrew, Christopher, and Nelson, Keith. "Tsarist Code-breakers and British Codes," *Intelligence and National Security* 1, no. 1, 1986.

Angevine, Robert G. "Gentlemen Do Read Each Other's Mail; American Intelligence in the Interwar Era," *Intelligence and National Security* 7, no. 2, 1992.

Armour, Ian D. "Colonel Redl: Fact and Fantasy," *Intelligence and National Security* 2, no 1, 1987.

Ascoli, Max. "The Case of Alger Hiss," *The Reporter*, August 30, 1949.

————. "The Lives and Deaths of Whittaker Chambers," *The Reporter*, July 8, 1952.

"The Atom Spy Hunt," *Time*, October 4, 1948.

"Away They Go!" *Time*, December 23, 1966.

"Baby Face," *Time*, March 14, 1949.

Bamford, James. "America's Supersecret Eyes in Space," New York *Times Magazine*, January 13, 1985.

Barmine, Alexander. "New Communist Conspiracy," *Reader's Digest*, October 1944.

Barron, John. "The KGB's Deepest Secret." *Reader's Digest*, November 1988.

"Basement in Chevy Chase," *Time*, August 23, 1948.

Becker, Henry. "The Nature and Consequences of Black Propaganda," *American Sociological Review*, April 1949.

Blake, Patricia. "This Is the Winter of Moscow's Dissent," New York *Times Magazine*, March 24, 1968.

Borland, Hal, "Diplomacy in Scrambled Words," *New York Times Magazine*, September 22, 1940.

Bosewell, Bryan. "Major Shake-up for French Spy Network," *The Weekend Australian*, November 20–21, 1982.

"The Boy from Virginia," *Time*, August 29, 1960.

Bratzel, John F., and Rout, Leslie B., Jr. "Pearl Harbor, Microdots, and J. Edgar Hoover," *American Historical Review*, December 1982.

Brinton, Crane. "Letters from Liberated France," *French Historical Studies*, Spring 1961.

"Britain's Pet Spy," *Newsweek*, May 28, 1945.

Broad, William J. "Evading the Soviet Ear at Glen Cove," *Science*, September 1982.

"The Brothers," *Time*, June 30, 1961.

Brower, Brock. "The Problems of Alger Hiss," *Esquire*, December 1960.

Bruce, David K. E. "The National Intelligence Authority," *Virginia Quarterly Review*, Summer 1946.

Bruce-Briggs, B. "Another Ride on Tricycle," *Intelligence and National Security* 7, no. 2, 1992.

Buckley, William F., Jr. "The End of Whittaker Chambers," *Esquire*, September 1962.

Budkevich, S. "The Credo of Richard Sorge," *New Times*, October 28, 1964.

Byrnes, Robert F. "American Scholars in Russia Soon Learn About the KGB," *New York Times Magazine*, November 16, 1969.

Cahn, Anne Hessing. "Team B: The Trillion Dollar Experiment," *Bulletin of the Atomic Scientists*, April 1993.

Calderon, Joseph. "How Can I Face Them?" *Commonweal*, May 10, 1946.

Carr, E. H. "The Origin and Status of the Cheka," *Soviet Studies*, July 1958.

Case, Lynn. "The Maquis Republic of Vercors," *Infantry Journal*, April 1947.

"Casey Vs. Moscow: Win and Lose," *Newsweek*, October 5, 1987.

Chakrabandhu, M. C. Karawik. "Force 136 and the Siamese Resistance Movement," *Asiatic Review*, April 1947.

Chamberlain, J. "OSS," Life, November 10, 1945.

Chandruang, Kumut, and Prabhu, C. "Our Siamese Underground," *Asia and the Americas*, November 1945.

Chapman, J. W. M. "No Final Solution: A Survey of the Cryptanalytical Capabilities of German Military Agencies, 1926–1935," *Intelligence and National Security* 1, no. 1, 1986.

Chekhonin, B. "Heroes Do Not Die," *Izvestia*, September 8, 1964.

Chernyavsky, V. "The Feat of Richard Sorge," *Pravda*, November 6, 1964.

Childs, John. "The Hiss Case and the American Intellectual," *The Reporter*, September 26, 1960.

Clark, Blake. "Spark Plugs of France's Secret Army," *Tricolor*, March 1945.

"Cleaning Up the Mess," *Newsweek*, October 12, 1987.

Cloud, Stanley W. "Holes in a Spy Scandal," *Time*, July 20, 1987.

"Cold War Candor," *Time*, May 16, 1960.

"Comrade, On to London," *Time*, July 13, 1962.

Conroy, Hilary. "Japan's War in China: Historical Paralllel to Vietnam," *Pacific Affairs*, Spring 1970.

Cook, Fred J. "The CIA," *The Nation*, June 24, 1961.

———. "Ghost of a Typewriter," *The Nation*, May 12, 1962.

Cookridge, E. H. "The Spy of the Century," *Daily Telegraph Magazine*, March 7, 1969.

"The Coplon Case," Time, February 4, 1952.

Corvo, Max. "America's Intelligence Dilemma," *Hartford Courant*, May 28, 1961.

Coster, Donald Q. "We Were Expecting You at Dakar," *The American Legion Magazine*, August 1946.

Countryman, Vernon. "Out Damned Spot: Judge Kaufman and the Rosenberg Case," *The New Republic*, October 8, 1977.

Cuelenaere, A. "A Short History of Microphotography," *Journal of Forensic Sciences*, January 1959.

Cyr, Paul. "We Blew the Yellow River Bridge," *The Saturday Evening Post*, March 23, 1946.

Davis, Forrest. "The Secret Story of a Surrender," *The Saturday Evening Post*, September 22, 1945.

Davis, Hope Hale. "A Memoir: Looking Back at My Years in the Party," *The New Leader*, February 11, 1980.

"Day of Judgment," *Time*, March 20, 1950.

"Death for the Saboteurs," *Time*, August 17, 1942.

Defourneaux, René. "Secret Encounter with Ho Chi Minh," *Look*, August 9, 1966.

Denniston, A. G. "The Government Code and Cypher School Between the Wars," *Intelligence and National Security* 1, no 1, 1986.

de Selding, Peter B. "Joxe: Spy Satellites Essential for France." *Space News*, May 13–19, 1991.

———. "French Firm Outlines Helios' Complex Encryption Plan." *Space News*, May 31–June 6, 1993.

"The Desperate Spy," *Time*, September 14, 1962.

De Toledano, Ralph. "The Alger Hiss Story," *American Mercury*, June 1953.

———. "Moscow Plotted Pearl Harbor," *The Freeman*, June 1962.

"Detour," *Time*, August 28, 1950.

Deutsch, Harold C. "Sidelights on the Redl Case: Russian Intelligence on the Eve of the Great War," *Intelligence and National Security* 4, no. 4, 1989.

"Disappointement," *Time*, February 26, 1945.

Dobbins, Charles. "China's Mystery Man," *Colliers*, February 1, 1946.

Donnelly, C. L. "The Soviet Desant Concept," *RUSI Journal*, December 1971.

Donovan, William J. "Intelligence: Key to Defense," *Life*, September 30, 1946.

Dorfman, Ben. "White Russians in the Far East," *Asia*, March 1935.

Dos Passos, John. "Mr. Chambers' Descent into Hell," *The Saturday Review*, May 24, 1952.

"Double Trouble," *Time*, November 5, 1951.

Du Berrier, Hilaire. "How We Helped Ho Chi Minh," *The Freeman*, April 19, 1954.

Eastman, Lloyd. "Fascism in Kuomintang China: The Blue Shirts," *The China Quarterly*, January–March, 1972.

"Edith of Malaya," *Time*, June 28, 1946.

"Eggshells & Espionage," *Time*, April 2, 1934.

Elliott, Lawrence. "Hitler's Undercover Invasion of the United States," *Reader's Digest*, March 1960.

"The Elusive Spy," *Time*, August 17, 1972.

"The Embassy Spy Case Fizzles," *Time*, November 23, 1987.

Erickson, John. "Shield 72: Warsaw Pact Military Exercises," *RUSI Journal*, December 1972.

Ernst, Morris. "Why I No Longer Fear the FBI," *Reader's Digest*, December 1950.

"Eruption at the Summit," *Time*, May 23, 1960.

"Escape into the Cold," *Newsweek*, November 7, 1966.

"Espionage," *Time*, March 7, 1938.

"The Faceless Men," *Time*, March 19, 1951.

Fallows, James. "America's High-Tech Weaponry," *Atlantic Monthly*, May 1981.

Ferris, John. "Whitehall's Black Chamber: British Cryptology and the Government Code and Cypher School, 1919–1929," *Intelligence and National Security* 2, no. 1, 1987.

Fischel, Edwin C. "The Mythology of Civil War Intelligence," *Civil War History*, December 1964 (Vol. X)

Ford, Franklin. "The 20th of July in the History of German Resistance," *American Historical Review*. July 1946.

French, David. "Spy Fever in Britain, 1900–1915," *Historical Journal*, 21, no. 2, 1978.

Funk, Arthur. "American Contacts with the Resistance in France," *Military Affairs*, February 1970.

Gerth, Hans. "The Nazi Party: Its Leadership and Composition," *The American Journal of Sociology*, January 1940.

Gervasi, Frank. "What's Wrong with Our Spy System?" *Colliers*, November 6, 1948.

Gilmore, Ken. "The Secret Keepers," *Popular Electronics*, August 1962.

Girard, André. "We Organized the French Underground," *Tricolor*, May 1944.

Glazer, Nathan. "Verdicts of History," *Commentary*, October 1983.

Glees, Anthony. "The Hollis Letters," London *Times*, April 3, 1982.

Goldberg, Arthur. "Top Secret," *The Nation*, March 23, 1946.

Goldsworthy, Frank. "Human Torpedoes at Gibraltar," *Reader's Digest*, November 1950.

"Goodbye to M," *The Economist*, November 20, 1982.

"The Great Impersonation," *Time*, April 28, 1961.

"The Great Western Spy Net," *Time*, May 17, 1963.

"The Greenglass Mechanism," *Time*, March 26, 1951.

Grell, William. "A Marine with OSS," *Marine Corps Gazette*, December 1945.

"Guilty!" *Time*, July 11, 1949.

"Guilty," *Time*, April 9, 1951.

"Guilty," *Time*, April 22, 1957.

"Guilty as Charged," *Time*, July 21, 1961.

Gunther, John. "Mystery Man of the A-Bomb," *Reader's Digest*, December 1953.

Hammant, Thomas R. "Communications Intelligence and Tsarist Russia," *Studies in Intelligence* 22, no. 2, 1976.

Hellman, Geoffrey. "That Was the War," *New Yorker*, November 18, 1947.

Hennessy, Peter, and Brownfeld, Gail. "Britain's Cold War Security Purge," *Historical Journal*, December 1982.

Henry, William A. III. "No Regrets: Kim Philby, 1912–1988," *Time*, May 23, 1988.

Hiley, Nicholas F. "The Failure of British Espionage Against Germany, 1907–1914," *Historical Journal* 26, no. 4, 1983.

"Himmler's Thriller," *Time*, December 4, 1939.

Hoover, J. Edgar. "The Enemy's Masterpiece of Espionage," *Reader's Digest*, April 1946.

———. "The Spy Who Double-Crossed Hitler," *The American Magazine*, May 1946.

———. (Fern Stukenbroeker actual writer). "The Crime of the Century," *Reader's Digest*, May 1951.

"How the Israelis Pulled It Off," *Newsweek*, July 19, 1976.

"'Idealist' on 'Bloodsuckers,'" *Time*, April 29, 1935.

"In Which We Serve," *Time*, January 6, 1947.

"It At First...," *Time*, January 15, 1945.

"Inside Ali's Suitcase," *Time*, September 20, 1954.

"It Was Love," *Time*, June 27, 1949.

Janesick, James R., and Blouke, Morely. "Sky on a Chip: The Fabulous CCD," *Sky & Telescope*, September 1987.

Johnson, Chalmers. "Again the Sorge Case." New York *Times Magazine*, October 11, 1964.

Johnson, Terry E. "Tarnished Honor," *Newsweek*, April 20, 1987.

Johnson, Thomas M. "Secrets of the Master Spies." *Popular Mechanics Magazine*, September 1932.

———. "How the War's Best-Kept Secret Was Kept," *Foreign Service*, October 1947.

———. "The Most Dangerous Man in Europe," *Argosy*, March 1949.

———. "Joey's Quiet War," *Reader's Digest*, August 1951.

———. "CIC: The Army's Spy-Hunters," *Reader's Digest*, January 1952.

"Judas, i, g." *Time*, November 12, 1951.

Kahn, David. "The Ultra Conference," *Cryptologia*, January 1979.

———. "Cryptology Goes Public," *Foreign Affairs*, Fall 1979.

Kaun, Alexander. "The Twilight of the Romanov Dynasty," *American Review*, vol. 3 (1925).

Kelly, Richard M. "Behind the Enemy Lines," *Blue Book*, January 1946.

———. "Torture Preferred," *Blue Book*. June 1946.

———. "With the Greek Underground," *Blue Book*, July 1947.

———. "Spy Work Ahead," *Blue Book*, August 1947.

———. "Secret Agent in Brussels," *Blue Book*, September 1947.

———. "Secret Agent in Munich," *Blue Book*, October 1947.

Kempner, Robert M. W. "The Highest Paid Spy in History," *The Saturday Evening Post*, January 28, 1950.

Kennan, George. "Russian Provincial Prisons," *Century Magazine*, January 1888.

Kent, George. "Shepherds of the Underground," *Reader's Digest*, April 1945.

———. "200,000 Persecutions Prevented," *Reader's Digest*, March 1963.

Klass, Philip J. "U.S. Monitoring Capability Impaired," *Aviation Week & Space Technology*, May 14, 1979.

Knight, Mary. "The Secret War of Censors vs Spies," *Reader's Digest*, March 1946.

Kobler, John. "He Runs a Private OSS," *The Saturday Evening Post*, May 21, 1955.

Kolcum, Edward H. "Night Launch of Discovery Boosts Secret Military Satellite Into Orbit," *Aviation Week & Space Technology*, November 27, 1989.

Korostovetz, Vladimir de, "The Black Cabinet," *Contemporary Review*, March 1945.

Krock, Arthur. "OSS Gets It Coming and Going," *New York Times*, July 31, 1945.

Kuznetsov, Anatoli (A. Anatol.) "Russian Writers and the Secret Police," London *Daily Telegram*, August 10, 1969.

Langer, William. "Scholarship and the Intelligence Problem," *American Philosophical Proceedings*, 1948.

"The Last Appeal," *Time*, June 29, 1953.

Lattimore, Owen. "New Road to Asia," *National Geographic Magazine*, December 1944.

Laue, T. H. von. "Count Witte and the Russian Revolution of 1905," *The American Slavic and Eastern European Review*, February 1958.

"Leaks in the Pipeline," *Time*, December 9, 1985.

Levine, Isaac Don. "Execution of Stalin's Spy in the Tower of London," *Plain Talk*, November 1948.

Lind, William S. "Some Doctrinal Questions for the United States Army," *Military Review*, 1977.

Lord, Walter. "Five Missed Chances at Pearl Harbor," *Reader's Digest*, December 1957.

Lyushkov, G. S. "The Far Eastern Red Army," *Contemporary Japan*, October 8, 1939.

"The Man with the Oval Face," *Time*, June 5, 1950.

Mann, Martin. "Our Secret Radar War with Russia," *Popular Science*, January 1961.

Mansfield, Walter. "Ambush in China," *Marine Corps Gazette*, March 1946.

"The Marine Verdict: Guilty," *Time*, August 31, 1987.

Markowitz, Gerald E., and Meeropol, Michael. "The 'Crime of the Century' Revisited: David Greenglass's Scientific Evidence in the Rosenberg Case." *Science and Society*, Spring 1980.

Marshal, Eliot. "Senate Skeptical on SALT Verifi-cation," *Science*, July 27, 1979.

"Marshall-Dewey Letters," *Life* Magazine, December 17, 1945.

Martin, David. "A CIA Spy in the Kremlin," *Newsweek*, July 21, 1980.

Massing, Hede. "The Almost Perfect Russian Spy," *True*, December 1951.

————. "Richard Sorge," *Deutsche Rundschau*, April 1953.

Mayer, Allen J., with Martin, David C. "Cracking a Soviet Cipher," *Newsweek*, May 19, 1980.

McElvoy, Anne. "We Have the Videos," *The Spectator*, September 29, 1990.

McGrath, Peter. "Death of a Double Agent," *Newsweek*, May 23, 1988.

Mecklin, J. M. "Of Our Sincere Gratitude," *New Republic*, July 29, 1946.

"Mercy and Justice," *Time*, February 23, 1953.

Michaelis, Karin. "The Thief and the Patriot," *Reader's Digest*, May 1946.

Michie, Allan A. "Forty Minutes That Changed the War," *Reader's Digest*, October 1944.

————. "The Greatest Hoax of the War," *Reader's Digest*, October 1946.

"Midsummer Dragnet," *Time*, July 19, 1963.

"The Missing Spies," *Time*, October 3, 1955.

"Mistaken Identities," *Time*, July 26, 1963.

"Model Spy," *Time*, April 2, 1934.

Morgan, Edward P. "The Spy the Nazis Missed," *True, The Man's Magazine*, July 1950.

Morganthau, Tom. "Once Again Controversy over Covert Operations," *Newsweek*, January 11, 1988.

"Mousy Mata Hari," *Time*, January 15, 1945.

Muller, Edwin. "The Inside Story of Pearl Harbor," *Reader's Digest*, April 1944.

————. "The Man Who Did Business with Himmler," *Reader's Digest*, January 1946.

————. "Exploits of the Navy's Frogmen," *The American Weekly*, March 16, 1952.

Munro, Neil, and Opall, Barbara. "Israeli Spy Satellite May Be Imminent," *Space News*, March 11–17, 1991.

————. "Intelligence Community Pushes Sensor Advances," *Space News*, September 6–12, 1993.

"My Friend, Yakovlev," *Time*, March 26, 1951.

"NATO's Secrets Up for Sale," *Newsweek*, September 5, 1988.

Navasky, Victor. "The Rosenberg Revival: Of 'Atom Spies' and Ambiguities," *The Nation*, October 22, 1983.

"Net Netted," *Time*, June 27, 1938.

"The Network," *Time*, August 8, 1948.

"The New Treason," *Time*, January 5, 1948.

Nikolaieff, A. M. "Secret Causes of German Successes on the Eastern Front," *Coast Artillery Journal*, September–October 1935.

"No. 4," *Time*, July 31, 1950.

Norton-Taylor, Duncan. "Wisdom Is the Most Terrible Ordeal," *National Review*, July 29, 1961.

Oberdorfer, Don. "The Playboy Sergeant Who Spied for Russia," *The Saturday Evening Post*, March 7, 1964.

"Off Base," *Time*, June 1, 1953.

"On His Socialist's Secret Service," *The Economist*, November 27, 1982.

"On the Way to Securing a World Position? Japan's Intelligence Agencies and Their Acitivities." *Japan Quarterly*, June 1982.

"One That Got Away," *Time*, March 31, 1961.

Packard, W. H. "ONI Centennial," *Naval Intelligence Newsletter*, October 1982.

Packer, Herbert. "The Strange Trial of the Rosenbergs," *The New York Review of Books*, February 3, 1966.

Painton, Frederick C. "Secret Mission to North Africa," *Reader's Digest*, May 1943.

————. "Fighting with Confetti," *The American Legion Magazine*, December 1943.

Parrish, Michael E. "Cold War Justice: The Supreme Court and the Rosenbergs," *The American Historical Review*, October 1977.

Parker, C. F. "Signals in the Sun," *Arizona Highways*, June 1967.

Paul, Anthony. "The Spy Who Loved Hanako," *Asia Week*, April 29, 1983.

Post, Melville Davisson. "German War Ciphers," *Everybody's Magazine*, June 1918.

Prange, Gordon W. "The Last Instand of Peace," *Reader's Digest*, Oct.–Nov. 1963.

————. "Master Spy," *Reader's Digest*, January 1967.

"The Premier Faints," *Time*, April 21, 1961.

"The Pretty Victim," *Time*, January 3, 1955.

"Pudgy Finger Points," *Time*, October 28, 1957.

"Punishment," *Time*, February 7, 1955.

"A Question of Identity," *Time*, November 4, 1966.

Radosh, Ronald, and Milton, Joyce. "Were the Rosenbergs Framed?" *The New York Review of Books*, July 21, 1983.

"Reagan Was the Target," *Newsweek*, October 5, 1987.

"Remorse & Punishment," *Time*, December 18, 1950.

Ripley, S. Dillon. "Incident in Siam," *Yale Review*, Winter 1947.

"The Rosenberg Diversion," *Time*, December 1, 1952.

Samrej, Nai. "That Thailand May Be Free," *Asia and the Americas*, February 1945.

Sanger, David E. "Journey to Isolation," New York *Times Magazine*, November 15, 1992.

"Scent for Secrets," *Time*, April 22, 1946.

Schapp, Dick. "The Strange Case of the Psycho Traitors," *True*, June 1961.

Schorreck, Henry F. "The Telegram That Changed History," *Cryptologic Spectrum*, Summer 1970.

"Secrets of the Deep," *Time*, February 17, 1961.

"7 Generals v. 8 Saboteurs," *Time*, July 20, 1942.

Shearer, Lloyd. "Master Spy," *Parade*, August 21, 1960.

Sheehan, Edward R. F. "The Rise and Fall of a Soviet Agent,.." *The Saturday Evening Post*, February 15, 1964.

"Shock," *Time*, February 13, 1950.

"The Smaller Ones," *Time*, June 26, 1950.

Smedley, Agnes. "The Tokyo Martyrs," *Far East Spotlight*, March 1949.

Snow, Edgar. "Japan Builds a New Colony," *The Saturday Evening Post*, February 24, 1934.

——. "Must the East Go Red?" *The Saturday Evening Post*, May 12, 1945.

——. "Secrets from Siam," *The Saturday Evening Post*, January 12, 1946.

Snyder, William J. "Inside Story of the Hess Flight," *American Mercury*, May 1943.

Sondern, Frederic, Jr. "This Spy-Catching Business," *American Mercury*, February 1942.

Sorge, Christiane. "Mein Mann—Richard Sorge," *Die Weltwoche,* December 11, 1964.

Spurr, Russell. "Enter the Spooks," *Far Eastern Economic Review*, February 25, 1977.

"Spy Business," *Time*, November 14, 1938.

"Spy, Spy, Spies," *Time*, July 12, 1963.

"Spy Trial," *Time*, December 2, 1941.

"The Spy Who Skipped," *Time*, July 6, 1962.

"Spy Swap?" *Newsweek*, February 29, 1988.

Steele, John L. "Assassin Disarmed by Love," *Life* Magazine, September 7, 1962.

Steiner, George. "The Cleric of Treason," *New Yorker*, December 8, 1980.

Stengers, Jean. "Le Guerre des Messages Codés (1930-1945)," *L'Histoire*, February 1981.

Stevens, Harley. "Prelude to Chinese Unity." *Pacific News Letter*, April 1946.

"Still Defiant," *Time*, January 12, 1953.

Stolberg, Benjamin. "Muddled Millions, Capitalist Angels of Left-Wing Propaganda," *The Saturday Evening Post*, February 15, 1941.

"A Strand in the Web," *Time*, February 4, 1957.

"The Strange Case of Amerasia," *Time*, June 12, 1950.

"The Tactful Servant," *Time*, December 9, 1957.

Taylor, John F. "The Rosenbergs—Our National Agony," *The Churchman*, August–September 1979.

Taylor, L. B. "OSS Mission," *Man's Magazine*, April 1965.

"Thank You, My Lord," *Time*, March 13, 1950.

"Theresa & Miss X," *Time*, February 15, 1963.

Thompson, Craig. "What Has Stalin Done With Noel Field?" *The Saturday Evening Post*, December 15, 1951.

"Timely Reminder," *Time*, February 21, 1949.

Toledano, Ralph de. "The Noel Field Story," *American Mercury*, April 1954.

Tolstoy, Ilia. "Across Tibet from India to China," *National* Geographic, August 1946.

Toombs, Alfred. "Washington Communication: Cryptographic Broadcasts," *Radio News*, January 1941.

"Top Secrets for Sale?" *Newsweek*, January 2, 1989.

"Tracked Toward Trouble," *Time*, May 23, 1960.

"Traitor's Day in Moscow," *Time*, September 19, 1960.

Trevor-Roper, Hugh. "The Philby Affair," *Encounter*, April 1968.

"Triple Double," *Time*, July 19, 1963.

Troy, Thomas F. "The British Assault on J. Edgar Hoover: The Tricycle Case," *International Journal of Intelligence and Counterintelligence* 3, no. 2, 1989.

"Two More Links," *Time*, August 7, 1950.

Turski, Roman. "Turn About," *Reader's Digest*, January 1953.

Ulmer, Alfred, Jr. "The Gulliver Mission." *Bluebook*, April 1946

"Unrepent Spy," *Time*, January 12, 1953.

Usui, Maoaki. "Group in Japan Recommends Spy Satellites," *Space News*, August 29–September 4, 1994.

Valtin, Jan (Richard Krebs). "Communist Agent," *American Mercury*, November 1939.

Varmaat, A. Emerson. "The East German Secret Service Structure and Operational Focus," *Conflict Quarterly*, Fall 1987.

Wager. Walter. "Slippery Giant of the OSS," *Men*, July 1961.

"Wages of Sin," *Time*, December 12, 1938.

Waldeck, Countess. "What Really Happened to Rommel," *Forum*, November 1948.

Walker, C. Lester. "China's Master Spy," *Colliers*, February 1, 1946.

Wall, Carl B. "The Hunt for a Spy," *The American Legion Magazine*, October 1945.

West, Rebecca. "Whittaker Chambers," *Atlantic Monthly*, June 1952.

Weyl, Nathaniel. "I Was in a Communist Unit with Hiss," *U.S. News & World Report*, January 9, 1953.

Weyland, Otto P. "The Air Campaign in Korea," *Air University Quarterly Review*, Fall 1953.

Wharton, Don. "Fooling Enemy Airmen," *Air Facts*, April 1942.

——. "How the North African Campaign was Organized," *Reader's Digest*, February 1943.

"What the FBI Heard," *Time*, January 9, 1950.

"The Whistler," *Time*, May 3, 1954.

White, William L. "Some Affairs of Honor," *Reader's Digest*, September 1945.

Winchester, James H. "The Soviets' Little Known 'Wet War,'" *Reader's Digest*, April 1962.

Wise, David. "The Spy Who Got Away," *Newsweek*, May 23, 1988.

"Without Mercy," *Time*, February 14, 1955.

Woodeman, Nathan X. "Yardley Revisited," *Studies in Intelligence* 27, no 2, 1983.

"The World of William Sebold," *Time*, September 22, 1941.

Wyden, Peter. "The Chances of Accidental War," *The Saturday Evening Post*, June 3, 1961.

"Yeah? Well, Take That!" *Time*, March 27, 1989.

Yegin, Daniel. "Victims of a Desperate Age," *New Times*, May 16, 1975.

Zoglin, Richard. "Did a Dead Man Tell No Tales?" *Time*, October 12, 1987.

Zuckerman, Laurence. "How Not to Silence a Spy," *Time*, August 17, 1987.

REPORTS

CIA: The Pike Report. Nottingham, Eng.: Spokesman Books, 1977.

Commonwealth of Australia. Report of the Royal Commission on Espionage. Sydney: Government Printer for New South Wales, 1955.

Cline, Ray S. *Washington Command Post: The Operation Division*. Washington, D.C.: Government Printing Office, 1951.

Franks, Lord. *Report on Official Secrets Act*. London: Her Majesty's Stationery Office, 1972.

Howe, George F. *Northwest Africa: Seizing the Initiative in the West.* Washington, D.C.: Government Printing Office, 1957.

International Civil Aviation Organization. *Report of the Completion of the Fact-Finding Investi-gation Regarding the Shooting Down of Korea Airlines Boeing 747 (Flight KE 007).* Montreal: ICAO, 1993.

Matloff, Maurice. *Strategic Planning for Coalition Warfare, 1943–1944.* Washington, D.C.: Government Printing Office, 1968.

Pipes, Richard. *Some Operational Principles of Soviet Foreign Policy.* Washington, D.C.: Government Printing Office, 1972.

Report Concerning the Disappearance of Two Former Foreign Office Officials. London: Her Majesty's Stationary Office, 1955.

Report of the Committee of Privy Councillors appointed to inquire into the interception of communications. London: Her Majesty's Stationery's Office, 1957.

Trials of Major War Criminals Before the Nuremberg Military Tribunals. (15 vols.) Washington, D.C.: Government Printing Office, 1949-1952.

U.S. Air Force (United States Strategic Bombing Survey, Pacific). *Japanese Military and Naval Intelligence Division.* Washington, D.C.: U.S. Government Printing Office, 1946.

U.S. Arms Control and Disarmament Agency. *Arms Control and Disarmanent Agrements: Text and Histories of Negotions.* Washington, D.C.: Government Printing Office, 1980.

U.S. Army, Far East Command, Military Intelligence Section. *The Sorge Spy Ring: A Case Study in International Espionage in the Far East.* U.S. 81st Congress, First Session. Washington, D.C.: Government Printing Office, 1949.

————. *A Partial Documentation of the Sorge Espionage Case.* Tokyo: Toppan Printing Co., 1950.

U.S. Central Intelligence Agency. *Israel: Foreign Intelligence and Security Services.* Washington, D.C.: Government Printing Office, 1979.

————. *Statement of Central Intelligence Agency Before the U.S. Senate Permanent Subcommittee on Investigations at Hearings of U.S. Government Personnel Security Program.* Washington, D.C.: Government Printing Office, 1985.

U.S. Committee on Foreign Affairs. *The New Strategy of Communism in the Caribbean.* Washington, D.C.: Government Printing Office, 1968.

U.S. Congress. *Hearings Before the Joint Committee on the Investigation of the Pearl Harbor Attack and Report.* Washington, D.C.: U.S. Government Printing Office, 1946.

————. *Alleged Assassination Plots Involving Foreign Leaders.* Washington, D.C.: Government Printing Office, 1975.

————. *Covert Action in Chile, 1963–1973.* Washington, D.C.: Government Printing Office, 1975.

————. *U.S. Intelligence Agencies and Activities.* Washington, D.C.: Government Printing Office, 1975

————. *Foreign and Military Intelligence.* Washington, D.C.: Government Printing Office, 1976.

————. *United States Military Installations and Objectives in Mediterranean.* Washington, D.C.: Government Printing Office, 1977.

————. *Fiscal Year 1980 International Security Assistance Authorization.* Washington, D.C.: Government Printing Office, 1979.

————. *Iran: Evaluation of U.S. Intelligence Performance Prior to November 1978.* Washington, D.C.: Government Printing Office, 1979.

————. *Intelligence Activities and the Rights of Americans.* Washington, D.C.: Government Printing Office, 1981.

————. *Compilation of Intelligence Laws and Related Laws and Executive Orders of Interest to the National Intelligence Community.* Washington, D.C.: Government Printing Office, 1983.

U.S. Counter Intelligence Corps School. *History and Mission of the Counter Intelligence Corps in World War II.* (Issued in 1951)

U.S. Department of Defense. *Military Space Projects.* Washington, D.C.: Government Printing Office, 1960.

————. *Soviet Intelligence Operations Against Americans and U.S. Installations Abroad.* Washington, D.C.: Government Printing Office, 1968.

————. *The 'Magic' Background of Pearl Harbor.* Washington, D.C.: Government Printing Office, 1977.

————. *Soviet Acquisition of Militarily Significant Western Technology: An Update.* Washington, D.C.: Government Printing Office, 1985.

————. *Conduct of the Persian Gulf War, Final Report to Congress.* Washington, D.C.: Government Printing Office, 1992.

————. *Security Awareness Bulletins, 1983–1995.*

U.S. Department of Justice. *Report of the Attorney General.* Washington, D.C.: Government Printing Office, 1927.

U.S. Department of State. *Nazi Conspiracy and Aggression* (10 vols.). Washington, D.C.: Government Printing Office, 1946–1948.

U.S. House Committee on Armed Services. *Intelligence Successes and Failures in Operations Desert Shield/ Storm.* Washington, D.C.: Government Printing Office, 1993.

U.S. House Committee on Un-American Activities. "Hearings regarding Communist espionage in the United States Government." Washington, D.C.: Government Printing Office, 1948.

————. "Hearings on American Aspects of the Richard Sorge Case." Washington, D.C.: Government Printing Office, 1951.

U.S. Joint Committee on Atomic Energy. *Soviet Atomic Espionage.* Washington, D.C.: Government Printing Office, 1951.

U.S. Office of Strategic Services (OSS). *Japanese Attempts of Infiltration Among the Muslims in Russia.* (Issued in 1944)

U.S. Senate Committee on the Judiciary. "Hearings on the Institute of Pacific Relations." Washington, D.C.: Government Printing Office, 1951–1952.

————. "Interlocking Subversion in Government Departments." Washington, D.C.: Government Printing Office, 1953–1955.

————. *Activities of Soviet Secret Service.* Washington, D.C.: Government Printing Office, 1954.

————. *The Episode of the Russian Seaman.* Washington, D.C.: Government Printing Office, 1956.

————. *Scope of Soviet Activity in the U.S.* Washington, D.C.: Government Printing Office, 1956.

————. *Speech of Nikita Khrushchev Before a Closed Session of the XXth Congress of the Communist Party of the Soviet Union on February 25, 1956.* Washington, D.C.: Government Printing Office, 1957.

————. *Exposé of Soviet Espionage.* (Prepared by the Federal Bureau of Investigation) Washington, D.C.: Government Printing Office, 1960.

————. Testimony of Richard Helms, Asst. Director, CIA. *Communist Forgeries.* Washington, D.C.: Government Printing Office, 1962.

————. Testimony of Alexander Orlov. Washington, D.C.: Government Printing Office, 1962.

————. *Communist Penetration and Exploitation of the Free Press.* Washington, D.C.: Government Printing Office, 1962.

————. *State Department Security: The Case of William Wieland, The New Passport Regulations.* Washington, D.C.: Government Printing Office, 1962.

————. *Communist International Youth and Student Apparatus.* Washington, D.C.: Government Printing Office, 1963.

————. *The Wennerstroem Spy Case.* Washington, D.C.: Government Printing Office, 1964.

————. Testimony of Peter Deriabin. *Murder International, Inc., Murder and Kidnapping as an Instrument of Soviet Policy.* Washington, D.C.: Government Printing Office, 1965.

————. Testimony of Rev. Richard Wurmbrand. *Communist Exploitation of Religion.* Washington, D.C.: Government Printing Office, 1966.

————. *Aspects of Intellectual Ferment and Dissent in the Soviet Union.* Washington, D.C.: Government Printing Office, 1968.

————. *Aspects of Intellectual Ferment and Dissent in the Soviet Union.* Washington, D.C.: Government Printing Office, 1969.

————. *Testimony of Yevgeny Y. Runge.* Washington, D.C.: Government Printing Office, 1970.

————. *The Amerasia Papers.* Washington, D.C.: Government Printing Office, 1971.

————. Testimony of Francisco Antonio Teira Alfonso. *Communist Threat to the United States Through the Caribbean.* Washington, D.C.: Government Printing Office, 1971.

————. *Soviet Intelligence and Security Services, 1964–1970.* Washington, D.C.: Government Printing Office, 1972.

Vigneras, Marcel. *Rearming the French.* Washington, D.C.: Government Printing Office, 1957.

NEWSPAPERS

THE FOLLOWING NEWSPAPERS WERE USED EXTENSIVELY in research; miscellaneous dates are too numerous to cite herein.

Atlanta *Constitution*
Baltimore *Sun*
Boston *Globe*
Chicago *American*
Chicago *Daily News*
Chicago *Sun-Times*
Chicago *Tribune*
Cincinnati *Enquirer*
Denver *Post*
Detroit *Free Press*
Detroit *News*
Frank Leslie's Weekly
Harper's Weekly
Kansas *City Star*
London *Daily Express*
London *Daily Telegraph*
London *Globe*
London *News Chronicle*
London *Times*
Los Angles *Daily News*
Los Angeles *Times*
Japan *Advertiser*
Japan *Times and Advertiser*
Japan *Times and Mail*
New Orleans *Picayune*
New York *Daily News*
New York *Herald*
New York *Post*
New York *Times*
New York *World*
Philadelphia *News*
Philadelphia *Inquirer*
St. Louis *Post-Dispatch*
San Francisco *Chronicle*
Toronto *Star*
Washington *Evening Star*
Washington *Post*
Washington *Times*

Index

In this annotated index, names in boldface indicate main text entries; page numbers in boldface indicate text wholly dedicated to entries.

Aquaviva, Cardinal, 139

Arabian Nights, 124

Arafat, Yassir, 352, 402

Araki, Gen. Sadao, 22

Arbenz Guzman, Jacobo, 98, 118, 152

Arcadia Conference, 135

Arcos, Ltd. (Soviet cover, a trading organization in London), 34, **42-43**, 289, 318

Arent, Albert, 27

Argonne Laboratory (Chicago, Ill.), 346

Argus (code name for CIA spy satellite), 114, 399

Arizona, USS, 311

Arlington, Lord Henry, 86

Arlington National Cemetery (U.S.), 185, 201

Armand, Major Le Comte (Alleged Austrian spy), **44**

Armand, Pauline, *See:* Granville, Christine

Armed Forces Courier Station (Orly Airport, Fr.), 283

Arnault, Jean-Claude (SOE spy in WW II), 502

Arnold, Benedict (infant), 44

Arnold, Benedict, 28, 36-40, **44-51**, 75, 82, 162, 165, 257, 355, 403, 475, 476, 481, 482, 503

Arnold, Edward, 50, 51

Arnold, Hannah (Benedict Arnold's mother), 44

Arnold, Hannah (Benedict Arnold's sister), 44

Arnold, Margaret Shippen (AKA: "Peggy"), 36, 48, 50, 51, 75

Arnold, Samuel B., 69

Arnold, Sophia, 51

Arnould, Rita (Soviet spy in WW II), 483, 484

Arrow Cross (Hungarian fascist party), 498, 499

Artamonov, Nicolai Fedorovich (Soviet double agent in U.S.), **51-52**

ASA (U.S. Army Security Agency), 372

Asahi Shimbun, 456, 458

Ascot, William (Pinkerton detective), 250, 251

Ashby, Turner (Confederate spymaster in Civil War), **52**, 83, 115, 281

Ashenden (book), 343

ASIO (Australian Security & Intelligence Organization), **52-53**

ASIS (Australian Secret Intelligence Service, a division of ASIO), 53

Assad, Hafez el, 53, 512

Assad, Rifaat (Syrian intelligence chief), **53**

Assembly of Russian Workingmen, The, 58, 227

Association of Free German Jurists, 452

Astbury, Peter J., 385

Astor, Vincent, 186

Athlumney, Lord, 323

Atkinson, Maj. John Wilder, 490

Atlantic Cable, 519, 526

Atlantic Charter, 134

Atlantic Wall Blueprint (Secret Nazi map of Normandy fortifications), **54**

Atomic Energy Commission, 88, 329, 488

Atomic Energy Establishment (Harwell, Eng.), 223

Attlee, Clement Richard, 244, 319

Atzerodt, George A., 69

Auden, W. H., 162

Augustus I (of Saxony, later Augustus II of Poland), 433

Augustenborg, Lon David (Alleged U.S. spy in Russia), **54**

Augustenborg, Mrs. Lon David, 54

Austerlitz (battle, 1805), 439

Australian Coast Watchers, *See:* Coast Watchers

Aylesbury Prison (London, Eng.), 139

Azar, Samuel (AKA: Jacques; Mossad spy in Egypt), 369, 370

Azev, Fischel, 55

Azev, Yevno (Okhrana and revolutionary spy in Russia), 7, 21, 22, **54-61**, 81, 110, 111, 227, 228, 229, 331, 374 412, 470, 528, 536

Baalsrud, Jan (SOE spy in WW II), 422

Ba'ath Party (Iraq), 22

Babington, Anthony (Catholic spy in England), **62**, 336, 501

Baca, Phil, 277, 278

Bacchus and Gambrini (ballet), 339

Bacon, Francis, 221

Baddlitt, USS, 212

Baden-Powell, Robert (British spy in Boer War), 9, **62-63**, 166, 168, 323

Baer, Israel, *See:* Beer, Israel

Bailey, Daniel, 140, 141

Baillie-Stewart, Norman (German spy in England), **63-64**

Baker, James A. III, 31

Baker, Josephine (French spy in WW II), **64**

Baker, Lafayette (AKA: Sam Munson; Union Spymaster in American Civil War), **65-71**, 116, 157, 391, 489

Baker, Luther B., 69

Baker, Rudy (AKA: Ralph Bowman; Soviet spy in U.S.), 20, **72**, 367

Bakhtiar, Gen. Teymur (Savak chief), 432

Buku (Rus.) oilfields, 454

Baldwin, Stanley, 43

Balfour, Arthur, 527

Ball, Dr. Desmond, 114

Ballard, John, 62

Ballard House (Richmond, Va.), 507

Balmashov, S. V., 57

Baltimore *Exchange*, 507

Bamler, Rudolf (Abwehr counterintelligence chief), 128

Bampfield, Col. Joseph, 86

Bancroft, Edward (British spy in American revolution), **72-73**, 82, 169, 206, 510, 516

Bandera, Stefan (AKA: Stefan Popel; SMERSH victim), 467, 468

Barbary Coast (San Francisco), 65

Barber of Seville, The (opera), 82

Barbie, Klaus (AKA: Klaus Altmann; "Butcher of Lyons"; Gestapo spycatcher), **73-74**, 360-61

Barcza, Margarete, 485

Barghoon, Frederick C. (Alleged U.S. spy in Russia), **74**, 292

Barker, Arizona Donnie Clark (AKA: Kate, Ma), 214

Barker, Arthur (AKA: Dock), 214

Barker, Bernard (Watergate plumber), 505

Barker, Fred, 214

Barker Gang, 271

Barnard College, 159, 398

Barth, Theodore H., 130

Bastian, 189

Bataan (Philippines), 24

Bates, Ann (British spy in American revolution), 36, **75**,

Batista, Fulgencio, 76

Batory, SS, 20, 72

Battle Organization (Russian Socialist Revolutionary Party), 22, 56, 57, 59, 229

Batz, Jean (Royalist spy in French revolution), **75-76**

Baucq, Phillippe, 143

Baun, Hermann, 231

"Bavarian Joe," 235

Bay of Pigs (abortive CIA-backed invasion of Cuba), **76-77**, 98, 152, 164, 200, 373

Bazna, Elyeza (AKA: Cicero; Abwehr spy in WW II), 7-8, **77-80**, 119, 134, 380, 426

BBC (British Broadcasting Company), 120, 453

BCRA (Central Bureau of Intelligence and Operations; Gaullist military intelligence in WW II), **80**, 117, 175, 521

Beach, Thomas (AKA: Henri Le Caron; British spy in U.S.), **81**

Bear Mountain State Park (N.Y.), 16

Beaumarchais, Pierre Augustin Caron de, **81-83** (French spy against the British), 169, 174

Beauregard, Gen. Pierre Goustave Toutant (Confederate general and spymaster), 52, 65, 66, **83**, 249, 250, 391, 506

Beautiful Blonde Woman of Antwerp, *See:* Kretschman, Maria von (in Mare Island Sabotage entry)

Beaverbrook, Lord, 192

Beck, Gen. Ludwig, 102, 103

Becker, Johann (Abwehr spymaster in Argentina in WW II), **83-84**

Beer Hall Putsch, 366

Beer, Israel (AKA: Baer; Soviet spy in Israel), **84-85**

Beer, Rebecca, 84

Begin, Menachem, 356

Behar, Albert William, 103

Behar, Catherine Beijdervellen, 103

Behar, George, *See:* Blake, George

Behn, Aphra (Aphra Johnson; AKA: Incomparable Astrea; British spy in Antwerp), **85-86**

Belard, Mathilde-Lucie, *See:* Carre, Mathilde

Beletsky, Police Chief, 331

Belgium Relief, 183

Belgrade (Serb.) Military Academy, 176

Bell, William (U.S. spy for Poland), **86-87**

Belleraphon, HMS, 166

Bellevue Hospital (N.Y.), 335, 442

Bellevue Hotel (Washington, D. C.), 305

Belotzerkovsky, Vadim, 255

Benedict XIII, Pope, 23

Benes, Eduard, 364

Ben-Gurion, David, 84, 85, 258, 259, 314, 356

Benjamin, Judah P., 507

Bensmann, Niko (Abwehr spymaster), 298

Bentley, Elizabeth (AKA: Helen Johnson; Soviet spy in U.S.), **87-89**

Ben-Tsur, Motke (Mossad spymaster in Paris), 369

Berg, Alexander, *See:* Orlov, Alexander

Berg, Jack (British double agent in WW II), **89-90**

Britton, Nan, 349
Broadway Limited, 304
Brockdorf, Ericka von (Soviet spy in WW II), 407, 408
Brooke, Gerald, 307
Brooklyn, USS, 137
Brooklyn Dodgers, 90
Brosselette, Pierre (AKA: Brumaire; French spy in WW II), **117-18**, 521-22
Brousse, Capt. Charles, 378
Browder, Earl, (American Communist Party leader), 26, 88
Brown, John, 52
Brown Shirts (German stormtroopers), *See:* SA
Bruce, David, 196
Brumaire, *See:* Brosselette, Pierre
Brundrett, Sir Frederick, 516
Brunswick, Duke of, 339
Brussels (battle, 1746), 434
BSC (British Security Coordination), 469
B-29 Bomber, 89
Buchanan, Sir George, 344
Buchanan, President James, 249
Buchenwald Concentration Camp, 522
Buckmaster, Col. Maurice (SOE director of operations), 139, 279, 454, 472
Buffham, Benson (NSA official), 400
Buford (AKA: The Soviet Ark), 270
Builot, Claude, *See:* DeFoe, Daniel
Bulenberg, Prince Philip von, 439
Bulganin, Nicolai, 164
Bulge, The (battle, WW II), 199
Bull Run, 1861 (AKA: First Manassas; Civil War battle), 8, 52, 83, 250, 281, 391, 489, 506
Bull Run, 1862 (AKA: Second Manassas; Civil War battle), 157
Bullitt, William C., 266
Bullock, Corrallie, 349
Bunaste (pro-Nazi German-American society), 130
Bunch of Grapes Pub (London, Eng.), 305
Bunke, Erich, 118
Bunke, Tamara (AKA: Laura Gutterez; Tania; KGB spy in Cuba), **118**
BUPO (Swiss intelligence), 217
Burchard, Adolph, 322
Burdiukov, Lev (Soviet spymaster in Canada), 362
Bureau Ha (Swiss intelligence agency), **119**
Bureau of Investigation (precursor to FBI), 184, 213, 270, 271, 334, 349, 424, 427
Burgess, Guy Francis de Moncy (British spy for Soviets), 8, 107, 108, 109, 112, **119-22**, 126, 192, 305, 319, 329, 330, 345, 350, 352, 353, 384, 384, 385, 386, 387, 388, 449, 450, 517, 532, 536, 538
Burgoyne, Gen. John, 36, 46, 47, 82
Burns Detective Agency, 270, 349
Burns, William J. (Bureau of Investigation director), 184, 214, 349, 424
Burnside, Gen. Ambrose, 158, 252, 281
Burr, Aaron (American conspirator and spymaster), **122-23**
Burrough, John (AKA: "Peanuts"), 68
Burt, Lt. Col. Leonard (Special Branch director), 346, 465
Burton, Richard (AKA: Mira Abdullah El Bushiri; British spy in India and Arabia), **123-24**
Burtzev, Vladimir, 61

Bush, President George Herbert Walker (CIA director), **125**
Bussy, Francois de (French spy for England), **125**
Butiki Prison, 415
Butler, Gen. Benjamin, 490, 491
Butler, Col. John, 355
Byers, Judge Mortimer W., 17
Bykov, Col. Boris (KGB spymaster), 144
Byrnes, James, 266
Bytchkov, A. E. (Soviet spy in Canada), 362

Cadogan, Sir Alexander, 185
Cafe Atlanta (Rotterdam), 193
Cagliostro, Count Alessandro (Joseph Balsamo), 140
Cahan, Samuel Borisovich (Soviet spy-master in England), **126**
Cairncross, John (British spy for Soviets), 120, **126**
Cairo Conference, 79
Cairo University, 154
Calhoun, John C., 249
California Institute of Technology, 242
Calvo, Luis (AKA: Garbo), 188
Cambridge University (Eng.), 8, 104, 107, 108, 119, 126, 150, 170, 305, 319, 329, 336, 345, 384, 400, 486, 500
Cambron, Jules, 340
Cameron, Dr. Archibald, 328
Cammaerts, Col. Francois (commander of *maquis* in WW II), 246, 247
Camorra, 100, 466
Camouflage Experimental Station (Eng.), 148
Canada
   Embassy in Paris, 374
Canadian Communist Party, 244
Canadian Pacific Railroad, 379
Canaris (film), 364
Canaris, Ericka Waag, 127
Canaris, Adm. Wilhelm (AKA: Reed Rosas; chief of Abwehr in WW II), 7, 10, 18, 102, 103, 110, **126-36**, 147, 169, 187, 198, 217, 230, 236, 262, 264, 289, 300, 301, 312, 313, 318, 335, 364, 365, 366, 368, 369, 376, 421, 425, 427, 430, 434, 435, 444, 454, 465, 534, 542
Carbonari (Italian underground organi-zation), **136**
Carchemish (archeological digs), 315
Cardano, Girolamo, 170
Carlos, *See:* Sanchez, Ilyich Ramirez
Carnegie Endowment for International Peace, 144, 266
Carol II (King of Rumania), 133
Caroline (Queen of England), 516
Caroline (play), 343
Carr, Sam, 244
Carranza, Ramon (AKA: Frederick W. Dobson; Spanish spymaster), **136-37**
Carranza, Venustiano, 225
Carre, Mathilde (Mathilde-Lucie Belard; AKA: The Cat; French double agent in WW II), **138-39**, 151
Carre, Maurice, 138
Carter, President James Earl Jr., 125, 153
Carve Her Name with Pride (film), 473
Carvell Hall Hotel (Annapolis, Md.), 211-12
Casablanca Conference, 79, 380
Casanova, Giovanni Giacomo (AKA: The Great Lover; Venetian spy for France), **139-40**

Casas, Cecilia Depuy, 30, 32
Casas, Maria del Rosario, *See:* Ames, Maria del Rosario Casas
Casas Santofimio, Pablo, 30
Casement, Roger (Irish spy against England), **140-41**
Casey, Sophia, 142
Casey, William J. (CIA director), **141-42**, 153, 154, 199
Casino de Paris, 339
Castle Thunder, Va. (Confederate prison), 489, 509
Castro, Fidel (Communist dictator of Cuba), 29, 76, 77, 98, 118, 152, 164, 200, 242-43, 337, 373, 431, 541
Cat, The, *See:* Carre, Mathilde
Cato (play), 257
Catherine II (Catherine the Great; Empress of Rus.), 140
Cauldwell, William Charles, *See:* Colepaugh, William Curtis
Cavell, Edith Louisa (Allied agent in WW I), 8, **142-43**
Cavendish Laboratory (Cambridge, Eng.), 345
Ceausecu, Nicolae, 352-53
Cecil, Lord Robert, 385
Cecil, William, 500
Censorship (U.S. Bureau in WW II), 26
Censorship Bureau (Ger. in WW I), 436
Censorship Office (Postal, London, WW I), 447, 465
Center, The (headquarters of all U.S.S.R. intelligence in Moscow), 14, 15, 16, 17, **143**, 217, 287, 291, 296, 353, 399, 405, 407, 417, 418, 440, 482, 483, 484, 485, 487
Central Committee (Communist Party, U.S.S.R.), 92, 455
Central Control Intelligence (div. of Central External Liaison Department), 143
Central External Liaison Department (Chinese intelligence service), **143**
Central High School (Washington, D.C.), 269
Central Intelligence Bureau (Ger.), 470, 472
Central Intelligence Group, *See:* CIG
Central Office of Information (U.S.), 375
CESID (*Centro Superior de Informacion de la Defensa*; Spanish intelli-gence service), **143**
Chamberlain, Sir Austin, 43
Chamberlain, Joseph, *See:* Hirsch, Willi
Chamberlain, Neville, 10, 120
Chambers, Esther Shemitz, 144
Chambers, Whittaker (AKA: George Crosley, Karl; American spy for Soviets), 35, 87, 89, **144-45**, 266-67, 347
Champagne Spy (book), 326
Chancellorsville (Va., battle), 281
Chancellory Building (Berlin, Ger.), 234
Chang Hsueh-liang, 26, 180, 181, 182, 204
Chang Tso-lin, 178, 179, 180, 459
Chao Kung, Abbot, *See:* Lincoln, Isaac Timothy Trebitsch
Chapelle, Fernand Bonnier de la, 186
Chapin, Dwight L., 506
Chapin, John H., 19
Chaplin, Charles, 303
Chapman, Eddie (AKA: Fritz, Zigzag; British double agent in WW II), 10, 90, **146-48**, 425
Charles I (Charles [Karl] Francis Joseph, Emperor of Austria), 44

Girty, Simon, 355
Gisevius, Hans Bernd, 198
Giskes, Hermann J. (Abwehr spymaster in WW II), **239-40**
Gizycki, Georg, 245
Glaser, Dr. Frederick Franz Ludwig, 398
Gleiwitz Incident (1939; Operation Canned Goods), 365-66
Glenn Martin Bomber, 130
Glienecker Bridge (Ger.), 17, 397
Glomar Explorer, 400, 401
"G-Men," 271
Goddard, Lord Chief Justice Rayner, 223
Goddard, Robert Hutchings, 130
Goebbels, Paul Joseph, 103, 264, 309, 407
Goerdeler, Dr. Carl, 102
Goering, Field Marshal Hermann, 89, 131, 234, 264, 407
Goertz, Dr. Hermann (Abwehr spy), 131, 313
Goetsch, Werner (SD agent), 364
Gold, Harry (Golodnotsky; American spy and courier for Soviets), 221, 222, 223, 224, **240-41**, 245, 248, 308, 347, 428, 429, 430
Goldberg, Arthur, 197
Goldfeder family, 245
Goldfus, Emil R., *See:* Abel, Rudolf Ivonovich
Goldman, Emma, 270
Goldsmith, Alexander, *See:* DeFoe, Daniel
Goleniewsky, Michael (KGB agent defecting to U.S.), 394
Gollnow, Herbert (Soviet spy in WW II), 407
Golos, Jacob, 88
Golytsin, Anatoli (KGB spymaster and defector to U.S.), 42, 52, **242**, 380, 388, 481
Gomez, Gen. Maximo, 106
Gone With the Wind, 9, 115
Gonse, Gen. Charles-Arthur, 191, 389
Gonzalez, Virgilio (White House plumber), 505
Gordievsky, Col. Oleg (AKA: Tickle; Soviet spy for the U.S.), 30
Gordon, Rev. William, 418
Gorky, Maxim, 519
Gottlieb, Dr. Sidney (AKA: Joseph Scheider; CIA chemist and poison expert), 98, **242-43**, 261, 514
Gouk, Arkady, 94
Gould, Frederick (German spy in WW I), 289
Gould, Lt. Joseph (OSS agent), 308
Gouzenko, Igor (Soviet spy and defector in Canada), **243-45**, 254, 266, 268, 346, 429, 526
Government Code and Cipher School (Bletchley, Eng.), 9, 90, 126, 221, 230, 350, 448, 487
Government Communications Headquarters (at Cheltenham, Eng.), *See:* GCHQ
GPU (U.S.S.R., State Political Administration, 1922-1923, Soviet intelligence), 92, 149, 201, 234, **245**, 291, 373, 374, 398, 413, 416, 417, 450, 515, 523
Gramisch, Walter (Gehlen spy in East Germany), 232, 515
Granatov, Major, *See:* Foote, Alexander Allan
Grande Patronne, *See:* Schragmüller, Elsbeth
Granger, Gen. Gordon, 167

Grant, Gen. [Hiram] Ulysses Simpson, 83, 490, 491
Granville, Christine (Kystyna Skarbek; AKA: Pauline Armand; SOE spy in WW II), **245-47**, 454
Graudenz, Johann (Soviet spy in WW II), 407
Graves, Dr. Armgaard (German spy in WW I), 289
Gray Bear Hotel (Innsbruck, Aus.), 87
Greek Memories (book), 328
Green, Edward George, *See:* Gimpel, Erich
Green House (Berlin, Ger. intelligence cover), 472
Green Mountain Boys, 45, 65
Greene, Graham, 328, 344
Greenglass, David (American spy for Soviets), 224, 241, 245, **247-48**, 347, 428, 429, 430
Greenglass, Ruth, 247, 248, 429
Greenhow, Gertrude, 249
Greenhow, Dr. Robert, 249
Greenhow, Rose, 249, 251, 253
Greenhow, Rose O'Neale (Confederate spy in U.S. Civil War), 8, 83, **248-54**, 281, 391, 506
Gregory, Thomas W., 269
Grese, Irma, 432
Gresham School (Eng.), 329
Grey, General Charles, 36
Gribinov, Gen. Oleg Mikhailovich, 292
Griebl, Dr. Ignatz Theodor (Abwehr spy in America), 129, 495
Grinev, Mikhail, 395, 397
Gripsholm, 237
Grishin, Boris Alexei, 114
Gromyko, Andre, 446
Groscurth, Helmuth (Abwehr sabotage chief), 128
Grosse, Heinrich (German spy in WW I), 289
Grosz, Armin, 331
Grotewohl, Otto, 515
Groves, Gen. Leslie R. (military commander of Manhattan Project), 346, 367
GRU (U.S.S.R., Chief Intelligence Directorate of the General Staff of the Red Army, Soviet military intelligence), 22, 143, 149, 217, 240, 244, **254**, 291, 304, 305, 378, 381, 382, 386, 393, 394, 404, 405, 451, 456, 457, 488, 526
Grunen, Capt. Stephen, 146, 147, 148
G-2 (U.S. Army Intelligence), 26, 135, 372, 375
Gubbins, Colin (SOE officer), 454
Gubitchev, Valentin, 160, 161, 162
Gudenberg, Werner Georg (Abwehr spy in America), 129, 495
Guellich, Gustav, 130
Guevara, Ernesto (AKA: Che), 118
Guibaud, Col. Louis, 292
Guillaume, Christel, 255
Guillaume, Gunther (Soviet spy in West Germany), 96 255, 278, 514
Guilot, Claude, *See:* DeFoe, Daniel
Guimet, Emile, 339
Guisan, Gen. Henri, 119, 435
Guise, Duke de, 336
Gurie, Sigrid, 260
Gustavus II (Gustavus Adolphus, King of Sweden), 420
Guthrum (King of the Danes), 24
Gutterez, Laura, *See:* Bunke, Tamara
Guttmann, Ingeborg, 131

Gyssling, George (Abwehr spymaster in U.S.), 226

Haakon VII (King of Norway), 403
Haarlen Prison, 240
Haegle, Anton, 130
Haganah (Israeli underground), 84, 258, 326
Hagiwara, Chuzo (Japanese spy in U.S.), 226
Haldeman, H(arry). R(obbins)., 506
Hale, Enoch (American spy in Revolution), 165, 257, 474, 481
Hale, Nathan (American spy in Revolution), 7, 40, 165, **256-57**, 474, 481, 502, 503, 509
Hall, James William III (American spy for Soviets), 372
Hall, T. W., 507
Hall, Capt. William Henry, 257
Hall, William Reginald (AKA: Blinker; chief of British naval intelligence), **257-58**, 288, 320, 379, 424, 428, 465, 468, 473, 480, 504, 516, 520, 526, 527
Halleck, Gen. H. W., 252
Halperin, Isser, *See:* Harel, Isser
Hambleton, Hugh, 542
Hambourg, R. A., 298
Hamburg-America Line, 131, 322, 425, 450
Hamburger, Rudolph, 307
Hamburger, Ursula Maria, *See:* Kuczynski, Ruth
Hamilton, Alexander, 50, 122
Hampden, Adm. Sir Hobart, 253, 254
Hancock, John, 149, 150, 418, 419
Handelsvertretung (Soviet trade organization in Germany), 34, 42
Hannibal, 312
Hansen, Hans, 133
Hansen, Joseph, 451
Hans Schaetzle Hotel (Berlin, Ger.), 282
Harbor Junior College, 113
Harding, President Warren G., 184, 214, 271, 349
Hardinge, Henry (British spymaster for Wellington), **258**, 509
Hardwick, Sen. Thomas, 270
Hardy, René, 360, 361
Harel, Isser (Isser Halperin; creator and director of Israel's Mossad intelligence agency), **258-59**, 357, 370
Harker, Gen. A. W. A., 318, 319
Harley, Robert, 170-72, 400
Harnack, Adolf, 259
Harnack, Arvid (German spymaster for Soviets in WW II), **259**, 407, 439, 440, 483, 484
Harnack, Mildred Fish, 259, 407, 408
Harnack, Otto, 259
Harper, Edward Durward, Jr. (American spy for Poland), **259**
Harper, Ruby Louise Schuler, 259
Harris, Clara, 68
Harrison, Sir Geoffrey, 292
Harrods (London, Eng.), 247
Harrow School (Eng.), 511
Hart, Basil Henry Liddell, *See:* Liddell Hart, Sir Basil Henry.
Harvard University, 88, 149, 188, 215, 265
Harvey's Restaurant (Washington, D.C.), 42
Harwell Atomic Energy Center, 319
Hassell, Ulrich von, 102
Hathaway, J., *See:* Bossard, Frank Clifton

Mitterrand, François, 441
Mixed Bureau (Allied counterintelligence agency in WW I), **354**
Miyagi, Yotoku (member of Sorge ring), 458, 459, 462
Miyake, 461
Miyazaki, Toshio (AKA: Tanni; Japanese spy in America), 477, 478, 479
MO5 (precursor to MI5, British counterintelligence), 169, 208, 288
Mokotow Prison, 322
Mola, Gen. Emilio, 131
"Mole Relief Fund," 42
Moll Flanders, 170
Molly Maguires (Secret Irish society in U.S.), 81, 348, 391
Molody, Konson Trofimovich, *See:* Lonsdale, Gordon Arnold
Molyneux (Paris, Fr.), 521
Monarchist Union of Central Russia, *See:* MUCR
Monat, Pawel (Polish spy for Soviets), **354**
Monjaret, Joseph, 359
Mons (battle, 1746), 434
Montagu, Lt. Comm. Ewen, 332-33
Montespan, Madame de (Francoise Athénais Rochechouart de Mortemart), 314
Montgaillard, Comte de (Maurice Rocques; French spy in Napoleonic era), **354-55**, 511
Montgomery, Gen. Sir Benard Law, 247, 334
Montgomery, Gen. Richard, 45, 46
Montgomery, Rev. William (cryptographer in Room 40), 526
Monthly Review, 72
Montieth, Robert, 140, 141
Montressor, Captain, 257
Moody, James (American spy for England in revolution), **355**
Moon and Sixpence, The (book), 345
Moore, Edwin G. II (American spy for Soviets), **355**
Moravec, Frantisek (Czech spymaster), **356**
Moreton, Andrew, *See:* DeFoe, Daniel
Morgan, Daniel, 46, 47
Morgan, Thomas A., 186
Morganthau, Henry Jr., 186
Mornard, Jacques, *See:* Mercader, Jaime
Mornet, Lt. Andre, 341
Morris, Mrs. Augusta Heath, 249, 252
Morris, James, 396
Morros, Boris (American spy for Soviets), 10, **356**
Morton, Sen. Jackson, 507
Moscow Casino, 518
Moses, 284
Moshinsky, Efim, 499
Moskva, 492
Moslem Brotherhood, 53
Mossad (AKA: Institute or Institution; Israeli intelligence service), 41, 110, 154-55, 232, 258, 259, 314, 326, **356-57**, 361, 369, 370, 371, 392, 406, 431, 432
Mossadegh, Mohammed, 152
"Motorboat" (code name for CIA agent), 31
Motorin, Sergein M. (Soviet spy for U.S.), 30
Moulin, Jean (AKA: Joseph-Jean Mercier, Jean Martel, Max; Free French spymaster in WW II), 8, 73, 80, 117, 175, **358-61**, 522

Mount Washington Female College (Baltimore, Md.), 115
Mountbatten, Louis, 333
Moyers, Charles H., 349
Moyzisch, L. C., 78-80
Mozart, Wolfgang Amadeus, 82
MUCR (Monarchist Union of Central Russia/Trust; cover for GPU/OGPU), 416
Mudd, Dr. Samuel, 68, 69, 70
Mueller, Ernst, 89
Mueller, Heinrich (Gestapo chief), 365
Mukhabaret El-Amm (General Intelligence Agency/GIA; Egyptian secret service), **361**, 369, 370, 371
Mulcahy, Kevin, 513
Mulder, 192
Muldowney, Dennis George, 247
Muller, Hans, *See:* Naujocks, Alfred Helmut
Müller, Lt. Joseph (Abwehr officer), 376
Munday, Anthony (spy for Francis Walsingham), **361**, 500
Munich Beer Hall Putsch (1923), 263
Munich (Ger.) Massacre (Olympic Games, 1972), 357, 406, 431
Munich Technological College (Ger.), 263
Munsinger Affair (Canadian sex and spy scandal), **362**
Munsinger, Gerda (Heseler), 362
Munson, Sam, *See:* Baker, Lafayette
Munthe, Malcolm (SOE agent), 454
Murat, Marshal Joachim, 439
Museum of Modern Art (New York City), 162
Mussert, Adrian, 192
Mussolini, Benito, 88, 101, 120, 135, 158, 159, 199, 321, 403
Muus, Flemming B. (Danish spymaster in WW II), **362**
Muzenberg, Willi (SMERSH victim), 287, 385
MVD (U.S.S.R., Ministry of Internal Affairs , Soviet intelligence, 1946-1954), 92, 149, 174, 245, 291, 295
My First Year in Prison, and the Abolition Rule in Washington, 253

Nagata, Gen. Tetsuzan, 459, 460
Naicho (Japanese intelligence), **363**
Napier, Gen. Sir Charles, 123, 124
Napoleon I (Napoleon Bonaparte, Emperor of France), 10, 76, 122, 136, 213, 218, 317, 330, 351, 354, 380, 383, 433, 437, 438, 439, 494, 495, 511, 546
Napoleon III, 106, 253, 471, 495
NASA (National Aeronautics and Space Administration), 395
Nash, Jay Robert, 517
Nassau Hotel (Long Island, N.Y.), 335
Nasser, Gamal Abdul, 314, 361, 369, 371, 402
Nassiri, Gen. Nematollah (Savak chief), 433
Nathanson, Philip (Mossad spy in Egypt), 369
National Aeronautics and Space Administration, *See:* NASA
National Archives (U.S.), 252
National Assistance (U.K.), 281
National Center (Russian émigré society), 195
National Council of the Resistance (Free French underground in WW II), 360
National Gallery of Art (Washington, D.C.), 88

National Observer, 517
National Press Building (Washington, D.C.), 213
National Republican, The, 252
National School of Agriculture (Grignon, Fr.), 279
National Security Act (U.S., 1947), 151, 363
National Security Agency, *See:* NSA
National Security Council (NSC, U.S.), 151, 152, **363**, 371, 373, 381
National Socialist Workers Party, *See:* Nazi Party
National Socialistische Beweging, 192
NATO (North Atlantic Treaty Organization), 84, 91, 149, 193, 242, 274, 284, 294, 327, 331, 351, 380, 387, 481, 510
Naujocks, Alfred Helmut (AKA: Hans Muller; SD agent provocateur), 132, **363-67**, 493
Naval Intelligence (U.K.), 288
Naval Intelligence (U.S.), *See:* ONI
Naval Investigative Service (U.S.), *See:* NIS
Naval Relief Society, 261
Navy Examining Board (U.S.), 211
Navy Yard, U.S. (San Diego), 176
Navy Yard, U.S. (San Francisco), 176
Nazi Party, 89, 128, 215, 263, 336, 363, 440, 462
Nazi Youth Party, 215
Nelson, George (Lester Gillis; AKA: Baby Face), 214
Nelson, Steve (Steve Mesarosch; Soviet spy in U.S.), 20, 72, **367-68**
Nero, 263
New China News Agency, 143, 285
New Masses, 18
New Mexico State Hospital (Santa Fe), 276
New Willard Hotel (Washington, D.C.), 210
New York *Herald*, 249
New York Public Library, 254
New York *Times*, 184
New York University, 359
New York *World*, 321
Newcombe, Capt. S. F., 315
Newgate Prison (Eng.), 170
Ney, Marshal Michel, 439
Niagra Falls, 497
Nicholas I (King of Montenegro), 176
Nicholas II (Russian czar), 21, 22, 57, 58-59, 60, 110, 111, 178, 227, 228, 229, 331-32, 344, 356, 415, 445
Nicolai, Walther (*Nachrichtendienst* director and Abwehr spymaster in WW I), 10, 17, 208, 320, 335, 339, 353, **368-69**, 409, 421, 423, 424, 436, 437, 464
Nicolaievich, Prince Nicholas (Rus.), 260
NID (British Naval Intelligence Department), 411
Niekisch, Ernst, 102
Nighthawk, 253
Nightingale, Florence, 142
Nikitushev, Col. Nikolai (KGB spymaster), 510
Nikolaev, Leonid V., 518
Nikolayev, Mikhail (GRU cutout), 233
Nimitz, USS, 464, 496
Ninio, Victorino (AKA: Marcelle; Mossad spy in Egypt), **369-70**
NIS (National Intelligence Service, South Afr.), 112

Venlo Incident (SD entrapment of British agents in WW II), 353, 434, 449, **492-94**
Veresanin, Gen. Marijan, 101
Versailles Peace Conference (1919), 196
Versailles Treaty (1919), 17, 264
Vespa, Amleto, 181
Vetterlein, Kurt, 535
Victoria (Queen of England), 124, 253
Victorica, Manual Gustave, 335
Victorica, Maria de, *See:* Kretschman, Maria von
Vidocq, **Eugene Francois** (French police spy), 314, **494-95**
Vienna University, 85
Vigilance Committee (San Francisco), 65
Villa, Pancho, 183, 225, 527
Villaverde, Raphael, 513
Vinogradov, Segei Alexandrovich, 386
Vita Nova Verlag, 426
Vitel, Charles, 213, 218, 383
Vittoria (battle, 1813), 258
Vladimir Prison, 500
Vogel, Jacob, 464
Vogel, Wolfgang, 500
Voice of the Mineworkers, 455
Voladarsky, V., 413
Volkov, Konstantin, 386
Voltaire (Francois-Marie Arouet), 140
Vomecourt, Pierre de, 139
Vonsiatsky, Anastase Andreyevich, 134
Voss, **Otto Herman** (Abwehr spy in America), 129, **495**
Vought Aviation, 129
Voynich, Ethel, 411
Vrinten, Adrianus, 193
Vukelic, Branko (member of Sorge ring), 458, 462, 463
Vukelic, Edith (member of Sorge ring), 458
Vulture, 37, 39, 50

Waberski, Pablo, *See:* Witzke, Lothar
Wadleigh, Julian, 145
Waem, Max, 246
Wagner, Gen. Eduard, 102
Wakefield Prison (Yorkshire, Eng.), 346
Waldgrave, Lord, 125
Waldstein, Graf von, 140
Walker, Arthur, 496, 497, 498
Walker, Mrs. Barbara, 496
Walker, **John Anthony, Jr.** (American spy for Soviets), 463, **496-98**
Walker, Laura, 496, 497
Walker, Michael Lance, 496, 497, 498
Wallenberg family, 135
Wallenberg, **Raoul** (Swedish diplomat and secret agent), **498-500**
Wallenstein, Albrecht von, 420
Wallinger, Maj. Sir John, 342-43, 344
Wallis, John, 480
Walpole, Horace, 334, 400
Walsingham, **Francis** (British spymaster for Elizabeth I), 9, 62, 170, 336, 353, 361, 465, 480, **500-02**
Walters, **Anne-Marie** (SOE spy in WW II), **502**
Wandsworth Prison (Eng.), 193
War Production Board (WPB, U.S.), 88
Warburg, James P., 186
Warne, Mrs. Kate, 391
Warren, Joseph, 149, 150, 418
Warsaw Pact, 382
Wartenburg, Count Peter Yorck von, 102

Washington, **George** (Commander of Continental Army in Revolution and Spymaster), 7, 10, 36, 37, 39, 40, 45, 46, 48, 50, 51, 72, 75, 82, 116, 117, 150, 165, 169, 268, 355, 426, 474, 475, 476, 477, 481, 482, **502-03**, 510, 515, 516
Washington, SS, 444
Washington Naval Conference (1921), 520
Washington *Post*, 212
Wassmuss, **Wilhelm** (German spymaster in WW I), 9, 428, 473, **503-05**, 526
Water on the Brain (book), 328
Watergate Scandal, 113, 152, 261, **505-06**
Waterloo (battle, Belg., Napoleonic wars, 1815), 76, 218, 258, 317, 433, 439, 509
Weber, Kurt, 295
Weber-Drohl, Ernst (Awehr spy), 313
Webster, **Timothy** (Union spy in Civil War), 65, 250, 390, 391, 490, **506-09**
Webster, William H. (CIA/FBI chief), 32, 154
Week at Westminster, The (Brit. radio program), 120
Weekly Journal (Jacobite organ, Eng.), 172
Wegman, Samuel J., 18
Weigels, Otto, 208
"Weigh" (code name for CIA agent), 31
Weinberg, Joseph Woodrow, 367, 368
Weinberger, Casper, 393
Weisenborn, Gunther (Soviet spy in WW II), 407
Weiskopf, Victor (American cryptologist), 520
Welch, Richard (CIA agent in Greece), 21
Welchman, Gordon, 486
Wellcome, Gwendolyn Maude Syrie, 342, 343, 344
Wellcome, Sir Henry, 344
Wellesley, Richard Colley, 509
Wellington, **Duke of** (Wellesley, Arthur, Wesley; British general and spymaster), 258, 449, **509**
Wennerstrom, **Stig** (Swedish spy for Soviets), **510**
Wentworth, **Paul** (British spymaster in American Revolution), 72, 73, 205-06, 476, **510-11**, 516
Wenzel, Johann (SOE/Soviet spy in WW II), 407, 484
Werner, Kurt, *See:* Wolf, Markus
Wesley, Garret (Earl of Mornington), 509
Wessell, Gen. Gerhard, 110, 232
West Point (N.Y.; fort, later U.S. Army Academy), 37, 39, 48, 249
Western Federation of Miners (U.S.), 349
Western Union, 71
Westminster School (Eng.), 384, 400
Weyler, Gen. Nicolau Valeriano (AKA: The Beast), 224
Whampoa Military Academy, 335
Wheeler Field (Oahu, Hawaii), 311
White, Harry Dexter, 88
White House (Washington, D. C.), 130
White House Plumbers, *See:* Watergate Scandal
White, Richard, 318
White Slave Traffic Act (U.S., 1910), 213
Whittier College, 317
Whitworth, Jerry Alfred (AKA: Wentworth; member of Walker ring), 496, 497, 498
Who's Who, 328
Wickersham, George W., 213

Wickham, **William** (British spymaster during French revolution), **511**
Wierner Neustadt Military Academy (Vienna, Aus.), 85
Wild Bill, *See:* Donovan, William Joseph
Wilde, Oscar, 168
Wilderness of Zin, The, 315
Wildprett, Wolfgang (SMERSH assassin), 453
Wilhelm I (Ger. Emperor), 470
Wilhelm II (Friedrich Wilhelm Victor Albert, Ger. Kaiser), 63, 127, 166, 176, 177, 208, 219, 317, 318, 320, 339, 412, 413, 444, 455, 503, 505
Wilhelm, Crown Prince, 339
Wilhelmina (Queen of the Netherlands), 193, 337
Wilhelmina Hotel (Venlo, Neth.), 493
Wilker, Haakon, 542
Wilkinson, Gen. James, 123
Wilkinson, Peter (SOE agent), 454
Will of the People, The (Russian revolutionary group), 57
Willard Hotel (Washington, D.C.), 88
William III, 400
Williams College, 261
Williams, David, 37-38
Willis, Sir Richard, 480
Willoughby, Lord Francis William, 85
Wilmer, George, 217
Wilmer, Joanna, 217
Wilmoth, **James R.** (American spy for Soviets), **511**
Wilson, **Edwin** (Spy and arms dealer for Muammar Qaddafi), 194, 403, **511-13**
Wilson, Harold, 288, 517
Wilson, Sen. Henry, 250
Wilson, Hugh, 196, 197
Wilson, President Woodrow, 196, 225, 258, 335, 424, 519, 527
Winchester Castle, 247
Winder, Gen. John H., 253, 489, 490, 491, 507, 508
Winter Palace (St. Petersburg, Rus.), 58, 227, 228, 229
Wirth, FBI Agent Robert J., 163
Wise, Det. Supt., 113
Wiseman, William (SIS spymaster), 344
Wisner, **Frank** (CIA deputy director), 261, **513-14**
Wissenger, Hans (GPU spymaster and SMERSH victim), 450
With Lawrence in Arabia (book), 316
Witkowski, Stanislaw, 246
Witt, Johan de, 188, 189
Witte, Count Sergius, 57
Witzke, Lothar (AKA: Pablo Waberski; Abwehr saboteur), 334, 335, 519
Witzleben, Field Marshal Erwin von, 102, 103
Wohlgemuth, Dr. Wolfgang, 282, 283
Woiziske, Wilhelm, 452
Wolf, **Gen. Markus** (AKA: Michael Storm, Kurt Werner; HVA/MfS director), 278, 283, 351, **514-15**
Wolfe, Gen. James, 268
Wolff, Gen. Karl, 199
Wolfinger, FBI Agent Joseph, 496
Wolkoff, Anna (Abwehr spy in England), 290, 291, 386
Wolkoff, Adm. Nicholas, 290
Wollweber, **Ernst** (HVA/MfS director), 232, 514, **515**
Women's Patriotic Society of Japan, 226
Wood, Harriet, *See:* Cushman, Pauline
Wood, Supt. William P., 252, 253